Contents

KU-484-409

Contents

Part 5 Special accounting procedures

Part 6 Partnership accounts and company accounts

Part 7 An introduction to financial analysis

Part 8 Other topics

Supporting resources

Visit **www.pearsoned.co.uk/wood** to find valuable online resources

Companion Website for students

- Learning objectives for each chapter
- Multiple choice questions to help test your learning
- Review questions and answers
- Links to relevant sites on the web
- Searchable online glossary
- Flashcards to test your knowledge of key terms and definitions

For instructors

- Complete, downloadable Solutions Manual
- PowerPoint slides that can be downloaded and used as OHTs

Also: The Companion Website provides the following features:

- Search tool to help locate specific items of content
- E-mail results and profile tools to send results of quizzes to instructors
- Online help and support to assist with website usage and troubleshooting

For more information please contact your local Pearson Education sales representative or visit **www.pearsoned.co.uk/wood**

Guided tour of the book

Part opening

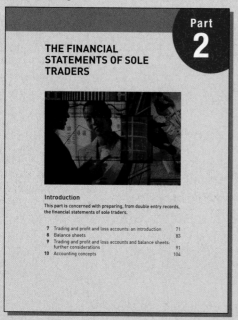

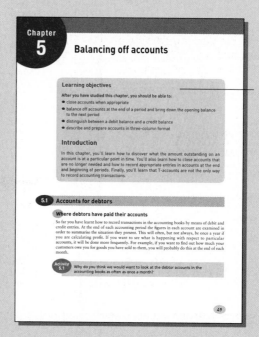

Learning objectives outline what you will need to have learned by the end of the chapter.

A wide range of **exhibits** offer clear examples of accounting practice and methodology.

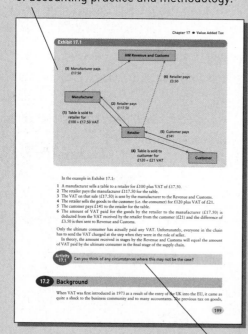

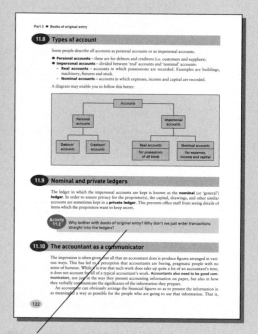

Activities occur frequently throughout the book to test your understanding of new concepts.

A number of **worked examples** are provided to guide you through more difficult concepts.

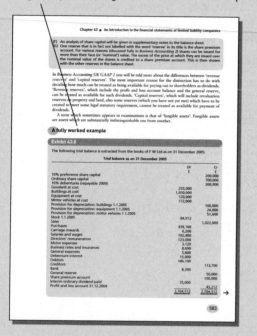

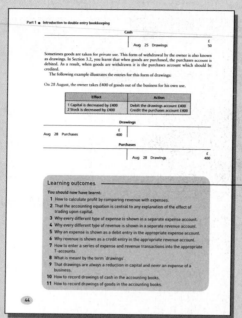

Learning outcomes revisit and reinforce the major topics covered in the chapter.

Each chapter ends with a selection of **review questions** to prepare you for your examinations.

Five sets of **multiple choice questions** allow you a quick and easy method of checking your own progress as you work through the book.

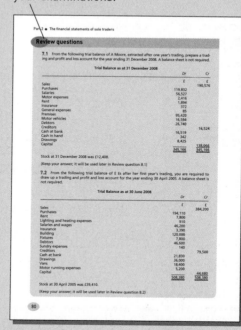

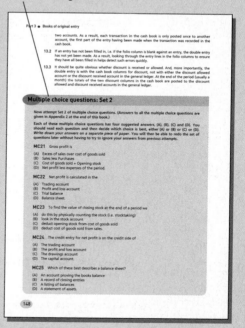

Guided tour of the companion website

Business Accounting is supported by a fully interactive Companion Website, available at **www.pearsoned.co.uk/wood**, that contains a range of additional learning material.

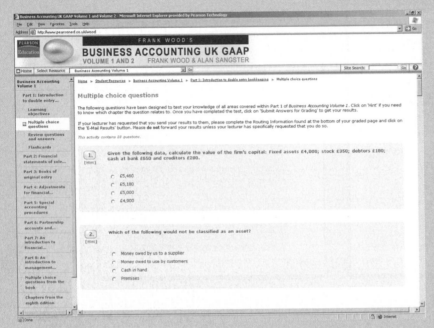

Multiple choice questions test your learning and provide helpful feedback to improve your results.

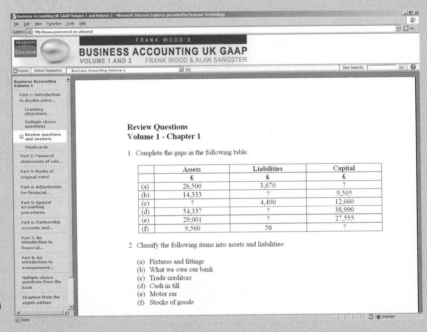

Review questions and answers provide practice at answering examination questions.

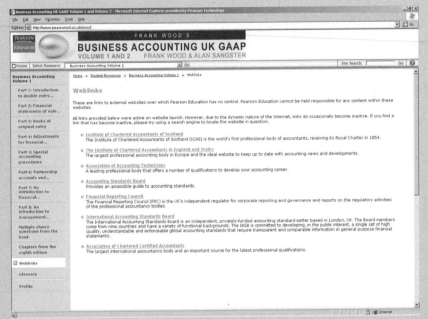

Weblinks to useful accounting sites.

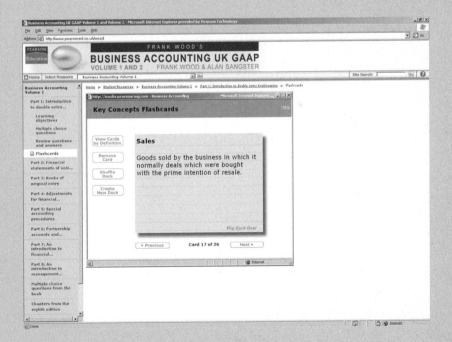

Flashcards provide an interactive revision tool for all key terms.

Notes for teachers and lecturers

This textbook has been written so that a very thorough introduction to accounting is covered in two volumes. The split into two volumes is a recognition of the fact that many students will find that Volume 1 contains all that they require. Volume 2 takes the studies of the remainder of the readers to a more advanced stage. As is discussed later, the decision to create two versions of this book, one for UK GAAP (this book) and one based on International GAAP (*Business Accounting UK GAAP 2*), is in response to changes that have been taking place in accounting over the past few years.

This textbook is suitable for anyone who wants to obtain a good grounding in financial accounting, for whatever purpose. It is ideal for students who are starting to study the subject for A level, Scottish Higher Grade, or General Certificate of Secondary Education examinations, and for those embarking on their studies for the Open University Certificate in Accounting, or for qualifications of the Association of Accounting Technicians, the Institute of Secretaries and Administrators, or any of the six UK and Irish Chartered Accountancy bodies. The financial accounting requirements for National Vocational Qualifications are also fully covered.

The book has the following features:

1 Each chapter:
   - starts with Learning Objectives;
   - contains Activities designed to broaden and reinforce students' understanding of the concepts being covered and, in some cases, to introduce new concepts in such a way that they do not come as a surprise when introduced formally later in the book;
   - ends with Learning Outcomes that can be mapped back to the Learning Objectives, reinforcing the major topics and concepts covered in the chapter;
   - contains answers to all the Activities immediately after the Learning Outcomes.
2 The book has an alphabetical Glossary (Appendix 3) of all the significant terms introduced. Each entry is referenced back to the chapter in which it appeared.
3 Five sets of 20 multiple choice questions are positioned in the book (in Chapters 6, 13, 25, 31, and 43) at the point they should be attempted, rather than as a group at the end of the book. The answers are all at the back of the book in Appendix 2.
4 At the end of Part 4 (Adjustments for financial statements), there are five Scenario questions which are designed to reinforce learning of the adjustments through their application in the preparation of financial statements previously learnt in Parts 1–3.
5 A set of Notes for Students appears at the front of the book. This covers how to use this book, how to tackle the end of chapter Review questions, and how to study for and sit examinations. It should be read by students before they start working through the main text.
6 Blue is used in the text so as to enhance readability and bring out key points in the text.

Some changes have been made to the content of the book:

- Chapter 1, *The accounting equation and the balance sheet*, has been expanded in order to provide some background information about the development and nature of accounting.
- There are 28 new questions in this edition.
- Depreciation is now dealt with in Chapters 24 and 25. The material on additional methods of depreciation that was part of Chapter 35 (Manufacturing accounts) has been moved into Chapter 24.
- All dates are now 'real' dates, such as 2008, rather than the artificial 20X8.

- Multi-column cash books has been added to Chapter 13 (cash books), so reflecting more real-istically the use of cash books in a manual accounting environment.
- A new chapter (46) has been added on the topic of International GAAP. This book is based on UK GAAP and this new chapter provides details of the different terminology used and of differences in the layout of some financial statements prepared under International GAAP.

The general public have tended to view accounting as a traditional, never-changing subject. This is not true; despite common appearances, accounting is a dynamic subject. A big change, which began in 2005 and is set to continue over the next few years, is the move in the UK from domestic accounting rules (UK GAAP) to international rules (International GAAP). Specifically, the rules that have been developed in the UK since 1970, known as Statements of Standard Accounting Practice (SSAPs) and Financial Reporting Standards (FRSs) are effectively being phased out. Coming in their place are International Financial Reporting Standards (IFRSs) and International Accounting Standards (IASs).

This change is being introduced gradually, with all companies across the European Union, including the UK, that are listed on a stock exchange in the EU, using the international set of standards from 2005 (later in the case of some stock exchanges). Other companies broadly the small and medium-sized ones, will continue to use UK GAAP for the time being. However, it seems likely that all companies will move to using international standards in the medium term and that UK GAAP will then presumably cease to exist. Indeed, the UK's standard setters are currently working on convergence of UK and international rules to that end.

This means that UK accounting is currently in the middle of a major transition and this book reflects that. The book is based on the terminology and rules of UK GAAP, although Chapter 46 (International GAAP) provides a bridge to that version of GAAP should a student's next stage of accounting study require its use. The sister book to this one, Business Accounting 1, applies International GAAP throughout.

We all know this is confusing (it is for all accountants during the current transition!) but we believe that by at least acknowledging the terminology and presentation formats in Chapter 46 that will become the norm over the next few years we will at least begin to prepare you for those years and beyond.

We hope that you find these changes helpful and appropriate and would welcome comments on these and any other changes you feel ought to be made in future editions. You can contact Alan Sangster by email at **a.j.a.sangster@btinternet.com** or by letter via the publishers.

We would like to thank all those teachers and lecturers who gave us their advice as to the changes they would like to see incorporated in this edition. Above all, we would like to acknow-ledge the assistance we have received from Graeme C Reid, FCA FCCA, lecturer in Financial Accounting, Auditing and Entrepreneurship at the University of Hull, who contributed questions for Chapters 6, 7, 8, 9, 13, 14, 16, 22, 23, 24, 25, 26, 28, 29, 30, 31, 32, 33, 35, 39, 41 and 43, plus the five scenario questions at the end of Part 4.

Frank Wood and Alan Sangster

Notes for students

This textbook is organised to provide you with what has been found to be the most appropriate sequencing of topics as you build the foundations of your accounting knowledge. You will find that a number of features of the book, properly used, will enhance your understanding and extend your ability to cope with what will possibly appear, at first, to be a mystifying array of rules and procedures.

To make best use of this resource, you should consider the following as being a proven path to success:

- At the start of each chapter, **read the Learning Objectives**. Then, while you work through the material, try to detect when you have achieved each of these objectives.
- At the end of each chapter **check what you have learnt against the Learning Outcomes** that follow the main text.
- If you find that you cannot say 'yes, I have learnt that' to any of the Learning Outcomes, look back through the chapter and reread the topic you have not yet learnt.
- **Learn the meaning of each new term as it appears**. Do not leave learning what terms mean until you are revising for an exam. Accounting is best learnt as a series of building blocks. If you don't remember what terms mean, your knowledge and ability to 'do' accounting will be very seriously undermined, in much the same way as a wall built without mortar is likely to collapse the first time someone leans against it.
- Attempt each of the Activities in the book *at the point at which they appear*. This is *very* important. They will reinforce your learning and help set in context some of the material that may otherwise appear very artificial and distant from the world you live in. The answers are at the end of each chapter. **Do not look at the answers before you attempt the questions – you'll just be cheating yourself**. Once you have answered one, check your answer against the answer provided in the book and be sure you understand it before moving on.
- Attempt each of the sets of multiple choice questions when you reach them in the book. There are five sets of twenty questions, one at the end of each of Chapters 6, 13, 25, 31, and 43. The answers are in Appendix 2 at the back of the book. **Do not look at the answers before you attempt the questions – you'll just be cheating yourself**. If you get any wrong, be sure you understand why before moving on to new material.
- Attempt the Scenario questions at the end of Part 4. They will help you see how the items covered in Part 4 affect the preparation of financial statements.
- **Learn the *accounting equation* when you first come across it in Chapter 1**. It is *the* key to understanding many of the aspects of accounting that students find difficult. Make sure that you learn it in both the forms presented to you or that you can rearrange it to produce the alternate form when appropriate.
- Do not be disillusioned by the mystery of double entry. The technique has been in common use for over 500 years and is probably the most tried and trusted technique for doing anything you are ever likely to encounter. It really is not difficult, so long as you remember the accounting equation and can distinguish between things that you own and things that you owe. Like riding a bike, once you understand it, you'll never forget it and, the more you do it, the easier it gets.
- Because of time pressure, some teachers and lecturers will need to omit Chapter 38 (*Joint venture accounts*). Make sure that you work through it on your own before you look at the material in Chapter 39, the first chapter on accounting for partnerships. This is very important, as accounting for joint ventures bridges the gap between accounting for sole traders and

accounting for partnerships and will make it much easier for you to understand the differences between them.

● Above all, remember that accounting is a vehicle for providing financial information in a form that assists decision-making. Work hard at presenting your work as neatly as possible and remember that pictures (in this case, financial figures) only carry half the message. When you are asked for them, words of explanation and insight are essential in order to make an examiner appreciate what you know and that you actually understand what the figures mean.

There are two subjects we would like you to consider very carefully – making best use of the end of chapter Review questions, and your examination technique.

Review questions: the best approach

We have set review questions at the end of most chapters for you to gauge how well you understand and can apply what you have learnt. **If you simply read the text without attempting the questions then we can tell you now that you will not pass your examinations.** You should first attempt each question, then check your answer fully against the answers at the back of the book.

What you should not do is perform a 'ticking' exercise. By this we mean that you should not simply compare the question with the answer and tick off the bits of the answer against the relevant part of the question. No one ever learnt to do accounting properly that way. It is tempting to save time in so doing but, believe us, you will regret it eventually. We have deliberately had the answers printed using a different page layout to try to stop you indulging in a 'ticking' exercise.

Need for practice

You should also try to find the time to answer as many exercises as possible. Our reasons for saying this are as follows:

1 Even though you may think you understand the text, when you come to answer the questions you may often find your understanding incomplete. The true test of understanding is whether or not you can tackle the questions competently.

2 It is often said that practice makes perfect, a sentiment we don't fully agree with. There is, however, enough sense in it in that, if you don't do quite a lot of accounting questions, you will almost certainly not become good at accounting.

3 You simply have to get up to a good speed in answering questions: you will always fail accounting examinations if you are a very slow worker. The history of accountancy examinations so far has always been that a ridiculously large amount of work has been expected from a student during a short time. However, examining boards maintain that the examination could be completed in the time by an adequately prepared student. You can take it for granted that *adequately prepared students* are those who not only have the knowledge, but have also been trained to work quickly and, at the same time, maintain accuracy and neatness.

4 Speed itself is not enough. You also have to be neat and tidy, and follow all the proper practices and procedures while working at speed. Fast but really scruffy work can also mean failing the exam. Why? At this level, the examiner is very much concerned with your practical ability in the subject. Accounting is a practical subject, and your practical competence is being tested. The examiner will, therefore, expect the answers to be neat and well set out. Untidy work with numbers spread over the page in a haphazard way, badly written numbers, and columns of figures in which the vertical columns are not set down in straight lines, will incur the examiner's displeasure.

5 Appropriate presentation of information is important. Learn how to present the various financial statements you may need to produce in an examination. Examiners expect to see the items in trading and profit and loss accounts, balance sheets, and cash flow statements in the

correct order and will probably deduct marks if you don't do this. Practise by writing down examples of these statements without any numbers until you always get the layout correct. One exam trick most students overlook is that the layout of a financial statement is often included in an examination paper as part of one question while another question asks you to produce a financial statement. **The one you need to produce will contain different numbers but the general layout should be very similar.**

Need for headings

The next thing is that work should not only be neat but also well laid out. Headings should always be given, and any dates needed should be inserted. The test you should apply is to imagine that you are a partner in a firm of professional accountants and you are away on holiday for a few weeks. During that time your assistants have completed all sorts of work including reports, drafting final accounts, various forms of other computations and so on. All of this work is deposited on your desk while you are away. When you return you look at each item in the pile awaiting your attention. Suppose the first item looks like a balance sheet as at 31 December in respect of one of your clients. When you look at it you can see that it is a balance sheet, but you don't know for which client, neither do you know which year it is for. Would you be annoyed with your staff? Of course you would. So, in an examination, why should the examiner accept as a piece of your work a balance sheet answer without the date or the name of the business or the fact that it is a balance sheet written clearly across the top? If proper headings are not given you will lose a lot of marks. Always put in the headings properly. Don't wait until your examination to start this correct practice. Similar attention should be paid to sub-totals which need showing, e.g. for Fixed assets or for Current assets.

We will be looking at examination technique in the next section.

The examiner

What you should say to yourself is: 'Suppose I were in charge of an office, doing this type of accounting work, what would I say if one of my assistants put on my desk a sheet of paper with accounting entries on it written in the same manner as my own efforts in attempting this question?' Just look at some of the work you have done in the past. Would you have told your assistant to go back and do the work again because it is untidy? If you say that about your own work, why should the examiner think any differently?

Anyone who works in accounting knows that untidy work leads to completely unnecessary errors. Therefore, the examiner's insistence on clear, tidy, well laid out work is not an outdated approach. Examiners want to ensure that you are not going to mess up the work of an accounting department. Imagine going to the savings bank and the manager saying to you: 'We don't know whether you've got £5 in the account or £5,000. You see, the work of our clerks is so untidy that we can never sort out exactly how much is in anybody's account.' We would guess that you would not want to put a lot of money into an account at that bank. How would you feel if someone took you to court for not paying a debt of £100 when, in fact, you owed them nothing? This sort of thing would happen all the time if we simply allowed people to keep untidy accounts. The examiner is there to ensure that the person to whom they give a certificate will be worthy of it, and will not continually mess up the work of any firm at which they may work in the future.

We can imagine quite a few of you groaning at all this, and if you do not want to pass the examination please give up reading here. If you do want to pass, and your work is untidy, what can you do about it? Well, the answer is simple enough: start right now to be neat and orderly in your work. Quite a lot of students have said to us over the years: 'I may be giving you untidy work now but, when I actually get into the exam room, I will then do my work neatly enough.' This is as near impossible as anything can be. You cannot suddenly become able to do accounting work neatly, and certainly not when you are under the stress and strain of an examination. Even the neatest worker may well find in an examination that their work may not be of its usual standard as nervousness will cause them to make mistakes. If this is true, and you are an untidy worker now, your work in an examination is likely to be even more untidy. Have we convinced you yet?

The structure of the questions

We have tried to build up the review questions in a structured way, starting with the easiest and then going on to more difficult ones. We would like to have omitted all the difficult questions, on the basis that you may well spend a lot of time doing them without adding very much to your knowledge about accounting. However, if all the questions were straightforward, the shock of meeting more complicated questions for the first time in an examination could lead you to fail it. We have, therefore, tried to include a mixture of straightforward and complicated questions to give you the maximum benefit.

The answers

At the back of the book, you will find answers to approximately half of the Review questions. The answers to the other review questions (indicated by the letter 'A' after the question number) are only available to you from your teacher or lecturer. Don't worry if you are studying this subject on your own. There are still more than sufficient review questions to ensure you know and understand the material in the book.

Examination technique

As authors, we can use the first person here, as we want to put across to you a message about examinations, and we want you to feel that we are writing this for you as an individual rather than simply as one of the considerable number of people who have read this book.

By the time you sit your first examination, you will have spent a lot of hours trying to master such things as double entry, balance sheets, final adjustments, and goodness knows what else. Learning accounting/bookkeeping does demand a lot of discipline and practice. Compared with the many hours learning the subject, most students spend very little time actually considering in detail how to tackle the examination. You may be one of them, and we would like you to start planning now for that day when you will need to be able to demonstrate what you have learnt and understood, and can apply, the material in this book.

Understanding examiners

Let's start by saying that if you want to understand anything about examinations then you have got to understand examiners, so let us look together at what these peculiar creatures get up to in an examination. The first thing is that when they set an examination they are looking at it on the basis that they want good students to get a pass mark. Obviously anyone who doesn't achieve the pass mark will fail, but the object of the exercise is to find those who will pass, not find the failures. This means that if you have done your work properly, and if you are not sitting for an examination well above your intellectual capabilities, you should manage to get a pass mark. It is important for us to stress this before we get down to the details of setting about the task.

There are, however, quite a large number of students who will fail, not because they haven't put in enough hours on their studies, nor because they are unintelligent, but simply because they throw away marks unnecessarily by poor examination technique. If you can read the rest of this piece, and then say honestly that you wouldn't have committed at least one of the mistakes that we are going to mention, then you are certainly well outside the ordinary range of students.

Punctuality

Before thinking about the examination paper itself, let us think about how you are going to get to the examination room. If it is at your own college then you have no problems as to how you will get there. On the other hand, it may be an external centre. Do you know exactly where the place is? If not, you had better have a trip there if possible. How are you going to get there? If you are going by bus or train, do you know which bus or train to catch? Will it be the rush hour when it may well take you much longer than if it were held at midday?

Quite a large proportion of students lose their way to the examination room, or else arrive, breathless and flustered, at the very last minute. They then start off the attempt at the examination in a somewhat nervous state: a recipe for disaster for a lot of students. So plan how you are going to get there and give yourself enough time.

Last minute learning for your examination will be of little use to you. The last few days before the examination should not be spent cramming. You can look at past examination papers and rework some of them. This is totally different from trying to cram new facts into your head.

On your way to the examination, if you can, try relaxation exercises. Deep breathing exercises in particular will put you into a relaxed mood. If you can't do anything like this, try reading the newspaper. Granted, you will need some adrenalin to spur you into action when you actually start answering the examination paper, but you do not want to waste it before the examination instead and then put yourself into a highly nervous state.

Read the rubric carefully and follow its instructions

The rubric appears at the start of the examination paper, and says something such as:

'Attempt five questions only: the *three* questions in Section A and *two* from Section B.'

That instruction from the examiner is to be followed exactly. The examinee (i.e. you) cannot change the instruction – it means what it says.

Now you may think that is so simple that it is not worthwhile our forcibly pointing it out to you. We wish that was the case for all students. However, you would be amazed at the quite high percentage of students who do not follow the instructions given in the rubric. Having been examiners for many years for examining bodies all over the world we can assure you that we are not overstating the case. Let us look at two typical examples where students have ignored the rubric above:

(a) A student answered *two* questions from Section A and *three* from Section B. Here the examiner will mark the two Section A answers plus the first two answers shown on the examinee's script in respect of Section B. He will not read any part of the third displayed answer to Section B. The student can therefore only get marks for four answers.

(b) A student answered *three* questions from Section A and *three* from Section B. Here he will mark the three answers to Section A plus the first two displayed answers to Section B. He will not look at the third answer to Section B.

In the case of (b), the student may have done it that way deliberately, thinking that the examiner would mark all three Section B answers, and then award the student the marks from the best two answered questions. Most examiners will not waste time marking an extra answer. Students have argued that examiners would do that, but they are simply deluding themselves.

If you have time and want to give an extra answer, thinking that you will get better marks than one answered previously, then do so. If you do, make certain that the examiner is fully aware that you have deleted the answer that you do not want to have marked. Strike lines right through it, and also state that you wish to delete it. Otherwise it is possible that the first answers only will be marked and your new answer ignored.

Always remember in examinations that you should try to make life easier for the examiner. Give the examiner what he/she wants, in the way that he/she wants it. If you do, you will get better marks. Make their job harder than it needs to be and you will suffer. Examiners are only human beings after all!

Time planning

We must now look at the way in which you should tackle the examination paper. One of the problems with bookkeeping/accounting examinations is that students are expected to do a lot of work in a relatively short time. We have campaigned against this attitude, but the tradition is longstanding and here to stay. It will be the same for every other student taking your examination, so it is not unfair so far as any one student is concerned. Working at speed does bring various disadvantages, and makes the way you tackle the examination of even greater importance than for examinations where the pace is more leisurely.

Time per question

The marks allotted to each question will indicate how long you should take in tackling the question. Most examinations are of three hours' duration, i.e. 180 minutes. This means that in a normal examination, with 100 marks in total, a 20-mark question should be allocated 20 per cent of the time, i.e. 20% × 180 = 36 minutes. Similarly, a question worth 30 marks should take up 30 per cent of the time, i.e. 30% × 180 = 54 minutes, and so on. Alternatively it is 1.8 minutes for each mark awarded for the question.

If the question is in parts, and the marks awarded are shown against each part, then that will give you a clue as to the time to be spent on each part. If part of the question asks for a description, for instance, and only 3 marks are awarded to that part, then you should not spend twenty minutes on a long and detailed description. Instead a brief description, taking about five minutes, is what is required.

Do the easiest questions first

Always tackle the easiest question first, then the next easiest question and so on. Leave the most difficult question as the last one to be attempted. Why is this good advice? The fact is, most examiners usually set what might be called 'warm-up' questions. These are usually fairly short, and not very difficult questions, and the examiner will expect you to tackle these first.

You may be able to do the easiest question in less than the time allocated. The examiner is trying to be kind to you. The examiner knows that there is a certain amount of nervousness on the part of a student taking an examination, and wants to give you the chance to calm down by letting you tackle these short, relatively easy questions first of all, and generally settle down to your work.

Even where all the questions are worth equal marks, you are bound to find some easier than others. It is impossible for an examiner to set questions which are equally as difficult as each other. So, remember, start with the easiest question. This will give you a feeling of confidence. It is very desirable to start off in this way.

Do not expect that these 'warm-up' questions will be numbered 1 and 2 on your examination paper. Most accounting examinations start off with a rather long question, worth quite a lot of marks, as question number 1 on the paper. Over the years we have advised students not to tackle these questions first. A lot of students are fascinated by the fact that such a question is number 1, that it is worth a lot of marks, and their thinking runs: 'If I do this question first, and make a good job of it, then I am well on the way to passing the examination.'

There is no doubt that a speedy and successful attempt at such a question could possibly lead to a pass. The trouble is that this doesn't usually happen, and many students have admitted afterwards that their failure could be put down to simply ignoring this advice. What happens very often is that the student starts off on such a question, things don't go very well, a few mistakes are made, the student then looks at the clock and sees that they are not 'beating the clock' in terms of possible marks, and then panic descends on them. Leaving that question very hastily, the student then proceeds to the next question, which normally might have been well attempted but, because of the state of mind, a mess is made of that one as well, and so students fail an examination which they had every right to think they could pass.

Attempt every required question

The last point concerning time allocation which we want to get through is that you should attempt each and every question as required. On each question the first few marks are the easiest to get. For instance, on an essay question it is reasonably easy to get, say, the first 5 marks in a 20-mark question. Managing to produce a perfect answer to get the last 5 marks, from 15 to 20, is extremely difficult. This applies also to computational questions.

This means that in an examination of, say, five questions with 20 marks possible for each question, there is not much point in tackling three questions only and trying to make a good job of them. The total possible marks would be 60 marks, and if you had not achieved full marks for each question, in itself extremely unlikely, you could easily fall below the pass mark of, say, 50 marks. It is better to leave questions unfinished when your allotted time, calculated as shown earlier, has expired, and to then go on immediately to the other questions. It is so easy, especially in an accounting examination, to find that one has exceeded the time allowed for a question by a considerable margin. So, although you may find it difficult to persuade yourself to do so, move on to the next question when your time for a question has expired.

Computations

When you sit an examination, you should be attempting to demonstrate how well you know the topics being examined. In accounting examinations, there are three things in particular to remember. If you fail to do so, you will probably earn less marks than your knowledge deserves. One of these things has already been mentioned – be neat and tidy. The other two have to do with computations: *show all your workings* and *don't worry if your balance sheet does not balance*.

Workings

One golden rule which should *always* be observed is to **show all of your workings.** Suppose you have been asked to work out the cost of goods sold, not simply as part of a trading account but for some other reason. On a scrap of paper you work out the answers below:

	£
Opening stock	4,000
Add Purchases	11,500
	15,500
Less Closing stock	(3,800)
	12,700

You put down the answer as £12,700. The scrap of paper with your workings on it is then crumpled up by you and thrown in the wastepaper basket as you leave the room. You may have noticed in reading this that in fact the answer should have been 11,700 and not 12,700 (the arithmetic was incorrect). The examiner may well have allocated, say, 4 marks for this bit of the question. What will he do when he simply sees your answer as £12,700? Will he say: 'I should imagine that the candidate mis-added to the extent of £1,000 and, as I am not unduly penalising for arithmetic, I will give the candidate 3½ marks'? Unfortunately the examiner cannot do this.

The candidate got the wrong answer, there is no supporting evidence, and so the examiner gives marks as nil. If you had only attached the workings to your answer, then we have no doubt that you would have got 3½ marks at least.

It is often better to put the workings on the face of the final accounts, if appropriate. For instance, if rent paid is £1,900 and £300 of it has been paid in advance, you can show it on the face of the profit and loss account as:

Rent (1,900 – 300)   £1,600

By showing the workings in brackets you are demonstrating that you realise that they would not be shown on the published accounts. It also makes it easier for the examiner to mark.

Do balance sheets have to balance?

Many students ask: 'What should I do if my balance sheet doesn't balance?' The answer is quite simple: leave it alone and get on with answering the rest of the examination paper.

One of the reasons for this is to try and ensure that you answer the required number of questions. You might take 20 minutes to find the error, which might save you 1 mark. In that time you might have gained, say, 10 marks if, instead, you had tackled the next question, for which you would not have had time if you had wasted it by searching for the error(s). That assumes that you actually find the error(s)! Suppose you don't, you have spent 20 minutes looking for it, have not found it, so how do you feel now? The answer is, of course: quite terrible. You may make an even bigger mess of the rest of the paper than you would have done if you had simply ignored the fact that the balance sheet did not balance. In any case, it is quite possible to get, say, 29 marks out of 30 even though the balance sheet does not balance. The error may be a very minor case for which the examiner deducts one mark only.

Of course, if you have finished all the questions, then by all means spend the rest of your time tracing the error and correcting it. Be certain, however, that your corrections are carried out neatly. Untidy crossings-out can result in the loss of marks. So, sometimes, an error found can get back one mark, which is then lost again because the corrections make an untidy mess of your paper, and examiners often deduct marks, quite rightly so, for untidy work. It might be better to write against the error 'see note', indicating exactly where the note is shown. You can then illustrate to the examiner that you know what the error is and how to correct it.

Essay questions

Until a few years ago, there were not many essay questions in accounting examinations at this level. This has changed, and you therefore need to know the approach to use in answering such questions.

Typical questions

Before discussing these, we want you to look at two recent examination questions. Having done that, visualise carefully what you would write in answer to them. Here they are:

(a) You are employed as a bookkeeper by G Jones, a trader. State briefly what use you would make of the following documents in relation to your bookkeeping records.
   (i)   A bank statement.
   (ii) A credit note received to correct an overcharge on an invoice.
   (iii) A pay-in slip.
   (iv) A petty cash voucher.
(b) Explain the term 'depreciation'. Name and describe briefly two methods of providing for depreciation of fixed assets.

Now we can test whether or not you would have made a reasonably good attempt at the questions. With question (a) a lot of students would have written down what a bank statement is, what a pay-in slip is, what a petty cash voucher is, and so on. Marks gained by you for an answer like that would be . . . virtually nil. Why is this? Well, you simply have not read the question properly. The question asked what *use* you would make of the documents, not to *describe* what the documents were. The bank statement would be used to check against the bank column in the Cash Book or cash records to see that the bank's entries and your own are in accordance with one another, with a bank reconciliation statement being drawn up to reconcile the two sets of records. The petty cash voucher would be used as a basis for entering up the payments columns in the Petty Cash Book. The *use* of the items was asked for, not the *descriptions* of the items.

Let us see if you have done better on question (b). Would you have written down how to calculate two methods of depreciation, probably the reducing balance method and the straight line method? But have you remembered that the question also asked you to *explain the term depreciation*? In other words, what is depreciation generally? A fair number of students will have omitted that part of the question. Our guess is that far more students would have made perhaps a poor attempt at question (a) rather than doing question (b).

Underline the key words

We have already illustrated that a large percentage of students fail to answer the question set, instead answering the question they imagine it to be. Too many students write down everything they know about a topic, rather than what the examiner has asked for.

To remedy this defect, *underline the key words* in a question. This brings out the meaning so that it is difficult to misunderstand the question. For instance, let us look at the following question:

'Discuss the usefulness of departmental accounts to a business.'

Many students will write down all they know about departmental accounts, how to draw them up, how to apportion overheads between departments, how to keep columnar sales and purchases journals to find the information, etc.

Number of marks gained . . . virtually nil.

Now underline the key words. They will be:

Discuss   usefulness   departmental accounts

The question is now seen to be concerned not with *describing* departmental accounts, but instead discussing the *usefulness* of departmental accounts.

Lastly, if the question says 'Draft a report on . . .' then the answer should be in the form of a *report*; if it says 'List the . . .' then the answer should consist of a *list*. Similarly 'Discuss . . .' asks for a *discussion*. 'Describe . . .' wants you to *describe* something, and so on.

You should therefore ensure that you are going to give the examiner

(*i*) What he is asking for *plus*
(*ii*) In the way that he wants it.

If you do not comply with (*i*) you may lose all the marks. If you manage to fulfil (*i*) but do not satisfy the examiner on (*ii*) you will still lose a lot of marks.

It is also just as important in computational questions to underline the key words to get at the meaning of a question, and then answer it in the manner required by the examiner. With computational questions it is better to look at what is required first before reading all of the rest of the question. That way, when you are reading the rest of the question, you are able to decide how to tackle it.

Never write out the question

Often – too often – students spend time writing out the text of essay questions before they set about answering them. This is a complete waste of time. It will not gain marks and should *never* be done.

Running out of time?

If your plans don't work out, you may find yourself with a question you could answer, but simply do not have the time to do it properly. It is better to write a short note to the examiner to that effect, and put down what you can of the main points in an abbreviated fashion. This will show that you have the knowledge and should gain you some marks.

Summary

Remember:

1 Read the instructions.
2 Plan your time before you start.
3 Tackle the easiest questions first.
4 Finish off answering each question when your time allocation for the question is up.
5 Hand in all your workings.
6 Do remember to be neat, also include all proper headings, dates, sub-totals, etc. A lot of marks can be lost if you don't.
7 Only answer as many questions as you are asked to tackle by the examiner. Extra answers will not normally be marked and certainly won't get credit.
8 Underline the *key* words in each question to ensure that you answer the question set, and not the question you wrongly take it to be.
9 Never write out the text of essay questions.

Best of luck with your examination. We hope you get the rewards you deserve!

Frank Wood and Alan Sangster

Publisher's acknowledgements

We are very grateful to teachers of accounting in many schools, colleges of further education and universities whose generous advice has contributed to the development of this new edition. We wish to thank, in particular:

Ann-Marie Ward, Queens University, Belfast
Bhagwan Moorjani, University of Westminster
Georgios Iatridis, Manchester University
Chris McMahon, Liverpool John Moores University
Adil Mahmood, Bradford College
Graeme Reid, Hull University
Rohan Chambers, University of Technology, Jamaica
Mike Rogers, Basingstoke College of Technology
Lindsay Whitlow, Dudley College
Paul Wertheim, Solihull College
David Gilding, Park Lane College, Leeds
Malcolm Rynn, Greencroft School, County Down
Eric Edwards, University of Northumberland
Helen Khoo, Sunway College, Petaling Jaya, Malaysia
Caroline Teh Swee Gaik, Inti College, Nilai, Malaysia
Christopher Foo, St George's School, Malaysia
Dave Knight, Leeds Met
Patrick Devlin, Glasgow Cale
Sally Nower, Colchester
Pushpa Kalu, Silpa
Penny Gardner, Napier
Sarah Knight, Huntingdon

We are grateful to the following for permission to reproduce examination questions:

Association of Accounting Technicians (AAT); Assessment and Qualifications Alliance (NEAB/AQA, SEB/AQA and AEB/AQA); Scottish Qualifications Authority (SQA); Association of Chartered Certified Accountants (ACCA); Oxford, Cambridge and RSA Examinations (MEG/OCR); Institute of Chartered Secretaries and Administrators (ICSA); London Qualifications Ltd trading as Edexcel and the Sage Group plc for Exhibit 21.1.

All answers to questions are the authors' own work and have not been supplied by any of the examining bodies.

Part 1

INTRODUCTION TO DOUBLE ENTRY BOOKKEEPING

Introduction

This part is concerned with the basic principles underlying the double entry system of bookkeeping.

The accounting equation and the balance sheet

Learning objectives

After you have studied this chapter, you should be able to:

- explain what accounting is about
- briefly describe the history of accounting
- explain the relationship between bookkeeping and accounting
- list the main users of accounting information and what accounting information they are interested in
- present and explain the accounting equation
- explain the relationship between the accounting equation and the layout of the balance sheet
- explain the meaning of the terms assets, capital, liabilities, debtors, and creditors
- describe how accounting transactions affect the items in the accounting equation
- draw up balance sheets after different accounting transactions have occurred

Introduction

In this chapter, you will learn: what accounting is; what led to its development into what it is today; who uses accounting information; and the relationship between the various components that, together, comprise what is known as the 'accounting equation'.

1.1 What is accounting?

What do *you* think of when you read or hear the word, 'accounting'? What do *you* believe it means or represents?

If you have already attended some accounting classes or if you have spoken with someone who knows something about accounting, you will probably have a fairly good idea of what accounting is and what it is used for. If not, you may find it useful to have this knowledge before you start studying the subject. During the course of the next few pages, let's see if you can gain that knowledge and learn what accounting is.

Accounting can be defined as 'the process of identifying, measuring, and communicating economic information to permit informed judgements and decisions by users of the information'. A bit of a mouthful really, but what it means is that accounting involves deciding what amounts of money are, were, or will be involved in transactions (often buying and selling transactions) and then organising the information obtained and presenting it in a way that is useful for decision making.

Despite what some people think, accounting is not a branch of mathematics, although the man credited with writing the first book to be printed on the subject, Fra Luca Pacioli (c. 1445–1517), was a mathematician and teacher. He wrote on the topic 'in order that the subjects of the most gracious Duke of Urbino [his sponsor or benefactor] may have complete instructions in the conduct of business', and to 'give the trader without delay information as to his assets and liabilities'. ('Assets' are things that you own; 'liabilities' are things that you owe.)

What Pacioli wrote is contained in 27 pages of a school textbook and reference manual for merchants on business and mathematics (*Summa de arithmetica, geometria, proportioni et proportionalita – Everything about Arithmetic, Geometry and Proportion*) which was first published in Italy in 1494. The bookkeeping treatise has been translated into many languages, including English and is acknowledged as the chief reason why we maintain accounts in the way we do today.

Accounting may not require a knowledge of mathematics but you do need to be able to add, subtract, multiply and divide – things you need to be able to do in your daily life anyway. Otherwise, you would not know how much money you had with you, how much you would have if you spent some of it, or whether the change you received was correct. So, let's remove one big misconception some people have concerning accounting: you do not need to be good at arithmetic to be good at accounting, though you will find it easier to 'do' accounting if you are.

The history of accounting

Accounting began because people needed to:

● record business transactions,
● know if they were being financially successful, and
● know how much they owned and how much they owed.

It is known to have existed in one form or another since at least 3,500 BC (records exist which indicate its use at that time in Mesopotamia). There is also considerable evidence of accounting being practised in ancient times in Egypt, China, India, Greece, and Rome. In England, the 'Pipe Roll', the oldest surviving accounting record in the English language, contains an annual description of rents, fines and taxes due to the King of England, from 1130 to 1830.

However, it was only when Paciloi wrote about it in 1494 or, to be more precise, wrote about a branch of accounting called 'bookkeeping' that accounting began to be standardised and recognised as a process or procedure.

No standard system for maintaining accounting records had been developed before this because the circumstances of the day did not make it practicable for anyone to do so – there was little point, for example, of anyone devising a formal system of accounting if the people who would be required to 'do' accounting did not know how to read or write.

One accounting scholar (A. C. Littleton) suggested that seven key ingredients which were required before a formal system could be developed existed when Pacioli wrote his treatise:

● *Private property*. The power to change ownership exists and there is a need to record the transaction.
● *Capital*. Wealth is productively employed such that transactions are sufficiently important to make their recording worthwhile and cost-effective.
● *Commerce*. The exchange of goods on a widespread level. The volume of transactions needs to be sufficiently high to motivate someone to devise a formal organised system that could be applied universally to record transactions.
● *Credit*. The present use of future goods. Cash transactions, where money is exchanged for goods, do not require that any details be recorded of who the customer or supplier was. The existence of a system of buying and selling on credit (i.e. paying later for goods and services

purchased today) led to the need for a formal organised system that could be applied universally to record credit transactions.

● *Writing*. A mechanism for making a permanent record in a common language. Writing had clearly been around for a long time prior to Pacioli but it was, nevertheless, an essential element required before accounting could be formalised.
● *Money*. There needs to be a common denominator for exchange. So long as barter was used rather than payment with currency, there was no need for a bookkeeping system based upon transactions undertaken using a uniform set of monetary values.
● *Arithmetic*. As with writing, this has clearly been in existence far longer than accounting. Nevertheless, it is clearly the case that without an ability to perform simple arithmetic, there was no possibility that a formal organised system of accounting could be devised.

When accounting information was being recorded in the Middle Ages it sometimes simply took the form of a collection of invoices (which each show the details of a transaction) and receipts (which each confirm that a payment has been made) which were used by the owner to calculate the profit or loss of the business up to some point in time. This practice persists to this day in many small businesses.

The accountant of the Middle Ages would be someone who had learnt how to convert the financial transaction data (i.e. the data recorded on invoices and receipts, etc.) into accounting information. Quite often, it would be the owner of the business who performed all the accounting tasks. Otherwise, an employee would be given the job of maintaining the accounting records.

As businesses grew in size, so it became less common for the owner to personally maintain the accounting records and more usual for someone to be employed as an accounts clerk. Then, as companies began to dominate the business environment, managers became separated from owners – the owners of companies (shareholders) often have no involvement in the day-to-day running of the business. This led to a need for some monitoring of the managers. Auditing of the financial records became the norm and this, effectively, established the accounting profession.

The first national body of accountants, the Institute of Chartered Accountants of Scotland, was formed in 1854 and other national bodies began to emerge gradually throughout the world, with the English Institute of Chartered Accountants being formed in 1880 and the first US national accounting body being formed in 1887.

If you wish to discover more about the history of accounting, you will find that it is readily available on the World Wide Web. Perform a search on either of the terms 'history of accounting' or 'accounting history' and you should find more information than you could ever realistically read on the subject.

The objectives of accounting

Accounting has many objectives, including letting people and organisations know:

● if they are making a profit or a loss;
● what their business is worth;
● what a transaction was worth to them;
● how much cash they have;
● how wealthy they are;
● how much they are owed;
● how much they owe to someone else;
● enough information so that they can keep a financial check on the things they do.

However, the primary objective of accounting is to provide information for decision-making. The information is usually financial, but can also be given in volumes, for example the number of cars sold in a month by a car dealership or the number of cows in a farmer's herd.

So, for example, if a business recorded what it sold, to whom, the date it was sold, the price at which it was sold, and the date it received payment from the customer, along with similar data concerning the purchases it made, certain information could be produced summarising what had taken place. The profitability of the business and the financial status of the business could also be identified, at any particular point in time. It is the primary objective of accounting to take such information and convert it into a form that is useful for decision-making.

People and businesses

Accounting is something that affects people in their personal lives just as much as it affects very large businesses. We all use accounting ideas when we plan what we are going to do with our money. We have to plan how much of it we will spend and how much we will save. We may write down a plan, known as a **budget**, or we may simply keep it in our minds.

Recording accounting data

However, when people talk about accounting, they are normally referring to accounting as used by businesses and other organisations. The owners cannot remember all the details so they have to keep records of it.

Organisations not only record cash received and paid out. They will also record goods bought and sold, items bought to use rather than to sell, and so on. This part of accounting is usually called the *recording of data*.

Classifying and summarising

When the data is being recorded it has to be organised so as to be most useful to the business. This is known as *classifying* and *summarising* data.

Following such classifications and summaries it will be possible to work out how much profit or loss has been made by the business during a particular period. It will also be possible to show what resources are owned by the business, and what is owed by it, on the closing date of the period.

Communicating information

From the data, people skilled in accounting should be able to tell whether or not the business is performing well financially. They should be able to ascertain the strengths and weaknesses of the business.

Finally, they should be able to tell or *communicate* their results to the owners of the business, or to others allowed to receive this information.

Accounting is, therefore, concerned with:

● recording data;
● classifying and summarising data;
● communicating what has been learnt from the data.

1.2 What is bookkeeping?

Until about one hundred years ago all accounting data was *kept* by being recorded manually in *books*. This is why the part of accounting that is concerned with recording data is often known as **bookkeeping**.

Nowadays, although hand-written books may be used (particularly by smaller organisations), most accounting data is recorded electronically and stored electronically using computers.

Bookkeeping is the process of recording data relating to accounting transactions in the accounting books.

1.3 Accounting is concerned with . . .

Accounting is concerned with the uses which accountants might make of the bookkeeping information given to them. This book will cover many such uses.

1.4 Users of accounting information

Possible users of accounting information include:

● *Managers*. These are the day-to-day decision-makers. They need to know how well things are progressing financially and about the financial status of the business.
● *Owner(s) of the business*. They want to be able to see whether or not the business is profitable. In addition they want to know what the financial resources of the business are.
● *A prospective buyer*. When the owner wants to sell a business the buyer will want to see such information.
● *The bank*. If the owner wants to borrow money for use in the business, then the bank will need such information.
● *Tax inspectors*. They need it to be able to calculate the taxes payable.
● *A prospective partner*. If the owner wants to share ownership with someone else, then the would-be partner will want such information.
● *Investors*, either existing ones or potential ones. They want to know whether or not to invest their money in the business.

There are many other users of accounting information – suppliers and employees, for example. One obvious fact is that without properly recorded accounting data a business would have many difficulties providing the information these various users (often referred to as '**stakeholders**') require.

However, the information produced by accounting needs to be a compromise – so many different groups of stakeholders make it impossible to produce accounting information at a reasonable cost in a form that suits them all. As a result, accounting focuses on producing information for owners. The other stakeholder groups often find the accounting information provided fails to tell them what they really want to know. However, if organisations made the effort to satisfy the information needs of all stakeholders, accounting would be a very costly exercise indeed!

1.5 The accounting equation

By adding up what the accounting records say belongs to a business and deducting what they say the business owes, you can identify what a business is worth according to those accounting records. The whole of financial accounting is based upon this very simple idea. It is known as the *accounting equation*.

It can be explained by saying that if a business is to be set up and start trading, it will need resources. Let's assume first that it is the owner of the business who has supplied all of the resources. This can be shown as:

> **Resources supplied by the owner = Resources in the business**

In accounting, special terms are used to describe many things. The amount of the resources supplied by the owner is called **capital**. The actual resources that are then in the business are called **assets**. This means that when the owner has supplied all of the resources, the accounting equation can be shown as:

$$\text{Capital} = \text{Assets}$$

Usually, however, people other than the owner have supplied some of the assets. **Liabilities** is the name given to the amounts owing to these people for these assets. The accounting equation has now changed to:

$$\text{Capital} = \text{Assets} - \text{Liabilities}$$

This is the most common way in which the accounting equation is presented. It can be seen that the two sides of the equation will have the same totals. This is because we are dealing with the same thing from two different points of view – the value of the owners' investment in the business and the value of what is owned by the owners.

Activity 1.1 What piece of useful information that is available from these three items is not directly shown by this equation? (*Hint*: you were introduced to it at the start of this section.)

Resources in the business

Unfortunately, with this form of the accounting equation, we can no longer see at a glance what value is represented by the resources in the business. You can see this more clearly if you switch assets and capital around to produce the alternate form of the accounting equation:

$$\text{Assets} = \text{Capital} + \text{Liabilities}$$

This can then be replaced with words describing the resources of the business:

$$\text{Resources: what they are} = \text{Resources: who supplied them}$$
$$\text{(Assets)} \qquad \text{(Capital + Liabilities)}$$

It is a fact that no matter how you present the accounting equation, the totals of both sides will *always* equal each other, and that this will *always* be true no matter how many transactions there may be. The actual assets, capital and liabilities may change, but the total of the assets will always equal the total of capital + liabilities. Or, reverting to the more common form of the accounting equation, the capital will always equal the assets of the business minus the liabilities.

Assets consist of property of all kinds, such as buildings, machinery, stocks of goods and motor vehicles. Other assets include debts owed by customers and the amount of money in the organisation's bank account.

Liabilities include amounts owed by the business for goods and services supplied to the business and for expenses incurred by the business that have not yet been paid for. They also include funds borrowed by the business.

Capital is often called the owner's **equity** or net worth. It comprises the funds invested in the business by the owner plus any profits retained for use in the business less any share of profits paid out of the business to the owner.

Activity 1.2 What else would affect capital? (*Hint*: this item causes the value of capital to fall.)

Inflation

1.6 The balance sheet and the effects of business transactions

The accounting equation is expressed in a financial position statement called the **balance sheet**.

> **Activity 1.3** Without looking back, write down the commonly used form of the accounting equation.

The balance sheet shows the financial position of an organisation at a point in time. In other words, it presents a snapshot of the organisation at the date for which it was prepared. The balance sheet is not the first accounting record to be made, nor the first that you will learn how to do, but it is a convenient place to start to consider accounting.

Let's now look at how a series of transactions affect the balance sheet.

1 The introduction of capital

On 1 May 2007, B Blake started in business and deposited £60,000 into a bank account opened specially for the business. The balance sheet would show:

B Blake
Balance Sheet as at 1 May 2007

	£
Assets: Cash at bank	60,000
Capital	60,000

Note how the top part of the balance sheet contains the assets and the bottom part contains the capital. This is always the way the information is presented in a balance sheet.

2 The purchase of an asset by cheque

On 3 May 2007, Blake buys a small shop for £32,000, paying by cheque. The effect of this transaction on the balance sheet is that the cash at the bank is decreased and the new asset, building, is added:

B Blake
Balance Sheet as at 3 May 2007

Assets	£
Shop	32,000
Cash at bank	28,000
	60,000
Capital	60,000

Note how the two parts of the balance sheet 'balance'. That is, their totals are the same. This is always the case with balance sheets.

3 The purchase of an asset and the incurring of a liability

On 6 May 2007, Blake buys some goods for £7,000 from D Smith, and agrees to pay for them some time within the next two weeks. The effect of this is that a new asset, **stock** of goods, is acquired, and a liability for the goods is created. A person to whom money is owed for goods is known in accounting language as a **creditor**. The balance sheet becomes:

B Blake
Balance Sheet as at 6 May 2007

Assets	£
Shop	32,000
Stock of goods	7,000
Cash at bank	28,000
	67,000
Less: Creditor	(7,000)
	60,000
Capital	60,000

Note how the liability (the creditor) is shown as a deduction from the assets. This is exactly the same calculation as is presented in the most common form of the accounting equation.

 Activity 1.4 Why do you think the £7,000 value for creditors is shown in brackets?

Now, let's return to our example.

4 Sale of an asset on credit

On 10 May 2007, goods which cost £600 were sold to J Brown for the same amount, the money to be paid later. The effect is a reduction in the stock of goods and the creation of a new asset. A person who owes the business money is known in accounting language as a **debtor**. The balance sheet is now:

B Blake
Balance Sheet as at 10 May 2007

Assets	£
Shop	32,000
Stock of goods	6,400
Debtor	600
Cash at bank	28,000
	67,000
Less: Creditor	(7,000)
	60,000
Capital	60,000

5 Sale of an asset for immediate payment

On 13 May 2007, goods which cost £400 were sold to D Daley for the same amount. Daley paid for them immediately by cheque. Here one asset, stock of goods, is reduced, while another asset, cash at bank, is increased. The balance sheet becomes:

B Blake
Balance Sheet as at 13 May 2007

Assets	£
Shop	32,000
Stock of goods	6,000
Debtor	600
Cash at bank	28,400
	67,000
Less: Creditor	(7,000)
	60,000
Capital	60,000

6 The payment of a liability

On 15 May 2007, Blake pays a cheque for £3,000 to D Smith in part payment of the amount owing. The asset of cash at bank is therefore reduced, and the liability to the creditor is also reduced. The balance sheet is now:

B Blake
Balance Sheet as at 15 May 2007

Assets	£
Shop	32,000
Stock of goods	6,000
Debtor	600
Cash at bank	25,400
	64,000
Less: Creditor	(4,000)
	60,000
Capital	60,000

Note how the total of each part of the balance sheet has not changed. The business is still worth £60,000 to the owner.

7 Collection of an asset

J Brown, who owed Blake £600, makes a part payment of £200 by cheque on 31 May 2007. The effect is to reduce one asset, debtor, and to increase another asset, cash at bank. The balance sheet becomes:

B Blake
Balance Sheet as at 31 May 2007

Assets	£
Shop	32,000
Stock of goods	6,000
Debtor	400
Cash at bank	25,600
	64,000
Less: Creditor	(4,000)
	60,000
Capital	60,000

1.7 Equality of the accounting equation

It can be seen that every transaction has affected two items. Sometimes it has changed two assets by reducing one and increasing the other. In other cases, the effect has been different. However, in each case other than the very first (when the business was started by the owner injecting some cash into it), no change was made to the total of either section of the balance sheet and the equality between their two totals has been maintained. The accounting equation has held true throughout the example, and it always will. The effect of each of these seven accounting transactions upon the two sections of the balance sheet is shown below:

Number of transaction as above	Assets	Capital and Liabilities	Effect on balance sheet totals
1	+	+	Each side added to equally
2	+ −		A *plus* and a *minus* both on the assets side *cancelling out* each other
3	+	+	Each side has equal increases
4	+ −		A *plus* and a *minus* both on the assets side *cancelling out* each other
5	+ −		A *plus* and a *minus* both on the assets side *cancelling out* each other
6	−	−	Each side has equal deductions
7	+ −		A *plus* and a *minus* both on the assets side *cancelling out* each other

These are not the only types of accounting transactions that can take place. Two other examples arise when the owner withdraws resources from the business for his or her own use; and where the owner pays a business expense personally.

A summary of the effect upon assets, liabilities and capital of each type of transaction you've been introduced to so far is shown below:

Example of transaction	Effect	
(1) Owner pays capital into the bank	↑ Increase asset (Bank)	↑ Increase capital
(2) Buy goods by cheque	↓ Decrease asset (Bank)	↑ Increase asset (Stock of goods)
(3) Buy goods on credit	↑ Increase asset (Stock of goods)	↑ Increase liability (Creditors)
(4) Sale of goods on credit	↓ Decrease asset (Stock of goods)	↑ Increase asset (Debtors)
(5) Sale of goods for cash (cheque)	↓ Decrease asset (Stock of goods)	↑ Increase asset (Bank)
(6) Pay creditor	↓ Decrease asset (Bank)	↓ Decrease liability (Creditor)
(7) Debtor pays money owing by cheque	↑ Increase asset (Bank)	↓ Decrease asset (Debtors)
(8) Owner takes money out of the business bank account for own use	↓ Decrease asset (Bank)	↓ Decrease capital
(9) Owner pays creditor from private money outside the firm	↓ Decrease liability (Creditor)	↑ Increase capital

These last two types of transaction do cause the totals of each part of the balance sheet to change (as did the very first, when capital was introduced to the business by the owner). When the capital changes, the totals of the two parts of the balance sheet both change.

1.8 More detailed presentation of the balance sheet

Let's now look at the balance sheet of B Blake as at 31 May 2007, presented in line with how you will learn to present the information later in the book:

B Blake
Balance Sheet as at 31 May 2007

	£	£
Fixed assets		
Shop		32,000
Current assets		
Stock of goods	6,000	
Debtor	400	
Cash at bank	25,600	
	32,000	
Less Current liabilities		
Creditor	(4,000)	
		28,000
		60,000
Capital		60,000

You will have noticed in this balance sheet the terms 'fixed assets', 'current assets' and 'current liabilities'. **Chapter 8 contains a full explanation of these terms.** At this point we will simply say:

● **Fixed assets** are assets which have a long life bought with the intention to use them in the business and not with the intention to simply resell them, e.g. buildings, machinery, fixtures, motor vehicles.
● **Current assets** are assets consisting of cash, goods for resale or items having a short life (i.e. no more than a year remaining on the date of the balance sheet). For example, the value of stock in hand goes up and down as it is bought and sold. Similarly, the amount of money owing to us by debtors will change quickly, as we sell more to them on credit and they pay their debts. The amount of money in the bank will also change as we receive and pay out money.
● **Current liabilities** are those liabilities which have to be paid within no more than a year from the date on the balance sheet, e.g. creditors for goods purchased.

Don't forget that there is a Glossary of accounting terms at the back of the book.

Learning outcomes

You should now have learnt that:

1 Accounting is concerned with the recording and classifying and summarising of data, and then communicating what has been learned from it.

2 Accounting has existed for at least 5,500 years but a formal, generally accepted method of recording accounting data has only been in existence for the last 500 years.

→

3 It may not only be the owner of a business who will need the accounting information. It may need to be shown to others, e.g. the bank or the Inspector of Taxes.

4 Accounting information can help the owner(s) of a business to plan for the future.

5 The accounting equation is: Capital = Assets − Liabilities.

6 The two sides of the accounting equation are represented by the two parts of the balance sheet.

7 The totals of one part of the balance sheet should always be equal to the total of the other part.

8 Every transaction affects two items in the accounting equation. Sometimes that may involve the same item being affected twice, once positively (going up) and once negatively (going down).

9 Every transaction affects two items in the balance sheet.

Note: Generally, the values used in exhibits and exercises have been kept down to relatively small amounts. This has been done deliberately to make the work of the student that much easier. Constantly handling large figures does not add anything to the study of the principles of accounting. Instead, it simply wastes a lot of the student's time, and he/she will probably make far more errors if larger figures are used.

Doing this may lead to the authors being accused of not being 'realistic' with the figures given, but we believe that it is far more important to make learning easier for the student.

Answers to activities

1.1 Who supplied the resources of the business.

1.2 Capital will be reduced if a business makes a loss. The loss means that assets have been reduced and capital is reduced by the same amount so as to maintain the balance in the accounting equation.

1.3 Capital = Assets − Liabilities

1.4 It is a negative number. In accounting, we <u>always</u> use brackets to indicate negative numbers.

Review questions

If you haven't already started answering them, you now have a set of graded review questions to try. 'Graded' means that they get more difficult as you go through them. Ideally, they should be done in the sequence they appear. *However, don't forget that the questions with an 'A' after the question number do not have any answers provided in this book.* Your teacher or lecturer will be able to provide you with the answers to those questions but be sure to attempt them first before asking for the answers! The answers to the other questions can be found at the back of the book.

We realise that you would like to have *all* the answers in the book. However, teachers and lecturers would not then be able to test your knowledge with questions from this book, as you would already possess the answers. It is impossible to please everyone, and the compromise reached is that of putting a large number of review questions in the book.

This means that appropriate reinforcement of what you have learnt can take place, even if you are studying on your own and have to miss out all the 'A' questions because you have no access to the answers.

Multiple choice questions. In addition to these review questions, there are questions relating to the material in this chapter among a bank of multiple choice questions at the end of Chapter 6. You should wait and attempt them when you reach them, not before.

1.1 Complete the gaps in the following table:

	Assets	Liabilities	Capital
	£	£	£
(a)	25,000	3,000	?
(b)	14,000	7,100	?
(c)	21,000	?	18,300
(d)	107,000	?	65,000
(e)	?	74,000	180,000
(f)	?	9,500	28,000

1.2A Complete the gaps in the following table:

	Assets	Liabilities	Capital
	£	£	£
(a)	55,000	16,900	?
(b)	?	17,200	34,400
(c)	36,100	?	28,500
(d)	119,500	15,400	?
(e)	88,000	?	62,000
(f)	?	49,000	110,000

1.3 Which of the items in the following list are liabilities and which of them are assets?

(a) Loan to C Shirley
(b) Bank overdraft
(c) Fixtures and fittings
(d) Printers
(e) We owe a supplier for goods
(f) Warehouse we own

1.4A Classify the following items into liabilities and assets:

(a) Motor vehicles
(b) Premises
(c) Creditors for goods
(d) Stock of goods
(e) Debtors
(f) Owing to bank
(g) Cash in hand
(h) Loan from D Jones
(i) Machinery

1.5 State which of the following are wrongly classified:

Assets	Liabilities
Loan from C Smith	Stock of goods
Cash in hand	Creditors
Machinery	Money owing to bank
Debtors	Computer
Premises	Land
Motor vehicles	

$A = C + L$

1.6A   Which of the following are shown under the wrong headings?

Assets	Liabilities
Cash at bank	Loan from J Graham
Fixtures	Machinery
Creditors	Motor vehicles
Building	
Stock of goods	
Debtors	
Capital	

1.7   B Wise is setting up a new business. Before actually selling anything, he bought a van for £4,500, a market stall for £2,000 and a stock of goods for £1,500. He did not pay in full for his stock of goods and still owes £1,000 in respect of them. He borrowed £5,000 from C Fox. After the events just described, and before trading starts, he has £400 cash in hand and £1,100 cash at bank. Calculate the amount of his capital.

1.8A   F Flint is starting a business. Before actually starting to sell anything, he bought fixtures for £1,200; a van for £6,000 and a stock of goods for £2,800. Although he has paid in full for the fixtures and the van, he still owes £1,600 for some of the goods. B Rub lent him £2,500. After the above, Flint has £200 in the business bank account and £175 cash in hand. You are required to calculate his capital.

1.9   Draw up G Putty's balance sheet from the following information as at 31 December 2008:

	£
Capital	7,200
Debtors	1,200
Van	3,800
Creditors	4,100
Fixtures	1,800
Stock of goods	4,200
Cash at bank	300

1.10A   Draw up M Kelly's balance sheet as at 30 June 2006 from the following items:

	£
Capital	10,200
Equipment	3,400
Creditors	4,100
Stock of goods	3,600
Debtors	4,500
Cash at bank	2,800

1.11   Complete the columns to show the effects of the following transactions:

	Effect upon		
	Assets	Liabilities	Capital
(a) We pay a creditor £340 in cash.			
(b) Bought PC £430 paying by cheque.			
(c) Bought goods on credit £1,300.			
(d) The proprietor introduces another £1,500 cash into the business.			
(e) J Walker lends the business £200 in cash.			
(f) A debtor pays us £318 by cheque.			
(g) We return goods costing £147 to a supplier whose bill we had not paid.			
(h) Bought additional shop fittings paying £1,900 by cheque.			

1.12A Complete the columns to show the effects of the following transactions;

	Effect upon		
	Assets	Liabilities	Capital

(a) Bought a van on credit £8,700.
(b) Repaid by cash a loan owed to F Duff £10,000.
(c) Bought goods for £1,400 paying by cheque.
(d) The owner puts a further £4,000 cash into the business.
(e) A debtor returns to us £150 goods. We agree to make an allowance for them.
(f) Bought goods on credit £760.
(g) The owner takes out £200 cash for his personal use
(h) We pay a creditor £1,150 by cheque.

1.13 E Silva has the following items in her balance sheet as on 7 April 2005: Capital £18,370; Creditors £2,100; Fixtures £2,800; Car £6,650; Stock of goods £3,180; Debtors £2,780; Bank £4,150; Cash in hand £910.

During the first week of April 2005

(a) She bought extra stock for goods £910 on credit.
(b) One of the debtors paid her £330 in cash.
(c) She bought a PC by cheque £560.

You are asked to draw up a balance sheet as on 7 April 2005 after the above transactions have been completed.

1.14A J. Hill has the following assets and liabilities as on 30 November 2009: Creditors £2,800; Equipment £6,200; Car £7,300; Stock of goods £8,100; Debtors £4,050; Cash at bank £9,100; Cash in hand £195.

You are not given the capital amount at that date.

During the first week of December 2009

(a) Hill bought extra equipment on credit for £110.
(b) Hill bought extra stock by cheque £380.
(c) Hill paid creditors by cheque £1,150.
(d) Debtors paid Hill £640 by cheque and £90 by cash.
(e) Hill put in an extra £1,500 into the business, £1,300 by cheque and £200 in cash.

You are to draw up a balance sheet as on 7 December 2009 after the above transactions have been completed.

You can find a range of additional self-test questions, as well as material to help you with your studies, on the website that accompanies this book at **www.pearsoned.co.uk/wood**

The double entry system for assets, liabilities and capital

Learning objectives

After you have studied this chapter, you should be able to:

- explain what is meant by 'double entry'
- explain how the double entry system follows the rules of the accounting equation
- explain why each transaction is recorded into individual accounts
- describe the layout of a 'T-account'
- explain what is meant by the terms debit and credit
- explain the phrase 'debit the receiver and credit the giver'
- prepare a table showing how to record increases and decreases of assets, liabilities and capital in the accounts
- enter a series of transactions into T-accounts

Introduction

In this chapter, you will learn how the double entry system is used to record financial transactions and how to use T-accounts, the traditional way to make such entries under the double entry system.

2.1 Nature of a transaction

In Chapter 1, you saw how various events had changed two items in the balance sheet. Events which result in such changes are known as 'transactions'. This means that if the proprietor asks the price of some goods, but does not buy them, then there is no transaction. If the proprietor later asks the price of some other goods, and then buys them, then there would be a transaction, and two balance sheet items would then have to be altered.

2.2 The double entry system

We have seen that every transaction affects two items. We need to show these effects when we first record each transaction. That is, when we enter the data relating to the transaction in the accounting books we need to ensure that the items that were affected by the transaction, and only those items, are shown as having changed. This is the bookkeeping stage of accounting and the process we use is called **double entry**. You will often hear it referred to as **double entry bookkeeping**. Either term is correct.

Activity 2.1 Why do you think it is called 'double entry'?

If we want to show the double effect of every transaction when we are doing our bookkeeping, we have to show the effect of each transaction on each of the two items it affects. For each transaction this means that a bookkeeping entry will have to be made to show an increase or decrease of one item, and another entry to show the increase or decrease of the other item. From this description, you will probably see that the term 'double entry bookkeeping' is a good one, as each entry is made twice (double entry).

At this point, you may be wondering why you can't just draw up a new balance sheet after each transaction, and so provide all the information required.

Activity 2.2 Why can't we just adjust the balance sheet and forget about making entries in any of the accounting books?

Instead of constantly drawing up balance sheets after each transaction what we have instead is the 'double entry' system. The basis of this system is that the transactions which occur are entered in a set of **accounts** within the accounting books. An account is a place where all the information referring to a particular asset or liability, or to capital, is recorded.

Thus, there will be an account where all the information concerning office equipment will be entered. Similarly, there will be an account for buildings, where all the information concerned with buildings will be shown. This will be extended so that every asset, every liability and capital will each have its own account for transactions involving that item.

2.3 The accounts for double entry

Each account should be shown on a separate page in the accounting books. The double entry system divides each page into two halves. The left-hand side of each page is called the **debit** side, while the right-hand side is called the **credit** side. The title of each account is written across the top of the account at the centre.

This is the layout of a page of an accounts book:

Title of account written here

Left-hand side of the page This is the 'debit' side.	*Right-hand side of the page* This is the 'credit' side.

Do you see how the shape resembles a 'T'? Not surprisingly, these are commonly referred to as **T-accounts**:

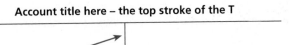

Account title here – the top stroke of the T

This line separates the two sides and is the downstroke of the T

Many students find it very difficult to make correct entries in the accounts because they forget that *debit* and *credit* have special accounting meanings. Don't fall into that trap. You must not confuse any other meanings you know for these two terms with the accounting ones.

You describe the entries in the accounts by saying something like 'debit account "x" with £z and credit account "y" with £z', inserting the names of the accounts and the actual amount in place of x, y, and z. So, for example, if you paid £10 by cheque for a kettle, you could say 'debit the kettle account with £10 and credit the bank account with £10'.

To actually make this entry, you enter £10 on the left-hand (i.e. debit) side of the kettle account and on the right-hand (i.e. credit) side of the bank account.

Kettle account		Bank account	
£ 10			£ 10

You learnt in Chapter 1 that transactions increase or decrease assets, liabilities, or capital. In terms of the assets, liabilities, and capital:

● to **increase** an **asset** we make a DEBIT entry
● to **decrease** an **asset** we make a CREDIT entry
● to **increase** a **liability/capital** account we make a CREDIT entry
● to **decrease** a **liability/capital** account we make a DEBIT entry.

Placing these in a table organised by type of item, the double entry rules for bookkeeping are:

Accounts	To record	Entry in the account
Assets	an increase a decrease	Debit Credit
Liabilities	an increase a decrease	Credit Debit
Capital	an increase a decrease	Credit Debit

Let's look once again at the accounting equation:

	Capital =	Assets −	Liabilities
To increase each item	Credit	Debit	Credit
To decrease each item	Debit	Credit	Debit

The double entry rules for liabilities and capital are the same, but they are the opposite of those for assets. Looking at the accounts the rules will appear as:

Capital account		Any asset account		Any liability account	
Decreases −	Increases +	Increases +	Decreases −	Decreases −	Increases +

In a real business, at least one full page would be taken for each account in the accounting books. However, as we have not enough space in this textbook to put each account on a separate page, we will list the accounts under each other.

2.4 Worked examples

The entry of a few transactions can now be attempted.

1 The owner starts the business with £10,000 in cash on 1 August 2008.

The effects of this transaction are entered as follows:

Effect	Action
1 Increases the *asset* of cash 2 Increases the capital	Debit the cash account Credit the capital account

Cash

2008		£		
Aug 1		10,000		

Capital

			2008		£
			Aug 1		10,000

The date of the transaction has already been entered. (**Never forget to enter the date of each transaction.**) Now there remains the description (often referred to as the 'narrative') which is to be entered alongside the amount. This is completed by a cross-reference to the title of the other account in which the double entry is completed. The double entry to the item in the cash account is completed by an entry in the capital account. Therefore the word 'Capital' will appear as the narrative in the cash account:

Cash

2008		£		
Aug 1	Capital	10,000		

Similarly, the double entry to the item in the capital account is completed by an entry in the cash account, so the word 'Cash' will appear in the capital account:

Capital

			2008		£
			Aug 1	Cash	10,000

2 A van is bought for £4,500 cash on 2 August 2008.

Effect	Action
1 Increases the *asset* of van 2 Decreases the *asset* of cash	Debit the van account Credit the cash account

Van

2008		£		
Aug 2	Cash	4,500		

Cash

		2008			£
		Aug	2	Van	4,500

3 Fixtures (e.g. shelves) are bought on credit from Shop Fitters for £1,250 on 3 August 2008.

Effect	Action
1 Increases the *asset* of fixtures	Debit the fixtures account
2 Increases the *liability* to Shop Fitters	Credit the Shop Fitters account

Fixtures

2008			£		
Aug	3	Shop Fitters	1,250		

Shop Fitters

			2008		£
			Aug 3 Fixtures		1,250

Note how the liability of creditors is split in the accounting books so that a separate account is maintained for each creditor.

4 Paid the amount owing to Shop Fitters in cash on 17 August 2008.

Effect	Action
1 Decreases the *liability* to Shop Fitters	Debit the Shop Fitters account
2 Decreases the *asset* of cash	Credit the cash account

Shop Fitters

2008			£		
Aug	17	Cash	1,250		

Cash

		2008			£
		Aug	17	Shop Fitters	1,250

5 Transactions to date.

Combining all four of these transactions, the accounts now contain:

Cash

2008			£	2008			£
Aug	1	Capital	10,000	Aug	2	Van	4,500
					17	Shop Fitters	1,250

Capital

		2008			£
		Aug	1	Cash	10,000

Van

2008		£			
Aug 2	Cash	4,500			

Shop Fitters

2008		£	2008		£
Aug 17	Cash	1,250	Aug 3	Fixtures	1,250

Fixtures

2008		£		
Aug 3	Shop Fitters	1,250		

Note how you enter each transaction in an account in date order and how, once you open an account (e.g. Shop Fitters), you continue to make entries in it rather than opening a new account for every entry.

> Before you read further, work through Review Questions 2.1 and 2.2A.

2.5 A further worked example

Have you noticed how each column of figures is headed by a '£' sign? This is important. You always need to indicate what the figures represent. In this case, it is £s, in other cases you will meet during this book, the figures may be thousands of pounds (represented by '£000') or they could be in a different currency altogether. **Always include appropriate column headings.**

Now you have actually made some entries in accounts, go carefully through the following example. Make certain you can understand every entry and, if you have any problems, reread the first four sections of this chapter until you are confident that you know and understand what you are doing.

First, here is a table showing a series of transactions, their effects and the double entry action to take:

Transactions	Effect	Action
2008 May 1 Started a household machines business putting £25,000 into a business bank account.	Increases *asset* of bank. Increases *capital* of owner.	Debit bank account. Credit capital account.
3 Bought equipment on credit from House Supplies £12,000.	Increases *asset* of equipment. Increases *liability* to House Supplies.	Debit equipment account. Credit House Supplies account.
4 Withdrew £150 cash from the bank and placed it in the cash box.	Increases *asset* of cash. Decreases *asset* of bank.	Debit cash account. Credit bank account.

Transactions	Effect	Action
2008 **May 7** Bought a van paying by cheque, £6,800.	↑ Increases *asset* of van. ↓ Decreases *asset* of bank.	Debit van account. Credit bank account.
10 Sold some equipment that was not needed at cost of £1,100 on credit to J Rose.	↑ Increases *asset* of money owing from J Rose. ↓ Decreases *asset* of equipment.	Debit J Rose account. Credit equipment account.
21 Returned some of the equipment costing £2,300 to House Supplies.	↓ Decreases *liability* to House Supplies. ↓ Decreases *asset* of equipment.	Debit House Supplies. Credit equipment account.
28 J Rose pays the amount owing of £1,100, by cheque.	↑ Increases *asset* of bank. ↓ Decreases *asset* of money owing by J Rose.	Debit bank account. Credit J Rose account.
30 Bought another van paying by cheque £4,300.	↑ Increases *asset* of vans. ↓ Decreases *asset* of bank.	Debit van account. Credit bank account.
31 Paid £9,700 to House Supplies by cheque.	↓ Decreases *liability* to House Supplies. ↓ Decreases *asset* of bank.	Debit House Supplies. Credit bank account.

You may find it worthwhile trying to enter all these transactions in T-accounts before reading any further. You will need to know that, similarly to creditors, the asset of debtors is split in the accounting books so that a separate account is maintained for each debtor. You will need accounts for Bank, Cash, Capital, Equipment, Vans, House Supplies, and J Rose.

In T-account form this is shown:

Bank

2008			£	2008			£
May	1	Capital	25,000	May	4	Cash	150
					7	Van	6,800
	28	J Rose	1,100		30	Van	4,300
					31	House Supplies	9,700

Cash

2008			£		
May	4	Bank	150		

Capital

2008				2008			£
				May	1	Bank	25,000

Equipment

2008			£	2008			£
May	3	House Supplies	12,000	May	10	J Rose	1,100
					21	House Supplies	2,300

Vans

2008			£		
May	7	Bank	6,800		
	30	Bank	4,300		

House Supplies

2008			£	2008			£
May	21	Equipment	2,300	May	3	Equipment	12,000
	31	Bank	9,700				

J Rose

2008			£	2008			£
May	10	Equipment	1,100	May	28	Bank	1,100

If you tried to do this before looking at the answer, be sure you understand any mistakes you made before going on.

2.6 Abbreviation of 'limited'

In this book, when we come across transactions with limited companies the letters 'Ltd' are used as the abbreviation for 'Limited Company'. So, if you see the name of a business is 'W Jones Ltd', it is a limited company. In our accounting books, transactions with W Jones Ltd will be entered in the same way as for any other customer or supplier. It will be seen later that some limited companies use plc (which stands for 'public limited company') instead of Ltd.

2.7 Value Added Tax (VAT)

You may have noticed that VAT has not been mentioned in the examples covered so far. This is deliberate, so you are not confused as you learn the basic principles of accounting. In Chapter 19, you will be introduced to VAT and shown how to make the entries relating to it.

Learning outcomes

You should now have learnt:

1 That double entry follows the rules of the accounting equation.

2 That double entry maintains the principle that every debit has a corresponding credit entry.

3 That double entries are made in accounts in the accounting books.

4 Why each transaction is entered into accounts rather than directly into the balance sheet.

→ **5** How transactions cause increases and decreases in asset, liability, and capital accounts.

6 How to record transactions in T-accounts.

Answers to activities

2.1 Each transaction is entered twice. In an accounting transaction, something always 'gives' and something 'receives' and both aspects of the transaction must be recorded. In other words, there is a double entry in the accounting books – each transaction is entered twice.

2.2 A balance sheet is a financial statement that summarises the financial position of an organisation at a point in time. It does not present enough information about the organisation to make it appropriate to enter each transaction directly on to the balance sheet. It does not, for instance, tell who the debtors are and how much each one of them owes the organisation, nor who the creditors are and the details of the amounts owing to each of them. We need to maintain a record of each individual transaction so that (a) we know what occurred and (b) we can check to see that it was correctly recorded.

Review questions

2.1 Complete the following table:

	Account to be debited	Account to be credited
(a) Bought office machinery on credit from D Isaacs Ltd.		
(b) The proprietor paid a creditor, C Jones, from his private funds.		
(c) A debtor, N Fox, paid us in cash.		
(d) Repaid part of loan from P Exeter by cheque.		
(e) Returned some of office machinery to D Isaacs Ltd.		
(f) A debtor, N Lyn, pays us by cheque.		
(g) Bought van by cash.		

2.2A Complete the following table:

	Account to be debited	Account to be credited
(a) Bought lorry for cash.		
(b) Paid creditor, T Lake, by cheque.		
(c) Repaid P Logan's loan by cash.		
(d) Sold lorry for cash.		
(e) Bought office machinery on credit from Ultra Ltd.		
(f) A debtor, A Hill, pays us by cash.		
(g) A debtor, J Cross, pays us by cheque.		
(h) Proprietor puts a further amount into the business by cheque.		
(i) A loan of £200 in cash is received from L Lowe.		
(j) Paid a creditor, D Lord, by cash.		

2.3 Write up the asset and liability and capital accounts to record the following transactions in the records of J Beanie:

2007
July 1 Started business with £25,000 in the bank.
      2 Bought office furniture by cheque £800.
      3 Bought printers £700 on credit from Fullcrop Ltd.
      5 Bought a van paying by cheque £8,100.

8 Sold some of the office furniture – not suitable for the business – for £90 on credit to P Dove Ltd.
15 Paid the amount owing to Fullcrop Ltd £700 by cheque.
23 Received the amount due from P Dove Ltd £90 in cash.
31 Bought machinery by cheque £800.

2.4 You are required to open the asset and liability and capital accounts and record the following transactions for June 2008 in the records of P Bernard:

2008
June 1 Started business with £12,000 in cash.
2 Paid £11,700 of the opening cash into a bank account for the business.
5 Bought office furniture on credit from Dream Ltd for £1,900.
8 Bought a van paying by cheque £5,250.
12 Bought equipment from Pearce & Sons on credit £2,300.
18 Returned faulty office furniture costing £120 to Dream Ltd.
25 Sold some of the equipment for £200 cash.
26 Paid amount owing to Dream Ltd £1,780 by cheque.
28 Took £130 out of the bank and added to cash.
30 F Brown lent us £4,000 – giving us the money by cheque.

2.5A Write up the asset, capital and liability accounts in the books of D Gough to record the following transactions:

2009
June 1 Started business with £16,000 in the bank.
2 Bought van paying by cheque £6,400.
5 Bought office fixtures £900 on credit from Old Ltd.
8 Bought van on credit from Carton Cars Ltd £7,100.
12 Took £180 out of the bank and put it into the cash till.
15 Bought office fixtures paying by cash £120.
19 Paid Carton Cars Ltd a cheque for £7,100.
21 A loan of £500 cash is received from B Berry.
25 Paid £400 of the cash in hand into the bank account.
30 Bought more office fixtures paying by cheque £480.

2.6A Write up the accounts to record the following transactions:

2007
March 1 Started business with £750 cash and £9,000 in the bank.
2 Received a loan of £2,000 from B Blane by cheque.
3 Bought a computer for cash £600.
5 Bought display equipment on credit from Clearcount Ltd £420.
8 Took £200 out of the bank and put it in the cash till.
15 Repaid part of Blane's loan by cheque £500.
17 Paid amount owing to Clearcount Ltd £420 by cheque.
24 Repaid part of Blane's loan by cash £250.
31 Bought a printer on credit from F Jones for £200.

You can find a range of additional self-test questions, as well as material to help you with your studies, on the website that accompanies this book at **www.pearsoned.co.uk/wood**

Stock

Learning objectives

After you have studied this chapter, you should be able to:

- explain why it is inappropriate to use a stock account to record increases and decreases in stock
- describe the two causes of stock increasing
- describe the two causes of stock decreasing
- explain the difference between a purchase account and a returns inwards account
- explain the difference between a sales account and a returns outwards account
- explain how to record increases and decreases of stock in the appropriate accounts
- explain the meanings of the terms 'purchases' and 'sales' as used in accounting
- explain the differences in recording purchases on credit as compared to recording purchases that are paid for immediately in cash
- explain the differences in recording sales on credit as compared to recording sales that are paid for immediately in cash

Introduction

In this chapter, you will learn how to record movements in stock in the appropriate ledger accounts and how to record purchases and sales on credit, as opposed to purchases and sales for cash.

3.1 Stock movements

In the examples in Chapter 1, goods were sold at the same price at which they were bought. This is, of course, extremely unusual. In fact, any new business doing this wouldn't last terribly long. Businesses need to make profits to survive, as many 'dot.com' Internet companies discovered in 2000 when their bubble burst and all the losses they had been making took effect.

Normally, goods and services are sold above cost price, the difference being **profit**. As you know, when goods and services are sold for less than their cost, the difference is a **loss**.

Activity 3.1

Let's think about the double entry implications if all sales were at cost price. Fill in the blanks in the following:

As we did in Chapter 1, it would be possible to have a stock account with goods purchased being _____ to the stock account (as purchases represent __ _____ in the asset, stock) and goods sold being _____ to it (as sales represent __ _____ in the asset, stock).

The difference between the two sides of the stock account would then represent the cost of the goods unsold at that date. (We'll ignore things like wastage, obsolescence, and losses of stock for now.)

However, most sales are not priced at cost and, therefore, the sales figures include elements of profit or loss. Because of this, in most cases, the difference between the two sides of the stock account would not represent the cost of the stock of goods. Maintaining a stock account on this basis would therefore serve no useful purpose.

To address this, we subdivide the way stock is reported into several accounts, each one showing a movement of stock. Firstly, we must distinguish between transactions that cause stock to increase and those that cause stock to decrease. Let's deal with each of these in turn.

1 **Increase in stock.** This can be due to one of two causes:
   (a) The purchase of additional goods.
   (b) The return in to the business of goods previously sold. The reasons for this are numerous. The goods may have been the wrong type; they may, for example, have been surplus to requirements or faulty.

To distinguish the two aspects of the increase of stocks of goods, two accounts are opened:
   (i) a **Purchases Account** – in which purchases of goods are entered; and
   (ii) a **Returns Inwards Account** – in which goods being returned in to the business are entered. (Another name for this account is the **Sales Returns Account**.)

So, for *increases* in stock, we need to choose which of these two accounts to use to record the *debit* side of the transaction.

2 **Decrease in stock.** Ignoring things like wastage and theft, this can be due to one of two causes:
   (a) The sale of goods.
   (b) Goods previously bought by the business now being returned to the supplier.

Once again, in order to distinguish the two aspects of the decrease of stocks of goods, two accounts are opened:
   (i) a **Sales Account** – in which sales of goods are entered; and
   (ii) a **Returns Outwards Account** – in which goods being returned out to a supplier are entered. (This is also known as the **Purchases Returns Account**.)

So, for *decreases* in stock, we need to choose which of these two accounts to use to record the *credit* side of the transaction.

As stock is an asset, and these four accounts are all connected with this asset, the double entry rules are those used for assets.

Activity 3.2

What are the double entry rules for assets?

Accounts	To record	Entry in the account
Assets	an increase	_____
	a decrease	_____

We shall now look at some entries in the following sections.

3.2 Purchase of stock on credit

On 1 August 2008, goods costing £165 are bought on credit from D Henry. First, the twofold effect of the transaction must be considered so that the bookkeeping entries can be worked out.

1 The asset of stock is increased. An increase in an asset needs a debit entry in an account. Here the account is one designed for this type of stock movement. It is clearly a 'purchase' movement so that the account to use must be the purchases account.
2 There is an increase in a liability. This is the liability of the business to D Henry because the goods bought have not yet been paid for. An increase in a liability needs a credit entry. In this case, it would be a credit entry to D Henry's account.

These two entries appear in the accounts as:

Purchases

2008		£	
Aug 1 D Henry		165	

D Henry

		2008		£
		Aug 1 Purchases		165

Note that these entries look identical to those you would make if you were using a stock account rather than a purchases account. (The word 'stock' would replace 'purchases' if a stock account were being used.)

3.3 Purchases of stock for cash

On 2 August 2008, goods costing £310 are bought, cash being paid for them immediately at the time of purchase.

1 As before, it is the asset of stock that is increased, so a debit entry will be needed. The movement of stock is that of a 'purchase', so the purchases account needs to be debited.
2 The asset of cash is decreased. To reduce an asset a credit entry is called for, and the asset is cash, so we need to credit the cash account.

Purchases

2008		£	
Aug 2 Cash		310	

Cash

		2008		£
		Aug 2 Purchases		310

3.4 Sales of stock on credit

On 3 August 2008, goods were sold on credit for £375 to J Lee.

1 An asset account is <u>increased.</u> The increase in the asset of debtors requires a debit and the debtor is J Lee, so that the account concerned is that of J Lee.

2 The asset of <u>stock</u> is decreased. For this a credit entry to reduce an asset is needed. The movement of stock is clearly the result of a 'sale' and so it is the sales account that needs to be credited.

J Lee

2008	£	
Aug 3 Sales	375	

Sales   *Credit*

	2008	£
	Aug 3 J Lee	375

3.5 Sales of stock for cash

On 4 August 2008, goods are sold for £55, cash being received immediately at the time of sale.

1 The asset of cash is increased, so the cash account must be debited.

2 The asset of stock is reduced. The reduction of an asset requires a credit and the movement of stock is represented by 'sales'. Thus the entry needed is a credit in the sales account.

Cash

2008	£	
Aug 4 Sales	55	

Sales

	2008	£
	Aug 4 Cash	55

So far, so good. Apart from replacing the stock account with the purchases account for stock increases and the sales account for stock decreases, you've done nothing different in your entries to the accounts compared with what you learnt in Chapters 1 and 2.

> Go back to Chapters 1 and 2, and refresh your understanding of account entries.

Now let's look at the other stock-related transactions that cause stocks to increase and decrease – returns inwards (sales that are being returned) and returns outwards (purchases that are being returned to the supplier).

3.6 Returns inwards

On 5 August 2008, goods which had been previously sold to F Lowe for £29 are now returned *to the business*. This could be for various reasons such as:

● we sent goods of the wrong size, the wrong colour or the wrong model;
● the goods may have been damaged in transit;
● the goods are of poor quality.

1 The asset of stock is increased by the goods returned. Thus, a debit representing an increase of an asset is needed. This time, the movement of stock is that of 'returns inwards'. The entry required is a debit in the *Returns Inwards account*.

2 There is a decrease in an asset. The debt of F Lowe to the business is now reduced. A credit is needed in F Lowe's account to record this.

Returns Inwards

2008		£	
Aug 5 F Lowe		29	

F Lowe

		2008		£
		Aug 5 Returns inwards		29

(Remember, another name for the Returns Inwards account is the 'Sales Returns account'.)

3.7 Returns outwards

On 6 August 2008, goods previously bought for £96 are returned *by the business* to K Howe.

1 The liability of the business to K Howe is decreased by the value of the goods returned. The decrease in a liability needs a debit, this time in K Howe's account.
2 The asset of stock is decreased by the goods sent out. Thus, a credit representing a reduction in an asset is needed. The movement of stock is that of 'returns outwards' so the entry will be a credit in the *Returns Outwards account*.

K Howe

2008		£	
Aug 6 Returns outwards		96	

Returns Outwards

		2008		£
		Aug 6 K Howe		96

(Remember, another name for the Returns Outwards account is the 'Purchases Returns account'.)

You're probably thinking this is all very straightforward. Well, let's see how much you have learnt by looking at two review questions.

Before you read further, work through Review Questions 3.1 and 3.2.

3.8 A worked example

2009
May   1   Bought goods on credit £220 from D Small.
2   Bought goods on credit £410 from A Lyon & Son.
5   Sold goods on credit to D Hughes for £60.
6   Sold goods on credit to M Spencer for £45.
10   Returned goods £15 to D Small.
11   Goods sold for cash £210.
12   Goods bought for cash £150.
19   M Spencer returned £16 goods to us.

21 Goods sold for cash £175.
22 Paid cash to D Small £205.
30 D Hughes paid the amount owing by him £60 in cash.
31 Bought goods on credit £214 from A Lyon & Son.

You may find it worthwhile trying to enter all these transactions in T-accounts before reading any further. You will need the following accounts: Purchases, Sales, Returns Outwards, Returns Inwards, D Small, A Lyon & Son, D Hughes, M Spencer, and Cash.

Purchases

2009			£	
May	1	D Small	220	
	2	A Lyon & Son	410	
	12	Cash	150	
	31	A Lyon & Son	214	

Sales

	2009			£
	May	5	D Hughes	60
		6	M Spencer	45
		11	Cash	210
		21	Cash	175

Returns Outwards

	2009			£
	May	10	D Small	15

Returns Inwards

2009			£	
May	19	M Spencer	16	

D Small

2009			£	2009			£
May	10	Returns outwards	15	May	1	Purchases	220
	22	Cash	205				

A Lyon & Son

			2009			£
			May	2	Purchases	410
				31	Purchases	214

D Hughes

2009			£	2009			£
May	5	Sales	60	May	30	Cash	60

M Spencer

2009			£	2009			£
May	6	Sales	45	May	19	Returns inwards	16

Cash

2009			£	2009			£
May	11	Sales	210	May	12	Purchases	150
	21	Sales	175		22	D Small	205
	30	D Hughes	60				

If you tried to do this before looking at the answer, be sure you understand any mistakes you made before going on.

3.9 Special meaning of 'sales' and 'purchases'

You need to remember that 'sales' and 'purchases' have a special meaning in accounting when compared to ordinary language usage.

Purchases in accounting means the *purchase of those goods which the business buys with the prime intention of selling*. Obviously, sometimes the goods are altered, added to, or used in the manufacture of something else, but it is the element of resale that is important. To a business that deals in computers, for instance, computers constitute purchases.

If something else is bought *which the business does not intend to sell*, such as a van, such an item cannot be called 'purchases', even though in ordinary language you would say that a van has been purchased. The van was bought to be used and *not* for resale.

Similarly, **sales** means the *sale of those goods in which the business normally deals and which were bought with the prime intention of resale*. The word 'sales' must never be given to the disposal of other items, such as vans or buildings that were purchased to be used and *not* to be sold.

If we did not keep to these meanings, we would find it very difficult to identify which of the items in the purchases and sales accounts were stock and which were assets that had been bought to be used.

Let's now look at another of the small complications accountants need to deal with – the differences between the treatment of cash transactions and credit transactions.

3.10 Comparison of cash and credit transactions for purchases and sales

As you saw in the last example, when goods are purchased for cash, the entries are:

● Debit the purchases account
● Credit the cash account.

On the other hand, the complete set of entries for the purchase of goods on credit can be broken down into two stages: first, the purchase of the goods, and second, the payment for them.

The first part is:

● Debit the purchases account
● Credit the supplier's account.

The second part is:

● Debit the supplier's account
● Credit the cash account.

Activity 3.3

What is the difference between the treatment of cash purchases and credit purchases?

A study of cash sales and credit sales reveals a similar difference in treatment:

Cash Sales	Credit Sales

Complete entry:
  Debit cash account
  Credit sales account
	First part:
	  Debit customer's account
	  Credit sales account
	Second part:
	  Debit cash account
	  Credit customer's account

Learning outcomes

You should now have learnt:

1 That it is *not* appropriate to use a stock account to record increases and decreases in stock because stock is normally sold at a price greater than its cost.

2 That stock increases either because some stock has been purchased or because stock that was sold has been returned by the buyer.

3 That stock decreases either because some stock has been sold or because stock previously purchased has been returned to the supplier.

4 That a purchase account is used to record purchases of stock (as debit entries in the account) and that a returns inwards account is used to record stock returned by customers (as debit entries in the account).

5 That a sales account is used to record sales of stock (as credit entries in the account) and that a returns outwards account is used to record stock returned to suppliers (as credit entries in the account).

6 How to record increases and decreases of stock in the appropriate accounts.

7 That in accounting, the term 'purchases' refers to purchases of stocks. Acquisitions of any other assets, such as vans, equipment and buildings, are *never* described as purchases.

8 That in accounting, the term 'sales' refers to sales of stocks. Disposals of any other assets, such as vans, equipment and buildings, are *never* described as sales.

9 That purchases for cash are *never* entered in the supplier's account.

10 That purchases on credit are *always* entered in the supplier's (creditor's) account.

11 That sales for cash are *never* entered in the customer's account.

12 That sales on credit are *always* entered in the customer's (debtor's) account.

Answers to activities

3.1 As we did in Chapter 1, it would be possible to have a stock account with goods purchased being DEBITED to the stock account (as purchases represent AN INCREASE in the asset, stock) and goods sold being CREDITED to it (as sales represent A DECREASE in the asset, stock).

3.2

Accounts	To record	Entry in the account
Assets	an increase a decrease	Debit Credit

3.3 With cash purchases, no entry is made in the supplier's account. This is because cash passes immediately and therefore there is no need to keep a check of how much money is owing to that supplier. On the other hand, with credit purchases, the records should show to whom money is owed until payment is made and so an entry is always made in the supplier's (creditor's) account.

Review questions

3.1 Complete the following table:

	Account to be debited	Account to be credited
(a) Goods bought on credit from J Reid.		
(b) Goods sold on credit to B Perkins.		
(c) Vans bought on credit from H Thomas.		
(d) Goods sold, a cheque being received immediately.		
(e) Goods sold for cash.		
(f) Goods purchased by us returned to supplier, H Hardy.		
(g) Machinery sold for cash.		
(h) Goods sold returned to us by customer, J Nelson.		
(i) Goods bought on credit from D Simpson.		
(j) Goods we returned to H Forbes.		

3.2A Complete the following table:

	Account to be debited	Account to be credited
(a) Goods bought on credit from T Morgan.		
(b) Goods returned to us by J Thomas.		
(c) Machinery returned to L Jones Ltd.		
(d) Goods bought for cash.		
(e) Van bought on credit from D Davies Ltd.		
(f) Goods returned by us to I Prince.		
(g) D Picton paid us his account by cheque.		
(h) Goods bought by cheque.		
(i) We paid creditor, B Henry, by cheque.		
(j) Goods sold on credit to J Mullings.		

3.3 You are to write up the following in the books:

2008
July   1   Started in business with £2,400 cash.
        3   Bought goods for cash £630.
        7   Bought goods on credit £980 from T Joop.
    10   Sold goods for cash £102.
    14   Returned goods to T Joop £42.
    18   Bought goods on credit £365 from B Topp.
    21   Returned goods to B Topp £24.
    24   Sold goods to J Lump £161 on credit.
    25   Paid T Joop account by cash £938.
    31   J Lump paid us his account in cash £161.

3.4A Enter the following transactions in the appropriate accounts:

2006
Aug
1   Started in business with £7,400 cash.
2   Paid £7,000 of the opening cash into the bank.
4   Bought goods on credit £410 from J Watson.
5   Bought a van by cheque £4,920.
7   Bought goods for cash £362.
10 Sold goods on credit £218 to L Less.
12 Returned goods to J Watson £42.
19 Sold goods for cash £54.
22 Bought fixtures on credit from Firelighters Ltd £820.
24 F Holmes lent us £1,500 paying us the money by cheque.
29 We paid J Watson his account by cheque £368.
31 We paid Firelighters Ltd by cheque £820.

3.5 Enter the following transactions in the accounts of L Linda:

2007
July
1   Started in business with £20,000 in the bank.
2   R Hughes lent us £5,000 in cash.
3   Bought goods on credit from B Brown £1,530 and I Jess £4,162.
4   Sold goods for cash £1,910.
6   Took £200 of the cash and paid it into the bank.
8   Sold goods on credit to H Rise £1,374.
*10 Sold goods on credit to P Taylor £341.
11 Bought goods on credit from B Brown £488.
12 H Rise returned goods to us £65.
14 Sold goods on credit to G Pate £535 and R Sim £262.
15 We returned goods to B Brown £94.
17 Bought van on credit from Aberdeen Cars Ltd £4,370.
18 Bought office furniture on credit from J Winter Ltd £1,800.
19 We returned goods to I Jess £130.
20 Bought goods for cash £390.
24 Goods sold for cash £110.
25 Paid money owing to B Brown by cheque £1,924.
26 Goods returned to us by G Pate £34.
27 Returned some of office furniture costing £180 to J Winter Ltd.
28 L Linda put a further £2,500 into the business in the form of cash.
29 Paid Aberdeen Cars Ltd £4,370 by cheque.
31 Bought office furniture for cash £365.

3.6A Enter the following transactions in the accounts:

2009
May
1   Started in business with £18,000 in the bank.
2   Bought goods on credit from B Hind £1,455.
3   Bought goods on credit from G Smart £472.
5   Sold goods for cash £210.
6   We returned goods to B Hind £82.
8   Bought goods on credit from G Smart £370.
10 Sold goods on credit to P Syme £483.
12 Sold goods for cash £305.
18 Took £250 of the cash and paid it into the bank.
21 Bought a printer by cheque £620.
22 Sold goods on credit to H Buchan £394.
23 P Syme returned goods to us £160.
25 H Buchan returned goods to us £18.
28 We returned goods to G Smart £47.
29 We paid Hind by cheque £1,373.
31 Bought machinery on credit from A Cobb £419.

The effect of profit or loss on capital and the double entry system for expenses and revenues

Learning objectives

After you have studied this chapter, you should be able to:

- calculate profit by comparing revenue with expenses
- explain how the accounting equation is used to show the effects of changes in assets and liabilities upon capital after goods or services have been traded
- explain why separate accounts are used for each type of expense and revenue
- explain why an expense is entered as a debit in the appropriate expense account
- explain why an item of revenue is entered as a credit in the appropriate revenue account
- enter a series of expense and revenue transactions into the appropriate T-accounts
- explain how the use of business cash and business goods for the owner's own purposes are dealt with in the accounting records

Introduction

In this chapter, you will learn how to calculate profits and losses and how to enter expense and revenue transactions into the ledger. You will also learn about drawings (i.e. amounts withdrawn from the business by the owner), and how to record them.

4.1 The nature of profit or loss

To an accountant, **profit** means the amount by which **revenue** is greater than **expenses** for a set of transactions. The term **revenue** means the sales value of goods and services that have been supplied to customers. The term **expenses** means the cost value of all the assets that have been used up to obtain those revenues.

If, therefore, we supplied goods and services valued for sale at £100,000 to customers, and the expenses incurred by us in order to supply those goods and services amounted to £70,000 the result would be a profit of £30,000:

		£
Revenue:	goods and services supplied to our customers for the sum of	100,000
Less Expenses:	value of all the assets used up to enable us to supply these goods and services	(70,000)
Profit is therefore:		30,000

On the other hand, it is possible for our expenses to exceed our revenues for a set of transactions. In this case the result is a **loss**. For example, a loss would be incurred given the following:

		£
Revenue:	what we have charged to our customers in respect of all the goods and services supplied to them	60,000
Less Expenses:	value of all the assets used up to supply these goods and services to our customers	(80,000)
Loss is therefore:		(20,000)

Activity 4.1 In each of these two examples, a different explanation was given for the terms 'revenue' and 'expenses'. What is the difference between the two explanations given for 'revenue'? What is the difference between the two explanations given for 'expenses'?

4.2 The effect of profit and loss on capital

Businesses exist to make profit and so increase their capital. Let's look at the relationship between profits and capital in an example.

On 1 January the assets and liabilities of a business are:

Assets: Fixtures £10,000; Stock £7,000; Cash at the bank £3,000.
Liabilities: Creditors £2,000.

The capital is found from the accounting equation:

$$\boxed{\text{Capital} = \text{Assets} - \text{Liabilities}}$$

In this case, capital is £10,000 + £7,000 + £3,000 − £2,000 = £18,000.

During January, the whole of the £7,000 stock is sold for £11,000 cash. On 31 January the assets and liabilities have become:

Assets: Fixtures £10,000, Stock nil, Cash at the bank £14,000.
Liabilities: Creditors £2,000.

The capital is now £22,000:

$$\text{Assets (£10,000 + £14,000)} - \text{Liabilities £2,000}$$

So capital has increased by £4,000 from £18,000 to £22,000. It has increased by £4,000 increase because the £7,000 stock was sold at a profit of £4,000 for £11,000. Profit, therefore, increases capital:

$$\boxed{\text{Old capital} + \text{Profit} = \text{New capital}}$$

$$£18,000 + £4,000 = £22,000$$

A loss, on the other hand, would reduce the capital:

$$\text{Old capital} - \text{Loss} = \text{New capital}$$

4.3 Profit or loss and sales

Profit will be made when goods or services are sold for more than they cost, while the opposite will result in a loss.

(You will learn later that there are different types of profit, some of which you may have heard of, such as 'gross profit' and 'net profit'. For now, we're not going to complicate things by going into that level of detail so, whatever you may already know about these different types of profit, try to focus for the time being on the simple definition of profit presented here.)

4.4 Profit or loss and expenses

Once profits or losses have been calculated, you can update the capital account. How often this will be done will depend on the business. Some only attempt to calculate their profits and losses once a year. Others do it at much more frequent intervals. Generally speaking, the larger the business, the more frequently profits are calculated.

In order to calculate profits and losses, revenues and expenses must be entered into appropriate accounts. All the expenses could be charged to one Expenses Account, but you would be able to understand the calculations of profit better if full details of each type of expense were shown in those profit calculations. The same applies to each type of revenue.

For this reason, a separate account is opened for each type of expense and for each type of revenue. For example, accounts in use may include:

Commissions Account	Subscriptions Account	Rent Account
Bank Interest Account	Motor Expenses Account	Postages Account
Royalties Receivable Account	Telephone Account	Stationery Account
Rent Receivable Account	General Expenses Account	Wages Account
Overdraft Interest Account	Audit Fees Account	Insurance Account

It is purely a matter of choice in a business as to the title of each expense or revenue account. For example, an account for postage stamps could be called 'Postage Stamps Account', 'Postages Account', 'Communication Expenses Account', and so on. Also different businesses amalgamate expenses, some having a 'Rent and Telephone Account', others a 'Rent, Telephone and Insurance Account', etc. Infrequent or small items of expense are usually put into a 'Sundry Expenses Account' or a 'General Expenses Account'.

Most organisations use names for their accounts that make it obvious which accounts are for revenue and which accounts are for expenses. However, some don't. When in doubt as to whether an account is for revenue or expenses, you have two obvious indicators to consult. The first is on which side the entries are mainly appearing in the account. If, for example, it is the debit side, the account is almost certainly an expense account. The other indicator is the nature of the business. For example, a commission account in the accounting books of a firm of stockbrokers is almost certainly a revenue account.

Activity 4.2 Identify which of the accounts listed in the three columns above are expense accounts and which ones are revenue accounts.

4.5 Debit or credit

You need to know whether expense accounts should be debited or credited with the amounts involved. You know that assets involve expenditure by the business and are shown as debit entries. Expenses also involve expenditure by the business and should, therefore, also be debit entries. Why? Because assets and expenses must ultimately be paid for. This payment involves a credit to the bank account (or to the cash account) so the original entry in the asset account or in the expense account must be a debit.

Even where an expense is incurred on credit, the creditor must eventually be paid. The first entry will be to credit the supplier's (i.e. creditor's) account and debit the expense account. When payment is made to the supplier, the bank account is credited and the supplier's account is debited.

For example, if you pay rent of £500 in cash, the asset cash is decreased by £500. The accounting equation tells you that this means that the capital is reduced by each expense – if assets decrease, so does capital; if liabilities increase, capital decreases (otherwise the accounting equation won't balance). Expense accounts contain debit entries for expenses. The second part of the entry will either be a credit against an asset account, such as cash, or it will be a credit against a liability account, such as creditors.

Activity 4.3 Some students find this explanation involving the capital account very difficult to understand, so try this example to ensure you have followed it. Write down the accounting equation and see if you can work out what happens to it if (a) a business spends £30 in cash hiring a van for a day and (b) if a business hires a van for a day at a cost of £30 and is given 1 month to pay the bill. Assume in each case that the business has assets of £200, liabilities of £80 and capital of £120 before the transaction. What happens to capital in each case?

Revenue is the opposite of expenses and is, therefore, treated in the opposite way – revenue entries appear on the credit side of the revenue accounts. You've already seen this when you've entered sales figures as credits into the sales account. Thus, revenue is collected together in appropriately named accounts, where it is shown as a credit until it is transferred to the profit calculations at the end of the period.

Consider too the use of funds to pay for expenses which are used up in the short term, or assets which are used up in the long term, both for the purpose of getting revenue. Both of these forms of transactions are entered on the debit side of the appropriate accounts (expense accounts or asset accounts respectively), while the revenue which they generate is shown on the credit side of the appropriate revenue accounts.

So, to summarise, profit belongs to the owners. Revenues increase profits, so they increase capital, and that makes them credits. Expenses decrease profits, so they reduce capital, and that makes them debits. The treatment of expenses is the same as the treatment of assets. Increases in expenses result in debit entries to the appropriate expense accounts, while decreases (such as refunds for overpayment of an electricity bill) result in credit entries to those same accounts. Revenue is treated the same as liabilities. Increases in revenue are credited to the appropriate revenue accounts, while decreases are debited to the same accounts.

In other words:

Debit	Credit
Expenses	Revenues
Losses	Profits
Assets	Liabilities
	Capital

Cash

				£
	Aug	25	Drawings	50

Sometimes goods are taken for private use. This form of withdrawal by the owner is also known as drawings. In Section 3.2, you learnt that when goods are purchased, the purchases account is debited. As a result, when goods are withdrawn it is the purchases account which should be credited.

The following example illustrates the entries for this form of drawings:

On 28 August, the owner takes £400 of goods out of the business for his own use.

Effect	Action
1 Capital is decreased by £400 2 Stock is decreased by £400	Debit the drawings account £400 Credit the purchases account £400

Drawings

				£
Aug	28	Purchases		400

Purchases

				£
	Aug	28	Drawings	400

Learning outcomes

You should now have learnt:

1 How to calculate profit by comparing revenue with expenses.

2 That the accounting equation is central to any explanation of the effect of trading upon capital.

3 Why every different type of expense is shown in a separate expense account.

4 Why every different type of revenue is shown in a separate revenue account.

5 Why an expense is shown as a debit entry in the appropriate expense account.

6 Why revenue is shown as a credit entry in the appropriate revenue account.

7 How to enter a series of expense and revenue transactions into the appropriate T-accounts.

8 What is meant by the term 'drawings'.

9 That drawings are *always* a reduction in capital and *never* an expense of a business.

10 How to record drawings of cash in the accounting books.

11 How to record drawings of goods in the accounting books.

Answers to activities

4.1 There is no difference between either the two meanings given for revenues or the two meanings given for expenses. In each case, you are being given a slightly different wording so as to help you understand what the two terms mean.

4.2 *Expense Accounts*
Rent Account
Postages Account
Commissions Account
Stationery Account
Wages Account
Insurance Account
Bank Interest Account
Motor Expenses Account
Telephone Account
General Expenses Account
Overdraft Interest Account
Audit Fees Account

Revenue Accounts
Subscriptions Account
Rent Receivable Account
Royalties Receivable Account

Note that the answer has assumed that *unless* words like 'received' or 'receivable' follow the name of an account, the account is an expense. For example, the Commission Account and the Bank Interest Account could easily be for revenue rather than expenses. However, accounting practice is that as most accounts are for expenses, where there may be some confusion as to whether an account is for revenue or expenses, the name of the revenue account should make it clear that it is for revenue, not expenses. You can see an example in this question if you compare the names of the two rent accounts. Accounts like Subscriptions tend to appear mainly in the accounting books of clubs and societies and so there is no need in that case to indicate in the name that it is a revenue account. You can tell whether subscriptions are revenue or expenditure items from the type of organisation whose accounting books you are looking at. The same would apply, but even more so, to Audit Fees which are only ever revenue accounts in the accounting books of a firm of accountants. In all other cases, they are expense accounts.

4.3 The accounting equation is Capital = Assets – Liabilities. In this example, it starts as £120 = £200 – £80. Each transaction is entered twice. In both cases, the debit entry is £30 to a van hire expense account. The credit in (a) is to the cash account. In (b) it is to the car hire company's account (the creditor's account). In order for the accounting equation to balance, in (a) an asset (i.e. cash) has been reduced by £30 so capital must be reduced by the same amount, £30. In the case of (b) liabilities (i.e. the van hire company's account) have increased by £30 and so capital must be also be reduced by that amount, £30. In the case of (a) the accounting equation becomes £90 = £170 – £80. In (b) it becomes £90 = £200 – £110. The effect on capital in both cases is that it decreases by the amount of the expense.

Review questions

4.1 Enter the following transactions, completing the double entry in the books for the month of May 2007:

2007
May
1 Started in business with £9,000 in the bank and £1,000 in cash.
2 Purchased goods £290 on credit from D James.
3 Bought fixtures and fittings £1,150 paying by cheque.
5 Sold goods for cash £140.
6 Bought goods on credit £325 from C Monty.
10 Paid rent by cash £200.
12 Bought stationery £45, paying in cash.
18 Goods returned to D James £41.
21 Received rent of £25 by cheque for sublet of corner space.

→

23 Sold goods on credit to G Cross for £845.
24 Bought a van paying by cheque £4,100.
30 Paid the month's wages by cash £360.
31 The proprietor took cash for his own personal use £80.

4.2 Write up the following transactions in the books of J Brown:

2008
March 1 Started in business with cash £9,600.
2 Bought goods on credit from J Harper £310.
3 Paid rent by cash £650.
4 Paid £3,000 of the cash of the business into a bank account.
5 Sold goods on credit to P Aisley £330.
7 Bought blank CDs for the PC £9 paying by cheque.
11 Cash sales £42.
14 Goods returned by us to J Harper £63.
17 Sold goods on credit to F Boggis £195.
20 Paid for repairs to the PC by cash £56.
22 P Aisley returned goods to us £30.
27 Paid J Harper by cheque £247.
28 Cash purchases £840.
29 Bought a second-hand motorbike paying by cheque £2,100.
30 Paid motor repairs in cash £101.
31 Bought office furniture £460 by cheque from D Simpson.

4.3A Prepare the double entries (*not* the T-accounts) for the following transactions using the format:

Date

	Dr	Cr
Account name	£x	
Account name		£x

July 1 Started in business with £5,000 in the bank and £1,000 cash.
2 Bought stationery by cheque £75.
3 Bought goods on credit from T Smart £2,100.
4 Sold goods for cash £340.
5 Paid insurance by cash £290.
7 Bought a computer on credit from J Hott £700.
8 Paid expenses by cheque £32.
10 Sold goods on credit to C Biggins £630.
11 Returned goods to T Smart £550.
14 Paid wages by cash £210.
17 Paid rent by cheque £225.
20 Received cheque £400 from C Biggins.
21 Paid J Hott by cheque £700.
23 Bought stationery on credit from News Ltd £125.
25 Sold goods on credit to F Tank £645.
31 Paid News Ltd by cheque £125.

4.4A Write up the following transactions in the T-accounts of F Fernandes:

Feb 1 Started in business with £11,000 in the bank and £1,600 cash.
2 Bought goods on credit: J Biggs £830; D Martin £610; P Lot £590.
3 Bought goods for cash £370.
4 Paid rent in cash £75.
5 Bought stationery paying by cheque £62.
6 Sold goods on credit: D Twigg £370; B Hogan £290; K Fletcher £410.
7 Paid wages in cash £160.
10 We returned goods to D Martin £195.

11 Paid rent in cash £75.
13 B Hogan returns goods to us £35.
15 Sold goods on credit to: T Lee £205; F Sharp £280; G Rae £426.
16 Paid business rates by cheque £970.
18 Paid insurance in cash £280.
19 Paid rent by cheque £75.
20 Bought van on credit from B Black £6,100.
21 Paid motor expenses in cash £24.
23 Paid wages in cash £170.
24 Received part of amount owing from K Fletcher by cheque £250.
28 Received refund of business rates £45 by cheque.
28 Paid by cheque: J Biggs £830; D Martin £415; B Black £6,100.

4.5 From the following statements which give the cumulative effects of individual transactions, you are required to state as fully as possible what transaction has taken place in each case. That is, write descriptions similar to those given in questions 4.1–4.4. There is no need to copy out the table. The first column of data gives the opening position. Each of the other columns represents a transaction. It is these transactions (A–I) that you are to describe.

Transaction:		A	B	C	D	E	F	G	H	I
Assets	£000	£000	£000	£000	£000	£000	£000	£000	£000	£000
Land and buildings	450	450	450	450	575	575	275	275	275	275
Motor vehicles	95	100	100	100	100	100	100	100	100	100
Office equipment	48	48	48	48	48	48	48	48	48	48
Stock	110	110	110	110	110	110	110	110	110	93
Debtors	188	188	188	188	188	108	108	108	108	120
Bank	27	22	22	172	47	127	427	77	77	77
Cash	15	15	11	11	11	11	11	11	3	3
	933	933	929	1,079	1,079	1,079	1,079	729	721	716
Liabilities										
Capital	621	621	621	621	621	621	621	621	621	616
Loan from Lee	200	200	200	350	350	350	350	–	–	–
Creditors	112	112	108	108	108	108	108	108	100	100
	933	933	929	1,079	1,079	1,079	1,079	729	721	716

Note: the sign *£000* means that all the figures shown underneath it are in thousands of pounds, e.g. Office Equipment book value is £48,000. It saves constantly writing out 000 after each figure, and is done to save time and make comparison easier.

4.6A The following table shows the cumulative effects of a succession of separate transactions on the assets and liabilities of a business. The first column of data gives the opening position.

Transaction:		A	B	C	D	E	F	G	H	I
Assets	£000	£000	£000	£000	£000	£000	£000	£000	£000	£000
Land and buildings	500	500	535	535	535	535	535	535	535	535
Equipment	230	230	230	230	230	230	230	200	200	200
Stocks	113	140	140	120	120	120	120	120	119	119
Trade debtors	143	143	143	173	160	158	158	158	158	158
Prepaid expenses*	27	27	27	27	27	27	27	27	27	27
Cash at bank	37	37	37	37	50	50	42	63	63	63
Cash on hand	9	9	9	9	9	9	9	9	9	3
	1,059	1,086	1,121	1,131	1,131	1,129	1,121	1,112	1,111	1,105
Liabilities										
Capital	730	730	730	740	740	738	733	724	723	717
Loan	120	120	155	155	155	155	155	155	155	155
Trade creditors	168	195	195	195	195	195	195	195	195	195
Accrued expenses*	41	41	41	41	41	41	38	38	38	38
	1,059	1,086	1,121	1,131	1,131	1,129	1,121	1,112	1,111	1,105

Required:
Identify clearly and as fully as you can what transaction has taken place in each case. Give two possible explanations for transaction I. Do not copy out the table but use the reference letter for each transaction.

(*Association of Accounting Technicians*)

Authors' Note: You have not yet been told about 'prepaid expenses' and 'accrued expenses'. Prepaid expenses are expenses that have been paid in advance, the benefits of which will only be felt by the business in a later accounting period. Because the benefit of having incurred the expense will not be received until a future time period, the expense is not included in the calculation of profit for the period in which it was paid. As it was not treated as an expense of the period when profit was calculated, the debit in the account is treated as an asset when the balance sheet is prepared, hence the appearance of the term 'prepaid expenses' among the assets in the question. Accrued expenses, on the other hand, are expenses that have not yet been paid for benefits which have been received. In F, £8,000 was paid out of the bank account of which £3,000 was used to pay off some of the accrued expenses.

You can find a range of additional self-test questions, as well as material to help you with your studies, on the website that accompanies this book at **www.pearsoned.co.uk/wood**

Balancing-off accounts

Learning objectives

After you have studied this chapter, you should be able to:

- close-off accounts when appropriate
- balance off accounts at the end of a period and bring down the opening balance to the next period
- distinguish between a debit balance and a credit balance
- describe and prepare accounts in three-column format

Introduction

In this chapter, you'll learn how to discover what the amount outstanding on an account is at a particular point in time. You'll also learn how to close accounts that are no longer needed and how to record appropriate entries in accounts at the end and beginning of periods. Finally, you'll learn that T-accounts are not the only way to record accounting transactions.

5.1 Accounts for debtors

Where debtors have paid their accounts

So far you have learnt how to record transactions in the accounting books by means of debit and credit entries. At the end of each accounting period the figures in each account are examined in order to summarise the situation they present. This will often, but not always, be once a year if you are calculating profit. If you want to see what is happening with respect to particular accounts, it will be done more frequently. For example, if you want to find out how much your customers owe you for goods you have sold to them, you will probably do this at the end of each month.

Activity 5.1
Why do you think we would want to look at the debtor accounts in the accounting books as often as once a month?

Let's look at the account of one of our customers, K Tandy, for transactions in August 2008:

K Tandy

2008			£	2008			£
Aug	1	Sales	144	Aug	22	Bank	144
	19	Sales	300		28	Bank	300

If you add up the figures on each side, you will find that they both sum to £444. In other words, during the month we sold a total of £444 worth of goods to Tandy, and have been paid a total of £444 by her. This means that at the end of August she owes us nothing. As she owes us nothing, we do not need her account to prepare the balance sheet (there is no point in showing a figure for debtors of zero in the balance sheet). We can, therefore, **close-off** her account on 31 August 2008. This is done by inserting the totals on each side:

K Tandy

2008			£	2008			£
Aug	1	Sales	144	Aug	22	Bank	144
	19	Sales	300		28	Bank	300
			444				444

Notice that totals in accounting are always shown with a single line above them, and a double line underneath. As shown in the following completed account for C Lee, totals on accounts at the end of a period are always shown on a level with one another, even when there are less entries on one side than on the other.

Now, let's look at the account for C Lee.

C Lee

2008			£	2008			£
Aug	11	Sales	177	Aug	30	Bank	480
	19	Sales	203				
	22	Sales	100				
			480				480

In this account, C Lee also owed us nothing at the end of August 2008, as he had paid us for all the sales we made to him.

Note: In handwritten accounts, you will often see this layout enhanced by two intersecting lines, one horizontal and one diagonal on the side which has less entries. If this were done, C Lee's account would look like this:

C Lee

2008			£	2008			£
Aug	11	Sales	177	Aug	30	Bank	480
	19	Sales	203				
	22	Sales	100				
			480				480

We won't use this layout in this book, but your teacher or lecturer may want you to use it whenever you are preparing T-accounts.

Activity 5.2 Why do you think we would want to draw these two extra lines on to the handwritten account?

If an account contains only one entry on each side and they are equal, you don't need to include totals. For example:

K Wood

2008		£	2008		£
Aug 6 Sales		214	Aug 12 Bank		214

Now let's look at what happens when the two sides do not equal each other.

Where debtors still owe for goods

It is unlikely that everyone will have paid the amounts they owe us by the end of the month. In these cases, the totals of each side would not equal one another. Let's look at the account of D Knight for August 2008:

D Knight

2008		£	2008		£
Aug 1 Sales		158	Aug 28 Bank		158
15 Sales		206			
30 Sales		118			

If you add the figures you will see that the debit side adds up to £482 and the credit side adds up to £158. You should be able to see what the difference of £324 (i.e. £482 – £158) represents. It consists of the last two sales of £206 and £118. They have not been paid for and so are still owing to us on 31 August 2008.

In double entry, we only enter figures as totals if the totals on both sides of the account agree. We do, however, want to **balance-off** the account for August showing that Knight owes us £324. (While there would be nothing wrong in using the term 'close-off', 'balance off' is the more appropriate term to use when there is a difference between the two sides of an account.)

If Knight owes us £324 at close of business on 31 August 2008, then the same amount will be owed to us when the business opens on 1 September 2008.

Balancing the accounts is done in five stages:

1 Add up both sides to find out their totals. Note: do not write anything in the account at this stage.
2 Deduct the smaller total from the larger total to find the balance.
3 Now enter the balance on the side with the smallest total. This now means the totals will be equal.
4 Enter totals level with each other.
5 Now enter the balance on the line below the totals on the *opposite* side to the balance shown above the totals.

Against the balance above the totals, complete the date column by entering the last day of that period – for August, this will always be '31' even if the business was shut on that date because it fell on a weekend or was a holiday. Below the totals, show the first day of the next period against the balance – this will always be the day immediately after the last day of the previous period, in this case, September 1. The balance above the totals is described as the **balance carried down** (often this is abbreviated to 'balance c/d'). The balance below the total is described as the **balance brought down** (often abbreviated to 'balance b/d').

Knight's account when 'balanced off' will appear as follows:

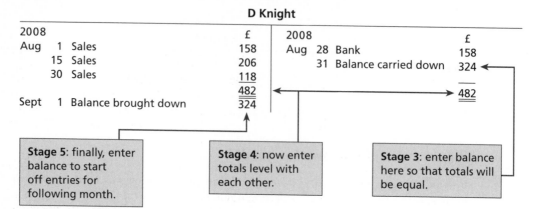

D Knight

2008			£	2008			£
Aug	1	Sales	158	Aug	28	Bank	158
	15	Sales	206		31	Balance carried down	324
	30	Sales	118				
			482				482
Sept	1	Balance brought down	324				

Stage 5: finally, enter balance to start off entries for following month.

Stage 4: now enter totals level with each other.

Stage 3: enter balance here so that totals will be equal.

Note for students

- From now on, we will use the abbreviations 'c/d' and 'b/d'.
- The date given to balance c/d is the last day of the period which is finishing, and balance b/d is given the opening date of the next period.
- As the total of the debit side originally exceeded the total of the credit side, **the balance is said to be a 'debit balance'**. This being a personal account (for a person), the person concerned is said to be a debtor – the accounting term for anyone who owes money to the business.

Just as when the two sides each have only one entry and the two sides are equal, if an account contains only one entry it is unnecessary to enter the total after entering the balance carried down (because the balance becomes the only entry on the other side and it is equal to the other entry). A double line ruled under the entry will mean that the entry is its own total. For example:

B Walters

2008			£	2008			£
Aug	18	Sales	51	Aug	31	Balance c/d	51
Sept	1	Balance b/d	51				

Note: T-accounts should *always* be closed-off at the end of each period, even when they contain only one entry.

5.2 Accounts for creditors

Exactly the same principles will apply when the balances are carried down to the credit side. **This balance is known as a 'credit balance'.** We can look at the accounts of two of our suppliers which are to be balanced off:

E Williams

2008			£	2008			£
Aug	21	Bank	100	Aug	2	Purchases	248
					18	Purchases	116

K Patterson

2008			£	2008			£
Aug	14	Returns outwards	20	Aug	8	Purchases	620
	28	Bank	600		15	Purchases	200

We now add up the totals and find the balance, i.e. Stages 1 and 2. When balanced off, these will appear as:

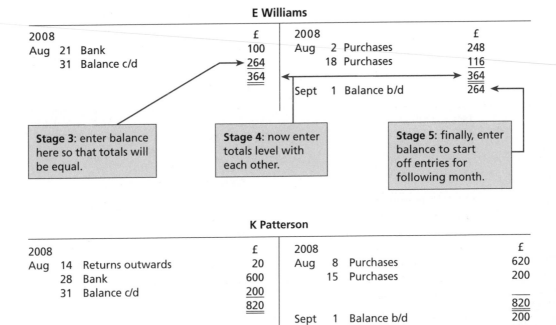

E Williams

2008			£	2008				£
Aug	21	Bank	100	Aug	2	Purchases		248
	31	Balance c/d	264		18	Purchases		116
			364					364
				Sept	1	Balance b/d		264

Stage 3: enter balance here so that totals will be equal.

Stage 4: now enter totals level with each other.

Stage 5: finally, enter balance to start off entries for following month.

K Patterson

2008			£	2008			£
Aug	14	Returns outwards	20	Aug	8	Purchases	620
	28	Bank	600		15	Purchases	200
	31	Balance c/d	200				
			820				820
				Sept	1	Balance b/d	200

The accounts of E Williams and K Patterson have credit balances. They are 'creditors' – the accounting term for someone to whom money is owed.

Before you read further attempt Review Questions 5.1 and 5.2.

5.3 Three-column accounts

Through the main part of this book, the type of account used is the T-account, where the left-hand side of the account is the debit side, and the right-hand side is the credit side. However, when computers are used the style of the ledger account is sometimes different. It appears as three columns of figures, one column for debit entries, another column for credit entries, and the last column for the balance. If you have a current account at a bank your bank statements will normally be shown using this three-column format method.

The accounts used in this chapter will now be redrafted to show the ledger accounts drawn up in this way.

K Tandy

2008			Debit	Credit	Balance (and whether debit or credit)	
			£	£	£	
Aug	1	Sales	144		144	Dr
	19	Sales	300		444	Dr
	22	Bank		144	300	Dr
	28	Bank		300	0	

C Lee

			Debit £	Credit £	Balance £	
2008						
Aug	11	Sales	177		177	Dr
	19	Sales	203		380	Dr
	22	Sales	100		480	Dr
	30	Bank		480	0	

K Wood

			Debit £	Credit £	Balance £	
2008						
Aug	6	Sales	214		214	Dr
	12	Bank		214	0	

D Knight

			Debit £	Credit £	Balance £	
2008						
Aug	1	Sales	158		158	Dr
	15	Sales	206		364	Dr
	28	Bank		158	206	Dr
	31	Sales	118		324	Dr

B Walters

			Debit £	Credit £	Balance £	
2008						
Aug	18	Sales	51		51	Dr

E Williams

			Debit £	Credit £	Balance £	
2008						
Aug	2	Purchases		248	248	Cr
	18	Purchases		116	364	Cr
	21	Bank	100		264	Cr

K Patterson

			Debit £	Credit £	Balance £	
2008						
Aug	8	Purchases		620	620	Cr
	14	Returns	20		600	Cr
	15	Purchases		200	800	Cr
	28	Bank	600		200	Cr

Note how the balance is calculated after every entry. This can be done quite simply when using a computer because the software can automatically calculate the new balance as soon as an entry is made.

When manual methods are being used it is often too much work to have to calculate a new balance after each entry. Also, the greater the number of calculations, the greater the possibility of errors. For these reasons, it is usual for students to use T-accounts *except* when required to use three-column accounts in an exam! However, it is important to note that there is no difference in principle – the final balances are the same using either method.

Learning outcomes

You should now have learnt:

1 How to close-off accounts upon which there is no balance oustanding.

2 How to balance-off accounts at the end of a period.

3 How to bring down the opening balance on an account at the start of a new period.

4 That when an opening balance on an account is a debit, that account is said to have a debit balance. It also has a debit balance during a period whenever the total of the debit side exceeds the total of the credit side.

5 That when an opening balance on an account is a credit, that account is said to have a credit balance. It also has a credit balance during a period whenever the total of the credit side exceeds the total of the debit side.

6 That 'debtors' are people or organisations whose account in your accounting books has a greater value on the debit side. They owe you money. They are included in the amount shown for debtors in the balance sheet.

7 That 'creditors' are people or organisations whose account in your accounting books has a greater value on the credit side. You owe them money. They are included in the amount shown for creditors in the balance sheet.

8 That both T-accounts and three-column accounts disclose the same balance, given identical information about transactions.

9 That three-column accounts update and show the balance on the account after every transaction.

10 How to prepare three-column accounts.

Answers to activities

5.1 In order to survive, business must, in the long term, make profits. However, even profitable businesses go 'bust' if they do not have enough funds to pay their bills when they are due. Debtors represent a resource that is not yet in the form of funds (e.g. cash) that can be used to pay bills. By regularly monitoring the position on the account of each debtor, a business can tell which debtors are being slow to pay and, very importantly, do something about it.

5.2 The purpose is to prevent any more entries being made in the account. The entries would *always* be made in ink, so as to prevent their being erased and replaced with different entries. In a computerised accounting system, there is no need for measures such as these as the controls and checks built into the computerised system prevent them from happening.

Review questions

5.1 Enter the following items in the appropriate debtors' accounts (i.e. your customers' accounts) only; do *not* write up other accounts. Then balance off each of these personal accounts at the end of the month. (Keep your answer; it will be used as a basis for question 5.3.)

2008
May
1 Sales on credit to J Fry £640; I Lee £920; K Rusch £530.
4 Sales on credit to A Davey £510; J Fry £130.
10 Returns inwards from J Fry £80; K Rusch £90.
18 I Lee paid us by cheque £920.
20 K Rusch paid us £440 in cash.

→

→
    24   J Fry paid us £250 by cheque.
    31   Sales on credit to A Davey £300.

5.2   Enter the following in the appropriate creditors' accounts (i.e. your suppliers' accounts) only. Do *not* write up the other accounts. Then balance off each of these personal accounts at the end of the month. (Keep your answer; it will be used as the basis for question 5.4.)

2008
June   1   Purchases on credit from J Saville £240; P Todd £390; J Fry £810.
       3   Purchases on credit from P Todd £470; J Mehan £1,450.
    10   We returned goods to J Fry £82; J Saville £65.
    15   Purchases on credit from J Saville £210.
    19   We paid J Mehan by cheque £1,450.
    28   We paid J Saville by cash £300.
    30   We returned goods to P Todd £39.

5.3   Redraft each of the accounts given in your answer to 5.1 in three-column ledger style accounts.

5.4   Redraft each of the accounts given in your answer to 5.2 in three-column ledger style accounts.

5.5   Enter the following in the personal accounts (i.e. the creditor and debtor accounts) only. Do *not* write up the other accounts. Balance off each personal account at the end of the month. After completing this, state which of the balances represent debtors and which represent creditors.

2008
Sept   1   Sales on credit to J Bee £520; T Day £630; J Soul £240.
      2   Purchases on credit D Blue £390; F Rise £510; P Lee £280.
      8   Sales on credit to T Day £640; L Hope £418.
    10   Purchases on credit from F Rise £92; R James £870.
    12   Returns inwards from J Soul £25; T Day £190.
    17   We returned goods to F Rise £12; R James £84.
    20   We paid D Blue by cheque £390.
    24   J Bee paid us by cheque £400.
    26   We paid R James by cheque £766.
    28   J Bee paid us by cash £80.
    30   L Hope pays us by cheque £418.

5.6A   Enter the following transactions in personal accounts only. Bring down the balances at the end of the month. After completing this, state which of the balances represent debtors and which represent creditors.

2007
May   1   Credit sales G Wood £310; K Hughes £42; F Dunn £1,100; M Lyons £309.
      2   Credit purchases from T Sim £190; J Leech £63; P Tidy £210; F Rock £190.
      8   Credit sales to K Hughes £161; F Dunn £224.
      9   Credit purchases from J Leech £215; F Rock £164.
    10   Goods returned to us by F Dunn £31; M Lyons £82.
    12   Cash paid to us by M Lyons £227.
    15   We returned goods to T Sim £15; F Rock £21.
    19   We received cheques from F Dunn £750; G Wood £310.
    21   We sold goods on credit to G Wood £90; K Hughes £430.
    28   We paid by cheque the following: T Sim £175; F Rock £100; P Tidy £180.
    31   We returned goods to F Rock £18.

5.7A   Redraft each of the accounts given in your answer to 5.6A in three-column style accounts.

The trial balance

Learning objectives

After you have studied this chapter, you should be able to:
- prepare a trial balance from a set of accounts
- explain why the debit and credit trial balance totals should equal one another
- explain why some of the possible errors that can be made when double entries are being entered in the accounts do not prevent the trial balance from 'balancing'
- describe uses for a trial balance other than to check for double entry errors

Introduction

In this chapter, you'll learn how to prepare a trial balance from the accounts in the accounting books. You'll discover that the alternate version of the accounting equation can be a useful guide to understanding why a trial balance must balance if all the double entries in the accounts are correct. You'll also learn that the trial balance is no guarantee that the double entries have all been recorded correctly. Finally, at the end of the chapter, you'll have the opportunity to do twenty multiple choice questions covering the material in Chapters 1–6.

6.1 Total debit entries = Total credit entries

You've learnt that under double entry bookkeeping
- for each debit entry there is a credit entry
- for each credit entry there is a debit entry.

Let's see if you can remember the basics of double entry.

Activity 6.1 What is the double entry for each of the following transactions:

(a) Purchase of a new van for £9,000 which was paid in full by cheque

Dr   £

    Cr   £

(b) Goods which cost £40 taken out by the owner for her own use

Dr   £

    Cr   £

The total of all the items recorded in all the accounts on the debit side should equal the *total* of all the items recorded on the credit side of the accounts.

 Activity 6.2 Do you remember the alternate form of the accounting equation you were shown in Chapter 1? What does it tell you has happened when it does not balance?

We need to check that for each debit entry there is also an equal credit entry. In order to check that there is a matching credit entry for every debit entry, we prepare something called a **trial balance**.

A type of trial balance could be drawn up by listing all the accounts and then entering the total of all the debit entries in each account in one column and the total of all the credit entries in each account into another column. Finally, you would add up the two columns of figures and ensure they are equal. Using the worked example in Section 3.8, this trial balance would be:

Trial Balance as at 31 May 2009		
	Dr £	Cr £
Purchases	994	
Sales		490
Returns outwards		15
Returns inwards	16	
D Small	220	220
A Lyon & Son		624
D Hughes	60	60
M Spencer	45	16
Cash	445	355
	1,780	1,780

6.2 Total debit balances = Total credit balances

The method described in Section 6.1 is *not* the accepted method of drawing up a trial balance, but it is the easiest to understand at first. The form of trial balance used by accountants is a list of account balances arranged according to whether they are debit balances or credit balances.

Let's balance off the accounts you saw in Section 3.8. The new entries are highlighted so that you can see the entries required to arrive at the closing balances that are used in the trial balance.

You may find it worthwhile trying to balance these accounts yourself before reading any further.

Purchases

2009			£	2009			£
May	1	D Small	220	May	31	Balance c/d	994
	2	A Lyon & Son	410				
	12	Cash	150				
	31	A Lyon & Son	214				
			994				994
June	1	Balance b/d	994				

Sales

2009			£	2009				£
May	31	Balance c/d	490	May	5	D Hughes		60
					6	M Spencer		45
					11	Cash		210
					21	Cash		175
			490					490
				June	11	Balance b/d		490

Returns Outwards

2009			£	2009			£
May	31	Balance c/d	15	May	10	D Small	15
				June	1	Balance b/d	15

Returns Inwards

2009			£	2009			£
May	19	M Spencer	16	May	31	Balance c/d	16
June	1	Balance b/d	16				

D Small

2009			£	2009			£
May	10	Returns outwards	15	May	1	Purchases	220
	22	Cash	205				
			220				220

A Lyon & Son

2009			£	2009			£
May	31	Balance c/d	624	May	2	Purchases	410
					31	Purchases	214
			624				624
				June	1	Balance b/d	624

D Hughes

2009			£	2009			£
May	5	Sales	60	May	30	Cash	60

M Spencer

2009			£	2009			£
May	6	Sales	45	May	19	Returns inwards	16
					31	Balance c/d	29
			45				45
June	1	Balance b/d	29				

Cash

2009			£	2009			£
May	11	Sales	210	May	12	Purchases	150
	21	Sales	175		22	D Small	205
	30	D Hughes	60		31	Balance c/d	90
			445				445
June	1	Balance b/d	90				

If you tried to do this before looking at the answer, be sure you understand any mistakes you made before going on.

If the trial balance was drawn up using the closing account balances, it would appear as follows:

Trial Balance as at 31 May 2009		
	Dr £	Cr £
Purchases	994	
Sales		490
Returns outwards		15
Returns inwards	16	
A Lyon & Son		624
M Spencer	29	
Cash	90	
	1,129	1,129

The trial balance always has the date of the *last* day of the accounting period to which it relates. It is a snapshot of the balances on the ledger accounts at that date.

Just like the trial balance you saw in Section 6.1, the two sides of this one also 'balance'. However, the totals are lower. This is because the £220 in D Small's account, £60 in D Hughes' account, £16 in M Spencer's account and £355 in the cash account have been cancelled out from each side of these accounts by taking only the *balances* instead of the *totals*. As equal amounts have been cancelled from each side, £651 in all, the new totals should still equal one another, as in fact they do at £1,129. (You can verify this if you subtract the new total of £1,129 from the previous one of £1,780. The difference is £651 which is the amount cancelled out from both sides.)

This form of trial balance is the easiest to extract when there are more than a few transactions during the period and it is the one accountants use.

Note that a trial balance can be drawn up at any time. However, it is normal practice to prepare one at the end of an accounting period before preparing a 'profit and loss account' and a 'balance sheet'. The profit and loss account shows what profit has been earned in a period. (You will be looking at profit and loss accounts in the next chapter.) The balance sheet shows what the assets and liabilities of a business are at the end of a period.

Go back to Chapter 1 to refresh your understanding of the balance sheet.

 Activity 6.3 What advantages are there in preparing a trial balance when you are about to prepare a profit and loss account and balance sheet?

As you've just learnt from Activity 6.3 trial balances are not just done to find errors.

6.3 Trial balances and errors

Many students new to accounting assume that when the trial balance 'balances', the entries in the accounts must be correct. **This assumption is incorrect.** While it means that certain types of error have not been made (such as forgetting to enter the credit side of a transaction), there are several types of error that will not affect the balancing of a trial balance – omitting a transaction altogether, for example.

Examples of the errors which would be revealed, provided there are no compensating errors which cancel them out, are addition errors, using one figure for the debit entry and another figure for the credit entry, and entering only one side of a transaction.

We shall consider addition errors in greater detail in Chapter 31.

Activity 6.4 If a trial balance fails to agree, what steps would you take in order to find the cause of the difference?

6.4 Multiple choice self-test questions

A growing practice of examining boards is to set multiple choice questions in accounting. In fact, this has become so popular with examiners that all the largest professional accounting bodies now use them, particularly in their first level examinations.

Multiple choice questions give an examiner the opportunity to cover large parts of the syllabus briefly, but in detail. Students who omit to study areas of the syllabus will be caught out by an examiner's use of multiple choice questions. It is no longer possible to say that it is highly probable a certain topic will not be tested – the examiner can easily cover it with a multiple choice question.

We have deliberately included sets of twenty multiple choice questions at given places in this textbook, rather than a few at the end of each chapter. Such questions are relatively easy to answer a few minutes after reading the chapter. Asking the questions later is a far better test of your powers of recall and understanding. It also gives you practice at answering questions covering a range of topics in one block, as in an examination.

Each multiple choice question has a 'stem' (a part which poses the problem), a 'key' (which is the one correct answer), and a number of 'distractors', i.e. incorrect answers. The key plus the distractors are known as the 'options'.

If you do not know the answer, you should guess. You may be right by chance, or you may remember something subconsciously. In any event, unless the examiner warns otherwise, you will be expected to guess if you don't know the answer.

Read through the Learning Outcomes for this chapter and then attempt Multiple Choice Set 1.

Answers to all the multiple choice questions are given in Appendix 2 at the end of this book.

6.5 Closing stock

Stock at the end of a period is not usually to be found in an account in the ledger. It has to be found from stock records and physical stocktaking. As it is not generally to be found in the ledger, it does not generally appear among the balances in a trial balance. However, opening stock is often recorded in a ledger account, in which case the stock balance at the start of a period would be included in the trial balance prepared at the end of that period.

Learning outcomes

You should now have learnt:

1 How to prepare a trial balance.

2 That trial balances are one form of checking the accuracy of entries in the accounts.

3 That errors can be made in the entries to the accounts that will not be shown up by the trial balance.

4 That the trial balance is used as the basis for preparing profit and loss accounts and balance sheets.

Answers to activities

6.1 (a) Dr   Van account   £9,000
             Cr   Bank account   £9,000
       (b) Dr   Drawings account   £40
             Cr   Purchases account   £40

6.2 The alternate form of the accounting equation is Assets = Capital + Liabilities. All the accounts with debit balances are assets and all the accounts with credit balances are either capital or liabilities. This means that so long as you enter a debit for every credit, the alternate accounting equation must always balance. If the alternate accounting equation does not balance, you've made an error somewhere, either in your double entries, or in your arithmetic within the individual accounts. Virtually all occurrences where the accounting equation does not balance that arise in practice are the result of double entry errors.

6.3 Firstly, you can verify whether the total of the debit balances equals the total of the credit balances. They need to be equal, or your profit and loss account and balance sheet will be incorrect and your balance sheet will not balance. (That is, the accounting equation will not balance.) Secondly, you need to know what the balance is on every account so that you can enter the appropriate figures into the profit and loss account and balance sheet. If you don't prepare a trial balance, you will find it much more difficult to prepare these two accounting statements.

6.4 You need to check each entry to verify whether or not it is correct but firstly, it is best to start by checking that the totals in the trial balance have been correctly summed. Then, check that no account has been omitted from the trial balance. Then, check each account in turn.

Multiple choice questions: Set 1

Each of these multiple choice questions has four suggested answers, (A), (B), (C) and (D). You should read each question and then decide which choice is best, either (A) or (B) or (C) or (D). *Write down your answers on a separate piece of paper.* You will then be able to redo the set of questions later without having to try to ignore your answers.

MC1   Which of the following statements is **incorrect**?

(A)   Assets – Capital = Liabilities
(B)   Liabilities + Capital = Assets
(C)   Liabilities + Assets = Capital
(D)   Assets – Liabilities = Capital

MC2   Which of the following is **not** an asset?

(A)   Buildings
(B)   Cash balance
(C)   Debtors
(D)   Loan from K Harris

MC3   Which of the following is a liability?

(A)   Machinery
(B)   Creditors for goods
(C)   Motor Vehicles
(D)   Cash at Bank

MC4 Which of the following is **incorrect**?

	Assets £	Liabilities £	Capital £
(A)	7,850	1,250	6,600
(B)	8,200	2,800	5,400
(C)	9,550	1,150	8,200
(D)	6,540	1,120	5,420

MC5 Which of the following statements is correct?

		Effect upon	
		Assets	Liabilities
(A)	We paid a creditor by cheque	−Bank	−Creditors
(B)	A debtor paid us £90 in cash	+Cash	+Debtors
(C)	J Hall lends us £500 by cheque	+Bank	−Loan from Hall
(D)	Bought goods on credit	+Stock	+Capital

MC6 Which of the following are correct?

	Accounts	To record	Entry in the account
(i)	Assets	an increase	Debit
		a decrease	Credit
(ii)	Capital	an increase	Debit
		a decrease	Credit
(iii)	Liabilities	an increase	Credit
		a decrease	Debit

(A) (i) and (ii)
(B) (ii) and (iii)
(C) (i) and (iii)
(D) (i), (ii) and (iii)

MC7 Which of the following are correct?

		Account to be debited	Account to be credited
(i)	Bought office furniture for cash	Office furniture	Cash
(ii)	A debtor, P Sangster, pays us by cheque	Bank	P Sangster
(iii)	Introduced capital by cheque	Capital	Bank
(iv)	Paid a creditor, B Lee, by cash	B Lee	Cash

(A) (i), (ii) and (iii) only
(B) (ii), (iii) and (iv) only
(C) (i), (ii) and (iv) only
(D) (i) and (iv) only

MC8 Which of the following are **incorrect**?

		Account to be debited	Account to be credited
(i)	Sold van for cash	Cash	Van
(ii)	Returned some of Office Equipment to Suppliers Ltd	Office Equipment	Suppliers Ltd
(iii)	Repaid part of loan from C Charles by cheque	Loan from C Charles	Bank
(iv)	Bought machinery on credit from Betterways Ltd	Betterways Ltd	Machinery

→

(A)   (*ii*) and (*iv*) only
(B)   (*iii*) and (*iv*) only
(C)   (*ii*) and (*iii*) only
(D)   (*i*) and (*iii*) only

MC9   Which of the following best describes the meaning of 'Purchases'?

(A)   Items bought
(B)   Goods bought on credit
(C)   Goods bought for resale
(D)   Goods paid for

MC10   Which of the following should not be called 'Sales'?

(A)   Office fixtures sold
(B)   Goods sold on credit
(C)   Goods sold for cash
(D)   Sale of item previously included in 'Purchases'

MC11   Of the following, which are correct?

		Account to be debited	Account to be credited
(*i*)	Goods sold on credit to R Williams	R Williams	Sales
(*ii*)	S Johnson returns goods to us	Returns inwards	S Johnson
(*iii*)	Goods bought for cash	Cash	Purchases
(*iv*)	We returned goods to A Henry	A Henry	Returns inwards

(A)   (*i*) and (*iii*) only
(B)   (*i*) and (*ii*) only
(C)   (*ii*) and (*iv*) only
(D)   (*iii*) and (*iv*) only

MC12   Which of the following are **incorrect**?

		Account to be debited	Account to be credited
(*i*)	Goods sold for cash	Cash	Sales
(*ii*)	Goods bought on credit from T Carter	Purchases	T Carter
(*iii*)	Goods returned by us to C Barry	C Barry	Returns outwards
(*iv*)	Van bought for cash	Purchases	Cash

(A)   (*i*) and (*iii*) only
(B)   (*iii*) only
(C)   (*ii*) and (*iv*) only
(D)   (*iv*) only

MC13   Given the following, what is the amount of Capital? Assets: Premises £20,000; Stock £8,500; Cash £100. Liabilities: Creditors £3,000; Loan from A Adams £4,000

(A)   £21,100
(B)   £21,600
(C)   £32,400
(D)   £21,400

MC14   Which of the following is correct?

(A)   Profit does not alter capital
(B)   Profit reduces capital
(C)   Capital can only come from profit
(D)   Profit increases capital

MC15 Which of the following are correct?

		Account to be debited	Account to be credited
(i)	Received commission by cheque	Bank	Commission received
(ii)	Paid rates by cash	Rates	Cash
(iii)	Paid motor expenses by cheque	Motor expenses	Bank
(iv)	Received refund of insurance by cheque	Insurance	Bank

(A) (i) and (ii) only
(B) (i), (ii) and (iii) only
(C) (ii), (iii) and (iv) only
(D) (i), (ii) and (iv) only

MC16 Of the following, which are **incorrect**?

		Account to be debited	Account to be credited
(i)	Sold van for cash	Cash	Sales
(ii)	Bought stationery by cheque	Stationery	Bank
(iii)	Took cash out of business for private use	Cash	Drawings
(iv)	Paid general expenses by cheque	General expenses	Bank

(A) (ii) and (iv) only
(B) (i) and (ii) only
(C) (i) and (iii) only
(D) (ii) and (iii) only

MC17 What is the balance on the following account on 31 May 2005?

C De Freitas

2005			£	2005			£
May	1	Sales	205	May	17	Cash	300
	14	Sales	360		28	Returns	50
	30	Sales	180				

(A) A credit balance of £395
(B) A debit balance of £380
(C) A debit balance of £395
(D) There is a nil balance on the account

MC18 What would have been the balance on the account of C De Freitas in MC17 on 19 May 2008?

(A) A debit balance of £265
(B) A credit balance of £95
(C) A credit balance of £445
(D) A credit balance of £265

MC19 Which of the following best describes a trial balance?

(A) Shows the financial position of a business
(B) It is a special account
(C) Shows all the entries in the books
(D) It is a list of balances on the books

MC20 Is it true that the trial balance totals should agree?

(A) No, there are sometimes good reasons why they differ
(B) Yes, except where the trial balance is extracted at the year end
(C) Yes, always
(D) No, because it is not a balance sheet

Review questions

6.1 You are to enter up the necessary accounts for the month of May from the following information relating to a small printing firm. Then balance off the accounts and extract a trial balance as at 31 May 2008.

2008
May   1   Started in business with capital in cash of £800 and £2,200 in the bank.
       2   Bought goods on credit from the following persons: J Ward £610; P Green £214;
           M Taylor £174; S Gemmill £345; P Tone £542.
       4   Sold goods on credit to: J Sharpe £340; G Boycott £720; F Titmus £1,152.
       6   Paid rent by cash £180.
       9   J Sharpe paid us his account by cheque £340.
       10 F Titmus paid us £1,000 by cheque.
       12 We paid the following by cheque: M Taylor £174; J Ward £610.
       15 Paid carriage by cash £38.
       18 Bought goods on credit from P Green £291; S Gemmill £940.
       21 Sold goods on credit to G Boycott £810.
       31 Paid rent by cheque £230.

6.2 Enter the following transactions of an antiques shop in the accounts and extract a trial balance as at 31 March 2008.

2008
March 1   Started in business with £10,000 in the bank.
       2   Bought goods on credit from the following persons: V Gott £490; S Trout £790; A
           Wills £870.
       5   Cash sales £920.
       6   Paid wages by cheque £120.
       7   Sold goods on credit to: T Blue £310; F Bin £430; K Loy £590.
       9   Bought goods for cash £230.
       10 Bought goods on credit from: S Trout £540; A Wills £1,190.
       12 Paid wages by cheque £120.
       13 Sold goods on credit to: F Bin £730; K Loy £380.
       15 Bought shop fixtures on credit from Shelf Ltd £610.
       17 Paid S Trout by cheque £1,330.
       18 We returned goods to A Wills £42.
       21 Paid Shelf Ltd a cheque for £610.
       24 K Loy paid us his account by cheque £970.
       27 We returned goods to V Gott £32.
       30 P Fair lent us £2,000 by cash.
       31 Bought a van paying by cheque £7,240.

6.3A Record the following details relating to a carpet retailer for the month of November 2007 and extract a trial balance as at 30 November 2007:

2007
Nov   1   Started in business with £15,000 in the bank.
       3   Bought goods on credit from: J Small £290; F Brown £1,200; T Rae £610; R Charles
           £530.
       5   Cash sales £610.
       6   Paid rent by cheque £175.
       7   Paid business rates by cheque £130.
       11 Sold goods on credit to: T Potts £85; J Field £48; T Gray £1,640.
       17 Paid wages by cash £290.
       18 We returned goods to: J Small £18; R Charles £27.

19   Bought goods on credit from: R Charles £110; T Rae £320; F Jack £165.
20   Goods were returned to us by: J Field £6; T Potts £14.
21   Bought van on credit from Turnkey Motors £4,950.
23   We paid the following by cheque: J Small £272; F Brown £1,200; T Rae £500.
25   Bought another van, paying by cheque immediately £6,200.
26   Received a loan of £750 cash from B. Bennet.
28   Received cheques from: T Potts £71; J Field £42.
30   Proprietor brings a further £900 into the business, by a payment into the business bank account.

6.4A Record the following transactions for the month of January of a small finishing retailer, balance-off all the accounts, and then extract a trial balance as at 31 January 2008:

2008
Jan
1   Started in business with £10,500 cash.
2   Put £9,000 of the cash into a bank account.
3   Bought goods for cash £550.
4   Bought goods on credit from: T Dry £800; F Hood £930; M Smith £160; G Low £510.
5   Bought stationery on credit from Buttons Ltd £89.
6   Sold goods on credit to: R Tong £170; L Fish £240; M Singh £326; A Tom £204.
8   Paid rent by cheque £220.
10 Bought fixtures on credit from Chiefs Ltd £610.
11 Paid salaries in cash £790.
14 Returned goods to: F Hood £30; M Smith £42.
15 Bought van by cheque £6,500.
16 Received loan from B Barclay by cheque £2,000.
18 Goods returned to us by: R Tong £5; M Singh £20.
21 Cash sales £145.
24 Sold goods on credit to: L Fish £130; A Tom £410; R Pleat £158.
26 We paid the following by cheque: F Hood £900; M Smith £118.
29 Received cheques from: R Pleat £158; L Fish £370.
30 Received a further loan from B Barclay by cash £500.
30 Received £614 cash from A Tom.

6.5 Note, this question should not be attempted until cash discounts and trade discounts have been covered (see Chapters 13 and 14). It should also be noted that this is an example of the exception to the rule that closing stock does not generally appear in a trial balance.

On 1 October 2009, the owner of the USS Enterprise, Mr Kirk, decided that he will boldly go and keep his records on a double entry system. His assets and liabilities at that date were:

	£
Fixtures and equipment	20,000
Stock including weapons	15,000
Balance at Universe Bank	17,500
Cash	375
Creditors – Spock	3,175
– Scott	200
– McCoy	500

Kirk's transactions during October were as follows:

1   Sold faulty phasers, original cost £500, to Klingon Corp, for cash £5,000
2   Bought Photon Torpedoes (weapons), on credit from Central Council £2,500
3   Sold goods to Aardvarks, original cost £250, on credit, £1,500
4   Bought Cloaking Device (Fixtures and Fittings) from Klingon Corp £3,500
5   Paid the balance owed to Spock at 1 October less a 5% cash discount
6   Paid Central Council full amount due by cheque

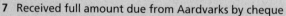

7 Received full amount due from Aardvarks by cheque
8 Paid Klingon Corp by cheque after deducting 20% trade discount
9 Paid, by bankers order, £10,000 for repairs to Enterprise following disagreement over amount owing to Klingon Corp and faulty phasers.

Required:
Open Enterprise's ledger accounts at 1 October, record all transactions for the month, balance the ledger accounts, and prepare a trial balance as at 31 October.

You can find a range of additional self-test questions, as well as material to help you with your studies, on the website that accompanies this book at **www.pearsoned.co.uk/wood**

THE FINANCIAL STATEMENTS OF SOLE TRADERS

Introduction

This part is concerned with preparing, from double entry records, the financial statements of sole traders.

Trading and profit and loss accounts: an introduction

Introduction

In this chapter, you will learn how to close down revenue and expenditure accounts in order to calculate profit and prepare a trading and profit and loss account. You will learn how to adjust purchases with stock and arrive at the cost of goods sold, and will discover the difference between gross profit and net profit. You will learn how to prepare a trading and profit and loss account and, finally, you will learn how to transfer net profit and drawings to the capital account at the end of a period.

7.1 Purpose of trading and profit and loss accounts

The main reason why people set up businesses is to make profits. Of course, if the business is not successful, it may well incur losses instead. The calculation of such profits and losses is probably the most important objective of the accounting function. The owners will want to know how the actual profits compare with the profits they had hoped to make. Knowing what profits are being made helps businesses to do many things, including:

- planning ahead
- obtaining loans from banks, other businesses, or from private individuals
- telling prospective business partners how successful the business is
- telling someone who may be interested in buying the business how successful the business is
- calculating the tax due on the profits so that the correct amount of tax can be paid to the tax authorities.

Chapter 4 dealt with the grouping of revenue and expenses prior to bringing them together to compute profit. In the case of a trader (someone who is mainly concerned with buying and selling goods), the profits are calculated by drawing up a special account called a **trading and profit and loss account**. Nowadays this is often simply called the 'profit and loss account' but, for now, we'll use the full title.

You may find it easier at this point if you try to remember that the trading and profit and loss account is a *financial statement.* **It is** *not* **an account in the sense that you have been using the term so far in this book.**

7.2 ● Gross profit

One of the most important uses of trading and profit and loss accounts is that of comparing the results obtained with the results expected. In a trading organisation, a lot of attention is paid to how much profit is made, before deducting expenses, for every £1 of sales revenue. As mentioned in Section 7.1, so that this can easily be seen in the profit calculation, the statement in which profit is calculated is split into two sections – one in which the **gross profit** is found (**this is the trading account section of the statement**), and the next section in which the **net profit** is calculated (**this is the 'profit and loss account' section of the statement**).

Gross profit is the excess of sales revenue over the **cost of goods sold**. Where the cost of goods sold is greater than the sales revenue, the result is a **gross loss**. By taking the figure of sales revenue less the cost of goods sold to generate that sales revenue, it can be seen that the accounting custom is to calculate a trader's profits **only on goods that have been sold**.

Both the trading account and the profit and loss account <u>are</u> part of the double entry system. At the end of a financial period, they are closed off. They are then summarised and the information they contain is then copied into the statement we call the 'trading and profit and loss account'. Sometimes this is abbreviated to, 'profit and loss account'. Trading and profit and loss accounts are <u>not</u> part of the double entry system.

Activity 7.1 What does this tell you about the costs and revenues that are included in the calculation of gross profit? (*Hint*: what do you not include in the calculation?)

To summarise:

Gross profit (calculated in the **trading account**)	is the excess of sales revenue over the cost of goods sold in the period.

Activity 7.2 Calculate the gross profit or gross loss of each of the following businesses:

	Cost of goods purchased £	Sales £	Gross profit/(Gross loss) £
A	9,820	10,676	_____
B	7,530	14,307	_____
C	10,500	19,370	_____
D	9,580	9,350	_____
E	8,760	17,200	_____

7.3 Net profit

Net profit, found in the **profit and loss account**, consists of the gross profit plus any revenue other than that from sales, such as rents received or commissions earned, less the total costs used up during the period other than those already included in the 'cost of goods sold'. Where the costs used up exceed the gross profit plus other revenue, the result is said to be a **net loss**. Thus:

Net profit (calculated in the profit and loss account)	is what is left of the gross profit after all other expenses have been deducted.

Activity 7.3

Using the answer to Activity 7.2, complete the following table:

	Other revenues £	Expenses £	Net profit/(Net loss) £
A	–	2,622	_____
B	4,280	2,800	_____
C	500	2,500	_____
D	–	1,780	_____
E	3,260	2,440	_____

7.4 Information needed

Before drawing up a trading and profit and loss account you should prepare the trial balance. This contains nearly all the information needed. (Later on in this book you will see that certain adjustments have to be made, but we will ignore these at this stage.)

We can now look at the trial balance of B Swift, drawn up as on 31 December 2008 after the completion of his first year in business.

Exhibit 7.1

B Swift
Trial Balance as at 31 December 2008

	Dr £	Cr £
Sales		38,500
Purchases	29,000	
Rent	2,400	
Lighting expenses	1,500	
General expenses	600	
Fixtures and fittings	5,000	
Debtors	6,800	
Creditors		9,100
Bank	15,100	
Cash	200	
Drawings	7,000	
Capital		20,000
	67,600	67,600

Note: **To make this easier to follow, we shall assume that purchases consist of goods that are resold without needing any further work. You'll learn later that these are known as 'finished goods' but, for now, we'll simply refer to them as 'goods'.**

We have already seen that gross profit is calculated as follows:

$$\boxed{\text{Sales} - \text{Cost of goods sold} = \text{Gross profit}}$$

It would be easier if all purchases in a period were always sold by the end of the same period. In that case, cost of goods sold would always equal purchases. However, this is not normally the case and so we have to calculate the cost of goods sold as follows:

What we bought in the period:	Purchases
Less Goods bought but not sold in the period:	(Closing stock)
	= Cost of goods sold

In Swift's case, there are goods unsold at the end of the period. However, there is no record in the accounting books of the value of this unsold stock. The only way that Swift can find this figure is by stocktaking at the close of business on 31 December 2008. To do this he would have to make a list of all the unsold goods and then find out their value. The value he would normally place on them would be the cost price of the goods, i.e. what he paid for them. Let's assume that this is £3,000.

The cost of goods sold figure will be:

	£
Purchases	29,000
Less Closing stock	(3,000)
Cost of goods sold	26,000

Based on the sales revenue of £38,500 the gross profit can be calculated:

$$\text{Sales} - \text{Cost of Goods Sold} = \text{Gross Profit}$$
$$£38,500 - £26,000 \qquad = £12,500$$

We now have the information we need to complete the trading account section of the trading and profit and loss account statement. Next, we need to close off the sales and purchases accounts at the end of the period so that they start the next period with no balance. To do so, we need to create a trading account (this is *not* the same as the trading part of the trading and profit and loss account, though it does produce the same gross profit figure) and then make the following entries:

(A) The balance of the sales account is transferred to the trading account by:

1 Debiting the sales account (thus closing it).
2 Crediting the trading account.

(B) The balance of the purchases account is transferred to the trading account by:

1 Debiting the trading account.
2 Crediting the purchases account (thus closing it).

(C) There is, as yet, no entry for the closing stock in the double entry accounts. This is achieved as follows:

1 Debit a closing stock account with the value of the closing stock.
2 Credit the trading account (thus completing the double entry).

The trading account will look like this:

Trading

2008			£	2008				£
Dec 31	Purchases	**(B)**	29,000	Dec 31	Sales	**(A)**		38,500
				31	Closing stock	**(C)**		3,000

We now close off the trading account in the normal way. In this case, revenues exceed costs so we describe the balance as 'gross profit'.

Trading

2008			£	2008			£
Dec 31	Purchases	**(B)**	29,000	Dec 31	Sales	**(A)**	38,500
	31	Gross profit	12,500		31	Closing stock	**(C)**	3,000
			41,500				41,500

Note that the balance shown on the trading account is described as 'gross profit' rather than being described as a balance. Also, note that the balance (i.e. the gross profit) is not brought down to the next period. The other accounts used in these double entries appear as shown below. (Note that there is no detail of the entries prior to the end of the period as all the information we have been given is the closing balances. These closing balances are simply described here as 'balance'.)

Sales

2008		£	2008		£
Dec 31	Trading	38,500	Dec 31	Balance	38,500

Purchases

2008		£	2008		£
Dec 31	Balance	29,000	Dec 31	Trading	29,000

Closing Stock

2008		£	2008		£
Dec 31	Trading	3,000	Dec 31	Balance	3,000

The entry of the closing stock on the credit side of the trading account is, in effect, a deduction from the purchases on the debit side. As you will see when we look later at the trading account section of the trading and profit and loss account statement, the closing stock is shown as a deduction from the purchases and the figure then disclosed is described as 'cost of goods sold'.

It must be remembered that we are concerned here with the very first year of trading when, for obvious reasons, there is no opening stock. In Chapter 9, we will examine how to account for stock in the later years of a business.

We can now draw up a profit and loss account (which is an 'account' opened so that the end of period double entries can be completed). Double entries are then prepared, firstly transferring the gross profit from the trading account to the credit of the profit and loss account. To do this, you would change the entry in the trading account to read 'Gross profit transferred to profit and loss':

Trading

2008			£	2008			£
Dec	31	Purchases	29,000	Dec	31	Sales	38,500
	31	Gross profit transferred to					
		Profit and loss	12,500		31	Closing stock	3,000
			41,500				41,500

Then, any revenue account balances, other than sales (which have already been dealt with in the trading account), are transferred to the credit of the profit and loss account. Typical examples are commissions received and rent received. In the case of B Swift, there are no such revenue accounts.

The costs used up in the year, in other words, the expenses of the year are then transferred to the debit of the profit and loss account. (It may also be thought, quite rightly, that as the fixtures and fittings have been used during the year with the subsequent deterioration of the assets, something should be charged for this use. **This charge is known as, 'depreciation'.** The methods for doing this are left until Chapter 24.)

The profit and loss account will now appear as follows:

Profit and Loss

2008			£	2008			£
Dec	31	Rent	2,400	Dec	31	Gross profit transferred	
	31	Lighting expenses	1,500			from Trading	12,500
	31	General expenses	600				
	31	Net profit	8,000				
			12,500				12,500

The expense accounts closed off will now appear as:

Rent

2008			£	2008			£
Dec	31	Balance	2,400	Dec	31	Profit and loss	2,400

Lighting Expenses

2008			£	2008			£
Dec	31	Balance	1,500	Dec	31	Profit and loss	1,500

General Expenses

2008			£	2008			£
Dec	31	Balance	600	Dec	31	Profit and loss	600

You now have all the information you need in order to prepare the trading and profit and loss account financial statement for the year ending 31 December 2008. It looks like this:

Exhibit 7.2

B Swift
Trading and Profit and Loss Account for the year ending 31 December 2008

	£	£
Sales		38,500
Less Cost of goods sold:		
Purchases	29,000	
Less Closing stock	(3,000)	
		(26,000)
Gross profit		12,500
Less Expenses		
Rent	2,400	
Lighting expenses	1,500	
General expenses	600	
		(4,500)
Net profit		8,000

7.5 Effect on the capital account

Although the net profit has been calculated at £8,000 and is shown as a balancing figure on the debit side of the profit and loss account, no credit entry has yet been made to complete the double entry. In other accounts, the credit entry would normally be the 'balance b/d' at the start of the next period. However, as net profit increases the capital of the owner, the credit entry must be made in the capital account by transferring the net profit from the profit and loss account. (You would change the entry in the profit and loss account from 'net profit' to read 'net profit transferred to capital'.)

The trading account and the profit and loss account, and, indeed, all the revenue and expense accounts, can thus be seen to be devices whereby the capital account is saved from being concerned with unnecessary detail. Every sale made at a profit increases the capital of the proprietor as does each item of revenue, such as rent received. On the other hand, each sale made at a loss, or each item of expense, decreases the capital of the proprietor.

Instead of altering the capital after each transaction, the respective bits of profit and loss, and of revenue and expense, are collected together using suitably described accounts. Then all the balances are brought together in one financial statement, the 'trading and profit and loss account', and the increase in the capital, i.e. the net profit, is determined. Alternatively, in the case of a net loss, the decrease in the capital is ascertained.

The fact that a separate drawings account has been in use can now also be seen to have been in keeping with the policy of avoiding unnecessary detail in the capital account. There will, therefore, only be one figure for drawings entered in the debit side of the capital account – the total of the drawings for the whole of the period.

The capital account, showing these transfers, and the drawings account now closed are as follows:

Capital

2008			£	2008			£
Dec	31	Drawings	7,000	Jan	1	Cash	20,000
	31	Balance c/d	21,000	Dec	31	Net profit	
							8,000
			28,000				28,000
				2009			
				Jan	1	Balance b/d	21,000

Drawings

2008			£	2008			£
Dec	31	Balance	7,000	Dec	31	Capital	7,000

Activity 7.4

Bertram Quigley opened a pet shop on 1 January 2008. He invested £10,000 in the business. The following information was obtained from his accounting records at the end of the year: Purchases of goods for resale £7,381; Sales £13,311; Expenses £1,172; Drawings £800; Stock in hand £410. What is the balance on Bertram Quigley's capital account at 31 December 2008?

7.6 The balances still in our books

It should be noticed that not all the items in the trial balance have been used in the trading and profit and loss account. The remaining balances are assets or liabilities or capital, they are not expenses or revenue. These will be used later when a balance sheet is drawn up. (You'll remember learning in Chapter 1 that assets, liabilities and capital are shown in balance sheets.)

Go back to Chapter 1 to refresh your understanding of assets, liabilities and capital.

Exhibit 7.3 shows the trial balance after the entries to the trading account and to the profit and loss account were made and the trading and profit and loss account was prepared. All the accounts that were closed off when the trading and profit and loss account was prepared have been removed, and drawings and net profit have been transferred to the capital account. Notice also that the stock account, which was not originally in the trial balance, is in the redrafted trial balance, as the item was not created as a balance in the books until the trading account was prepared. We will be using this trial balance when we start to look at balance sheets in the next chapter.

Note: As the trading and profit and loss account financial statement was prepared using all this information, the trial balance shown in Exhibit 7.3 can also be described as having been prepared following preparation of the trading and profit and loss account financial statement.

Exhibit 7.3

B Swift
Trial Balance as at 31 December 2008
(after the Trading Account and the Profit and Loss Account have been completed and the Trading and Profit and Loss Account prepared and the capital account adjusted for net profit and drawings)

	Dr	Cr
	£	£
Fixtures and fittings	5,000	
Debtors	6,800	
Creditors		9,100
Stock	3,000	
Bank	15,100	
Cash	200	
Capital		21,000
	30,100	30,100

Note for students: Now that you have learnt how to prepare a T-account for the trading account and a T-account for the profit and loss account, we will only rarely ask you to prepare them again. You should remember how they are used to calculate gross profit and net profit and the typical entries they may contain. From now on, we will concentrate on producing the financial statement that combines and summarises these two accounts: the trading and profit and loss account (which we will often refer to as simply the profit and loss account).

Learning outcomes

You should now have learnt:

1 Why the trading and profit and loss account is not part of the double entry system.
2 Why profit is calculated.
3 How to calculate cost of goods sold, gross profit and net profit.
4 The double entries required in order to close off the relevant expense and revenue accounts at the end of a period and post the entries to the trading account and to the profit and loss account.
5 How to deal with stock at the end of a period.
6 How to prepare a trading and profit and loss account from a trial balance.
7 How to transfer the net profit and drawings to the capital account at the end of a period.
8 That balances on accounts not closed off in order to prepare the trading and profit and loss account are carried down to the following period, that these balances represent assets, liabilities and capital, and that they are entered in the balance sheet.

Answers to activities

7.1 You only include the costs that were incurred in creating those goods that were sold. These costs include the cost of buying those goods and any costs incurred in converting goods purchased into the goods that were sold – for example, the costs of converting raw materials into finished goods. The only costs you include are those that relate to the goods sold. The costs relating to goods that have not yet been sold are not included. You do not include other costs of the business, such as postage, motor expenses, office expenses, salaries of managers, and advertising costs. Nor do you include any costs relating to the purchase or use of any assets, such as motor vehicles, computers, machinery, fixtures and fittings, and buildings.

7.2

	Cost of goods purchased £	Sales £	Gross profit/(Gross loss) £
A	9,820	10,676	856
B	7,530	14,307	6,777
C	10,500	19,370	8,870
D	9,580	9,350	(230)
E	8,760	17,200	8,440

7.3

	Other revenues £	Expenses £	Net profit/(Net loss) £
A	–	2,622	(1,766)
B	4,280	2,800	8,257
C	500	2,500	6,870
D	–	1,780	(2,010)
E	3,260	2,440	9,260

7.4 £14,368. That is, £10,000 + £13,311 – (£7,381 – £410) – £1,172 – £800.

Review questions

7.1 From the following trial balance of A Moore, extracted after one year's trading, prepare a trading and profit and loss account for the year ending 31 December 2008. A balance sheet is not required.

Trial Balance as at 31 December 2008

	Dr	Cr
	£	£
Sales		190,576
Purchases	119,832	
Salaries	56,527	
Motor expenses	2,416	
Rent	1,894	
Insurance	372	
General expenses	85	
Premises	95,420	
Motor vehicles	16,594	
Debtors	26,740	
Creditors		16,524
Cash at bank	16,519	
Cash in hand	342	
Drawings	8,425	
Capital		138,066
	345,166	345,166

Stock at 31 December 2008 was £12,408.

(Keep your answer; it will be used later in Review question 8.1)

7.2 From the following trial balance of E Es after her first year's trading, you are required to draw up a trading and profit and loss account for the year ending 30 April 2005. A balance sheet is not required.

Trial Balance as at 30 June 2008

	Dr	Cr
	£	£
Sales		384,200
Purchases	194,110	
Rent	7,800	
Lighting and heating expenses	910	
Salaries and wages	46,200	
Insurance	3,390	
Building	120,000	
Fixtures	7,800	
Debtors	46,600	
Sundry expenses	140	
Creditors		79,500
Cash at bank	21,830	
Drawings	36,000	
Vans	18,400	
Motor running expenses	5,200	
Capital		44,680
	508,380	508,380

Stock at 30 April 2005 was £39,410.

(Keep your answer; it will be used later in Review question 8.2)

7.3A From the following trial balance of B Morse drawn-up on conclusion of his first year in business, draw up a trading and profit and loss account for the year ending 31 December 2008. A balance sheet is not required.

Trial Balance as at 31 December 2008

	Dr	Cr
	£	£
General expenses	305	
Business rates	2,400	
Motor expenses	910	
Salaries	39,560	
Insurance	1,240	
Purchases	121,040	
Sales		235,812
Car	4,300	
Creditors		11,200
Debtors	21,080	
Premises	53,000	
Cash at bank	2,715	
Cash in hand	325	
Capital		23,263
Drawings	23,400	
	270,275	270,275

Stock at 31 December 2008 was £14,486.

(Keep your answer; it will be used later in Review question 8.3A)

7.4A Extract a trading and profit and loss account for the year ending 30 June 2008 for G Graham. The trial balance as at 30 June 2008 after his first year of trading was as follows:

	Dr	Cr
	£	£
Equipment rental	940	
Insurance	1,804	
Lighting and heating expenses	1,990	
Motor expenses	2,350	
Salaries and wages	48,580	
Sales		382,420
Purchases	245,950	
Sundry expenses	624	
Lorry	19,400	
Creditors		23,408
Debtors	44,516	
Fixtures	4,600	
Shop	174,000	
Cash at bank	11,346	
Drawings	44,000	
Capital		194,272
	600,100	600,100

Stock at 30 June 2008 was £29,304.

(Keep your answer; it will be used later in Review question 8.4A)

→

7.5 Henry York is a sole trader who keeps records of his cash and bank transactions. His transactions for the month of March were as follows:

March

1 Cash in hand £100, Cash at bank £5,672
4 York received a cheque for £1,246 from W Abbot which was paid directly into the bank. This represented sales.
6 Paid wages in cash £39
8 Sold goods for cash £152
10 Received cheque from G Smart for £315, in full settlement of a debt of £344; this was paid directly into the bank.
11 Paid sundry expenses in cash £73
14 Purchased goods by cheque for £800
18 Paid J Sanders a cheque of £185 in full settlement of a debt of £201
23 Withdrew £100 from the bank for office purposes
24 Paid wages in cash £39
26 Sold goods for cash £94
28 Paid salaries by cheque £230
31 Retained cash amounting to £150 and paid the remainder into the bank

Required:
(a) Enter the above transactions within T-accounts and bring down the balances.
(b) Assuming no opening debtors, creditors or stock, prepare a trading and profit and loss account for the month ending 31 March.

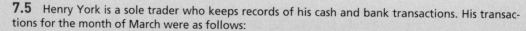

You can find a range of additional self-test questions, as well as material to help you with your studies, on the website that accompanies this book at **www.pearsoned.co.uk/wood**

Balance sheets

Learning objectives

After you have studied this chapter, you should be able to:

- explain why balance sheets are not part of the double entry system
- explain why it is important that account balances are shown under appropriate headings in the balance sheet
- explain the meanings of the terms fixed asset, current asset, current liability, and long-term liability
- describe the sequence in which each of the five main categories of items appear in the balance sheet
- describe the sequence in which each fixed asset is entered in the balance sheet
- describe the sequence in which each current asset is entered in the balance sheet
- draw up a balance sheet from information given in a trial balance

Introduction

In this chapter, you'll learn how to present asset, liability, and capital balances in a balance sheet and of the importance of adopting a consistent and meaningful layout.

8.1 Contents of the balance sheet

In Chapter 1, you learnt that balance sheets contain details of assets, liabilities and capital. The items and amounts to be entered in the balance sheet are found in the accounting books. As shown in the last chapter, they comprise those **accounts with balances** that were *not* included in the trading and profit and loss account. All these accounts that continue to have balances must be assets, capital or liabilities.

 Activity 8.1 Why have the accounts entered into the trading and profit and loss account been removed from the trial balance? (*Hint*: it is *not* just because they were entered in that statement.)

8.2 Drawing up a balance sheet

Let's look again at the post-trading and profit and loss account trial balance of B Swift (from Exhibit 7.3):

While the balance sheet layout used in Exhibit 8.2 could be considered useful, it can be improved. Let's look at a how we can do this. Firstly, we'll look at how assets could be presented in a more helpful and more meaningful way.

Assets

We are going to show the assets under two headings, fixed assets and current assets.

Fixed assets

These are assets that

1 were not bought primarily to be sold; but
2 are to be used in the business; and
3 are expected to be of use to the business for a long time.

Examples: buildings, machinery, motor vehicles, fixtures and fittings.

Fixed assets are listed first in the balance sheet starting with those the business will keep the longest, down to those which will not be kept so long. For instance:

Fixed Assets
1 Land and buildings
2 Fixtures and fittings
3 Machinery
4 Motor vehicles

Current assets

These are assets that are likely to change in the short term and certainly within twelve months of the balance sheet date. They include items held for resale at a profit, amounts owed by debtors, cash in the bank, and cash in hand.

These are listed in increasing order of liquidity. That is, starting with the asset furthest away from being turned into cash, finishing with cash itself. For instance:

Current Assets
1 Stock
2 Debtors
3 Cash at bank
4 Cash in hand

Some students feel that debtors should appear before stock because, at first sight, stock would appear to be more easily realisable (i.e. convertible into cash) than debtors. In fact, debtors can normally be more quickly turned into cash – you can often **factor** them by selling the rights to the amounts owed by debtors to a finance company for an agreed amount.

As all retailers would confirm, it is not so easy to quickly turn stock into cash. Another advantage of using this sequence is that it follows the order in which full realisation of the assets in a business takes place: before there is a sale, there must be a stock of goods which, when sold on credit, turns into debtors and, when payment is made by the debtors, turns into cash.

Liabilities

There are two categories of liabilities, current liabilities and long-term liabilities.

Current liabilities

These are items that have to be paid within a year of the balance sheet date.

Examples: bank overdrafts, amounts due to creditors for the purchase of goods for resale.

Long-term liabilities

Long-term liabilities are items that have to be paid more than a year after the balance sheet date.

Examples: bank loans, loans from other businesses.

8.5 A properly drawn up balance sheet

Exhibit 8.3 shows Exhibit 8.2 drawn up in a more appropriate way. Also read the notes following the exhibit.

Exhibit 8.3

B Swift
Balance Sheet as at 31 December 2005

	£	£
Fixed assets		
Fixtures and fittings		5,000
Current assets		
Stock	3,000	
Debtors	6,800	
Bank	15,100	
Cash	200	
	25,100	
Less Current liabilities		
Creditors	(9,100)	
Net assets		16,000
		21,000
Capital		
Cash introduced		20,000
Add Net profit for the year		8,000
		28,000
Less Drawings		(7,000)
		21,000

Notes:

(*a*) There are four categories of entries shown in this balance sheet. In practice, the fifth, long-term liabilities, often appears. It is positioned after the current liabilities; and its total appears as a deduction under the figure depicting the difference between the totals of the fixed and current assets and the current liabilities. Exhibit 8.4 shows where this would be if B Swift had any long-term liabilities.

(b) The figure for each item within each category should be shown and a total for the category produced. An example of this is the £25,100 total of current assets. The figure for each asset is listed, and the total is shown below them.

(c) The total for current liabilities is subtracted from the total for current assets and the net figure is then placed under the figure for fixed assets.

This net figure is an important one in accounting. It is known as **net current assets** or **working capital** and it shows the amount of resources the business has in a form that is readily convertible into cash.

(d) You do not write the word 'account' after each item.

(e) The owners will be most interested in their capital and the reasons why it has changed during the period. To show only the final balance of £21,000 means that the owners will not know how it was calculated. So we show the full details of the capital account.

(f) Look at the date on the balance sheet. Now compare it with the dates put on the top of the trading and profit and loss account in the last chapter. The balance sheet is a position statement – it is shown as being at one point in time, i.e. 'as at 31 December 2008'. The trading and profit and loss account is different. It is for a period of time, in this case for a whole year, and so it uses the phrase 'for the year ended 31 December 2008'.

Exhibit 8.4

B Swift
Balance Sheet as at 31 December 2008
(showing the position of long-term liabilities and net current assets)

	£	£
Fixed assets		
Fixtures and fittings		5,000
Current assets		
Stock	3,000	
Debtors	6,800	
Bank	15,100	
Cash	200	
	25,100	
Less Current liabilities		
Creditors	(9,100)	
Net current assets		16,000
		21,000
Less Long-term liabilities		(–)
Net assets		21,000
Capital		
Cash introduced		20,000
Add Net profit for the year		8,000
		28,000
Less Drawings		(7,000)
		21,000

Learning outcomes

You should now have learnt:

1 That all balances remaining on a trial balance after the trading and profit and loss account for a period has been drawn up are displayed in a balance sheet dated 'as at' the last day of the period.

2 That the balance sheet is *not* part of double entry.

3 That the balance sheet starts with fixed assets at the top, then current assets, then current liabilities, then long-term liabilities, then capital.

4 The meanings of the terms fixed asset, current asset, current liability, and long-term liability.

5 That you list fixed assets in descending order starting with those that will remain in use in the business for the longest time.

6 That you list current assets top to bottom in increasing order of liquidity.

7 That current assets less current liabilities is known as 'net current assets' or 'working capital'.

8 Why net current assets is a very important figure.

Answers to activities

8.1 All these accounts should have been closed off when the trading account and the profit and loss account were completed and the trading and profit and loss account prepared. Only accounts with balances appear in a trial balance.

8.2 A balance sheet is a financial statement that summarises the position at the end of a period. It contains all the balances on the accounts held in the accounting books at that time. As it is prepared after the trading and profit and loss account, all the accounts have already been balanced off. All we do with the balance sheet is lift the balances carried forward from the accounts and place them in an appropriate position in the statement.

Review questions

8.1 Return to question 7.1 and prepare a balance sheet as at 31 December 2008.

8.2 Return to question 7.2 and prepare a balance sheet as at 30 April 2005.

8.3A Return to question 7.3A and prepare a balance sheet as at 31 December 2008.

8.4A Return to question 7.4A and prepare a balance sheet as at 30 June 2008.

8.5 A Manny started in business on 1 January 2007, with £74,000 capital in cash. During the first year he kept very few records of his transactions.
   The assets and liabilities of the business at 31 December 2007 were:

	£
Premises	130,000
Mortgage on the premises	90,000
Stock	37,000
Debtors	4,100
Cash and bank balances	8,600
Creditors	11,300

→

→ During the year, Hope withdrew £18,000 cash for his personal use but he also paid £9,000 received from the sale of his private car into the business bank account.

Required:
From the above information, prepare a balance sheet showing the financial position of the business at 31 December 2007 and indicating the net profit for the year.

8.6A The following information relates to A Trader's business:

Assets and liabilities at	1 January 2009	31 December 2009
	£	£
Fixtures	18,000	16,200
Debtors	4,800	5,800
Stock	24,000	28,000
Creditors	8,000	11,000
Cash	760	240
Balance at bank	15,600	4,600
Loan from B Burton	6,000	2,000
Motor vehicle	–	16,000

During the year, Trader had sold private investments for £4,000 which he paid into the business bank account, and he had drawn out £200 weekly for private use.

Required:
Prepare a balance sheet as at 31 December 2009 and give the net profit as at that date.

You can find a range of additional self-test questions, as well as material to help you with your studies, on the website that accompanies this book at **www.pearsoned.co.uk/wood**

Trading and profit and loss accounts and balance sheets: further considerations

Learning objectives

After you have studied this chapter, you should be able to:

- explain the terms returns inwards, returns outwards, carriage inwards, and carriage outwards
- record returns inwards and returns outwards in the trading and profit and loss account
- explain the difference between the treatment of carriage inwards and carriage outwards in the trading and profit and loss account
- explain why carriage inwards is treated as part of the cost of purchasing goods
- explain why carriage outwards is *not* treated as part of the cost of purchasing goods
- prepare a stock account showing the entries for opening and closing stock
- prepare a trading and profit and loss account and a balance sheet containing the appropriate adjustments for returns, carriage, and other items that affect the calculation of the cost of goods sold
- explain why the costs of putting goods into a saleable condition should be charged to the trading account

Introduction

This chapter contains material that *many* students get wrong in examinations. Take care as you work through it to understand and learn the points as they are presented to you.

In this chapter, you'll learn how to treat goods returned from customers and goods returned to suppliers in the trading account. You'll also learn how to deal with the costs of transporting goods into and out of a business. You will learn how to record stock in a stock account and then carry it forward in the account to the next period. You'll also learn how to enter opening stock in the trading account. You'll learn that there are other costs that must be added to the cost of goods in the trading account. Finally, you'll learn how to prepare a trading and profit and loss account and a balance sheet when any of these items are included in the list of balances at the end of a period.

9.1 Returns inwards and returns outwards

In Chapter 3, the idea of different accounts for different movements of stock was introduced. There are four accounts involved. The sales account and the **returns inwards account** deal with goods sold and goods returned by customers. The purchases account and the **returns outwards account** deal with goods purchased and goods returned to the supplier respectively. In our first look at the preparation of a trading account in Chapter 7, returns inwards and returns outwards were omitted. This was done deliberately, so that your first sight of trading and profit and loss accounts would be as straightforward as possible.

Activity 9.1	Why do you think organisations bother with the two returns accounts? Why don't they just debit sales returned to the sales account and credit purchases returned to the purchases account?

Just as you may have done yourself, a large number of businesses return goods to their suppliers (**returns outwards**) and will have goods returned to them by their customers (**returns inwards**). When the gross profit is calculated, these returns will have to be included in the calculations.

Let's look again at the trial balance shown in Exhibit 7.1:

Exhibit 7.1 (extract)

B Swift Trial Balance as at 31 December 2008	Dr	Cr
	£	£
Sales		38,500
Purchases	29,000	

Now suppose that in Exhibit 7.1 the trial balance of B Swift, rather than simply containing a sales account balance of £38,500 and a purchases account balance of £29,000 the balances included those for returns inwards and outwards.

Exhibit 9.1

B Swift Trial Balance as at 31 December 2008 (extract)	Dr	Cr
	£	£
Sales		40,000
Purchases	31,200	
Returns inwards	1,500	
Returns outwards		2,200

Comparing these two exhibits reveals that they amount to the same thing as far as gross profit is concerned. Sales were £38,500 in the original example because the returns inwards had already been deducted in arriving at the amount shown in Exhibit 7.1. In the amended version, returns inwards should be shown separately in the trial balance and then deducted on the face of the trading and profit and loss account to get the correct figure for goods sold to customers and *kept* by them, i.e. £40,000 – £1,500 = £38,500. Purchases were originally shown as being £29,000. In the new version, returns outwards should be deducted to get the correct figure of purchases *kept* by Swift. Both the returns accounts are included in the calculation of gross profit, which now becomes:

> (Sales *less* Returns inwards) – (Cost of goods sold *less* Returns outwards) = Gross profit

The gross profit is therefore unaffected and is the same as in Chapter 7: £12,500.

The trading account section of the trading and profit and loss account will appear as in Exhibit 9.2:

Exhibit 9.2

B Swift
Trading Account section of the Trading and Profit and Loss Account for the year ending 31 December 2008

	£	£
Sales		40,000
Less Returns inwards		(1,500)
		38,500
Less Cost of goods sold:		
Purchases	31,200	
Less Returns outwards	(2,200)	
	29,000	
Less Closing stock	(3,000)	
		(26,000)
Gross profit		12,500

9.2 Carriage

If you have ever purchased anything by telephone, by letter, or over the Internet, you have probably been charged for 'postage and packing'. When goods are delivered by suppliers or sent to customers, the cost of transporting the goods is often an additional charge to the buyer. In accounting, this charge is called 'carriage'. When it is charged for delivery of goods purchased, it is called **carriage inwards**. Carriage charged on goods sent out by a business to its customers is called **carriage outwards**.

When goods are purchased, the cost of carriage inwards may either be included as a hidden part of the purchase price, or it may be charged separately. For example, suppose your business was buying exactly the same goods from two suppliers. One supplier might sell them for £100 and not charge anything for carriage. Another supplier might sell the goods for £95, but you would have to pay £5 to a courier for carriage inwards, i.e. a total cost of £100. In both cases, the same goods cost you the same total amount. It would not be appropriate to leave out the cost of carriage inwards from the 'cheaper' supplier in the calculation of gross profit, as the real cost to you having the goods available for resale is £100.

As a result, in order to ensure that the true cost of buying goods for resale is *always* included in the calculation of gross profit, **carriage inwards is *always* added to the cost of purchases in the trading account.**

Carriage outwards is not part of the selling price of goods. Customers could come and collect the goods themselves, in which case there would be no carriage out expense for the seller to pay or to recharge customers. **Carriage outwards is *always* entered in the profit and loss account section of the trading and profit and loss account. It is *never* included in the calculation of gross profit.**

Suppose that in the illustration shown in this chapter, the goods had been bought for the same total figure of £31,200 but, in fact, £29,200 was the figure for purchases and £2,000 for carriage inwards. The trial balance extract would appear as in Exhibit 9.3.

Exhibit 9.3

B Swift
Trial Balance as at 31 December 2008 (extract)

	Dr	Cr
	£	£
Sales		40,000
Purchases	29,200	
Returns inwards	1,500	
Returns outwards		2,200
Carriage inwards	2,000	

The trading account section of the trading and profit and loss account would then be as shown in Exhibit 9.4:

Exhibit 9.4

B Swift
Trading Account section of the Trading and Profit and Loss Account for the year ending 31 December 2008

	£	£
Sales		40,000
Less Returns inwards		(1,500)
		38,500
Less Cost of goods sold:		
Purchases	29,200	
Less Returns outwards	(2,200)	
	27,000	
Carriage inwards	2,000	
	29,000	
Less Closing stock	(3,000)	
		(26,000)
Gross profit		12,500

It can be seen that the three versions of B Swift's trial balance have all been concerned with the same overall amount of goods bought and sold by the business, at the same overall prices. Therefore, in each case, the same gross profit of £12,500 has been found.

Before you proceed further, attempt Review questions 9.1 and 9.2A.

9.3 The second year of a business

At the end of his second year of trading, on 31 December 2009, B Swift draws up another trial balance.

Exhibit 9.5

B Swift Trial Balance as at 31 December 2009	Dr	Cr
	£	£
Sales		67,000
Purchases	42,600	
Lighting and heating expenses	1,900	
Rent	2,400	
Wages: shop assistant	5,200	
General expenses	700	
Carriage outwards	1,100	
Buildings	20,000	
Fixtures and fittings	7,500	
Debtors	12,000	
Creditors		9,000
Bank	1,200	
Cash	400	
Drawings	9,000	
Capital		31,000
Stock (at 31 December 2008)	3,000	
	107,000	107,000

Adjustments needed for stock

So far, we have been looking at new businesses only. When a business starts, it has no stock brought forward. B Swift started in business in 2008. Therefore, when we were preparing Swift's trading and profit and loss account for 2008, there was only closing stock to worry about.

When we prepare the trading and profit and loss account for the second year we can see the difference. If you look back to the trading and profit and loss account in Exhibit 9.4, you can see there was closing stock of £3,000. This is the opening stock figure for 2009 that we will need to incorporate in the trading account. It is also the figure for stock that you can see in the trial balance at 31 December 2009.

The closing stock for one period is *always* brought forward as the opening stock for the next period.

Swift undertook a stocktake at 31 December 2009 and valued the closing stock at that date at £5,500.

We can summarise the opening and closing stock account positions for Swift over the two years as follows:

Trading Account for period ——→	Year to 31 December 2008	Year to 31 December 2009
Opening stock 1.1.2008	None	
Closing stock 31.12.2008	£3,000	
Opening stock 1.1.2009		£3,000
Closing stock 31.12.2009		£5,500

Financial statements

Financial statements is the term given to all the summary statements that accountants produce at the end of accounting periods. They are often called **final accounts**, but this term is quite misleading (as none of the financial statements are 'accounts' in the accounting sense). Nevertheless, some do still refer to them as the 'final accounts' or simply as **the accounts** of a business. You will, therefore, need to be aware of these terms, just in case you read something that uses these terms, or your teacher or lecturer, or an examiner, uses them at some time.

Other expenses in the trading account

You already know that carriage inwards is added to the cost of purchases in the trading account. You also need to add to the cost of goods in the trading account any costs incurred in converting purchases into goods for resale. In the case of a trader, it is very unusual for any additional costs to be incurred getting the goods ready for sale.

Activity 9.2 What sort of costs do you think a trader may incur that would need to be added to the cost of the goods in the trading account?

For goods imported from abroad it is usual to find that the costs of import duty and insurance are treated as part of the cost of the goods, along with any costs incurred in repackaging the goods. Any such additional costs incurred in getting goods ready for sale are debited to the trading account.

Note: Students often find it difficult to remember how to treat returns and carriage when preparing the trading and profit and loss account. You need to be sure you learn and remember that all returns, inwards and outwards, and carriage inwards appear in the calculation of gross profit. Carriage outwards appears as an expense in the profit and loss section of the statement.

9.4 A warning

Students lose a lot of marks on the topics covered in this chapter because they assume that the topics are easy and unlikely to be things that they will forget. Unfortunately, they are fairly easy to understand, and that is why they are easily forgotten and confused. You would be wise to make sure that you have understood and learnt everything presented to you in this chapter before you go any further in the book.

9.5 Review questions: the best approach

Before you attempt the review questions at the end of this chapter, you should read the section on review questions in the *Notes for Students* (pp. xv–xxiv).

Learning outcomes

You should now have learnt:

1 That returns *inwards* should be deducted from sales in the *trading* account.

2 That returns *outwards* should be deducted from purchases in the *trading* account.

3 That carriage *inwards* is shown as an expense item in the *trading* account.

4 That carriage *outwards* is shown as an expense in the *profit and loss* account.

5 How to prepare the stock account and carry forward the balance from one period to the next.

6 That in the second and later years of a business, both opening and closing stocks are brought into the trading account.

7 That it is normal practice to show cost of goods sold as a separate figure in the trading account.

8 How to prepare a trading and profit and loss account that includes the adjustments for carriage inwards and both opening and closing stock in the trading section and carriage outwards as an expense in the profit and loss section.

9 That expense items concerned with getting goods into a saleable condition are charged in the trading account.

10 That where there is import duty or insurance charged on goods purchased, these costs are treated as part of the cost of goods sold.

Answers to activities

9.1 Organisations want to know how much they sold as a separate item from how much of those goods sold were returned. The same goes for purchases and the goods sent back to the supplier. It is useful to know what proportion of goods sold are returned and whether there is any pattern in which customers are returning them. On the purchases side, knowing how many times goods have been returned and the proportion of purchases from individual suppliers that are being returned helps with monitoring the quality of the goods being purchased. While this information could be gathered if returns accounts were not used, it would be a more complicated task obtaining it. Most of all, however, the sales account is a revenue account. Entering returns inwards amounts in the sales account is contrary to the nature of the sales account. The same holds for returns outwards and the purchases account, which is an expense account.

9.2 In the case of a trader, it is very unusual for any additional costs to be incurred getting the goods ready for sale. However, a trader who sells clocks packed in boxes might buy the clocks from one supplier, and the boxes from another. Both of these items would be charged in the trading account as purchases. In addition, if someone was paid to pack the clocks into the boxes, then the wages paid for that to be done would also be charged in the trading account as part of the cost of those goods. Be careful not to confuse this with the wages of shop assistants who sell the clocks. Those wages *must* be charged in the profit and loss account because they are selling costs rather than extra costs incurred getting the goods ready for sale. The wages of the person packing the clocks would be the only wages in this case that were incurred while 'putting the goods into a saleable condition'.

Review questions

9.1 From the following information, draw up the trading account section of the trading and profit and loss account of J Bell for the year ending 31 December 2007, which was his first year in business:

	£
Carriage inwards	980
Returns outwards	840
Returns inwards	1,290
Sales	162,918
Purchases	121,437
Stocks of goods: 31 December 2007	11,320

9.2A The following information is available for the year ending 31 March 2008. Draw up the trading account section of the trading and profit and loss account of P Frank for that year.

	£
Stocks: 31 March 2008	52,400
Returns inwards	16,220
Returns outwards	19,480
Purchases	394,170
Carriage inwards	2,490
Sales	469,320

9.3 From the following trial balance of O Veneto, draw up a trading and profit and loss account for the year ending 30 April 2006, and a balance sheet as at that date.

	Dr	Cr
	£	£
Stock: 1 May 2005	80,000	
Carriage outwards	3,000	
Carriage inwards	4,000	
Returns inwards	2,000	
Returns outwards		3,000
Purchases	320,000	
Sales		610,000
Salaries and wages	90,000	
Warehouse rent	15,000	
Insurance	2,000	
Motor expenses	3,600	
Office expenses	700	
Lighting and heating expenses	1,200	
General expenses	400	
Premises	170,000	
Motor vehicles	18,000	
Fixtures and fittings	2,600	
Debtors	72,000	
Creditors		58,000
Cash at bank	7,800	
Drawings	38,000	
Capital		159,300
	830,300	830,300

Stock at 30 April 2006 was £79,530.

9.4 The following trial balance was extracted from the books of F Sorley on 30 April 2007. From it, and the note about stock, prepare his trading and profit and loss account for the year ending 30 April 2007, and a balance sheet as at that date.

	Dr	Cr
	£	£
Sales		210,420
Purchases	108,680	
Stock: 1 May 2006	9,410	
Carriage outwards	1,115	
Carriage inwards	840	
Returns inwards	4,900	
Returns outwards		3,720
Salaries and wages	41,800	
Motor expenses	912	
Rent	6,800	
Sundry expenses	318	
Motor vehicles	14,400	
Fixtures and fittings	912	
Debtors	23,200	
Creditors		14,100
Cash at bank	4,100	
Cash in hand	240	
Drawings	29,440	
Capital		18,827
	247,067	247,067

Stock at 30 April 2007 was £11,290.

9.5A The following is the trial balance of T Owen as at 31 March 2009. Draw up a set of financial statements for the year ended 31 March 2009.

	Dr	Cr
	£	£
Stock: 1 April 2008	52,800	
Sales		276,400
Purchases	141,300	
Carriage inwards	1,350	
Carriage outwards	5,840	
Returns outwards		2,408
Wages and salaries	63,400	
Business rates	3,800	
Communication expenses	714	
Commissions paid	1,930	
Insurance	1,830	
Sundry expenses	208	
Buildings	125,000	
Debtors	45,900	
Creditors		24,870
Fixtures	1,106	
Cash at bank	31,420	
Cash in hand	276	
Drawings	37,320	
Capital		210,516
	514,194	514,194

Stock at 31 March 2009 was £58,440.

→

9.6A F Brown drew up the following trial balance as at 30 September 2008. You are to draft the trading and profit and loss account for the year ending 30 September 2008 and a balance sheet as at that date.

	Dr	Cr
	£	£
Capital *P and L*		49,675
Drawings *P*	28,600	
Cash at bank *B*	4,420	
Cash in hand *B*	112	
Debtors *B*	38,100	
Creditors *B*		26,300
Stock: 30 September 2007 *P and L*	72,410	
Van *B*	5,650	
Office equipment *B — fixed asset*	7,470	
Sales *P*		391,400
Purchases *P*	254,810	
Returns inwards *P*	2,110	
Carriage inwards *P*	760	
Returns outwards *P*		1,240
Carriage outwards *P*	2,850	
Motor expenses *P*	1,490	
Rent *P*	8,200	
Telephone charges *P*	680	
Wages and salaries *P*	39,600	
Insurance *P P*	745	
Office expenses *P*	392	
Sundry expenses *P*	216	
	468,615	468,615

Stock at 30 September 2008 was £89,404. *— C.S*

9.7 Enter the following transactions in the ledger of A Baker and prepare a trial balance at 31 May, together with a calculation of the profit for the month and a balance sheet at 31 May.

May 1	Started in business with £1,500 in the bank and £500 cash
2	Purchased goods to the value of £1,750 from C Dunn, agreeing credit terms of 60 days
3	Bought fixtures and fittings for the bakery for £150, paying by cheque
6	Bought goods on credit from E Farnham for £115
10	Paid rent of £300 paying cash
12	Bought stationery – cash book and invoices – for £75 – paying by cash
14	Sold goods on credit, value £125, to G Harlem
20	Bought an old van for deliveries for £2,000 on credit from I Jumpstart
30	Paid wages of £450 net for the month by cheque
31	Summarised cash sales for the month and found them to be £2,500. Took a cheque for £500 as own wages for the month. Banked £2,000 out of the cash sales over the month
31	Closing stock was £500

98,051 ST
105 736 – Net current ST
111 386 – Total ST

9.8A Ms Porter's business position at 1 July was as follows:

	£
Stock	5,000
Equipment	3,700
Creditor (OK Ltd)	500
Debtor (AB Ltd)	300
Bank balance	1,200

During July, she:

	£
Sold goods for cash – paid to bank	3,200
Sold goods to AB Limited	600
Bought goods from OK Ltd on credit	3,900
Paid OK Ltd by cheque	3,000
Paid general expenses by cheque	500
AB Ltd paid by cheque	300

Stock at 31 July was £6,200

Required:
(a) Open ledger accounts (including capital) at 1 July
(b) Record all transactions
(c) Prepare a trial balance
(d) Prepare a trading and profit and loss account for the period
(e) Prepare a balance sheet as at 31 July

9.9 From the following trial balance of Kingfire, extracted after one year of operations, prepare a trading and profit and loss account for the year ending 30 June 2008, together with a balance sheet as at that date.

	£	£
Sales		35,800
Purchases	14,525	
Salaries	2,325	
Motor expenses	9,300	
Rent and business rates	1,250	
Insurances – building	750	
– vehicles	1,200	
Motor vehicles	10,000	
Fixtures	17,500	
Cash in hand	500	
Cash at bank		1,250
Drawings	12,000	
Long-term loan		15,000
Capital		19,275
Debtors	11,725	
Creditors		9,750
	81,075	81,075

Stock on 30 June 2008 was £3,000.

Accounting concepts and assumptions

Learning objectives

After you have studied this chapter, you should be able to:

- describe the assumptions which are made when recording accounting data
- explain why one set of financial statements has to serve many purposes
- explain the implications of objectivity and subjectivity in the context of accounting
- explain what accounting standards are and why they exist
- explain the underlying concepts of accounting
- explain how the further overriding concepts of materiality, going concern, consistency, prudence, accruals, separate determination and substance over form affect the recording and adjustment of accounting data and the reporting of accounting information

Introduction

What you have been reading about so far has been concerned with the recording of transactions in the books and the subsequent preparation of trial balances, trading and profit and loss accounts, and such recording has been based on certain assumptions. Quite deliberately, these assumptions were not discussed in detail at the time. This is because it is much easier to look at them with a greater understanding *after* basic double entry has been covered. These assumptions are known as the *concepts of accounting*.

The trading and profit and loss accounts and balance sheets shown in the previous chapters were drawn up for the owner of the business. As shown later in the book, businesses are often owned by more than just one person and these accounting statements are for the use of all the owners.

If the financial statement were solely for the use of the owner(s), there would be no need to adopt a common framework for the preparation and presentation of the information contained within them. However, as you learnt at the start of this book, there are a lot of other people who may be interested in seeing these financial statements and they need to be able to understand them. It is for this reason that there has to be a commonly established practice concerning how the information in the financial statements is prepared and presented.

In this chapter, you will learn about some of the agreed practices that underpin the preparation of accounting information, and about some of the regulations that have been developed to ensure that they are adhered to.

10.1 Objectives of financial statements

Financial statements should provide information about the financial position, performance, and changes in the financial position of an entity that is useful to a wide range of users in making economic decisions.

In order to do so, financial statements present information on the basis of a number of accounting concepts and assumptions and in accordance with various rules and procedures laid down in accounting standards.

10.2 One set of financial statements for all purposes

If it had always been the custom to draft different kinds of financial statements for different purposes, so that one version was given to a banker, another to someone wishing to buy the business, etc., then accounting would be very different from what it is today. However, this has not occurred. Identical copies of the financial statements are given to all the different external stakeholders, irrespective of why they wish to look at them.

This means that the banker, the prospective buyer of the business, the shareholders, etc. all see the same trading and profit and loss account and balance sheet. This is not an ideal situation as the interests of each party are different and each party seeks different kinds of information from those wanted by the others. For instance, the bank manager would really like to know how much the assets would sell for if the business ceased trading. She could then see what the possibility would be of the bank obtaining repayment of its loan or the overdraft. Other people would also like to see the information in the way that is most useful to them.

> **Activity 10.1** This doesn't sound very ideal for anyone, does it? What benefits do you think there may be that outweigh these disadvantages of one set of financial statements for all?

Because everyone receives the same trading and profit and loss account and balance sheet, in order to be of any use, all the various stakeholders have to believe that the assumptions upon which these financial statements are based are valid and appropriate. If they don't, they won't trust the financial statements.

Assume that you are in a class of students and that you have the problem of valuing your assets, which consist of four textbooks. The first value you decide is based upon how much you could sell them for. Your own guess is £60, but the other members of your class may suggest they should be valued at anything from £30 to £80.

Suppose that you now decide to put a value on their use to you. You may well think that the use of these textbooks will enable you to pass your examinations and that you will then be able to get a good job. Another person may have the opposite idea concerning the use of the textbooks. The use value placed on the textbooks by others in the class will be quite different. Your value may be higher than those of some of your colleagues and lower than others.

Finally, you decide to value them by reference to cost. You take out the receipts you were given when you purchased the textbooks, which show that you paid a total of £120 for them. If the rest of the class does not think that you have altered the receipts, then they will all agree with you that the value of the books, expressed at original cost, is £120. At last, you have found a way of valuing the textbooks where everyone agrees on the same figure. As this is the only valuation that you can all agree upon, each of you decides to use the idea of valuing the asset of textbooks at their cost price so that you can have a meaningful discussion about what you are worth (in terms of your assets, i.e. your textbooks) compared with everyone else in the class. It probably won't come as a surprise to you to learn that this is precisely the basis upon which the assets of a business are valued. Accountants call it the **historical cost concept**.

10.3 Objectivity and subjectivity

The use of a method which arrives at a value that everyone can agree to *because it is based upon a factual occurrence* is said to be **objective**. Valuing your textbooks at their cost is, therefore, objective – you are adhering to and accepting the facts. You are not placing your own interpretation on the facts. As a result, everyone else knows where the value came from and can see that there is very good evidence to support its adoption.

If, instead of being objective, you were **subjective**, you would use your own judgement to arrive at a cost. This often results in the value you arrive at being biased towards your own views and preferences – as in the example above when the usefulness of the textbooks to you for examinations was the basis of their valuation. Subjective valuations seem right to the person who makes them, but many other people would probably disagree with the value arrived at, because it won't appear to them to be objectively based.

The desire to provide the same set of financial statements for many different parties, and so provide a basis for measurement that is generally acceptable, means that objectivity is sought in financial accounting. If you are able to understand this desire for objectivity, then many of the apparent contradictions in accounting can be understood because it (objectivity) is at the heart of the financial accounting methods we all use.

Financial accounting, therefore, seeks objectivity and it seeks consistency in how information is prepared and presented. To achieve this, there must be a set of rules which lay down the way in which the transactions of the business are recorded. These rules have long been known as 'accounting concepts'. A group of these have become known as 'fundamental accounting concepts' or 'accounting principles' and have been enforced through their incorporation in accounting standards issued on behalf of the accountancy bodies by accounting standard boards and by their inclusion in the relevant legislation governing companies.

10.4 Accounting Standards and Financial Reporting Standards in the UK and Ireland

At one time, there used to be quite wide differences in the ways that accountants calculated profits. In the late 1960s a number of cases led to a widespread outcry against this lack of uniformity in accounting practice.

In response, the UK accounting bodies formed the Accounting Standards Committee (ASC). It issued a series of accounting standards, called *Statements of Standard Accounting Practice* (SSAPs). The ASC was replaced in 1990 by the Accounting Standards Board (ASB), which also issued accounting standards, this time called *Financial Reporting Standards* (FRSs). Both forms of accounting standards were compulsory, enforced by company law.

By April 2008, 27 FRSs had been issued and seven of the SSAPs were in force. From time to time, the ASB also issues *Urgent Issue Task Force Abstracts* (UITFs). These are generally intended to be in force only while a standard is being prepared or an existing standard amended to cover the topic dealt with in the UITF. Of course, some issues do not merit a full standard and so 26 of the 45 UITFs issued to date are still in force. UITFs carry the same weight as accounting standards and their application is compulsory for financial statements prepared under UK GAAP.

SSAPs and FRSs were generally developed with the larger company in mind. In an effort to make adherence to standards more manageable for smaller companies, in 1997 the ASB issued a third category of standard – the *Financial Reporting Standard for Smaller Entities* (FRSSE). The

FRSSE was the ASB's response to the view that smaller entities should not have to apply all the cumbersome rules contained in the SSAPs and FRSs. It is, in effect, a collection of some of the rules from virtually all the other accounting standards. Small entities can choose whether to apply it or continue to apply all the other accounting standards.

The authority, scope and application of each document issued by the ASB is announced when the document is issued. Thus, even though each accounting standard and UITF must be applied by anyone preparing financial statements under UK GAAP, in some cases certain classes of organisations are exempted from applying some or all of the rules contained within them. You can find out more about the work of the ASB and the standards and UITFs currently in issue at its website: **www.frc.org.uk/asb/technical/standards/accounting.cfm**

The use of accounting standards does not mean that two identical businesses will show exactly the same revenue, expenditure and profits year by year in their financial statements. It does, however, considerably reduce the possibilities of very large variations in financial reporting.

From 2005, all entities can switch to International Accounting Standards.

10.5 International Accounting Standards

The Accounting Standards Board deals with the United Kingdom and Ireland. Besides this and other national accounting boards, there is an international organisation concerned with accounting standards. The International Accounting Standards Committee (IASC) was established in 1973 and changed its name to the International Accounting Standards Board (IASB) in 2000.

The need for an IASB has been said to be mainly due to:

(a) The considerable growth in international investment. This means that it is desirable to have similar accounting methods the world over so that investment decisions are more compatible.
(b) The growth in the number of multinational organisations. These organisations have to produce financial statements covering a large number of countries. Standardisation between countries makes the accounting work that much easier, and reduces costs.
(c) As quite a few countries now have their own standard-setting bodies, it is desirable that their efforts should be harmonised.
(d) The need for accounting standards in countries that cannot afford a standard-setting body of their own.

The work of the IASB is overseen by 22 trustees, six from Europe, six from North America, six from Asia/Pacific. The remaining four can be from anywhere so long as geographical balance is retained. The IASB has 12 full-time members and two part-time members. Its members must reflect an appropriate balance of auditors, financial statement preparers, users of financial statements, and academics.

The IASC issued International Accounting Standards (IASs) and the IASB issues International Financial Reporting Standards (IFRSs). When the IASC was founded, it had no formal authority and IASs were entirely voluntary and initially intended for use in countries that either did not have their own accounting standards or, which had considerable logistical difficulty in establishing and maintaining the infrastructure necessary to sustain a national accounting standards board.

Up until 2005, SSAPs and FRSs had precedence over IASs in the UK and Ireland. This has all changed. From 2005, it is mandatory for all listed companies within the European Union preparing consolidated financial statements (i.e. the financial statements of a group of companies of which they are the overall parent company) to publish them in accordance with IASs and IFRSs.

This means that there is now a dual set of standards in force in the UK and Ireland, some of which apply to a small number of large companies (IASs and IFRSs), and the rest (SSAPs and FRSs) which apply to all other entities. (Companies that prefer to apply International GAAP may also do so.) While the ASB has been at pains to ensure that most of the provisions of the relevant IASs are incorporated in existing SSAPs or FRSs and each FRS indicates the level of compliance with the relevant IAS, there do remain some differences between the two sets of standards. This textbook describes and discusses the contents of UK and Ireland accounting standards and the terminology used throughout the book is that typically used under those standards.

10.6 Accounting Standards and the legal framework

Accounting standards are given legal status under the Companies Acts and comply with European Union Directives. This ensures that there is no conflict between the law and accounting standards. Anyone preparing financial statements which are intended to show a 'true and fair view' (i.e. truly reflect what has occurred and the financial position of the organisation) must observe the rules laid down in the accounting standards.

10.7 Underlying accounting concepts

A number of accounting concepts have been applied ever since financial statements were first produced for external reporting purposes. These have become second nature to accountants and are not generally reinforced, other than through custom and practice.

The historical cost concept

The need for this has already been described in the textbook valuation example. It means that assets are normally shown at cost price, and that this is the basis for valuation of the asset.

The money measurement concept

Accounting information has traditionally been concerned only with those facts covered by (*a*) and (*b*) which follow:

(*a*) it can be measured in monetary units, and
(*b*) most people will agree to the monetary value of the transaction.

This limitation is referred to as the **money measurement concept**, and it means that accounting can never tell you everything about a business. For example, accounting does not show the following:

(*c*) whether the business has good or bad managers;
(*d*) whether there are serious problems with the workforce;
(*e*) whether a rival product is about to take away many of the best customers;
(*f*) whether the government is about to pass a law which will cost the business a lot of extra expense in future.

The reason that (*c*) to (*f*) or similar items are not recorded is that it would be impossible to work out a monetary value for them which most people would agree to.

Some people think that accounting and financial statements tell you everything you want to know about a business. The above shows that this is not the case.

The business entity concept

The **business entity concept** implies that the affairs of a business are to be treated as being quite separate from the non-business activities of its owner(s).

The items recorded in the books of the business are, therefore, restricted to the transactions of the business. No matter what activities the proprietor(s) get up to outside the business, they are completely disregarded in the books kept by the business.

The only time that the personal resources of the proprietor(s) affect the accounting records of a business is when they introduce new capital into the business, or take drawings out of it.

The dual aspect concept

This states that there are two aspects of accounting, one represented by the assets of the business and the other by the claims against them. The concept states that these two aspects are always equal to each other. In other words, this is the alternate form of the accounting equation:

$$\text{Assets} = \text{Capital} + \text{Liabilities}$$

As you know, double entry is the name given to the method of recording transactions under the **dual aspect concept**.

The time interval concept

One of the underlying principles of accounting, the **time interval concept**, is that financial statements are prepared at regular intervals of one year. For internal management purposes they may be prepared far more frequently, possibly on a monthly basis or even more frequently.

10.8 Fundamental accounting concepts

These comprise a set of concepts considered so important that they have been enforced through accounting standards and/or through the Companies Acts. Five were enforced through the Companies Act 1985, and a sixth through an accounting standard, FRS 5 (*Reporting the substance of transactions*).

The five enforced through the Companies Act are the going concern concept, the consistency concept, the prudence concept, the accruals concept, and the separate determination concept.

1 Going concern

Under the UK and Ireland accounting standards (normally referred to as 'UK GAAP'), the **going concern concept** implies that the business will continue to operate for the foreseeable future. As a result, if there is no going concern problem, it is considered sensible to keep to the use of the historical cost concept when arriving at the valuations of assets.

Suppose, however, that a business is drawing up its financial statements at 31 December 2008. Normally, using the historical cost concept, the assets would be shown at a total value of £100,000. It is known, however, that the business will be forced to close down in February 2009, only two months later, and the assets are expected to be sold for only £15,000.

In this case it would not make sense to keep to the going concern concept, and so we can reject the historical cost concept for asset valuation purposes. In the balance sheet at 31 December 2008 the assets will therefore be shown at the figure of £15,000. Rejection of the going concern concept is the exception rather than the rule.

Examples where the going concern assumption should be rejected are:

● if the business is going to close down in the near future;
● where shortage of cash makes it almost certain that the business will have to cease trading;
● where a large part of the business will almost certainly have to be closed down because of a shortage of cash.

2 Consistency

Even if we do everything already listed under the concepts, there will still be quite a few different ways in which items could be recorded. This is because there can be different interpretations as to the exact meaning of a concept.

Each business should try to choose the methods which give the most reliable picture of the business.

This cannot be done if one method is used in one year and another method in the next year, and so on. Constantly changing the methods would lead to misleading profits being calculated from the accounting records. Therefore the convention of consistency is used. **The consistency concept says that when a business has once fixed a method for the accounting treatment of an item, it will enter all similar items that follow in exactly the same way.**

However, it does not mean that the business has to follow the method until the business closes down. A business can change the method used, but such a change is not made without a lot of consideration. When such a change occurs and the profits calculated in that year are affected by a material amount (i.e. one that makes a noticeable difference to the figures shown in the financial statements) then, either in the profit and loss account itself or in one of the reports that accompany it, the effect of the change should be stated.

3 Prudence

Very often accountants have to use their judgement to decide which figure to take for an item. Suppose a debt has been owing for quite a long time, and no one knows whether it will ever be paid. Should the accountant be an optimist in thinking that it will be paid, or be more pessimistic?

It is the accountant's duty to see that people get the proper facts about a business. The accountant should make certain that assets are not valued too highly. Similarly, liabilities should not be shown at values that are too low. Otherwise, people might inadvisedly lend money to a business, which they would not do if they had been provided with the proper facts.

The accountant should always exercise caution when dealing with uncertainty while, at the same time, ensuring that the financial statements are neutral – that gains and losses are neither overstated nor understated – and this is known as **prudence**.

It is true that, in applying the prudence concept, an accountant will normally make sure that all losses are recorded in the books, but that profits and gains will not be anticipated by recording them before they should be recorded. Although it emphasises neutrality, many people feel that the prudence concept means that accountants will normally take the figure relating to un-realised profits and gains which will understate rather than overstate the profit for a period. That is, they believe that accountants tend to choose figures that will cause the capital of the business to be shown at a lower amount rather than at a higher amount.

 Activity 10.2 Do you agree with this view that the prudence concept results in accountants producing financial statements that understate profits and gains and therefore present a value for capital that is lower than it should be? Justify your answer.

The recognition of profits at an appropriate time has long been recognised as being in need of guidelines and these have long been enshrined in what is known as the **realisation concept**. This is not a separate concept. Rather, it is a part of the broader concept of prudence. Its meaning was clarified by FRS 18 which was issued in 2000 and superseded SSAP 2, the accounting standard that first laid down most of the accounting concepts in use today.

The realisation concept holds to the view that profit and gains can only be taken into account when realisation has occurred and that realisation occurs only when the ultimate cash realised is capable of being assessed (i.e. determined) with reasonable certainty. Several criteria have to be observed before realisation can occur:

● goods or services are provided for the buyer;
● the buyer accepts liability to pay for the goods or services;
● the monetary value of the goods or services has been established;
● the buyer will be in a situation to be able to pay for the goods or services.

Notice that it is not the point in time

● when the order is received; or
● when the customer pays for the goods.

However, **it is only when you can be reasonably certain as to how much will be received that you can recognise profits or gains**.

Of course, recognising profits and gains now that will only be 100 per cent known in future periods is unlikely to ever mean that the correct amount has been recognised. Misjudgements can arise when, for example, profit is recognised in one period, only to discover later that this was incorrect because the goods involved have been returned in a later period because of some deficiency. Also, where services are involved rather than goods, the services might turn out to be subject to an allowance being given in a later period owing to poor performance.

Activity 10.3 What do you think the accountant should do about these possibilities when applying the realisation concept?

The accountant needs to take every possibility into account yet, at the same time, **the prudence concept requires that the financial statements are 'neutral', that is, that neither gains nor losses should be overstated or understated**.

As you will see if you take your studies to a more advanced stage, there are times other than on completion of a sale when profit may be recognised. These could include profits on long-term contracts spanning several years, such as the building of a hotel or a very large bridge. In this case, profit might be calculated for each year of the contract, even though the work is not finished at that date.

4 The accruals concept

The **accruals concept** says that net profit is the difference between revenues and the expenses incurred in generating those revenues, i.e.

$$\text{Revenues} - \text{Expenses} = \text{Net profit}$$

Determining the expenses used up to obtain the revenues is referred to as *matching* expenses against revenues. The key to the application of the concept is that all income and charges relating to the financial period to which the financial statements relate should be taken into account without regard to the date of receipt or payment.

This concept is particularly misunderstood by people who have not studied accounting. To many of them, actual payment of an item in a period is taken as being matched against the revenue of the period when the net profit is calculated. The fact that expenses consist of the assets used up in a particular period in obtaining the revenues of that period, and that cash paid in a period and expenses of a period are usually different, as you will see later, comes as a surprise to a great number of them.

5 Separate determination

In determining the aggregate amount of each asset or liability, the amount of each individual asset or liability should be determined separately from all other assets and liabilities. For example, if you have three machines, the amount at which machinery is shown in the balance sheet should be the sum of the values calculated individually for each of the three machines. Only when individual values have been derived should a total be calculated.

This concept is, perhaps, best described in relation to potential gains and potential losses. If a business is being sued by a customer for £10,000 and there is a high probability that the business will lose the case, the prudence concept requires the £10,000 to be included as a liability in the financial statements. The same business may, itself, be suing a supplier for £6,000 and may have a good probability of winning the case. It might be tempting to offset the two claims, leaving a net liability of £4,000 to appear in the financial statements. Yet, this would be contrary to the realisation concept which would not allow the probable £6,000 gain to be realised until it was viewed with reasonable certainty that it was going to be received. The **separate determination concept** prohibits the netting-off of potential liabilities and potential gains. As a result, only the probable £10,000 expense would be recognised in the financial statements.

The remaining fundamental accounting concept, that of **substance over form**, was established by the issue of FRS 5.

6 Substance over form

It can happen that the legal form of a transaction can differ from its real substance. Where this happens, accounting should show the transaction in accordance with its real substance which is, basically, how the transaction affects the economic situation of the business. This means that accounting in this instance will not reflect the exact legal position concerning that transaction.

You have not yet come across the best and easiest illustration of this concept. Later in your studies you may have to learn about accounting for fixed assets being bought on hire purchase. We will take a car as an example.

● From a legal point of view, the car does not belong to the business until all the hire purchase instalments have been paid, and an option has been taken up whereby the business takes over legal possession of the car.
● From an economic point of view, you have used the car for business purposes, just as any other car owned by the business which was paid for immediately has been used. In this case, the business will show the car being bought on hire purchase in its ledger accounts and balance sheet as though it were legally owned by the business, but also showing separately the amount still owed for it.

In this way, therefore, the substance of the transaction has taken precedence over the legal form of the transaction.

10.9 Materiality

The accounting concepts already discussed have become accepted in the business world, their assimilation having taken place over many years. However, there is one overriding rule applied to anything that appears in a financial accounting statement – that of **materiality** – it should be 'material'. That is, it should be of interest to the stakeholders, those people who make use of financial accounting statements. It need not be material to every stakeholder, but it must be material to a stakeholder before it merits inclusion.

Accounting does not serve a useful purpose if the effort of recording a transaction in a certain way is not worthwhile. Thus, if a box of paper-clips was bought it would be used up over a period of time, and this cost is used up every time someone uses a paper-clip. It is possible to record this as an expense every time a paper-clip is used but, obviously, the price of a paper-clip is so small that it is not worth recording it in this fashion, nor is the entire box of paper-clips. The paper-clips are not a material item and, therefore, the box would be charged as an expense in the period it was bought, irrespective of the fact that it could last for more than one account-ing period. In other words, **do not waste your time in the elaborate recording of trivial items.**

Similarly, the purchase of a cheap metal ashtray would also be charged as an expense in the period it was bought because it is not a material item, even though it may in fact last for twenty years. A lorry would, however, be deemed to be a material item in most businesses, and so, as will be seen in Chapter 26, an attempt is made to charge each period with the cost consumed in each period of its use.

> **Activity 10.4**
>
> Which fundamental accounting concept is what is being described in the previous paragraph an example of?

Businesses fix all sorts of arbitrary rules to determine what is material and what is not. There is no law that lays down what these should be – the decision as to what is material and what is not is dependent upon judgement. A business may well decide that all items under £100 should be treated as expenses in the period in which they were bought, even though they may well be in use in the business for the following ten years. Another business, especially a large one, may fix the limit at £1,000. Different limits may be set for different types of item.

It can be seen that the size and the type of business will affect the decisions as to which items are material. With individuals, an amount of £1,000 may well be more than you, as a student, possess. For a multi-millionaire, what is a material item and what is not will almost certainly not be comparable. Just as individuals vary, then, so do businesses. Some businesses have a great deal of machinery and may well treat all items of machinery costing less than £1,000 as not being material, whereas another business which makes about the same amount of profit, but has very little machinery, may well treat a £600 machine as being a material item as they have fixed their materiality limit at £250.

10.10 The assumption of the stability of currency

You don't have to be very old to remember that a few years ago many goods could be bought with less money than today. If you listen to any older relative, you are likely to hear many stories of how little this item or the other could be bought for x years ago. The currencies of the coun-tries of the world are not stable in terms of what each unit of currency can buy over the years.

Accounting, however, uses the historical cost concept, which states that the asset is normally shown at its cost price. This means that accounting statements will be distorted because assets will be bought at different points in time at the price then ruling, and the figures totalled up to show the value of the assets in cost terms. For instance, suppose that you had bought a building twenty years ago for £20,000. You now decide to buy an identical additional building, but the price has now risen to £190,000. You buy it, and the buildings account now shows buildings at a figure of £210,000. One building is measured cost-wise in terms of the currency of twenty years ago, while the other is taken at today's currency value. The figure of a total of £210,000 is historically correct, but, other than that, the total figure cannot be said to be particularly valid for any other use.

This means that to make a correct assessment of accounting statements one must bear in mind the distorting effects of changing price levels upon the accounting entries as recorded. There are techniques for adjusting accounts so as to try and eliminate these distortions, but they fall out-side the scope of this book and are dealt with in *Business Accounting 2*.

10.11 FRS 18

SSAP 2 was the first UK accounting standard to cover the disclosure of accounting policies which include accounting concepts. It dealt with four of the fundamental accounting concepts, going concern, accruals, consistency, and prudence. When FRS 18 was issued in 2000, it superseded SSAP 2. As mentioned in Section 10.8, one change it brought concerned the clarification of what was meant by 'realisation' and so clarified the position concerning recognition of profits and gains. The other main change it introduced was to amend the SSAP 2 definition of prudence by stating that **financial statements must be neutral**. Various matters dealt with in this standard have not yet been examined, and are covered in later chapters.

> A fuller discussion of FRS 18 is left until Chapter 45.

10.12 Accounting concepts in action

This is too early a stage in your studies for you to be able to appreciate more fully how these concepts work in practice. It is far better left towards the end of this book and, therefore, we consider this topic further in Chapter 45.

Learning outcomes

You should now have learnt:

1 Why one set of financial statements has to serve many purposes.

2 Why the need for general agreement has given rise to the concepts and conventions that govern accounting.

3 The implications of objectivity and subjectivity in the context of accounting.

4 What accounting standards are and why they exist.

5 The assumptions which are made when recording accounting data.

6 The underlying concepts of accounting.

7 How the further overriding concepts of materiality, going concern, consistency, prudence, accruals, separate determination and substance over form affect the recording and adjustment of accounting data and the reporting of accounting information.

8 That an assumption is made that monetary measures remain stable, i.e. that normally accounts are not adjusted for inflation or deflation.

Answers to activities

10.1 Although this is hardly ideal, at least everyone receives the same basic financial information concerning an organisation and, because all financial statements are prepared in the same way, comparison between them is reasonably straightforward. Also, some of the users of these financial statements have other sources of information, financial and otherwise, about a business – the banker, for example, will also have access to the financial statements produced for use by the managers of the business. These 'management accounts' are considerably more detailed than the financial statements and most bankers insist upon access to them when large sums of money are involved. (The financial statements produced for internal use are dealt with in Chapter 43.) The banker will also have information about other businesses in the same industry and about the state of the market in which the business operates, and will thus be able to compare the performance of the business against those of its competitors.

10.2 Although accountants do include all the losses that have been identified in the financial statements, they also include all the gains that can be identified with reasonable certainty. In effect, by doing so, an accountant is being neutral and so, in practice, the amount of capital shown in the balance sheet should be a true reflection of the position as known when the financial statements were produced.

10.3 When applying the realisation concept, the accountant will endeavour to estimate as accurately as possible the returns or allowances that are reasonably likely to arise and will build that information into the calculation of the profit and gains to be recognised in the period for which financial statements are being prepared.

10.4 The accruals concept.

Review questions

10.1 What is meant by the 'money measurement concept'?

10.2 Explain the concept of prudence in relation to the recognition of profits and losses.

10.3 Explain the term 'materiality' as it is used in accounting.

10.4 'The historical cost convention looks backwards but the going concern convention looks forwards.'

Required:
(a) Explain clearly what is meant by:
   (i) the historical cost convention;
   (ii) the going concern convention.
(b) Does traditional financial accounting, using the historical cost convention, make the going concern convention unnecessary? Explain your answer fully.
(c) Which do you think a shareholder is likely to find more useful – a report on the past or an estimate of the future? Why?

(*Association of Chartered Certified Accountants*)

You can find a range of additional self-test questions, as well as material to help you with your studies, on the website that accompanies this book at **www.pearsoned.co.uk/wood**

Part 3

Part 3

BOOKS OF ORIGINAL ENTRY

Introduction

This part is concerned with the books into which transactions are first entered; it also includes chapters on VAT, the banking system in the UK, employees' pay, and two chapters on computers and computerised accounting systems.

Chapter
11

Books of original entry and ledgers

Learning objectives

After you have studied this chapter, you should be able to:

- justify the need for books of original entry
- explain what each book of original entry is used for
- describe the process of recording transactions in a book of original entry and then recording a summary of the transactions involving similar items in a ledger
- distinguish between personal and impersonal accounts
- list the ledgers most commonly used and distinguish between those that are used for personal accounts and those that are used for impersonal accounts
- explain the broader role of an accountant, the communicator role that lies beyond the recording and processing of data about transactions

Introduction

In this chapter, you will learn about the books in which details of accounting transactions are recorded. You will learn that day books and journals are used to record all transactions made on credit and that the cash book is used to record all cash and bank transactions. Then, you will learn that these entries are transferred from the books of original entry to a set of books called ledgers and that each ledger is for a particular type of item and that, by having a set of ledgers, entries in accounts of items of a similar nature are recorded in the same place.

11.1 The growth of the business

When a business is very small, all the double entry accounts can be kept in one book, which we would call a 'ledger'. As the business grows it would be impossible just to use one book, as the large number of pages needed for a lot of transactions would mean that the book would be too big to handle. Also, suppose we have several bookkeepers. They could not all do their work properly if there were only one ledger.

The answer to this problem is for us to use more books. When we do this, we put similar types of transactions together and have a book for each type. In each book, we will not mix together transactions which are different from one another.

11.2 Books of original entry

When a transaction takes place, we need to record as much as possible of the details of the transaction. For example, if we sold four computers on credit to a Mr De Souza for £1,000 per computer, we would want to record that we sold four computers for £1,000 each to Mr De Souza on credit. We would also want to record the address and contact information of Mr De Souza and the date of the transaction. Some businesses would also record information like the identity of the person who sold them to Mr De Souza and the time of the sale.

Books of original entry are the books in which we first record transactions, such as the sale of the four computers. We have a separate book for each kind of transaction.

Thus, the nature of the transaction affects which book it is entered into. Sales will be entered in one book, purchases in another book, cash in another book, and so on. We enter transactions in these books recording:

● the date on which each transaction took place – the transactions should be shown in date order;
● details relating to the sale (as listed in the computer example above) are entered in a 'details' column;
● a folio column entry is made cross-referencing back to the original 'source document', e.g. the invoice;
● the monetary amounts are entered in columns included in the books of original entry for that purpose.

11.3 Types of books of original entry

Books of original entry are known as either 'journals' or 'day books'. However, in the case of the last book of original entry shown below, it is always a 'journal' and the second last is always known as the 'cash book'. The term 'day book' is, perhaps, more commonly used, as it more clearly indicates the nature of these books of original entry – entries are made to them every day. The commonly used books of original entry are:

● **Sales day book** (or *sales journal*) – for credit sales.
● **Purchases day book** (or *purchases journal*) – for credit purchases.
● **Returns inwards day book** (or *returns inwards journal*) – for returns inwards.
● **Returns outwards day book** (or *returns outwards journal*) – for returns outwards.
● **Cash book** – for receipts and payments of cash and cheques.
● General journal (or **journal** if the term 'day book' is used for the other books of original entry) – for other items.

Most students find it less confusing if 'day book' is used rather than 'journal', as it makes it very clear what is meant when someone refers to 'the journal'. **During the remainder of this book, we will use the term 'day book'. However, never forget that the term 'day book' can always be substituted with the word 'journal'. Be sure to remember this. Examiners may use either term.**

11.4 Using more than one ledger

Entries are made in the books of original entry. The entries are then summarised and the summary information is entered, using double entry, to accounts kept in the various ledgers of the business. One reason why a set of ledgers is used rather than just one big ledger is that this makes it easier to divide the work of recording all the entries between different bookkeepers.

Activity 11.1   Why else do you think we have more than one ledger?

11.5   Types of ledger

The different types of ledger most businesses use are:

● **Sales ledger**. This is for customers' personal accounts.
● **Purchases ledger**. This is for suppliers' personal accounts.
● **General ledger**. This contains the remaining double entry accounts, such as those relating to expenses, fixed assets, and capital.

11.6   A diagram of the books commonly used

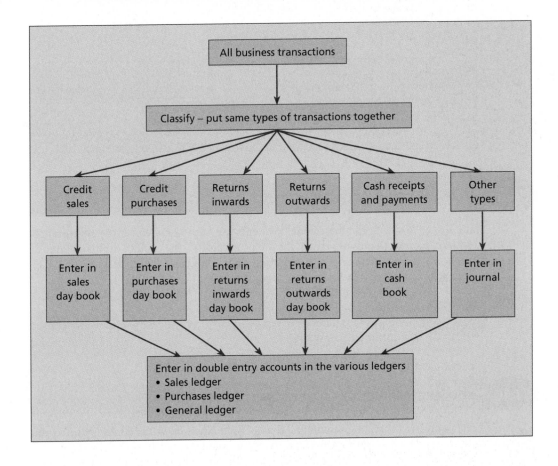

11.7   Description of books used

In the next few chapters we will look at the books used in more detail.

11.8 Types of account

Some people describe all accounts as personal accounts or as impersonal accounts.

● **Personal accounts** – these are for debtors and creditors (i.e. customers and suppliers).
● **Impersonal accounts** – divided between 'real' accounts and 'nominal' accounts:
 – **Real accounts** – accounts in which possessions are recorded. Examples are buildings, machinery, fixtures and stock.
 – **Nominal accounts** – accounts in which expenses, income and capital are recorded.

A diagram may enable you to follow this better:

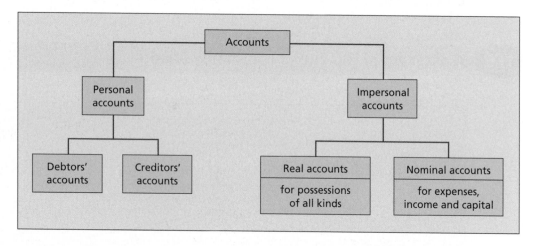

11.9 Nominal and private ledgers

The ledger in which the impersonal accounts are kept is known as the **nominal** (or 'general') **ledger**. In order to ensure privacy for the proprietor(s), the capital, drawings, and other similar accounts are sometimes kept in a **private ledger**. This prevents office staff from seeing details of items which the proprietors want to keep secret.

Activity 11.2 Why bother with *books of original entry*? Why don't we just enter transactions straight into the ledgers?

11.10 The accountant as a communicator

The impression is often given that all that an accountant does is produce figures arranged in various ways. This has led to a perception that accountants are boring, pragmatic people with no sense of humour. While it is true that such work does take up quite a lot of an accountant's time, it does not account for all of a typical accountant's work. **Accountants also need to be good communicators,** not just in the way they present accounting information on paper, but also in how they verbally communicate the significance of the information they prepare.

An accountant can obviously arrange the financial figures so as to present the information in as meaningful a way as possible for the people who are going to use that information. That is, after all, what accountants are trained to do. If the financial figures are to be given to several people, all of whom are very knowledgeable about accounting, an accountant will simply apply all the conventions and regulations of accounting in order to present the information in the 'normal' accounting way, knowing full well that the recipients of the information will understand it.

On the other hand, accounting figures may well be needed by people who have absolutely no knowledge at all of accounting. In such a case, a typical accounting statement would be of little or no use to them. They would not understand it. In this case, an accountant might set out the figures in a completely different way to try to make it easy for them to grasp. For instance, instead of preparing a 'normal' trading and profit and loss account, the accountant might show the information as follows:

	£	£
In the year ended 31 December 2009 you sold goods for		100,000
Now, how much had those goods cost you to buy?		
At the start of the year you had stock costing	12,000	
+ You bought some more goods in the year costing	56,000	
So altogether you had goods available to sell that cost	68,000	
– At the end of the year, you had stock of goods unsold that cost	(6,000)	
So, the goods you had sold in the year had cost you	62,000	
Let us deduct this from what you had sold the goods for		(62,000)
This means that you had made a profit on buying and selling goods, before any other expenses had been paid, amounting to		38,000
(We call this type of profit the **gross** profit)		
But, during the year, you suffered other expenses such as wages, rent, and electricity. The amount of these expenses, not including anything you took for yourself, amounted to		(18,000)
So, in this year your sales value exceeded all the costs involved in running the business (so that the sales could be made) by		20,000
(We call this type of profit the **net** profit)		

An accountant is failing to perform his or her role appropriately and effectively if the figures are not arranged so as to make them meaningful to the recipient. The accountant's job is not just to produce figures for the accountant's own consumption, it is to communicate the results to other people, many of whom know nothing about accounting.

 Activity 11.3 Reconcile this observation with the standardisation of the presentation of financial accounting information as contained in accounting standards and the Companies Acts.

Nowadays, communication skills are a very important part of the accountant's role. Very often, the accountant will have to talk to people in order to explain the figures, or send a letter or write a report about them. The accountant will also have to talk or write to people to find out exactly what sort of accounting information is needed by them, or to explain to them what sort of information could be provided.

If accounting examinations contained only computational type questions, they would not test the ability of candidates to communicate in any way other than writing down accounting figures and, as a result, the examinations would fail to examine these other important aspects of the job. **In recent years much more attention has been paid by examining boards to these other aspects of an accountant's work.**

Learning outcomes

You should now have learnt:

1 That transactions are classified and details about them are entered in the appropriate book of original entry.

2 That the books of original entry are used as a basis for posting the transactions in summary form to the double entry accounts in the various ledgers.

3 That there is a set of books of original entry, each of which serves a specific purpose.

4 That there is a set of ledgers, each of which serves a specific purpose.

5 That accountants need to be good communicators.

Answers to activities

11.1 The most important reason is to aid analysis by keeping similar items together.

11.2 Books of original entry contain all the important information relating to a transaction. Ledgers just contain a summary. In fact, some of the entries in the ledgers are often just one-line entries covering an entire month of transactions.

11.3 There really is no conflict so far as financial information prepared for internal use is concerned. Financial statements produced for consumption by users outside the business do have to conform to the conventions relating to content and layout. However, those prepared for internal use do not. There is no reason why they could not be prepared along the lines of the unconventionally laid-out trading and profit and loss example shown on page 123. External stakeholders will never receive their financial statements in this highly user-friendly form. It is simply too much work to customise the financial statement for every class of stakeholder.

You can find a range of additional self-test questions, as well as material to help you with your studies, on the website that accompanies this book at **www.pearsoned.co.uk/wood**

The banking system in the UK

Learning objectives

After you have studied this chapter, you should be able to:

- describe the changes that have occurred in the UK since the late 1960s in the ways payments can be made
- describe the many alternatives to cheques and cash that currently exist
- describe the cheque clearing system
- write a cheque
- explain the effect of various kinds of crossings on cheques
- explain how to endorse a cheque over to someone else
- complete bank pay-in slips
- explain the timing differences between entries in a cash book and those on a bank statement

Introduction

In this chapter, you'll learn about the current UK system for payment of money out of and into bank accounts. You'll learn about the range of plastic cards in use and about various alternatives to cheques that have arisen since the 1960s. You will also learn about the cheque clearing system and how to prepare cheques and bank pay-in slips.

12.1 Twenty-first-century banking

Until quite recently, if individuals wanted money out of their bank accounts, they had to go to their local branch and use a cheque to withdraw the amount they needed. Now they can go into their bank, hand over their **debit card** and withdraw money from their account. Alternatively, they can use virtually any cash machine to do the same thing.

This alternative to cheques first started in 1967 when Barclays Bank introduced the first 'automatic teller machines' (ATMs) or 'cash machines'. These early ATMs gave cash in exchange for tokens. In the early 1970s, **plastic cards** were introduced with magnetic strips that enabled the ATMs to read the account details and process transactions directly with the accounts held in the bank. This marked the start of the plastic card revolution in banking and transaction payment.

By the mid 1970s a number of banks had ATMs in the wall outside major branches where cash could be withdrawn using a **Personal Identification Number** or 'PIN'.

At that time, ATMs offered a very limited service – some, for example, only allowed you to withdraw £10, no matter how much you had in your bank account.

Activity 12.1 Why do you think they only offered a limited service at that time?

Gradually, cash machines became more common and by the mid 1980s the facilities they offered began to include the options to print a mini statement, provide a receipt, and vary the amount you wished to withdraw. However, you could only use the machines at some of the branches of your own bank.

ATM facilities now are very much better than thirty years ago. In addition to allowing withdrawal of funds and informing customers of the balance on their accounts, some ATMs also allow customers to order cheque books, change their PIN, request statements, pay bills, deposit funds and order mini statements; and most ATMs allow access to funds '24/7', i.e. 24 hours a day, 7 days a week. And, for some time, many banks and building societies have allowed their customers access to their accounts via cash machines owned by other institutions, principally through the Link network (**www.link.co.uk**), of which 38 UK financial institutions and 13 non-financial institutions are members.

It is hardly surprising that nearly half of all personal cash withdrawals from bank accounts are now done through an ATM and that over 75 per cent of all cash in circulation comes from an ATM. In fact, over 35 million people make an average of six withdrawals, each of an average of £66, from one of the UK's 61,000 ATMs each month. In a move towards widening accessibility, over a quarter of ATMs are *not* located at banks, but in places such as shopping centres, supermarkets, railway stations and airports where obtaining money quickly is important.

Outside the UK, customers of many UK banks can continue to use their plastic cards in ATMs through the Visa 'Plus' and MasterCard 'Cirrus' networks.

Cash is still the most popular method of making payments, but use of debit and credit cards is growing. **Direct debits** are the most popular form of non-cash payment and debit cards are the most popular form of payment by plastic card. The situation is changing significantly, as can be seen by the way it changed between 2002 and 2005, shown in Exhibit 12.1:

Exhibit 12.1

Payment transactions by medium in 2005	Number (billion)	% change on 2002
Debit card purchases	4.08	36.4
Credit and charge card purchases	1.92	14.0
Store cards (estimate)	0.08	(41.7)
Plastic card withdrawals at ATMs and branch counters	2.81	19.9
Direct debits, standing orders, direct credits and CHAPS	5.38	36.8
Cheques	1.93	(19.3)
Total non-cash (plastic card, automated and paper)	*16.21*	*20.2*
Cash payments (estimate)	23.97	(10.0)
Post Office order book payments and passbook withdrawals	0.26	(62.6)
TOTAL	40.43	(0.9)

Activity 12.2 How many different forms of plastic cards do you think there are? Think about this for a minute and then list as many forms of plastic card as you can. (Note: this is *not* a question about how many different credit cards there are. It is about different forms of plastic cards, of which a credit card is but one example.)

Now let's look in more detail at some of the features of the UK banking and payments system.

12.2 Debit cards

Debit cards were first introduced into the UK in 1967. The most basic debit cards have an ATM facility. However, many also serve as cheque guarantee cards and as **Switch** cards. Switch is a debit card system that is rapidly replacing cheques as a way to pay for in-store purchases. It allows holders to pay for purchases and, in some shops, withdraw cash at the checkout till. Similarly to cheques, the money spent is automatically withdrawn from the shopper's bank account within three days. More than half the adults in the UK use a debit card. The use of these cards increased by over 500 per cent between 1993 (660 million transactions) and 2005 (4.08 billion transactions).

12.3 Direct debits

Direct debits are the most popular form of non-cash payment and their use was forecast to double by the end of the decade. They were introduced as a paper-based system in 1967. The scheme is managed by BACS Limited, the UK's automated clearing house. They enable payments to be made automatically into a bank account for whatever amount the recipient requests. (This differs from another similar payment medium, the **standing order**, which pays only an amount agreed by the payer.)

12.4 Internet banking

Increasingly, people are making non-cash payments by using credit cards on the Internet. Individuals can also operate their bank accounts in this way, with most banks now offering a 24/7 facility to check account balances, set up standing orders, view direct debits, pay bills and transfer funds between current accounts and savings accounts. In 2006, 42 per cent of 28 million UK adults who went on to the Internet accessed their current accounts in this way.

12.5 Clearing

Clearing involves the transmission and settlement of cheque payments between accounts held at different banks and different branches of the same bank. Clearing generally takes three working days:

Day 1   Cheques are processed by the bank into which they were paid. Information about each cheque is then sent electronically through a secure data exchange network (the Inter Bank Data Exchange) to the clearing centre of the bank on which the cheque is drawn.

Day 2   Each cheque is physically delivered to an Exchange Centre, where each bank collects all the cheques drawn on accounts held with it.

Day 3   Bank staff review the cheques presented for payment and decide whether to authorise payment; and the banks pay each other the net value of the cheques transferred between them.

APACS

The Association for Payment Clearing Services was set up in 1985. It is the umbrella body for the UK payments industry and it oversees the major UK payment clearing systems and maintains their operational efficiency and financial integrity.

Cheque and Credit Clearing Company

The Cheque and Credit Clearing Company is responsible for the bulk clearing of cheques and paper credits throughout Great Britain. Cheque and credit payments in Northern Ireland are processed locally.

Members of the Cheque and Credit Clearing Company, under the umbrella of APACS, are individually responsible for processing cheques drawn by or credited to the accounts of their customers. In addition, several hundred other institutions, such as smaller building societies, provide cheque facilities for their customers and obtain indirect access to the cheque clearing mechanisms by means of commercially negotiated agency arrangements with one of the full members of APACS.

You can find further information about many of the topics so far covered in this chapter at the APACS website: www.apacs.org.uk and at the National Statistics website: www.statistics.gov.uk

Let's look now at the types of bank account typically in use and at how cheque payments are made.

12.6   Types of account

There are two main types of bank account: current accounts and deposit accounts.

Current accounts

Current accounts may be used for regular payments into and out of a bank account. A **cheque book** will be given by the bank to the holder of the account. The cheque book will be used by the account holder to make payments out of the current account.

So that the account holder can pay money into his/her current account, the holder may also be given a pay-in book.

Holders of current accounts are usually also given a multiple use plastic card incorporating a cheque guarantee card, debit card and ATM card.

Many years ago, banks discovered that customers normally don't change banks once they have opened accounts. Their initial response in the 1970s was to encourage students to do so by offering free gifts, such as loose-leaf folders and note pads. Things have moved on a lot and they now offer reduced facility current accounts to children, young adults and students, often with free gifts such as toys, personal organisers, calculators, discount vouchers to be used in retail stores, and even cash.

Current accounts often earn little or no interest. To gain more interest on funds deposited in a bank, it is necessary to also open a **deposit account**.

Deposit accounts

These accounts generally earn more interest than current accounts and are intended for funds that will not be accessed on a frequent or regular basis. However, this is now changing with many banks linking current accounts to deposit accounts (also known as 'savings accounts') so that funds can be transferred from one to the other whenever it is appropriate. Some banks operate this automatically but most leave it to the account holder to notify the bank, often by telephone, that a transfer should be made between the accounts.

12.7 Cheques

Use of cheques peaked in 1990, since when debit cards and direct debits have swiftly established themselves as favourite alternatives among private individuals. Nevertheless, they remain the most common form of payment used by businesses.

Activity 12.3 Why do you think businesses still prefer to use cheques?

The cheque system

1 When the bank has agreed to let someone open a current account it obtains a copy of the new customer's signature. This allows the bank to verify that cheques used are, in fact, signed by the customer. The bank then normally issues the new customer with a cheque book. (Note: some current accounts only offer a debit card and customers have to request a cheque book in addition if they intend writing cheques.)

2 The cheques can then be used to make payments out of the account. Account holders need to ensure that they do not make out a cheque for more than they have in their account – post-dating cheques (i.e. putting a future date on them when sufficient funds will be available) is not permitted and banks will not process such cheques. If a customer wishes to pay out more money than is available they should contact the bank first and request an **overdraft**. The bank is not obliged to grant an overdraft, though many grant all their customers a minimal one – perhaps £100 – when they open the current account that they can use if they wish. (Businesses often have very large overdrafts as this is a cheaper way of financing short-term borrowing than taking out a formal **bank loan**.)

3 The person filling in the cheque and using it for payment is known as the **drawer**. The person to whom the cheque is paid is known as the **payee**.

Activity 12.4 Why do you think an overdraft is cheaper than a bank loan?

The features of a cheque

Exhibit 12.2 shows a blank cheque before it is filled in.

On the face of the cheque are various sets of numbers. These are:

914234   Every cheque printed for the Cheshire Bank for your account will be given a different number, so that individual items can be traced.

09-07-99 Each branch of every bank in the United Kingdom has a different number given to it. Thus this branch has a 'code' number 09-07-99.

Exhibit 12.2

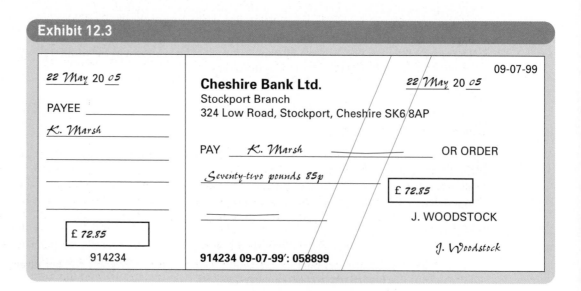

| | 20__ | | **Cheshire Bank Ltd.** | 09-07-99 |
| PAYEE _____ | | | Stockport Branch | __ 20__ |

058899   Each account with the bank is given a different number. This particular number is kept only for the account of J Woodstock at the Stockport branch.

If a cheque has a counterfoil attached, it can be filled in at the same time as the cheque, showing the information that was entered on the cheque. The counterfoil is then kept as a note of what was paid, to whom, and when. (Many cheque books don't have counterfoils. Instead they contain separate pages where the details can be entered.)

We can now look at the completion of a cheque. Let's assume that we are paying seventy-two pounds and eighty-five pence to K Marsh on 22 May 2005. Exhibit 12.3 shows the completed cheque.

Exhibit 12.3

In Exhibit 12.3, the drawer is J Woodstock, and the payee is K Marsh.

The two parallel lines across the face of the cheque are drawn as a safeguard. If this had not been done, the cheque would have been an 'uncrossed cheque'. If this cheque had not been crossed, a thief could have gone to the Stockport branch of the Cheshire Bank and obtained cash in exchange for the cheque. When the cheque is crossed it *must* be paid into a bank account. Normally, a more secure type of crossing is used.

Cheque crossings

Cheques can be further safeguarded by using a specific crossing, i.e. writing a form of instruction within the crossing on the cheques as shown in Exhibit 12.4:

Exhibit 12.4

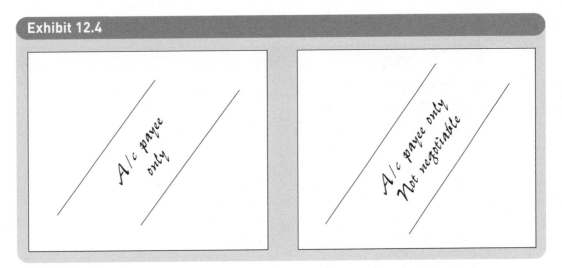

These both mean the same thing. They are specific instructions to the banks about the use of the cheque. There is a third, more common crossing that also means the same thing, '**Account Payee**'. As it is shorter, it is the one most commonly used. The use of any of these three crossings means the cheques should be paid only into the account of the payee named. If cheques (whether crossed or not) are lost or stolen, the drawer must advise their bank immediately and the cheques will be 'stopped', i.e. payment will not be made on these cheques, provided the drawer acts swiftly. In addition, if a crossed cheque is lost or stolen it will be of no use to the thief or finder. This is because it is impossible for this cheque to be paid into any bank account other than that of the named payee. For obvious reasons, cheques are often printed with the 'Account Payee' crossing on them.

Cheque endorsements

Cheques with the above crossings can only be paid into the bank account of the payee. However, if the crossing does not contain any of these three terms, a cheque received by someone can be **endorsed** over to someone else. The person then receiving the cheque could bank it. This means that if Adam Smith receives a cheque from John Wilson, he can 'endorse' the cheque and hand it to Petra Jones as payment of money by Smith to Jones. Jones can then pay it into her bank account.

To endorse the cheque, Smith would write the words 'Pay P Jones or order' on the reverse side of the cheque and then sign underneath it. Jones would then usually bank the cheque, but she could endorse it over to someone else by adding yet another endorsement and signing it.

A cheque which has been paid to someone, and has passed through their bank account or been endorsed over by that person to someone else, is legal proof of the fact that payment had been made. However, cheques do not indicate what the payment was for, and so do not legally carry the same weight as a receipt.

12.8 Pay-in slips

When we want to pay money into a current account, either cash or cheques, or both, we use a **pay-in slip**. When the payment is into an account held in a different bank, the form is called a **bank giro credit**. The two types of form are virtually identical. A bank giro credit can be used instead of a pay-in slip, but not the other way around, as the details of the other bank need to be entered on the bank giro credit. Exhibit 12.5 shows a completed bank giro credit:

Exhibit 12.5

Face of bank giro credit

	pounds	pence
£5 notes and over	20	
£1 coins	3	
50p coins		50
Other silver		30
Bronze coins		12
Total cash	23	92
Cheques, PO's etc. (see over)	249	59
	273	51

Date 22 May 20 05 — Cashier's stamp and initials

bank giro credit — Destination Branch Code number: 09-07-99

Bank: Cheshire Bank
Branch: Stockport

Account Name (Block letters) & A/c. No: J. WOODSTOCK 058899

A/c J. WOODSTOCK
Cash 23.92
Cheques PO's etc 249.59
£ 273.51

Paid in by J Woodstock

Details for advice to recipient

Counterfoil retained by Woodstock
Bank giro credit and cash and cheques handed in to bank

Reverse side of bank giro credit

Details of Cheques, POs etc

for cheques please specify Drawer's name	and Bank Code Number as shown in top right corner				
E. KANE & SON	02-58-76	184	15	184	15
J. GALE	05-77-85	65	44	65	44
In view of the risk of loss in course of clearing, customers are advised to keep an independent record of the drawers of cheques.	Total carried over £	249	59	249	59

Reverse of counterfoil

J Woodstock has banked the following items:

Four	£5 notes	
Three	£1 coins	
One	50p coin	
Other silver	30p	
Bronze coins	12p	
Cheques received from:		Code numbers:
E Kane & Son	£184.15	02-58-76
J Gale	£65.44	05-77-85

12.9 Cheque clearing

In Section 12.5, you learnt about the cheque clearing system. Let's now look at an example of how cheques paid from one person's bank account pass into another person's bank account. We'll use the cheque from Exhibit 12.3.

2005
May 22 Woodstock, in Stockport, sends the cheque to K Marsh, who lives in Leeds. Woodstock enters the payment in his cash book.
23 Cheque received by Marsh. He deposits it the same day in his bank account at Barclays Bank in Leeds. Marsh shows the cheque in his cash book as being received and banked on 23 May.
24 The Exchange Centre in London receives it, where the Cheshire Bank collects it. The Cheshire Bank sends the cheque to their Stockport branch.
25 Staff at the Stockport branch of the Cheshire Bank examine the cheque. If there is nothing wrong with it, the cheque can now be debited by the bank to J Woodstock's account.

In Chapter 30, we'll be looking at bank reconciliation statements.

What we have looked at so far:

2005
May 22 the day on which Woodstock has made the entry in his cash book
25 the day when the bank makes an entry in Woodstock's account in respect of the cheque

will become an important part of your understanding of such statements.

Learning outcomes

You should now have learnt:

1 That the banking sector has been revolutionised by the developments in computers and information technology over the last 40 years.

2 That where previously payments could usually only be made by cash or cheque, there is now a wide range of alternatives, ranging from plastic cards to direct debits and direct transfers into bank accounts.

3 That the use of cheques is falling but that they are still a very common form of payment in business.

4 That cheque clearing is the way in which a cheque goes through the banking system and is credited to its rightful owner and charged against the drawer's bank account.

→

→

5 That it usually takes three days for a cheque payment to reach the account of the payee.

6 That it usually takes three days for a debit card payment to reach the account of the payee.

7 That cash is still the most common form of medium for payments.

8 That holders of a current account will be normally be issued with a cheque book and a multiple use plastic card incorporating a cheque guarantee card, debit card and ATM card.

9 How to write a cheque.

10 That crossings on cheques indicate that they must be banked before cash can be collected for them.

11 That special crossings on cheques act as instructions to the banker, and are usually used to ensure that the cheque cannot be used by anyone other than its rightful owner.

12 That cheque endorsements enable the rightful owner of the cheque to give it to someone else.

13 How to complete a bank pay-in slip.

14 How to complete a bank giro credit.

Answers to activities

12.1 Computers were still very limited in what they could do, particularly in terms of the size of computer needed for even the smallest task. Without the sophisticated programming flexibility of modern computers, these first age cash machines could only have very limited facilities. There was also the fairly obvious point that cash machines were a new invention and no one knew at that time whether the general public would actually use them!

12.2 There are many varieties of plastic cards. A list based on one produced by the Association for Payment Clearing Services (APACS) is listed below:

● **Affinity card**. A credit card where the card issuer makes a donation to an organisation (often a charity) every time the card is used.

● **ATM card**. A plastic card used in an ATM for cash withdrawals and other bank services.

● **Business card**. Also known as a company or corporate card. A card which companies issue to staff to pay for business expenses like travel costs.

● **Charge card**. A payment card that requires the cardholder to settle the account in full at the end of a specified period, such as American Express and Diners cards. Holders have to pay an annual fee for the card. (Compare this to a credit card.)

● **Cheque guarantee card**. A card that guarantees settlement of cheques of up to a specified amount.

● **Credit card**. A card enabling the holder to make purchases and to draw cash up to a pre-arranged limit. The credit granted in a period can be settled in full or in part by the end of a specified period. Many credit cards carry no annual fee. (Compare this to a charge card.)

● **Debit card**. A card linked to a bank or building society account and used to pay for goods and services by debiting the holder's account. Debit cards are usually combined with other facilities such as ATM and cheque guarantee functions.

● **Electronic purse**. Also known as a pre-payment card. This card has a stored cash value which can be used to purchase goods and services – it is an alternative to cash. The card can be disposable or re-loadable. Examples include Mondex and VisaCash.

● **Loyalty card**. Cards issued by retailers to promote customer loyalty. Holders earn cash back, vouchers, or discounts. Examples include the Tesco Clubcard and the Boots Advantage card.

- **Payment card**. A generic term for any plastic card (credit, debit, charge, etc.) which may be used on its own to pay for goods and services or to withdraw cash.
- **Purchasing card**. A payment card issued to businesses, companies or government departments to make supplier and/or trade payments.
- **Smart card**. A card that holds details on a computer chip instead of a traditional magnetic stripe. (This is expected to be the normal form of all credit and debit cards in the future.)
- **Shareholder card**. A special form of store card issued to shareholders that operates like a credit card but gives the holder a discount off all purchases charged to the card. These cards can only be used in shops owned by the company that issued the card. An example is the Arcadia Group card.
- **Store card**. Also known as a retailer card. A plastic payment card that can be used only in a specified retailer or group of retailers. An example is the John Lewis Partnership card.
- **Travel & entertainment card**. A plastic payment card which operates similarly to a charge card.

12.3 Businesses can't send employees round to all their suppliers with debit cards. Nor can they insist that one-off suppliers allow them to pay by direct transfer into the supplier's bank account. Cheques remain more convenient in many cases, though there is a definite shift towards using more modern methods. The most obvious indicator of this is the attempt by many companies to encourage shareholders to accept their dividend payments as electronic transfers into the shareholders' bank accounts.

Customers also still often use cheques, particularly for postal payments for goods purchased by telephone or mail order and to send deposits on, for example, holidays – and to pay credit card bills!

12.4 It is not because the rate of interest is lower on overdrafts, it isn't, it is higher! It is because interest on overdrafts is charged daily on the amount of the overdraft on that date. Bank loans are for fixed amounts and interest is paid on the full amount each day whether or not the money has been spent. With an overdraft, customers have the freedom to use as much or as little of the overdraft as they wish (and so incur interest only on the amount they are overdrawn). In many cases, they will never actually use the overdraft facility. Also, bank loans must be repaid on a stated date. Overdrafts are only payable to the bank when the bank demands repayment, which is rare, unless the individual or business looks likely to have problems paying back the overdraft at some future date. Thus, overdrafts are cheaper to use than bank loans, they are more flexible, and the borrower doesn't have to regularly look for other funds to replace them.

You can find a range of additional self-test questions, as well as material to help you with your studies, on the website that accompanies this book at **www.pearsoned.co.uk/wood**

Effect	Action
1 Asset of cash is decreased	Credit the asset account, i.e. the cash account which is represented by the cash column in the cash book.
2 Asset of bank is increased	Debit the asset account, i.e. the bank account which is represented by the bank column in the cash book.

A cash receipt of £100 from M Davies on 1 August 2008 which was followed by the banking on 3 August of £80 of this amount would appear in the Cash Book as follows:

Cash Book						
	Cash	Bank			Cash	Bank
	£	£			£	£
2008				2008		
Aug 1 M Davies	100			Aug 3 Bank	80	
3 Cash		80				

The details column shows entries against each item stating the name of the account in which the completion of double entry has taken place. Against the cash payment of £80 appears the word 'bank', meaning that the debit of £80 is to be found in the bank column, and the opposite applies.

2 Where the whole of the cash received is banked immediately the receipt can be treated in exactly the same manner as a cheque received, i.e. it can be entered directly into the bank column.

3 If the business requires cash, it may withdraw cash from the bank. Assuming this is done by use of a cheque, the business would write out a cheque to pay itself a certain amount in cash. The bank will give cash in exchange for the cheque over the counter. It could also be done using a cash card. The effect on the accounts is the same.

The twofold effect and the action required is:

Effect	Action
1 Asset of bank is decreased	Credit the asset account, i.e. the bank column in the cash book.
2 Asset of cash is increased	Debit the asset account, i.e. the cash column in the cash book.

A withdrawal of £75 cash on 1 June 2008 from the bank would appear in the cash book as:

Cash Book						
	Cash	Bank			Cash	Bank
	£	£			£	£
2008				2008		
June 1 Bank	75			June 1 Cash		75

Both the debit and credit entries for this item are in the same book. When this happens it is known as a **contra** item.

13.3 The use of folio columns

As you have already seen, the details column in an account contains the name of the account in which the other part of the double entry has been entered. Anyone looking through the books should, therefore, be able to find the other half of the double entry in the ledgers.

However, when many books are being used, just to mention the name of the other account may not be enough information to find the other account quickly. More information is needed, and this is given by using **folio columns**.

In each account and in each book being used, a folio column is added, always shown on the left of the money columns. In this column, the name of the other book and the number of the page in the other book where the other part of the double entry was made is stated against each and every entry.

So as to ensure that the double entry is completed, **the folio column should only be filled in when the double entry has been completed.**

An entry for receipt of cash from C Kelly whose account was on page 45 of the sales ledger, and the cash recorded on page 37 of the cash book, would have the following folio column entries:

● in the cash book, the folio column entry would be SL 45
● in the sales ledger, the folio column entry would be CB 37.

Note how each of the titles of the books is abbreviated so that it can fit into the space available in the folio column. Each of any contra items (transfers between bank and cash) being shown on the same page of the cash book would use the letter '¢' (for 'contra') in the folio column. There is no need to also include a page number in this case.

The act of using one book as a means of entering transactions into the accounts, so as to perform or complete the double entry, is known as **posting**. For example, you 'post' items from the sales day book to the appropriate accounts in the sales ledger and to the sales account and you 'post' items from the cash book to the appropriate accounts in the sales ledger.

Activity 13.1 Why do you think only one account is posted to from the cash book rather than two, which is what happens with postings from the other day books (i.e. the other books of original entry)?

13.4 Advantages of folio columns

As described in 13.3, folio entries speed up the process of finding the other side of the double entry in the ledgers.

Activity 13.2 What other advantage can you think of for using a folio column?

13.5 Example of a cash book with folio columns

The following transactions are written up in the form of a cash book. The folio columns are filled in as though all the double entries had been completed to other accounts.

2008				£
Sept	1	Proprietor puts capital into a bank account for the business.		10,940
	2	Received cheque from M Boon.		315
	4	Cash sales.		802
	6	Paid rent by cash.		135
	7	Banked £50 of the cash held by the business.		50
	15	Cash sales paid direct into the bank.		490
	23	Paid cheque to S Wills.		277
	29	Withdrew cash from bank for business use.		120
	30	Paid wages in cash.		518

Cash Book											(page 1)
			Folio	*Cash*	*Bank*				*Folio*	*Cash*	*Bank*
2008				£	£	2008				£	£
Sept	1	Capital	GL1		10,940	Sept	6	Rent	GL65	135	
	2	M Boon	SL98		315		7	Bank	¢	50	
	4	Sales	GL87	802			23	S Wills	PL23		277
	7	Cash	¢		50		29	Cash	¢		120
	15	Sales	GL87		490		30	Wages	GL39	518	
	29	Bank	¢	120			30	Balances	c/d	219	11,398
				922	11,795					922	11,795
Oct	1	Balances	b/d	219	11,398						

The abbreviations used in the folio column are:

GL = General Ledger   SL = Sales Ledger   ¢ = Contra   PL = Purchases Ledger

13.6 Cash discounts

Businesses prefer it if their customers pay their accounts quickly. A business may accept a smaller sum in full settlement if payment is made within a certain period of time. The amount of the reduction of the sum to be paid is known as a 'cash discount'. The term 'cash discount' thus refers to the allowance given for quick payment. It is still called cash discount, even if the account is paid by cheque or by direct transfer into the bank account.

The rate of cash discount is usually stated as a percentage. Full details of the percentage allowed, and the period within which payment is to be made, are quoted on all sales documents by the seller. A typical period during which discount may be allowed is one month from the date of the original transaction.

Note: Cash discounts *always* appear in the profit and loss section of the trading and profit and loss account. They are not part of the cost of goods sold. Nor are they a deduction from selling price. Students often get this wrong in examinations – be careful!

13.7 Discounts allowed and discounts received

A business may have two types of cash discounts in its books. These are:

1 **Discounts allowed:** cash discounts allowed by a business to its customers when they pay their accounts quickly.

2 **Discounts received**: cash discounts received by a business from its suppliers when it pays what it owes them quickly.

We can now see the effect of discounts by looking at two examples.

Example 1

W Clarke owed us £100. He pays us in cash on 2 September 2008, which is within the time limit applicable for a 5 per cent cash discount. He pays £100 − £5 = £95 in full settlement of his account.

Effect	Action
1 Of cash: Cash is increased by £95. Asset of debtors is decreased by £95.	Debit cash account, i.e. enter £95 in debit column of cash book. Credit W Clarke £95.
2 Of discounts: Asset of debtors is decreased by £5. (After the cash was paid there remained a balance of £5. As the account has been paid, this asset must now be cancelled.) Expense of discounts allowed increased by £5.	Credit W Clarke £5. Debit discounts allowed account £5.

Example 2

The business owed S Small £400. It pays him by cheque on 3 September 2008, which is within the time limit laid down by him for a $2^1/_2$ per cent cash discount. The business will pay £400 − £10 = £390 in full settlement of the account.

Effect	Action
1 Of cheque: Asset of bank is reduced by £390. Liability of creditors is reduced by £390.	Credit bank, i.e. entry in the credit bank column for £390. Debit S Small's account £390.
2 Of discounts: Liability of creditors is reduced by £10. (After the cheque was paid, a balance of £10 remained. As the account has been paid the liability must now be cancelled.) Revenues of discounts received increased by £10.	Debit S Small's account £10. Credit discounts received account £10.

The entries made in the business's books would be:

Cash Book								(page 32)
	Folio	Cash	Bank			Folio	Cash	Bank
		£	£				£	£
2008		95		2008				390
Sept 2 W Clarke	SL12			Sept 3 S Small		PL75		

Discounts Received (General Ledger *page 18*)

			Folio	£
	2008			
	Sept 2 S Small		PL75	10

Discounts Allowed (General Ledger *page 17*)

	Folio	£	
2008			
Sept 2 W Clarke	SL12	5	

W Clarke (Sales Ledger *page 12*)

	Folio	£			*Folio*	£
2008			2008			
Sept 1 Balance	b/d	100	Sept 2 Cash		CB32	95
		<u>100</u>	2 Discount		GL17	<u>5</u>
						<u>100</u>

S Small (Purchases Ledger *page 75*)

	Folio	£		*Folio*	£
2008			2008		
Sept 3 Bank	CB32	390	Sept 1 Balance	b/d	400
3 Discount	GL18	<u>10</u>			
		<u>400</u>			<u>400</u>

It is the accounting custom to enter the word 'Discount' in the personal accounts without stating whether it is a discount received or a discount allowed.

Activity 13.3 Why do you think it is accounting custom only to enter the word 'Discount' in the personal accounts?

13.8 Discounts columns in cash book

The *discounts allowed account* and the *discounts received account* are in the general ledger along with all the other revenue and expense accounts. It has already been stated that every effort should be made to avoid too many entries in the general ledger. To avoid this, we add two columns for discount in the cash book.

An extra column is added on each side of the cash book in which the amounts of discounts are entered. Discounts received are entered in the discounts column on the credit side of the cash book, and discounts allowed in the discounts column on the debit side of the cash book.

The cash book, if completed for the two examples so far dealt with, would be:

Cash Book									(page 32)
	Folio	*Discount*	*Cash*	*Bank*		*Folio*	*Discount*	*Cash*	*Bank*
2008		£	£	£	2008		£	£	£
Sept 2 W Clarke	SL12	5	95		Sept 3 S Small	PL75	10		390

There is no alteration to the method of showing discounts in the personal accounts.

To make entries in the discounts accounts in the general ledger

At the end of the period:

Total of discounts column on receipts side of cash book } Enter on **debit** side of discounts allowed account

Total of discounts column on payments side of cash book } Enter on **credit** side of discounts received account

13.9 A worked example

2008		£
May	1 Balances brought down from April:	
	Cash balance	29
	Bank balance	654
	Debtors accounts:	
	B King	120
	N Campbell	280
	D Shand	40
	Creditors accounts:	
	U Barrow	60
	A Allen	440
	R Long	100
	2 B King pays us by cheque, having deducted 2½ per cent cash discount £3.	117
	8 We pay R Long his account by cheque, deducting 5 per cent cash discount £5.	95
	11 We withdrew £100 cash from the bank for business use.	100
	16 N Campbell pays us his account by cheque, deducting 2½ per cent discount £7.	273
	25 We paid office expenses in cash.	92
	28 D Shand pays us in cash after having deducted 5 per cent cash discount.	38
	29 We pay U Barrow by cheque less 5 per cent cash discount £3.	57
	30 We pay A Allen by cheque less 2½ per cent cash discount £11.	429

Folio numbers have been included in the solution to make the example more realistic.

Cash Book (page 64)

2008	Folio	Discount £	Cash £	Bank £	2008		Folio	Discount £	Cash £	Bank £
May 1 Balance	b/d		29	654	May	8 R Long	PL58	5		95
2 B King	SL13	3		117		11 Cash	¢			100
11 Bank	¢		100			25 Office	GL77		92	
16 N Campbell	SL84	7		273		expenses				
28 D Shand	SL91	2	38			29 U Barrow	PL15	3		57
						30 A Allen	PL98	11		429
						31 Balances	c/d		75	363
		12	167	1,044				19	167	1,044
Jun 1 Balances	b/d		75	363						

Sales Ledger
B King (page 13)

2008		Folio	£	2008			Folio	£
May	1 Balance	b/d	120	May	2 Bank		CB64	117
					2 Discount		CB64	3
			120					120

N Campbell (page 84)

2008		Folio	£	2008			Folio	£
May	1 Balance	b/d	280	May	16	Bank	CB64	273
			___		16	Discount	CB64	7
			280					280

D Shand (page 91)

2008		Folio	£	2008			Folio	£
May	1 Balance	b/d	40	May	28	Cash	CB64	38
			___		28	Discount	CB64	2
			40					40

Purchases Ledger
U Barrow (page 15)

2008			Folio	£	2008		Folio	£
May	29	Bank	CB64	57	May	1 Balance	b/d	60
	29	Discount	CB64	3				___
				60				60

R Long (page 58)

2008			Folio	£	2008		Folio	£
May	8	Bank	CB64	95	May	1 Balance	b/d	100
	8	Discount	CB64	5				___
				100				100

A Allen (page 98)

2008			Folio	£	2008		Folio	£
May	30	Bank	CB64	429	May	1 Balance	b/d	440
	30	Discount	CB64	11				___
				440				440

General Ledger
Office Expenses (page 77)

2008		Folio	£		
May	25 Cash	CB64	92		

Discounts Received (page 88)

			2008			Folio	£
			May	31	Total for the month	CB64	19

Discounts Allowed (page 89)

2008			Folio	£		
May	31	Total for the month	CB64	12		

Is the above method of entering discounts correct?

You can easily check. See the following:

Discounts in Ledger Accounts	Debits		Credits	
		£		
Discounts Received	U Barrow	3	Discounts Received	£19
	R Long	5		
	A Allen	11		
		19		
				£
Discounts Allowed	Discounts Allowed	£12	B King	3
			N Campbell	7
			D Shand	2
				12

You can see that proper double entry has been carried out. Equal amounts, in total, have been entered on each side of the two discount accounts.

13.10 Bank overdrafts

A business may borrow money from a bank by means of a **bank overdraft**. This means that the business is allowed to pay more out of its bank account than the total amount it has deposited in the account.

Up to this point, the bank balances have all been money at the bank, so they have all been assets, i.e. debit balances. When the bank account is overdrawn, the business owes money to the bank, so the account is a liability and the balance becomes a credit one.

Taking the cash book last shown, suppose that the amount payable to A Allen was £1,429 instead of £429. The amount in the bank account of £1,044, is exceeded by the amount withdrawn. We will take the discount for Allen as being £11. The cash book would appear as follows:

Cash Book							(page 64)	
	Discount £	Cash £	Bank £			Discount £	Cash £	Bank £
2008				2008				
May 1 Balances b/d		29	654	May 8 R Long		5		95
2 B King	3		117	11 Cash				100
11 Bank		100		25 Office			92	
16 N Campbell	7		273	expenses				
28 D Shand	2	38		29 U Barrow		3		57
31 Balance c/d				30 A Allen		11		1,429
			637	31 Balance c/d			75	
	12	167	1,681			19	167	1,681
Jun 1 Balance b/d		75		Jun 1 Balance b/d				637

On a balance sheet, a bank overdraft is shown as an item included under the heading 'current liabilities'.

13.11 Multi-column cash books

For many years, it has been normal practice for cash books to have many more columns than those you have seen so far. Once again, the reason for having a column for every commonly occurring transaction is to reduce the number of entries in the ledgers. The process adopted at the end of each period (typically, each month) is to add-up all the columns and post the column totals to the appropriate ledger account. Most businesses that operate a cash book use one of this type. An example of a multi-column cash book is shown below.

Cash Book

Debit (Receipts) side

2008	Ref	Cash	Bank	VAT	Discount allowed	Sales	Debtors	Carriage Out	Rent
May 1 Balances	b/d	490	4,240						
3 J Park			660				660		
4 I Collie		120					120		
5 R Bundy		470		70		400			
6 G Gall		310					310		
8 J Fall			160						160
8 W Watt		658		98		560			
10 Cash	¢		1,200						
14 Post		15						15	
15 T Gore			534		6		534		
22 J Fall			160						160
22 M Prat		878					878		
22 L Jones		962					962		
23 Cash	¢		1,400						
25 B Hill		752		112		640			
26 N Mole		1,128		168		960			
28 Post		12						12	
31 K Dixon		376		56	5	325			
31 Cash	¢		2,000						
		6,171	10,354	504	11	2,885	3,464	27	320
June 1 Balances	b/d	562	7,036						

Credit (Payments) side

2008	Ref	Cash	Bank	VAT	Discount received	Purchases	Creditors	Wages	Motor	Adverts
May 3 Wages	56		320					320		
5 R Frank	57		611	91		520				
8 B Todd	58		690		10		690			
8 Truckstop		141		21					120	
10 Bank	¢	1,200								
14 J Twigg							210			
17 Wages		320						320		
19 B Lime	59		470	70	8	408				
22 Le Garage	60		564	84					480	
23 Bank	¢	1,400								
24 Weges		320						320		
27 Printo Ltd	61		94	14						80
28 A Moss		75					75			
29 I Syme	62		249	49	2	280				
29 R Trip		47		7						40
30 Signs Ltd		106					106			
31 Wages	63		320					320		
Balances	c/d	562	7,036							
		6,171	10,354	336	20	1,208	391	1,280	600	120

Notes:

1 Each entry in the creditor column is entered in the individual creditor account, and the entries in the debtor column are entered in the individual debtor account.

2 Discount received from individual creditors is debited to the appropriate creditor account and the total is credited to the discount received account.

3 Discount allowed from individual debtors is credited to the appropriate debtor account and the total is debited to the discount allowed account.

4 The total of the other revenue and expenditure columns and the two VAT columns is entered in the appropriate ledger account.

5 The columns headed 'Ref' can be used to enter ledger folios. The numbers in the Ref column on the credit side is the cheque number.

6 Discount allowed is not included in the amount entered in the bank or cash column. When debtors are given discount, only the amount they pay is shown in the debtor column. VAT is calculated on the amount of the sale net of cash discount.

7 When discount is allowed on sales it is the amount received plus the discount that is shown in the sales column.

8 For discount received on purchases and on payments to creditors, the process is the same as for discount allowed.

13.12 Petty cash books

In the United Kingdom, many organisations use a separate book called a 'petty cash book' for payments of small amounts of cash. Its format is similar to that of a multi-column cash book (*see* Chapter 16).

This move away from three-column cash books is not yet evident in many other countries, especially where banking systems are not as developed or as efficient as in the UK.

Learning outcomes

You should now have learnt:

1 That a cash book consists of a cash account and a bank account put together into one book.

2 How to enter up and balance a two-column cash book, i.e. one containing a debit and a credit column for the bank account, and a debit and a credit column for the cash account.

3 That the bank columns in the cash book are for cheques and any other transfers of funds that have been made into or out of the bank account.

4 That a folio column is included in the cash book so as to help trace entries made into accounts in the ledgers and so as to provide assurance that the double entries have been made.

5 That cash discounts are given to encourage people to pay their accounts within a stated time limit.

6 That 'cash discount' is the name given for discount for quick payment even where the payment was made by cheque or by direct transfer into the bank account, rather than by payment in cash.

7 That cash discounts appear in the profit and loss part of the trading and profit and loss account.

8 How to enter up and balance a three-column cash book, i.e. one containing a debit and a credit column for the bank account, a debit and a credit column for the cash account, and a debit and a credit column for discount.

9 That the discounts columns in the cash book make it easier to enter up the books. They act as a collection point for discounts allowed and discounts received, for which double entry into the general ledger is completed when the totals are transferred to the discount accounts in the general ledger, usually at the end of the month.

10 That a multiple-column cash book is often used in order to further reduce the number of entries made in the general ledger.

11 How to add additional columns to the cash book for frequently recurring items and make the appropriate entries in them and in the ledgers.

Answers to activities

13.1 Although the cash book is a book of original entry, it is also where the cash account and bank account are recorded. In effect, it is both a book of original entry and a ledger dedicated to those two accounts. As a result, each transaction in the cash book is only posted once to another account, the first part of the entry having been made when the transaction was recorded in the cash book.

13.2 If an entry has not been filled in, i.e. if the folio column is blank against an entry, the double entry has not yet been made. As a result, looking through the entry lines in the folio columns to ensure they have all been filled in helps detect such errors quickly.

13.3 It should be quite obvious whether discount is received or allowed. And, more importantly, the double entry is with the cash book columns for discount, not with either the discount allowed account or the discount received account in the general ledger. At the end of the period (usually a month) the totals of the two discount columns in the cash book are posted to the discount allowed and discount received accounts in the general ledger.

Multiple choice questions: Set 2

Now attempt Set 2 of multiple choice questions. (Answers to all the multiple choice questions are given in Appendix 2 at the end of this book.)

Each of these multiple choice questions has four suggested answers, (A), (B), (C) and (D). You should read each question and then decide which choice is best, either (A) or (B) or (C) or (D). *Write down your answers on a separate piece of paper.* You will then be able to redo the set of questions later without having to try to ignore your answers from previous attempts.

MC21 Gross profit is

(A) Excess of sales over cost of goods sold
(B) Sales less Purchases
(C) Cost of goods sold + Opening stock
(D) Net profit less expenses of the period.

MC22 Net profit is calculated in the

(A) Trading account
(B) Profit and loss account
(C) Trial balance
(D) Balance sheet.

MC23 To find the value of closing stock at the end of a period we

(A) do this by physically counting the stock (i.e. stocktaking)
(B) look in the stock account
(C) deduct opening stock from cost of goods sold
(D) deduct cost of goods sold from sales.

MC24 The credit entry for net profit is on the credit side of

(A) The trading account
(B) The profit and loss account
(C) The drawings account
(D) The capital account.

MC25 Which of these best describes a balance sheet?

(A) An account proving the books balance
(B) A record of closing entries
(C) A listing of balances
(D) A statement of assets.

MC26 The descending order in which current assets should be shown in the balance sheet is

(A) Stock, Debtors, Bank, Cash
(B) Cash, Bank, Debtors, Stock
(C) Debtors, Stock, Bank, Cash
(D) Stock, Debtors, Cash, Bank.

MC27 Which of these best describes fixed assets?

(A) Items bought to be used in the business
(B) Items which will not wear out quickly
(C) Expensive items bought for the business
(D) Items of long life that are not bought specifically for resale.

MC28 Carriage inwards is charged to the trading account because

(A) It is an expense connected with buying goods
(B) It should not go in the balance sheet
(C) It is not part of motor expenses
(D) Carriage outwards goes in the profit and loss account.

MC29 Given figures showing: Sales £8,200; Opening stock £1,300; Closing stock £900; Purchases £6,400; Carriage inwards £200, the cost of goods sold figure is

(A) £6,800
(B) £6,200
(C) £7,000
(D) Another figure.

MC30 The costs of putting goods into a saleable condition should be charged to

(A) Trading account
(B) Profit and loss account
(C) Balance sheet
(D) None of these.

MC31 Suppliers' personal accounts are found in the

(A) Nominal ledger
(B) General ledger
(C) Purchases ledger
(D) Sales ledger.

MC32 The sales day book is best described as

(A) Part of the double entry system
(B) Containing customers' accounts
(C) Containing real accounts
(D) A list of credit sales.

MC33 Which of the following are personal accounts?

(*i*) Buildings
(*ii*) Wages
(*iii*) Debtors
(*iv*) Creditors

→

→

(A) (*i*) and (*iv*) only
(B) (*ii*) and (*iii*) only
(C) (*iii*) and (*iv*) only
(D) (*ii*) and (*iv*) only.

MC34 When Lee makes out a cheque for £50 and sends it to Young, then Lee is known as

(A) The payee
(B) The banker
(C) The drawer
(D) The creditor.

MC35 If you want to make sure that your money will be safe if cheques sent are lost in the post, you should

(A) Not use the postal service
(B) Always pay by cash
(C) Always take the money in person
(D) Cross your cheques 'Account Payee only, Not Negotiable'.

MC36 When depositing money in your current account you can use

(A) A cheque book
(B) A paying-in slip
(C) A cash book
(D) A general ledger.

MC37 A debit balance of £100 in a cash account shows that

(A) There was £100 cash in hand
(B) Cash has been overspent by £100
(C) £100 was the total of cash paid out
(D) The total of cash received was less than £100.

MC38 £50 cash taken from the cash till and banked is entered

(A) Debit cash column £50: Credit bank column £50
(B) Debit bank column £50: Credit cash column £50
(C) Debit cash column £50: Credit cash column £50
(D) Debit bank column £50: Credit bank column £50.

MC39 A credit balance of £200 on the cash columns of the cash book would mean

(A) We have spent £200 more than we have received
(B) We have £200 cash in hand
(C) The bookkeeper has made a mistake
(D) Someone has stolen £200 cash.

MC40 'Posting' the transactions in bookkeeping means

(A) Making the first entry of a double entry transaction
(B) Entering items in a cash book
(C) Making the second entry of a double entry transaction
(D) Something other than the above.

Review questions

13.1 Write up a two-column cash book for a small furniture shop from the following details, and balance it off as at the end of the month:

2008
May 1 Started in business with capital of £1,000 in cash and £ 3,000 in the bank.
2 Paid rent by cash £450.
3 G Luke lent us £4,000, paid by cheque.
4 We paid R Owen by cheque £1,200.
5 Cash sales £340.
7 M Smart paid for purchase by cheque £70.
9 We paid supplier, T Trump, in cash £290.
11 Sales paid for by debit card £410.
15 W Sharp, a customer, paid us in cash £185.
16 We took £80 out of the till and paid it into the bank account.
19 We repaid part of the loan from G Luke £2,000 by cheque.
22 Cash sales paid direct into the bank £370.
26 Paid motor expenses by cheque £65.
30 Withdrew £300 cash from the bank for business use.
31 Paid wages in cash £240.

13.2A Write up a two-column cash book for a second-hand bookshop from the following:

2009
Nov 1 Balance brought forward from last month: Cash £295; Bank £4,240.
2 Cash sales £310.
3 Took £200 out of the cash till and paid it into the bank.
4 F Bell paid us by cheque £194.
5 We paid for postage stamps in cash £80.
6 Bought office equipment by cheque £310.
7 We paid L Root by cheque £94.
9 Received business rates refund by cheque £115.
11 Withdrew £150 from the bank for business use.
12 Paid wages in cash £400.
13 Cash sales £430.
14 Paid motor expenses by cheque £81.
16 J Bull lent us £1,500 in cash.
20 K Brown paid us by cheque £174.
28 We paid general expenses in cash £35.
30 Paid insurance by cheque £320.

13.3 A three-column cash book for a wine wholesaler is to be written up from the following details, balanced off, and the relevant discount accounts in the general ledger shown.

2008
Mar 1 Balances brought forward: Cash £620; Bank £7,142.
2 The following paid their accounts by cheque, in each case deducting 5 per cent cash discounts: G Slick £260; P Fish £320; T Old £420 (all amounts are pre-discount).
4 Paid rent by cheque £430.
6 F Black lent us £5,000 paying by cheque.
8 We paid the following accounts by cheque in each case deducting a 2½ per cent cash discount: R White £720; G Green £960; L Flip £1,600 (all amounts are pre-discount).
10 Paid motor expenses in cash £81.

→

Day books and returns day books

Learning objectives

After you have studied this chapter, you should be able to:

- distinguish between a cash sale and a credit sale and between the way they are recorded in the accounting books
- distinguish between a cash purchase and a credit purchase and between the way they are recorded in the accounting books
- explain the differences between the processes of recording credit sales and credit purchases in the books
- explain why, when credit card payments are received at the time of sale, details of the customer are not recorded even though a debtor is created at the same time
- draw up a sales invoice
- explain why multiple copies are often made of each sales invoice
- make the appropriate entries relating to credit sales in a sales day book
- make the appropriate entries relating to credit purchases in a purchases day book
- make the correct postings from the sales day book to the sales ledger and general ledger
- make the correct postings from the purchases day book to the purchases ledger and general ledger
- explain how trade discounts differ from cash discounts, both in nature and in the way they are treated in the accounting books
- describe measures that may be taken to exercise credit control over debtors
- make the appropriate entries relating to returns outwards in the returns outwards day book
- make the appropriate entries relating to returns inwards in the returns inwards day book
- make the correct postings from the returns day books to the purchases ledger, sales ledger and general ledger
- explain the differences between a credit note and a debit note
- describe how a debtor should use statements received from suppliers
- enter up the accounts for credit card transactions
- explain the need for internal checks on all sales and purchases invoices and credit notes
- describe what use may be made of factoring

Introduction

In Chapter 11, you learnt that, rather than having only one book of original entry and only one ledger, most businesses use a set of day books (or journals) and a set of ledgers. In this chapter, you'll learn more about the sales day book (or sales journal) and the sales ledger; the purchases day book (or purchases journal), and the purchases ledger; the returns inwards day book (or returns inwards journal); and the returns outwards day book (or returns outwards journal). You'll also learn how cash and credit sales and purchases are entered in these books, and about trade discounts and how to record them. We shall start by looking at the sales day book, then we'll look at the purchase day book and, finally, we'll look at the two returns day books.

Section A Sales day books

14.1 Cash sales

As you have already learnt, when goods are paid for immediately they are described as 'cash sales', even where the payment has been made by cheque or transfer of funds from the customer's bank account into the seller's bank account. For accounting purposes, in such cases we do not need to know the names and addresses of customers nor what has been sold to them and, as a result, there is no need to enter such sales in the sales day book. **The sales day book (and all the other day books) are *only* used for credit transactions.**

> **Activity 14.1** Other than for accounting purposes, can you think of anything a business might want to record somewhere outside the accounting records concerning these transactions?

Credit card payments

When customers pay immediately by credit card, so far as recording details of the customer is concerned, this is treated as if it were a payment made by cash. No record is required for accounting purposes concerning the contact details of the customer. However, it is still a credit transaction and it does result in a debtor being created – the credit card company. The double entry would be a credit to the sales account and a debit to the credit card company's account in the sales ledger.

14.2 Credit sales

In all but the smallest business, most sales will be made on credit. In fact, the sales of many businesses will consist entirely of credit sales. The only major exceptions to this are Internet businesses (such as Amazon) and retailers (e.g. corner shops, supermarkets, department stores, fast food outlets, and small businesses) where all sales are paid for at the time of sale.

For each credit sale, the selling business will give or send a document to the buyer showing full details of the goods sold and the prices of the goods. This document is an 'invoice'. It is known to the buyer as a 'purchase invoice' and to the seller as a **sales invoice**. The seller will keep one or more copies of each sales invoice for his or her own use.

Activity 14.2 What uses would the seller have for these copies of the sales invoice?

Exhibit 14.1 is an example of an invoice:

Exhibit 14.1

Your Purchase Order: 10/A/980				J Blake
	INVOICE No 16554			7 Over Warehouse
				Leicester LE1 2AP
				1 September 2009
To: D Poole & Co				
45 Charles Street				
Manchester M1 5ZN				

	Per unit	Total
	£	£
21 cases McBrand Pears	20	420
5 cartons Kay's Flour	4	20
6 cases Joy's Vinegar	20	120
		560
Terms 1¼% cash discount if paid within one month		

You must not think that all invoices will look exactly like the one shown in Exhibit 14.1. Each business will have its own design. All invoices will be uniquely numbered, usually sequentially, and they will contain the names and addresses of both the supplier and the customer. In this case, the supplier is J Blake and the customer is D Poole. (A 'purchase order' – there's one referred to in the top left-hand corner of this sales invoice – is the record or document drawn up by the customer that the customer referred to or gave the seller when the order was placed with the seller. It is used by the buyer to check the details of the order against the invoice and against the goods delivered.)

14.3 Copies of sales invoices

As soon as the sales invoices for the goods being sold have been made out, they are given or sent to the customer. The copies kept by the seller are created at the same time as the original.

14.4 Making entries in the sales day book

From the copy of the sales invoice, the seller enters up the transaction in the sales day book. This book is merely a list of details relating to each credit sale:

● Date
● Name of customer

● Invoice number
● Folio column
● Final amount of invoice.

There is no need to show details of the goods sold in the sales day book. This can be found by looking at copy invoices.

We can now look at Exhibit 14.2, which shows page 26 of a sales day book, starting with the record of the sales invoice already shown in Exhibit 14.1. (These could have been on any page. In this example, we are assuming they have been entered on page 26 as pages 1–25 have been filled with details of earlier transactions.)

Exhibit 14.2

Sales Day Book				**(page 26)**
		Invoice No	Folio	Amount £
2009				
Sept	1 D Poole	16554		560
	8 T Cockburn	16555		1,640
	28 C Carter	16556		220
	30 D Stevens & Co	16557		1,100
				3,520

14.5 Posting credit sales to the sales ledger

Instead of having one ledger for all accounts, we now have a separate sales ledger for credit sale transactions. This was described in Chapter 11.

1 The credit sales are now posted, one by one, to the debit side of each customer's account in the sales ledger.
2 At the end of each period the total of the credit sales is posted to the credit of the sales account in the general ledger.

This is now illustrated in Exhibit 14.3:

Exhibit 14.3 Posting credit sales

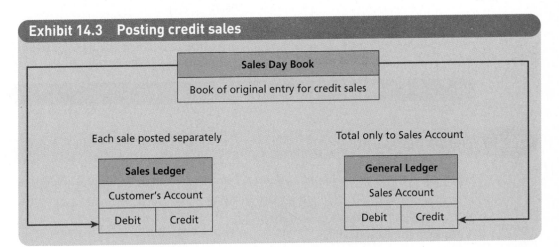

14.6 An example of posting credit sales

The sales day book in Exhibit 14.2 is now shown again. This time, posting is made to the sales ledger and the general ledger. Notice the completion of the folio columns with the reference numbers.

Sales Day Book				(page 26)
		Invoice No	Folio	Amount £
2009				
Sept	1 D Poole	16554	SL 12	560
	8 T Cockburn	16555	SL 39	1,640
	28 C Carter	16556	SL 125	220
	30 D Stevens & Co	16557	SL 249	1,100
	Transferred to Sales Account		GL 44	3,520

Sales Ledger
D Poole
(page 12)

2009		Folio	£	
Sept	1 Sales	SB 26	560	

T Cockburn
(page 39)

2009		Folio	£	
Sept	8 Sales	SB 26	1,640	

C Carter
(page 125)

2009		Folio	£	
Sept	28 Sales	SB 26	220	

D Stevens & Co
(page 249)

2009		Folio	£	
Sept	30 Sales	SB 26	1,100	

General Ledger
Sales
(page 44)

				2009		Folio	£
				Sept	30 Credit sales for the month	SB 26	3,520

Before you continue you should attempt Review question 14.1.

14.7 Trade discounts

Suppose you are the proprietor of a business. You are selling to three different kinds of customer:

1 Traders who buy a lot of goods from you.
2 Traders who buy only a few items from you.
3 Direct to the general public.

The traders themselves have to sell the goods to the general public in their own areas. They have to make a profit to help finance their businesses, so they will want to pay you less than retail price (i.e. the price at which the goods are sold to the general public).

The traders who buy in large quantities will not want to pay as much as those traders who buy in small quantities. You want to attract large customers like these, so you are happy to sell to these traders at a lower price than the price you charge the other customers.

This means that your selling prices are at three levels:

1 to traders buying large quantities,
2 to traders buying small quantities, and
3 to the general public.

Let's use an example to illustrate this. You are selling a make of food mixing machine. The basic price is £200. The traders who buy in large quantities are given 25 per cent trade discount. The other traders are given 20 per cent, and the general public get no trade discount. The price paid by each type of customer would be:

		Trader 1		Trader 2	General Public
		£		£	£
Basic price		200		200	200
Less Trade discount	(25%)	(50)	(20%)	(40)	nil
Price to be paid by customer		150		160	200

You could deal with this by having three price lists, and many businesses do. However, some use trade discounts instead. This involves having only one price list but giving a **trade discount** to traders so that they are invoiced for the correct price.

Exhibit 14.4 is an example of an invoice for a food manufacturer and retailer that shows how trade discount is presented clearly and the trade discounted price easily identified. It is for the same items as were shown in Exhibit 14.1 as having been sold to D Poole. In that example, the seller operated a different price list for each category of customer. This time the seller is R Grant and trade discount is used to adjust the selling price to match the category of customer.

Exhibit 14.4

Your Purchase Order: 11/A/G80	INVOICE No 30756	R Grant Higher Side Preston PR1 2NL 2 September 2009
To: D Poole & Co 45 Charles Street Manchester M1 5ZN		Tel (01703) 33122 Fax (01703) 22331

	Per unit	Total
	£	£
21 cases McBrand Pears	25	525
5 cartons Kay's Flour	5	25
6 cases Joy's Vinegar	25	150
		700
Less 20% trade discount		(140)
		560

By comparing Exhibits 14.1 and 14.4, you can see that the amount paid by D Poole was the same. It is simply the method of calculating and showing it that is different.

14.8 No double entry for trade discounts

As trade discount is simply a way of calculating sales prices, no entry for trade discount should be made in the double entry records, nor in the sales day book. The recording of Exhibit 14.4 in R Grant's sales day book and D Poole's personal account will be:

Sales Day Book			(page 87)
	Invoice No	Folio	Amount £
2009			
Sept 2 D Poole	30756	SL 32	560

Sales Ledger
D Poole   (page 32)

2009		Folio	£	
Sept 2 Sales		SB 87	560	

To compare with cash discounts:

● Trade discounts: *never* shown in double entry accounts, nor in the trading and profit and loss account.
● Cash discounts: *always* shown in double entry accounts and in the profit and loss part of the trading and profit and loss account.

Be very careful about this topic. Students often get confused between the treatment of trade discount and the treatment of cash discount. Remember, it is trade discount that is not entered anywhere in either the ledger accounts or the financial statements. Cash discount appears in the cash book and is always shown in the financial statements.

14.9 Manufacturer's recommended retail price

Looking at an item displayed in a shop window, you will frequently see something like the following:

50 inch HD LCD TV	
Manufacturer's Recommended Retail Price	£2,300
less discount of 20 per cent	(460)
You pay only	£1,840

Very often the manufacturer's recommended retail price is a figure above what the manufacturer would expect the public to pay for its product. In the case of the TV, the manufacturer would probably have expected the public to pay around £1,840 for the TV.

The inflated figure used for the 'manufacturer's recommended retail price' is simply a sales gimmick. Most people like to feel they are getting a bargain. Most people feel happier about making a purchase like this if they are told they are getting '20 per cent discount' and pay £1,840 than when they are told that the price is £1,840 and that they cannot get any discount.

14.10 Credit control

Any organisation which sells goods on credit should keep a close check to ensure that debtors pay their accounts on time. If this is not done properly, the amount of debtors can grow to a level that will make the business short of cash. Businesses that grow too short of cash will fail, no matter how profitable they may be.

The following procedures should be carried out:

1 A credit limit should be set for each debtor. Debtors should not be allowed to owe more than their credit limit. The amount of the limit will depend on the circumstances. Such things as the size of the customer's business and the amount of business done with it, as well as its past record of payments, will help guide the choice of credit limit. Credit rating agencies may be used to assess the creditworthiness of customers before credit is granted.

2 As soon as the payment date set by the seller has been reached, a check should be made to verify whether the debtor has paid the amount due. Failure to pay on time may trigger a refusal to supply any more goods to the customer until payment is received, even if the customer's credit limit has not been reached.

3 Where payment is not forthcoming, after investigation it may be necessary to take legal action to sue the customer for the debt. This will depend on the circumstances.

4 It is important that the customer is aware of what will happen if the amount due is not paid by the deadline set by the seller.

Now, let's look at the 'other side of the coin', the purchases day book.

Section B   Purchases day books

14.11   Purchases invoices

An invoice is called a 'sales invoice' when it is entered in the books of the seller. When an invoice is entered in the books of the buyer, it is called a '**purchase invoice**'. For example, in Exhibit 14.1:

● in the books of J Blake, the seller, it is a sales invoice, and
● in the books of D Poole, the buyer, it is a purchases invoice.

14.12   Making entries in the purchases day book

There is virtually no difference in the process involved from those you make in the sales day book. From the purchases invoices for goods bought on credit, the purchaser enters the details in the purchases day book (or purchases journal).

 Activity 14.3 Think back to what you learnt about the list of items contained in the sales day book. What do you think is the list of items recorded in the purchases day book?

There is no need to show details of the goods bought in the purchases day book. This can be found by looking at the invoices themselves. Exhibit 14.5 is an example of a purchases day book.

Exhibit 14.5

Purchases Day Book			(page 49)
	Invoice No	Folio	Amount £
2009			
Sept 1 J Blake	9/101		560
8 B Hamilton	9/102		1,380
19 C Brown	9/103		230
30 K Gabriel	9/104		510
			2,680

Activity 14.4 Note the entry for 1 September and compare it to the entry on the same date shown in the sales day book of J Blake in Exhibit 14.2. What differences are there between the entries in the two day books? Why do you think these differences arise?

14.13 Posting credit purchases to the purchases ledger

We have a separate purchases ledger. The double entry is as follows:

1 The credit purchases are posted, one by one, to the credit of each supplier's account in the purchases ledger.
2 At the end of each period the total of the credit purchases is posted to the debit of the purchases account in the general ledger. This is now illustrated in Exhibit 14.6:

Exhibit 14.6 Posting credit purchases

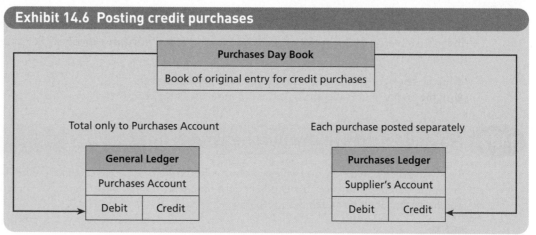

Look at how similar it is to Exhibit 14.3, where the posting of credit sales was shown. The entry to the general ledger is a debit for purchases, so that ledger is now on the left of the exhibit. The entry to the purchases ledger is a credit, so that ledger is on the right, the opposite side from the sales ledger in Exhibit 14.3.

14.14 An example of posting credit purchases

The purchases day book in Exhibit 14.5 is now shown again in Exhibit 14.7 but, this time, posting is made to the purchases ledger and the general ledger. Note the completion of the folio columns indicating that the posting had been completed.

Exhibit 14.7

Purchases Day Book			(page 49)
	Invoice No	Folio	Amount £
2009			
Sept 1 J Blake	9/101	PL 16	560
8 B Hamilton	9/102	PL 29	1,380
19 C Brown	9/103	PL 55	230
30 K Gabriel	9/104	PL 89	510
Transferred to Purchases Account		GL 63	2,680

Purchases Ledger
J Blake   (page 16)

	2009	Folio	£
	Sept 1 Purchases	PB 49	560

B Hamilton   (page 29)

	2009	Folio	£
	Sept 8 Purchases	PB 49	1,380

C Brown   (page 55)

	2009	Folio	£
	Sept 19 Purchases	PB 49	230

K Gabriel   (page 89)

	2009	Folio	£
	Sept 30 Purchases	PB 49	510

General Ledger
Purchases   (page 63)

2009	Folio	£
Sept 30 Credit purchases for the month	PB 49	2,680

Now, let's consider what happens when credit sales are returned by customers or when we return credit purchases to our suppliers.

Section C Returns day books

14.15 Returns inwards and credit notes

You know that businesses allow customers to return goods they've bought. You've probably done so yourself at some time or other. Some retail businesses give every customer the right to do so within a few days of the sale and won't ask why they are being returned. It is a means of assuring the customer that the seller believes that the goods are of good quality and will do what the customer wants. Whatever the rights of return granted by the seller, in the UK there are also legal rights of return that permit retail customers to return goods for a refund should the goods prove to have been unfit for the purpose that was intended.

Businesses that deal with trade customers may operate a similar policy, but that would be more unusual and would normally include a proviso that the customer had a justifiable and reasonable reason for returning the goods.

Activity 14.5 List as many reasons as you can think of why (a) retail customers and (b) trade customers may return goods to the seller.

Sometimes sellers may agree to keep the goods returned, even when they don't normally do so, but won't provide a full refund. Sometimes buyers will agree to keep goods they had wanted to return if the seller offers to refund some of the price they paid.

When the seller agrees to take back goods and refund the amount paid, or agrees to refund part or all of the amount the buyer paid, a document known as a **credit note** will be sent to the customer, showing the amount of the allowance given by the seller.

It is called a credit note because the customer's account will be credited with the amount of the allowance, to show the reduction in the amount owed.

Referring back to Exhibit 14.4, if D Poole returns two of the cases of McBrand Pears, a credit note like the one shown in Exhibit 14.8 would be issued by R Grant, the seller.

Exhibit 14.8

To: D Poole & Co
45 Charles Street
Manchester M1 5ZN

R Grant
Higher Side
Preston PR1 2NL
8 September 2009

Tel (01703) 33122
Fax (01703) 22331

CREDIT NOTE No 9/37

	Per unit	Total
	£	£
2 cases McBrand Pears	25	50
Less 20% trade discount		(10)
		40

To stop them being mistaken for invoices, credit notes are sometimes printed in red.

14.16 Returns inwards day book

The credit notes are listed in a returns inwards day book (or returns inwards journal). This is then used for posting the items, as follows:

1 Sales ledger: credit the amount of credit notes, one by one, to the accounts of the customers in the ledger.

2 General ledger: at the end of the period the total of the returns inwards day book is posted to the debit of the returns inwards account.

14.17 Example of a returns inwards day book

Exhibit 14.9 presents an example of a returns inwards day book showing the items to be posted to the sales ledger and the general ledger followed by the entries in the ledger accounts.

Exhibit 14.9

Returns Inwards Day Book			(page 10)
	Note No	Folio	Amount
2009			£
Sept 8 D Poole	9/37	SL 12	40
17 A Brewster	9/38	SL 58	120
19 C Vickers	9/39	SL 99	290
29 M Nelson	9/40	SL 112	160
Transferred to Returns Inwards Account		GL 114	610

Sales Ledger
D Poole (page 12)

				Folio	£
	2009				
	Sept 8	Returns inwards		RI 10	40

A Brewster (page 58)

				Folio	£
	2009				
	Sept 17	Returns inwards		RI 10	120

C Vickers (page 99)

				Folio	£
	2009				
	Sept 19	Returns inwards		RI 10	290

M Nelson (page 112)

				Folio	£
	2009				
	Sept 29	Returns inwards		RI 10	160

General Ledger
Returns Inwards (page 114)

		Folio	£	
2009				
Sept 30 Returns for the month		RI 10	610	

The returns inwards day book is sometimes known as the sales returns day book, because it is goods that were sold that are being returned.

14.18 Returns outwards and debit notes

If the supplier agrees, goods bought previously may be returned. When this happens a **debit note** is sent by the customer to the supplier giving details of the goods and the reason for their return.

The credit note received from the supplier will simply be evidence of the supplier's agreement, and the amounts involved.

Also, an allowance might be given by the supplier for any faults in the goods. Here also, a debit note should be sent to the supplier. Referring back to Exhibit 14.8, Exhibit 14.10 shows an example of the debit note that Poole, the buyer, may have sent to Grant, the seller.

Exhibit 14.10

			D Poole & Co 45 Charles Street Manchester M1 5ZN 7 September 2009 Tel (0161) 488 2142 Fax (0161) 488 2143

To: R Grant
   Higher Side
   Preston PR1 2NL			

DEBIT NOTE No 9.22			
		Per Unit	Total
		£	£
2 cases McBrand Pears damaged in transit		25	50
Less 20% trade discount			(10)
			40

Note the differences between this debit note and the credit note in Exhibit 14.8: the names and addresses have swapped places and the document is described as 'Debit Note No 9.22' rather than 'Credit Note No 9/37', because Poole uses its own debit note numbering sequence. Also, the dates are different. In this case, it is assumed that Poole raised the debit note on 7 September and sent it and the goods to Grant. Grant received the goods on 8 September and raised the credit note on that date. Finally, the reason for the return of the goods is given.

14.19 Returns outwards day book

The debit notes are listed in a returns outwards day book (or returns outwards journal). This is then used for posting the items, as follows:

1 Purchases ledger: debit the amounts of debit notes, one by one, to the personal accounts of the suppliers in the ledger.
2 General ledger: at the end of the period, the total of the returns outwards day book is posted to the credit of the returns outwards account.

14.20 Example of a returns outwards day book

Exhibit 14.11 presents an example of a returns outwards day book showing the items to be posted to the purchases ledger and the general ledger followed by the entries in the ledger accounts.

Exhibit 14.11

Returns Outwards Day Book			(page 7)
	Note No	Folio	Amount £
2009			
Sept 7 R Grant	9.22	PL 29	40
16 B Rose	9.23	PL 46	240
28 C Blake	9.24	PL 55	30
30 S Saunders	9.25	PL 87	360
Transferred to Returns Outwards Account		GL 116	670

Purchases Ledger
R Grant *(page 29)*

2009		Folio	£
Sept 7 Returns outwards		RO 7	40

B Rose *(page 46)*

2009		Folio	£
Sept 16 Returns outwards		RO 7	240

C Blake *(page 55)*

2009		Folio	£
Sept 28 Returns outwards		RO 7	30

S Saunders *(page 87)*

2009		Folio	£
Sept 30 Returns outwards		RO 7	360

General Ledger
Returns Outwards *(page 116)*

	2009		Folio	£
	Sept 30 Returns for the month		RO 7	670

The returns outwards day book is sometimes known as the purchases returns day book, because it is goods that were purchased that are being returned.

14.21 Double entry and returns

Exhibit 14.12 shows how the entries are made for returns inwards and returns outwards.

The double entry needed is:

Sale of items via credit cards:	Dr: Credit card company
	Cr: Sales
Receipt of money from credit card company:	Dr: Bank
	Cr: Credit card company
Commission charged by credit card company:	Dr: Selling expenses
	Cr: Credit card company

Note: the commission is *not* a deduction from the selling price. It is treated in the same way as cash discounts. That is, it is a selling expense and is entered in the profit and loss part of the trading and profit and loss account.

14.24 Internal check

When sales invoices are prepared, they should be very carefully checked. A system is usually set up so that each stage of the preparation of an invoice is checked by someone other than the person whose job is to send out the invoice.

Activity 14.7 What sort of things could occur that make checking of all invoices, both those for sales and those for purchases, something that all businesses should do?

A system should, therefore, be set up whereby invoices are checked at each stage by someone other than the person who sends out the invoices or is responsible for paying them.

For purchase invoices, checks should be established, such as using a rubber stamp to stamp each incoming invoice with a mini form with spaces for ticks as each stage of the check on them is completed. The spaces in the stamp will be filled in by the people responsible for making each of the checks on the purchase invoices received, e.g.:

● one person certifying that the goods were actually received;
● a second person certifying that the goods were ordered;
● a third person certifying that the prices and calculations on the invoice are correct, and in accordance with the order originally placed and agreed;
● a fourth person certifying that the goods are in good condition and suitable for the purpose for which ordered.

Naturally, in a small business, simply because the office staff might number only a few, this cross-check may be in the hands of only one person other than the person who will pay the invoice.

A similar sort of check will be made in respect of sales invoices being sent out and on credit notes, both those being sent out and those being received.

14.25 Factoring

You've already learnt that one of the problems that many businesses face is the time taken by debtors to pay their accounts. Few businesses have so much cash available to them that they do not mind how long debtors take to pay. It is a rather surprising fact that a lot of businesses which fail do so, not because the business is not making a profit, but because it has run out of cash funds. Once that happens, confidence in the business evaporates, and the business then finds that very few people will supply it with goods. It also cannot pay its employees. Closure of the business then happens fairly quickly in many cases.

As mentioned in Chapter 8, in the case of debtors, the cash flow problem may be alleviated by using the services of a financial intermediary called a **factor**.

Factoring is a financial service designed to improve the cash flow of healthy, growing companies, enabling them to make better use of management time and the money tied up in trade credit to customers.

In essence, factors provide their clients with three closely integrated services covering sales accounting and collection, credit management which can include protection against bad debts, and the availability of finance against sales invoices.

14.26 E&OE

On some invoices and other documents you will see 'E&OE' printed at the bottom. This abbreviation stands for 'Errors and Omissions Excepted'. Basically, this is a warning that there may possibly be errors or omissions which could mean that the figures shown could be incorrect, and that the recipient should check carefully the figures before taking any action concerning them.

Learning outcomes

You should now have learnt:

1 That 'sales day book' and 'sales journal' are different names for the same book.

2 That cash sales are not entered in the sales day book.

3 That when credit card payments are received at the time of sale, details of the customer are not recorded even though a debtor is created at the same time.

4 That the sales day book (or sales journal) contains information relating to each credit sale made in each period.

5 That the sales day book is used for posting credit sales to the sales ledger.

6 That the total of the sales day book for the period is posted to the credit of the sales account in the general ledger.

7 How to make the appropriate entries relating to credit sales in a sales day book and make the correct postings from it to the sales ledger and general ledger.

8 How to prepare a sales invoice.

9 Why multiple copies are often made of each sales invoice.

10 That no entry is made for trade discounts in the double entry accounts.

11 That all businesses should operate a sound system of credit control over their debtors.

12 Some measures that may be taken to exercise credit control over debtors.

13 That 'purchases day book' and 'purchases journal' are different names for the same book.

14 That cash purchases are not entered in the purchases day book.

15 That the purchases day book is a list of all credit purchases.

16 That the purchases day book is used to post the items to the personal accounts in the purchases ledger.

→

→ **17** That the total of credit purchases for the period is posted from the purchases day book to the debit of the purchases account in the general ledger.

18 How to make the appropriate entries relating to credit purchases in a purchases day book and make the correct postings from it to the purchases ledger and general ledger.

19 That the process of making entries in the books of the purchaser is very similar to that of making those in the books of the seller.

20 That 'returns inwards day book', 'returns inwards journal', 'sales returns journal' and 'sales returns day book' are different names for the same book.

21 That 'returns outwards day book', 'returns outwards journal', 'purchases returns journal' and 'purchases returns day book' are different names for the same book.

22 That goods returned by customers are all entered in a returns inwards day book.

23 That the returns inwards day book is used to post each item to the credit of the personal account of the customer in the sales ledger.

24 That the total of the returns inwards day book is debited at the end of the period to the returns inwards account in the general ledger.

25 That goods returned to suppliers are all entered in a returns outwards day book.

26 What the difference is between a credit note and a debit note.

27 That the returns outwards day book is used to debit the personal account of each supplier in the purchases ledger.

28 That the total of the returns outwards day book is credited at the end of the period to the returns outwards account in the general ledger.

29 How to make the appropriate entries relating to returns in the returns inwards and returns outwards day books and make the correct postings from them to the purchases ledger, sales ledger and general ledger.

30 That the process of making entries for returns in the books of purchasers and sellers is the mirror image of those made in their books for purchases and sales.

31 That statements are used by debtors to check the entries made in their books.

32 Of a range of causes for differences that can arise between statements and the seller's account in the debtor's purchases ledger and that such differences may not all be the result of an error.

33 How credit card transactions are recorded in the books and how commission charged to sellers by the credit card companies is treated in the trading and profit and loss account.

34 Why an effective system of invoice checking should be used by all businesses.

35 Why factoring is an attractive option for some businesses.

Answers to activities

14.1 A business may want to know the contact details of cash customers for marketing purposes. In fact, most businesses of any size would like to keep records in a database of all their cash customers for this reason. Businesses may also want to encourage cash customers to open credit accounts with the business so that they may be more likely to buy from the business in future. Also, where the goods sold are to be delivered to the customer, the customer's contact details will need to be recorded, but this will be in a record held elsewhere than in the accounting books.

14.2 Sellers keep copies of sales invoices for a number of reasons including: to prove that a sale took place; to enable the entries in the books to be correctly recorded and checked; to pass to the stock department so that the correct goods can be selected for shipping to the customer; to pass to the delivery department, so that the correct goods will be shipped to the customer and to the correct address, and to enable the goods to be shipped accompanied by a copy of the sales invoice so that the customer can acknowledge receipt of the correct goods.

14.3 Similarly to the sales day book, the purchases day book is merely a list of details relating to each credit purchase. The list of items is virtually identical to those recorded in the sales day book, the only differences being that it is the name of the supplier that is recorded, not the purchaser, and that the invoice number is replaced with the buyer's own internally generated reference number:

- date
- name of supplier
- the reference number of the invoice
- folio column
- final amount of invoice.

14.4 Apart from the name of the day books, there are two differences. Firstly, the description of the entry in each case contains the name of the other party to the transaction. This is the personal account in the respective ledger (sales or purchases) where details of the transaction will be entered. The second difference is in the entry in the Invoice Number column. In the case of the seller, Blake, the number entered was the number of the invoice that Blake gave to the invoice and is the invoice number shown on the invoice in Exhibit 14.1. In the case of the buyer, Poole, the invoice number is one Poole gave the invoice when it was received from the seller, Blake. As with the number assigned to it by the seller, the buyer also gives each purchase invoice a unique number relating to its place in the sequence of purchase invoices that the buyer has received so far in the period. '9/101' probably means 'month nine' (9), 'purchase invoice' (1) 'number one' (01).

14.5 In either case, the reasons why goods may be returned include:

- they were of the wrong type (e.g. the wrong model number of replacement remote control for a TV)
- the item purchased was one that was already owned by the customer (e.g. a CD)
- they were the wrong colour (e.g. paint doesn't match the existing colour)
- they were the wrong size (e.g. a pair of trousers was too tight)
- they were faulty (e.g. a computer kept crashing)
- a customer bought more than was needed (newsagents returning unsold newspapers)
- a customer changed her mind (e.g. hire purchase agreement on a DVD player)
- a customer saw the same goods elsewhere at a cheaper price
- a customer found the goods too difficult to use (e.g. the instructions for setting up and operating a video recorder were too complicated)
- (for trade customers) a customer had returned a faulty item to them and they were now returning it to their supplier
- items received damaged by the customer (e.g. fruit delivered to a supermarket)
- the seller had asked all customers to return a specific item (e.g. when an electrical good or a child's toy is found to be dangerous).

14.6 Differences could be due to a number of things having occurred, including the following:

- a purchase had been omitted from the books of either the seller or the debtor
- a purchase had been incorrectly entered in the books of either the seller or the debtor
- a purchase had been made at the end of the month but only entered in the books of either the seller or the debtor in the following month

- goods returned had been entered in the books of the seller but not in the books of the debtor
- goods returned had been incorrectly entered in the books of either the seller or the debtor
- the debtor had entered goods as having been returned in the books when, in fact, the goods were not returned to the seller
- a purchase had been recorded in the books of the seller in the debtor's account when it should have been entered in the account of another customer
- a purchase had been recorded in the books of the debtor in the seller's account when it should have been entered in the account of another seller
- a payment made to the supplier and entered in the books of the debtor had not yet been received by the seller
- goods had been despatched by the seller and entered in the books of the seller but had not yet been received by the debtor.

14.7 If this were not done then it would be possible for someone inside a business to send out an invoice at a price less than the true price. Any difference could then be split between that person and the outside business. For example, if an invoice was sent to Ivor Twister & Co for £2,000 but the invoice clerk made it out deliberately for £200 then, if there was no cross-check, the difference of £1,800 could be split between the invoice clerk and Ivor Twister & Company.

Similarly, outside businesses could send invoices for goods which were never received by the business. This might be in collaboration with an employee within the business, but there are businesses sending false invoices which rely on the businesses receiving them being inefficient and paying for items never received. There have been cases of businesses sending invoices for such items as advertisements which have never been published. The cashier of the business receiving the invoice, if the business is an inefficient one, might possibly think that someone in the business had authorised the advertisements and would pay the bill. Besides these there are, of course, genuine errors that an invoice checking system helps to avoid.

Review questions

14.1 You are to enter up the sales day book from the following details. Post the items to the relevant accounts in the sales ledger and then show the transfer to the sales account in the general ledger.

2006			£
Mar	1	Credit sales to A Bell	520
	3	Credit sales to J Tom	310
	6	Credit sales to C Oak	74
	10	Credit sales to A Bell	102
	17	Credit sales to J Tom	841
	19	Credit sales to F Lyle	135
	27	Credit sales to M Sole	62
	31	Credit sales to T Gaul	190

14.2A Enter up the sales day book from the following details. Post the items to the relevant accounts in the sales ledger and then show the transfer to the sales account in the general ledger.

2008			£
Mar	1	Credit sales to I Hood	520
	3	Credit sales to S Bell	318
	5	Credit sales to J Smart	64
	7	Credit sales to K Byers	165
	16	Credit sales to T Todd	540
	23	Credit sales to W Morris	360
	30	Credit sales to F Lock	2,040

14.3 F Benjamin of 10 Lower Street, Plymouth, is selling the following items at the recommended retail prices as shown: white tape £10 per roll, green felt at £4 per metre, blue cotton at £6 per sheet, black silk at £20 per dress length. He makes the following sales:

2007

May   1   To F Gray, 3 Keswick Road, Portsmouth: 3 rolls white tape, 5 sheets blue cotton, 1 dress length black silk. Less 25 per cent trade discount.

   4   To A Gray, 1 Shilton Road, Preston: 6 rolls white tape, 30 metres green felt. Less 33$^1/_3$ per cent trade discount.

   8   To E Hines, 1 High Road, Malton: 1 dress length black silk. No trade discount.

   20   To M Allen, 1 Knott Road, Southport: 10 rolls white tape, 6 sheets blue cotton, 3 dress lengths black silk, 11 metres green felt. Less 25 per cent trade discount.

   31   To B Cooper, 1 Tops Lane, St Andrews: 12 rolls white tape, 14 sheets blue cotton, 9 metres green felt. Less 33$^1/_3$ per cent trade discount.

You are to (a) draw up a sales invoice for each of the above sales, (b) enter them up in the sales day book and post to the personal accounts, and (c) transfer the total to the sales account in the general ledger.

14.4A J Fisher, White House, Bolton, is selling the following items at the retail prices as shown: plastic tubing at £1 per metre, polythene sheeting at £2 per length, vinyl padding at £5 per box, foam rubber at £3 per sheet. She makes the following sales:

2009

June   1   To A Portsmouth, 5 Rockley Road, Worthing: 22 metres plastic tubing, 6 sheets foam rubber, 4 boxes vinyl padding. Less 25 per cent trade discount.

   5   To B Butler, 1 Wembley Road, Colwyn Bay: 50 lengths polythene sheeting, 8 boxes vinyl padding, 20 sheets foam rubber. Less 20 per cent trade discount.

   11   To A Gate, 1 Bristol Road, Hastings: 4 metres plastic tubing, 33 lengths of polythene sheeting, 30 sheets foam rubber. Less 25 per cent trade discount.

   21   To L Mackeson, 5 Maine Road, Bath: 29 metres plastic tubing. No trade discount is given.

   30   To M Alison, Daley Road, Box Hill: 32 metres plastic tubing, 24 lengths polythene sheeting, 20 boxes vinyl padding. Less 33$^1/_3$ per cent trade discount.

Required:

(a) Draw up a sales invoice for each of the above sales.

(b) Enter them up in the sales day book and post to the personal accounts.

(c) Transfer the total to the sales account in the general ledger.

14.5 B Gray has the following purchases for the month of May 2008:

2008

May   1   From M Day: 4 DVD players at £36 each, 3 mini hi-fi units at £122 each. Less 20 per cent trade discount.

   3   From L Hope: 2 tumble driers at £200 each, 5 vacuum cleaners at £40 each, 2 dishwashers at £160 each. Less 25 per cent trade discount.

   15   From G Hill: 1 hi-fi unit at £400, 2 washing machines at £260 each. Less 15 per cent trade discount.

   20   From R Vine: 6 DAB radios at £50 each. Less 30 per cent trade discount.

   30   From E Brig: 4 dishwashers at £180 each. Less 10 per cent trade discount.

Required:

(a) Enter up the purchases day book for the month.

(b) Post the transactions to the suppliers' accounts.

(c) Transfer the total to the purchases account.

14.6A J Glen has the following purchases for the month of June 2009:

2009
June 2 From F Day: 2 sets golf clubs at £800 each, 5 footballs at £40 each. Less 25 per cent trade discount.
11 From G Smith: 6 cricket bats at £60 each, 6 ice skates at £35 each, 4 rugby balls at £30 each. Less 20 per cent trade discount.
18 From F Hope: 6 sets golf trophies at £90 each, 4 sets golf clubs at £900. Less 33⅓ per cent trade discount.
25 From L Todd: 5 cricket bats at £52 each. Less 25 per cent trade discount.
30 From M Moore: 8 goal posts at £80 each. Less 40 per cent trade discount.

Required:
(a) Enter up the purchases day book for the month.
(b) Post the items to the suppliers' accounts.
(c) Transfer the total to the purchases account.

14.7 C Phillips, a sole trader specialising in material for Asian clothing, has the following purchases and sales for March 2009:

Mar 1 Bought from Smith Stores: silk £40, cotton £80. All less 25 per cent trade discount.
8 Sold to A Grantley: lycra goods £28, woollen items £44. No trade discount.
15 Sold to A Henry: silk £36, lycra £144, cotton goods £120. All less 20 per cent trade discount.
23 Bought from C Kelly: cotton £88, lycra £52. All less 25 per cent trade discount.
24 Sold to D Sangster: lycra goods £42, cotton £48. Less 10 per cent trade discount.
31 Bought from J Hamilton: lycra goods £270. Less 33⅓ per cent trade discount.

Required:
(a) Prepare the purchases and sales day books of C Phillips from the above.
(b) Post the items to the personal accounts.
(c) Post the totals of the day books to the sales and purchases accounts.

14.8A A Henriques has the following purchases and sales for May 2006:

2006
May 1 Sold to M Marshall: brass goods £24, bronze items £36. Less 25 per cent trade discount.
7 Sold to R Richards: tin goods £70, lead items £230. Less 33 per cent trade discount.
9 Bought from C Clarke: tin goods £400. Less 40 per cent trade discount.
16 Bought from A Charles: copper goods £320. Less 50 per cent trade discount.
23 Sold to T Young: tin goods £50, brass items £70, lead figures £80. All less 20 per cent trade discount.
31 Bought from M Nelson: brass figures £100. Less 50 per cent trade discount.

Required:
(a) Write up the sales and purchases day books.
(b) Post the items to the personal accounts.
(c) Post the totals of the day books to the sales and purchases accounts.

14.9 A Jones has the following credit purchases and credit sales for May:

May 1 Sold to M Marshall: brass goods £24, bronze items £36. All less 25 per cent trade discount
Sold to R Richards: tin goods £70, lead items £230. All less 33⅓ per cent trade discount
9 Bought from C Clarke: tin goods £400 less 40 per cent trade discount
16 Bought from A Charles: copper goods £320 less 50 per cent trade discount
23 Sold to T Young: tin goods £50, brass items £70, lead figures £80. All less 20 per cent trade discount
31 Bought from M Nelson: brass figures £100 less 50 per cent trade discount

Required:
(a) Write up sales and purchases day books.
(b) Post the items to the personal accounts.
(c) Post the totals of the day books to the sales and purchases accounts.
(d) What are the books of prime entry within a business and why are they so called? Illustrate your answer with suitable examples.

14.10 You are to enter up the purchases day book and the returns outwards day book from the following details, then to post the items to the relevant accounts in the purchases ledger and to show the transfers to the general ledger at the end of the month.

2007

May 1 Credit purchase from L Hoy £419.

4 Credit purchases from the following: N Hill £320; G Fry £140; L Pacioli £14; S Umma £94.

7 Goods returned by us to the following: L Hoy £38; N Hill £16.

10 Credit purchase from G Fry £315.

18 Credit purchases from the following: A Mole £190; S Fey £678; C Dod £532; G Ray £217.

25 Goods returned by us to the following: B Fell £161; G Fry £52.

31 Credit purchases from: L Pacioli £203; M Show £317.

14.11A Enter up the sales day book and the returns inwards day book from the following details. Then post to the customers' accounts and show the transfers to the general ledger.

2008

June 1 Credit sales to: B Dock £240; M Ryan £126; G Soul £94; F Trip £107.

6 Credit sales to: P Coates £182; L Job £203; T Mann £99.

10 Goods returned to us by: B Dock £19; F Trip £32.

20 Credit sales to B Uphill £1,790.

24 Goods returned to us by L Job £16.

30 Credit sales to T Kane £302.

14.12 You are to enter up the sales, purchases, returns inwards and returns outwards day books from the following details, then to post the items to the relevant accounts in the sales and purchase ledgers. The total of the day books are then to be transferred to the accounts in the general ledger.

2009

May 1 Credit sales: T Thompson £56; L Rodriguez £148; K Barton £145.

3 Credit purchases: P Potter £144; H Harris £25; B Spencer £76.

7 Credit sales: K Kelly £89; N Mendes £78; N Lee £257.

9 Credit purchases: B Perkins £24; H Harris £58; H Miles £123.

11 Goods returned by us to: P Potter £12; B Spencer £22.

14 Goods returned to us by: T Thompson £5; K Barton £11; K Kelly £14.

17 Credit purchases: H Harris £54; B Perkins £65; L Nixon £75.

20 Goods returned by us to B Spencer £14.

24 Credit sales: K Mohammed £57; K Kelly £65; O Green £112.

28 Goods returned to us by N Mendes £24.

31 Credit sales: N Lee £55.

14.13A You are to enter the following items in the books, post to personal accounts, and show the transfers to the general ledger.

2009

July 1 Credit purchases from: K Hill £380; M Norman £500; N Senior £106.

3 Credit sales to: E Rigby £510; E Phillips £246; F Thompson £356.

5 Credit purchases from: R Morton £200; J Cook £180; D Edwards £410; C Davies £66.

8 Credit sales to: A Green £307; H George £250; J Ferguson £185.

12 Returns outwards to: M Norman £30; N Senior £16.

14 Returns inwards from: E Phillips £18; F Thompson £22.

20 Credit sales to: E Phillips £188; F Powell £310; E Lee £420.

24 Credit purchases from: C Ferguson £550; K Ennevor £900.

31 Returns inwards from: E Phillips £27; E Rigby £30.

31 Returns outwards to: J Cook £13; C Davies £11.

Learning objectives

After you have studied this chapter, you should be able to:

- explain the purpose of having a journal
- enter up the journal
- post from the journal to the ledgers
- complete opening entries for a new set of accounting books in the journal and make the appropriate entries in the ledgers
- describe and explain the accounting cycle

Introduction

In this chapter, you will learn about the book of original entry that sweeps up all the transactions that have not been entered fully in the other five books of original entry – the journal. You'll learn about the sort of transactions that are entered in the journal and how to make those entries. You'll also learn how to transfer those entries to the accounts in the ledgers. Finally, you will learn what the accounting cycle consists of and see how it links all the material you have learnt so far in this book.

15.1 Main books of original entry

We have seen in earlier chapters that most transactions are entered in one of the following books of original entry:

- cash book
- Sales day book
- Purchases day book
- Returns inwards day book
- Returns outwards day book.

These books are each devoted to a particular form of transaction. For example, all credit sales are in the sales day book. To trace any of the transactions entered in these five books would be relatively easy, as we know exactly which book of original entry would contain the information we are looking for.

15.2　The journal: the other book of original entry

The other items which do not pass through these five books are much less common, and sometimes much more complicated. It would be easy for a bookkeeper to forget the details of these transactions if they were made directly into the ledger accounts from the source documents and, if the bookkeeper left the business, it could be impossible to understand such bookkeeping entries.

Activity 15.1　If these five books are used to record all cash and bank transactions, and all credit purchase and sales items, what are these other items that need to be recorded in a sixth book of original entry?

What is needed is a form of diary to record such transactions, before the entries are made in the double entry accounts. This book is called the **journal**. For each transaction it will contain:

● the date
● the name of account(s) to be debited and the amount(s)
● the name of the account(s) to be credited and the amount(s)
● a description and explanation of the transaction (this is called a **narrative**)
● a folio reference to the source documents giving proof of the transaction.

The use of a journal makes fraud by bookkeepers more difficult. It also reduces the risk of entering the item once only instead of having double entry. Despite these advantages there are many businesses which do not have such a book.

15.3　Typical uses of the journal

Some of the main uses of the journal are listed below. It must not be thought that this is a complete list.

1　The purchase and sale of fixed assets on credit.
2　Writing-off bad debts.
3　The correction of errors in the ledger accounts.
4　Opening entries. These are the entries needed to open a new set of books.
5　Adjustments to any of the entries in the ledgers.

The layout of the journal is:

The Journal				
Date	Details	Folio	Dr	Cr
	The name of the account to be debited. 　The name of the account to be credited. The narrative.			

On the first line in the entry is the account to be debited. The second line gives the account to be credited. It is indented so as to make it obvious that it is the credit part of the double entry. The final line is a description of what is being done and provides a permanent record of the reason(s) for the entry.

　　You should remember that the journal is not a double entry account. It is a form of diary, just as are the day books you learnt about in Chapter 14. Entering an item in the journal is not the same as recording an item in an account. Once the journal entry is made, the entry in the double entry accounts can then be made.

Note for students

The vertical lines have been included above in order to illustrate how the paper within the journal may be printed. You may find it useful to rule your paper according to this layout when attempting examples and questions on this topic.

15.4 Journal entries in examination questions

If you were to ask examiners what type of bookkeeping and accounting questions are always answered badly by students they would certainly include 'questions involving journal entries'. This is not because they are difficult, but because many students seem to suffer some sort of mental block when doing such questions. The authors, who have been examiners for a large number of accounting bodies around the world, believe that this occurs because students fail to view the journal as a document containing instructions, three per transaction:

1 The account(s) to be debited.
2 The account(s) to be credited.
3 A description of the transaction.

To help you avoid this sort of problem with journal entries, you will first of all see what the entries are in the accounts, and then be shown how to write up the journal for each of these entries. Let's now look at a few examples.

In practice, the folio reference entered in the T-accounts is often that of the other account involved in the transaction; rather than that of a journal entry. However, this is done when no journal entry has been prepared. When a journal entry has been prepared, it is always the journal entry folio reference that appears in the T-accounts.

1 Purchase and sale on credit of fixed assets

1 A milling machine is bought on credit from Toolmakers Ltd for £10,550 on 1 July 2008.

The transaction involves the acquisition of an asset matched by a new liability. From what you have learnt in earlier chapters, you will know that the acquisition of an asset is represented by a debit entry in the asset account. You will also know that a new liability is recorded by crediting a liability account. The double entries would be:

	Machinery			Folio	GL1
2008			£		
July 1 Toolmakers Ltd	J1	10,550			

	Toolmakers Ltd			Folio	PL55
	2008				£
	July 1 Machinery	J1	10,550		

 Activity 15.2 All the folio numbers have been entered in these ledger accounts. You do need to enter them at some time so that you can trace the other side of the entries, but why have they already been entered?

Now what we have to do is to record those entries in the journal. Remember, the journal is simply a kind of diary, not in account form but in ordinary written form. It says which account has been debited, which account has been credited, and then gives the narrative which simply describes the nature of the transaction. For the transaction above, the journal entry will appear as follows:

The Journal					(page 1)
Date	Details	Folio	Dr	Cr
2008 July 1	Machinery Toolmakers Ltd Purchase of milling machine on credit, Capital purchases invoice No 7/159	GL 1 PL55	£ 10,550	£ 10,550

2 Sale of a van no longer required for £800 on credit to K Lamb on 2 July 2008.

Here again it is not difficult to work out what entries are needed in the double entry accounts. They are as follows:

K Lamb   Folio   SL79

2008 July 2 Van	J2	£ 800	

Van   Folio   GL51

	2008 July 2 K Lamb	J2	£ 800

The journal entry will appear as follows:

The Journal					(page 2)
Date	Details	Folio	Dr	Cr
2008 July 2	K Lamb Van Sales of a van no longer required See letter ref. KL3X8g	SL79 GL51	£ 800	£ 800

2 Bad debts

A debt of £78 owing to us from H Mander is written off as a bad debt on 31 August 2008.

As the debt is now of no value we have to stop showing it as an asset. This means that we will credit H Mander to cancel it out of his account. A bad debt is an expense, and so we will debit it to a bad debts account. The double entry for this is shown as:

Bad Debts   Folio   GL16

2008 Aug 31 H Mander	J3	£ 78	

H Mander   Folio   SL99

	2008 Aug 31 Bad debts	J3	£ 78

The journal entry is:

The Journal					(page 3)
Date	Details	Folio	Dr	Cr
2008 Aug 31	Bad debts H Mander Debt written-off as bad. See letter in file HM2X8	GL16 SL99	£ 78	£ 78

3 Correction of errors

This is explained in detail in Chapters 30 and 31.

However, the same procedures are followed as in the case of these other types of journal entries.

4 Opening entries

J Brew, after being in business for some years without keeping proper records, now decides to keep a double entry set of books. On 1 July 2008 he establishes that his assets and liabilities are as follows:

Assets: Van £3,700; Fixtures £1,800; Stock £4,200.
  Debtors – B Young £95; D Blake £45; Bank £860; Cash £65.
Liabilities: Creditors – M Quinn £129; C Walters £410.

The Assets therefore total £3,700 + £1,800 + £4,200 + £95 + £45 + £860 + £65 = £10,765; and the Liabilities total £129 + £410 = £539

The Capital consists of Assets – Liabilities, i.e. £10,765 – £539 = £10,226.

1 July 2008 will be the first day of the accounting period, as that is the date on which all the asset and liability values were established.

We start the writing up of the books on 1 July 2008. To do this we:

1 Open the journal and make the journal entries to record the opening assets, liabilities and capital.
2 Open asset accounts, one for each asset. Each opening asset is shown as a debit balance.
3 Open liability accounts, one for each liability. Each opening liability is shown as a credit balance.
4 Open an account for the capital. Show it as a credit balance.

The journal records what you are doing, and why. Exhibit 15.1 shows:

● The journal
● The opening entries in the double entry accounts.

Exhibit 15.1

The Journal				(page 5)
Date	Details	Folio	Dr	Cr
2008			£	£
July 1	Van	GL1	3,700	
	Fixtures	GL2	1,800	
	Stock	GL3	4,200	
	Debtors – B Young	SL1	95	
	D Blake	SL2	45	
	Bank	CB1	860	
	Cash	CB1	65	
	Creditors – M Quinn	PL1		129
	C Walters	PL2		410
	Capital	GL4		10,226
	Assets and liabilities at this date			
	entered to open the books.		10,765	10,765

General Ledger
Van (page 1)

2008		Folio	£				
July 1	Balance	J 5	3,700				

Fixtures (page 2)

2008		Folio	£				
July 1	Balance	J 5	1,800				

Stock (page 3)

2008		Folio	£				
July 1	Balance	J 5	4,200				

Capital (page 4)

				2008		Folio	£
				July 1	Balance	J 5	10,226

Sales Ledger
B Young (page 1)

2008		Folio	£				
July 1	Balance	J 5	95				

D Blake (page 2)

2008		Folio	£				
July 1	Balance	J 5	45				

Purchases Ledger
M Quinn (page 1)

				2008		Folio	£
				July 1	Balance	J 5	129

C Walters (page 2)

				2008		Folio	£
				July 1	Balance	J 5	410

Cash Book

			Cash	Bank	(page 1)	

2008		Folio	£	£		
July 1	Balances	J 5	65	860		

Once these opening balances have been recorded in the books, the day-to-day transactions can be entered in the normal manner.

At the elementary level of examinations in bookkeeping, questions are often asked which require you to open a set of books and record the day-by-day entries for the ensuing period.

Activity 15.3 Do you think you will ever need to do this again for this business? (Hint: think about the entries to be made at the start of the next accounting period.)

5 Adjustments to any of the entries in the ledgers

These can be of many types and it is impossible to write out a complete list. Several examples are now shown:

1 K Young, a debtor, owed £2,000 on 1 July 2009. He was unable to pay his account in cash, but offers a five-year-old car in full settlement of the debt. The offer is accepted on 5 July 2009.

The personal account has now been settled and needs to be credited with the £2,000. On the other hand, the business now has an extra asset, a car, resulting in the car account needing to be debited with the £2,000 value that has been placed upon the new car.

The double entry recorded in the ledgers is:

	Car			GL171
2009		£		
July 5 K Young	J6	2,000		

	K Young			SL333
2009	£	2009		£
July 1 Balance b/d	2,000	July 5 Motor car	J6	2,000

The journal entry is:

The Journal					(page 6)
Date	Details		Folio	Dr	Cr
2009				£	£
July 5	Car		GL171	2,000	
	K Young		SL333		2,000
	Accepted car in full settlement of debt				
	per letter dated 5/7/2009				

2 T Jones is a creditor. On 10 July 2009 his business is taken over by A Lee to whom the debt of £150 is now to be paid.

Here one creditor is just being exchanged for another one. The action needed is to cancel the amount owing to T Jones by debiting his account, and to show it owing to Lee by opening an account for Lee and crediting it.

The entries in the ledger accounts are:

	T Jones			SL92
2009	£	2009		£
July 10 A Lee	J7 150	July 1 Balance b/d		150

	A Lee			SL244
		2009		£
		July 10 T Jones	J7	150

The journal entry is:

The Journal				(page 7)	
Date	Details	Folio	Dr	Cr	
2009 July 10	T Jones A Lee Transfer of indebtedness as per letter ref G/1335	SL 92 SL244	£ 150	£ 150	

3 We had not yet paid for an office printer we bought on credit for £310 because it was not working properly when installed. On 12 July 2009 we returned it to the supplier, RS Ltd. An allowance of £310 was offered by the supplier and accepted. As a result, we no longer owe the supplier anything for the printer.

The double entry in the ledger accounts is:

RS Ltd   PL124

2009			£	2009				£
July	12	Office machinery	J8	310	2009 July	1	Balance b/d	310

Office Machinery   GL288

2009			£	2009				£
July	1	Balance b/d	310	July	12	RS Ltd	J8	310

The journal entry is:

The Journal				(page 8)	
Date	Details	Folio	Dr	Cr	
2009 July 12	RS Ltd Office machinery Faulty printer returned to supplier. Full allowance given. See letter 10/7/2009.	PL124 GL288	£ 310	£ 310	

15.5 Examination guidance

Later on in your studies, especially in *Business Accounting 2*, you may find that some of the journal entries become rather more complicated than those you have seen so far. The best plan for nearly all students is to follow this advice:

1 **On your examination answer paper write a heading 'Workings'. Then show the double entry accounts under that heading.**
2 **Now put a heading 'Answer', and show the answer in the form of the journal, as shown in this chapter.**

If the question asks for journal entries you must *not* fall into the trap of just showing the double entry accounts, as you could get no marks at all *even though your double entry records are correct*. The examiner wants to see the journal entries, and you *must* show those in your answer.

15.6 The basic accounting cycle

Now that we have covered all aspects of bookkeeping entries, we can show the whole **accounting cycle** in the form of the diagram in Exhibit 15.2.

Note that the 'accounting cycle' refers to the sequence in which data is recorded and processed until it becomes part of the financial statements at the end of the period.

Exhibit 15.2 The accounting cycle for a profit-making organisation

Source documents

Where original information is to be found

- Sales and purchases invoices
- Debit and credit notes for returns
- Bank pay-in slips and cheque counterfoils
- Receipts for cash paid out and received
- Correspondence containing other financial information

Original entry

What happens to it

Classified and then entered in books of original entry:

- The Cash Books*
- Sales and Purchases Day Books
- Returns Inwards and Outwards Day Books
- The Journal

Double entry

How the dual aspect of each transaction is recorded

Double entry accounts

General Ledger	Sales Ledger	Purchases Ledger	Cash Books*
Real and nominal accounts	Debtors' accounts	Creditors' accounts	Cash Book and Petty Cash Book

(*Note: Cash Books fulfil both the roles of books of original entry and double entry accounts)

Check arithmetic

Checking the arithmetical accuracy of double entry accounts

Trial balance

Profit or Loss

Calculation of profit or loss for the accounting period shown in a financial statement

Trading and Profit and Loss Account

Closing financial position

Financial statement showing liabilities, assets and capital at the end of the accounting period

Balance sheet

> **Activity 15.4** What are the six books of original entry?

Learning outcomes

You should now have learnt:

1 What the journal is used for.

2 That the journal is the collection place for items that do not pass fully through the other five books of original entry.

3 That there is a range of possible types of transactions that must be entered in the journal.

4 That the opening double entries made on starting a set of books for the first time are done using the journal.

5 How to make the opening entries for a new set of books in the journal and in the ledger accounts.

6 That the main parts of the accounting cycle are as follows:

(a) Collect source documents.
(b) Enter transactions in the books of original entry.
(c) Post to ledgers.
(d) Extract trial balance.
(e) Prepare the trading and profit and loss account.
(f) Draw up the balance sheet.

Answers to activities

15.1 All transactions relating to fixed assets. Also, entries have to be recorded somewhere when errors in the books have to be corrected, or when any figures in the ledger accounts need to be changed. Also, any transfers involving the capital account, such as when funds are set aside from the capital account to provide resources should a building need to be repaired or replaced.

15.2 You are looking at the ledger accounts after the details have been entered in them from the journal and you always enter the folio number in the ledger account as you make each entry, not afterwards. The check that the entries has been completed is made by only entering the folio numbers *in the journal* as each entry is written in the appropriate ledger account. You could, therefore, see a journal entry in the journal that has no folio numbers entered against it. This would signify that the journal entry has not yet been fully recorded in the appropriate ledger accounts. As mentioned above, you should *never* see this in a ledger account as the folio number is always entered *at the same time* as the rest of the details from the journal are entered.

15.3 The need for opening entries will not occur very often. They will not be needed each year as the balances from the previous period will have been brought forward. They will only be required a second time if the business goes through a change in status, for example, if it becomes a limited company.

15.4 Cash book, sales day book, purchases day book, returns inwards day book, returns outwards day book, and the journal.

Review questions

15.1 You are to show the journal entries necessary to record the following items which occurred in 2008:

(*a*) March 1 Bought a van on credit from Fring's Wheels for £7,200.

(*b*) March 3 A debt of £90 owing from A Collins was written off as a bad debt.

(*c*) March 8 Office equipment bought by us for £430 was returned to the supplier Comfort Ltd, as it was faulty. Full allowance will be given to us.

(*d*) March 12 We are owed £491 by J Smith. He is declared bankrupt and we received £49 in full settlement of the debt.

(*e*) March 14 We take goods costing £73 out of the business stock without paying for them.

(*f*) March 28 Some time ago we paid an insurance bill thinking that it was in respect of the business. We now discover that £98 of the amount paid was in fact insurance of our private house.

(*g*) 2008 March 28 Bought two PCs for £1,186 on credit from Findler Brothers.

15.2A Show the journal entries necessary to record the following items:

2007

Apr 1 Bought fixtures on credit from Bell and Co £1,153.

4 We take goods costing £340 out of the business stock without paying for them.

9 £68 of the goods taken by us on 4 April is returned back into stock by us. We do not take any money for the return of the goods.

12 H Cowes owes us £640. He is unable to pay his debt. We agree to take some computer equipment from him at that value and so cancel the debt.

18 Some of the fixtures bought from Bell and Co, £42 worth, are found to be unsuitable and are returned to them for full allowance.

24 A debt owing to us by P Lees of £124 is written off as a bad debt.

30 Office equipment bought on credit from Furniture Today Ltd for £1,710.

15.3 You are to open the books of F Polk, a trader, via the journal to record the assets and liabilities, and are then to record the daily transactions for the month of May. A trial balance is to be extracted as on 31 May 2009.

2009

May 1 *Assets*: Premises £34,000; Van £5,125; Fixtures £810; Stock £6,390. Debtors: P Mullen £140; F Lane £310. Cash at bank £6,240; Cash in hand £560.
Liabilities: Creditors: S Hood £215; J Brown £460.

1 Paid storage costs by cheque £40.

2 Goods bought on credit from: S Hood £145; D Main £206; W Tone £96; R Foot £61.

3 Goods sold on credit to: J Wilson £112; T Cole £164; F Syme £208; J Allen £91; P White £242; F Lane £77.

4 Paid for motor expenses in cash £47.

7 Cash drawings by proprietor £150.

9 Goods sold on credit to: T Cole £68; J Fox £131.

11 Goods returned to Polk by: J Wilson £32; F Syme £48.

14 Bought another van on credit from Abel Motors Ltd £4,850.

16 The following paid Polk their accounts by cheque less 5 per cent cash discount: P Mullen; F Lane; J Wilson; F Syme.

19 Goods returned by Polk to R Foot £6.

22 Goods bought on credit from: L Mole £183; W Wright £191.

24 The following accounts were settled by Polk by cheque less 5 per cent cash discount: S Hood; J Brown; R Foot.

27 Salaries paid by cheque £480.

30 Paid business rates by cheque £132.

31 Paid Abel Motors Ltd a cheque for £4,850.

The analytical petty cash book and the imprest system

Learning objectives

After you have studied this chapter, you should be able to:

- explain why many organisations use a petty cash book
- make entries in a petty cash book
- transfer the appropriate amounts from the petty cash book to the ledgers at the end of each period
- explain and operate the imprest system for petty cash
- explain why some organisations use a bank cash book
- make entries in a bank cash book

Introduction

You may remember that you learnt in Chapter 13 that there is a second type of cash book, called the **petty cash book**, which many businesses use to record small amounts paid for in cash. (It was included in the accounting cycle diagram in Chapter 15.) In this chapter, you'll learn of the type of items that are recorded in the petty cash book, and how to make the entries to it. You'll also learn how to transfer financial data from the petty cash book into the ledgers. Finally, you will learn about bank cash books and how they differ from the cash books you learnt about in Chapter 13.

16.1 Division of the cash book

As businesses continue to grow, some now having a commercial value in excess of that of many smaller countries, you have learnt that, for many, it has become necessary to have several books instead of just one ledger. In fact, nowadays all but the very smallest organisations use sets of ledgers and day books.

Activity 16.1 Why do we have day books? Why don't we just enter every transaction directly into the appropriate ledger accounts?

The cash book became a book of original entry so that all cash and bank transactions could be separated from the rest of the accounts in the general ledger. It is for much the same reason that many organisations use a petty cash book. Every business has a number of transactions of very small value which, were they all recorded in the cash book, would only serve to make it more difficult to identify the important transactions that businesses need to keep a close eye upon. **Just like the cash book, the petty cash book is both a book of original entry and a ledger account.**

The advantages of using a petty cash book can be summarised as follows:

● The task of handling and recording small cash payments can be given by the cashier (the person responsible for recording entries in the cash book) to a junior member of staff. This person is known as the 'petty cashier'. The cashier, who is a more senior and, consequently, higher paid member of staff would be saved from routine work.

● If small cash payments were entered into the main cash book, these items would then need posting one by one to the ledgers. For example, if travelling expenses were paid to staff on a daily basis, this could mean approximately 250 postings to the staff travelling expenses account during the year, i.e. 5 days per week × 50 working weeks per year. However, by using a petty cash book, it would only be the monthly totals for each period that need posting to the general ledger. If this were done, only twelve entries would be needed in the staff travelling expenses account instead of approximately 250.

When a petty cashier makes a payment to someone, then that person will have to fill in a voucher showing exactly what the payment was for. They usually have to attach bills, e.g. for petrol, to the petty cash voucher. They would sign the voucher to certify that their expenses had been received from the petty cashier.

16.2 The imprest system

It is all very well having a petty cash book but, where does the money paid out from it come from? The **imprest system** is one where the cashier gives the petty cashier enough cash to meet the petty cash needs for the following period. Then, at the end of the period, the cashier finds out the amounts spent by the petty cashier, by looking at the entries in the petty cash book. At the same time, the petty cashier may give the petty cash vouchers to the cashier so that the entries in the petty cash book may be checked. The cashier then passes cash to the value of the amount spent on petty cash in the period to the petty cashier. In other words, the cashier tops up the amount remaining in petty cash to bring it back up to the level it was at when the period started. This process is the imprest system and this topped-up amount is known as the petty cash **float**.

Exhibit 16.1 shows an example of this method.

Exhibit 16.1

		£
Period 1	The cashier gives the petty cashier	100
	The petty cashier pays out in the period	(78)
	Petty cash now in hand	22
	The cashier now gives the petty cashier the amount spent	78
	Petty cash in hand at the end of Period 1	100
Period 2	The petty cashier pays out in the period	(84)
	Petty cash now in hand	16
	The cashier now gives the petty cashier the amount spent	84
	Petty cash in hand at the end of Period 2	100

It may be necessary to increase the petty cash float to be held at the start of each period. In the above case, if we had wanted to increase the float at the end of the second period to £120, then the cashier would have given the petty cashier an extra £20, i.e. £84 + £20 = £104.

In some small organisations, no petty cash book is kept. Instead, at the end of each period, the amount left in petty cash is reconciled (i.e. checked and verified as correct) with the receipts held by the petty cashier. The amount spent is then given to the petty cashier in order to restore the float to its agreed level. However, this is not an ideal method to adopt. Businesses need to control the uses of all their resources, including petty cash, and so virtually every organisation that operates a petty cash float maintains a petty cash book. The most common format adopted is the 'analytical petty cash book'.

16.3 Illustration of an analytical petty cash book

An analytical petty cash book is shown in Exhibit 16.2. This example shows one for an elementary school.

Exhibit 16.2

Petty Cash Book											*(page 31)*
Receipts	Folio	Date	Details	Voucher No	Total	Motor Expenses	Staff Travelling Expenses	Postages	Cleaning	Ledger Folio	Ledger Accounts
£					£	£	£	£	£		£
300	CB 19	Sept 1	Cash								
		2	Petrol	1	16	16					
		3	J Green	2	23		23				
		3	Postage	3	12			12			
		4	D Davies	4	32		32				
		7	Cleaning	5	11				11		
		9	Petrol	6	21	21					
		12	K Jones	7	13		13				
		14	Petrol	8	23	23					
		15	L Black	9	5		5				
		16	Cleaning	10	11				11		
		18	Petrol	11	22	22					
		20	Postage	12	12			12			
		22	Cleaning	13	11				11		
		24	G Wood	14	7		7				
		27	C Brown	15	13					PL18	13
		29	Postage	16	12			12			
					244	82	80	36	33		13
						GL	GL	GL	GL		
244	CB 22	30	Cash			17	29	44	64		
		30	Balance	c/d	300						
544					544						
300		Oct 1	Balance	b/d							

The Receipts column is the debit side of the petty cash book. On giving £300 to the petty cashier on 1 September, the credit entry is made in the cash book while the debit entry is made in the petty cash book. A similar entry is made on 30 September for the £244 paid by the head-teacher to the petty cashier. As this amount covers all the expenses paid by the petty cashier, the float is now restored to its earlier level of £300. The credit side is used to record all the payments made by the petty cashier.

The transactions that were recorded in the petty cash book were:

2008		Voucher No.		£
Sept	1	–	The headteacher gives £300 as float to the petty cashier	
			Payments out of petty cash during September:	
	2	1	Petrol: School bus	16
	3	2	J Green – travelling expenses of staff	23
	3	3	Postage	12
	4	4	D Davies – travelling expenses of staff	32
	7	5	Cleaning expenses	11
	9	6	Petrol: School bus	21
	12	7	K Jones – travelling expenses of staff	13
	14	8	Petrol: School bus	23
	15	9	L Black – travelling expenses of staff	5
	16	10	Cleaning expenses	11
	18	11	Petrol: School bus	22
	20	12	Postage	12
	22	13	Cleaning expenses	11
	24	14	G Wood – travelling expenses of staff	7
	27	15	Settlement of C Brown's account in the Purchases Ledger	13
	29	16	Postage	12
	30	–	The headteacher reimburses the petty cashier the amount spent in the month.	

The process followed during the period that led to these entries appearing in the petty cash book as shown in Exhibit 16.2 is:

1 Enter the date and details of each payment. Put the amount paid in the Total column.
2 Put the same amount in the column for that type of expense.
3 At the end of each period, add up the Total column.
4 Add up each of the expense columns. The total found in step 3 should equal the total of all the expense columns. In Exhibit 16.2 this is £244.
5 Enter the amount reimbursed to make up the float in the Receipts column.
6 Balance off the petty cash book, carrying down the petty cash in hand balance to the next period.

To complete the double entry for petty cash expenses paid:

1 The total of each expense column is debited to the appropriate expense account in the general ledger.
2 The folio number of each expense account in the general ledger is entered under the appropriate expense column in the petty cash book. (This signifies that the double entry to the ledger account has been made.)
3 The last column in the petty cash book is a ledger column. It contains entries for items paid out of petty cash which need posting to a ledger other than the general ledger. (This might arise, for example, if a purchases ledger account was settled out of petty cash.)

Activity 16.2

Where is the other side of the double entry for all these expense postings to the ledgers recorded?

The double entry for all the items in Exhibit 16.2 are shown in Exhibit 16.3.

Exhibit 16.3

Cash Book
(Bank and Folio columns only)   (page 19)

					2008			Folio	£
					Sept	1	Petty cash	PCB 31	300
						30	Petty cash	PCB 31	244

General Ledger
School Bus Expenses   (page 17)

2008			Folio	£	
Sept	30	Petty cash	PCB 31	82	

Staff Travelling Expenses   (page 29)

2008			Folio	£	
Sept	30	Petty cash	PCB 31	80	

Postages   (page 44)

2008			Folio	£	
Sept	30	Petty cash	PCB 31	36	

Cleaning   (page 64)

2008			Folio	£	
Sept	30	Petty cash	PCB 31	33	

Purchases Ledger
C Brown   (page 18)

2008			Folio	£	2008				£
Sept	30	Petty cash	PCB 31	13	Sept	1	Balance	b/d	13

Note how the Folio column is used to enter 'b/d'. You may have noticed previously that this is done for both 'b/d' and 'c/d' in all ledger accounts and in the cash book where contra entries are also indicated in the folio column by use of the symbol '¢'.

16.4 Bank cash book

Nowadays, many businesses have only a small number of sales that are paid for with cash. The rest of the 'cash' sales are actually paid using credit cards, cheques, and direct transfers into the business bank account using systems like Switch (which, as you learnt in Chapter 12, is operated by UK banks and involves a customer's bank card being swiped into a special machine in the same way that credit card payments are processed). Switch is used in retail transactions and results in the payment being transferred immediately from the customer's bank account into the business bank account.

Organisations which have only a small number of sales for cash may use a different form of cash book from the one you learnt about in Chapter 13. If they do, they will use a petty cash book and a **bank cash book**. The bank cash book is given this name because *all* payments in cash are entered in the petty cash book, and the bank cash book contains *only* bank columns and discount columns.

In a bank cash book (it could also be done in an 'ordinary' cash book), an extra column may be added. The extra column would show the details of the cheques and direct transfers banked, with just the total of the banking being shown in the total column.

Exhibit 16.4 shows the receipts side of a bank cash book containing this extra column. The totals of the deposits made into the bank on each of the three days were £192, £381 and £1,218. The details column shows what the bankings are made up of.

Exhibit 16.4

Bank Cash Book (Receipts side)

Date 2009	Details	Discount £	Items £	Total Banked £
May 14	G Archer	5	95	
14	P Watts	3	57	
14	C King		40	192
20	K Dooley	6	114	
20	Cash Sales		55	
20	R Jones		60	
20	P Mackie	8	152	381
31	J Young		19	
31	T Broome	50	950	
31	Cash Sales		116	
31	H Tiller	7	133	1,218

Learning outcomes

You should now have learnt:

1 That the petty cash book saves (a) the cash book and (b) the ledger accounts from containing a lot of trivial detail.

2 That the use of the petty cash book enables the cashier or a senior member of staff to delegate this type of work to a more junior member of staff.

3 That the cashier should periodically check the work performed by the petty cashier.

4 That all payments made by the petty cashier should have petty cash vouchers as evidence of proof of expense.

5 How to enter petty cash transactions into the petty cash book.

6 How to transfer the totals for each expense recorded in the petty cash book to the appropriate ledger accounts.

7 How to operate a float system for petty cash.

8 The difference between a cash book and a bank cash book.

9 Why some organisations use a bank cash book instead of a cash book.

Answers to activities

16.1 One reason why we have day books is to avoid too much detail being entered in the ledgers.

16.2 In the petty cash book. Like the cash book, the petty cash book is not only a book of original entry, it is also an account that would otherwise appear in the general ledger.

Review questions

16.1 The following is a summary of the petty cash transactions of Jockfield Ltd for May 2008.

May			£
	1	Received from cashier £300 as petty cash float	
	2	Postage	18
	3	Travelling	12
	4	Cleaning	15
	7	Petrol for delivery van	22
	8	Travelling	25
	9	Stationery	17
	11	Cleaning	18
	14	Postage	5
	15	Travelling	8
	18	Stationery	9
	18	Cleaning	23
	20	Postage	13
	24	Delivery van 5,000 mile service	43
	26	Petrol	18
	27	Cleaning	21
	29	Postage	5
	30	Petrol	14

You are required to:
(a) Rule up a suitable petty cash book with analysis columns for expenditure on cleaning, motor expenses, postage, stationery, travelling.
(b) Enter the month's transactions.
(c) Enter the receipt of the amount necessary to restore the imprest and carry down the balance for the commencement of the following month.
(d) State how the double entry for the expenditure is completed.

(*Association of Accounting Technicians*)

16.2

(a) Why do some businesses keep a petty cash book as well as a cash book?
(b) Kathryn Rochford keeps her petty cash book on the imprest system, the imprest being £25. For the month of April 2009 her petty cash transactions were as follows:

			£
Apr	1	Petty cash balance	1.13
	2	Petty cashier presented vouchers to cashier and obtained cash to restore the imprest	23.87
	4	Bought postage stamps	8.50
	9	Paid to Courtney Bishop, a creditor	2.35
	11	Paid bus fares	1.72
	17	Bought envelopes	0.70
	23	Received cash for personal telephone call	0.68
	26	Bought petrol	10.00

(*i*) Enter the above transactions in the petty cash book and balance the petty cash book at 30 April, bringing down the balance on 1 May.
(*ii*) On 1 May Kathryn Rochford received an amount of cash from the cashier to restore the imprest. Enter this transaction in the petty cash book.

(c) Open the ledger accounts to complete the double entry for the following:

(*i*) The petty cash analysis columns headed *Postage and Stationery* and *Travelling Expenses*;
(*ii*) The transactions dated 9 and 23 April 2009.

(*Northern Examinations and Assessment Board: GCSE*)

→

Value Added Tax

Introduction

In this chapter, you'll learn about the UK system of Value Added Tax. You will learn about how the concept that *the final consumer pays all* underlies the system and of how VAT is collected in stages as goods pass their way down the supply chain. You'll learn about the different rates of VAT and of the different ways VAT has to be recorded as a result. Finally, you will learn how to prepare a VAT Account and complete a VAT Return.

17.1 What is VAT?

Value Added Tax (VAT) is a tax charged on the supply of most goods and services in the United Kingdom. Some goods and services are not taxable, for example postal services. In addition some persons and businesses are exempted, such as those with low levels of turnover. Value Added Tax is administered in the UK by HM Revenue and Customs.

The concept underlying VAT is that the tax is paid by the ultimate consumer of the goods or services *but* that everyone in the supply chain must account for and settle up the net amount of VAT they have received in the VAT tax period, usually three months. If they have received more in VAT than they have paid out in VAT, they must send that difference to HM Revenue and Customs. If they have paid out more than they have received, they will be reimbursed the difference.

Goods typically pass through at least two sellers (the manufacturer and the retailer) before they are finally sold to the consumer. These intermediate-stage VAT payments will be cancelled out when the final stage in the chain is reached and the good or service is sold to its ultimate consumer.

Exhibit 17.1 shows, through an example, how the system works.

Exhibit 17.1

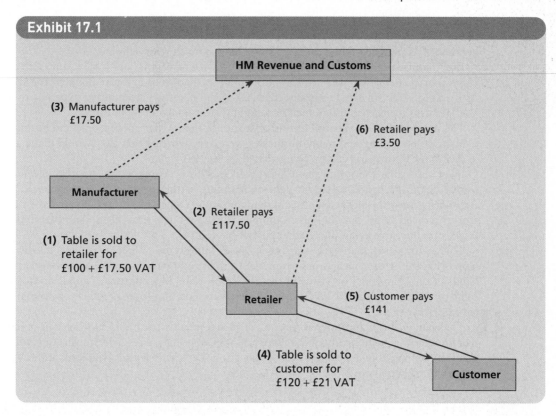

In the example in Exhibit 17.1:

1 A manufacturer sells a table to a retailer for £100 plus VAT of £17.50.
2 The retailer pays the manufacturer £117.50 for the table.
3 The VAT on that sale (£17.50) is sent by the manufacturer to the Revenue and Customs.
4 The retailer sells the goods to the customer (i.e. the consumer) for £120 plus VAT of £21.
5 The customer pays £141 to the retailer for the table.
6 The amount of VAT paid for the goods by the retailer to the manufacturer (£17.50) is deducted from the VAT received by the retailer from the customer (£21) and the difference of £3.50 is then sent to Revenue and Customs.

Only the ultimate consumer has actually paid any VAT. Unfortunately, everyone in the chain has to send the VAT charged at the step when they were in the role of seller.

In theory, the amount received in stages by the Revenue and Customs will equal the amount of VAT paid by the ultimate consumer in the final stage of the supply chain.

Activity 17.1 Can you think of any circumstances where this may not be the case?

17.2 Background

When VAT was first introduced in 1973 as a result of the entry of the UK into the EU, it came as quite a shock to the business community and to many accountants. The previous tax on goods,

Purchase Tax, had only applied to manufacturers and wholesalers whose goods were liable to the tax. VAT, on the other hand, applied to virtually all goods and services and all but a few organisations suddenly found they had something extra to worry about.

Every entity responsible for accounting for VAT found that it had 'VAT Returns' to complete every quarter. Being late was not an option and they had to be accurate down to the last penny. As a result, some smaller businesses that lacked the necessary accounting expertise to do their VAT Returns themselves found their accountant's fees going up significantly.

The press of the day was full of horror stories of the impact upon people and businesses of a VAT inspector calling and many businesses were very worried that they would make a mistake in their VAT Return and end up being visited by the 'VAT man'.

Over the years, the initial panic has given way to acceptance that another piece of paper simply has to be processed and a debt outstanding settled or an amount receivable received. Accounting records and accounting systems now deal with VAT routinely and the additional work involved in all but the most complex businesses has now been absorbed and become largely unnoticeable as simply another part of the routine.

This is not to say that VAT is a simple tax to understand. While consumers hardly notice it (goods have to be sold clearly indicating the total price to pay), some organisations suffer at the hands of the complexity by virtue of their being involved in a mixture of goods and/or services, some of which are liable to VAT, some of which are not, and some of which are, but at a different rate of the tax.

Thankfully, this complexity is beyond the scope of this textbook. However, it is important that you know something about the nature of VAT and that, necessarily, means that you need to know something about the range of its application. Let's start with a brief look at the VAT rates and what they apply to.

17.3　VAT rates

The **standard rate** of VAT is decided by Parliament. It has been changed from time to time. At the time of writing it is 17.5 per cent. There is also currently a **reduced rate** of 5 per cent on domestic fuel and power, one of 5 per cent on the installation of some energy-saving materials, and a **zero rate** on items like food sold in a supermarket.

17.4　Standard-rated businesses

You've already seen an example in Exhibit 17.1 of what happens to the VAT when a manufacturer sells to a retailer who then sells to a consumer. Another common example involves a business selling its own product direct to the final consumer.

Imagine that Trader A (a farmer) sells some of the plants they have grown to the general public.

Trader A sells goods to Jones for £100 + VAT of 17.5%:

		£
The sales invoice is for:	Price	100.00
	+ VAT 17.5%	17.50
	= Total price	117.50

Trader A will then pay the £17.50 she has collected to the Revenue and Customs.

Note: VAT has to be recorded and included in the VAT Return *to the penny*.

In both this example and the one shown in Exhibit 17.1, you can see that the full amount of VAT has fallen on the person who finally buys the goods. The sellers have merely acted as unpaid collectors of the tax for HM Revenue and Customs.

The value of goods sold and/or services supplied by a business is known as the **outputs**. VAT on such items is called **output tax**. The value of goods bought in and/or services supplied to a business is known as the **inputs**. The VAT on these items is, therefore, called **input tax**.

17.5 Exempted businesses

Some businesses are exempted from accounting for VAT. They do not add VAT to the amount at which they sell their products or supply their services, nor do they get a refund of the VAT they have themselves paid on goods and services bought by them.

The types of businesses exempted can be listed under two headings:

1 Nature of business. Various types of business do not have to add VAT to charges for goods or services. A bank, for instance, does not have to add VAT on to its bank charges, nor do credit card companies.
2 Small businesses. If small businesses do register for VAT then they will have to keep full VAT records in addition to charging out VAT. To save very small businesses the costs and effort of keeping such records, provided that their turnover is below a certain amount (at the time of writing, £64,000 in a 12-month period), they don't need to register unless they want to. They can also deregister if their turnover falls below a certain level (at the time of writing, £62,000).

 Activity 17.2 Apart from not having to keep VAT records, what advantages might there be for a business that does not register for VAT?

17.6 Zero-rated businesses

This special category of business

1 does not have to add VAT on to the selling price of products, and
2 can obtain a refund of all VAT paid on the purchase of goods or services.

If, therefore, £100,000 worth of goods are sold by the business, nothing has to be added for VAT but, if £8,000 VAT had been paid by it on goods or services bought, then the business would be able to claim a full refund of the £8,000 paid.

It is 2 above which distinguishes it from an exempted business. A zero-rated business is, therefore, in a better position than an exempted business. Examples of zero-rated businesses are those selling young children's clothing and shoes.

17.7 Partly exempt businesses

Some businesses sell some goods which are exempt, some that are zero-rated, and others that are standard-rated. These traders will have to apportion their turnover accordingly, and follow the rules already described for each separate part of their turnover.

17.8 Different methods of accounting for VAT

If a business is exempted from registering for VAT (an **unregistered business**), it need not keep any VAT records. The amount it enters in its accounting records relating to expenditure would be the total amount paid to suppliers including any VAT. For example, if it purchased goods for £235 that included £35 for VAT, it would enter £235 in its purchases account and make no separate entries for the £35 VAT. It would not charge VAT on its sales. As a result, VAT will not appear anywhere in its accounting records or in its financial statements.

The VAT Account

All **registered businesses** must account for VAT on all the taxable supplies they make and all the taxable goods and services they receive. This includes standard-rated, reduced rate and zero-rated supplies. They must also keep records of any exempt supplies they make. They must also keep a summary (called a 'VAT Account') of the totals of input tax and output tax for each VAT tax period. All these records must be kept up to date.

Exhibit 17.2 shows an example of a 'VAT Account'* in the format suggested by HM Revenue and Customs in Notice 700/21.

Exhibit 17.2

2003	£	2003	£
Input Tax: January	1,000.10	Output Tax: January	1,645.40
February	1,240.60	February	2,288.15
March	845.85	March	1,954.80
	3,086.55		5,888.35
VAT allowable on acquisitions	45.10	VAT due on acquisitions	45.10
Net overclaim of input tax		Net understatement of output	
from previous returns	(130.65)	tax on previous returns	423.25
Bad debt relief	245.90	Annual adjustment: Retail Scheme D	91.69
Sub-total	3,246.90	Sub-total	6,448.39
Less: VAT on credits received		Less: VAT on credits allowed	
from suppliers	(18.20)	to customers	(14.90)
Total tax deductible	3,228.70	Total tax payable	6,433.49
		Less total tax deductible	(3,228.70)
		Payable to Revenue and Customs	3,204.79

Note: Although this is described as a 'VAT Account' and it is set-out with two sides like a T-account, it is not ruled off in the way that T-accounts are ruled off. It is a memorandum item and is *not* part of the double entry system.

VAT in the ledger accounts and financial statements

How VAT appears in the ledger accounts and in the financial statements depends on which of the following categories businesses fall into:

1 **Exempted businesses**. Do not record VAT. VAT does not appear in the financial statements.
2 **Standard-rated businesses**. Need to record all output and input VAT. VAT will not appear in the profit and loss account, though it will appear in the balance sheet among either current assets or current liabilities.
3 **Partially exempt businesses**. Need to record all output and input VAT. In the case of input VAT, they must distinguish between (a) expenditure relating to taxable supplies and (b) expenditure relating to exempt supplies. Only (a) can be reclaimed; (b) is added to the net cost to arrive at the cost of each item of expenditure of type (b) to enter in the financial statements.

VAT will not appear in the profit and loss account, though it will appear in the balance sheet among either current assets or current liabilities.

4 **Zero-rated businesses**. Need to record all *input* VAT. VAT will not appear as an expense in the profit and loss account, though it will appear in the balance sheet among the current assets.

The following discussion of the accounting entries needed will, therefore, distinguish between these two types of business: those which can recover VAT paid, and those which cannot get refunds of VAT.

Note: For simplicity, most of the examples in this book use a VAT rate of 10 per cent.

17.9 Entries for businesses which can recover VAT paid

1 Standard-rated and reduced-rated businesses

Value Added Tax and sales invoices

These businesses will have to add VAT to the value of the sales invoices. It must be pointed out that this is based on the amount of the invoice *after* any trade discount has been deducted. Exhibit 17.3 is an invoice drawn up from the following details:

On 2 March 2008, W Frank & Co, Hayburn Road, Stockport, sold the following goods to R Bainbridge Ltd, 267 Star Road, Colchester. Bainbridge's Order Number was A/4/559, for the following items:

200 Rolls T56 Black Tape at £6 per 10 rolls
600 Sheets R64 Polythene at £10 per 100 sheets
7,000 Blank Perspex B49 Markers at £20 per 1,000

All of these goods are subject to VAT at the rate of 10 per cent. A trade discount of 25 per cent is given by Frank & Co. The sales invoice is numbered 8851.

Exhibit 17.3

```
                        W Frank & Co
                        Hayburn Road
                        Stockport SK2 5DB
                        VAT No: 454 367 821

To: R Bainbridge Ltd                              Date: 2 March 2008
    267 Star Road          INVOICE No: 8851
    Colchester CO1 1BT                            Your order no A/4/559
                                                                    £
    200 Rolls T56 Black Tape @ £6 per 10 rolls                    120
    600 Sheets R64 Polythene @ £10 per 100 sheets                  60
    7,000 Blank Perspex B49 Markers @ £20 per 1,000               140
                                                                  320
    Less Trade Discount 25%                                      ( 80)
                                                                  240
    Add VAT 10%                                                    24
                                                                  264
```

Note how VAT is calculated on the price *after* deducting trade discount.

The sales day book will normally have an extra column for the VAT contents of the sales invoice. This is needed to make it easier to account for VAT. Let's now look at the entry of several sales invoices in the sales day book and in the ledger accounts.

Employees' pay

Learning objectives

After you have studied this chapter, you should be able to:

● explain the basic system of PAYE income tax

● explain the difference between employee's and employer's National Insurance Contributions

● calculate the net pay of an employee given details of his or her gross pay and PAYE income tax and other deductions

● calculate the amount of the employer's National Insurance Contribution that would have to be paid on behalf of an employee given details of the employee's gross pay and PAYE income tax and other deductions

● explain how basic pensions and additional pensions are determined

Introduction

In this chapter, you'll learn about the calculation of pay and the deductions that are made from it by an employer for tax and National Insurance. You'll also learn about two forms of state pensions that an employee may be eligible for upon retirement, and about a number of items that reduce an employee's liability to income tax. You'll learn about some benefits that employees can receive as a result of their having made National Insurance Contributions. Finally, you'll learn how to calculate the net payment received by employees after adjusting their gross pay by the reliefs available and deductions, both statutory and voluntary, that have to be made.

19.1 Pay

Employees are paid either a wage or a salary. If you see an advert for a job and it mentions that the rate of pay will be £4 per hour, that is an example of a wage. If, on the other hand, an advert refers to an annual amount, that is a salary. In the UK, we normally talk about wages per hour or per week, and salaries per year.

Activity 19.1 Write down what you think would be good definitions for the term 'wage' and the term 'salary'.

In the UK, every employee is taxed under a system called **PAYE (Pay As You Earn)**. This means that for every employee, employers are required by law to make various deductions for tax and National Insurance (effectively a contribution towards some of the benefits people who have made these contributions receive from the state, such as money paid by the state to someone who is out of work or retired). As a result, a distinction is made between:

● **Gross pay**, which is the amount of wages or salary *before* deductions are made, and
● **Net pay**, which is the amount of wages or salary *after* deductions.

Many employees talk about 'take-home pay'. This is, in fact, the same as their net pay.

 Activity 19.2 What other deductions might be made from gross pay by an employer?

19.2 Methods of calculating gross pay

The methods employers use to calculate gross pay vary widely, not just between employers but also for employees in the same organisation. The main methods are:

● a fixed amount per period of time, usually a year;
● piece rate: pay based on the number of units produced by the employee;
● commission: a percentage based on the value of sales made by the employee;
● basic hourly rate: a fixed rate multiplied by number of hours worked.

Arrangements for rewarding people for working overtime (time exceeding normal hours worked) will vary widely. The rate will usually be in excess of that paid during normal working hours. Many people who are being paid salaries are not paid for working overtime.

In addition, bonuses may be paid on top of these 'normal' earnings. Bonus schemes will also vary widely, and may depend on the amount of net profit made by the company, or on the amount of work performed, or on the quality of performance by the employee, or on production levels achieved, either by the whole company or by the department in which the employee works. In some cases, these bonuses can amount to many times an employee's 'normal' salary.

Activity 19.3 Can you think of any examples where these extremely high bonuses have been paid?

19.3 Income tax deductions

In the UK, the wages and salaries of all employees are liable to have income tax deducted from them. It does not mean that everyone will pay income tax – some may not earn enough to be liable for any tax. However, if income tax is found to be payable, under the PAYE system the employer deducts the tax due from the employee's wages or salary and sends it to the Inland Revenue, the government department in charge of the collection of income tax.

Each person in the UK is allowed to subtract various amounts called 'allowances' from their earnings when calculating how much they are liable to pay in income tax. Many people pay no tax because they earn less than their total allowance. The amounts given for each person depend upon his or her personal circumstances, but everyone is entitled to a personal allowance. For the income tax year ending on 5 April 2008, that allowance was £5,225.

An extra allowance is given to blind people. Anyone aged over 65 receives an additional allowance, as do married couples born before 6 April 1935. Other allowances available may depend on the type of job. For example, some people can claim allowances for special clothing they need for their job. The totals of these allowances are known as a person's 'personal reliefs'

National Insurance Contributions are split into two parts:

(*a*) the part that employees have to suffer by it being deducted from their pay;

(*b*) the part that the employer has to suffer. This is not deductible from pay.

The rates change from time to time but, assuming a total national insurance rate of 19 per cent, of which the employee's contribution is 9 per cent and the employer's contribution 10 per cent, then £38 total contribution will have to be paid in respect of an employee who has earned £200 in the period, i.e. £200 × 19% = £38.

Of this, £18 (9%) can be deducted from the employee's pay, whilst £20 (10%) is a cost to the employer.

Pensions

Paying National Insurance Contributions results in employees receiving a state pension when they retire. Where an employee qualifies for a 'basic pension', the pension paid is based upon the number of years in which the 'minimum amount' of contributions were paid. This minimum amount is based on employees needing to have paid contributions on earnings of at least 52 times the weekly lower earnings limit during a tax year. If the weekly lower earnings limit is £100, the employee would need to have earned £5,200 in the year for that year to be included in the calculation of the basic pension. The number of years when this occurred is then multiplied by the basic pension per year to arrive at the amount of basic pension the individual will receive.

Where employees pay more than the minimum amount required for a basic pension, they will be entitled to an extra pension on top of their basic pension. This is known as 'additional pension' (AP). It is based upon earnings during the employee's working life from the year 1978–79 to that ending before the one in which the employee reaches retirement age.

Where an employee belongs to a contracted-out (superannuation or) occupational pension scheme (one operated by or on behalf of their employer) or a personal pension scheme (one run by, for example, an insurance company to which the employee makes contributions out of net pay), that scheme will provide a pension wholly or partly in place of any additional pension the individual may have otherwise been eligible to receive.

19.6 Other deductions from pay

Pensions contributions

An employee may belong to a company's occupational pension scheme. The money paid into the fund will be paid partly by the company and partly by the employee. For example, in many cases the employee's contribution will be 6 per cent, with the company paying whatever is necessary to give the employee the agreed amount of pension.

The amount of the contribution payable by the employee will, therefore, be deducted in calculating the net pay due to them.

Voluntary contributions

These include items such as charitable donations, subscriptions to the business's social club, union subscriptions and payments under a 'Save As You Earn' (SAYE) scheme.

19.7 Statutory Sick Pay and Statutory Maternity Pay

1 Statutory Sick Pay (SSP) is a payment made to employees when they are ill and absent from work. At present, it is not paid for the first three days of illness, and is limited to a total of 28 weeks' maximum.

2 Statutory Maternity Pay (SMP) is a payment made for up to 39 weeks to an employee away from work on maternity leave.

SSP and SMP are paid to employees in the same way as ordinary wages. They are both liable to have income tax and National Insurance deducted from them.

19.8 Calculation of net wages/salary payable

UK students who need to know how to use PAYE tax and National Insurance tables will need to study this further.

For general guidance for all readers, and for those who do not want to know about the use of income tax and National Insurance tables, we can look at two general examples of the calculation of net pay. The percentages used are for illustrative purposes only.

(A) G Jarvis:

	£
Gross earnings for the week ended 8 May 2008	500
Income tax: found by consulting tax tables and employee's code number	60
National Insurance: 9% of gross pay	45

G Jarvis: Payslip week ended 8 May 2008

	£	£
Gross pay for the week		500
Less Income tax	60	
National Insurance	45	
		(105)
Net pay		395

(B) H Reddish:

	£
Gross earnings for the month of May 2008	6,000
Income tax (from tax tables)	1,120
Superannuation: 6% of gross pay	360
National Insurance: 9% of gross pay	540

H Reddish: Payslip month ended 31 May 2008

	£	£
Gross pay for the month		6,000
Less Income tax	1,120	
Superannuation	360	
National Insurance	540	
		(2,020)
Net pay		3,980

The total costs to the employer in each of the above cases will be as follows, assuming the employer's part of National Insurance Contributions to be £50 for Jarvis and £600 for Reddish:

	G Jarvis	H Reddish
	£	£
Gross pay	500	6,000
Employer's share of National Insurance	50	600
Total cost to the employer	550	6,600

It will be the figures of £550 and £6,600 that will be incorporated in the trading and profit and loss account as expenses shown under wages and salaries headings.

You can find out more about income tax and National Insurance Contributions at the Revenue and Customs website: www.hmrc.gov.uk

Learning outcomes

You should now have learnt:

1 That the PAYE system ensures that employees pay tax on their earnings.

2 That the amount of tax paid varies between employees and depends on their eligibility for the various reliefs available.

3 That tax codes are used by employers to calculate tax due by employees.

4 That National Insurance Contributions are deducted from earnings at the same time as income tax.

5 That superannuation (i.e. pension) contributions are deducted from earnings to find taxable pay.

6 That the level of state pension is dependent upon the individual having paid sufficient employee's National Insurance Contributions before reaching retirement age.

7 That employees who are members of a superannuation (or occupational pension) scheme pay lower levels of National Insurance Contributions.

8 That employers pay an employer's National Insurance Contribution on behalf of each employee.

9 How to calculate net pay given the gross pay, PAYE, and NIC amounts.

Answers to activities

19.1 There is no exact definition of 'wage' or of 'salary'. In general, it is accepted that wages are earnings paid on a weekly basis, whilst salaries are paid monthly. In accounting, you will see this distinction taken a step further when you look at types of costs in Chapter 47. In effect, accounting assumes that salaries are fixed amounts paid monthly and that people who are paid a salary do not receive any extra payment should they happen to work extra hours in the month. Those who earn wages are assumed to be paid extra when they work extra hours.

19.2 Other deductions include contributions to a superannuation scheme (i.e. a pension scheme), charitable contributions (where the employee has agreed to give some of the wage or salary to a charity and has asked the employer to deduct the money from the amount earned), and subscriptions to a trade union (where the employer has asked that this be done). None of these are compulsory, but they all affect the amount the employee is left with as 'take-home pay'.

19.3 People working as traders in the financial markets can earn huge amounts in bonus payments – figures in excess of £1 million are not unusual – if they or their business have had a particularly successful year. However, very few people perform this type of work, and some of those who do receive very small bonuses if, indeed, they receive any bonus at all.

Review questions

Note: These questions are for general use only. They have been designed to be able to be done without the use of tax and National Insurance tables. The National Insurance given is the employee's part only.

19.1 H Smith is employed at a rate of £5 per hour. During the week to 18 May 2009 he worked his basic week of 40 hours. According to the requisite tables the income tax due on his wages was £27, and National Insurance £16. Calculate his net wages.

19.2 B Charles has a basic working week of 40 hours, paid at the rate of £4 per hour. For hours worked in excess of this he is paid 1½ times basic rate. In the week to 12 March 2006 he worked 45 hours. The first £80 per week is free of income tax, on the next £50 he pays at the 20% rate and above that he pays at the 25% rate. National Insurance amounted to £17. Calculate his net wages.

19.3 B Croft has a job as a car salesman. He is paid a basic salary of £200 per month, with a commission extra of 2% on the value of his car sales. During the month of April 2006 he sells £30,000 worth of cars. The first £450 per month is free of income tax, on the next £50 he pays at the 20% rate and above that he pays at the 25% rate. He also pays National Insurance for the month of £66. Calculate his net pay for the month.

19.4 T Penketh is an accountant with a salary of £2,000 per month plus bonus, which for May 2006 was £400. He pays superannuation contributions of 5% of gross pay, and these are allowed as reliefs against income tax. In addition to this he has further reliefs of £430. The taxable pay is taxed at the rate of 20% on the first £250, whilst the remainder suffers the 25% tax rate. In addition he pays National Insurance of £190. Calculate his net pay for the month.

19.5A K Blake is employed at the rate of £6 per hour. During the week to 25 May 2006 he works 35 hours. According to the tax and National Insurance tables he should pay income tax £28 and National Insurance £18. Calculate his net wages.

19.6A R Kennedy is a security van driver. He has a wage of £200 per week, plus danger money of £2 per hour extra spent in transporting gold bullion. During the week ended 15 June 2006 he spends 20 hours taking gold bullion to London Airport. The first £90 per week of his pay is free of income tax, whilst on the next £50 he pays at the 20% rate, and at the 25% rate above that figure. He pays National Insurance for the week of £19. Calculate his net pay for the week.

19.7A Mrs T Hulley is paid monthly. For part of April 2006 she earns £860 and then goes on maternity leave, her maternity pay for April being £90. She has pay free of tax £320, whilst on the next £250 she pays at the 20% tax rate, and 25% above that. She pays £79 National Insurance. Calculate her net pay for the month.

19.8A P Urmston is paid monthly. For June 2006 he earns £1,500 and also receives statutory sick pay of £150. He pays £90 superannuation which is allowed as a relief against income tax and he has further reliefs (free pay) of £350. The taxable pay is taxed at the rate of 20% on the first £250 and 25% thereafter. He pays National Insurance of £130 for the month. Calculate his net pay for the month.

You can find a range of additional self-test questions, as well as material to help you with your studies, on the website that accompanies this book at **www.pearsoned.co.uk/wood**

Computers and accounting

Learning objectives

After you have studied this chapter, you should be able to:

- explain that different computer hardware configurations are used, depending largely upon company size
- explain why financial accounting packages tend to be bought 'off-the-shelf', possibly customised to the business, or the software (particularly in larger companies) may be commissioned from computer software specialists either within the business or from external agencies
- explain why accountants use spreadsheets to write many of their own computer programs, particularly for managerial accounting purposes
- explain that an accounting information system is just one part of the management information system
- describe the structure and flexibility of spreadsheets
- explain why a database package is a useful tool
- explain the importance of backing up data in a computerised environment
- explain the importance of and benefits of the use of passwords
- describe the requirements and implications of the Data Protection Act 1998

Introduction

In this chapter, you'll learn about how computers can be used to input and process data and produce output from an accounting system for decision-making. You'll learn about how computers are linked together and of the differences between buying ready-made accounting software and writing the accounting program from scratch. You'll be introduced to spreadsheets and database packages and you will learn of the importance of backing up data and using passwords. Finally, you will learn about the regulations relating to the storage of personal data on computer.

20.1 Background

Nowadays, there are very few businesses which do not use a computer for at least some of their data processing tasks. In some cases, this may simply involve the accountant using a spreadsheet as an extended trial balance, the data being input having been obtained, in the first place, from the manually maintained ledgers. Once the final adjustments to the trial balance have been made, the spreadsheet would then be used to produce the financial statements. (You will be learning about these accounting activities in the next few chapters.)

In other cases, computers may be used for most, or even all, of the accounting tasks. Whatever the level of use of computers in accounting, accountants need to be able to understand how data is being entered and processed so that they can understand and have faith in the reliability of the figures produced. It has been suggested, for example, that over 60 per cent of spreadsheet programs have errors. This is something accountants need to guard against.

Auditors have special computer programs designed to test the reliability of computerised accounting systems but it is obviously better to ensure that the computers are being used appropriately and correctly in the first place, rather than relying on an auditor to discover that some aspect of the system is not operating correctly – you would not, for example, wish to discover that for the previous year you have been giving all your customers a 10 per cent cash discount, even when they haven't paid you the amount they owe you! Thus, when computers are used in accounting, the accountant involved needs to ensure that they are being used appropriately and that the records they are creating and the output they produce is both valid and meaningful.

20.2 Large versus small systems

The technology when computers are used in an accounting system will vary in size to meet the volume of data processing required by the business. Very large businesses may use a large and extremely powerful central computer for handling bulk data and workstations and/or stand-alone PCs for a number of purposes such as data entry, producing departmental accounts and **financial modelling** (i.e. **forecasting** and **what if** or **sensitivity analysis**). Other businesses will use PCs for all accounting purposes.

Whatever the hardware used, where more than one person is using the computerised part of the accounting system some mechanism has to be in place to enable data to be entered and accessed by everyone who is responsible for that aspect of the system. This is unlikely to be done by sharing the same PC, so some appropriate organisation of the hardware is required.

Networks

When a central computer is used, the **workstations** used to interrogate the data held on the central computer may be **dumb terminals** – i.e. they have no processing capabilities of their own – or PCs. In either case, they need to be networked (i.e. linked together through wires that run from their workstations to the central computer; or via phone lines over the Internet; or connected using a wireless network).

In some cases, these groupings of central computer with workstations will be a **local area network** (LAN) (i.e. internal to the location). In other cases, they will be part of a **wide area network** (WAN) (i.e. connected outside the location of the workstation to, for example, a computer located at the business's head office in another city). It is quite common for a workstation to be connected to both a local area network and a wide area network.

Being linked together has the advantage that data and information can be passed directly from one computer to another. Thus, although they can operate independently of any other computer, PC-based systems may also be connected together on a local area network, and have links to wide area networks.

Special forms of these networks emerged over the last few years as a result of the extension of the Internet. It is now becoming increasingly common for businesses to have an '**intranet**', a network based on Internet technologies where data and information private to the business is made available to employees of the business. Some also have **extranets**, where data and information private to the business is made available to a specific group of outsiders, for example making a company's stock records available online to major customers. Of course, most now have **websites** where they place information for the use of anyone who happens to want to look at it. In many cases, these contain copies of the latest financial statements of the business and a part of the website is devoted to promoting and selling goods and services.

Software

The software used may be developed in-house (by employees) or written under contract with an outside business or agency. Such systems are tailored to exactly what the business wants and are sometimes referred to as 'bespoke' systems. A large supermarket chain, for example, could have software developed incorporating the EPOS (electronic point of sale) system and you see this being used when barcodes on goods are scanned at supermarket checkouts. Not only do these checkout systems keep an accurate check on what is sold, in the form of an electronic cash book, but such information can be fed into the central computer to assist the process of reordering stock from warehouses, and to keep a check on cash sales. They also provide data for stock analysis and marketing purposes.

Expensive, specially designed software (often called 'customised' software) of this type will be used, generally, only by large businesses. Many medium-sized and smaller businesses will not require such special solutions, and will rely on 'off-the-shelf' software packages, most of which are flexible enough to be adapted to meet the major needs of most businesses.

Most financial accounting and bookkeeping programs are purchased off-the-shelf and then developed in-house, often by the accountants working, in the case of ledger systems, with their organisation's IT department.

Besides the main accounting system, the part used for recording transactions, adjustments and producing financial statements, accountants also use the accounting system to tackle other problems not yet discussed in this textbook. These will include matters such as forecasting the cash flows of a business (i.e. how much money will leave the organisation and how much will be received), stock ordering, deciding on capital expenditure investment, how to find the sales volume at which the business moves into profit (breakeven analysis) and costing.

For such purposes, irrespective of the size of the business, accountants can use PC-based spreadsheets (see Section 20.5), such as Excel, and databases, such as Access. Such systems will change fairly rapidly over the years as new ones are developed.

The cost of computer hardware and software has been falling in real terms for many years – it has been suggested that had the same relative cost reduction applied to a Rolls-Royce car, it would now be cheaper to throw the car away once it ran out of petrol than to fill up the petrol tank! Consequently, computerisation is now affordable for all businesses. In fact, such has been the increase in data processing and power and range of analysis available as a result of businesses seeking to maximise the use of their computing power that many businesses now process such large volumes of data, they would find it impossible to revert to a manual system.

20.3 Benefits from computers

Time-saving with respect to transaction processing, increased accuracy and the production of a whole series of reports are obvious desirable and realistic benefits when computers are used for accounting. The basic principle of any accounting system is depicted in Exhibit 20.1.

Computers can be used in all aspects of the accounting system. When computers are used for some or all of these activities they can do everything that can be done with a manual system, but computers often do them faster, more accurately, and more efficiently.

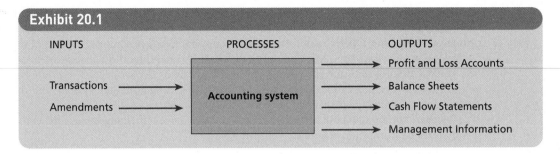

Exhibit 20.1

INPUTS	PROCESSES	OUTPUTS
		Profit and Loss Accounts
Transactions ⟶	Accounting system	Balance Sheets
Amendments ⟶		Cash Flow Statements
		Management Information

Increased job satisfaction

Increased job satisfaction and more effective use of operator time can be an added bonus of computerisation. For example, if a business computerises its stock records, an operator's job of keeping records properly maintained will be much the same as in the manual system. However, with instant reporting facilities available, such as a list of all stock items that may be in short supply, the operator can produce details almost instantly. This will allow an operator the facility of keeping a much closer check on stock levels. Also, if time can be saved in producing stock reports, the operator may have more time to 'chase up' suppliers who are not delivering on time or 'shop around' the market for better suppliers and products. Obviously, these are more interesting tasks than entering data into the accounting records and then ploughing through them in order to produce the reports.

Activity 20.1 Is it always going to be the case that employees experience greater satisfaction of working in a computerised environment?

Overall

Many more benefits of computerisation tend to become apparent as businesses develop their systems. It is worth noting that the extent of the benefits will vary from business to business, with each one deriving different benefits. It may well be the case that a business can derive no benefit at all from computerisation.

Some benefits bring problems of their own. For example, once computers are being used effectively in an accounting system, managers will often find themselves extracting reports that under a manual system could not be achieved within a timescale that would serve a useful purpose. The improved reporting and analysis that can be achieved by computerisation should improve the whole decision-making process within a business, but it can also lead to information overload as decision-makers suddenly find they have too much information for them to fully understand and apply.

20.4 Management information systems

All computer systems, whether purchased off-the-shelf or custom-made for a particular business, will need to supply information in a form that management can use to assist in its decision-making. Whether the output is on paper, via computer screens, on disk, or available online, the information system centred upon the computer is generally referred to as the 'management information system' (MIS). The MIS contains far more information than the accounting information system – production data and marketing statistics, for example, would be included in the MIS. The accounting information system is a component within the MIS, and must be capable of integration with the other functional information systems that together comprise the rest of the MIS.

Beyond standard reports, MISs are normally flexible enough to allow management to extract the kind of reports that may be unique to their business or department. These reports can be extracted in a very short time compared with that taken using a manual system, and they serve to enhance the control management have over their business.

However, two things should be emphasised, and they have not changed since the early days of computerised information systems:

1 The reports and information extracted from a computer can only be as good as the data placed into it – the well-known 'garbage in, garbage out' situation. If the full benefits of computerisation are to be enjoyed, regular checks need to be made to ensure that the data input is accurate and timely.

2 Computerisation allows infinite instant access to data. It is a straightforward way of designing and producing a new report, and it can be easier to print all possible types of reports across all functions than to limit the reports produced to those actually needed by the people they are sent to. If report generation is not controlled, information overload will occur and decision-makers may have difficulty seeing the wood because of all the trees.

20.5 Use of spreadsheets

The spreadsheet is the software tool most used by accountants. Spreadsheets first appeared in 1979 and within only a handful of years surveys were showing that of those accountants who had access to PCs, virtually 100 per cent were using them for some task or other. The name derives from the appearance of the computer *spreading* data across a *sheet*, allowing the user to directly enter numbers, formulae or text into the cells. Exhibit 20.2 shows an example of an empty spreadsheet.

As you can see, the screen is divided into vertical columns and horizontal rows to form a grid of cells. Each cell is referred to by its co-ordinate, like a map reference or point on a graph. For example, cell C12 is in column C row 12. Formulae can be entered to link cells. An example of linking cells is where a cell entry reads:

$$=B5*C12$$

(Note the use of an asterisk to represent a multiplication sign.)

This expression makes the value of the contents of the cell it is in equal to the value of cell B5 multiplied by the value of cell C12. Thus, if the formula was entered in cell D16 and B5 contained the number 6 and C12 contained the number 4, D16 would display the value 24. A spreadsheet is, effectively, a very powerful screen-based calculator and report generator whose output, both text and graphs, can be printed or electronically transmitted to another computer.

Any item in a spreadsheet can be changed at any time and the new results will instantly and automatically be shown. This makes it very easy to perform **what if** or **sensitivity analysis** (for example, what would the result be if sales were to increase by 10 per cent?) and has led to a far higher level of understanding of the effects of decisions than was ever possible when all such recalculations could involve several days work. It is this facility of being able to quickly recalculate formulae that makes the spreadsheet a powerful, useful and popular analytical tool.

Spreadsheets can be used in order to seek goals, such as specific profit figures. For example, spreadsheets can depict the sales and costs of a business and the goal seeking function can then be used to determine what selling price will be required in order to achieve a specific net profit.

Spreadsheets tend to be written by accountants for their own use, rather than by computer programmers. Some other examples of uses for spreadsheets include:

Exhibit 20.2

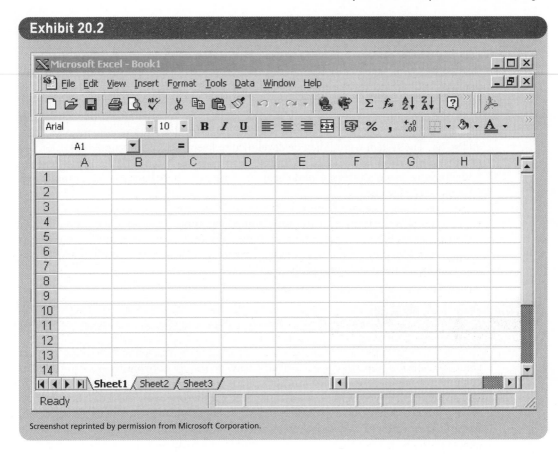

Screenshot reprinted by permission from Microsoft Corporation.

- financial plans and budgets can be represented as a table, with columns for time periods (e.g. months) and rows for different elements of the plan (e.g. costs and revenue);
- tax, investment and loan calculations can be made with ease;
- statistics using built-in functions such as averages, standard deviations, time series and regression analysis can be calculated;
- consolidation – merging branch or departmental accounts to form overall company (consolidated) financial statements;
- multi-dimensional spreadsheets can be created, enabling far deeper analysis of data – the 'sheet' tabs at the foot of the spreadsheet in Exhibit 20.2 can each be a 'dimension' that can be linked to other sheets, thus permitting views to be developed across various dimensions of a business activity. Even without this facility, the number of rows and columns available in a spreadsheet make this type of data modelling relatively simple for all but the most complex of scenarios;
- currency conversion is simple – useful for an organisation with overseas interests such as a multinational company;
- timetabling and roster planning of staff within organisations or departments can be performed.

It is hardly surprising that spreadsheets are so widely used by accountants.

Activity 20.2 Why do you think that accountants frequently write their own spreadsheet programs rather than having them written by an IT specialist?

20.6 Use of databases

Instead of being specifically designed for the types of tasks that accountants perform a lot, databases are designed for a more general purpose. A database is organised into a collection of related files into which go records. For example, a stock system could be developed where a stock file contains a record for each item of stock. The records are further broken down into fields. Hence, there could be a field for reference, one for description, a quantity, reordering level and so on. The system would then be developed to keep such records updated.

This application is favoured by many businesses as it tends to be more flexible than an accounting package and easier and cheaper to put together than a set of programs specifically written for the business.

Such database packages require a little more computing expertise and a sound knowledge of the accounting system in order to create something appropriate. In such instances, while many would be written by an accountant, it is possible that computing and accounting personnel would work together on the development, particularly where the accountant had no previous experience of using the database software.

20.7 Data back-ups

One of the most important principles in computing is the discipline of backing up data held on computer. Backing up is now performed easily by simply copying the relevant files to another computer or on to a storage medium, such as a CD or even a floppy disk.

This serves the purpose that, if anything ever goes wrong with the data, then the business can always revert to a back-up copy of the data. If, for example, a company backs up its data at mid-day and there is a loss of data later that afternoon, then the worst that could happen is that the company has to restore the data from the midday back-up and then re-enter the data since that time. Clearly, therefore, the more often a business backs up its data, the less work is needed in the event of data loss.

Many of the software packages routinely used by accountants, such as spreadsheets, can be programmed to automatically back up work every few minutes so that it is not all lost should the computer or program crash.

20.8 Passwords

When computers are being used along with an accounting package, it is normally possible for passwords to be set up to restrict which personnel have access to certain parts of the computerised elements of the accounting system. This assists management in maintaining tighter control on the system and avoids over-complicating operations for operators. It ensures that operators do not have access to parts of a wider system than they need in order to do their job adequately, and avoids the risks inherent in exposing all parts of the system to all operators. As an extra benefit, if the functions available to operators are limited, it becomes easier and quicker to train the operators.

Activity 20.3 What has happened in recent years to make the use of passwords more important than ever?

20.9 Data security and the Data Protection Act 1998

Most businesses that make extensive use of computers for accounts, payroll, and any other applications that involve personal details of individuals, need to register with the **Office of the Information Commissioner**.

The Data Protection Act defines a **data controller** as someone who determines how and for which purposes **personal data** is used. A **data subject** is anyone on whom data is held on a computer that can be identified as relating to them. Such data on a computer has to be processed by the computer's software before it can serve the purpose of information. It is this information that the **Information Commissioner** wants to know about.

Essentially, data users must declare what information they have access to on data subjects and the uses they will put that information to. The main objective of the Act is to ensure that individuals are aware of what is being held about them on business computers and allow them access to this information.

If a business is only using the sales ledger or purchases ledger for preparing and sending invoices and statements and does not use the comment details for a contact name then registration may not be necessary. Also, if customers and suppliers are companies, and individuals cannot be identified in the data, registration is not necessary. In the same way, if all a business does with payroll data is to pay wages and prepare statutory returns, registration is not necessary.

If customer and supplier lists are used for sending out sales promotions, the business must register. Likewise, registration is required if a business uses data on the payroll for management information about staff sickness or any form of staff monitoring.

Forms for registration require the business to reveal the kind of data it holds on individuals and the purpose for which it wants to use it. The business must also give details on how data subjects can find out what data is held on computer about them.

In addition to the possible need to register, businesses must comply with certain practices with regard to holding personalised data on computer. Many of these legal requirements simply define good computing practice and should be applied, where applicable, to all data used on a computer. These legal principles are contained in Schedule I of the Act:

1 Personal data shall be processed fairly and lawfully and, in particular, shall not be processed unless certain conditions contained in Schedules 2 and 3 of the Act have been met.
2 Personal data shall be obtained only for one or more specified and lawful purposes, and shall not be further processed in any manner incompatible with that purpose or those purposes.
3 Personal data shall be adequate, relevant and not excessive in relation to the purpose or purposes for which they are processed.
4 Personal data shall be accurate and, where necessary, kept up to date.
5 Personal data processed for any purpose or purposes shall not be kept for longer than is necessary for that purpose or those purposes.
6 Personal data shall be processed in accordance with the rights of data subjects under this Act.
7 Appropriate technical and organisational measures shall be taken against unauthorised or unlawful processing of personal data and against accidental loss or destruction of, or damage to, personal data.
8 Personal data shall not be transferred to a country or territory outside the European Economic Area unless that country or territory ensures an adequate level of protection for the rights and freedoms of data subjects in relation to the processing of personal data.

The website of the Information Commissioner's Office can be found at www.ico.gov.uk and the text of the Data Protection Act 1998 can be found at www.opsi.gov.uk/acts/acts1998/ 19980029.htm

Computerised accounting systems

Learning objectives

After you have studied this chapter, you should be able to:

- explain how computerised accounting systems mimic manual accounting systems and can do everything that is done by a manual accounting system
- describe how computerised accounting systems automate most of the entries required in a manual accounting system including, in some cases, the initial entry for each transaction
- describe and explain the advantages and pitfalls of using a computerised accounting system
- explain the importance of fully integrating a computerised accounting system
- explain the importance of full compatibility between the various components of a computerised accounting system
- explain the need to take great care when converting from a manual accounting system to a computerised one

Introduction

In this chapter, you'll learn about the differences between manual and computerised accounting information systems and about the benefits of using computerised accounting systems to produce output for decision-making. You will also learn of the variety of output that can be produced by a computerised information system. In addition, you will learn of the importance of integration and compatibility of all the components of a computerised accounting system and of the need to take great care when switching from a manual system to a computerised one.

21.1 Background

Most businesses, except the very smallest, now use computers to handle their accounting data. When businesses switch to computerised accounting, they soon discover that bookkeeping and accounting skills are more important than computing ones. This is because users of many computerised accounting systems have very little to learn in order to use them. In Windows-based software, as you can see from the entry screen of the *Sage Instant Accounting 2000* accounting package shown in Exhibit 21.1, the interfaces look fairly familiar – the file menu is usually in the top left, for example, and many of the icons are the same and have the same meanings across a whole range of software produced by different companies.

Exhibit 21.1

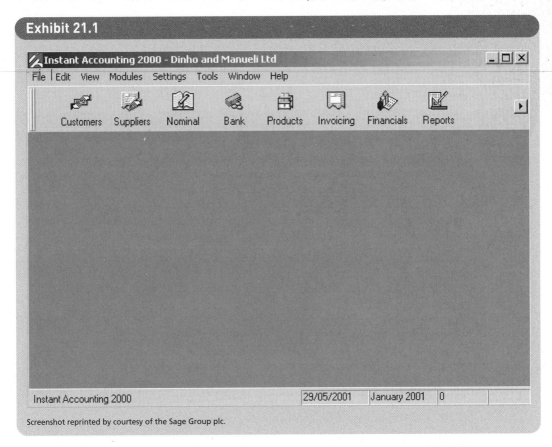

Screenshot reprinted by courtesy of the Sage Group plc.

Activity 21.1   Not very long ago, only the largest businesses used computers to handle their accounting data. Why do you think the situation is so different now?

The methods adopted in computer-based accounting adhere to the fundamental principles of accounting covered in this and other accounting textbooks. No matter how sophisticated and easy to use a computerised accounting system is, it will not overcome the need for bookkeeping and accounting knowledge by those in control. Imagine, for example, how anyone who does not know how to prepare journal entries could correct an error in an original entry correctly from an accounting point of view and, just as importantly, understand why it is important not to erase the original entry.

Apart from a need for knowledge of accounting principles in order to best convert a business from manual to computer-based accounting, some accounting knowledge is required to help understand the significance of many of the outputs from a computerised accounting system, just as it is required in respect of output from a manual accounting system.

Thus, computerised accounting systems do not remove the need for some accounting knowledge among those responsible for key accounting tasks or from those who use the output from the accounting systems. In fact, some accountants working in practice would tell you that they believe there is an even greater need for accounting knowledge among those who record the transactions in a computerised accounting system than in a manual one.

Activity 21.2

What do you think? Is there an even greater need for accounting knowledge among those that record the transactions in a computerised accounting system? Why?/Why not?

21.2 Benefits of using a computerised accounting system

As you learnt in Chapter 20, there are many benefits from using a computerised accounting system. Overall, probably the greatest benefit comes from the fact that a computerised accounting system can do the same things as a manual system, but does them better. Thus all the features in a manual system, such as the one shown in Exhibit 21.2, can be replicated in a computerised accounting system which not only does them quicker, more accurately, and 100 per cent consistently, but can also do them more frequently *and* do other things as well.

Exhibit 21.2

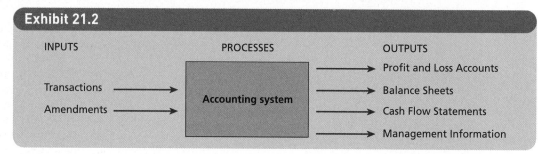

Let's look at some of these benefits in more detail.

Speed and accuracy

The main aim of computerising an accounting system is to perform the processing stage electronically, much more quickly, consistently and accurately than if it were done manually. However, transactions and amendment details have to be input into the process (1) in the correct form, (2) in the correct order, and (3) in a timely manner. Although there is scope to use electronic methods of entering some of this information (e.g. EPOS systems and document scanning), it requires a good deal of initiative and an organised way of doing things in order to do so. Nevertheless, improved accuracy is one of the more obvious benefits of any kind of computerised accounting system.

Further time-saving can be achieved by immediate output of reports, such as customer statements, purchase analysis, cash and bank statements, and details about whether the business is meeting sales targets. Such reports and statements can be produced both on request and, automatically, by the computer searching through information generated and saved within the accounting system and then producing whatever report is required.

Error detection

Effective error detection improves the decision-making process. For example, a computerised accounting system should be capable of detecting when a customer appears to be running up excessive debts with the business, so offering the chance for the credit controller to take remedial action.

Another area is the need to remain within budgets. Many business expenses can get out of hand if they are not checked at regular intervals. A computerised accounting system should be capable of an activity called **exception reporting**, a process of issuing a warning message to decision-makers when something unexpected is happening: for example, when expenditure against a budget is higher than it should be. In a manual accounting system, the situation can occur that errors or unwanted transactions go unnoticed until it is too late, resulting in unnecessary costs being incurred by the business.

Enhanced reporting

For many businesses, the task of producing reports on a regular basis, such as VAT Returns, payroll processing, cash flow analysis, and financial statements, can be time-consuming, tedious and unrewarding. The use of a computerised accounting system speeds up the process to the point, in some cases, where it is done automatically thus reducing the monotony of producing lengthy reports requiring extensive preparatory analysis of data. In many cases, such as VAT Returns and payslips, businesses find that they can use computer printouts or electronic output, e.g. on computer disks, instead of having to manually complete official or standard forms.

21.3 Computerised accounting records

Many businesses now make good use of accounting packages which are readily available and have been well tested. Such packages are commonly modularised with, typically, the sales ledger, purchase ledger, general ledger, stock control, sales invoicing, sales order processing, purchases order processing, fixed assets, payroll, bill of materials, and job costing all being offered as separate modules in their own right. When a business decides to computerise its accounting system, it acquires only the modules it needs. For example, a sole trader would have no use for a payroll module.

The various ledgers and accounts maintained in a computerised accounting system mimic those kept in a manual system. The general ledger, for example, will adhere to the basic rules of double entry bookkeeping in that each debit entry has a corresponding credit entry – if a customer is issued with an invoice, the transaction giving precise details of the invoice will be stored in the credit sales records to form part of the customer history and then the double entry is made by crediting sales accounts and debiting a debtor's account.

The difference lies in the method of entry – each transaction is entered only once (accountants refer to this as a 'single entry' system) and the software automatically completes the double entry. This has a down-side, however: some computerised accounting packages will post various amounts into suspense accounts when it is unclear where postings are to be made. These require manual intervention and journal entries to remove each item from the suspense account and complete the original double entry.

(Suspense accounts are the topic of Chapter 31.)

Flexibility

The information stored in a computerised accounting system is available instantly and can be used to produce statements, ledger account details, analysis of how long debts have been outstanding, etc. immediately it is requested. For example, the computerised sales ledger will hold all details about customers. The starting point would be to enter the details concerning the customer (name, address, etc.) along with the balance brought forward from the manual system (if such a transfer is occurring; otherwise, if it is a new customer, an opening zero balance will be created automatically by the software).

All transactions relating to a customer, such as the issue of an invoice or receipt of payment, are entered into the system and automatically posted to the customer's account. Customers can, at any time, be issued with a statement of their account, and the business can always obtain an up-to-date and complete history of trading with any particular customer. The purchase ledger will operate in exactly the same way in that supplier details are held and, once entered through the purchases module, all transactions relating to individual purchasers will automatically be posted to the appropriate creditor account.

Bank payments and receipts are a central feature of computerised accounting systems. The modules can be operated by someone with virtually no bookkeeping knowledge. For example, if an electricity bill is paid, the system will prompt for the details of the transaction that are required to process and record the double entry. The system will not assume any knowledge of double entry on the part of the individual making the entries.

Account codes

In order to use a computerised accounting system efficiently and effectively, someone with both accounting skills and a good knowledge of the business will be required to organise the accounts and ledgers in the first instance. Some of these packages are not written for specific businesses and need to be 'tailored' to the one that is going to use it. Most require businesses to define what accounts they are to have in their general ledger and how such accounts are to be grouped.

For example, fixed asset accounts may have account references commencing with 'F', while expense accounts commence with 'E'. The package will probably have its own default set of **account codes** (the computerised equivalent of the folio references in a manual system), and it may be necessary to override the defaults in the accounting package in order to use the business's own account code list (also known as the '**chart of accounts**'). In addition, part of the setting up of a computer system will require the tailoring of the package for certain reports such as the profit and loss account and balance sheet.

Knowledge of double entry

Most packages are capable of allowing businesses to set up their preferred methods for dealing with depreciation of fixed assets and regular payments of, for example, rent and rates. However, as you saw with the need to correct entries in a suspense account arising from the computer not knowing how to complete a double entry, such packages do require a good 'knowledge' of double entry so that adjustments can be made through their journal entries. For example, the computer will not overcome some errors and omissions, such as the operator misreading an amount on an invoice or crediting a payment to the wrong customer account. Anyone correcting these errors will require a full knowledge of the relevant part of the accounting system as well as bookkeeping and accounting principles.

21.4 Computerised stock control and modular integration

Automation of much of the data processing can be taken further when integrating other modules. Stock control offers the benefit of keeping very close tabs on stock levels. If an invoicing package is also in use, then an invoice can be generated in such a way that an operator can collect the details of the business or person to invoice from the sales ledger and details of all stock to be invoiced from the stock files. Once the invoice has been raised, the recorded stock levels fall accordingly, the sales ledger is updated and the nominal entries are made by crediting sales and debiting debtors' control (a topic which will be covered in Chapter 29).

Sales order processing

Sales order processing allows an order to be placed into the system which can then be used at a later stage to generate an invoice. Sales order processing is important to many businesses as it gives them an indication about what stock levels are required. Having sales orders on computer also offers the advantage of being able to monitor sales orders outstanding and so ensure they are supplied on time to the customers. Computers can produce outstanding order reports and such things as 'picking lists' (a list of items to be taken out of storage and given or shipped to customers) very quickly.

Purchase order processing

Purchase order processing allows an operator to print an order to send off to a supplier or, in some more advanced systems, it may be transmitted over a direct link into the supplier's accounting system where it will be recorded and converted into an issue from stock. The computerised purchase order system also serves the useful purpose of allowing instant access to information about what is on order. This prevents duplicates of the same order being processed by mistake.

Modular integration

The full use of all modules in this integrated manner allows a business to access stock details and get a complete profile on its status in terms of what is left in stock, what is on order, what has been ordered by customers. Furthermore, most packages keep a history of stock movements so helping the business to analyse specific stock turnovers. When integrated in this fashion, the processing structure may be as depicted in Exhibit 21.3.

Exhibit 21.3 An integrated computerised accounting system

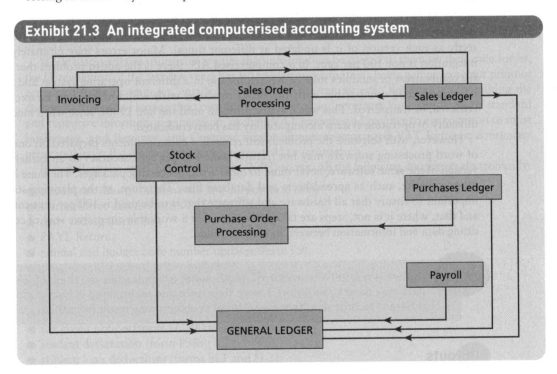

Exhibit 21.3 includes a payroll module. Businesses with a large number of employees would find this particularly useful as payroll systems require a good deal of regular processing. Again, a reasonable knowledge of payroll is required in order to set up the system in the first place.

21.5 Accounting information systems

An **accounting information system (AIS)** is the total suite of components that, together, comprise all the inputs, storage, transaction processing, collating, and reporting of financial

- lower administration costs;
- greater security;
- less use of paper;
- immediate acknowledgement of receipt.

Benefits of electronic transmission of funds

Of course, if electronic submission of documents is a recent phenomenon, electronic transmission of funds has been around a good deal longer. Among the benefits attributed to it and again, potentially, to a computerised AIS are:

- certainty of payment on a specific date;
- certainty that exactly the amount due to be paid is paid;
- immediate acknowledgement of receipt;
- lower administration costs;
- lower bank charges;
- greater security.

Benefits of linking AISs

Another significant recent change brought about by computerisation of AISs is the growth in electronic data exchange between supplier and customer. Some very large companies now insist that their suppliers link their stock systems to the customer's AIS. The customer can then interrogate the stock records of the supplier to see if items are available and place orders directly into the supplier's AIS without any need for physical transmission of an order document. This has helped the growth of just-in-time stock keeping by customers who, rather than holding their own stock, simply order it from their suppliers when required.

Among the benefits attributed to linking AISs and again, potentially, to a computerised AIS are:

- speed;
- lower administration costs;
- greater awareness of the current position;
- improved control of related risks;
- greater security of a continuing relationship between the parties.

21.6 Issues to consider when introducing a fully computerised AIS

When you computerise an accounting system, you have some decisions to make. These include:

1 Deciding whether to mimic what you have been doing manually or start from scratch and redesign everything. For example, you may only have been using one ledger in the manual system, but may choose to use three or four in the computerised system. You may have had a two-column cash book in the manual system but decide to have a columnar cash book in the computerised system.

2 Deciding whether to buy a general accounting package 'off-the-shelf' or create one from scratch. Depending on the size of the business, creating one from scratch may be done using a spreadsheet and a database package or it may involve having computer programmers writing the entire system.

3 If you decide to buy one off-the-shelf, you need to decide how much to customise it, if at all.

4 If you decide not to customise it, or aren't able to customise parts of it, you may need to change the terminology you use when referring to parts of the accounting system. For example, you may need to refer to the nominal ledger rather than the general ledger and to the purchases journal rather than the purchases day book. For example, *Sage* uses the term 'Customers Module' rather than sales ledger and 'Suppliers Module' instead of a purchases ledger.

5 You need to decide who is going to be responsible for overseeing the project.
6 You need to decide how long you are going to allow for the new system to be developed and make plans to introduce it accordingly.
7 You need to decide who is to be trained in using it and when.
8 You need to decide how long you will run the new system in parallel with the existing manual system before you stop using the manual system.
9 You need to identify the hardware you will need and ensure that it is in place at the appropriate time.
10 You need to identify who is going to test the new system and what data is to be used to do so.
11 You need to weigh up the costs and benefits of computerising the accounting system and decide whether it is actually worth doing it.

These are just some of the issues you need to deal with. Many more will appear as each of these questions is answered and many more will materialise as the project proceeds.

The most popular software used by small and medium-sized businesses in the UK is *Sage*. However, you should look at a range of available alternatives, such as *Pegasus*, *Quickbooks*, and *Microsoft Dynamics GP*, before proceeding to purchase the package you intend using. Factors to consider obviously include price, but they also include capacity, hardware requirements, ease of use, reliability, appropriateness of the way data is entered, stored and secured, and the range and style of reports that can be produced. You also need to consider compatibility of the package with any other systems or packages you might wish to link it to if that is, in fact, a possibility in the first place. Accountants are not normally the most knowledgeable people to answer these technical questions and guidance from an IT specialist is often advisable.

Once the package is installed and fully operational, you need to monitor its effectiveness and reliability and need to have contingency plans in place should it ultimately prove to have been a mistake. (In other words, you need to ensure you can revert to the previous system if necessary.)

When you come to review your hardware or operating system with a view to upgrading it, you need to ensure the package will continue to run without any problems when you upgrade. You also need to consider carefully before committing to an upgrade of the accounting package, in case things that used to work no longer function or need to be done in very different ways.

You also need to ensure that the data stored in the system is backed up regularly and that password or other security devices are in place in order to prevent unauthorised access to it.

Overall, you need to think the whole thing through very carefully before committing to the switch and you need to ensure you have all the controls over the system in place before it starts to be used.

Nevertheless, although great care and a lot of effort must be expended when converting to a computerised accounting system, there is no doubt that the benefits of having an appropriate one will vastly improve the quality and reliability of the accounting data and information produced.

Learning outcomes

You should now have learnt that:

1 Bookkeeping and accounting skills and knowledge are more important than computing skills and knowledge when a switch is made from a manual accounting system to a computerised accounting system.

2 The user interface of an accounting package often looks similar to those of other frequently used Windows-based software packages.

→

3 Computerised accounting systems can do everything a manual accounting system can do, but does them quicker, more accurately, more consistently, and with greater flexibility.

4 A considerably enhanced ability to obtain reports is available from a computerised accounting system compared to a manual accounting system.

5 The various records maintained in a computerised accounting system mimic those in a manual accounting system, though the names of some of the records may be different.

6 Acccount codes are used in computerised accounting systems instead of folio numbers.

7 Maximised integration of the various components in a computerised accounting system generates the maximum benefits.

8 Compatibility between the various components in a computerised accounting system is essential if it is to operate effectively.

9 One of the major benefits of computerised accounting systems is the ability to generate electronic output.

10 Implementing a switch to a computerised accounting system is a non-trivial task that should never be done lightly and needs to be done with the greatest of care.

Answers to activities

21.1 This question can be answered from many perspectives including:

- vastly lower relative cost of computer technology and IT in general
- greater ease of use thanks to a graphical rather than a text-based visual interface (this only really became the norm in the mid 1990s)
- wide range of available software to choose from
- the current high flexibility in (even off-the-shelf) software enabling customisation to suit the needs of the business
- a vastly greater level of IT literacy
- pressure from accountants to modernise methods and so increase control over the accounting records
- greater financial awareness among business people generally (e.g. the enormous growth in MBA holders over the last twenty years)
- pressures from the authorities to maintain up-to-date accounting records (e.g. VAT)
- pressure from competitors (i.e. the need to keep up)
- deeper insight that can be gained by using computers and information technology (C&IT) to present views of the business and business opportunities virtually instantly when they could only be produced manually after weeks of effort
- a desire to appear 'modern and up-to-date'.

21.2 Most accountants would disagree with the comment in a general sense but agree with it in the context of (a) knowing the accounts to use (b) knowing whether an entry looks correct and, most importantly, (c) knowing how to make appropriate entries when an error has occurred.

21.3 One example would be where the stock control system is not integrated with the sales ledger. A customer could return goods that were recorded in the stock control system immediately. However, it might take a few hours, even days for the credit entry to be made in the customer's account in the sales ledger. During the delay period, the customer might be refused credit because the account showed that the customer's credit limit had been reached when, in fact, the customer had no outstanding debt to the business as a result of having returned the items purchased. The customer might also be sent a statement of the account that did not show the credit entry but was accompanied by a letter demanding immediate payment as the account was now overdue. If the reverse happened and the first entry was made in the sales ledger, orders from other customers for the same items might be rejected because the stock records showed a zero amount of those items in stock when, in fact, the ones returned by the customer were in the warehouse.

Another problem of non-integration relates to customer details. If they are changed, for example by a change of address, and only entered in the sales ledger and not in the records maintained by the delivery department, goods ordered by the customer could be sent to the wrong address.

If the cash book is not fully integrated with the sales ledger, customers may pay their accounts but still be shown as debtors when the system is asked to print an aged list of debtors in the middle of a month. Time and effort might then be expended chasing a debt that didn't exist and, of course, the customer would not be exactly pleased either.

21.4 There were a number of issues at that time:

● The output was sometimes inaccurate, mainly due to the inexperience of the people who were keying data into the AIS, but also due to errors in programming. Also, until the late 1970s, much of the input was by punched card and cards in a batch had to be entered into the computer in the same order as they were produced. If a batch of cards was dropped before being put into the card reader that then transferred the data into the computer, all sorts of nonsense could result. This type of situation gave rise to the phrase 'garbage in, garbage out' which was often used by those who favoured traditional manual systems when explaining why computers were 'useless'. It still applies today, but for different reasons, such as the original data being incorrect or out-of-date.

● Many early AISs were developed by computer specialists, not accountants. They often produced reports that were less meaningful than they might have been, frequently omitting key information. The decision-makers did not know what rules had been followed in generating numbers in the reports and so would sometimes reach a decision assuming the data meant one thing when, in fact, it meant something else. (For example, the scrap value of a fixed asset may have been ignored when calculating whether it should be used for one more year or replaced.) They also often gave everything possible to the decision-makers, resulting in huge piles of reports being received of which only a few pages were actually of any interest.

In other words, the output from early computerised AISs was often less than useful and often could not be relied upon.

Review questions

21.1 What benefits for the whole accounting system can follow from using a computer for accounting work?

21.2 Why is the need for accounting skills and knowledge important when the accounting system is computerised?

21.3 Why is the need to fully integrate a computerised accounting system so important?

21.4 What issues need to be considered when making the switch from a manual accounting system to a computerised accounting system?

You can find a range of additional self-test questions, as well as material to help you with your studies, on the website that accompanies this book at **www.pearsoned.co.uk/wood**

ADJUSTMENTS FOR FINANCIAL STATEMENTS

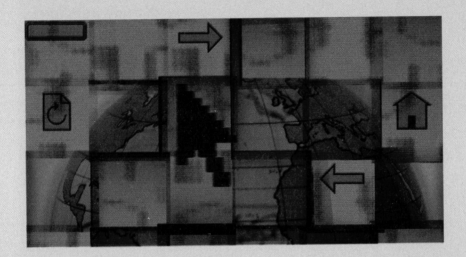

Introduction

This part is concerned with all the adjustments that have to be made before financial statements can be prepared.

The Scenario questions take the knowledge you have acquired in Parts 1 to 3 and apply it to what you have learnt in Part 4.

15 was issued in 1999, that is. FRS 15 allows interest directly attributable to the construction of a tangible fixed asset to be capitalised as part of the cost of that asset. Note that FRS 15 *does not* permit capitalisation of interest incurred on the funds used to purchase a fixed asset, only interest incurred *on the construction* of one.

Review questions

22.1

(a) What is meant by 'capital expenditure', and 'revenue expenditure'?

(b) Some of the following items should be treated as capital and some as revenue. For each of them state which classification applies:

  (i)   The purchase of machinery for use in the business.
  (ii) Carriage paid to bring the machinery in (i) above to the works.
  (iii) Complete redecoration of the premises at a cost of £1,500.
  (iv) A quarterly account for heating.
  (v)   The purchase of a soft drinks vending machine for the canteen with a stock of soft drinks.
  (vi) Wages paid by a building contractor to his own workmen for the erection of an office in the builder's stockyard.

22.2A   Indicate which of the following would be revenue items and which would be capital items in a wholesale bakery:

(a) Purchase of a new van.
(b) Purchase of replacement engine for existing van.
(c) Cost of altering interior of new van to increase carrying capacity.
(d) Cost of motor tax for new van.
(e) Cost of motor tax for existing van.
(f) Cost of painting business's name on new van.
(g) Repair and maintenance of existing van.

22.3   State the type of expenditure, capital or revenue, incurred in the following transactions

(a) Break-down van purchased by a garage.
(b) Repairs to a fruiterer's van.
(c) The cost of installing a new machine.
(d) Cost of hiring refrigeration plant in a butcher's shop.
(e) Twelve dozen sets of cutlery, purchased by a catering firm for a new dining-room.
(f) A motor vehicle bought for re-sale by a motor dealer.
(g) The cost of acquiring patent rights.

22.4A   On what principles would you distinguish between capital and revenue expenditure? Illustrate your answer by reference to the following:

(a) The cost of repairs and an extension to the premises.
(b) Installation of a gas central heating boiler in place of an oil-fired central heating boiler.
(c) Small but expensive alterations to a cigarette manufacturing machine which increased the machine's output by 20%.

22.5   Explain clearly the difference between capital expenditure and revenue expenditure. State which of the following you would classify as capital expenditure, giving your reasons:

(a) Cost of building extension to factory.
(b) Purchase of extra filing cabinets for sales office.
(c) Cost of repairs to accounting machine.
(d) Cost of installing reconditioned engine in delivery van.
(e) Legal fees paid in connection with factory extension.

22.6A The data which follows was extracted from the books of account of H Kirk, an engineer, on 31 March 2006, his financial year end.

	£
(a) Purchase of extra milling machine (includes £300 for repair of an old machine)	2,900
(b) Rent	750
(c) Electrical expenses (includes new wiring £600, part of premises improvement)	3,280
(d) Carriage inwards (includes £150 carriage on new cement mixer)	1,260
(e) Purchase of extra drilling machine	4,100

You are required to allocate each or part of the items above to either 'capital' or 'revenue' expenditure.

22.7 For the business of J Charles, wholesale chemist, classify the following between 'capital' and 'revenue' expenditure:

(a) Purchase of an extra van.
(b) Cost of rebuilding warehouse wall which had fallen down.
(c) Building extension to the warehouse.
(d) Painting extension to warehouse when it is first built.
(e) Repainting extension to warehouse three years later than that done in (d).
(f) Carriage costs on bricks for new warehouse extension.
(g) Carriage costs on purchases.
(h) Carriage costs on sales.
(i) Legal costs of collecting debts.
(j) Legal charges on acquiring new premises for office.
(k) Fire insurance premium.
(l) Costs of erecting new machine.

22.8A For the business of H Ward, a food merchant, classify the following between 'capital' and 'revenue' expenditure:

(a) Repairs to meat slicer.
(b) New tyre for van.
(c) Additional shop counter.
(d) Renewing signwriting on shop.
(e) Fitting partitions in shop.
(f) Roof repairs.
(g) Installing thief detection equipment.
(h) Wages of shop assistant.
(i) Carriage on returns outwards.
(j) New cash register.
(k) Repairs to office safe.
(l) Installing extra toilet.

22.9

(a) Distinguish between capital and revenue expenditure.
(b) Napa Ltd took delivery of a PC and printer on 1 July 2006, the beginning of its financial year. The list price of the equipment was £4,999 but Napa Ltd was able to negotiate a price of £4,000 with the supplier. However, the supplier charged an additional £340 to install and test the equipment. The supplier offered a 5% discount if Napa Ltd paid for the equipment and the additional installation costs within seven days. Napa Ltd was able to take advantage of this additional discount. The installation of special electrical wiring for the computer cost £110. After initial testing certain modifications costing £199 proved necessary. Staff were sent on special training courses to operate the PC and this cost £990. Napa Ltd insured the machine against fire and theft at a cost of £49 per annum. A maintenance agreement was entered into

→

→ with Sonoma plc. Under this agreement Sonoma plc promised to provide 24 hour breakdown cover for one year. The cost of the maintenance agreement was £350.

Required:
Calculate the acquisition cost of the PC to Napa Ltd.

(c) The following costs were also incurred by Napa Ltd during the financial year ended 30 June 2007:

(1) Interest on loan to purchase PC.
(2) Cost of software for use with the PC.
(3) Cost of customising the software for use in Napa Ltd's business.
(4) Cost of paper used by the computer printer.
(5) Wages of computer operators.
(6) Cost of ribbons used by the computer printer.
(7) Cost of adding extra memory to the PC.
(8) Cost of floppy disks used during the year.
(9) Costs of adding a manufacturer's upgrade to the PC equipment.
(10) Cost of adding air conditioning to the computer room.

Required:
Classify each of the above as capital expenditure or revenue expenditure.

(*Association of Accounting Technicians*)

22.10A Classify the following items as either revenue or capital expenditure:

(a) An extension to an office building costing £24,000.
(b) The cost of replacement valves on all the labelling machines in a canning factory.
(c) Repairs to the warehouse roof.
(d) Annual service costs for a courier firm's fleet of vans.
(e) Replacement of rubber tread on a printing press with a plastic one that has resulted in the useful economic life of the printing press being extended by three years.
(f) A new bicycle purchased by a newsagent for use by the newspaper delivery boy.
(g) Repairs to a refrigeration system of a meat wholesaler.
(h) Repainting of the interior of a bar/restaurant which has greatly improved the potential for finding a buyer for the bar/restaurant as a going concern.
(i) Wages paid to employees who worked on the construction of their company's new office building.

22.11 A Bloggs, a building contractor, had a wooden store shed and a brick-built office which have balances b/d in the books of £850 and £179,500 respectively. During the year, the wooden shed was pulled down at a cost of £265, and replaced by a brick building. Some of the timber from the old store shed was sold for £180 and the remainder, valued at £100, was used in making door frames, etc., for the new store. The new brick-built store was constructed by the builder's own employees, the expenditure thereon being materials (excluding timber from the old store shed) £4,750; wages £3,510; and direct expenses of £85.

At about the same time, certain repairs and alterations were carried out to the office, again using the builder's own materials, the cost of which was: wages £290 and materials £460. It was estimated that £218 of this expenditure, being mainly that incurred on providing additional windows, represented improvements, 50% of this was wages, 50% materials.

Required:
Prepare the following four ledger accounts as they would appear after giving effect to all the above matters:
(a) Wooden store shed account
(b) Office buildings account
(c) New store account
(d) Office buildings repairs account

22.12 At the beginning of the financial year on 1 April 2005, a company had a balance on plant account of £372,000 and on provision for depreciation of plant account of £205,400.

The company's policy is to provide depreciation using the reducing balance method applied to the fixed assets held at the end of the financial year at the rate of 20% per annum.

On 1 September 2005 the company sold for £13,700 some plant which it had acquired on 31 October 2001 at a cost of £36,000. Additionally, installation costs totalled £4,000. During 2003 major repairs costing £6,300 had been carried out on this plant and, in order to increase the capacity of the plant, a new motor had been fitted in December 2003 at a cost of £4,400. A further overhaul costing £2,700 had been carried out during 2004.

The company acquired new replacement plant on 30 November 2005 at a cost of £96,000, inclusive of installation charges of £7,000.

Required:
Calculate:
(a) the balance of plant at cost at 31 March 2006
(b) the provision for depreciation of plant at 31 March 2006
(c) the profit or loss on disposal of the plant.

(*Association of Chartered Certified Accountants*)

22.13A Sema plc, a company in the heavy engineering industry, carried out an expansion programme in the 2006 financial year, in order to meet a permanent increase in contracts.

The company selected a suitable site and commissioned a survey and valuation report, for which the fee was £1,500. On the basis of the report the site was acquired for £90,000.

Solicitor's fees for drawing up the contract and conveyancing were £3,000.

Fees of £8,700 were paid to the architects for preparing the building plans and overseeing the building work. This was carried out partly by the company's own workforce (at a wages cost of £11,600), using company building materials (cost £76,800), and partly by subcontractors who charged £69,400, of which £4,700 related to the demolition of an existing building on the same site.

The completed building housed two hydraulic presses.

The cost of press A was £97,000 (*ex-works*), payable in a single lump sum two months after installation. Sema was given a trade discount of 10% and a cash discount for prompt payment of 2%. Hire of a transporter to collect the press and to convey it to the new building was £2,900. Installation costs were £2,310, including hire of lifting gear, £1,400.

Press B would have cost £105,800 (delivered) if it had been paid in one lump sum. However, Sema opted to pay three equal annual instalments of £40,000, starting on the date of acquisition. Installation costs were £2,550, including hire of lifting gear, £1,750.

The whole of the above expenditure was financed by the issue of £500,000 7% Debentures (on which the annual interest payable was £35,000).

Before the above acquisitions were taken into account, the balances (at cost) on the fixed asset accounts for premises and plant were £521,100 and £407,500 respectively.

Required:
(a) Using such of the above information as is relevant, post and balance the premises and plant accounts for the 2006 financial year.
(b) State, with reasons, which of the given information you have not used in your answer to (a) above.

(*Association of Chartered Certified Accountants*)

22.14 Why is the difference between classifying something as capital expenditure rather than revenue expenditure, and vice versa, so important to the users of financial statements?

22.15A John Boggis saw a computer for sale in a local store for £1,499. This was much cheaper than he'd seen it for sale elsewhere. He needed five of these PCs and also needed the cabling to

→

→ network them. Following negotiations with the retailer, he obtained the machines for a total of £7,000. However, the cost of the cabling was £300 and the supplier was going to charge £500 to install the network. If John paid the total amount due before installation, he would receive a discount of 2½ per cent. He liked this idea and paid immediately.

Subsequently, he purchased three printers costing £125 each and software costing £350, together with CDs and other consumables costing a total of £250. The supplier gave a discount of £50 on the consumables due to the size of the order.

All of John's staff were sent on a customised training course organised by the retailer at a total cost of £500.

Required:
(a) Calculate the amount capitalised in the balance sheet and also the amount to be charged to revenue accounts.
(b) 'Materiality' is a concept which sometimes has an effect on the capitalisation of amounts within a balance sheet. Give examples of how this may be done.

You can find a range of additional self-test questions, as well as material to help you with your studies, on the website that accompanies this book at **www.pearsoned.co.uk/wood**

Bad debts, provisions for doubtful debts, and provisions for discounts on debtors

Learning objectives

After you have studied this chapter, you should be able to:

- explain and show how bad debts are written-off
- explain why provisions for doubtful debts are made
- make the necessary entries to record a provision for doubtful debts in the books
- calculate and make provisions for discounts on debtors
- make all the entries in the profit and loss account and balance sheet for bad debts, provisions for doubtful debts, and provisions for cash discount

Introduction

In this chapter, you'll learn how businesses deal with bad debts and how they provide for the possibility that other debts will not be paid. You'll learn how to record increases and decreases in the provision for doubtful debts. Finally, you'll learn how to make and adjust provisions for cash discounts.

23.1 Bad debts

With many businesses a large proportion, if not all, of the sales are on credit. The business is therefore taking the risk that some of the customers may never pay for the goods sold to them on credit. This is a normal business risk and such **bad debts** are a normal business expense. They must be charged to profit and loss as an expense when calculating the profit or loss for the period. The other thing that needs to be done is to remove the bad debt from the asset account. Usually, this will mean closing the debtor's account.

When a debt is found to be 'bad', the asset as shown by the debt in the debtor's account is worthless. It must be eliminated from the account. If doing so reduces the balance to zero, the debtor's account is closed.

To record a bad debt, you credit the debtor's account to cancel the asset and increase the expense account by debiting it to the bad debts account.

 Activity 23.1 What circumstances might lead you to write off a debt as bad and *not* close the debtor's account?

23.5 The reason for reinstating the debt in the ledger account of the debtor is to have a detailed history of the debtor's account as a guide for granting credit in future. When a debt is written off as bad, it is recorded in the debtor's ledger account. Therefore, when a bad debt is recovered, it should also be shown in the debtor's ledger account, so as to provide the full picture.

23.6 (c) an increase in net profit.

Review questions

23.1 In a new business during the year ended 31 December 2006 the following debts are found to be bad, and are written off on the dates shown:

31 March	G Frank	£180
30 June	B Will	£219
31 October	R Stot	£42

On 31 December 2006 the schedule of remaining debtors totalling £17,162 is examined and it is decided to make a provision for doubtful debts of £343.

You are required to show:
(a) The bad debts account, and the provision for doubtful debts account.
(b) The charge to the profit and loss account.
(c) The relevant extracts from the balance sheet as at 31 December 2006.

23.2 A business had always made a provision for doubtful debts at the rate of 4% of debtors. On 1 January 2008 the amount, brought forward from the previous year was £320.
   During the year to 31 December 2008 the bad debts written off amounted to £680.
   On 31 December 2008 the remaining debtors totalled £16,800 and the usual provision for doubtful debts is to be made.

You are to show:
(a) The bad debts account for the year ended 31 December 2008.
(b) The provision for doubtful debts account for the year.
(c) Extract from the profit and loss account for the year.
(d) The relevant extract from the balance sheet as at 31 December 2008.

23.3 A business started trading on 1 January 2007. During the two years ended 31 December 2007 and 2008 the following debts were written off to the bad debts account on the dates stated:

31 May 2007	F Lamb	£175
31 October 2007	A Clover	£230
31 January 2008	D Ray	£190
30 June 2008	P Clark	£75
31 October 2008	J Will	£339

On 31 December 2007 there had been a total of debtors remaining of £52,400. It was decided to make a provision for doubtful debts of £640.
   On 31 December 2008 there had been a total of debtors remaining of £58,600. It was decided to make a provision for doubtful debts of £710.

You are required to show:
(i) The bad debts account and the provision for doubtful debts account for each of the two years.
(ii) The relevant extracts from the balance sheets as at 31 December 2007 and 2008.

23.4A A business, which started trading on 1 January 2007, adjusted its doubtful debt provision at the end of each year on a percentage basis, but each year the percentage rate is adjusted in accordance with the current 'economic climate'. The following details are available for the three years ended 31 December 2007, 2008 and 2009.

	Bad debts written off year to 31 December	Debtors at 31 December after bad debts written-off	Percentage provision for doubtful debts
	£	£	
2007	1,240	41,000	4
2008	2,608	76,000	6
2009	5,424	88,000	5

You are required to show:
(a) Bad debts accounts for each of the three years.
(b) Provision for doubtful debts accounts for each of the three years.
(c) Balance sheet extracts as at 31 December 2007, 2008 and 2009.

23.5 A business which prepares its financial statements annually to 31 December suffered bad debts which were written off:

   2007 £530
   2008 £490
   2009 £320

The business had a balance of £300 on the provision for doubtful debts account on 1 January 2007.
   At the end of each year, the business considered which of its debtors appeared doubtful and carried forward a provision:

   2007 £600
   2008 £800
   2009 £700

Show the entries in the profit and loss account and prepare the provision for doubtful debts account for each of the three years.

23.6A

(a) Businesses often create a provision for doubtful debts.

   (i)   Of which concept (or convention) is this an example? Explain your answer.
   (ii) What is the purpose of creating a provision for doubtful debts?
   (iii) How might the amount of a provision for doubtful debts be calculated?

(b) On 1 January 2008 there was a balance of £500 in the provision for doubtful debts account, and it was decided to maintain the provision at 5% of the debtors at each year end.
   The debtors on 31 December each year were:

	£
2008	12,000
2009	8,000
2000	8,000

Show the necessary entries for the **three** years ended 31 December 2008 to 31 December 2010 inclusive in the following:

   (i)   the provision for doubtful debts account;
   (ii) the profit and loss accounts.

(c) What is the difference between bad debts and provision for doubtful debts?
(d) On 1 January 2010 Warren Mair owed Jason Dalgleish £130. On 25 August 2010 Mair was declared bankrupt. A payment of 30p in the £ was received in full settlement. The remaining balance was written off as a bad debt. Write up the account of Warren Mair in Jason Dalgleish's ledger.

(*Northern Examinations and Assessment Board: GCSE*)

→

23.7 The balance sheet as at 31 May 2007 of Forest Traders Limited included a provision for doubtful debts of £2,300. The company's accounts for the year ended 31 May 2008 are now being prepared. The company's policy now is to relate the provision for doubtful debts to the age of debts outstanding. The debts outstanding at 31 May 2008 and the required provisions for doubtful debts are as follows:

Debts outstanding	Amount	Provision for doubtful debts
	£	%
Up to 1 month	24,000	1
More than 1 month and up to 2 months	10,000	2
More than 2 months and up to 3 months	8,000	4
More than 3 months	3,000	5

Customers are allowed a cash discount of $2^{1}/_{2}$% for settlement of debts within one month. It is now proposed to make a provision for discounts to be allowed in the company's accounts for the year ended 31 May 2008.

Required:
Prepare the following accounts for the year ended 31 May 2008 in the books of Forest Traders Limited to record the above transactions:

(a) Provision for doubtful debts;
(b) Provision for discounts to be allowed on debtors.

(*Association of Accounting Technicians*)

23.8A A business makes a provision for doubtful debts of 3% of debtors, also a provision of 1% for discount on debtors.
   On 1 January 2008 the balances brought forward on the relevant accounts were provision for doubtful debts £930 and provision for discounts on debtors £301.

You are required to:
(a) Enter the balances in the appropriate accounts, using a separate provision for doubtful debts account.
(b) During 2008 the business incurred bad debts £1,110 and allowed discounts £362. On 31 December 2008 debtors amounted to £42,800. Show the entries in the appropriate accounts for the year 2008, assuming that the business's accounting year ends on 31 December 2008, also extracts from the profit and loss account statement at 31 December 2008.

23.9 J Blane commenced business on 1 January 2006 and prepares her financial statements to 31 December every year. For the year ended 31 December 2006, bad debts written-off amounted to £1,400. It was also found necessary to create a provision for doubtful debts of £2,600.
   In 2007, debts amounting to £2,200 proved bad and were written-off. J Sweeny, whose debt of £210 was written off as bad in 2006, settled her account in full on 30 November 2007. As at 31 December 2007 total debts outstanding were £92,000. It was decided to bring the provision up to 4% of this figure.
   In 2008, £3,800 debts were written-off during the year, and another recovery of £320 was made in respect of debts written-off in 2006. As at 31 December 2008, total debts outstanding were £72,000. The provision for doubtful debts is to be increased to 5% of this figure.

You are required to show for the years 2006, 2007 and 2008, the
(a) Bad debts account.
(b) Bad debts recovered account.
(c) Provision for doubtful debts account.
(d) Extract from the profit and loss account statement.

23.10

(A) Explain why a provision may be made for doubtful debts.

(B) Explain the procedure to be followed when a customer whose debt has been written-off as bad subsequently pays the amount originally owing.

(C) On 1 January 2007 D Watson had debtors of £25,000 on which he had made a provision for doubtful debts of 3%.

During 2007,

(*i*) A Stewart who owed D Watson £1,200 was declared bankrupt and a settlement of 25p in the £ was made, the balance being treated as a bad debt.

(*ii*) Other bad debts written-off during the year amounted to £2,300.

On 31 December 2007 total debtors amounted to £24,300 but this requires to be adjusted as follows:

(*a*) J Smith, a debtor owing £600, was known to be unable to pay and this amount was to be written off.

(*b*) A cheque for £200 from S McIntosh was returned from the bank unpaid.

D Watson maintained his provision for doubtful debts at 3% debtors.

Required:

(1) For the financial year ended 31 December 2007, show the entries in the following accounts:
   (*i*) Provision for doubtful debts
   (*ii*) Bad debts

(2) What is the effect on net profit of the change in the provision for doubtful debts?

(*Scottish Qualifications Authority*)

23.11A

D Faculti started in business buying and selling law textbooks, on 1 January 2003. At the end of each of the next three years, his figures for debtors, before writing-off any bad debts, were as follows:

    31 December 2003   £30,000
    31 December 2004   £38,100
    31 December 2005   £4,750

Bad debts to be written-off are as follows:

    31 December 2004   £2,100
    31 December 2005   £750

The provision for doubtful debts in each year is 5% of outstanding debtors.

Required:

(*a*) Prepare Faculti's bad debts expense account and provision for doubtful debts account for 2003, 2004 and 2005.

(*b*) The amounts due from debtors B Roke (£70) and HA Ditt (£42) became irrecoverable in 2006 and were written off. Show the entries in the ledger accounts to record these write-offs.

You can find a range of additional self-test questions, as well as material to help you with your studies, on the website that accompanies this book at **www.pearsoned.co.uk/wood**

Exhibit 24.3

The business starts in business on 1 January 2006.

	£
In its first year it buys crates costing	800
Their estimated value at 31 December 2006	540
Crates bought in the year ended 31 December 2007	320
Estimated value of all crates in hand on 31 December 2007	530
Crates bought in the year ended 31 December 2008	590
Estimated value of all crates in hand on 31 December 2008	700

Crates

2006			£	2006			£
Dec	31	Cash (during the year)	800	Dec	31	Profit and loss	260
					31	Stock c/d	540
			800				800
2007				2007			
Jan	1	Stock b/d	540	Dec	31	Profit and loss	330
Dec	31	Cash (during the year)	320		31	Stock c/d	530
			860				860
2008				2008			
Jan	1	Stock b/d	530	Dec	31	Profit and loss	420
Dec	31	Cash (during the year)	590		31	Stock c/d	700
			1,120				1,120
2009							
Jan	1	Stock b/d	700				

Profit and Loss Account for the year ended 31 December

		£
2006	Use of crates	260
2007	Use of crates	330
2008	Use of crates	420

The balance of the crates account at the end of each year is shown as a fixed asset in the balance sheet.

Sometimes the business may make its own items such as tools or crates. In these instances the tools account or crates account should be debited with labour costs and material costs.

Revaluation is also used, for instance, by farmers for their cattle. Like other fixed assets depreciation should be provided for, but during the early life of an animal it will be appreciating in value, only to depreciate later. The task of calculating the cost of an animal becomes virtually impossible if it has been born on the farm, and reared on the farm by grazing on the pasture land and being fed on other foodstuffs, some grown on the farm and others bought by the farmer.

To get over this problem the revaluation method is used. Because of the difficulty of calculating the cost of the animals, they are valued at the price which they would fetch if sold at market. This is an exception to the general rule of assets being shown at cost price.

Depletion unit method

With fixed assets such as a quarry from which raw materials are dug out to be sold to the building industry, a different method is needed: the depletion unit method.

If a quarry was bought for £5,000 and it was expected to contain 1,000 tonnes of saleable materials, then for each tonne taken out we would depreciate it by £5, i.e. £5,000 ÷ 1,000 = £5.

This can be shown as:

$$\frac{\text{Cost of fixed asset}}{\text{Expected total contents in units}} \times \text{Number of units taken in period}$$

$$= \text{Depreciation for that period.}$$

Machine hour method

With a machine the depreciation provision may be based on the number of hours that the machine was operated during the period compared with the total expected running hours during the machine's life with the business. A business which bought a machine costing £2,000 having an expected running life of 1,000 hours, and no scrap value, could provide for depreciation of the machine at the rate of £2 for every hour it was operated during a particular accounting period.

Sum of the years' digits method

This method is popular in the USA but not common in the UK. It provides for higher depreciation to be charged early in the life of an asset with lower depreciation in later years.

Given an asset costing £3,000 which will be in use for 5 years, the calculations will be:

From purchase the asset will last for	5 years
From the second year the asset will last for	4 years
From the third year the asset will last for	3 years
From the fourth year the asset will last for	2 years
From the fifth year the asset will last for	1 year
Sum of these digits	15

	£
1st year 5/15 of £3,000 is charged =	1,000
2nd year 4/15 of £3,000 is charged =	800
3rd year 3/15 of £3,000 is charged =	600
4th year 2/15 of £3,000 is charged =	400
5th year 1/15 of £3,000 is charged =	200
	3,000

Units of output method

This method establishes the total expected units of output expected from the asset. Depreciation, based on cost less salvage value, is then calculated for the period by taking that period's units of output as a proportion of the total expected output over the life of the asset.

An instance of this could be a machine which is expected to be able to produce 10,000 widgets over its useful life. It has cost £6,000 and has an expected salvage value of £1,000. In year 1 a total of 1,500 widgets are produced, and in year 2 the production is 2,500 widgets.

The depreciation per period is calculated:

$$(\text{Cost} - \text{salvage value}) \times \left(\frac{\text{period's production}}{\text{total expected production}} \right)$$

$$\text{Year 1:} \quad £5,000 \times \frac{1,500}{10,000} = £750 \text{ depreciation}$$

$$\text{Year 2:} \quad £5,000 \times \frac{2,500}{10,000} = £1,250 \text{ depreciation}$$

Learning outcomes

You should now have learnt:

1 That depreciation is an expense of the business and has to be charged against any period during which a fixed asset has been in use.

2 That the main causes of depreciation are: physical deterioration, economic factors, the time factor and depletion.

3 How to calculate depreciation using the straight line method.

4 How to calculate depreciation using the reducing balance method.

5 How to calculate depreciation on assets bought or sold within an accounting period.

6 That there are other methods of calculating depreciation in addition to the straight line and reducing balance methods.

Answers to activities

24.1 Fixed assets are those assets of material value which are:

- of long life, and
- to be used in the business, and
- not bought with the main purpose of resale.

24.2 Firstly, financial statements must show a true and fair view of the financial performance and position of the business. If depreciation was not provided for, both fixed assets and profits would be stated in the financial statements at inflated amounts. This would only mislead the users of those financial statements and, so, depreciation must be charged. Secondly, FRS 15 requires that fixed assets are depreciated.

24.3 Just as with the depreciation percentage, you round it to the nearest whole number.

Review questions

24.1 A Gill, purchased a notebook PC for £1,211. It has an estimated life of three years and a scrap value of £50.

She is not certain whether she should use the straight line or the reducing balance basis for the purpose of calculating depreciation on the computer.

You are required to calculate the depreciation (to the nearest £) using both methods, showing clearly the balance remaining in the computer account at the end of each of the four years under each method. (Assume that 65 per cent per annum is to be used for the reducing balance method.)

24.2 A machine costs £8,000. It will be kept for five years, and then sold for an estimated figure of £2,400. Show the calculations of the figures for depreciation (to nearest £) for each of the five years using (a) the straight line method, (b) the reducing balance method, for this method using a depreciation rate of 20 per cent.

24.3 A car costs £9,600. It will be kept for three years, and then sold for £2,600. Calculate the depreciation for each year using (a) the reducing balance method, using a depreciation rate of 50 per cent, (b) the straight line method.

24.4A A photocopier costs £23,000. It will be kept for four years, and then traded-in for £4,000. Show the calculations of the figures for depreciation for each year using (a) the straight line method, (b) the reducing balance method, for this method using a depreciation rate of 35 per cent.

24.5A A printer costs £800. It will be kept for five years and then scrapped. Show your calculations of the amount of depreciation each year if (a) the reducing balance method at a rate of 60 per cent was used, (b) the straight line method was used.

24.6A A bus is bought for £56,000. It will be used for four years, and then sold back to the supplier for £18,000. Show the depreciation calculations for each year using (a) the reducing balance method with a rate of 25 per cent, (b) the straight line method.

24.7 A company, which makes up its financial statements annually to 31 December, provides for depreciation of its machinery at the rate of 15 per cent per annum using the reducing balance method.
  On 31 December 2008, the machinery consisted of three items purchased as shown:

	£
On 1 January 2006 Machine A	Cost 2,000
On 1 September 2007 Machine B	Cost 4,000
On 1 May 2008 Machine C	Cost 3,000

Required:
Your calculations showing the depreciation provision for the year 2008.

24.8 A motor vehicle which cost £12,000 was bought on credit from Trucks Ltd on 1 January 2006. Financial statements are prepared annually to 31 December and depreciation of vehicles is provided at 25 per cent per annum under the reducing balance method.

Required:
Prepare the motor vehicle account and the accumulated provision for depreciation on motor vehicles account for the first two years of the motor vehicle's working life.

24.9 Ivor Innes has supplied you with the following information:

	1 April 2007	31 March 2008
	£	£
Cash	840	700
Fixtures	7,600	7,600
Balance at bank	5,500	8,320
Stock	17,800	19,000
Debtors	8,360	4,640
Creditors	5,200	8,800

During the year to 31 March 2008, Ivor withdrew £11,400 from the business for private purposes. In November 2008, Ivor received a legacy of £18,000 which he paid into the business bank account.
  Ivor agrees that £600 should be provided for depreciation of fixtures and £200 for doubtful debts.

Required:
Prepare a balance sheet as at 31 March 2008 which clearly indicates the net profit for the year.

24.10A On 10 August 2003 Joblot, a computer software retailer, bought a fixed asset which cost £100,000. It had an anticipated life of four years and an estimated residual value of £20,000. Due to unforeseen events in the computer industry, the asset was suddenly sold on 10 March 2006 for £45,000.
  The policy of the company is to provide depreciation in full in the year of purchase and none in the year of sale.

→

→

Required:

(a) Calculate the charge for depreciation for each of the years using both the straight line method and the reducing balance method, showing clearly the net book values as at the end of each of the years.

(b) Calculate the profit or loss on the disposal of the asset under both of the above methods.

(c) Explain why assets are depreciated and provide an example where it would be more appropriate to use straight line and another example where it would be more appropriate to use reducing balance.

(d) Explain what the figures for net book value that are shown in the balance sheet represent.

24.11A Black and Blue Ltd depreciates its forklift trucks using a reducing balance rate of 30 per cent. Its accounting year end is 30 September. On 30 September 2006, it owned four forklift trucks:

(A) Purchased on 1 January 2003 for £2,400
(B) Purchased on 1 May 2004 for £2,500
(C) Purchased on 1 October 2004 for £3,200
(D) Purchased on 1 April 2006 for £3,600

Required:
Calculate the depreciation provision for the year ending 30 September 2006.

24.12 State which depreciation method will be the most appropriate in the case of each of the following assets and why. Also, indicate to what extent obsolescence will affect each of the assets.

(a) A delivery van used by a baker.

(b) A filing cabinet.

(c) A shop held on a 20-year lease.

(d) A plastic moulding machine to manufacture a new novelty – plastic fireguards. It is expected that these will be very popular next Christmas and that sales will continue for a year of two thereafter but at a very much lower level.

(e) Machine X. This machine is used as a standby when the normal machines are being maintained. Occasionally it is used to increase capacity when there is a glut of orders. Machine X is of an old type and is inefficient compared with new machines. When used on a full-time basis, the machine should last for approximately four years.

You can find a range of additional self-test questions, as well as material to help you with your studies, on the website that accompanies this book at **www.pearsoned.co.uk/wood**

Chapter

25

Double entry records for depreciation

Learning objectives

After you have studied this chapter, you should be able to:

● incorporate depreciation calculations into the accounting records
● record the entries relating to disposal of fixed assets
● make depreciation entries using either a one-stage or a two-stage approach to recording depreciation

Introduction

Now that you know what depreciation is and how it may be calculated, in this chapter you'll learn how to make the appropriate entries for depreciation in the accounting books. You'll also learn how to make the appropriate period-end entries in the financial statements.

25.1 Recording depreciation

Previously, the charge for depreciation on a fixed asset was recorded in the account for that fixed asset. This is no longer done.

 Activity 25.1 Why do you think this is no longer done?

Recording depreciation now involves maintaining each fixed asset at its cost in the ledger account while operating another ledger account where the depreciation to date is recorded. This account is known as the 'accumulated provision for depreciation account', often shortened to the **accumulated depreciation account** (or sometimes, confusingly, known as the 'provision for depreciation account').

 Activity 25.2 Why do you think it would be confusing to call the accumulated provision for depreciation account the 'provision for depreciation account'?

Let's look at how this is done by first looking at the double entry required and then looking at how it is used in an example shown in Exhibit 25.1.

The depreciation is posted directly into the cumulative provision for depreciation account. The double entry is:

Debit the profit and loss account
Credit the accumulated provision for depreciation account

Exhibit 25.1

A business has a financial year end of 31 December. A computer is bought for £2,000 on 1 January 2005. It is to be depreciated at the rate of 20 per cent using the reducing balance method. The records for the first three years are:

Computer

2005			£	
Jan	1	Cash	2,000	

Accumulated Provision for Depreciation – Computer

2005			£	2005			£
Dec	31	Balance c/d	400	Dec	31	Profit and loss	400
2006				2006			
Dec	31	Balance c/d	720	Jan	1	Balance b/d	400
				Dec	31	Profit and loss	320
			720				720
2007				2007			
Dec	31	Balance c/d	976	Jan	1	Balance b/d	720
				Dec	31	Profit and loss	256
			976				976
				2008			
				Jan	1	Balance b/d	976

Profit and Loss

2005			£
Dec	31	Accumulated provision for depreciation – Computer	400
2006			
Dec	31	Accumulated provision for depreciation – Computer	320
2007			
Dec	31	Accumulated provision for depreciation – Computer	256

Profit and Loss Account (extracts) for the years ending 31 December

		£
2005	Depreciation	400
2006	Depreciation	320
2007	Depreciation	256

Note: In this case, the depreciation for the period being posted to the profit and loss account is being described as 'depreciation' in the financial statement and *not* by the name of the account it originated from (the accumulated provision for depreciation account).

Activity 25.3 What advantages are there in making this exception to the rule by using 'depreciation' rather than 'accumulated provision for depreciation' in the profit and loss account entry?

Now the balance on the computer account is shown on the balance sheet at the end of each year less the balance on the accumulated provision for depreciation account.

Balance Sheets (extracts)

	£	£
As at 31 December 2005		
Computer at cost	2,000	
Less Accumulated depreciation	(400)	
		1,600
As at 31 December 2006		
Computer at cost	2,000	
Less Accumulated depreciation	(720)	
		1,280
As at 31 December 2007		
Computer at cost	2,000	
Less Accumulated depreciation	(976)	
		1,024

25.2 The disposal of a fixed asset

Reason for accounting entries

Upon the sale of a fixed asset, we will want to remove it from our ledger accounts. This means that the cost of that asset needs to be taken out of the asset account. In addition, the accumulated depreciation on the asset which has been sold will have to be taken out of the accumulated provision. Finally, the profit and loss on sale, if any, will have to be calculated and posted to the profit and loss account.

When we charge depreciation on a fixed asset we are having to make an informed guess. We will not often guess correctly. This means that, when we dispose of an asset, the amount received for it is usually different from our estimate.

Activity 25.4 List as many things as you can think of in one minute that could cause the amount charged for depreciation to have been incorrect.

Accounting entries needed

On the sale of a fixed asset, in this example a computer, the following entries are needed:

(A) Transfer the cost price of the asset sold to an assets disposal account (in this case a computer disposals account):

> Debit computer disposals account
> > Credit computer account

(B) Transfer the depreciation already charged to the assets disposal account:

> Debit accumulated provision for depreciation: computer
> > Credit computer disposals account

(C) For the amount received on disposal:

> Debit cash book
> > Credit computer disposals account

(D) Transfer the difference (i.e. the amount needed to balance the computer disposals account) to the profit and loss account.

   (i) If the computer disposals account shows a difference on the debit side (i.e. if more has been credited to the account than has been debited to it), there is a profit on the sale:

> Debit computer disposals account
> > Credit profit and loss account

   (ii) If the computer disposals account shows a difference on the credit side, there is a loss on sale:

> Debit profit and loss account
> > Credit computer disposals account

These entries can be illustrated by looking at those needed if the computer already shown in Exhibit 25.1 was sold on 2 January 2008. At 31 December 2007, the cost was £2,000 and a total of £976 had been written off as depreciation leaving a net book value of £2,000 − £976 = £1,024. If the computer is sold in 2008 for *more* than £1,024 a profit on sale will be made. If, on the other hand, the computer is sold for *less* than £1,024 then a loss will be incurred.

Exhibit 25.2 shows the entries needed when the computer has been sold for £1,070 and a profit of £46 on sale has, therefore, been made. Exhibit 25.3 shows the entries where the computer has been sold for £950, thus incurring a loss on sale of £74. In both cases, the sale is on 2 January 2008 and no depreciation is to be charged for the two days' ownership in 2008. (The letters in brackets refer to the accounting double entries, A–D, above.)

Exhibit 25.2 Fixed asset sold at a profit

Computer

2005				£	2008				£
Jan	1	Cash		2,000	Jan	2	Machinery disposals	(A)	2,000

Accumulated Provision for Depreciation: Computer

2008				£	2008				£
Jan	2	Machinery disposals	(B)	976	Jan	1	Balance b/d		976

Computer Disposals

2008				£	2008				£
Jan	2	Computer	(A)	2,000	Jan	2	Accumulated provision		
Dec	31	Profit and loss	(D)	46			for depreciation	(B)	976
					Jan	2	Cash	(C)	1,070
				2,046					2,046

Profit and Loss

			£
2008			
Dec	31	Computer disposals (gain) (D)	46

Profit and Loss Account (extract) for the year ending 31 December 2008

		£
Gross profit		XXX
Add Profit on sale of computer	(D)	46

Exhibit 25.3 Fixed asset sold at a loss

Computer

2005			£	2008				£
Jan	1	Cash	2,000	Jan	2	Computer disposals	(A)	2,000

Accumulated Provision for Depreciation: Computer

2008				£	2008			£
Jan	2	Computer disposals	(B)	976	Jan	1	Balance b/d	976

Computer Disposals

2008				£	2008				£
Jan	2	Computer	(A)	2,000	Jan	2	Accumulated provision for depreciation	(B)	976
					Jan	2	Cash	(C)	950
					Dec	31	Profit and loss	(D)	74
				2,000					2,000

Profit and Loss (extract)

2008				£
Dec	31	Computer disposal (loss) (D)		74

Profit and Loss Account (extract) for the year ending 31 December 2008

		£
Gross profit		xxx
Less Loss on sale of computer	(D)	(74)

In many cases, the disposal of an asset will mean that we have sold it. This will not always be the case. For example, a car may be given up in part payment for a new car. Here the disposal value is the exchange value. If a new car costing £10,000 was to be paid for by £6,000 in cash and an allowance of £4,000 for the old car, then the disposal value of the old car is £4,000.

Similarly a car may have been in an accident and now be worthless. If it was insured, the disposal value will be the amount received from the insurance company. If an asset is scrapped, the disposal value is that received from the sale of the scrap, which may be nil.

25.3 Change of depreciation method

It is possible to make a change in the method of calculating depreciation. This should not be done frequently, and it should only be undertaken after a thorough review. Where a change is made, if material (*see* Chapter 10 on materiality), the effect of doing so upon the figures reported should be shown as a note to the financial statements in the year of change.

Further examples

So far, the examples have deliberately been kept simple. Only one fixed asset has been shown in each case. Exhibits 25.4 and 25.5 give examples of more complicated cases.

Exhibit 25.4

A machine is bought on 1 January 2005 for £1,000 and another one on 1 October 2006 for £1,200. The first machine is sold on 30 June 2007 for £720. The business's financial year ends on 31 December. The machinery is to be depreciated at 10 per cent, using the straight line method. Machinery in existence at the end of each year is to be depreciated for a full year. No depreciation is to be charged on any machinery disposed of during the year.

Machinery

2005			£	2005				£
Jan	1	Cash	1,000	Dec	31	Balance c/d		1,000
2006				2006				
Jan	1	Balance b/d	1,000	Dec	31	Balance c/d		2,200
Oct	1	Cash	1,200					
			2,200					
								2,200
2007				2007				
Jan	1	Balance b/d	2,200	Jun	30	Machinery disposals		1,000
				Dec	31	Balance c/d		1,200
			2,200					2,200
2008								
Jan	1	Balance b/d	1,200					

Accumulated Provision for Depreciation: Machinery

2005			£	2005				£
Dec	31	Balance c/d	100	Dec	31	Profit and loss		100
2006				2006				
Dec	31	Balance c/d	320	Jan	1	Balance b/d		100
				Dec	31	Profit and loss		220
			320					320
2007				2007				
Jun	30	Disposals of machinery (2 years × 10 per cent × £1,000)	200	Jan	1	Balance b/d		320
				Dec	31	Profit and loss		120
Dec	31	Balance c/d	240					
			440					
								440
				2008				
				Jan	1	Balance b/d		240

Machinery Disposals

2007			£	2007			£
Jun	30	Machinery	1,000	Jun	30	Cash	720
					30	Accumulated provision for depreciation	200
				Dec	31	Profit and loss	80
			1,000				1,000

Profit and Loss (extracts)

2005			**£**
Dec	31	Acc Provn for Depn: Machinery	100
2006			
Dec	31	Acc Provn for Depn: Machinery	220
2007			
Dec	31	Acc Provn for Depn: Machinery	120
Dec	31	Machinery disposals (loss)	80

Profit and Loss Account (extracts) for the years ending 31 December

		£
Gross profit		xxx
Less Expenses:		
2005	Depreciation: Machinery	(100)
2006	Depreciation: Machinery	(220)
2007	Depreciation: Machinery	(120)
	Loss on machinery sold	(80)

Balance Sheet (extracts) as at 31 December

		£	£
2005	Machinery at cost	1,000	
	Less Accumulated provision for depreciation	(100)	
			900
2006	Machinery at cost	2,200	
	Less Accumulated provision for depreciation	(320)	
			1,880
2007	Machinery at cost	1,200	
	Less Accumulated provision for depreciation	(240)	
			960

Another example can now be given. This is somewhat more complicated. Firstly, it involves a greater number of items. Secondly, the depreciation provisions are calculated on a proportionate basis, i.e. one month's depreciation for one month's ownership.

Exhibit 25.5

A business with its financial year end on 31 December buys two vans on 1 January 2001, No 1 for £8,000 and No 2 for £5,000. It also buys another van, No 3, on 1 July 2003 for £9,000 and another, No 4, on 1 October 2003 for £7,200. The first two vans are sold, No 1 for £2,290 on 30 September 2004, and No 2 for scrap for £50 on 30 June 2005.

Depreciation is on the straight line basis, 20 per cent per annum, ignoring scrap value in this particular case when calculating depreciation per annum. Show the extracts from the assets account, provision for depreciation account, disposal account and profit and loss account for the years ended 31 December 2001, 2002, 2003, 2004, and 2005, and the balance sheets as at those dates.

→

→

Vans

2001			£	2001			£
Jan	1	Cash	13,000	Dec	31	Balance c/d	13,000
2002				2002			
Jan	1	Balance b/d	13,000	Dec	31	Balance c/d	13,000
2003				2003			
Jan	1	Balance b/d	13,000				
July	1	Cash	9,000				
Oct	1	Cash	7,200	Dec	31	Balance c/d	29,200
			29,200				29,200
2004				2004			
Jan	1	Balance b/d	29,200	Sept	30	Disposals	8,000
				Dec	31	Balance c/d	21,200
			29,200				29,200
2005				2005			
Jan	1	Balance b/d	21,200	June	30	Disposals	5,000
				Dec	31	Balance c/d	16,200
			21,200				21,200
2006							
Jan	1	Balance b/d	16,200				

Accumulated Provision for Depreciation: Vans

2001			£	2001			£
Dec	31	Balance c/d	2,600	Dec	31	Profit and loss	2,600
2002				2002			
				Jan	1	Balance b/d	2,600
Dec	31	Balance c/d	5,200	Dec	31	Profit and loss	2,600
			5,200				5,200
2003				2003			
				Jan	1	Balance b/d	5,200
Dec	31	Balance c/d	9,060	Dec	31	Profit and loss	3,860
			9,060				9,060
2004				2004			
Sept	30	Disposals	6,000	Jan	1	Balance b/d	9,060
Dec	31	Balance c/d	8,500	Dec	31	Profit and loss	5,440
			14,500				14,500
2005				2005			
June	30	Disposals	4,500	Jan	1	Balance b/d	8,500
Dec	31	Balance c/d	7,740	Dec	31	Profit and loss	3,740
			12,240				12,240
				2006			
				Jan	1	Balance b/d	7,740

Workings – depreciation provisions

		£	£
2001	20% of £13,000		2,600
2002	20% of £13,000		2,600
2003	20% of £13,000 × 12 months	2,600	
	20% of £9,000 × 6 months	900	
	20% of £7,200 × 3 months	360	
			3,860
2004	20% of £21,200 × 12 months	4,240	
	20% of £8,000 × 9 months	1,200	
			5,440
2005	20% of £16,200 × 12 months	3,240	
	20% of £5,000 × 6 months	500	
			3,740

Workings – transfers of depreciation provisions to disposal accounts

Van 1   Bought Jan 1 2001 Cost £8,000
         Sold Sept 30 2004
         Period of ownership $3\frac{3}{4}$ years
         Depreciation provisions $3\frac{3}{4} \times 20\% \times £8,000 = £6,000$

Van 2   Bought Jan 1 2001 Cost £5,000
         Sold June 30 2005
         Period of ownership $4\frac{1}{2}$ years
         Depreciation provisions $4\frac{1}{2} \times 20\% \times £5,000 = £4,500$

Disposals of Vans

2004			£	2004			£
Sept	30	Van	8,000	Sept	30	Accumulated provision for depreciation	6,000
						Cash	2,290
Dec	31	Profit and loss	290				8,290
			8,290				
2005				2005			
Jun	30	Van	5,000	Jun	30	Accumulated provision for depreciation	4,500
						Cash	50
				Dec	31	Profit and loss	450
			5,000				5,000

Profit and Loss (extracts)

2001			£				£
Dec	31	Acc Provn for Depn: Vans	2,600				
2002							
Dec	31	Acc Provn for Depn: Vans	2,600				
2003							
Dec	31	Acc Provn for Depn: Vans	3,860				
2004				2004			
Dec	31	Acc Provn for Depn: Vans	5,440	Dec	31	Disposal of Vans (Gain)	290
2005							
Dec	31	Acc Provn for Depn: Vans	3,740				
		Dsiposal of Vans (loss)	450				

Profit and Loss Account (extracts) for the years ending 31 December

		£	£
Gross profit (each year 2001, 2002, 2003)			xxx
	Less Expenses:		
2001	Depreciation: vans		(2,600)
2002	Depreciation: vans		(2,600)
2003	Depreciation: vans		(3,860)
2004	Gross profit		x,xxx
	Add Profit on van sold		290
			x,xxx
	Less Expenses:		
	Depreciation: vans		(5,440)
			x,xxx
2005	Gross profit		x,xxx
	Less Expenses:		
	Depreciation: vans	3,740	
	Loss on van sold	450	
			(4,190)

→

Balance Sheets (extracts) as at 31 December

		£	£
2001	Vans at cost	13,000	
	Less Accumulated provision for depreciation	(2,600)	
			10,400
2002	Vans at cost	13,000	
	Less Accumulated provision for depreciation	(5,200)	
			7,800
2003	Vans at cost	29,200	
	Less Accumulated provision for depreciation	(9,060)	
			20,140
2004	Vans at cost	21,200	
	Less Accumulated provision for depreciation	(8,500)	
			12,700
2005	Vans at cost	16,200	
	Less Accumulated provision for depreciation	(7,740)	
			8,460

25.4 Depreciation provisions and the replacement of assets

Making a provision for depreciation does not mean that money is invested somewhere to finance the replacement of the asset when it is put out of use. It is simply a bookkeeping entry, and the end result is that lower net profits are shown because the provisions have been charged to the profit and loss account.

It is not surprising to find that many people – especially students – who have not studied accounting, misunderstand the situation. They often think that a provision is the same as money kept somewhere with which to replace the asset eventually. Never make that mistake. It may cost you a lot of marks in an exam!

A cautious owner may take out less drawings if the net profit is lower, but that is no justification for arguing that depreciation results in funds being available to replace the fixed asset later!

25.5 Another approach

In this chapter, you've learnt how to perform the double entries necessary to record the periodic charge for depreciation. The approach you learnt about is known as the 'one-stage approach'. It was based upon the use of one double entry, a credit to the accumulated provision for depreciation account and a debit to the profit and loss account.

There is another approach which is widely used in practice. It involves using a '**provision for depreciation account**', often shortened to '**depreciation account**', as well as the 'accumulated provision for depreciation account'. At the end of the period, you calculate the depreciation for the period and make the following double entries:

1 Debit the depreciation account
      Credit the accumulated provision for depreciation account
2 Debit the profit and loss account
      Credit the depreciation account

Compare this two-stage approach to the one-stage approach you learnt earlier:

Debit the profit and loss account
Credit the accumulated provision for depreciation account

Note how the double entry you learnt earlier combines the two entries used in the two-stage approach by cancelling out the debit and credit to the depreciation account. This makes it much simpler to record the entries required, but adopting the two-stage approach has the advantage that it actually shows what has happened rather than compressing the two double entries that theory says should be used into one.

However, some accountants still prefer to keep recording the entries as simple as possible and so use only the 'accumulated provision for depreciation account' (i.e. the 'one-stage approach').

Nevertheless, you need to be aware of and able to do the two-stage approach described above, just in case you should be asked to use it by an examiner. If you are *not* asked for two accounts (a depreciation account *plus* an accumulated provision for depreciation account) you should assume that the one-stage approach is the one you are expected to use.

Note: **As in Review questions 25.7A, 25.8 and 25.9A, examiners sometimes ask for a 'depreciation' account to be shown in an answer and they do not mention an 'accumulated provision for depreciation' account. When this happens it is usually the 'accumulated provision for depreciation' account they are looking for. That is, they expect the balance on it to be carried forward to the next period, as in the case of the one-stage approach. It is the one-stage approach they want you to use but they have given the account the 'wrong' name. Use the name they used ('depreciation') but treat it as if it were an 'accumulated provision for depreciation' account. When examiners want you to prepare both a 'depreciation' account and an 'accumulated provision for depreciation' account, it will be obvious from the wording of the question.**

25.6 Finally

This chapter has covered all the principles involved. Obviously examiners can present their questions in their own way. In fact, in order to better test your understanding, examiners do tend to vary the way questions involving depreciation are presented. Practise all the questions in this book, including the exhibits, and compare them with the answers shown in full. Doing so will demonstrate the truth of this statement and prepare you better for your examination when you can be virtually guaranteed that you will need to be able to calculate and make appropriate entries for depreciation.

Learning outcomes

You should now have learnt:

1 That the method of showing depreciation in the asset account is now used only by some small organisations, and should be avoided.

2 That fixed asset accounts should show only the cost of each asset. Depreciation is credited to an accumulated provision for depreciation account.

3 That when we sell a fixed asset, we must transfer both the cost and the accumulated depreciation to a separate disposal account.

4 That it is very rare for the depreciation provided to have been accurate.

5 That a profit on the disposal of a fixed asset is transferred to the credit of the profit and loss account.

→

→ The machinery bought was:

2008	1 January	1 machine costing £1,200
2009	1 August	2 machines costing £672 each
	1 November	1 machine costing £1,920
2011	1 May	1 machine costing £300

Depreciation is over eight years, using the straight line method, machines being depreciated for the proportion of the year that they are owned.

25.3A A company maintains its fixed assets at cost. Depreciation provision accounts, one for each type of asset, are in use. Machinery is to be depreciated at the rate of 15% per annum, and fixtures at the rate of 5% per annum, using the reducing balance method. Depreciation is to be calculated on assets in existence at the end of each year, giving a full year's depreciation even though the asset was bought part of the way through the year. The following transactions in assets have taken place:

2005	1 January	Bought machinery £2,800, fixtures £290
	1 July	Bought fixtures £620
2006	1 October	Bought machinery £3,500
	1 December	Bought fixtures £130

The financial year end of the business is 31 December.

You are to show:
(a) The machinery account.
(b) The fixtures account.
(c) The two separate provision for depreciation accounts.
(d) The fixed assets section of the balance sheet at the end of each year, for the years ended 31 December 2005 and 2006.

25.4 A company depreciates its plant at the rate of 25 per cent per annum, straight line method, for each month of ownership. From the following details draw up the plant account and the provision for depreciation account for each of the years 2004, 2005, 2006 and 2007.

2004	Bought plant costing £2,600 on 1 January.
	Bought plant costing £2,100 on 1 October.
2006	Bought plant costing £2,800 on 1 September.
2007	Sold plant which had been bought for £2,600 on 1 January 2004 for the sum of £810 on 31 August 2007.

You are also required to draw up the plant disposal account and the extracts from the balance sheet as at the end of each year.

25.5 A company maintains its fixed assets at cost. Depreciation provision accounts for each asset are kept.

At 31 December 2008 the position was as follows:

	Total cost to date £	Total depreciation to date £
Machinery	94,500	28,350
Office furniture	3,200	1,280

The following additions were made during the financial year ended 31 December 2009:
Machinery £16,000, office furniture £460.
A machine bought in 2005 for £1,600 was sold for £360 during the year.
The rates of depreciation are:
Machinery 20 per cent, office furniture 10 per cent, using the straight line basis, calculated on the assets in existence at the end of each financial year irrespective of the date of purchase.

You are required to show the asset and depreciation accounts for the year ended 31 December 2009 and the balance sheet entries at that date.

25.6 A vehicle bought on 1 January 2010 cost £16,000. Its useful economic life is estimated at 4 years and its trade-in value at that point is estimated as being £4,000.

During 2012 a review of the vehicle's probable useful economic life suggested that it should be retained until 1 January 2015 and its residual value should be £2,500.

Required:
What is the amount of straight line depreciation charged in the profit and loss account in the year ending 31 December 2012 and the amount included in the balance sheet for accumulated depreciation at that date?

25.7A

(a) What is the meaning of depreciation?
(b) Give **three** reasons why depreciation may occur.
(c) Name **two** methods of depreciation.
(d) In what way do you think the concept of consistency applies to depreciation?
(e) 'Since the calculation of depreciation is based on estimates, not facts, why bother to make the calculation?'
Explain briefly why you think that the calculation of depreciation is based on estimates.
(f) If depreciation was omitted, what effects would this have on the final accounts?
(g) 'Some assets increase (appreciate) in value, but normal accounting procedure would be to ignore any such appreciation.'
Explain why bringing appreciation into account would go against the prudence concept.
(h) A business whose financial year ends at 31 December purchased on 1 January 2007 a machine for £5,000. The machine was to be depreciated by ten equal instalments. On 4 January 2009 the machine was sold for £3,760.
Ignoring any depreciation in the year of sale, show the relevant entries for each of the following accounts for the years ended 31 December 2007, 2008 and 2009:
(i) Machinery
(ii) Provision for depreciation of machinery[Authors' Note]
(iii) Machinery disposals
(iv) Profit and loss

(*Northern Examinations and Assessment Board: GCSE*)

Authors' Note: **this is the accumulated provision for depreciation of machinery account.**

25.8

(a) Identify the four factors which cause fixed assets to depreciate.
(b) Which one of these factors is the most important for each of the following assets?
(i) a gold mine,
(ii) a lorry,
(iii) a 50 year lease on a building,
(iv) land,
(v) a ship used to ferry passengers and vehicles across a river following the building of a bridge across the river,
(vi) a franchise to market a new computer software package in a certain country.
(c) The financial year of Ochre Ltd will end on 31 December 2006. At 1 January 2006 the company had in use equipment with a total accumulated cost of £135,620 which had been depreciated by a total of £81,374. During the year ended 31 December 2006 Ochre Ltd purchased new equipment costing £47,800 and sold off equipment which had originally cost £36,000, and which had been depreciated by £28,224, for £5,700. No further purchases or sales of equipment are planned for December. The policy of the company is to depreciate equipment at 40% using the diminishing balance method. A full year's depreciation is provided for on all equipment in use by the company at the end of each year.

Required:
Show the following ledger accounts for the year ended 31 December 2006:

→

→   (*i*)   the equipment account;
       (*ii*)   the provision for depreciation on equipment account;^{Authors' Note}
       (*iii*) the assets disposals account.

(*Association of Accounting Technicians*)

***Authors' Note*: this is the accumulated provision for depreciation account.**

25.9A   Mavron plc owned the following motor vehicles as at 1 April 2006:

Motor Vehicle	Date Acquired	Cost £	Estimated Residual Value £	Estimated Life (years)
AAT 101	1 October 2003	8,500	2,500	5
DJH 202	1 April 2004	12,000	2,000	8

Mavron plc's policy is to provide at the end of each financial year depreciation using the straight line method applied on a month-by-month basis on all motor vehicles used during the year.

During the financial year ended 31 March 2007 the following occurred:

(*a*) On 30 June 2006 AAT 101 was traded in and replaced by KGC 303. The trade-in allowance was £5,000. KGC 303 cost £15,000 and the balance due (after deducting the trade-in allowance) was paid partly in cash and partly by a loan of £6,000 from Pinot Finance. KGC 303 is expected to have a residual value of £4,000 after an estimated economic life of 5 years.

(*b*) The estimated remaining economic life of DJH 202 was reduced from 6 years to 4 years with no change in the estimated residual value.

Required:
(*a*) Show any journal entries necessary to give effect to the above.
(*b*) Show the journal entry necessary to record depreciation on motor vehicles for the year ended 31 March 2007.
(*c*) Reconstruct the motor vehicles account and the provision for depreciation account for the year ended 31 March 2007.*

Show the necessary calculations clearly.

(*Association of Accounting Technicians*)

***Authors' Note*: this is the accumulated provision for depreciation account.**

25.10   A business buys a fixed asset for £10,000. The business estimates that the asset will be used for 5 years. After exactly 2½ years, however, the asset is suddenly sold for £5,000. The business always provides a full year's depreciation in the year of purchase and no depreciation in the year of disposal.

Required:
(*a*) Write up the relevant accounts (including disposal account but not profit and loss account) for each of Years 1, 2 and 3:
    (*i*)   Using the straight line depreciation method (assume 20% pa);
    (*ii*) Using the reducing balance depreciation method (assume 40% pa).
(*b*) (*i*)   What is the purpose of depreciation? In what circumstances would each of the two methods you have used be preferable?
    (*ii*) What is the meaning of the net figure for the fixed asset in the balance sheet at the end of Year 2?
(*c*) If the asset was bought at the beginning of Year 1, but was not used at all until Year 2 (and it is confidently anticipated to last until Year 6), state under each method the appropriate depreciation charge in Year 1, and briefly justify your answer.

(*Association of Chartered Certified Accountants*)

25.11A Contractors Ltd was formed on 1 January 2006 and the following purchases and sales of machinery were made during the first 3 years of operations.

Date	Asset	Transaction	Price
1 January 2006	Machines 1 and 2	purchase	£40,000 each
1 October 2006	Machines 3 and 4	purchase	£15,200 each
30 June 2008	Machine 3	sale	£12,640
1 July 2008	Machine 5	purchase	£20,000

Each machine was estimated to last 10 years and to have a residual value of 5% of its cost price. Depreciation was by equal instalments, and it is company policy to charge depreciation for every month an asset is owned.

Required:
(a) Calculate
   (i)   the total depreciation on Machinery for each of the years 2006, 2007, and 2008;
   (ii) the profit or loss on the sale of Machine 3 in 2008.
(b) Contractors Ltd depreciates its vehicles by 30% per annum using the diminishing balance method. What difference would it have made to annual reported profits over the life of a vehicle if it had decided instead to depreciate this asset by 20% straight line?

(*Scottish Qualifications Authority*)

25.12 A friend of the family believes that depreciation provides him with a reserve to purchase new assets. His secretary has blown up his computer, but he knows he has the funds to replace it in the accumulated depreciation account. You know he is wrong and have grown tired of listening to him going on about it, but he won't listen to what you have to say. You decide to put him out of his misery by writing a letter to him about it that he may actually read before he realises that it is telling him things he does not want to hear.

Write him a letter, using fictitious names and addresses, which defines depreciation and explains why his view is incorrect.

25.13A A machine cost £40,000 on 1 January 2007. The reducing balance depreciation method is used at 25% per annum. Year end is 31 December. During 2009, it was decided that a straight line method would be more appropriate. At that time, the remaining useful economic life of the machine was seven years with a residual value of £1,500.

Required:
The accumulated provision for depreciation account for the years 2007 to 2009 inclusive together with the relevant balance sheet extract on 31 December in each of those years.

25.14 (a) A machine was bought on credit for £15,000 from the XY Manufacturing Co Ltd, on 1 October 2001. The estimated useful economic life of the machine was seven years and the estimated scrap value £1,000. The machine account is to be maintained at cost. Financial statements are prepared annually to 30 September and the straight line depreciation method is used on machines.

Required:
(a) Prepare the journal entries and ledger accounts to record the machine and its depreciation for the first two years of its working life.
(b) Illustrate how the machine would appear in the balance sheet at 30 September, 2003.

(b) The machine was sold for £7,500 cash to another manufacturer on 1 October 2004. A new replacement machine was bought on credit for £18,000 from the XY Manufacturing Co Ltd. It also has an estimated useful economic life of seven years but its estimated scrap value is £1,200.

Required:
(a) Prepare the machine account, the accumulated provision for depreciation account and the machine disposal account for the year to 30 September 2005.
(b) Repeat (a) but this time assume that the selling price of the old machine was £12,000.

→

→ **25.15A** Distance Limited owned three lorries at 1 April 2006:

A Purchased 21 May 2002 Cost £31,200
B Purchased 20 June 2004 Cost £19,600
C Purchased 1 January 2006 Cost £48,800

Depreciation is charged annually at 20% on cost on all vehicles in use at the end of the year.

During the year ended 31 March 2007, the following transactions occurred:

(*i*) 1 June 2006 lorry B was involved in an accident and considered to be a write-off by the insurance company which paid £10,500 in settlement.
(*ii*) 7 June 2006 lorry D was purchased for £32,800
(*iii*) 21 August 2006 lorry A was sold for £7,000
(*iv*) 30 October 2006 lorry E was purchased for £39,000
(*v*) 6 March 2007 lorry E was considered not to be suitable for carrying the type of goods required and was exchanged for lorry F. The value of lorry F was deemed to be £37,600.

Required:
Prepare the ledger T-accounts recording these transactions for the year ending 31 March 2007 and bring down the balances at 1 April.

25.16 XY Ltd provides for depreciation of its machinery at 20% per annum on cost; it charges for a full year in the year of purchase but no provision is made in the year of sale/disposal.

Financial statements are prepared annually to 31 December.

2005
January 1 Bought machine 'A' £10,000
July 1 Bought machine 'B' £6,000.

2006
March 31 Bought machine 'C' £8,000

2007
October 7 Sold machine 'A' – proceeds £5,500
November 5 Bought machine 'D' £12,000

2008
February 4 Sold machine 'B' – proceeds £3,000
February 6 Bought machine 'B' £9,000
October 11 Exchanged machine 'D' for machinery valued at £7,000

Prepare
(*a*) The machinery account for the period 1 January 2005 to 31 December 2008.
(*b*) The accumulated provision for depreciation on machinery account, for the period 1 January 2005 to 31 December 2008.
(*c*) The disposal of machinery accounts showing the profit/loss on sale for each year.
(*d*) The balance sheet extract for machinery at (i) 31 December 2007 and (ii) 31 December 2008.

25.17A A company maintains its fixed assets at cost. Accumulated provision for depreciation accounts are kept for each asset.

At 31 December 2008 the position was as follows:

	Total Cost To Date	Total Depreciation To Date
	£	£
Machinery	52,950	25,670
Office furniture	2,860	1,490

The following transactions were made in the year ended 31 December 2009:

(*a*) Purchased – machinery £2,480 and office furniture £320
(*b*) Sold machinery which had cost £2,800 in 2005 for £800

Depreciation is charged, on a straight line basis, at 10% on machinery and at 5% on office furniture on the basis of assets in use at the end of the year irrespective of the date of purchase.

Required:

Show the asset and accumulated provision for depreciation accounts for the year 31 December 2009 and the relevant balance sheet entries at that date.

25.18 Alice Burke prepares her financial statements on 31 December each year and maintains a plant and equipment register at cost. She provides depreciation for the full year on fixed assets which are in use at the end of the year, and none in the year of disposal.

At 31 December 2003 the plant account balance was £180,000 and the balance on the accumulated provision for depreciation account was £70,000. Depreciation is provided on the reducing balance method at 20%.

Early in 2006, an item of plant which had cost £20,000 on 1 March 2004 was sold for £14,000.

At the end of 2006, it was decided that for that and all succeeding years the straight line method of calculating depreciation should be used. It was assumed that all the plant would be sold at the end of 2009 for approximately £30,000.

Required:

Prepare the ledger accounts recording all of the above. You are not required to prepare the profit and loss account.

25.19A

(a) The following trial balance was extracted from the books of M Jackson on 30 April 2007. From it, and the note below it, prepare his trading and profit and loss account for the year ending 30 April 2007, and a balance sheet as at that date.

	Dr £	Cr £
Sales		18,614
Purchases	11,570	
Stock 1 May 2006	3,776	
Carriage outwards	326	
Carriage inwards	234	
Returns inwards	440	
Returns outwards		355
Salaries and wages	2,447	
Motor expenses	664	
Rent	576	
Sundry expenses	1,202	
Motor vehicles	3,400	
Fixtures and fittings	600	
Debtors	4,577	
Creditors		3,045
Cash at bank	3,876	
Cash in hand	120	
Drawings	2,050	
Capital		13,844
	35,858	35,858

Note:

Closing stock amounted to £4,000. Depreciation is to be charged at rates of 10% on cost for Fixtures and Fittings and 25% on cost for Motor Vehicles. Bad debts of £800 are to be written-off.

(b) Michael has indicated that he thinks that the debtor amounts that have been written-off will be paid eventually. He is also querying why adjustments are made in the financial statements for bad debts and depreciation. Write a short note to him, making appropriate references to accounting concepts, outlining why these adjustments are made.

25.20 On 1 April 2006 a business purchased a machine costing £112,000. The machine can be used for a total of 20,000 hours over an estimated life of 48 months. At the end of that time the machine is expected to have a trade-in value of £12,000.

→

→   The financial year of the business ends on 31 December each year. It is expected that the machine will be used for:

4,000 hours during the financial year ending 31 December 2006
5,000 hours during the financial year ending 31 December 2007
5,000 hours during the financial year ending 31 December 2008
5,000 hours during the financial year ending 31 December 2009
1,000 hours during the financial year ending 31 December 2010

Required:
(a) Calculate the annual depreciation charges on the machine on each of the following bases for each of the financial years ending on 31 December 2006, 2007, 2008, 2009 and 2010:
   (i)   the straight line method applied on a month for month basis,
   (ii) the diminishing balance method at 40% per annum applied on a full year basis, and
   (iii) the units of output method.
(b) Suppose that during the financial year ended 31 December 2007 the machine was used for only 1,500 hours before being sold for £80,000 on 30 June.
   Assuming that the business has chosen to apply the straight line method on a month for month basis, show the following accounts for 2007 only:
   (i)   the machine account,
   (ii) the provision for depreciation – machine account, and
   (iii) the assets disposals account.

(*Association of Accounting Technicians*)

25.21A   On 1 January 2001 a business purchased a laser printer for £1,800. The printer has an estimated life of 4 years after which it will have no residual value.
   It is expected that the output from the printer will be:

Year	Sheets printed
2001	35,000
2002	45,000
2003	45,000
2004	55,000
	180,000

Required:
(a) Calculate the annual depreciation charges for 2001, 2002, 2003 and 2004 on the laser printer on the following bases:
   (i)   the straight line basis,
   (ii) the diminishing balance method at 60% per annum, and
   (iii) the units of output method.

   Note: Your workings should be to the nearest £.

(b) Suppose that in 2004 the laser printer were to be sold on 1 July for £200 and that the business had chosen to depreciate it at 60% per annum using the diminishing balance method applied on a month for month basis.
   Reconstruct the following accounts for 2004 only:
   (i)   the laser printer account,
   (ii) the provision for depreciation – laser printer account, and
   (iii) the assets disposals account.

(*Association of Accounting Technicians*)

You can find a range of additional self-test questions, as well as material to help you with your studies, on the website that accompanies this book at **www.pearsoned.co.uk/wood**

Accruals and prepayments and other adjustments for financial statements

Learning objectives

After you have studied this chapter, you should be able to:

● adjust expense accounts for accruals and prepayments
● adjust revenue accounts for amounts owing
● show accruals, prepayments and revenue debtors in the balance sheet
● ascertain the amounts of expense and revenue items to be shown in the profit and loss account after making adjustments for accruals and prepayments
● make the necessary end of period adjustments relating to drawings that have not yet been entered in the books
● explain what an extended trial balance is and describe what it looks like
● prepare accrual and prepayment entries to the accounts using two different methods

Introduction

In this chapter, you'll continue to learn about adjustments made to the ledger accounts at the end of a period. You'll learn how to make the appropriate entries in the accounts for outstanding balances on expense and income accounts and make the appropriate entries in the profit and loss account and balance sheet.

26.1 Financial statements so far

The trading and profit and loss accounts you have looked at so far have taken the sales for a period and deducted all the expenses for that period, the result being a net profit or a net loss.

Up to this part of the book it has always been assumed that the expenses incurred belong to the period of the trading and profit and loss account when they took place. That is, if the trading and profit and loss account for the year ending 31 December 2008 was being prepared, then the rent paid as shown in the trial balance was all treated as relating to 2008. There was no rent owing at the beginning of 2008 nor any owing at the end of 2008, nor had any rent been paid in advance relating to 2009.

This was done to make your first meeting with financial statements as straight forward as possible.

The amounts owing for expenses could be called expense creditors, expenses owing or accrued expenses. However, we'll use the term 'accruals'. They represent *very* current liabilities – they will have to be paid in the very near future.

The items prepaid could be called prepaid expenses or payments in advance, but we'll call them 'prepayments'. Similarly to accruals, they represent *very* current assets as they should be received very soon.

Activity 26.2 From your knowledge of accounting, how should all the expense account debit and credit balances appear in the balance sheet – as one debit entry and one credit entry or as a separate entry for each item? Why?

Activity 26.3
(a) where in the current asset sequence do you place prepayments?
(b) where in the current liability sequence do you place accruals?
(c) why?

Amounts owing for rents receivable or other revenue owing are a special case. If you look back at the T-account in Section 26.5, you'll see that they are described as 'accrued'. However, they are not accrued expenses, as they represent amounts receivable. They are, therefore, **accrued income**.

Activity 26.4 Where do you think these items of accrued income go in the balance sheet?

The part of the balance sheet in respect of the accounts so far seen in this chapter is therefore:

Balance Sheet as at 31 December 2008 (extract)

	£	£	£
Current assets			
Stock		xxx	
Accrued income		450	
Prepayments (400 + 210)		610	
Bank		xxx	
Cash		xxx	
		x,xxx	
Less Current liabilities			
Trade creditors	xxx		
Accrued expenses	1,000		
		(x,xxx)	
Net current assets			x,xxx

26.7 Expenses and revenue accounts covering more than one period

So far we've only looked at accounts where there were closing accruals or prepayments. In real life, you will also expect to see some opening accruals and prepayments, such as is shown in the final version of the rent receivable account in Section 26.5. This is something that students are often asked to deal with in examinations as it tests their knowledge and ability to distinguish the treatment of these items at the beginning and end of a period. Typically, they may be asked to draw up an expense or revenue account for a full year which has amounts owing or prepaid at both the beginning and end of the year. We can now see how this is done.

Example A

The following details are available:

(A) On 31 December 2004, three months' rent amounting to a total of £3,000 was owing.
(B) The rent chargeable per year was £12,000.
(C) The following rent payments were made in the year 2008:
   6 January £3,000; 4 April £3,000; 7 July £3,000; 18 October £3,000.
(D) The final three months' rent for 2008 is still owing.

Now we can look at the completed rent account. The letters (A) to (D) give reference to the details above.

Rent

2008				£	2008				£
Jan	6	Bank	(C)	3,000	Jan	1	Accrued b/d	(A)	3,000
Apr	4	Bank	(C)	3,000	Dec	31	Profit and loss	(B)	12,000
Jul	7	Bank	(C)	3,000					
Oct	18	Bank	(C)	3,000					
Dec	**31**	**Accrued c/d**	(D)	3,000					
				15,000					15,000
					2009				
					Jan	1	Accrued b/d		3,000

Example B

The following details are available:

(A) On 31 December 2004, packing materials in hand amounted to £1,850.
(B) During the year to 31 December 2008, we paid £27,480 for packing materials.
(C) There were no stocks of packing materials on 31 December 2008.
(D) On 31 December 2008, we still owed £2,750 for packing materials already received and used.

The packing materials account will appear as:

Packing Materials

2008				£	2008			£
Jan	1	Stocks b/d	(A)	1,850	Dec	31	Profit and loss	32,080
Dec	31	Bank	(B)	27,480				
	31	Owing c/d	(D)	2,750				
				32,080				32,080
					2009			
					Jan	1	Owing b/d	2,750

The figure of £32,080 is the difference on the account, and is transferred to the profit and loss account.
   We can prove it is correct:

	£	£
Stock at start of year		1,850
Add Bought and used:		
Paid for	27,480	
Still owed for	2,750	
Cost of packing materials bought and used in the year		30,230
Cost of packing materials used in the year		32,080

hairdressing, chimney sweeping, piano tuning, and banks, football clubs, health clubs, gyms, and leisure centres.

As they do not deal in 'goods' there is no point in their attempting to draw up trading accounts. While it is quite possible for, say, a dentist to treat depreciation on equipment, the costs of materials consumed, and the dental assistant's salary as deductions from income in order to arrive at a figure for gross profit, such information is likely to be of little benefit in terms of decision-making. They will, however, prepare a profit and loss account (containing only the items that pass through the profit and loss account in the ledger) and a balance sheet.

The first item in the profit and loss account will be the revenue which might be called 'work done', 'fees', 'charges', 'accounts rendered', 'takings', etc., depending on the nature of the organisation. Any other items of income will be added, e.g. rent receivable, and then the expenses will be listed and deducted to arrive at a net profit or net loss.

An example of the profit and loss account of a solicitor might be as per Exhibit 26.1:

Exhibit 26.1

J Plunkett, Solicitor
Profit and Loss Account for the year ending 31 December 2008

	£	£
Revenue:		
Fees charged		87,500
Insurance commissions		1,300
		88,800
Less Expenses:		
Wages and salaries	29,470	
Rent and rates	11,290	
Office expenses	3,140	
Motor expenses	2,115	
General expenses	1,975	
Depreciation	2,720	
		(50,710)
Net profit		38,090

Other than for the descriptions given in the revenue section, it doesn't look very different from the ones you've prepared for traders. In effect, if you can prepare a trading and profit and loss account for a trader, you can do so for a service organisation. You just need to remember that it will contain no trading account items and that the income will need to be appropriately described.

26.11 Extended trial balances

Instead of drafting a set of financial statements in the way shown so far in this textbook, you could prepare them using an 'extended trial balance', or 'worksheet'. It can be very useful when there are a large number of adjustments to be made. Professional accountants use them a lot for that very reason.

Extended trial balances are usually drawn up on specially preprinted types of stationery with suitable vertical columns printed across the page. You start with the trial balance extracted from the ledgers and then enter adjustments in the columns to the right. Columns for the trading account, the profit and loss account, and the balance sheet then follow.

Exhibit 26.2 shows an example of the extended trial balance that could have been drawn up as an answer to Review question 26.11. Once you have attempted the question yourself, compare your answer to the one shown in Exhibit 26.2. The gross profits and net profits are the same in each case; it is simply the method of displaying the information that is different.

Exhibit 26.2

JOHN BROWN WORKSHEET

See Review question 26.11

	Trial Balance 1 Dr	Trial Balance 2 Cr	Adjustments 3 Dr	Adjustments 4 Cr	Trading Account 5 Dr	Trading Account 6 Cr	Profit and Loss Account 7 Dr	Profit and Loss Account 8 Cr	Balance Sheet 9 Dr	Balance Sheet 10 Cr
Sales		400,000				400,000				
Purchases	350,000				350,000					
Sales returns	5,000				5,000					
Purchases returns		6,200				6,200				
Stock 1.1.2007	100,000				100,000					
Stock 31.12.2007 – Cost of goods sold				120,000 (i)		120,000				
Provision for doubtful debts		800		180 (iv)						980
Wages and salaries	30,000		5,000 (ii)				35,000			
Rates	6,000			500 (iii)			5,500			
Telephone	1,000		220 (v)				1,220			
Shop fittings	40,000			4,000 (vi)					36,000	
Van	30,000			6,000 (vi)					24,000	
Debtors	9,800								9,800	
Creditors		7,000								7,000
Bad debts	200						200			
Capital		179,000								179,000
Bank	3,000								3,000	
Drawings	18,000								18,000	
	593,000	593,000								
Stock 31.12.2007 – Asset			120,000 (i)						120,000	
Accrued expenses				5,000 (ii)						5,000
				220 (v)						220
Provision for doubtful debts – change			180 (iv)				180			
Prepaid expenses			500 (iii)						500	
Depreciation shop fittings			4,000 (vi)				4,000			
Depreciation van			6,000 (vi)				6,000			
			135,900	135,900						
Gross profit (balancing figure)					71,200			71,200		
					526,200	526,200				
Net profit (balancing figure)							19,100			19,100
							71,200	71,200	211,300	211,300

If you were an accountant, the financial statements you prepare and give to the owner and to anyone else who was an interested party, such as the Inspector of Taxes or the bank, would not be in the style of an extended trial balance. Instead, having completed the extended trial balance, the figures for the trading account, profit and loss account, and balance sheet would be transferred to the financial statements prepared using the conventional style of presentation.

To provide such special stationery in an examination is unusual, though it has been known to happen. In addition, for students to draw up an extended trial balance from scratch could be very time-consuming. Therefore, it is very rare for examiners to ask for one to be prepared from scratch. However, the examiner may ask you something about extended trial balances (or worksheets) or provide a partially completed one to work on, if this topic is included in the syllabus. You should note, however, that nowadays spreadsheets are often used to produce financial statements in this way. If your course includes use of spreadsheets to prepare financial statements, you are more likely to be asked to prepare an extended trial balance in your examination or as part of your assessed coursework.

26.12 Definition of accounting

In Chapter 1, you were given a definition of bookkeeping as being concerned with the work of entering information into accounting records and afterwards maintaining such records properly. This definition does not need to be amended.

However, **accounting** was not fully defined in Chapter 1. It would probably not have meant much to you at that stage in your studies. The following is a commonly used definition: *'The process of identifying, measuring, and communicating economic information to permit informed judgements and decisions by users of the information.'*

26.13 An alternative way to record accruals and prepayments

After learning in Chapter 25 that there was a second commonly used way to record provisions for depreciation, it will come as no surprise to you to learn that there is a second commonly used way to record accruals and prepayments. Just as with the two-stage method of recording depreciation provisions, the alternative way to record accruals and prepayments requires that you create additional ledger accounts. You open an accruals account and a prepayments account and post any balances on expense accounts at the period end to the appropriate one of the two new accounts.

The balance carried down in an expense account under the method you learnt earlier in this chapter is described as either 'accrued c/d' or 'prepaid c/d'. Under the alternative method, there would be no balance in the expense account after the double entry to the accruals account or prepayments account. Instead, there will be a balance on these two accounts which is then entered in the balance sheet in exactly the same way as you did under the other method.

At the start of the next period, you reverse the entry by crediting the prepayments account and debiting each of the expense accounts that had debit balances. Similarly, the accruals account is debited and the expense accounts that had credit balances are credited with the appropriate amounts.

For example, in the insurance account from Section 26.4, the entries in the insurance account were:

Insurance

2008			£	2008				£
Feb	28	Bank	210	Dec	31	Profit and loss		840
Aug	31	Bank	420		31	Prepaid c/d		210
Nov	18	Bank	420					
			1,050					1,050
2009								
Jan	1	Prepaid b/d	210					

The same information if a prepayments account were used would be entered:

Insurance

2008			£	2008			£
Feb	28	Bank	210	Dec	31	Profit and loss	840
Aug	31	Bank	420			Prepayments	210
Nov	18	Bank	420				
			1,050				1,050

Prepayments

2008			£	2008			£
Dec	31	Insurance	210	Dec	31	Balance c/d	210
2009							
Jan	1	Balance b/d	210				

Then, once the relevant date had been extracted for the financial statements, the prepayment is reversed back to the insurance account:

Insurance

2008			£	2008			£
Feb	28	Bank	210	Dec	31	Profit and loss	840
Aug	31	Bank	420			Prepayments	210
Nov	18	Bank	420				
			1,050				1,050
2009							
Jan	1	Prepayments	210				

Prepayments

2008			£	2008			£
Dec	31	Insurance	210	Dec	31	Balance c/d	210
2009				2009			
Jan	1	Balance b/d	210	Jan	1	Insurance	210

In reality, it doesn't matter which of these two methods you use. Examiners will accept them both unless they specifically ask for one of them to be used. Your teacher or lecturer will know whether this is likely to happen. Follow the guidance of your teacher or lecturer and use whichever method he or she indicates is more appropriate.

In order not to confuse things by switching back and forth between the two methods, all examples of accruals and prepayments and all questions involving accruals and prepayments in the rest of this textbook will use the first method that has been covered in detail in this chapter. Should you be using the second method, as you will have seen above, it is very obvious what the equivalent entries would be when you look at examples prepared using the method adopted in this textbook.

Learning outcomes

You should now have learnt:

1 That adjustments are needed so that the expenses and income shown in the financial statements equal the expenses incurred in the period and the revenue that has arisen in the period.

2 That the balances relating to the adjustments will be shown on the balance sheet at the end of the period as current assets and current liabilities.

3 That goods taken for the owner's own use without anything being recorded in the books will necessitate a transfer from purchases to the drawings account, plus an adjustment for VAT if appropriate.

4 How to record appropriate entries in the accounts and financial statements at the end of a period for accrued expenses, prepaid expenses, accrued income, and drawings.

5 That private expenses should not be charged as an expense in the trading and profit and loss accounts, but should be charged to the drawings account.

6 That an extended trial balance is an alternative way of arriving at the figures to be included in the financial statements.

7 That there are two common ways to prepare accruals and prepayments.

Answers to activities

26.1 Don't worry if you didn't know what names to give the accounts other than the rent account. What is important is that you thought about it and that you knew which side the entries should be in the rent account.

(a) *Dr* Rent account £1,000   *Cr* Accruals account £1,000
(b) *Dr* Prepayments account £500   *Cr* Rent account £500

Note how the two entries in the rent account are on opposite sides. The £200 rent owing at the end of the year is an expense that has not yet been entered in the books, but it must be as it relates to the current year. The £100 paid in advance for next year is not an expense of the current year, so you need to reduce the amount you have currently in the rent account so that the correct expense will be included in the profit and loss account. The accruals account is similar to a creditor's account, but it is used for expenses unpaid at the year end. Similarly, the prepayments account is like a debtor's account, but it is used to record amounts paid for expenses in advance of the accounting period in which the benefit (i.e. what was paid for) is received.

26.2 All the debit entries should be added together and shown as one entry called 'prepayments' within current assets. Similarly, all the credit entries should be added together and shown as one entry called 'accruals' under current liabilities. This is done so as to minimise the clutter in the balance sheet while providing enough information for anyone looking at the financial statement to be able to identify the figure for accruals and the figure for prepayments.

26.3 (a) between debtors and bank
(b) between creditors and bank overdraft
(c) their degree of liquidity.

26.4 They are usually added to debtors. This is because these represent a regular source of income and, even though the income has nothing to do with the goods or services that form the main activity of the business, they are in every other sense another form of customer account. It makes sense, therefore, to include them in the debtor balance shown in the balance sheet.

26.5

	£
Rates due during the year	4,000
Add: Rates accrued at the start of the year	400
	4,400
Less: Rates paid during the year	(5,000)
Rates prepaid at the end of the year	(600)

Review questions

26.1 The financial year of L Pacioli ended on 31 December 2007. Show the ledger accounts for the following items including the balance transferred to the necessary part of the financial statements, also the balances carried down to 2008:

(a) Motor expenses: Paid in 2007 £620; Owing at 31 December 2007 £410.
(b) Insurance: Paid in 2007 £730; Prepaid as at 31 December 2007 £90.   2006
(c) Stationery: Paid during 2007 £410; Owing as at 31 December 2009 £170; Owing as at 31 December 2008 £320. ↘2007
(d) Business rates: Paid during 2007 £1,840; Prepaid as at 31 December 2009 £80; Prepaid as at 31 December 2007 £60.   2006
(e) Pacioli sub-lets part of the premises. He receives £1,600 during the year ended 31 December 2007. Robb, the tenant, owed Pacioli £200 on 31 December 2009 and £220 on 31 December 2007.

26.2A W Hope's year ended on 30 June 2008. Write up the ledger accounts, showing the transfers to the financial statements and the balances carried down to the next year for the following:

(a) Stationery: Paid for the year to 30 June 2008 £240; Inventory of stationery at 30 June 2007 £60; at 30 June 2008 £95.
(b) General expenses: Paid for the year to 30 June 2008 £470; Owing at 30 June 2007 £32; Owing at 30 June 2008 £60.
(c) Rent and business rates (combined account): Paid in the year to 30 June 2008 £5,410; Rent owing at 30 June 2007 £220; Rent paid in advance at 30 June 2008 £370; Business rates owing 30 June 2007 £191; Business rates owing 30 June 2008 £393.
(d) Motor expenses: Paid in the year to 30 June 2008 £1,410; Owing as at 30 June 2007 £92; Owing as at 30 June 2008 £67.
(e) Hope earns commission from the sales of one item. Received for the year to 30 June 2008 £1,100; Owing at 30 June 2007 £50; Owing at 30 June 2008 £82.

26.3 On 1 January 2009 the following balances, among others, stood in the books of G Pierce, a sole trader:

(a) Business rates, £340 (Dr);
(b) Packing materials, £610 (Dr).

During the year ended 31 December 2009 the information related to these two accounts is as follows:

(i)   Business rates of £2,400 were paid to cover the period 1 April 2009 to 31 March 2010;
(ii) £4,300 was paid for packing materials bought;
(iii) £360 was owing on 31 December 2009 in respect of packing materials bought on credit;
(iv) Old materials amounting to £94 were sold as scrap for cash;
(v)   Closing stock of packing materials was valued at £770.

You are required to write up the two accounts showing the appropriate amounts transferred to the Profit and Loss Account at 31 December 2009, the end of the financial year of the trader.

Note: Individual accounts are not opened for creditors for packing materials bought on credit.

→

26.4A On 1 January 2009 the following balances, among others, stood in the books of B Baxter:

(a) Lighting and heating, (Dr) £192.
(b) Insurance, (Dr) £1,410.

During the year ended 31 December 2009 the information related to these two accounts is as follows:

(i) Fire insurance, £1,164 covering the year ended 31 May 2007 was paid.
(ii) General insurance, £1,464 covering the year ended 31 July 2007 was paid.
(iii) An insurance rebate of £82 was received on 30 June 2009.
(iv) Electricity bills of £1,300 were paid.
(v) An electricity bill of £162 for December 2009 was unpaid as on 31 December 2009.
(vi) Oil bills of £810 were paid.
(vii) Stock of oil as on 31 December 2009 was £205.

You are required to write up the accounts for lighting and heating, and for insurance, for the year to 31 December 2009. Carry forward necessary balances to 2007.

26.5 Three of the accounts in the ledger of Charlotte Williams indicated the following balances at 1 January 2010:

Insurance paid in advance £562;
Wages outstanding £306;
Rent receivable, received in advance £36.

During 2010 Charlotte:

Paid for insurance £1,019, by bank standing order;
Paid £15,000 wages, in cash;
Received £2,600 rent, by cheque, from the tenant.

At 31 December 2010, insurance prepaid was £345. On the same day rent receivable in arrears was £105 and wages accrued amounted to £419.

(a) Prepare the insurance, wages and rent receivable accounts for the year ended 31 December 2010, showing the year end transfers and the balances brought down.
(b) Prepare the profit and loss account extract showing clearly the amounts transferred from each of the above accounts for the year ending 31 December 2010.
(c) Explain the effects on the financial statements of accounting for (i) expenses accrued and (ii) income received in advance at year end.
(d) What are the purposes of accounting for (i) expenses accrued and (ii) income received in advance at year end?

(*Edexcel Foundation, London Examinations: GCSE*)

26.6A The two accounts below were taken from the books of a retailer at the end of his financial year, 31 December 2007.

Insurance Account

Dr			£				Cr £
2007				2007			
Jan	1	Balance	80	Dec	31	Profit and loss	530
Jan–Dec		Bank	540	Dec	31	Balance c/d	90
			620				620
2008							
Jan	1	Balance b/d	90				

Rent Receivable Account

Dr						Cr
2007		£	2007			£
Dec 31	Profit and loss	885	Jan 1	Balance		60
Dec 31	Balance c/d	75	Jan–Dec	Bank		900
		960				960
			2008			
			Jan 1	Balance b/d		75

Required:
Answers to the following questions.

1 What type of account is the insurance account?
2 What type of account is the rent receivable account?
3 In which subdivision of the ledger will these accounts be found?
4 Under which heading will the closing balance of the insurance account be found on the balance sheet?
5 Under which heading will the closing balance of the rent receivable account be found on the balance sheet?
6 In which subsidiary book (book of prime entry) will the entries transferring amounts to the profit and loss account be found?
7 Which document will be the source of information for the entry in the insurance account 'bank £540'?
8 Which document will be the source of information for the entry in the rent receivable account 'bank £900'?
9 What amount for insurance will appear in the trial balance dated 31 December 2007 prepared prior to the preparation of financial statements?
10 What amount for rent receivable will appear in the trial balance dated 31 December 2007 prepared prior to the preparation of financial statements?
11 If the adjustment in the insurance account for £90 on 31 December had been overlooked, would the net profit have been under- or overstated and by how much?
12 If the adjustment in the rent receivable account for £75 on 31 December had been overlooked, would the net profit have been under- or overstated and by how much?

(*Southern Examining Group: GCSE*)

26.7A The owner of a small business selling and repairing cars which you patronise has just received a copy of his accounts for the current year.

He is rather baffled by some of the items and as he regards you as a financial expert, he has asked you to explain certain points of difficulty to him. This you have readily agreed to do. His questions are as follows:

(a) What is meant by the term 'assets'? My mechanical knowledge and skill is an asset to the business but it does not seem to have been included.
(b) The house I live in cost £130,000 five years ago and is now worth £160,000, but that is not included either.
(c) What is the difference between 'fixed assets' and 'current assets'?
(d) Why do amounts for 'vehicles' appear under both fixed asset and current asset headings?
(e) Why is the 'bank and cash' figure in the balance sheet different from the profit for the year shown in the profit and loss account?
(f) I see the profit and loss account has been charged with depreciation on equipment etc. I bought all these things several years ago and paid for them in cash. Does this mean that I am being charged for them again?

Required:
Answer each of his questions in terms which he will be able to understand.

(*Association of Chartered Certified Accountants*)

→ **26.8** The following trial balance was extracted from the books of R Giggs at the close of business on 28 February 2007.

	Dr £	Cr £
Purchases and sales	92,800	157,165
Cash at bank	4,100	
Cash in hand	324	
Capital account 1 March 2006		11,400
Drawings	17,100	
Office furniture	2,900	
Rent	3,400 − 230	
Wages and salaries	31,400 + 340	
Discounts	820	160
Debtors and creditors	12,316	5,245
Stock 1 March 2006	4,120	
Provision for doubtful debts 1 March 2006		405 + 91
Delivery van	3,750	
Van running costs	615 + 72	
Bad debts written off	730 + 91	
	174,375	174,375

Notes:
(a) Stock 28 February 2007 £2,400. − *closing Stock.*
(b) Wages and salaries accrued at 28 February 2007 £340. *Accrual in BS. + Adjust →*
(c) Rent prepaid at 28 February 2007 £230. − *Prepayment in bs. + Adjust −*
(d) Van running costs owing at 28 February 2007 £72. *Accrual + Adjust*
(e) Increase the provision for doubtful debts by £91.
(f) Provide for depreciation as follows: Office furniture £380; Delivery van £1,250.

Required:
Draw up the trading and profit and loss account for the year ending 28 February 2007 together with a balance sheet as at 28 February 2007.

26.9 The trial balance for a small business at 31 August 2008 is as follows:

	£	£
Stock 1 September 2007	8,200	
Purchases and Sales	26,000	40,900
Rent	4,400	
Business rates	1,600	
Sundry expenses	340	
Motor vehicle at cost	9,000	
Debtors and creditors	1,160	2,100
Bank	1,500	
Provision for depreciation on motor vehicle		1,200
Capital at 1 September 2007		19,700
Drawings	11,700	
	63,900	63,900

At 31 August 2008 there was:

● Stock valued at cost prices £9,100
● Accrued rent of £400
● Prepaid business rates of £300
● The motor vehicle is to be depreciated at 20% of cost

Required:
1 The adjustments to the ledger accounts for rent and business rates for the year to 31 August 2008.
2 A trading profit and loss account for the year ending 31 August 2008, together with a balance sheet as at that date.

26.10A J Wright, a sole trader, extracted the following trial balance from his books at the close of business on 31 March 2009:

	Dr £	Cr £
Purchases and sales	61,420	127,245
Stock 1 April 2008	7,940	
Capital 1 April 2008		25,200
Bank overdraft		2,490
Cash	140	
Discounts	2,480	62
Returns inwards	3,486	
Returns outwards		1,356
Carriage outwards	3,210	
Rent and insurance	8,870	
Provision for doubtful debts		630
Fixtures and fittings	1,900	
Van	5,600	
Debtors and creditors	12,418	11,400
Drawings	21,400	
Wages and salaries	39,200	
General office expenses	319	
	168,383	168,383

Notes:
(a) Stock 31 March 2009 £6,805.
(b) Wages and salaries accrued at 31 March 2009 £3,500; Office expenses owing £16.
(c) Rent prepaid 31 March 2009 £600.
(d) Increase the provision for doubtful debts by £110 to £740.
(e) Provide for depreciation as follows: Fixtures and fittings £190; Van £1,400.

Required:
Prepare the trading and profit and loss accounts for the year ending 31 March 2009 together with a balance sheet as at that date.

26.11 This question also relates to extended trial balances (see Exhibit 26.2)
From the following trial balance of John Brown, store owner, prepare a trading account and profit and loss account for the year ending 31 December 2007, and a balance sheet as at that date, taking into consideration the adjustments shown below:

Trial Balance as at 31 December 2007

	Dr £	Cr £
Sales		400,000
Purchases	350,000	
Sales returns	5,000	
Purchases returns		6,200
Opening stock at 1 January 2007	100,000	
Provision for doubtful debts		800
Wages and salaries	30,000	
Rates	6,000	
Telephone	1,000	
Shop fittings at cost	40,000	
Van at cost	30,000	
Debtors and creditors	9,800	7,000
Bad debts	200	
Capital		179,000
Bank balance	3,000	
Drawings	18,000	
	593,000	593,000

➡ (i)   Closing stock at 31 December 2007 £120,000.
(ii) Accrued wages £5,000.
(iii) Rates prepaid £500.
(iv) The provision for doubtful debts to be increased to 10 per cent of debtors.
(v) Telephone account outstanding £220.
(vi) Depreciate shop fittings at 10 per cent per annum, and van at 20 per cent per annum, on cost.

26.12A The following trial balance has been extracted from the ledger of Mr Yousef, a sole trader.

Trial Balance as at 31 May 2009

	Dr £	Cr £
Sales		138,078
Purchases	82,350	
Carriage	5,144	
Drawings	7,800	
Rent, rates and insurance	6,622	
Postage and stationery	3,001	
Advertising	1,330	
Salaries and wages	26,420	
Bad debts	877	
Provision for doubtful debts		130
Debtors	12,120	
Creditors		6,471
Cash in hand	177	
Cash at bank	1,002	
Stock as at 1 June 2008	11,927	
Equipment		
at cost	58,000	
accumulated depreciation		19,000
Capital		53,091
	216,770	216,770

The following additional information as at 31 May 2009 is available:

(a) Rent is accrued by £210.
(b) Rates have been prepaid by £880.
(c) £2,211 of carriage represents carriage inwards on purchases.
(d) Equipment is to be depreciated at 15% per annum using the straight line method.
(e) The provision for doubtful debts to be increased by £40.
(f) Stock at the close of business has been valued at £13,551.

Required:
Prepare a trading and profit and loss account for the year ending 31 May 2009 and a balance sheet as at that date.

(Association of Accounting Technicians)

26.13 Mr Chai has been trading for some years as a wine merchant. The following list of balances has been extracted from his ledger as at 30 April 2007, the end of his most recent financial year.

	£
Capital	83,887
Sales	259,870
Trade creditors	19,840
Returns out	13,407
Provision for doubtful debts	512
Discounts allowed	2,306
Discounts received	1,750
Purchases	135,680
Returns inwards	5,624
Carriage outwards	4,562
Drawings	18,440
Carriage inwards	11,830
Rent, rates and insurance	25,973
Heating and lighting	11,010
Postage, stationery and telephone	2,410
Advertising	5,980
Salaries and wages	38,521
Bad debts	2,008
Cash in hand	534
Cash at bank	4,440
Stock as at 1 May 2009	15,654
Trade debtors	24,500
Fixtures and fittings – at cost	120,740
Provision for depreciation on fixtures and fittings – as at 30 April 2007	63,020
Depreciation	12,074

The following additional information as at 30 April 2007 is available:

(a) Stock at the close of business was valued at £17,750.
(b) Insurances have been prepaid by £1,120.
(c) Heating and lighting is accrued by £1,360.
(d) Rates have been prepaid by £5,435.
(e) The provision for doubtful debts is to be adjusted so that it is 3% of trade debtors.

Required:
Prepare Mr Chai's trading and profit and loss account for the year ending 30 April 2007 and a balance sheet as at that date.

(*Association of Accounting Technicians*)

You can find a range of additional self-test questions, as well as material to help you with your studies, on the website that accompanies this book at **www.pearsoned.co.uk/wood**

27.6 Thomas Brown and Partners, a business of practising accountants, have several clients who are retail distributors of the Allgush Paint Spray guns.

The current price list of Gushing Sprayers Limited, manufacturers, quotes the following whole-sale prices for the Allgush Paint Spray guns:

    Grade A distributors   £500 each
    Grade B distributors   £560 each
    Grade C distributors   £600 each

The current normal retail price of the Allgush Paint Spray gun is £750.

Thomas Brown and Partners are currently advising some of their clients concerning the valuation of stock in trade of Allgush Paint Spray guns.

1   Charles Gray – Grade B distributor
    On 30 April 2009, 15 Allgush Paint Spray guns were in stock, including 1 gun which was slightly damaged and expected to sell at half the normal retail price. Charles Gray considers that this gun should remain in stock at cost price until it is sold.
        K. Peacock, a customer of Charles Gray, was expected to purchase a spray gun on 30 April 2009, but no agreement was reached owing to the customer being involved in a road accident and expected to remain in hospital until late May 2009.
        Charles Gray argues that he is entitled to regard this as a sale during the year ended 30 April 2009.

2   Jean Kim – Grade C distributor
    On 31 May 2009, 22 Allgush Paint Spray guns were in stock. Unfortunately Jean Kim's business is suffering a serious cash flow crisis. It is very doubtful that the business will survive and therefore a public auction of the stock in trade is likely. Reliable sources suggest that the spray guns may be auctioned for £510 each; auction fees and expenses are expected to total £300.
        Jean Kim has requested advice as to the basis upon which her stock should be valued at 31 May 2009.

3   Peter Fox – Grade A distributor
    Peter Fox now considers that stock valuations should be related to selling prices because of the growing uncertainties of the market for spray guns.
        Alternatively, Peter Fox has suggested that he uses the cost prices applicable to Grade C distributors as the basis for stock valuations – 'after all, this will establish consistency with Grade C distributors'.

Required:
A brief report to each of Charles Gray, Jean Kim and Peter Fox concerning the valuation of their stocks in trade.

Note: Answers should include references to appropriate accounting concepts.

(*Association of Accounting Technicians*)

27.7A Mary Smith commenced trading on 1 September 2009 as a distributor of the Straight Cut garden lawnmower, a relatively new product which is now becoming increasingly popular.

Upon commencing trading, Mary Smith transferred £7,000 from her personal savings to open a business bank account.

Mary Smith's purchases and sales of the Straight Cut garden lawnmower during the three months ended 30 November 2009 are as follows:

2009	Bought	Sold
September	12 machines at £384 each	–
October	8 machines at £450 each	4 machines at £560 each
November	16 machines at £489 each	20 machines at £680 each

Assume all purchases are made in the first half of the month and all sales are in the second half of the month.

At the end of October 2009, Mary Smith decided to take one Straight Cut garden lawnmower out of stock for cutting the lawn outside her showroom. It is estimated that this lawnmower will be used in Mary Smith's business for 8 years and have a nil estimated residual value. Mary Smith wishes to use the straight line basis of depreciation.

Additional information:

1 Overhead expenses paid during the three months ended 30 November 2009 amounted to £1,520.
2 There were no amounts prepaid on 30 November 2009, but sales commissions payable of 2½% of the gross profit on sales were accrued due on 30 November 2009.
3 Upon commencing trading, Mary Smith resigned a business appointment with a salary of £15,000 per annum.
4 Mary Smith is able to obtain interest of 10% per annum on her personal savings.
5 One of the lawnmowers not sold on 30 November 2009 has been damaged in the showroom and is to be repaired in December 2009 at a cost of £50 before being sold for an expected £400.

Note: Ignore taxation.

Required:
(a) Prepare, in as much detail as possible, Mary Smith's trading and profit and loss account for the quarter ending 30 November 2009 using:
   (i) the first in first out basis of stock valuation, and
   (ii) the last in first out basis of stock valuation.
(b) Using the results in (a) (i) above, prepare a statement comparing Mary Smith's income for the quarter ended 30 November 2009 with that for the quarter ended 31 August 2009.
(c) Give one advantage and one disadvantage of each of the bases of stock valuations used in (a) above.

(*Association of Accounting Technicians*)

27.8 'The idea that stock should be included in accounts at the lower of historical cost and net realisable value follows the prudence convention but not the consistency convention.'

Required:
(a) Do you agree with the quotation?
(b) Explain, with reasons, whether you think this idea (that stocks should be included in accounts at the lower of historical cost and net realisable value) is a useful one. Refer to at least two classes of user of financial accounting reports in your answer.

(*Association of Chartered Certified Accountants*)

27.9 After stocktaking for the year ended 31 May 2009 had taken place, the closing stock of Cobden Ltd was aggregated to a figure of £87,612.
   During the course of the audit which followed, the undernoted facts were discovered:

(a) Some goods stored outside had been included at their normal cost price of £570. They had, however, deteriorated and would require an estimated £120 to be spent to restore them to their original condition, after which they could be sold for £800.
(b) Some goods had been damaged and were now unsaleable. They could, however, be sold for £110 as spares after repairs estimated at £40 had been carried out. They had originally cost £200.
(c) One stock sheet had been over-added by £126 and another under-added by £72.
(d) Cobden Ltd had received goods costing £2,010 during the last week of May 2009 but, because the invoices did not arrive until June 2009, they have not been included in stock.
(e) A stock sheet total of £1,234 had been transferred to the summary sheet as £1,243.
(f) Invoices totalling £638 arrived during the last week of May 2009 (and were included in purchases and in creditors) but, because of transport delays, the goods did not arrive until late June 2009 and were not included in closing stock.
(g) Portable generators on hire from another company at a charge of £347 were included, at this figure, in stock.

→

(h) Free samples sent to Cobden Ltd by various suppliers had been included in stock at the catalogue price of £63.

(i) Goods costing £418 sent to customers on a sale or return basis had been included in stock by Cobden Ltd at their selling price, £602.

(j) Goods sent on a sale or return basis to Cobden Ltd had been included in stock at the amount payable (£267) if retained. No decision to retain had been made.

Required:
Using such of the above information as is relevant, prepare a schedule amending the stock figure as at 31 May 2009. State your reason for each amendment or for not making an amendment.

(*Association of Chartered Certified Accountants*)

27.10A Yuan Ltd has an accounting year ended 29 February 2008. Due to staff shortages, the stocktaking had not been undertaken until 9 March 2008 and the stock valued at this date is £100,600. This value was also used in the company draft accounts for the year ended 29 February 2008 which showed a net profit of £249,600 and a current asset total of £300,000. The selling price of goods is based on cost plus 25%.

During the auditing period, the following errors were discovered:

1 Sales invoices for goods dispatched to customers during the period 1–9 March 2008 amounted to £43,838 which include carriage on sales of 5%.

2 Goods costing £14,000 were delivered to the company during the period 1–9 March 2008.

3 During the period 1–9 March 2008, returns from customers at selling price were £4,170, and returns to suppliers amounted to £850.

4 The stock valuation of 9 March 2008 included the stock of the company's office cleaning materials. These materials had all been bought during February 2000 at a cost of £600.

5 Stock with a selling price of £1,650 had been borrowed by the marketing department on 27 February 2008 to be displayed at an exhibition from 28 February to 16 March. This had helped to attract orders of £27,400 for delivery in April 2008.

6 Stocks with a selling price of £800 were sent to a customer on sale or return basis on 14 February 2008. On 23 February 2008, the customer sold half of the consignment. This credit sale had not yet been recorded ini Yuan Ltd's accounts for the year ended 29 February 2008. On 9 March 2008, the remaining half of the consignment had not been returned to Yuan Ltd and the customer had not signified its acceptance.

7 On 3 March 2008, Yuan Ltd received a batch of free samples which had been included in the stock valuation at the list price of £20.

Required:
(a) Prepare a schedule amending the stock figure as at 29 February 2008.
(b) Calculate the revised net profit for the year ending 29 February 2008 and the correct value of current assets at that date.

You can find a range of additional self-test questions, as well as material to help you with your studies, on the website that accompanies this book at **www.pearsoned.co.uk/wood**

Bank reconciliation statements

Learning objectives

After you have studied this chapter, you should be able to:

- explain why bank reconciliations are prepared
- reconcile cash book balances with bank statement balances
- reconcile ledger accounts to suppliers' statements
- make the necessary entries in the accounts for dishonoured cheques

Introduction

In this chapter, you'll learn how to prepare a bank reconciliation statement and why you need to do this when a bank statement is received from the bank. You will also learn how to deal with dishonoured cheques in the ledger accounts.

28.1 Completing entries in the cash book

In the books of a business, funds paid into and out of the bank are entered into the bank columns of the cash book. At the same time, the bank will also be recording the flows of funds into and out of the business bank account.

If all the items entered in the cash book were the same as those entered in the records held by the bank, the balance on the business bank account as shown in the cash book and the balance on the account as shown by the bank's records would be the same.

Unfortunately, it isn't usually that simple, particularly in the case of a current account. There may be items paid into or out of the business bank account which have not been recorded in the cash book. And there may be items entered in the cash book that have not yet been entered in the bank's records of the account. To see if any of these things have happened, the cash book entries need to be compared to the record of the account held by the bank. Banks usually send a copy of that record, called a **bank statement**, to their customers on a regular basis, but a bank statement can be requested by a customer of the bank at any time.

Bank statements should *always* be checked against the cash book entries! (And you would be wise to do so yourself with your own bank account.)

Activity 28.1 What might cause the two balances to be different? Spend two minutes making a list.

2 **Direct Debits.** These are payments which have to be made, such as gas bills, electricity bills, telephone bills, rates, and insurance premiums. Instead of asking the bank to pay the money, as with standing orders, you give permission to the creditor to obtain the money directly from your bank account. This is particularly useful if the amounts payable may vary from time to time, as it is the creditor who changes the payments, not you. With standing orders, if the amount is ever to be changed, *you* have to inform the bank. With direct debits it is *the creditor* who informs the bank.

Just as with anything else omitted from the cash book, items of these types need to be included in the reconciliation and entered in the cash book before balancing it off at the end of the period.

28.6 Bank overdrafts

The adjustment needed to reconcile a bank overdraft according to the firm's books (shown by a credit balance in the cash book) with that shown in the bank's records are the same as those needed when the account is not overdrawn.

Exhibit 28.4 is of a cash book and a bank statement both showing an overdraft. Only the cheque for G Cumberbatch (A) £106 and the cheque paid to J Kelly (B) £63 need adjusting. Work through the reconciliation statement and then read the note after it. Because the balance shown by the cash book is correct (and, therefore, the balance that will appear in the balance sheet), you can use the form of bank reconciliation statement shown in Section 28.2.

Exhibit 28.4

Cash Book

2008			£	2008				£
Dec	5	I Howe	308	Dec	1	Balance b/d		709
	24	L Mason	120		9	P Davies		140
	29	K King	124		27	J Kelly	(B)	63
	31	G Cumberbatch (A)	106		29	United Trust		77
	31	Balance c/d	380		31	Bank charges		49
			1,038					1,038

Bank Statement

2008			Dr £	Cr £	Balance £
Dec	1	Balance b/d			709 O/D
	5	Cheque		308	401 O/D
	14	P Davies	140		541 O/D
	24	Cheque		120	421 O/D
	29	K King: Credit transfer		124	297 O/D
	29	United Trust: Standing order	77		374 O/D
	31	Bank charges	49		423 O/D

Note: An overdraft is often shown with the letters 'O/D' following the amount. Alternatively, some banks use 'Dr' and 'Cr' after every balance entry to indicate whether the account is overdrawn.

Activity 28.4 Will the bank statement show 'Dr' or 'Cr' if an account is overdrawn?

Bank Reconciliation Statement as at 31 December 2008

	£
Overdraft as per cash book	(380)
Add Unpresented cheque	63
	(317)
Less Bank lodgement not on bank statement	(106)
Overdraft per bank statement	(423)

Note: You may find it confusing looking at this bank reconciliation statement because the opening entry is an overdraft, i.e. a negative number. Don't be, the adjusting entries are the same as those you make when it is positive:

	£
Balance/overdraft per cash book	xxxx
Adjustments	
Unpresented cheque	Plus
Bank lodgement not on bank statement	Less
Balance/overdraft per bank statement	xxxx

28.7 Dishonoured cheques

When a cheque is received from a customer and paid into the bank, it is recorded on the debit side of the cash book. It is also shown on the bank statement as a deposit increasing the balance on the account. However, at a later date it may be found that the customer's bank will not pay the amount due on the cheque. The customer's bank has failed to 'honour' the cheque. The cheque is described as a **dishonoured cheque**.

There are several possible reasons for this. Imagine that K King paid a business with a cheque for £5,000 on 20 May 2009. The business deposits it at the bank but, a few days later, the bank contacts the business and informs it that the cheque has been dishonoured. Typical reasons are:

1 King had put £5,000 in figures on the cheque, but had written it in words as 'five thousand *five hundred* pounds'. A new cheque correctly completed will need to be provided by King.
2 Normally cheques are considered *stale* six months after the date on the cheque. In other words, banks will not honour cheques that are more than six months old. If King had put the year 2008 on the cheque instead of 2009, then King's bank would dishonour the cheque and King would need to be asked for a correctly dated replacement.
3 King simply did not have sufficient funds in her bank account. Suppose she had previously a balance of only £2,000 and yet she has made out a cheque for £5,000. Her bank has not allowed her an overdraft in order to honour the cheque. As a result, the cheque has been dishonoured. The bank inform the business that this has happened and the business would have to contact King, explain what has happened and ask for valid payment of the account.

In all of these cases, the bank would record the original entry in its records as being reversed. This is shown on the bank statement, for example, by the entry 'dishonoured cheque £5,000'. The business then makes the equivalent credit entry in the cash book while, at the same time, debiting King's account by the same amount.

When King originally paid the £5,000 the accounts in the ledger and cash book would have appeared as:

K King

2009		£	2009			£
May	1 Balance b/d	5,000	May	20	Bank	5,000

Bank Account

2009		£	
May 20	K King	5,000	

After recording the dishonoured cheque, the accounts would be:

K King

2009			£	2009			£
May 1	Balance b/d		5,000	May 20	Bank		5,000
May 25	**Bank: cheque dishonoured**		**5,000**				

Bank Account

2009			£	2009			£
May 20	K King		5,000	**May 25**	**K King: cheque dishonoured**		**5,000**

In other words, King is once again shown as owing the business £5,000.

Learning outcomes

You should now have learnt:

1 Why it is important to perform a bank reconciliation when a bank statement is received.

2 That a bank reconciliation statement should show whether or not errors have been made either in the bank columns of the cash book or on the bank statement.

3 That a bank reconciliation statement can be prepared either before or after updating the cash book with items omitted from it that are shown on the bank statement.

4 That a bank reconciliation statement prepared after updating the cash book with items omitted from it that are shown on the bank statement shows that you know why the bank statement balance is different from that shown in the cash book and balance sheet.

5 That a bank reconciliation statement prepared before updating the cash book with items omitted from it that are shown on the bank statement is reconciled from cash book to balance sheet amount and then to the bank statement. It shows the amount to be entered in the balance sheet and also shows that you know why the bank statement balance is different from the balances shown in the cash book and in the balance sheet.

6 That in the case of bank overdrafts, the reconciliation statement adjustments are the same as those shown when there is a positive bank balance, but the opening and closing balances are negative.

7 How to prepare a bank reconciliation statement *after* updating the cash book with items omitted from it that are shown on the bank statement.

8 How to prepare a bank reconciliation statement *before* updating the cash book with items omitted from it that are shown on the bank statement.

9 Why cheques may be dishonoured and what the effect is upon the bank balance.

10 How to make the appropriate entries to the accounts when a cheque is dishonoured.

Answers to activities

28.1 There is quite a long list of possible causes, including:

- a business may take a day or two to deposit some cheques that it has already entered in the cash book
- a cheque may take a few days to be entered in the account of the business held at the bank after it is deposited (because the bank won't recognise the amount received until a few days later, in case there is a problem with it)
- bank interest paid and bank charges often aren't known by a business until a bank statement is received
- bank interest received won't be known by a business until it receives a bank statement
- standing orders may not be written up in the cash book of the business until they are identified on the bank statement
- the amount of a direct debit is sometimes not known and so should not be entered in the cash book until it is confirmed how much was paid out of the bank account
- customers may pay their accounts by direct transfer from their bank account or by paying cash directly into the business bank account and the business may only learn of their having done so some time later
- there may have been an error made in the cash book entries
- the bank may have made an error in operating the account, such as adding funds to it instead of to the account of the person depositing the funds
- a cheque paid into the bank may have 'bounced' (i.e. there were insufficient funds in the writer of the cheque's bank account to make the payment).

28.2 It is wise to wait until receiving the bank statement before balancing off the bank account in the cash book at the end of the accounting period. In a manual accounting system, if a cash book is balanced on a regular basis, balancing off is usually done at the end of the time period selected and any additional entries are recorded along with the other entries made in the following day, week, month, or quarter. However, at the end of the accounting year, the balancing off is often done in pencil (so that financial statements can be drafted) and then done in ink after any missing entries and corrections of errors have been entered following receipt of the bank statement.

28.3 M Peck £200 and J Soames £470.

28.4 'Dr' indicates an overdraft. The customer is a debtor of the bank. In the customer's balance sheet, the overdraft is included in the current liabilities, indicating that the bank is a creditor. Always remember that a bank is looking at the relationship from the opposite side to the view seen by the customer.

Review questions

28.1 From the following, draw up a bank reconciliation statement from details as on 31 December 2006:

	£
Cash at bank as per bank column of the cash book	2,910
Unpresented cheques	730
Cheques received and paid into the bank, but not yet entered on the bank statement	560
Credit transfers entered as banked on the bank statement but not entered in the cash book	340
Cash at bank as per bank statement	3,420

28.2A Draw up a bank reconciliation statement, after writing the cash book up to date, ascertaining the balance on the bank statement, from the following as on 31 March 2009:

	£
Cash at bank as per bank column of the cash book (Dr)	2,740
Bankings made but not yet entered on bank statement	410
Bank charges on bank statement but not yet in cash book	32
Unpresented cheques W Shute	131
Standing order to Giffy Ltd entered on bank statement, but not in cash book	93
Credit transfer from B Barnes entered on bank statement, but not yet in cash book	201

28.3 The following are extracts from the cash book and the bank statement of F Perry.

You are required to:
(a) Write the cash book up to date, and state the new balance as on 31 December 2009, and
(b) Draw up a bank reconciliation statement as on 31 December 2009.

Cash Book

2009	Dr	£	2009	Cr	£
Dec	1	Balance b/d	3,419	Dec	8	B Young	462
	7	F Lamb	101		15	F Gray	21
	22	G Brock	44		28	T Errant	209
	31	W Terry ✓	319		31	Balance c/d	3,437
	31	S Miller ✓	246				
			4,129				4,129

Bank Statement

2009			Dr £	Cr £	Balance £
Dec	1	Balance b/d			3,419
	7	Cheque		101	3,520
	11	B Young	462		3,058
	20	F Gray	21		3,037
	22	Cheque		44	3,081
	31	Credit transfer: T Morris ✓		93	3,174
	31	Bank charges ✓	47		3,127

28.4A The bank columns in the cash book for June 2007 and the bank statement for that month for D Hogan are as follows:

Cash Book

2007	Dr	£	2007	Cr	£
Jun	1	Balance b/d	1,410	Jun	5	L Holmes	180
	7	J May	62		12	J Rebus	519
	16	T Wilson	75		16	T Silver	41
	28	F Slack	224		29	Blister Disco	22
	30	G Baker	582		30	Balance c/d	1,591
			2,353				2,353

Bank Statement

2007			Dr £	Cr £	Balance £
Jun	1	Balance b/d			1,410
	7	Cheque		62	1,472
	8	F Lane	180		1,292
	16	Cheque		75	1,367
	17	J Rebus	519		848
	18	T Silver	41		807
	28	Cheque		224	1,031
	29	SLM standing order	52		979
	30	Flynn: trader's credit		64	1,043
	30	Bank charges	43		1,000

You are required to:
(a) Write the cash book up to date to take the above into account, and then
(b) Draw up a bank reconciliation statement as on 30 June 2007.

28.5 Read the following and answer the questions below.

On 31 December 2008 the bank column of C Tench's cash book showed a debit balance of £1,500.
   The monthly bank statement written up to 31 December 2008 showed a credit balance of £2,950.
   On checking the cash book with the bank statement it was discovered that the following transactions had not been entered in the cash book:

   Dividends of £240 had been paid directly to the bank.
   A credit transfer – Revenue and Customs VAT refund of £260 – had been collected by the bank.
   Bank charges £30.
   A direct debit of £70 for the RAC subscription had been paid by the bank.
   A standing order of £200 for C Tench's loan repayment had been paid by the bank.
   C Tench's deposit account balance of £1,400 was transferred into his bank current account.

A further check revealed the following items:

Two cheques drawn in favour of T Cod £250 and F Haddock £290 had been entered in the cash book but had not been presented for payment.
Cash and cheques amounting to £690 had been paid into the bank on 31 December 2008 but were not credited by the bank until 2 January 2009.

(a) Starting with the debit balance of £1,500, bring the cash book (bank columns) up to date and then balance the bank account.
(b) Prepare a bank reconciliation statement as at 31 December 2008.

(Midland Examining Group: GCSE)

28.6A In the draft accounts for the year ended 31 October 2009 of Thomas P Lee, garage proprietor, the balance at bank according to the cash book was £894.68 in hand.

Subsequently the following discoveries were made:

(1) Cheque number 176276 dated 3 September 2009 for £310.84 in favour of G Lowe Limited has been correctly recorded in the bank statement, but included in the cash book payments as £301.84.
(2) Bank commission charged of £169.56 and bank interest charged of £109.10 have been entered in the bank statement on 23 October 2009, but not included in the cash book.
(3) The recently received bank statement shows that a cheque for £29.31 received from T Andrews and credited in the bank statements on 9 October 2009 has now been dishonoured and debited in the bank statement on 26 October 2009. The only entry in the cash book for this cheque records its receipt on 8 October 2009.
(4) Cheque number 177145 for £15.10 has been recorded twice as a credit in the cash book.
(5) Amounts received in the last few days of October 2009 totalling £1,895.60 and recorded in the cash book have not been included in the bank statements until 2 November 2009.
(6) Cheques paid according to the cash book during October 2009 and totalling £395.80 were not presented for payment to the bank until November 2009.
(7) Traders' credits totalling £210.10 have been credited in the bank statement on 26 October 2009, but not yet recorded in the cash book.
(8) A standing order payment of £15.00 on 17 October 2009 to Countryside Publications has been recorded in the bank statement but is not mentioned in the cash book.

Required:
(a) Prepare a computation of the balance at bank to be included in Thomas P Lee's balance sheet as at 31 October 2009.

(b) Prepare a bank reconciliation statement as at 31 October 2009 for Thomas P Lee.
(c) Briefly explain why it is necessary to prepare bank reconciliation statements at accounting year ends.

(*Association of Accounting Technicians*)

28.7 The bank statement for R Hood for the month of March 2006 is:

2006		Dr £	Cr £	Balance £
Mar	1 Balance			4,200 O/D
	8 T MacLeod	184		4,384 O/D
	16 Cheque		292	4,092 O/D
	20 W Milne	160		4,252 O/D
	21 Cheque		369	3,883 O/D
	31 G Frank: trader's credit		88	3,795 O/D
	31 TYF: standing order	32		3,827 O/D
	31 Bank charges	19		3,846 O/D

The cash book for March 2006 is:

2006	Dr	£	2006	Cr	£
Mar 16	G Philip	292	Mar 1	Balance b/d	4,200
21	J Forker	369	6	T MacLeod	184
31	S O'Hare	192	30	W Milne	160
31	Balance c/d	4,195	30	S Porter	504
		5,048			5,048

You are required to:
(a) Write the cash book up to date, and
(b) Draw up a bank reconciliation statement as on 31 March 2006.

28.8A The following is the cash book (bank columns) of F King for December 2007:

2007	Dr	£	2007	Cr	£
Dec 6	P Pan	230	Dec 1	Balance b/d	1,900
20	C Hook	265	10	J Lamb	304
31	W Britten	325	19	P Wilson	261
31	Balance c/d	1,682	29	K Coull	37
		2,502			2,502

The bank statement for the month is:

2007		Dr £	Cr £	Balance £
Dec	1 Balance			1,900 O/D
	6 Cheque		230	1,670 O/D
	13 J Lamb	304		1,974 O/D
	20 Cheque		265	1,709 O/D
	22 P Wilson	261		1,970 O/D
	30 Tox: standing order	94		2,064 O/D
	31 F Ray: trader's credit		102	1,962 O/D
	31 Bank charges	72		2,034 O/D

You are required to:
(a) Write the cash book up to date to take the necessary items into account, and
(b) Draw up a bank reconciliation statement as on 31 December 2007.

28.9 The following is a summary of a cash book as presented by George Ltd for the month of October:

	£		£
Receipts	1,469	Balance b/d	761
Balance c/d	554	Payments	1,262
	2,023		2,023

All receipts are banked and all payments are made by cheque.

On investigation you discover:

(1) Bank charges of £136 entered on the bank statement have not been entered in the cash book.
(2) Cheques drawn amounting to £267 had not been presented to the bank for payment.
(3) Cheques received totalling £762 had been entered in the cash book and paid into the bank, but had not been credited by the bank until 3 November.
(4) A cheque for £22 for sundries had been entered in the cash book as a receipt instead of as a payment.
(5) A cheque received from K Jones for £80 had been returned by the bank and marked 'No funds available'. No adjustment has been made in the cash book.
(6) A standing order for a business rates instalment of £150 on 30 October had not been entered in the cash book.
(7) All dividends received are credited directly to the bank account. During October amounts totalling £62 were credited by the bank but no entries were made in the cash book.
(8) A cheque drawn for £66 for stationery had been incorrectly entered in the cash book as £60.
(9) The balance brought forward in the cash book should have been £711, not £761.

Required:
(a) Show the adjustments required in the cash book.
(b) Prepare a bank reconciliation statement as at 31 October.

You can find a range of additional self-test questions, as well as material to help you with your studies, on the website that accompanies this book at **www.pearsoned.co.uk/wood**

Control accounts

29.1 The benefits of accounting controls

In any but the smallest business, the accounting information system (which you read about in Chapter 21) is set up so as to include controls that help ensure that errors are minimised and that nothing occurs that shouldn't, such as the cashier embezzling funds. One of the tasks undertaken by auditors is to check the various controls that are in place to ensure they are working satisfactorily and one of the things they will look out for is segregation of duties. So, for example, the same person will not both invoice customers and act as cashier when payment is received and, if someone claims reimbursement of an expense, it will be authorised for payment by someone else. Another form of control you've already learnt about involves whether or not customers are allowed to purchase goods on credit.

All these controls are 'organisational'. That is, they do not directly impose controls over the accounting data, nor do they ensure that accounting entries are correct. One control measure that does these things was covered in Chapter 28 – the process of bank reconciliation. In this chapter, we'll look at another type of accounting control which is used mainly in manual accounting systems, **control accounts**.

When all the accounts were kept in one ledger a trial balance could be drawn up as a test of the arithmetical accuracy of the accounts. If the trial balance totals disagree, the books of a small business could easily and quickly be checked so as to find the errors. Of course, as you know, even when the totals do agree, certain types of error may still have occurred, the nature of which makes it impossible for them to be detected in this way. Nevertheless, using a trial balance ensures that all the double entries appear, at least, to have been recorded correctly.

Activity 29.1 How do you find errors of the types that a trial balance cannot detect?

When a business has grown and the accounting work has been so divided up that there are several ledgers, any errors could be very difficult to find if a trial balance was the only device used to try to detect errors. Every item in every ledger may need to be checked just to find one error that caused the trial balance not to balance. What is required is a type of trial balance for each ledger, and this requirement is met by control accounts. A control account is a summary account that enables you to see at a glance whether the general ledger balance for the ledger to which that control account belongs agrees with the total of all the individual accounts held within that ledger.

If you use control accounts, only the ledgers whose control accounts do not balance need detailed checking to find errors.

29.2 Principle of control accounts

The principle on which the control account is based is simple and is as follows: if the opening balance of an account is known, together with information of the additions and deductions entered in the account, the closing balance can be calculated.

Applying this to a complete ledger, the total of opening balances together with the additions and deductions during the period should give the total of closing balances. This can be illustrated by reference to a sales ledger for entries for a month.

	£
Total of opening balances, 1 January 2006	3,000
Add Total of entries which have increased the balances	9,500
	12,500
Less Total of entries which have reduced the balances	(8,000)
Total of closing balances should be	4,500

Because totals are used, control accounts are sometimes known as 'total accounts'. Thus, a control account for a sales ledger could be known as either a '**sales ledger control account**' or as a '**total debtors account**'.

Similarly, a control account for a purchases ledger could be known either as a '**purchases ledger control account**' or as a '**total creditors account**'.

A control account is a memorandum account. It is not part of the double entry system. It will be prepared in either the general ledger or in the ledger to which it relates, i.e. the purchases ledger or the sales ledger.

A control account looks like any other T-account:

Sales Ledger Control

2006			£	2006			£
Jan	1	Balances b/d	x,xxx	Jan	31	Returns Inwards Day Book (total of all goods returned from debtors in the period)	xxx
	31	Sales day book (total of sales invoiced in the period)	xx,xxx		31	Cash book (total of all cash received from debtors in the period)	x,xxx
					31	Cash book (total of all cheques received from debtors in the period)	xx,xxx
					31	Balances c/d	x,xxx
			xx,xxx				xx,xxx

29.3 Information for control accounts

Exhibits 29.1 and 29.2 list from where information is obtained with which to draw up control accounts.

Exhibit 29.1

Sales Ledger Control	Source
1 Opening debtors	List of debtors balances drawn up at the end of the previous period
2 Credit sales	Total from the Sales Day Book
3 Returns inwards	Total of the Returns Inwards Day Book
4 Cheques received	Cash Book: bank column on received side. List extracted or the total of a special column for cheques which has been included in the Cash Book
5 Cash received	Cash Book: cash column on received side. List extracted or the total of a special column for cash which has been included in the Cash Book
6 Discounts allowed	Total of discounts allowed column in the Cash Book
7 Closing debtors	List of debtors balances drawn up at the end of the period

Exhibit 29.2

Purchases Ledger Control	Source
1 Opening creditors	List of creditors balances drawn up at the end of the previous period
2 Credit purchases	Total from Purchases Day Book
3 Returns outwards	Total of Returns Outwards Day Book
4 Cheques paid	Cash Book: bank column on payments side. List extracted or total of a special column for cheques which has been included in the Cash Book
5 Cash paid	Cash Book: cash column on payments side. List extracted or total of a special column for cash which has been included in the Cash Book
6 Discounts received	Total of discounts received column in the Cash Book
7 Closing creditors	List of creditors balances drawn up at the end of the period

29.4 Form of control accounts

As shown in Section 29.2, control accounts kept in the general ledger are normally prepared in the same form as an account, with the totals of the debit entries in the ledger on the left-hand side of the control account, and the totals of the various credit entries in the ledger on the right-hand side.

The process is very straightforward. Take the sales ledger as an example. The first two steps are identical to those you learnt in Chapters 13 (cash books) and 14 (day books).

1 Individual amounts received from debtors are transferred from the cash book into the personal accounts in the sales ledger. (The double entry is completed automatically in the normal way, because the cash book is, in itself, a ledger account.)
2 Individual invoice amounts are transferred from the sales day book into the personal accounts in the sales ledger. (You would complete the double entry in the normal way, by crediting the sales account.)
3 The sales ledger control account would open each period with the total of the debtor balances at the start of the period.
4 Then, post the total of the returns inwards day book to the credit side of the sales ledger control account. (This is new.)
5 At the end of the period, you post the totals of all the payments from debtors received during the period from the cash book to the credit side of the sales ledger control account. (This is new.)
6 This is followed by posting to the debit side of the sales ledger control account the totals of all new sales during the period shown in the sales day book. (This is new.)
7 Balance off the control account.
8 Check whether the balance on the control account is equal to the total of all the balances in the sales ledger.

If the balance is not the same as the total of all the balances in the sales ledger, there is an error either in the totals entered in the control account from the books of original entry or, more likely, somewhere in the sales ledger.

Note: You do _not_ enter the total of the balances from the sales ledger in the control account. Instead, you balance-off the control account and check whether the balance c/d is the same as the total of all the individual balances in the sales ledger.

Activity 29.2

If you look at these eight steps, you can see that the first three are those you learnt to do earlier in the book, so you know that the other part of the double entry has been completed in the normal way. However, what about the double entries for (4), (5) and (6)? What is the other side of the double entry in each case?

Exhibit 29.3 shows an example of a sales ledger control account for a sales ledger in which all the entries are arithmetically correct and the totals transferred from the books of original entry are correct.

Exhibit 29.3

Sales Ledger Control Account data:	£
Debit balances on 1 January 2006	1,894
Total credit sales for the month	10,290
Cheques received from customers in the month	7,284
Cash received from customers in the month	1,236
Returns inwards from customers during the month	296
Debit balances on 31 January as extracted from the Sales Ledger	3,368

Sales Ledger Control

2006			£	2006				£
Jan	1	Balances b/d	1,894	Jan	31	Bank		7,284
	31	Sales	10,290		31	Cash		1,236
					31	Returns inwards		296
					31	Balances c/d		3,368
			12,184					12,184

We have proved the ledger to be arithmetically correct, because the control account balances with the amount equalling the total of the balances extracted from the sales ledger.

Like a trial balance, if the totals of a control account are not equal and the entries made to it were correct (i.e. the amounts transferred to it from the books of original entry have been corrrectly summed), this shows that there is an error somewhere in the ledger.

Exhibit 29.4 shows an example where an error is found to exist in a purchases ledger. The ledger will have to be checked in detail, the error found, and the control account then corrected.

Exhibit 29.4

Purchases Ledger Control Account data:	£
Credit balances on 1 January 2006	3,890
Cheques paid to suppliers during the month	3,620
Returns outwards to suppliers in the month	95
Bought from suppliers in the month	4,936
Credit balances on 31 January as extracted from the Purchases Ledger	5,151

Purchases Ledger Control

2006			£	2006			£
Jan	31	Bank	3,620	Jan	1	Balances b/d	3,890
	31	Returns outwards	95		31	Purchases	4,936
	31	Balances c/d	5,151				
			8,866[(Note)]				8,826[(Note)]

Note: Providing all the totals transferred into the Purchases Ledger Control Account from the books of original entry were correct, there is a £40 difference between the debit and credit entries in the Purchases Ledger.

We will have to check the purchases ledger in detail to find the error. A double line has not yet been drawn under the totals. We will do this (known as 'ruling-off the account') when the error has been found and the totals corrected.

Note: You need to be sure that the totals transferred from the books of original entry were correct before assuming that an out-of-balance control account means that the ledger is incorrect.

29.5 Other advantages of control accounts in a manual accounting system

Control accounts are usually only maintained in a manual accounting system. They are not normally maintained in a computerised accounting system.

Control accounts have merits other than that of locating errors. When used the control accounts are normally under the charge of a responsible official, and fraud is made more difficult because transfers made (in an effort) to disguise frauds will have to pass the scrutiny of this person.

The balances on the control account can always be taken to equal debtors and creditors without waiting for an extraction of individual balances. Management control is thereby aided, for the speed at which information is obtained is one of the prerequisites of efficient control.

29.6 Other sources of information for control accounts

With a large organisation there may well be more than one sales ledger or purchases ledger. The accounts in the sales ledgers may be divided up in ways such as:

● Alphabetically. Thus we may have three sales sub-ledgers split A–F, G–O and P–Z.
● Geographically. This could be split: Europe, Far East, Africa, Asia, Australia, North America and South America.

For each of these sub-ledgers we must have a separate control account. An example of a columnar sales day book is shown as Exhibit 29.5:

Exhibit 29.5

Columnar Sales Day Book

Date	Details	Total		Ledgers	
			A–F	G–O	P–Z
2006		£	£	£	£
Feb 1	J Archer	58	58		
3	G Gaunt	103		103	
4	T Brown	116	116		
8	C Dunn	205	205		
10	A Smith	16			16
12	P Smith	114			114
15	D Owen	88		88	
18	B Blake	17	17		
22	T Green	1,396		1,396	
27	C Males	48		48	
		2,161	396	1,635	130

The total of the A–F column will be the total sales figures for the sales ledger A–F control account, the total of the G–O column for the G–O control account, and so on.

A similar form of analysis can be used in the purchases day book, returns inwards day book, returns outwards day book and the cash book. The *totals* necessary for each of the control accounts can be obtained from the appropriate columns in these books.

Other items, such as bad debts written off or transfers from one ledger to another, will be recorded in the journal.

29.7 Other transfers

Transfers to bad debt accounts will have to be recorded in the sales ledger control account as they involve entries in the sales ledger.

Similarly, a contra account, whereby the same entity is both a supplier and a customer, and inter-indebtedness is set off, will also need to be entered in the control accounts. An example of this follows:

(A) The business has sold A Hughes £600 goods.
(B) Hughes has supplied the business with £880 goods.
(C) The £600 owing by Hughes is set off against £880 owing to him.
(D) This leaves £280 owing to Hughes.

Sales Ledger
A Hughes

		£	
Sales	(A)	600	

Purchases Ledger
A Hughes

					£
			Purchases	(B)	880

The set-off now takes place following the preparation of a journal entry in the journal:

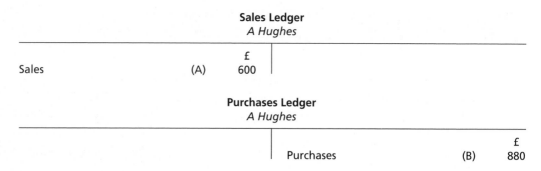

Sales Ledger
A Hughes

		£			£
Sales	(A)	600	Set-off: Purchases ledger	(C)	600

Purchases Ledger
A Hughes

		£			£
Set-off: Sales ledger	(C)	600	Purchases	(B)	880
Balance c/d	(D)	280			
		880			880
			Balance b/d	(D)	280

The set-off will be posted from the journal to the credit side of the sales ledger control account and to the debit side of the purchases ledger control account.

29.8 A more complicated example

Exhibit 29.6 shows a worked example of a more complicated control account.

You will see that there are sometimes credit balances in the sales ledger as well as debit balances. Suppose for instance we sold £500 goods to W Young, he then paid in full for them, and then afterwards he returned £40 goods to us. This would leave a credit balance of £40 on the account, whereas usually the balances in the sales ledger are debit balances.

Exhibit 29.6

2006			£
Aug	1	Sales ledger – debit balances	3,816
	1	Sales ledger – credit balances	22
	31	Transactions for the month:	
		Cash received	104
		Cheques received	6,239
		Sales	7,090
		Bad debts written off	306
		Discounts allowed	298
		Returns inwards	664
		Cash refunded to a customer who had overpaid his account	37
		Dishonoured cheques	29
		Interest charged by us on overdue debt	50
		At the end of the month:	
		Sales ledger – debit balances	3,429
		Sales ledger – credit balances	40

Sales Ledger Control Account

2006			£	2006			£
Aug	1	Balances b/d	3,816	Aug	1	Balances b/d	22
	31	Sales	7,090		31	Cash	104
		Cash refunded	37			Bank	6,239
		Bank: dishonoured cheques	29			Bad debts	306
		Interest on debt	50			Discounts allowed	298
		Balances c/d	40			Returns inwards	664
						Balances c/d	3,429
			11,062				11,062

Note that you do *not* net-off the debit and credit balances in the sales ledger.

29.9 Control accounts as part of double entry in larger organisations

In larger organisations, control accounts may be an integral part of the double entry system, the balances of the control accounts being taken for the purpose of extracting a trial balance. In this case, the control accounts are always kept in the general ledger. When control accounts are part of the double entry system, the personal accounts are being used as subsidiary records and the sales and purchases ledgers are memorandum books lying outside the double entry system.

The same entries are made to the control accounts at the end of the period as are made if they are not part of the double entry system.

29.10 Self-balancing ledgers and adjustment accounts

Because ledgers which have a control account system are proved to be correct as far as the double entry is concerned they used to be called '**self-balancing ledgers**'. The control accounts were often called '**adjustment accounts**'. These terms are very rarely used nowadays but you should remember them in case an examiner mentions them.

29.11 Reconciliation of control accounts

Errors and omissions can occur when entering information into the accounting records. We have seen in Chapter 28 how these are identified and used to reconcile differences between the bank account and the bank statement balances. When a ledger control account is not in balance, it indicates that something has gone wrong with the entries made to the accounting records. This leads to an investigation which (hopefully) reveals the cause(s). Then, in order to verify whether the identified item(s) caused the failure to balance the control account, a reconciliation is carried out.

Exhibit 29.7 shows an example of a **purchases ledger control account reconciliation**. It takes the original control account balance and adjusts it to arrive at an amended balance which should equal the revised total of the source amounts that, together, equal the control account balance.

It can be seen that the general approach is similar to that adopted for bank reconciliation statements when trying to explain the difference between the balance shown on a bank statement with that shown in the cash book. However, as each control account may be constructed using information from a number of sources (*see* Section 29.3) the extent of the investigation to identify the cause of the control account imbalance is likely to be far greater than that undertaken when performing a bank reconciliation.

Exhibit 29.7

An example of a Purchases Ledger Control Account Reconciliation

	£
Original purchases ledger control account balance	xxx
Add Invoice omitted from control account, but entered in Purchases Ledger	xxx
Supplier balance excluded from Purchases Ledger total because the account had been included in the Sales Ledger by mistake	xxx
Credit sale posted in error to the debit of a Purchases Ledger account instead of the debit of an account in the Sales Ledger	xxx
Under-casting error in calculation of total end of period creditors' balances	xxx
	xxx
Less Customer account with a credit balance included in the Purchases Ledger that should have been included in the Sales Ledger	(xxx)
Return inwards posted in error to the credit of a Purchases Ledger account instead of the credit of an account in the Sales Ledger	(xxx)
Credit note entered in error in the Returns Outwards Day Book as £223 instead of £332	(xxx)
Revised purchases ledger control account balance obtained from revised source amounts	xxx

---

29.12 A cautionary note

Students often get the following wrong: only credit purchases are recorded in a Purchase Ledger control account. Also, in Sales Ledger control accounts, do not include cash sales or provisions for doubtful debts.

29.13 Finally

Control accounts are used in manual accounting systems. Most computerised accounting systems automatically provide all the benefits of using control accounts without the necessity of actually maintaining them. This is because computerised accounting systems automatically ensure that all double entries are completed, so ensuring that the ledgers all balance. Of course, errors can still arise, such as a posting made to the wrong ledger account, but not of the type that control accounts can detect.

Learning outcomes

You should now have learnt:

1 How to prepare control accounts.

2 How to prepare a control account reconciliation.

3 That control accounts enable errors to be traced down to the ledger that does not balance. Thus there will be no need to check all the books in full to find an error.

4 That transfers between sales and purchases ledgers should be prepared in the journal and shown in the control accounts.

5 That control accounts for most businesses are outside the double entry system, and are kept as memorandum accounts in the general ledger or in the individual ledgers.

6 That control accounts of large organisations may be part of the double entry system, which means that the sales ledger and purchases ledger are treated as memorandum books outside the double entry system. The entries to such control accounts are the same as for control accounts that lie outside the double entry system.

7 That control accounts are normally only used in manual accounting systems.

Answers to activities

29.1 These errors tend to be detected either as the result of someone drawing attention to an entry that appears to be incorrect or as the result of sample checking of the entries that have been made in the accounting books. A debtor may, for example, question whether the amount on an invoice is correctly summed or suggest that one of the invoices listed in the debtor's monthly statement had nothing to do with the debtor. One of the tasks that auditors carry out involves checking a sample of the transactions during a period so as to determine the level of errors within the entries made relating to them. If the level of error detected is considered material, a more extensive check will be carried out.

29.2 (4) The other side of this double entry was to the debit of the returns inwards account.

(5) The other side of the double entry was done earlier at the time when the individual amounts received from debtors were posted as credits to the individual debtor accounts in the sales ledger. That is, *the other side of this double entry was all the debit entries to the cash book* (see Chapter 13). The posting of each receipt as a credit to the individual debtor accounts done in step (1) is actually a memorandum entry and does not form part of the double entry system. So, in effect, the sales ledger has been taken out of the double entry system and is now a memorandum book. *To summarise, step (5) is actually the credit side of the double entry whose debit side is all the debit entries in the cash book.*

(6) The other side of the double entry was done earlier at the time when each sale was posted from the sales day book to the individual debtors accounts in the sales ledger. That is, *the other side of this double entry was the credit entry made when the total of the sales shown in the sales day book was posted to the sales account in the general ledger* (see Chapter 14). The posting of each sale as a debit to the individual debtor accounts done in step (2) is actually a memorandum entry and does not form part of the double entry system. *To summarise, step (6) is actually the debit side of the double entry whose credit side is all the credit entries in the sales account.*

→ During the half year, debit balances in the sales ledger, amounting to £438, were transferred to the purchases ledger.

Required:
Prepare the sales ledger control account and the purchases ledger control account for the half-year to 31 December 2009.

29.8A The following extracts have been taken from the subsidiary books of the business owned by D Jenkinson for the month of April 2010.

Purchases Day Book		£
Apr	3 W Allen	480
	7 J Morris	270
	17 T Sage	410
	24 F Wilding	650

Returns Outwards Day Book		£
Apr	14 W Allen	50
	29 T Sage	80

Cash Book (Credit side)

		Discounts received £	Bank £
Apr	9 T Sage	30	690
	18 F Wilding	5	195
	24 J Morris	31	389
	27 W Allen	18	322

Journal

		£	£
Apr 30	Creditor W Allen	180	
	Debtor W Allen		180
	being transfer		
	from sales ledger		
	to purchases ledger		

It should be noted that the balances in the accounts of D Jenkinson's suppliers on 1 April 2010 were as follows:

	£
W Allen	360
J Morris	140
T Sage	720
F Wilding	310

Required:
(a) The name of the source document which will have been used for making entries in the
 (i) purchases day book
 (ii) returns outwards day book.
(b) The name of **two** subsidiary books (other than those shown in the extracts above) which could form part of D Jenkinson's accounting system. In the case of **one** of the subsidiary books chosen, explain its purpose.
(c) The account of T Sage in D Jenkinson's purchases ledger for the month of April 2010. (The account should be balanced at the end of the month.)
(d) D Jenkinson's purchases ledger control account for the month of April 2010. (The account should be balanced at the end of the month.)
(e) Advice for D Jenkinson on **two** ways in which he might find the purchases ledger control account useful.

(*Southern Examining Group: GCSE*)

29.9 The financial year of The Better Trading Company ended on 30 November 2007. You have been asked to prepare a total debtors account and a total creditors account in order to produce end-of-year figures for debtors and creditors for the draft final accounts.

You are able to obtain the following information for the financial year from the books of original entry:

	£
Sales – cash	344,890
– credit	268,187
Purchases – cash	14,440
– credit	496,600
Total receipts from customers	600,570
Total payments to suppliers	503,970
Discounts allowed (all to credit customers)	5,520
Discounts received (all from credit suppliers)	3,510
Refunds given to cash customers	5,070
Balance in the sales ledger set off against balance in the purchases ledger	70
Bad debts written-off	780
Increase in the provision for bad debts	90
Credit notes issued to credit customers	4,140
Credit notes received from credit suppliers	1,480

According to the audited financial statements for the previous year debtors and creditors as at 1 December 2006 were £26,555 and £43,450 respectively.

Required:
Draw up the relevant Total Accounts entering end-of-year totals for debtors and creditors.

(*Association of Accounting Technicians*)

29.10

(*a*) Why are many accounting systems designed with a purchases ledger (creditors ledger) control account, as well as with a purchases ledger (creditors ledger)?

(*b*) The following errors have been discovered:

    (*i*)   An invoice for £654 has been entered in the purchases day book as £456;

    (*ii*) A prompt payment discount of £100 from a creditor had been completely omitted from the accounting records;

    (*iii*) Purchases of £250 had been entered on the wrong side of a supplier's account in the purchases ledger;

    (*iv*) No entry had been made to record an agreement to contra an amount owed to X of £600 against an amount owed by X of £400;

    (*v*) A credit note for £60 had been entered as if it was an invoice.

State the numerical effect on the purchases ledger control account balance of correcting each of these items (treating each item separately).

(*c*) Information technology and computerised systems are rapidly increasing in importance in data recording. Do you consider that this trend will eventually remove the need for control accounts to be incorporated in the design of accounting systems? Explain your answer briefly.

(*Association of Chartered Certified Accountants*)

29.11 Control accounts are used mainly for debtors and creditors. Explain:

(*a*) Why it may be appropriate to use control accounts.
(*b*) The advantages of using them.

You can find a range of additional self-test questions, as well as material to help you with your studies, on the website that accompanies this book at www.pearsoned.co.uk/wood

(marginal text, partially visible)

A Smaile
Sales
Correctic

6 Com

A paym
error an
come th
the corr
is so:
    What

Cash

was ente

M Dickso

We can r

M Dickso

Cash (err

Overall,
credit of
As the fi
now corr

C Sim
C S
Purcl

The e

Sept

3 E

The [
to a r
that a

Mach
Pur
Corre

4 C

In the
and t
theref

Sales
Wa
Corre
accoul

5 Er

A sale

The accounts now appear as Exhibit 31.2:

Exhibit 31.2

Suspense

2009			£	2009			£
Mar	31	Sales	40	Jan	1	Balance b/d	40

Sales

				2009			£
				Mar	31	Suspense	40

This can be shown in journal form as:

The Journal

				Dr	Cr
2009				£	£
Mar	31	Suspense		40	
		Sales			40
		Correction of undercasting of sales by £40 last year			

Here's another example.

Example 2

The trial balance on 31 December 2009 had a difference of £168. It was a shortage on the debit side.

A suspense account is opened, and the difference of £168 is entered on the debit side in the account. On 31 May 2010 the error was found. We had made a payment of £168 to K Leek to close his account. It was correctly entered in the cash book, but was not entered in K Leek's account.

First of all, the account of K Leek is debited with £168, as it should have been in 2009. Second, the suspense account is credited with £168 so that the account can be closed.

Exhibit 31.3

K Leek

2010			£	2010			£
May	31	Bank	168	Jan	1	Balance b/d	168

The account of K Leek is now correct.

Suspense

2010			£	2010			£
Jan	1	Balance b/d	168	May	31	K Leek	168

The Journal entry is:

The Journal

				Dr	Cr
2010				£	£
May	31	K Leek		168	
		Suspense			168
		Correction of non-entry of payment last year in K Leek's account			

More than one error

Let's now look at Example 3 where the suspense account difference was caused by more than one error.

Example 3

The trial balance at 31 December 2007 showed a difference of £77, being a shortage on the debit side. A suspense account is opened, and the difference of £77 is entered on the debit side of the account.

On 28 February 2008 all the errors from the previous year were found.

(A) A cheque of £150 paid to L Kent had been correctly entered in the cash book, but had not been entered in Kent's account.
(B) The purchases account had been undercast by £20.
(C) A cheque of £93 received from K Sand had been correctly entered in the cash book, but had not been entered in Sand's account.

These three errors resulted in a net error of £77, shown by a debit of £77 on the debit side of the suspense account. These are corrected as follows:

(a) Make correcting entries in accounts for (A), (B) and (C).
(b) Record double entry for these items in the suspense account.

Exhibit 31.4

L Kent

2008				£	
Feb	28	Suspense	(A)	150	

Purchases

2008				£	
Feb	28	Suspense	(B)	20	

K Sand

					2008				£
					Feb	28	Suspense	(C)	93

Suspense

2008				£	2008				£
Jan	1	Balance b/d		77	Feb	28	L Kent	(A)	150
Feb	28	K Sand	(C)	93		28	Purchases	(B)	20
				170					170

The Journal

			Dr	Cr
2008			£	£
Feb	28	L Kent	150	
		Suspense		150
		Cheque paid omitted from Kent's account		
	28	Purchases	20	
		Suspense		20
		Undercasting of purchases by £20 in last year's accounts		
	28	Suspense	93	
		K Sand		93
		Cheque received omitted from Sand's account		

Note: Only those errors which make the trial balance totals different from each other can be corrected via the suspense account.

31.5 The effect of errors on profits

Some of the errors will have meant that original profits calculated will be wrong. Other errors will have no effect upon profits.

Exhibit 31.5 shows a set of financial statements in which errors have been made.

Exhibit 31.5

K Davis
Trading and Profit and Loss Account for the year ending 31 December 2005

		£	£
Sales			180,000
Less	Cost of goods sold:		
	Opening stock	15,000	
	Add Purchases	92,000	
		107,000	
	Less Closing stock	(18,000)	
			(89,000)
Gross profit			91,000
Add Discounts received			1,400
			92,400
Less	Expenses:		
	Rent	8,400	
	Insurance	1,850	
	Lighting	1,920	
	Depreciation	28,200	
			(40,370)
Net profit			52,030

Balance Sheet as at 31 December 2005

	£	£
Fixed assets		
Equipment at cost		62,000
Less Depreciation to date		(41,500)
		20,500
Current assets		
Stock	18,000	
Debtors	23,000	
Bank	19,000	
	60,000	
Less Current liabilities		
Creditors	(14,000)	
Net current assets		46,000
Suspense account		80
		66,580
Capital		
Balance as at 1.1.2005		46,250
Add Net profit		52,030
		98,280
Less Drawings		(31,700)
		66,580

The errors that have been made may be of three types.

1 Errors which do not affect profit calculations

If an error affects items only in the balance sheet, then the original calculated profit will not need to be changed. Example 1 shows this.

Example 1

Assume that in Exhibit 31.5 the £80 debit balance on the suspense account was because of the following error:

On 1 November 2005 we paid £80 to a creditor T Monk. It was correctly entered in the cash book. It was not entered anywhere else. The error was identified on 1 June 2006.

The journal entries to correct it will be:

The Journal

	Dr	Cr
2006	£	£
June 1 T Monk	80	
Suspense		80
Payment to T Monk on 1 November 2005 not entered in his account. Correction now made.		

Both of these accounts appeared in the balance sheet only with T Monk as part of creditors. The net profit of £52,030 does not have to be changed.

2 Errors which do affect profit calculations

If the error is in one of the figures shown in the trading and profit and loss account, then the original profit will need to be amended. Example 2 shows this.

Example 2

Assume that in Exhibit 31.5 the £80 debit balance was because the rent account was added up incorrectly. It should be shown as £8,480 instead of £8,400. The error was identified on 1 June 2006. The journal entries to correct it are:

The Journal

	Dr	Cr
2006	£	£
Jun 1 Rent	80	
Suspense		80
Correction of rent undercast last year		

Rent last year should have been increased by £80. This would have reduced net profit by £80. A statement of corrected profit for the year is now shown.

K Davis
Statement of Corrected Net Profit for the year ending 31 December 2005

	£
Net profit per the financial statements	52,030
Less Rent understated	(80)
Corrected net profit for the year	51,950

3 Where there have been several errors

If in Exhibit 31.5 there had been four errors in the ledger accounts of K Davis, found on 31 March 2006, their correction can now be seen. Assume that the net difference had also been £80.

		£
(A)	Sales overcast by	£90
(B)	Insurance undercast by	£40
(C)	Cash received from a debtor entered in the cash book only	£50
(D)	A purchase of £59 is entered in the books, debit and credit entries as	£95

Note: Error (D) is known as an error of transposition, as the correct figures have been shown in the wrong order, i.e. they have been 'transposed'.

The entries in the suspense account and the journal entries will be as follows:

Suspense Account

2006				£	2006					£
Jan	1	Balance b/d		80	Mar	31	Sales	(A)	90
Mar	31	Debtor	(C)	50		31	Insurance	(B)	40
				130						130

The Journal

					Dr	Cr
	2006				£	£
1	Mar	31	Sales		90	
			Suspense			90
			Sales overcast of £90 in 2005			
2	Mar	31	Insurance		40	
			Suspense			40
			Insurance expense undercast by £40 in 2005			
3	Mar	31	Suspense		50	
			Debtor's account			50
			Cash received omitted from debtor's account in 2005			
4	Mar	31	Creditor's account		36	
			Purchases			36
			Credit purchase of £59 entered both as debit and credit as £95 in 2005			

Note: In (D), the correction of the overstatement of purchases does *not* pass through the suspense account.

Now we can calculate the corrected net profit for the year 2005. Only items (A), (B) and (D) affect figures in the trading and profit and loss account. These are the only adjustments to be made to profit.

K Davis
Statement of Corrected Net Profit for the year ending 31 December 2005

			£
Net profit per the financial statements			52,030
Add Purchases overstated	(D)		36
			52,066
Less Sales overcast	(A)	90	
Insurance undercast	(B)	40	
			(130)
Corrected net profit for the year			51,936

Error (C), the cash not posted to a debtor's account, did not affect profit calculations.

31.6 Suspense accounts: businesses and examinations

Businesses

Every attempt should be made to find errors. A suspense account should be opened only if all other efforts have failed, and they *never* should!

Examinations

Unless it is part of a question, *do not* make your balance sheet totals agree by using a suspense account. The same applies to trial balances. Examiners are very likely to penalise you for showing a suspense account when it should not be required.

Overall

Suspense accounts have probably been used ever since people first started keeping accounts and using them to produce financial statements. However, just because suspense accounts have been used for a very long time does not mean that they should still be used today.

Long ago, accounting records were very poorly maintained. The people maintaining them were frequently untrained. Errors were fairly common, and no one was very concerned when it proved difficult to find out what had caused a trial balance not to balance, if they even went to the extent of preparing one.

Businesses were largely owned by one person who would often also prepare the financial statements, more out of interest than in order to make much use of what they showed which, before there was some regulation concerning what they presented, was frequently little more than the excess or shortfall of revenue over expenditure.

Nowadays, accounting is far more sophisticated and the people maintaining the accounting records are much better trained. Many organisations use computerised accounting systems and very few organisations of any complexity continue to do everything manually. When they do, their records will be good enough to make tracing an error reasonably straightforward.

Errors of the types that cause trial balances not to balance are, therefore, much less common and much easier to detect. As a result, it is inconceivable that a suspense account will ever be needed in practice when an accountant is involved in preparing or auditing the financial statements.

Nevertheless, circumstances may make it impossible for a sole trader's financial statements to be ready in time, for example, to show the bank manager when asking for a loan. It is probably only in circumstances of this type that you may find suspense accounts still in use, albeit rarely. An example may be when money is received by post or credited into the business bank account with no explanation and no information. It needs to be put somewhere in the ledger accounts, so a suspense account is used while the reason it was sent to the business is identified.

Learning outcomes

You should now have learnt:

1 How to make the appropriate entries in setting up a suspense account.
2 How to make the correcting entries involving the suspense account when the cause of an error is identified.
3 That some errors may cause the profits originally calculated to have been incorrect.
4 That errors that do not affect profit calculations will have an effect only on items in the balance sheet.
5 That nowadays suspense accounts very rarely need to be used, if at all.

→
(A) (*i*) and (*iv*)
(B) (*ii*) and (*iii*)
(C) (*iii*) and (*iv*)
(D) (*ii*) and (*iv*).

MC72 The journal is

(A) Part of the double entry system
(B) A supplement to the cash book
(C) Not part of the double entry system
(D) Used when other journals have been mislaid.

MC73 Given a desired cash float of £200, if £146 is spent in the period, how much will be reimbursed at the end of the period?

(A) £200
(B) £54
(C) £254
(D) £146.

MC74 When a petty cash book is kept there will be

(A) More entries made in the general ledger
(B) Fewer entries made in the general ledger
(C) The same number of entries in the general ledger
(D) No entries made at all in the general ledger for items paid by petty cash.

MC75 Which of the following do *not* affect trial balance agreement?

(*i*) Sales £105 to A Henry entered in P Henry's account
(*ii*) Cheque payment of £134 for motor expenses entered only in cash book
(*iii*) Purchases £440 from C Browne entered in both accounts as £404
(*iv*) Wages account added up incorrectly, being totalled £10 too much.

(A) (*i*) and (*iv*)
(B) (*i*) and (*iii*)
(C) (*ii*) and (*iii*)
(D) (*iii*) and (*iv*).

MC76 Which of the following are *not* errors of principle?

(*i*) Motor expenses entered in motor vehicles account
(*ii*) Purchases of machinery entered in purchases account
(*iii*) Sale of £250 to C Phillips completely omitted from books
(*iv*) Sale to A Henriques entered in A Henry's account.

(A) (*ii*) and (*iii*)
(B) (*i*) and (*ii*)
(C) (*iii*) and (*iv*)
(D) (*i*) and (*iv*).

MC77 Errors are corrected via the journal because

(A) It saves the bookkeeper's time
(B) It saves entering them in the ledger
(C) It is much easier to do
(D) It provides a good record explaining the double entry records.

MC78   Which of these errors would be disclosed by the trial balance?

(A)   Cheque £95 from C Smith entered in Smith's account as £59
(B)   Selling expenses had been debited to sales account
(C)   Credit sales of £300 entered in both double entry accounts as £30
(D)   A purchase of £250 was omitted entirely from the books.

MC79   If the two totals of a trial balance do *not* agree, the difference must be entered in

(A)   The profit and loss account
(B)   A suspense account
(C)   A nominal account
(D)   The capital account.

MC80   What should happen if the balance on a suspense account is of a material amount?

(A)   Should be written off to the balance sheet
(B)   Carry forward the balance to the next period
(C)   Find the error(s) before publishing the final accounts
(D)   Write it off to profit and loss.

Review questions

31.1   A trial balance was extracted from the books of V Baker, and it was found that the debit side exceeded the credit side by £40. This amount was entered in the suspense account. The following errors were later discovered and corrected:

(*i*)   Purchases were over-summed by £20.
(*ii*)   An amount paid to B Simpkins was debited to the control account as £98 instead of £89.
(*iii*)   Sales were under-summed by £11.

Required:
Write up and rule off the suspense account as it would appear in Baker's ledger.

31.2   Your bookkeeper extracted a trial balance on 31 December 2005 which failed to agree by £210, a shortage on the credit side of the trial balance. A suspense account was opened for the difference.

In January 2006 the following errors made in 2005 were found:

(*i*)   Sales day book had been undercast by £200.
(*ii*)   Sales of £610 to T Vantuira had been debited in error to T Ventura's account.
(*iii*)   Rent account had been undercast by £90.
(*iv*)   Discounts allowed account had been overcast by £100.
(*v*)   The sale of a computer at net book value had been credited in error to the sales account £230.

You are required to:
(*a*)   Show the journal entries necessary to correct the errors.
(*b*)   Draw up the suspense account after the errors described have been corrected.
(*c*)   If the net profit had previously been calculated at £31,400 for the year ending 31 December 2005, show the calculations of the corrected net profit.

31.3A   You have extracted a trial balance and drawn up accounts for the year ended 31 December 2007. There was a shortage of £78 on the credit side of the trial balance, a suspense account being opened for that amount.

During 2008 the following errors made in 2007 were found:

(*i*)   £125 received from sales of old office equipment has been entered in the sales account.
(*ii*)   Purchases day book had been overcast by £10.

→

Scenario questions

The following questions are designed to reinforce learning of the adjustments covered in Part 4 through their application in the preparation of financial statements previously learnt in Parts 1–3.

The answers to these questions are to be found on page 703.

SQ1

Michael Angelo owns Picta Simpla, a company specialising in selling painting by numbers by mail order. The packs are purchased from a wholesaler and then resold. The public have no access to the wholesaler and so there is no competition.

During the year ended 30 June 2007 Michael sold 2,900 units at £89 each, having started the year with £19,250 of stock (600 units). During the year, he purchased a total of 3,150 packs from the wholesaler at £59 each. Michael wants to value his stock using the FIFO basis.

Staff have been paid wages totalling £14,500, which is only slightly less than the advertising bills paid of £15,000. Michael is upset since the advertising agency has yet to send a final bill, estimated to be £500. Postage per unit sent out was £2. The packing costs were £0.50 per unit.

Rent was £1,000 per month. Insurance of £3,500 has been paid but £650 of this relates to the year ending 30 June 2008. Electricity bills amounted to £2,900, but the bill for the final quarter is still outstanding and is expected to be approximately £500.

The business has a computer which was purchased about two years ago and which Michael reckons has about another three years of useful life left, at which point it will be worthless. It cost £4,000 and Michael uses the straight line method when calculating the depreciation charge. He also has a fax machine which he uses to communicate with his suppliers.

Stationery charges have amounted to £1,350 and he has had telephone bills of £3,500, of which £200 relates to July and August 2007. In the year ending 30 June 2006, he paid £150 for July and August 2006.

Michael has also paid £5,000 from the business bank account for a month long holiday in Florida. He has asked you whether he can class this as business expenses since it has enabled him to recover from the stresses and strain of running his own business.

Required:
(a) Prepare a profit and loss account for the year ending 30 June 2007.
(b) Write a brief letter to Michael explaining what drawings are in relation to a small business and answering his query concerning his holiday.

406

SQ2

The following balance sheet has been prepared by your client, Mr Conman, proprietor of the Sleasy Cars second-hand car dealership:

Balance Sheet as at 31 December 2006

	£	£	£
Fixed Assets			
Freehold Land, at valuation			10,000
Offices			1,000
Breakdown truck			5,000
			16,000
Current Assets			
Stock		23,000	
Debtors and prepayments		3,500	
Cash in hand		100	
		26,600	
Current Liabilities			
Creditors and accruals	8,200		
Bank Overdraft	6,400		
		(14,600)	
Working Capital			12,000
Net assets			28,000
Financed By			
Capital Introduced			15,500
Add Profit for the year			23,500
			39,000
Less Drawings			(11,000)
			28,000

This was the first year of trading for Sleasy Cars. Mr Conman acquired a field in Hull (which had previously been used for a rubbish tip and then filled in) for £5,000 on 1 January 2006 and erected a portacabin on the site to be used as an office at a cost of £500. He then bought ten second-hand cars from a national dealership for £10,000. He has some accountancy training and has taken a lot of care in producing the balance sheet but confesses that he did not produce a profit and loss account. Instead, as it must be the correct figure, the amount shown for profit in the balance sheet was the amount required to make it balance.

The following points have come to light in your discussion:

(*i*) The office was bought at a discount from a friend who had acquired it from a builder's yard and Conman has included it in the balance sheet at the proper price as he knows that accountants like original costs to be shown. The office should last for five years and Conman agrees that maybe that thing called depreciation should be included at straight line. The office will be worthless at the end of the five years.

(*ii*) The land was a bargain. Conman heard on the grapevine that the council were going to take the previous owners to court as it was an environmental hazard. The owners put it up for sale at £10,000 so he made an offer to the owners of £5,000 which was accepted. He is ignoring the court order to clean up the site since this would cost approximately £3,000. His reason for ignoring it is that although the order was made in December 2005 (i.e. before he bought the land), he did not receive the notice until January 2007 (i.e. after he had bought the land).

(*iii*) The breakdown truck is very old and was bought at the start of the year. It has been shown at cost although it is probably only going to last another year and will have no residual value.

(*iv*) Stocks have all been valued at cost although on one car there is a good chance that it will sell at a loss of £500. Another one was sold in January 2007 for £3,000 but the new owner has not picked it up yet – the profit was £1,500 so this has been included in the valuation of the car. As he has included the car, Conman has not included the debtor in the balance sheet.

(*v*) A customer has owed £2,000 for six months and Mr Conman is becoming slightly bothered. The customer has moved away from the address she gave Mr Conman and he thinks that this debt might not be recoverable.

(vi) After hearing the above, you have decided to check the figures and have found that the cash, overdraft and drawings figures are correct and also that there has been no adjustment for the fact that he has not paid his electricity bill of £250 nor his telephone bill of £150. The reason for this is that he is subletting part of the field and is owed £400 in rent and, therefore, the two cancel each other out.

Required
(a) A revised balance sheet after taking into account all of the above.
(b) A description of each of the adjustments that have been made and why each of them is necessary.

SQ3

The following represents the trial balance extracted from the books of Mr Jones, a small businessman based in Aboyne. The books are well maintained and there is no reason to doubt the accuracy of the entries:

	£	£
Sales		430,000
Purchases	293,500	
Carriage in	2,100	
Drawings	31,000	
Rent	5,200	
Business rates	2,600	
Insurance	550	
Postage	250	
Stationery	986	
Advertising	250	
Wages	10,500	
Bad debts	400	
Provision for doubtful debts		400
Debtors	5,120	
Creditors		3,600
Cash in hand	120	
Cash at Bank	3,257	
Stock	6,520	
Equipment at cost	150,000	
Accumulated depreciation – equipment		35,000
Capital		43,353
	512,353	512,353

Following a discussion with Mr Jones, the following points have come to light:

(a) Accruals are necessary for rent (£150), business rates (£200), and stationery (£16).
(b) Insurance has been prepaid by £150, advertising by £50.
(c) Stock at the year end is £7,000.
(d) Depreciation is to be charged on the equipment at a rate of 10% on cost.
(e) The doubtful debt provision is to be increased to 10% of the year-end balance.
(f) Purchase invoices to the value of £12,000 were found in a desk drawer the day before the meeting with Mr Jones. Half of them have been paid by cheque (but no record made in the cash book) and the rest are outstanding.

Required
(a) Prepare a trading and profit and loss account for the year ending on the date of extraction of the trial balance together with a balance sheet as at that date.
(b) Mr Jones has kept accurate records (with the exception of point (f)) and yet the accountant must still adjust the figures in the trial balance before preparing the financial statements. As the accountant, write a letter to Mr Jones outlining why the accountant must adjust the figures to convey meaningful information.

SQ4

The following balances were extracted from the books of Mr Try, a window cleaner. He has no knowledge of double entry bookkeeping but records everything correctly. His year end is 30 June and the following balances relate to the year ended 30 June 2007:

	£
Accounts to be paid	100
Cleaning income	17,644
Cash balance	35
Own wages	10,600
Ladders and equipment	750
Repairs to customers' houses due to damage	230
Miscellaneous expenses	110
Owed by customers	220
Insurances	350
Accountancy fees (relating to 2006 – paid in this year)	250
Postage and stationery	50
Bank	2,345
Cleaning materials and cloths	3,400

He has not included the following items as he is not sure how to record them:

(i) Bank charges are to be levied for the year of £45 – they are to be processed by the bank in September 2007.

(ii) Insurances have been prepaid by £50.

(iii) None of the amounts owed by customers can be realistically recovered but Mr Try wants to keep on trying and therefore wants a provision to be made of 50% of the balances.

(iv) Accountancy charges for the current year ended 2007 are to be £275.

(v) The ladders, including the ones bought in the year, will only last until the end of 2008 and are to be depreciated using the straight line method with no residual value.

Required

(a) Prepare a trading and profit and loss account for the year ending 30 June 2007.

(b) Prepare a balance sheet at that date.

(c) Mr Try has heard about a treatment of fixed assets which he thinks is 'consumables'. He wonders if his ladders could be treated as consumables and not depreciated. Write a letter, using fictitious names and addresses to Mr Try to answer his query.

SQ5

Michael Baldwin owns *B's Casuals*, a company specialising in low-quality, high-priced clothing. The material is purchased from Canada, made up into the finished garments in his own factory, and then sold in the local markets through stallholders.

During the year ended 30 June 2007 Michael made sales of £260,040.

Stock levels have remained relatively consistent over the years, the starting stock being £21,500 and the closing stock £22,500.

Michael is not very generous to his staff. This is reflected in the wages paid during the year of only £24,500.

Business rates are a problem, since there is a dispute with the local council. He has paid a total of £7,500 but there is a good chance that he will have to pay a further £2,450.

Postage and advertising is another problem area. For the imports from Canada it is necessary to pay all of the flight costs. These amounted to £5,200 over the year.

He delivers all of his invoices to the stallholders in person and is paid promptly, with the exception of one debtor who owes £2,000 and who has been declared bankrupt. This amount is to be written off.

Advertising is minimal and is done in the local pub: £20 per week is paid to the landlord in return for permission to pin leaflets on the walls and an agreement that the landlord will place a leaflet every day on each table in the bar.

Insurance of £3,500 has been paid, but £650 of this relates to the year ending 30 June 2008.

Electricity bills amounted to £2,900, but the bill for the final quarter is still outstanding and is expected to be approximately £500. Purchases of cloth from Canada for the year are currently recorded as being £65,000, but there is an outstanding bill of £3,500 which is not yet included in that figure.

The factory and the machinery were bought at the same time and originally cost £400,000. Depreciation has accumulated to the sum of £100,000. The current year charge is 5% on the reducing balance basis.

The business had a computer which was purchased about three years ago and which Michael reckons has about another two years of life left. It cost £4,000 and Michael uses the straight line method of calculating the depreciation charge. The computer will be worthless at the end of that time.

Stationery charges amounted to £1,350 and he had telephone bills of £3,500, £200 of which relates to July and August 2007. In the year ending 30 June 2006, he had paid £150 which related to telephone charges in the year ending 30 June 2007.

Michael has also paid £5,000 for a top of the range digital home cinema system. He has enquired as to whether he can class this as a business expense as it has enabled him to unwind after long days at the office.

His salary for the year was £50,000.

Cash in hand at 30 June 2007 was £600 which he borrowed from his wife temporarily on 30 June when he realised that there was no cash available to pay any expenses.

Required

(a) Prepare a profit and loss account for the year ending 30 June 2007.

(b) Prepare a balance sheet at 30 June 2007 showing clearly Mr Baldwin's opening capital, working capital and the profit for the year.

(c) Michael has enquired why he should include the amounts owing to both the council and the Canadians in the current year's financial statements and also why he cannot include his own wages within expenses since they have been paid out from the business. Write a letter to Michael explaining these points and answering his query concerning the home cinema system.

SPECIAL ACCOUNTING PROCEDURES

Introduction

This part is concerned with the accounting procedures that have to be followed with different forms of organisations, and commences with a chapter outlining the basic accounting ratios which may be found necessary at this stage.

Introduction to accounting ratios

Learning objectives

After you have studied this chapter, you should be able to:

● calculate some basic accounting ratios
● use accounting ratios to calculate missing figures in financial statements
● offer some explanations for changes in these ratios over time

Introduction

In this chapter, you'll learn about the relationship between mark-up and margin and how to use the relationship between them and sales revenue and gross profit to find figures that are missing in the trading account. You will also learn how to calculate the stock turnover ratio and some explanations for why these ratios change over time.

32.1 The need for accounting ratios

We will see in, Chapter 45, that accounting ratios are used to enable us to analyse and interpret accounting statements.

This chapter has been inserted at this point in the book simply so that you will be able to deal with the material in Chapter 33 which includes the drawing up of financial statements from incomplete records. The ratios described in this chapter will be sufficient for you to deduce the data needed to make the incomplete records into a complete set of records, so that you can then prepare the financial statements. Without the use of such accounting ratios, the construction of financial statements from incomplete records would often be impossible.

 Activity 32.1 What do you think is meant by the term 'incomplete records'?

32.2 Mark-up and margin

The purchase cost, gross profit and selling price of goods or services may be shown as:

> Cost price + Gross profit = Selling price

When shown as a fraction or percentage of the *cost price*, the gross profit is known as the **mark-up**.

When shown as a fraction or percentage of the *selling price*, gross profit is known as the **margin**. We can calculate mark-up and margin using this example:

$$\text{Cost price} + \text{Gross profit} = \text{Selling price}$$
$$£4 \quad + \quad £1 \quad = £5$$

$$\text{Mark-up} = \frac{\text{Gross profit}}{\text{Cost price}} \text{ as a fraction, or if required as a percentage, multiply by 100:}$$

$$\frac{1}{4} = \frac{1}{4}, \quad \text{or } \frac{1}{4} \times 100 = 25 \text{ per cent.}$$

$$\text{Margin} = \frac{\text{Gross profit}}{\text{Selling price}} \text{ as a fraction, or if required as a percentage, multiply by 100:}$$

$$\frac{1}{5} = \frac{1}{5}, \quad \text{or } \frac{1}{5} \times 100 = 20 \text{ per cent.}$$

Activity 32.2 Can you see a simple rule connecting mark-up to margin?

32.3 Calculating missing figures

Now we can use these ratios to complete trading accounts where some of the figures are missing. In all the examples in this chapter, we shall:

● assume that all the goods in a business have the same rate of mark-up, and
● ignore wastages and theft of goods.

Example 1

The following figures are for the year 2005:

	£
Stock 1.1.2005	400
Stock 31.12.2005	600
Purchases	5,200

A uniform rate of mark-up of 20% is applied.

Required: find the gross profit and the sales figures.

Firstly, you prepare the trading account section of the trading and profit and loss account with the various missing figures shown as blank (or highlighted with a highlight pen, or with '?' inserted where the missing number should go):

**Trading Account Section of the Trading and Profit and Loss Account
for the year ending 31 December 2005**

	£	£
Sales		?
Less Cost of goods sold:		
Stock 1.1.2005	400	
Add Purchases	5,200	
	5,600	
Less Stock 31.12.2005	(600)	
		(5,000)
Gross profit		?

Answer:

It is known that: Cost of goods sold + Gross profit   = Sales
and you know that you can use
   mark-up to find the profit, because: Cost of goods sold + Percentage mark-up = Sales

So: £5,000   + 20%   = Sales
and Sales =   £5,000   + £1,000   = £6,000

The trading account can be completed by inserting the Gross profit £1,000 and £6,000 for Sales:

Trading Account Section of the Trading and Profit and Loss Account
for the year ending 31 December 2005

	£	£
Sales		6,000
Less Cost of goods sold:		
Stock 1.1.2005	400	
Add Purchases	5,200	
	5,600	
Less Stock 31.12.2005	(600)	
		(5,000)
Gross profit		1,000

Example 2

Another business has the following figures for 2006:

	£
Stock 1.1.2006	500
Stock 31.12.2006	800
Sales	6,400

A uniform rate of margin of 25% is in use.

Required: find the gross profit and the figure for purchases.

Trading Account Section of the Trading and Profit and Loss Account
for the year ending 31 December 2006

	£	£
Sales		6,400
Less Cost of goods sold:		
Stock 1.1.2006	500	
Add Purchases	?	
	?	
Less Stock 31.12.2006	800	?
Gross profit		?

Answer: Cost of goods sold + Gross profit = Sales
Moving items about: Sales   – Gross profit = Cost of goods sold
                      Sales   – 25% margin   = Cost of goods sold
                      £6,400   – £1,600   = £4,800

Now the following figures are known:

		£	£
Sales			6,400
Less Cost of goods sold:			
Stock 1.1.2006		500	
Add Purchases	(1)	?	
	(2)	?	
Less Stock 31.12.2006		(800)	
			(4,800)
Gross profit			1,600

Exhibit 32.1 illustrates this:

Exhibit 32.1

Trading Account Section of the Trading and Profit and Loss Accounts for the years ending 31 December

		2006		2007
	£	£	£	£
Sales		7,000		8,000
Less Cost of goods sold:				
Opening stock	500		900	
Add Purchases	6,000		7,200	
	6,500		8,100	
Less Closing stock	(900)		(1,100)	
		(5,600)		(7,000)
Gross profit		1,400		1,000

In the year 2006 the gross profit as a percentage of sales was

$$\frac{1,400}{7,000} \times \frac{100}{1} = 20 \text{ per cent.}$$

In the year 2007 it became

$$\frac{1,000}{8,000} \times \frac{100}{1} = 12\frac{1}{2} \text{ per cent.}$$

Sales had increased but, as the gross profit percentage had fallen by a relatively greater amount, the gross profit has fallen. There can be many reasons for such a fall in the gross profit percentage, including:

1 Perhaps the goods being sold have cost more, but the selling price of the goods has not risen to the same extent.
2 There may have been a greater wastage or theft of goods.
3 There could be a difference in how much has been sold of each sort of goods, called the sales-mix, between this year and last, with different kinds of goods carrying different rates of gross profit per £100 of sales.
4 Perhaps in order to increase sales, reductions have been made in the selling price of goods.

(This last one was the example used in Activity 32.4, but any of these possible causes could have been used instead.) These are only some of the possible reasons for the decrease. The idea of calculating the ratio is to show that the profitability per £100 of sales has changed. The business would then try to find out why and how such a change has taken place.

As the figure of sales revenue less returns inwards is also known as 'turnover', the ratio is sometimes referred to as 'gross profit percentage on turnover'. However, the most frequently used names for it are 'gross profit on sales' and 'gross margin'.

Stock turnover

If we always kept just £100 of stock at cost which, when we sold it, would always sell for £125, and we sold this amount eight times in a year, we would make 8 × £25 = £200 gross profit. The quicker we sell our stock (we could say the quicker we turnover our stock) the more the profit we will make, if our gross profit percentage stays the same.

To check on how quickly we are turning over our stock we can use the formula:

$$\frac{\text{Cost of goods sold}}{\text{Average stock}} = \text{Number of times stock is turned over within a period}$$

Activity 32.5 Spend a minute thinking about this and then write down why you think it might be useful to know how many times we turn over our stock in a period.

It would be best if the average stock held could be calculated by valuing the stock quite a few times each year, then dividing the totals of the figures obtained by the number of valuations. For instance, monthly stock figures are added up and then divided by twelve. This would provide a far more meaningful figure for 'average' stock. However, it is quite common, especially in examinations or in cases where no other information is available, to calculate the average stock as the opening stock plus the closing stock and the answer divided by two. Using the figures in Exhibit 32.1 we can calculate the stock turnover for 2006 and 2007:

$$2006 \quad \frac{5,600}{(500 + 900) \div 2} = 8 \text{ times per year}$$

$$2007 \quad \frac{7,000}{(900 + 1,100) \div 2} = 7 \text{ times per year}$$

Instead of saying that the stock turnover is so many times per year, we could say on average how long we keep stock before we sell it. We do this by the formula:

To express it in months: $12 \div \text{Stock turnover} = x \text{ months}$
To express it in days: $365 \div \text{Stock turnover} = x \text{ days}$

From Exhibit 32.1:

	2006	2007
In months	$\frac{12}{8} = 1.5$ months	$\frac{12}{7} = 1.7$ months
In days	$\frac{365}{8} = 45.6$ days	$\frac{365}{7} = 52.1$ days

All the above figures are rounded to one decimal place.

When the rate of stock turnover is falling it can be due to such causes as a slowing down of sales activity, or to keeping a higher figure of stock than is really necessary. The ratio does not prove anything by itself, it merely prompts inquiries as to why it should be changing.

This chapter has introduced ratios so as to help you understand the material in the next chapter.

Current ratio

This ratio is current assests:current liabilities and indicates whether there are sufficient relatively liquid (i.e. convertible to cash) assets to meet short term debts when due. It is discussed in greater detail in Chapter 15.

In Chapter 45, we will return again to ratios, and cover the topic with a more advanced and detailed survey of what a range of ratios can be used for.

Learning outcomes

You should now have learnt:

1 That accounting ratios can be used to deduce missing figures, given certain assumptions.

2 That if the mark-up is known, the margin can easily be calculated.

3 That if the margin is known, the mark-up can easily be calculated.

4 How to calculate the gross profit on sales and stock turnover ratios.

5 What may cause these ratios to change over time.

Answers to activities

32.1 Incomplete records exist where a business does not keep detailed accounting records. Perhaps it only operates a cash book, maybe not even that. In these circumstances, accountants have to construct the records that would have existed had a proper set of books been maintained, so that they can then prepare the financial statements. This involves working through invoices, receipts, and bank records, plus any records the business actually kept and trying to identify and record what actually occurred during the period. Because of the logical relationships that exist between many of the items in financial statements, and because of the unambiguous rule of double entry, ratios defining the relationship between various items can be used to assist in this investigation. So, for example, if you know what stock was held at the start, what was purchased and you know what is left in stock at the end, you can easily work out what was sold.

32.2 If you take mark-up and add one to the denominator (the bottom part of the fraction), you get the margin. This is *always* the case when the numerator (the top line) is '1'.

32.3 As you will remember from Chapter 17 (page 209), you use the same formula but replace both the '5s' in the example with '17.5' and 'Profit before commission' with the total amount of the bill:

$$\frac{17.5}{100 + 17.5} \times £235 = £35$$

This is a *very* useful formula to know. You would be wise to remember it.

32.4 Gross profit may increase at the same rate as sales revenue because demand absorbed more units at the original price. This is normally the case if you make relatively small increases in the volume offered for sale when demand is currently exceeding supply. However, when sales volume increases, it is often partly because selling price has been reduced. Even though total sales volume has increased, sales revenue per unit is less than previously and so gross profit as a percentage of sales revenue will be lower than previously. Unless enough additional units were sold to recover the profit lost as a result of cutting the selling price, total gross profit will fall, not increase.

When a business is in trouble and cutting selling prices to try to make more profits by selling more units, it can often look as if it is doing much better if you only look at the sales revenue and gross profit figures. However, when you calculate the gross profit as a percentage of sales (i.e. the gross margin) and compare it with the previous gross margin, you can see that the business is possibly doing less well than before in terms of overall profitability.

32.5 It is useful to know as you can compare how quickly stock is turning over now compared to the past. If it is turning over more slowly now (i.e. less times in a period than before), stock levels may have grown higher, which may mean that the costs of holding stocks have risen. This rise in stock levels may be due to our now buying more stock every time we place an order – perhaps suppliers are offering discounts for larger sized orders. This may be good, or it may be bad. You need to investigate the situation and find out. Hence, checking the trend in stock turnover alerts you to the possibility that costs may be rising and that they may exceed any savings being made. You can also check your rate of stock turnover with those of your competitors, enabling you to detect if your ordering and storing practices are significantly different from theirs. If they are, you would then investigate what is happening so as to ensure you are not wasting resources unnecessarily.

Review questions

32.1 G Flynn is a trader who sells all of his goods at 20% above cost. His books give the following information at 31 December 2007:

	£
Stock 1 January 2007	19,400
Stock 31 December 2007	26,660
Sales for year	155,880

You are required to:
(a) Ascertain cost of goods sold.
(b) Show the value of purchases during the year.
(c) Calculate the profit made by Flynn.

Show your answer in the form of the trading account section of the trading and profit and loss account.

32.2A R Jack gives you the following information as at 31 March 2005:

	£
Stock 1 April 2004	14,000
Purchases	82,000

Jack's mark-up is 40% on 'cost of goods sold'. His average stock during the year was £17,000. Draw up a trading and profit and loss account for the year ending 31 March 2005.

(a) Calculate the closing stock as at 31 March 2005.
(b) State the total amount of profit and loss expenditure Jack must not exceed if he is to maintain a *net* profit on sales of 8%.

32.3 L Hope's business has a rate of stock turnover of 8 times per year. Average stock is £16,240. Mark-up is 60%. Expenses are 70% of gross profit.

You are to calculate:
(a) Cost of goods sold.
(b) Gross profit.
(c) Turnover.
(d) Total expenses.
(e) Net profit.

32.4A The following figures relate to the retail business of A Bell for the month of July 2003. Goods which are on sale fall into two categories, X and Y.

	Category X	Category Y
Sales to the public at manufacturer's recommended list price	£9,000	£24,000
Trade discount allowed to retailers	15%	18%
Total expenses as a percentage of sales	14%	14%
Annual rate of stock turnover	10	16

You are to calculate for each category of goods:
(a) Cost of goods sold.
(b) Gross profit.
(c) Total expenses.
(d) Net profit.
(e) Average stock at cost, assuming that sales are distributed evenly over the year, and that each month is of the same length.

32.5 The following trading account is extracted from the trading and profit and loss account for the year ending 31 December 2008 and is given to you by the owner of the business, M Pole:

	£	£
Sales		271,400
Less Cost of goods sold:		
Opening stock	34,000	
Add Purchases	237,000	
	271,000	
Less Closing stock	(41,000)	
		(230,000)
Gross profit		41,400

Pole says that normally he adds 20% to the cost of goods to fix the sales price. However, this year there were some arithmetical errors in these calculations.

(a) Calculate what his sales would have been if he had not made any errors.
(b) Given that his expenses remain constant at 9% of his sales, calculate his net profit for the year 2008.
(c) Work out the rate of stock turnover for 2008.
(d) He thinks that next year he can increase his mark-up to 25%, selling goods which will cost him £260,000. If he does not make any more errors in calculating selling prices, you are to calculate the expected gross and net profits for 2009.

32.6A   **Trading Account for the year ended 31 December 2009**

	£		£
Stock 1 January 2009	3,000	Sales	60,000
Purchases	47,000		
	50,000		
Stock 31 December 2009	(4,500)		
Cost of sales	45,500		
Gross profit	14,500		
	60,000		60,000

R Sheldon presents you with the trading account set out above.[Authors' Note] He always calculates his selling price by adding 33⅓% of cost on to the cost price.

(a) If he has adhered strictly to the statement above, what should be the percentage of gross profit to sales?
(b) Calculate his actual percentage of gross profit to sales.
(c) Give two reasons for the difference between the figures you have calculated above.
(d) His suppliers are proposing to increase their prices by 5%, but R Sheldon considers that he would be unwise to increase his selling price. To obtain some impression of the effect on gross profit if his costs should be increased by 5% he asks you to reconstruct his trading account to show the gross profit if the increase had applied from 1 January 2009.
(e) Using the figures given in the trading account at the beginning of the question, calculate R Sheldon's rate of stock turnover.
(f) R Sheldon's expenses amount to 10% of his sales. Calculate his net profit for the year ending 31 December 2009.
(g) If all expenses remained unchanged, but suppliers of stock increased their prices by 5% as in (d) above, calculate the percentage reduction in the amount of net profit which R Sheldon's accounts would have shown.

(*Edexcel, London Examinations: GCSE*)

Authors' Note: The trading account shown in the question has been prepared in an unconventional way. It is, in effect, a different form of presentation of the trading account section of the trading and profit and loss account. Do not adopt this layout yourself.

32.7 L Mann started business with £5,000 in the bank on 1 April. The business transactions during the month were as follows:

(*i*)   Took £300 out of the bank for petty cash
(*ii*)   Bought a second-hand van and paid by cheque £3,500
(*iii*) Bought goods on credit from A Supplier for £2,500
(*iv*)   Sold goods for cash for £300
(*v*)   Sold goods on credit for £1,000 to B Safe
(*vi*)   Returned faulty goods to A Supplier £500
(*vii*) Paid sundry expenses of £50 in cash
(*viii*) Paid the rent of £500 by cheque
(*ix*)   Withdrew cash drawings of £500

Stock at cost at 30 April was £1,250.

Required:
(a) Prepare the ledger accounts recording the transactions.
(b) Prepare the trial balance at 30 April.
(c) Prepare a trading, profit and loss account for April.
(d) Prepare a balance sheet as at 30 April.
(e) Calculate the percentages of:
   (i) Gross profit to sales.
   (ii) Net profit to opening capital.
(f) Comment on:
   (i) The relationship between drawings and net profit and why it is important that Mann keeps an eye on it.
   (ii) Working capital.

32.8A Arthur deals in bicycles. His business position at 1 October was as follows:

Capital £3,369
Stock £306 (3 x Model A bicycles @ £54 and 3 x Model B @ £48)
Balance at bank £3,063

Having established good relations with his supplier he is able to obtain bicycles on one month's credit. He kept notes of all transactions during October which he then summarised as follows:

(*i*)   Purchased on credit from Mr Raleigh: 12 Model A at £54 and 10 Model B at £48. Total purchase £1,128.
(*ii*) Sales for cash were: 11 Model A at £81 and 8 Model B at £72.
(*iii*) Paid Rent by cheque £60, advertising £66 and miscellaneous expenses £12.
(*iv*) Drawings were £150.

Arthur's valuation of the closing stock was £456 as at 31 October.

Required:
(a) Prepare a statement showing the bank transactions during October.
(b) Check the closing stock valuation.
(c) Prepare a statement showing the gross profit and net profit for October and calculate the percentages of gross profit to sales and net profit to sales.
(d) Prepare a trading, profit and loss account for the month of October together with a balance sheet as at 31 October.
(e) Prepare a statement to show where the profit for the month has gone.

→

32.9 The following information is available for the years 2007, 2008, and 2009:

	2007 £	2008 £	2009 £
Opening stock	10,000	20,000	28,000
Purchases	70,000	86,000	77,000
	80,000	106,000	105,000
Less Closing stock	(20,000)	(28,000)	(23,000)
Cost of sales	60,000	78,000	82,000
Sales	90,000	125,000	120,000
Gross profit	30,000	47,000	38,000

The stock valuations used above at the end of 2007 and at the end of 2008 were inaccurate. The stock at 31 December 2007 had been under-valued by £1,000, whilst that at 31 December 2008 had been over-valued by £3,000.

Required:
(a) Give the corrected figures of gross profit for each of the years affected by the errors in stock valuation.
(b) Using the figures in the revised trading accounts, calculate for each year:
  (i) the percentage of gross profit to sales, and
  (ii) the rate of turnover of stock.

You can find a range of additional self-test questions, as well as material to help you with your studies, on the website that accompanies this book at **www.pearsoned.co.uk/wood**

Single entry and incomplete records

Learning objectives

After you have studied this chapter, you should be able to:

- deduce the figure of profits where only the increase in capital and details of drawings are known
- draw up a trading and profit and loss account and balance sheet from records not kept on a double entry system
- deduce the figure for cash drawings when all other cash receipts and cash payments are known
- deduce the figures of sales and purchases from incomplete records

Introduction

In this chapter, you'll learn about single entry and incomplete records. You will learn how to use the accounting equation to identify the profit for a period when only the opening and closing capital figures and drawings are known. You will also learn how to find the figure for cash drawings or the figure for cash expenses when all other cash receipts and payments are known. And you will learn how to find the figures for purchases and sales from incomplete records.

33.1 Why double entry is not used

For every small shopkeeper, market stall, internet cafe, or other small business to keep its books using a full double entry system would be ridiculous. Apart from anything else, a large number of the owners of such businesses would not know how to write up double entry records, even if they wanted to.

It is more likely that they would enter details of a transaction once only, using a single entry system. Many of them would fail to record every transaction, resulting in incomplete records.

It is, perhaps, only fair to remember that accounting is supposed to be an aid to management – accounting *is not* something to be done as an end in itself. Therefore, many small firms, especially retail shops, can have all the information they want by merely keeping a cash book and having some form of record, not necessarily in double entry form, of their debtors and creditors.

However, despite many small businesses not having any need for accounting records, most do have to prepare financial statements or, at least, calculate their sales or profits once a year. How can these be calculated if the bookkeeping records are inadequate or incomplete?

Activity 33.1 What may cause these accounting statements and figures to need to be calculated?

(*i*) profits
(*ii*) sales
(*iii*) financial statements

33.2 Profit as an increase in capital

From your knowledge of the accounting equation, you know that unless there has been an introduction of extra cash or resources into a business, the only way that capital can be increased is by making profits.

Identifying profits when opening and closing capital are known

If you know the capital at the start of a period and the capital at the end of the period, profit is the figure found by subtracting capital at the start of the period from that at the end of the period.

Let's look at a business where capital at the end of 2004 was £20,000. During 2005 there have been no drawings, and no extra capital has been brought in by the owner. At the end of 2005 the capital was £30,000.

$$\text{Net profit} = \underset{\text{capital}}{\underset{\text{This year's}}{£30,000}} - \underset{\text{capital}}{\underset{\text{Last year's}}{£20,000}} = £10,000$$

If drawings had been £7,000, the profits must have been £17,000:

$$\underset{£20,000}{\text{Last year's capital}} + \underset{?}{\text{Profits}} - \underset{£7,000}{\text{Drawings}} = \underset{£30,000}{\text{This year's capital}}$$

We can see that £17,000 profits is the figure needed to complete the formula:

$$£20,000 + £17,000 - £7,000 = £30,000$$

Identifying profits when you only have a list of the opening and closing assets and liabilities

In this case, you use the accounting equation.

Activity 33.2 What is the formula for the accounting equation? Write down both (a) the normal form and (b) the alternate form.

Exhibit 33.1 shows the calculation of profit where insufficient information is available to draft a trading and profit and loss account. The only information available is about the assets and liabilities.

Exhibit 33.1

H Taylor has not kept proper bookkeeping records, but she has kept notes in diary form of the transactions of her business. She is able to give you details of her assets and liabilities as at 31 December 2005 and 31 December 2006:

At 31 December 2005
Assets: Van £6,000; Fixtures £1,800; Stock £3,000; Debtors £4,100; Bank £4,800; Cash £200.
Liabilities: Creditors £1,200; Loan from J Ogden £3,500.

At 31 December 2006
Assets: Van (after depreciation) £5,000; Fixtures (after depreciation) £1,600; Stock £3,800; Debtors £6,200; Bank £7,500; Cash £300.
Liabilities: Creditors £1,800; Loan from J Ogden £2,000.

Drawings during 2006 were £5,200.
You need to put all these figures into a format that will enable you to identify the profit. Firstly, you need to draw up a **statement of affairs** as at 31 December 2005. This is really just a balance sheet, but is the name normally used when you are dealing with incomplete records.

From the accounting equation, you know that capital is the difference between the assets and liabilities.

H Taylor
Statement of Affairs as at 31 December 2005

	£	£
Fixed assets		
Van		6,000
Fixtures		1,800
		7,800
Current assets		
Stock	3,000	
Debtors	4,100	
Bank	4,800	
Cash	200	
	12,100	
Less Current liabilities		
Creditors	(1,200)	
Net current assets		10,900
		18,700
Less: Long-term liability		
Loan from J Ogden		(3,500)
Net assets		15,200
Financed by:		
Capital(Note)		15,200

Note: the accounting equation tells you that this must be the figure to use.

You now draw up a second statement of affairs, this time as at the end of 2006. The formula of *Opening capital + Profit – Drawings = Closing capital* is then used to deduce the figure of profit.

→

→

H Taylor
Statement of Affairs as at 31 December 2006

	£	£
Fixed assets		
Van		5,000
Fixtures		1,600
		6,600
Current assets		
Stock	3,800	
Debtors	6,200	
Bank	7,500	
Cash	300	
	17,800	
Less Current liabilities		
Creditors	(1,800)	
Net current assets		16,000
		22,600
Less: Long-term liability		
Loan from J Ogden		(2,000)
Net assets		20,600

Financed by:		
Capital		
Balance at 1.1.2006		15,200
Add Net profit	(C)	?
	(B)	?
Less Drawings		(5,200)
	(A)	

Deduction of net profit:

Opening capital + Net profit − Drawings = Closing capital. Finding the missing figures (A), (B) and (C) by deduction:

(A) is the same as the total of the top half of the statement of affairs, i.e. £20,600;
(B) is therefore £20,600 + £5,200 = £25,800;
(C) is therefore £25,800 − £15,200 = £10,600.

To check:

Capital		
Balance at 1.1.2006		15,200
Add Net profit	(C)	10,600
	(B)	25,800
Less Drawings		(5,200)
	(A)	20,600

Obviously, this method of calculating profit is very unsatisfactory. It is much more informative when a trading and profit and loss account can be drawn up. Therefore, whenever possible, this 'comparisons of capital method' of ascertaining profit should be avoided and a full set of financial statements should be drawn up from the available records.

It is important to realise that a business should have exactly the same trading and profit and loss account and balance sheet whether they kept their books by single entry or double entry. However, as you will see, whereas the double entry system uses the trial balance in preparing the financial statements, the single entry system will have to arrive at the same answer by different means.

33.3 Drawing up the financial statements

The following example shows the various stages of drawing up financial statements from a single entry set of records.

The accountant has found the following details of transactions for J Frank's shop for the year ended 31 December 2005.

(a) The sales are mostly on credit. No record of sales has been kept, but £61,500 has been received from persons to whom goods have been sold – £48,000 by cheque and £13,500 in cash.

(b) Amount paid by cheque to suppliers during the year = £31,600.

(c) Expenses paid during the year: by cheque: Rent £3,800; General Expenses £310; by cash: Rent £400.

(d) J Frank took £250 cash per week (for 52 weeks) as drawings.

(e) Other information is available:

	At 31.12.2004	At 31.12.2005
	£	£
Debtors	5,500	6,600
Creditors for goods	1,600	2,600
Rent owing	–	350
Bank balance	5,650	17,940
Cash balance	320	420
Stock	6,360	6,800

(f) The only fixed asset consists of fixtures which were valued at 31 December 2004 at £3,300. These are to be depreciated at 10 per cent per annum.

We'll now prepare the financial statements in five stages.

Stage 1

Draw up a statement of affairs on the closing day of the earlier accounting period:

J Frank
Statement of Affairs as at 31 December 2004

	£	£
Fixed assets		
Fixtures		3,300
Current assets		
Stock	6,360	
Debtors	5,500	
Bank	5,650	
Cash	320	
	17,830	
Less Current liabilities		
Creditors	(1,600)	
Net current assets		16,230
		19,530
Financed by:		
Capital (difference)		19,530

All of these opening figures are then taken into account when drawing up the financial statements for 2005.

Stage 2

Prepare a cash and bank summary, showing the totals of each separate item, plus opening and closing balances.

	Cash	Bank		Cash	Bank
	£	£		£	£
Balances 31.12.2004	320	5,650	Suppliers		31,600
Receipts from debtors	13,500	48,000	Rent	400	3,800
			General Expenses		310
			Drawings	13,000	
			Balances 31.12.2005	420	17,940
	13,820	53,650		13,820	53,650

Stage 3

Calculate the figures for purchases and sales to be shown in the trading account. Remember that the figures needed are the same as those which would have been found if double entry records had been kept.

Purchases: In double entry, 'purchases' are the goods that have been bought in the period irrespective of whether they have been paid for or not during the period. The figure of payments to suppliers must, therefore, be adjusted to find the figure for purchases.

	£
Paid during the year	31,600
Less Payments made, but which were for goods purchased in a previous year	
(creditors at 31.12.2004)	(1,600)
	30,000
Add Purchases made in this year for which payment has not yet been made	
(creditors at 31.12.2005)	2,600
Goods bought in this year, i.e. purchases	32,600

The same answer could have been obtained if the information had been shown in the form of a total creditors account, the figure for purchases being the amount required to make the account totals agree.

Total Creditors

	£		£
Cash paid to suppliers	31,600	Balances b/d	1,600
Balances c/d	2,600	Purchases (missing figure)	32,600
	34,200		34,200

Sales: The sales figure will only equal receipts where all the sales are for cash. Therefore, the receipts figures need adjusting to find sales. This can only be done by constructing a total debtors account, the sales figure being the one needed to make the totals agree.

Total Debtors

	£		£
Balances b/d	5,500	Receipts: Cash	13,500
Sales (missing figure)	62,600	Cheque	48,000
		Balances c/d	6,600
	68,100		68,100

Stage 4

Expenses. Where there are no accruals or prepayments either at the beginning or end of the accounting period, then expenses paid will equal expenses used up during the period. These figures will be charged to the trading and profit and loss account.

On the other hand, where such prepayments or accruals exist, an expense account should be drawn up for that particular item. When all known items are entered, the missing figure will be the expenses to be charged for the accounting period. In this case, only the rent account needs to be drawn up.

Rent

	£		£
Bank	3,800	Profit and loss (missing figure)	4,550
Cash	400		
Accrued c/d	350		
	4,550		4,550

Stage 5

Now draw up the financial statements.

J Frank
Trading and Profit and Loss Account for the year ending 31 December 2005

	£	£
Sales (stage 3)		62,600
Less Cost of goods sold:		
Stock at 1.1.2005	6,360	
Add Purchases (stage 3)	32,600	
	38,960	
Less Stock at 31.12.2005	(6,800)	
		(32,160)
Gross profit		30,440
Less Expenses:		
Rent (stage 4)	4,550	
General expenses	310	
Depreciation: Fixtures	330	
		(5,190)
Net profit		25,250

Balance Sheet as at 31 December 2005

	£	£	£
Fixed assets			
Fixtures at 1.1.2005			3,300
Less Depreciation			(330)
			2,970
Current assets			
Stock		6,800	
Debtors		6,600	
Bank		17,940	
Cash		420	
		31,760	
Less Current liabilities			
Creditors	2,600		
Rent owing	350		
		(2,950)	
Net current assets			28,810
Net assets			31,780
Financed by:			
Capital			
Balance 1.1.2005 (per Opening Statement of Affairs)			19,530
Add Net profit			25,250
			44,780
Less Drawings			13,000
			31,780

33.4 Incomplete records and missing figures

In practice, part of the information relating to *cash* receipts or payments is often missing. If the missing information is in respect of one type of payment, then it is normal to assume that the missing figure is the amount required to make both totals agree in the *cash* column of the cash and bank summary. (This does not happen with bank items owing to the fact that another copy of the bank statement can always be obtained from the bank.)

Exhibit 33.2 shows an example where the figure for Drawings is unknown. The exhibit also shows the contra entry made in the cash book when cash receipts are banked.

Exhibit 33.2

The following information on cash and bank receipts and payments is available:

	Cash	Bank
	£	£
Cash paid into the bank during the year	35,500	
Receipts from debtors	47,250	46,800
Paid to suppliers	1,320	44,930
Drawings during the year	?	–
Expenses paid	150	3,900
Balances at 1.1.2004	235	11,200
Balances at 31.12.2004	250	44,670

Now, you need to enter this information in a cash book:

	Cash	Bank		Cash	Bank
	£	£		£	£
Balances 1.1.2004	235	11,200	Bank ¢	35,500	
Received from debtors	47,250	46,800	Suppliers	1,320	44,930
Cash ¢		35,500	Expenses	150	3,900
			Drawings	?	
			Balances 31.12.2004	250	44,670
	47,485	93,500		47,485	93,500

The amount needed to make the two sides of the cash columns agree is £10,265 i.e. £47,485 minus £(35,500 + 1,320 + 150 + 250). This is the figure for drawings.

Exhibit 33.3 shows an example where the amount of cash received from debtors is unknown.

Exhibit 33.3

Information on cash and bank transactions is available as follows:

	Cash	Bank
	£	£
Receipts from debtors	?	78,080
Cash withdrawn from the bank for business use (this is the amount which is used besides cash receipts from debtors to pay drawings and expenses)		10,920
Paid to suppliers	–	65,800
Expenses paid	640	2,230
Drawings	21,180	315
Balances at 1.1.2007	40	1,560
Balances at 31.12.2007	70	375

	Cash	Bank		Cash	Bank
	£	£		£	£
Balances 1.1.2007	40	1,560	Suppliers		65,800
Received from debtors	?	78,080	Expenses	640	2,230
Bank ¢	10,920		Cash ¢		10,920
			Drawings	21,180	315
			Balances 31.12.2007	70	375
	21,890	79,640		21,890	79,640

As it is the only missing item, receipts from debtors is, therefore, the amount needed to make each side of the cash column agree, £10,930 i.e. £21,890 minus £(10,920 + 40).

It must be emphasised that the use of balancing figures is acceptable *only* when all the other figures have been verified. Should, for instance, a cash expense be omitted when cash received from debtors is being calculated, this would result in an understatement not only of expenses but also, ultimately, of sales.

33.5 Where there are two missing pieces of information

Quite often, the only cash expense item for which there is some doubt is drawings. Receipts will normally have been retained for all the others.

If both cash drawings and cash receipts from debtors (or from cash sales) were not known, it would not be possible to deduce both of these figures separately. The only course available would be to estimate whichever figure was more capable of being accurately assessed, use this as if it were a 'known' figure, then deduce the other figure. However, this is a most unsatisfactory position as both of the figures are estimates, the accuracy of each one relying entirely upon the accuracy of the other.

Activity 33.3 Why is arriving at a figure for drawings that is as accurate as possible *very* important for the owner of a business?

33.6 Cash sales and purchases for cash

Where there are cash sales as well as sales on credit terms, then the cash sales must be added to sales on credit to give the total sales for the year. This total figure of sales will be the one shown in the trading account section of the trading and profit and loss account.

Similarly, purchases for cash will need to be added to credit purchases in order to produce the figure of total purchases for the trading account.

33.7 Stock stolen, lost or destroyed

When stock is stolen, lost or destroyed, its value will have to be calculated. This could be needed to justify an insurance claim or to settle problems concerning taxation, etc.

If the stock had been valued immediately before the fire, burglary, etc., then the value of the stock lost would obviously be known. Also, if a full and detailed system of stock records were

Exhibit 34.1

The Haven Running Club
Receipts and Payments Account for the year ended 31 December 2005

Receipts	£	Payments	£
Bank balance at 1.1.2005	2,360	Groundsman's wages	7,280
Subscriptions received in 2005	11,480	Sports ground rental	2,960
Rent received	1,160	Committee expenses	580
		Printing and stationery	330
		Bank balance at 31.12.2005	3,850
	15,000		15,000

Activity 34.1

Why do you think non-profit-oriented organisations prepare receipts and payments accounts when they have all this information in the cash book already?

34.3 Income and expenditure accounts

When assets are owned and/or there are liabilities, the receipts and payments account is not sufficient. Other than the cash received and paid out, it shows only the cash balances. The other assets and liabilities are not shown at all. What is required is:

1 a balance sheet, and
2 a statement showing whether the association's capital has increased.

In a profit-oriented organisation, 2 would be a trading and profit and loss account. In a non-profit-oriented organisation, 2 would be an **income and expenditure account**.

An income and expenditure account follows the same rules as a trading and profit and loss account. The only differences are the terms used.

A comparison between the terminology of financial statements produced by profit-oriented and non-profit-oriented organisations now follows.

Terms used

Profit-oriented organisation	Non-profit-oriented organisation
1 Trading and profit and loss account	1 Income and expenditure account
2 Net profit	2 Surplus of income over expenditure
3 Net loss	3 Deficit of income over expenditure

34.4 Profit or loss for a special purpose

Sometimes there are reasons why a non-profit-oriented organisation would want to prepare either a trading account or a full trading and profit and loss account.

This is where something is done by it in order to make a profit. The profit is not to be kept, but is used to pay for the main purpose of the organisation.

For instance, a football club may organise and run dances which people pay to go to. Any profit from these helps to pay football expenses. For these dances, either a trading account or a full trading and profit and loss account would be drawn up. Any profit (or loss) would be transferred to the income and expenditure account.

34.5 Accumulated fund

A sole trader has a capital account. A non-profit-oriented organisation has an **accumulated fund**. In effect, it is the same as a capital account, as it is the difference between the assets and liabilities.

For a sole trader

$$\boxed{\text{Capital} = \text{Assets} - \text{Liabilities}}$$

For a non-profit-oriented organisation

$$\boxed{\text{Accumulated Fund} = \text{Assets} - \text{Liabilities}}$$

34.6 Drawing up income and expenditure accounts

We can now look at the preparation of an income and expenditure account and a balance sheet of a club in Exhibit 34.2. A separate trading account is to be prepared for a bar, where refreshments are sold to make a profit.

The majority of clubs and associations keep their accounts using single entry methods. This example will therefore be from single entry records, using the principles described in the previous chapter.

Exhibit 34.2

The treasurer of the Long Lane Football Club has prepared a receipts and payments account, but members have complained about the inadequacy of such an account. She therefore asks an accountant to prepare a trading account for the bar, and an income and expenditure account and a balance sheet. The treasurer gives the accountant a copy of the receipts and payments account together with information on assets and liabilities at the beginning and end of the year:

Long Lane Football Club
Receipts and Payments Account for the year ended 31 December 2006

Receipts	£	Payments	£
Bank balance at 1.1.2006	524	Payment for bar supplies	38,620
Subscriptions received for		Wages:	
2005 (arrears)	1,400	Groundsman and assistant	19,939
2006	14,350	Barman	8,624
2007 (in advance)	1,200	Bar expenses	234
Bar sales	61,280	Repairs to stands	740
Donations received	800	Ground upkeep	1,829
		Secretary's expenses	938
		Transport costs	2,420
		Bank balance at 31.12.2006	6,210
	79,554		79,554

→

Additional information:	31.12.2005	31.12.2006
1	£	£
Stocks in the bar – at cost	4,496	5,558
Owing for bar supplies	3,294	4,340
Bar expenses owing	225	336
Transport costs	–	265

2 The land and football stands were valued at 31 December 2005 at: land £40,000; football stands £20,000; the stands are to be depreciated by 10 per cent per annum.
3 The equipment at 31 December 2005 was valued at £2,500, and is to be depreciated at 20 per cent per annum.
4 Subscriptions owing by members amounted to £1,400 on 31 December 2005, and £1,750 on 31 December 2006.

From this information, in the following three stages, the accountant drew up the appropriate accounts and statements:

Stage 1

Draw up a statement of affairs at the end of the previous period in order to identify the balance on the Accumulated Fund brought forward to 2006.

Statement of Affairs as at 31 December 2005

	£	£	£
Fixed assets			
Land			40,000
Stands			20,000
Equipment			2,500
Current assets			62,500
Stock in bar		4,496	
Debtors for subscriptions		1,400	
Cash at bank		524	
Less Current liabilities		6,420	
Creditors	3,294		
Bar expenses owing	225		
		(3,519)	
Net current assets			2,901
			65,401
Financed by:			
Accumulated fund (difference)			65,401

 Activity 34.2 Why do you think this statement was described as being a 'statement of affairs' rather than a 'balance sheet'?

Stage 2

Draw up a bar trading account.

Long Lane Football Club
Bar Trading Account for the year ending 31 December 2006

	£	£
Sales		61,280
Less Cost of goods sold:		
Stock 1.1.2006	4,496	
Add Purchases[Note 1]	39,666	
	44,162	
Less Stock 31.12.2006	(5,558)	
		(38,604)
Gross profit		22,676
Less Bar expenses[Note 2]	345	
Barman's wages	8,624	
		(8,969)
Net profit to income and expenditure account		13,707

Notes:

1 **Purchases Control**

	£		£
Cash	38,620	Balances (creditors) b/d	3,294
Balances c/d	4,340	Trading account (difference)	39,666
	42,960		42,960

2 **Bar Expenses**

	£		£
Cash	234	Balance b/d	225
Balance c/d	336	Trading account (difference)	345
	570		570

Stage 3

Draw up the financial statements.

Long Lane Football Club
Income and Expenditure Account for the year ending 31 December 2006

	£	£	£
Income			
Subscriptions for 2006[Note 1]			**16,100**
Profit from the bar			13,707
Donations received			800
			30,607
Less Expenditure			
Wages – Groundsman and assistant		19,939	
Repairs to stands		740	
Ground upkeep		1,829	
Secretary's expenses		938	
Transport costs[Note 2]		2,685	
Depreciation			
Stands	2,000		
Equipment	500		
		2,500	
			(28,631)
Surplus of income over expenditure			1,976

Notes:

1   **Subscriptions Received**

	£		£
Balance (debtors) b/d	1,400	Cash 2005	1,400
Income and expenditure		2006	14,350
account (difference)	16,100	2007	1,200
Balance (in advance) c/d	1,200	Balance (owing) c/d	1,750
	18,700		18,700

2   **Transport Costs**

	£		£
Cash	2,420	**Income and expenditure**	
Accrued c/d	265	account (difference)	2,685
	2,685		2,685

Note that subscriptions received in advance are carried down as a credit balance to the following period.

The Long Lane Football Club
Balance Sheet as at 31 December 2006

	£	£	£
Fixed assets			
Land at valuation			40,000
Football stands at valuation		20,000	
Less Depreciation		(2,000)	
			18,000
Equipment at valuation		2,500	
Less Depreciation		(500)	
			2,000
			60,000
Current assets			
Stock of bar supplies		5,558	
Debtors for subscriptions		1,750	
Cash at bank		6,210	
		13,518	
Less Current liabilities			
Creditors for bar supplies	4,340		
Bar expenses owing	336		
Transport costs owing	265		
Subscriptions received in advance	1,200		
		(6,141)	
Net current assets			7,377
Net assets			67,377
Financed by:			
Accumulated fund			
Balance as at 1.1.2006			65,401
Add Surplus of income over expenditure			1,976
			67,377

34.7   Outstanding subscriptions and the prudence concept

So far we have treated subscriptions owing as being an asset. However, as any treasurer of a club would tell you, most subscriptions that have been owing for a long time are never paid – members lose interest or simply go somewhere else. As a result, many clubs do not include unpaid subscriptions as an asset in the balance sheet.

Activity 34.3

Does this policy of ignoring subscriptions due when preparing the financial statements comply with the prudence concept? Why/Why not?

In an examination, you should assume that subscriptions owing are to be brought into the financial statements, unless instructions to the contrary are given.

Exhibit 34.3 shows an instance where subscriptions in arrears and in advance occur at the beginning and end of a period.

Exhibit 34.3

An amateur theatrical group charges its members an annual subscription of £20 per member. It accrues for subscriptions owing at the end of each year and also adjusts for subscriptions received in advance.

(A) On 1 January 2002, 18 members had not yet paid their subscriptions for the year 2001.
(B) In December 2001, 4 members paid £80 for the year 2002.
(C) During the year 2002 it received £7,420 in cash for subscriptions:

	£
For 2001	360
For 2002	6,920
For 2003	140
	7,420

(D) At 31 December 2002, 11 members had not paid their 2002 subscriptions.

Subscriptions

2002			£	2002			£
Jan 1	Owing b/d	(A)	360	Jan 1	Prepaid b/d	(B)	80
Dec 31	Income and expenditure*		7,220	Dec 31	Bank	(C)	7,420
	Prepaid c/d	(C)	140		Owing c/d	(D)	220
			7,720				7,720
2003				2003			
Jan 1	Owing b/d	(D)	220	Jan 1	Prepaid b/d	(C)	140

*This is the difference between the two sides of the account.

34.8 Life membership

In some clubs and societies, members can make a payment for life membership. This means that by paying a fairly large amount now members can enjoy the facilities of the club for the rest of their lives.

Such a receipt should not be treated as income in the income and expenditure account solely in the year in which the member paid the money. It should be credited to a life membership account, and transfers should be made from that account to the credit of the income and expenditure account of an appropriate amount annually.

Exactly what is meant by an 'appropriate amount' to transfer each year is decided by the committee of the club or society. The usual basis is to establish, on average, how long members will continue to use the benefits of the club. To take an extreme case, if a club was in existence which could not be joined below the age of 70, then the expected number of years' use of the club on average per member would be relatively few. Another club, such as a golf club, where a fair proportion of the members joined when reasonably young, and where the game is capable of being played by members until and during old age, would expect a much higher average of years of use per member. In the end, the club has to decide for itself.

As a club has to provide amenities for life members without any further payment, the credit balance remaining on the account, after the transfer of the agreed amount has been made to the credit of the income and expenditure account, should be shown on the balance sheet as a liability.

In an examination, be sure to follow the instructions set by the examiner.

34.9 Donations

Any donations received are usually shown as income in the year that they are received.

34.10 Entrance fees

When they first join a club, in addition to the membership fee for that year, new members often have to pay an entrance fee. Entrance fees are normally included as income in the year that they are received. A club could, however, decide to treat them differently, perhaps by spreading the income over a number of years. It all depends on the circumstances.

Learning outcomes

You should now have learnt:

1 That a receipts and payments account does not show the full financial position of an organisation, except for one where the only asset is cash and there are no liabilities.

2 That an income and expenditure account is drawn up to show either the surplus of income over expenditure or the excess of expenditure over income. These are the same as 'profit' or 'loss' in a profit-oriented organisation.

3 That the accumulated fund is basically the same as a capital account.

4 That although the main object of the organisation is non-profit-oriented, certain activities may be run at a profit (or may lose money) in order to help finance the main objectives of the organisation.

5 That in an examination you should treat subscriptions owing at the end of a period in the same way as debtors, unless told otherwise.

6 That donations are usually treated as income in the period in which they are received.

7 That entrance fees are usually treated as income in the year in which they are received.

8 That the treatment of life membership fees is purely at the discretion of the organisation, but that they are usually amortised over an appropriate period.

Answers to activities

34.1 Just as you would prepare a balance sheet for a profit-oriented organisation in order to summarise its financial position at a specific point in time, so non-profit-oriented organisations that deal only in cash, own no assets and have no liabilities may prepare a receipts and payments account in order to show what happened over a period and the amount of funds left at the end. Non-profit-oriented organisations with assets and liabilities may also prepare them but only, normally, in order to help prepare their main financial statements.

34.2 You could just as easily draw up a balance sheet but you're trying to summarise the financial statement even more than in a balance sheet. You would not, for example, show provision for doubtful debts being subtracted from debtors in a statement of affairs, but you would in the balance sheet of a sole trader. To avoid confusion, the title 'statement of affairs' is used when performing any preparatory work prior to preparing the balance sheet. (It must be said, however, that you would not be wrong if you called the statement of affairs a balance sheet.)

34.3 It does not comply with the prudence concept. You will remember from your coverage of the prudence concept in Chapter 10 that you should not overstate *or* understate income and expenditure. While this practice ensures the figure for subscriptions due is not overstated, it does understate them.

Review questions

34.1 A summary of the Downline Rugby Club's cash book is shown below. From it, and the additional information, you are to construct an income and expenditure account for the year ending 31 December 2006, and a balance sheet as at that date.

Cash Book Summary

	£		£
Balance at 1.1.2006	1,440	Purchase of equipment	380
Collections at matches	4,218	Rent for pitch	1,600
Profit on sale of refreshments	5,520	Printing and stationery	104
		Secretary's expenses	220
		Repairs to equipment	210
		Groundsman's wages	6,400
		Miscellaneous expenses	96
		Balance at 31.12.2006	2,168
	11,178		11,178

Further information:
(*i*) At 1.1.2006 equipment was valued at £2,000.
(*ii*) Depreciate all equipment 20 per cent for the year 2006.
(*iii*) At 31.12.2006 rent paid in advance was £400.
(*iv*) At 31.12.2006 there was £25 owing for printing.

34.2A The following trial balance of the Shire Golf Club was extracted from the books as on 31 December 2003:

	Dr £	Cr £
Clubhouse	142,000	
Equipment	18,600	
Profits from raffles		6,508
Subscriptions received		183,400
Wages of bar staff	29,200	
Bar stocks 1 January 2003	9,400	
Bar purchases and sales	41,300	84,600
Greenkeepers' wages	21,500	
Golf professional's salary	37,000	
General expenses	910	
Cash at bank	3,924	
Accumulated fund at 1 January 2003		29,326
	303,834	303,834

→

→

Notes:

(*i*) Bar purchases and sales were on a cash basis. Bar stocks at 31 December 2003 were valued at £6,410.

(*ii*) Subscriptions paid in advance by members at 31 December 2003 amounted to £1,870.

(*iii*) Provide for depreciation of equipment £2,400.

You are required to:

(*a*) Draw up the bar trading account for the year ending 31 December 2003.

(*b*) Draw up the income and expenditure account for the year ending 31 December 2003, and a balance sheet as at 31 December 2003.

34.3 Read the following and answer the questions below.

On 1 January 2008 the Happy Haddock Angling Club had the following assets:

	£
Cash at bank	200
Snack bar stocks	800
Club house buildings	12,500

During the year to 31 December 2008 the Club received and paid the following amounts:

Receipts	£	Payments	£
Subscriptions 2008	3,500	Rent and rates	1,500
Subscriptions 2009	380	Extension to club house	8,000
Snack bar income	6,000	Snack bar purchases	3,750
Visitors' fees	650	Secretarial expenses	240
Loan from bank	5,500	Interest on loan	260
Competition fees	820	Snack bar expenses	600
		Games equipment	2,000

Notes: The snack bar stock on 31 December 2008 was £900.
The games equipment should be depreciated by 20%.

(*a*) Prepare an income and expenditure account for the year ending 31 December 2008. Show, either in this account or separately, the snack bar profit or loss.

(*b*) Prepare a balance sheet as at 31 December 2008.

(Midland Examining Group: GCSE)

34.4A The treasurer of the Plumpton Leisure Centre has produced the following receipts and payments account for the year ended 31 December 2004:

Receipts	£	Payments	£
Balance at bank 1 January 2004	3,900	Refreshment supplies bought	4,320
Subscriptions received	45,060	Wages of attendants and cleaners	31,400
Profits from dances	4,116	Rent of building	8,700
Profit on exhibition	890	New equipment bought	18,200
Refreshment takings	16,290	Travelling expenses of teams	1,900
Sale of equipment	340	Balance at bank 31 December 2004	6,076
	70,596		70,596

Notes:

(*i*) Refreshment stocks were valued: 31 December 2003 £680; 31 December 2004 £920. There was nothing owing for refreshment stocks on either of these dates.

(*ii*) On 1 January 2004 the club's equipment was valued at £32,400. Included in this figure, valued at £420, was the equipment sold during the year for £340.

(*iii*) The amount to be charged for depreciation of equipment for the year is £5,200. This is in addition to the loss on equipment sold during the year.

(*iv*) Subscriptions owing by members at 31 December 2003 nil; at 31 December 2004 £860.

You are required to:

(a) Draw up the refreshment trading account for the year ending 31 December 2004. For this purpose £4,680 of the wages is to be charged to this account; the remainder is to be charged in the income and expenditure account.

(b) Calculate the accumulated fund as at 1 January 2004.

(c) Draw up the income and expenditure account for the year ending 31 December 2004, and a balance sheet as at 31 December 2004.

34.5 The following is a summary of the receipts and payments of the Miniville Rotary Club during the year ended 31 July 2009.

Miniville Rotary Club
Receipts and Payments Account for the year ended 31 July 2009

	£		£
Cash and bank balances b/d	210	Secretarial expenses	163
Sales of competition tickets	437	Rent	1,402
Members' subscriptions	1,987	Visiting speakers' expenses	1,275
Donations	177	Donations to charities	35
Refund of rent	500	Prizes for competitions	270
Balance c/d	13	Stationery and printing	179
	£3,324		£3,324

The following valuations are also available:

as at 31 July	2008	2009
	£	£
Equipment (original cost £1,420)	975	780
Subscriptions in arrears	65	85
Subscriptions in advance	10	37
Owing to suppliers of competition prizes	58	68
Stocks of competition prizes	38	46

Required:

(a) Calculate the value of the accumulated fund of the Miniville Rotary Club as at 1 August 2008.

(b) Reconstruct the following accounts for the year ended 31 July 2009:

   (i) the subscriptions account,

   (ii) the competition prizes account.

(c) Prepare an income and expenditure account for the Miniville Rotary Club for the year ending 31 July 2009 and a balance sheet as at that date.

(Association of Accounting Technicians)

34.6A The Milham Theatre Club has been in existence for a number of years. Members pay an annual subscription of £15 which entitles them to join trips to professional productions at a reduced rate.

On 1 February 2007 the Club's assets and liabilities were as follows:

Cash in hand £80, Bank balance (overdrawn) £180, Subscriptions in arrears £150, Savings account £1,950, Amount owing for coach hire £60.

Required:

(a) A *detailed* calculation of the Milham Theatre Club's accumulated fund at 1 February 2007.

→ The Club's treasurer was able to present the following information at 31 January 2008:

Receipts and Payments Accounts for year ended 31 January 2008

	£	£
Opening balances		
Cash in hand	80	
Cash at bank (overdrawn)*	(180)	
		(100)
Receipts		
Subscriptions		
For year ended 31 January 2007	120	
For year ended 31 January 2008	1,620	
For year ended 31 January 2009	165	
Gift from member	1,000	
Interest on savings account	140	
Theatre outings		
Receipts from members for theatre tickets	2,720	
Receipts from members for coach travel	1,240	
		7,005
		6,905
Payments		
Transfer to savings account	1,210	
Theatre trips		
Tickets	3,120	
Coach hire	1,540	
Secretarial and administrative expenses	55	
		(5,925)
		980
Closing balances		
Cash in hand	35	
Cash at bank	945	
		980

- On 31 January 2008 the club committee decided to write off any arrears of subscriptions for the year ended 31 January 2007; the membership secretary reported that £75 is due for subscriptions for the year ended 31 January 2008.
- The treasurer has calculated that the full amount of interest receivable on the savings account for the year ended 31 January 2008 is £155.
- The club committee has decided that the gift should be capitalised.

Required:
(b) An account showing the surplus or deficit made by the Milham Theatre Club on theatre trips.
(c) An income and expenditure account for the Milham Theatre Club for the year ending 31 January 2008.
(d) An extract from the Milham Theatre Club's balance sheet as at 31 January 2008, showing the accumulated fund and current liability sections only.

The club committee have been concerned by the fact that the club's income has been steadily declining over recent years.

Required:
(e) Advice for the committee on *four* ways in which they could improve the club's income.

(*Southern Examining Group: GCSE*)

*Note: Figures in brackets represent negative amounts.

34.7 The accounting records of the Happy Tickers Sports and Social Club are in a mess. You manage to find the following information to help you prepare the accounts for the year to 31 December 2008.

Summarised Balance Sheet as at 31 December 2007

	£
Half-share in motorised roller	600
New sports equipment unsold	1,000
Used sports equipment at valuation	700
Rent prepaid (2 months)	200
Subscriptions 2007	60
Café inventory	800
Cash and bank	1,210
	4,570
Life subscriptions	1,400
Subscriptions 2008	120
Insurance accrued (3 months)	150
Accumulated fund	2,900
	4,570

Receipts in the year to 31 December 2008:	£
Subscriptions – 2007	40
– 2008	1,100
– 2009	80
– Life	200
From sales of new sports equipment	900
From sales of used sports equipment	14
Café takings	4,660
	6,994

Payments in the year to 31 December 2008:	
Rent (for 12 months)	1,200
Insurance (for 18 months)	900
To suppliers of sports equipment	1,000
To café suppliers	1,900
Wages of café manager	2,000
Total cost of repairing motorised roller	450
	7,450

Notes:
(i) Ownership and all expenses of the motorised roller are agreed to be shared equally with the Carefree Conveyancers Sports and Social Club which occupies a nearby site. The roller cost a total of £2,000 on 1 January 2006 and had an estimated life of 10 years.
(ii) Life subscriptions are brought into income equally over 10 years, in a scheme begun 5 years ago in 2003. Since the scheme began the cost of £200 per person has been constant. Prior to 31 December 2007 10 life subscriptions had been received.
(iii) Four more annual subscriptions of £20 each had been promised relating to 2008, but not yet received. Annual subscriptions promised but unpaid are carried forward for a maximum of 12 months.
(iv) New sports equipment is sold to members at cost plus 50%. Used equipment is sold off to members at book valuation. Half the sports equipment bought in the year (all from a cash and carry supplier) has been used within the club, and half made available for sale, new, to members. The 'used equipment at valuation' figure in the 31 December 2008 balance sheet is to remain at £700.
(v) Closing café stocks are £850, and £80 is owed to suppliers at 31 December 2008.

→

Required:
(a) Calculate the profit on café operations and the profit on sale of sports equipment.
(b) Prepare a statement of subscription income for 2008.
(c) Prepare an income and expenditure statement for the year ending 31 December 2008, and balance sheet as at 31 December 2008.
(d) Why do life subscriptions appear as a liability?

(*Association of Chartered Certified Accountants*)

You can find a range of additional self-test questions, as well as material to help you with your studies, on the website that accompanies this book at **www.pearsoned.co.uk/wood**

Manufacturing accounts

Learning objectives

After you have studied this chapter, you should be able to:

- calculate prime cost and production cost of goods manufactured
- draw up a manufacturing account and appropriate trading and profit and loss accounts
- adjust the manufacturing account in respect of work-in-progress

Introduction

In this chapter, you'll learn how to prepare manufacturing accounts and the reasons for doing so.

35.1 Manufacturing: not retailing

We now have to deal with businesses which are manufacturers. For these businesses, a **manufacturing account** is prepared in addition to the trading and profit and loss accounts. **It is produced for internal use only.** People other than the owners and managers of the organisation rarely see a manufacturing account.

If a business is using manufacturing accounts, instead of a figure for purchases (of finished goods) the trading account will contain the cost of manufacturing the goods that were manufactured during the period. The manufacturing account is used to calculate and show the cost of manufacturing those goods. The figure it produces that is used in the trading account is known as the **production cost**.

35.2 Divisions of costs

In a manufacturing business the costs are divided into different types. These may be summarised in chart form as follows:

```
Direct materials  ⎫
Direct labour      ⎬  Prime cost   ⎫
Direct expenses   ⎭              ⎪
     Plus                         ⎬  Production cost  ⎫
Indirect manufacturing costs   ──⎭                  ⎪
     Plus                                            ⎬  Total cost
Administration expenses                              ⎪
Selling and distribution expenses                    ⎪
Financial charges                                  ──⎭
```

The prime cost items and the other production cost items are shown in the manufacturing account. The administration expenses, selling and distribution expenses and the financial charges appear in the profit and loss account.

35.3 Direct and indirect costs

With reference to the above chart, when you see the word *direct* followed by a type of cost, you know that it has been possible to trace the costs to an item being manufactured.

As shown in the chart, the sum of all the **direct costs** is known as the **prime cost**. If a manufacturing-related cost cannot easily be traced to the item being manufactured, then it is an indirect cost and will be included under **indirect manufacturing costs** (which are also sometimes known as 'factory overhead expenses'). 'Production cost' is the sum of prime cost plus the indirect manufacturing costs.

For example, the wages of a machine operator making a particular item will be direct labour. The wages of a foreman in charge of many men on different jobs will be indirect labour, and will be part of the indirect manufacturing costs. Other examples of costs being direct costs would be:

1 Cost of raw materials including carriage inwards on those raw materials.
2 Hire of special machinery for a job.

 Activity 35.1 Think about it for a minute and then list five costs you think are direct and five that you think are indirect.

35.4 Indirect manufacturing costs

'Indirect manufacturing costs' are all those costs which occur in the factory or other place where production is being done, but which cannot easily be traced to the items being manufactured. Examples are:

● wages of cleaners
● wages of crane drivers
● rent of a factory
● depreciation of plant and machinery
● costs of operating forklift trucks
● factory power
● factory lighting

35.5 Administration expenses

'Administration expenses' consist of such items as managers' salaries, legal and accountancy charges, the depreciation of accounting machinery and secretarial salaries.

35.6 Selling and distribution expenses

'Selling and distribution expenses' are items such as sales staff's salaries and commission, carriage outwards, depreciation of delivery vans, advertising and display expenses.

35.7 Financial charges

'Financial charges' are expense items such as bank charges and discounts allowed.

Activity 35.2

Place a tick in the appropriate column for each of the following cost items:

	Direct materials	Direct labour	Direct expenses	Indirect manufacturing costs	Administration expenses	Selling and distribution expenses	Financial charges
(a) Purchases of raw materials							
(b) Direct wages							
(c) General factory expenses							
(d) Depreciation of machinery							
(e) Commission on sales							
(f) Factory rent							
(g) Carriage inwards of raw materials							
(h) Royalties paid							
(i) Stock of raw materials							
(j) Administration salaries							
(k) Indirect labour							
(l) Bank charges							
(m) Carriage outwards							
(n) Discounts allowed							
(o) Factory lighting							

35.8 Format of the financial statements

Manufacturing account section

This is debited with the production cost of goods completed during the accounting period. It contains costs of:

- Direct materials
- Direct labour
- Direct expenses
- Indirect manufacturing costs

The manufacturing account includes all purchases of raw materials, including the stock adjustments for raw materials. It also includes stock adjustments for **work in progress** (goods that are part-completed at the end of a period). Let's put this into a series of steps:

1 Add opening stock of raw materials to purchases and subtract the closing stock of raw materials.
2 Add in all the direct costs to get the prime cost.

3 Add in all the indirect manufacturing costs.
4 Add the opening stock of work in progress and subtract the closing stock of work in progress to get the production cost of all goods completed in the period.

Thus, when completed, the manufacturing account shows the total of production cost that relates to those manufactured goods that have been available for sale during the period. This figure will then be transferred down to the profit and loss account where it will replace the entry for purchases.

Trading account section

This account includes:

● Production cost brought down from the manufacturing account
● Opening and closing stocks of finished goods
● Sales

When completed, this account shows the gross profit. This is then carried down to the profit and loss account section.

The manufacturing account and the trading account can be shown in the form of a diagram:

Manufacturing Account

	£
Production costs for the period:	
Direct materials	xxx
Direct labour	xxx
Direct expenses	xxx
Prime cost	xxx
Indirect manufacturing costs	xxx
Production cost of goods completed c/d to trading account	xxx

Trading Account

		£	£
Sales			xxx
Less Production cost of goods sold:			
Opening stock of finished goods	(A)	xxx	
Add Production costs of goods completed b/d		xxx	
		xxx	
Less Closing stock of finished goods	(B)	(xxx)	
Gross profit			(xxx)
			xxx

(A) is production costs of goods unsold in previous period.
(B) is production costs of goods unsold at end of the current period.

Profit and loss account section

This is prepared in the way you learnt in earlier chapters in this book. You know, therefore, that it includes:

● Gross profit brought down from the trading account
● All administration expenses
● All selling and distribution expenses
● All financial charges

However, some of the items you would normally put in the profit and loss account part are already included in the manufacturing account, e.g. depreciation on machines, and canteen wages. When completed, this account will show the net profit.

Activity 35.3 Why do you think some expenses have been moved to the manufacturing account?

35.9 A worked example of a manufacturing account

Exhibit 35.1 shows the necessary details for a manufacturing account. It has been assumed that there were no partly completed units (work in progress) either at the beginning or end of the period.

Exhibit 35.1

Details of production costs for the year ended 31 December 2007:

	£
1 January 2007, stock of raw materials	5,000
31 December 2007, stock of raw materials	7,000
Raw materials purchased	80,000
Manufacturing (direct) wages	210,000
Royalties	1,500
Indirect wages	90,000
Rent of factory – excluding administration and selling and distribution blocks	4,400
Depreciation of plant and machinery in factory	4,000
General indirect expenses	3,100

Manufacturing Account for the year ending 31 December 2007

	£	£
Stock of raw materials 1.1.2007		5,000
Add Purchases		80,000
		85,000
Less Stock of raw materials 31.12.2007		(7,000)
Cost of raw materials consumed		78,000
Manufacturing wages		210,000
Royalties		1,500
Prime cost		289,500
Indirect manufacturing costs		
Rent	4,400	
Indirect wages	90,000	
General expenses	3,100	
Depreciation of plant and machinery	4,000	
		101,500
Production cost of goods completed c/d		391,000

Sometimes, if a business has produced less than the customers have demanded, it may buy in some finished goods. In this case, the trading account will have both a figure for purchases of finished goods and a figure for production cost of goods completed.

An example of this could be the rent expense. If the rent is paid separately for each part of the organisation, then it is easy to charge the rent to each sort of expense. However, only one figure of rent may be paid, without any indication as to how much is for the factory, how much is for the selling and distribution building and how much is for the administration building.

How the rent expense will be apportioned in the latter case will depend on the circumstances, using the most equitable way of doing it. A range of methods may be used. Common ones include on the basis of:

● floor area
● property valuations of each part of the buildings and land.

35.13 Full set of financial statements

A complete worked example is now given. Note that in the profit and loss account section the expenses have been separated so as to show whether they are administration expenses, selling and distribution expenses, or financial charges.

The trial balance in Exhibit 35.3 has been extracted from the books of J Jarvis, Toy Manufacturer, as at 31 December 2007.

Exhibit 35.3

J Jarvis
Trial Balance as at 31 December 2007

	Dr	Cr
	£	£
Stock of raw materials 1.1.2007	21,000	
Stock of finished goods 1.1.2007	38,900	
Work in progress 1.1.2007	13,500	
Wages (direct £180,000; factory indirect £145,000)	325,000	
Royalties	7,000	
Carriage inwards (on raw materials)	3,500	
Purchases of raw materials	370,000	
Productive machinery (cost £280,000)	230,000	
Administration computers (cost £20,000)	12,000	
General factory expenses	31,000	
Lighting	7,500	
Factory power	13,700	
Administration salaries	44,000	
Sales reps' salaries	30,000	
Commission on sales	11,500	
Rent	12,000	
Insurance	4,200	
General administration expenses	13,400	
Bank charges	2,300	
Discounts allowed	4,800	
Carriage outwards	5,900	
Sales		1,000,000
Debtors and creditors	142,300	64,000
Bank	16,800	
Cash	1,500	
Drawings	60,000	
Capital as at 1.1.2007		357,800
	1,421,800	1,421,800

Notes at 31.12.2007:

1 Stock of raw materials £24,000; stock of finished goods £40,000; work in progress £15,000.
2 Lighting, rent and insurance are to be apportioned: factory ⁵/₆, administration ¹/₆.
3 Depreciation on productive and administration computers at 10 per cent per annum on cost.

J Jarvis
Manufacturing, Trading and Profit and Loss Account for the year ending 31 December 2007

	£	£	£
Stock of raw materials 1.1.2007			21,000
Add Purchases			370,000
Carriage inwards			3,500
			394,500
Less Stock of raw materials 31.12.2007			(24,000)
Cost of raw materials consumed			370,500
Direct labour			180,000
Royalties			7,000
Prime cost			557,500
Indirect manufacturing costs:			
General factory expenses		31,000	
Lighting ⁵/₆		6,250	
Power		13,700	
Rent ⁵/₆		10,000	
Insurance ⁵/₆		3,500	
Depreciation of productive machinery		28,000	
Indirect labour		145,000	
			237,450
			794,950
Add Work in progress 1.1.2007			13,500
			808,450
Less Work in progress 31.12.2007			(15,000)
Production cost of goods completed c/d			793,450
Sales			1,000,000
Less Cost of goods sold:			
Stock of finished goods 1.1.2007		38,900	
Add Production cost of goods completed		793,450	
		832,350	
Less Stock of finished goods 31.12.2007		(40,000)	
			(792,350)
Gross profit			207,650
Administration expenses			
Administration salaries	44,000		
Rent ¹/₆	2,000		
Insurance ¹/₆	700		
General expenses	13,400		
Lighting ¹/₆	1,250		
Depreciation of administration computers	2,000		
		63,350	
Selling and distribution expenses			
Sales reps' salaries	30,000		
Commission on sales	11,500		
Carriage outwards	5,900		
		47,400	
Financial charges			
Bank charges	2,300		
Discounts allowed	4,800		
		7,100	
			(117,850)
Net profit			89,800

→

J Jarvis
Balance Sheet as at 31 December 2007

	£	£
Fixed assets		
Productive machinery at cost	280,000	
Less Depreciation to date	(78,000)	
		202,000
Administration computers at cost	20,000	
Less Depreciation to date	(10,000)	
		10,000
		212,000
Current assets		
Stock		
Raw materials	24,000	
Finished goods	40,000	
Work in progress	15,000	
Debtors	142,300	
Bank	16,800	
Cash	1,500	
	239,600	
Less Current liabilities		
Creditors	(64,000)	
Net current assets		175,600
		387,600
Financed by		
Capital		
Balance as at 1.1.2007		357,800
Add Net profit		89,800
		447,600
Less Drawings		(60,000)
		387,600

35.14 Market value of goods manufactured

The financial statements of Jarvis are subject to the limitation that the respective amounts of the gross profit which are attributable to the manufacturing side or to the selling side of the business are not known. A technique is sometimes used to bring out this additional information. This method uses the cost which would have been involved if the goods had been bought in their finished state instead of being manufactured by the business. This figure is credited to the manufacturing account and debited to the trading account so as to throw up two figures of gross profit instead of one. It should be pointed out that the net profit will remain unaffected. All that will have happened will be that the figure of £207,650 gross profit will be shown as two figures instead of one. When added together, they will total £207,650.

Assume that the cost of buying the goods instead of manufacturing them had been £950,000. The relevant parts of the Manufacturing Trading and Profit and Loss Account will then be:

Manufacturing, Trading and Profit and Loss Account (extracts) for the year ending 31 December 2007

	£	£
Market value of goods completed c/d		950,000
Less Production cost of goods completed (as before)		(793,450)
Gross profit on manufacture c/d		156,550
Sales		1,000,000
Stock of finished goods 1.1.2007	38,900	
Add Market value of goods completed b/d	950,000	
	988,900	
Less Stock of finished goods 31.12.2007	(40,000)	
		(948,900)
Gross profit on trading c/d		51,100
Gross profit		
On manufacturing	156,550	
On trading	51,100	
		207,650

Learning outcomes

You should now have learnt:

1 Why manufacturing accounts are used.

2 How to prepare a manufacturing, trading and profit and loss account.

3 That the trading account section of the manufacturing, trading and profit and loss account statement is used for calculating the gross profit made by selling the goods manufactured.

4 That the profit and loss account section of the manufacturing, trading and profit and loss account statement shows as net profit what is left of gross profit after all administration, selling and distribution and finance costs incurred have been deducted.

5 That work in progress, both at the start and the close of a period, must be adjusted so as to identify the production costs of goods completed in the period.

Answers to activities

35.1 You may have included some of the following:

Direct costs	*Indirect costs*
(1) raw materials	canteen wages
(2) machine operator's wages	business rates
(3) packer's wages	rent
(4) machine set-up costs	insurance
(5) crane hire for building contract	storage of finished goods costs

However, you can only really do a split like this if you have a specific job or product in mind. You must first identify the 'cost object', that is, the item you are making or providing. Taking the example of a construction company building a hotel (it is engaged in other similar projects at the same time). The direct and indirect costs may include:

Direct costs	Indirect costs
(1) concrete	site canteen wages
(2) forklift truck operator's wages	company lawyer's salary
(3) bricklayer's wages	company architect's salary
(4) steel girders	company headquarters insurance
(5) windows	company warehousing costs

Now you should see that the indirect costs are not solely incurred in order to build the hotel. This is the key. Direct costs are those costs you can specifically link to a specific job. All the other costs of a job are indirect.

35.2 Direct materials (a) (g) (i)
Direct labour (b)
Direct expenses (h)
Indirect manufacturing costs (c) (d) (f) (k) (o)
Administration expenses (j)
Selling and distribution expenses (e) (m)
Financial charges (l) (n)

35.3 Because only administration expenses, selling and distribution expenses and financial charges appear in the profit and loss account part when a manufacturing account is being used. The rest all arose because manufacturing was taking place and can be directly or indirectly attributed to the products being produced, so they appear in the manufacturing account.

Review questions

35.1 A business both buys loose tools and also makes some itself. The following data is available concerning the years ending 31 December 2007, 2008 and 2009.

		£
2007		
Jan 1	Stock of loose tools	2,400
	During the year:	
	Bought loose tools from suppliers	3,800
	Made own loose tools: the cost of wages of employees being £490 and the materials cost £340	
Dec 31	Loose tools valued at	5,100
2008		
	During the year:	
	Loose tools bought from suppliers	1,820
	Made own loose tools: the cost of wages of employees being £610 and the materials cost £420	
Dec 31	Loose tools valued at	5,940
2009		
	During the year:	
	Loose tools bought from suppliers	2,760
	Made own loose tools: the cost of wages of employees being £230 and the materials cost £370. Received refund from a supplier for faulty tools returned to him	142
Dec 31	Loose tools valued at	5,990

You are to draw up the loose tools account for the three years, showing the amount transferred as an expense in each year to the manufacturing account.

35.2 Using whichever of the following figures are required, prepare a manufacturing account and a trading account for 2003. The manufacturing account should show clearly the prime cost of manufacture and the production cost of finished goods produced.

	£
Stocks, 1 January 2003:	
Raw materials	13,500
Partly finished goods	11,800
Finished goods	13,400
Stocks, 31 December 2003:	
Raw materials	14,100
Partly finished goods	11,450
Finished foods	14,160
Purchases of raw materials	82,700
Carriage on raw materials	4,430
Salaries and wages: factory (including £22,700 for management and supervision)	75,674
Salaries and wages: general office	14,200
Rent and business rates (three-quarters works, one-quarter office)	1,600
Lighting and heating (seven-eighths works, one-eighth office)	2,960
Repairs to machinery	1,527
Depreciation of machinery	2,700
Factory direct expenses	365
Insurance of plant and machinery	440
Sales	202,283

Note: partly finished goods are valued at their production cost.

35.3A From the following information, prepare a manufacturing, trading and profit and loss account for the year ending 31 December 2006 and the balance sheet as at 31 December 2006 for the firm of J Jones Limited.

	£	£
Purchase of raw materials	258,000	
Fuel and light	21,000	
Administration salaries	17,000	
Factory wages	59,000	
Carriage outwards	4,000	
Rent and business rates	21,000	
Sales		482,000
Returns inward	7,000	
General office expenses	9,000	
Repairs to plant and machinery	9,000	
Stock at 1 January 2006:		
Raw materials	21,000	
Work in progress	14,000	
Finished goods	23,000	
Sundry creditors		37,000
Capital account		457,000
Freehold premises	410,000	
Plant and machinery	80,000	
Debtors	20,000	
Accumulated provision for depreciation on plant and machinery		8,000
Cost in hand	11,000	
	984,000	984,000

Make provision for the following:

(*i*) Stock in hand at 31 December 2006:
   Raw materials £25,000
   Work in progress £11,000
   Finished goods £26,000.

→

→ Prepare the manufacturing, trading and profit and loss account for the year ending 31 December 2002 and a balance sheet as at that date. Give effect to the following adjustments:

1 Stocks at 31 December 2002: raw materials £14,510; finished goods £44,490. There is no work in progress.
2 Depreciate machinery £3,000; office equipment £600; van £1,200.
3 Manufacturing wages due but unpaid at 31 December 2002 £550; office rent prepaid £140.

35.8 The financial year end of Mendip Limited is 30 June. At 30 June 2002, the following balances are available:

	£
Freehold land and buildings at cost	143,000
Plant and machinery at cost	105,000
Accumulated depreciation on plant and machinery	23,000
Purchase of raw materials	130,100
Sales	317,500
Factory rates	3,000
Factory heat and light	6,500
Debtors	37,200
Creditors	30,900
Wages (including £15,700 for supervision)	63,000
Direct factory expenses	9,100
Selling expenses	11,000
Office salaries and general expenses	43,000
Bank	24,500
General reserve	30,000
Profit and loss account	18,000
Stocks 1 July 2001: Raw materials	20,000
Finished goods	38,000
Dividends paid: Preference shares	840
Ordinary shares	20,000

(i) The stocks at 30 June 2002 were: raw materials £22,000; finished goods £35,600.
(ii) Salaries include £6,700 for directors' fees.
(iii) Depreciation is to be charged at 10% on cost of plant and machinery.

Required
Prepare a manufacturing, trading and profit and loss account for the year ending 30 June 2002.

35.9A Jean Marsh owns a small business making and selling children's toys. The following trial balance was extracted from her books on 31 December 2009.

	Dr £	Cr £
Capital		15,000
Drawings	2,000	
Sales		90,000
Stocks at 1 January 2009:		
Raw materials	3,400	
Finished goods	6,100	
Purchases of raw materials	18,000	
Carriage inwards	800	
Factory wages	18,500	
Office salaries	16,900	
J Marsh: salary and expenses	10,400	
General expenses:		
Factory	1,200	
Office	750	
Lighting	2,500	
Rent	3,750	
Insurance	950	
Advertising	1,400	
Bad debts	650	
Discount received		1,600
Carriage outwards	375	
Plant and machinery, at cost less depreciation	9,100	
Car, at cost less depreciation	4,200	
Bank	3,600	
Cash in hand	325	
Debtors and creditors	7,700	6,000
	112,600	112,600

You are given the following additional information.
1   Stocks at 31 December 2009
    Raw materials   £2,900
    Finished goods   £8,200
    There was no work in progress.
2   Depreciation for the year is to be charged as follows:
    Plant and machinery   £1,500
    Car   £500
3   At 31 December 2009 Insurance paid in advance was £150 and Office general expenses unpaid
    were £75.
4   Lighting and rent are to be apportioned: ⁴/₅ Factory, ¹/₅ Office
    Insurance is to be apportioned: ³/₄ Factory, ¹/₄ Office
5   Jean is the business's salesperson and her salary and expenses are to be treated as a selling
    expense. She has sole use of the business's car.

Questions:
For the year ended 31 December 2009 prepare:
(a) the manufacturing account showing prime cost and factory cost of production;
(b) the trading account;
(c) the profit and loss account, distinguishing between administrative and selling costs;
(d) a balance sheet as at 31 December 2009. [Authors' Note]

(Midland Examining Group: GCSE)

Authors' Note: Part (d) of the question was not in the original examination question. It has been added
to give you further practice.

If we knew the above information, we could see how well, or how badly, each part of the business was doing. If we closed down Department D we could make a greater total gross profit of £180,000. Perhaps we could replace Department D with a department which would make a gross profit instead of a gross loss.

Activity 36.1 Why do you think we have only mentioned gross profit and haven't referred to net profit?

You would have to know more about the business before you could be certain what the figures in the account mean. For example, some stores deliberately allow parts of their business to lose money, so that customers come to the store to buy the cheap goods and then spend money in the other departments.

Accounting information seldom tells all the story. It serves as one measure, but there are other non-accounting factors to be considered before a relevant decision for action can be made.

The various pros and cons of the actions to be taken to increase the overall profitability of a business cannot therefore be properly considered until the departmental gross profits or gross losses are known. It must not be thought that departmental accounts can be prepared only for department stores, such as Marks & Spencer or Debenhams. They can be prepared for the various departments or sections of any business.

The reputation of many a successful business person has been built up on an ability to utilise the departmental account principle to guide decision-making and so increase the profitability of a business. The lesson still has to be learned by many medium-sized and small businesses. It is one of accounting's greatest and simplest aids to business efficiency.

To find out how profitable each part of the business is, we have to prepare departmental accounts to give us the facts for each department.

36.2 Allocation of expenses

The expenses of a business can be split between the various departments, and then the net profit for each department calculated. Each expense is divided between the departments on what is considered to be the most logical basis. This will differ considerably between businesses. An example of a departmental trading and profit and loss account drawn up in such a manner is shown in Exhibit 36.1:

Exhibit 36.1

Northern Stores has three departments:

	(a) Jewellery £	(b) Hairdressing £	(c) Clothing £
Stock of goods or materials at 1 January 2008	20,000	15,000	30,000
Purchases	110,000	30,000	150,000
Stock of goods or materials at 31 December 2008	30,000	25,000	40,000
Sales and work done	180,000	90,000	270,000
Wages of assistants in each department	28,000	55,000	60,000

The following expenses cannot be traced to any particular department:

	£
Rent	8,200
Administration expenses	48,000
Air conditioning and lighting	6,000
General expenses	2,400

It is decided to apportion (i.e. spread) the cost of rent together with air conditioning and lighting in accordance with the floor space occupied by each department. These were taken up in the ratios of (a) one-fifth, (b) half, (c) three-tenths. Administration expenses and general expenses are to be split in the ratio of sales and work done.

Northern Stores
Departmental Trading and Profit and Loss Accounts for the year ending 31 December 2008[Note]

	(a) Jewellery		(b) Hairdressing		(c) Clothing	
	£	£	£	£	£	£
Sales and work done		180,000		90,000		270,000
Less: Cost of goods or materials:						
Stock 1.1.2008	20,000		15,000		30,000	
Add Purchases	110,000		30,000		150,000	
	130,000		45,000		180,000	
Less Stock 31.12.2008	(30,000)		(25,000)		(40,000)	
		(100,000)		(20,000)		(140,000)
Gross profit		80,000		70,000		130,000
Less Expenses:						
Wages	28,000		55,000		60,000	
Rent	1,640		4,100		2,460	
Administration expenses	16,000		8,000		24,000	
Air conditioning and lighting	1,200		3,000		1,800	
General expenses	800		400		1,200	
		(47,640)		(70,500)		(89,460)
Net profit/(loss)		32,360		(500)		40,540

The overall net profit is, therefore, £32,360 − £500 + £40,540 = £72,400.

Note: this has been prepared on the gross profit basis.

This way of calculating net profits and losses seems to imply a precision that is, in fact, lacking. This can lead to the mistaken interpretation that the loss of £500 by the Hairdressing Department would be saved if the department were closed down. This is not what the loss of £500 implies. It has already been stated that different departments are very often dependent on one another, and the answer to Activity 36.1 explained why. Therefore, you should realise that this amount of loss would not necessarily be saved by closing the Hairdressing Department.

To explain this further, the calculation of departmental net profits and losses is dependent on the arbitrary division of indirect costs. It is by no means certain that the indirect costs of the Hairdressing Department would be avoided if it were closed down. Assuming that the sales staff of the department could be discharged without compensation, then £55,000 would be saved in wages. The other expenses shown under the Hairdressing Department would not, however, necessarily disappear.

The rent may still be payable in full even if the department were closed down. The administration expenses may turn out to be only slightly down, say from £48,000 to £46,100 – a saving of £1,900; air conditioning and lighting may fall by £300 to £5,700; general expenses may be reduced by £100 to £2,300. None of these reductions are obvious from the departmental trading and profit and loss accounts.

Taking these cost reductions as what would actually happen were the Hairdressing Department to be closed, indicates that there would be a saving of £57,300:

	£
Administration expenses	1,900
Air conditioning and lighting	300
General expenses	100
Wages	55,000
	57,300

But when open, assuming this year is typical, the Hairdressing Department makes £70,000 gross profit. The business is therefore £12,700 a year better off (i.e. £70,000 minus £57,300) when the department is open than when it is closed, subject to certain assumptions, such as:

(a) That the remaining departments would not be profitably expanded into the space vacated to give greater proportionate benefits than the Hairdressing Department.
(b) That a new type of department which would be more profitable than hairdressing could not be set up.
(c) That the floor space could not be leased to another business at a more profitable figure than that shown by hairdressing – you can see examples of this in many large stores where a part of the store has been leased to a coffee house like Starbucks or Costa Coffee.

Activity 36.2 What other possible events that can only occur if the department is closed could make it profitable to close the Hairdressing Department?

There are also other factors which, though not easily seen in an accounting context, are still extremely pertinent. They are concerned with the possible loss of confidence in the business by customers generally – what appears to be an ailing business does not usually attract large numbers of customers.

Also, the effect on the remaining staff should not be ignored. The fear that the dismissal of the hairdressing staff may also happen to them may result in the loss of other staff, especially the most competent members who could easily find work elsewhere, and so the general quality of the staff may decline with serious consequences for the business.

36.3 Allocation of expenses: a better method

It is less misleading to show costs split as follows:

First section of trading and profit and loss account	**Direct costs** allocated entirely to the department (i.e. costs which would *not* be paid if the department closed down)
Second section of trading and profit and loss account	Costs not directly traceable to the department or which would still be payable even if the department closed down (i.e. **indirect costs** and **fixed costs**)

The *surpluses* brought down from the first of these two sections represent the **contribution** that each department has made to cover the remaining costs, the remainder being the net profit for the whole of the business. If direct costs of a department were greater than the sales figure then the result would be a **negative contribution**.

From the figures given in Exhibit 36.1 the departmental trading and profit and loss accounts prepared on the basis of contribution rather than gross profit would appear as in Exhibit 36.2:

Exhibit 36.2

Northern Stores
Departmental Trading and Profit and Loss Accounts for the year ending
31 December 2008 (Contribution basis)

	(a) Jewellery		(b) Hairdressing		(c) Clothing	
	£	£	£	£	£	£
Sales and work done		180,000		90,000		270,000
Less Cost of goods or materials:						
Stock 1.1.2008	20,000		15,000		30,000	
Add Purchases	110,000		30,000		150,000	
	130,000		45,000		180,000	
Less Stock 31.12.2008	(30,000)		(25,000)		(40,000)	
	100,000		20,000		140,000	
Wages	28,000		55,000		60,000	
		(128,000)		(75,000)		(200,000)
Contribution c/d		52,000		15,000		70,000

All Departments

	£	£
Contribution b/d:		
Jewellery	52,000	
Hairdressing	15,000	
Clothing	70,000	
		137,000
Less		
Rent	8,200	
Administration expenses	48,000	
Air conditioning and lighting	6,000	
General expenses	2,400	
		(64,600)
Net profit		72,400

As you can see, this is the same overall net profit as found in Exhibit 36.1 and now no department is seen as making a loss.

The contribution of a department is the result of activities which are under the control of a departmental manager. The efficiency of their control will affect the amount of the contribution. If a department's contribution is negative, it would be a strong candidate for closure, or for a change in its management. Similarly, if a department has a far lower contribution to revenue ratio than the others, it may be a candidate for closure if doing so would allow other departments to expand.

The costs in the second section, such as rent, insurance or lighting, cannot be affected by the departmental manager. It is therefore only fair if the departmental manager is judged by the *contribution* of his or her department rather than the net profit of the department.

In examinations, students must answer the questions as set, and not give their own interpretations of what the question should be. Therefore, if examiners give details of the methods of apportionment of expenses, then they are really looking for an answer in the same style as Exhibit 36.1. However, if you are then asked to comment on the performance of individual departments, it would be wise to indicate that, had a contribution approach been adopted, a different view of their performance may have been obtained which would have been more meaningful and useful than the one produced using the approach taken in Exhibit 36.1.

36.4 The balance sheet

The balance sheet does not usually show assets and liabilities split between different departments.

36.5 Interdepartmental transfers

Purchases made for one department may be subsequently sold in another department. In such a case, the items should be deducted from the figure for purchases of the original purchasing department, and added to the figure for purchases for the subsequent selling department.

Learning outcomes

You should now have learnt:

1 How to prepare departmental trading and profit and loss accounts on the gross profit basis.

2 How to prepare departmental trading and profit and loss accounts on the contribution basis.

3 That it is desirable for the contribution of each section of a business to be calculated to aid management decisions and that the contribution-based trading and profit and loss account is more appropriate for departmental closure decisions than the gross-profit-based statement.

4 That costs should be divided between those which can logically be allocated to departments and those which cannot.

5 That a negative contribution is only one guide as to whether a section of a business should be closed. There may be other factors which would go against such a closure, and others that would suggest that even departments with positive contributions should be closed.

Answers to activities

36.1 Indirect costs and fixed costs. Net profit includes them. Unlike a manufacturing company, in a trading company, the only costs that are included in the calculation of gross profit are the purchase costs of the items that were sold.

Indirect costs and direct wages and direct expenses appear in the profit and loss account as deductions from gross profit. So far as the direct costs are concerned, it would be appropriate to include them in any comparison between departments because they were definitely incurred for and by the department to which their cost is charged. However, it is not appropriate to include the indirect costs because they have to be spread across all the departments on a basis that is subjective rather than objective. That is, you cannot be certain that they were incurred in respect of the department to which they are charged.

Fixed costs can be direct expenses (e.g. lease of a cash register) or indirect expenses (e.g. rates). They are period costs of the business. They cannot be changed in the timescale you are looking at. If you wanted to know the net profit of a department, you would need to spread the indirect fixed costs across all the departments. This results in charges that are, at best, a close approximation to the extent to which each department merits that level of indirect fixed cost.

Often it has very little to do with appropriateness of the charge made on each department. If you tried to use net profit to make comparisons, you would be basing any conclusion on figures that could easily have been very different had another, possibly, more appropriate method of spreading the indirect fixed costs been used. In addition to all this, there is also the question of what happens to the fixed costs, both direct and indirect, that you have charged to a department that you have decided to close because it is making a net loss. Perhaps the other departments are only profitable because the loss-making department is absorbing some of the fixed costs.

36.2 There is a large range of possibilities. You may have suggested some of the following:
● a restaurant could be opened by the store, attracting more shoppers and, therefore, boosting the sales of the remaining departments;
● the floor space could be used for a children's play area, thereby making the store more attractive to shoppers with young children;
● the floor space could be converted to contain chairs, tables, plants and sculptures where shoppers can relax and chat to each other during the time they are in the store – you can see examples of this in many modern shopping centres.

Review questions

36.1 From the following you are to draw up a departmental trading account for Fine's Department Store for the year ending 30 June 2006.

Stocks:	1.7.2005		30.6.2006
	£		£
Carpet Department	16,100		18,410
White Goods Department	37,916		35,119
Music Department	31,222		40,216
Sales for the year:		£	
Carpet Department		62,400	
White Goods Department		151,300	
Music Department		94,820	
Purchases for the year:			
Carpet Department		43,600	
White Goods Department		118,260	
Music Department		55,924	

→

36.2 J Horner is the proprietor of a shop selling paintings and ornaments. For the purposes of his financial statements he wishes the business to be divided into two departments:

Department A   Paintings
Department B   Ornaments

The following balances have been extracted from his nominal ledger at 31 August 2007:

	Dr	Cr
	£	£
Sales Department A		75,000
Sales Department B		50,000
Stocks Department A, 1 September 2006	1,250	
Stocks Department B, 1 September 2006	1,000	
Purchases Department A	51,000	
Purchases Department B	38,020	
Wages of sales assistants Department A	7,200	
Wages of sales assistants Department B	6,800	
Picture framing costs	300	
General office salaries	13,200	
Fire insurance – buildings	360	
Lighting and heating	620	
Repairs to premises	175	
Internal telephone	30	
Cleaning	180	
Accountancy charges	1,490	
General office expenses	510	

Stocks at 31 August 2007 were valued at:
    Department A £1,410
    Department B £912

The proportion of the total floor area occupied by each department was:
    Department A two-fifths
    Department B three-fifths

Prepare J Horner's departmental trading and profit and loss account for the year ending 31 August 2007, apportioning the costs, where necessary, to show the net profit or loss of each department. The apportionment should be made by using the methods as shown:

Area – Fire insurance, Lighting and heating, Repairs, Telephone, Cleaning; Turnover – General office salaries, Accountancy, General office expenses.

36.3A From the following list of balances you are required to prepare a departmental trading and profit and loss account for the year ending 31 March 2005, in respect of the business carried on under the name of Jack's Superstores:

			£	£
Rent and business rates				9,300
Delivery expenses				3,600
Commission				10,000
Insurance				1,800
Purchases:	Dept.	A	101,300	
		B	81,200	
		C	62,900	
				245,400
Discounts received				2,454
Salaries and wages				91,200
Advertising				2,307
Sales:	Dept.	A	180,000	
		B	138,000	
		C	82,000	
				400,000
Depreciation				4,200
Opening stock:	Dept.	A	27,100	
		B	21,410	
		C	17,060	
				65,570
Administration and general expenses				19,800
Closing stock:	Dept.	A	23,590	
		B	15,360	
		C	18,200	
				57,150

Except as follows, expenses are to be apportioned equally between the departments.

Delivery expenses – proportionate to sales.
Commission – 2½ per cent of sales.
Salaries and wages; Insurance – in the proportion of 3:2:1.
Discounts received – 1 per cent of purchases.

You can find a range of additional self-test questions, as well as material to help you with your studies, on the website that accompanies this book at **www.pearsoned.co.uk/wood**

Cash flow statements

Learning objectives

After you have studied this chapter, you should be able to:

- draw up a cash flow statement for any type of organisation
- explain how cash flow statements can give a different view of a business to that simply concerned with profits
- describe the contents of Financial Reporting Standard 1 (FRS 1) and the format to be used when preparing cash flow statements using FRS 1
- describe some of the uses that can be made of cash flow statements

Introduction

In this chapter, you'll learn about cash flow statements, how to prepare them and the requirements of FRS 1, the accounting standard that regulates their preparation under UK GAAP.

37.1 Need for cash flow statements

For any business it is important to ensure that:

- Sufficient profits are made to finance the business activities.
- Sufficient cash funds are available as and when needed.

Activity 37.1   What do you think is meant by 'cash' in this context? (*Hint*: which are the truly liquid assets?)

We ascertain the amount of profits in a profit and loss account. We also show what the assets, capital and liabilities are at a given date by drawing up a balance sheet. Although the balance sheet shows the cash balance (*see* definition given in the solution to Activity 37.1) at a given date, it does not show us how we have used our cash funds during the accounting period.

What we really need, to help throw some light on to the cash situation, is some form of statement which shows us exactly where the cash has come from during the year, and exactly what we have done with it. The statement that fulfils these needs is called a **cash flow statement**.

37.2 Financial Reporting Standard 1: Cash Flow Statements

This standard, as its title suggests, concerns the preparation of cash flow statements. This focus on cash flow has not always been considered so important. An earlier SSAP (which FRS 1 replaced) had favoured the use of 'source and application of funds statements'. These funds were concerned with working capital and not cash. FRS 1 changed all of this, with cash as the central item.

The Accounting Standards Board requires all but the smallest companies to include cash flow statements with their published financial statements. It does, however, encourage all other organisations preparing financial statements to use them.

37.3 Businesses other than companies

Although small companies, partnerships and sole traders do not have to prepare them, cash flow statements can be of considerable use to all organisations.

FRS 1 prescribes a format for cash flow statements. An example is shown later in Exhibit 37.7. This is suitable for a company but, obviously, there are factors concerning partnerships and sole traders which do not occur in companies. It will be of help to students if the cash flow statements for sole traders and partnerships are fashioned to be similar to those for companies as is possible. Consequently, the layouts for cash flow statements of sole traders and partnerships in this book will follow the style of layout presented in FRS 1.

37.4 Profit and liquidity are not directly related

Many people think that if we are making profits then there should be no shortage of cash. As you have learnt earlier in this book, this is not necessarily so. Let's look at a few instances where, although reasonable profits are being made by each of the following businesses, they could find themselves short of cash, maybe not now, but at some time in the future.

- A sole trader is making £40,000 a year profits. However, his drawings have been over £60,000 a year for some time.
- A company has been over-generous with credit terms to debtors, and last year extended the time in which debtors could pay from one month to three months. In addition it has taken on quite a few extra customers who are not creditworthy and such sales may result in bad debts in the future.
- A partnership whose products will not be on the market for quite a long time has invested in some very expensive machinery. A lot of money has been spent now, but no income will result in the near future.

In all of these cases, each of the businesses could easily run out of cash. In fact many businesses fail and are wound up because of cash shortages, despite adequate profits being made. Cash flow statements can help to signal the development of such problems.

> **Activity 37.2** Can you think of any more examples? Spend a minute thinking about this and then write down any you come up with.

37.5 Where from: where to

Basically a cash flow statement shows where the cash resources came from, and where they have gone to. Exhibit 37.1 shows details of such cash flows.

Exhibit 37.1

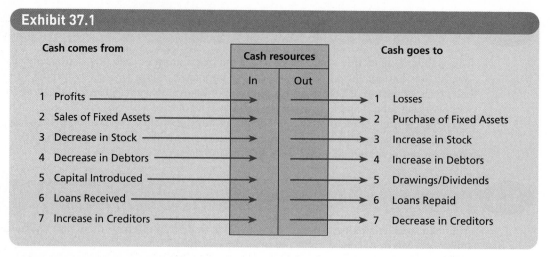

These can be explained as follow:

1 Profits bring a flow of cash into the business. Losses take cash out of it.
2 The cash received from sales of fixed assets comes into the business. A purchase of fixed assets takes it out.
3 Reducing stock in the normal course of business means turning it into cash. An increase in stock ties up cash funds.
4 A reduction in debtors means that the extra amount paid comes into the business as cash. Letting debtors increase stops that extra amount of cash coming in.
5 An increase in a sole proprietor's capital, or issues of shares in a company, brings cash in. Drawings or dividends take it out.
6 Loans received bring in cash, while their repayment reduces cash.
7 An increase in creditors keeps the extra cash in the business. A decrease in creditors means that the extra payments take cash out.

If, therefore, we take the cash (and bank) balances at the start of a financial period, and adjust for cash flows in and out during the financial period, then we should arrive at the cash (and bank) balances at the end of the period. This can be shown as:

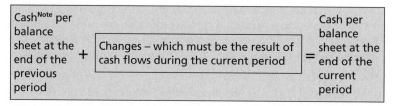

Note: 'Cash' in this context includes amounts held in bank accounts. We don't usually refer to 'cash and bank', but simply to 'cash'.

37.6 UK companies and cash flow statements

We have already stated that UK companies, except the very smallest, have to publish a cash flow statement for each accounting period. Students whose level of studies terminates with the conclusion of *Business Accounting UK GAAP 1* will not normally need to know more than has already been written in this chapter. However, some will need to know the basic layout given in FRS 1.

There are two approaches available under the standard: the 'direct' method, which shows the operating cash receipts and payments summing to the net cash flow from operating activities – in effect, it summarises the cash book; and the 'indirect' method, which identifies the net cash flow via a reconciliation to operating profit. As the reconciliation has also to be shown when the direct method is used, it is hardly surprising that the indirect method is the more commonly adopted one. Although the ASB prefer the direct method to be used, the indirect method is permitted because the cost of producing the data required for the direct method is likely to be greater than the benefit of doing so, in most cases. The direct method is too advanced for this book and is dealt with in *Business Accounting UK GAAP 2*.

For FRS 1, it is the indirect method that most examining bodies wish you to know. The basic layout prescribed by FRS 1 is shown in Exhibit 37.2:

Exhibit 37.2

X Limited
Cash Flow Statement for the year ending 31 December 2007 (FRS 1)

	£000	£000
1 Net cash inflow/(outflow) from operating activities (*see* Note 1)		XXX
2 *Dividends from joint ventures and associates*		XXX
3 *Returns on investments and servicing of finance*		
Interest received	XXX	
Interest paid	(XXX)	
Preference dividends paid	(XXX)	
Net cash inflow/(outflow) from returns on investments and servicing		
of finance		XXX
4 *Taxation*		XXX
5 *Capital expenditure and financial investment*		
Payments to acquire intangible fixed assets	(XXX)	
Payments to acquire tangible fixed assets	(XXX)	
Receipts from sales of tangible fixed assets	XXX	
Net cash inflow/(outflow) from capital expenditure and financial investment		(XXX)
6 *Acquisitions and disposals*		
Purchase of subsidiary undertaking	(XXX)	
Sale of business	XXX	
Net cash inflow/(outflow) from acquisitions and disposals		XXX
7 *Equity dividends paid*		(XXX)
8 *Management of liquid resources*		
Cash withdrawn from 7 day deposit	XXX	
Purchase of government securities	(XXX)	
Sale of corporate bonds	XXX	
Net cash inflow/(outflow) from management of liquid resources		XXX
9 *Financing*		
Issue of ordinary share capital	XXX	
Repurchase of debenture loan	(XXX)	
Expenses paid in connection with share issues	(XXX)	
		XXX
Increase/(decrease) in cash in the period		XXX
Reconciliation of net cash flow to movement in net debt/funds		
Increase/(decrease) in cash in the period	XXX	
Cash inflow/(outflow) from increase/decrease in debt and lease financing	XXX	
Cash inflow/(outflow) from decrease/increase in liquid resources	XXX	
Change in net debt resulting from cash flows		XXX
Loans and finance leases acquired with subsidiary		(XXX)
New finance leases		(XXX)
Exchange rate translation differences		XXX
Movement in net debt in the period		XXX
Net debt at 1 January 2007		XXX
Net debt at 31 December 2007		XXX

→ *Note to the cash flow statement:*

1 *Reconciliation of operating profit to net cash inflow/(outflow) from operating activities*

	£000
Operating profit	XXX
Depreciation charges	XXX
(Profit)/Loss on sale of tangible fixed assets	XXX
(Increase)/Decrease in stocks	XXX
(Increase)/Decrease in debtors	XXX
Increase/(Decrease) in creditors	XXX
Net cash inflow/(outflow) from operating activities	XXX

Each of the nine headings of the cash flow statement can be shown as one line in the statement and the detail in a note. (The numbers have been shown on the left in Exhibit 37.2 in order to make it clear what the nine headings are. These line numbers would not normally be included in the cash flow statement.)

The first seven headings should be in the sequence shown. The eighth and ninth can be combined under one heading, so long as their cash flows are shown separately and separate sub-totals are given for each of them within it.

The reconciliation to net debt does not form part of the cash flow statement, nor does the reconciliation of operating profit to net cash flow from operating activities. Either can be shown in a separate note (as the reconciliation of operating profit to net cash flow from operating activities is shown above) or adjoining the cash flow statement (as in the case of the reconciliation of the movement of cash to net debt above).

37.7 Construction of a cash flow statement

We will first of all look at a cash flow statement drawn up for a sole trader's business, as this will be easier than looking at the more complicated example of a limited company.

We will start from Exhibit 37.3 and construct Exhibit 37.4, a cash flow statement using the format prescribed by FRS 1.

Exhibit 37.3

The following are the balance sheets of T Holmes as at 31 December 2006 and 31 December 2007:

	31.12.2006		31.12.2007	
	£	£	£	£
Fixed assets				
Premises at cost		25,000		28,800
Current assets				
Stock	12,500		12,850	
Debtors	21,650		23,140	
Cash and bank balances	4,300		5,620	
	38,450		41,610	
Less Current liabilities				
Creditors	(11,350)		(11,120)	
Working capital		27,100		30,490
		52,100		59,290
Financed by:				
Capital				
Opening balances b/d		52,660		52,100
Add Net profit for year		16,550		25,440
		69,210		77,540
Less Drawings		(17,110)		(18,250)
		52,100		59,290

Note: For simplicity, no depreciation has been charged.

Exhibit 37.4

T Holmes
Cash Flow Statement for the year ending 31 December 2007

	£
Net cash inflow from operating activities (see Note 1)	23,370
Dividends from joint ventures and associates	–
Returns on investments and servicing of finance	–
Taxation	–
Capital expenditure and financial investment	
Payments to acquire extra premises	(3,800)
Acquisitions and disposals	–
Equity dividends paid	–
Management of liquid resources	–
Financing	
Drawings	(18,250)
Increase in cash	1,320

Note:

1 Reconciliation of net profit to net cash inflow:	£	£
Net profit		25,440
Less cash used for:		
Increase in stock	350	
Increase in debtors	1,490	
Decrease in creditors	230	
		(2,070)
Net cash flow from operating activities		23,370

37.8 Note on the use of brackets

As you know, in accounting it is customary to show a figure in brackets if it is a minus figure. This would be deducted from the other figures to arrive at the total of the column. These are seen very frequently in cash flow statements. For example, instead of bringing out a sub-total of the deductions, Note 1 accompanying Exhibit 37.4 would normally be shown as:

	£
Net profit	25,440
Increase in stock	(350)
Increase in debtors	(1,490)
Decrease in creditors	(230)
Net cash flow from operating activities	23,370

37.9 Adjustments needed to net profit

You saw in the cash flow statement in Exhibit 37.4 that when net profit is included as a source of cash funds, the net profit figure has to be adjusted to take account of items included which do not involve a movement of cash *in the period covered by the cash flow statement*. The most common examples are depreciation, provisions for doubtful debts, and book profits and losses on the sale or disposal of fixed assets.

Depreciation

For example, suppose we bought equipment costing £3,000 in the year ended 31 December 2006. It is depreciated at £1,000 per annum for 3 years and then scrapped, disposal value being nil. This would result in the following:

	Years to 31 December		
	2006	2007	2008
	£	£	£
(i) Item involving flow of cash: Cost of equipment (as this is purchase of an asset this is not part of the net profit calculation)	3,000		
(ii) Net profit before depreciation	12,000	13,000	15,000
(iii) Items not involving flow of cash: Depreciation	(1,000)	(1,000)	(1,000)
(iv) Net profit after depreciation	11,000	12,000	14,000

Now the question arises as to which of figures (*i*) to (*iv*) are the ones to be used in cash flow statements. Let's consider items (*i*) to (*iv*):

(*i*) **A payment of £3,000 is made to buy equipment. This** *does* **involve a flow of cash and should therefore be included in the cash flow statement for 2006.**

(*ii*) **Net profit before depreciation. This brings cash flowing into the business and therefore** *should* **be shown in cash flow statements.**

(*iii*) **Depreciation does not involve a flow of cash. It is represented by a bookkeeping entry:**
   Debit profit and loss: Credit provision for depreciation.
   As this does not involve any outflow of cash, it *should not* **be shown in a cash flow statement.**

(*iv*) **Net profit after depreciation. Depreciation does not involve cash flow, and therefore (*ii*) is the net profit we need.**

In most examination questions (*ii*) will not be shown. As we will show you, the figure for net profit before depreciation is calculated in the cash flow statement itself.

Doubtful debts provisions

A provision for doubtful debts is similar to a provision for depreciation. The cash flow occurs when a debt is paid, *not* when provisions are made in case there may be bad debts in the future. As a result, **when preparing the cash flow statement, you need to add back to net profit any increase in doubtful debt provision or deduct from net profit any decrease in the doubtful debt provision.**

If an examination question gives you the net profits *after* doubtful debts provision, then the provision has to be added back to exclude it from the profit calculations.

 Activity 37.3 What about bad debts? Should you make similar adjustments in the cash flow statement for them? Why/why not?

Book profit/loss on sales of fixed assets

If a fixed asset with a book value (after depreciation) of £5,000 is sold for £6,400 cash, then the flow of cash is £6,400. The fact that there has been a book profit of £1,400 does not provide any more cash above the figure of £6,400. Similarly, the sale of an asset with a book value of £3,000 for £2,200 cash produces a flow of cash of £2,200. **Book profits and losses of this type need to be eliminated by adjusting the net profit when preparing the cash flow statement.**

37.10 Example of adjustments

As the net profit figure in accounts is

(*i*) *after* adjustments for depreciation,
(*ii*) *after* adjustment to provisions for doubtful debts, and
(*iii*) *after* book profits/losses on sales of fixed assets,

net profit needs to be adjusted in cash flow statements for these three events. However, the adjustments are only for depreciation in *that period*, and for fixed asset book profits/losses for *that period*. No adjustments are needed with reference to previous periods. Exhibit 37.5 shows examples of three businesses.

Exhibit 37.5

	Business A £	Business B £	Business C £
Depreciation for the year	2,690	4,120	6,640
Increase in doubtful debt provision	540	360	
Decrease in doubtful debt provision			200
Book loss on sale of fixed assets	1,200		490
Book profit on sale of fixed assets		750	
Net profit after the above items are included	16,270	21,390	32,410
Reconciliation of net profit to net cash inflow	£	£	£
Net profit	16,270	21,390	32,410
Adjustment for items not involving the movement of cash:			
Depreciation	2,690	4,120	6,640
Book profit on sale of fixed assets		(750)	
Book loss on sale of fixed assets	1,200		490
Increase in doubtful debt provision	540	360	
Decrease in doubtful debt provision			(200)
Net cash flow from operating activities	20,700	25,120	39,340

You will notice that the items in brackets, i.e. (750) and (200), had been credits in the profit and loss accounts and need to be deducted, while the other items were debits and need to be added back.

37.11 A comprehensive example

Exhibit 37.6

The balance sheets of R Lester are as follows:

	31.12.2007			31.12.2008		
	£	£	£	£	£	£
Fixed assets						
Equipment at cost		28,500			26,100	
Less Depreciation to date		(11,450)			(13,010)	
			17,050			13,090
Current assets						
Stock		18,570			16,250	
Debtors	8,470			14,190		
Less Doubtful debts provision	(420)			(800)		
		8,050			13,390	
Cash and bank balances		4,060			3,700	
		30,680			33,340	
Less Current liabilities						
Creditors		(4,140)			(5,730)	
Net current assets			26,540			27,610
			43,590			40,700
Loan from J Gorsey			(10,000)			(4,000)
			33,590			36,700
Financed by:						
Capital						
Opening balances b/d			35,760			33,590
Add Net profit			10,240			11,070
Add Cash introduced			–			600
			46,000			45,260
Less Drawings			(12,410)			(8,560)
			33,590			36,700

Note: Equipment with a book value of £1,350 was sold for £900. Depreciation written off equipment during the year was £2,610.

The cash flow statement will be as follows:

Exhibit 37.7

R Lester
Cash Flow Statement for the year ending 31 December 2008 (FRS 1)

	£	£
Net cash inflow from operating activities (see Note 1)		12,700
Dividends from joint ventures and associates		–
Returns on investments and servicing of finance		–
Taxation		–
Capital expenditure and financial investment		
Receipts from sale of fixed assets		900
Acquisitions and disposals		–
Equity dividends paid		–
Management of liquid resources		–
Financing		
Capital introduced	600	
Loan repaid to J Gorsey	(6,000)	
Drawings	(8,560)	
		(13,960)
Decrease in cash in the year		(360)

Note:

1 Reconciliation of net profit to net cash inflow:	£
Net profit	11,070
Depreciation	2,610
Loss on sale of fixed assets	450
Increase in provision for doubtful debts	380
Decrease in stock	2,320
Increase in creditors	1,590
Increase in debtors	(5,720)
Net cash inflow from operating activities	12,700

37.12 Uses of cash flow statements

Cash flow statements have many uses other than the legal need for some companies to prepare them.

Cases where a business might find them useful in helping to answer their queries include:

(a) A small businessman wants to know why he now has an overdraft. He started off the year with money in the bank, he has made profits, and yet he now has a bank overdraft.

(b) Another businessman wants to know why the bank balance has risen even though the business is losing money.

(c) The partners in a business have put in additional capital during the year. Even so, the bank balance has fallen dramatically. They want an explanation as to how this has happened.

A study of the other financial statements themselves would not provide the information they needed. However, a study of the cash flow statement in each case will reveal the answers to their questions.

37.2A

Gerry Peace
Balance Sheets as at 31 December

	2002				2003	
	£	£	£	£	£	£
Fixed assets						
Buildings			50,000			50,000
Fixtures *less* Depreciation			1,800			2,000
Van *less* Depreciation			3,920			7,400
			55,720			59,400
Current Assets						
Stocks		5,600			12,400	
Trade debtors		6,400			8,200	
Bank		900			–	
Cash		220			200	
		13,120			20,800	
Current Liabilities						
Creditors	6,300			3,006		
Bank overdraft	–			94		
		(6,300)			(3,100)	
			6,820			17,700
			62,540			77,100
Loan (repayable in 10 years' time)			(10,000)			(15,000)
			52,540			62,100
Represented by						
Capital account:						
Balance at 1 January			37,040			52,540
Add Net profit for the year			35,200			21,160
Cash introduced			–			10,000
			72,240			83,700
Less Drawings			(19,700)			(21,600)
			52,540			62,100

Draw up a cash flow statement for Gerry Peace for the year ending 31 December 2003 using the FRS 1 layout. You are told that fixtures bought in 2003 cost £400, whilst a van was bought for £5,500.

37.3 Malcolm Phillips is a sole trader who prepares his accounts annually to 30 April. His summarised balance sheets for the last two years are shown below.

Balance Sheets as at 30 April

	2008 £	2008 £	2008 £	2009 £	2009 £	2009 £
Fixed assets			15,500			18,500
Less Provision for depreciation			(1,500)			(1,700)
			14,000			16,800
Current assets						
Stocks		3,100			5,900	
Trade debtors		3,900			3,400	
Bank		1,500			–	
		8,500			9,300	
Current liabilities						
Trade creditors	2,000			2,200		
Bank overdraft	–			900		
		(2,000)			(3,100)	
			6,500			6,200
			20,500			23,000
Represented by						
Capital account:						
Balance at 1 May			20,000			20,500
Add Net profit for the year			7,000			8,500
Additional capital introduced			–			2,000
			27,000			31,000
Less Drawings			(6,500)			(8,000)
			20,500			23,000

Malcolm is surprised to see that he now has an overdraft, in spite of making a profit and bringing in additional capital during the year.

Questions:

(a) Draw up a suitable financial statement which will explain to Malcolm how his overdraft has arisen.

(b) The following further information relates to the year ended 30 April 2009.

	£
Sales (all on credit)	30,000
Cost of sales	22,500

Calculate Malcolm's
(i) gross profit margin
(ii) rate of stock turnover.

(*Midland Examining Group: GCSE*)

→

37.4 From the following details you are to draft a cash flow statement for D Duncan for the year ending 31 December 2005: using the FRS 1 layout.

D Duncan
Profit and Loss Account for the year ending 31 December 2005

	£	£
Gross profit		44,700
Add Discounts received	410	
Profit on sale of van	620	1,030
		45,730
Less Expenses		
Motor expenses	1,940	
Wages	17,200	
General expenses	830	
Bad debts	520	
Increase in doubtful debt provision	200	
Depreciation: Van	1,800	22,490
		23,240

Balance Sheets as at 31 December

	2004		2005	
	£	£	£	£
Fixed assets				
Vans at cost		15,400		8,200
Less Depreciation to date		(5,300)		(3,100)
		10,100		5,100
Current assets				
Stock	18,600		24,000	
Debtors less provision*	8,200		6,900	
Bank	410		720	
	27,210		31,620	
Less Current liabilities				
Creditors	(5,900)		(7,200)	
		21,310		24,420
		31,410		29,520
Less Long-term liability				
Loan from J Fry		(10,000)		(7,500)
		21,410		22,020
Capital				
Opening balance b/d		17,210		21,410
Add Net profit		21,200		23,240
		38,410		44,650
Less Drawings		(17,000)		(22,630)
		21,410		22,020

*Debtors 2004 £8,800 – provision £600.
 Debtors 2005 £7,700 – provision £800.
Note: A van was sold for £3,820 during 2005. No new vans were purchased during the year.

37.5A You are required to draw up a cash flow statement for K Rock for the year ending 30 June 2009 from the following information using the FRS 1 layout.

K Rock
Profit and Loss Account for the year ending 30 June 2009

	£	£
Gross profit		155,030
Add Reduction in doubtful debt provision		200
		155,230
Less Expenses:		
Wages and salaries	61,400	
General trading expenses	15,200	
Equipment running costs	8,140	
Motor vehicle expenses	6,390	
Depreciation: Motor vehicles	5,200	
Equipment	6,300	
Loss on sale of equipment	1,600	
		(104,230)
Net profit		51,000

Balance Sheets as at 30 June

	2008 £	2008 £	2009 £	2009 £
Fixed assets				
Equipment at cost	40,400		30,800	
Less Depreciation to date	(24,600)		(20,600)	
		15,800		10,200
Motor vehicles at cost	28,300		28,300	
Less Depreciation to date	(9,200)		(14,400)	
		19,100		13,900
		34,900		24,100
Current assets				
Stock	41,700		44,600	
Debtors *less* provision*	21,200		19,800	
Bank	12,600		28,100	
	75,500		92,500	
Less Current liabilities				
Creditors	(14,300)		(17,500)	
		61,200		75,000
		96,100		99,100
Less Long-term liability				
Loan from T Pine		(20,000)		(10,000)
		76,100		89,100
Capital				
Opening balance		65,600		76,100
Add Net profit		42,500		51,000
		108,100		127,100
Less Drawings		(32,000)		(38,000)
		76,100		89,100

*Debtors 2008 £22,100 – provision £900.
 Debtors 2009 £20,500 – provision £700.
Note: Equipment was sold for £15,800. Equipment costing £18,100 was purchased during the year.

Joint venture accounts

Learning objectives

After you have studied this chapter, you should be able to:

- explain what is meant by the term 'joint venture'
- explain why separate joint venture accounts are kept by each of the parties to a joint venture
- make the entries in the accounts for a joint venture
- calculate and enter the profits of the joint venture into the accounts of the parties to the joint venture
- identify the amount owing to or owed by each of the parties to the other parties in the joint venture and make the appropriate entries in the joint venture accounts when payment is made and received
- name the accounting standard relating to joint ventures

Introduction

Joint ventures, which were the reason why the system of bookkeeping we use today was developed in the thirteenth century, are becoming increasingly common. In this chapter, you'll learn how to record joint ventures in the books of the parties to a joint venture. You'll learn how to calculate profits and identify how much each of the parties must pay to the other parties at the end of the joint venture. Finally you'll learn that an accounting standards has been issued to regulate accounting for longer-term and larger joint ventures.

38.1 Nature of joint ventures

Sometimes a particular business venture can best be done by two or more businesses joining together to do it instead of doing it separately. The joining together is for that one venture only, it is not joining together to make a continuing business.

Such projects are known as **joint ventures**. For instance, a merchant might provide the capital, the transport to the markets and the selling skills. The farmer grows the produce. The profits or losses are then shared between them in agreed ratios. It is like a partnership, but only for this one venture. There may be several joint ventures between the same businesses, but each one is a separate venture. The agreements for each venture may be different from each other.

38.2 Accounting for large joint ventures

For large-scale or long-term joint ventures, a separate bank account and separate set of books are kept. In such cases the calculation of profit is not difficult. It is similar to preparing a set of financial statements for an ordinary business.

38.3 Accounting for smaller joint ventures

No separate set of books or separate bank accounts are kept for smaller joint ventures. Each of the parties will record in their own books only those transactions with which they have been concerned. Exhibit 38.1 gives an example of such a joint venture.

Exhibit 38.1

White of London and Green of Glasgow enter into a joint venture. White is to supply the goods and pay some of the expenses. Green is to sell the goods and receive the cash, and pay the remainder of the expenses. Profits are to be shared equally.
  Details of the transactions are as follows:

	£
White supplied the goods costing	1,800
White paid wages	200
White paid for storage expenses	160
Green paid transport expenses	120
Green paid selling expenses	320
Green received cash from sales of all the goods	3,200

Stage 1

White and Green will each have entered up their own part of the transactions. White will have opened an account named 'Joint Venture with Green'. Similarly, Green will have opened a 'Joint Venture with White' account. The double entry to these joint venture accounts will be:

In White's books:
  Payments by White: Debit joint venture with Green
                                        Credit cash book

  Goods supplied to Green: Debit joint venture with Green
                                        Credit purchases

In Green's books:
  Payments by Green: Debit joint venture with White
                                        Credit cash book

  Cash received by Green: Debit cash book
                                        Credit joint venture with White

At this point the joint venture accounts in each of their books will appear as follows:

White's books (in London):

Joint Venture with Green

	£	
Purchases	1,800	
Cash: wages	200	
Cash: storage expenses	160	

Activity 38.2 Can you remember what is meant by a debit balance? Is it where the balance c/d is a debit or where the balance b/d is a debit?

Finally, the parties in the joint venture need to settle their debts to each other. They know whether they are to pay money or receive money when they look at the side of their copy of the joint venture account and see whether the balance is a debit or a credit:

(a) If the balance brought down is a credit balance, money is owing to the other party in the joint venture. In this case, Green owes White the amount shown by the credit balance, £2,460.

(b) If the balance brought down is a debit balance, money is due from the other party in the joint venture. In this case White is owed the amount of the balance, £2,460 by Green.

The payment is now made by Green to White and the final entry is made in each of the joint venture accounts, closing off the accounts.

White's books (in London):

Joint Venture with Green

	£		£
Purchases	1,800	Balance c/d	2,460
Cash: wages	200		
Cash: storage expenses	160		
Profit and loss: share of profit	300		
	2,460		2,460
Balance b/d	2,460	Cash: settlement from Green	2,460

Green's books (in Glasgow):

Joint Venture with White

	£		£
Cash: transport expenses	120	Cash: sales	3,200
Cash: selling expenses	320		
Profit and loss: share of profit	300		
Balance c/d	2,460		
	3,200		3,200
Cash: settlement to White	2,460	Balance b/d	2,460

38.4 FRS 9: Associates and Joint Ventures

In 1997, in response to a growing number of joint ventures, the ASB issued FRS 9. For the first time, a UK accounting standard existed laying out the accounting treatment for joint ventures. It was aimed more at accounting for long-term joint ventures, which were mentioned briefly in Section 38.2. However, it confirmed that the above treatment of short-term joint ventures is appropriate by stating that participants should account for their own assets, liabilities and cash flows measured according to the agreement governing the arrangement.

Learning outcomes

You should now have learnt:

1 That when two or more businesses join together for a particular business venture, and do not form a permanent business entity, they have entered into a joint venture.

2 That larger and long-term joint ventures operate a separate bank account and books dedicated to the project.

3 That the participants in smaller joint ventures rely on their own bank accounts and books to run and record their part of the project, using a *memorandum joint venture account* to pass the details of their part of the project to the other participant(s).

4 Why separate joint venture accounts are kept by each party to smaller and short-term joint ventures.

5 How to make the appropriate entries in the books of the parties to the joint venture, calculate the profit, share that profit among the parties to the joint ventures and close off the joint venture accounts at the end of the joint venture.

6 That FRS 9 regulates accounting for long-term joint ventures.

Answers to activities

38.1 It's quite simple really, isn't it? You take each debit entry in the first of the T-accounts (joint venture with Green) and copy it as a debit entry into the memorandum joint venture account. You then do the same with the debits in the second T-account (joint venture with White). Then you do exactly the same with the credit entries. The order you do this in doesn't matter. All you need to ensure is that you have replicated all the T-account entries from the individual joint venture accounts in the memorandum joint venture account. You have to do this because the memorandum joint venture account lies outside the double entry system.

38.2 An account with a debit balance has more value on the debit side. That is, it is the side on which the balance b/d figure lies that tells you whether the balance is a debit or a credit. In this case, the joint venture account in White's books has a debit balance. The one in Green's books has a credit balance. Therefore, Green owes White £2,460.

Review questions

38.1 Stanley and Barclay enter a joint venture to share profits or losses equally resulting from dealings in second-hand digital TVs. Both parties take an active part in the business, each recording his own transactions. They have no joint banking account or separate set of books.

2003
July 1 Stanley buys four TVs for a total of £1,100.
3 Stanley pays for repairs £840.
4 Barclay pays office rent £300 and advertising expenses £90.
6 Barclay pays for packaging materials £34.
7 Barclay buys a TV in excellent condition for £600.
31 Stanley sells the five TVs to various customers, the sales being completed on this date, and totalling £3,100.

Show the relevant accounts in the books of both joint venturers.

38.2A Frank entered into a joint venture with Graham for the purchase and sale of robot mowers. They agreed that profits and losses should be shared equally.

The following transactions took place:

(a) Frank purchased mowers for £120,400 and paid carriage £320.
(b) Graham purchased mowers for £14,860 and paid carriage £84.
(c) Graham paid to Frank £70,000.
(d) Frank sold mowers for £104,590 and sent a cheque for £50,000 to Graham.
(e) Graham sold for £19,200 all the mowers he had purchased.
(f) The unsold mowers in the possession of Frank were taken over by him at a valuation of £40,000.
(g) The amount due from one venturer to the other was paid and the joint venture was dissolved.

You are required to prepare:
(i) a statement to show the net profit or loss of the joint venture, and
(ii) the accounts for the joint venture in the books of Frank and Graham.

38.3 Bull, Craig and Finch entered into a joint venture for dealing in strawberries. The transactions connected with this venture were:

2009
May	1	Bull rented land for two months for £600.
	2	Craig supplied plants costing £510.
	3	Bull employed labour for planting £260.
	16	Craig charged motor expenses £49.
	19	Bull employed labour for fertilising £180.
	29	Bull paid the following expenses: Sundries £19, Labour £210, Fertiliser £74.
June	11	Finch employed labour for lifting strawberries £416.
	24	Sale expenses paid by Finch £318.
	26	Finch received cash from sale proceeds £2,916.

Required:
Show the joint venture accounts in the books of Bull, Craig and Finch. Also show in full the method of arriving at the profit on the venture which is to be apportioned: Bull four-sevenths; Craig two-sevenths; Finch one-seventh.

Any outstanding balances between the parties are settled by cheque on 31 July.

38.4A Rock, Hill and Pine enter into a joint venture for dealing in paintings. The following transactions took place:

2004
May	1	Rock rented a shop paying 3 months rent £2,100.
	3	Hill bought a van for £2,200.
	5	Hill bought paintings for £18,000.
	17	Pine received cash from sale proceeds of paintings £31,410.
	23	Rock bought paintings for £317,000.
June	9	Van broke down. Pine agreed to use his own van for the job until cessation of the joint venture at an agreed charge of £600.
	14	Van bought on May 3 was sold for £1,700. Proceeds were kept by Rock.
	17	Sales of paintings, cash being paid by Hill £4,220.
	25	Lighting bills paid for shop by Pine £86.
	29	Pine bought paintings for £1,700.
July	3	General expenses of shop paid for £1,090, Pine and Rock paying half each.
	16	Paintings sold by Pine £2,300, proceeds being kept by him.
	31	Joint venture ended. The paintings still in stock were taken over at an agreed valuation of £6,200 by Hill.

Required:
Show the joint venture accounts in the books of the three parties. Show in full the workings needed to arrive at the profit on the venture. The profit or loss was to be split: Hill one-half; Rock one-third; Pine one-sixth. Any outstanding balances between the parties were settled on 31 July 2004.

Part

6

PARTNERSHIP ACCOUNTS AND COMPANY ACCOUNTS

Introduction

This part is concerned with accounting procedures, particularly those affecting partnerships; gives an introduction to goodwill in relation to partnerships and other business organisations; and introduces the accounts of limited liability companies.

Partnership accounts: an introduction

Learning objectives

After you have studied this chapter, you should be able to:

- explain what a partnership is and how it differs from a joint venture
- explain the rules relating to the number of partners
- distinguish between limited partners and general partners
- describe the main features of a partnership agreement
- explain what will happen if no agreement exists on how to share profits or losses
- draw up the ledger accounts and financial statements for a partnership

Introduction

In this chapter, you'll learn about the nature of partnerships and the regulations governing them. You'll learn that there are two types of partner, limited and general, and about the difference between them, and about the difference between those that are limited partnerships and those that are not. Finally, you'll learn how to prepare partnership ledger accounts and how to prepare partnership financial statements.

39.1 The need for partnerships

So far we have mainly considered businesses owned by only one person. We've also looked at joint ventures, which are temporary projects involving two or more parties where they work together to make a profit and then disband the venture. When a more permanent possibility exists, two or more people may form themselves into a **partnership**. This is a long-term commitment to operate in business together. The people who own a partnership are called **partners**. They do not have to be based or work in the same place, though most do. However, they maintain one set of accounting records and share the profits and losses.

Activity 39.1 From your general knowledge, can you think of any well-known partnerships where the partners are located, not just in different cities, but in different countries? What line of business are they in?

There are various reasons for multiple ownership of a business.

Years	1	2	3	4	5	Total
	£	£	£	£	£	£
Net profits	36,000	48,000	60,000	60,000	72,000	276,000
Shared:						
Allen ⅔	24,000	32,000	40,000	40,000	48,000	184,000
Beet ⅓	12,000	16,000	20,000	20,000	24,000	92,000

Overall, Allen would receive £184,000, i.e. £92,000 more than Beet. As the duties of the partners are the same, in order to treat each partner fairly, the difference between the two shares of profit should be adequate to compensate Allen for putting extra capital into the firm. It should not be excessive. It is obvious that £92,000 extra profits is excessive, as Allen only put in an extra £20,000 as capital.

Consider too the position of capital ratio sharing of profits if one partner puts in £99,000 and the other puts in £1,000 as capital.

To overcome the difficulty of compensating fairly for the investment of extra capital, the concept of **interest on capital** was devised.

3 Interest on capital

If the work to be done by each partner is of equal value but the capital contributed is unequal, it is reasonable to pay interest on the partners' capitals out of partnership profits. This interest is treated as a deduction prior to the calculation of profits and their distribution among the partners according to the profit sharing ratio.

The rate of interest is a matter of agreement between the partners. Often it will be based upon the return which they would have received if they had invested the capital elsewhere.

Taking Allen and Beet's partnership again, but sharing the profits equally after charging 5 per cent per annum interest on capital, the division of profits would become:

Years	1	2	3	4	5		Total
	£	£	£	£	£		£
Net profit	36,000	48,000	60,000	60,000	72,000		276,000
Interest on capitals							
Allen	2,000	2,000	2,000	2,000	2,000	=	10,000
Beet	1,000	1,000	1,000	1,000	1,000	=	5,000
Remainder shared:							
Allen ½	16,500	22,500	28,500	28,500	34,500	=	130,500
Beet ½	16,500	22,500	28,500	28,500	34,500	=	130,500

Summary	Allen	Beet
	£	£
Interest on capital	10,000	5,000
Balance of profits	130,500	130,500
	140,500	135,500

Allen has thus received £5,000 more than Beet, this being adequate return (in the partners' estimation) for having invested an extra £20,000 in the partnership for five years.

4 Interest on drawings

It is obviously in the best interests of the partnership if cash is withdrawn from it by the partners in accordance with the two basic principles of: (*a*) as little as possible, and (*b*) as late as possible.

The more cash that is left in the partnership, the more expansion can be financed, the greater the economies of having ample cash to take advantage of bargains and of not missing cash discounts because cash is not available and so on.

To deter the partners from taking out cash unnecessarily the concept can be used of charging the partners interest on each withdrawal, calculated from the date of withdrawal to the end of the financial year. The amount charged to them helps to swell the profits divisible between the partners. The rate of interest should be sufficient to achieve this without being too harsh.

Suppose that Allen and Beet have decided to charge **interest on drawings** at 5 per cent per annum, and that their year end was 31 December. The following drawings are made:

Allen

Drawings	£	Interest		£
1 January	2,000	£2,000 × 5% × 12 months	=	100
1 March	4,800	£4,800 × 5% × 10 months	=	200
1 May	2,400	£2,400 × 5% × 8 months	=	80
1 July	4,800	£4,800 × 5% × 6 months	=	120
1 October	1,600	£1,600 × 5% × 3 months	=	20
		Interest charged to Allen	=	520

Beet

Drawings	£	Interest		£
1 January	1,200	£1,200 × 5% × 12 months	=	60
1 August	9,600	£9,600 × 5% × 5 months	=	200
1 December	4,800	£4,800 × 5% × 1 month	=	20
		Interest charged to Beet	=	280

5 Partnership salaries

One partner may have more responsibility or tasks than the others. As a reward for this, rather than change the profit and loss sharing ratio, the partner may have a **partnership salary** which is deducted before sharing the balance of profits.

6 Performance-related payments to partners

Partners may agree that commission or performance-related bonuses be payable to some or all the partners linked to their individual performance. As with salaries, these would be deducted before sharing the balance of profits.

39.7 An example of the distribution of profits

Taylor and Clarke have been in partnership for one year sharing profits and losses in the ratio of Taylor $^3/_5$, Clarke $^2/_5$. They are entitled to 5 per cent per annum interest on capitals, Taylor having £20,000 capital and Clarke £60,000. Clarke is to have a salary of £15,000. They charge interest on drawings, Taylor being charged £500 and Clarke £1,000. The net profit, before any distributions to the partners, amounted to £50,000 for the year ended 31 December 2007.

The way in which the net profit is distributed among the partners can be shown as:

	£	£	£
Net profit			50,000
Add Charged for interest on drawings:			
Taylor		500	
Clarke		1,000	
			1,500
			51,500
Less Salary: Clarke		15,000	
Interest on capital:			
Taylor	1,000		
Clarke	3,000		
	4,000		
			(19,000)
Balance of profits			32,500
Shared:			
Taylor ³/₅		19,500	
Clarke ²/₅		13,000	
			32,500

The £50,000 net profits have therefore been shared:

	Taylor	Clarke
	£	£
Balance of profits	19,500	13,000
Interest on capital	1,000	3,000
Salary	–	15,000
	20,500	31,000
Less Interest on drawings	(500)	(1,000)
	20,000	30,000
		£50,000

39.8 The financial statements

If the sales, stock and expenses of a partnership were exactly the same as that of a sole trader, then the trading and profit and loss account would be identical with that as prepared for the sole trader. However, a partnership would have an extra section at the end of the trading and profit and loss account. This section is called the **profit and loss appropriation account,** and it is in this account that the distribution of profits is shown. The heading to the trading and profit and loss account for a partnership does not normally include the words 'appropriation account'. It is purely an accounting custom not to include it in the heading. (**Sometimes examiners ask for it to be included in the heading, in which case, you need to do so!**)

The profit and loss appropriation account of Taylor and Clarke from the details given would be:

Taylor and Clarke
Trading and Profit and Loss Account for the year ending 31 December 2007

(Trading Account section – same as for sole trader)

(Profit and Loss Account section – same as for sole trader)

Profit and Loss Appropriation Account

	£	£	£
Net profit (from the Profit and Loss Account section)			50,000
Interest on drawings:			
Taylor		500	
Clarke		1,000	
			1,500
			51,500
Less: Salary: Clarke		15,000	
Interest on capitals			
Taylor	1,000		
Clarke	3,000		
		4,000	(19,000)
			32,500
Balance of profits shared:			
Taylor ³/₅		19,500	
Clarke ²/₅		13,000	
			32,500

39.9 Fixed and fluctuating capital accounts

There are two choices open to partnerships: **fixed capital accounts** plus current accounts, and **fluctuating capital accounts**.

1 Fixed capital accounts plus current accounts

The capital account for each partner remains year by year at the figure of capital put into the partnership by the partners. The profits, interest on capital and the salaries to which the partner may be entitled are then credited to a separate current account for the partner, and the drawings and the interest on drawings are debited to it. The balance of the current account at the end of each financial year will then represent the amount of undrawn (or withdrawn) profits. A credit balance will be undrawn profits, while a debit balance will be drawings in excess of the profits to which the partner was entitled.

For Taylor and Clarke, capital and current accounts, assuming drawings of £15,000 for Taylor and £26,000 for Clarke will be:

Taylor – Capital

	2007			£
	Jan	1	Bank	20,000

Clarke – Capital

	2007			£
	Jan	1	Bank	60,000

Taylor – *Current Account*

2007			£	2007			£
Dec	31	Cash: Drawings	15,000	Dec	31	Profit and loss	
	31	Profit and loss				appropriation account:	
		appropriation account:				Interest on capital	1,000
		Interest on drawings	500			Share of profits	19,500
	31	Balance c/d	5,000				
			20,500				20,500
				2008			
				Jan	1	Balance b/d	5,000

Clarke – *Current Account*

2007			£	2007			£
Dec	31	Cash: Drawings	26,000	Dec	31	Profit and loss	
	31	Profit and loss				appropriation account:	
		appropriation account:				Salary	15,000
		Interest on drawings	1,000			Interest on capital	3,000
	31	Balance c/d	4,000			Share of profits	13,000
			31,000				31,000
				2008			
				Jan	1	Balance b/d	4,000

Notice that the salary of Clarke was not paid to him, it was merely credited to his current account. If instead it was paid in addition to his drawings, the £15,000 cash paid would have been debited to the current account, changing the £4,000 credit balance into a £11,000 debit balance.

Note also that the drawings have been posted to the current accounts at the end of the year. The amounts withdrawn which add up to these amounts were initially recorded in the cash book. Only the totals for the year are posted to the current account, rather than each individual withdrawal.

Examiners often ask for the capital accounts and current accounts to be shown in columnar form rather than as T-accounts. For Taylor and Clarke, these would appear as follows:

Capital Accounts

			Taylor	Clarke				Taylor	Clarke
			£	£	2007			£	£
					Jan	1	Bank	20,000	60,000

Current Accounts

			Taylor	Clarke				Taylor	Clarke
2007			£	£	2007			£	£
Dec	31	Cash: Drawings	15,000	26,000	Dec	31	Salary	19,500	15,000
	31	Interest on drawings	500	1,000		31	Interest on capital	1,000	3,000
	31	Balances c/d	5,000	4,000		31	Share of profits		13,000
			20,500	31,000				20,500	31,000
					2008				
					Jan	1	Balances b/d	5,000	4,000

2 Fluctuating capital accounts

The distribution of profits would be credited to the capital account, and the drawings and interest on drawings debited. Therefore the balance on the capital account will change each year, i.e. it will fluctuate.

If fluctuating capital accounts had been kept for Taylor and Clarke they would have appeared:

Taylor – *Capital*

2007			£	2007				£
Dec	31	Cash: Drawings	15,000	Jan	1	Bank		20,000
	31	Profit and loss		Dec	31	Profit and loss		
		appropriation account:				appropriation account:		
		Interest on drawings	500			Interest on capital		1,000
	31	Balance c/d	25,000			Share of profits		19,500
			40,500					40,500
				2008				
				Jan	1	Balance b/d		25,000

Clarke – *Capital*

2007			£	2007				£
Dec	31	Cash: Drawings	26,000	Jan	1	Bank		60,000
	31	Profit and loss		Dec	31	Profit and loss		
		appropriation account:				appropriation account:		
		Interest on				Salary		15,000
		drawings	1,000			Interest on capital		3,000
	31	Balance c/d	64,000			Share of profit		13,000
			91,000					91,000
				2008				
				Jan	1	Balance b/d		64,000

Fixed capital accounts preferred

The keeping of fixed capital accounts plus current accounts is considered preferable to fluctuating capital accounts. When partners are taking out greater amounts than the share of the profits that they are entitled to, this is shown up by a debit balance on the current account and so acts as a warning.

39.10 Where no partnership agreement exists

As mentioned in the answer to Activity 39.4, where no partnership agreement exists, express or implied, Section 24 of the Partnership Act 1890 governs the situation. The accounting content of this section states:

(a) Profits and losses are to be shared equally.
(b) There is to be no interest allowed on capital.
(c) No interest is to be charged on drawings.
(d) Salaries are not allowed.
(e) Partners who put a sum of money into a partnership in excess of the capital they have agreed to subscribe are entitled to interest at the rate of 5 per cent per annum on such an advance.

Section 24 applies where there is no agreement. There may be an agreement not by a partnership deed but in a letter, or it may be implied by conduct, for instance when a partner signs a balance sheet which shows profits shared in some other ratio than equally. Where a dispute arises as to whether an agreement exists or not, and this cannot be resolved by the partners, only the courts are competent to decide.

39.11 The balance sheet

For the partnership, the capital part of the balance sheet will appear:

Taylor and Clarke
Balance Sheet as at 31 December 2007 (extract)

						£	£
Capital accounts	Taylor					20,000	
	Clarke					60,000	
							80,000

Current accounts		*Taylor*		*Clarke*			
		£	£	£	£		
Salary			–		15,000		
Interest on capital			1,000		3,000		
Share of profits			19,500		13,000		
			20,500		31,000		
Less Drawings	15,000			26,000			
Interest on drawings	500			1,000			
			(15,500)		(27,000)		
			5,000		4,000		
							9,000

If one of the current accounts had finished in debit, for instance if the current account of Clarke had finished up as £400 debit, the figure of £400 would appear in brackets and the balances would appear net in the totals column:

	Taylor	*Clarke*	
	£	£	£
Closing balance	5,000	(400)	4,600

If the net figure turned out to be a debit figure then this would be deducted from the total of the capital accounts.

Learning outcomes

You should now have learnt:

1 That there is no limited liability in partnerships except for 'limited partners'.

2 That limited partners cannot withdraw any of the capital they invested in the partnership or take part in the management of the partnership.

3 That apart from some professions, if more than twenty owners of an organisation are needed, a limited company would need to be formed, not a partnership.

4 That the contents of a partnership agreement will override anything written in this chapter. Partners can agree to anything they want to, in as much or as little detail as they wish.

5 That if there is no partnership agreement, then the provisions of the Partnership Act 1890 (details shown in section 39.10) will apply.

6 That partners can agree to show their capital accounts using either the fixed capital or fluctuating capital methods.

7 How to prepare the ledger accounts and financial statements of partnerships.

Answers to activities

39.1   The best example is accounting partnerships. Some of them have offices all over the world.

39.2   Your answer could have included some of the following:
- The capital required is more than one person can provide.
- The experience or ability required to manage the business cannot be found in one person alone.
- Many people want to share management instead of doing everything on their own.
- Very often the partners will be members of the same family.

39.3   Limited partners contribute capital. They may also contribute expertise. Either of these is a benefit to the general partners – they have to contribute less capital and they can rely on the additional expertise when appropriate without needing to seek assistance from people outside the partnership. Also, because limited partners cannot be involved in the management of the partnership, general partners can take decisions without consulting a limited partner, thus saving time and effort when, in many instances, the limited partner will be busy doing other things that have nothing to do with the partnership business.

39.4   The Partnership Act 1890 imposes a standard partnership agreement upon partnerships that do not draw up a partnership agreement. See Section 39.10.

Review questions

39.1   Black, Brown and Cook are partners. They share profits and losses in the ratios of $^2/_9$, $^1/_3$ and $^4/_9$ respectively.
   For the year ended 31 July 2002, their capital accounts remained fixed at the following amounts:

	£
Black	60,000
Brown	40,000
Cook	20,000

They have agreed to give each other 6 per cent interest per annum on their capital accounts.
   In addition to the above, partnership salaries of £30,000 for Brown and £18,000 for Cook are to be charged.
   The net profit of the partnership, before taking any of the above into account was £111,000.
   You are required to draw up the appropriation account of the partnership for the year ending 31 July 2002.

39.2A   Gray, Wilkes and Booth are partners. They share profits and losses in the ratios of $^3/_8$, $^3/_8$ and $^1/_4$ respectively.
   For the year ended 31 December 2003 their capital accounts remained fixed at the following amounts:

	£
Gray	50,000
Wilkes	40,000
Booth	30,000

They have agreed to give each other 5 per cent interest per annum on their capital accounts.
   In addition to the above, partnership salaries of £32,000 for Wilkes and £14,000 for Booth are to be charged.
   The net profit of the partnership before taking any of the above into account was £84,800.

Required:
Draw up the appropriation account of the partnership for the year ending 31 December 2003.

39.3   I Skip and U Jump sell toys. Their individual investments in the business on 1 January 2004 were: Skip £80,000, Jump £40,000.
   For the year to 31 December 2004, the net profit was £30,000 and the partners' drawings were: Skip £8,000, Jump £9,000.

→ For 2004 (their first year), the partners agreed to share profits and losses equally, but they decided that from 1 January 2005:

(*i*) The partners should be entitled to annual salaries of: Skip £10,000; Jump £14,000.
(*ii*) Interest should be allowed on capital at 7% per annum.
(*iii*) The profit remaining should be shared equally (as should losses).

| | Net trading profit before dealing with partners' items | Drawings | |
		Skip	Jump
	£	£	£
2005	38,000	13,000	17,000
2006	29,000	12,000	20,000

Required:
Prepare the profit and loss appropriation accounts and the partners' current accounts for the three years.

39.4 Draw up a profit and loss appropriation account for the year ending 31 December 2007 and balance sheet extract at that date, from the following:

(*i*) Net profits £111,100.
(*ii*) Interest to be charged on capitals: Blair £3,000; Short £2,000; Steel £1,500.
(*iii*) Interest to be charged on drawings: Blair £400; Short £300; Steel £200.
(*iv*) Salaries to be credited: Short £20,000; Steel £25,000.
(*v*) Profits to be shared: Blair 70%; Short 20%; Steel 10%.
(*vi*) Current accounts: balances b/d Blair £18,600; Short £9,460; Steel £8,200.
(*vii*) Capital accounts: balances b/d Blair £100,000; Short £50,000; Steel £25,000.
(*viii*) Drawings: Blair £39,000; Short £27,100; Steel £16,800.

39.5A Draw up a profit and loss appropriation account for Cole, Knox and Lamb for the year ending 31 December 2005, and a balance sheet extract at that date, from the following:

(*i*) Net profits £184,800.
(*ii*) Interest to be charged on capitals: Cole £3,600; Knox £2,700; Lamb £2,100.
(*iii*) Interest to be charged on drawings: Cole £1,200; Knox £900; Lamb £500.
(*iv*) Salaries to be credited: Knox £22,000; Lamb £28,000.
(*v*) Profits to be shared: Cole 55%; Knox 25%; Lamb 20%.
(*vi*) Current accounts: Cole £18,000; Knox £8,000; Lamb £6,000.
(*vii*) Capital accounts: Cole £60,000; Knox £45,000; Lamb £35,000.
(*viii*) Drawings: Cole £27,000; Knox £23,000; Lamb £17,000.

39.6A Penrose and Wilcox are in partnership, sharing profits and losses in the ratio 3 : 2. The following information was taken from their books for the year ending 31 December 2009, before the completion of their profit and loss appropriation account.

		£	
Current accounts (1 January 2009)			
	Penrose	640	(*Dr*)
	Wilcox	330	(*Cr*)
Drawings	Penrose	3,000	
	Wilcox	2,000	
Net trading profit		6,810	
Interest on capital	Penrose	540	
	Wilcox	720	
Salary	Penrose	2,000	
Interest on drawings	Penrose	270	
	Wilcox	180	

(a) Prepare, for the year ending 31 December 2009:
    (i) the profit and loss appropriation account of Penrose and Wilcox;
    (ii) the current accounts in the ledger for Penrose and Wilcox.
(b) Why in many partnerships are current accounts prepared as well as capital accounts?
(c) At 1 January 2009 Penrose had a debit balance in his current account. What does this mean?
(d) In partnership accounts what is the purpose of preparing:
    (i) a profit and loss account?
    (ii) a profit and loss appropriation account?
(e) In partnership accounts why is:
    (i) interest allowed on capital?
    (ii) interest charged on drawings?

(*Northern Examinations and Assessment Board: GCSE*)

39.7A A and B are in partnership sharing profits and losses 3:2. Under the terms of the partnership agreement, the partners are entitled to interest on capital at 5 per cent per annum and B is entitled to a salary of £4,500. Interest is charged on drawings at 5 per cent per annum and the amounts of interest are given below. No interest is charged or allowed on current accounts.

The partners' capitals at 1 July 2006 were: A £30,000 and B £10,000.

The net trading profit of the firm, before dealing with partners' interest or B's salary for the year ended 30 June 2007 was £25,800. Interest on drawings for the year amounted to A £400, B £300.

At 1 July 2006, there was a credit balance of £1,280 on B's current account, while A's current account balance was a debit of £500. Drawings for the year to 30 June 2007 amounted to £12,000 for A and £15,000 for B.

Required:
Prepare, for the year to 30 June 2007:
(a) The profit and loss appropriation account.
(b) The partners' current accounts.

39.8 Bee, Cee and Dee have been holding preliminary discussions with a view to forming a partnership to buy and sell antiques.

The position has now been reached where the prospective partners have agreed the basic arrangements under which the partnership will operate.

Bee will contribute £40,000 as capital, and up to £10,000 as a long-term loan to the partnership, if needed. He has extensive other business interests and will not therefore be taking an active part in the running of the business.

Cee is unable to bring in more than £2,000 as capital initially, but, because he has an expert knowledge of the antique trade, will act as the manager of the business on a full-time basis.

Dee is willing to contribute £10,000 as capital. He will also assist in running the business as the need arises. In particular, he is prepared to attend auctions anywhere within the United Kingdom in order to acquire trading stock which he will transport back to the firm's premises in his van. On occasions he may also help Cee to restore the articles prior to sale to the public.

At the meeting, the three prospective partners intend to decide upon the financial arrangements for sharing out the profits (or losses) made by the firm, and have approached you for advice.

You are required to prepare a set of explanatory notes, under suitable headings, of the considerations which the prospective partners should take into account in arriving at their decisions at the next meeting.

(*Association of Chartered Certified Accountants*)

→

39.9 Frame and French are in partnership sharing profits and losses in the ratio $^3/_5$: $^2/_5$, respectively. The following is their trial balance as at 30 September 2009.

	Dr £	Cr £
Buildings (cost £210,000)	160,000	
Fixtures at cost	8,200	
Provision for depreciation: Fixtures		4,200
Debtors	61,400	
Creditors		26,590
Cash at bank	6,130	
Stock at 30 September 2008	62,740	
Sales		363,111
Purchases	210,000	
Carriage outwards	3,410	
Discounts allowed	620	
Loan interest: P Prince	3,900	
Office expenses	4,760	
Salaries and wages	57,809	
Bad debts	1,632	
Provision for doubtful debts		1,400
Loan from P Prince		65,000
Capitals: Frame		100,000
French		75,000
Current accounts: Frame		4,100
French		1,200
Drawings: Frame	31,800	
French	28,200	
	640,601	640,601

Required:
Prepare a trading and profit and loss appropriation account for the year ending 30 September 2009, and a balance sheet as at that date.

(a) Stock at 30 September 2009: £74,210.
(b) Expenses to be accrued: Office Expenses £215; Wages £720.
(c) Depreciate fixtures 15 per cent on reducing balance basis, buildings £5,000.
(d) Reduce provision for doubtful debts to £1,250.
(e) Partnership salary: £30,000 to Frame. Not yet entered.
(f) Interest on drawings: Frame £900; French £600.
(g) Interest on capital account balances at 5 per cent.

39.10A Scot and Joplin are in partnership. They share profits in the ratio: Scot 70 per cent; Joplin 30 per cent. The following trial balance was extracted as at 31 December 2007.

	Dr £	Cr £
Office equipment at cost	9,200	
Motor vehicles at cost	21,400	
Provision for depreciation at 31.12.2006:		
Motor vehicles		12,800
Office equipment		3,600
Stock at 31 December 2006	38,410	
Debtors and creditors	41,940	32,216
Cash at bank	2,118	
Cash in hand	317	
Sales		180,400
Purchases	136,680	
Salaries	27,400	
Office expenses	2,130	
Discounts allowed	312	
Current accounts at 31.12.2006		
Scot		7,382
Joplin		7,009
Capital accounts: Scot		50,000
Joplin		20,000
Drawings: Scot	17,500	
Joplin	16,000	
	313,407	313,407

Required:

Draw up a set of financial statements for the year ended 31 December 2007 for the partnership. The following notes are applicable at 31 December 2007.

(a) Stock at 31 December 2007: £41,312.
(b) Office expenses owing £240.
(c) Provide for depreciation: motor 25 per cent of cost, office equipment 20 per cent of cost.
(d) Charge interest on capitals at 5 per cent.
(e) Charge interest on drawings: Scot £300; Joplin £200.

→

39.11 Sage and Onion are trading in partnership, sharing profits and losses and equally. Interest at 5% per annum is allowed or charged on both the capital account and the current account balances at the beginning of the year. Interest is charged on drawings at 5% per annum. The partners are entitled to annual salaries of: Sage £12,000; Onion £8,000.

Required:

From the information given below, prepare the partnership profit and loss account for the year ending 31 December 2001, and the balance sheet as at that date.

Sage and Onion
Trial Balance as at 31 December 2001

	Dr £	Cr £
Capital accounts: Sage		100,000
Onion		50,000
Current accounts: Sage		2,000
Onion	600	
Cash drawings for the year: Sage	15,000	
Onion	10,000	
Freehold premises at cost	50,000	
Stock at 1 January 2001	75,000	
Fixtures and fittings at cost	15,000	
Purchases and purchase returns	380,000	12,000
Bank	31,600	
Sales and sales returns	6,000	508,000
Trade debtors and trade creditors	52,400	33,300
Carriage inwards	21,500	
Carriage outwards	3,000	
Staff salaries	42,000	
VAT		8,700
Office expenses	7,500	
Provision for doubtful debts		2,000
Advertising	5,000	
Discounts received		1,000
Discounts allowed	1,200	
Bad debts	1,400	
Rent and business rates	2,800	
Accumulated provision for depreciation of fixtures and fittings		3,000
	720,000	720,000

At 31 December 2001:

(a) Stock on hand was valued at £68,000.

(b) Purchase invoices amounting to £3,000 for goods included in the stock valuation at (a) above had not been recorded.

(c) Staff salaries owing £900.

(d) Business rates paid in advance £200.

(e) Provision for doubtful debts to be increased to £2,400.

(f) Goods withdrawn by partners for private use had not been recorded and were valued at: Sage £500, Onion £630. No interest is to be charged on these amounts.

(g) Provision is to be made for depreciation of fixtures and fittings at 10% on cost.

(h) Interest on drawings for the year is to be charged: Sage £360, Onion £280.

39.12A Bush, Home and Wilson share profits and losses in the ratios 4:1:3 respectively. Their trial balance as at 30 April 2004 was as follows:

	Dr £	Cr £
Sales		334,618
Returns inwards	10,200	
Purchases	196,239	
Carriage inwards	3,100	
Stock 30 April 2003	68,127	
Discounts allowed	190	
Salaries and wages	54,117	
Bad debts	1,620	
Provision for doubtful debts 30 April 2003		950
General expenses	1,017	
Business rates	2,900	
Postage	845	
Computers at cost	8,400	
Office equipment at cost	5,700	
Provisions for depreciation at 30 April 2003:		
Computers		3,600
Office equipment		2,900
Creditors		36,480
Debtors	51,320	
Cash at bank	5,214	
Drawings: Bush	39,000	
Home	16,000	
Wilson	28,000	
Current accounts: Bush		5,940
Home	2,117	
Wilson		9,618
Capital accounts: Bush		60,000
Home		10,000
Wilson		30,000
	494,106	494,106

Draw up a set of financial statements for the year ending 30 April 2004. The following notes are relevant at 30 April 2004:

(*i*) Stock 30 April 2004, £74,223.
(*ii*) Business rates in advance £200; Stock of postage stamps £68.
(*iii*) Increase provision for doubtful debts to £1,400.
(*iv*) Salaries: Home £18,000; Wilson £14,000. Not yet recorded.
(*v*) Interest on Drawings: Bush £300; Home £200; Wilson £240.
(*vi*) Interest on Capitals at 8 per cent.
(*vii*) Depreciate Computers £2,800; Office equipment £1,100.

→

39.13 Reid and Benson are in partnership as lecturers and tutors. Interest is to be allowed on capital and on the opening balances on the current accounts at a rate of 5% per annum and Reid is to be given a salary of £18,000 per annum. Interest is to be charged on drawings at 5% per annum (see notes below) and the profits and losses are to be shared Reid 60% and Benson 40%.

The following trial balance was extracted from the books of the partnership at 31 December 2003.

	£	£
Capital account – Benson		50,000
Capital account – Reid		75,000
Current account – Benson		4,000
Current account – Reid		5,000
Drawings – Reid	17,000	
Drawings – Benson	20,000	
Sales – goods and services		541,750
Purchases of textbooks for distribution	291,830	
Returns inwards and outwards	800	330
Carriage inwards	3,150	
Staff salaries	141,150	
Rent	2,500	
Insurance – general	1,000	
Insurance – public indemnity	1,500	
Compensation paid due to Benson error	10,000	
General expenses	9,500	
Bad debts written off	1,150	
Fixtures and fittings – cost	74,000	
Fixtures and fittings – depreciation		12,000
Debtors and creditors	137,500	23,400
Cash	400	
Total	711,480	711,480

● A provision for doubtful debts is to be created of £1,500.
● Insurances paid in advance at 31 December 2002 were General £50; Professional Indemnity £100.
● Fixtures and fittings are to be depreciated at 10% on cost.
● Interest on drawings are: Benson £550, Reid £1,050.
● Stock of books at 31 December 2003 was £1,500.

Required:
Prepare a profit and loss account together with an appropriation account at 31 December 2003 together with a balance sheet as at that date.

Goodwill for sole traders and partnerships

Learning objectives

After you have studied this chapter, you should be able to:

- describe a range of methods for arriving at the selling price of a business
- explain and calculate super profits
- explain why goodwill exists
- explain why goodwill has a monetary value
- distinguish between purchased and non-purchased goodwill
- calculate purchased goodwill
- calculate the adjustments needed when there is some form of change in a partnership

Introduction

In this chapter, you'll learn about purchased goodwill and its treatment in the books and financial statements of sole traders and partnerships. You will also learn how to make adjustments to the partnership capital accounts when circumstances change.

40.1 Nature of goodwill

Suppose you have been running a business for some years and you wanted to sell it. How much would you ask as the total sale price of the business? You decide to list how much you could get for each asset if sold separately. This list might be as follows:

	£
Buildings	225,000
Machinery	75,000
Debtors	60,000
Stock	40,000
	400,000

Note: if there are any liabilities, you would deduct them from the total value of the assets to arrive at the value of the net assets, which is the net amount you would have left if you sold all the assets and paid off all the creditors.

So, if you sold off everything separately, you would expect to receive £400,000.

Exhibit 42.1

The last balance sheet of X and Y, who share profits X two-thirds : Y one-third is shown below. On this date they are to dissolve the partnership.

Balance Sheet at 31 December 2009

	£	£
Fixed assets		
Buildings		100,000
Motor vehicle		12,000
		112,000
Current assets		
Stock	6,000	
Debtors	8,000	
Bank	2,000	
	16,000	
Current liabilities		
Creditors	(5,000)	
		11,000
		123,000
Capitals: X		82,000
Y		41,000
		123,000

The buildings were sold for £105,000 and the stock for £4,600. £6,800 was collected from debtors. The motor vehicle was taken over by X at an agreed value of £9,400, but he did not pay any cash for it. £5,000 was paid to creditors. The £400 cost of the dissolution was paid.

The accounting entries needed are:

(A) Transfer book values of all assets to the realisation account:
     Debit realisation account
       Credit asset accounts

(B) Amounts received from disposal of assets:
     Debit bank
       Credit realisation account

(C) Values of assets taken over by partner without payment:
     Debit partner's capital account
       Credit realisation account

(D) Creditors paid:
     Debit creditors' accounts
       Credit bank

(E) Costs of dissolution:
     Debit realisation account
       Credit bank

(F) Profit or loss on realisation to be shared between partners in profit and loss sharing ratios:
     If a profit: Debit realisation account
                 Credit partners' capital accounts
     If a loss: Debit partners' capital accounts
                 Credit realisation account

(G) Pay to the partners their final balances on their capital accounts:
    Debit capital accounts
      Credit bank

The entries are now shown. The letters (A) to (G) as above are shown against each entry:

Buildings

		£				£
Balance b/d		100,000	Realisation	(A)		100,000

Motor Vehicle

		£				£
Balance b/d		12,000	Realisation	(A)		12,000

Stock

		£				£
Balance b/d		6,000	Realisation	(A)		6,000

Debtors

		£				£
Balance b/d		8,000	Realisation	(A)		8,000

Realisation

		£				£
Assets to be realised:			Bank: Assets sold			
Buildings	(A)	100,000	Buildings	(B)		105,000
Motor vehicle	(A)	12,000	Stock	(B)		4,600
Stock	(A)	6,000	Debtors	(B)		6,800
Debtors	(A)	8,000	Taken over by partner A:			
Bank:			Motor vehicle	(C)		9,400
Dissolution costs	(E)	400	Loss on realisation		£	
			X $^2/_3$	(F)	400	
			Y $^1/_3$	(F)	200	
						600
		126,400				126,400

Creditors

		£			£
Bank	(D)	5,000	Balance b/d		5,000

X: Capital

		£		£
Realisation: Motor	(C)	9,400	Balance b/d	82,000
Realisation: Share of loss	(F)	400		
Bank: to close	(G)	72,200		
		82,000		82,000

The debtors realised £8,200, the buildings £66,000 and the tools and fixtures £1,800. The expenses of dissolution were £400 and discounts totalling £300 were received from creditors.

Required:
Prepare the accounts necessary to show the results of the realisation and of the disposal of the cash.

42.2 X, Y and Z have been in partnership for several years, sharing profits and losses in the ratio 3 : 2 : 1. Their last balance sheet which was prepared on 31 October 2009 is as follows:

Balance Sheet of X, Y and Z as at 31 October 2009

	£	£	£
Fixed assets			
At cost			20,000
Less Depreciation			(6,000)
			14,000
Current assets			
Stock		5,000	
Debtors		21,000	
		26,000	
Current liabilities			
Bank	13,000		
Creditors	17,000		
		(30,000)	
			(4,000)
			10,000
Capital			
X			4,000
Y			4,000
Z			2,000
			10,000

Despite making good profits during recent years they had become increasingly dependent on one credit customer, Smithson, and in order to retain his custom they had gradually increased his credit limit until he owed the partnership £18,000. It has now been discovered that Smithson is insolvent and that he is unlikely to repay any of the money owed by him to the partnership. Reluctantly X, Y and Z have agreed to dissolve the partnership on the following terms:

(*i*) The stock is to be sold to Nelson Ltd for £4,000.
(*ii*) The fixed assets will be sold for £8,000 except for certain items with a book value of £5,000 which will be taken over by X at an agreed valuation of £7,000.
(*iii*) The debtors, except for Smithson, are expected to pay their accounts in full.
(*iv*) The costs of dissolution will be £800 and discounts received from creditors will be £500. Z is unable to meet his liability to the partnership out of his personal funds.

Required:
(*a*) the realisation account;
(*b*) the capital accounts to the partners recording the dissolution of the partnership.

(*Associated Examining Board*)

42.3A The following trial balance has been extracted from the books of Gain and Main as at 31 March 2008; Gain and Main are in partnership sharing profits and losses in the ratio 3 to 2:

	£	£
Capital accounts:		
Gain		10,000
Main		5,000
Cash at bank	1,550	
Creditors		500
Current accounts:		
Gain		1,000
Main	2,000	
Debtors	2,000	
Depreciation: Fixtures and fittings		1,000
Motor vehicles		1,300
Fixtures and fittings	2,000	
Land and buildings	30,000	
Motor vehicles	4,500	
Net profit (for the year to 31 March 2008)		26,250
Stock, at cost	3,000	
	£45,050	£45,050

In appropriating the net profit for the year, it has been agreed that Main should be entitled to a salary of £9,750. Each partner is also entitled to interest on his opening capital account balance at the rate of 10 per cent per annum.

Gain and Main have decided to convert the partnership into a limited company, Plain Limited, as from 1 April 2008. The company is to take over all the assets and liabilities of the partnership, except that Gain is to retain for his personal use one of the motor vehicles at an agreed transfer price of £1,000.

The purchase consideration will consist of 40,000 ordinary shares of £1 each in Plain Limited, to be divided between the partners in profit-sharing ratio. Any balance on the partners' current accounts is to be settled in cash.

You are required to:
Prepare the main ledger accounts of the partnership in order to close off the books as at 31 March 2008.

(*Association of Accounting Technicians*)

42.4A A, B and C are partners sharing profits and losses in the ratio 2 : 2 : 1. The balance sheet of the partnership as at 30 September 2007 was as follows:

	£	£
Freehold premises		18,000
Equipment and machinery		12,000
Cars		3,000
		33,000
Inventory^{Authors' Note}	11,000	
Debtors	14,000	
Bank	9,000	
	34,000	
Creditors	(10,000)	
		24,000
		57,000
Loan account – A		(7,000)
		50,000
Capital accounts		
A		22,000
B		18,000
C		10,000
		50,000

→ ***Authors' Note*: Inventory is another word for stock.**

The partners agreed to dispose of the business to CNO Limited with effect from 1 October 2007 under the following conditions and terms:

(*i*)   CNO Limited will acquire the goodwill, all fixed assets and the inventory for the purchase consideration of £58,000. This consideration will include a payment of £10,000 in cash and the issue of 12,000 10 per cent preference shares of £1 each at par, and the balance by the issue of £1 ordinary shares at £1.25 per share.

(*ii*) The partnership business will settle amounts owing to creditors.

(*iii*) CNO Limited will collect the debts on behalf of the vendors.

Purchase consideration payments and allotments of shares were made on 1 October 2007.

The partnership creditors were paid off by 31 October 2007 after the taking of cash discounts of £190.

CNO Limited collected and paid over all partnership debts by 30 November 2007 except for bad debts amounting to £800. Discounts allowed to debtors amounted to £400.

Required:

(*a*) Journal entries (including those relating to cash) necessary to close the books of the partnership, and

(*b*) Set out the basis on which the shares in CNO Limited are allotted to partners. Ignore interest.

(*Institute of Chartered Secretaries and Administrators*)

42.5   Amis, Lodge and Pym were in partnership sharing profits and losses in the ratio 5 : 3 : 2. The following trial balance has been extracted from their books of account as at 31 March 2008:

	£	£
Bank interest received		750
Capital accounts (as at 1 April 2007):		
Amis		80,000
Lodge		15,000
Pym		5,000
Carriage inwards	4,000	
Carriage outwards	12,000	
Cash at bank	4,900	
Current accounts:		
Amis	1,000	
Lodge	500	
Pym	400	
Discounts allowed	10,000	
Discounts received		4,530
Drawings:		
Amis	25,000	
Lodge	22,000	
Pym	15,000	
Motor vehicles:		
at cost	80,000	
accumulated depreciation (at 1 April 2007)		20,000
Office expenses	30,400	
Plant and machinery:		
at cost	100,000	
accumulated depreciation (at 1 April 2007)		36,600
Provision for doubtful debts (at 1 April 2007)		420
Purchases	225,000	
Rent, rates, heat and light	8,800	
Sales		404,500
Stock (at 1 April 2007)	30,000	
Trade creditors		16,500
Trade debtors	14,300	
	£583,300	£583,300

Additional information:
(a) Stock at 31 March 2008 was valued at £35,000.
(b) Depreciation on the fixed assets is to be charged as follows:
   Motor vehicles – 25 per cent on the reduced balance.
   Plant and machinery – 20 per cent on the original cost.
   There were no purchases or sales of fixed assets during the year to 31 March 2008.
(c) The provision for doubtful debts is to be maintained at a level equivalent to 5 per cent of the total trade debtors as at 31 March 2008.
(d) An office expense of £405 was owing at 31 March 2008, and some rent amounting to £1,500 had been paid in advance as at that date. These items had not been included in the list of balances shown in the trial balance.
(e) Interest on drawings and on the debit balance on each partner's current account is to be charged as follows:

	£
Amis	1,000
Lodge	900
Pym	720

(f) According to the partnership agreement, Pym is allowed a salary of £13,000 per annum. This amount was owing to Pym for the year to 31 March 2008, and needs to be accounted for.
(g) The partnership agreement also allows each partner interest on his capital account at a rate of 10 per cent per annum. There were no movements on the respective partners' capital accounts during the year to 31 March 2008, and the interest had not been credited to them as at that date.

Note: The information given above is sufficient to answer part (a) (i) and (ii) of the question, and notes (h) and (i) below are pertinent to requirements (b) (i), (ii) and (iii) of the question.

(h) On 1 April 2008, Fowles Limited agreed to purchase the business on the following terms:
   (i) Amis to purchase one of the partnership's motor vehicles at an agreed value of £5,000, the remaining vehicles being taken over by the company at an agreed value of £30,000;
   (ii) the company agreed to purchase the plant and machinery at a value of £35,000 and the stock at a value of £38,500;
   (iii) the partners to settle the trade creditors: the total amount agreed with the creditors being £16,000;
   (iv) the trade debtors were not to be taken over by the company, the partners receiving cheques on 1 April 2008 amounting to £12,985 in total from the trade debtors in settlement of the outstanding debts;
   (v) the partners paid the outstanding office expense on 1 April 2008, and the landlord returned the rent paid in advance by cheque on the same day;
   (vi) as consideration for the sale of the partnership, the partners were to be paid £63,500 in cash by Fowles Limited, and to receive £75,000 in £1 ordinary shares in the company, the shares to be apportioned equally amongst the partners.
(i) Assume that all the matters relating to the dissolution of the partnership and its sales to the company took place on 1 April 2008.

Required:
(a) Prepare:
   (i) Amis, Lodge and Pym's trading, profit and loss and profit and loss appropriation account for the year ending 31 March 2008;
   (ii) Amis, Lodge and Pym's current accounts (in columnar format) for the year to 31 March 2008 (the final balance on each account is to be then transferred to each partner's respective capital account);
   and
(b) Compile the following accounts:
   (i) the partnership realisation account for the period up to and including 1 April 2008;
   (ii) the partners' bank account for the period up to and including 1 April 2008; and
   (iii) the partners' capital accounts (in columnar format) for the period up to and including 1 April 2008.

Note: Detailed workings should be submitted with your answer.

(Association of Accounting Technicians)

→

42.6A Proudie, Slope and Thorne were in partnership sharing profits and losses in the ratio 3 : 1 : 1. The draft balance sheet of the partnership as at 31 May 2009 is shown below:

	£000 Cost	£000 Depreciation	£000 Net book value
Fixed assets			
Land and buildings	200	40	160
Furniture	30	18	12
Motor vehicles	60	40	20
	290	98	192
Current assets			
Stocks		23	
Trade debtors	42		
Less Provision for doubtful debts	(1)		
		41	
Prepayments		2	
Cash		10	
		76	
Less Current liabilities			
Trade creditors	15		
Accruals	3		
		(18)	
			58
			250
Loan			
Proudie			(8)
			242
Financed by:			
Capital accounts			
Proudie		100	
Slope		60	
Thorne		40	
			200
Current accounts			
Proudie		24	
Slope		10	
Thorne		8	
			42
			242

Additional information:

1 Proudie decided to retire on 31 May 2009. However, Slope and Thorne agreed to form a new partnership out of the old one, as from 1 June 2009. They agreed to share profits and losses in the same ratio as in the old partnership.

2 Upon the dissolution of the old partnership, it was agreed that the following adjustments were to be made to the partnership balance sheet as at 31 May 2009.
 (a) Land and buildings were to be revalued at £200,000.
 (b) Furniture was to be revalued at £5,000.
 (c) Proudie agreed to take over one of the motor vehicles at a value of £4,000, the remaining motor vehicles being revalued at £10,000.
 (d) Stocks were to be written down by £5,000.
 (e) A bad debt of £2,000 was to be written off, and the provision for doubtful debts was then to be adjusted so that it represented 5 per cent of the then outstanding trade debtors as at 31 May 2009.
 (f) A further accrual of £3,000 for office expenses was to be made.
 (g) Professional charges relating to the dissolution were estimated to be £1,000.

3 It has not been the practice of the partners to carry goodwill in the books of the partnership, but on the retirement of a partner it had been agreed that goodwill should be taken into account. Goodwill was to be valued at an amount equal to the average annual profits of the three years expiring on the retirement. For the purpose of including goodwill in the dissolution arrangement when Proudie retired, the net profits for the last three years were as follows:

	£000
Year to 31 May 2007	130
Year to 31 May 2008	150
Year to 31 May 2009	181

The net profit for the year to 31 May 2009 had been calculated before any of the items listed in 2 above were taken into account. The net profit was only to be adjusted for items listed in 2(*d*), 2(*e*) and 2(*f*) above.

4 Goodwill is not to be carried in the books of the new partnership.

5 It was agreed that Proudie's old loan of £8,000 should be repaid to him on 31 May 2009, but any further amount owing to him as a result of the dissolution of the partnership should be left as a long-term loan in the books of the new partnership.

6 The partners' current accounts were to be closed and any balances on them as at 31 May 2009 were to be transferred to their respective capital accounts.

Required:

(*a*) Prepare the revaluation account as at 31 May 2009.

(*b*) Prepare the partners' capital accounts as at the date of dissolution of the partnership, and bring down any balances on them in the books of the new partnership.

(*c*) Prepare Slope and Thorne's balance sheet as at 1 June 2009.

(*Association of Accounting Technicians*)

42.7 Lock, Stock and Barrel have been in partnership as builders and contractors for many years. Owing to adverse trading conditions it has been decided to dissolve the partnership. Profits are shared Lock 40 per cent, Stock 30 per cent, Barrel 30 per cent. The partnership deed also provides that in the event of a partner being unable to pay off a debit balance the remaining partners will treat this as a trading loss.

The latest partnership balance sheet was as follows:

	Cost	Depreciation	
	£	£	£
Fixed tangible assets			
Freehold yard and buildings	20,000	3,000	17,000
Plant and equipment	150,000	82,000	68,000
Motor vehicles	36,000	23,000	13,000
	206,000	108,000	98,000
Current assets			
Stock of land for building		75,000	
Houses in course of construction		115,000	
Stocks of materials		23,000	
Debtors for completed houses		62,000	
		275,000	
Current liabilities			
Trade creditors	77,000		
Deposits and progress payments	82,000		
Bank overdraft	132,500		
		(291,500)	
Excess of current liabilities over current assets			(16,500)
			81,500
Partners' capital accounts			
Lock		52,000	
Stock		26,000	
Barrel		3,500	
			81,500

→ During the six months from the date of the latest balance sheet to the date of dissolution the following transactions have taken place:

	£
Purchase of materials	20,250
Materials used for houses in course of construction	35,750
Payments for wages and subcontractors on building sites	78,000
Payments to trade creditors for materials	45,000
Sales of completed houses	280,000
Cash received from customers for houses	225,000
Payments for various general expenses	12,500
Payments for administration salaries	17,250
Cash withdrawn by partners: Lock	6,000
Stock	5,000
Barrel	4,000

All deposits and progress payments have been used for completed transactions.

Depreciation is normally provided each year at £600 on the freehold yard and buildings, at 10 per cent on cost for plant and equipment and 25 per cent on cost for motor vehicles.

The partners decide to dissolve the partnership on 1 February 2007 and wish to take out the maximum cash possible, as items are sold. At this date there are no houses in course of construction and one-third of the stock of land had been used for building.

It is agreed that Barrel is insolvent and cannot bring any money into the partnership. The partners take over the partnership cars at an agreed figure of £2,000 each. All other vehicles were sold on 28 February 2007 for £6,200. At the same date stocks of materials were sold for £7,000, and the stock of the land realised £72,500. On 30 April 2007 the debtors paid in full and all the plant and equipment was sold for £50,000.

The freehold yard and buildings realised £100,000 on 1 June 2007, on which date all remaining cash was distributed.

There are no costs of realisation or distribution.

Required:

(a) Prepare a partnership profit and loss account for the six months ending 1 February 2007, partners' capital accounts for the same period and a balance sheet at 1 February 2007.

(b) Show calculations of the amounts distributable to the partners.

(c) Prepare a realisation account and the capital accounts of the partners to the final distribution.

(*Association of Chartered Certified Accountants*)

42.8A Grant and Herd are in partnership sharing profits and losses in the ratio 3 to 2. The following information relates to the year to 31 December 2008:

	Dr £000	Cr £000
Capital accounts (at 1 January 2008):		
Grant		300
Herd		100
Cash at bank	5	
Creditors and accruals		25
Debtors and prepayments	18	
Drawings during the year: Grant (all at 30 June 2008)	40	
Herd (all at 31 March 2008)	40	
Fixed assets: at cost	300	
accumulated depreciation (at 31 December 2008)		100
Herd – salary	10	
Net profit (for the year to 31 December 2008)		60
Stocks at cost (at 31 December 2008)	90	
Trade creditors		141
Trade debtors	223	
	726	726

Additional information:

1 The partnership agreement allows for Herd to be paid a salary of £20,000 per annum, and for interest of 5 per cent per annum to be paid on the partners' capital account balances as at 1 January in each year. Interest at a rate of 10 per cent per annum is charged on the partners' drawings.
2 The partners decide to dissolve the partnership as at 31 December 2008, and the business was then sold to Valley Limited. The purchase consideration was to be 400,000 £1 ordinary shares in Valley at a premium of 25p per share. The shares were to be issued to the partners on 31 December 2008, and they were to be shared between them in their profit-sharing ratio.

   The sale agreement allowed Grant to take over one of the business cars at an agreed valuation of £10,000. Apart from the car and the cash and bank balances, the company took over all the other partnership assets and liabilities at their book values as at 31 December 2008.
3 Matters relating to the appropriation of profit for the year to 31 December 2008 are to be dealt with in the partners' capital accounts, including any arrears of salary owing to Herd.

Required:
(a) Write up the following accounts for the year to 31 December 2008:
   (*i*)   the profit and loss appropriation account;
   (*ii*) Grant and Herd's capital accounts; and
   (*iii*) the realisation account.
(b) Prepare Valley's balance sheet as at 1 January 2009 immediately after the acquisition of the partnership and assuming that no further transactions have taken place in the meantime.

(Association of Accounting Technicians)

You can find a range of additional self-test questions, as well as material to help you with your studies, on the website that accompanies this book at **www.pearsoned.co.uk/wood**

An introduction to the financial statements of limited liability companies

Learning objectives

After you have studied this chapter, you should be able to:

- explain how limited companies differ from sole traders and partnerships
- explain the differences between different classes of shares
- calculate how distributable profits available for dividends are divided between the different classes of shares
- explain the differences between shares and debentures
- prepare the trading and profit and loss accounts for a company for internal purposes
- prepare the balance sheet for a company for both internal and external purposes
- explain what an audit report is
- explain how to present goodwill in company financial statements

Introduction

In this chapter, you'll learn about the different types of companies that can exist and about the different types of long-term funds they can raise in order to finance their activities. You'll learn how to prepare the financial statements for companies and about the differences between the treatment of goodwill in company accounts and its treatment in the accounts of sole traders and partnerships.

43.1 Need for limited companies

Limited liability companies, more commonly referred to as **limited companies**, came into existence originally because of the growth in the size of businesses, and the need to have a lot of people investing in the business who would not be able to take part in its management.

Activity 43.1 Why do you think a partnership was not an appropriate form of business in this case?

The UK law governing companies, their formation and the duties relating to their members (i.e. shareholders), directors, auditors, and officials is contained in the Companies Act 2006 and in the Companies Acts of 1985, 1989 and 2004. Much of the requirements concerning financial statements are in the 1985 Act, as amended by the 1989 and 2004 Acts.

43.2 Limited liability

The capital of a limited company is divided into **shares**. Shares can be of any nominal value – 10p, 25p, £1, £5, £10, or any other amount per share. To become a member of a limited company, or a shareholder, a person must buy one or more of the shares.

If shareholders have paid in full for their shares, their liability is limited to what they have already paid for those shares. If a company loses all its assets, all those shareholders can lose is their shares. They cannot be forced to pay anything more in respect of the company's losses.

Shareholders who have only partly paid for their shares can be forced to pay the balance owing on the shares, but nothing else.

Shareholders are therefore said to have 'limited liability' and this is why companies are known as 'limited liability' or, more usually, simply 'limited' companies. By addressing the need for investors to have limited risk of financial loss, the existence of limited liability encourages individuals to invest in these companies and makes it possible to have both a large number of owners and a large amount of capital invested in the company.

There are a few companies which have unlimited liability, but these are outside the scope of this book.

43.3 Public and private companies

In the UK, there are two main classes of company, the **public company** and the **private company**. Private companies far outnumber public companies. In the Companies Acts, a public company is defined as one which fulfils the following conditions:

● Its memorandum (a document that describes the company) states that it is a public company, and that it has registered as such.
● It has an authorised share capital of at least £50,000.
● Minimum membership is one. There is no maximum.
● Its name must end with the words 'public limited company' or the abbreviation 'PLC'. It can have the Welsh equivalent if registered in Wales ('CCC').

PLCs can, but don't have to, offer their shares for sale on the Stock Exchange. It is through the Stock Exchange that a large ownership base can be established.

A private company is usually, but not always, a smaller business, and may be formed by one or more persons. It is defined by the Act as a company which is not a public company. The main differences between a private company and a public company are that a private company

● can have an authorised capital of less than £50,000 and
● *cannot* offer its shares for subscription to the public at large, whereas public companies can.

This means that if you were to walk into a bank, or similar public place, and see a prospectus offering anyone the chance to take up shares in a company, then that company would be a public company, i.e. a PLC.

The shares that are dealt in on the Stock Exchange are all of public limited companies. This does not mean that shares of all public companies are traded on the Stock Exchange. For various reasons, some public companies have either chosen not to, or have not been allowed to have their shares traded there. The ones whose shares are traded are known as 'quoted companies' meaning that their shares have prices quoted on the Stock Exchange. They have to comply with

Stock Exchange requirements in addition to those laid down by the Companies Acts and accounting standards.

Activity 43.2

Apart from not having to worry about complying with the Stock Exchange requirements, what other reasons can you think of that would explain why some PLCs do not wish to offer their shares on the Stock Market?

43.4 Directors of the company

The day-to-day business of a company is *not* carried out by the shareholders. The possession of a share normally confers voting rights on the holder, who is then able to attend general meetings of the company. At one of these general meetings, normally the **Annual General Meeting** or AGM, the shareholders vote for **directors**, these being the people who will be entrusted with the running of the business. At each AGM, the directors report on their stewardship, and this report is accompanied by a set of financial statements and other documents – the 'annual report'.

43.5 Legal status of a limited company

A limited company is said to possess a 'separate legal identity' from that of its shareholders. Put simply, this means that a company is not seen as being exactly the same as its shareholders. For instance, a company can sue one or more of its shareholders, and similarly, a shareholder can sue the company. This would not be the case if the company and its shareholders were exactly the same thing, as one cannot sue oneself. This concept is often referred to as the **veil of incorporation**.

Note: This is an extremely important concept. The most frequently cited example of the strength of the veil of incorporation is a case that went to the House of Lords in 1897. The case is known as *Saloman* v *Saloman & Co Ltd*. It involved a company formed by a Mr Saloman. The company was run by Mr Saloman in the same way as when he was operating as a sole trader. He received all the profits and made all the decisions. However, the *veil of incorporation* meant that the company was treated as completely separate from him. When the business failed owing a large amount of money, Mr Saloman did not have to pay for the business debts personally. The debts were the responsibility of the company, not of Mr Saloman. This was held to be the case even though Mr Saloman had lent some money to the company in the form of secured debentures. This meant that any funds left in the company when it failed were first used to repay *those* debentures (because they were 'secured' on the assets of the company) and the rest of the creditors (who were not 'secured') received nothing.

43.6 Share capital

Shareholders of a limited company obtain their reward in the form of a share of the profits, known as a **dividend**. The directors decide on the amount of profits which are placed in reserves (i.e. retained). Of the remaining profits the directors then propose the payment of a certain amount of dividend. It is important to note that the shareholders cannot propose a higher dividend for themselves than that already proposed by the directors. They can, however, propose that a lesser dividend should be paid, although this is very rare indeed. If the directors propose that no dividend be paid, then the shareholders are powerless to alter the decision.

The decision by the directors as to the amount proposed as dividends is a very complex one and cannot be fully discussed here. Such points as government directives to reduce dividends, the effect of taxation, the availability of bank balances to pay the dividends, the possibility of takeover bids and so on will all be taken into account.

The dividend is usually expressed as a percentage. A dividend of 10 per cent in Business A on 500,000 ordinary shares of £1 each will amount to £50,000. A dividend of 6 per cent in Business B on 200,000 ordinary shares of £2 each will amount to £24,000. A shareholder having 100 shares in each business would receive £10 from Business A and £12 from Business B.

There are two main types of shares:

1 **Preference shares.** Holders of these shares get an agreed percentage rate of dividend before the ordinary shareholders receive anything.
2 **Ordinary shares.** Holders of these shares receive the remainder of the total profits available for dividends. There is no upper limit to the amounts of dividends they can receive.

For example, if a company had 50,000 5 per cent preference shares of £1 each and 200,000 ordinary shares of £1 each, then the dividends would be payable as in Exhibit 43.1:

Exhibit 43.1

Year	1	2	3	4	5
	£	£	£	£	£
Profits appropriated for dividends	6,500	10,500	13,500	28,500	17,500
Preference dividends (5%)	2,500	2,500	2,500	2,500	2,500
Ordinary dividends	(2%)4,000	(4%)8,000	(5½%)11,000	(13%)26,000	(7½%)15,000
	6,500	10,500	13,500	28,500	17,500

The two main types of preference shares are non-cumulative preference shares and cumulative preference shares:

1 **Non-cumulative preference shares.** These can receive a dividend up to an agreed percentage each year. If the amount paid is less than the maximum agreed amount, the shortfall is lost by the shareholder. The shortfall cannot be carried forward and paid in a future year.
2 **Cumulative preference shares.** These also have an agreed maximum percentage dividend. However, any shortfall of dividend paid in a year can be carried forward. These arrears of preference dividends will have to be paid before the ordinary shareholders receive anything.

 Activity 43.3 Why do you think an investor might purchase preference shares rather than ordinary shares in a company?

Exhibit 43.2

A company has 500,000 £1 ordinary shares and 100,000 5 per cent non-cumulative preference shares of £1 each. The profits available for dividends are: year 1 £145,000, year 2 £2,000, year 3 £44,000, year 4 £118,000, year 5 £264,000. Assuming all profits are paid out in dividends, the amounts paid to each class of shareholder are:

Year	1	2	3	4	5
	£	£	£	£	£
Profits appropriated for dividends	145,000	2,000	44,000	118,000	264,000
Preference dividend (non-cumulative) (limited in year 2)	5,000	2,000	5,000	5,000	5,000
Dividends on ordinary shares	140,000	–	39,000	113,000	259,000
	145,000	2,000	44,000	118,000	264,000

Exhibit 43.3

Assume that the preference shares in Exhibit 43.2 had been cumulative. The dividends would have been:

Year	1	2	3	4	5
	£	£	£	£	£
Profits appropriated for dividends	145,000	2,000	44,000	118,000	264,000
Preference dividend	5,000	2,000	8,000*	5,000	5,000
Dividends on ordinary shares	140,000	–	36,000	113,000	259,000
	145,000	2,000	44,000	118,000	264,000

*including arrears.

Note: **This exhibit shows how much of the profit made in each year was paid out as dividend. The dividends are shown in the financial statements in the year they are paid, which may be a year later than the year in which the profit used to pay them was earned – see Section 43.12, especially Exhibit 43.5.**

43.7 Share capital: different meanings

The term 'share capital' can have any of the following meanings:

1 **Authorised share capital.** Sometimes known as 'registered capital' or 'nominal capital'. This is the total of the share capital which the company is allowed to issue to shareholders.
2 **Issued share capital.** This is the total of the share capital actually issued to shareholders.

Note: **Some students mix up these two terms and throw away marks in examinations as a result. In order to remember which is which, you only need to think about what the words 'authorised' and 'issued' mean.**

If all of the authorised share capital has been issued, then 1 and 2 above would be the same amount.

3 **Called-up capital.** Where only part of the amount payable on each issued share has been asked for, the total amount asked for on all the issued shares is known as the called-up capital.
4 **Uncalled capital.** This is the total amount which is to be received in future relating to issued share capital, but which has not yet been asked for.
5 **Calls in arrears.** The total amount for which payment has been asked for (i.e. 'called for'), but has not yet been paid by shareholders.
6 **Paid-up capital.** This is the total of the amount of share capital which has been paid for by shareholders.

Exhibit 43.4 illustrates these different meanings.

Exhibit 43.4

1 Better Enterprises Ltd was formed with the legal right to issue 1 million shares of £1 each.
2 The company has actually issued 750,000 shares.
3 None of the shares has yet been fully paid up. So far, the company has made calls of 80p (£0.80) per share.
4 All the calls have been paid by shareholders except for £200 owing from one shareholder.

(a)	Authorised or nominal share capital is:	1	£1 million.
(b)	Issued share capital is:	2	£750,000.
(c)	Called-up share capital is:	3	750,000 × £0.80 = £600,000.
(d)	Calls in arrears amounted to:	4	£200.
(e)	Paid-up share capital is:	(c)	£600,000 less (d) £200 = £599,800.

43.8 Bonus shares

The issue of **bonus shares** would appear to be outside the scope of syllabuses at this level. However, some examinations have included a minor part of a question concerned with bonus shares. All that is needed here is a very brief explanation only, leaving further explanations for a later stage in your studies.

Bonus shares are 'free' shares issued to shareholders without their having to pay anything for them. The reserves (e.g. retained profits shown in the balance sheet) are utilised for the purpose. Thus, if before the bonus issue there were £20,000 of issued share capital and £12,000 reserves, and a bonus issue of 1 for 4 was then made (i.e. 1 bonus share for every 4 shares already held) the bonus issue would amount to £5,000. The share capital then becomes £25,000 and the reserves become £7,000.

A proper and fuller explanation appears in *Business Accounting UK GAAP 2*. An issue of bonus shares is often referred to as a **scrip issue**.

43.9 Debentures

You will recall the note about the veil of incorporation where debentures had been issued to the owner of a company. The term **debenture** is used when a limited company receives money on loan, and a document called a debenture certificate is issued to the lender. Interest will be paid to the holder, the rate of interest being shown on the certificate. They are not always called debentures; they are often known as loan stock, loan notes, or as loan capital.

Interest has to be paid on debentures whether profits are made or not. They are, therefore, different from shares, where dividends depend on profits being made. A debenture may be either:

● Redeemable, i.e. repayable at or by a particular date, or
● Irredeemable, normally repayable only when the company is officially terminated by its going into liquidation. (Also sometimes referred to as 'perpetual' debentures.)

If a date is shown on a debenture, e.g. 2005/2012, it means that the company can redeem it in any of the years covered by the date(s) shown, in this case 2005 to 2012 inclusive.

People lending money to companies in the form of debentures will be interested in how safe their investment will be. Some debentures are assigned the legal right that on certain happenings the debenture holders will be able to take control of specific assets, or of the whole of the assets. They can then sell the assets and recoup the amount due under their debentures, or deal with the assets in ways specified in the deed under which the debentures were issued. Such debentures are said to be 'secured' against the assets – this was the case in the veil of incorporation note. (The term 'mortgage' debenture is sometimes used instead of 'secured'.) Other debentures have no prior right to control the assets under any circumstances. These are known as 'simple' or 'naked' debentures.

> **Activity 43.4**
> Why do you think a debenture might be 'secured' rather than being designated as a 'simple' debenture? (*Hint*: think about Mr Saloman.)

43.10 FRS 10: Goodwill and Intangible Assets (Companies)

This standard applies to companies; it does not apply to partnerships or sole traders.

1 Purchased goodwill and purchased intangible assets (e.g. patents, trade marks, etc.) should be capitalised as assets.

2 If goodwill has not been purchased then there should not be any entry of it in the company's books. (This is different from the situation applicable to partnerships.)

3 Internally developed intangible assets should be capitalised (i.e. entered in the company's books as an asset) only when they have a readily ascertainable market value.

4 The calculation of goodwill should be the excess of the value of the consideration given (the price paid) over the total of the fair values of the net assets acquired.

FRS 10 requires that goodwill and intangible assets are amortised (i.e. depreciated) over their useful economic life. However, when goodwill or intangible assets are regarded as having indefinite useful economic lives, they should not be amortised.

43.11 Trading and profit and loss accounts of companies

The trading and profit and loss accounts for both private and public companies are drawn up in exactly the same way.

The trading account section of a company's trading and profit and loss account for internal use is no different from that of a sole trader or a partnership. However, some differences may be found in the profit and loss account section. Two main expenses that would be found only in company accounts are directors' remuneration and debenture interest.

Directors' remuneration

As directors exist only in companies, this type of expense is found only in company accounts.

Directors are legally employees of the company, appointed by the shareholders. Their re-muneration is charged to the profit and loss account.

Debenture interest

The interest payable for the use of the money borrowed is an expense of the company, and is payable whether profits are made or not. This means that debenture interest is charged as an expense in the profit and loss account itself. Contrast this with dividends which are dependent on profits having been made.

43.12 The appropriation account

As with partnership profit and loss accounts, below the profit and loss account for a company is a section called the 'profit and loss appropriation account'. The appropriation account shows how the net profits are to be appropriated, i.e. how the profits are to be used. However, what it contains within it differs greatly from that of a partnership.

We may find any of the following in the appropriation account of a company:

Credit side

1 **Net profit for the year.** This is the net profit brought down from the main profit and loss account.

2 **Balance brought forward from last year.** As you will see, all the profits may not be appropri-ated during a period. This then will be the balance on the appropriation account, as brought forward from the previous year. It is usually called retained profits.

Debit side

3 **Transfers to reserves.** The directors may decide that some of the profits should not be included in the calculation of how much should be paid out as dividends. These profits are transferred to **reserve accounts**.

There may be a specific reason for some profits being transferred to reserves, such as a need to replace fixed assets. (In this case, an amount would be transferred to a fixed assets replacement reserve.)

When there is no specific reason for the transfer of an amount of profit, the transfer is to a general reserve.

4 **Amounts written off as goodwill.** Goodwill, in a company, may have amounts written off it from time to time. When this is done the amount written off should be shown in the appropriation account and not in the main profit and loss account.

5 **Preliminary expenses.** When a company is formed, there are many kinds of expenses concerned with its formation. These include, for example, legal expenses and various government taxes. These cannot be shown as an asset in the balance sheet, but can be charged to the appropriation account.

6 **Taxation payable on profits.** At this point in your studies you do not need to know very much about taxation. However, it does affect the preparation of accounts, and so we will tell you here as much as you need to know now. Sole traders and partnerships pay income tax based on their profits. Such income tax, when paid, is simply charged as drawings – it is not an expense of the business.

In the case of companies, the taxation levied upon them is called **corporation tax**. It is also based on the amount of profits made. In the later stages of your examinations you will learn how to calculate it. At this point you will be told how much it is, or be given a simple arithmetical way of calculating the amount.

Corporation tax is *not* an expense of the business, it is an appropriation of profits. This was established by two legal cases many years ago. However, for the sake of presentation and to make the financial statements more understandable to the reader, it is not shown with the other appropriations. Instead, as in Exhibit 43.5 it is shown as a deduction from net profit to show the net result, i.e. profit for the year after taxation.

7 **Dividends paid during the year.**

8 **Balance carried forward to next year.** After the dividends have been proposed there will probably be some profits that have not been appropriated. These retained profits will be carried forward to the following year.

Exhibit 43.5 contains an example showing the profit and loss appropriation account of a new business for its first three years of trading.

Exhibit 43.5

IDC Ltd has share capital of 400,000 ordinary shares of £1 each and 200,000 5 per cent preference shares of £1 each.

● The net profits for the first three years of business ended 31 December are: 2004, £109,670; 2005 £148,640; and 2006 £158,220.
● Transfers to reserves are made as follows: 2004 nil; 2005, general reserve, £10,000; and 2006, fixed assets replacement reserve, £22,500.
● Dividends proposed for each year on the preference shares at 5 per cent and on the ordinary shares at: 2004, 10 per cent; 2005, 12.5 per cent; 2006, 15 per cent. The dividends were all paid in the year after the one in which they were proposed.
● Corporation tax, based on the net profits of each year, is 2004 £41,000; 2005 £52,500; 2006 £63,000.

→

IDC Ltd
Profit and Loss Appropriation Accounts
(1) For the year ending 31 December 2004

	£	£
Profit for the year before taxation		109,670
Less Corporation tax		(41,000)
Profit for the year after taxation		68,670
Less Dividends paid:		–
Retained profits carried forward to next year		68,670

Note: *Dividends proposed and unpaid:

Preference dividend of 5%	10,000	
Ordinary dividend of 10%	40,000	
	50,000	

*The Note is not part of the appropriation account. It will be one of (probably) many notes to the financial statements.

(2) For the year ending 31 December 2005

	£	£	£
Profit for the year before taxation			148,640
Less Corporation tax			(52,500)
Profit for the year after taxation			96,140
Add Retained profits from last year			68,670
			164,810
Less Transfer to general reserve		10,000	
Dividends paid:			
Preference dividend of 5%	10,000		
Ordinary dividend of 10%	40,000		
		50,000	
			(60,000)
Retained profits carried forward to next year			104,810

Note: Dividends proposed and unpaid:

Preference dividend of 5%	10,000	
Ordinary dividend of 12$\frac{1}{2}$%	50,000	
	60,000	

(3) For the year ending 31 December 2006

	£	£	£
Profit for the year before taxation			158,220
Less Corporation tax			(63,000)
Profit for the year after taxation			95,220
Add Retained profits from last year			104,810
			200,030
Less Transfer to fixed assets replacement reserve		22,500	
Dividends paid			
Preference dividend of 5%	10,000		
Ordinary dividend of 12$\frac{1}{2}$%	50,000		
		60,000	
			(82,500)
Retained profits carried forward to next year			117,530

Note: Dividends proposed and unpaid:

Preference dividend of 5%	10,000	
Ordinary dividend of 15%	60,000	
	70,000	

Note: In the balance sheet, corporation tax owing is normally shown as a current liability.

43.13 The balance sheet

Prior to the UK Companies Act 1981, provided it disclosed the necessary information, a company could draw up its balance sheet and profit and loss account for publication in any way that it wished. The 1981 Act stopped this and laid down the precise details to be shown. These are unchanged in the Companies Act 2006 and the current legal requirements are largely to be found in the Companies Act 1985. We will cover this topic in more detail in *Business Accounting UK GAAP 2*.

Exhibits 43.6 and 43.7 present two versions of a balance sheet. They both comply with UK GAAP. Exhibit 43.6 shows more detail. The detail that is omitted from Exhibit 43.7 would be shown separately as a note. Both these balance sheets would be prepared by companies for their own use. Balance sheets prepared for publication (i.e. for external users) contain much less detail and will be covered in detail in *Business Accounting UK GAAP 2*.

If you are asked in an examination to prepare a balance sheet for internal use and choose to present a balance sheet similar to Exhibit 43.7, you should include the omitted detail (that you would have shown had you prepared it using the layout in Exhibit 43.6) in a note.

Exhibit 43.6 Greater detail for internal use

Balance Sheet as at 31 December 2007

		Cost	Depreciation to date (*b*)	Net book value
Fixed assets	(*a*)	£000	£000	£000
Goodwill		15,000	5,000	10,000
Buildings		15,000	6,000	9,000
Machinery		8,000	2,400	5,600
Motor vehicles		4,000	1,600	2,400
		42,000	15,000	27,000
Current assets				
Stock			6,000	
Debtors			3,000	
Bank			4,000	
			13,000	
Less Current liabilities				
Creditors		4,000		
Corporation tax owing		2,000		
			(6,000)	
Net current assets				7,000
				34,000
Debentures				
Six per cent debentures: repayable 2009				(8,000)
				26,000
Financed by:				
Share capital				
Authorised 30,000 shares of £1 each	(*c*)			30,000
Issued 20,000 ordinary shares of £1 each, fully paid	(*d*)			20,000
Reserves	(*e*)			
Share premium			1,200	
General reserve			3,800	
Profit and loss account			1,000	
				6,000
	(*f*)			26,000

Notes:

(*a*) Fixed assets should normally be shown either at cost or alternatively at some other valuation. In either case, the method chosen should be clearly stated.

(*b*) The total depreciation from date of purchase to the date of the balance sheet should be shown.

→

(c) The authorised share capital, where it is different from the issued share capital, is shown as a note.

(d) Where shares are only partly called up, then it is the amount actually called up that appears in the balance sheet and not the full amount.

(e) Reserves consist either of those unused profits remaining in the appropriation account, or those transferred to a reserve account appropriately titled, e.g. general reserve, fixed assets replacement reserve. At this juncture all that needs to be said is that any account labelled as a reserve has originated by being charged as a debit in the appropriation account and credited to a reserve account with an appropriate title. These reserves are shown in the balance sheet after share capital under the heading of 'Reserves'.

(f) The share capital and reserves should be totalled so as to show the book value of all the shares in the company. Either the term 'shareholders' funds' or 'members' equity' is often given to the total of share capital plus reserves.

Exhibit 43.7 Less detail for internal use

Letters in brackets (A) to (G) refer to notes following the balance sheet.

Balance Sheet as at 31 December 2007

		£000	£000	£000
Fixed assets				
Intangible assets	(A)			
Goodwill				10,000
Tangible assets	(B)			
Buildings			9,000	
Machinery			5,600	
Motor vehicles			2,400	
				17,000
				27,000
Current assets				
Stock			6,000	
Debtors			3,000	
Bank			4,000	
			13,000	
Creditors: Amounts falling due within one year	(C)			
Creditors		4,000		
Corporation tax owing		2,000		
			(6,000)	
Net current assets	(D)			7,000
Total assets less current liabilities				34,000
Creditors: amounts falling due after more than one year	(E)			
Debenture loans				(8,000)
				26,000
Capital and reserves				
Called-up share capital	(F)			20,000
Share premium account	(G)			1,200
Other reserves				
General reserve				3,800
Profit and loss account				1,000
				26,000

Notes:

(A) Intangible assets are those not having a 'physical' existence; for instance, you can see and touch tangible assets under (B), i.e. buildings, machinery etc., but you cannot see and touch goodwill.

(B) Tangible fixed assets under a separate heading. Note that figures are shown net after depreciation. In a note accompanying the accounts the cost and depreciation on these assets would be given.

(C) Only items payable within one year go under this heading.

(D) The term 'net current assets' replaces the more familiar term of 'working capital'.

(E) These particular debentures are repayable several years hence. If they had been payable within one year they would have been shown under (C).

(F) An analysis of share capital will be given in supplementary notes to the balance sheet.
(G) One reserve that is in fact not labelled with the word 'reserve' in its title is the share premium account. For various reasons (discussed fully in *Business Accounting 2*) shares can be issued for more than their face (or 'nominal') value. The excess of the price at which they are issued over the nominal value of the shares is credited to a share premium account. This is then shown with the other reserves in the balance sheet.

In *Business Accounting UK GAAP 2* you will be told more about the differences between 'revenue reserves' and 'capital reserves'. The most important reason for the distinction has to do with deciding how much can be treated as being available for paying out to shareholders as dividends. 'Revenue reserves', which include the profit and loss account balance and the general reserve, can be treated as available for such dividends. 'Capital reserves', which will include revaluation reserves on property and land, also some reserves (which you have not yet met) which have to be created to meet some legal statutory requirement, cannot be treated as available for payment of dividends.

A term which sometimes appears in examinations is that of 'fungible assets'. Fungible assets are assets which are substantially indistinguishable one from another.

A fully worked example

Exhibit 43.8

The following trial balance is extracted from the books of F W Ltd as on 31 December 2005:

Trial balance as on 31 December 2005

	Dr £	Cr £
10% preference share capital		200,000
Ordinary share capital		700,000
10% debentures (repayable 2009)		300,000
Goodwill at cost	255,000	
Buildings at cost	1,050,000	
Equipment at cost	120,000	
Motor vehicles at cost	172,000	
Provision for depreciation: buildings 1.1.2005		100,000
Provision for depreciation: equipment 1.1.2005		24,000
Provision for depreciation: motor vehicles 1.1.2005		51,600
Stock 1.1.2005	84,912	
Sales		1,022,000
Purchases	439,100	
Carriage inwards	6,200	
Salaries and wages	192,400	
Directors' remuneration	123,000	
Motor expenses	3,120	
Business rates and insurances	8,690	
General expenses	5,600	
Debenture interest	15,000	
Debtors	186,100	
Creditors		113,700
Bank	8,390	
General reserve		50,000
Share premium account		100,000
Interim ordinary dividend paid	35,000	
Profit and loss account 31.12.2004		43,212
	2,704,512	2,704,512

→

→ **(c)** Balance sheet in less detail for internal use

F W Ltd
Balance Sheet as at 31 December 2005

		£	£	£
Fixed assets				
Intangible assets				
Goodwill				225,000
Tangible assets	(A)			
Buildings			940,000	
Equipment			84,000	
Motor vehicles			102,400	
				1,126,400
				1,351,400
Current assets				
Stock			91,413	
Debtors			186,100	
Bank			8,390	
			285,903	
Creditors: amounts falling due within one year				
Creditors		113,700		
Debenture interest accrued		15,000		
Taxation		50,000		
			(178,700)	
Net current assets				107,203
Total assets less current liabilities				1,458,603
Creditors: amounts falling due after more than one year				
10% Debentures				(300,000)
				1,158,603
Capital and reserves	(B)			
Called-up share capital	(C)			900,000
Share premium account				100,000
Other reserves				
General reserve				60,000
Profit and loss				98,603
				1,158,603

The proposed dividends will be shown as a note.

(A) Notes to be given in an appendix as to cost, acquisitions and sales in the year and depreciation.
(B) Reserves consist either of those unused profits remaining in the appropriation account, or those transferred to a reserve account appropriately titled, e.g. general reserve, fixed assets replacement reserve, etc.

   One reserve that is in fact not labelled with the word 'reserve' in its title is the share premium account. This is shown with the other reserves in the balance sheet.
   The closing balance on the profit and loss appropriation account is shown under reserves. These are profits not already appropriated, and therefore 'reserved' for future use.

(C) The authorised share capital, where it is different from the issued share capital, is shown as a note. Notice that the total figure of £1,200,000 for authorised capital is not included when adding up the balance sheet sides. Only the issued capital amounts are included in balance sheet totals.

Note: the difference between the two balance sheets is solely that of detail. You should use whichever layout is more appropriate.

43.14 True and fair view

When the financial statements of a company are published no one, neither the directors nor the auditors, ever states that 'the financial statements are correct'. This is because in preparing company financial statements many subjective estimates and judgements affect the figures. The valuation of stock, or the estimates of depreciation cannot be said to be 'correct', just as it is impossible to say that the provision for doubtful debts is 'correct'. Only time will tell whether these estimates and judgements will turn out to have been 'correct'.

The expression that is used is that, in the opinion of the auditors, the financial statements give a **true and fair view** of the state of affairs and financial performance of the company.

43.15 FRS 3: Reporting Financial Performance

Accounting is not a static subject. Changes occur over the years as they are seen to be necessary, and also get general agreement as to their usefulness. Since the introduction of accounting standards, the number of changes that practitioners and students have had to learn has increased at a very fast rate. A prime example of this is the introduction of FRS 3, which necessitated changes to the formats of company profit and loss accounts when certain events have occurred.

Suppose that you are considering the affairs of a business over the years. The business has not changed significantly, there have been no acquisitions, no discontinued operations, no fundamental reorganisation or restructuring of the business, nor have there been any extraordinary items affecting the financial statements. In these circumstances, when comparing the financial statements over the years, you are comparing like with like, subject to the problem of the effects of inflation or deflation.

On the other hand, suppose that some of the things mentioned above have occurred. When trying to see what the future might hold for the company, simply basing your opinions on what has happened in the past can be very confusing.

To help you to distinguish the past and the future, and to give you some idea as to what changes have occurred, FRS 3 requires that the following are highlighted in the profit and loss account if they are material in amount:

(a) *What the results of continuing operations are, including the results of acquisitions.* Obviously acquisitions affect future results, and are therefore included in continuing operations.
(b) *What the results have been of discontinued operations.* This should help distinguish the past from the future.
(c) *The profits or losses on the sale or termination of an operation, the costs of fundamental reorganisation or restructuring* and *the profits and losses on the disposal of fixed assets.* The profits and losses concerning these matters are not going to happen again, and so this also helps us distinguish the past from the future.

We can see in Exhibit 43.9 how FRS 3 requires (a), (b) and (c) to be shown on the face of the profit and loss account. Not only is the turnover split to show the figures relevant to continuing operations, acquisitions and discontinued operations, the operating profit is split in a similar fashion. In addition any profit or loss on the disposal of the discontinued operations would also be shown.

Exhibit 43.9

Block PLC
Profit and Loss Account for the year ending 31 December 2006 (extract)

		£000	£000
1	Turnover		
	Continuing operations	520	
	Acquisitions	110	
		630	
	Discontinued operations	170	
			800
2	Cost of sales		(500)
3	Gross profit		300
4	Distribution costs	60	
5	Administrative expenses	40	
	Operating profit		(100)
	Continuing operations	160	
	Acquisitions	60	
	(A)	220	
	Discontinued operations (loss) (B)	(20)	
			200
	Profit on disposal of discontinued operations (C)		10
			210
6	Other operating income		20
	Profit or loss on ordinary activities before interest		230

The items marked (A), (B) and (C) can be described as exceptional items. They are material in amount, they fall within the ordinary activities of the business, and need to be shown so that the accounts will give a 'true and fair view'.

They are exceptional in that they are not the ordinary daily occurrence, but remember that they fall within the ordinary activities of the company. FRS 3 requires that three categories of exceptional items be shown separately on the face of the profit and loss account after operating profit and before interest, and included under the appropriate heading of continued or discontinued operations:

● profits or losses on the sale or termination of an operation;
● costs of a fundamental reorganisation or restructuring having a material effect on the nature and focus of the reporting entity's operations;
● profits or losses on the disposal of fixed assets.

Other exceptional items should be credited or charged in arriving at the profit or loss on ordinary activities by inclusion under the heading to which they relate. The amount of each exceptional item should be disclosed in a note, or on the face of the profit and loss account, if necessary, in order to give a true and fair view.

Some other items are also contained in FRS 3. These are:

(*a*) Where assets have been revalued there may be a material difference in the results shown in the accounts using such revalued figures, which obviously affects depreciation. If this is the case, then FRS 3 requires that there should also be shown as a note what the profit and loss account would have been if it had been prepared using historical (i.e. not revalued) figures.

There should also be a statement (the *statement of total recognised gains and losses*) which shows how the reported profit on ordinary activities (calculated using revalued asset values) can be reconciled with that calculated using historical figures.

(*b*) A note should be given reconciling the opening and closing totals of shareholders' funds of the period. This shows how such items as the profit for the year or a new share issue have increased the funds, whereas dividends and items written off capital reserves have reduced the funds.

43.16 The Audit Report

The Companies Act requires that all companies other than dormant companies (i.e. companies that have not traded during the year) and small companies be audited every year. ('Small' is currently defined as having a turnover of not more than £5.6 million and a balance sheet total (of assets) of not more than £2.8 million.)

The auditors are appointed each year by the shareholders at the company annual general meeting (AGM). The auditors complete the report after examining the books and accounts and, in the report, they must say whether or not they agree that the accounts give a true and fair view. The report is presented to the shareholders at the same time as the financial statements are presented to them at the AGM.

In preparing the audit report, the auditor must consider whether

● the accounts have been prepared in accordance with the Companies Act;
● the balance sheet shows a true and fair view of the state of the company's affairs at the end of the period and the profit and loss account shows a true and fair view of the results for the period;
● proper accounting records have been kept and proper returns received from parts of the company not visited by the auditor;
● the accounts are in agreement with the accounting records;
● the directors' report is consistent with the accounts.

While smaller companies (those with turnover below £5.6 million) are exempt from the requirement to have their financial statements audited, they may still do so, if they wish.

Organisations that are not required to have their financial statements audited, such as sole traders, partnerships, clubs and societies, can still have their accounts audited. In this case, the audit is described as a *non-statutory audit*.

A qualified audit report indicates that the auditor is not satisfied that the financial statements present a true and fair view. When a company receives a qualified audit report, it acts as a signal to all stakeholders that something may be amiss. As such, it is a vitally important safeguard of the interests of the shareholders.

Contrary to what most of the public think, auditors do not guarantee to discover any fraud that may have occurred. That is not what the audit is for. Following such financial scandals as Enron, the Maxwell affair, BCCI bank, Polly Peck and Barlow Clowes there has been pressure exerted upon the accounting profession to reconsider its position regarding the discovery of fraud when auditing the financial statements of a company.

Learning outcomes

You should now have learnt:

1 That limited companies exist because of the disadvantages and constraints arising from partnerships.

2 That a fully paid-up shareholder's liability is limited to the shares he or she holds in the company. Shareholders cannot then be asked to pay any other company debt from their private resources.

3 The difference between public and private companies.

4 That there are far more private companies than public companies.

5 The difference between a PLC and a company that is not a PLC.

6 That a limited company has a 'separate legal entity' from that of its members.

7 The difference between ordinary shares and preference shares.

8 How dividends are calculated.

9 The difference between shares and debentures.

10 The contents of and purpose of a company's appropriation account.

11 That directors' remuneration is charged to the main part of the profit and loss account.

12 That debenture interest is charged to the main part of the profit and loss account.

13 That transfers to reserves, dividends paid and taxation are charged to the appropriation part of the profit and loss account.

14 That any balance of profits unappropriated at the end of a period is carried forward as a balance to the next period.

15 How to prepare company trading and profit and loss accounts for internal purposes.

16 How to prepare company balance sheets for internal purposes.

17 How goodwill is treated in company financial statements.

Answers to activities

43.1 Partnerships were not suitable for such businesses because:

● normally they cannot have more than twenty partners, not counting limited partners.
● if a partnership business fails, partners could lose part, or all, of their private assets to pay the debts of the business.

Limited companies do not have restrictions on the number of owners. Nor do the owners of limited companies generally run the risk of losing everything they own if the company fails.

43.2 There may be any number of explanations, including:

● they may not wish a wide ownership base
● they may feel the costs of doing so are prohibitive
● they may feel there would not be sufficient demand for the shares to make it worthwhile
● the directors may be concerned that it would make it easier for the company to be taken over

● they may wish to wait until the Stock Market is at a higher level, i.e. they wish to wait until they can maximise the amount they can sell the shares for when they first offer them for sale on the Stock Market

● the Stock Market may be very volatile, making choosing a price at which to sell the shares very difficult – if the company gets it wrong, they may not sell all the shares they wanted to sell or they may not receive as much for each share as they could have done had they waited for the Stock Market to stabilise.

43.3 There is less risk for the investor. The annual preference dividend is known and it will be paid before any funds left over are used to pay a dividend on the ordinary shares. Even when an ordinary dividend is paid, it is not known in advance how much this will be, as it depends on how profitable the business has been over the financial period. It could be more than the preference dividend (which is normally the case) or it could be less. Although the preference dividend will often be at a lower rate than an ordinary dividend (i.e. a preference shareholder will receive less of a dividend for the same investment as an ordinary shareholder) the reduced risk results in some people preferring to purchase preference shares.

43.4 The lender may require it or the company may offer secured debenture status in order to attract funds at a more favourable rate of interest.

Multiple choice questions: Set 5

Now attempt Set 5 of multiple choice questions. (Answers to all the multiple choice questions are given in Appendix 2 at the end of this book.)

Each of these multiple choice questions has four suggested answers, (A), (B), (C) and (D). You should read each question and then decide which choice is best, either (A) or (B) or (C) or (D). *Write down your answers on a separate piece of paper.* You will then be able to redo the set of questions later without having to try to ignore your answers.

MC81 Given opening debtors of £11,500, Sales £48,000 and receipts from debtors £45,000, the closing debtors should total

(A) £8,500
(B) £14,500
(C) £83,500
(D) £18,500

MC82 In a Sales Ledger Control Account the Bad Debts written off should be shown in the account

(A) As a debit
(B) As a credit
(C) Both as a debit and as a credit
(D) As a balance carried down

MC83 If cost price is £90 and selling price is £120, then

(i) Mark-up is 25 per cent
(ii) Margin is 33$\frac{1}{3}$ per cent
(iii) Margin is 25 per cent
(iv) Mark-up is 33$\frac{1}{3}$ per cent

(A) (i) and (ii)
(B) (i) and (iii)
(C) (iii) and (iv)
(D) (ii) and (iv)

→

→ **MC84** Given cost of goods sold £16,000 and margin of 20 per cent, then sales figure is

(A) £20,160
(B) £13,600
(C) £21,000
(D) £20,000

MC85 If opening stock is £3,000, closing stock £5,000, sales £40,000 and margin 20 per cent, then stockturn is

(A) 8 times
(B) 7½ times
(C) 5 times
(D) 6 times

MC86 If creditors at 1 January 2003 were £2,500, creditors at 31 December 2003 £4,200 and payments to creditors £32,000, then purchases for 2003 are

(A) £30,300
(B) £33,700
(C) £31,600
(D) £38,700

MC87 Given opening capital of £16,500; closing capital as £11,350; and drawings of £3,300, then

(A) Loss for the year was £1,850
(B) Profit for the year was £1,850
(C) Loss for the year was £8,450
(D) Profit for the year was £8,450

MC88 A Receipts and Payments Account is one

(A) Which is accompanied by a balance sheet
(B) In which the profit is calculated
(C) In which the opening and closing cash balances are shown
(D) In which the surplus of income over expenditure is calculated

MC89 Prime cost includes

(*i*) Direct labour
(*ii*) Factory overhead expenses
(*iii*) Raw materials consumed
(*iv*) Direct expenses

(A) (*i*), (*ii*) and (*iii*)
(B) (*ii*), (*iii*) and (*iv*)
(C) (*i*), (*iii*) and (*iv*)
(D) (*i*), (*ii*) and (*iv*)

MC90 Which of the following should be charged in the Profit and Loss Account?

(A) Office rent
(B) Work-in-progress
(C) Direct materials
(D) Carriage on raw materials

MC91 In the Manufacturing Account is calculated

(A) The production costs paid in the year
(B) The total cost of goods produced
(C) The production cost of goods completed in the period
(D) The gross profit on goods sold

MC92 The recommended method of departmental accounts is

(A) To allocate expenses in proportion to sales
(B) To charge against each department its controllable costs
(C) To allocate expenses in proportion to purchases
(D) To charge against each department its uncontrollable costs

MC93 Where there is no partnership agreement then profits and losses

(A) Must be shared in same proportion as capitals
(B) Must be shared equally
(C) Must be shared equally after adjusting for interest on capital
(D) None of these

MC94 If it is required to maintain fixed capitals then the partners' shares of profits must be

(A) Debited to capital accounts
(B) Credited to capital accounts
(C) Debited to partners' current accounts
(D) Credited to partners' current accounts

MC95 You are to buy an existing business which has assets valued at Buildings £50,000, Motor vehicles £15,000, Fixtures £5,000 and Stock £40,000. You are to pay £140,000 for the business. This means that

(A) You are paying £40,000 for Goodwill
(B) Buildings are costing you £30,000 more than their value
(C) You are paying £30,000 for Goodwill
(D) You have made an arithmetical mistake

MC96 Assets can be revalued in a partnership change because

(A) The law insists upon it
(B) It helps prevent injustice to some partners
(C) Inflation affects all values
(D) The depreciation charged on them needs to be reversed

MC97 Any loss on revaluation is

(A) Credited to old partners in old profit-sharing ratios
(B) Credited to new partners in new profit-sharing ratios
(C) Debited to old partners in old profit-sharing ratios
(D) Debited to new partners in new profit-sharing ratios

MC98 In a limited company which of the following are shown in the Appropriation Account?

(*i*) Debenture interest
(*ii*) Proposed dividend
(*iii*) Transfers to reserves
(*iv*) Directors' remuneration

→

→

(A) *(i)*
(B) *(ii)*
(C) *(iii)*
(D) *(iv)*

MC99 The Issued Capital of a company is

(A) Always the same as the Authorised Capital
(B) The same as Preference Share Capital
(C) Equal to the reserves of the company
(D) None of the above

MC100 A company wishes to pay out all available profits as dividends. Net profit is £26,600. There are 20,000 8% Preference shares of £1 each, and 50,000 Ordinary shares of £1 each. £5,000 is to be transferred to General Reserve. What Ordinary dividends are to be paid, in percentage terms?

(A) 20 per cent
(B) 40 per cent
(C) 10 per cent
(D) 60 per cent

Review questions

43.1 Flyer Ltd started in business on 1 April 2004. Its issued share capital was 200,000 ordinary shares of £1 each and 100,000 5 per cent preference shares of £1 each. The following information is available:

● Its net profits for the first two years of business were: 2004/5 £90,200; 2005/6 £84,600.
● Preference dividends were paid for each of these years, whilst ordinary dividends were proposed as 2004/5 8 per cent and 2005/6 6 per cent.
● Corporation tax, based on the profits of these two years, was: 2004/5 £18,000; 2005/6 £16,000.
● Transfers to general reserve took place: 2004/5 £20,000; 2005/6 £15,000.

Draw up profit and loss appropriation accounts for each of the years ending 31 March 2005 and 2006.

43.2 Trainsign Ltd has an authorised capital of £500,000, consisting of 350,000 ordinary shares of £1 each and 150,000 7 per cent preference shares of £1 each. Of these, 260,000 ordinary shares and 90,000 preference shares had been issued when the company first started trading. The following information is available:

● The company has a financial year end of 31 December. The first three years of business resulted in net profit as follows: 2002 £62,400; 2003 £81,900; 2004 £114,190.
● Dividends were paid each year on the preference shares. Dividends on the ordinary shares were proposed as follows: 2002 6 per cent; 2003 8 per cent; 2004 12 per cent.
● Corporation tax, based on the profits of each year, was: 2002 £12,000; 2003 £16,000; 2004 £22,000.
● Transfers to reserves were: general reserve 2002 £10,000, 2003 £18,000, and foreign exchange reserve 2004 £15,000.

You are to show the profit and loss appropriation accounts for each of the years 2002, 2003 and 2004.

43.3 A balance sheet is to be drawn up from the following information as at 30 September 2002:

	£
Issued share capital: ordinary shares £1 each	200,000
Authorised share capital: ordinary shares of £1 each	500,000
6 per cent debentures (repayable 30 September 2006)	40,000
Buildings at cost	330,000
Motor vehicles at cost	74,000
Fixtures at cost	9,200
Profit and loss account	32,000
Fixed assets replacement reserve	30,000
Stock	21,400
Debtors	10,300
General reserve	50,000
Creditors	13,700
Depreciation to date: Buildings	40,000
Motor vehicles	41,000
Fixtures	5,100
Bank (balancing figure for you to ascertain)	?

43.4 The following balances remained in the ledger of OK Ltd after preparation of the profit and loss account for the year ending 31 March 2006

	£000s
Stock	52
Debtors	24
Ordinary share capital	100
8% preference share capital	50
Creditors	37
Balance at bank	14
General reserve	30
Profit and loss account balance 2005	11
Net profit for the year to 31 March 2006	29
Fixed assets at cost, less depreciation	167

The directors propose:
(*i*) a transfer to general reserve of £10,000;
(*ii*) payment of the preference dividend and a 12% dividend on the ordinary shares.

Required:
(*a*) Prepare a profit and loss appropriation account for the year ended 31 March 2006.
(*b*) Prepare a balance sheet as at 31 March 2006, showing clearly the ordinary shareholders' equity, the total shareholders' funds and the working capital.

→

→

43.5A Developing Ltd has an authorised capital of 50,000, 10% preference shares of £1 each and 200,000 ordinary shares of 50p each. After preparation of the profit and loss account for 2004, the following balances remained in the ledger

	£000s
Share capital: fully paid-up:	
Preference	30
Ordinary	80
Debentures	20
Share premium account	4
General reserve	7
Unappropriated profit 2003	3
Net profit for 2004	27
Fixed assets	140
Current assets	50
Creditors	19

The directors recommend:
(*i*) that £10,000 be transferred to general reserve,
(*ii*) payment of the preference dividend,
(*iii*) an ordinary dividend of 15%.

Required:
Prepare the appropriation account for 2004 and a balance sheet as at 31 December 2004.

43.6 Select Ltd is registered with an authorised capital of 300,000 ordinary shares of £1. The following trial balance was extracted from the books of the company on 31 March 2001, after the preparation of the trading account:

	Dr £	Cr £
Ordinary share capital, fully paid		200,000
Land and buildings at cost	170,000	
Sundry debtors	38,300	
Furniture and fittings at cost	80,000	
VAT	3,800	
Sundry Creditors		25,000
Stock at 31 March 2000	42,000	
Bank	12,000	
Trading account: gross profit		98,050
Office salaries and expenses	25,000	
Accumulated provision for depreciation on furniture and fittings		32,000
Share premium account		20,000
Advertising and selling expenses	5,000	
Bad debts	250	
Provision for doubtful debts		600
Profit and loss account		12,000
Directors' fees	11,300	
	387,650	387,650

Required:
Prepare the profit and loss account of the company for the year ending 31 March 2001, and balance sheet as at that date, after taking into account the following adjustments:

(*i*) The provision for doubtful debtors is to be adjusted to £700.
(*ii*) Depreciation is to be provided in respect of furniture and fittings at 10% per annum on cost.
(*iii*) £25,000 is to be transferred from profit and loss to general reserve.
(*iv*) Provide for a proposed dividend on share capital at 10%.

Present the balance sheet in a form which shows the shareholders' equity and the working capital.

43.7A

	£000
Fixed assets, at cost	160
Stock	40
Bank overdraft	30
Ordinary share capital	100
Creditors	45
Unappropriated profit	22
Accumulated depreciation	50
Debtors	47

Required:

(a) From the above information, prepare the balance sheet of Budgie Limited indicating clearly the shareholders' funds and working capital.

(b) Comment on the capital position disclosed by the balance sheet you have prepared.

43.8 The trial balance extracted from the books of Tailor Times Ltd at 31 December 2003 was as follows:

	£	£
Share capital		200,000
Profit and loss account 31 December 2002		27,500
Freehold premises at cost	271,000	
Provision for depreciation on freehold premises at 31 December 2002		54,000
Machinery at cost	84,000	
Provision for depreciation on machinery account as at 31 December 2002		21,000
Purchases	563,700	
Sales		925,300
General expenses	14,600	
Wages and salaries	179,400	
Business rates	6,100	
Electricity	4,800	
Bad debts	1,400	
Provision for doubtful debts at 31 December 2002		1,200
Debtors	74,200	
Creditors		68,300
Stock in trade 31 December 2002	81,900	
Bank balance	16,200	
	1,297,300	1,297,300

You are given the following additional information:

(i) The authorised and issued share capital is divided into 400,000 ordinary shares of 50p each.

(ii) Stock in trade at 31 December 2003, £94,300.

(iii) Wages and salaries due at 31 December 2003 amounted to £1,800.

(iv) Business rates paid in advance at 31 December 2003 amounted to £700.

(v) A dividend of £20,000 is proposed for 2003.

(vi) The provision for doubtful debts is to be increased to £1,500.

(vii) A depreciation charge is to be made on freehold premises of £25,000 and machinery at the rate of 25 per cent per annum on cost.

Required:

A trading and profit and loss account for 2003 and a balance sheet as at 31 December 2003.

→

→ **43.9A** The following is the trial balance of Tully Ltd as on 31 December 2005:

	Dr £	Cr £
Share capital issued: ordinary shares 20p		375,000
Debtors and creditors	169,600	74,900
Stock 31 December 2004	81,300	
Bank	17,900	
Premises at cost	265,000	
Machinery at cost	109,100	
Motor vehicles at cost	34,700	
Depreciation provisions at 31.12.2004:		
Premises		60,000
Machinery		41,400
Motor vehicles		18,200
Sales		975,600
Purchases	623,800	
Motor expenses	4,300	
Repairs to machinery	3,600	
Sundry expenses	2,900	
Wages and salaries	241,500	
Directors' remuneration	82,600	
Profit and loss account as at 31.12.2004		31,200
General reserve		60,000
	1,636,300	1,636,300

Given the following information, you are to draw up a trading and profit and loss account for the year ending 31 December 2005, and a balance sheet as at that date:

(*i*) Authorised share capital: £500,000 in ordinary shares of 20p.
(*ii*) Stock at 31 December 2005 £102,400.
(*iii*) Motor expenses owing £280.
(*iv*) Ordinary dividend proposed of 5 per cent.
(*v*) Transfer £7,500 to general reserve.
(*vi*) Provide for depreciation: motor vehicles and machinery 20% on cost; premises 5% on cost.

43.10 You are to draw up a trading and profit and loss account for the year ending 31 December 2002, and a balance sheet as at that date from the following trial balance and details of Partido Ltd:

	Dr £	Cr £
Bank	8,100	
Debtors	321,219	
Creditors		237,516
Stock at 31 December 2001	290,114	
Buildings at cost	800,000	
Equipment at cost	320,000	
Profit and loss account as at 31 December 2001		136,204
General reserve		120,000
Foreign exchange reserve		20,000
Authorised and issued share capital		800,000
Purchases	810,613	
Sales		1,606,086
Carriage inwards	2,390	
Carriage outwards	13,410	
Salaries	384,500	
Business rates	14,800	
Office expenses	9,100	
Sundry expenses	2,360	
Provisions for depreciation at 31 December 2001:		
Buildings		80,000
Equipment		96,000
Directors' remuneration	119,200	
	3,095,806	3,095,806

Notes at 31 December 2002:

(*i*)   Stock £317,426.
(*ii*) Business rates owing £1,700; Office expenses owing £245.
(*iii*) Dividend of 15 per cent proposed.
(*iv*) Transfers to reserves: General £70,000; Foreign exchange £30,000.
(*v*)   Depreciation on cost: Buildings 5 per cent; Equipment 15 per cent.

→

→ on sales returns account has inadvertently been omitted from the trial balance, though correctly entered in the ledger records.

(*ii*) A standing order received from a regular customer for £2,000, and bank charges of £1,000, have been completely omitted from the records.

(*iii*) A debtor for £1,000 is to be written off. The provision for doubtful debts balance is to be adjusted to 1% of debtors.

(*iv*) The opening stock figure had been overstated by £1,000 and the closing stock figure had been understated by £2,000.

(*v*) Any remaining balance on suspense account should be treated as purchases if a debit balance and as sales if a credit balance.

(*vi*) The debentures were issued three months before the year end. No entries have been made as regards interest.

(*vii*) A dividend of 10% of share capital is to be proposed.

Required:
(*a*) Prepare journal entries to cover items in notes (*i*) to (*v*) above. You are NOT to open any new accounts and may use only those accounts included in the trial balance as given.
(*b*) Prepare financial statements for internal use in good order within the limits of the available information. For presentation purposes all the items arising from notes (*i*) to (*vii*) above should be regarded as material.

(*Association of Chartered Certified Accountants*)

43.14 'The historical cost convention looks backwards but the going concern convention looks forwards.'

Required:
(*a*) Explain clearly what is meant by:
  (*i*) the historical cost convention;
  (*ii*) the going concern convention.
(*b*) Does traditional financial accounting, using the historical cost convention, make the going concern convention unnecessary? Explain your answer fully.
(*c*) Which do you think a shareholder is likely to find more useful – a report on the past or an estimate of the future? Why?

(*Association of Chartered Certified Accountants*)

43.15 The chairman of a public limited company has written his annual report to the shareholders, extracts of which are quoted below.

Extract 1
'In May 2006, in order to provide a basis for more efficient operations, we acquired PAG Warehousing and Transport Ltd. The agreed valuation of the net tangible assets acquired was £1.4 million. The purchase consideration, £1.7 million, was satisfied by an issue of 6.4 million equity shares, of £0.25 per share, to PAG's shareholders. These shares do not rank for dividend until 2007.'

Extract 2
'As a measure of confidence in our ability to expand operations in 2007 and 2008, and to provide the necessary financial base, we issued £0.5 million 8% Redeemable Debenture Stock, 2001/2007, 20 million 6% £1 Redeemable Preference Shares and 4 million £1 equity shares. The opportunity was also taken to redeem the whole of the 5 million 11% £1 Redeemable Preference Shares.'

Required:
Answer the following questions on the above extracts.

Extract 1
(*a*) What does the difference of £0.3 million between the purchase consideration (£1.7m) and the net tangible assets value (£1.4m) represent?
(*b*) What does the difference of £0.1 million between the purchase consideration (£1.7m) and the nominal value of the equity shares (£1.6m) represent?

(c) What is the meaning of the term 'equity shares'?

(d) What is the meaning of the phrase 'do not rank for dividend'?

Extract 2

(e) In the description of the debenture stock issue, what is the significance of
   (i) 8%?
   (ii) 2001/2007?

(f) In the description of the preference share issue, what is the significance of
   (i) 6%?
   (ii) Redeemable?

(g) What is the most likely explanation for the company to have redeemed existing preference shares but at the same time to have issued others?

(h) What effect will these structural changes have had on the gearing of the company?^{Authors' Note}

(j) Contrast the accounting treatment in the company's profit and loss accounts, of the interest due on the debentures with dividends proposed on the equity shares.

(k) Explain the reasons for the different treatments you have outlined in your answer to (j) above.

(Association of Chartered Certified Accountants)

Authors' Note: Part (h) of the question is covered in the text in Section 45.4.

43.16 The directors of the company by which you are employed as an accountant have received the forecast profit and loss account for 2009 which disclosed a net profit for the year of £36,000.

This is considered to be an unacceptably low figure and a working party has been set up to investigate ways and means of improving the forecast profit.

The following suggestions have been put forward by various members of the working party:

(a) 'Every six months we deduct income tax of £10,000 from the debenture interest and pay it over to Revenue & Customs. If we withhold these payments, the company's profit will be increased considerably.'

(b) 'I see that in the three months August to October 2009 we have forecast a total amount of £40,000 for repainting the exterior of the company's premises. If, instead, we charge this amount as capital expenditure, the company's profit will be increased by £40,000.'

(c) 'In November 2009, the replacement of a machine is forecast. The proceeds from the sale of the old machinery should be credited to profit and loss account.'

(d) 'There is a credit balance of £86,000 on general reserve account. We can transfer some of this to profit and loss account to increase the 2009 profit.'

(e) 'The company's £1 ordinary shares, which were originally issued at £1 per share, currently have a market value of £1.60 per share and this price is likely to be maintained. We can credit the surplus £0.60 per share to the 2009 profit and loss account.'

(f) 'The company's premises were bought many years ago for £68,000, but following the rise in property values, they are now worth at least £300,000. This enhancement in value can be utilised to increase the 2009 profit.'

You are required, as the accounting member of the working party, to comment on the feasibility of each of the above suggestions for increasing the 2009 forecast profit.

(Association of Chartered Certified Accountants)

43.17 Explain what you understand by the accounting term 'debentures' and indicate the circumstances under which a debenture issue would or would not be an appropriate form of financing.

(Scottish Qualifications Authority)

You can find a range of additional self-test questions, as well as material to help you with your studies, on the website that accompanies this book at **www.pearsoned.co.uk/wood**

Purchase of existing partnership and sole traders' businesses

Learning objectives

After you have studied this chapter, you should be able to:

● enter up the purchase of a business in the purchaser's books

● draw up the balance sheet of the purchaser after taking over the assets and liabilities of the vendor

Introduction

In this chapter, you'll learn how to record the entries in the accounting books when a sole trader or a partnership is taken over by individuals, sole trader businesses, partnerships, and companies.

44.1　Types of purchase

You learnt in Chapter 40 that a sole trader's business may be sold as a going concern, rather than being broken up and its assets sold off one by one. The seller normally prefers to sell the business as a going concern, as more money is usually generated arising from the goodwill of the business. Buyers often prefer to purchase a going concern as it saves them all the problems of building markets and reputation.

In that chapter we also looked at the calculation of partnership goodwill when there was a change in the partners. We didn't consider what happens when a partnership is sold as a going concern. This happens relatively frequently. Now that you've learnt how to maintain partnership accounts, we're going to look further at the accounting treatment of sole traders being taken over as going concerns. **While we will focus on sole traders, everything you will learn in this chapter applies also to partnerships when they are taken over as going concerns.**

There are many ways in which a sole trader or a partnership may be taken over as a going concern. For example, an individual may purchase the business of a sole trader (this was the example used at the start of Chapter 40) or a sole trader may take over a partnership.

Activity 44.1 Think about this for a minute and then write down as many different entities (i.e. a person or persons, or a type of business) as you can think of that might purchase a sole trader or a partnership as a going concern.

44.2　Value of assets bought in purchaser's books

It must not be thought that because the assets bought are shown in the selling firm's books at one value, that the purchaser must record the assets taken over in its own books at the same value – you learnt about recording changes in asset values in Chapter 41 when you looked at revaluation of partnership assets but, in that case, you were looking at what you do when you revalue the assets of a partnership that is continuing in business, not when it is sold.

When a business is sold, the seller has no need to revalue the assets and adjust the values shown in the balance sheet. However the buyer really ought to show the assets (and liabilities) of the business it has taken over at their current values.

Activity 44.2 Why does the seller not need to revalue the assets of the business and change the values shown in the balance sheet?

The values shown in the books of the purchaser are, therefore, those values at which it is buying the assets, such values being frequently quite different from those shown in the selling firm's books. As an instance of this, the selling firm may have bought premises many years ago for £10,000 which are now worth £50,000. The purchaser buying the premises will obviously have to pay £50,000 for them. It is, therefore, this value that is recorded in the books of the purchaser.

Activity 44.3 Why would an accounting firm want to purchase another accounting firm?

44.3 Goodwill on purchase

As you might have guessed, when the total purchase price is *greater* than the new valuation made by the purchaser of the assets taken over, the difference is goodwill in the eyes of the purchaser. (The seller may have a very different view concerning the value of the assets.) This can be shown as:

	£
Total purchase consideration	90,000
Less New valuation of assets taken over (not usually the same values as per the old balance sheet)	(75,000)
Goodwill	15,000

The revised balance sheet of the purchaser will include goodwill as an intangible asset at the calculated figure. It will also include the assets bought at their new valuations.

44.4 Capital reserve on purchase

Where the total purchase price is *less* than the new valuations of the assets taken over, the difference can either be treated in the purchaser's sole trader or partnership books as **negative goodwill** or as a **capital reserve**. (Companies *must* treat it as negative goodwill.) When treated as a capital reserve, it can be shown as:

	£
Total purchase consideration	55,000
Less New valuation of assets taken over (not usually the same values as per the old balance sheet)	(75,000)
Capital reserve	(20,000)

The new valuations of the assets will appear in the revised balance sheet of the purchaser. Any capital reserve arising will be shown in the capital section of the balance sheet.

44.5 **Taking over a sole trader's business**

It is easier to start with the takeover of the simplest sort of business unit, that of a sole trader. Some of the balance sheets shown will be deliberately simplified so that the principles involved are not hidden behind a mass of complicated calculations.

To illustrate the takeover of a business, given varying circumstances, the same business will be assumed to be taken over in different ways. The balance sheet of this business is that of A Brown, as shown in Exhibit 44.1:

Exhibit 44.1

A Brown
Balance Sheet as at 31 December 2006

	£	£
Fixed assets		
Fixtures		30,000
Current assets		
Stock	8,000	
Debtors	7,000	
Bank	1,000	
	16,000	
Less: Current liabilities		
Creditors	(3,000)	
		13,000
		43,000
Capital		43,000

1 An individual purchases the business of a sole trader

(**a**) Assume that the assets and liabilities of A Brown, with the exception of the bank balance, are taken over by D Towers. He is to take over the assets and liabilities at the valuations as shown in Brown's balance sheet. The price to be paid is £52,000.

The opening balance sheet of Towers will be as shown in Exhibit 44.2:

Exhibit 44.2

D Towers
Balance Sheet as at 1 January 2007

	£	£
Fixed assets		
Goodwill		10,000
Fixtures		30,000
		40,000
Current assets		
Stock	8,000	
Debtors	7,000	
	15,000	
Less: Current liabilities		
Creditors	(3,000)	
		12,000
		52,000
Capital		52,000

As £52,000 has been paid for the net assets (assets less liabilities) valued at £30,000 + £8,000 + £7,000 − £3,000 = £42,000, the excess £10,000 represents the amount paid for goodwill.

(b) Suppose that, instead of the information just given, the same amount (£52,000) has been paid by Towers, but the assets were taken over at a value of Fixtures £37,000; Stock £7,500; Debtors £6,500.

The opening balance sheet of D Towers would be as shown in Exhibit 44.3:

Exhibit 44.3

D Towers
Balance Sheet as at 1 January 2007

	£	£
Fixed assets		
Goodwill		4,000
Fixtures		37,000
		41,000
Current assets		
Stock	7,500	
Debtors	6,500	
	14,000	
Less: Current liabilities		
Creditors	(3,000)	
		11,000
		52,000
Capital		52,000

As £52,000 had been paid for net assets valued at £37,000 + £7,500 + £6,500 − £3,000 = £48,000, the excess £4,000 represents the amount paid for goodwill. The other assets are shown at their value to the purchaser, Towers.

2 A partnership acquires the business of a sole trader

Assume instead that the business of Brown had been taken over by M Ukridge and D Allen. The partners are to introduce £30,000 each as capital. The price to be paid for the net assets, other than the bank balance, is £52,000. The purchasers placed the following values on the assets taken over: Fixtures £40,000; Stock £7,000; Debtors £6,000.

The opening balance sheet of Ukridge and Allen will be as in Exhibit 44.4:

Exhibit 44.4

M Ukridge and D Allen
Balance Sheet as at 1 January 2007

	£	£
Fixed assets		
Goodwill		2,000
Fixtures		40,000
		42,000
Current assets		
Stock	7,000	
Debtors	6,000	
Bank*	8,000	
	21,000	
Less: Current liabilities		
Creditors	(3,000)	
		18,000
		60,000
Capitals		
M Ukridge		30,000
D Allen		30,000
		60,000

*The bank balance is made up of £30,000 + £30,000 introduced by the partners, less £52,000 paid to Brown = £8,000.

The sum of £52,000 has been paid for net assets of £40,000 + £7,000 + £6,000 − £3,000 = £50,000. This makes goodwill to be the excess of £2,000.

3 Amalgamation of existing sole traders

Now assume that Brown was to enter into partnership with T Owens whose last balance sheet is shown in Exhibit 44.5:

Exhibit 44.5

T Owens
Balance Sheet as at 31 December 2006

	£	£
Fixed assets		
Premises		20,000
Fixtures		5,000
		25,000
Current assets		
Stock	6,000	
Debtors	9,000	
Bank	2,000	
	17,000	
Less: Current liabilities		
Creditors	(5,000)	
		12,000
		37,000
Capital		37,000

(a) If the two traders were to amalgamate all their business assets and liabilities, at the values as shown, the opening balance sheet of the partnership would be as in Exhibit 44.6 (remember that Brown's balance sheet is shown above in Exhibit 44.1).

Exhibit 44.6

A Brown & T Owens
Balance Sheet as at 1 January 2007

	£	£
Fixed assets		
Premises		20,000
Fixtures		35,000
		55,000
Current assets		
Stock	14,000	
Debtors	16,000	
Bank	3,000	
	33,000	
Less: Current liabilities		
Creditors	(8,000)	
		25,000
		80,000
Capitals		
Brown		43,000
Owens		37,000
		80,000

(b) Suppose that instead of both parties agreeing to amalgamation at the asset values as shown, the following values had been agreed to:

Owens' premises to be valued at £25,000 and his stock at £5,500; other items as per the balance sheet in Exhibit 44.6. Brown's fixtures to be valued at £33,000; his stock at £7,200 and debtors at £6,400. It is also to be taken that Brown has goodwill of £7,000 whereas Owens' goodwill was considered valueless. Other items are as per the balance sheet in Exhibit 44.6.

The opening balance sheet will be at the revised figures, and is shown as Exhibit 44.7:

Exhibit 44.7

A Brown & T Owens
Balance Sheet as at 1 January 2007

	£	£
Fixed assets		
Goodwill		7,000
Premises		25,000
Fixtures		38,000
		70,000
Current assets		
Stock	12,700	
Debtors	15,400	
Bank	3,000	
	31,100	
Less: Current liabilities		
Creditors	(8,000)	
		23,100
		93,100
Capitals		
Brown		51,600
Owen		41,500
		93,100

Brown's capital can be seen to be £43,000 + £3,000 (fixtures) − £800 (stock) − £600 (debtors) + £7,000 (goodwill) = £51,600.

Owens' capital is £37,000 + £5,000 (premises) − £500 (stock) = £41,500.

4 A limited company acquires the business of a sole trader

In this book, only an elementary treatment of this topic will be considered. More complicated examples will be covered in *Business Accounting UK GAAP 2*.

This time, D Lucas Ltd is taking over Brown's business. For Brown, you need to use the balance sheet shown in Exhibit 44.1. Before the acquisition, the balance sheet of D Lucas Ltd was as shown in Exhibit 44.8:

Exhibit 44.8

D Lucas Ltd
Balance Sheet as at 1 January 2007

	£	£
Fixed assets		
Fixtures		36,000
Current assets		
Stock	23,000	
Debtors	14,000	
Bank	6,000	
	43,000	
Less: Current liabilities		
Creditors	(11,000)	
		32,000
		68,000
Capital and reserves		
Preference shares		20,000
Ordinary shares		40,000
Profit and loss		8,000
		68,000

(a) Assume that Brown's business had been acquired, except for the bank balance, goodwill being valued at £8,000 and the other assets and liabilities at balance sheet values. D Lucas Ltd is to issue an extra 32,000 £1 ordinary shares at par and 18,000 £1 preference shares at par to Brown, in full settlement of the £50,000 net assets taken over.

Exhibit 44.9 presents the summarised balance sheet of the company before and after the acquisition. (Note that the increase in the creditors amount is shown as a minus adjustment as it increases the amount to be deducted from the assets.)

Exhibit 44.9

D Lucas Ltd
Summarised Balance Sheet

	Before £	+ or − £	After £
Goodwill	–	+8,000	8,000
Fixtures	36,000	+30,000	66,000
Stock	23,000	+8,000	31,000
Debtors	14,000	+7,000	21,000
Bank	6,000		6,000
	79,000		132,000
Creditors	(11,000)	−3,000	(14,000)
	68,000		118,000

	Before £	+ or − £	After £
Capital and reserves			
Preference shares	20,000	+18,000	38,000
Ordinary shares	40,000	+32,000	72,000
Profit and loss	8,000		8,000
	68,000		118,000

(b) If instead we assume that the business of Brown was acquired as follows:
The purchase price to be satisfied by Brown being given £5,000 cash and issue an extra 50,000 ordinary shares at par and £10,000 debentures at par. The assets taken over to be valued at Fixtures £28,000; Stock £7,500; Debtors £6,500. The bank balance is not taken over.

Exhibit 44.10 shows the summarised balance sheet of the company after the acquisition. (Note that both the increase in the creditors amount and the debentures are shown as minus adjustments as they increase the amount to be deducted from the assets.)

Exhibit 44.10

D Lucas Ltd
Summarised Balance Sheet

	Before £	+ or − £	After £
Goodwill		+26,000	26,000
Fixtures	36,000	+28,000	64,000
Stock	23,000	+7,500	30,500
Debtors	14,000	+6,500	20,500
Bank	6,000	−5,000	1,000
	79,000		142,000
Creditors	(11,000)	−3,000	(14,000)
	68,000		128,000
Debentures	–	−10,000	(10,000)
	68,000		118,000

	Before £	+ or − £	After £
Capital and reserves			
Preference shares	20,000		20,000
Ordinary shares	40,000	+50,000	90,000
Profit and loss	8,000		8,000
	68,000		118,000

Goodwill is calculated: Purchase consideration is made up of ordinary shares £50,000 + debentures £10,000 + bank £5,000 = £65,000.

Net assets bought are: Fixtures £28,000 + Stock £7,500 + Debtors £6,500 – Creditors £3,000 = £39,000.

Therefore, Goodwill is £65,000 – £39,000 = £26,000.

44.6 Business purchase account

In this chapter, to economise on space and descriptions, only the balance sheets have been shown. However, in the books of the purchaser the purchase of a business should pass through a business purchase account.

This would be as follows:

Business Purchase Account

Debit		*Credit*	
Each liability taken over	(B)	Each asset taken over	
Vendor: net amount of		at values placed on it,	
purchase price	(C)	including goodwill	(A)

Vendor's Account (Name of seller/s)

Debit		*Credit*	
Bank (or share capital)		Amount to be paid	
Amount paid	(D)	for business	(C)

Various Asset Accounts

Debit			
Business purchase (value placed			
on asset taken over)	(A)		

Various Liability Accounts

		Credit	
		Amount of liability	
		taken over	(B)

Bank (or Share Capital)

		Credit	
		Amount paid to vendor	(D)

Learning outcomes

You should now have learnt:

1 That assets purchased when a business is taken over are shown in the purchaser's balance sheet at their valuation, not at the value shown in the closing balance sheet of the seller.

2 That where a greater price is paid than the total valuation of identifiable net assets then the difference is shown as goodwill.

3 That where the purchase price is less than the total valuation of identifiable net assets then the difference is shown as a capital reserve or as negative goodwill (except for limited companies, which *must* show it as negative goodwill).

4 That a limited company may use shares or debentures, as well as cash, to pay for the acquisition of another business.

5 How to enter up the purchase of a business in the purchaser's books.

6 How to draw up the balance sheet of the purchaser after taking over the assets and liabilities of the vendor.

Answers to activities

44.1 These include:

- an individual purchases the business of a sole trader
- an existing sole trader buys the business of another sole trader
- a partnership acquires the business of a sole trader
- a partnership acquires the business of another partnership (this happens quite a lot in accounting partnerships)
- existing businesses of sole traders join together to form a partnership
- a limited company takes over the business of a sole trader
- a limited company takes over the business of a partnership.

44.2 Goodwill. The total amount received less the value of net assets shown in the balance sheet represents the goodwill paid by the purchaser. Adjusting the asset values first simply increases the accounting work to be done by the seller. (In a partnership, the change in value of the assets would need to be shared among the partners, and then followed by a similar series of entries to account for the goodwill.)

44.3 There could be many reasons, including:

- to gain the specialist expertise of the other firm – one may specialise in small business accounts and the other in tax. Combining them removes the need to pay a specialist when they need the expertise the other firm specialises in.
- to save money by relocating the staff of one firm into the offices of the other, enabling the existing offices of the other firm to be sold.

However, the most common reason is to achieve growth. The number of times over the last 15 years or so that the list by size of the largest accounting firms in the UK has changed is testimony to this drive for market dominance through growth.

Review questions

44.1

V A Fraga
Balance Sheet as at 31 March 2006

	£	£
Fixed assets		
Premises		190,000
Current assets		
Stock	39,200	
Debtors	18,417	
Bank	828	
	58,445	
Less: Current liabilities		
Creditors	(23,216)	
		35,229
		225,229
Capital		225,229

Required:

(a) The business of V A Fraga is taken over by T Malloy in its entirety. The assets are deemed to be worth the balance sheet values as shown. The price paid by Malloy is £260,000. Show the opening balance sheet of Malloy.

(b) Suppose instead that F Templar had taken over Fraga's business. He does not take over the bank balance, and values premises at £205,000 and stock at £36,100. The price paid by him is also £260,000. Show the opening balance sheet of Templar.

44.2A I Dodgem's balance sheet as at 31 December 2008 was as follows:

	£	£	£
Fixed assets			
Premises			55,000
Plant and machinery at cost *less* depreciation			21,000
Fixtures and fittings at cost *less* depreciation			4,000
			80,000
Current assets			
Stock		17,000	
Trade debtors		9,500	
Cash		4,500	
		31,000	
Less Current liabilities			
Trade creditors	8,000		
Bank overdraft	15,800		
Expenses owing	200		
		(24,000)	
			7,000
			87,000
Capital			87,000

An opportunity had arisen for Dodgem to acquire the business of A Swing who is retiring.

A Swing
Balance Sheet as at 31 December 2008

	£	£
Fixed assets		
Premises		25,000
Plant		9,000
Motor vehicle		3,500
		37,500
Current assets		
Stock	11,000	
Trade debtors	6,000	
Bank	8,000	
Cash	500	
	25,500	
Less Current liabilities		
Trade creditors	(9,000)	
		16,500
		54,000
Capital		54,000

Dodgem agreed to take over Swing's premises, plant, stock, trade debtors and trade creditors.

For the purpose of his own records Dodgem valued the premises at £35,000, plant at £6,000 and stock at £8,000.

The agreed purchase price was £50,000 and in order to finance the purchase Dodgem had obtained a fixed loan for 5 years from his bank, for one half of the purchase price on the condition that he contributed the same amount from his own private resources in cash. The purchase price was paid on 1 January 2009.

Dodgem also decided to scrap some of his oldest plant and machinery which cost £9,000 with depreciation to date £8,000. This was sold for scrap for £300 cash on 1 January 2009. On the same date he bought one new plant for £4,000, paying in cash.

Required:
(*a*) The purchase of business account in I Dodgem's books.
(*b*) I Dodgem's balance sheet as at 1 January 2009 after all the above transactions have been completed.

(*Associated Examining Board*)

44.3 Spectrum Ltd is a private company with an authorised capital of £700,000 divided into shares of £1 each. 500,000 shares have been issued and are fully paid. The company has been formed to acquire small retail shops and establish a chain of outlets.

The company made offers to three sole traders and purchased the businesses run by Red, Yellow and Blue.

The assets acquired, liabilities taken over, and prices paid are listed below:

	Red	Yellow	Blue
	£	£	£
Premises	75,000	80,000	90,000
Delivery vans	7,000	–	10,000
Furniture and fittings	12,000	13,000	13,000
Stock	8,000	7,000	12,000
Creditors	6,000	8,000	7,000
Purchase price	120,000	130,000	150,000

The company also purchased a warehouse to be used as a central distribution store for £60,000. This has been paid.

Preliminary expenses (formation expenses) of £15,000 have also been paid.

→

→ The company took over the three shops outlined above and started trading on 1 January 2002.
Approaches have also been made to Green for the purchase of his business for £100,000. Green
has accepted the offer and the company will take over in the near future the following assets and
liabilities:

	£
Premises	70,000
Stock	18,000
Creditors	3,000

The transaction had not been completed on 1 January 2002 and Green was still running his own
business.

(a) Prepare the opening balance sheet of Spectrum Ltd as at 1 January 2002.
(b) How would you advise Spectrum Ltd to finance the purchase of Green's business when the deal
is completed?

(*Edexcel Foundation, London Examinations (University of London)*)

44.4 Dinho and Manueli are in partnership sharing profits and losses equally after interest of
10% on each partner's capital account in excess of £100,000. At 31 December 2008, the partnership
trial balance was:

	Dr £	Cr £
Ban		56,700
Capital accounts: Dinho		194,000
Manueli		123,000
Creditors		85,800
Debtors	121,000	
Equipment, at cost	85,000	
Long-term loan		160,000
Freehold property	290,000	
Provision for depreciation on equipment		20,000
Stocks	143,500	
	639,500	639,500

On 31 December 2008, the partnership was converted to a limited company, Bin Ltd. All the partnership assets and liabilities were taken over by the company in exchange for shares in Bin Ltd valued
at £304,000. The share capital was allocated so as to preserve the rights previously enjoyed by the
partners under their partnership agreement.

The assets and liabilities and shares issued were all entered in the books of Bin Ltd at
31 December. In the company's books, the debtors were recorded at £116,000 and the freehold
property was valued at £260,000.

On 1 January 2009, Pa invested £120,000 in the company and was issued shares on the same
basis as had been applied when deciding the share allocations to Dinho and Manueli – i.e. as if he
had been an equal partner in the partnership.

Pa had previously been an employee of the partnership earning £40,000 per annum. The
£120,000 he invested in the company had been earning interest of 6% per annum from the bank.
His salary will continue to be paid.

Assume that all profits will be paid as dividends. Ignore taxation.

Required:
(a) Prepare the partnership realisation account after the sale of the business to Bin Ltd had been
completed and recorded in the partnership books.
(b) Prepare Bin Ltd's balance sheet as at 1 January 2009 after the purchase of shares by Pa.
(c) Calculate the annual profit that Bin Ltd needs to make before it pays any dividends if Pa is to
receive the same amount of income as he was receiving before buying shares in Bin Ltd.

Part 7

AN INTRODUCTION TO
FINANCIAL ANALYSIS

Introduction

This part deals with the interpretation of figures contained in
financial statements using ratio analysis.

An introduction to the analysis and interpretation of accounting statements

Learning objectives

After you have studied this chapter, you should be able to:

- explain how the use of ratios can help to analyse the profitability, liquidity, efficiency and capital structure of businesses
- calculate the main accounting ratios
- interpret the results of calculating accounting ratios
- explain the advantages and disadvantages of the gearing of an organisation being high or low
- explain how the proportion of costs that are fixed and variable impacts profit at different levels of activity
- explain the relevance of FRS 18 and accounting standards in general to the preparation of financial statements

Introduction

In this chapter, you'll learn how to calculate and interpret the most commonly used accounting ratios. You'll learn how to assess an organisation's profitability, liquidity, efficiency, and capital structure using ratio analysis. In addition, you'll learn more about FRS 18 and its importance and that of accounting standards in general to the preparation of financial statements.

45.1 The need for ratios

Without ratios, financial statements would be largely uninformative to all but the very skilled. With ratios, financial statements can be interpreted and usefully applied to satisfy the needs of the reader.

For example, let's take the performance of four companies, all dealing in the same type of goods:

	Gross profit £	Sales £
Company A	200,000	848,000
Company B	300,000	1,252,000
Company C	500,000	1,927,500
Company D	350,000	1,468,400

policies have been used when preparing such statements. This FRS was issued to help continue the improvement in the quality of financial reporting that had been started in 1971 by the accounting standard it replaced, SSAP 2.

The FRS focuses upon **accounting policies** and considers the **estimation techniques** used in implementing them. It also looks in detail at the various accounting concepts that you covered earlier when you worked through Chapter 10.

Accounting policies

These are defined in FRS 18 as:

those principles, bases, conventions, rules and practices applied by an entity that specify how the effects of transactions and other events are to be reflected in its financial statements through:

(i)   recognising,
(ii) selecting measurement basis for, and
(iii) presenting

assets, liabilities, gains, losses and changes to shareholders' funds.

Accounting policies, therefore, define the processes whereby transactions and other events are reflected in the financial statements. The accounting policies selected should enable the financial statements to give a true and fair view and should be consistent with accounting standards, UITFs, and company legislation.

When selecting an accounting policy, its appropriateness should be considered in the context of four 'objectives' that financial information must possess:

● **Relevance** – Does it produce information that is useful for assessing stewardship and for making economic decisions?
● **Reliability** – Does it reflect the substance of the transaction and other events that have occurred? Is it free of bias, i.e. neutral? Is it free of material error? If produced under uncertainty, has prudence been exercised?
● **Comparability** – Can it be compared with similar information about the entity for some other period or point in time?
● **Understandability** – Is it capable of being understood by users who have a reasonable knowledge of business and economic activities and accounting?

Estimation techniques

These are the methods adopted in order to arrive at estimated monetary amounts for items that appear in the financial statements.

Activity 45.3 From your knowledge of accounting, what do you think these methods may include? Think about this for a minute and then write down as many examples of estimation techniques as you can think of.

Examples of accounting policies

● The treatment of gains and losses on disposals of fixed assets – they could be applied to adjust the depreciation charge for the period, or they may appear as separate items in the financial statements.

● The classification of overheads in the financial statements – for example, some indirect costs may be included in the trading account section of the trading and profit and loss account, or they may be included in administration costs in the profit and loss account section of the trading and profit and loss account.
● The treatment of interest costs incurred in connection with the construction of fixed assets – these could be charged to profit and loss as a finance cost, or they could be capitalised and added to the other costs of creating the fixed assets (this is permitted by the relevant accounting standard, FRS 15).

Identifying whether an accounting policy has changed

This is done by considering whether any of three aspects have changed:

● **Recognition** – some items may be recognised in more than one way. For example, SSAP 13 allows expenditure on developing new products to be recognised either as a profit and loss expense or as an asset in the balance sheet.
● **Presentation** – how something is presented in the financial statements. For example, where certain indirect costs appear in the profit and loss account.
● **Measurement basis** – the monetary aspects of the items in the financial statements, such as the basis of the stock valuation, say FIFO or LIFO.

If any of these three aspects have changed, it represents a change in accounting policy. If they haven't, something else has occurred, for example, the estimation technique in use. If depreciation was changed from straight line to reducing balance this would be **a change in estimation technique**, not a change in accounting policy. On the other hand, a decision to switch from valuing stock using FIFO to LIFO would constitute **a change in accounting policy** as the measurement basis had changed.

45.10 Further thoughts on concepts and conventions

In Chapter 10, you were introduced to the concepts and conventions used in accounting. Since then further chapters have consolidated your knowledge on specific points.

In recent years there has been a considerable change in the style of examinations in accounting at all levels. At one time nearly every examination question was purely computational, requiring you to prepare financial statements, draft journal entries, extract a trial balance and so on. Now, *in addition* to all that (which is still important) there are quite a lot of questions asking such things as:

● **Why do we do it?**
● **What does it mean?**
● **How does it relate to the concepts and conventions of accounting?**

Such questions depend very much on the interests and ingenuity of examiners. They like to set questions worded to find out those who can understand and interpret financial information, and eliminate those who cannot and simply try to repeat information learned by rote.

The examiners will often draw on knowledge from any part of the syllabus. It is therefore impossible for a student (or an author) to guess exactly how an examiner will select a question and how he will word it.

An example of this is where the examiner could ask you to show how different concepts contradict one another. Someone who has just read about the concepts, and memorised them, could not answer this unless they had thought further about it. **Think about whether or not you could have answered that question before you read further.**

One instance is the use of the concept of consistency. Basically it says that one should keep to the same method of entering an item each year. Yet if the net realisable value of stock is less than cost, then the normal method of showing it at cost should be abandoned and the net realisable value used instead. Thus, at the end of one period, stock may be shown at cost and at the end of the next period it will be shown at net realisable value. In this case the concept of prudence has overridden the concept of consistency.

Another instance of this is that of calculating profit based on sales whether they have been paid for or not. If the prudence concept were taken to extremes, then profit would only be calculated on a sale when the sale had been paid for. Instead, the realisation concept has overridden the prudence concept so you recognise a sale when it is reasonably certain that it will be paid for.

Review questions 45.11 to 45.20 are typical examination questions which obviously relate to concepts and conventions, and to general understanding of the subject.

45.11 Other accounting standards

As well as the accounting standards that you have read about in this book, there are some other standards which may appear in your examinations. We will cover them briefly here.

SSAP 13: Research and Development and IAS 38: Intangible Assets

Money spent on research and development presents a problem for accountants. You could argue that:

● Such costs are incurred so that profits can be earned in the future, and should therefore be carried forward to those future periods.
● Just because you have incurred such costs, you cannot be certain about future profitability occurring. It should therefore be written off as an expense in the period when the costs are incurred.

The costs can be divided between:

● **Pure (basic) research.** This is carried out to advance scientific and technical knowledge, but without any specific objective.
● **Applied research.** This utilises pure research undertaken so that a specific objective can be attained.
● **Development.** Work undertaken to develop new or existing products or services. This has to be carried out before commercial operations can begin.

SSAP 13 requires that both pure research and applied research costs be written off in the year they are incurred.

However, with development costs, if certain conditions are met, then they may be carried forward to future periods.

FRS 21: Events after the Balance Sheet Date

The balance sheet is supposed to reflect the financial position of an organisation at the balance sheet date. However, between the balance sheet date and the date when the financial statements are authorised for issue, certain events may occur. These may mean that the financial statements need to be amended.

The events can be divided between:

● **Adjusting events.** When these exist, the financial statements must be amended.
● **Non-adjusting events.** These do not lead to amendments to the financial statements, but they may be shown as notes accompanying the financial statements.

FRS 12: Provisions, Contingent Liabilities and Contingent Assets

FRS 12 defines a provision as

a liability that is of uncertain timing or amount, to be settled by the transfer of economic benefits.

A provision should only be recognised when it is probable that a transfer of economic benefits will have to occur and a reasonable estimate can be made of the amount involved.

FRS 12 defines a contingent liability as:

either a possible obligation arising from past events whose existence will be confirmed only by the occurrence of one or more uncertain future events not wholly within the entity's control; or a present obligation that arises from past events but is not recognised because it is not probable that a transfer of economic benefits will be required to settle the obligation or because the amount of the obligation cannot be measured with sufficient reliability.

An example of this could be where a legal action is being carried on, but the case has not yet been decided. For instance, a company may have been sued for £10 million damages, but the case is not yet over. The company may or may not have to pay the damages, but the case is so complex that it has no way of knowing.

FRS 12 defines a contingent asset as:

a possible asset arising from past events whose existence will be confirmed only by the occurrence of one or more uncertain events not wholly within the entity's control.

Neither contingent liabilities nor contingent assets should be recognised. This is consistent with the prudence concept, as defined in FRS 18.

FRSSE: Financial Reporting Standard for Smaller Entities

This accounting standard provides a simplified version of the body of UK accounting standards and is for use by 'smaller entities', i.e. small companies and other organisations that would be classified as 'small' were they companies. According to the Companies Act 2006, a 'small' company is one that does not exceed two or more of the following criteria:

Turnover	£5.6 million
Balance sheet total	£2.8 million
Average number of employees	50

The FRSSE is applicable to the great majority of companies and will, undoubtedly, feature increasingly in both examinations and in the work undertaken by accountants. There is no direct equivalent international accounting standard.

Learning outcomes

You should now have learnt:

1 That comparing the trends to see if the ratios are getting better or worse as each period passes is essential for proper control. Prompt action needs to be taken where the trend in a ratio is deteriorating.

2 The importance of interpreting ratios in their context: that is, against those of other similar businesses or against the same ratios calculated for the same organisation using data from other time periods.

3 That a business must be both profitable *and* sufficiently liquid to be successful. One factor without the other can lead to serious trouble.

4 That careful credit control to ensure that the debtor/sales ratio is not too high is usually essential to the well-being of any business.

5 That gearing affects the risk factor for ordinary share investors. High gearing means greater risk whilst low gearing means lower risks.

6 How to calculate and interpret the most commonly used ratios.

7 The relevance of ratio analysis to an assessment of liquidity, efficiency, profitability and capital structure.

8 That the relative amounts of fixed and variable costs can affect profit significantly when there are swings in business activity.

9 The importance of FRS 18, and accounting standards in general to the preparation of financial statements.

Answers to activities

45.1 The only difference in the items involved between the two ratios is that the acid test (or 'quick') ratio does not include stock. Otherwise, it is identical to the current ratio, comparing current assets *other than stock* to current liabilities.

45.2 Stock is omitted as it is considered to be relatively illiquid, because it depends upon prevailing and future market forces and may be impossible to convert to cash in a relatively short time.

45.3 All depreciation methods and methods used to estimate doubtful debts are the main ones we have encountered so far in this book. However, we've also looked at asset revaluation, another aspect of accounting for which the methods adopted in arriving at the valuation would be considered estimation techniques. Basically, any method used to arrive at an *estimated* figure shown in the financial statements is an estimation technique. So, to answer the question fully, you need to make a list of all those items that appear in financial statements that are estimates. The methods used to arrive at the value used for those figures are all estimation techniques. This would include, for example, the method used in order to arrive at the proportion of an electricity bill spanning the period end that belongs in the period for which the financial statements are being prepared. More obviously, estimates may be required for bad debts, inventory obsolescence, and the useful lives or consumption pattern of fixed assets.

Review questions

45.1 You are to study the following financial statements for two furniture stores and then answer the questions which follow.

Financial Statements

	X		Y	
	£	£	£	£
Profit and loss accounts				
Sales		555,000		750,000
Less Cost of goods sold				
Opening stock	100,000		80,000	
Add Purchases	200,000		320,000	
	300,000		400,000	
Less Closing stock	(60,000)	(240,000)	(70,000)	(330,000)
Gross profit		315,000		420,000
Less Depreciation	5,000		15,000	
Wages, salaries and commission	165,000		220,000	
Other expenses	45,000	(215,000)	35,000	(270,000)
Net profit		100,000		150,000
Balance sheets				
Fixed assets				
Equipment at cost	50,000		100,000	
Less Depreciation to date	(40,000)	10,000	(30,000)	70,000
Current assets				
Stock	60,000		70,000	
Debtors	125,000		100,000	
Bank	25,000		12,500	
	210,000		182,500	
Less Current liabilities				
Creditors	(104,000)	106,000	(100,500)	82,000
		116,000		152,000
Financed by:				
Capitals				
Balance at start of year		76,000		72,000
Add Net profit		100,000		150,000
		176,000		222,000
Less Drawings		(60,000)		(70,000)
		116,000		152,000

Required:

(a) Calculate the following ratios for each business:
  (i)   gross profit as percentage of sales;
  (ii) net profit as percentage of sales;
  (iii) expenses as percentage of sales;
  (iv) stock turnover;
  (v)   rate of return of net profit on capital employed (use the average of the capital account for this purpose);
  (vi) current ratio;
  (vii) acid test ratio;
  (viii) debtor/sales ratio;
  (ix) creditor/purchases ratio.

(b) Drawing upon all your knowledge of accounting, comment upon the differences and similarities of the accounting ratios for X and Y. Which business seems to be the most efficient? Give possible reasons.

→

→ **45.4** The summarised accounts of Hope (Eternal Springs) Ltd for the years 2008 and 2009 are given below.

Trading and Profit and Loss Accounts for the years ended 31 December

	2008		2009	
	£000	£000	£000	£000
Sales		200		280
Less Cost of sales		(150)		(210)
Gross profit		50		70
Less				
Administration expenses	38		46	
Debenture interest	–		4	
		(38)		(50)
Net profit		12		20

Balance Sheets as at 31 December

	2008		2009	
	£000	£000	£000	£000
Fixed assets at cost *less* depreciation		110		140
Stock	20		30	
Debtors	25		28	
Bank	–		5	
	45		63	
Creditors	(15)		(12)	
Bank	(10)		–	
		20		51
		130		191
8% Debentures		(–)		(50)
		130		141
Ordinary share capital		100		100
Profit and Loss Account		30		41
		130		141

Stock at 1 January 2008 was £50,000.

Required:

(a) Calculate the following ratios for 2008 and 2009:
   (i) Gross profit: Sales
   (ii) Stock turnover
   (iii) Net profit: Sales
   (iv) Quick ('acid test')
   (v) Working capital
   (vi) Net profit: Capital employed

(b) State the possible reasons for and significance of any changes in the ratios shown by your calculations.

(*Midland Examining Group: GCSE*)

45.5A The following figures are for AB Engineering Supplies Ltd at 31 December 2009:

	£000	£000
Turnover		160
Gross profit		40
Average stock at cost price		10
Expenses		8
Fixed assets		108
Current assets		
Stock	10	
Debtors	8	
Bank	2	
		20
		128
Current liabilities		(10)
		118
Capital		118

(a) Calculate:
   (i) gross profit as a percentage of the sales;
   (ii) rate of stock turnover;
   (iii) net profit as a percentage of sales;
   (iv) net profit as a percentage of total capital employed (fixed assets plus current assets);
   (v) current ratio;
   (vi) quick asset (acid test) ratio.

(b) The following figures are for another firm in the same line of business, CD Engineering Services Ltd, for the year ended 31 December 2009.

	CD Engineering Services Ltd
Gross profit as a percentage of the sales	25%
Rate of stock turnover	9
Net profit as a percentage of sales	10%
Net profit as a percentage of total capital employed	$12\frac{1}{2}$%
Current ratio	1 : 1
Quick asset (acid test) ratio	0.5 : 1

Compare your results in (a) with those given for CD Engineering Services Ltd.

As a result of your comparison, say which you think was the more successful business during 2009, giving your reasons.

(*Northern Examinations and Assessment Board: GCSE*)

→

45.6A Galloway Ltd has an authorised capital of 250,000 ordinary shares of £1 each.

(a) At the end of its financial year, 30 April 2008, the following balances remained in the company's books after preparation of trading and profit and loss accounts.

	£
Motor vehicles:	
at cost	38,400
provision for depreciation	16,300
Net profit for year	36,600
Freehold premises at cost	190,000
Stock in trade	32,124
Share capital: 200,000 ordinary shares of £1 each, fully paid	200,000
Insurance prepaid	280
Profit and loss account balance brought forward	3,950
Wages and salaries due	774
General reserve	24,000
Trade creditors	3,847
Trade debtors	4,782
8% debentures	15,000
Rent receivable outstanding	175
Bank overdraft	1,830
Furniture and equipment:	
at cost	44,000
provision for depreciation	7,460

The directors have proposed

(i) the transfer of £5,000 to the general reserve
(ii) a final dividend on the ordinary shares of 12.5%.

(b) Galloway Ltd's directors are making an assessment of the company's performance for the year. They are concerned by a decline in both profitability and liquidity despite an increase in turnover.

Required:
1 THREE significant differences between ordinary shares and debentures.
2 For Galloway Ltd
  (i) a profit and loss appropriation account for the year ended 30 April 2008
  (ii) a balance sheet as at 30 April 2008 in a form which shows clearly:
    total shareholders' funds
    working capital.
3 Concerning the company's performance
  (i) Name ONE ratio which could be used to assess profitability.
  (ii) State TWO possible reasons why the profitability ratio may have declined despite increased turnover.
  (iii) Name ONE ratio, other than working capital ratio, which could be used to assess liquidity.
  (iv) Give FOUR suggestions as to how working capital could be increased during the year ahead.

(*Southern Examining Group: GCSE*)

45.7 The trading stock of Joan Street, retailer, has been reduced during the year ended 31 March 2008 by £6,000 from its commencing figure of £21,000.

A number of financial ratios and related statistics have been compiled relating to the business of Joan Street for the year ended 31 March 2008. These are shown below alongside comparative figures for a number of retailers who are members of the trade association to which Joan Street belongs:

	Joan Street	Trade association
	%	%
Net profit as % net capital employed[Authors' Note]	15	16
$\dfrac{\text{Net profit}}{\text{Sales}}$	9	8
$\dfrac{\text{Sales}}{\text{Net capital employed}}$	$166^2/_3$	200
$\dfrac{\text{Fixed assets}}{\text{Sales}}$	45	35
Working capital ratio:		
$\dfrac{\text{Current assets}}{\text{Current liabilities}}$	400	$287^1/_2$
Acid test ratio:		
$\dfrac{\text{Bank} + \text{Debtors}}{\text{Current liabilities}}$	275	$187^1/_2$
$\dfrac{\text{Gross profit}}{\text{Sales}}$	25	26
Debtors collection period:		
$\dfrac{\text{Debtors} \times 365}{\text{Sales}}$	$36^1/_2$ days	$32^{17}/_{20}$ days
Stock turnover (based on average stock for the year)	10 times	8 times

Joan Street has supplied all the capital for her business and has had no drawings from the business during the year ending 31 March 2008.

Required:
(a) Prepare the trading and profit and loss account for the year ending 31 March 2008 and balance sheet as at that date of Joan Street in as much detail as possible.
(b) Identify two aspects of Joan Street's results for the year ending 31 March 2008 which compare favourably with the trade association's figures and identify two aspects which compare unfavourably.
(c) Outline two drawbacks of the type of comparison used in this question.

Authors' Note: **take the closing figure at 31 March 2008.**

(*Association of Accounting Technicians*)

45.8A Harold Smart, who is a small manufacturer trading as Space Age Projects, is very pleased with his recently completed financial results which show that a planned 20% increase in turnover has been achieved in the last accounting year.

→

The summarised results relating to the last three financial years are as follows:

Year ended 30 September		2007	2008	2009
		£	£	£
Sales		90,000	100,000	120,000
Cost of sales		(74,000)	(75,000)	(92,000)
Gross profit		16,000	25,000	28,000
Administrative overheads		(3,000)	(5,000)	(6,000)
Net profit		13,000	20,000	22,000

As at 30 September	2006	2007	2008	2009
	£	£	£	£
Fixed assets:				
At cost	155,000	165,000	190,000	206,000
Provision for depreciation	(42,000)	(45,000)	(49,000)	(53,000)
	113,000	120,000	141,000	153,000
Current assets:				
Stock	3,000	4,000	7,000	30,000
Debtors	14,000	19,000	15,000	10,000
Balance at bank	2,000	1,000	3,000	–
	19,000	24,000	25,000	40,000
Current liabilities:				
Creditors	5,000	4,000	6,000	9,000
Bank overdraft	–	–	–	2,000
	5,000	4,000	6,000	11,000

Since 30 September 2006, Harold Smart has not taken any drawings from the business.

Harold Smart has been invited recently to invest £150,000 for a 5-year fixed term in government loan stock earning interest at $12\frac{1}{2}$% per annum.

Note: Taxation is to be ignored.

Notwithstanding his response to these financial results, Harold Smart is a very cautious person and therefore has asked a financial consultant for a report.

Required:
(a) A schedule of six accounting ratios or measures of resource utilisation covering each of the three years ended 30 September 2009 of Space Age Projects.
(b) As financial consultant prepare a report to Harold Smart on the financial results of Space Age Projects given above including comments on the alternative future actions that he might take.

Note: Reports should utilise the information given in answers to part (a) of this question.

(Association of Accounting Technicians)

45.9 Business A and Business B are both engaged in retailing, but seem to take a different approach to this trade according to the information available. This information consists of a table of ratios, shown below:

Ratio	Business A	Business B
Current ratio	2 : 1	1.5 : 1
Quick assets (acid test) ratio	1.7 : 1	0.7 : 1
Return on capital employed (ROCE)	20%	17%
Return on shareholders' funds (ROSF)	30%	18%
Debtors turnover	63 days	21 days
Creditors turnover	50 days	45 days
Gross profit percentage	40%	15%
Net profit percentage	10%	10%
Stock turnover	52 days	25 days

Required:
(a) Explain briefly how each ratio is calculated.
(b) Describe what this information indicates about the differences in approach between the two businesses. If one of them prides itself on personal service and one of them on competitive prices, which do you think is which and why?

(*Association of Chartered Certified Accountants*)

45.10A You are given summarised information about two firms in the same line of business, A and B, as follows.

Balance sheets at 30 June		A			B	
	£000	£000	£000	£000	£000	£000
Land			80			260
Buildings		120			200	
Less: Depreciation		(40)			–	
			80			200
Plant		90			150	
Less: Depreciation		(70)			(40)	
			20			110
			180			570
Stocks		80			100	
Debtors		100			90	
Bank		–			10	
		180			200	
Creditors	110			120		
Bank	50			–		
		(160)			(120)	
			20			80
			200			650
Capital at start of year			100			300
Add: Profit for year			30			100
			130			400
Less: Drawings			(30)			(40)
			100			360
Land revaluation			–			160
Loan (10% p.a.)			100			130
			200			650
Sales			1,000			3,000
Cost of sales			400			2,000

Required:
(a) Produce a table of eight ratios calculated for both businesses.
(b) Write a report briefly outlining the strengths and weaknesses of the two businesses. Include comment on any major areas where the simple use of the figures could be misleading.

(*Association of Chartered Certified Accountants*)

45.11 The following letter has been received from a client. 'I gave my bank manager those audited accounts you prepared for last year. But he says he needs more information before he will agree to increase my overdraft. What could he possibly want to know that he can't get from those accounts? If they are not good enough why bother to prepare them?'

Required:
Outline the major points which should be included in a reply to this letter.

(*Association of Chartered Certified Accountants*)

→

→ **45.12** An acquaintance of yours, H Gee, has recently set up in business for the first time as a general dealer.

The majority of his sales will be on credit to trade buyers but he will sell some goods to the public for cash.

He is not sure at which point of the business cycle he can regard his cash and credit sales to have taken place.

After seeking guidance on this matter from his friends, he is thoroughly confused by the conflicting advice he has received. Samples of the advice he has been given include:

The sale takes place when:

(*i*) 'you have bought goods which you know you should be able to sell easily';
(*ii*) 'the customer places the order';
(*iii*) 'you deliver the goods to the customer';
(*iv*) 'you invoice the goods to the customer';
(*v*) 'the customer pays for the goods';
(*vi*) 'the customer's cheque has been cleared by the bank'.

He now asks you to clarify the position for him.

Required:
(a) Write notes for Gee, setting out, in as easily understood a manner as possible, the accounting conventions and principles which should generally be followed when recognising sales revenue.
(b) Examine each of the statements (*i*) to (*vi*) above and advise Gee (stating your reasons) whether the method advocated is appropriate to the particular circumstances of his business.

(*Association of Chartered Certified Accountants*)

45.13 The annual final accounts of businesses are normally prepared on the assumption that the business is a going concern.

Required:
Explain and give a simple illustration of:

(a) the effect of this convention on the figures which appear in those final accounts.
(b) the implications for the final accounts figures if this convention were deemed to be inoperative.

(*Association of Chartered Certified Accountants*)

45.14 One of the well known accounting concepts is that of materiality.

Required:
(a) Explain what is meant by this concept.
(b) State and explain three types of situation to which this concept might be applicable.
(c) State and explain two specific difficulties in applying this concept.

(*Association of Chartered Certified Accountants*)

45.15 State three classes of people, other than managers and owners, who are likely to need to use financial accounting information. Discuss whether you think their requirements are compatible.

(*Association of Chartered Certified Accountants*)

45.16 A business produces a standard manufactured product. The stages of the production and sale of the product may be summarised as follows:

Stage	A	B	C	D
Activity	Raw material	WIP-I	WIP-II	Finished product
	£	£	£	£
Costs to date	100	120	150	170
Net realisable value	80	130	190	300
Stage	E	F	G	H
Activity	For sale	Sale agreed	Delivered	Paid for
	£	£	£	£
Costs to date	170	170	180	180
Net realisable value	300	300	300	300

Required:
(a) What general rule do accountants apply when deciding when to recognise revenue on any particular transaction?
(b) Apply this rule to the above situation. State and explain the stage at which you think revenue will be recognised by accountants.
(c) How much would the gross profit on a unit of this product be? Why?
(d) Suggest arguments in favour of delaying the recognition of revenue until Stage H.
(e) Suggest arguments in favour of recognising revenue in appropriate successive amounts at Stages B, C and D.

(Association of Chartered Certified Accountants)

45.17

(a) In accounting practice a distinction is drawn between the terms 'reserves' and 'provisions' and between 'accrued expenses' and 'creditors'.

Required:
Briefly define each of the four terms quoted and explain the effect of each on the preparation of accounts.

(b) While preparing the final accounts for year ended 30 September 2007, the accountant of Lanep Lighting Ltd had to deal with the following matters:
(i) the exterior of the company's premises was being repaired. The contractors had started work in August but were unlikely to finish before the end of November 2007. The total cost would not be known until after completion. Cost of work carried out to 30 September 2007 was estimated at £21,000;
(ii) the company rented a sales showroom from Commercial Properties plc at a rental of £6,000 per annum payable half yearly in arrears on 1 August and 1 February;
(iii) on 3 October 2007 an invoice was received for £2,500 less a trade discount of 30 per cent, from Lucifer Ltd for goods for resale supplied during September 2007;
(iv) the directors of Lanep Lighting Ltd have decided that an annual amount of £5,000 should be set aside, starting with year ended 30 Sept 2007, for the purpose of plant replacement.

Required:
State the accounting treatment which should be accorded to each of the above matters in the Lanep Lighting Ltd profit and loss account for year ending 30 September 2007 and balance sheet at that date.

(Association of Chartered Certified Accountants)

45.18 Bradwich plc is a medium-sized engineering company whose shares are listed on a major Stock Exchange.
It has recently applied to its bankers for a 7-year loan of £500,000 to finance a modernisation and expansion programme.

Mr Whitehall, a recently retired civil servant, is contemplating investing £10,000 of his lump sum pension in the company's ordinary shares in order to provide both an income during his retirement and a legacy to his grandchildren after his death.

The bank and Mr Whitehall have each acquired copies of the company's most recent annual report and accounts.

Required:

(*a*) State, separately for each of the two parties, those aspects of the company's performance and financial position which would be of particular interest and relevance to their respective interests.

(*b*) State, separately for each of the two parties, the formula of four ratios which would assist in measuring or assessing the matters raised in your answer to (*a*).

(*Association of Chartered Certified Accountants*)

45.19 Explain what you understand by the accounting term 'capital gearing', showing clearly the benefits of, and the potential problems associated with, high gearing.

(*Scottish Qualifications Authority*)

45.20A What benefits can result through the use of ratios and what limitations should be imposed on any conclusions drawn from their use?

You can find a range of additional self-test questions, as well as material to help you with your studies, on the website that accompanies this book at **www.pearsoned.co.uk/wood**

OTHER TOPICS

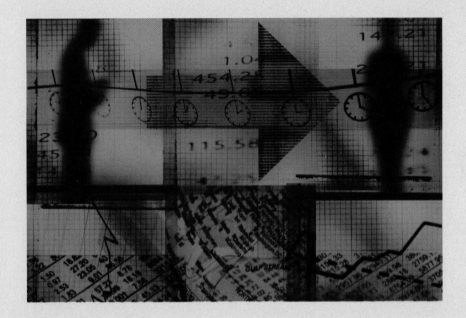

Introduction

This part presents some of the differences between UK GAAP and International GAAP; and introduces the management accounting side of accounting and looks at how costs can be gathered and utilised in decision-making within an organisation.

46

International GAAP

Learning objectives

After you have studied this chapter, you should be able to:

- explain some major differences in terminology between UK GAAP and International GAAP
- explain the differences between trading, profit and loss accounts and income statements
- explain the differences between UK GAAP balance sheets and International GAAP balance sheets
- explain the differences between UK GAAP cash flow statements and International GAAP statements of cash flows

Introduction

The International Accounting Standards Board was mentioned briefly in Chapter 10. The IASB is responsible for issuing International Financial Reporting Standards and International Accounting Standards (the previous name used). There are (November 2007) 8 IFRSs and 29 IASs currently in use. International GAAP is the underlying regulatory framework established by those standards.

Since, 2005, International GAAP must be adopted in the UK and Ireland by all companies listed on the Stock Exchange preparing consolidated financial statements. All other reporting entities may adopt International GAAP in place of UK GAAP (which is the underlying regulatory framework followed in this book) if they wish. To date, most entities have continued to apply UK GAAP but, eventually, all entities will use International GAAP.

This chapter will introduce you to the terminology differences between International GAAP and UK GAAP and then show you the differing layouts used under International GAAP for some of the main financial statements.

46.1 Terminology differences

The following table shows the most important terminological differences between the two versions of GAAP.

Table 46.1 Differences in terminology: UK GAAP and International GAAP

UK GAAP	International GAAP
Cash flow statement	Statement of cash flows
Creditors	Accounts payable
Debentures	Loan notes
Debtors	Accounts receivable
Exceptional item	– (does not exist)
Fixed assets	Non-current assets
Long-term liabilities	Non-current liabilities
Profit and loss account (in the balance sheet)	Retained profits
Provision for doubtful debts	Allowance for doubtful debts
Sales	Revenue
Stock	Inventory
Trading and profit and loss account	Income statement

46.2 Differences in presentation of the financial statements

Trading and profit and loss account v Income statement

Below are two financial statements (Exhibits 46.1 and 46.2). Other than for the positioning of goodwill, they contain the same information down to the figure for profit for the year. The first is under UK GAAP and the second is under International GAAP.

Exhibit 46.1 UK GAAP

Trading and Profit and Loss Account for the year ending 31 December 2008

	£	£
Sales		1,022,000
Less Cost of goods sold:		
Opening stock	84,912	
Add Purchases	439,100	
Add Carriage inwards	6,200	
	530,212	
Less Closing stock	(91,413)	
		(438,799)
Gross profit		583,201
Less Expenses:		
Salaries and wages	192,400	
Motor expenses	3,120	
Business rates and insurances	8,690	
General expenses	5,600	
Directors' remuneration	123,000	
Debenture interest	30,000	
Depreciation: Buildings	10,000	
Equipment	12,000	
Motor vehicles	18,000	
		(402,810)
Profit for the year before taxation		180,391
Less Corporation tax		(50,000)
Profit for the year after taxation		130,391
Add Retained profits from last year		43,212
		173,603
Less Appropriations:		
Transfer to general reserve	10,000	
Goodwill part written off	30,000	
Ordinary share dividends:		
Interim	35,000	
		(75,000)
Retained profits carried forward		98,603

Exhibit 46.2 International GAAP

Income Statement for the year ending 31 December 2008

	£	£
Revenue		1,022,000
Less Cost of goods sold:		
Opening inventory	84,912	
Add Purchases	439,100	
Add Carriage inwards	6,200	
	530,212	
Less Closing inventory	(91,413)	
		(438,799)
Gross profit		583,201
Less Expenses:		
Salaries and wages	192,400	
Motor expenses	3,120	
Business rates and insurances	8,690	
General expenses	5,600	
Directors' remuneration	123,000	
Loan note interest	30,000	
Goodwill impairment	30,000	
Depreciation: Buildings	10,000	
Equipment	12,000	
Motor vehicles	18,000	
		(432,810)
Profit for the year before taxation		150,391
Less Corporation tax		(50,000)
Profit for the year		100,391

The appropriations of dividends paid and transfers to other reserves are shown in a Statement of Changes in Equity.

An introduction to management accounting

Learning objectives

After you have studied this chapter, you should be able to:

- explain why cost accounting is needed for there to be an effective management accounting system
- explain why the benefits of operating a costing system should always outweigh the costs of operating it
- explain what characteristic must exist before anything can be described as information
- explain why different costs are often needed when making decisions about the future compared to those that are used to calculate profit in the past
- explain which costing approach is the relevant one to use when considering a change in what and/or how much is produced
- explain what is meant by marginal cost and why selling prices should always exceed it
- explain why budgets are prepared
- describe the role of management accountants in the budgetary process
- describe the relationship between financial accounting data and management accounting data

Introduction

In this chapter, you'll learn about the importance of data being suitable for the purpose for which it is to be used and of the need for information to be useful. You'll learn how costs are recorded and of two of the most used approaches to costing. You'll also learn about systems of costing and of the importance of budgeting, not just to business but also to the role of the management accountant. Finally, you will learn about how management accounting data often forms the basis of data used in financial accounting.

47.1 Background

So far, you have learnt about bookkeeping and the preparation of financial statements. In accounting, these are the two components of what is known as financial accounting. The information that is produced by financial accounting is usually historical, backwards looking and, mainly, for the use of decision-makers external to the organisation to which the data relates. You learnt about the sort of things that are done with this information in Chapter 45.

> **Activity 47.1** What sort of things are done with this information?

There is a second side to accounting. This one looks forwards and the output from it is used by decision-makers within the organisation. It also consists of two components: one where costs are recorded and one where the data is processed and converted into reports for managers and other decision-makers. The cost recording component is called **cost accounting** and the processing and reporting component is called **management accounting**, which is also the name used to refer to this side of accounting. It is also sometimes referred to as 'managerial accounting'.

47.2 Cost accounting

Cost accounting is needed so that there can be an effective management accounting system. Without a study of costs such a system could not exist. Before entering into any detailed description of costs it is better if we first ask what use we are going to make of information about costs in the business.

This can best be done by referring to something which is not accounting, and then relating it to accounting. Suppose that your employer asked you to 'measure the distance between Manchester and London', but walked away from you without giving any further information. As you thought about the request the following thoughts might go through your head:

1 *How* is the distance to be measured? – e.g. by road, rail, plane, or train.
2 The *costs* and *benefits* of obtaining the information – how much can you spend finding out the information without making it cost more to find out than will be saved by knowing the information we seek?
3 What is the *purpose* for which the measurement will be used? – e.g. to travel there by car, to walk there, to have goods shipped there by train or by road.

The lesson to be learned from this is that measurement depends entirely on the use that is to be made of the data. Too often businesses make measurements of financial and other data without looking first at the use that is going to be made of it. In fact, it could be said that 'information' is useful data that is provided for someone.

Data given to someone which is not relevant to the purpose required is just not information. Data which is provided for a particular purpose, and which is completely wrong for the purpose, is worse than having no data at all. At least when there is no data, the manager knows the best that can be done is to guess.

When useless data is collected it has cost money to collect, in itself a waste of money. Secondly, it is often assumed to be useful and so misleads a manager into taking decisions that are completely inappropriate. Third, it clogs up the communication system within a business, so that other data is not acted on properly because of the general confusion that has been caused.

When looking at costs, you need to consider the following:

1 What is the data on costs wanted for?
2 How are the costs to be measured? and
3 That the cost of obtaining costing data should not exceed the benefits to be gained from having it.

When it is known what the costs are for, and how much is to be spent on studying them, the appropriate method for measuring them can be decided.

47.3 Costs

There are many classifications of cost. Let's briefly summarise those that you already know about.

Historical costs

These are the foundation of financial accounting. Exhibit 47.1 shows costs flowing through the financial accounting system.

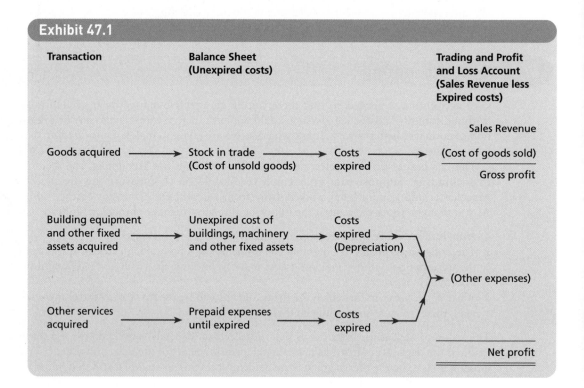

Exhibit 47.1

| Transaction | Balance Sheet (Unexpired costs) | | Trading and Profit and Loss Account (Sales Revenue less Expired costs) |

Sales Revenue

Goods acquired ⟶ Stock in trade (Cost of unsold goods) ⟶ Costs expired ⟶ (Cost of goods sold) / Gross profit

Building equipment and other fixed assets acquired ⟶ Unexpired cost of buildings, machinery and other fixed assets ⟶ Costs expired (Depreciation)

(Other expenses)

Other services acquired ⟶ Prepaid expenses until expired ⟶ Costs expired

Net profit

Product costs

These are the costs attributed to the units of goods manufactured. They are charged up to the cost of goods manufactured in the trading account, and would normally be part of the valuation of unsold goods if the goods to which they refer had not been sold by the end of the period. Product costs are therefore matched up against revenue as and when the goods are sold and not before.

Period costs

Period costs are those of a non-manufacturing nature and represent the selling and distribution, administration and financial expenses. They are treated as expenses of the period in which they were incurred irrespective of the volume of goods sold.

Combining all this, you arrive at the manufacturing accounts you covered in Chapter 35. Exhibit 47.2 shows the flow of costs through to finished products.

Exhibit 47.2

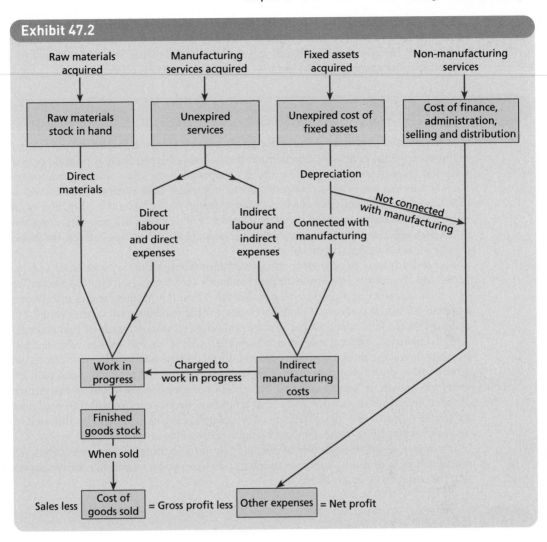

This, therefore, is what you use costs information for in financial accounting – to produce the information you need in order to prepare the financial statements. In management accounting, there is a different emphasis, some of which overlaps with the needs of financial accounting but some of which is for something quite different.

For example, most businesses want to know how much each item has cost to make. This means that the total costs for the whole business are not sufficient, and so these costs must be analysed further. They also want to know what costs are likely to be in the future. Again, more analysis is needed. Cost accounting is the process of measuring and recording all these costs.

Many advantages are gained by having a cost accounting system that provides this detail of cost information. When armed with the cost information that management accounting techniques can provide, managers and other internal decision-makers are far more able to make sensible decisions about what should be done to aid the progress of the business towards its objectives.

For example, imagine trying to decide which item to stop producing out of twelve items made by a business if you have little information as to the amount each item contributes towards the profitability of the business. Very often the solution will be that a new layout in the factory is needed; special training given to certain employees; changes made in the system of remunerating employees; and so on. The information provided by accounting is, therefore, only one part of the whole story for any problem requiring a decision to be made. Sometimes *it will be the least important information* available, as far as the decision-maker is concerned.

47.4 Cost control

One of the most important features of cost accounting is its use for control purposes, meaning, in this context, the control of expenditure. But control of expenditure is possible only if you can trace the costs down to employees who are responsible for such costs. A convenient and frequently adopted approach to collecting costs is through **cost centres** – production or service locations, functions, activities, or items of equipment. Costs are collected from cost centres for individual **cost units** – units of product or service. For example, in a manufacturing business, all direct materials, direct labour and direct expenses are traced to cost centres. (In this case, they may be known as 'product centres'.)

A cost centre may be a single machine used for jobbing work, i.e. quite a lot of separate jobs performed specially to conform with the customer's specifications. It could, however, be a group of similar machines or a production department. Thus, if a business makes metal boxes on one machine, all the costs incurred directly relating to that machine (cost centre) would be gathered and then shared (allocated) among all the metal boxes (cost units) made by that machine.

By comparison, factory indirect expenses are 'indirect' and so cannot be traced (or it is not worthwhile tracing them) to product centres. Instead, these are traced to cost centres which give service rather than being concerned with work directly on the products. Such cost centres are, therefore, known as 'service centres'. Examples of service centres would be the factory canteen or the maintenance department. The costs from these service centres will then need allocating to the product centres in a logical fashion – for example, canteen costs may be allocated to product cost centres according to the number of employees working at each of them.

In practice, there are a number of possible ways of allocating costs to cost centres. What must not be lost sight of is the endeavour to trace costs to a person responsible for the expenditure so that the costs can be controlled.

47.5 Costing approaches

There are a number of ways costs can be gathered and collated. The two most commonly used are **absorption costing** and **marginal costing**.

Absorption costing

This involves allocating all direct costs and factory indirect expenses to products. The factory indirect expenses are seen as adding to the value of work in progress and, therefore, to finished goods. The production cost of any article is thus comprised of direct materials, direct labour, any direct expenses and a share of factory indirect expense.

After the financial year end, it is possible to look back and calculate exactly what the factory indirect expenses were. This means that this figure is used when calculating the valuation of the closing stock. For a business which had produced 1,000 units, of which 200 units have not yet been sold, with a total production cost of £100,000, the closing stock valuation becomes:

$$\frac{\text{Unsold units}}{\text{Total units produced}} \times \text{Production cost of goods completed} = \frac{200}{1,000} \times £100,000$$

$$= £20,000 \text{ closing stock valuation}$$

Cost data is, however, used for purposes other than that of valuing stock. The question is, therefore, often asked as to whether or not this method is suitable for all costing purposes. The short answer is that it is not. A fuller consideration of this question is beyond the scope of this book and is covered in *Business Accounting UK GAAP 2*.

Marginal costing

Where costing is used which takes account of only the variable cost of products rather than the full production cost, this is known as **marginal costing**. By ignoring the fixed costs, it is possible to see how much something contributes towards the profitability of a business. So, for example, if an order was received to buy 100 tables from a business for £65 each and the absorption cost of a table was £70, the order would be rejected but, if marginal costing was used and the marginal cost was £60, the order might be accepted as every table sold contributed £5 towards the overall profitability of the business. Whether it is or not will depend upon whether there is any spare production capacity.

When using marginal costing for decisions like this, care needs to be taken that over all the decisions taken, sufficient additional income is generated to pay for all the fixed costs that are ignored by marginal costing.

47.6 Costing systems

Having decided which costing approach to adopt, you then need to decide which costing system to adopt. The one you choose will depend upon how your products or services are produced. There are two main types of costing system, **job costing** and **process costing**.

Job costing

This is used when production consists of separate jobs. For instance, where a Rolls-Royce is made to each customer's specifications, each car can be regarded as a separate job. When a job is long-term, the term 'project costing' is often used.

Job costing also applies where batches of items are made. For example, a jam bottling company may make jam in batches of 10,000 bottles and then switch over to making a different type of jam for the next batch. A printer may print a batch of 2,000 copies of a book. The 'job' can thus be one item or a batch of similar items. When a batch is involved, it is usually referred to as 'batch costing'.

Process costing

Process costing is used where production is regarded as a continuous flow. It is applicable to industries such as oil, paint manufacturing, steel, textiles, and food processing, where production is repetitive and continuous. For example, an oil refinery where crude oil is processed continually, emerging as different grades of petrol, paraffin, motor oil, etc. would use process costing, as would a salt works where sea water is pumped into the works, and the resulting product is slabs or packets of salt. Another example would be a car manufacturer that produced one model of car for an extended period.

Overall

Job costing treats production as a number of separate jobs being performed, each of which needs to have costs allocated to it. Process costing, on the other hand, sees production as a continuous flow and no attempt is made to allocate costs to specific units being produced because the same thing is being produced continuously. As a result, costs per unit produced can always be calculated by dividing the costs for the period by the number of units produced.

> **Activity 47.2**
>
> For which of the following would you use job costing and for which would you use process costing? Split the job costing ones between job, batch, and project costing.
>
> Newspaper printing
> School meals
> A film in a cinema
> Making a film
> Manufacturing computer memory chips
> A play in a theatre
> Egg production
> Building a space satellite

47.7 Budgeting and budgetary control

Management accounting is concerned with providing information for planning and control so that organisations can achieve their objectives. One of the central supporting devices of both of these aims is budgeting.

When a plan is expressed quantitatively it is known as a **budget** and the process of converting plans into budgets is known as **budgeting**.

The budgeting process may be quite formal in a large organisation with committees set up to perform the task. On the other hand in a very small business the owner may jot down the budget on a piece of scrap paper or even on the back of a used envelope. Some even manage without writing anything down at all – they have done the budgets in their heads and can easily remember them.

The methodology of budgetary control is probably accountancy's major contribution to management. Budgets are drawn up by management and recorded by management accountants. Actual results are compared against the budgets by the management accountants who pass reports to management concerning the extent to which budgets are being met. This enables managers to control activities and to step in and stop situations where the budget is being ignored or overlooked.

When budgets are being drawn up, two main objectives must be uppermost in the minds of management and management accountants – that budgets are for planning and for control. Management accountants must, therefore, operate a system of budgeting that enables these two aims to be achieved. They do so mainly through a system called variance analysis, which compares actual data to budgeted data and endeavours to identify what has given rise to any differences that are found. For example, if the gross profit on an item is lower than was budgeted, this could be because costs have risen or because the selling price has fallen. The management accountant uses special formulae to pinpoint the cause and passes the information to management so that they can exercise control if required.

47.8 Other aspects of management accounting

Management accounting is, therefore, all about gathering costs appropriately so that businesses can take appropriate decisions relating to manufacturing and selling their goods and services. Management accountants are primarily involved in establishing the costs incurred in producing the output of a business and in maintaining a budgeting system that provides managers with the capability to plan and control activity and so meet the objectives of the organisation.

Apart from the activities mentioned already in this chapter, management accountants are also involved in preparing any information of a financial nature that managers and other decision-makers require and which is not considered part of the role of the financial accountant. This can range from identifying the cost of a component part to the expected returns on a twenty-year project to build a chain of hotels. Their work can be very much more varied than that of a financial accountant, and they are not tied by any rules and regulations concerning either how they perform calculations or how they present information.

However, as much of the cost information they produce is also used in the financial accounting system, they do need to ensure that their cost data are capable of being used in that medium. As it is easier to simply have one set of costs for an entire business, rather than one calculated for the management accountants and one calculated for the financial accountants, most management accountants follow the rules relating to cost determination that financial accountants are obliged to follow.

This chapter has been very much an introduction to management accounting. The topic is covered in detail in *Business Accounting UK GAAP 2*.

Learning outcomes

You should now have learnt that:

1 Cost accounting is needed for there to be an effective management accounting system.

2 The benefits of operating a costing system should always outweigh the costs of operating it.

3 Information is data prepared for a purpose. To qualify as 'information', the 'information' must be useful.

4 Different costs will often be needed when making decisions about the future than were used when calculating profit in the past.

5 Marginal cost, not absorption cost, is the relevant cost when considering a change in what and/or how much is produced.

6 Selling prices should exceed marginal costs. (Almost the only exception to this would be where a product was being promoted as a 'loss leader'.)

7 In the long term, the total of all the differences between revenue and marginal cost must exceed the fixed costs of the business.

8 Budgets are prepared in order to guide the business towards its objectives.

9 Budgets should be drawn up within the context of *planning* and *control*.

Answers to activities

47.1 It is used for ratio analysis, particularly for trend analysis and benchmarking against appropriate comparators such as the previous year's figures or the equivalent figures relating to competitors.

47.2

Job costing	*Process costing*
Newspaper printing (batch)	Egg production
School meals (batch)	Manufacturing computer memory chips
A film in a cinema (job)	
Making a film (project)	
A play in a theatre (job)	
Building a space satellite (project)	

Review questions

47.1 What makes information useful?

47.2 What is the difference between absorption costing and marginal costing?

47.3 What is the difference between job costing, batch costing, project costing, and process costing?

47.4 What are the two main objectives of budgeting?

47.5 What role do management accountants play in the budgetary process?

You can find a range of additional self-test questions, as well as material to help you with your studies, on the website that accompanies this book at **www.pearsoned.co.uk/wood**

Answers to review questions

Note: All the answers are the work of the author. None has been supplied by an examining body. The examining bodies accept no responsibility whatsoever for the accuracy or method of working in the answers given.

Note: In order to save space, in most cases brackets have not been entered to indicate negative numbers. Also, £ signs have been omitted from columns of figures, except where the figures refer to £000, or where the denomination needs to be specified.

1.1

(a) 22,000	(b) 6,900	(c) 2,700	(d) 42,000
(e) 106,000	(f) 18,500		

1.3

(a) Asset	(b) Liability	(c) Asset
(d) Asset	(e) Liability	(f) Asset

1.5

Wrong: Assets: Loan from C Smith. Liabilities: Stock of goods, Computer, Land.

1.7

Assets: Van 4,500; Market stall 2,000; Stock 1,500; Bank 1,100; Cash 400 = total 9,500.
Liabilities: Loan 5,000; Creditors 1,000 = total 6,000.
Capital: 9,500 − 6,000 = 3,500.

1.9

G Putty
Balance Sheet as at 31 December 2008

Fixed assets		
Fixtures	1,800	
Van	3,800	
		5,600
Current assets		
Stock of goods	4,200	
Debtors	1,200	
Cash at bank	300	
	5,700	
Less Current liabilities		
Creditors	4,100	
		1,600
		7,200
Capital		7,200

1.11

	Assets	Liabilities	Capital
(a)	− Cash	− Creditors	
(b)	− Bank + Fixtures		
(c)	+ Stock	+ Creditors	
(d)	+ Cash		+ Capital
(e)	+ Cash		
(f)	+ Bank − Debtors		
(g)	− Stock	− Creditors	
(h)	+ Premises − Bank		

1.13

E Silva
Balance Sheet as at 7 April 2005

Fixed assets		
Fixtures	2,800	
Car	6,650	
PC	560	
		10,010
Current assets		
Stock	4,090	
Debtors	2,450	
Bank	3,590	
Cash	1,240	
	11,370	
Less Current liabilities		
Creditors	3,010	
		8,360
		18,370
Capital		18,370

2.1

	Debited	Credited
(a)	Office machinery	D Isaacs Ltd
(b)	C Jones	Capital
(c)	Cash	N Fox
(d)	Loan: P Exeter	Bank
(e)	D Isaacs Ltd	Office machinery
(f)	Bank	Cash
(g)	Van	Cash

2.3

Bank
(1) Capital 25,000 (2) Office furn. 800 (23) P Dove 800
(5) Van 8,100 (15) Bank 700
(15) Fullcrop 700 (31) Machinery 800
(31) Machinery 800

Cash
(5) Bank 8,100 (8) Off. furn. 90

Capital
(1) Bank 25,000

Office furniture
(2) Bank 800 (8) Cash 90

Machinery
(31) Bank 800

Fullcrop Ltd
(15) Bank 700 (3) Printers 700

Van
(5) Bank 8,100

P Dove Ltd
(23) Bank 800 (2) ... 800

Printers
(3) Fullcrop Ltd 700

2.4

Cash
(1) Capital 12,000 (2) Bank 11,700
(25) Equipment 200 (30) F Brown 130

Bank
(1) Capital 12,000 (8) Van 5,250
(2) Cash 11,700 (26) Dream 1,780
(30) F Brown 130 (28) Cash 130

Capital
(1) Cash 12,000 (18) Office furn. 1,900

Office Furniture
(18) Cash 1,900 (26) Bank 120
(5) Office furn. 1,900

Van
(5) Dream 1,780 (8) Bank 5,250

Dream Ltd
(26) Bank 1,780 (5) Office furn. 1,900

Pearce & Sons
(12) Equipment 2,300

Equipment
(8) Bank 5,250 (12) Equipment 2,300
(12) Pearce & Sons 2,300 (25) Cash 200

F Brown (Loan)
(30) Bank 130

3.1

	Debited	Credited
(a)	Purchases	J Reid
(b)	B Perkins	Sales
(c)	Van	H Thomas
(d)	Bank	Sales
(e)	Cash	Sales
(f)	H Hardy	Returns Outwards
(g)	Cash	Machinery
(h)	Returns Inwards	J Nelson
(i)	Purchases	D Simpson
(j)	H Forbes	Returns Outwards

3.3

Cash
(1) Capital 2,400 (3) Purchases 630
(10) Sales 102 (25) T Joop 938
(31) J Lump 161

Purchases
(3) Cash 630
(7) T Joop 980
(18) B Topp 365

Returns Outwards
(14) T Joop 42
(21) B Topp 24

J Lump
(24) Sales 161 (31) Cash 161

T Joop
(14) Returns 42 (7) Purchases 980
(25) Cash 938

B Topp
(21) Returns 24 (18) Purchases 365

Sales
(10) Cash 102
(24) J Lump 161

Capital
(1) Cash 2,400

3.5

Bank
(1) Capital 20,000 (25) B Brown 1,924
(6) Cash 200 (29) Aberdeen Cars 4,370

Cash
(6) Bank 200
(20) Purchases 390
(31) Office Furn 365

R Hughes (Loan)
(2) Bank 5,000

Sales
(4) Cash 1,910
(8) H Rise 1,374
(10) P Taylor 341
(14) G Pate 535
(14) R Sim 262
(24) Cash 110

Purchases
(4) Cash 1,530
(3) B Brown 1,530
(3) I Jess 4,162
(11) B Brown 488
(20) Cash 390

Returns Inwards
(12) H Rise 65
(26) G Pate 34

Van
(17) Aberdeen Cars 4,370

Office Furniture
(18) J Winter 1,800
(31) Cash 365

Returns Outwards
(15) B Brown 94
(19) I Jess 130

Aberdeen Cars
(17) Van 4,370 (29) Bank 4,370

J Winter Ltd
(18) Office furn. 1,800 (27) Office furn. 180

Capital
(1) Bank 20,000
(28) Cash 2,500

B Brown
(15) Returns 94 (3) Purchases 1,530
(25) Bank 1,924 (11) Purchases 488

P Taylor
(10) Sales 341

I Jess
(19) Returns 130 (3) Purchases 4,162

G Pate
(14) Sales 535 (26) Returns 34

R Hughes (Loan)
(2) Cash 5,000

H Rise
(8) Sales 1,374 (12) Returns 65

R Sim
(14) Sales 262

4.1

Bank
| (1) Capital | 9,000 | (3) Fixtures | 1,150 |
| (21) Rent received | 25 | (24) Van | 4,100 |

Cash
(1) Capital	1,000	(2) Purchases	290
(5) Sales	140	(10) Rent	200
		(12) Stationery	45
		(30) Wages	360
		(31) Drawings	80

Purchases
| (2) D James | 290 | | |
| (6) C Monty | 325 | | |

Sales
| | | (23) G Cross | 845 |

Fixtures
| (3) Bank | 1,150 | | |

Rent
| (10) Cash | 200 | | |

Stationery
| (12) Cash | 45 | | |

D James
| (18) Returns out | 41 | (2) Purchases | 290 |

C Monty
| | | (6) Purchases | 325 |

G Cross
| (23) Sales | 845 | | |

Returns Out
| | | (18) D James | 41 |

Van
| (24) Bank | 4,100 | | |

Wages
| (30) Cash | 360 | | |

Drawings
| (31) Cash | 80 | | |

Rent Received
| | | (21) Bank | 25 |

4.2

Cash
(1) Capital	9,600	(3) Rent	650
(11) Sales	42	(4) Bank	3,000
		(20) B Repairs	56
		(28) Purchases	840
		(30) Motor exps	101

Bank
(4) Cash	3,000	(7) Stationery	9
		(27) J Harper	247
		(29) Van	2,150
		(31) Off furn.	460

Purchases
| (2) W Young | 310 | | |
| (28) Cash | 840 | | |

Sales
		(5) P Aisley	330
		(11) Cash	42
		(17) F Boggis	195

PC Supplies
| (7) Bank | 9 | | |

Returns Outwards
| | | (14) J Harper | 63 |

Office furniture
| (31) Bank | 460 | | |

Capital
| | | (1) Cash | 9,600 |

Rent
| (3) Cash | 650 | | |

PC Repairs
| (20) Cash | 56 | | |

Motor Repairs
| (30) Cash | 101 | | |

Motorbike
| (29) Bank | 2,150 | | |

J Harper
| (14) Returns out | 63 | (2) Purchases | 310 |
| (27) Bank | 247 | | |

P Aisley
| (5) Sales | 330 | (22) Returns in | 30 |

F Boggis
| (17) Sales | 195 | | |

Returns Inwards
| (22) P Aisley | 30 | | |

4.5

(A) Bought motor vehicle £5,000 paying by bank.
(B) Paid off £4,000 creditors in cash.
(C) Lee lent us £150,000 this being paid into the bank.
(D) Bought land and buildings £125,000 paying by bank.
(E) Debtors paid cheques £80,000 being paid into bank.
(F) Land and buildings sold for £300,000 the proceeds being paid into the bank.
(G) Loan from Lee repaid out of the bank.
(H) Creditors £8,000 paid in cash.
(I) Stock costing £17,000 sold for £12,000 on credit. Loss of £5,000 shown deducted from Capital.

5.1

J Fry
(1) Sales	640	(10) Returns	80
(4) Sales	130	(24) Bank	250
		(31) Balance c/d	440
	770		770
(1) Balance b/d	440		

I Lee
| (18) Bank | 920 | (1) Sales | 920 |

K Rusch
(1) Sales	530	(10) Returns	90
		(20) Cash	440
	530		530

A Davey
(4) Sales	510	(31) Balance c/d	810
(31) Sales	300		
	810		810
(1) Balance b/d	810		

5.2

J Saville
(10) Returns	65	(1) Purchases	240
(28) Cash	300	(15) Purchases	210
(30) Balance c/d	85		
	450		450
		(1) Balance b/d	85

P Todd
(30) Returns	39	(1) Purchases	390
(30) Balance c/d	821	(3) Purchases	470
	860		860
		(1) Balance b/d	821

J Fry
(10) Returns	82	(1) Purchases	810
(30) Balance c/d	728		
	810		810
		(1) Balance b/d	728

J Mehan
| (19) Bank | 1,450 | (3) Purchases | 1,450 |

23.3 (cont'd)

Provision for Doubtful Debts

2007			2007		
Dec 31 Balance c/d		640	Dec 31 Profit and loss		640
2008			2008		
Dec 31 Balance c/d		710	Jan 1 Balance b/d		640
			Dec 31 Profit and loss		70
		710			710

(ii)

Balance Sheet (extracts)

	2007		2008
Debtors	52,400		57,890
	58,600		
Less Provision for doubtful debts	640		710
	51,760		

23.5

Provision for Doubtful Debts

2007		2007	
Dec 31 Balance c/d	600	Jan 1 Balance b/d	600
		Dec 31 Profit and loss	
	600		600
2008		2008	
Dec 31 Balance c/d	800	Jan 1 Balance b/d	600
		Dec 31 Profit and loss	200
	800		800
2009		2009	
Dec 31 Profit and loss	100	Jan 1 Balance b/d	800
Dec 31 Balance c/d	700		
	800		800

Profit and Loss Account Extract for the year ending 31 December

2007

Gross profit		xxx
Less Expenses		
Provision for doubtful debts	300	
Bad debts	420	

2008

Gross profit		xxx
Less Expenses		
Provision for doubtful debts	200	
Bad Debts	490	

2009

Gross profit		xxx
Add Reduction in provision for doubtful debts		100
		xxx
Less Expenses		
Bad Debts	530	

23.7

(a)

Provision for Doubtful Debts

2008			2007		
May 31 Profit and loss (W1)		1,390	Jun 1 Balance b/d		2,300
31 Balance c/d		910			
		2,300			2,300
			2008		
			Jun 1 Balance b/d		910

(b)

Provision for Discounts Allowed

	2008		
	May 31 Profit and loss (W2)		594

Workings

(W1) Provision 1.6.2007 ... 2,300

Less Provision 31.5.2008:

1% × 24,000	240
2% × 10,000	200
4% × 8,000	320
5% × 3,000	150
	910

Reduction in Provision ... 1,390

(W2) Debtors liable for discounts ... 24,000

Less Provision for doubtful debts ... 240

Provision for discounts allowed $2\frac{1}{2}\% \times 23{,}760 = 594$ ... 23,760

23.9

(days and months omitted)

(a)

Bad Debts

2006 Debtors	1,400	2006 Profit and loss	1,400
2007 Debtors	2,200	2007 Profit and loss	2,200
2008 Debtors	3,800	2008 Profit and loss	3,800

(b)

Bad Debts Recovered

2007 Profit and loss	210	2007 J Sweeny	210
2008 Profit and loss	320	2008 Various debtors	320

(c)

Provision for Doubtful Debts

2006 Balance c/d	2,600	2006 Profit and loss	2,600
2007 Balance c/d	3,680	2007 Balance b/d	2,600
		Profit and loss	1,080
	3,680		3,680
2008 Profit and loss	80	2008 Balance b/d	3,680
Balance c/d	3,600		
	3,680		3,680

(d)

Profit and Loss Account (extracts)

(2006) Bad debts	1,400		
Provision for doubtful debts	2,600		
(2007) Bad debts	2,200	(2007) Bad debt recovered	210
Provision for doubtful debts	1,080		
(2008) Bad debts	3,800	(2008) Reduction in provision for doubtful debts	80
		Bad debt recovered	320

23.10

(A) See text.
(B) See text.
(C) (1) (i)

2007	
Dec 31 Profit and loss	750*
	750

Provision for Doubtful Debts

		2007	
		Jan 1 Balance b/d	33
			717**
			750

Bad Debts

2007		2007	
? Debtors – A Stewart	900	Dec 31 Profit and loss	3,800
? Debtors	2,300		3,800
Dec 31 Debtors – J Smith	600		
	3,800		

(2) the net profit will increase by £33.

*3% 25,000 = 750; **3% 23,900

24.1

Straight Line		Reducing Balance	
Cost	1,211	Cost	1,211
Yr 1 Depreciation*	387	Yr 1 Depn 65% of 1,211	787
	824		424
Yr 2 Depreciation	387	Yr 2 Depn 65% of 424	276*
	437		148
Yr 3 Depreciation	387	Yr 3 Depn 65% of 148	96
	50		50

*1,211 − 50 = 1,161 ÷ 3 = 387

24.2

(a) Straight Line		(b) Reducing Balance	
Cost	8,000	Cost	8,000
Yr 1 Depreciation*	1,120	Yr 1 Depn 20% of 8,000	1,600
	6,880		6,400
Yr 2 Depreciation	1,120	Yr 2 Depn 20% of 6,400	1,280
	5,760		5,120
Yr 3 Depreciation	1,120	Yr 3 Depn 20% of 5,120	1,024
	4,640		4,096
Yr 4 Depreciation	1,120	Yr 4 Depn 20% of 4,096	819
	3,520		3,277
Yr 5 Depreciation	1,120	Yr 5 Depn 20% of 3,277	655
	2,400		2,622

$$\frac{8,000 - 2,400}{5} = 1,120$$

24.3

(a) Reducing Balance		(b) Straight Line	
Cost	9,600	Cost	9,600
Yr 1 Depn 50% of 9,600	4,800	Yr 1 Depreciation*	2,333
	4,800		7,267
Yr 2 Depn 50% of 4,800	2,400	Yr 2 Depreciation	2,333
	2,400		4,934
Yr 3 Depn 50% of 2,400	1,200	Yr 3 Depreciation	2,333
	1,200		2,601

$$* \frac{9,600 - 2,600}{3} = 2,333$$

24.7

	A	B	C
		Machines	
Brought 1.1.2006	2,000		
2006 Depreciation 15% for 12 months	300		
	1,700		
Brought 1.9.2007		4,000	
2007 Depreciation 15% × 1,700	255		
Depreciation 15% for 4 months		200	
	1,445	3,800	
Brought 1.4.2008			3,000
2008 Depreciation 15% × 1,445	217		
Depreciation 15% × 3,800		570	
Depreciation 15% for 8 months			300
	1,662	3,230	2,700

2008 Total depreciation provision 217 + 570 + 300 = 1,087

24.8

Motor Vehicle

2006	
Jan 1 Trucks Ltd	12,000

Accumulated provision for depreciation on motor vehicles

2006		2006	
Dec 31 Balance c/d	3,000	Dec 31 Depreciation	3,000
2007		2007	
Dec 31 Balance c/d	5,250	Jan 1 Balance b/d	3,000
		Dec 31 Depreciation	2,250
	5,250		5,250

24.9

Ivor Innes
Balance Sheet as at 31 March 2008

Fixed Assets		
Fixtures		7,000
Current Assets		
Stock	19,000	
Debtors	4,440	
Bank	8,320	
Cash	700	
	32,460	
Less: Current liabilities—Creditors	8,800	
		23,660
		30,660
Capital		
Balance at 1 April 2007*		34,900
Capital introduced		18,000
		52,900
Less: Net loss	10,840	
Drawings	11,400	
		22,240
		30,660

*840 + 7,600 + 5,500 + 17,800 + 8,360 − 5,200 = 34,900

24.12

(a) Reducing balance. Obsolescence probably very slow and not relevant.
(b) Straight line. Obsolescence very slow and probably not relevant.
(c) Straight line. Obsolescence depends on the market and growth of the business.
(d) Reducing balance (as it is likely to be more efficient in the early years of use and susceptible to sudden obsolescence).
(e) Machine hours. Already obsolete.

25.1

Vans

2006			2006		
Jan 1	Bank	16,600	Dec 31	Balance c/d	25,240
Sept 1	Bank	8,640			
		25,240			25,240

Provision for Depreciation: Vans

2006			2006		
Dec 31	Balance c/d	4,870	Dec 31	Profit and loss	4,870*

*16,600 × 25% = £4,150
8,640 × 25% × 4/12 = 720
  4,870

25.2

(a)

Machinery

2008			2008		
Jan 1	Bank	1,200	Dec 31	Balance c/d	1,200
2009			**2009**		
Jan 1	Balance b/d	1,200	Dec 31	Balance c/d	4,464
Aug 1	Bank	1,344			
Nov 1	Bank	1,920			
		4,464			4,464
2010			**2010**		
Jan 1	Balance b/d	4,464	Dec 31	Balance c/d	4,464
2011			**2011**		
Jan 1	Balance b/d	4,464	Dec 31	Balance c/d	4,764
May 1	Bank	300			
		4,764			4,764

(b)

Provision for Depreciation: Machinery

2008			2008		
Dec 31	Balance c/d	150	Dec 31	Profit and loss	150
2009			**2009**		
Dec 31	Balance c/d	410	Jan 1	Balance b/d	150
			Dec 31	Profit and loss	260*
		410			410
2010			**2010**		
Dec 31	Balance c/d	968	Jan 1	Balance b/d	410
			Dec 31	Profit and loss	558
		968			968
2011			**2011**		
Dec 31	Balance c/d	1,551	Jan 1	Balance b/d	968
			Dec 31	Profit and loss	583**
		1,551			1,551

*1,200 × 1/8 = 150
1,344 × 1/8 × 5/12 = 70
1,920 × 1/8 × 1/6 = 40
  260

**4,464 × 1/8 = 558
300 × 1/8 × 2/3 = 25
  583

(c)

Balance Sheet Extracts

31 December 2003		
Machinery at cost	1,400	
Less Depreciation	140	1,260
31 December 2004		
Machinery at cost	3,600	
Less Depreciation to date	365	3,235
31 December 2005		
Machinery at cost	3,600	
Less Depreciation to date	725	2,875
31 December 2006		
Machinery at cost	4,000	
Less Depreciation to date	1,115	2,885

25.4

Plant

2004			2004		
Jan 1	Bank	2,600	Dec 31	Balance c/d	4,700
Oct 1	Bank	2,100			
		4,700			4,700
2006			2006		
Jan 1	Balance b/d	4,700	Dec 31	Balance c/d	7,500
Sep 1	Bank	2,800			
		7,500			7,500
2007			2007		
Jan 1	Balance b/d	7,500	Aug 31	Disposals	2,600
			Dec 31	Balance c/d	4,900
		7,500			7,500

Provision for Depreciation: Plant

2004			2004		
Dec 31	Balance c/d	781	Dec 31	Profit and loss	781*
					781

$2,600 \times 25\% = 650$
$2,100 \times 25\% \times 3/12 = 131.25$
= 781

2005			2005		
Dec 31	Balance c/d	1,956	Jan 1	Balance b/d	781
			Dec 31	Profit and loss	1,175
		1,956			1,956

$*4,700 \times 25\% = 1,175$
$2,800 \times 25\% \times 4/12 = 233.33$
= 1,408

2006			2006		
Dec 31	Balance c/d	3,364	Jan 1	Balance b/d	1,956
			Dec 31	Profit and loss	1,408*
		3,364			3,364

$*2,600 \times 25\% \times 8/12 = 433.33$
$2,100 \times 25\% = 525$
$2,800 \times 25\% = 700$
= 1,658

2007			2007		
Sep 30	Plant Disposals	2,383	Jan 1	Balance b/d	3,364
Dec 31	Balance c/d	2,639	Dec 31	Profit and loss	1,658*
		5,022			5,022

Plant Disposals

2007			2007		
Sep 30	Plant	2,600	Sep 30	Provn for depn	2,383
Dec 31	Profit and loss	593	30	Bank	810
		3,193			3,193

Balance Sheets

	2004	2005	2006	2007
Plant at cost	4,700	4,700	7,500	4,900
Less depn to date	781	1,956	3,364	2,639
	3,919	2,744	4,136	2,261

25.5

Machinery

2009			2009		
Jan 1	Balance b/d	94,500	Dec 31	Machinery disposals	1,600
Dec 31	Bank	16,000	31	Balance c/d	108,900
		110,500			110,500

Office Furniture

2009			2009		
Jan 1	Balance b/d	3,200	Dec 31	Balance c/d	3,660
Dec 31	Bank	460			
		3,660			3,660

Provision for Depreciation: Machinery

2009			2009		
Dec 31	Machinery disposals	1,280	Jan 1	Balance b/d	28,350
31	Balance c/d	48,850	Dec 31	Profit and loss	21,780
		50,130			50,130

Provision for Depreciation: Office Furniture

2009			2009		
Dec 31	Balance c/d	1,646	Jan 1	Balance b/d	1,280
			Dec 31	Profit and loss	366
		1,646			1,646

Machinery Disposals

2009			2009		
Dec 31	Machinery	1,600	Dec 31	Provision for depn	1,280
31	Profit and loss: Gain on sale	40	31	Bank	360
		1,640			1,640

Balance Sheet as at 31 December 2009

Machinery at cost		108,900
Less Depreciation to date		48,850
		60,050
Office furniture at cost		3,660
Less Depreciation to date		1,646
		2,014

25.6

£2,500 and £8,500.

25.8

(a) (i) Time factor (ii) Economic factors (iii) Deterioration physically (iv) Depletion.

(b) (i) Depletion (ii) Physical deterioration (iii) Time (iv) Not usually subject to depletion, but depends on circumstances (v) Economic factors, obsolescence for example (vi) Time factor.

(c)

Equipment

Balance b/d	135,620	Asset disposals	36,000
Bank	47,800	Balance c/d	147,420
	183,420		183,420
Balance b/d	147,420		

Provision for Depreciation – Equipment

Asset disposals	28,224	Balance b/d	81,374
Balance c/d	90,858	Profit and loss	37,708
	119,082		119,082
		Balance b/d	90,858

Asset Disposals

Equipment	36,000	Provision for depreciation	28,224
		Bank	5,700
		Profit and loss	2,076
	36,000		36,000

25.10

(a) (i) Straight line depreciation method

Fixed Asset

Year 1 Bank	10,000	Year 3 Asset disposals	10,000

Provision for Depreciation

		Year 1 Profit and loss	2,000
Year 2 Balance c/d	4,000	Year 2 Profit and loss	2,000
	4,000		4,000
Year 3 Asset disposals	4,000	Year 3 Balance b/d	4,000

Asset Disposals

Year 3 Fixed asset	10,000	Year 3 Bank	5,000
		3 Provision for depn.	4,000
		3 Profit and loss	1,000
	10,000		10,000

(ii) Reducing balance method

Fixed Asset

Year 1 Bank	10,000	Year 3 Asset disposals	10,000

Provision for Depreciation

		Year 1 Profit and loss	4,000
Year 2 Balance c/d	6,400	2 Profit and loss	2,400
	6,400		6,400
Year 3 Asset disposals	6,400	Year 3 Balance b/d	6,400

Asset Disposals

Year 3 Fixed asset	10,000	Year 3 Bank	5,000
3 Profit and loss	1,400	3 Provision for depn.	6,400
	11,400		11,400

(b) (i) The purpose of depreciation provisions is to apportion the cost of a fixed asset over the useful years of its life to the organisation.

The matching concept concerns the matching of costs against the revenues which those costs generate. If the benefit to be gained is equal in each year then the straight line method is to be preferred. If the benefits are greatest in year 1 and then falling year by year, then the reducing balance method would be preferred. The impact of maintenance costs of the fixed asset, if heavier in later years, may also give credence to the reducing balance method.

(ii) The net figure at the end of year 2 is the amount of original cost not yet expensed against revenue.

(c) The charge in year 1 should be nil in this case. The matching concept concerns matching costs against revenues. There have been no revenues in year 1, therefore there should be no costs.

25.12 Your letter should include the following:

● depreciation is an expense;
● it allows the expense of an asset to be spread over its useful economic life;
● it is only a book figure and therefore 'real' money is not set aside when you depreciate an asset;
● it is not a reserve, and never can be as there are no assets of the business underpinning it.

25.14

(a) (a)

		Dr	Cr
2001	Machines	15,000	
	XY Manufacturing Co		15,000
2002	Depreciation	2,000	
	Acc. provn for depn-m/c		2,000
2003	Depreciation	2,000	
	Acc. provn for depn-m/c		2,000

(b) *Balance Sheet extract as 30 September 2003*

Machine	11,000

(b) (a)

Machine

2004			2004	
Oct 1 Balance b/d	15,000		Oct 1 Machine disposal	15,000

Accumulated Provision for Depreciation-Machine

2004			2004	
Oct 1 Machine disposal	6,000		Oct 1 Balance b/d	6,000

Machine Disposal

2004			2004		
Oct 1	Machine	15,000	Oct 1	Acc provn for depn	6,000
			1	Cash	7,500
			2005		
			Sept 30	Profit and loss	1,500
		15,000			15,000

(b)

Machine Account and Accumulated Provision for Depreciation Account are as in (a)

Machine Disposal

2004			2004		
Oct 1	Machine	15,000	Oct 1	Acc provn for depn	6,000
			1	Cash	12,000
2005					
Sept 30	Profit and loss	3,000			
		18,000			18,000

25.16

Machinery

2005			2005		
Jan 1	Bank	10,000	Dec 31	Balance c/d	16,000
July 1	Bank	6,000			
		16,000			16,000
2006			2006		
Jan 1	Balance b/d	16,000	Dec 31	Balance c/d	24,000
March 31	Bank	8,000			
		24,000			24,000
2007			2007		
Jan 1	Balance b/d	24,000	Oct 7	Machinery disposal	10,000
Nov 5	Bank	12,000	Dec 31	Balance c/d	26,000
		36,000			36,000
2008			2008		
Jan 1	Balance b/d	26,000	Feb 4	Machinery disposal	6,000
Feb 6	Bank	9,000	Oct 11	Machinery disposal	12,000
Oct 11	Machinery disposal	7,000	Dec 31	Balance c/d	24,000
		42,000			42,000

Accumulated provision for depreciation

2005			2005		
Dec 31	Balance c/d	3,200	Dec 31	Depreciation	3,200
2006			2006		
Dec 31	Balance c/d	8,000	Jan 1	Balance b/d	3,200
			Dec 31	Depreciation	4,800
		8,000			8,000
2007			2007		
Oct 7	Machinery disposal	4,000	Jan 1	Balance b/d	8,000
Dec 31	Balance c/d	9,200	Dec 31	Depreciation	5,200
		13,200			13,200
2008			2008		
Feb 4	Machinery disposal	3,600	Jan 1	Balance b/d	9,200
Oct 11	Machinery disposal	2,400	Dec 31	Depreciation	4,800
Dec 31	Balance c/d	7,000			
		13,000			13,000

Machinery Disposal

2007			2007		
Oct 7	Machinery	10,000	Oct 7	Acc provn for depn	4,000
			7	Bank	5,500
			Dec 31	Profit and loss (loss on sale)	500
		10,000			10,000
2008			2008		
Feb 4	Machinery	6,000	Feb 4	Acc provn for depn	3,600
Oct 11	Machinery	12,000	4	Bank	3,000
			Oct 11	Acc provn for depn	2,400
			11	Machinery	7,000
			Dec 31	Profit and loss (loss on disposal)	2,000
		18,000			18,000

X Y Ltd

Balance Sheet extract as at 31 December

2007		
Machinery at cost		26,000
Less: Accumulated depreciation		9,200
		16,800

2008		
Machinery at cost		24,000
Less: Accumulated depreciation		7,000
		17,000

25.18

Plant and machinery

2004			2004		
Jan 1	Balance b/d	180,000	Dec 31	Balance c/d	200,000
Mar 1	Bank	20,000			
		200,000			200,000
2005			2005		
Jan 1	Balance b/d	200,000	Dec 31	Balance c/d	200,000
		200,000			200,000
2006			2006		
Jan 1	Balance b/d	200,000	Jan	Plant and m/c disposal	20,000
			Dec 31	Balance c/d	180,000
		200,000			200,000

25.18 (cont'd)

Accumulated provision for depreciation

2004		2004	
Dec 31 Balance c/d	96,000	Jan 1 Balance b/d	70,000
		Dec 31 Depreciation	26,000
	96,000		96,000
2005		2005	
Dec 31 Balance c/d	116,800	Jan 1 Balance b/d	96,000
		Dec 31 Depreciation	20,800
	116,800		116,800
2006		2006	
Jan Plant and machinery** disposal	7,200	Jan 1 Balance b/d	116,800
Dec 31 Balance c/d	123,067	Dec 31 Depreciation*	13,467
	130,267		130,267

*180,000 − (116,800 − 7,200) − 30,000 = 41,400 ÷ 3 = 13,467
**[(20,000 × 0.2) + [(20,000 − (20,000 × 0.2)) × 0.2] = 4,000 + 3,200 = 7,200

Plant and Machinery Disposal

2006		2006	
Mar 1 Plant and machinery	20,000	Mar 1 Acc provn for depn	7,200
Dec 31 Profit and loss	1,200	Bank	14,000
	21,200		21,200

25.20

(a) (i) Straight line
Cost £112,000 − trade-in £12,000 = £100,000
Per month £100,000 ÷ 48 = 2,083.33

2006	9 months	=	18,750
2007	12 months	=	25,000
2008	12 months	=	25,000
2009	12 months	=	25,000
2010	3 months	=	6,250
			100,000

(ii) Diminishing (Reducing) Balance:

Cost	112,000
Depreciation 2006 (40%)	44,800
	67,200
Depreciation 2007	26,880
	40,320
Depreciation 2008	16,128
	24,192
Depreciation 2009	9,677
	14,515
Depreciation 2010	5,806
	8,709

(iii) Units of output (Total £100,000)

2006	4,000/20,000	=	20,000
2007	5,000/20,000	=	25,000
2008	5,000/20,000	=	25,000
2009	5,000/20,000	=	25,000
2010	1,000/20,000	=	5,000

(b) (i)

Machine

2007		2007	
Jan 1 Balance b/d	112,000	Dec 31 Assets disposal	112,000

(ii)

Provision for Depreciation

2007		2007	
Dec 31 Assets disposal	31,250	Jan 1 Balance b/d	18,750
		Dec 31 Profit and loss	12,500
	31,250		31,250

(iii)

Assets Disposals

2007		2007	
Dec 31 Machine	112,000	Jun 30 Bank	80,000
		Dec 31 Depreciation	31,250
		31 Profit and loss	750
	112,000		112,000

26.1

(a)

Motor Expenses

2007		2007	
Dec 31 Cash and bank	620	Dec 31 Profit and loss	1,030
31 Accrued c/d	410		
	1,030		1,030
		2008	
		Jan 1 Accrued b/d	410

(b)

Insurance

2007		2007	
Dec 31 Cash and bank	730	Dec 31 Prepaid c/d	90
		31 Profit and loss	640
	730		730
2008			
Jan 1 Prepaid b/d	90		

(c)

Stationery

2007		2007	
Dec 31 Cash and bank	410	Jan 1 Accrued b/d	170
31 Accrued c/d	320	Dec 31 Profit and loss	560
	730		730
		2008	
		Jan 1 Accrued b/d	320

(d)

Business Rates

2007		2007	
Jan 1 Prepaid b/d	80	Dec 31 Profit and loss	1,860
Dec 31 Cash and bank	1,840	31 Prepaid c/d	60
	1,920		1,920
2008			
Jan 1 Prepaid b/d	60		

(e)

Rent Received

2007		2007	
Jan 1 Accrued b/d	200	Dec 31 Cash and bank	1,600
Dec 31 Profit and loss	1,620	31 Accrued c/d	220
	1,820		1,820
2008			
Jan 1 Accrued b/d	220		

26.3

Business Rates

2009		2009	
Jan 1 Balance b/d	340	Dec 31 Profit and loss	2,140
Dec 31 Bank	2,400	31 Prepaid c/d	600*
	2,740		2,740

*2,400 × $^3/_{12}$ = 600

Packing Materials

2009		2009	
Jan 1 Balance b/d	610	Dec 31 Profit and loss	4,406
Dec 31 Bank	4,300	31 Cash: Scrap	94
31 Owing c/d	360	31 Stock c/d	770
	5,270		5,270

26.5

(a)

Insurance

2010		2010	
Jan 1 Prepaid b/d	562	Dec 31 Profit and loss	1,236
Dec 31 Bank	1,019	31 Prepaid c/d	345
	1,581		1,581
2011			
Jan 1 Prepaid b/d	345		

Wages

2010		2010	
Dec 31 Cash	15,000	Jan 1 Accrued b/d	306
31 Accrued c/d	419	Dec 31 Profit and loss	15,113
	15,419		15,419
		2011	
		Jan 1 Accrued b/d	419

Rent Receivable

2010		2010	
Dec 31 Profit and loss	2,741	Jan 1 In advance b/d	36
		Dec 31 Bank	2,600
		31 Arrears c/d	105
	2,741		2,741
2011			
Jan 1 Arrears b/d	105		

(b)

Profit and Loss (extract)

Insurance	1,236
Wages	15,113
Rent receivable	(2,741)

(c) (i) Expenses accrued increases the amount charged as expense for that period. It reduces the recorded net profit. It shows as a current liability in the balance sheet.

(ii) Income received in advance reduces the revenue to be recorded for that period. It reduces the recorded net profit. It shows as a current liability in the balance sheet.

(d) (i) To match up expenses charged in the profit and loss account with the expense cost used up in the period.

(ii) To match up revenue credited to profit and loss with revenue earned for the period.

26.8

R Giggs

Trading and Profit and Loss Account for the year ending 28 February 2007

Sales			157,165
Less Cost of goods sold:			
Opening stock		4,120	
Add Purchases		92,800	
		96,920	
Less Closing stock		2,400	94,520
Gross profit			62,645
Add Discounts received			160
			62,805
Less Expenses:			
Wages and salaries (31,400 + 340)		31,740	
Rent (3,400 − 230)		3,170	
Discounts allowed		820	
Van running costs (615 + 72)		687	
Bad debts		730	
Doubtful debt provision		91	
Depreciation:			
Office furniture	380		
Delivery van	1,250	1,630	38,868
Net profit			23,937

Balance Sheet as at 28 February 2007

Fixed assets			
Office furniture		2,900	
Less Depreciation		380	2,520
Delivery van		3,750	
Less Depreciation		1,250	2,500
			5,020
Current assets			
Stock		2,400	
Debtors	12,316		
Less Provision for doubtful debts	496	11,820	
Prepaid expenses		230	
Cash at bank		4,100	
Cash in hand		324	
		18,874	
Less Current liabilities			
Creditors	5,245		
Expenses owing (340 + 72)	412	5,657	
Net current assets			13,217
			18,237
Financed by:			
Capital			
Balance at 1.3.2006			11,400
Add Net profit			23,937
			35,337
Less Drawings			17,100
			18,237

26.9

Rent

Aug 31 Balance b/d	4,400	Aug 31 Profit and Loss	4,800
31 Accrual c/d	400		
	4,800		4,800
		Sept 1 Accrual b/d	400

26.11   John Brown
Trading and Profit and Loss Account for the year ending 31 December 2007

Sales		400,000
Less Returns in		5,000
		395,000
Less Cost of goods sold		
Stock at 1.1.2007		100,000
Add Purchases	350,000	
Less Returns out	6,200	
	343,800	
	443,800	
Less Stock at 32.12.2007	120,000	323,800
Gross profit		71,200
Less Wages	35,000	
Rates	5,500	
Telephone	1,220	
Bad debts	200	
Provision for doubtful debts	180	
Depreciation: Shop fittings	4,000	
Van	6,000	52,100
Net profit		19,100

Balance Sheet as at 31 December 2007

Fixed assets			
Shop fittings at cost		40,000	
Less Depreciation		4,000	36,000
Van at cost		30,000	
Less Depreciation		6,000	24,000
			60,000
Current assets			
Stock		120,000	
Debtors	9,800		
Less Provision	980	8,820	
Prepayments		500	
Bank		3,000	
		132,320	
Less Current liabilities			
Creditors	7,000		
Expenses accrued	5,220	12,220	
Net current assets			120,100
			180,100
Financed by:			
Capital			
Balance as at 1.1.2007			179,000
Add Net profit			19,100
			198,100
Less Drawings			18,000
			180,100

26.9 *(cont'd)*

Rates

Aug 31 Balance b/d	1,600	Aug 31 Prepaid c/d	300
		31 Profit and loss	1,300
	1,600		1,600
Sept 1 Prepaid b/d	300		

Trading Profit and Loss Account for the year ending 31 August 2008

Sales		40,900
Less Cost of goods sold		
Opening stock	8,200	
Add Purchases	26,000	
	34,200	
Less Closing stock	9,100	25,100
Gross profit		15,800
Less expenses:		
Rent	4,800	
Business rates	1,300	
Sundry expenses	340	
Depreciation	1,800	8,240
Net profit		7,560

Balance Sheet as at 31 August 2008

Fixed Assets			
Motor vehicles		9,000	
Less Depreciation		3,000	6,000
Current Assets			
Debtors		1,160	
Stock		9,100	
Bank		1,500	
Prepayment		300	
		12,060	
Less Current Liabilities			
Creditors	2,100		
Accrual	400	2,500	9,560
			15,560
Capital			
Opening balance			19,700
Add Net profit			7,560
			27,260
Less: Drawings			11,700
			15,560

26.13 Mr Chai
Trading and Profit and Loss Account for the year ended 30 April 2007

Sales (259,870 − 5,624)			254,246
Less Cost of goods sold			
Stock 1.5.2006		15,654	
Purchases (135,680 − 13,407)		122,273	
Carriage inwards		11,830	
		149,757	
Less Stock 30.4.2007		17,750	132,007
Gross profit			122,239
Discounts received			1,750
			123,989
Less Expenses			
Salaries and wages		38,521	
Rent, rates and insurances (25,973 − 1,120 − 5,435)		19,418	
Heating and lighting (11,010 + 1,360)		12,370	
Carriage out		4,562	
Advertising		5,980	
Postage, stationery and telephone		2,410	
Bad debts		2,008	
Provision for doubtful debts		223	
Discounts allowed		2,306	
Depreciation		12,074	99,872
Net profit			24,117

Balance Sheet as at 30 April 2007

Fixed assets			
Fixtures and fittings at cost		120,740	
Less Depreciation to date		63,020	57,720
Current assets			
Stock		17,750	
Debtors	24,500		
Less Provision for doubtful debts	735	23,765	
Prepaid expenses		6,555	
Bank		4,440	
Cash		534	53,044
Less Current liabilities			
Creditors	19,840		
Expenses accrued	1,360	21,200	
Net current assets			31,844
			89,564
Financed by:			
Capital: Balance as at 1.5.2006			83,887
Add Net profit			24,117
			108,004
Less Drawings			18,440
			89,564

27.1

(i) FIFO Closing Stock 190 × £19 = £3,610

(ii)

LIFO	Received	Issued	Stock after each transaction		
Mar	100 × £16		100 × £16	1,600	1,600
Sept	220 × £19		100 × £16	1,600	
			220 × £19	4,180	5,780
Dec		130 × £24	100 × £16	1,600	
			90 × £19	1,710	3,310

(iii)

AVCO	Received	Issued	Average cost per unit stock held	No. of units in stock	Total value of stock
Mar	100 × £16		£16	100	£1,600
Sept	220 × £19		£18.0625	320	£5,780
Dec		130	£18.0625	190	£3,432*

*3,431.875 rounded to nearest £

27.2 Trading Account for the year ended 31 December 2010

	FIFO	LIFO	AVCO
Sales	3,120	3,120	3,120
Less Cost of sales			
Purchases	5,780	5,780	5,780
	3,610	3,310	3,432
Less Closing stock	(2,170)	(2,470)	(2,348)
Gross profit	950	650	772

27.5 (a) (dates and calculations omitted)

Cash

Loan: School fund	200.00	Purchases	
Sales	53.50		
		Purchases	
Cash	51.36		
		Sales	
		Cash	

(b) Stock valuation:

Break × 16p =	34
Brunch × 12p =	15
Stock	7.24
Trading account	

(c) Broadway School
Trading Account for the month ending 31 December 2009

Sales		53.50
Less Cost of sales		
Purchases	51.36	
Less Closing stock	−51.36 7.24	44.12
Gross profit	7.24	9.38

697

27.5 *(cont'd)*

(d)

	Break	Brunch
Purchases (units)	240	108
Less Sold	200	90
Stock should have been	40	18
Actual stock	34	15
Missing items	6	3

If there have been no arithmetical errors, one can only assume that someone has stolen 6 Breaks and 3 Brunches.

27.6

(This is a brief answer showing the main points to be covered. In the examination the answer should be in report form and elaborated.)

1 For Charles Gray

(i) The concept of prudence says that stock should be valued at lower of cost or net realisable value. As 50% of the retail price £375 is lower than cost £560, then £375 will be taken as net realisable value and used for stock valuation.

(ii) The sale has not taken place by 30 April 2009. The prudence concept does not anticipate profits and therefore the sale will not be assumed. The gun should therefore be included in stock, at cost price £560.

2 For Jean Kim

It appears that it is doubtful if the business can still be treated as a going concern.

If the final decision is that the business cannot continue, then the stock valuation should be £510 each, as this is less than cost, with a further overall deduction of auction fees and expenses £300.

3 For Peter Fox

Stock must be valued at the lower of cost or net realisable value in this case.

The cost to be used is the *cost* for Peter Fox. It is quite irrelevant what the cost may be for other distributors.

It would also be against the convention of consistency to adopt a different method. The consistency applies to Peter Fox, it is not a case of consistency with other businesses. Using selling prices as a basis is not acceptable to the vast majority of businesses.

27.8

(a) In one respect the consistency convention is not applied, as at one year end the stock may be shown at cost whereas the next year end may see stock valued at net realisable value.

On the other hand, as it is prudent to take the lower of cost or net realisable value, it can be said to be consistently prudent to consistently take the lower figure.

(b) Being prudent can be said to be an advantage. For instance, a shareholder can know that stocks are not overvalued: if they were, it would give him a false picture of his investment.

Someone to whom money is owed, such as a creditor, will know that the stocks in the balance sheet are realisable at least at that figure.

It is this knowledge that profits are not recorded because of excessive values placed on stocks that gives outside parties confidence to rely on reported profits.

27.9

Cobden Ltd

Computation of inventory as at 31 May 2009

	Increase	Decrease
(a) No adjustment needed	–	–
(b) Cost lower than net realisable value		130
Reduction to net realisable value		126
(c) Arithmetic corrected	72	
(d) Omitted items	2,010	
(e) Transposition error		9
(f) Goods omitted	638	
(g) Hired item not to be included		347
(h) Samples to be excluded		63
(i) Sale or return items reduced to cost		184
(j) Goods held simply on sale or return		267
	2,720	1,126

Net increase	1,594
	87,612
Inventory as originally computed	89,206

28.1

Bank Reconciliation as at 31 December 2006

Cash at bank as per cash book	2,910
Add Credit transfers	340
	3,250
Cash at book per balance sheet	
Less Bank lodgements	560
	2,690
Add Unpresented cheques	730
Cash at bank as per bank statement	3,420

Note for students

Both in theory and in practice you can start with the cash book balance working to the bank statement balance, or you can reverse this method. Many teachers have their preferences, but this is a personal matter only. Examiners sometimes ask for them using one way, sometimes the other. Students should therefore be able to tackle them both ways.

28.3

(a)

Cash Book

2009 (Totals so far)	4,129	2009 (Totals so far)	692
Dec 31 T Morris	93	Dec 31 Bank Charges	47
		31 Balance c/d	3,483
	4,222		4,222

(b)

Bank Reconciliation Statement as on 31 December 2009

Balance per cash book	3,483
Add Unpresented cheque	209
	3,692
Less Bankings not yet on bank statement (319 + 246)	565
Balance per bank statement	3,127

or

Bank Reconciliation Statement as at 31 December 2009

Balance per bank statement		3,127
Add Bankings not yet on bank statement (319 + 246)		565
		3,692
Less Unpresented cheque		209
Balance per cash book		3,483

28.5

(a) *Cash Book (bank columns)*

2008			2008		
Dec 31 Balance b/d	1,500		Dec 31 Bank charges	30	
Dec 31 Dividends	240		Dec 31 RAC	70	
Dec 31 Customs and Excise	260		Dec 31 Loan repayment	200	
Dec 31 Deposit account	1,400		Dec 31 Balance c/d	3,100	
	3,400			3,400	

(b) *Bank Reconciliation Statement as on 31 December 2008*

Balance per cash book		3,100
Add Unpresented cheques (250 + 290)		540
		3,640
Less Bankings not entered on statement		690
Balance per bank statement		2,950

28.7

Cash Book

2006	(Totals so far)	853	2006	(Totals so far)	5,048
Mar 31 G Frank		88	Mar 31 TYF		32
31 Balance c/d		4,158	31 Bank charges		19
		5,099			5,099

Bank Reconciliation Statement as at 31 March 2006

Overdraft per cash book		4,158
Add Bankings not yet in bank statement		192
		4,350
Less Unpresented cheques		504
Overdraft per bank statement		3,846

28.9

(a) Balance per Cash Book at 31 October		(554)
Less: Bank charges	136	
Sundries cheque	44	
Cheque returned – Jones	80	
Rates standing order	150	
Incorrect entry	6	
		(416)
		(970)
Add Dividends received not entered	62	
Error in calculation of opening balance	50	
		112
Corrected Cash Book balance		(858)

George Ltd
Bank Reconciliation Statement as at 31 October

(b) Balance per Bank Statement*		(1,353)
Add Outstanding lodgements		762
		(591)
Less Unpresented cheques		(267)
Balance per cash book		(858)

*This is the balancing figure.

29.1 *Sales Ledger Control*

Balances b/d	23,220	Returns inwards	826	
Sales Day Book	14,194	Cheques and cash	17,918	
		Discounts allowed	312	
		Balances c/d	18,358	
	37,414		37,414	

29.3 *Sales Ledger Control*

2009		2009		
March 1 Balances b/d	12,271	March 31 Cash and bank	11,487	
March 31 Sales	9,334	March 31 Discounts allowed	629	
		March 31 Set-offs:		
March 31 Balances c/d	47	Purchases ledger	82	
		March 31 Balances c/d	9,454	
	21,652		21,652	

29.5 *Purchases Ledger Control*

Returns outwards	1,452	Balances b/d	19,420	
Bank	205,419	Purchases Day Book	210,416	
Petty cash	62			
Discounts received	1,721			
Set-offs against sales ledger	640			
Balances c/d	20,210			
	*229,504		*229,836	

*Difference between two sides 332

Sales Ledger Control

Balances b/d	28,227	Returns inwards	3,618	
Sales Day Book	305,824	Bank and cash	287,317	
		Discounts allowed	4,102	
		Set-offs against		
		Purchase ledger	640	
		Balances c/d	38,374	
	334,051		334,051	

29.6

Debtors' Ledger Control

	£		£
Balance b/d	46,462	Balance b/d	245
Sales	126,024	Contra	455
Cash	52	Bad debt	1,253
		Discount	746
		Cash	120,464
		Balance c/d	49,375
	172,538		172,538
Balance b/d	49,375		

Creditor's Ledger Control

	£		£
Balance b/d	1,472	Balance b/d	25,465
Returns	2,154	Purchases	76,474
Contra	455		
Discount received	1,942		
Cash	70,476		
Balance c/d	25,440		
	101,939		101,939
		Balance b/d	25,440

29.9

Total Debtors Account

	£		£
Balance b/d	26,555	Cash (600,570 − 344,890)	255,680
Credit sales	268,187	Discounts allowed	5,520
		Set-offs (Total debtors)	70
		Bad debts	780
		Returns inwards	4,140
		Balances c/d	28,552
	294,742		294,742
Balances b/d	28,552		

Total Creditors Account

	£		£
Cash (503,970 − 14,440)	489,530	Balances b/d	43,450
Discounts received	3,510	Credit purchases	496,600
Set-offs (total creditors)	70		
Returns outwards	1,480		
Balances c/d	45,460		
	540,050		540,050
		Balances b/d	45,460

Note: the provision for doubtful debts does not affect the control account.

29.10

(a) To ensure an arithmetical check on the accounting records. The agreement of total of individual creditors balances with that of the balance on control account provides that check.

If control account and ledger are kept by separate personnel, then a check on their work and honesty is provided.

(b) (i) Increase £198 (ii) Decrease £100 (iii) No effect (iv) Decrease £400 (v) Decrease £120.

(c) A computer will automatically enter two figures in different directions and will then confirm it in total fashion. As such there may seem at first sight for there to be no need for control accounts.

However, there is still the need to check on the accuracy of data input. It is important that both the skill and the honesty of the programmer are checked.

Accordingly there will still be a need for control accounts.

29.11

(a) See Section 29.1.
(b) See Section 29.5.

30.1

(a) Error of omission – a credit purchase omitted from the books.
(b) Error of commission – a credit sale to J Briggs entered in the account of H Briggs.
(c) Error of principle – repairs debited to the asset account.
(d) Compensating errors – prepayments £15 too high and accruals £15 too high.
(e) Errors of original entry – a credit purchase for £100 recorded in the books as £10.
(f) Complete reversal of entries – payment of advertising debited to bank and credited to advertising.
(g) Transposition error – sales invoice for £263 entered as £236 in both ledger accounts.

30.2

To economise on space, all narratives for journal entries are omitted.

		£			£
(a) T More	Dr	412	T Mone	Cr	412
(b) Machinery	Dr	619	J Frank	Cr	619
(c) Computer	Dr	550	Office expenses	Cr	550
(d) B Wood	Dr	18	Sales	Cr	18
(e) Sales	Dr	164	Commissions rec'd	Cr	164
(f) Cash (needs double the amount)	Dr	136	T Blair	Cr	136
(g) Purchases	Dr	372	Drawings	Cr	372
(h) Discounts allowed	Dr	48	Discounts received	Cr	48

30.4

(a) 100 units × £1.39 = £139 *not* £1.390.
(b) (i) Stock overstated by £1,251 (i.e. 1,390 − 139).
(ii) Cost of goods sold understated by £1,251.
(iii) Net profit overstated by £1,251.
(iv) Current Assets overstated by £1,251.
(v) Owner's Capital overstated by £1,251.

30.5

		£			£
(a) Sales	Dr	5,000	Capital	Cr	5,000
(b) Drawings	Dr	72	Sundry expenses	Cr	72
(c) Drawings	Dr	191	Rent	Cr	191
(d) D Pine	Dr	180	Purchases	Cr	180
(e) Bank	Dr	820	Cash	Cr	820
(f) Bank	Dr	120	Cash	Cr	120
(g) T Young	Dr	195	G Will	Cr	195
(h) Office expenses	Dr	100	Printer disposals	Cr	100

31.1

	Dr	Cr
(i) Purchases		
(ii) Creditors		
(iii) Sales		

Suspense

	20	Balance b/d 9
		11
	40	40

31.2

The Journal (narratives omitted)

(a)

	Dr	Cr
(i) Suspense	200	
Sales		200
(ii) T Vantura	610	
T Ventura		610
(iii) Rent	90	
Suspense		90
(iv) Suspense	100	
Discounts allowed		100
(v) Sales	230	
Computer disposals		230

(b)

Suspense Account

Sales	200	Balance b/d	210
Discounts allowed	100	Rent	90
	300		300

(c)

Net profit per financial statements		31,400
Add (i) Sales undercast	200	
(iv) Discounts overcast	100	300
		31,700
Less (iii) Rent undercast	90	
(v) Reduction in sales	230	320
Corrected net profit		31,380

31.5   Trial Balance as at 31 January 2003

	Dr	Cr
Drawings	19,500	
Stock	8,410	
Debtors (34,517 − 8)	34,509	
Furniture (2,400 + 407)	2,807	
Cash	836	
Returns inwards	2,438	
Business expenses	3,204	
Purchases (72,100 − 407)	71,693	
Discounts allowed	42	
Capital		7,845
Creditors (6,890 − 315)		6,575
Sales (127,510 + 90)		127,600
Discounts received		1,419
	143,439	143,439

31.6

(a) (i)   The Journal

C Thomas

	Dr	Cr
Thomasson Manufacturing Ltd	450	450
Suspense	100	
Telephone		100
Suspense	2,000	
Sales account		2,000
Machine repairs	390	
Machinery		390
Suspense	1,500	
Rent received*		1,500
Purchases account	765	
P Brooks		765

* Assumed not invoiced to Atlas Ltd

(ii) Computation of Corrected Profit for year ending 31 December 2008

Profit as originally reported		47,240
Add Telephone expense overstated	100	
Sales understated	2,000	
Rent received omitted	1,500	3,600
		50,840
Less Machinery repairs understated	390	
Purchases omitted	765	1,155
Corrected profit figure		49,685

(b) (i) Per text (ii) Per text

31.4

Item	If no effect state 'No'	Debit side exceeds credit side by	Credit side exceeds debit side by
(i)	No		
(ii)	No		
(iii)	No		
(iv)		£290	
(v)			£188
(vi)			£317
(vii)	No		

701

31.8

(a)   Difference on Trial Balance Suspense

Per trial balance	2,513	J Winters	198
Discounts received	324	Wages	2,963
Discounts allowed	324		
	3,161		3,161

(b)   **Computation of Corrected Net Profit for year ending 30 April 2007**

Net profit per draft accounts			24,760
	–	+	
(i) Discounts	–	648	
(ii) Wages	2,963		
(iv) Stationery stock		1,500	
(vi) Remittance	3,000		
	5,963	2,148	
Correct net profit			3,815
			20,945

(iii) and (v) did not affect profit

(c) Per text

31.11

(a) (i) Van | 6,000 |
Motor vehicle expenses		6,000
(ii) Fuel	250	
Drawings		250
(iii) B Struton	300	
B Burton Ltd		300
(iv) Drawings	750	
Business rates		750
(v) Drawings	720	
Wages		720
(vi) Purchases	500	
K Jarman		500

(b) Net profit per draft financial statements | | 23,120 |
Add (i)	6,000	
(iv)	750	
(v)	720	
	7,470	
		30,590
Less (ii)	250	
(vi)	500	
	750	
		29,840

31.12

(a) (i) Suspense | 10 | |
Sales		10
(ii) Discount allowed	2	
Suspense		2
(iii) Discount allowed	140	
Suspense		140
(iv) D Bird	10	
Suspense		10
(v) Suspense	3	
J Flyn		3

(b) The overall effect on the trial balance is that the following changes have been made:

		Dr	Cr
(i)	Sales	142	10
(ii) and (iii)	Discount allowed	7	
(iv) and (v)	Debtors		
(i) to (v)	Suspense		139

31.14   Workings

(i) Purchases	10	
Suspense		10
(ii) A Supplier	45	
Suspense		45
(iii) Plant and Machinery	70	
Repairs		70
(iv) Suspense	20	
S Kane		20
(v) Sales	300	
Plant and Machinery disposals		300
(vi) Debtors	60	
Suspense		60
(vii) Suspense	2	
B Luckwood		2
(viii) Business rates	45	
Prepayments		45

(a)   Suspense

Balance	93	(i) Purchases	10
(iv) S Kane	20	(ii) A Supplier	45
(vii) B Luckwood	2	(vi) Debtors	60
	115		115

(b) (i) The suspense account is shown in the balance sheet, not the profit and loss account. The following item increases net profit:

(iii)   70

The following items reduce net profit:

(i)   10
(viii)   45
    (55)
    15

Overall, net profit is increased by   15

Note: (v) has no effect or net profit. Sales are reduced by 300 and the loss on disposal of the plant and machinery is reduced by 300.

(ii) The following items are changed in the balance sheet

Suspense	Dr	Cr
		93
(ii) Creditors	45	
(iii) Plant and Machinery	70	
(iv), (vi), (vii) Debtors	38	
(viii) Prepayments		45
Net profit		15
	153	153

Answers to Scenario Questions

SQ1 (a)

Picta Simpla
Profit and Loss Account for the year ending 30 June 2007

	£	£
Sales		258,100
Less Cost of goods sold		
Opening stock	19,250	
Purchases	185,850	
	205,100	
Less: Closing stock	50,150	
		154,950
Gross profit		103,150
Less Expenses		
Wages	14,500	
Advertising	15,500	
Postage and packing	7,250	
Rent	12,000	
Insurance	2,850	
Electricity	3,400	
Depreciation	800	
Stationery	1,350	
Telephone	3,450	
		61,100
Net profit		42,050

(b) Your note should explain that the business is a separate entity from him and so the cost of having a holiday has nothing to do with the business, but must be treated as drawings. It should also explain that drawings represent the amount of business assets taken out of the business by the owner for the owner's, not the business's use. Drawings are *never* an expense of the business.

SQ2
(a)

Sleasy Cars
Balance Sheet as at 31 December 2006

	£	£	£
Fixed Assets			
Land			5,000
Offices		500	
Less Depreciation		100	400
Truck		5,000	
Less Depreciation		2,500	2,500
			7,900
Current Assets			
Stock	21,000		
Debtors and prepayments	1,900		
Cash	100		
	23,000		
Current Liabilities			
Creditors and accruals	8,600		
Bank overdraft	6,400		
		15,000	
Working capital			8,000
			15,900
Long-term Liability			3,000
			12,900
Capital			
Opening balance*		15,500	
Add Net profit**		8,400	
		23,900	
Less Drawings		11,000	
			12,900

*5,000 + 10,000 + 500 = 15,500
**23,500 − 500 − 100 − 3,000 − 2,500 − 500 − 2,000 − 400 − 5,000 − 1,500 + 400 = 8,400

SQ2 (cont'd)

(b)

	Dr £	Cr £
Office overvalued: Net profit	500	
Office		500
Office depreciation: Net profit	100	
Depreciation–Office		100
Land overvalued: Net profit	5,000	
Land		5,000
Provision for long-term liability: Net profit	3,000	
Long-Term liability		3,000
Depreciation on truck: Net profit	2,500	
Depreciation–Truck		2,500
Car overvalued: Net profit	500	
Stock		500
Bad debt: Net profit	2,000	
Debtors		2,000
Accruals: Net profit	400	
Accruals		400
Prepayment: Prepayment	400	
Net profit		400
Car overvalued: Net profit	1,500	
Stock		1,500

SQ3

Mr Jones

Trading Profit and Loss Account for the year ending XXXX

	£	£
Sales		430,000
Less Cost of goods sold		
Opening stock	6,520	
Purchases	305,500	
Carriage in	2,100	
	314,120	
Less Closing stock	7,000	307,120
Gross profit		122,880
Less: Expenses		
Rent	5,350	
Business rates	2,800	
Insurance	400	
Postage	250	
Stationery	1,002	
Advertising	200	
Salaries and wages	10,500	
Bad debts	400	
Provision for doubtful debts	112	
Depreciation	15,000	36,014
Net profit		86,866

Balance Sheet as at XXXX

	£	£	£
Fixed Assets			
Equipment			150,000
Less: Depreciation			50,000
			100,000
Current Assets			
Stock		7,000	
Debtors		4,608	
Prepayment		200	
Cash in hand		120	
		11,928	
Current Liabilities			
Creditors	9,600		
Bank overdraft	2,743		
Accrual	366		
		12,709	781
			99,219
Capital			
Balance			43,353
Net profit			86,866
			130,219
Less Drawings			31,000
			99,219

SQ4

(a) *Trading and Profit and Loss Account for the year ending 30 June 2007*

Mr Try

	£	£
Sales		17,644
Less Expenses		
Repairs	230	
Miscellaneous	110	
Insurance (350 − 50)	300	
Accounting fees (250 − 250 + 275)	275	
Postage and stationery	50	
Depreciation	375	
Doubtful debt provision	110	
Bank charges	45	1,495
Net profit		16,149

(b)

Balance Sheet as at 30 June 2007

	£	£	£
Fixed Assets			
Ladders and equipment		750	
Less: Depreciation		375	
			375
Current Assets			
Cleaning materials and cloths		3,400	
Debtors		110	
Prepayments		50	
Bank		2,345	
Cash		35	
		5,940	
Current Liabilities			
Creditors	100		
Accruals	320		
		420	
			5,520
			5,895
Capital			
Balance at 1 July 2006			16,149
Net profit			346
			16,495
Less Drawings			10,600
			5,895

(c) Your letter should explain that consumables are items purchased with the intention of using them in the short-term, after which they will either have been used up (e.g. printer ink) or no longer useable (e.g. carbon paper). The ladders do not fall into the category of consumables. They were purchased for use in the long-term, in this case, more than one accounting period. As such, they are fixed assets and must be depreciated.

SQ5 (a)

B's Casuals

Profit and Loss Account for the year ending 30 June 2007

Sales		260,040
Less: Cost of goods sold		
Opening stock	21,500	
Purchases	68,500	
Carriage in	5,200	
	95,200	
Less: Closing stock	22,500	
		72,700
		187,340
Gross profit		187,340
Less: Expenses		
Wages	24,500	
Business rates	9,950	
Bad debt	2,000	
Advertising	1,040	
Insurance	2,850	
Electricity	3,400	
Depreciation	15,800	
Stationery	1,350	
Telephone	3,450	
	64,340	
		123,000

(b)

Balance Sheet as at 30 June 2007

Fixed Assets		
Factory and Machinery	400,000	
Less Depreciation	115,000	
		285,000
Computer	4,000	
Less Depreciation	2,400	
		1,600
		286,600
Current Assets		
Prepayments:		
Insurance	650	
Telephone	200	
Cash in hand	600	
	1,450	
Current liabilities		
Creditors	3,500	
Rates Accrual	2,450	
Electricity Accrual	500	
Loan from Mrs Baldwin	600	
	7,050	
		5,600
		281,000
Capital		
Balance at 1 July 2006		213,000*
Net profit		123,000
Less Drawings		(55,000)
		281,000

*balancing figure

(c) You need to explain how the accrual system operates and why it is used (see text Section 10.7). You also need to explain that drawings are assets withdrawn from the business for the owner's personal use, which is what his 'wages' and his home cinema system purchase are. Drawings are never expenses of a business.

32.1

G Flynn

Trading Account for the year ended 31 December 2007

Sales		155,880
Less Cost of goods sold:		
Stock 1.1.2007	19,400	
Add Purchases	137,160	(D)
	156,560	(C)
Less Stock 32.12.2007	26,660	
	129,900	(B)
Gross profit	25,980	(A)

Missing figures found in the order (A) to (D).

(A) Mark-up is 20%. Therefore Margin is 16.67%. Sales are 155,880 so Margin is 16.67% or 1/6; 1/6 × 155,880 = 25,980 Gross Profit

(B) + (A) = 155,880. Therefore (B) + 25,980 = 155,880 and accordingly (B) is 129,900.

(C) − 26,660 = 129,900. Therefore (C) is 156,560.

(D) + 19,400 = 156,500. Therefore (D) is 137,160.

Van

Bank	3,500	Balance c/d	3,500
	3,500		3,500
Balance b/d	3,500		

Purchases

A. Supplier	2,500	Balance c/d	2,500
	2,500		2,500
Balance b/d	2,500		

A. Supplier

Returns	500	Purchases	2,500
Balance c/d	2,000		
	2,500		2,500
		Balance b/d	2,000

Sales

Balance c/d	1,300	Cash	300
		B. Safe	1,000
	1,300		1,300
		Balance b/d	1,300

B. Safe

Sales	1,000	Balance c/d	1,000
	1,000		1,000
Balance b/d	1,000		

Returns out

Balance c/d	500	A. Supplier	500
	500		500
		Balance b/d	500

Sundry Expenses

Cash	50	Balance c/d	50
	50		50
Balance b/d	50		

32.3

(a) We know that

$$\frac{\text{Cost of goods sold}}{\text{Average stock}} = \text{Rate of stock turnover}$$

Substituting $\dfrac{x}{16,240} = 8$

$x = $ Cost of goods sold $= 129,920$.

(b) If mark-up is 60%, gross profit is 60% of the cost of sales $= 77,952$.

(c) Turnover is (a) + (b) = 129,920 + 77,952 = 207,872.

(d) 70% × 77,952 = 54,566.40.

(e) Gross profit − Expenses = Net profit = 23,385.60.

32.5

(a) Sales = 230,000 + (20% × 230,000) = 276,000.

(b) 41,400 − (9% × 271,400) = 16,974.

(c) $\dfrac{230,000}{(34,000+41,000) \div 2} = \dfrac{230,000}{37,500} = 6.13$

(d) Gross profit is 25% × 260,000 = 65,000.
Sales are 260,000 + 65,000 = 325,000.
Expenses are 9% of sales = 29,250.
Net profit = 65,000 − 29,250 = 35,750.

32.7

(a)

Capital

Balance c/d	5,000	Bank	5,000
	5,000		5,000
		Balance b/d	5,000

Bank

Capital	5,000	Cash	300
		Van	3,500
		Rent	500
		Balance c/d	700
	5,000		5,000
Balance b/d	700		

Cash

Bank	300	Sundry Expenses	50
Sales	300	Drawings	500
		Balance c/d	50
	600		600
Balance b/d	50		

Rent

Bank	500	Balance c/d	500
	500		500
Balance b/d	500		

Drawings

Cash	500	Balance c/d	500
	500		500
Balance b/d	500		

(b)

L. Mann
Trial Balance as at 30 April

Bank	700	
Cash	50	
Van	3,500	
Purchases	2,500	
Debtors	1,000	
Sundry expenses	50	
Rent	500	
Drawings	500	
Capital		5,000
Creditors		2,000
Sales		1,300
Returns out		500
	8,800	8,800

(c) *Trading, Profit and Loss Account for the month ending 30 April*

Sales		1300
Purchases	2,500	
– Returns out	500	
	2,000	
– Closing stock	750	
Cost of sales		750
Gross profit		550
Less Expenses		
Sundry expenses	50	
Rent	500	
		550
		0

(d) *Balance Sheet as at 30 April*

Fixed Assets		
Van		3,500
Current Assets		
Stock	1,250	
Debtors	1,000	
Bank	700	
Cash	50	
	3,000	
Current Liabilities		
Creditors	2,000	
		1,000
		4,500
Capital		5,000
Less Drawings		500
		4,500

(e) (i) $\dfrac{550}{1,300} = 42.3\%$

(ii) $\dfrac{0}{5,000} = 0\%$

(f) (i) As there has been neither a profit or a loss, the £500 drawings are eating into capital. This is not a good sign. Drawings must not exceed net profit in the long-term, or the business will fail.

(ii) Working capital is £1,000. The current ratio is 1.5, which ought to be adequate, though this would need to be confirmed by comparison with other businesses operating in the same sector.

32.9 (a)

	2007	2008	2009
Opening stock	10,000	21,000	25,000
Purchases	70,000	86,000	77,000
	80,000	107,000	102,000
Less Closing stock	21,000	25,000	23,000
Cost of goods sold	(59,000)	(82,000)	(79,000)
Sales	90,000	125,000	120,000
Gross profit	31,000	43,000	41,000

(b) Gross profit/sales

(i) 2007

$\dfrac{31,000}{90,000} = 34\%$

2008

$\dfrac{43,000}{125,000} = 34\%$

2009

$\dfrac{41,000}{120,000} = 34\%$

707

32.9 (cont'd)

(ii) Stock turnover = $\dfrac{\text{Cost goods sold}}{\text{Average stock}}$

2007

$\dfrac{59,000}{(10,000 + 21,000) \div 2} = 3.8$ times

2008

$\dfrac{82,000}{(21,000 + 25,000) \div 2} = 3.5$ times

2009

$\dfrac{79,000}{(25,000 + 23,000) \div 2} = 3.2$ times

33.1

F Lee
Statement of Affairs as at 31 December 2002

Fixed assets			
Van at cost		6,400	
Less Depreciation		1,600	
			4,800
Current assets			
Stock		6,200	
Debtors		15,200	
Prepaid expenses		310	
Bank		33,490	
Cash		270	
		55,470	
Less Current liabilities			
Trade creditors	7,100		
Expenses owing	640		
		7,740	
Net current assets			47,730
			52,530
Capital			
Cash introduced		35,000	(C)
Add Net profit			(B)
Less Drawings		20,870	(A)

Missing figures (A), (B) and (C) deduced in that order. (A) to balance is 52,530, thus (B) has to be 73,400 and (C) becomes 38,400.

33.2

$500 \times 4 = 2,000 =$ Costs
$\qquad\qquad \times 5$
$\qquad\qquad = 10,000 =$ Fees

Fees	10,000
Costs	2,000
Profit	8,000

33.4

Workings:

Purchases Bank	67,360
Cash	4,940
	72,300
– Creditors 31.12.2001	12,700
	59,600
+ Creditors 31.12.2002	14,100
Purchases for 2002	73,700

Sales Banked	91,190
Cash	17,400
	108,590
– Debtors 31.12.2001	21,200
	87,390
+ Debtors 31.12.2002	19,800
Sales for 2002	107,190

Opening Capital:

Bank	4,100
Stock	10,800
Debtors	21,200
Insurance prepaid	420
Fixtures	1,800
	38,320
Less Creditors	12,700
Rent owing	390
	13,090
	25,230

Jane
Trading and Profit and Loss Account for the year ending 31 December 2002

Sales			107,190
Less Cost of goods sold:			
Opening stock		10,800	
Add Purchases		73,700	
		84,500	
Less Closing stock		12,200	
			72,300
Gross profit			34,890
Less Expenses:			
Wages		11,260	
Rent (3,950 − 390)		3,560	
Insurance (1,470 + 420 − 440)		1,450	
Sundry expenses		610	
Depreciation: Fixtures		200	
			17,080
Net profit			17,810

Balance Sheet as at 31 December 2002

Fixed assets		
Fixtures at valuation	1,800	
Less Depreciation	200	1,600
Current assets		
Stock	12,200	
Debtors	19,800	
Prepayments	440	
	32,440	
Less Current liabilities		
Trade creditors	14,100	
Bank overdraft	6,300	
	20,400	
Net current assets		12,040
		13,640
Capital		
Balance at 1.1.2002		25,230
Add Net profit		17,810
		43,040
Less Drawings (1,200 + 28,200)		29,400
		13,640

33.6

Jenny Barnes

Trading and Profit and Loss Account for the year ending 30 April 2009

Sales*		102,908
Less: Opening stock	9,500	
Purchases	78,100	
	87,600	
Less: Closing stock	13,620	73,980
Gross profit		28,928
Less: Expenses		
Sales assistants' wages	5,620	
Vehicle running expenses	1,020	
Bad debts	150	
Miscellaneous expenses**	1,370	
Light and heat	940	
Depreiation: Equipment	720	
Vehicles	1,000	10,460
Net profit		18,468

*Sales 96,500 + takings in cash later spent 6,408
(drawings 6,000 + expenses 408)
**Bank 962 + cash 408 = 1,370

33.8

(a)

Creditors Control

Bank	101,500	Balances b/d	7,400
Cash	1,800	Drawings: Goods	600
Balances c/d	8,900	Purchases (difference)	104,200
	112,200		112,200

(b)

Janet Lambert

Trading and Profit and Loss Account for the year ending 31 August 2009

Sales (deduced – as margin is 25% = 4 × gross profit)		128,000
Opening stock	8,600	
Add Purchases	104,200	
	112,800	
Less Closing stock	16,800	
Cost of goods sold		96,000
Gross profit (33⅓% of Cost of goods sold)		32,000
Less: Casual labour (1,200 + 6,620)	7,820	
Rent (5,040 + 300 – 420)	4,920	
Delivery costs	3,000	
Electricity (1,390 + 160 – 210)	1,340	17,080
Net profit		14,920

Balance Sheet as at 31 August 2009

Current assets		
Stock	16,800	
Debtors	4,300	
Prepayments	420	
Bank	1,650	
Cash	330	
	23,500	
Less Current liabilities		
Creditors	8,900	
Expenses owing	160	
	9,060	
		14,440
Capital:		
Balance as at 1 September 2008 (Workings 1)		7,850
Add Net profit		14,920
		22,770
Less Drawings (Workings 2)		8,330
		14,440

Workings:
(1) Capital as on 1.9.2008. Stock 8,600 + Debtors 3,900 + Prepaid 300 + Bank 2,300 + Cash 360 = 15,460 – Creditors 7,400 – Accruals 210 = 7,850.
(2) Cash drawings. Step (A) find cash received from sales. Debtors b/d 3,900 + Sales 128,000 – Debtors c/d 4,300 = 127,600 cash received.

33.8 (cont'd)

Step (B) find cash banked. Balance b/d 2,300 + cash received? – payments 117,550 = balance c/d 1,650. Therefore cash banked? = 116,900. Step (C) draw up cash account:

Balance b/d	360	Labour	1,200
Sales receipts	127,600	Purchases	1,800
		Banked	116,900
		Drawings (difference)	7,730
		Balance c/d	330
	127,960		127,960

(c) Per text.

33.10 David Denton

Profit and Loss Account for the year ending 31 December 2010

Work done: Credit accounts		29,863	
For cash		3,418	33,281
Less Expenses:			
Materials (9,600 – 580)		9,020	
Secretarial salary		3,000	
Rent		225	
Rates (180 – 45)		135	
Insurance (800 – 200)		600	
Electricity (1,122 + 374 estimated)		1,496	
Motor expenses		912	
General expenses (1,349 + 295)		1,644	
Loan interest (4,000 × 10% × $^3/_4$)		300	
Provision for doubtful debts		425	
Accounting fee		250	
Amortisation of lease (650 × $^3/_4$)		487	
Depreciation: Equipment	960		
Van	900	1,860	20,354
Net profit			12,927

Balance Sheet as at 31 December 2010

	Cost	Depreciation	
Fixed assets			
Lease	6,500	487	6,013
Equipment	4,800	960	3,840
Vehicle	3,600	900	2,700
	14,900	2,347	12,553
Current assets			
Stock		580	
Debtors	4,250		
Less Provision for doubtful debts	425	3,825	
Prepaid expenses (75 + 200)		275	
Bank (see workings)		6,084	
Cash		123	
		10,887	
Less Current liabilities			
Trade creditors	714		
Interest owing	300		
Accountancy fee owing	250		
Rates owing	135		
Electricity owing	374	1,773	
Net current assets			9,114
			21,667
Less Loan			4,000
			17,667
Financed by:			
Capital			10,100
Introduced (6,500 + 3,600)			
Add Net profit			12,927
			23,027
Less Drawings (4,680 + 280 + 400)			5,360
			17,667

Workings:

Bank (6,500 + 25,613 + 2,600 + 4,000) = 38,713 – 4,680 – 280 – 6,500 – 300 – 3,000 – 8,886 – 4,800 – 1,122 – 912 – 1,349 – 800 = 6,084

33.11

(a)

J Duncan

Capital Account on 1 January 2008

Bank		8,000
Cash		300
Stock		4,100
Machinery		12,600
Rent prepaid		200
Debtors		6,300
		31,500
Less: Creditors	2,400	
Loan	5,000	(7,400)
		24,100

(b)

J Duncan
Trading and Profit and Loss Account for the year ending 31 December 2008

Sales			40,450
Less: Sales returns			1,200
			39,250
Less: Cost of Sales			
Opening Stock at 1 January 2008		4,100	
Add: Purchases		18,950	
		23,050	
Less: Withdrawn by the owner	300		
Less: Closing stock at 31 December 2008	3,200	3,500	
			19,550
Gross profit			19,700
Add: Discount received			350
			20,050
Less: Expenses			
Rent		1,850	
Bad debts written-off		400	
Wages		6,100	
Insurance		1,450	
Loan interest		400	
Depreciation		4,200	
Repairs		300	
Electricity		750	
			15,450
Net profit			4,600

Workings:
Sales 26,000 − 250 + 14,000 + 400 − 6,300 + 5,000 + 1,200 + 400 = 40,450
Purchases 18,500 − 2,400 − 2,500 + 2,400 + 350 = 18,950
Depreciation = balancing figure.

33.12

J Duncan
Balance Sheet as at 31 December 2008

Fixed Assets				
Machinery at 1 January 2008			12,600	
Add: Additions			7,500	
			20,100	
Less: Depreciation			4,200	
				15,900
Current assets				
Stock			3,200	
Debtors			5,000	
Bank			2,600	
Cash			50	
			10,850	
Current liabilities				
Creditors		2,500		
Accrued charges				
Loan interest	100			
Rent	250	350		
		2,850		
			8,000	
			23,900	
Less: Long-term liabilities				
Bank loan 8%			5,000	
			18,900	
Capital Account				
Balance at 1 January 2008			24,100	
Add: Net profit			4,600	
			28,700	
Less: Drawings			9,800	
			18,900	

33.15

Stock value per stocktake on 3 May 2005	124,620
Less Purchases (1,510 − 530)	980
	123,640
Less Sales returns (222 @ 80%)	176
	123,464
Less Obsolete stock	300
	123,164
Add Stock sold (2,300 @ 80%)	1,840
Value of stock on 30 April 2005	125,004

34.1 Downline Rugby Club
Income and Expenditure Account for the year ending 31 December 2006

Income		
Collections at matches		4,218
Profit on refreshments		5,520
		9,738
Less Expenditure		
Rent for pitch (1,600 – 400)	1,200	
Printing and stationery (104 + 25)	129	
Secretary's expenses	210	
Repairs to equipment	210	
Groundsman's wages	6,400	
Miscellaneous expenses	96	
Depreciation of equipment	476	
		8,731
Surplus of income over expenditure		1,007

Balance Sheet as at 31 December 2006

Fixed assets		
Equipment	2,380	
Less Depreciation	476	
		1,904
Current assets		
Prepayment	400	
Cash	2,168	
	2,568	
Less Current liabilities		
Expenses owing	25	
Net current assets		2,543
Net assets		4,447
Financed by:		
Accumulated fund		
Balance at 1.1.2006 (2,000 + 1,440)		3,440
Add Surplus of income over expenditure		1,007
		4,447

34.3 The Happy Haddock Angling Club
(a) Income and Expenditure Account for the year ending 31 December 2008

Income:		
Subscriptions		3,500
Visitors' fees		650
Competition fees		820
Snack bar profit (see workings)		1,750
		6,720
Less Expenditure:		
Rent and rates	1,500	
Secretarial expenses	240	
Loan interest	260	
Depreciation on games equipment	400	
		2,400
Surplus of income over expenditure		4,320

Workings: Snack bar profit: 6,000 – (800 + 3,750 – 900) – 600 = 1,750

(b) Balance Sheet as at 31 December 2008

Fixed assets		
Clubhouse buildings		20,500
Games equipment	2,000	
Less Depreciation	400	1,600
		22,100
Current assets		
Snack bar stocks	900	
Bank	700	
	1,600	
Less Current liabilities		
Subscriptions received in advance	380	
		1,220
		23,320
Less Loan from bank		5,500
		17,820
Financed by:		
Accumulated fund		
Balance 1.1.2008 (see workings)	13,500	
Add surplus for year	4,320	
		17,820

Workings: 200 + 800 + 12,500 = 13,500

34.5
(a) Accumulated fund 1 August 2008

Equipment		975
Stocks of prizes		38
Arrears of subscriptions		65
Cash and bank		210
		1,288
Less Subscriptions in advance	10	
Prizes suppliers	58	
		68
		1,220

(b)
(i) *Subscriptions*

In arrears b/d	65	In advance b/d	10
In advance c/d	37	Cash	1,987
Income and expenditure	1,980	In arrears c/d	85
	2,082		2,082

(ii) *Competition prizes*

Stocks b/d	38	Creditors b/d	58
Cash	270	Stock c/d	46
Creditors c/d	68	Cost of prizes given	272
	376		376

(c)

Miniville Rotary Club
Income and expenditure account for the year ended 31 July 2009

Income

Subscriptions		1,980
Ticket sales	437	
Less Cost of prizes	272	165
Donations received		177
		2,322

Less Expenditure

Rent (1,402 − 500)	902	
Visiting speakers' expenses	1,275	
Secretarial expenses	163	
Stationery and printing	179	
Donations to charities	35	
Depreciation	195	2,749
Excess of expenditure over income		427

Balance sheet as at 31 July 2009

Fixed assets

Equipment at cost		1,420
Less Depreciation		640
		780

Current assets

Stocks of prizes	46	
Arrears of subscriptions	85	
	131	

Less Current liabilities

Creditors for prizes	68	
Advance subscriptions	37	
Bank overdraft	13	118
		13
		793

Accumulated fund

Balance 1.8.2008		1,220
Less Excess of expenditure over income		427
		793

34.7

(a) Café operations:

Takings		4,660
Less Cost of supplies:		
Opening stock	800	
Add purchases (1,900 + 80)	1,980	
	2,780	
Less Closing stock	850	1,930
		2,730
Wages		2,000
Profit		730

Sports equipment:

Sales		900
Less Cost of goods sold:		
Opening stock	1,000	
Add Purchases (1,000 × 50%)	500	
	1,500	
Less Closing stock (see note)	900	600
Profit		300

Note: To find closing sports equipment stock: 900 is sales at 50% on cost so cost of sales is 600. By arithmetical deduction closing stock is found to be 900.

(b)

Subscriptions

Owing b/d	60	In advance b/d		120
		Cash: 2007		40
Income and expenditure	1,280	2008		1,100
		2009		80
In advance c/d	80	Owing c/d		80
	1,420			1,420

Life Subscriptions

Income and expenditure	220	Balance b/d	1,400
(11 × 20)		Cash	200
Balance c/d	1,380		
	1,600		1,600

(c)

Happy Tickers & Social Club
Income and Expenditure Account for the year ended 31 December 2008

Income:

Subscriptions (1,280 + 220)		1,500
Profit on café operations		730
Profit on sports equipment		300
		2,530

Less Expenditure

Rent	1,200	
Insurance	600	
Repairs to roller ($\frac{1}{2} \times 450$)	225	
Sports equipment depreciation (see note 1)	486	
Depreciation of roller ($\frac{1}{2} \times 200$)	100	2,611
Excess of expenditure over income		81

34.7 (cont'd) Balance Sheet as at 31 December 2008

Fixed assets

Share in motor roller at cost	1,000	
Less Depreciation to date	500	
		500
Used sports equipment at valuation		700
		1,200

Current assets

Stock of new sports equipment (see note 2)	900
Stock of café supplies	850
Subscriptions owing	80
Carefree Conveyancers: owing for expenses	225
Prepaid expenses	350
Cash and bank (note 3)	754
	3,159

Less Current liabilities

Café suppliers	80	
Advance subscriptions	80	
		160
		2,999
Less Life subscriptions		1,380
		4,199
		2,819

Accumulated fund

Balance at 1.1.2008	2,900
Less Excess of expenditure	81
	2,819

Notes:

1 Stock b/d

Used Sports Equipment

Stock b/d	700	Cash		14
Transferred from purchases	500	Income and expenditure a/c		486
		Stock c/d		700
	1,200			1,200

2 b/d 1,000 + bought (1,000 × ½) 500 = 1,500 − sold 600 = 900

3 b/d 1,210 + receipts 6,994 − paid 7,450 = 754

(d) To most people probably the best description of the item would be 'deferred income', i.e. income paid in advance for future benefits.

It could, however, be described as a liability of the club. The club in future will have to provide and finance amenities for life members, but they do not have to pay any more money for it. This is therefore the liability of the future to provide these services without further payment.

35.1

Loose Tools

2007				2007		
Jan 1 Stock	b/d	2,400		Dec 31 Manufacturing		1,930
Dec 31 Bank		3,800		31 Stock	c/d	5,100
31 Wages		490				
31 Materials		340				
		7,030				7,030

2008				2008		
Jan 1 Stock	b/d	5,100		Dec 31 Manufacturing	c/d	2,010
Dec 31 Bank		1,820		31 Stock		5,940
31 Wages		610				
31 Materials		420				
		7,950				7,950

2009				2009		
Jan 1 Stock	b/d	5,940		Dec 31 Bank: Refund		142
Dec 31 Bank		2,760		31 Manufacturing		3,168
31 Wages		230		31 Stock	c/d	5,990
31 Materials		370				
		9,300				9,300

35.2 Manufacturing and Trading Account for 2003

Sales			202,283
Less: Cost of goods sold			
Opening stock of raw materials		13,500	
Purchases of raw materials		82,700	
Carriage in of raw materials		4,430	
		100,630	
Closing stock raw materials		14,100	
Cost of materials consumed		86,530	
Direct expenses			
Salaries and wages (75,674 − 22,700)		52,974	
Factory direct expenses		365	
Prime cost		139,869	
Indirect expenses			
Salaries and wages	22,700		
Rent and rates	1,200		
Light and heat	2,590		
Repairs to machinery	1,527		
Depreciation – machinery	2,700		
Insurance – plant and machinery	440		
		171,026	
Add Work in progress at 1 Jan 2003		11,800	
		182,826	
Less Work in progress at 31 Dec 2003		11,450	
Production cost of goods produced		171,376	
Add Opening stock of finished goods		13,400	
		184,776	
Less Closing stock of finished goods		14,160	
		170,616	
Gross profit		31,667	

35.4

W Miller
Manufacturing, Trading and Profit and Loss Accounts for the year ending 31 December 2003

Stock raw materials 1.1.2003		25,400
Add Purchases		91,535
Add Carriage inwards		1,960
		118,895
Less Stock raw materials 31.12.2003		28,900
Cost of raw materials consumed		89,995
Direct labour		84,208
Prime cost		174,203
Factory overhead expenses		
Rent $3/4$	3,900	
Fuel and power	8,120	
Depreciation: Machinery	10,200	
		22,220
		196,423
Add Work in progress 1.1.2003		31,100
		227,523
Less Work in progress 31.12.2003		24,600
Production cost of goods completed		202,923
Sales		318,622
Less Cost of goods sold		
Stock finished goods 1.1.2003	23,260	
Add Production cost of goods completed	202,923	
	226,183	
Less Stock finished goods 31.12.2003	28,840	
		197,343
Gross profit		121,279
Less Expenses:		
Office salaries	33,419	
Rent $1/4$	1,300	
Lighting and heating	4,420	
Depreciation: Office equipment	2,300	
		41,439
Net profit		79,840

35.5

Manufacturing and Trading Account for the six months ending 30 September 2005

Raw materials		
Opening stock		2,990
Purchases		15,630
Carriage in		126
		18,746
Less Closing stock		4,200
(a) Cost of raw materials consumed		14,546
Direct wages		48,648
(b) Prime cost of production		63,194
Indirect expenses		
Factory general expenses	7,048	
Depreciation–Factory equipment	4,200	
Rent and business rates	2,100	
		13,348
		16,542
Add Opening work in progress		3,900
		80,442
Less Closing work in progress		3,600
(c) Production cost of finished goods		76,842
Sales		112,410
Less Cost of goods sold		
Opening stock of finished goods	15,300	
Add Production cost of finished goods	76,842	
	92,142	
Less Closing stock of finished goods	17,700	
		74,442
Gross profit		37,968
(d) Gross profit on sales = $\dfrac{37,968}{112,410}$ = 33.8%		

35.7

E Wilson
Manufacturing Trading and Profit and Loss Account for the year ending
31 December 2002

Stock of raw materials 1.1.2002		13,260
Add Purchases		57,210
		70,470
Less Stock of raw materials 31.12.2002		14,510
Cost of raw materials consumed		55,960
Manufacturing wages (72,100 + 550)		72,650
Prime cost		128,610
Factory overhead expenses:		
Factory lighting and heating	7,220	
General expenses: factory	8,100	
Rent of factory	6,100	
Depreciation: Machinery	3,000	24,420
Production cost of goods completed		153,030
Sales		194,800
Less Cost of goods sold:		
Stock of finished goods 1.1.2002	41,300	
Add Production cost of goods completed	153,030	
	194,330	
Less Stock of finished goods 31.12.2002	44,490	149,840
Gross profit		44,960
Less Expenses:		
Office salaries	17,740	
General expenses: office	1,940	
Office rent (2,700 – 140)	2,560	
Office heating and lighting	1,490	
Sales reps' commission	11,688	
Delivery van expenses	1,760	
Depreciation: Office equipment	600	
Van	1,200	38,978
Net profit		5,982

Balance Sheet as at 31 December 2002

	Cost	Depreciation	Net
Fixed assets			
Machinery	40,000	14,400	25,600
Office Equipment	9,000	1,400	7,600
Van	6,800	1,800	5,000
	55,800	17,600	38,200
Current Assets			
Stocks: Finished goods		44,490	
Raw materials		14,510	
Debtors		34,200	
Prepaid expenses		140	
Bank		16,142	
		109,482	
Less current liabilities			
Creditors	9,400		
Expenses owing	550	9,950	
Net current assets			99,532
			137,732
Capital			
Balance 1.1.2002			155,950
Add Net profit			5,982
			161,932
Less Drawings			24,200
			137,732

35.8

Mendip Ltd
Manufacturing, Trading and Profit and Loss Account for the year ending 30 June 2002

Raw materials
Opening stock		20,000
Purchases		130,100
		150,100
Less Closing stock		22,000
Cost of raw materials consumed		128,100
Direct wages (63,000 − 15,700)		47,300
Direct factory expenses		9,100
Prime cost of production		184,500
Factory overheads		
Rates	3,000	
Heat and light	6,500	
Supervision	15,700	
Depreciation Plant and Machinery	10,500	
		35,700
Production cost of finished goods		220,200
Sales		317,500
Less: Cost of goods sold		
Opening stock of finished goods	38,000	
Production cost of finished goods	220,200	
	258,200	
Less Closing stock of finished goods	35,600	
		222,600
Gross profit		94,900
Less: Office salaries	36,300	
Directors fees	6,700	
Selling expenses	11,000	
		54,000
Net profit		40,900

Note: The dividends are not charged against revenue in the calculation of net profit. They are an appropriation of profit.

35.10

(a)

Jane Seymour
Manufacturing, Trading and Profit and Loss Account for the year ending 31 July 2006

Direct materials purchased		43,000	
Less Stock 31 July 2006		7,000	
		36,000	
Direct factory wages		39,000	
Prime cost		75,000	
Factory overhead expenses:			
Indirect factory wages		8,000	
Machinery repairs		1,600	
Rent and insurance (11,600 − 800) × $^2/_3$		7,200	
Light and power (5,000 + 1,000) × $^2/_3$		4,000	
Loose tools (9,000 − 5,000)		4,000	
Motor vehicle running expenses (12,000 × $^1/_2$)		6,000	
Depreciation: Plant and machinery		6,000	
Motor vehicles (7,500 × $^1/_2$)		3,750	40,550
			115,550
Less Work in progress 31 July 2006			12,300
			103,250
Transfer of goods manufactured to trading account			95,000
Loss on manufacturing			8,250
Sales			170,000
Less Goods manufactured transferred		95,000	
Stock at 31 July 2006		10,000	85,000
Gross profit			85,000
Less Administrative staff salaries		31,000	
Administrative expenses		9,000	
Sales and distribution staff salaries		13,000	
Rent and insurance (11,600 − 800) × $^1/_3$		3,600	
Motor vehicle running expenses (12,000 × $^1/_3$)		6,000	
Light and power (5,000 + 1,000) × $^1/_3$		2,000	
Depreciation: Motors (7,500 × $^1/_2$)		3,750	68,350
Net profit in trading			16,650
Loss on manufacturing			8,250
Overall net profit			8,400

(b) *Conservatism.* The valuation of stock or work in progress does not include any element of expected future profit.

Matching. All of the prepayments and accruals adjusted for are examples of matching expenses against the time period, as also are the depreciation provisions.

Going Concern. When valuing stocks and work in progress, it has been assumed that the business is going to carry on indefinitely, and that they will be sold in the normal course of business rather than being sold because of cessation of activities.

36.1

Fine's Department Store
Departmental Trading Account for the year ending 30 June 2006

	Carpet		White Goods		Music	
Sales		62,400		151,300		94,820
Less Cost of good sold:						
Stock 1.7.2005	16,100		37,916		31,222	
Add Purchases	43,600		118,260		55,924	
	59,700		156,176		87,146	
Less Stock 30.6.2006	18,410	41,290	35,119	121,057	40,216	46,930
		21,110		30,243		47,890

36.2

J Horner
Departmental Trading and Profit and Loss Account for the year ending 31 August 2007

	A		B	
Sales		75,000		50,000
Less Cost of goods sold:				
Stock 1.9.2006	1,250		1,000	
Add Purchases	51,000		38,020	
	52,250		39,020	
Less Stock 31.8.2007	1,410	50,840	912	38,108
Gross profits		24,160		11,892
Less Expenses:				
Wages	7,200		6,800	
Picture framing costs	300		–	
General office salaries	7,920		5,280	
Fire insurance	144		216	
Lighting and heating	248		372	
Repairs to premises	70		105	
Internal telephone	12		18	
Cleaning	72		108	
Accountancy changes	894		596	
General office expenses	306	17,166	204	13,699
Net profits/(losses)		6,994		(1,807)

37.1 FRS1

F Black
Cash Flow Statement for the year ending 31 December 2006

Net cash flow from operating activities (note 1)		21,750
Returns on investments and servicing of finance		
Payments to acquire tangible fixed assets		(6,000)
Financing		
Loan received	20,000	
Drawings	(15,000)	
		5,000
Increase in cash		20,750

Notes:
1 Reconciliation of net profit to net cash inflow:

Net profit	22,000
Depreciation	4,650
Decrease in stock	300
Decrease in creditors	(10,400)
Decrease in debtors	5,200
Net cash flow from operating activities	21,750

2 Analysis of changes in cash during the year:

Balance at 1 January 2006	(13,650)
Net cash inflow	20,750
Balance at 31 December 2006	7,100

37.3 FRS1

Malcolm Phillips
Cash Flow Statement for the year ending 30 April 2009

Net cash flow from operating activities (note 1)		6,600
Returns on investments and servicing of finance		
Payments for fixed assets		(3,000)
Financing		
Capital introduced	2,000	
Drawings	(8,000)	
		(6,000)
Decrease in cash		(2,400)

Notes:
1 Reconciliation of net profit to net cash inflow:

Net profit	8,500
Depreciation	200
Increase in creditors	200
Increase in stock	(2,800)
Decrease in debtors	500
	(1,900)
	6,600

2 Analysis of changes in cash during the year:

Balance at 1.5.2008	1,500
Net cash outflow	(2,400)
Balance at 30.4.2009	(900)

(b) (i) $\dfrac{7,500}{30,000} \times \dfrac{100}{1} = 25\%$ (ii) $\dfrac{22,500}{(3,100 + 5,900) \div 2} = \dfrac{22,500}{4,500} = 5$

37.4 FRS1

D Duncan
Cash Flow Statement for the year ending 31 December 2005

Net cash flow from operating activities (note 1)		21,620
Returns on investments and servicing of finance		
Receipts from sale of fixed assets		3,820
Financing		
Loan repaid to J Fry	(2,500)	
Drawings	(22,630)	
		(25,130)
Increase in cash		310

Notes:

1 Reconciliation of net profit to net cash inflow:

Net profit	23,240
Depreciation	1,800
Profit on sale of van	(620)
Increase in doubtful debt provision	200
Increase in stock	(5,400)
Decrease in debtors (8,800 – 7,700)	1,100
Increase in creditors	1,300
	21,620

2 Analysis of changes in cash during the year:

Balance at 1 January 2005	410
Net cash inflow	310
Balance at 31 December 2005	720

38.1

Stanley's Books (dates ignored)
Joint Venture with Barclay

TVs	1,100	Sales	3,100
Repairs	840		
Profit on venture	68		
Balance c/d	1,092		
	3,100		3,100
Cash to Barclay	1,092	Balance b/d	1,092

Barclay's Books
Joint Venture with Stanley

Office rental	300	Balance c/d	1,092
Advertising	90		
Packaging materials	34		
TV	600		
Profit on venture	68		
	1,092		1,092
Balance b/d	1,092	Cash from Stanley	1,092

Memorandum Joint Venture Account

TVs	1,700	Sales	3,100
Repairs	840		
Office rental	300		
Advertising	90		
Packaging materials	34		
Profit on venture			
Stanley ½	68		
Barclay ½	68	136	
	3,100		3,100

38.3

Bull Books
Joint Venture with Craig and Finch

Rent	600	Balance c/d	1,503
Labour: Planting	260		
Labour: Fertilising	180		
Sundries	19		
Labour	210		
Fertiliser	74		
Profit and loss	160		
	1,503		1,503
Balance c/d	1,503	Cash from Finch	1,503

Craig's Books
Joint Venture with Bull and Finch

Plants	510	Balance c/d	639
Motor expenses	49		
Profit and loss	80		
	639		639
Balance b/d	639	Cash from Finch	639

38.3 (cont'd)

Finch's Books
Joint Venture with Bull and Craig

Lifting	416	Sales	2,916
Sale expenses	318		
Profit and loss	40		
Balance c/d	2,142		
	2,916		2,916
Cash to Bull	1,503	Balance b/d	2,142
Cash to Craig	639		
	2,142		2,142

Memorandum Joint Venture Account

Rent	600	Sales	2,916
Labour: Planting	260		
Labour: Fertilising	180		
Labour: Sundry	210		
Labour: Lifting	416		
Fertiliser	74		
Motor expenses	49		
Plants	510		
Sale expenses	318		
Sundries	19		
Profit shared: Bull 4/7	160		
Craig 2/7	80		
Finch 1/7	40		
	280		
	2,916		2,916

39.1

Black, Brown and Cook
Appropriation Account for the year ending 31 July 2002

Net profit b/d		111,000
Less Salaries: Brown	30,000	
Cook	18,000	48,000
Interest on capitals: Black	3,600	
Brown	2,400	
Cook	1,200	7,200
Balance of profits		55,800
Shared: Black 2/9	12,400	
Brown 1/3	18,600	
Cook 4/9	24,800	55,800

39.3

I Skip and U Jump

Profit and Loss Appropriation Account 2004

Net profit			30,000
Profit shared	I. Skip	15,000	
	U. Jump	15,000	
		30,000	30,000

Profit and Loss Appropriation Account 2005

Net profit			38,000
Salaries	I. Skip	10,000	
	U. Jump	14,000	
Interest on capital	I. Skip	5,600	
	U. Jump	2,800	
Profit shared	I. Skip	2,800	
	U. Jump	2,800	
		38,000	38,000

Profit and Loss Appropriation Account 2006

Net profit			29,000
Salaries	I. Skip	10,000	
	U. Jump	14,000	
Interest on capital	I. Skip	5,600	
	U. Jump	2,800	
Loss shared	I. Skip	(1,700)	
	U. Jump	(1,700)	
		29,000	29,000

Current Account – I Skip

2004				
Drawings	8,000		Profit share	15,000
Bal c/d	7,000			
	15,000			15,000
2005			**2005**	
Drawings	13,000		Bal b/d	7,000
Bal c/d	12,400		Salary	10,000
			Interest on capital	5,600
			Profit share	2,800
	25,400			25,400
2006			**2006**	
Loss share	1,700		Bal b/d	12,400
Drawings	12,000		Salary	10,000
Bal c/d	14,300		Interest on capital	5,600
	28,000			28,000
			2007	
			Bal b/d	14,300

Current Account – U Jump

2004				
Drawings	9,000		Profit share	15,000
Bal c/d	6,000			
	15,000			15,000
2005			**2005**	
Drawings	17,000		Bal b/d	6,000
Bal c/d	8,600		Salary	14,000
			Interest on capital	2,800
			Profit share	2,800
	25,600			25,600
2006			**2006**	
Loss share	1,700		Bal b/d	8,600
Drawings	20,000		Salary	14,000
Bal c/d	3,700		Interest on capital	2,800
	25,400			25,400
			2007	
			Bal b/d	3,700

39.4

Blair, Short and Steel
Appropriation Account for the year ending 31 December 2007

Net profit b/d			111,100
Add Interest on drawings:	Blair	400	
	Short	300	
	Steel	200	900
			112,000
Less Interest on Capitals:	Blair	3,000	
	Short	2,000	
	Steel	1,500	6,500
Salaries:	Short	20,000	
	Steel	25,000	45,000
			51,500
			60,500
Balance of Profits			
Shared: Blair 70%		42,350	
Short 20%		12,100	
Steel 10%		6,050	60,500

Balance Sheet as at 31 December 2007 (extract)

Capital Accounts:	Blair	100,000	
	Short	50,000	
	Steel	25,000	175,000

Current Accounts:	Blair	Short	Steel
Balances 1.4.2007	18,600	9,460	8,200
Add Interest on capital	3,000	2,000	1,500
Salaries		20,000	25,000
Share of profits	42,350	12,100	6,050
	63,950	43,560	40,750
Less Interest on drawings	400	300	200
Drawings	39,000	27,100	16,800
	24,550	16,160	23,750
			64,460

39.8

Considerations

(a) *Legal position re Partnership Act 1890*: Partners can agree to anything. The main thing is that of mutual agreement. The agreement can either be very formal in a partnership deed drawn up by a lawyer or else it can be evidenced in other ways.

The Act lays down the provisions for profit sharing if agreement has not been reached, written or otherwise.

(b) As Bee is not taking active part in the running of the business he could be registered as a limited partner under the 1907 Limited Partnership Act. This has the advantage that his liability is limited to the amount of capital invested by him; he can lose that but his personal possessions cannot be taken to pay any debts of the firm.

As Bee is a 'sleeping partner' you will have to decide whether his reward should be in the form of a fixed amount, or should vary according to the profits made. In this context you should also bear in mind whether or not he would suffer a share of losses if they occurred.

If he were to have a fixed amount, irrespective as to whether profits had been made or not, then the question arises as to whether his reward required. This is obviously a more risky investment than, say, government securities. He therefore would naturally expect to get a higher return.

Bee would probably feel aggrieved if the profits rose sharply, but he was still limited to the amounts already described. There could be an arrangement for extra payments if the profits exceeded a given figure.

Cee is the expert conducting the operations of the business. He will consequently expect a major share of the profits.

One possibility would be to give him a salary, similar to his current salary, before dividing whatever profits then remain.

(c) Dee is making himself available, as well as bringing in some capital. Because of this active involvement he will affect the profits made. It would seem appropriate to give him a salary commensurate with such work, plus a share of the profits.

(d) *Interest on capital*: Whatever is decided about profit-sharing, it would seem appropriate for each of the partners to be given interest on their capitals before sharing the balance of the profits.

39.9

Frame and French

Trading and Profit and Loss Account for the year ending 30 September 2009

Sales			363,111
Less Cost of goods sold:			
Opening stock		62,740	
Add Purchases		210,000	
		272,740	
Less Closing stock		74,210	198,530
Gross profit			164,581
Add Reduction in provision for doubtful debts			150
			164,731
Less Salaries and wages (57,809 + 720)		58,529	
Office expenses (4,760 + 215)		4,975	
Carriage outwards		3,410	
Discounts allowed		620	
Bad debts		1,632	
Loan interest		3,900	
Depreciation: Fixtures	600		
Buildings	5,000	5,600	78,666
Net profit			86,065
Add Interest on drawings: Frame		900	
French		600	1,500
			87,565
Less Interest on capitals: Frame		5,000	
French		3,750	8,750
Salary: Frame			30,000
Balance of Profits			48,815
Shared: Frame		29,289	
French		19,526	48,815

Balance Sheet as at 30 September 2009

		Cost	Depn	N.B.V.
Fixed assets				
Buildings		210,000	55,000	155,000
Fixtures		8,200	4,800	3,400
		218,200	59,800	158,400
Current assets				
Stock			74,210	
Debtors		61,400		
Less Provision for doubtful debts		1,250	60,150	
Bank			6,130	
			140,490	
Less Current liabilities				
Creditors		26,590		
Expenses owing		935	27,525	
Net current assets				112,965
				271,365
Less Loan from P Prince				65,000
				206,365
Financed by				
Capital Accounts: Frame			100,000	
French			75,000	175,000
		Frame	*French*	
Current Accounts				
Balance 1.10.2008		4,100	1,200	
Add Interest on capital		5,000	3,750	
Salary		30,000	–	
Balance of profit		29,289	19,526	
		68,389	24,476	
Less Drawings		31,800	28,200	
Interest on drawings		900	600	
		35,689	(4,324)	31,365
				206,365

39.11

Sage and Onion

Profit and Loss Appropriation Account for the year ending 31 December 2001

Sales (508,000 – 6,000)			502,000
Opening stock		75,000	
Purchases (380,000 + 3,000)		383,000	
Carriage in		21,500	
		479,500	
Returns		12,000	
		467,500	
Closing stock	68,000		
Drawings (500 + 630)	1,130	69,130	398,370
Gross profit			103,630
Discounts received			1,000
			104,630
Expenses			
Salaries (42,000 + 900)		42,900	
Office		7,500	
Carriage out		3,000	
Adverts		5,000	
Discount allowed		1,200	
Repairs and renewals (2,800 – 200)		2,600	
Bad debt		1,400	
Depreciation – Fixtures and fittings		1,500	
Provision for doubtful debts		400	
			65,500
Net profit			39,130
Add Interest on drawings (360 + 280)			640
Interest on current account			30
			39,800
Less Interest on capital (5,000 + 2,500)		7,500	
Interest on current account		100	
Salaries (12,000 + 8,000)		20,000	
			27,600
Balance of Profits			12,200
Shared: Sage		6,100	
Onion		6,100	
			12,200

Balance Sheet as at 31 December 2001

Fixed assets			
Freehold – Cost			50,000
Fixtures and fittings – Cost		15,000	
– Depreciation		4,500	10,500
			60,500
Current assets			
Stock		68,000	
Debtors (52,400 – 2,400)		50,000	
Bank		31,600	
Prepayments		200	
		149,800	
Current liabilities			
Creditors (33,300 + 3,900)		37,200	
VAT		8,700	
		45,900	103,900
			164,400
Financed by			
Capital Accounts			
Sage		100,000	
Onion		50,000	
			150,000

Current Accounts	Sage	Onion
Balance b/d	2,000	(600)
Interest on capital	5,000	2,500
Interest on current account	100	(30)
Salaries	12,000	8,000
Profit	6,100	6,100
Drawings/Int/Goods	(15,860)	(10,910)
	9,340	5,060

		14,400
		164,400

42.7 (cont'd)

(c) First distribution

	Lock	Stock	Barrel
Capital balances before dissolution	39,680	16,260	(5,240)
Loss if no further assets realised			
(85,700 + 92,500 − 6,000 − 6,200 −			
7,000 − 72,500 − 35,000 − 50,000) = 1,500			
Loss shared in profit/loss ratios	(600)	(450)	(450)
Cars taken over	(2,000)	(2,000)	(2,000)
	37,080	13,810	(7,690)
	4,394	3,296	7,690
Barrel's deficiency shared profit/loss ratio			
Paid to partners	32,686	10,514	—

Second and final distribution

Capital balances before dissolution	39,680	16,260	(5,240)
Profit finally ascertained			
100,000 − 1,500 = 98,500			
Shared	39,400	29,550	29,550
	79,080	45,810	24,310
Less Distribution and cars	34,686	12,514	2,000
Final distribution (100,000)	44,394	33,296	22,310

43.1

Flyer Ltd
Profit and Loss Appropriation Accounts

(1) For the year ending 31 March 2005

Profit for the year before taxation		90,200
Less Corporation tax		18,000
Profit for the year after taxation		72,200
Less: Transfer to general reserve	20,000	
Preference dividend of 5%	5,000	25,000
Retained profits carried forward to next year		47,200

(2) For the year ending 31 March 2006

Profit for the tax year before taxation		84,600
Less Corporation tax		16,000
Profit for the year after taxation		68,600
Add Retained profits from last year		47,200
		115,800
Less: Transfer to general reserve	15,000	
Preference dividend of 5%	5,000	
Ordinary dividend of 8%	16,000	36,000
Retained profits carried forward to next year		79,800

43.2

Trainsign Ltd
Profit and Loss Appropriation Accounts

(1) For the year ended 31 December 2002

Profit for the year before taxation		62,400
Less Corporation tax		12,000
Profit for the year after taxation		50,400
Less: Transfer to general reserve	10,000	
Preference dividend 7%	6,300	16,300
Retained profits carried forward to next year		34,100

(2) For the year ended 31 December 2003

Profit for the year before taxation		81,900
Less Corporation tax		16,000
Profit for the year after taxation		65,900
Add Retained profits from last year		34,100
		100,000
Less: Transfer to general reserve	18,000	
Preference dividend 7%	6,300	
Ordinary dividend 6%	15,600	39,900
Retained profits carried forward to next year		60,100

(3) For the year ended 31 December 2004

Profit for the year before taxation		114,190
Less Corporation tax		22,000
Profit for the year after taxation		92,190
Add Retained profits from last year		60,100
		152,290
Less: Transfer to foreign exchange reserve	15,000	
Preference dividend 7%	6,300	
Ordinary dividend 8%	20,800	42,100
Retained profits carried forward to next year		110,190

43.3 Balance Sheet as at 30 September 2002

	Cost	Depn	
Fixed assets			
Buildings	330,000	40,000	290,000
Motors	74,000	41,000	33,000
Fixtures	9,200	5,100	4,100
	413,200	86,100	327,100

Current assets
Stock	21,400	
Debtors	10,300	
Bank (difference)	6,900	
	38,600	

Less Current liabilities
Creditors	13,700	
Net current assets		24,900
Total assets *less* current liabilities		352,000
Less Debentures: repayable 30.9.2006		40,000
		312,000

Capital and reserves
Called-up share capital	200,000
Fixed assets replacement reserve	30,000
General reserve	50,000
Profit and loss account	32,000
	312,000

43.4 OK Limited
Profit and Loss Appropriation Account for the year ended 31 March 2006

Net profit	29
Balance b/d	11
	40
Less:	
Transfer to general reserve	10
Balance c/d	30

Balance Sheet as at 31 March 2006

Fixed assets		167
Current assets		
Stock	52	
Debtors	24	
Bank	14	
	90	
Current liabilities		
Creditors	37	
Working capital		53
		220
Share Capital and Reserves		
8% preference share capital		50
Ordinary shares	100	
General reserve	40	
Profit and loss	30	
Ordinary shareholders' equity		170
Total shareholders' equity		220

Note: the proposed dividend will be shown as a note.

43.6 Select Limited
Profit and Loss Account for the year ending 31 March 2001

Gross Profit		98,050
Office salaries and expenses	25,000	
Advertising	5,000	
Directors' fees	11,300	
Doubtful debts provision	350	
Provision for depreciation	8,000	
		49,650
Net profit		48,400
Profit and Loss balance b/d		12,000
		60,400
Less:		
Transfer to general reserve	25,000	
Profit and loss c/d		35,400

Note: the proposed dividend will be shown as a note.

43.6 (cont'd)

Balance Sheet as at 31 March 2010

	Cost	Depreciation	
Fixed Assets			
Land and Buildings	170,000	–	170,000
Fixtures and fittings	80,000	40,000	40,000
	250,000	40,000	210,000
Current Assets			
Stock		42,000	
Debtors		37,600	
VAT		3,800	
Bank		12,000	
		95,400	
Creditors: Amounts falling due within one year			
Sunday creditors		25,000	
Net Current Assets			70,400
			280,400
Share Capital			
Authorised; 300,000 ordinary shares of £1			200,000
Alloted, called up and fully paid			
Reserves			
Share premium		20,000	
General reserve		25,000	
Profit and loss		35,400	
			80,400
			280,400

43.8 Tailor Times Ltd

Trading and Profit and Loss Account for the year ending 31 December 2003

Sales			925,300
Less Cost of goods sold			
Opening stock		81,900	
Add Purchases		563,700	
		645,600	
Less Closing stock		94,300	
			551,300
Gross profit			374,000
Less expenses			
Wages and salaries (179,400 + 1,800)		181,200	
Business rates (6,100 – 700)		5,400	
Electricity		4,800	
Bad debts		1,400	
Provision for doubtful debts		300	
General expenses		14,600	
Depreciation: Freehold premises		25,000	
Machinery		16,800	
			249,500
Net profit			124,500
Add Unappropriated profits from last year			27,500
			152,000

Balance Sheet as at 31 December 2003

Fixed assets			
Premises		271,000	
Less Depreciation		79,000	192,000
Machinery		84,000	
Less Depreciation		37,800	46,200
			238,200
Current assets			
Stock		94,300	
Debtors	74,200		
Less Provision	1,500	72,700	
Prepayments		700	
Bank		16,200	
		183,900	
Less Current liabilities			
Creditors	68,300		
Expenses owing	1,800	70,100	
Net current assets			113,800
			352,000
Financed by:			
Authorised and issued capital			200,000
Revenue reserves: Profit and loss			152,000
			352,000

Partido Ltd

43.10 Trading and Profit and Loss Account for the year ending 31 December 2002

Sales			1,606,086
Less Cost of goods sold			
Opening stock		290,114	
Add Purchases		810,613	
Add Carriage inwards		2,390	
		1,103,117	
Less Closing stock		317,426	
			785,691
Gross profit			820,395
Less Expenses			
Salaries		384,500	
Business rates		16,500	
Carriage outwards		13,410	
Office expenses		9,345	
Sundry expenses		2,360	
Depreciation: Buildings		40,000	
Equipment		48,000	
Directors' remuneration		119,200	
			633,315
Net profit			187,080
Add Unappropriated profits from last year			136,204
			323,284
Less Appropriations			
General reserve		70,000	
Foreign exchange		30,000	
			100,000
Unappropriated profits carried to next year			223,284

Note: the proposed dividend will be shown as a note.

Balance Sheet as at 31 December 2002

	Cost	Depn	Net
Fixed assets			
Buildings	800,000	120,000	680,000
Equipment	320,000	144,000	176,000
	1,120,000	264,000	856,000
Current assets			
Stock		317,426	
Debtors		321,219	
Bank		8,100	
		646,745	
Less Current liabilities			
Creditors	237,516		
Expenses owing	1,945		
		239,461	
Net current assets			407,284
			1,263,284
Financed by:			
Share capital: authorised and issued			800,000
Reserves			
Foreign exchange		50,000	
General reserve		190,000	
Profit and loss		223,284	
			463,284
			1,263,284

43.12

1   Burden plc: Computation of corrected net profit

Recorded net profit		58,070
Add Profit on sale of equipment		500
		58,570
Less Bad debt written off	300	
Stock reduced to net realisable value	700	
		1,000
Correct figure of net profit		57,570

Burden plc

2   Profit and Loss Appropriation Account for the year ending 31 May 2009

Net profit for the year brought down		57,570
Add Retained profits from last year		36,200
		93,770
Less Transfer to general reserve		50,000
Retained profits carried forward to next year		43,770

3 (i)   Current assets

Stock	17,100	
Debtors	6,540	
Prepayments	760	
	24,400	
Less Current liabilities		
Trade creditors	28,500	
Accrued expenses	430	
Bank overdraft	2,400	
	31,330	
Net current assets deficit		(6,930)

Note: Figures in brackets are negative.

(ii)   Capital and reserves

Ordinary share capital: called up	200,000
Share premium	25,000
General reserve	70,000
Profit and loss	23,770
Shareholders' funds	318,770

4   *Examples:*

Issue of shares: + Bank; + Share capital.
Sales of fixed assets: + Bank; − Fixed assets.
Debentures issued: + Bank; + Debentures.

43.14

(a) See text.

(b) The historical cost convention does not make the going concern convention unnecessary. Several instances illustrate this:

(i) Fixed assets are depreciated over the useful life of the assets. This presupposes that the business will continue to operate during the years of assumed useful life.

(ii) Prepayments also assume that the benefits available in the future will be able to be claimed, because the business is expected to continue.

(iii) Stocks are valued also on the basis that it will be disposed of during the future ordinary running of the business.

(iv) The accruals concept itself assumes that the business is to continue. All of this shows that the two concepts complement each other.

(c) A shareholder wants financial statements so that he can decide what to do with his shareholding, whether he should sell his shares or hold on to them.

To enable him to decide upon his actions, he would really like to know what is going to happen in the future. To help him in this he also would like information which shows him what happened in the past. Ideally therefore he would like both types of report, those on the past and on the future.

If he had a choice, the logical choice would be to receive a report on the future providing that it could be relied on.

43.15

Extract 1

(a) The amount paid for goodwill.

(b) The excess represents share premium.

(c) Equity shares generally means ordinary shares.

(d) That although issued in 2006 a dividend will not be paid in that year. The first year that dividends *could* be paid is 2007.

Extract 2

(e) (i) A rate of 8% per annum interest will be paid on them, irrespective of whether profits are made or not.

(ii) These are the years within which the debentures could be redeemed, if the company so wished.

(f) (i) This is the rate per annum at which preference dividends will be paid, subject to there being sufficient distributable profits.

(ii) That the shares could be bought back by the company.

(g) Probably because there was currently a lower interest rate prevailing at the time of redemption and the company took advantage of it.

(h) Large amounts of both fixed interest and fixed dividend funds have resulted in a raising of the gearing.

(j) Debenture interest gets charged before arriving at net profit. Dividends are an appropriation of profits in the period in which they are actually paid.

(k) Shareholders are owners and help decide appropriations. Debenture holders are external lenders and interest expense has to be paid.

43.16

(a) This is incorrect. The tax portion has to be counted as part of the total cost, which is made up of debenture interest paid plus tax. Holding back payment will merely see legal action taken by Revenue & Customs to collect the tax.

(b) This cannot be done. The repainting of the exterior does not improve or enhance the original value of the premises. It cannot therefore be treated as capital expenditure.

(c) This is not feasible. Only the profit on the sale of the old machinery, found by deducting net book value from sales proceeds, can be so credited to the profit and loss account. The remainder is a capital receipt and should be treated as such.

(d) This is an incorrect view. Although some of the general reserve could, if circumstances allowed it, be transferred back to the profit and loss account, it could not be shown as affecting the operating profit for 2009. This is because the general reserve was built up over the years before 2009.

(e) This is not feasible. The share capital has to be maintained at nominal value as per the Companies Act. A share premium cannot be created in this fashion, and even if it could, it would still have to be credited to the *share premium account* and not the profit and loss account.

(f) Incorrect. Although the premises could be revalued the credit for the increase has to be to a capital reserve account. This cannot then be transferred to the credit of the profit and loss account.

43.17

See text. Points to be made include that there must be an expectation that sufficient profits will be made in future to make the debenture interest payments when due; also, there may be cheaper sources of finance available; also, if secured debentures are to be issued, there must be sufficient assets available to act as security over the issue. Gearing is also an issue to be considered – see text.

44.1

Balance Sheet as at 31 March 2006

	(a) T Malloy	(b) F Templar
Goodwill	34,771	23,699
Premises	190,000	205,000
Stock	39,200	36,100
Debtors	18,417	18,417
Bank	828	–
	283,216	283,216
Less Creditors	(23,216)	(23,216)
	260,000	260,000
Capital	260,000	260,000

44.3

(a)

Spectrum Ltd
Balance Sheet as at 1 January 2002

Fixed assets		
Goodwill (note 1)		94,000
Premises (75,000 + 80,000 + 90,000 + 60,000)		305,000
Delivery vans (7,000 + 10,000)		17,000
Furniture and fittings (12,000 + 13,000 + 13,000)		38,000
		454,000
Current assets		
Stock (8,000 + 7,000 + 12,000)	27,000	
Bank (note 2)	25,000	
	52,000	
Less Current liabilities		
Creditors (6,000 + 8,000 + 7,000)	21,000	
Net current assets		31,000
		485,000
Financed by:		
Share capital		
Authorised 700,000 shares £1	700,000	
Issued 500,000 shares £1		500,000
Reserves		
Profit and loss		(15,000)
		485,000

Notes:

1 Goodwill:

Red – paid	120,000	
Net assets taken over		
75,000 + 7,000 + 12,000 + 8,000 – 6,000 =	96,000	24,000
Yellow – paid	130,000	
Net assets taken over		
80,000 + 13,000 + 7,000 – 8,000 =	92,000	38,000
Blue – paid	150,000	
Net assets taken over		
90,000 + 10,000 + 13,000 + 12,000 – 7,000 =	118,000	32,000
		94,000

2 Bank:

Shares issued		500,000
Less: Preliminary expenses		
Warehouse	15,000	
Red	60,000	
Yellow	120,000	
Blue	130,000	
	150,000	475,000
		25,000

(b) Spectrum Ltd can issue part or the remainder of the authorised capital, i.e. 700,000 – 500,000 = £200,000. £100,000 will buy the business but some extra Net current assets is also needed.

44.4

(a)

Dinho and Manueli
Realisation Account

Property	290,000	Creditors	85,800
Equipment	65,000	Bank	56,700
Stock	143,500	Loan	160,000
Debtors	121,000	Bin Ltd	304,000
		Loss: Dinho	6,500
		Manueli	6,500
	619,500		619,500

(b)

Bin Ltd

Goodwill [write downs (30,000 + 5,000) – realisation loss (13,000)]	22,000
Property	260,000
Equipment	65,000
Stocks	143,500
Debtors	116,000
Bank (120,000 – 56,700)	63,300
Creditors	(85,800)
	584,000
Loan	160,000
	424,000
Ordinary Share Capital	300,000
10% Preference shares (D = 87,500; M = 16,500; P = 20,000)	124,000

(c) (salary as before, therefore not relevant; earnings on savings were 120,000 @ 6% = 7,200; preference dividend will be 20,000 @ 10% = 2,000, therefore 5,200 needed from profit after preference dividend. Profit must be 3 × 5,200 = 15,600 + the total preference dividend of 12,400 = 28,000.

45.1

(a)

	X	Y
(i) Gross profit as % of sales	$\dfrac{315,000}{555,000} \times \dfrac{100}{1} = 56.8\%$	$\dfrac{420,000}{750,000} \times \dfrac{100}{1} = 56\%$
(ii) Net profit as % of sales	$\dfrac{100,000}{555,000} \times \dfrac{100}{1} = 18\%$	$\dfrac{150,000}{750,000} \times \dfrac{100}{1} = 20\%$
(iii) Expenses as % of sales	$\dfrac{215,000}{555,000} \times \dfrac{100}{1} = 38.7\%$	$\dfrac{270,000}{750,000} \times \dfrac{100}{1} = 36\%$
(iv) Stock turnover	$\dfrac{240,000}{(100,000+60,000)\div 2} = 3 \text{ times}$	$\dfrac{330,000}{(80,000+70,000)\div 2} = 4.4 \text{ times}$
(v) Rate of return	$\dfrac{100,000}{(76,000+116,000)\div 2} \times \dfrac{100}{1} = 104.2\%$	$\dfrac{150,000}{(72,000+152,000)\div 2} \times \dfrac{100}{1} = 133.9\%$

45.1 (*cont'd*)

(*vi*) Current ratio $\dfrac{210{,}000}{104{,}000} = 2.02$ $\dfrac{182{,}500}{100{,}500} = 1.82$

(*vii*) Acid test ratio $\dfrac{145{,}000}{104{,}000} = 1.44$ $\dfrac{112{,}500}{100{,}500} = 1.12$

(*viii*) Debtor/sales ratio $\dfrac{125{,}000}{555{,}000} \times 12 = 2.7$ months $\dfrac{100{,}000}{750{,}000} \times 12 = 1.6$ months

(*ix*) Creditor/purchases ratio $\dfrac{104{,}000}{200{,}000} \times 12 = 6.24$ months $\dfrac{100{,}500}{320{,}000} \times 12 = 3.77$ months

(*b*) Business Y is the most profitable, both in terms of actual net profit, £150,000 compared to £100,000, but also in terms of capital employed; Y has managed to achieve a return of £133.90 for every £100 invested compared with £104.20 for X. Reasons – possibly only – as not until you know more about the business could you give a definite answer:

(*i*) Possibly managed to sell far more merchandise because of lower prices, but the margins are so similar (56.8%-v-56%) that this is unlikely.

(*ii*) Maybe more efficient use of mechanised means in the business. Note that Y has more equipment and, perhaps as a consequence, kept other expenses down to £35,000 as compared with X's £45,000.

(*iii*) Did not have as much stock lying idle. Turned over stock 4.4 times in the year as compared with 3 for A.

(*iv*) X's current ratio of 2.02 is not much higher than Y's (1.82) so it is unlikely that this has contributed significantly to the difference in profitability through money sitting around doing nothing to increase profits.

(*v*) Following on from (*iv*) the Acid Test ratio for X may be higher than necessary. Part of the reason for (*v*) is that X waited (on average) 2.7 months to be paid by customers. Y managed to collect them on average in 1.2 months. Money represented by debts is money lying idle.

(*vii*) Another reason for (*v*) is that X took almost twice as long to pay its creditors (6.24 months v 3.77). However, this may be a 'good' sign for X as long as suppliers do not object and start refusing to sell to X.

Put all these factors together, and it appears that Y may be being run more efficiently, and is more profitable as a consequence.

45.3

(*a*)

Durham Limited
Profit and Loss Appropriation Account for the year ending 30.4.2009

Net profit for the year b/d		16,500
Add Retained profits from last year		14,500
		31,000
Less Transfer to general reserve	5,000	
Preference dividend	2,000	7,000
Retained profits carried forward to next year		24,000

(*b*)

Balance Sheet as at 30.4.2009

Fixed assets			
Premises at cost			86,000
Machinery and plant at cost		60,000	
Less Depreciation		40,000	20,000
			106,000
Current assets			
Stock			60,000
Debtors		20,000	
Less Provision for doubtful debts		4,000	16,000
Prepayments			900
Bank			13,100
			90,000
Less Current liabilities			
Creditors		12,900	
Expenses owing		100	13,000
Working capital			77,000
			183,000
Capital and reserves			
8% preference shares			50,000
Ordinary shares			100,000
			150,000
General reserve			9,000
Profit and loss account			24,000
Shareholders' funds			183,000

(*c*) (*i*) *Return on Capital Employed (ROCE)*
This is the amount of profit earned compared with the amount of capital employed to earn it. Calculated:

$$\dfrac{\text{Net profit}}{\text{Average of shareholders' funds}} \times \dfrac{100}{1} = \dfrac{16{,}500}{(168{,}500 + 183{,}000) \div 2} \times \dfrac{100}{1}$$
$$= 9.39\%$$

(*ii*) *Current Ratio*
This calculates how well the current assets can finance current liabilities. Calculated:

$$\dfrac{\text{Current assets}}{\text{Current liabilities}} = \dfrac{90{,}000}{13{,}000} = 6.9 : 1$$

Acid Test Ratio
This calculates whether the business has sufficient liquid resources to meet its current liabilities. Calculated:

$$\dfrac{\text{Current assets} - \text{Stock}}{\text{Current liabilities}} = \dfrac{30{,}000}{13{,}000} = 2.3 : 1$$

(*d*) ROCE. The return of 9.39% would appear to be adequate, but we cannot really comment further without more information.
Current Ratio. A figure of 2 : 1 is often reckoned as adequate. In this case a 6.9 : 1 figure is more than adequate.
Acid Test Ratio. All current liabilities can be met and the return is therefore adequate.

(*e*) 1 Previous years' figures.
2 We would need to know ratios for other similar businesses.

45.4

(a) (i) Gross profit: Sales

2008	2009
$\frac{50}{200} \times \frac{100}{1} = 25\%$	$\frac{70}{280} \times \frac{100}{1} = 25\%$

(ii) Stock turnover

2008	2009
$\frac{150}{(50+20) \div 2} = 4.29$	$\frac{210}{(20+30) \div 2} = 8.4$

(iii) Net profit: Sales

2008	2009
$\frac{12}{200} \times \frac{100}{1} = 6\%$	$\frac{20}{280} \times \frac{100}{1} = 7.14\%$

(iv) Quick ratio

2008	2009
$\frac{25}{25} = 1$	$\frac{33}{12} = 2.75$

(v) Working capital (current ratio)

2008	2009
$\frac{45}{25} = 1.8$	$\frac{63}{12} = 5.25$

(vi) Net profit: Capital employed

2008	2009
$\frac{12}{130} \times \frac{100}{1} = 9.23\%$	$\frac{20}{191} \times \frac{100}{1} = 10.47\%$

(b) (Brief answer, but you should expand in an exam)

(i) No change.

(ii) Increase caused by lowering average stocks; also probably better sales management.

(iii) An increase in sales, without a larger increase in expenses, has led to a better return.

(iv) Issue of debentures has improved the cash situation and therefore a better quick ratio.

(v) Net current assets have increased largely due to issue of debentures, although partly offset by fixed assets bought.

(vi) Increasing sales and better stock turnover brought about better ROCE.

45.7

(a)

Joan Street

Trading and Profit and Loss Account for the year ending 31 March 2008

Sales			(W3)	240,000
Cost of sales				
Opening stock	(W6)	21,000		
Add Purchases	(W7)	174,000		
		195,000		
Less Closing stock		15,000		
			(W1)	180,000
Gross profit			(W2)	60,000
Sundry expenses			(W5)	38,400
Net profit			(W4)	21,600

Balance Sheet as at 31 March 2008

Fixed assets			(W9)	108,000
Current assets				
Stock	(W8)	15,000		
Debtors	(W14)	24,000		
Bank	(W13)	9,000		
		48,000		
Less *Current liabilities*	(W13)	12,000		
Net current assets			(W13)	36,000
			(W12)	144,000
Financed by:				
Capital:				
Balance at 1.4.2007			(W11)	122,400
Add Net profit			(W10)	21,600
				144,000

Workings (could possibly find alternatives)

(W1) As average stock $21,000 + 15,000 \div 2 = 18,000$ and stock turnover is 10, this means that cost of sales $= 18,000 \times 10 = 180,000$

(W2) As gross profit is 25% of sales, it must therefore be $33\frac{1}{3}\%$ of cost of sales

(W3) As (W1) is 180,000 & (W2) is 60,000 therefore sales = (W1) + (W2) = 240,000

(W4) Net profit = 9% of sales = 21,600

(W5) Missing figure, found by arithmetical deduction

(W6) & (W7) Missing figures – found by arithmetical deduction

(W8) $\text{Debtors (?)} \times 365 \div \text{Sales} = 36\frac{1}{2}$, i.e.

$\dfrac{? \times 365}{240,000} = 36\frac{1}{2}$, by arithmetic

$\dfrac{24,000 \times 365}{240,000} = 36\frac{1}{2}$. Proof $\dfrac{24,000 \times 365}{240,000} = 36\frac{1}{2}$

debtors = 24,000.

45.7 (cont'd)

(W9) 45% × 240,000 = 108,000

(W10) Knowing that net profit 21,600 is 15% of W10, so W10 = 21,600 × 100/15 = 144,000

(W11) Missing figure

(W12) Put in after (W11)

(W13) If Net current assets ratio is 4, it means a factor of current assets 4, current liabilities 1 = Net current assets 3 which is W12 – W9 = 36,000. Current assets therefore:

4/3 × 36,000 = 48,000

and current liabilities

1/3 × 36,000 = 12,000

(W14) Is new missing figure.

(b) Question asked for two favourable aspects and two unfavourable aspects but four of each are given here

Favourable: Stock turnover, liquidity, net current assets, net profit on sales

Unfavourable: Gross profit to sales, debtors collection, return on capital employed, turnover to net capital employed.

(c) Drawbacks include:

(i)   No access to trends over recent years.

(ii) No future plans etc. given.

(iii) Each business is often somewhat different.

(iv) Size of businesses not known.

45.9

(a) (i)   Current ratio: by dividing current assets by current liabilities.

(ii) Quick assets ratio: by dividing current assets less stock by current liabilities.

(iii) Return on capital employed (ROCE): can have more than one meaning. One in common use is net profit divided by capital plus long-term liabilities (e.g. loans), and shown as a percentage.

(iv) Return on shareholders' funds (ROSF): net profit divided by capital, shown as a percentage.

(v)   Debtors turnover: Sales divided by average debtors, expressed in days or months.

(vi) Creditors turnover: Purchases divided by average creditors, expressed in days or months.

(vii) Gross profit percentage: Gross profit divided by sales, expressed as a percentage.

(viii) Net profit percentage: Net profit divided by sales.

(ix) Stock turnover: Cost of goods sold, divided by average stock, expressed in days.

(b) (This part of the question tests your ability to be able to deduce some conclusions from the information given. You have to use your imagination.)

First, an assumption, we do not know relative sizes of these two businesses. We will assume that they are approximately of the same size.

A has a higher current ratio, 2 to 1.5, but the quick assets ratio shows a much greater disparity, 1.7 to 0.7. As stock is not included in the quick assets ratio, it can be deduced that B has relatively greater stocks. Expected also from these ratios is that A has high amounts of debtors, this being seen because debtors turnover is 3 times as great for A as for B.

The return on shareholders' funds (ROSF) is much greater for A than for B, 30% to 18%, but the ROCE for A is not that different for B, 20% to 17%. This shows that A has far more in long-term borrowings than B. The ROCE indicates that A is somewhat more efficient than B, but not by a considerable amount.

Gross profit percentage is far greater for A than B, but net profit percentage is the same. Obviously A has extremely high operating expenses per £100 of sales.

The last ratio shows that stock in A lies unsold for twice as long a period as for B.

A summary of the above shows that A has lower stocks, greater debtors, sells at a slower rate, and has high operating expenses. B has greater stocks, sells its goods much quicker but at lower prices as shown by the gross profit percentage.

All the evidence points to A being a firm which gives emphasis to personal service to its customers. B on the other hand emphasises cheap prices and high turnover, with not as much concentration on personal service.

45.11

(There is no set answer. In addition, as a large number of points could be mentioned, the examiner cannot expect every aspect to be covered.)

The main points which could be covered are:

(i)   The financial statements are for last year whereas, in fact, the bank is more interested in what might happen to the business in the future.

(ii) The financial statements are usually prepared on a historic cost basis. These therefore do not reflect current values.

(iii) The bank manager would want a cash budget to be drawn up for the ensuing periods. This would give the manager an indication as to whether or not the business will be able to meet its commitments as they fall due.

(iv) The bank manager wants to ensure that bank charges and interest can be paid promptly, also that a bank loan or overdraft will be able to be paid off. He will want to see that these commitments can still be met if the business has to cease operations. This means that the market value of assets on cessation, rather than the cost of them, is of much more interest to the bank manager.

To say that the financial statements are 'not good enough' is misleading. What the manager is saying is that the financial statements do not provide him with what he would really like to know. One could argue that there should be other types of financial statements drawn up in addition to those drawn up on a historic basis.

45.12

(a) The basis on which financial statements are prepared is that of 'accruals'. By this it is meant that the recognition of revenue and expenditure takes place not at the point when cash is received or paid out, but instead at the point when the revenue is earned or the expenditure is incurred.
To establish the point of recognition of a sale, several criteria are necessary:

(i) The product, or the service, must have been supplied to the customer.

(ii) The buyer must have indicated his willingness to pay for the product or services and to have accepted liability to do so.

(iii) A monetary value of the goods or services must have been agreed to by the buyer.

(iv) Ownership of the goods must have passed to the buyer.

(b) (i) This cannot be recognised as a sale. It does not comply with any of the four criteria above.

(ii) This also cannot be recognised as a sale. Neither criterion (i) nor (iv) has been covered.

(iii) If this was a cash sale, all of the above criteria would probably be achieved on delivery, and therefore it could be appropriate to recognise the sale.
If it was a credit sale, if the invoice was sent with the goods and a delivery note stating satisfaction by the customer is signed by him, then it would also probably be appropriate to recognise the sale.

(iv) Usually takes place after the four criteria have been satisfied. If so, the sale should be recognised.

(v) In the case of cash sales this would be the point of recognition.
In the case of credit sales it would depend on whether or not criteria (a) (i) and (iv) had also been satisfied.

(vi) This would only influence recognition of sales if there was serious doubt about the ability of the customer to pay his debts.

45.13

Obviously there is no set answer to this question. However, the following may well be typical:

(a) If the business is going to carry on operating, then the going concern concept comes into operation. Consequently, fixed assets are valued at cost, less depreciation to date. Stocks will be valued at lower of cost or net realisable value. The 'net realisable value' will be that based on the business realising stock through normal operations.

(b) Should the business be deemed as a case for cessation, then the going concern concept could not be used. The values on fixed assets and stocks will be their disposal values. This should be affected by whether or not the business could be sold as a whole or whether it would have to be broken up. Similarly, figures would be affected by whether or not assets had to be sold off very quickly at low prices, or sold only when reasonable prices could be achieved.
It is not only the balance sheet that would be affected, as the profit and loss account would reflect the changes in values.

45.14

(a) See text, Chapter 10.

(b) Various illustrations are possible, but the following are examples:

(i) Apportionment of expenses between one period and another. For instance, very rarely would very small stocks of stationery be valued at the year end. This means that the stationery gets charged against one year's profits even though it may not all have been used up in that year.

(ii) Items expensed instead of being capitalised. Small items which are, in theory, capital expenditure will often be charged up to an expense account.

(iii) The value of assets approximated, instead of being measured with absolute precision.

(c) (i) An illustration could be made under (b) (iii). A stock of oil could well be estimated; the true figure, if known, might be one or two litres out. The cost of precise measurement would probably not be worth the benefit of having such information.

(ii) What is material in one company may not be material in another.

45.15

No set answer. Question is of a general nature rather than being specific. A variety of answers is therefore acceptable.
The examiner might expect to see the following covered (this is not a model answer):

(a) Different reports needed by different outside parties, as they have to meet different requirements. Might find they therefore include:

(i) for bankers – accounts based on 'break-up' value of the assets if they have to be sold off to repay loans or overdrafts;

(ii) for investors – to include how business has fared against budgets set for that year to see how successful business is at meeting targets;

(iii) for employees – include details of number of employees, wages and salaries paid, effect on pension funds;

(iv) for local community – to include reports showing amounts spent on pollution control, etc.
And any similar instances.

(b) The characteristics of useful information have been stated in the ASB Statement of Principles, and the accounting reports should be measured against this.

(c) Presentation (additional) in form of pie charts, bar charts, etc., as these are often more easily understood by readers.

45.16

(a) Accountants follow the realisation concept when deciding when to recognise revenue on any particular transaction. This states that profit is normally regarded as being earned at the time when the goods or services are passed to the customer and he incurs liability for them. For a service business it means when the services have been performed.

(b) The stage at which revenue is recognised could be either F or G. The normal rule is that the goods have been despatched, not delivered. For instance the goods may be shipped to Australia and take several weeks to get there.
Exactly where this fits in with F or G in the question cannot be stipulated without further information.

45.16 (cont'd)

(c) If F is accepted as point of recognition, then £130 will be gross profit. If G is accepted as point of recognition the gross profit recognised will be £120.

(d) The argument that can be advanced is to take the prudence concept to its final conclusion, in that the debtor should pay for the goods before the profit can be recognised.

Until H is reached there is always the possibility that the goods will not be paid for, or might be returned because of faults in the goods.

(e) If the goods are almost certain to be sold, it could give a better picture of the progress of the firm up to a particular point in time, if profit could be recognised in successive amounts at stages B, C and D.

45.17

(a) A 'provision' is an amount written off or retained by way of providing for depreciation, renewals or diminution in value of assets, or retained by way of providing for any known liability of which the amount cannot be determined with 'substantial' accuracy. This therefore covers such items as provisions for depreciation. A 'liability' is an amount owing which can be determined with substantial accuracy.

Sometimes, therefore, the difference between a provision and a liability hinges around what is meant by 'substantial' accuracy. Rent owing at the end of the financial year would normally be known with precision; this would obviously be a liability. Legal charges for a court case which has been heard, but for which the lawyers have not yet submitted their bill, would be a provision.

Accrued expenses are those accruing from one day to another, but not paid at the year end. Such items as rates, electricity, telephone charges will come under this heading.

Creditors are persons to whom money is owed for goods and services.

Reserves consist of either undistributed profits, or else sums that have been created to comply with the law. An example of the first kind is a *general reserve*, whilst a *share premium account* is of the second type.

Provisions, accrued expenses and creditors would all be taken into account before calculating net profit. Reserves do not interfere with the calculation of net profit, as they are appropriations of profit or, as in the case of capital reserves, do not pass through the profit and loss account.

(b) (i) Provision made for £21,000. Charge to profit and loss and show in balance sheet under current liabilities.

(ii) Accrued expenses, $^2/_{12}$ £6,000 = £1,000. Charge in profit and loss account and show as current liability in balance sheet.

(iii) Creditor £2,500. Bring into purchases in trading account and show as current liability in balance sheet.

(iv) Reserve £5,000. Transfer from retained profits to plant replacement reserve and show the transfer in the profit and loss appropriation account and in the balance sheet under reserves.

45.18

(a) *The bank*

The bank will be interested in two main aspects. The first is the ability to repay the loan as and when it falls due. The second is the ability to pay interest on the due dates.

Mr Whitehall

He will be interested in the expected return on his investment. This means that recent performance of the company and its plans will be important to him. In addition the possible capital growth of his investment would be desirable.

(b) Note: For your information, more than four ratios for bank are given, below despite your having been asked for four.

Bank

Long-term ability to repay loan

(i) Members' equity/Total assets

(ii) Loan capital/Members' equity

(iii) Total liabilities/Members' equity

(iv) Operating profit/Loan interest.

Short-term liquidity

(i) Liquid assets/Current liabilities.

(ii) Current assets/Current liabilities.

Mr Whitehall

Return on investment

(i) Price per share/Earnings per share

(ii) Trends of (i) for past few years.

(iii) Net profit – Preference dividend/Ordinary dividend.

(iv) Trends of (iii) for past few years.

45.19
See text.

47.1
See text.

47.2
See text.

47.3
See text.

47.4
See text.

47.5
See text.

Answers to multiple choice questions

Set 1 (pages 62–5)

1	(C)	2	(D)	3	(B)	4	(C)	5	(A)
6	(C)	7	(C)	8	(A)	9	(C)	10	(A)
11	(B)	12	(D)	13	(B)	14	(D)	15	(B)
16	(C)	17	(C)	18	(A)	19	(D)	20	(C)

Set 2 (pages 148–50)

21	(A)	22	(B)	23	(A)	24	(D)	25	(C)
26	(A)	27	(D)	28	(A)	29	(C)	30	(A)
31	(C)	32	(D)	33	(C)	34	(C)	35	(D)
36	(B)	37	(A)	38	(B)	39	(C)	40	(C)

Set 3 (pages 307–9)

41	(A)	42	(C)	43	(A)	44	(D)	45	(A)
46	(A)	47	(B)	48	(C)	49	(D)	50	(C)
51	(A)	52	(D)	53	(C)	54	(C)	55	(D)
56	(C)	57	(A)	58	(A)	59	(B)	60	(C)

Set 4 (pages 396–9)

61	(B)	62	(A)	63	(D)	64	(A)	65	(C)
66	(A)	67	(D)	68	(D)	69	(B)	70	(A)
71	(D)	72	(C)	73	(D)	74	(B)	75	(B)
76	(C)	77	(D)	78	(A)	79	(B)	80	(C)

Set 5 (pages 591–4)

81	(B)	82	(B)	83	(C)	84	(D)	85	(A)
86	(B)	87	(A)	88	(C)	89	(C)	90	(A)
91	(C)	92	(B)	93	(B)	94	(D)	95	(C)
96	(B)	97	(C)	98	(C)	99	(D)	100	(B)

Glossary

Absorption costing (Chapter 47): The method of allocating all factory indirect expenses to products. (All fixed costs are allocated to cost units.)

Account (Chapter 2): Part of double entry records, containing details of transactions for a specific item.

Account codes (Chapter 21): The computerised equivalent of the folio references used in a manual accounting system, whereby each ledger account is given a unique number.

Accounting (Chapter 26): The process of identifying, measuring and communicating economic information to permit informed judgements and decisions by users of the information.

Accounting cycle (Chapter 15): The sequence in which data is recorded and processed until it becomes part of the financial statements at the end of the period.

Accounting information system (AIS) (Chapter 21): The total suite of components that, together, comprise all the inputs, storage, transformation processing, collating, and reporting of financial transaction data. It is, in effect, the infrastructure that supports the production and delivery of accounting information.

Accounting policies (Chapter 45): Those principles, bases, conventions, rules and practices applied by an entity that specify how the effects of transactions and other events are to be reflected in its financial statements.

Accounts (or **Final Accounts**) (Chapter 9): This is a term previously used to refer to statements produced at the end of accounting periods, such as the trading and profit and loss account and the balance sheet. Nowadays, the term 'financial statements' is more commonly used.

Accruals concept (Chapter 10): The concept that profit is the difference between revenue and the expenses incurred in generating that revenue.

Accrued expense (Chapter 26): An expense for which the benefit has been received but which has not been paid for by the end of the period. It is included in the balance sheet under current liabilities as 'accruals'.

Accrued income (Chapter 26): Income (normally) from a source other than the main source of business income, such as rent receivable on an unused office in the company headquarters, that was due to be received by the end of the period but which has not been received by that date. It is added to debtors in the balance sheet.

Accumulated depreciation account (Chapter 25): The account where depreciation is accumulated for balance sheet purposes. It is used in order to leave the cost (or valuation) figure as the balance in the fixed asset account. (It is sometime confusingly referred to as the 'provision for depreciation account'.)

Accumulated fund (Chapter 34): A form of capital account for a non-profit-oriented organisation.

Acid test ratio (Chapter 45): A ratio comparing current assets less stock with current liabilities.

Amortisation (Chapter 24): A term used instead of depreciation when assets are used up simply because of the passing of time.

Assets (Chapter 1): Resources owned by a business.

AVCO (Chapter 27): A method by which the goods used are priced out at average cost.

Bad debt (Chapter 23): A debt that a business will not be able to collect.

Balance brought down (Chapter 5): The difference between both sides of an account that is entered below the totals on the opposite side to the one on which the balance carried down was entered. (This is normally abbreviated to 'balance b/d'.)

Balance carried down (Chapter 5): The difference between both sides of an account that is entered above the totals and makes the total of both sides equal each other. (This is normally abbreviated to 'balance c/d'.)

Balance off the account (Chapter 5): Insert the difference (called a 'balance') between the two sides of an account and then total and rule off the account. This is normally done at the end of a period (usually a month, a quarter, or a year).

Balance sheet (Chapter 1): A statement showing the assets, liabilities, and capital of a business.

Bank cash book (Chapter 16): A cash book that only contains entries relating to payments into and out of the bank.

Bank giro credit (Chapter 12): A type of pay-in slip usually used when the payment is into an account held in a different bank. The two types of form are virtually identical – a bank Giro credit can be used instead of a pay-in slip, but not the other way around, as the details of the other bank need to be entered on the bank Giro credit.

Bank Giro credit (Chapter 28): An amount paid by someone directly into someone else's bank account.

Bank loan (Chapter 12): An amount of money advanced by a bank that has a fixed rate of interest that is charged on the full amount and is repayable on a specified future date.

Bank reconciliation statement (Chapter 28): A calculation comparing the cash book balance with the bank statement balance.

Bank statement (Chapter 13): A copy issued by a bank to a customer showing the customer's current account maintained at the bank.

Bookkeeping (Chapter 1): The process of recording data relating to accounting transactions in the accounting books.

Books of original entry (Chapter 11): Books where the first entry recording a transaction is made. (These are sometimes referred to as 'books of prime entry'.)

Bought ledger (Chapter 18): A variant of a purchases ledger where the individual accounts of the creditors, whether they be for goods or for expenses such as stationery or motor expenses, can be kept together in a single ledger.

Budget (Chapters 1 and 47): A plan quantified in monetary terms in advance of a defined time period – usually showing planned income and expenditure and the capital employed to achieve a given objective.

Business entity concept (Chapter 10): Assumption that only transactions that affect the firm, and not the owner's private transactions, will be recorded.

Capital (Chapter 1): The total of resources invested and left in a business by its owner.

Capital expenditure (Chapter 22): When a business spends money to buy or add value to a fixed asset.

Capital reserve (Chapter 44): An account that can be used by sole traders and partnerships to place the amount by which the total purchase price paid for a business is less than the valuation of the net assets acquired. Limited companies cannot use a capital reserve for this purpose. Sole traders and partnerships can instead, if they wish, record the shortfall as negative goodwill.

Carriage inwards (Chapter 9): Cost of transport of goods into a business.

Carriage outwards (Chapter 9): Cost of transport of goods out to the customers of a business.

Cash (Chapter 37): Cash balances and bank balances, plus funds invested in 'cash equivalents'.

Cash book (Chapter 11): A book of original entry for cash and bank receipts and payments.

Cash equivalents (Chapter 37): Temporary investments of cash not required at present by the business, such as funds put on short-term deposit with a bank. Such investments must be readily convertible into cash, or available as cash within three months.

Cash flow statement (Chapter 37): A statement showing how cash has been generated and disposed of by an organisation. The layout is regulated by FRS 1.

Casting (Chapter 30): Adding up figures.

Charge card (Chapter 12): A payment card that requires the cardholder to settle the account in full at the end of a specified period, e.g. American Express and Diners cards. Holders have to pay an annual fee for the card. (Compare this to a credit card.)

Chart of accounts (Chapter 21): The list of account codes used in a computerised accounting system.

Cheque book (Chapter 12): Book containing forms (cheques) used to pay money out of a current account.

Clearing (Chapter 12): The process by which amounts paid by cheque from an account in one bank are transferred to the bank account of the payee.

Close off the account (Chapter 5): Totalling and ruling off an account on which there is no outstanding balance.

Columnar purchases day book (Chapter 18): A purchases day book used to record all items obtained on credit. It has analysis columns so that the various types of expenditure can be grouped together in a column. Also called a purchases analysis book.

Columnar sales day book (Chapter 18): A sales day book used to show the sales for a period organised in analysis columns according to how the information recorded is to be analysed. Also called a sales analysis book.

Compensating error (Chapter 30): Where two errors of equal amounts, but on opposite sides of the accounts, cancel each other out.

Consistency (Chapter 10): Keeping to the same method of recording and processing transactions.

Contra (Chapter 13): A contra, for cash book items, is where both the debit and the credit entries are shown in the cash book, such as when cash is paid into the bank.

Contribution (Chapter 36): The surplus of revenue over direct costs allocated to a section of a business.

Control account (Chapter 29): An account which checks the arithmetical accuracy of a ledger.

Cost centre (Chapter 46): A production or service location, function, activity, or item of equipment whose costs may be attributed to cost units.

Cost unit (Chapter 46): A unit of product or service in relation to which costs are ascertained.

Credit (Chapter 2): The right-hand side of the accounts in double entry.

Credit card (Chapter 12): A card enabling the holder to make purchases and to draw cash up to a pre-arranged limit. The credit granted in a period can be settled in full or in part by the end of a specified period. Many credit cards carry no annual fee. (Compare this to a charge card.)

Credit note (Chapter 14): A document sent to a customer showing allowance given by a supplier in respect of unsatisfactory goods.

Creditor (Chapter 1): A person to whom money is owed for goods or services.

Creditor/purchases ratio (Chapter 45): A ratio assessing how long a business takes to pay creditors.

Current account (Chapter 12): A bank account used for regular payments in and out of the bank.

Current assets (Chapter 8): Assets consisting of cash, goods for resale or items having a short life.

Current liabilities (Chapter 8): Liabilities to be paid for within a year of the balance sheet date.

Current ratio (Chapter 45): A ratio comparing current assets with current liabilities.

Day books (Chapter 11): Books in which credit sales, purchases, and returns inwards and outwards of goods are first recorded. The details are then posted from the day books to the ledger accounts.

Debenture (Chapter 43): Loan to a company.

Debit (Chapter 2): The left-hand side of the accounts in double entry.

Debit card (Chapter 12): A card linked to a bank or building society account and used to pay for goods and services by debiting the holder's account. Debit cards are usually combined with other facilities such as ATM and cheque guarantee functions.

Debit note (Chapter 14): A document sent to a supplier showing allowance to be given for unsatisfactory goods.

Debtor (Chapter 1): A person who owes money to a business for goods or services supplied to him.

Debtor/sales ratio (Chapter 45): A ratio assessing how long it takes debtors to pay their debts.

Depletion (Chapter 24): The wasting away of an asset as it is used up.

Deposit account (Chapter 12): A bank account for money to be kept in for a long time.

Depreciation (Chapter 24): The part of the cost of a fixed asset consumed during its period of use by the firm. It represents an estimate of how much of the overall economic usefulness of a fixed asset has been used up in each accounting period. It is charged as a debit to profit and loss and a credit against fixed asset accounts in the general ledger.

Direct costs (Chapter 35): Costs that can be traced to the item being manufactured.

Direct debit (Chapter 12): A medium used to enable payments to be made automatically into a bank account for whatever amount the recipient requests.

Directors (Chapter 43): Officials appointed by shareholders to manage the company for them.

Discounts allowed (Chapter 13): A deduction from the amount due given to customers who pay their accounts within the time allowed.

Discounts received (Chapter 13): A deduction from the amount due given to a business by a supplier when their account is paid before the time allowed has elapsed. It appears as income in the profit and loss part of the trading and profit and loss account.

Dishonoured cheque (Chapter 28): A cheque which the writer's bank has refused to make payment upon.

Dissolution (Chapter 42): When a partnership firm ceases operations and its assets are disposed of.

Dividends (Chapter 43): The amount given to shareholders as their share of the profits of the company.

Double entry bookkeeping (Chapter 2): A system where each transaction is entered twice, once on the debit side and once on the credit side.

Drawer (Chapter 12): The person making out a cheque and using it for payment.

Drawings (Chapter 4): Funds or goods taken out of a business by the owners for their private use.

Dual aspect concept (Chapter 10): The concept of dealing with both aspects of a transaction.

Dumb terminal (Chapter 20): A computer screen with keyboard (and, perhaps, a mouse) that has no processing power of its own but uses the processing power of a central computer to carry out tasks involving the data held on that central computer.

Endorsement (Chapter 12): A means by which someone may pass the right to collect money due on a cheque.

Equity (Chapter 1): Another name for the capital of the owner.

Error of commission (Chapter 30): Where a correct amount is entered, but in the wrong person's account.

Error of omission (Chapter 30): Where a transaction is completely omitted from the books.

Error of original entry (Chapter 30): Where an item is entered, but both the debit and credit entries are of the same incorrect amount.

Error of principle (Chapter 30): Where an item is entered in the wrong type of account, e.g. a fixed asset in an expense account.

Estimation techniques (Chapter 45): The methods adopted in order to arrive at estimated monetary amounts for items that appear in the financial statements.

Exception reporting (Chapter 21): A process of issuing a warning message to decision-makers when something unexpected is happening: for example, when expenditure against a budget is higher than it should be.

Exempted businesses (Chapter 17): Businesses which do not have to add VAT to the price of goods and services supplied to them. They cannot obtain a refund of VAT paid on goods and services purchased by them.

Expenses (Chapter 4): The value of all the assets that have been used up to obtain revenues.

Extranet (Chapter 20): A network based on Internet technologies where data and information private to the business is made available to a specific group of outsiders, such as suppliers.

Factoring (Chapter 8): Selling the rights to the amounts owing by debtors to a finance company for an agreed amount (which is less than the figure at which they are recorded in the accounting books because the finance company needs to be paid for providing the service).

FIFO (Chapter 27): A method by which the first goods to be received are said to be the first to be sold.

Final accounts (or 'the accounts') (Chapter 9): This is a term previously used to refer to statements produced at the end of accounting periods, such as the trading and profit and loss account and the balance sheet. Nowadays, the term 'financial statements' is more commonly used.

Financial modelling (Chapter 20): Manipulating accounting data to generate forecasts and perform sensitivity analysis.

Financial statements (Chapter 9): The more common term used to refer to statements produced at the end of accounting periods, such as the trading and profit and loss account and the balance sheet (sometimes referred to as 'final accounts' or simply 'the accounts').

Fixed assets (Chapter 8): Assets which have a long life bought with the intention to use them in the business and not with the intention to simply resell them.

Fixed capital accounts (Chapter 39): Capital accounts which consist only of the amounts of capital actually paid into the firm.

Fixed costs (Chapter 45): Expenses which remain constant whether activity rises or falls, within a given range of activity.

Float (Chapter 16): The amount at which the petty cash starts each period.

Fluctuating capital accounts (Chapter 39): Capital accounts whose balances change from one period to the next.

Folio columns (Chapter 13): Columns used for entering reference numbers.

Forecasting (Chapter 20): Taking present data and expected future trends, such as growth of a market and anticipated changes in price levels and demand, in order to arrive at a view of what the likely economic position of a business will be at some future date.

Garner v Murrary rule (Chapter 42): If one partner is unable to make good a deficit on his capital account, the remaining partners will share the loss in proportion to their last agreed capitals, not in the profit/loss sharing ratio.

Gearing (Chapter 45): The ratio of long-term loans and preference shares shown as a percentage of total shareholders' funds, long-term loans, and preference shares.

General ledger (Chapter 11): A ledger for all accounts other than those for customers and suppliers.

Going concern concept (Chapter 10): The assumption that a business is to continue for the foreseeable future.

Goodwill (Chapter 40): An amount representing the added value to a business of such factors as customer loyalty, reputation, market penetration, and expertise.

Gross loss (Chapter 7): Where the cost of goods sold exceeds the sales revenue.

Gross profit (Chapter 7): Where the sales revenue exceeds the cost of goods sold.

Historical cost concept (Chapter 10): Assets are normally shown at cost price.

Impersonal accounts (Chapter 11): All accounts other than debtors' and creditors' accounts.

Imprest system (Chapter 16): A system where a refund is made of the total paid out in a period in order to restore the float to its agreed level.

Income and expenditure account (Chapter 34): An account for a non-profit-oriented organisation to find the surplus or loss made during a period.

Indirect manufacturing costs (Chapter 35): Costs relating to manufacture that cannot be economically traced to the item being manufactured (also known as 'indirect costs' and, sometimes, as 'factory overhead expenses').

Input tax (Chapter 17): VAT added to the net price of inputs (i.e. purchases).

Inputs (Chapter 17): Purchases of goods and services.

Intangible asset (Chapter 40): An asset, such as goodwill, that has no physical existence.

Interest on capital (Chapter 39): An amount at an agreed rate of interest which is credited to a partner based on the amount of capital contributed by him/her.

Interest on drawings (Chapter 39): An amount at an agreed rate of interest, based on the drawings taken out, which is debited to the partners.

Intranet (Chapter 20): A network based on Internet technologies where data and information private to the business is made available to employees of the business.

Job costing (Chapter 46): A costing system that is applied when goods or services are produced in discrete jobs, either one item at a time, or in batches.

Joint ventures (Chapter 38): Business agreements under which two businesses join together for a set of activities and agree to share the profits.

Journal (Chapter 11): A book of original entry for all items not contained in the other books of original entry.

Liabilities (Chapter 1): Total of funds owed for assets supplied to a business or expenses incurred not yet paid.

LIFO (Chapter 27): A method by which the goods sold are said to have come from the last lot of goods received.

Limited company (Chapter 43): An organisation owned by its shareholders, whose liability is limited to their share capital.

Limited partner (Chapter 39): A partner whose liability is limited to the capital he or she has put into the firm.

Liquidity ratios (Chapter 45): Those ratios that relate to the cash position in an organisation and hence its ability to pay liabilities when due.

Local area network (LAN) (Chapter 20): A group of workstations linked together locally through wires.

Long-term liabilities (Chapter 8): Liabilities that do not have to be paid within twelve months of the balance sheet date.

Loss (Chapter 4): The result of selling goods for less than they cost.

Manufacturing account (Chapter 35): An account in which production cost is calculated.

Margin (Chapter 32): Profit shown as a percentage or fraction of selling price.

Marginal costing (Chapter 46): An approach to costing that takes account of the variable cost of products rather than the full production cost. It is particularly useful when considering utilisation of spare capacity.

Mark-up (Chapter 32): Profit shown as a percentage or fraction of cost price.

Materiality (Chapter 10): That something should only be included in the financial statements if it would be of interest to the stakeholders, i.e. to those people who make use of financial accounting statements. It need not be material to every stakeholder, but it must be material to a stakeholder before it merits inclusion.

Measurement basis (Chapter 45): The monetary aspects of the items in the financial statements, such as the basis of the stock valuation, say FIFO or LIFO.

Memorandum joint venture account (Chapter 38): A memorandum account outside the double entry system where the information contained in all the joint venture accounts held by the parties to the joint ventures are collated, the joint venture profit is calculated and the share of profit of each party is recorded in order to close off the account.

Money measurement concept (Chapter 10): The concept that accounting is concerned only with facts measurable in monetary terms, and for which purpose measurements can be used that obtain general agreement as to their suitability.

Narrative (Chapter 15): A description and explanation of the transaction recorded in the journal.

Negative contribution (Chapter 36): The excess of direct costs allocated to a section of a business over the revenue from that section.

Negative goodwill (Chapter 44): The name given to the amount by which the total purchase price for a business a limited company has taken over is less than the valuation of the assets at that time. The amount is entered at the top of the fixed assets in the balance sheet as a negative amount. (Sole traders and partnerships can use this approach instead of a capital reserve.)

Net current assets (Chapter 8): Current assets minus current liabilities. The figure represents the amount of resources the business has in a form that is readily convertible into cash. Same as working capital.

Net loss (Chapter 7): Where the cost of goods sold plus expenses is greater than the revenue.

Net profit (Chapter 7): Where sales revenue plus other income, such as rent received, exceeds the sum of cost of goods sold plus other expenses.

Net realisable value (Chapter 27): The value of goods calculated as their selling price less expenses before sale.

Nominal accounts (Chapter 11): Accounts in which expenses, revenue and capital are recorded.

Nominal ledger (Chapter 11): Another name for the general ledger.

Objectivity (Chapter 10): Using a method that everyone can agree to based on some clear and indisputable fact.

Obsolescence (Chapter 24): Becoming out of date.

Ordinary shares (Chapter 43): Shares entitled to dividends after the preference shareholders have been paid their dividends.

Output tax (Chapter 17): VAT added to the net price of outputs (i.e. sales).

Outputs (Chapter 17): Sales of goods and services.

Overdraft (Chapter 12): A facility granted by a bank that allows a customer holding a current account with the bank to spend more than the funds in the account. Interest is charged daily on the amount of the overdraft on that date and the overdraft is repayable at any time upon request from the bank.

Partnership (Chapter 39): A firm in which two or more people are working together as owners with a view to making profits.

Partnership salaries (Chapter 39): Agreed amounts payable to partners in respect of duties undertaken by them.

PAYE (Pay As You Earn) (Chapter 19): The system whereby income tax is deducted from wages and salaries by employers and sent to Revenue & Customs.

Payee (Chapter 12): The person to whom a cheque is paid.

Pay-in slip (Chapter 12): A form used for paying money into a bank account with the same bank.

Personal accounts (Chapter 11): Accounts for creditors and debtors.

Personal allowances (Chapter 19): Amounts each person may subtract from income in order to arrive at taxable income. The value of each allowance is set by Parliament following the Budget each year. They are for things like being married, caring for a dependent relative, etc.

Personal Identification Number or **PIN** (Chapter 12): A secret number issued by a bank to a customer so that the customer may use a debit card in an ATM.

Petty cash book (Chapter 16): A cash book for small payments.

Plastic card (Chapter 12): The generic name for the range of payment-related cards.

Posting (Chapter 13): The act of transferring information into ledger accounts from books of original entry.

Preference shares (Chapter 43): Shares that are entitled to an agreed rate of dividend before the ordinary shareholders receive anything.

Preliminary expenses (Chapter 43): All the costs that are incurred when a company is formed.

Prepaid expense (Chapter 26): An expense which has been paid in advance, the benefits from which will be received in the next period. It is included in the balance sheet under current assets as 'prepayments'.

Prime cost (Chapter 35): Direct materials plus direct labour plus direct expenses.

Private company (Chapter 43): A limited company that must issue its shares privately.

Private ledger (Chapter 11): A ledger for capital and drawings accounts.

Process costing (Chapter 46): A costing system that is applied when goods or services are produced in a continuous flow.

Production cost (Chapter 35): Prime cost plus indirect manufacturing costs.

Profit (Chapter 4): The result of selling goods or services for more than they cost.

Profit and loss account (Chapter 7): An account in which net profit is calculated.

Provision for doubtful debts (Chapter 23): An account showing the expected amounts of debtors at the balance sheet date who will not be able to pay their accounts.

Prudence (Chapter 10): Ensuring that profit is not shown as being too high, or that assets are shown at too high a value and that the financial statements are neutral: that is, that neither gains nor losses are understated or overstated.

Public company (Chapter 43): A company that can issue its shares publicly, and for which there is no maximum number of shareholders.

Purchased goodwill (Chapter 40): The difference between the amount paid to acquire a part or the whole of a business as a going concern and the value of the net assets owned by the business.

Purchases (Chapter 3): Goods bought by the business for the prime purpose of selling them again.

Purchases day book (Chapter 11): Book of original entry for credit purchases. Also called the purchases journal.

Purchases invoice (Chapter 14): A document received by a purchaser showing details of goods bought and their prices.

Purchases ledger (Chapter 11): A ledger for suppliers' personal accounts.

Real accounts (Chapter 11): Accounts in which property of all kinds is recorded.

Realisation concept (Chapter 10): Only profits and gains realised at the balance sheet date should be included in the profit and loss account. For a gain to be realised, it must be possible to be reasonably certain that it exists and that it can be measured with sufficient reliability.

Receipts and payments account (Chapter 34): A summary of the cash book of a non-profit-oriented organisation.

Reduced rate (of VAT) (Chapter 17): A lower VAT rate applicable to certain goods and services.

Reducing balance method (Chapter 24): A method of calculating depreciation based on the principle that you calculate annual depreciation as a percentage of the net-of-depreciation-to-date balance brought forward at the start of the period on the fixed asset.

Registered business (Chapter 17): A business that has registered for VAT. It must account for VAT and submit a VAT Return at the end of every VAT tax period.

Reserve accounts (Chapter 43): The transfer of apportioned profits to accounts for use in future years.

Residual value (Chapter 24): The net amount receivable when a fixed asset is put out of use by the business.

Return on capital employed (Chapter 45): Net profit as a percentage of capital employed, often abbreviated as ROCE.

Return on owners' equity (Chapter 45): Net profit as a percentage of ordinary share capital plus all reserves, often abbreviated as ROOE. The more common term in use for this is 'return on shareholders' funds'.

Return on shareholders' funds (Chapter 45): Net profit as a percentage of ordinary share capital plus all reserves, often abbreviated as ROSF and more commonly used than the alternative term, return on owners' equity.

Returns inwards (Chapter 9): Goods returned by customers. (Also known as 'sales returns'.)

Returns inwards day book (Chapter 11): Book of original entry for goods returned by customers. Also called the returns inwards journal or the sales returns book.

Returns outwards (Chapter 9): Goods returned to suppliers. (Also known as 'purchases returns'.)

Returns outwards day book (Chapter 11): Book of original entry for goods returned to suppliers. Also called the returns outwards journal or the purchases returns book.

Revaluation account (Chapter 41): An account used to record gains and losses when assets are revalued.

Revenue expenditure (Chapter 22): Expenses needed for the day-to-day running of the business.

Revenues (Chapter 4): The financial value of goods and services sold to customers.

Sale or return (Chapter 27): Goods passed to a customer on the understanding that a sale will not occur until they are paid for. As a result, these goods continue to belong to the seller.

Sales (Chapter 3): Goods sold by the business in which it normally deals which were bought with the prime intention of resale.

Sales day book (Chapter 11): Book of original entry for credit sales. Also called the sales journal.

Sales invoice (Chapter 14): A document showing details of goods sold and the prices of those goods.

Sales ledger (Chapter 11): A ledger for customers' personal accounts.

Sensitivity analysis (Chapter 20): Altering volumes and amounts so as to see what would be likely to happen if they were changed. For example, a company may wish to know the financial effects of cutting its selling price by £1 a unit. Also called 'what if' analysis.

Separate determination concept (Chapter 10): The amount of each asset or liability should be determined separately.

Shares (Chapter 43): The division of the capital of a limited company into parts.

Smart card (Chapter 12): A card that holds details on a computer chip instead of a traditional magnetic stripe.

Standard cost (Chapter 27): What you would expect something to cost.

Standard rate (of VAT) (Chapter 17): The VAT rate usually used.

Standard-rated business (Chapter 17): A business that charges VAT at the standard rate on its sales.

Standing order (Chapter 12): A medium used to enable payments to be made automatically at given dates into a bank account for an amount agreed by the payer.

Statement (Chapter 14): A copy of a customer's personal account taken from the supplier's books.

Statement of Affairs (Chapter 33): A statement from which the capital of the owner can be found by estimating assets and liabilities. Then Capital = Assets – Liabilities. It is the equivalent of the balance sheet.

Stock (Chapter 1): Goods in which the business normally deals that are held with the intention of resale. They may be finished goods, partly finished goods, or raw materials awaiting conversion into finished goods which will then be sold. (Also known as inventory.)

Stock turnover (Chapter 32): The number of times stock is sold in an accounting period. (Also known as 'stockturn'.)

Stocktaking (Chapter 27): The process of physically identifying the stock on hand at a given point in time.

Straight line method (Chapter 24): A method of calculating depreciation that involves deducting the same amount every accounting period from the original cost of the fixed asset.

Subjectivity (Chapter 10): Using a method that other people may not agree to, derived from one's own personal preferences.

Substance over form (Chapter 10): Where real substance takes precedence over legal form.

Super profits (Chapter 40): Net profit less the opportunity costs of alternative earnings and alternative returns on capital invested that have been foregone.

Suspense account (Chapter 31): An account in which you can enter the amount equal to the difference in the trial balance while you try to find the cause of the error(s) that resulted in the failure of the trial balance to balance.

Switch (Chapter 12): A system that allows a debit card to be used to pay for goods and services in the UK. In effect, it is the electronic version of paying by cheque.

T-account (Chapter 2): The layout of accounts in the accounting books.

Tax code (Chapter 19): The number found by adding up an individual's personal allowances which is used to calculate that individual's tax liability.

Time interval concept (Chapter 10): Financial statements are prepared at regular intervals.

Total cost (Chapter 35): Production cost plus administration, selling and distribution expenses and finance expenses.

Trade discount (Chapter 14): A deduction in price given to a trade customer when calculating the price to be charged to that customer for some goods. It does not appear anywhere in the accounting books and so does not appear anywhere in the financial statements.

Trading account (Chapter 7): An account in which gross profit is calculated.

Trading and profit and loss account (Chapter 7): A financial statement in which both gross profit and net profit are calculated.

Transposition error (Chapter 30): Where the characters within a number are entered in the wrong sequence.

Trial balance (Chapter 6): A list of account titles and their balances in the ledgers, on a specific date, shown in debit and credit columns.

True and fair view (Chapter 43): The expression that is used by auditors to indicate whether, in their opinion, the financial statements fairly represent the state of affairs and financial performance of a company.

Unpresented cheque (Chapter 28): A cheque which has been given to a creditor but which has not yet been received and processed by the writer's bank.

Unregistered business (Chapter 17): A business that ignores VAT and treats it as part of the cost of purchases. It does not charge VAT on its outputs. It does not need to maintain any record of VAT paid.

Value Added Tax (VAT) (Chapter 17): A tax charged on the supply of most goods and services.

Variable costs (Chapter 45): Expenses which change in response to changes in the level of activity.

Website (of a business) (Chapter 20): A location on the Internet where businesses place information for the use of anyone who happens to want to look at it. In many cases, a business website contains copies of the latest financial statements of the business and a part of the website is devoted to promoting and selling goods and services.

'What if' analysis (Chapter 20): Altering volumes and amounts so as to see what would be likely to happen if they were changed. For example, a company may wish to know the financial effects of cutting its selling price by £1 a unit. Also called sensitivity analysis.

Wide area network (WAN) (Chapter 20): A group of workstations not all of which are based locally that are linked together by wires and over telephone lines.

Work in progress (Chapter 35): Items not completed at the end of a period.

Working capital (Chapter 8): Current assets minus current liabilities. The figure represents the amount of resources the business has in a form that is readily convertible into cash. Same as net current assets.

Workstation (Chapter 20): A dumb terminal or a PC that is used to access data held in a database on a central computer.

Zero rate (of VAT) (Chapter 17): The VAT rate (of zero) that applies to supply of certain goods and services.

Zero-rated business (Chapter 17): A business that only supplies zero-rated goods and services. It does not charge VAT to its customers but it receives a refund of VAT on goods and services it purchases.

Index

Advanced Financial Accounting

Visit the *Advanced Financial Accounting* Companion Website at
www.pearsoned.co.uk/kothari to find valuable **student**
learning material including:

- Practice questions to reinforce learning
- Bonus chapter content to broaden understanding

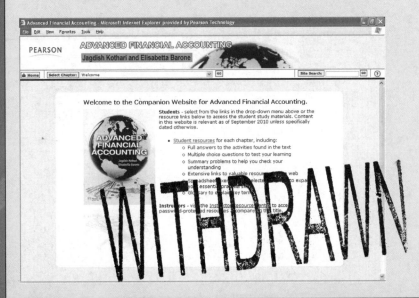

We work with leading authors to develop the
strongest educational materials in accounting,
bringing cutting-edge thinking and best
learning practice to a global market.

Under a range of well-known imprints, including
Financial Times Prentice Hall, we craft high quality print and
electronic publications which help readers to understand
and apply their content, whether studying or at work.

To find out more about the complete range of our
publishing, please visit us on the World Wide Web at:
www.pearsoned.co.uk

Jagdish Kothari
Elisabetta Barone

Advanced Financial Accounting

An International Approach

**Financial Times
Prentice Hall
is an imprint of**

Harlow, England • London • New York • Boston • San Francisco • Toronto • Sydney • Singapore • Hong Kong
Tokyo • Seoul • Taipei • New Delhi • Cape Town • Madrid • Mexico City • Amsterdam • Munich • Paris • Milan

Pearson Education Limited
Edinburgh Gate
Harlow
Essex CM20 2JE
England

and Associated Companies throughout the world

Visit us on the World Wide Web at:
www.pearsoned.co.uk

First published 2011

ISBN: 978-0-273-71274-9

British Library Cataloguing-in-Publication Data
A catalogue record for this book is available from the British Library

Library of Congress Cataloging-in-Publication Data
Kothari, Jagdish.
    Advanced financial accounting : an international approach / Jagdish Kothari,
Elisabetta Barone. – 1st ed.
        p. cm.
    ISBN 978-0-273-71274-9 (pbk.)
    1. Accounting – Standards. 2. International finance. I. Barone, Elisabetta, 1970–
II. Title.
    HF5626.K67 2010
    657'.046—dc22

                                                                        2010009904

10 9 8 7 6 5 4 3 2 1
15 14 13 12 11

Typeset in 9.25/12pt Stone Serif by 35
Printed and bound in Great Britain by Ashford Colour Press Ltd., Gosport, Hants

To my grandchildren James Arun and
Amber Joyce
– Jagdish Kothari

To my parents Ezio and Dora, my niece Diletta and
my nephews Daniele, Emanuele, Francesco, Lorenzo and Luca
– Elisabetta Barone

Contents

Supporting resources

Visit www.pearsoned.co.uk/kothari to find valuable online resources

Companion Website for students
- Practice questions to reinforce learning
- Bonus chapter content to broaden understanding

For instructors
- Downloadable PowerPoint slides for use in lectures
- Downloadable Instructors Manual

Also: The Companion Website provides the following features:

- Search tool to help locate specific items of content
- Online help and support to assist with website usage and troubleshooting

For more information please contact your local Pearson Education sales representative or visit www.pearsoned.co.uk/kothari

List of International Financial Reporting Standards (IFRS) and International Accounting Standards (IAS)

A full list of the International Financial Reporting Standards (IFRS) and International Accounting Standards (IAS) which are in force at the time of writing this book is given below.

It is important to note that new or modified standards are issued fairly often. The reader who wishes to keep up-to-date is advised to consult the website of the International Accounting Standards Board (IASB) at www.iasb.org.

International Financial Reporting Standards (IFRS)

		Chapter
IFRS 1	First-Time Adoption of International Financial Reporting Standards	4
IFRS 2	Share-Based Payments	13
IFRS 3	Business Combinations	19
IFRS 4	Insurance Contracts	–
IFRS 5	Non-Current Assets Held for Sale and Discontinued Operations	–
IFRS 6	Exploration for and Evaluation of Mineral Resources	–
IFRS 7	Financial Instruments: Disclosures	14–15
IFRS 8	Operating Segments	17
IFRS for SMEs	International Financial Reporting Standard for Small and Medium-Sized Entities	1

International Accounting Standards (IAS)

It should be noted that some of these standards are beyond the scope of this book and are not considered hereafter. These are IFRS 4, 5 and 6, IAS 20, 21, 26, 29, 34 and 41.

The IASB has published a *Framework for the Preparation and Presentation of Financial Statements* (see Chapters 2 and 3) which sets out a number of concepts that underlie financial reporting. This document is not itself a standard but it is referred to by the IASB during the development of new and amended standards.

List of figures

List of tables

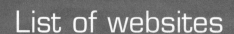

List of websites

adidas Group	http://www.adidas-group.com/en/investorrelations/reports/annualreports.aspx
Agfa-Gevaert NV	http://www.agfa.com/en/co/investor_relation/reports_presentations/index.jsp
Amer Sports	http://www.amersports.com/media/reports/annual_reports/
Avis Europe	http://ir.avis-europe.com/avisplc/
Barloworld Limited	http://ir.barloworld.com/phoenix.zhtml?c=69979&p=irol-reports
Bayer	http://www.investor.bayer.com/en/
British Airways Plc	http://www.bashares.com/phoenix.zhtml?c=69499&p=irol-reportsannual
Cavotec MSL	http://www.cavotec.com/corporate/21/annual-reports/
CEZ Group	http://www.cez.cz/en/investors/financial-reports.html
Diageo plc	http://www.diageo.com/investor/Pages/financialreports.aspx
EADS	http://www.eads.com/eads/int/en/investor-relations.html
Electrolux	http://www.electrolux.com/investors_and_media.aspx
FLSmidth	http://www.flsmidth.com/FLSmidth/English/Investor/Reports/default.htm
Groupe Danone	http://finance.danone.com/phoenix.zhtml?c=95168&p=irol-irHome
HOCHTIEF Aktiengesellschaft	http://www.hochtief.com/hochtief_en/604.jhtml
HSBC Holdings plc	http://www.hsbc.com/1/2/investor-relations/financial-results
Invensys	http://www.invensys.com/isys/publications/default.asp?top_nav_id=4&nav_id=45&prev_id=41
J Sainsbury plc	http://www.j-sainsbury.co.uk/index.asp?pageid=4
Lonmin Plc	http://www.lonmin.com/investorpresentations.aspx?pageId=211
Lufthansa	http://investor-relations.lufthansa.com/en/finanzberichte.html
Millicom International Cellular SA	http://www.millicom.com/investors/annuals.cfm
Nokia	http://investors.nokia.com/phoenix.zhtml?c=107224&p=irol-productFactSheets

Novo Nordisk	http://novonordisk.com/investors/download-centre/default.asp
Puma	http://about.puma.com/?cat=19
Roche	http://www.roche.com/investors/annual_reports.htm
Roll Royce	http://www.rolls-royce.com/investors/financial_reporting/
Skandia	http://www.skandia.com/financials/annual_reports_and_supplements.asp
Smith & Nephew	http://global.smith-nephew.com/master/investor_centre_2738.htm
Syngenta	http://www2.syngenta.com/en/investor_relations/financial_information.html
TeliaSonera	http://www.teliasonera.com/
Telkom SA Limited	https://secure1.telkom.co.za/ir/financial/financial_review_summary.jsp
The Emirates Group	http://www.theemiratesgroup.com/english/facts-figures/annual-reports.aspx?TYPE=ANNUALREPORT
Thomson Reuters	http://thomsonreuters.com/investor_relations/
Vodafone Group Plc	http://www.vodafone.com/start/investor_relations.html
Yell Group plc	http://www.yellgroup.com/english/investors

Acknowledgements

Our thanks go to Richard Macve, Jill Solomon, Robert Bruce, Paolo Caccini, Gandenzio Albertinazzi, Sabrina Barone, Sheila Ellwood and Jim Klein. Special thanks to Richard Laughlin and John Plender for their active encouragement and for their valuable inputs.

We should also like to thank our editors, Matthew Smith, Robin Lupton, Tim Parker, Anna Faherty and their colleagues at Pearson Education for their infinite patience and for all the hard work that they have put into producing this book. It has been tough going for everyone involved in the process. We alone remain responsible for any errors and for the thoughts and views that are expressed.

Publisher's acknowledgements

We are grateful to the following for permission to reproduce copyright material:

Figures

Figure 1.1 courtesy of Mary Ann Sullivan; Figure 1.2 from http://www.iasb.org/ Use+around+the+world/Use+around+the+world.htm, Copyright © 2010 International Accounting Standards Committee Foundation. All rights reserved. No permission granted to reproduce or distribute; Figure 3.4 extract from HSBC Holdings plc Annual Report 2008, http://www.hsbc.com/1/PA_1_1_S5/content/assets/ investor_relations/hsbc2008ara0.pdf, reproduced with permission from HSBC Holdings plc Annual Report and Accounts 2008; Figures 3.6b and 6.5 from Extract from Novo Nordisk Annual Report 2008, http://annualreport2008.novonordisk.com/; Figure 5.2 extract from Adidas Group Annual Report 2008: Accounting Policies, http://www.adidasgroup.com/en/investorrelations/assets/pdf/annual_reports/2008/ GB_2008_En.pdf; Figure 5.4 extract from Vodafone Group Plc Annual Report 2008, http://www.vodafone.com/etc/medialib/attachments/agm_2008.Par.77336.File.dat/ 2008_Annual_Report_FINAL.pdf; Figure 6.1 from *Introduction to Financial Accounting*, 8th ed., Pearson Education (Horngren, C.T., Sundem, G.L. and Elliott, J.A. 2002);

Figures 6.5, 7.2 extract from Bayer Annual Report 2008, http://www.annualreport2008.bayer.com/en/homepage.aspx; Figure 6.6 extract from Electrolux Annual Report 2008, http://www.electrolux.com/annual_reports.aspx; Figures 7.3, 8.2 and 8.5 extract from The Emirates Group Annual Report 2008–2009, http://www.theemiratesgroup.com/english/facts-figures/annual-reports.aspx; Figure 7.9 from HOCHTIEF Aktiengesellschaft Annual Report 2008, http://www.reports.hochtief.com/ar08/0.jhtml; Figure 8.3 from Agfa-Gevaert NV, Annual Report 2008, http://www.agfa.com/en/co/investor_relation/reports_presentations/annual_reports/index.jsp; Figure 9.4 extract from Syngenta Financial Report 2008, http://www.syngenta.com/en/investor_relations/pdf/Syngenta_FR2008_English.pdf; Figure 10.3 extract from Vodafone Group Plc Annual Report 2010, Copyright © Vodafone Group 2010; Figure 10.4 extract from SAP Annual Report 2008, http://www.sap.com/germany/about/investor/reports/gb2008/files/downloads/en/00-Annual_Report_2008-Full_Version.pdf, © 2008. SAP AG. All rights reserved. The publication contains references to the products of SAP AG. SAP, R/3, SAP NetWeaver, Duet, PartnerEdge, ByDesign, Clear Enterprise, SAP BusinessObjects Explorer, and other SAP products and services mentioned herein as well as their respective logos are trademarks or registered trademarks of SAP AG in Germany and other countries. Business Objects and the Business Objects logo, BusinessObjects, Crystal Reports, Crystal Decisions, Wen Intelligence, Xcelsius and other Business Objects products and services mentioned herein as well as their respective logos are trademarks or registered trademarks of SAP France in the United States and in other countries. SAP AG is neither the author nor the publisher of this publication and is not responsible for its content. SAP Group shall not be liable for errors or omissions with respect to the materials. The only warranties for SAP Group products and services are those that are set forth in the express warranty statements accompanying such products and services, if any. Nothing herein should be construed as constituting an additional warranty; Figure 11.1 from *IAS 37 Provisions, Contingent liabilities and contingent assets*, International Accounting Standards Board (2009) Copyright © 2010 International Accounting Standards Committee Foundation. All rights reserved. No permission granted to reproduce or distribute; Figure 11.2 extract from CEZ Group Annual Report 2008, http://www.cez.cz/edee/content/file/investors/inside-information/2009-04/cez-039-2009_en.pdf; Figure 11.3 extract from J. Sainsbury plc Annual Report 2009, http://www.j-sainsbury.co.uk/ar09/; Figure 13.2 extract from Telkom SA Limited Annual Report 31 March 2009, http://telkom.investoreports.com/telkom_ar_2009/downloads/telkom_ar_2009.pdf.

Tables

Table 1.1 from *Comparative International Accounting*, 10th ed., Pearson Education (Nobes, C. and Parker, R.B. 2008); Tables 3.1, and 3.3 from *IAS 1 (revised) Presentation of Financial Statements*, International Accounting Standards Board (2007) Copyright © 2010 International Accounting Standards Committee Foundation. All rights reserved. No permission granted to reproduce or distribute; Table 3.4 after *IAS 1 (revised) – Presentation of Financial Statements*, International Accounting Standards Board (2007) Copyright © 2010 International Accounting Standards Committee Foundation. All rights reserved. No permission granted to reproduce or distribute; Table 6.7 adapted from *Annual Statement Studies*, The Risk Management Association

(2007) © 2007 by RMA – The Risk Management Association. All rights Reserved. No part of this table may be reproduced or utilized in any form or by any means, electronic or mechanical, including photocopying, recording or by any information storage and retrieval system, without permission in writing from the RMA-Risk Management Association. Please refer to www.rmahq.org for further warranty, copyright, and use of data information; Tables 6.12, 6.13, 6.14 from *Introduction to Financial Accounting*, 8th ed., Pearson Education (Horngren, C.T., Sundem, G.L. and Elliott, J.A. 2002).

Text

Extract on page 44 from *IAS 1 – Presentation of financial statements paragraphs 25–26*, International Accounting Standards Board (2007) Copyright © 2010 International Accounting Standards Committee Foundation. All rights reserved. No permission granted to reproduce or distribute; Extract on pages 47–48 from *Exposure draft (ED): Conceptual Framework for Financial Reporting: The Objective of Financial Reporting and Qualitative Characteristics and Constraints of Decision-Useful Financial Reporting Information*, International Accounting Standards Board (2008) Copyright © 2010 International Accounting Standards Committee Foundation. All rights reserved. No permission granted to reproduce or distribute; Exam Board Question 2.9 from *International Financial Reporting Standards, A practical guide*, 4 ed., World Bank (Van Greuning, H. 2005) p. 10; Extract on page 76 from *IAS 1 (revised) Presentation of Financial Statements*, International Accounting Standards Board (2007) Copyright © 2010 International Accounting Standards Committee Foundation. All rights reserved. No permission granted to reproduce or distribute; Extract on page 79 from *IAS 1 (revised) – Presentation of Financial Statements, paragraph 32*, International Accounting Standards Board (2007) Copyright © 2010 International Accounting Standards Committee Foundation. All rights reserved. No permission granted to reproduce or distribute; Example 4.1 from *International Financial Reporting*, 1st ed., Pearson Education (Melville, A. 2008) pp. 60–62; Extract on pages 165–7 adapted from *Corporate Financial Accounting and Reporting*, 2nd ed., Pearson Education (Sutton, T. 2004); Examples 11.1, 11.2 from *International Financial Reporting*, 1st ed., Pearson Education (Melville, A. 2008); Example 11.3 adapted from *IAS 37 Provisions, Contingent Liabilities and Contingent Assets*, International Accounting Standards Board (2009) Copyright © 2010 International Accounting Standards Committee Foundation. All rights reserved. No permission granted to reproduce or distribute; Extract 12.4 adapted from *International Financial Reporting Standards, A practical guide*, 4th ed., World Bank (Van Greuning, H. 2005) p. 117; Example 13.2 adapted from *International Financial Reporting*, 1st ed., Pearson Education (Melville, A. 2008) pp. 217–218; Extract on page 384 from *IAS 32 Financial Instruments: Presentation*, International Accounting Standards Board (2009) para 11, Copyright © 2010 International Accounting Standards Committee Foundation. All rights reserved. No permission granted to reproduce or distribute; Example 14.1 from *International Financial Reporting*, 1st ed., Pearson Education (Melville, A. 2008); Example 14.3 from *IAS 39 Financial Instruments: Recognition and Measurement*, International Accounting Standards Board (2009) IG B16, Copyright © 2010 International Accounting Standards Committee Foundation. All rights reserved. No permission granted to reproduce or distribute; Extract on pages 463–4 from *IAS 7 Statement of*

Cash Flows, International Accounting Standards Board (2009) para 18 (b), Copyright © 2010 International Accounting Standards Committee Foundation. All rights reserved. No permission granted to reproduce or distribute; Extract on page 599 from *IAS 31 Interests in Joint Ventures*, International Accounting Standards Board (2009) para 3, Copyright © 2010 International Accounting Standards Committee Foundation. All rights reserved. No permission granted to reproduce or distribute; Extracts on page 601, page 602 from *IAS 31 Interests in Joint Ventures*, International Accounting Standards Board (2009) para 13, Copyright © 2010 International Accounting Standards Committee Foundation. All rights reserved. No permission granted to reproduce or distribute; Extract 20.1 from *IAS 28 Investments in associates*, International Accounting Standards Board (2009) para 2, Copyright © 2010 International Accounting Standards Committee Foundation. All rights reserved. No permission granted to reproduce or distribute.

The Financial Times

Exhibit 1.1 from EU backs accounting rule change, *Financial Times*, 16/10/2008 (Tait, N. and Hughes, J.); Exhibit 1.2 from Danger of a shift from principles to rules highlighted, *Financial Times*, 12/10/2006 (Bruce, R.); Exhibit 2.2 from Lost through destructive creation, *Financial Times*, 9/03/2009 (Tett, G.); Exhibit 15.1 from Disclose the fair value of complex securities *Financial Times*, 17/08/2009 (Kaplan, R., Merton, R. and Richard, S.).

In some instances we have been unable to trace the owners of copyright material, and we would appreciate any information that would enable us to do so.

Part One Introduction to IFRS

1

Introduction to international financial reporting

Contents

Figure 1.1 Tax return in ancient Egypt.
High relief of Prince Mereruka's tomb in Sakkara (beginning of the Sixth Dynasty, 2315–2190 BC)

effective use of accounting and auditing to control the generals of conquered territories. The role of *quaestores*, or financial officers, was introduced in about 200 BC. They were responsible to Rome and had custody of the treasury, supervised the scribes in their duties of recording treasury receipts and disbursements, and examined the accounts of the governors of subjugated countries. The *quaestores* were required to report periodically to Rome and have their records 'heard' by an examiner. The word 'auditor' came into use through this practice.

The Roman Empire made use of a complete system of checks and cross-checks. They separated the duties of collecting revenue, authorising expenditures, maintaining custody of cash, and recording financial transactions. Expenditures were required to be supported by documents disclosing the identity and title of the creditor and attesting the completion of the work or receipt of the goods ordered. Magistrates authorised payment on the basis of these documents and treasury scribes recorded all transactions. *Quaestores* supervised and audited all government financial transactions. Tax examiners in Rome played a prominent role in the collection of government revenues. Cato advised private land owners to count the cash and take inventories of grain, fodder, wine and oil on each visit to their farms and to check the accounts of their stewards frequently.

Accounting was an important part of government in the Byzantine world, the Eastern Roman Empire. Constantine founded a school at Constantinople which taught accounting among other subjects for the training of government officials.

In the Middle Ages, accounting, along with the other arts, suffered a decline because of the general disorganised condition of government and the economy throughout Europe. Gradually, however, accounting was re-established, as Durant (1950) explains:

The complicated operations of the bankers, the papacy, and the monarchies required a careful system of bookkeeping. Archives and account books swelled with records of rents, tax, receipts, expenditures, audits and debits. The accounting methods of imperial Rome, lost in Western Europe in the seventh century, continued in Constantinople, were adopted by the Arabs and were revived in Italy during the Crusades. A fully developed system of double-entry bookkeeping appears in the communal accounts of Genoa in 1340; the loss of Genoese records for the years from 1278 to 1340 leaves open the probability that this advance was also an achievement of the thirteenth century.

Several prerequisites have been identified as contributing towards the emergence of accounting as we know it today. These include:

- a system of writing, necessary to keep records;
- arithmetic, necessary for simple computations;
- money within the economy as all transactions are denoted in this denominator;
- the existence of credit (if all transactions are immediately completed there is little need to record them);
- commerce, as trade on a very small scale would be unlikely to result in the innovative development of complicated systems;
- capital, the availability of which ensures that trade expands beyond a very small scale.

1.1.3 Luca Pacioli and the basis of modern accounting

Double-entry bookkeeping (a system which records two aspects of every transaction) progressed in Italy around the thirteenth and fourteenth centuries as a result of the growth of maritime trade and of banking institutions. Merchants required details of voyages to be kept, in order to calculate and share profits from overseas trading. The first bank with customer facilities opened in Venice in 1149. Balance sheets were evident from around 1400 and the Medici family had accounting records of 'cloth manufactured and sold'. Regular audits of the records of the Medici Bank were performed during the period 1397 to 1494. The main office in Florence required that an annual balance sheet be submitted by each branch. The general manager and his assistants audited these statements which are still found in the archives of Florence. Raymond de Roover (1963) describes one:

This balance [sheet] is of special interest because it throws a great deal of light on the procedure followed in auditing and checking statements. Each item is accompanied by a comment on the prospects of obtaining payment in the case of receivables and on the likelihood of having to repay in the case of deposits. A typical comment, for instance, is the following: 'This customer has such great difficulty in making a living that he is unable to pay us, and selling the contents of his shop will involve much trouble and not bring enough to cover his debt . . .' Many of the ecclesiastics attending the Council had deposit accounts on which they drew to meet living expenses. A frequent comment is: 'he withdraws his funds little by little'. On the basis of annotations made on the balance sheet, one comes to the conclusion that at least twenty-two items appearing as assets and totalling 575 florins [the Florentine gold florin contained 3.53 grams of gold] represent overdue accounts which should have been written off.

Luca Pacioli, a Franciscan monk, is widely believed to be the inventor of double-entry bookkeeping. However, a rudimentary system of double-entry bookkeeping was used in Genoa around 1340, which predates Pacioli's contribution by over 100 years. In 1494, Pacioli documented the double-entry system being practised at the time by merchants in Venice in his famous book *Summa de arithmetica, geometria, proportioni et proportionalita* (The Collected Knowledge of Arithmetic, Geometry, Proportion and Proportionality). Pacioli wrote the *Summa* in an attempt to redress the poor state of the teaching of mathematics in his time. The section of the book which made him famous was *Particularis de Computis et Scripturis*, a treatise on accounting. *De Scripturis* has been described as 'a catalyst that launched the past into the future' (Jackson *et al.* 1990). Double-entry accounting became known as the 'Venetian method'. Pacioli's new system was state-of-the-art. *Summa* made Pacioli 'The Father of Accounting'. It was the most widely read mathematical work in all Italy, and became one of the first books published by the Gutenberg press. It was translated into several languages. The Venetian method became the standard for not only the Italians, but also the Dutch, German and English authors on accounting.

Much of the language of accounting has Latin roots. 'Debtor' comes from the Latin *debitum*, something that is owed; 'assets' from the Latin *ad* 'to' + *satis* 'enough', i.e. to pay obligations; 'liability' from *ligare*, to bind; 'capital' from *caput*, a head (of wealth). Even 'account' derives initially from the Latin *computare*, to count, while 'profit' comes from *profectus*, advance or progress.

1.1.4 Development of accounting after Luca Pacioli

During the 1550s the rise of nation-states and the need to manage public finances underpinned the importance of good accounting practice.

> The rise of nation-states and the need to manage public finances increased the importance of good accounting practice. However, a major change was the decline of Italy as a world commercial power. As commercial traffic shifted from the ports of Venice to the Atlantic shipping routes, Italy slipped in importance and relatively few new developments took place in accounting. [. . .] The French Revolution in the late 1700s marked the beginning of a great social upheaval that affected governments, finances, laws, and customs. Italy came under the influence of the French and then the Austrians, and their system of double-entry accounting was also influenced. It is interesting to note that Napoleon was surprised at how efficient the Italian system of accounting was.
>
> (Radebaugh *et al.* 2006: 4–5)

Development of accounting theory also began in this period and has continued to the present day. However, the influence of Pacioli's *Summa* continues to be felt in the double-entry bookkeeping we use today. The British, who acquired their knowledge of double-entry accounting soon after Pacioli's *Summa* was published, did not begin adopting the double-entry system until the Industrial Revolution (1760–1830). At that point, the importance of accounting grew substantially. As the scale of enterprise increased by technological breakthroughs such as mass production, and fixed costs grew in importance compared to the variable costs, it became necessary to account for depreciation, the allocation of overheads, and inventory. In addition, the basic form of business organisation shifted from proprietorships and partnerships to limited liability companies and ultimately to listed companies. Accounting had to adapt to satisfy all these new needs. Moreover, increased government regulation of business made new demands on enterprises, and so generated new accounting systems.

Since the early 1900s, the rapidity of change and the increasing complexity of the world's industrial economies necessitated still more changes in accounting. Mergers, acquisitions, and the growth of multinational corporations fostered new internal and external reporting and control systems. With widespread ownership of modern corporations came new audit and reporting procedures, and new agencies became involved in promulgating accounting standards: namely, stock exchanges, securities regulation commissions, internal revenue agencies, and so on. Finally, with the dramatic increase in foreign investment and world trade and the formation of regional economic groups such as the European Union, problems arose concerning the international activities of business. This phenomenon remains particularly complex, for it involves reconciling the accounting practices of different nations in which each multinational operates, as well as dealing with accounting problems unique to international business. [. . .] Furthermore, there is growing public concern about the impact of corporations, especially in relation to so-called externalities (e.g. pollution of the environment and the influence of large corporations on national economic and social policies).

(Radebaugh *et al.* 2006: 5)

1.2   From national accounting standards to global standards

A company, or an entity, that receives capital from investors and creditors or one that is seeking new capital has an obligation to keep its capital providers informed about its performance, condition and prospects. In other words, this entity is *accountable* to its investors and creditors. It is also accountable to others who provide resources or an environment in which to operate, such as employees, governments and the community at large. Making this information available in an accurate and understandable format is the role of financial accounting and reporting.

Historically, the rules for what information should be provided and the format that information should take have evolved country by country. By the 1990s, a mechanism for developing and adopting accounting standards had been established in most countries.

1.2.1   Legal systems and accounting rules

Some countries have a legal system that relies upon a limited amount of statute law, which is then interpreted by courts, which build up large numbers of case law to supplement the statutes. Such a 'common law' system developed in England, primarily after the Norman Conquest, by judges acting on the king's behalf (see R.C. van Caenegem, *The Birth of the English Common Law*, Cambridge University Press, Cambridge, 1988). A common law rule seeks to provide an answer to a specific case rather than to formulate a general rule for the future. Although this common law system emanates from England, it may be found in similar forms in many countries influenced by England. Thus, the federal law of the United States, the laws of Ireland, India, Australia, and so on are to a greater or less extent modelled on English common law. This naturally influences commercial law, which traditionally does not prescribe rules regarding how companies should prepare their financial statements. To a large extent accounting within such a context is not specified in detail in law. Instead accountants themselves establish rules for accounting practice, which may come to be written down as recommendations or standards as explained in section 1.2.2 below.

Other countries have a system of law that is based on the Roman *ius civile* as compiled by Justinian in the sixth century and developed by European universities in the twelfth century. Here, rules are linked to ideas of justice and morality; they become doctrine. The word 'codified' may be associated with such a system. This difference has the important effect that company law or commercial codes need to establish rules for accounting and financial reporting. For example, in Germany and in Italy, company accounting under domestic rules is to a large extent a branch of company law.

Table 1.1 illustrates the way in which major developed countries' legal systems fall into these two categories.

Table 1.1 Western legal systems

Common law	Codified Roman law
England and Wales	France
Ireland	Italy
United States	Germany
Canada	Spain
Australia	Netherlands
New Zealand	Portugal
	Japan (commercial)

Note: the laws of Scotland, Israel, South Africa, Quebec, Louisiana and the Philippines embody elements of both systems.
Source: Nobes and Parker (2008).

1.2.2 Towards global accounting standards

It is clear from section 1.2.1 that the nature of accounting regulation in a country is affected by its general system of laws.

In some cases, standard setting is the responsibility of the public accounting profession, with enforcement of the standards often achieved by law or government regulation. For example, accounting standards are set by the private sector professional accounting bodies in Austria, Brazil, Canada, Denmark, Hong Kong, Indonesia, the Netherlands, New Zealand, the Philippines, South Africa, Sweden, Switzerland and Taiwan.

In other cases, standard setting is the responsibility of the government. For example, there are government-sponsored accounting standards boards in Argentina, Australia, China, Finland, France, Greece, Malaysia, Poland and Saudi Arabia. In particular, the Australian Accounting Standards Board (AASB) is a government agency, with a government-appointed oversight body, the Financial Reporting Council, whose members include representatives from a range of government and private-sector users and preparers of financial statements, including the accounting profession. The chairman of the board is appointed by the government, with other members being appointed by the Financial Reporting Council. In certain major countries, such as Germany, Italy, Japan, the United Kingdom and the United States, a private-sector standard setter is established that is independent of the public accounting profession and of government.

National accounting standards made sense when companies raised money, and investors and lenders looked for investment opportunities, in their home country. As the capital markets of the industrialised countries began to globalise rapidly since the 1980s, the investment community and the accounting profession quickly became aware of the need to develop international accounting standards and of the benefits of a common global accounting language.

Nowadays, investors seek investment opportunities all over the world. Similarly, companies seek capital at the lowest price anywhere. Almost every day you can open a financial newspaper and read about a sizable cross-border merger or investment transaction. The problem that this creates for investors, of course, is that accounting differences can completely obscure comparisons and other analyses that they must make in order to assess various investment opportunities.

Therefore, the development of a global set of comprehensive, high-quality accounting standards is welcome as it would serve investors by making it easier for them to compare investment options and reduce costs for issuers by no longer requiring them to prepare financial statements under more than one standard. A common financial language, applied consistently, will enable investors to compare the financial results of companies operating in different jurisdictions more easily and provide greater opportunity for investment and diversification. The removal of a major investment risk – the concern that the nuances of different national accounting regimes have not been fully understood – should reduce the cost of capital and open new opportunities for diversification and improved investment returns. A single set of global accounting standards would imply, *inter alia*, the following advantages (see also Ball 2006: 5–27):

- *More accurate and timely information.* IFRS promise more accurate, comprehensive and timely financial statement information relative to the national standards they replace for public financial reporting in most of the countries adopting them. To the extent that financial statement information is not obtained from other sources, this should lead to more informed valuation in the equity markets and hence lower risk for investors.

- *Lower risk for small investors.* Small investors are less likely than investment professionals to be able to access financial statement information from other sources. Improved financial reporting quality allows them to compete better with professionals, and hence reduces the risk they are trading with a better informed professional.

- *Easier access to foreign capital markets.* Reduction of differences in accounting standards internationally assists to some degree in removing barriers to cross-border acquisitions and divestitures, which in theory should reward investors with higher takeover premiums.

- *Increased credibility of domestic capital markets* among foreign capital providers and potential foreign merger partners.

- *Increased credibility of financial statements of companies* in less-developed countries among capital providers and potential lenders.

- *Lower cost of capital for companies.*

- *No need for reconciliation to another country's accounting standards,* for example US GAAP.

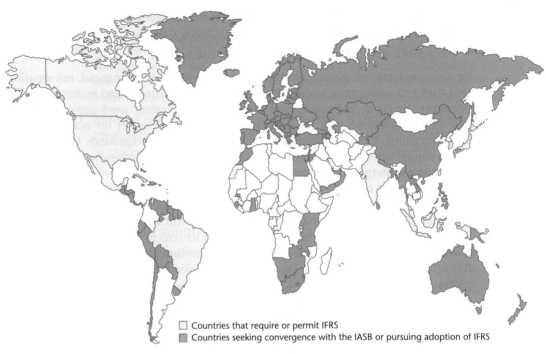

Figure 1.2 Global IFRS adoption
Source: IASB website (January 2010).

Convergence *de facto* is less certain than convergence *de jure*: convergence in actual financial reporting practice is a different thing than convergence in financial reporting standards (Ball 2006). We will return to this issue in section 1.4 below.

1.3.1 Convergence of US GAAP and IFRS

In July 2007 the SEC in the USA announced two important initiatives relating to US GAAP and IFRS. The first initiative related to a new rule, which was then introduced at the end of 2007, that eliminated the 'US GAAP reconciliation' – that is, the reconciliation required to be given by foreign private issuers (FPIs) from home country GAAP, which are often IFRS, to US GAAP. These reconciliations are a cost and burden to FPIs and yet the general view is that hardly any use is made of them by investors or others. It should be noted, however, that the SEC states that the home country GAAP – the principal financial reporting convention – should be IFRS as issued by the IASB, not another variant of IFRS.

This alone was a big step but the second initiative of the July 2007 announcement was more dramatic. The SEC proposed that IFRS might be permitted in the US markets as an alternative to US GAAP. The timescale is somewhat lengthy (confirmation of the decision in 2011, implementation possibly in 2014) and subject to various conditions.

There has been a major strategic shift in the world of accounting as a result of these two SEC announcements.

There is a perception today that IFRS has started to suffer from the importing of specific US rules and the adoption of US-style detailed prescription. The USA has been setting detailed accounting rules over 70 years and recent decades have witnessed more and more detailed rules being written in response to the combination of a complex business environment and a litigious society (see section 1.3.4; refer also to Global Accounting Alliance 2008). US GAAP suit the US environment; they are essentially written for listed (i.e. SEC-registered) companies. Hence, a problem with IFRS/US GAAP harmonisation is that US GAAP is in danger of being exported, via IFRS, to many countries that have a different business environment to the USA, have smaller economies and a smaller accounting infrastructure. In many of those countries IFRS are often being applied across the whole economy, not just to the listed sector. So, there is a potential problem of unsuitability of standards for the contexts in which they are being applied. It is important, therefore, that the IASB remembers that convergence with US GAAP, although an important objective, should not be carried out in such a way as to make its standards unsuitable for its widespread and varied constituency.[1]

1.3.2 Where are we today?

The movement towards IFRS as a single set of globally accepted accounting standards presents many challenges. Perhaps the biggest challenge is a cultural one. Bringing together accounting standards may be easier than coordinating a variety of cultural differences and perspectives involved in interpreting and applying IFRS.

With IFRS, companies, auditors, regulators and users need to adapt to an accounting and financial reporting framework that requires greater professional judgment and less reliance on detailed rules. This requires a change in behaviour by all market participants and more focus on understanding the substance underlying a transaction or event and how it aligns with primary principles and objectives. The challenge is to ensure that although different outcomes may result from the application of IFRS, such outcomes are within the conceptual parameters of the standards.

Given the impending move to IFRS in the USA, Deloitte in November 2008 surveyed over 200 senior finance managers and officers of the US listed companies on various issues related to the adoption of IFRS. Survey participants were self-selected, and responded through a web-based survey. Overall, 42 per cent of the companies surveyed indicated that, if permitted, they would consider implementing IFRS sooner than 2014, the initial mandatory date within the SEC proposed roadmap.[2]

The sample of respondents included companies of all sizes that operate in various industries – such as financial services; health services and government; consumer products, retail; manufacturing; energy and resources; and technology, media and telecommunications.

Those who would consider adopting IFRS at an earlier date are from companies operating predominantly in telecommunications, manufacturing, and financial services industries. Fifty-seven per cent of the respondents from companies operating in the telecommunications industry would consider adopting before 2014. For financial services, 42 per cent of respondents would consider early adoption.

1.3.3 Arguments against convergence

As one can easily guess, not everyone is in agreement that a global standard is a good idea. In fact, several groups oppose the convergence for the following main reasons:

- the emphasis in IFRS on **fair value** accounting is a concern, particularly in relation to reporting in lesser-developed countries. We will return to this issue in Chapter 2, section 2.5;
- uneven implementation, auditing and enforcement of international rules make it difficult to ensure credible **financial statements**;
- there are high costs related to the convergence to IFRS;
- uniform international standards reduce competition among systems;
- the long run implication of global politics could well be that the IASB becomes a representative, politicised and bureaucratic body.

In order for the convergence in accounting standards to work effectively, there has to be a convergence of auditing standards throughout the world. Moreover, the regulatory authorities throughout the world, such as the SEC in the USA, the Securities and Exchange Board in India (SEBI), and so on, need to get together and come to an agreement as to how IFRS are going to be enforced. This is especially important because IFRS are principle-based standards (see section 1.3.4) so there is a lot of judgement involved in applying the standards as we have mentioned above.

The regulatory authorities need to have a common set of enforcement standards. Otherwise, the convergence of accounting standards will not work. For example, if Infosys files its consolidated financial statements under IFRS with SEBI in India and SEBI approves the filing, but the SEC in the USA does not agree with Infosys's interpretation of IFRS then it will be a big issue for Infosys. Effectively, Infosys would end up preparing two sets of financial statements.

As pointed out by Ball (2006), 'there are overwhelming political and economic reasons to expect IFRS enforcement to be uneven around the world, including within Europe. Substantial international differences in financial reporting practice and financial reporting quality are inevitable', independently of IFRS. Ball's conclusion is based on the premise that – despite increased globalisation – most political and economic influences on financial reporting *practice* remain local. One concern that arises from widespread IFRS adoption is that investors will be misled into believing that there is more uniformity in practice than actually is the case and that, even to sophisticated investors, international differences in the quality of reporting will be obscured under the banner of seemingly uniform standards. In addition, uneven implementation curtails the ability of uniform standards to reduce information costs and information risk, described above in section 1.2.2 as an advantage of convergence. Uneven implementation could increase information processing costs to transnational investors – by burying accounting inconsistencies at a deeper and less transparent level than differences in standards.

Markets and politics remain primarily local, not global

Ball (2006) notes that the fundamental reason for being sceptical about uniformity of implementation in practice is that the incentives of preparers (managers) and enforcers (auditors, courts, regulators, boards, block shareholders, politicians, analysts, rating agencies, the press) remain primarily local. All accounting accruals (versus simply counting cash) involve judgements about future cash flows. Consequently, there is much leeway in implementing accounting rules. Powerful local economic and political forces therefore determine how managers, auditors, courts, regulators and other parties influence the implementation of rules. These forces have exerted a substantial influence on financial reporting practice historically, and are unlikely to suddenly cease doing so, IFRS or no IFRS. Achieving uniformity in accounting standards seems easy compared with achieving uniformity in actual reporting behaviour. The latter would require radical change in the underlying economic and political forces that determine actual behaviour. Sir David Tweedie, the IASB chairman, advocates the case for international uniformity in accounting standards on global integration of markets: 'As the world's capital markets integrate, the logic of a single set of accounting standards is evident. A single set of international standards will enhance comparability of financial information and should make the allocation of capital across borders more efficient. The development and acceptance of international standards should also reduce compliance costs for corporations and improve consistency in audit quality'. But this logic works both ways. One can change the underlying premise to make a case *against* uniformity. Because capital markets are not perfectly integrated (debt markets in particular), and because more generally economic and political integration are both far from being complete, the logic of national *differences* should be equally evident. While increased internationalisation of markets and politics can be expected to reduce some of the diversity in accounting practice across nations, nations continue to display clear and substantial domestic facets in both their politics and how their markets are structured, so increased internationalisation cannot be expected to eliminate diversity in practice. Important dimensions in which the world still looks considerably more local than global include:

- extent and nature of government involvement in the economy;
- politics of government involvement in financial reporting practices (e.g. political influence of managers, corporations, labour unions, banks);
- legal systems (e.g. common versus code law; shareholder litigation rules);
- securities regulation and regulatory bodies;
- depth of financial markets;
- financial market structure (e.g. closeness of relationship between banks and client companies);
- the role of the press, financial analysts and rating agencies;
- size of the corporate sector;
- structure of corporate governance (e.g. relative roles of labour, management and capital);
- extent of private versus public ownership of corporations;
- extent of family-controlled businesses;
- extent of corporate membership in related-company groups (e.g. Japanese *keiretsu* or Korean *chaebol*);
- extent of financial intermediation;
- the role of small shareholders versus institutions and corporate insiders;

- the use of financial statement information, including earnings, in management compensation; and
- the status, independence, training and compensation of auditors.

The above list is far from complete, but it gives some sense of the extent to which financial reporting occurs in a local, non-global, context. Despite increased global-isation, the clear majority of economic and political activity remains *intra*national, the implication being that the primary driving forces behind the majority of actual accounting practices seem likely to remain domestic in nature for the foreseeable future. The most visible effect of local political and economic factors on IFRS lies at the level of the national standard adoption decision (see Ball 2006). This already has occurred in the EU. For example, the European version of IAS 39 – *Financial Instruments: Recognition and Measurement* emerged in response to considerable polit-ical pressure from the French government, which responded to pressure from domestic banks concerned about **balance sheet** volatility. After a lengthy political process, a so-called carve-out version of IAS 39 was approved: the November 2004 EU-endorsed version of IAS 39 excluded a few paragraphs to which some EU banks objected. More recently, in October 2008, calls for relaxing fair value accounting came from banks and politicians, particularly the French and Italian. They claimed that fair value had undermined banks' balance sheets by forcing them to report assets at current weak market prices even though the banks have no intention of selling them and in fact expect values to recover. The IASB made the change relax-ing controversial fair value accounting practices, to avoid what was considered the bigger danger of the threatened carve-out by the Commission (see Exhibit 1.1). A further example is the controversy which arose in connection with the endorsement of IFRS 8 – *Operating Segments*, although the standard was eventually endorsed. Politically, the process is highly significant as it introduces the prospect that, with one or more future standards, there may emerge a more fundamental difference between EU IFRS and IFRS as promulgated by the IASB.

Exhibit 1.1

Accounting rules blamed by some banks for exacerbating the financial turmoil were eased in the European Union yesterday, bringing its 27 countries in line with changes agreed by international accounting rulemakers.

An EU regulators' committee in Brussels voted unanimously to accept Monday's emergency changes made by the International Accounting Standards Board. These will give banks more leeway in how they value certain assets whose prices have plunged.

Lawmakers in the European Parliament soon endorsed the vote and member states gave their unanimous support. This means the changes, which are optional, can apply to calculations of banks' third quarter results if they wish.

Under the rule changes, banks and other financial institutions would be able to 'reclassify' certain financial instruments. In effect, this means they could move them from their trading books, where they must be marked at 'fair', or current, market values, to their banking books.

In banking books, they can be reported at 'amortised' cost, so financial institu-tions would not have to report further falls in market prices, and gains would be spread evenly over the lifetime of the assets.

The IASB changes followed heavy pressure from European banks and politicians. European companies had complained, in particular, that US rules gave US rivals more flexibility than they had. EU finance ministers took up the issue last week. They urged international accounting standard boards to work together and 'welcomed the readiness' of Brussels to take action 'as soon as possible'. They demanded the reclassification issue be solved by the end of the month.

The commission plans further meetings in the next few days to discuss accounting issues, related in particular to the mark-to-market issue, derivatives and insurance issues.

Source: from 'EU backs accounting rule change', *Financial Times*, 16/10/2008 (Tait, N. and Hughes, J.)

Another level at which local political and economic factors are likely to visibly influence IFRS adoption stems from the latitude IFRS give to entities to choose among alternative accounting methods. Local factors make it unlikely that this discretion will be exercised uniformly across countries, and across firms within countries.

Another issue which may lead to uneven implementation of IFRS relates to accounting accruals, which generally require at least some element of subjective judgement and hence can be influenced by the incentives of managers and auditors. Consider for example the case of IAS 36 – *Impairment of Assets* and IAS 38 – *Intangible Assets* which require periodic review of non-current **tangible** and **intangible assets** for possible **impairment losses**. It is very hard to believe that managers and auditors will comb through a company's asset portfolios to discover economically impaired assets with the same degree of diligence and ruthlessness in all the countries that adopt IFRS. Will auditors, regulators, courts, boards, analysts, rating agencies and all the other participants to the financial reporting supply chain provide the same degree of oversight in all IFRS-adopting countries? Moreover, it should be noted that in many countries the available information needed to implement the asset impairment standards is meagre and not readily available to auditors and other monitors.

IFRS enforcement mechanisms

Under its constitution, the IASB is a standard setter and does not have an enforcement mechanism for its standards: it can cajole countries and companies to adopt IFRS in name, but cannot require their enforcement in practice. It cannot penalise individual companies or countries that adopt its standards, but in which financial reporting practice is of low quality because managers, auditors and local regulators fail to fully implement the standards. Nor has it shown any interest in disallowing or even dissuading low-quality companies or countries from using its brand name. Individual countries remain primarily regulators of their own financial markets, EU member states included. That exposes IFRS to the risk of adoption in name only.

Costs of implementation

There are significant costs with respect to the convergence to one international set of accounting rules. These costs are related to 'dismantling' the standard-setting infrastructure in each country, to uniform accountancy qualifications, to training of accountants, auditors and regulators. Needless to say, the university faculty in each country has to learn IFRS and teach it to students, and the textbooks in each country have to be rewritten.

Long-term effects

There are also concerns about longer-term effects. One concern is that allowing unfettered use of the IFRS brand name by any country discards information about differences in reporting quality, and does not allow high-quality financial reporting regimes to signal that they follow better standards than low-quality regimes. Therefore, the only available quality signal could become the quality of enforcement of standards, not standards per se.

Another concern is that international standards reduce competition among alternative financial reporting systems, and hence reduce innovation. International competition among economic systems in general is healthy; imposing worldwide standards therefore is a risky centralisation process in any sphere of economic activity. There are some arguments about the long run implications of countries downgrading the resources and status – and even eliminating – their national standard-setting bodies. Therefore, 'convergence' rather than outright IFRS adoption would be more desirable.

The final longer-term concern is the risk of the IASB becoming a representative, politicised, polarised and bureaucratic body. The current membership representation (six trustees from the Asia/Oceania region, six from Europe, six from North America, and four from any region) seems likely to face challenges in the longer term. Over time, each of the 150 IFRS adopting countries will have a politically legitimate argument that they deserve some sort of representation in the standard-setting process. Do not the standards that are issued by the IASB affect those same countries, after all? (see Ball 2006).

Table 1.2 summarises the pros and cons of having uniform accounting standards internationally.

1.3.4 Principle- versus rule-based accounting

Over the last few years, a broad consensus of support seems to have emerged for 'principle-based standards'. However, there is a range of different interpretations as to what this term really means. There are also major and varying challenges faced in different jurisdictions from the implementation of principle-based standards.

A principle is a general statement, with widespread support, which is intended to support the true and fair presentation of the economic consequences of business transactions and acts as a guide to action. Principles cannot be replaced by mechanical rules. Sometimes a set of rules may be proposed to guide the observance of a principle, but it will always be a matter of judgement whether following these rules will actually achieve conformity to the principle. This definition emphasises the importance of judgement in interpreting the rules. A rule is a means of establishing an unambiguous decision-making method. There can be no doubt about when and how it is to be applied. Rules represent specific instructions – like a computer programme. Rules are sometimes arbitrary and may not always reflect the underlying principles. Compliance with a rule-based accounting framework does not necessarily result in financial statements that show a true and fair presentation of an organisation's

Table 1.2 Pros and cons of uniform accounting standards

Pros/advantages	Cons/challenges
Improved transparency and management information together with consistency in reporting between jurisdictions and sectors	Excessive emphasis on fair value accounting
More accurate, comprehensive and timely financial information	Uneven implementation of IFRS make it difficult to ensure credible financial statements
More informed valuation of the equity markets and hence lower risk for investors	Lack of enforcement mechanisms
Easier access to foreign capital markets	High cost of convergence to IFRS
Increased credibility of domestic capital markets among foreign capital providers and potential foreign merger partners	Reduced competition among alternative financial reporting systems
Increased credibility of financial statements of companies in less developed countries among capital providers and potential lenders	The IASB could become a representative, politicised and bureaucratic body
Lower cost of capital for companies	
No need for reconciliation to another country's accounting standards	
Comparability of financial data across borders	
Increased market efficiency	
Reduced national standard-setting costs	
Ease of regulation of securities markets	
Portability of knowledge and education across national boundaries	
Improved auditing standards for listed companies	

commercial situation. Maintaining and adhering to a large, complex set of accounting rules creates insurmountable problems for standard setters, preparers of financial statements, auditors and users and, it is argued, the overriding objective of true and fair presentation can get lost in the quest for 'compliance' (ICAS 2006).

Exhibit 1.2

There is a fundamental difficulty with accounting in general that is a particular problem in financial reporting. While the outside world's perception is that it is an exact science, anyone in accounting knows that this is far from the truth. This mismatch in perception increasingly makes financial reporting fraught. Judgement is at the heart of accounting. And judgment can only thrive in a system based on principles. If you try to apply specific rules, all that happens is lawyers become even richer and the figures become less trustworthy.

Source: from 'Danger of a shift from principles to rules highlighted',
Financial Times, 12/10/2006 (Bruce, R.)

The contrast between principles and rules came to prominence because it was highlighted in the Sarbanes-Oxley Act of 2002. Following the failure of Enron, the initial reaction of governments and regulatory bodies across a range of countries having significant capital markets tended to be either to call for some form of review or to adapt an existing review process in order to confirm that a principle-based approach to accounting was already in place, albeit perhaps submersed under details of rules in some instances.

In the debate on accounting standards in the immediate aftermath of Enron and WorldCom, opinions were divided on the relative merits and demerits of rule-based accounting standards. The arguments were presented from a range of perspectives, including the freedom to exercise professional judgement, enforceability, comparability, complexity, prevention of creative accounting and the representation of economic reality. From each perspective there are arguments for and against rules as summarised in Table 1.3, below.

US GAAP are rule-based compared to principle-based IFRS. However, the difference between principles and rules is not always clear-cut and a combination of both approaches might be necessary and appropriate. Therefore, characterising standard setters or jurisdictions as principle-based or as rule-based does not result in an accurate description of the current situation. For example, the UK is a hybrid: principles but also rules.

We believe that the debate about principles and rules is misleading as it suggests that standards should be either all principles or all rules. Thus, 'principles vs rules' is a false distinction and a balance is needed between principles and supporting

Table 1.3 Pros and cons of rule-based standards

Pros	Cons
Rule-based standards provide detailed guidance and clarification and precise answers to questions.	Rule-based standards reduce or eliminate the exercise of professional judgement and lead to de-skilling of the profession.
Rule-based standards are authoritative and enforceable.	Rule-based standards do not prevent dishonest practice, but in fact they encourage interested parties to find loopholes.
Rule-based standards provide greater comparability.	Rule-based standards do not guarantee comparability. In fact, financial statements should be capable of comparison when the economic reality of similar transactions and events are understood in a similar way by the users of those financial statements. The disclosure by the preparer of judgements made is key to that understanding.
The complexity of rule-based standards is only a consequence of the complexity of the underlying business.	Rule-based standards cause complexity and delay in keeping abreast of change. A well-defined set of principles provides the framework for dealing with complexity as it arises, retaining a strong focus on representing the economic reality.
Rule-based standards offer equal access to emerging opinions.	Rule-based standards can never be comprehensive. A system of principle-based standards is not static. Discussion of the principles brings out emerging opinions.
Rule-based standards deter creative accounting.	Rule-based standards foster creative accounting by diverting judgement from economic reality to the detail of application.
Rule-based standards set out greater detail, which is especially important where translation is needed.	Greater detail in rules requires translation, with corresponding greater difficulties.

Source: This table is based on ICAS (2006a and 2006b).

guidance or 'rules'. So the idea is to have principles and rules that are both simple and effective, but this is difficult to achieve. It is not realistic to have no rules, but at the same time, standards need to be based on a framework (as we will discuss in Chapter 2), so we need principles and then high level guidance (i.e. rules) and examples for the application of those principles.

There are also cultural and behavioural issues, particularly involving regulators and auditors that need to be addressed. The complexity of structured business trans-actions led to more complex standards, and this in turn led to greater length and attempts to deal with every possible situation. There is a big behavioural issue here in the form of a mindset which has developed over time. This stems in particular from the litigious culture of the USA. Directors, preparers and auditors want protection in their decision-making processes. They want someone to tell them that what they are doing is the right thing to do: they need detailed rules to back up their decision.

> *We are a heavily litigious society. We are a lawyer-laden society, and that manifests itself in a belief that piling on layers and layers of rules will somehow eradicate improper human conduct. Of course, nothing could be further from the truth. What influences human conduct is not simply rules, what influences human conduct is culture.*
> (From an interview of Michael Young, Willkie Farr & Gallagher, in GAA 2008)

1.4 EU implementation of IFRS and its benefits

The EU Regulation of 2002 requires the use of IFRS in the consolidated financial statements of publicly traded companies established in EU member states. Each member state may also permit or require the use of IFRS in the legal entity financial statements of companies and the consolidated financial statements of non-publicly traded companies.

The EU Regulation has been effective in achieving the core objective of all pub-licly traded entities preparing consolidated financial statements in accordance with IFRS, subject to the deferral of implementation in some countries to 2007 for enti-ties with only debt securities admitted to trading or those entities listed on a non-EU market and using internationally accepted standards.

Allowing member states discretion over the extent to which IFRS was to be used outside the consolidated financial statements of publicly traded entities has inevitably resulted in legal positions varying significantly. Some member states are prescriptive on the use of IFRS in the consolidated and legal entity financial state-ments, others allow some choice.

A common theme is a more prescriptive regime for specific types of entity, par-ticularly financial institutions. In many cases the legal position has changed from 2005.

As mentioned above, the EU Regulation requires publicly traded companies to present consolidated financial statements in conformity with IFRS adopted by the European Union for each financial year starting on or after 1 January 2005. Bringing IFRS into EU law takes place through a complex *endorsement mechanism*, which has been made even more elaborate by introducing a role for the European Parliament and creating the Standards Advice Review Group whose role is to advise the Commission before it takes a decision on endorsement of an IFRS.

The endorsement mechanism has proven to be somewhat problematic. In section 1.3.3 we discussed the politics related to the endorsement of IAS 39. An interesting example of the interaction of accounting and EU politics arose during the credit crunch of 2007–9 in connection with the practice of stating certain assets, mainly of banks, at fair values. As a result, there have been calls for the suspension of fair value accounting[3].

Despite initial difficulties and uncertainties, EU listed companies went through first-time adoption of IFRS reasonably well. There were numerous issues of interpretation, many pieces of additional information that needed to be collected in order to be disclosed and a considerable effort in terms of explaining the transition to the market. The fact that there were no major disasters is a tribute to the amount of time and effort put in by companies and auditors alike.

In 2006, at the request of the European Commission, the **Institute of Chartered Accountants in England and Wales** (ICAEW) embarked on an assessment of compliance with the requirements of IFRS and the overall quality of IFRS financial reporting, evaluating the application of IFRS across EU industries, markets and member states.

The study involved a number of work streams, including: a detailed review of the 2005 **financial statements** of 200 listed companies drawn from across 25 member states; evaluation of the reactions to the transition of preparers, users and auditors through an online survey; and roundtables with stakeholders held across the EU.

The following were the key findings from the online survey:

- There was widespread agreement that IFRS has made financial statements easier to compare across countries, across competitors within the same industry sector and across industry sectors.

- Sixty-three per cent of investors thought that IFRS had improved the quality of consolidated financial statements against 24 per cent who thought that IFRS had made it worse. The corresponding figures for preparers were 60 per cent and 14 per cent respectively and for auditors 80 per cent and 8 per cent, respectively.

- Forty-nine per cent of investors thought that the switch to IFRS accounting had made financial statements more difficult to understand, although 32 per cent disagreed. Investors found the majority of accounting areas easier to understand, but some specific accounting policies caused difficulty in understanding – particularly financial instruments.

- The move to consolidated IFRS financial statements had influenced the investment decisions of 41 per cent of investors.

- A majority of 51 per cent of preparers was either very or fairly confident that fund managers and analysts fully understand the impact of IFRS but a 36 per cent minority was not confident and 13 per cent did not know.

- Preparers' views on board understanding of the financial impact of IFRS were broadly positive, although significant minorities were not confident of the board's understanding or did not express a view.

- Sixty-nine per cent of the preparers used IFRS accounting for internal reporting and 25 per cent stated that IFRS financial statements had impacted the way the business was run.

These findings are summarised in Figure 1.5.

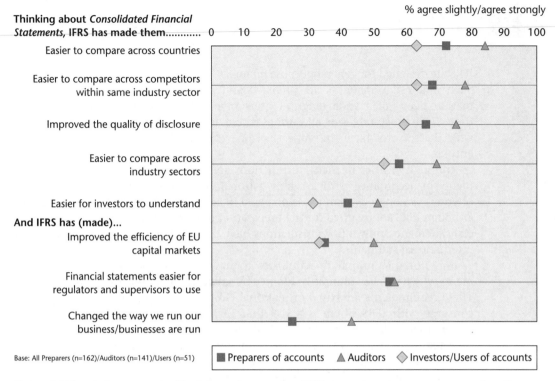

Thinking about *Consolidated Financial*
Statements, **IFRS has made them............**

% agree slightly/agree strongly

Easier to compare across countries

Easier to compare across competitors
within same industry sector

Improved the quality of disclosure

Easier to compare across
industry sectors

Easier for investors to understand

And IFRS has (made)...

Improved the efficiency of EU
capital markets

Financial statements easier for
regulators and supervisors to use

Changed the way we run our
business/businesses are run

Base: All Preparers (n=162)/Auditors (n=141)/Users (n=51)

■ Preparers of accounts   ▲ Auditors   ◇ Investors/Users of accounts

Figure 1.5 Level of agreement with statements regarding IFRS among investors, preparers and auditors
Source: ICAEW (2007).

Naturally enough there are some less positive findings. The study draws attention to examples of poor disclosure, for example in relation to defined benefit pension plans, and too much standard wording or 'boilerplating' in the disclosure of accounting policies. It also highlights the degree of choice in IFRS, on transition, in the selection of accounting policies, and in terms of presentation – choices which do not necessarily sit comfortably with the objective of comparability. In fact, many participants to the roundtables and telephone interviews pointed to the requirements of national legislation and national regulators and the enduring strengths of national accounting traditions as factors contributing to the 'local accents' found in IFRS reporting in the EU.

It was also notable that concerns were expressed at the roundtables about complexity of IFRS and over the likely increase in the pace and future direction of change in IFRS, referring in particular to the greater use of fair values and the possibility that convergence with US GAAP may lead to more rule-based standards. These concerns, coupled with an awareness of the scale and effort involved in implementation, were reflected in a general lack of appetite for any wider application of full IFRS.

1.5 IFRS for small and medium-sized entities (SMEs)

IFRS are designed for general purpose financial statements of profit-oriented entities. Such financial statements are prepared and presented with the common information needs of a wide range of users in mind. While the IASB believes that these IFRS are suitable for all entities, there are numerous smaller entities worldwide that do not have the same level of public accountability as listed or larger entities.

Although entities in many jurisdictions are required to prepare financial statements in accordance with a set of national accounting requirements, these are often far less onerous than those prepared in accordance with IFRS. Within the EU, although IFRS are required for the preparation of listed entities' consolidated financial statements, only a few jurisdictions have encouraged unlisted entities to adopt international standards.

It is not uncommon for countries to have less onerous accounting requirements which can be voluntarily adopted by small and medium-sized entities (SMEs). These requirements are based on national GAAP in each jurisdiction. As countries converge with IFRS, there is a risk that each jurisdiction will develop its own national requirements for SMEs which may or may not be based on IFRS. Where such requirements are based on IFRS, this may lead to numerous versions of the same IFRS. Consequently, the IASB decided to develop international standards for SMEs. This standard, *IFRS for Small and Medium-sized Entities*, was published in July 2009.

SMEs are entities that:

(a) do not have *public accountability*, and

(b) publish general purpose financial statements for external users. Examples of external users include owners who are not involved in managing the business, existing and potential creditors, and credit rating agencies.

An entity has public accountability if:

(a) its debt or equity instruments are traded in a public market or it is in the process of issuing such instruments for trading in a public market (a domestic or foreign stock exchange or an over-the-counter market, including local and regional markets), or

(b) it holds assets in a fiduciary capacity for a broad group of outsiders as one of its primary businesses. This is typically the case for banks, credit unions, insurance companies, securities brokers/dealers, mutual funds and investment banks.

Because 'full' IFRS are designed to meet the needs of equity investors in capital markets, they cover a wide range of issues, include extensive implementation guidance and disclosures appropriate for public companies. Many SMEs say that 'full' IFRS impose a burden on them – a burden that has been growing as IFRS have become more detailed and more countries have begun to use them. Thus, in developing the IFRS for SMEs, IASB's twin goals were to meet user needs while balancing costs and benefits from a preparer perspective.

The aim of the proposed standard is to provide a simplified, self-contained set of accounting principles that are appropriate for smaller, non-listed companies and are based on IFRS, developed primarily for listed companies.

Some topics such as earnings per share, operating segments and interim reporting have been omitted from the IFRS for SMEs as irrelevant to private entities. Most of the complex options in 'full' IFRS have also been omitted (for example, only the cost method is permitted for property, plant and equipment, and borrowing costs are required to be expensed in all circumstances). In the IFRS for SMEs there are simplified principles for recognising and measuring assets, liabilities, income and expense (for example, goodwill is amortised, the cost method is used for associates and joint ventures, all research and development costs are expensed and there is much less use of fair value) and requirements for reduced disclosures (roughly 400 as compared to 3,000 in full IFRSs).

By removing choices for accounting treatment, eliminating topics that are not generally relevant to SMEs and simplifying methods for recognition and measurement, the resulting standard reduces the volume of accounting guidance applicable to SMEs by more than 85 per cent when compared with the 'full' set of IFRS. As a result, the IFRS for SMEs offers a workable, self contained set of accounting standards that would allow investors for the first time to compare SMEs' financial performance across international boundaries on a like for like basis. The standard is stand-alone, with no cross-references to IFRS. No quantitative test has been set out by the IASB for entities eligible to use such standards; this decision is to be made by each national jurisdiction. Small listed entities are not included in the intended scope of the IFRS for SMEs.

The adoption of the IFRS for SMEs will be attractive to private companies for many reasons, including:

- improved access to capital;

- improved comparability;

- improved quality of reporting as compared to existing national GAAP (in many countries, local GAAPs for private entities are very limited);

- the focus on the needs of users of SME financial statements;

- less of a burden for entities in jurisdictions where 'full' IFRS or full national GAAP are required at present.

1.6   Note on terminology

Many readers of this book will aim not only to master a subject relatively new to them, but also to do so in a language that is not their first. One added difficulty is that UK terms and US terms are considerably different for accounting issues. The IASB issues its standards in English using a mixture of UK and US terms. Some examples of different terminology used by the standard setters are shown in Table 1.4, below.

Table 1.4 Examples of the UK, US and IASB terms

UK	USA	IASB
Balance sheet	Balance sheet	Statement of financial position
Profit and loss account	Income statement	Statement of comprehensive income
Cash flow statement	Statement of cash flows	Statement of cash flows
Stock	Inventory	Inventory
Shares	Stock	Shares
Ordinary shares	Common stock	Share capital
Shareholders' equity, Shareholders' funds, Capital and reserves	Shareholders' equity	Shareholders' equity
Own shares	Treasury stock	Treasury shares
Debtors	Accounts receivable	Trade and other receivables
Creditors	Accounts payable	Trade and other payables
Bad debts, Doubtful debts	Doubtful accounts	Bad debts
Provision for doubtful debts	Allowance for doubtful accounts	Allowance for bad debts
Finance lease	Capital lease	Finance lease
Creditors: amounts falling due after more that one year	Long-term liabilities	Non-current liabilities
Creditors: amounts falling due within one year	Current liabilities	Current liabilities
Turnover	Sales (or revenue)	Sales (or revenue)
Acquisition	Purchase	Acquisition
Fixed assets	Long-term assets	Non-current assets
Tangible fixed assets	Property, plant and equipment	Property, plant and equipment
Profit and loss account	Income statement	Income statement
Reducing-balance depreciation method	Declining-balance method	Diminishing-balance depreciation method
Company	Corporation	Entity
Prudence	Conservatism	Prudence

Summary

- There is evidence of some sort of accounting in ancient civilisations dating back to around 3600 BC. Luca Pacioli, an Italian Franciscan monk, is widely considered to be the inventor of double-entry bookkeeping, which is the basis of current financial accounting.

- Much of the regulatory and legal framework of financial reporting that we have today has resulted from past events. Historically, the rules for the type of information to be provided and the format that information should take have evolved country by country. By the 1990s, a mechanism for developing and adopting accounting standards was established in most countries.

- The nature of accounting regulation in a country is affected by its general system of laws. In some countries, standard setting is the responsibility of the public accounting profession; enforcement of the standards is often achieved by law or government regulation. In other countries, standard setting is the responsibility of the government.

- National accounting standards made sense when companies raised money, and investors and lenders looked for investment opportunities, in their home country. The globalisation of capital markets of the industrialised countries raised the need for high-quality accounting standards which would make it easier for investors to compare investment options and reduce costs for issuers by no longer requiring them to prepare financial statements under more than one standard.

- A single set of global accounting standards would (i) make it easy to access foreign capital markets; (ii) increase credibility of domestic capital markets among foreign capital providers and potential foreign merger partners; (iii) increase credibility of financial statements of entities in less-developed countries among capital providers and potential lenders; (iv) lower cost of capital for companies; (v) improve comparability of financial data across borders.

- The main disadvantages of having uniform accounting standards internationally are represented by (i) the emphasis in IFRS on fair value accounting, particularly in relation to reporting in lesser-developed countries; (ii) the effects of their uneven implementation, auditing and enforcement; (iii) high cost of convergence; and (iv) reduced competition among systems.

- In the debate on accounting standards in the immediate aftermath of Enron and Worldcom, opinions are divided on the merits and demerits of principle- and rule-based accounting standards. However, 'principles vs rules' is a false distinction and a balance is needed between principles and supporting guidance or 'rules'.

- IFRS are now used by listed companies for reporting purposes in more than 100 countries, ranging from Australia to the United Kingdom. Other countries are expected to follow suit over the next few years and the IASB expects nearly 150 countries to use IFRS by 2011.

- In July 2002, the EU mandated that its listed companies abandon home country GAAP and prepare and issue financial statements using IFRS as from 2005. Also in 2002, the FASB and IASB signed the Norwalk Agreement in which each pledged to work together to make their competing standards compatible.

- In July 2007 the SEC introduced a new rule which eliminated the requirement for foreign private issuers using IFRS to reconcile their filings with the SEC to US GAAP (the so-called 'US GAAP reconciliation') and proposed that IFRS should be permissible in the US markets as an alternative to US GAAP.

- In 2009, the IASB issued an IFRS for SMEs. SMEs are entities that do not have public accountability and publish general purpose financial statements for external users. By removing choices for accounting treatment, eliminating topics that are not generally relevant to SMEs and simplifying methods for recognition and measurement, the resulting standard reduces the volume of accounting guidance applicable to SMEs by more than 85 per cent when compared with the 'full' set of IFRS.

- The adoption of IFRS for SMEs will be attractive to private companies for many reasons: (i) improved access to capital; (ii) improved comparability; (iii) improved quality of reporting as compared to existing national GAAP; (iv) focus on the needs of users of SME financial statements.

Research and references

The IASB document relevant for this chapter is IFRS for Small and Medium-sized Entities (SMEs).

The following are examples of papers, books and reports that take the issues of this chapter further:

- Ball, R. (2006) 'International Financial Reporting Standards (IFRS): pros and cons for investors', *Accounting and Business Research*, International Accounting Policy Forum.
- Benston, G., Bromwich, M., Litan, L.E. and Wagenhofer, A. (2006) *Worldwide Financial Reporting: The Development and Future of Accounting Standards*. Oxford: OUP.
- Biondi, Y. and Suzuki, T. (2007) 'Socio-economic impact of international accounting standards: an international socio-economic review', *Socio-Economic Review*, (5).
- Bromwich, M., Macve, R.H. and Sunder, S. (2005) *The Conceptual Framework: Revisiting the Basics. A Comment on Hicks and the Concept of Income in the Conceptual Framework*, LSE Working Paper (pdf file available from: http://www2.lse.ac.uk/accounting/facultyAndStaff/Conceptual%20framework-Revisiting%20the%20Basics_mbrmv__Fri4Jan08_.pdf).
- Bush, T. (2005) *'Divided by Common Language'. Where Economics Meets the Law: US versus Non-US Financial Reporting Models*. ICAEW, June.
- Ciesielski, J. (2008) 'It's not a small world, after all: The SEC goes international', *The Analyst's Accounting Observer*, 16(11), July.
- Deloitte (2008) *2008 IFRS Survey. Where Are We Today?* (pdf file available from: http://www.deloitte.com/dtt/cda/doc/content/us_assurance_IFRS_2008%20IFRS%20Survey.pdf).
- Durant, W. (1935) *The History of Civilization. Our Oriental Heritage*, Vol. I. Simon and Schuster.
- Durant, W. (1950) *The History of Civilization. The Age of Faith*, Vol. IV. Simon and Schuster.
- Felloni, G. and Guido, L. (2004) *Genova e la storia della finanza: una serie di primati? Genoa and the history of finance: A series of firsts*. Brigati Glauco, Genova Pontedecimo (pdf file available from: http://www.giuseppefelloni.it/img/ASeriesofFirsts.pdf).
- Global Accounting Alliance (2008) *Getting to the Heart of the Issue: Can Financial Reporting Be Made Simpler and More Useful?*, December.
- Hussey, R. and Ong, A. (2005) 'The lord of global standards: the twin towers', *Financial Reporting, Regulation & Governance*.
- ICAEW (Institute of Chartered Accountants in England and Wales) (2007) *EU Implementation of IFRS and the Fair Value Directive. A Report for the European Commission*. October (pdf file available from: www.icaew.com/ecifrsstudy).
- ICAS (2006a) *Principles-based or Rules-based Accounting Standards? A Question of Judgement*, April (pdf file available from: http://www.icas.org.uk/site/cms/download/rs_PVR_Literature_Review_pw.pdf).
- ICAS (2006b) *Principles not Rules: A Question of Judgement*, April (pdf file available from: http://www.icas.org.uk/site/cms/download/rs_Principles_v_Rules.pdf).

- Jackson, P., Tinius, D. and Weis, W. (1990) *Luca Pacioli: Unsung Hero of the Renaissance*. South-Western Publishing.
- Most, K.S. (1959) 'Accounting by the ancients', *The Accountant*, May.
- Nobes, C. and Parker, R.B. (2008) *Comparative International Accounting*, 10th edn. Financial Times Press, Chapter 2.
- Parks, T. (2005) *Medici Money: Banking, Metaphysics and Art in Fifteenth-Century Florence*. London: Profile Books.
- PricewaterhouseCoopers (2005) *IFRS. The Investors' View*. November (pdf file available from: http://download.pwc.com/ie/pubs/ifrs_survey.pdf).
- Radebaugh, L.H., Gray, S.J. and Black, E.L. (2006) *International Accounting and Multinational Enterprises*, 6th edn. Wiley, Chapter 1.
- Rayman, R.A. (2007) 'Fair value accounting and the present value fallacy: the need for an alternative conceptual framework', *British Accounting Review*, 39(3), September, pp. 211–25.
- de Roover, R. (1963) *The Rise and Decline of the Medici Bank*, 1397–1494. Harvard University Press.
- Stone, W.E. (1969) 'Antecedents of the accounting profession', *The Accounting Review*, 44(2), April (pdf file available from: http://uk.jstor.org/).
- Zeff, S. (2007) 'The SEC rules historical cost accounting: 1934 to the 1970s', *Accounting and Business Research*, Special Issue: International Accounting Policy Forum, pp. 49–62.
- Zeff, S. (ed.) (2009) *The ICAEW's Recommendations on Accounting Principles: 1942 to 1969*. London: ICAEW.

Discussion questions

1.1 Convergence in financial reporting

'If markets are to function properly and capital is to be allocated efficiently, investors require transparency and must have confidence that financial information accurately reflects economic performance. Investors should be able to make comparisons among companies in order to make rational investment decisions. In a rapidly globalising world, it only makes sense that the same economic transactions are accounted for in the same manner across various jurisdictions' (from a statement by Paul Volcker, former chairman of the US Federal Reserve Board and former chairman of the IASC Foundation, before the Capital Markets, Insurance and Government Sponsored Enterprises Sub-committee of the US House of Representatives in Washington, 7 June 2001).

Do you agree? Explain why.

1.2 Principle- versus rule-based accounting

Einstein once said that 'Everything should be made as simple as possible, but not simpler'. This perfectly captures the view that accounting standards should be firmly governed by high-level principles with only the absolute minimum additional guidance required to make the standard operational. Preparers and auditors, therefore, would need the courage to exercise and defend their judgements in this simplified accounting world. Users and regulators would need the wisdom to accept that there may be more than one answer and over time all parties would have to build the trust that this state of the world implies (from the ICAS 2006b).

Do you agree? Explain why.

1.3   Convergence in financial reporting and principle-based accounting

Convergence cannot be achieved if the basis for convergence is detailed rules-driven standards as this will be difficult to roll out across different jurisdictions and cultures around the world.

Do you agree? Explain why.

1.4   Regulation and accounting rules

'The basic cause of international differences in financial reporting practices is the different degree of interference by governments in accounting.'

Discuss.

1.5   Differences in financial reporting

History is primarily responsible for international differences in corporate financial reporting.

Do you agree? Explain why.

1.6   From national accounting standards to global standards

'Accounting is shaped by economic and political forces. It follows that increased worldwide integration of both markets and politics (driven by reductions in communications and information processing costs) makes increased integration of financial reporting standards and practice almost inevitable. But most market and political forces will remain local for the foreseeable future, so it is unclear how much convergence in actual financial reporting practice will (or should) occur' (Ball 2006).

Discuss.

1.7   Advantages and disadvantages of accounting convergence

Explain the purpose of accounting standards (national or international) and identify the advantages that stem from the convergence of accounting practice. Describe disadvantages, if any.

Notes

1 In this regard, in July 2009 the IASB issued an IFRS for Small and Medium-sized Entities (SMEs) (see section 1.6) which simplified recognition and measurement rules and reduced disclosures. Accordingly, the IASB has made its standards available to companies in a form that is suitable to their scale and sophistication.
2 An earlier Deloitte IFRS study showed that 30 per cent of respondents would consider adopting IFRS, if given a choice. These two Deloitte studies demonstrate changing attitudes and growing interest for IFRS in the USA.
3 Further examples of interaction of politics and accounting were seen during 2009. The G8 and G20 heads of state and finance ministers took an interest in accounting, as part of their work in connection with global financial stability. They put pressure on the IASB and FASB to accelerate their work on improving and simplifying IAS 32 – *Financial Instruments: Presentation* and IAS 39 – *Financial Instruments: Recognition and Measurement*. As a result, in July 2009 the IASB published an exposure draft *Financial Instruments: Classification and Measurement*, followed by IFRS 9 – *Financial Instruments* in November 2009, which will be applicable from 2013.

2 Conceptual framework for financial reporting

Contents

2.2.1 The objective of financial statements

The objective of a general purpose financial report is to provide financial information about the reporting entity that is useful to present and potential investors and creditors in making decisions in their capacity as capital providers. The objective refers to financial reporting as a whole, not just financial statements.

The objective of financial reporting is focused on meeting the information needs of the primary user group. The primary user group is made up of those who have a claim (or potentially may have a claim) on an entity's resources – its present and potential equity investors, lenders, and other creditors (capital providers).

The primary user group is interested in financial information because that information is useful in making decisions that equity investors, lenders, and other creditors make in their capacity as capital providers.

The decisions made by capital providers include whether and how to allocate their resources to a particular entity and how to protect or enhance their holdings. When making these decisions, capital providers are interested in assessing an entity's ability to generate net cash inflows and management's stewardship (see section 2.2.2 for a discussion on stewardship as an objective of financial statements).

Capital providers use information about an entity's resources, claims to those resources, and changes in resources and claims as inputs into the decision-making process.

Other potential user groups are represented by governmental and regulatory bodies, as shown in Figure 2.1.

Figure 2.1 shows that, according to the IASB *Framework* the users of financial statements include present and potential investors, employees, lenders, suppliers and other trade creditors, customers, governments and their agencies and the public.

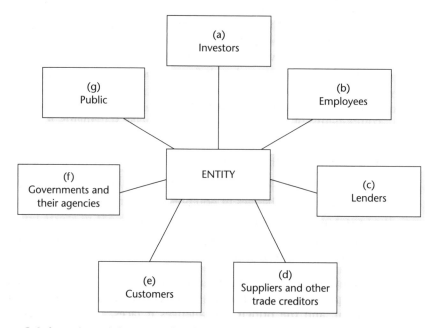

Figure 2.1 An entity and the users of its financial information according to the IASB *Framework*

Financial statements satisfy many of their users' different needs for information. These needs include the following:

(a) *Owners* (or investors) need financial information relating to the entity to assess how effectively the managers are running it and to make judgements about likely levels of risk and return in the future. Shareholders need information to assess the ability of the entity to pay them a return (dividend). The same applies to potential shareholders.

(b) *Employees and their representative groups* are interested in information about the stability and profitability of their employers. They too need information which enables them to assess the ability of the entity to provide remuneration, retirement benefits and employment opportunities.

(c) *Lenders* (such as banks) need financial information about an entity in order to assess its ability to meet its obligations, to pay interest and to repay the amount borrowed.

(d) *Suppliers and other trade creditors* need information that enables them to determine whether amounts owed to them will be paid when due. Trade creditors are likely to be interested in an entity over a shorter period than lenders unless they are dependent upon the continuation of the entity as a major customer.

(e) *Customers* have an interest in information about the continuance of an entity, especially when they have a long-term involvement with, or are dependent on, the entity.

(f) *Governments and their agencies* need information in order to regulate the activities of entities, to assess whether they comply with agreed pricing policies, whether financial support is needed, and how much tax they should pay. They also require information in order to determine taxation policies and as the basis for national income and statistics.

(g) *Public*. Entities affect members of the public in a variety of ways. For example, entities may make a substantial contribution to the local economy in many ways including the number of people they employ and their patronage of local suppliers. Financial statements may assist the public by providing information about the trends and recent developments in the prosperity of the entity and the range of its activities.

Though not mentioned by the IASB *Framework*, other users and their information needs include the following:

- *Investment analysts* need financial information relating to an entity to assess the risks and returns associated with the entity in order to determine its investment potential and to advise clients accordingly.

- *Competitors* need financial information relating to an entity to assess the threat to sales and profits posed by those businesses and to provide a benchmark against which the competitor's performance can be measured.

- *Managers* need financial information relating to an entity to help make decisions and plans for the business and to exercise control so that the plans come to fruition.

While all the information needs of these users cannot be met by financial statements, there are needs which are common to all users. As investors are providers of risk capital to the entity, the publication of financial statements that meet their needs will also meet most of the needs of other users.

> *It is unlikely that one piece of information, such as a single profit figure, will meet all of the wide variety of needs which financial accounting is meant to satisfy. For example, it is not necessary that the measure of profit used for tax purposes should be the same as that used for setting an upper limit to the dividends which can be distributed to shareholders: the fact that taxable profit and distributable profit differ under current British legislation is evidence of this.*

(Whittington 1983: 3)

2.2.2 Stewardship as an objective of financial statements: the current debate

The IASB and FASB are currently developing a common conceptual framework. This would improve upon the existing conceptual frameworks of each board and provide a sound foundation for the development of accounting standards which might attain global acceptance.[1]

In May 2008, IASB and FASB published an exposure draft (ED), *Conceptual Framework for Financial Reporting: The Objective of Financial Reporting and Qualitative Characteristics and Constraints of Decision-Useful Financial Reporting Information*, in which it was proposed that:

- the converged framework should specify only one objective of financial reporting, that of providing information that is useful to users in making investment, credit and similar resource allocation decisions ('the resource allocation decision-usefulness objective'); and
- information relevant to assessing stewardship will be encompassed in that objective.

In this section, we argue that stewardship and decision-usefulness for investors are parallel objectives, which do not necessarily conflict, but which have different emphases and therefore they should be defined as separate objectives. Stewardship, which is linked to agency theory, should be considered as a broader notion than resources allocation as it focuses on both past performance and how the entity is positioned for the future. It should therefore be retained as a separate objective of financial reporting to ensure that there is appropriate emphasis on company performance as a whole and not just on potential future cash flows. As noted by Andrew Lennard (2007):

> *Stewardship contributes an important dimension to financial reporting, which should be reflected by specific acknowledgement in the objectives of financial reporting. Moreover, stewardship should not be characterised simply as information to assist an assessment of the competence and integrity of 'stewards' (i.e. management, directors) but as the provision of information that provides a foundation for a constructive dialogue between management and shareholders.*

Meaning of 'stewardship' and 'accountability'

The previous IASB *Framework* issued in 1989 referred to '**stewardship**' as follows:

> *Financial statements also* [i.e. in addition to providing information that is useful in making economic decisions] *show the results of the stewardship of management, or the accountability of*

management for the resources entrusted to it. Those users who wish to assess the stewardship or accountability of management do so in order that they make economic decisions; these decisions may include, for example, whether to hold or sell their investment in the entity or whether to re-appoint or replace the management.

(*Framework* para 14)

Thus, the previous *Framework* argued that stewardship accounting is implicit in a decision-relevance objective. Moreover, the previous *Framework* seemed to imply that the terms *stewardship* and *accountability* are synonymous. However, 'accountability' refers directly to the fact that, not only do management have the responsibility to use the assets entrusted to them for the benefit of shareholders, they also have the overriding obligation to provide those shareholders with an account of what it has done with those assets.

The view of 'stewardship' given in the current ED is somewhat different. It mentions that management are accountable to the entity's capital providers for the custody and safekeeping of the entity's economic resources and for their efficient and profitable use, including protecting them from unfavourable economic effects such as inflation and technological changes. Management are also responsible for ensuring compliance with laws, regulations and contractual provisions.

Stewardship and agency theory

In the context of business entities, the need for accounting is often rationalised in terms of agency theory.

The main focus of the agency theory is the conflict that arises when ownership is different from management. Agency theory is concerned with resolving two problems that can occur in an agency relationship. The first problem arises when:

(a) the desires or goals of the principal and agent conflict; and

(b) it is difficult or expensive for the principal to verify what the agent is actually doing.

The problem here is that the principal cannot verify that the agent has behaved appropriately. The second problem is that of risk sharing when the principal and the agent have different attitudes towards risk and therefore prefer different actions.[2]

When a company is listed (quoted) on the **stock exchange**, control and ownership are separated. The company is controlled, at least on a day-to-day basis, by its management (the directors or management board) but owned by its shareholders (or proprietors). This involves obvious benefits for both parties but also risks. These risks may be controlled or reduced by various means: one of the most obvious, and widely used, strategies is for a requirement on management to provide regular accounts that are available to the shareholders. Financial statements therefore provide a key condition for the existence of a modern company: it is difficult to imagine how companies with widely held and traded shares would be managed if credible accounts were not generally prepared. A stewardship objective emphasises this role of financial reporting as explained below.

Shareholders, in their capacity as owners of the business, make decisions other than to buy, sell or hold. The other decisions include a consideration of whether they, as owners of the business, need to intervene in its management. The shareholders look to financial reporting to access information relating to management's stewardship of the business. Most accounts of agency theory stress the possibility of a divergence of interest between management and shareholders, both of which are assumed to be relentlessly pursuing their economic self-interest. Perhaps it is for this reason that the ED characterises stewardship as a demand for information on management's safe custody of the assets, and compliance with laws and regulations. The stress is on whether management have behaved properly and not for example, unjustly enriched themselves at the company's expense.

If owners assign stewardship of their company to management, they wish to have the ability to oversee management behaviour to ensure that:

- it is aligned to the owners' objectives;
- management are devising strategies aimed at making the best use of company assets; and
- no misappropriation of the company assets takes place.

The owners attempt to ensure alignment to their objectives by monitoring the company against some criteria e.g. at its simplest the increase in profits and net assets over the year. However, they also need information that enables them to review the company's performance in light of the risks management took in order to obtain the results and to assist them in making decisions about the future direction of the business.

Company law in many jurisdictions also interprets what is now commonly known as agency theory as discussed above. Stewardship was originally the primary objective of financial reporting which is why company law initially sought to ensure that management provide an account of their performance over a given period and show how they have utilised the resources entrusted to them by the owners. It was only after the development of capital markets that a further focus for financial reporting developed, i.e. on cash flow generation that would assist in buy, sell or hold decisions (the main focus of the resource allocation decision-usefulness objective as described in the ED).

For many investors in unlisted companies, selling the shares in a readily available, liquid market is not an option (due to a lack of capital markets or otherwise). The only alternatives available to such investors are intervention or removal of management. As a result, the main objective of financial reporting for these investors is stewardship. Such equity investors are interested in the following:

- how management have performed in the past so they can gauge their likely performance in the future;
- ability to gauge the extent to which transactions similar to those already undertaken might recur in the future; and
- how the management performance and transactions undertaken, including related party transactions, might affect the entity's performance.

Thus, we consider stewardship as a separate objective of financial reporting. In fact, an investor first assesses how an entity has performed in a given period, and secondly to make a judgement about how it is likely to perform in the future (so that he can make resource-allocation decisions). We believe that one of the first assessments an investor makes is to take a view on stewardship and as such this should have equal prominence with the resource-allocation decisions. Therefore, the stewardship objective that financial reporting has is broader than the resource-allocation decision-usefulness objective described in the ED. The stewardship objective is about providing information about the past (including, for example, the transactions entered into, the decisions taken and the policies adopted) at a level of detail and in a way that enables an entity's past performance to be assessed in its own right, rather than just as part of an assessment about likely future performance. And it is about providing information about how an entity has been positioned for the future.

2.2.3 Underlying assumptions

There are two assumptions underlying financial statements. These are the **accrual basis** and the going concern conventions.[3]

Accrual basis

Financial statements of an entity are prepared on an accrual basis of accounting. Under this basis, the effects of transactions and other events are recognised when they occur (and not as cash or its equivalent is received or paid) and they are recorded in the accounting records and reported in the financial statements of the periods to which they relate. Financial statements prepared on an accrual basis inform users not only of past transactions involving the payment and receipt of cash but also of obligations to pay **cash** in the future and of resources that represent cash to be received in the future. Hence, they provide the type of information about past transactions and other events that is most useful to users in making economic decisions.

Going concern

The financial statements are normally prepared on the assumption that an entity will continue in operation for the foreseeable future. Hence, it is assumed that the entity has neither the intention nor the need to liquidate or curtail materially the scale of its operations; if such an intention or need exists, the financial statements may have to be prepared on a different basis and, if so, the basis used should be disclosed.

> *The going concern assumption is a fundamental principle in the preparation of financial statements. Under the going concern assumption, an entity is ordinarily viewed as continuing in business for the foreseeable future with neither the intention nor the necessity of liquidation, ceasing trading or seeking protection from creditors pursuant to laws or regulations. Accordingly, unless the going concern assumption is inappropriate in the circumstances of the entity, assets and liabilities are recorded on the basis that the entity will be able to realize its assets, discharge its liabilities, and obtain refinancing (if necessary) in the normal course of business.*
>
> (IAASB 2009)

2.2.4 A note on the 'going concern' assumption[4]

The assessment of an entity's ability to continue as a going concern is the responsibility of the entity's management; and the appropriateness of management's use of the going concern assumption is a matter for the auditor to consider on *every* audit engagement. Some financial reporting frameworks contain an explicit requirement for management to make a specific assessment of the entity's ability to continue as a going concern, and include guidance regarding matters to be considered and disclosures to be made in connection with going concern. For example, IAS 1 (revised) paras 25 and 26 require management to make an assessment of an entity's ability to continue as a going concern:

> *When preparing financial statements, management shall make an assessment of an entity's ability to continue as a going concern. An entity shall prepare financial statements on a going concern basis unless management either intends to liquidate the entity or to cease trading, or has no realistic alternative but to do so. When management is aware, in making its assessment, of material uncertainties related to events or conditions that may cast significant doubt upon the entity's ability to continue as a going concern, the entity shall disclose those uncertainties. When an entity does not prepare financial statements on a going concern basis, it shall disclose that fact, together with the basis on which it prepared the financial statements and the reasons why the entity is not regarded as a going concern.*
>
> *In assessing whether the going concern assumption is appropriate, management takes into account all available information about the future, which is at least, but is not limited to, twelve months from the end of the reporting period. The degree of consideration depends on the facts in each case. When an entity has a history of profitable operations and ready access to financial resources, the entity may reach a conclusion that the going concern basis of accounting is appropriate without detailed analysis. In other cases, management may need to consider a wide range of factors relating to current and expected profitability, debt repayment schedules and potential sources of replacement financing before it can satisfy itself that the going concern basis is appropriate.*

Other standards and guidance may also be relevant, such as those relating to disclosures of risks and uncertainties or to supplementary statements such as management discussion and analysis or similar.

Management's assessment of the going concern assumption involves making a judgement, at a particular point in time, about the future outcome of events or conditions which are inherently uncertain. Where management have made a preliminary assessment, it will be probably necessary to update it at year-end given the speed with which economic conditions are changing as a result of the credit crunch. The information available at the time at which the judgement is made, the size and complexity of the entity, the nature and condition of its business and the degree to which it is affected by external factors all affect the judgement regarding the outcome of events or conditions.

Consideration of the going concern assumption

IAS 1 and International Standard on Auditing (ISA) 570 acknowledge that entities with a history of profitable operations and ready access to financial resources *may not* need a detailed analysis to support the going concern assumptions. However, the effect of the credit crisis and economic downturn is likely to be that such an approach will no longer be appropriate for many entities. In particular, the implicit assumptions behind such an approach may no longer be valid in the current economic environment (2007–10). Issues surrounding liquidity and credit risk may create new uncertainties, or may exacerbate those already existing. Even many well-respected entities with a long-standing history of profits and availability of credit may find it difficult to obtain or renew financing, either at all or on comparable terms. Further, entities that have typically relied on extensions of debt payments or waivers of debt covenants at year-end may find that these reliefs are no longer available from their lenders. In addition, the economic crisis may undermine the previous assumptions about profitability.

Consequently, entities that have not previously found the need to prepare a detailed analysis in support of the going concern assumption may need to give the matter further consideration. In many cases, the management of smaller entities may not have historically prepared a detailed assessment of the entity's ability to continue as a going concern, but instead may have relied on in-depth knowledge of the business and anticipated future prospects.

Disclosures in the financial statements

In addition to specific disclosures that may be required regarding a material uncertainty about the entity's ability to continue as a going concern, disclosures of risks and uncertainties are required in order to assist users of the financial statements to better understand the entity's financial position, financial performance and cash flows.

For those entities that are significantly affected by the prevailing economic conditions, management need to consider how to address the risks arising from such economic conditions in their financial statements.

Under IFRS, financial statements should provide sufficient disclosures to enable users to understand the effects of material transactions and events on the information conveyed in the financial statements. Moreover, entities are required to disclose the nature and extent of risks arising from financial instruments to which the entity is exposed during the period and at the reporting date, and how the entity manages those risks (for example, IFRS 7 – *Financial Instruments: Disclosures*[5]). A combination of qualitative and quantitative disclosures should provide an overview of the entity's use of financial instruments and the exposures to risks they create.

Historically, when management has concluded that the entity is a going concern without any material uncertainty, this conclusion has not usually been expressly stated in the financial statements. However, even in such cases management may nevertheless consider it appropriate, or in fact may be required by the applicable financial reporting framework, to make disclosures in the financial statements to set out the challenges management are facing in the prevailing economic environment, how this affects the outlook for the entity and any uncertainties that could have an effect on the entity, whether material or not. These could include, for example:

- concerns over availability of credit, in particular if there are facilities due for renewal soon after the issuance of the financial statements;
- developments in the industry and region in which the entity operates;
- uncertainties regarding plans to sell assets or dispose of businesses; and
- potential impairments of **fixed assets** and **intangibles**.

Further discussion in an entity's annual report (such as Management's Discussion and Analysis section; Business Review section of the Directors' Report; or equivalent) of management's assessment of the entity's funding position will be particularly relevant to users of the financial statements. Such discussion, when combined with required disclosures regarding debt maturities, help to provide a fuller view of an entity's outlook and risks (see Figure 2.2).

Corporate governance and responsibility (extract)

Description of directors' responsibilities in respect of the Annual Report, the Remuneration report and the financial statements

The directors are responsible for preparing the Annual Report, the Remuneration report and the financial statements in accordance with applicable law and regulations.

Company law requires the directors to prepare financial statements for each financial year that give a true and fair view of the state of affairs of the Company and the Group and of the profit or loss of the Group for that period.

In preparing those financial statements the directors are required to:

- Select suitable accounting policies and then apply them consistently.
- Make judgements and estimates that are reasonable and prudent.
- State that the financial statements conform with IFRSs as adopted by the European Union.
- Prepare the financial statements on a *going concern basis* unless it is inappropriate to presume that the Company will continue in business.

(. . .)

Independent auditors' report to the members of XYZ plc (extract)

Emphasis of matter – Going concern

In forming our opinion on the financial statements, which is not qualified, we have considered the adequacy of the disclosures made in note 1 to the financial statements concerning the ability of the Company to continue as a going concern. There is a risk that the Group may need to renegotiate its financial covenants with its lenders. If the Group needed to but were unable to agree amendments to the covenants and those covenants were breached, the syndicate of lenders would have the right to demand, with a two-thirds majority vote, immediate repayment of all amounts due to them. This right, together with other remedies available to lenders, creates doubt about the future capital funding of the Group. These conditions, along with the other matters explained in note 1 to the financial statements, indicate the existence of a material uncertainty which may cast significant doubt about the Company's ability to continue as a going concern. The financial statements do not include the adjustments that would result if the company was unable to continue as a going concern.

Notes (extract)

1. Basis of preparation and consolidation, accounting policies and critical accounting estimates and judgements

Basis of preparation and consolidation

XYZ plc (the Company) is a public limited company incorporated, listed and domiciled in the UK.

The financial statements have been prepared under the historical cost convention as modified by the revaluation of financial instruments (including derivative instruments) at fair value in accordance with International Financial Reporting Standards (IFRSs) as adopted by the European Union (EU), and the Companies Act 1985. Accordingly, these financial statements have been prepared in accordance with IFRSs as adopted by the European Union and therefore comply with Article 4 of the EU IAS Resolution. A summary of the more important Group accounting policies is set out below.

(. . .)

The financial statements have been prepared on a going concern basis. The Group is currently in full compliance with the financial covenants contained in all of its borrowing agreements.

However, as a consequence of the increasingly uncertain trading conditions there is a risk that the Group would need to reset its financial covenants with its lenders. Details of our covenants and our management of the risks associated with meeting those covenants are set out in our risk management disclosures.

If the Group were required but not able to agree amendments to the covenants such that undertakings to the Group's lenders were breached, then the syndicate of lenders would have

Figure 2.2 Example of disclosure on going concern

the right to demand immediate repayment of all amounts due to them, but only after a two-thirds majority vote for such action.

Whilst this eventuality would, if it arose, cast doubt on the future capital funding of the Group, the Group's cash flow forecasts show that in the year ahead interest payments will be fully met, with further cash generated to repay debt. For this reason the directors believe that adopting the going concern basis in preparing the consolidated financial statements is appropriate.

Nevertheless, the directors are making full disclosure, as required by accounting standards, to indicate the existence of a material uncertainty, which may cast significant doubt about the Group's ability to continue as a going concern. The financial statements do not include the adjustments that would result if the Group was unable to continue as a going concern.

(. . .)

21. Loans, other borrowings and net debt
We manage the capital requirements of the Group by maintaining leverage of the Group within the terms of our debt Facility Agreement. The Group's objectives when managing capital are:

- To safeguard the entity's ability to continue as a going concern, so that it can continue to provide returns for shareholders and benefits for other stakeholders.
- To provide an adequate return to shareholders by pricing products and services commensurately with the level of risk.

The Group sets the amount of capital in proportion to risk. The Group manages the capital structure and makes adjustments to it in the light of changes in economic conditions and the risk characteristics of the underlying assets. In order to maintain or adjust the capital structure, the Group may adjust the amount of dividends paid to shareholders, return capital to shareholders, issue new shares, or sell assets to reduce debt.

Under the Articles of Association, the directors are required to ensure that the total of all amounts borrowed by group companies do not exceed five times capital and reserves. This ratio is currently exceeded following the significant goodwill impairment during the year. Resolutions to authorise the exceeding of this restriction in the Articles will be put to shareholders at the Annual General Meeting.

Consistently with others in the industry, the Group monitors capital on the basis of the debt-to-profit ratio. This ratio is calculated as net debt ÷ profit. Net debt is calculated as total debt (as shown in the balance sheet) less cash and cash equivalents. Adjusted profit is defined by lending institutions in our Facilities Agreement.

Figure 2.2 (*Cont'd*)

The current economic conditions (2010) are likely to increase the level of uncertainty existing when management make their judgement about the outcome of future events or conditions. However, while the effect of the current market conditions on individual entities requires careful evaluation, it should not automatically be assumed that a material uncertainty exists to cast significant doubt on the ability of the entity to continue as a going concern.

2.2.5 Qualitative characteristics of financial reporting information

Qualitative characteristics are the attributes that make the information provided in financial statements useful to users. According to the IASB ED *Conceptual Framework for Financial Reporting: The Objective of Financial Reporting and Qualitative Characteristics and Constraints of Decision-Useful Financial Reporting Information* (29 May 2008), for financial information to be useful, it should possess two fundamental qualitative characteristics:

some other period or some other point in time. Comparability is not a quality of an individual item of information but, rather, a quality of the relationship between two or more items of information.

Comparability should not be confused with uniformity. For information to be comparable, like things must look alike and different things must look different. An overemphasis on uniformity may reduce comparability by making unlike things look alike. Comparability of financial reporting information is not enhanced by making unlike things look alike any more than it is by making like things look different.

Verifiability. This quality helps assure users that information faithfully represents the economic phenomena that it purports to represent. Verifiability implies that different knowledgeable and independent observers could reach general consensus, although not necessarily complete agreement, that either:

(a) the information represents the economic phenomena that it purports to represent without material error or bias; or

(b) an appropriate recognition or measurement method has been applied without material error or bias.

To be verifiable, information need not be a single point estimate. A range of possible amounts and the related probabilities also can be verified.

Verification may be direct or indirect. With *direct verification*, an amount or other representation itself is verified, such as by counting cash or observing marketable securities and their quoted prices. With *indirect verification*, the amount or other representation is verified by checking the inputs and recalculating the outputs using the same accounting convention or methodology. An example is verifying the carrying amount of inventory by checking the inputs (quantities and costs) and recalculating the ending inventory using the same cost flow assumption (e.g. average cost or first-in, first-out).

Timeliness. Information should be available to decision makers before it loses its capacity to influence decisions. Having relevant information available sooner can enhance its capacity to influence decisions, and a lack of timeliness can rob information of its potential usefulness. Some information may continue to be timely long after the end of a reporting period because some users may continue to consider it when making decisions. For example, users may need to assess trends in various items of financial reporting information in making investment or credit decisions.

Understandability. This quality of information enables users to comprehend its meaning. Understandability is enhanced when information is classified, characterised, and presented clearly and concisely. Comparability also can enhance understandability. Although presenting information clearly and concisely helps users to comprehend it, the actual comprehension or understanding of financial information depends largely on the users of the financial report. Users of financial reports are assumed to have a reasonable knowledge of business and economic activities and to be able to read a financial report. In making decisions, users also should review and analyse the information with reasonable diligence. However, when underlying economic phenomena are particularly complex, fewer users may understand the financial information depicting those phenomena. In these cases, some users may need to seek the aid of an adviser. Information that is relevant and faithfully represented should not be excluded from financial reports solely because it may be too complex or difficult for some users to understand without assistance.

2.2.6 Constraints on financial reporting

Two pervasive constraints limit the information provided by financial reporting:

- materiality; and
- cost as shown in Figure 2.4.

Materiality. Information is material if its omission or misstatement could influence the decisions that users make on the basis of an entity's financial information. Because materiality depends on the nature and amount of the item judged in the particular circumstances of its omission or misstatement, it is not possible to specify a uniform quantitative threshold at which a particular type of information becomes material. When considering whether financial information is a faithful representation of what it purports to represent, it is important to take into account materiality because material omissions or misstatements will result in information that is incomplete, biased, or not free from error.

Cost. Financial reporting imposes costs; the benefits of financial reporting should justify those costs. Assessing whether the benefits of providing information justify the related costs will usually be more qualitative than quantitative. In addition, the qualitative assessment of benefits and costs often will be incomplete. The costs of providing information include costs of collecting and processing the information,

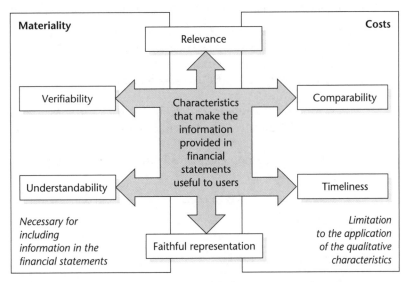

Figure 2.4 Qualitative characteristics of accounting information and constraints on financial reporting

The figure shows that there are six qualitative characteristics that influence the usefulness of financial information. In addition, however, financial information should be material and the benefits of providing the information should outweigh the costs.

costs of verifying it, and costs of disseminating it. Users incur the additional costs of analysis and interpretation. Omission of decision-useful information also imposes costs, including the costs that users incur to obtain or attempt to estimate needed information using incomplete data in the financial report or data available elsewhere.

Preparers expend the majority of the effort towards providing financial information. However, capital providers ultimately bear the cost of those efforts in the form of reduced returns.

Financial reporting information helps capital providers make better decisions, which result in more efficient functioning of capital markets and a lower cost of capital for the economy as a whole. Individual entities also enjoy benefits, including improved access to capital markets, favourable effect on public relations, and perhaps lower costs of capital. The benefits also may include better management decisions because financial information used internally often is based at least partly on information prepared for general-purpose financial reporting.

2.3 Elements of financial statements

Financial statements portray the financial effects of transactions and other events by grouping them into broad classes according to their economic characteristics. These broad classes are termed the elements of financial statements (*Framework* para 47). There are two main groups of elements:

- The first is associated with the measurement of an entity's **financial position**: assets, liabilities and equity.
- The second is related to the measurement of performance: income and expenses.

Within these main categories there are sub-classifications. For example, assets and liabilities may be classified by their nature or function in the business of the entity in order to display information in the manner most useful to users for purposes of making economic decisions (*Framework* para 48).

Assets. An asset is a resource controlled by the entity as a result of past events and from which future economic benefits are expected to flow to the entity (*Framework* para 49(a)).

The following example explains better the above definition.

Example 2.1

Recognition of an asset

Entity X enters into a legal arrangement to act as trustee for entity Y by holding listed shares on entity Y's behalf. Entity Y makes all investment decisions and entity X will act according to entity Y's instructions. Entity X will earn a trustee fee for holding the shares. Any dividends or profit/(loss) from the investments belong to entity Y.

Entity X should not recognise the listed shares as its asset even though it is in possession of the shares.

Entity X does not control the investment's future economic benefits. Benefits from the investments flow to entity Y and entity X earns a trustee fee for holding the shares regardless of how the shares perform. The listed shares, therefore, do not meet the criteria of an asset in entity X's balance sheet.

In assessing whether an item meets the definition of an asset (or a liability or equity), attention needs to be given to its underlying substance and economic reality and not merely its legal form. Thus, for example, in the case of finance leases, the substance and economic reality are that the lessee acquires the economic benefits of the use of the leased asset for the major part of its useful life in return for entering into an obligation to pay for that right an amount approximating to the fair value of the asset and the related finance charge. Hence, the finance lease gives rise to items that satisfy the definition of an asset and a liability and are recognised as such in the lessee's balance sheet (*Framework* para 51). Thus, the Framework stresses economic substance over legal form and reminds us that not all assets and liabilities will meet the criteria for recognition.

Many assets, for example, property, plant and equipment, have a physical form. However, physical form is not essential to the existence of an asset; hence patents and copyrights, for example, are assets if future economic benefits are expected to flow from them to the entity and if they are controlled by the entity (*Framework* para 56).

Many assets, for example, receivables and property, are associated with legal rights, including the right of ownership. In determining the existence of an asset, the right of ownership is not essential; thus, for example, property held on a lease is an asset if the entity controls the benefits which are expected to flow from the property. Although the capacity of an entity to control benefits is usually the result of legal rights, an item may nonetheless satisfy the definition of an asset even when there is no legal control. For example, know-how obtained from a development activity may meet the definition of an asset when, by keeping that know-how secret, an entity controls the benefits that are expected to flow from it (*Framework* para 57).

The assets of an entity result from past transactions or other past events. Entities normally obtain assets by purchasing or producing them, but other transactions or events may generate assets; examples include property received by an entity from the government as part of a programme to encourage economic growth in an area and the discovery of mineral deposits. Transactions or events expected to occur in the future do not in themselves give rise to assets; hence, for example, an intention to purchase inventory does not, of itself, meet the definition of an asset (*Framework* para 58).

There is a close association between incurring expenditure and generating assets but the two do not necessarily coincide. Hence, when an entity incurs expenditure, this may provide evidence that future economic benefits were sought but is not conclusive proof that an item satisfying the definition of an asset has been obtained. Similarly the absence of a related expenditure does not preclude an item from satisfying the definition of an asset and thus becoming a candidate for recognition in the balance sheet; for example, items that have been donated to the entity may satisfy the definition of an asset (*Framework* para 59).

Liabilities. A liability is a present obligation of an entity arising from past events, the settlement of which is expected to result in an outflow from the entity of resources embodying economic benefits (*Framework* para 49(b)).

Obligations may be legally enforceable as a consequence of a binding contract or statutory requirement. This is normally the case, for example, with amounts payable for goods and services received. However, obligations do not have to be legally binding. If, for example, an entity decides as a matter of policy to rectify faults in its products even when these become apparent after the warranty period has expired, the costs that are expected to be incurred in respect of goods already sold are liabilities. Obligations do not include future commitments (*Framework* paras 60 to 63).

Some liabilities can be measured only by using a substantial degree of estimation. Some entities describe these liabilities as provisions. In some countries, such provisions are not regarded as liabilities because the concept of a liability is defined narrowly so as to include only amounts that can be established without making estimates. The definition of a liability in paragraph 49 follows a broader approach. Thus, when a provision involves a present obligation and satisfies the rest of the definition, it is a liability even if the amount has been estimated. Examples include provisions for payments to be made under existing warranties and provisions to cover pension obligations (*Framework* para 64).

Equity. Equity represents the residual amount after all the liabilities have been deducted from the assets of an entity. Although equity is defined as a residual, it may be sub-classified in the balance sheet into various types of capital and reserves, such as shareholders' capital, retained earnings, statutory reserves, tax reserves, etc. Such classifications can be relevant to the decision-making needs of the users of financial statements when they indicate legal or other restrictions on the ability of the entity to distribute or otherwise apply its equity. They may also reflect the fact that parties with ownership interests in an entity have differing rights in relation to the receipt of dividends or the repayment of contributed capital (*Framework* paras 65 and 66).

Performance. The income and expense elements of performance are also measured in terms of assets and liabilities. Income is measured by increases in assets or decreases in liabilities, other than those relating to contributions from equity participants. Expenses, on the other hand, are measured by increases in liabilities or decreases in assets (*Framework* para 70).

Income and expenses may be presented in the income statement in different ways so as to provide information that is relevant for economic decision making. For example, it is a common practice to distinguish between those items of income and expenses that arise in the course of the ordinary activities of the entity and those that do not (*Framework* para 72).

Distinguishing between items of income and expense and combining them in different ways also permit several measures of entity performance to be displayed. These have differing degrees of inclusiveness. For example, the income statement could display gross margin, profit from ordinary activities before taxation, profit from ordinary activities after taxation, and net profit (*Framework* para 73). We illustrate in depth the income statement layouts in Chapter 3.

Recognition. IASB *Framework* para 83 calls for recognition of elements when:

(a) it is probable that any future economic benefit associated with the item will flow to or from the entity; and

(b) the item has a cost or value that can be measured reliably.

It is possible for an item to meet the definition of an asset, but not the recognition criteria as illustrated below.

Example 2.2

Asset recognition

Entity W is in the beverage business and its brand name is known throughout the world. Its main products command premium prices and the product names represent considerable future economic benefits. The brand has a market value and may be sold.

Management should not recognise its brand name as an asset, although it meets the definition of one. Management is prohibited from recognising internally generated brands, mastheads, publishing titles, customer lists and items similar in substance (IAS 38 para 63). The recognition criteria for intangible assets are more narrowly defined by IAS 38, limiting recognition of assets for which cost can be measured reliably (IAS 38 para 21(b)). The standard takes the view that the cost of brand generated internally cannot be distinguished from the cost of developing the business as a whole. Such items should not be recognised as intangible assets since the cost cannot be reliably measured.

When similar assets are acquired from a third party, the consideration given to acquire those assets is clearly distinguishable from the general costs of developing the business as a whole and, therefore, should be recognised, provided that they also meet the criteria of control and the probable flow of future economic benefits.

Uncertainty surrounds the meaning of *probable*. The concept of probability used in the recognition criteria refers to the degree of uncertainty that the future economic benefits associated with the item will flow to or from the entity. The concept is in keeping with the uncertainty that characterises the environment in which an entity operates. Assessments of the degree of uncertainty attaching to the flow of future economic benefits are made on the basis of the evidence available when the financial statements are prepared. For example, when it is probable that a receivable owed by a customer will be paid, it is then legitimate, in the absence of any evidence to the contrary, to recognise the receivable as an asset (*Framework* para 85). Some see 'probable' as representing 51 per cent likelihood, while others consider that a higher threshold is required for asset or income recognition. This is an area where there is little explicit guidance, so professional judgement should be exercised.

The second criterion for recognition is reliability. The *Framework* notes that the use of reasonable estimates is an essential part of the preparation of financial statements and that estimates in themselves do not undermine the reliability of financial information. Where an item has the characteristics of an element, but does not meet the recognition criteria, then it may be that disclosure in the notes is required (*Framework* paras 86 to 88).

The *Framework* takes an asset and liability approach rather than focusing on matching of income and expenses. This is borne out by the recognition criterion for income and expenses: Income is recognised in the income statement when an increase in future economic benefits related to an increase in an asset or a decrease in a liability has arisen that can be measured reliably. This means, in effect, that recognition of income occurs simultaneously with the recognition of increases in assets or decreases in liabilities (for example, the net increase in assets arising on a sale of goods or services or the decrease in liabilities arising from the waiver of a debt payable) (*Framework* para 92)[6]. The example below illustrates this concept.

Example 2.3

Accrued revenue

Entity T, a telecom company, invoices its customers for call charges on a monthly basis. At the beginning of March the total value of invoices that entity T sent out to its customers was EUR 1m. The invoices relate to calls customers made during the month of February. The invoices are payable by customers by the end of April.

Entity T should recognise revenue of EUR 1m in the income statement of February. A corresponding increase in assets (Sales invoice to be issued, under Other receivables, or **Trade receivables** should be recognised in the balance sheet.

The effects of transactions and other events are recognised as they occur. They are reported in the financial statements of the periods to which they relate (*Framework* para 22). Revenue is not deferred to match the timing of the receipt of cash or the raising of the invoices.

The recognition criterion for expenses is the mirror of the recognition criterion for income. Expenses are recognised in the income statement when a decrease in future economic benefits related to a decrease in an asset or an increase in a liability has arisen that can be measured reliably. This means, in effect, that recognition of expenses occurs simultaneously with the recognition of an increase in liabilities or a decrease in assets (for example, the accrual of employee entitlements or the depreciation of equipment) (*Framework* para 94).

Expenses are recognised in the income statement on the basis of a direct association between the costs incurred and the earning of specific items of income. This process, commonly referred to as the matching of costs with revenues, involves the simultaneous or combined recognition of revenues and expenses that result directly and jointly from the same transactions or other events; for example, the various components of expense making up the cost of goods sold are recognised at the same time as the income derived from the sale of the goods. However, the application of the matching concept under this framework does not allow the recognition of items in the balance sheet which do not meet the definition of assets or liabilities (*Framework* para 95).

When economic benefits are expected to arise over several accounting periods and the association with income can only be broadly or indirectly determined, expenses are recognised in the income statement on the basis of systematic and rational allocation procedures. This is often necessary in recognising the expenses associated with the using up of assets such as **property, plant, equipment**, patents and **trade marks**; in such cases the expense is referred to as **depreciation** or amortisation. These allocation procedures are intended to recognise expenses in the accounting periods in which the economic benefits associated with these items are consumed or expire (*Framework* para 96).

An expense is recognised immediately in the income statement when an expenditure produces no future economic benefits or when, and to the extent that, future economic benefits do not qualify, or cease to qualify, for recognition in the balance sheet as an asset. An expense is also recognised in the **income statement** in those cases when a liability is incurred without the recognition of an asset, as when a liability under a product warranty arises (*Framework* paras 97 and 98).

2.4 Measurement of the elements of financial statements

Measurement is the process of determining the monetary amounts at which the elements of the financial statements are to be recognised and carried in the balance sheet and income statement. This involves the selection of the particular basis of measurement (*Framework* para 99).

The IASB *Framework* para 100 lists a number of different measurement bases which are employed in different degrees and in varying combinations in financial statements:

(a) **Historical cost.** Assets are recorded at the amount of cash or cash equivalents paid or the fair value of the consideration given to acquire them at the time of their acquisition. Liabilities are recorded at the amount of proceeds received in exchange for the obligation, or in some circumstances (for example, income taxes), at the amounts of cash or cash equivalents expected to be paid to satisfy the liability in the normal course of business.

(b) **Current cost.** Assets are carried at the amount of cash or cash equivalents that would have to be paid if the same or an equivalent asset was acquired currently. Liabilities are carried at the undiscounted amount of cash or cash equivalents that would be required to settle the obligation currently.

(c) **Realisable (settlement) value.** Assets are carried at the amount of cash or cash equivalents that could currently be obtained by selling the asset in an orderly disposal. Liabilities are carried at their settlement values; that is, the undiscounted amounts of cash or cash equivalents expected to be paid to satisfy the liabilities in the normal course of business.

(d) *Present value.* Assets are carried at the present discounted value of the future net cash inflows that the item is expected to generate in the normal course of

(IAS 39 para 9). Although this definition states the measurement objective, it lacks sufficient specificity to ensure consistent application.

As regards verifiability of fair value, verifiability is a component of faithful representation. A concern over verifiability of fair value often is expressed in relation to assets and liabilities that do not have observable market prices. For such assets and liabilities, fair value must be estimated, which raises the possibility that the estimates may not be verifiable.

The effect of incentives on fair value estimates by management is also of concern when observable market prices are unavailable.

The fact that fair value estimates incorporate and, thus, reflect managers' detailed information that is not necessarily available to others is a desirable aspect of fair value. Reflecting such information in financial statements mitigates the need for market participants to develop noisy estimates based only on public information. Nonetheless, the concern about the effects of management incentives is valid. But, it is not unique to fair value. A large body of research shows that managers find ways to manage earnings regardless of the accounting regime.

(Barth 2007)

Lastly, concerning potential circularity, it is unlikely that even if all recognised assets and liabilities are measured at fair value, recognised equity would equal the market value of equity. This is because only assets and liabilities that meet the Framework definitions are candidates for recognition. Market value of equity reflects investors' assessments of, among other things, growth options and managerial skill that do not meet the asset definitions (Barth 2007).

Notwithstanding the above, the use of fair value would minimise the undesirable effects of the mixed measurement approach to financial reporting that we have today (Barth 2007). Presently, financial statement amounts are determined using a variety of measurement bases. These include, for example, historical cost (used for cash), amortised historical cost (used for loans receivable and long-term debt), impaired amortised historical cost (used for purchased property, plant, and equipment), accumulated amortised and impaired historical cost (used for self-constructed property, plant, and equipment), fair value (used for derivatives and asset revaluations), and entity-specific value (used for impaired inventories and impaired property, plant, and equipment). These differences in measurement bases do not result from differences specified in the *Framework*. Rather, they result from conventions and differences in practice that have evolved over time. Thus, when viewed in terms of the Framework, these differences cause financial statements to be internally inconsistent. Not only is use of multiple measurement bases conceptually unappealing, but it also creates difficulties for financial statement users. Measuring financial statement amounts in different ways complicates the interpretation of accounting summary amounts such as profit or loss (Barth 2007).

Support for fair value accounting is also backed by a study on mark-to-market accounting standards carried out in the last quarter of 2008 by the US SEC. Most *investors and other users of financial reports* indicated a view that fair value accounting transparently reflects, under the prevailing economic conditions, the value of assets and liabilities of the companies in which they invest. Most indicated that suspending fair value accounting would result in a loss of information and investor confidence: fair value is the most relevant measurement attribute for financial instruments in the prevailing market environment. However, fair value reporting can pose challenges, particularly in the absence of active markets. Users also expressed the need to supplement fair value accounting with robust disclosure on the methods used, of the underlying assumptions and sensitivities, particularly when fair value estimates are necessary in the absence of quoted prices. There is little evidence to suggest investors and other users generally believe an alternative to fair value, such as amortised cost, would be a superior approach. *Preparers of financial statements* held mixed views about the usefulness of fair value accounting in the prevailing market conditions. Preparers that manage their businesses based on fair values, such as investment banks and mutual funds, indicated that fair value for financial instruments is always the most relevant measure. Preparers whose business activities include managing financial assets based on a longer-term profit expectation, for instance insurance companies and commercial banks, questioned the relevance of measuring securities based on current illiquid prices when those prices do not reflect the company's ultimate cash flow expectations (see US SEC 2008).

2.4.2 Alternatives to fair value

As mentioned earlier, there are opponents to a more comprehensive use of fair value especially in the economic climate of 2007–10. As pointed out in the article from the *Financial Times* (Exhibit 2.2), fair values sometimes are the output of such complex mathematical models, that not only are they not verifiable, but are also so abstract and practically incomprehensible.

Exhibit 2.2

> [. . .] Another problem was at play: the extraordinary complexity and opacity of modern finance. During the past two decades, a wave of innovation has reshaped the way markets work, in a manner that once seemed able to deliver huge benefits for all concerned. But this innovation became so intense that it outran the comprehension of most ordinary bankers – not to mention regulators.
>
> As a result, not only is the financial system plagued with losses of a scale that nobody foresaw, but the pillars of faith on which this new financial capitalism were built have all but collapsed. That has left everyone from finance minister or central banker to small investor or pension holder bereft of an intellectual compass, dazed and confused. [. . .] The current crisis stems from changes that have been quietly taking root in the west for many years. Half a century ago, banking appeared to be a relatively simple craft. When commercial banks extended loans, they typically kept those on their own books – and they used rudimentary calculations (combined with knowledge of their customers) when deciding whether to lend or not.
>
> From the 1970s onwards, however, two revolutions occurred: banks started to sell their credit risk on to third-party investors in the blossoming capital markets; and they adopted complex computer-based systems for measuring credit risk that were often imported from the hard sciences. [. . .] In reality, many of the new products were so specialized that they were never traded in 'free' markets at all. An instrument known as 'collateralised debt obligations of

▶

asset-backed securities' was a case in point. [. . .] In 2006 and early 2007, no less than $450bn worth of these 'CDO of ABS' securities were produced. Instead of being traded, most were sold to banks' off-balance-sheet entities such as SIVs – 'structured investment vehicles' – or simply left on the books.

That made a mockery of the idea that innovation had helped to disperse credit risk. *It also undermined any notion that banks were using 'mark to market' accounting systems: since most banks had no market price for these CDOs (or much else), they typically valued them by using theoretical calculations from models. The result was that a set of innovations that were supposed to create freer markets actually produced an opaque world in which risk was being concentrated – and in ways almost nobody understood. By 2006, it could 'take a whole weekend' for computers to perform the calculations needed to assess the risks of complex CDOs* [. . .] Most investors were happy to buy products such as CDOs because they trusted the value of credit ratings. Meanwhile, the banks were making such fat profits they had little incentive to question their models [. . .] In July 2007, this blind faith started to crack. [. . .] So did faith in banks. Then, as models lost credibility, investors shunned all forms of complex finance. [. . .]

Source: from 'Lost through destructive creation', *Financial Times*, 9/03/2009 (Tett, G.)

Some opponents of comprehensive use of fair value advocate *historical cost*. However, we do not use historical cost comprehensively in financial statements today. Items initially recognised at cost typically are subsequently measured at amortised and impaired amounts; these are not historical cost. Thus, one would need to specify how these items should be measured subsequent to initial recognition. Also, it is unclear whether historical cost has the qualitative characteristics of accounting information specified in the *Framework*. For example, although an historical cost measure can be a faithful representation, historical cost may not be as relevant for users making economic decisions. However, cost is not always clearly identifiable, for example for self-constructed assets or assets acquired in a basket purchase, which raises concerns about verifiability. Also, the present convention of recognising decreases in asset values, i.e. impairments, but not increases in asset values, is inconsistent with neutrality. Moreover, some assets and liabilities have no cost – notably derivatives. This raises the question of how such assets and liabilities should be reflected in historical cost financial statements without either leaving them unrecognised or creating a mixed measurement approach.

Value in use, or entity-specific value, is another possible measurement alternative. Value in use requires inclusion of future cash flows that the entity expects to receive, discounted at a rate that reflects the entity's cost of capital, even if these differ from those of other entities. Thus, entity-specific value differs from fair value in that entity-specific value includes cash inflows or outflows expected by the entity that would not be expected by other market participants, such as expected inflows related to superior management talent. Thus, entity-specific value can result in embedding the measure of an intangible asset, e.g. superior management talent, in the measure of another asset, e.g. property, plant, and equipment. As with all measurement bases, measuring assets and liabilities at entity-specific value also has implications for profit or loss measurement. Because entity-specific value measures, assets and liabilities are based on what the entity expects to accomplish with the assets, the value of the entity's special rights or skills are recognised when the assets are recognised, not when the entity realises the benefits associated with those special rights or skills. In contrast, using fair value would result in profit or loss reflecting how the entity performed during the period given the assets at its disposal relative to other market participants' expected performance. If the entity makes better use of the assets, profit will be greater than the return expected based on the risk of its net assets; if it makes worse use of the assets, profit will be less than the expected return (Barth 2007).

2.5   Concepts of capital and capital maintenance

All accounting systems depend on the capital maintenance concept adopted, the basis used to value assets and the unit of measurement used.

Capital maintenance is central to the measurement of total accounting profit. Disregarding additions to capital or repayments of capital and distributions, accounting profit is the difference between a company's capital at the start of the period and at the end of the period. A company can only be considered to have made a profit if it has increased its net assets, which are represented by its capital, over and above that necessary to maintain its opening capital. Thus, total accounting profit can be measured only once a definition has been established as to what capital is to be maintained.

There are at least two different concepts of capital maintenance:

- operating (or physical) capital maintenance; and
- financial capital maintenance.

Operating capital maintenance, although it can be measured in a variety of different ways, generally seeks to ensure that the business's physical operating capacity is preserved.

Financial capital maintenance attempts to conserve the value of the funds that shareholders have invested in the business. Financial capital maintained can either be the monetary value of capital attributable to shareholders or a value adjusted by a general purchasing power index to maintain capital as a fund of real purchasing power.

The principal difference between the two concepts of capital maintenance is the treatment of the effects of changes in the prices of assets and liabilities of the entity. In general terms, an entity has maintained its capital if it has as much capital at the end of the period as it had at the beginning of the period. Any amount over and above that required to maintain the capital at the beginning of the period is profit (*Framework* para 107).

Under the concept of financial capital maintenance where capital is defined in terms of nominal monetary units, profit represents the increase in nominal money capital over the period. Thus, increases in the prices of assets held over the period, conventionally referred to as holding gains, are, conceptually, profits. They may not

The results of this formula are summarised in a present value factor table:

(n) Periods	2%	3%	4%	5%	6%	7%	8%	9%	10%
1	0.9804	0.9709	0.9615	0.9524	0.9434	0.9346	0.9259	0.9174	0.9091
2	0.9612	0.9426	0.9246	0.9070	0.8900	0.8734	0.8573	0.8417	0.8265
3	0.9423	0.9151	0.8890	0.8638	0.8396	0.8163	0.7938	0.7722	0.7513
4	0.9239	0.8885	0.8548	0.8227	0.7921	0.7629	0.7350	0.7084	0.6830
5	0.9057	0.8626	0.8219	0.7835	0.7473	0.7130	0.6806	0.6499	0.6209

Example

Suppose one wishes to determine the amount needed to invest today to have EUR 10,000 in five years if the sum invested would earn 8 per cent.

Looking across the row with $n = 5$ and finding the present value factor for the $r = 8\%$ column, the factor of 0.6806 would be identified. Multiplying EUR 10,000 by 0.6806 results in EUR 6,806, the amount needed to invest today to have EUR 10,000 at the end of five years.

Alternatively, using a calculator and applying the present value of a single sum formula, one could multiply EUR 10,000 by $1 \div (1 + 0.08)^5$, which would also give the same answer, EUR 6,806.

Present value of a series of equal payments (an annuity)

Often in business transactions a series of equal payments paid at equal time intervals is required. Examples of these include payments of semiannual bond interest and principal or lease payments. The present value of each of these payments could be added up to find the present value of this annuity, or alternatively a much simpler approach is available. The formula for calculating the present value of an annuity of EUR 1 payments over n periodic payments, at a periodic interest rate of r is:

$$PV \text{ Annuity} = 1 - \frac{1}{(1 + r)^n}$$

The results of this formula are summarised in an annuity present value factor table.

(n) Periods	2%	3%	4%	5%	6%	7%	8%	9%	10%
1	0.9804	0.9709	0.9615	0.9524	0.9434	0.9346	0.9259	0.9174	0.9091
2	1.9416	1.9135	1.8861	1.8594	1.8334	1.8080	1.7833	1.7591	1.7355
3	2.8839	2.8286	2.7751	2.7233	2.6730	2.6243	2.5771	2.5313	2.4869
4	3.8077	3.7171	3.6299	3.5460	3.4651	3.3872	3.3121	3.2397	3.1699
5	4.7135	4.5797	4.4518	4.3295	4.2124	4.1002	3.9927	3.8897	3.7908

Example

Suppose four annual payments of EUR 1,000 are needed to satisfy an agreement with a supplier. What would be the amount of the liability today if the interest rate the supplier charges is 6 per cent per year?

Using the table to get the present value factor, $n = 4$ periods row, and the 6 per cent column, gives you a factor of 3.4651. Multiply this by EUR 1,000 and you get a liability of EUR 3,465.10 that should be recorded. Using the formula would also give you the same answer with $r = 6\%$ and $n = 4$.

Caution should be exercised when payments are not to be made on an annual basis. If payments are on a semiannual basis $n = 8$, but r is now 3 per cent. This is because r is the periodic interest rate, and the semiannual rate would not be 6 per cent, but half of the 6 per cent annual rate. Note that this is somewhat simplified, since due to the effect of compound interest 3 per cent semiannually is slightly more than a 6 per cent annual rate.

Present value of a perpetuity

An important, special type of annuity is a perpetual annuity or perpetuity. A perpetuity is a stream of cash flows that lasts forever. The classic example is the 'consol' bonds issued by the British government or Rendita Italiana issued by the Italian Treasury in the nineteenth century which pay interest each year on the stated face value of the bonds but have no maturity date. Another example is a preference share that pays a fixed cash dividend each year and never mature.

A feature of any perpetual annuity is that you cannot compute the future value of its cash flows because it is infinite. Nevertheless, it has a perfectly well-defined and determinable present value. Consider a perpetual stream of EUR 100 per year: if the interest rate is 10 per cent per year, how much is this perpetuity worth today? The answer is EUR 1,000. To see why, consider how much money you would have to put into a bank account offering interest at 10 per cent per year in order to be able to take out EUR 100 every year for ever. If you put EUR 1,000 then at the end of the first year you would have EUR 1,100 in the account. You would take out EUR 100, leaving EUR 1,000 for the second year. Clearly, if the interest rate stayed at 10 per cent per year, you could go on doing this forever.

More generally, the formula for the present value for a perpetual annuity is:

$$PV \text{ perpetuity} = \frac{C}{r}$$

where C is the periodic payment and r is the interest rate. This is the present value of an ordinary annuity with $n = \infty$.

Summary

- The IASB *Framework* describes the basic concepts that underlie financial statements prepared in conformity with International Financial Reporting Standards.

- The *Framework*, which identifies the principal classes of users of an entity's general-purpose financial statements, states that the objective of financial statements is to provide information about the financial position, performance and changes in financial position of an entity that is useful to a wide range of users in making economic decisions; and to show the results of management's stewardship (i.e. accountability for resources entrusted to them).

- The *Framework* specifies the qualities that make financial information useful; namely, understandability, relevance, reliability and comparability. It also defines the basic elements of financial statements (assets, liabilities, equity, income and expenses) and discusses the criteria for recognising and measuring them.

- The IASB and FASB are jointly working on a project to revise and conform their conceptual Frameworks. It has been proposed that the converged framework should specify only one objective of financial reporting, that of providing information that is useful to users in making investment, credit and similar resource allocation decisions ('the resource allocation decision-usefulness objective'). We consider that stewardship and decision-usefulness for investors are parallel objectives, which do not necessarily conflict, but which are equally important and therefore they should be defined as separate objectives.

- The elements of financial statements are assets, liabilities, equity, income and expenses. Each of these elements is defined in the IASB *Framework*.

- An element is recognised in the financial statements if it is probable that any economic benefits associated with the element will flow to or from the entity and if the element has a cost or value which can be reliably measured.

- Elements may be measured at their historical cost, current cost, realisable value, present value and fair value. The measurement basis most commonly adopted by entities in preparing their financial statements is historical cost, which is usually combined with other measurement bases.

- Profits and losses may be measured in terms of changes in the amount of an entity's net assets (financial capital maintenance) or in terms of changes in the entity's physical operating capability (physical capital maintenance).

Research and references

The IASB documents relevant for this chapter are:

- *Framework for the Preparation and Presentation of Financial Statements*, 1989.
- *Discussion Paper (DP): Preliminary Views on an improved Conceptual Framework for Financial Reporting: Objective of Financial Reporting and Qualitative Characteristics of Decision-Useful Financial Reporting Information*, July 2006.

- Exposure Draft (ED): *Conceptual Framework for Financial Reporting: The Objective of Financial Reporting and Qualitative Characteristics and Constraints of Decision-Useful Financial Reporting Information*, May 2008.

The following are examples of books, research and discussion papers that take the issues of this chapter further:

- Accounting Standards Board, Foreningen af Statsautoriserede Revisor, Deutsches Rechnungslegungs Standards Committee, Komitet Standardów Rachunkowoci and EFRAG (2007) *Stewardship/Accountability as an Objective of Financial Reporting. A Comment on the IASB/FASB Conceptual Framework Project*, June.
- Ball, R. (2006) 'International Financial Reporting Standards (IFRS): pros and cons for investors', *Accounting and Business Research*, Special Issue: International Accounting Policy Forum.
- Barth, M.E. (2007) 'Standard-setting measurement issues and the relevance of research', *Accounting and Business Research*, Special Issue: International Accounting Policy Forum.
- Barth, M.E., Beaver, W.H. and Landsman, W.R. (2001) 'The relevance of the value relevance literature for financial accounting standard setting: another view', *Journal of Accounting and Economics*, 31: 77–104.
- Baxter, W.T. and Davidson, S. (eds) (1962) *Studies in Accounting Theory*. London: Sweet and Maxwell.
- Bush, T. (2005) *'Divided by a common language' where economics meets the law: US versus non-US financial reporting models*, ICAEW, June.
- Eisenhardt, M.K. (1989) 'Agency theory: an assessment and review', *Academy of Management Review*, 14(1), 57.
- Ellwood, S. and Newbury, S. (2006) 'A bridge too far: a common conceptual framework for commercial and public benefit entities', *Accounting and Business Research*, 36(1).
- FRC (Financial Reporting Council) (2009) *Going concern and liquidity risk: guidance for directors of UK companies*, October.
- Institut der Wirtschaftsprüfer in Deutschland e.V. (2007) *Additional Issues in Relation to a Conceptual Framework for Financial Reporting*.
- ICAEW (2006) *Improved Conceptual Framework for Financial Reporting*, Memorandum of comment submitted in November 2006 in response to the IASB's Discussion Paper 'Preliminary Views on an Improved Conceptual Framework for Financial Reporting: The Objective of Financial Reporting and Qualitative Characteristics of Decision-Useful Financial Reporting Information'.
- IAASB (International Auditing and Assurance Standards Board) (2009) *Audit considerations in respect of going concern in the current economic environment*, January.
- Landsman, W.R. (2005) 'Fair value accounting for financial instruments: some implications for bank regulation'. Working Paper. Chapel Hill: University of North Carolina.
- Landsman, W.R. (2006) 'Fair value and value relevance: what do we know?'. Working Paper. Chapel Hill: University of North Carolina.
- Lennard, A. (2007) 'Stewardship and the objectives of financial statements: A comment on IASB's Preliminary Views on an improved conceptual framework for financial reporting: The objective of financial reporting and qualitative characteristics of decision-useful financial reporting information', *Accounting in Europe*, 4(1), 51–66.
- Macve, R.H. (1997) *A Conceptual Framework for Financial Accounting and Reporting: Vision, Tool or Threat?* New York: Garland.
- Macve, R.H., Bromwich, M. and Sunder, S. (2008) *The Conceptual Framework: Revisiting the Basics. A Comment on Hicks and the Concept of 'Income' in the Conceptual Framework*. London: London School of Economics and Political Science (pdf file available from: http://www.lse.ac.uk/collections/accounting/facultyAndStaff/Conceptual%20framework-Revisiting%20the%20Basics_mbrmv_Fri4Jan08_.pdf).
- Morris, C.R. (2008) *The Trillion Dollar Meltdown: Easy Money, High Rollers and the Great Credit Crash*. London: PublicAffairs Ltd.

- Nobes, C. and Parker, R. (2008) *Comparative International Accounting*, 10th edn. Prentice Hall-Financial Times, Chapter 6.
- Peasnell, K.V. (1982) 'The function of a conceptual framework for corporate financial reporting', *Accounting and Business Research*, Autumn.
- PricewaterhouseCoopers (2009) *IFRS Manual of Accounting 2010. Global Guide to International Financial Reporting Standards*. CCH, November, Chapter 2.
- Schuetze, W.P. (1993) 'What is an Asset?', *Accounting Horizons*, 7(3), September, pp. 66–70.
- Underdown, B. and Taylor, P.J. (1985) *Accounting Theory and Policy Making*. London: Heinemann.
- US SEC (Securities and Exchange Commission) (2008) *Report and Recommendations Pursuant to Section 133 of the Emergency Economic Stabilization Act of 2008: Study on Mark-to-Market Accounting*, December.
- Whittington, G. (1983) *Inflation Accounting*. Cambridge: CUP.
- Zeff, S. (ed.) (2009) *The ICAEW's Recommendations on Accounting Principles: 1942 to 1969*. London: ICAEW.

Discussion questions

2.1 Conceptual framework

(a) Why do we need a conceptual framework when we have a comprehensive set of accounting standards such as IFRS?

(b) Who are the primary users of general-purpose financial statements?

(c) IASB does not include management of a company as one of the primary users of general-purpose financial statements. Why do you suppose that is?

(d) Should financial information be only 'decision useful'? Explain why.

2.2 Qualitative characteristics of financial information

(a) Illustrate the qualitative characteristics of useful financial information. Describe the factors which contribute to the achievement of each characteristic.

(b) Relevance is one of the key qualities of the information in financial statements. What does relevance mean?

(c) What is the difference between consistency of accounting information and comparability of accounting information?

2.3 Probable future economic benefits

Under the IASB *Framework*, an asset is recognised 'when it is probable that the future economic benefits will flow to the entity'.

(a) Which future economic benefits does that principle refer to? Illustrate your answer with examples.

(b) How would you interpret 'probable' in this context?

2.4 Recognition of asset

A company buys a costly item of electronic equipment that it expects will have a useful life of eight years, and it depreciates the asset over that period.

By the end of the fourth year, the item of equipment is obsolete and the company is no longer using it. It is still in the company's balance sheet at the remaining undepreciated one-half of original cost, which the company says (i) is a faithful representation of its circumstances since the company still owns the asset, and (ii) is a reliable measure of the asset.

Comment on the company's view.

2.5 General-purpose financial statements

In some countries, income tax authorities require companies to prepare accounts that conform to national laws for measuring taxable income.

Are those financial statements 'general-purpose financial statements'? Why?

2.6 Conceptual framework and IFRS

A company's senior financial officer says, 'I always follow IFRSs in preparing my company's financial statements. But the IASB *Framework* is a lot of conceptual theory that doesn't affect me directly. It is not an accounting standard, so I have never read it.'

Is the IASB *Framework* a standard? Is it relevant to preparing IFRS financial statements? If so, how?

2.7 Going concern assumption

An entity has incurred losses during the last four years and its current liabilities exceed its total assets. The entity was in breach of its loan covenants and has been negotiating with the related financial institutions in order to ensure their continuing support. These factors raise substantial doubt that the entity will be able to continue as a going concern.

How should management deal with this matter?

2.8 Definition and recognition of an asset

(a) Give examples of resources that might be treated as assets in a balance sheet but normally are not. How helpful is the *Framework* definition of assets in making clear that they are not included?

(b) Give examples of resources that are normally treated as assets in a balance sheet. How helpful is the *Framework* definition of assets in deciding the monetary amount at which they should be recorded?

2.9 Definition and recognition criteria for an asset

Chemco Ltd. is engaged in the production of chemical products and selling them locally. The company wishes to extend its market and export some of its products. It has come to the attention of the financial director that compliance with international environmental requirements is a significant precondition if it wishes to sell products overseas. Although Chemco Ltd. has during the past put in place a series of environmental policies, it is clear that it is also common practice to have an environmental audit done from time to time, which will cost approximately EUR 120,000. The audit will encompass the following:

- a full review of all environmental policy directives;
- a detailed analysis of compliance with these directives;
- a report containing in-depth recommendations of those physical and policy changes that would be necessary to meet international requirements.

The financial director of Chemco Ltd has suggested that the amount be capitalised as an asset and then written off against the revenues generated from export activities so that the matching of income and expense will occur.

Do you agree with the financial director? Explain why.

Notes

1 The progress of this project may be followed on the website www.iasb.org.
2 See Eisenhardt, M.K. (1989).
3 The IASB's ED of 2008 proposes to remove the concept of 'underlying assumptions'. The accruals concept becomes part of relevant information. The going concern convention is not mentioned in the ED, but it is dealt with in the revised version of IAS 1 – *Presentation of Financial Statements*, para 17.
4 This section is based on IAASB (2009).
5 The standard incorporates simple financial instruments, such as **trade receivables** and **trade payables**, as well as more complex instruments, such as **derivatives**.
6 For a different opinion see Jim Leisenring's presentation (Conceptual Framework CD-Rom 2004, IASB: London). Jim Leisenring, IASB member, compares the IASB *Framework* with the FASB's conceptual framework for financial accounting and reporting. He argues that the IASB *Framework* has an income statement approach.
7 Readers who are not familiar with the concepts of discounting and present value should refer to the appendix at the end of this chapter where these concepts are explained.
8 This section is based on Ball (2007) and US SEC (2008).
9 See Barth *et al.* (2001), Landsman (2005), Landsman (2006) and Barth (2007) for summaries of empirical research relating to the value relevance of fair values.

Part Two Reporting and presentation

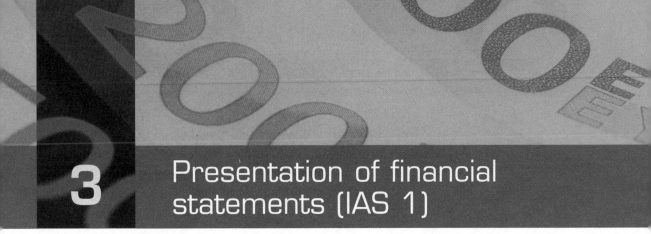

3

Presentation of financial statements (IAS 1)

Contents

Objectives

When you have completed this chapter you should be able to:

- Identify the components of a complete set of financial statements
- Explain the overall considerations which should be taken into account when preparing financial statements
- Explain the structure and content of each component of a set of financial statements
- Distinguish between current and non-current assets and between current and non-current liabilities
- Prepare a statement of financial position, a statement of comprehensive income and a statement of changes in equity in accordance with the requirement of IAS 1 – *Presentation of Financial Statements*
- Outline the main requirements of IAS 34 – *Interim Financial Reporting*.

3.1 Introduction

Guidance on the overall structure of financial statements, including minimum requirements for each primary statement (balance sheet, income statement, statement of changes in equity and **statement of cash flows**) and notes to the financial statements, is provided by IAS 1 – *Presentation of Financial Statements*.

On 6 September 2007 the IASB issued a revised IAS 1 – *Presentation of Financial Statements* (hereinafter: 'IAS 1 (revised)') to replace the 2005 version of IAS 1 for annual periods beginning on or after 1 January 2009. The revisions to the standard form part of a larger project being undertaken jointly by the IASB and the FASB. This project seeks to establish a common, high quality standard for presenting information in the financial statements, including the classification and display of line items and the aggregation of line items into subtotals and totals. IAS 1 (revised) is the first phase of the project and its requirements on the presentation of the statement of comprehensive income are similar to those of FASB Statement No. 130 – *Reporting Comprehensive Income*. In this chapter, references to IAS 1 are to the revised version of IAS 1.

The IASB *Framework* defines the objective of financial statements and this definition is repeated in IAS 1 (revised) para 9: '[. . .] The objective of financial statements is to provide information about the financial position, financial performance and cash flows of an entity that is useful to a wide range of users in making economic decisions. Financial statements also show the results of the management's stewardship of the resources entrusted to it [. . .]'. This objective is met by providing information on assets, liabilities, equity, income and expenses (including gains and losses), other changes in equity and cash flows. Although financial statements are a historical record and not a forecast, the standard recognises that financial statements have a predictive value in that past performance can be an indicator of likely future performance.

3.2   Components of financial statements

IAS 1 (revised) para 10 states that a complete set of financial statements should comprise:

(a) a statement of financial position as at the end of the period (i.e. balance sheet in the previous version);

(b) a statement of comprehensive income for the period (i.e. income statement in the previous version);

(c) a statement of changes in equity for the period;

(d) a statement of cash flows for the period;

(e) notes, comprising a summary of significant accounting policies and other explanatory information; and

(f) a statement of financial position as at the beginning of the earliest comparative period when an entity applies an accounting policy retrospectively or makes a retrospective restatement of items in its financial statements, or when it reclassifies items in its financial statements.

An entity may use titles for the statements other than those listed above[1].

One of the most significant changes introduced by IAS 1 (revised) is that it requires entities to present a statement of comprehensive income. Entities can choose whether to present this statement as a single statement, or two, presenting an income statement and separate statement, displaying components of other comprehensive income.

3.3   General features of financial statements

IAS 1 (revised) sets out a number of general rules which relate to the presentation of financial statements. Some of these are based upon the principles established in the IASB *Framework* (see Chapter 2). The main areas dealt with in this part of IAS 1 (revised) are:

- fair presentation and compliance with IFRS;
- **going concern** basis and accrual basis of accounting;
- **materiality** and aggregation;
- **offsetting**;
- frequency of reporting;
- comparative information;
- consistency of presentation.

Each of these is considered below with the exception of going concern and accrual basis which have been dealt with in Chapter 2, sections 2.3.3 and 2.3.4.

3.3.1 Fair presentation and compliance with IFRS

Financial statements should present fairly the financial position, financial performance and cash flows of an entity. Fair presentation requires the faithful representation of the effects of transactions, other events and conditions in accordance with the definitions and recognition criteria for assets, liabilities, income and expenses set out in the *Framework*. The application of IFRS, with additional disclosure when necessary, is presumed to result in financial statements that achieve a fair presentation (IAS 1 (revised) para 15).

The requirements of IAS 1 (revised) reflect the qualitative characteristics of financial statements set out in the IASB Framework (see Chapter 2). IAS 1 (revised) states that, in virtually all circumstances, a fair presentation is achieved by compliance with applicable IFRS. A fair presentation also requires an entity:

(a) to select and apply accounting policies in accordance with IAS 8 – *Accounting Policies, Changes in Accounting Estimates and Errors*. IAS 8 sets out a hierarchy of authoritative guidance that management should consider in the absence of an IFRS that specifically applies to an item.

(b) to present information, including accounting policies, in a manner that provides relevant, reliable, comparable and understandable information.

(c) to provide additional disclosures when compliance with the specific requirements in IFRS is insufficient to enable users to understand the impact of particular transactions, other events and conditions on the entity's financial position and financial performance (IAS 1 (revised) para 17).

Under IFRS, there is a basic principle that a fair presentation is achieved if financial statements are prepared in compliance with each applicable standard and interpretation. However, an entity may depart from the specific requirements of an IFRS in the extremely rare circumstances in which management conclude that compliance with the specific requirement would be so misleading that it would conflict with the objective of financial statements set out in the *Framework*, if the relevant regulatory framework requires, or otherwise does not prohibit, such a departure (IAS 1 (revised) para 19). An item is only considered to conflict with this objective if it does not represent faithfully the transactions, other events and conditions it purports to, or could reasonably be expected to, represent. Consequently, a departure from an IFRS will be necessary only when the treatment required by an IFRS is clearly inappropriate and thus a fair presentation cannot be achieved either by applying an IFRS or through additional disclosure alone. Such departures are rare indeed and should be handled with care.

3.3.2 Materiality

IAS 1 (revised) para 29 states that an entity should present separately each material class of similar items and should present separately items of dissimilar nature or function unless they are immaterial.

IAS 1 (revised) para 31 explicitly states that there is no need to satisfy the disclosure requirements of an IFRS if the information disclosed would not be material. This means that compliance with the standards can be achieved without having to disclose immaterial items, whether on the face of the financial statements or in the accompanying notes.

3.3.3 Offsetting

In general, assets and liabilities should be reported separately in the balance sheet and not offset against one another. Similarly, income and expenses should be reported separately in the income statement. IAS 1 (revised) takes the view that offsetting should not be allowed, since this would normally detract from users' ability to understand transactions and other events.

However, this general rule does not apply in a specific instance if another IFRS permits or requires offsetting in that instance: 'An entity should not offset assets and liabilities or income and expenses, unless required or permitted by an IFRS' (IAS 1 (revised) para 32).

An entity should report separately both assets and liabilities, and income and expenses. Offsetting in the financial statements, except when offsetting reflects the substance of the transaction or other event, detracts from the ability of users both to understand the transactions, other events and conditions that have occurred and to assess the entity's future cash flows. Measuring assets net of valuation allowances – for example, obsolescence allowances for inventories and doubtful debts allowances for receivables – is not offsetting (IAS 1 (revised) para 33).

Items that would not be considered to be offsetting of assets and liabilities include:

- accumulated depreciation of property, plant and equipment;
- impairment provisions;
- accumulated **amortisation** of intangible assets;
- allowances for inventory obsolescence;
- allowances for bad debts.

Items that would be considered to be acceptable offsetting of income and expenses include:

- income and related expenses on transactions that do not generate revenue and are incidental to the main revenue-generating activities (where that presentation reflects the substance of the transaction or event);
  - ❐ disposal proceeds and carrying value on disposal of non-current investment and operating assets;
  - ❐ expenditure and related reimbursement under a **contractual** agreement (for example, a supplier's warranty agreement);
- gains and losses arising from a group of similar items:
  - ❐ foreign exchange gains and losses (unless material);
  - ❐ gains and losses arising on **financial instruments** held for trading (unless material);
- releases of provisions against expenses incurred.

Example 3.1

Presentation and calculation of gains arising on the sale of property, plant and equipment

An entity is a manufacturing business. During the period it sells one of its buildings and realises a gain on the sale.

How should management present the gain on sale of the building in the income statement?

Management should present the gain by netting the disposal income with the **carrying amount** of the building and other related expenses. The gain on this transaction should be presented within operating profit (where operating profit is voluntarily disclosed). Proceeds or gains should not be classified as revenue.

Management should aggregate the gain, if appropriate, with amounts of similar nature or function, for instance other gains or losses on sale of other property, plant and equipment. The gain or loss should be presented separately when the size, nature or incidence is such that separate disclosure is required.

3.3.4 Frequency of reporting

An entity should present a complete set of financial statements (including comparative information) at least annually. When an entity changes the end of its reporting period and presents financial statements for a period longer or shorter than one year, it should also disclose:

- the reason for using a longer or shorter period;
- the fact that amounts presented in the financial statements are not entirely comparable (IAS 1 (revised) para 36).

Normally, an entity consistently prepares financial statements for a one-year period. However, for practical reasons, some entities prefer to report, for example, for a 52-week period (IAS 1 (revised) para 37).

3.3.5 Comparative information

Except when IFRS permit or require otherwise, an entity should disclose comparative information in respect of the previous period for all amounts reported in the current period's financial statements. An entity should include comparative information for narrative and descriptive information when it is relevant to an understanding of the current period's financial statements (IAS 1 (revised) para 38).

When an entity changes the presentation or classification of items in its financial statements, the entity should reclassify comparative amounts unless reclassification is impracticable. When the entity reclassifies comparative amounts, the entity should disclose:

(a) the nature of the reclassification;

(b) the amount of each item or class of items that is reclassified; and

(c) the reason for the reclassification (IAS 1 (revised) para 41).

Figure 3.1 is an example of a change in presentation with a change in comparatives.

In addition to these requirements, IAS 1 (revised) requires an entity to present a statement of financial position (or balance sheet) as at the beginning of the earliest comparative period when the entity applies an accounting policy retrospectively or makes a retrospective restatement (that is, when it makes a prior period adjustment) or when it reclassifies items in its financial statements. This statement of financial position should be presented in addition to those at the end of the current period and at the end of the previous period (IAS 1 (revised) para 39). However, as a practical matter, where the retrospective change in accounting policy (or restatement) has no effect on this earliest balance sheet, entities may wish merely to disclose that fact, rather than reproducing the previously presented unchanged balance sheet. The requirement for comparative information for the other primary statements is unchanged.

3.3.6 Consistency of presentation

IFRS require entities to present the financial statements in a consistent manner. IAS 1 (revised) para 45 states that an entity should retain the presentation and classification of items in the financial statements from one period to the next unless:

(a) it is apparent, following a significant change in the nature of the entity's operations or a review of its financial statements, that another presentation or classification would be more appropriate having regard to the criteria for the selection and application of accounting policies referred to in IAS 8; or

(b) an IFRS requires a change in presentation.

Once management have selected a particular presentation, they should use it consistently. Most entities will seldom have good reasons to change their presentation and so they should select carefully the presentation that they wish to adopt when they prepare their first set of financial statements after incorporation or transition to IFRS. Unless a standard or interpretation requires a change in presentation, an entity may only change its presentation if the changed presentation provides reliable and more relevant information; that is, the new presentation should be an improvement on the previous presentation. Just as entities should not change an accounting policy to another equally acceptable, but not improved, accounting policy, they should not change presentation to another equally acceptable, but not improved, presentation. So that comparability is not impaired, entities should only change to a presentation that is likely to continue to be used in future periods (IAS 1 (revised) para 46).

Where an entity changes the presentation or classification of items, the notes to the financial statements should disclose the nature, amount of, and reason for the reclassification. IAS 1 (revised) specifies additional presentation requirements when such changes are made. If an entity does change its presentation, it may incur a considerable amount of extra work, because it will have to restate the corresponding amounts for the previous year in accordance with the new format. In certain

---

Notes (extract)

Presentation of income statement (extract)

The income statement for the year ended 31 December 2005 has been restated following the changes in IFRS that were adopted effective 1 January 2006. In addition the Group has made certain presentational changes to further improve comparability of its results to those of other healthcare companies and to allow readers to make a more accurate assessment of the sustainable earnings capacity of the Group. These changes, which have been applied retrospectively, are listed below.

- Support costs for leased diagnostics instruments are now reported as part of 'Cost of sales' instead of 'Marketing and distribution'. In 2006 these were 114 million Swiss francs (2005: 76 million Swiss francs).

Figure 3.1 Change in presentation

Source: Roche Group Annual Report 2006.

circumstances, it may be impracticable to restate the corresponding amounts, but disclosures are still required in these rare cases.

Figure 3.1 illustrates the disclosure relating to a change of presentation of certain costs in the income statement.

3.4   Structure and content of financial statements

IAS 1 (revised) specifies disclosures required in the statement of financial position or comprehensive income, in the separate income statement (if presented), or in the statement of changes in equity and requires disclosure of other line items either in those statements or in the notes. IAS 7 – *Statement of Cash Flows* sets out requirements for the presentation of cash flow information. This statement is covered in depth in Chapter 16.

Identification of financial statements

An entity should clearly identify the financial statements and distinguish them from other information in the same published document. IFRS apply only to financial statements, and not necessarily to other information presented in an annual report, a regulatory filing, or another document. Therefore, it is important that users can distinguish information that is prepared using IFRS from other information that may be useful to users but is not the subject of those requirements (IAS 1 (revised) paras 49 and 50).

Similarly, it is important that the audited IFRS compliant financial statements are distinguished from unaudited information that may or may not be in compliance with IFRS. The use of non-GAAP measures of performance has been of particular concern to regulators and users, particularly in the USA and the UK. Frequently these measures give a more flattering picture of the entity's financial performance than that determined in accordance with IFRS.

An entity should clearly identify each financial statement and the notes. In addition, an entity should display the following information prominently, and repeat it when necessary for the information presented to be understandable:

(a) the name of the reporting entity or other means of identification, and any change in that information from the end of the preceding reporting period;

(b) whether the financial statements are of an individual entity or a group of entities;

(c) the date of the end of the reporting period or the period covered by the set of financial statements or notes;

(d) the presentation currency, as defined in IAS 21; and

(e) the level of rounding used in presenting amounts in the financial statements (IAS 1 (revised) para 51).

An entity meets the requirements set out above by presenting appropriate headings for pages, statements, notes, columns and the like. Judgement is required in determining the best way of presenting such information (IAS 1 (revised) para 52).

An entity often makes financial statements more understandable by presenting information in thousands or millions of units of the presentation currency. This is acceptable as long as the entity discloses the level of rounding and does not omit material information (IAS 1 (revised) para 53).

3.5 Statement of financial position (or balance sheet)

As a minimum, a statement of financial position should include line items that present the following amounts:

(a) **property, plant and equipment;**

(b) **investment property;**

(c) **intangible assets;**

(d) **financial assets** (excluding amounts shown under (e), (h) and (i));

(e) investments accounted for using the equity method;

(f) biological assets;

(g) **inventories;**

(h) **trade and other receivables;**

(i) **cash** and **cash equivalents;**

(j) the total of assets classified as held for sale and assets included in disposal groups classified as held for sale in accordance with IFRS 5 – *Non-Current Assets Held for Sale and Discontinued Operations*;

(k) **trade and other payables;**

(l) **provisions;**

(m) **financial liabilities** (excluding amounts shown under (k) and (l));

(n) liabilities and assets for current tax, as defined in IAS 12 – *Income Taxes*;

(o) deferred tax liabilities and deferred tax assets, as defined in IAS 12;

(p) liabilities included in disposal groups classified as held for sale in accordance with IFRS 5;

(q) non-controlling interests, presented within equity; and

(r) issued capital and reserves attributable to owners of the parent (IAS 1 (revised) para 54).

3.5.1 Current/non-current distinction

An entity should present current and non-current assets, and current and non-current liabilities, as separate classifications in its statement of financial position (or balance sheet) except when a presentation based on liquidity provides information that is reliable and more relevant. When that exception applies, an entity shall present all assets and liabilities in order of liquidity (IAS 1 (revised) para 60).

When an entity supplies goods or services within a clearly identifiable operating cycle, separate classification of current and non-current assets and liabilities in the statement of financial position provides useful information by distinguishing the net assets that are continuously circulating as working capital from those used in the entity's long-term operations. It also highlights assets that are expected to be realised within the current operating cycle, and liabilities that are due for settlement within the same period (IAS 1 (revised) para 62). The operating cycle of an entity is the time between the acquisition of assets for processing and their realisation in cash or cash equivalents. When an entity's normal operating cycle is not clearly identifiable, it is assumed to be twelve months (IAS 1 (revised) para 68).

Most industrial and retail entities would present a current/non-current classified balance sheet because significant amounts of their assets and liabilities would be realised or settled within a relatively short period. Property developers may be less likely to use a current/non-current classified balance sheet as their assets and liabilities are typically realised or settled over a long period, sometimes over several years. An asset recoverable within the normal operating cycle of more than one year is still a current asset under IAS 1 (revised); similarly, a liability to be settled within the normal operating cycle of more than one year is a current liability. That is, although it is common practice to consider normal operating cycle to be one year or less, the period of one year after balance sheet date is not an inflexible cut-off point for determining the current/non-current status of assets and liabilities.

For some entities, such as financial institutions, a presentation of assets and liabilities in increasing or decreasing order of liquidity provides information that is reliable and more relevant than a current/non-current presentation because the entity does not supply goods or services within a clearly identifiable operating cycle (IAS 1 (revised) para 63).

Whichever method of presentation is adopted (current/non-current classified or a liquidity-based balance sheet), an entity should disclose the amount expected to be recovered or settled after more than 12 months for each asset and liability line item that combines amounts expected to be recovered or settled:

(a) no more than twelve months after the reporting period, and

(b) more than twelve months after the balance sheet date (IAS 1 (revised) para 61).

Information about expected dates of realisation of assets and liabilities is useful in assessing the liquidity and solvency of an entity. IFRS 7 – *Financial Instruments: Disclosures* requires disclosure of the maturity dates of financial assets and financial liabilities. Financial assets include trade and other receivables, and financial liabilities include trade and other payables. Information on the expected date of recovery of non-monetary assets such as inventories and expected date of settlement for liabilities such as provisions is also useful, whether assets and liabilities are classified as current or as non-current. For example, an entity discloses the amount of inventories that are expected to be recovered more than twelve months after the reporting period (IAS 1 (revised) para 65). An example of such disclosures is given in Figure 3.2.

Figure 3.3 shows an example of a current/non-current classified statement of financial position, whilst Figure 3.4 shows an example of a liquidity-based statement of financial position.

6. Trade Receivables

This item consists of the following:

	2008 € million	2007 € million
Trade receivables, gross	427.4	418.2
net of value adjustments	−30.9	−28.6
Trade receivables, net	396.5	389.6

Value adjustments concerning trade receivables developed as follows:

	2008 € million	2007 € million
Status of value adjustments as of January 1	28.6	31.9
Price differences	−0.4	−1.1
Additions	17.7	13.5
Utilization	−10.6	−9.3
Release	−4.4	−6.4
Status of value adjustments December 31	30.9	28.6

2007	Total			Gross values Thereof not value-adjusted					Thereof value-adjusted
		Not due	0–30 days	31–60 days	61–90 days	91–180 days	more than 180 days		
€ million	418.2	307.4	37.0	12.3	4.1	4.6	3.3		49.6

2008	Total			Gross values Thereof not value-adjusted					Thereof value-adjusted
		Not due	0–30 days	31–60 days	61–90 days	91–180 days	more than 180 days		
€ million	427.4	296.9	39.6	16.5	8.1	6.8	7.4		52.2

Withe respect to non-adjusted trade receivables, the Company assumes that the debtors will meet their payment obligations.

Figure 3.2 Current/non-current distinction and disclosure of amounts due after one year

Source: Puma Annual Report 2008.

Consolidated Balance Sheet

	2008 € million	2007 € million
ASSETS		
Cash and cash equivalents	375.0	522.5
Inventories	430.8	373.6
Trade receivables	396.5	389.6
Other current assets	159.8	109.7
Current assets	**1,362.0**	**1,395.3**
Deferred taxes	80.5	77.4
Property, plant and equipment	245.1	194.9
Intangible assets	189.8	180.3
Other non-current assets	21.2	15.0
Non-current assets	**536.6**	**467.7**
Total assets	**1,898.7**	**1,863.0**
LIABILITIES AND SHAREHOLDERS' EQUITY		
Current bank liabilities	49.7	61.3
Trade payables	269.1	234.0
Tax provisions	27.6	18.1
Other current provisions	91.0	79.2
Liabilities from acquisitions	40.0	52.7
Other current liabilities	137.5	157.8
Current liabilities	**614.8**	**603.1**
Deferred taxes	26.5	22.7
Pension provisions	21.3	17.9
Liabilities from acquisitions	53.3	58.6
Other non-current liabilities	5.6	5.9
Non-current liabilities	**106.7**	**105.1**
Subscribed capital	41.0	41.0
Group reserves	174.2	153.9
Retained earnings	1,175.6	986.7
Treasury stock	−216.1	−34.7
Minority interest	2.5	8.0
Shareholders' equity	**1,177.2**	**1,154.8**
Total liabilities and shareholders' equity	**1,898.7**	**1,863.0**

Figure 3.3 Current/non-current classified statement of financial position (or balance sheet)
Source: Puma Annual Report 2008.

Consolidated balance sheet at 31 December 2008

	2008 US$m	2007 US$m
ASSETS		
Cash and balances at central banks	52,396	21,765
Items in the course of collection from other banks	6,003	9,777
Hong Kong Government certificates of indebtedness	15,358	13,893
Trading assets	427,329	445,968
Financial assets designated at fair value	28,533	41,564
Derivatives	494,876	187,854
Loans and advances to banks	153,766	237,366
Loans and advances to customers	932,868	981,548
Financial investments	300,235	283,000
Interests in associates and joint ventures	11,537	10,384
Goodwill and intangible assets	27,357	39,689
Property, plant and equipment	14,025	15,694
Other assets	37,822	39,493
Current tax assets	2,552	896
Deferred tax assets	7,011	5,284
Prepayments and accrued income	15,797	20,091
Total assets	2,527,465	2,354,266
LIABILITIES AND EQUITY		
Liabilities		
Hong Kong currency notes in circulation	15,358	13,893
Deposits by banks	130,084	132,181
Customer accounts	1,115,327	1,096,140
Items in the course of transmission to other banks	7,232	8,672
Trading liabilities	247,652	314,580
Financial liabilities designated at fair value	74,587	89,939
Derivatives	487,060	183,393
Debt securities in issue	179,693	246,579
Retirement benefit liabilities	3,888	2,893
Other liabilities	72,384	35,013
Current tax liabilities	1,822	2,559
Liabilities under insurance contracts	43,683	42.606
Accruals and deferred income	15,448	21,766
Provisions	1,730	1,958
Deferred tax liabilities	1,855	1,859
Subordinated liabilities	29,433	24,819
Total liabilities	2,427,236	2,218,850
Equity		
Called up share capital	6,053	5,915
Share premium account	8,463	8,134
Other equity instruments	2,133	–
Other reserves	(3,747)	33,014
Retained earnings	80,689	81,097
Total shareholders' equity	93,591	128,160
Minority interests	6,638	7,256
Total equity	100,229	135,416
Total equity and liabilities	2,527,465	2,354,266

Figure 3.4 Liquidity-based statement of financial position (or balance sheet)

Source: from HSBC Holdings plc Annual Report 2008, http://www.hsbc.com/1/PA_1_1_S5/content/assets/ investor_relations/hsbc2008ara0.pdf, reproduced with permission from HSBC Holdings plc Annual Report and Accounts 2008.

Current assets

According to IAS 1 (revised) para 66, an entity should classify an asset as current when:

(a) it expects to realise the asset, or intends to sell or consume it, in its normal operating cycle;

(b) it holds the asset primarily for the purpose of trading;

(c) it expects to realise the asset within 12 months after the reporting period; or

(d) the asset is cash or a cash equivalent (as defined by IAS 7; see Chapter 16) unless the asset is restricted from being exchanged or used to settle a liability for at least 12 months after the reporting period.

An entity should classify all other assets as non-current. IAS 1 (revised) uses the term 'non-current' to include tangible, intangible and financial assets of long-term nature. However, it does not prohibit the use of alternative descriptions as long as the meaning is clear (IAS 1 (revised) para 67).

As explained earlier, the operating cycle of an entity is the time between the acquisition of assets for processing and their realisation in cash or cash equivalents. When the entity's normal operating cycle is not clearly identifiable, it is assumed to be 12 months (IAS 1 (revised) para 68).

A current asset is, therefore, not necessarily one that is recoverable within 12 months of the balance sheet date. Where the company's operating cycle is such that inventory or trade receivables are normally not realised in cash within 12 months, they will still be traded as current asset.

Example 3.2

Classification based on normal operating cycle

A company produces aeroplanes. The length of time between first purchasing raw materials to make the planes and the date the company completes the production and delivery is 10 months. The company receives payment for the planes six months after delivery.

(a) How should the company show its inventory and trade receivables in its classified balance sheet?

(b) Would the answer be different if the production time was 14 months and the time between delivery and payment was 15 months?

(a) The time between the first purchase of goods and the realisation of those goods in cash is 16 months (10 months + 6 months). The age of inventory held by the company at the year-end will range between zero months to 10 months, and once the goods are delivered, it will take a further six months to receive payment. All of the inventory should be classified as a current asset, even though some of the inventory will not be realised in cash within 12 months of the balance sheet date. This is because the inventory is realised in the entity's normal operating cycle, as envisaged by IAS 1 (revised). However, the expected date of recovery of the inventory should be disclosed by the company. The trade receivables will be realised in cash within 12 months of the balance sheet date and should, therefore, be included as a current asset.

(b) No, the inventory and the trade receivables should still be classified as a current asset. In this case, the inventory is, on average, older but nevertheless it is realised in cash in the entity's normal operating cycle. Similarly, the trade receivables are realised in cash as part of the operating cycle and should be classified as a current asset, even though they will not be realised in cash within 12 months of the balance sheet date. In addition to disclosing the maturity date of the trade receivables, a financial asset, will require disclosure under IFRS 7 – *Financial Instruments: Disclosures*.

Current liabilities

An entity should classify a liability as current when:

(a) it expects to settle the liability in its normal operating cycle;

(b) it holds the liability primarily for the purpose of trading;

(c) the liability is due to be settled within twelve months after the reporting period; or

(d) the entity does not have an unconditional right to defer settlement of the liability for at least 12 months after the reporting period.

An entity should classify all other liabilities as non-current (IAS 1 (revised) para 69).

Some current liabilities, such as trade payables and some accruals for employee and other operating costs, are part of the **working capital** used in the entity's normal operating cycle. An entity should classify such operating items as current liabilities even if they are due to be settled more than 12 months after the balance sheet date. The same normal operating cycle applies to the classification of an entity's assets and liabilities. When an entity's normal operating cycle is not clearly identifiable, it is assumed to be 12 months (IAS 1 (revised) para 70).

An entity should classify its financial liabilities as current when they are due to be settled within 12 months after the reporting period, even if:

(a) the original term was for a period longer than 12 months, and

(b) an agreement to refinance, or to reschedule payments, on a long-term basis is completed after the reporting period and before the financial statements are authorised for issue (IAS 1 (revised) para 72).

If an entity expects, and has the discretion, to refinance or roll over an obligation for at least 12 months after the balance sheet date under an existing loan facility, it should classify the obligation as non-current, even if it would otherwise be due within a shorter period. However, when refinancing or rolling over the obligation is not at the discretion of the entity (for example, there is no arrangement for refinancing), the entity should not consider the potential to refinance the obligation as current (IAS 1 (revised) para 73).

Example 3.3

Classification of bank debt

An entity has entered into a facility arrangement with a bank. It has a committed facility that the bank cannot cancel unilaterally and the scheduled maturity of this facility is three years from the balance sheet date. The entity has drawn down funds on this facility and these funds are due to be repaid six months after the balance sheet date. The entity intends to roll over this debt through the three year facility arrangements.

How should this borrowing be shown in the company's balance sheet?

Would the answer be different if the facility and existing loan were with different banks?

The borrowing should be shown as non-current. Although the loan is due for repayment within six months of the balance sheet date, the entity is entitled to roll over this borrowing into a 'new loan'. The substance is, therefore, that the debt is not repayable until three years after the balance sheet date when the committed facility expires.

The position would be different if the facility and loan were with different banks. In that case the entity would have a loan repayable in six months, but would be entitled to take out a new loan to settle its existing debt. These two loans are separate and the new loan is not, either in substance or in fact, an extension of the existing loan. The existing loan would, therefore, be shown as current in the entity's balance sheet.

It is common practice for financial institutions to include borrowing covenants in the terms of loans. Under these borrowing covenants a loan, which would otherwise be long-term in nature, becomes immediately repayable if certain items relating to the borrower's financial condition are breached. Typically, these items are measures of liquidity or solvency based on ratios derived from the entity's financial statements.

When an entity breaches a provision of a long-term loan arrangement on or before the end of the reporting period with the effect that the liability becomes payable on demand, it classifies the liability as current even if the lender agreed, after the reporting period and before the authorisation of the financial statements for issue, not to demand payment as a consequence of the breach. An entity classifies the liability as current because, at the end of the reporting period, it does not have an unconditional right to defer its settlement for at least 12 months after that date (IAS 1 (revised) para 74). An example of disclosure of a breach of covenant disclosed in an interim report and events subsequent to the interim reporting date is given in Figure 3.5.

An entity classifies the liability as non-current if the lender agreed by the end of the reporting period to provide a period of grace ending at least 12 months after the reporting period, within which the entity can rectify the breach and during which the lender cannot demand immediate repayment (IAS 1 (revised) para 75). In respect of loans classified as current liabilities, if the following events occur between

14. Bank overdrafts and loans

	Six months ended 31st October 2005	Six months ended 31st October 2004	Year ended 30th April 2005
	£'m	£'m	£'m
Bank overdrafts	0.6	5.6	2.0
Bank loans	224.8	222.8	210.6
	225.4	228.4	212.6
Repayable: On demand or within one year	225.4		
In the second year	–	97.8	94
In the third year	–	16.2	15.6
In the fourth year	–	16.2	15.6
In the fifth year	–	82.4	75
	225.4	228.4	212.6
Less: Amount due for settlement within 12 months (shown under current liabilities)	(225.4)	(15.8)	(12.4)
Amounts due for settlement after more than 12 months		212.6	200.2

The Group's principal source of debt at 31st October 2005 was a multi-currency syndicated bank loan ('the Facilities') entered into with a group of seven banks in May 2004 in connection with the Group's offer for BWT. The Facilities comprised three tranches: a US$75 million revolving credit facility; a term loan of up to US$75 million and a US$ 100 million revolving credit facility. The Facilities were repayable between May 2006 and May 2009. The Facilities were unsecured and initially carried interest at a margin of 1.5% over LIBOR (or EURIBOR for amounts advanced in Euros), plus mandatory costs. The applicable margin was variable (ranging from a minimum of 0.875% up to a maximum of 1.75%) according to the ratio of consolidated net borrowings to EBITDA.

The Facilities were subject to three financial covenants, which were tested quarterly. On 17th August 2005, First Technology PLC informed its bankers that it had failed to meet one of these covenants with respect to the test for the period ended 26th July 2005. As a result of the covenant breach, the Facilities technically became repayable on demand.

On 12th December 2005, the Group signed an agreement for a new bank loan ('the new Facility') with its two principal bankers, HSBC Bank plc and The Royal Bank of Scotland plc, the proceeds of which are being used to repay the existing Facilities. The new Facility comprises two tranches: a US$80 million revolving credit facility and a US$140 million term loan, each available until December 2006. Both tranches, under certain circumstances can be extended at the Company's option for a further twelve months to December 2007. The new Facility carries interest at a margin of 1.5% over LIBOR, plus mandatory costs. The new Facility is unsecured, although certain of First Technology PLC's wholly-owned subsidiaries have given guarantees with respect to First Technology PLC's obligations under the agreement. However, in the event

Figure 3.5 Breach of covenant resulting in loans restated as current at period end, post balance sheet refinancing

Source: First Technology plc, Interim report, 31 October 2005.

that the offer-announced on 19th December, or any other offer, for the entire issued share capital of the Company does not become wholly unconditional or that the Company has not completed an equity issue raising proceeds of at least £40 million and used such amount to repay the new Facility, the Company will be required to give security by 30th September 2006. Any net proceeds of an equity issue must be applied to repay the new Facility. If the amount prepaid is more than £40 million, the Company has the option to extend the new Facility for an additional one year term. Under all circumstances, the Company retains the flexibility to re-finance this new Facility.

In July 2004, First Technology PLC entered into an interest rate swap lo fix the rate of interest that it would pay under the US$75 million term loan tranche of the syndicated loan. The interest rate swap fixed for the whole term the rate of interest at 3.605% plus the applicable margin for this element of the Group's debt. This swap is now being used to fix the rate of interest payable under a proportion of the new Facility.

Figure 3.5 (*Cont'd*)

the end of the reporting period and the date the financial statements are authorised for issue, those events are disclosed as non-adjusting events:

(a) refinancing on a long-term basis;

(b) rectification of a breach of a long-term loan arrangement; and

(c) granting by the lender of a period of grace to rectify a breach of a long-term loan arrangement ending at least 12 months after the reporting period (IAS 1 (revised) para 76).

The key to this approach is that the presentation of the loan is dictated by the condition of that loan at the balance sheet date. Events after the balance sheet date may give evidence of that condition but they do not change it. This is consistent with IAS 10 – *Events after the Reporting Period*.

The standard approach to breaches of borrowing covenants should focus on the legal rights of an entity, but in dealing with situations where an entity has the discretion to roll over or refinance loans, the entity's expectations on the timing of settlement also play a part in deciding the liability's classification. The liability's classification is, however, unaffected by the entity's intentions in the case of a breach of a loan agreement. If the entity breaches the loan agreement before the balance sheet date and the lender grants a period of grace of more than 12 months from the balance sheet date, then the loan may be classified as non-current.

Although post balance sheet events may not alter the classification of a liability, they may require disclosure as a **non-adjusting event**, as we will see in Chapter 4.

3.5.2 Format of the statement of financial position (or balance sheet)

Although IAS 1 does not prescribe a format for the balance sheet, the implementation guidance which accompanies (but is not part of) the standard includes an illustration which shows one way in which a balance sheet may be presented. A slightly simplified version of this illustration is shown in Table 3.1, below. This illustrative format is not prescriptive and other formats may be used if appropriate.

Table 3.1 Illustrative format of the statement of financial position (or balance sheet)

XYZ Group – Statement of financial position as at 31 December 20X9 (in thousands of euro)		
	20X9	*20X8*
ASSETS		
Non-current assets		
Property, plant and equipment	X	X
Goodwill	X	X
Other intangible assets	X	X
Investments in associates	X	X
Available-for-sale investments	X	X
Total non-current assets	X	X
Current assets		
Inventories	X	X
Trade receivables	X	X
Other current assets	X	X
Cash and cash equivalents	X	X
Total current assets		
Total assets	X	X
EQUITY AND LIABILITIES		
Equity attributable to owners of the parent		
Share capital	X	X
Retained earnings	X	X
Other components of equity	X	X
	X	X
Minority interest	X	X
Total equity	X	X
Non-current liabilities		
Long-term borrowings	X	X
Deferred tax	X	X
Long-term provisions	X	X
Total non-current liabilities	X	X
Current liabilities		
Trade and other payables	X	X
Short-term borrowings	X	X
Current portion of long-term borrowings	X	X
Current tax payable	X	X
Short-term provisions	X	X
Total current liabilities	X	X
Total liabilities	X	X
Total equity and liabilities	X	X

Source: IAS 1 (revised) IG6.

In €m	2008	2007
Traffic revenue	19,998	17,568
Other revenue	4,872	4,852
Total revenue	**24,870**	**22,420**
Changes in inventories and work performed by the enterprise and capitalised	178	119
Other operating income	1,969	1,571
Cost of materials and services	−13,707	−11,553
Staff costs	−5,692	−5,498
Depreciation, amortisation and impairment	−1,289	−1,204
Other operating expenses	−4,946	−4,269
Profit from operating activities	**+1,383**	**+1,586**
Result of equity investments accounted for using the equity method	−22	+223
Result from other equity investments	+42	+131
Interest income	202	177
Interest expense	−374	−371
Other financial items	−427	−133
Financial result	**−579**	**+27**
Profit before income taxes	**+804**	**+1,613**
Income taxes	−195	−356
Profit from continuing operations	**+609**	**+1,257**
Profit from the discontinued Leisure Travel segment	**–**	**+503**
Profit after income taxes	**+609**	**+1,760**
Minority interests	−10	−105
Net profit attributable to shareholders of Lufthansa AG	**+599**	**+1,655**

Figure 3.6(a) Example of an income statement presenting expenses by nature
Source: Lufthansa Annual Report 2008.

An entity classifying expenses by function should disclose additional information on the nature of expenses, including depreciation and amortisation expense and employee benefits expense (IAS 1 (revised) para 104).

The choice between the function of expense method and the nature of expense method depends on historical and industry factors and the nature of the entity. Both methods provide an indication of those costs that might vary, directly or indirectly, with the level of sales or production of the entity. Because each method of presentation has merit for different types of entities, management should select the presentation that is reliable and more relevant. However, because information on the nature of expenses is useful in predicting future cash flows, additional disclosure is required when the function of expense classification is used (IAS 1 (revised) para 105).

DKK million	2008	2007	2006
Sales	45,553	41,831	38,743
Cost of goods sold	10,109	9,793	9,585
Gross profit	35,444	32,038	29,158
Sales and distribution costs	12,866	12,371	11,608
Research and development costs	7,856	8,538	6,316
– hereof costs related to discontinuation of all pulmonary diabetes projects	(325)	(1,325)	–
Administrative expenses	2,635	2,508	2,387
Licence fees and other operating income (net)	286	321	272
Operating profit	12,373	8,942	9,119
Share of profit/(loss) in associated companies	(124)	1,233	(260)
Financial income	1,127	1,303	931
Financial expenses	681	507	626
Profit before income taxes	12,695	10,971	9,164
Income taxes	3,050	2,449	2,712
Net profit	9,645	8,522	6,452

Figure 3.6(b) Example of an income statement presenting expenses by function
Source: Novo Nordisk Annual Report 2008.

Example of income statements based on the 'nature of expense' and 'function of expense' methods are shown in Figure 3.6(a) and Figure 3.6(b).

Example 3.4

Mix of expenses by function and nature

Entity A has five subsidiaries, the largest of which, entity B, represents 40 per cent of the group's results. Entity B represents a separate business segment. All entities in the group present a functional analysis of expenses in their separate financial statements prepared in accordance with IFRS, except entity B, which uses the 'nature of expense' method.

As a functional analysis of entity B's expenses has not been prepared, entity A's management would like to present the consolidated income statement on a split-method basis: entity B's results will be presented using the 'nature of expense' method, whereas the rest of the group's results will be presented on a functional basis. Entity A's management argue that because entity B's business is from a different segment and, therefore, non-comparable with the rest of the group, the use of a different presentation basis should be acceptable.

Can management mix different analysis of expenses in the group's income statement?

No, management should not adopt a mix of the two types of analysis in the group's financial statements. Management should choose the classification of expenses, by nature or by function, most appropriate for the consolidated financial statements. The results of all entities within the group should be prepared on the chosen basis, which will require part of the group to prepare, for consolidation purposes, additional analysis to that used in their separate financial statements so that the aggregate disclosures in the consolidated financial statements are presented on a consistent basis.

3.6.2 Classification of expenses: examples

Cost of sales will normally include:

- opening (less closing) inventories;
- direct materials;
- other external charges (such as the hire of plant and machinery or the cost of casual labour used in the productive process);
- direct labour;
- all direct production overheads, including depreciation and indirect overheads that can reasonably be allocated to the production function;
- amortisation of development expenditure previously capitalised as an intangible asset;
- cash discounts received on 'cost of sales' expenditure (that is not an offsetting, but an effective reduction in the purchase price of an item);
- inventory write-downs.

Distribution costs are generally interpreted more widely than the name suggests and often include selling and marketing costs. Items normally included in this caption comprise:

- payroll costs of the sales, marketing and distribution functions
- advertising;
- salespersons' travel and entertaining;
- warehouse costs for finished goods;
- transport costs arising on the distribution of finished goods;
- all costs of maintaining sales outlets;
- agents' commission payable.

Administrative expenses will normally include:

- the cost of general management;
- all costs of maintaining administration buildings;

- bad debts;
- professional costs.

In some specific instances, the above analyses may not be appropriate. For example, in the context of a mail order company, agents' commission payable may be regarded as a cost of sale rather than as a distribution cost.

The way in which an entity analyses its costs will depend on the nature of its business. Where an entity incurs significant operating expenses that it considers do not fall under any one of the headings 'cost of sales', 'distribution costs' and 'administrative expenses', there is nothing to prevent the company including an additional item for these expenses, provided that it does not mix the two classification methods (by nature and by function).

Other income (or *other expenses*, as appropriate) will normally include:

- interest income on investments;
- lessor's finance income on finance leases;
- dividend income;
- fair value gains and losses on financial assets at fair value through income statement;
- gains and losses on trading derivatives;
- licence fees.

Finance costs will normally include:

- interest payable on bank overdrafts and current and non-current borrowings (IFRS 7 para 20);
- unwinding of discounts on financial liabilities (IAS 37 para 60);
- finance charges in respect of finance leases (IAS 17 para 25);
- dividends on preference shares classified as debt (IAS 32 paras 35 and 40);
- amortisation of discounts and premiums on debt instruments that are liabilities (IAS 39 paras 9 and 47);
- foreign exchange differences on foreign currency borrowings;
- changes in the fair value of certain derivative financial instruments;
- interest on tax payable where the interest element can be identified separately.

Finance income should not be netted against finance costs. This does not preclude an entity from presenting finance revenue followed by finance costs and a subtotal (for example, 'net finance costs') on the face of the income statement. However, where earning interest income is part of the entity's main business objectives, rather than an incidental benefit, that interest income should be included within the main 'revenue' heading. For example, a retailer who, as a principal business objective, earns interest income from offering extended credit arrangements should include this interest income in 'revenue'. Similarly, a diversified conglomerate which has a financing business should include its finance revenue in the main 'revenue' heading. *Finance revenue* normally includes items such as:

- interest income on cash and cash equivalents;
- unwinding of discounts on financial assets.

3.6.3 A note on operating profit, EBIT and EBITDA

Under IAS 1 (revised), it is not mandatory to disclose results from operating activities. The IASB decided against requiring disclosure of 'operating profit' because 'operating profit' is not defined in the standard. However, entities are not prohibited from disclosing operating profit, or a similar line item.

An entity should not present any items of income or expense as extraordinary items, in the statement of comprehensive income or the separate income statement (if presented), or in the notes (IAS 1 (revised) para 87).

As with the balance sheet additional line items, headings and subtotals should be shown on the face of the statement of comprehensive income and the separate income statement when such presentation is relevant to understanding the entity's financial performance (IAS 1 (revised) para 85). Management should exercise judgement in determining whether additional line items or subtotals are necessary.

As discussed above, where operating profit is disclosed, it should include all operating items. Earnings before interest and tax (EBIT) may be an appropriate sub-heading in the income statement. This line item usually distinguishes between the pre-tax

Consolidated Income Statement

	2008 € million	2007 € million
Sales	2,524.2	2,373.5
Cost of sales	1,217.6	1,131.8
Gross profit	1,306.6	1,241.7
Royalty and commission income	25.7	35.6
	1,332.4	1,277.2
Other operating income and expenses	1,007.0	905.2
EBIT	325.4	372.0
Financial result	1.1	10.5
EBT	326.4	382.5
Taxes on income	94.8	110.9
Net earnings before attribution	231.6	271.6
attributable to: Minorities	−1.1	2.6
Equity holders of the parent (net earnings)	232.8	269.0
Earnings per share (€)	15.15	16.80
Earnings per share (€) – diluted	15.15	16.78
Weighted average shares outstanding	15.360	16.018
Weighted average shares outstanding, diluted	15.360	16.031

Figure 3.7 Earnings before interest and tax (EBIT) (function of expense method)

Source: Puma Annual Report 2008.

Table 3.3 Earnings before interest, taxes, depreciation and amortisation (EBITDA) (nature of expense method)

XYZ plc – income statement for the year ended 31 December 20X9		
	20X9 *€000*	*20X8* *€000*
Revenue	xxx	xxx
Other income	xxx	xxx
Changes in inventories of finished goods and work in progress	(xxx)	xxx
Work performed by the entity and capitalised	xxx	xxx
Raw material and consumables used	(xxx)	(xxx)
Employee benefits expense	(xxx)	(xxx)
Other expenses	(xxx)	(xxx)
Earnings before interest, taxes, depreciation and amortisation (EBITDA)	xxx	xxx
Depreciation of property, plant and equipment	(xxx)	(xxx)
Amortisation of intangible assets	(xxx)	(xxx)
Operating profit	xxx	xxx
Finance costs	(xxx)	(xxx)
Share of profit of associates	xxx	xxx
Profit before tax	xxx	xxx
Tax expense	(xxx)	(xxx)
Net profit for the year	xxx	xxx

profits arising from operating items and those arising from financing activities. Puma, for example, uses EBIT as a sub-heading (see Figure 3.7).

Earnings before interest, tax, depreciation and amortisation (EBITDA) is a measure that many financial analysts use. When permitted by local practice and not otherwise prohibited by applicable regulation, some entities disclose EBITDA in their income statements. EBITDA is sometimes disclosed as a footnote to the income statement. Where an entity presents its expenses by nature, it would be possible for EBITDA to be presented as a sub-total within the income statement. The presentation of EBITDA within the income statement can be more problematic when an entity presents its expenses by function as in that case 'cost of sales' and 'distribution expenses', for example, could both include depreciation.

Table 3.3 above shows the presentation of EBITDA on the face of the income statement for an entity presenting its expenses by nature.

3.6.4 Other comprehensive income for the period

As discussed earlier, an entity should present its income and expense items for a period in a single statement of comprehensive income or in two statements (i.e. an income statement and a statement of comprehensive income which begins with profit or loss from the income statement and then lists other comprehensive income, such as revaluation gains) (IAS 1 (revised) para 81). Table 3.4 below

Table 3.4 Statement of comprehensive income

XYZ plc – Statement of comprehensive income for the year ended 31 December 20X9		
	20X9 €000	20X8 €000
Revenue	xxx	xxx
Cost of sales	(xxx)	(xxx)
Gross profit	xxx	xxx
Other income	xxx	xxx
Distribution costs	(xxx)	(xxx)
Administrative expenses	(xxx)	(xxx)
Other expenses	(xxx)	(xxx)
Finance costs	(xxx)	(xxx)
Net profit before tax	xxx	xxx
Tax expense	(xxx)	(xxx)
Net profit for the year	xxx	xxx
Other comprehensive income:		
Gain/(loss) on property revaluation	(xxx)	xxx
Gain/(loss) on available-for-sale investments	xxx	(xxx)
Other comprehensive income for the year	xxx	xxx
Total comprehensive income for the year	xxx	xxx

Source: based on IAS 1 (revised) IG6.

illustrates a statement of comprehensive income in one single statement and the classification of expenses by function.

3.7   Statement of changes in equity

A statement of changes in equity shows how each component of equity has changed during an accounting period.

An entity should present a statement of changes in equity showing:

(a) total comprehensive income for the period, showing separately the total amounts attributable to owners of the parent and to non-controlling interests;

(b) for each component of equity, the effects of retrospective application or retrospective restatement recognised in accordance with IAS 8 (see Chapter 4);

(c) for each component of equity, a reconciliation between the carrying amount at the beginning and the end of the period, separately disclosing changes resulting from:

(i)   profit or loss;

(ii) each item of other comprehensive income;

Table 3.5 Statement of changes in equity

XYZ plc – Statement of changes in equity for the year ended 31 December 20X9				
	Share capital *€000*	*Other reserves* *€000*	*Retained earnings* *€000*	*Total equity* *€000*
Balance at 31 December 20X8	xxx	xxx	xxx	xxx
Changes in accounting policy			xxx	xxx
Restated balance	xxx	xxx	xxx	xxx
Change in equity for the year				
Total comprehensive income		xxx	xxx	xxx
Dividends			(xxx)	(xxx)
Issue of share capital	xxx			xxx
Total changes in equity	xxx	xxx	xxx	xxx
Balance at 31 December 20X9	xxx	xxx	xxx	xxx

Source: based on IAS 1 (revised) IG6.

(iii) transactions with owners (e.g. share issue and dividends) (IAS 1 (revised) para 106).

A statement of changes in equity which complies with the revised version of IAS 1 is illustrated in Table 3.5.

An entity should present, either in the statement of changes in equity or in the notes, the amount of dividends recognised as distributions to owners during the period, and the related amount per share (IAS 1 (revised) para 107).

Changes in an entity's equity between the beginning and the end of the reporting period reflect the increase or decrease in its net assets during the period. Except for changes resulting from transactions with owners in their capacity as owners (such as equity contributions, reacquisitions of the entity's own equity instruments and dividends) and transaction costs directly related to such transactions, the overall change in equity during a period represents the total amount of income and expense, including gains and losses, generated by the entity's activities during that period (IAS 1 (revised) para 109).

3.8 Notes to financial statements

Notes which accompany the financial statements (statement of financial position, statement of comprehensive income, statement of cash flows and statement of changes in equity) are an integral part of the financial statements. IAS 1 (revised) para 112 states that the notes should:

- provide information about the basis of preparation of the financial statements and the **accounting policies** which have been used, including:
  - ❐ the measurement bases used in preparing the financial statements;
  - ❐ other accounting policies used that are relevant to an understanding of the financial statements;

- disclose information as required by IFRS to the extent that this is not presented elsewhere in the financial statements;

- provide any additional information which is relevant to an understanding of any of the financial statements.

The notes should be presented in a systematic manner and should be cross-referenced to the four primary financial statements. The notes which normally should begin with a statement of compliance with IFRS, should have a summary of significant accounting policies, followed by supporting information for line items presented in the four primary statements and further disclosures as necessary (IAS 1 (revised) paras 113 and 114).

3.9   Interim financial reporting (IAS 34)

IAS 34 – *Interim Financial Reporting* applies if an entity publishes an interim financial report that is stated to comply with IFRS. An interim financial report is a financial report containing either a complete set of financial statements or a set of condensed financial statements for an interim period. An interim period is a period which is less than a full financial year.

IFRS do not actually require entities to publish interim financial reports. But entities whose shares are publicly traded are generally required to do so by local legislation or stock exchanges. Interim financial reports may be presented quarterly or half-yearly in addition to the main annual report. Interim financial reports that are stated to comply with international standards should satisfy the requirements of IAS 34. These requirements are summarised below:

- An interim financial report may consist of a complete set of financial statements as prescribed by IAS 1 (revised). Alternatively, an entity may provide a condensed set of financial statements consisting of:

  - a condensed statement of financial position;
  - a condensed statement of comprehensive income;
  - a condensed statement of changes in equity;
  - a condensed statement of cash flows;
  - selected explanatory notes.

  These condensed financial statements should include, at a minimum, each of the headings and subtotals that are included in the entity's most recent annual financial statements. Additional items should be presented if their omission would make the condensed statements misleading. The term 'headings and subtotals' is not defined in IAS 34 and so is open to interpretation. In practice, condensed financial statements tend to follow the same format as complete financial statements, so that the 'condensed' nature of the statements is confined largely to notes.

- Basic and diluted earnings per share should be presented on the face of the income statement, whether complete or condensed.

- The main explanatory notes which should be provided (if the information concerned is material and is not disclosed elsewhere in the interim report) include:

  - ❑ a statement that the same accounting policies have been used in the interim financial statements as in the recent annual statements, or a description of the nature and effect of any changes in policy;
  - ❑ explanatory comments about the seasonality of the entity's operations;
  - ❑ the nature and amount of any unusual items;
  - ❑ the nature and amount of any changes made to estimates from previous periods, if these have a material effect on the interim financial statements;
  - ❑ issues and repayments of debt securities (e.g. loan stock) or shares;
  - ❑ dividends paid;
  - ❑ certain **segment** information;
  - ❑ any material events that have occurred subsequent to the end of the interim period;
  - ❑ any changes to the composition of the entity during the interim period, including business combinations;
  - ❑ any changes in **contingent assets** or **contingent liabilities** since the last annual balance sheet date.

  The entity should also disclose any further transactions or events that are material to an understanding of the interim period.

Summary

- IAS 1 (revised) – *Presentation of Financial Statements* defines a complete set of financial statements as consisting of a statement of financial position (or balance sheet), a statement of comprehensive income (or income statement), a statement of changes in equity, a statement of cash flows and a set of notes.

- The effects of transactions and other items should be faithfully represented in the financial statements. The application of international standards will normally ensure that this is the case.

- Financial statements should be prepared on a going concern basis and on an accruals basis.

- The way in which items are presented and classified in the financial statements should generally be consistent from one accounting period to the next. Comparative information should normally be disclosed in respect of the previous period for all amounts reported in the financial statements.

- Financial statements should be clearly identified as such and each statement should be clearly labelled. Financial statements should normally be presented at least annually.

- In general, current and non-current assets and current and non-current liabilities should be shown separately in the statement of financial position.

- IAS 1 lists the main line items that should be presented in the statement of comprehensive income and requires an analysis of expenses (by nature or by function) to be shown on the face of the income statement or in the notes.

- A statement of changes in equity shows the changes in each component of equity during an accounting period and provides detailed information about transactions between the entity and its owners.

- IAS 1 does not require any particular format for the financial statements but does provide illustrative examples.

- Notes to the financial statements provide information about measurement bases and accounting policies, together with supporting information for line items in the main financial statements and further information required by IFRS or which is relevant to an understanding of the financial statements.

- IAS 34 – *Interim Financial Reporting* prescribes the minimum content of an interim financial report (if one is published) but does not require entities to publish such a report. Interim financial reports are generally required for listed companies by local legislators or stock exchange regulation.

Research and references

The IASB documents relevant for this chapter are:

- IAS 1 (revised) – *Presentation of Financial Statements*, September 2007.
- *Framework for the Preparation and Presentation of Financial Statements*, 1989.
- IAS 34 – *Interim Financial Reporting*.

The following are examples of books, research and discussion papers that take the issues of this chapter further:

- Alexander, D., Britton, A. and Jorissen, A. (2007) *International Financial Reporting and Analysis,* 3rd edn. Thomson, Chapters 9 and 10.
- Elliott, B. and Elliott, J. (2009) *Financial Accounting and Reporting,* 13th edn. Financial Times-Prentice Hall, Chapters 8 and 9.
- Epstein, B.J. and Jermakowicz, E.K. (2009) *IFRS 2009: Interpretation and Application of International Accounting and Financial Reporting Standards.* Wiley.
- European Financial Reporting Advisory Group (EFRAG) and Instituto de Contabilidad y Auditoría de Cuentas (2006) *The Performance Reporting Debate – What (If Anything) Is Wrong with the Good Old Income Statement?*, November (available on www.efrag.org).
- PricewaterhouseCoopers (2009) *IFRS Manual of Accounting – 2010. Global Guide to International Financial Reporting Standards.* CCH, Chapter 4.
- Stolowy, H. and Lebas, M.J. (2006) *Corporate Financial Reporting. A Global Perspective,* 2nd edn. Thomson, September, Chapter 3.
- Sutton, T. (2004) *Corporate Financial Accounting and Reporting,* 2nd edn. Financial Times-Prentice Hall, Part I.

Discussion questions and exercises

3.1 IAS 1 requirements

(a) IAS 1 (revised) lists six 'overall considerations' relating to the presentation of financial statements. Explain the main requirements of IAS 1 in relation to three of them.

(b) Explain the purpose of a statement of changes in equity and list the main items that should be shown in this statement.

(c) List the main types of information which should be provided in the notes which accompany and form an integral part of the financial statements.

3.2 Classification of assets and liabilities

(a) Distinguish between current assets and non-current assets.

(b) Distinguish between current liabilities and non-current liabilities.

(c) Explain why these distinctions are useful.

(d) A parent provides a loan to a subsidiary. Interest of 8 per cent is paid annually. The loan is repayable on demand. How should the loan be classified in the parent's balance sheet?

(e) A subsidiary holds cash and cash equivalent balances with domestic banks. It operates in a country where the host government has the power to prevent or restrict the remittance of cash abroad to fellow subsidiaries and to the parent. The amount of cash held is neither excessive nor short of the subsidary's operating needs. How should the subsidiary's cash and cash equivalent balances be classified in the group's consolidated balance sheet?

3.3 Statement of comprehensive income

The trial balance of Sabrina plc includes the following accounts as at 30 September 2010:

- Sales revenue   €2,400,000
- Interest income   €48,000
- Gain on disposal of PPE   €10,000
- Valuation gain on trading investments   €40,000
- Dividends revenue   €10,000
- Cost of sales   €1,680,000
- Interest expense   €36,000
- Selling, distribution and administrative expenses   €222,000
- Tax expense   €170,000

Additional information:

- The loss on valuation of available-for-sale investments recognised directly in equity was EUR 2,000 net of taxes.
- Sabrina plc uses the single statement format for the statement of comprehensive income.

Assume you are the accountant of Sabrina plc, responsible for the preparation of the statement of comprehensive income of the company for the year ended 30 September 2010. The company classifies expenses by function.

Prepare the statement of comprehensive income of Sabrina plc, showing the analysis of expenses in the statement of comprehensive income.

3.4   Statement of changes in equity

The equity section of the statement of financial position of Lorenzo plc as at 30 September 2010 is as follows (amounts in thousands of euro):

	2010	2009
Share capital	400	320
Retained earnings	340	320
Revaluation reserve	148	120
Other reserves	100	80
Total equity	988	840

Additional information:

- Lorenzo plc issued 16,000 shares at EUR 5 each on 31 August 2010 for cash.
- A transfer of EUR 20,000 was made from retained earnings to other reserves.
- Comprehensive income for the year ended 30 September 2010 was EUR 288,000, including a revaluation gain of EUR 28,000 net of tax.
- Dividends for the year comprised interim dividends of EUR 100,000 and final dividends provided for EUR 120,000.

Prepare the statement of changes in equity of Lorenzo plc for the year ended 30 September 2010 in accordance with IAS 1 (revised).

3.5   Preparation of financial statements

The data given below are available for ABC SpA for the year ended 31 December 2009.

Trial balance of ABC SpA as at 31 December 2009 (amounts in thousands of euro)

	Dr	Cr
Interest expense on bank overdraft	2,300	
Bank overdraft		17,250
Cash in hand	9,200	
Long-term loans		126,500
Trade and other receivables	57,500	
Accumulated depreciation on equipment		6,900
Accumulated depreciation on motor vehicles		18,400
Directors' remuneration	2,300	
Dividends	3,450	
Equipment	29,900	
Audit fees	2,300	
Land	115,000	
Buildings	115,000	
Hire charges	600	
Interest on long-term loans	12,650	
Share capital		34,500
Lighting and power	1,840	
Miscellaneous expense	550	
Motor expenses	18,400	
Motor vehicles	41,400	
Postage, telephone, courier	3,680	
Retained earnings		115,000
Provision for income taxes		11,500
Purchases	517,500	
Insurance	6,900	
Repairs and maintenance	5,520	
Salaries and wages	36,110	
Income tax	11,500	
Sales		690,000
Inventory at 1 January 2009	86,250	
Trade and other payables		59,800
	1,079,850	1,079,850

The following information has not yet been taken into account in the amounts shown in the trial balance:

- *Inventory* at cost at 31 December 2009 was EUR 45,750,000. Inventory of certain items at net realisable value (NRV) at 31 December 2009 was EUR 6m. The cost of this inventory was EUR 8m.
- *Depreciation* is to be provided as follows:
  2 per cent on buildings using the straight-line method
  10 per cent on equipment using the reducing balance method
  25 per cent on motor vehicles using the reducing balance method
- EUR 4,600,000 was prepaid for repairs and EUR 10,350,000 was payable for wages at 31 December 2009.

Help the financial controller to prepare a statement of comprehensive income for 2009 and a statement of financial position as at 31 December 2009 according to IAS 1 (revised).

When allocating expenses to distribution, selling and marketing costs or to administrative expenses, use the following assumptions:

	Distribution	Administrative
Directors' remuneration	–	100%
Audit fees	–	100%
Hire charges	50%	50%
Lighting and power	50%	50%
Miscellaneous expense	50%	50%
Motor expenses	100%	–
Postage, telephone, courier	50%	50%
Insurance	50%	50%
Repairs and maintenance	50%	50%
Salaries and wages	50%	50%
Depreciation	70%	30%

3.6   Preparation of financial statements

The following trial balance is extracted from the books of Walrus plc as at 31 March 2010:

	Dr €000	Cr €000
Land, at cost	240	
Buildings, at cost	500	
Equipment, at cost	392	
Vehicles, at cost	568	
Goodwill, at cost	600	
Accumulated depreciation at 1 April 2009:		
Buildings		180
Equipment		152
Vehicles		264
Inventory at 1 April 2009	214	
Trade receivables	366	
Trade payables		234
Allowance and receivables		16
Bank balance		114
Corporation tax		12
Ordinary shares of €2 each		400
Retained earnings at 1 April 2009		1,006
Sales		2,864
Purchases	976	
Directors' fees	300	
Wages and salaries	552	
General distribution costs	202	
General administrative expenses	372	
Dividend paid	40	
Rents received		60
Disposal of vehicle		20
	5,322	5,322

Additional information:

- The company's non-depreciable land was valued at EUR 600,000 on 31 March 2010 and this valuation is to be incorporated into the accounts for the year ended 31 March 2010.
- The company's depreciation policy is as follows:

Buildings	4% p.a. straight line
Equipment	40% p.a. reducing balance
Vehicles	25% p.a. straight line

In all cases, a full year's depreciation is charged in the year of acquisition and no depreciation is charged in the year of disposal. None of the assets had been fully depreciated by 31 March 2009.

On 1 February 2010, a vehicle used entirely for administrative purposes was sold for EUR 20,000 for cash. The vehicle had cost EUR 88,000 in August 2006. This was the only disposal of a non-current asset, made during the year ended 31 March 2010.

- Depreciation is apportioned as follows:

	Distribution costs	Administrative expenses
Buildings	50%	50%
Equipment	25%	75%
Vehicles	70%	30%

- The company's inventory at 31 March 2010 is valued at EUR 238,000.
- Trade receivables include a receivable of EUR 16,000 which is to be written off. The allowance for receivables is to be adjusted to 4 per cent of the receivables which remain after the writing off of the receivable.
- Corporation tax for the year ended 31 March 2009 was over-estimated by EUR 12,000. The corporation tax liability for the year ended 31 March 2010 is estimated at EUR 60,000.
- One-quarter of wages and salaries were paid to distribution staff and the remaining three-quarters were paid to administrative staff.
- General administrative expenses include bank overdraft interest of EUR 18,000.
- A dividend of EUR 0.20 per ordinary share was paid on 31 December 2009. No further dividends are proposed for the year ended 31 March 2010.

Prepare the following financial statements for Walrus plc in accordance with the requirements of IAS 1 (revised):

(a) a statement of comprehensive income for the year ended 31 March 2010;
(b) a statement of financial position as at 31 March 2010;
(c) a statement of changes in equity for the year ended 31 March 2010.

Note

1 In this chapter we have used the new titles for the financial statements introduced by IAS 1 (revised), though in the subsequent chapters we have used the captions 'balance sheet' and 'income statement'.

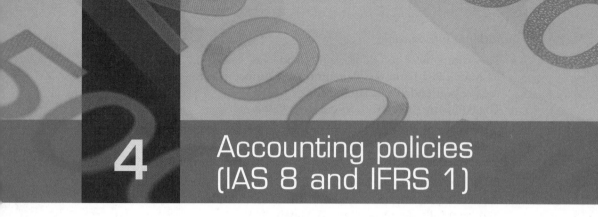

4 Accounting policies (IAS 8 and IFRS 1)

Contents

When you have completed this chapter you should be able to:

Objectives

- Define the term 'accounting policy' and explain how an entity should select its accounting policies
- Explain the circumstances in which an entity may change an accounting policy
- Account for a change in an accounting policy and list the disclosures which should be made when an accounting policy is changed
- Explain what is meant by an 'accounting estimate' and account for a change in an accounting estimate
- Define the term 'prior period error'
- Account for the correction of a prior period error and list the disclosures which should be made when a prior period error is corrected.

4.1   Introduction

IAS 8 – *Accounting Policies, Changes in Accounting Estimates and Errors* defines accounting policies as the specific principles, bases, conventions, rules and practices applied by an entity in preparing and presenting financial statements (IAS 8 para 5). Use of the word 'policy' suggests that the entity has made a choice between alternative accounting treatments. However, some of an entity's accounting policies will be dictated by international standards which permit no choice of treatment. For instance:

- IAS 2 – *Inventories* requires that inventories are measured at the lower of the cost and **net realisable value** (see Chapter 6).
- IAS 38 – *Intangible Assets* prohibits entities from recognising internally generated **goodwill** in their financial statements (see Chapter 9).
- IAS 37 – *Provisions, Contingent Liabilities and Contingent Assets* prohibits entities from **recognising contingent assets** and liabilities (see Chapter 11).

But certain standards do permit a choice. For instance:

- IAS 16 – *Property, Plant and Equipment* allows items of **property, plant and equipment** to be measured using the cost or revaluation models (see Chapter 7).
- Similarly, IAS 38 – *Intangible Assets* allows intangible assets to be measured using the cost or revaluation models (see Chapter 9).

- IAS 1 (revised) requires entities to disclose their significant accounting policies in the notes which form an integral part of the financial statements (see Chapter 3).

4.2   Selection and application of accounting policies

IAS 8 paras 10 and 11 provide the following guidance on the selection of accounting policies:

(a) If an international standard (or IFRIC interpretation) specifically applies to the item under consideration, the accounting policy which is applied to that item should be determined by applying the relevant standard or interpretation.

(b) If there is no international standard or interpretation which specifically applies to the item, management should use its judgement in selecting an accounting policy that results in information which is relevant and reliable. In making this judgement, management should refer to:

   (i) the guidance provided by international standards and interpretations which deal with similar and related issues;

   (ii) the definitions, recognition criteria and measurement concepts for assets, liabilities, income and expenses given in the IASB *Framework*.

Management may also consider the pronouncements of other standard-setting bodies which use a similar conceptual framework to the IASB *Framework* and may refer to accounting literature and accepted industry practices, to the extent that these do not conflict with international standards, interpretations or the *Framework* (IAS 8 para 12).

IAS 8 para 13 also stresses the need for *consistent* application of accounting policies. Having selected an accounting policy in relation to an item, that policy should be applied consistently to all similar items.

IAS 8 allows an entity to change one of its accounting policies only if the change:

(a) is required by an international standard or interpretation; or

(b) results in the financial statements providing reliable and more relevant information than would be the case if the accounting policy were not changed.

An example of changes in accounting policies required by the revised version of certain standards is given in Figure 4.1.

The users of financial statements should be able to compare an entity's financial statements from one accounting period to another. Therefore the same accounting policies should be used from one period to the next unless the above conditions are satisfied.

If a change in accounting policy results from the initial application of an international standard or interpretation, the change should be accounted for in accordance with the transitional provisions (if any) provided in that standard or interpretation.

However, if there are no transitional provisions or if the change in policy has been made voluntarily so as to improve the relevance of the financial statements,

> **Notes to the XYZ Group Consolidated Financial Statements (extract)**
>
> In 2007 the Group early adopted IFRS 8 'Operating Segments' and IAS 23 (revised) 'Borrowing Costs' which were required to be implemented from 1 January 2009 at the latest. In 2008 the Group early adopted the revised versions of IFRS 3 'Business Combinations' and IAS 27 'Consolidated and Separate Financial Statements' which are required to be implemented from 1 January 2010 at the latest.
>
> In 2009 the Group has implemented revisions to IAS 1 'Presentation of Financial Statements' the effects of which are described below. The Group has also implemented various other amendments to existing standards and interpretations, which have no material impact on the Group's overall results and financial position.
>
> IAS 1 (revised) 'Presentation of Financial Statements' – Amongst other matters, the revised standard requires some changes to the format of the statement of comprehensive income, the statement of changes in equity and requires some additional disclosures in the Notes to the Financial Statements, notably disclosing the pre-tax and tax impact of items of other comprehensive income (. . .). The balance sheet also includes the opening balances as at the beginning of the comparative period, and this is also reflected in the relevant Notes to the Financial Statements. The Group has also simplified the presentation of its equity by reporting 'own equity instruments' together with 'retained earnings'. The changes from the implementation of the revised standard are purely presentational and have no impact on the Group's overall results and financial position.
>
> The Group is currently assessing the potential impacts of the other new and revised standards and interpretations that will be effective from 1 January 2010 and beyond, and which the Group has not early adopted. The Group does not anticipate that these will have a material impact on the Group's overall results and financial position.

Figure 4.1 Changes in accounting policies

IAS 8 requires that the change should be accounted for *retrospectively* (IAS 8 para 19). This means that comparative figures for the previous period (or previous periods if comparatives are provided for more than one period) should be adjusted and presented *'as if the new accounting policy had always been applied'* (IAS 8 para 5). Retrospective application maintains comparability between accounting periods and this approach should usually be adopted unless it is impracticable to do so.

An important exception to the requirement for retrospective application arises in the case of property, plant and equipment (IAS 16) and intangible assets (IAS 38) where an entity changes from the cost model to the revaluation model. In this case, the relevant standards require that the change is accounted for prospectively rather than retrospectively.

Example 4.1

Application of a change in accounting policy retrospectively

During 2010, entity A changed its accounting policy for training costs in order to comply with IAS 38 – *Intangible Assets*. Previously, entity A had capitalised certain training costs. Under IAS 38, it cannot capitalize training costs and, according to the transitional provisions of the standard, it must apply the change in accounting policy retrospectively.

During the year ended 30 June 2009, entity A had capitalised training costs of EUR 18,000. In periods before 2009, it had capitalised training costs of EUR 36,000. In 2010, it incurred training costs of EUR 13,500.

Entity A's statement of comprehensive income for 2009 reported profit of EUR 147,000 net of income taxes of EUR 63,000. Its statement of comprehensive income for 2010 reported income of EUR 168,000 after income taxes of EUR 72,000. The training costs of EUR 13,500 were expensed in 2010.

Entity A's retained earnings were EUR 1.8m at July 2009 and EUR 1,947,000 at 30 June 2009. It had EUR 300,000 in share capital throughout 2009 and 2010, representing 100,000 ordinary shares, and there were no other reserves.

Entity A's tax rate was 30 per cent for both 2009 and 2010. The end of its accounting period is 30 June.

Applying the change in accounting policy retrospectively, entity A's statement of comprehensive income for the year ended 30 June 2010, with comparative figures, shows the following:

	2010 €000	2009 (restated) €000
Profit before income taxes	240,000	192,000[a]
Deduct: Income taxes	72,000	57,600[b]
Net profit for the year	168,000	134,400
Other items of comprehensive income	–	–
Comprehensive income	168,000	134,400

Notes:
a. €210,000 – €18,000
b. €63,000 – €18,000 × 30%

Entity A's statement of changes in equity is shown in Table 4.1.

Table 4.1 Statement of changes in equity

	Share capital €	Retained earnings €	Total €
Balance as at 30 June 2008 as previously reported	300,000	1,800,000	2,100,000
Change in accounting policy for capitalisation of training costs: €36,000 × (1–30%)	–	25,200	25,200
Balance as at 30 June 2008 as restated	300,000	1,774,800	2,074,800
Comprehensive income for the year ended 30 June 2009 (restated)	–	134,400	134,400
Balance as at 30 June 2009	300,000	1,909,200	2,209,200
Comprehensive income for the year ended 30 June 2010	–	168,000	168,000
Balance as at 30 June 2010	300,000	2,077,200	2,377,200

Except where driven by a change in circumstances, a change in the classification of an item within the balance sheet or the income statement often represents a change in accounting policy. There would be no effect on profit or loss for the period or on net assets; the only effect is to restate comparative amounts on a consistent basis. IAS 1 – *Presentation of Financial Statements* requires that when the presentation or classification of items is changed, the comparative figures should be restated (unless it is impracticable; see section 4.5) and it sets out disclosure requirements (IAS 1 (revised) para 41). An example of a change in presentation is given in Figure 4.2 below.

Accounting policies (extract)

Revenue and expense recognition: Sales are recognised when the significant risks and rewards of ownership of the assets have been transferred to a third party and are reported net of sales taxes and rebates. Provisions for rebates to customers are recognised in the same period that the related sales are recorded, based on the contract terms. Expenses of research and service contracts in progress are recognised based on their percentage of completion. Sales have been restated for all periods presented to treat certain sales incentives and discounts to retailers as sales deductions instead of marketing and distribution expenses.

Income statement (extract) **for the years ended 31 December 20X9 and 20X8**

	20X9	20X8
	€m	€m
Sales	xxx	yyy
Cost of sales	(xx)	(yy)[(1)]
Gross profit	XXX	YYY
Marketing & distribution	(xxx)	(yyy)[(1)]
Research & development	(xxx)	(yyy)
Administration & general overheads	(xxx)	(yyy)
Operating income	XX	YY

[(1)] Restated to reflect a change in classification of certain sales incentives and discounts to retailers. 20X8 sales and marketing & distribution expenses have both been reduced by €ZZZ.

Figure 4.2 Change in presentation

4.3   Changes in accounting estimates

As a result of uncertainties inherent in business activities, many items in financial statements cannot be measured with precision but can only be estimated. Estimation involves judgements based on the latest available reliable information. For example, estimates may be required of:

(a) bad debts;

(b) inventory obsolescence;

(c) the fair value of financial assets or financial liabilities;

(d) the useful lives of, or expected pattern of consumption of the future economic benefits embodied in, depreciable assets; and

(e) warranty obligations (IAS 8 para 32).

The use of reasonable estimates is an essential part of the preparation of financial statements and does not undermine their reliability (IAS 8 para 33).

An estimate may need revision if changes occur in the circumstances on which the estimate was based or as a result of new information or more experience. By its nature, the revision of an estimate does not relate to prior periods and is not a correction of an error (IAS 8 para 34).

A change in the measurement basis applied is a change in an accounting policy, and is not a change in an accounting estimate. When it is difficult to distinguish a change in an accounting policy from a change in an accounting estimate, the change is treated as a change in an accounting estimate (IAS 8 para 35).

The effect of a change in an accounting estimate should be recognised *prospectively* by including it in the income statement in:

(a) the period of the change, if the change affects that period only; or

(b) the period of the change and future periods, if the change affects both (IAS 8 para 36).

To the extent that a change in an accounting estimate gives rise to changes in assets and liabilities, or relates to an item of equity, it should be recognised by adjusting the carrying amount of the related asset, liability or equity item in the period of the change (IAS 8 para 37).

Prospective recognition of the effect of a change in an accounting estimate means that the change is applied to transactions, other events and conditions from the date of the change in estimate. A change in an accounting estimate may affect only the current period's profit or loss, or the profit or loss of both the current period and future periods. For example, a change in the estimate of the amount of bad debts affects only the current period's profit or loss and therefore is recognised in the current period. However, a change in the estimated useful life of, or the expected pattern of consumption of the future economic benefits embodied in, a depreciable asset affects depreciation expense for the current period and for each future period during the asset's remaining useful life. In both cases, the effect of the change relating to the current period is recognised as income or expense in the current period. The effect, if any, on future periods is recognised as income or expense in those future periods (IAS 8 para 38).

Disclosure of changes in accounting estimates

An entity should disclose the nature and amount of a change in an accounting estimate that has an effect in the current period or is expected to have an effect in future periods, except for the disclosure of the effect on future periods when it is impracticable to estimate that effect. If the amount of the effect in future periods is not disclosed because estimating it is impracticable, an entity should disclose that fact (IAS 8 paras 39 and 40).

Example 4.2 below illustrates how to account for a change in an accounting estimate and the related disclosure.

Example 4.2

Accounting for a change in an accounting estimate and the relevant disclosure

Entity B has always depreciated its factory plant and equipment assuming a useful life of 15 years. In 2010, entity B's directors determined that, due to technological developments in its industry, the factory plant and equipment should be depreciated over a shorter period: 10 years. The end of entity B's accounting period is 30 September.

The balance of factory plant and equipment as at 1 October 2009 was as follows:

	€
Cost	450,000
Accumulated depreciation	(120,000)
Carrying amount	330,000

For the year ended 30 September 2010, entity B's depreciation expense should be determined dividing the carrying amount of the asset at the date of the change in estimate by the remaining useful life, as shown below:

$$€330,000 \div 6 \text{ years} = €55,000$$

Since the total useful life is reassessed to 10 years, and four years have already elapsed, the remaining useful life is six years.

Entity B's financial statements for the year ended 30 September 2010 (extract)

Entity B has historically depreciated its factory plant and equipment over 15 years. As at 1 October 2009, the entity's directors determined that, due to technological developments in its industry, the factory plant and equipment should be depreciated over a shorter period: 10 years. The effect of the change in accounting estimate in the current year is an increase in depreciation expense and accumulated depreciation of EUR 25,000. In future, annual depreciation expense will be EUR 55,000.

4.4   Prior period errors

Errors can arise in respect of the recognition, measurement, presentation or disclosure of elements of financial statements. Financial statements do not comply with IFRS if they contain either material errors or immaterial errors made intentionally to achieve a particular presentation of an entity's financial position, financial performance or cash flows. Potential current period errors discovered in that period are corrected before the financial statements are authorised for issue. However, material errors are sometimes not discovered until a subsequent period, and these prior period errors are corrected in the comparative information presented in the financial statements for that subsequent period (IAS 8 para 41).

An entity should correct material prior period errors retrospectively in the first set of financial statements authorised for issue after their discovery by:

(a) restating the comparative amounts for the prior period(s) presented in which the error occurred; or

(b) if the error occurred before the earliest prior period presented, restating the opening balances of assets, liabilities and equity for the earliest prior period presented (IAS 8 para 42).

Example 4.3

Prior period errors

Whilst preparing its financial statements for the year ended 31 December 2009, an entity discovers that its inventory at 31 December 2008 was overstated by EUR 100,000. This is a material amount.

The entity's draft income statement for the year ended 31 December 2009 (before correcting the error) shows the following:

	2009 €000	2008 €000
Sales	1,880	1,580
Cost of sales	(1,500)	(1,080)
Gross profit	380	500
Other expenses	(240)	(220)
Profit before taxation	140	280
Taxation	(28)	(56)
Profit after taxation	112	224

Retained earnings were reported to be EUR 540,000 at 31 December 2007. No dividends were paid in either 2008 or 2009. It may be assumed that the entity's taxation expense is always equal to 20 per cent of its profit before tax.

We will show:

(a) The entity's income statement for the year ended 31 December 2009, showing restated comparative figures for 2008.

(b) The entity's retained earnings at 31 December 2009 and the restated retained earnings at 31 December 2008.

(a) Income statement for the year ended 31 December 2009:

	2009 €000	(restated) 2008 €000
Sales	1,880	1,580
Cost of sales	(1,400)	(1,180)
Gross profit	480	400
Other expenses	(240)	(220)
Profit before taxation	240	180
Taxation	(48)	(36)
Profit after taxation	192	144

(b) Retained earnings:

	€000
Balance at 31 December 2007	540
Restated profit for the year ended 31 December 2008	144
Restated balance at 31 December 2008	684
Profit for the year ended 31 December 2009	192
Balance at 31 December 2009	876

Note: Retrospective adjustment of the prior period error reveals that the profit after tax has increased in 2009. If the comparatives for 2008 had not been restated, the financial statements would have given the incorrect impression that the profit after tax had decreased in 2009.

4.4.1 Limitations on retrospective restatement

A prior period error should be corrected by retrospective restatement except to the extent that it is impracticable to determine either the period-specific effects or the cumulative effect of the error (IAS 8 para 43).

When it is impracticable to determine the period-specific effects of an error on comparative information for one or more prior periods presented, the entity should restate the opening balances of assets, liabilities and equity for the earliest period for which retrospective restatement is practicable (which may be the current period) (IAS 8 para 44).

When it is impracticable to determine the cumulative effect, at the beginning of the current period, of an error on all prior periods, the entity should restate the comparative information to correct the error prospectively from the earliest date practicable (IAS 8 para 45).

The correction of a prior period error is excluded from the income statement for the period in which the error is discovered. Any information presented about prior periods, including any historical summaries of financial data, is restated as far back as is practicable (IAS 8 para 46).

When it is impracticable to determine the amount of an error (e.g. a mistake in applying an accounting policy) for all prior periods, the entity should restate the comparative information prospectively from the earliest date practicable. It therefore should disregard the portion of the cumulative restatement of assets, liabilities and equity arising before that date (IAS 8 para 47).

Corrections of errors are distinguished from changes in accounting estimates. Accounting estimates by their nature are approximations that may need revision as additional information becomes known. For example, the gain or loss recognised on the outcome of a contingency is not a correction of an error (IAS 8 para 48).

4.4.2 Disclosure of prior period errors

When an entity corrects material prior period errors, it should disclose the following:

(a) the nature of the prior period error;

(b) for each prior period presented, to the extent practicable, the amount of the correction:

    (i) for each financial statement line item affected; and

    (ii) if IAS 33 applies to the entity, for basic and diluted earnings per share;

(c) the amount of the correction at the beginning of the earliest prior period presented;

(d) if retrospective restatement is impracticable for a particular prior period, the circumstances that led to the existence of that condition and a description of how and from when the error has been corrected.

Financial statements of subsequent periods need not repeat these disclosures (IAS 8 para 49).

4.5   Impracticability of retrospective application or restatement

Retrospective application relates to changes in accounting policies and retrospective restatement relates to the correction of material prior period errors. In both cases it is sometimes impracticable to adjust prior years retrospectively. IAS 8 gives additional guidance relating to situations for which retrospective application or restatement is impracticable.

IAS 8 paras 5 and 52 define *impracticable* in the following terms: Applying a requirement is impracticable when the entity cannot apply it after making every reasonable effort to do so. For a particular prior period, it is impracticable to apply a change in an accounting policy retrospectively or to make a retrospective restatement to correct an error if:

(a) the effects of the retrospective application or retrospective restatement are not determinable;

(b) the retrospective application or retrospective restatement requires assumptions about what management's intent would have been in that period; or

(c) the retrospective application or retrospective restatement requires significant estimates of amounts and it is impossible to distinguish objectively information about those estimates that:

    (i) provides evidence of circumstances that existed on the date(s) as at which those amounts are to be recognised, measured or disclosed; and

    (ii) would have been available when the financial statements for that prior period were authorised for issue from other information.

One circumstance that might give rise to impracticability is where data may not have been collected in the prior period in a way that enables retrospective application of a new accounting policy or retrospective restatement of a prior period error and where it may not be practicable to create, or recreate, the information (IAS 8 para 50).

Making estimates is a major part of the process of preparing financial statements. In order to adjust prior periods for changes in policy or for correction of errors it is necessary, when making estimates, to try and recreate the circumstances that existed in the prior period. However, with the passage of time it becomes increasingly difficult to develop estimates that reflect the circumstances that existed in a prior period and such estimates are more and more likely to be coloured and distorted by knowledge of events and circumstances that have arisen since that prior period. However, the objective of estimates relating to prior period remains the same as for estimates made in the current period, namely, for the estimate to reflect the circumstances that existed when the transaction, other event or condition occurred (IAS 8 para 51).

The definition of *impracticable* reproduced above requires information to have been available at the time of issue of the prior period's financial statements and that gives evidence of circumstances that existed at the time when the transaction, or event or condition existed. Such information should be capable of being distinguished from other information, such as information that only became available after the financial statements for that period had been issued. The standard notes that, for some types of estimate, such as an estimate of fair value that is not based on an observable price or observable inputs, it is not possible to distinguish these different sorts of information. This is presumably because such valuations would be highly subjective and it would be impossible to reliably recreate the subjective considerations that would have been taken into account when making the original estimate in the earlier period. Where it is not practicable to distinguish the type of information that was available and that was needed to recreate the circumstances in the earlier period from other information, retrospective application or restatement is not practicable (IAS 8 para 52).

Use of hindsight is not permitted when applying a new accounting policy or correcting prior period errors, either to second guess management's intentions in the earlier period or in estimating amounts recognised, measured or disclosed in the prior period. The standard gives as an example of the former restriction, a correction of an error in the measurement of held-to-maturity investments and points out that a decision by management in a subsequent period not to hold the investments to maturity should not be taken into account in making the correction. Similarly, it gives as an example the correction of a prior period error in calculating an employee healthcare liability and points out that information about an unusually severe influenza epidemic in a later period should not be taken into account in making the correction to the earlier period's financial statements (IAS 8 para 53).

Despite these restrictions, the standard emphasises that, although significant estimates are often required when adjusting comparative information for prior periods, this does not in itself prevent reliable adjustments or correction of the comparative amounts (IAS 8 para 53).

4.6   First-time adoption of IFRS (IFRS 1)

An entity should prepare and present an opening IFRS statement of financial position at the date of transition to IFRS. This is the starting point for its accounting under IFRSs (IFRS 1 para 6). According to the definition given in Appendix A of IFRS 1, *date of transition to IFRS* is 'the beginning of the earliest period for which an entity presents full comparative information under IFRS in its first IFRS financial statements'. Therefore, the date of transition to IFRS depends on two factors: the date of adoption of IFRS and the number of years of comparative information that the entity decides to present along with the financial information of the year of adoption, as shown in Example 4.4.

Example 4.4

Opening IFRS statement of financial position

Trevelyan Ltd presents its financial statements under its previous GAAP annually as at 31 December each year. The most recent financial statements it presented under its previous GAAP were as at 31 December 2008. Trevelyan Ltd decided to adopt IFRS as at 31 December 2009 and to present one-year comparative information for the year 2008. When should Trevelyan Ltd prepare its opening IFRS statement of financial position?

The beginning of the earliest period for which Trevelyan Ltd should present full comparative information would be 1 January 2008. In this case, the opening IFRS balance sheet that the entity would need to prepare under IFRS 1 would be as at 1 January 2008.

Alternatively, if Trevelyan Ltd decided to present two-year comparative information (i.e. for 2008 and 2007), then the beginning of the earliest period for which the entity should present full comparative information would be 1 January 2007. In this case, the opening IFRS statement of financial position that Trevelyan Ltd would need to prepare under IFRS 1 would be as at 1 January 2007.

An entity should use the same accounting policies in its opening IFRS statement of financial position and throughout all periods presented in its first IFRS financial statements. Those accounting policies should comply with each IFRS effective at the end of its first IFRS reporting period (IFRS 1 para 7).

An entity should not apply different versions of IFRSs that were effective at earlier dates. An entity may apply a new IFRS that is not yet mandatory if it permits early application (IFRS 1 para 8).

Example 4.5

Consistent application of latest version of IFRS

Entity A adopted IFRS as from December 2010 and decided to present comparative information in those financial statements for one year only. Therefore, the date of transition to IFRS is the beginning of business on 1 January 2009 (or, equivalently, close of business on 31 December 2008). Entity A presented financial statements under its previous GAAP annually to 31 December each year up to, and including, 31 December 2009.

Entity A should apply the IFRS effective for the year ended 31 December 2010 in:

(a) preparing and presenting its opening IFRS statement of financial position at 1 January 2009; and

(b) preparing and presenting its statement of financial position as at 31 December 2010 (including comparative amounts for 2009), statement of comprehensive income, statement of changes in equity and statement of cash flows for the year ended 31 December 2010 (including comparative amounts for 2009) and disclosures (including comparative information for 2009).

If a new IFRS is not yet mandatory but permits early application, entity A is permitted, but not required, to apply that IFRS in its first IFRS financial statements.

When preparing its opening IFRS statement of financial position, an entity should:

(a) recognise all assets and liabilities whose recognition is required by IFRS;

(b) not recognise items as assets or liabilities if IFRS do not permit such recognition;

(c) reclassify items that it recognised under previous GAAP as one type of asset, liability or component of equity, but are a different type of asset, liability or component of equity under IFRS; and

(d) apply IFRS in measuring all recognised assets and liabilities (IFRS 1 para 10).

The accounting policies that an entity uses in its opening IFRS statement of financial position may differ from those that it used for the same date using its previous GAAP. The resulting adjustments arise from events and transactions before the date of transition to IFRS. Therefore, an entity should recognise those adjustments directly in retained earnings (or, if appropriate, another category of equity) at the date of transition to IFRS (IFRS 1 para 11).

Example 4.6

Adjustments required in preparing the opening IFRS statement of financial position

Fashionable Co presented its financial statements under the national GAAP of Exuberance, a little island in the Mediterranean, until 2009. It adopted IFRS from 2010 and is required to prepare an opening IFRS balance sheet as at 1 January 2009. In preparing the opening IFRS balance sheet Fashionable Co noted the following issues:

- under its previous GAAP, Fashionable Co had deferred advertising costs of EUR 2m and had classified proposed dividends of EUR 1m as a current liability;

- it had not made a provision for warranty of EUR 400,000 in the financial statements presented under previous GAAP since the concept of *constructive obligation* was not recognised under its previous GAAP;

- in arriving at the amount to be capitalised as part of costs necessary to bring an asset to its working condition, Fashionable Co had not included professional fees of EUR 600,000 paid to engineers at the time when the building it currently occupies as its head office was being constructed.

The tax rate in Exuberance is 30 per cent.

We will illustrate how Fashionable Co should treat all the above items under IFRS 1.

In order to prepare the opening IFRS balance sheet as at 1 January 2009, Fashionable Co would need to make these adjustments to its balance sheet as at 31 December 2008, presented under its previous GAAP:

(a) IAS 38 does not allow advertising costs to be deferred whereas Fashionable Co's previous GAAP allowed this treatment. Thus, EUR 2m of such deferred costs should be derecognised (i.e. expensed) under IFRS.

(b) IAS 37 requires recognition of a provision for warranty but Fashionable Co's previous GAAP did not allow a similar treatment. Thus, a provision for warranty of EUR 400,000 should be recognised under IFRS.

(c) IAS 10 does not allow proposed dividends to be recognised as a liability; instead, under the latest revision to IAS 10, they should be disclosed in footnotes. Fashionable Co's previous GAAP allowed proposed dividends to be treated as a current liability. Therefore, proposed dividends of EUR 1m should be disclosed in footnotes.

(d) IAS 16 requires all directly attributable costs of bringing an asset to its working condition for its intended use to be capitalised as part of the carrying cost of PPE. Thus, EUR 600,000 of engineers' fees should be capitalised as part of (i.e., used in the measurement of) PPE under IFRS.

Table 4.2 (below) summarises the adjustments described above.

Table 4.2 Adjustments required for the opening IFRS statement of financial position*

Dr (Cr)	Opening equity @1 Jan 2009	Income statement result 2009	Other equity movements 2009	Closing equity @31 Dec 2009
	€m	€m	€m	€m
Reported under local GAAP	55.0	8.0	(1.0)	62.0
Advertising costs	(2.5)	0.5		(2.0)
Warranty provision	(0.3)	(0.1)		(0.4)
Engineers fees	0.5	0.1		0.6
			–	
Tax effect (@30% rate)	0.7	(0.2)	–	0.5
Proposed dividends	1.5		(0.5)	1.0
IFRS adjusted	54.9	8.4	(1.5)	61.7

* Assumptions have been made relating to the opening equity and to the income statement results for 2009.

4.6.1 Comparative information

To comply with IAS 1, an entity's first IFRS financial statements should include at least three statements of financial position, two statements of comprehensive income, two separate income statements (if presented), two statements of cash flows and two statements of changes in equity and related notes, including comparative information (IFRS 1 para 36).

Many listed entities give five-year historical summaries of key financial data. IFRS 1 does not require historical summaries to comply with IFRS (IFRS 1 para 37). This is because the IASB felt that the cost of doing so would outweigh the benefits to users. Although IFRS 1 does not require historical summaries to be restated, it does require disclosure of the main adjustments to comply with IFRS. The entity should also label the previous GAAP information prominently as not being prepared under IFRS (IFRS 1 para 37(a)). An example of disclosure is given in Figure 4.3, below.

Five-year summary (extract)

The figures for 2004 and 2005 are extracted from this Annual Report and thus prepared under IFRS. The figures for 2001, 2002 and 2003 are UK GAAP figures presented in the same fomat as the 2004 and 2005 figures. The principal differences between UK GAAP and IFRS are described in note 50 to the financial statements which provides an explanation of the transition to IFRS.

Group income statements year ended 31 December	UK GAAP 2001 £million	UK GAAP 2002 £million	UK GAAP 2003 £million	IFRS 2004 £million	IFRS 2005 £million
Revenue	7,089.4	7,771.6	8,799.3	8,898.4	9,171.2
Operating profit before amortisation of goodwill including:					
Share of associates' operating profit	198.1	227.0	263.1	289.7	331.8
Less: share of associates' operating profit	(17.4)	(21.5)	(36.8)	(46.1)	(70.8)
Operating profit before amortisation of goodwill	180.7	205.5	226.3	243.6	261.0
Costs in relation to proposed merger	–	–	–	–	(3.8)
Share of associates' post tax earnings	9.4	14.8	27.0	34.0	45.3
Profit on disposal of businesses	–	–	–	19.2	7.8
(Amounts written off)/profit on disposal of investments	–	–	–	(1.9)	2.1
Amortisation of goodwill	(10.7)	(12.2)	(13.3)	–	–
Profit from operations	179.4	208.1	240.0	294.9	312.4

Figure 4.3 Transition to IFRS: historical summaries

Source: Alliance UniChem PLC Report and Accounts 31 December 2005.

4.6.2 Reconciliations

IFRS 1 requires the following reconciliations between previous GAAP and IFRS. These form part of the standard's overall requirement for explanation of the transition to IFRS: An entity should explain how the transition from previous GAAP to IFRS affected its reported financial position, financial performance and cash flows (IFRS 1 para 38). IFRS 1 para 39 prescribes the disclosures an entity should give as follows:

(a) reconciliations of its equity reported under previous GAAP to its equity under IFRS for both of the following dates:

    (i) the date of transition to IFRSs; and

    (ii) the end of the latest period presented in the entity's most recent annual financial statements under previous GAAP.

(b) a reconciliation to its total comprehensive income under IFRSs for the latest period in the entity's most recent annual financial statements. The starting point for that reconciliation should be total comprehensive income under previous GAAP for the same period or, if an entity did not report such a total, profit or loss under previous GAAP.

(c) if the entity recognised or reversed any impairment losses for the first time in preparing its opening IFRS statement of financial position, the disclosures that IAS 36 – Impairment of Assets would have required if the entity had recognised those impairment losses or reversals in the period beginning with the date of transition to IFRS.

For example, an entity that prepared its first IFRS financial statements for the year ended 31 December 2009 and one year of comparative information, should present reconciliations for:

- equity as at 1 January 2008 and 31 December 2008; and
- profit for the year ended 31 December 2008.

The reconciliation should give enough information to enable users to understand the material adjustments to the income statement, balance sheet and statement of cash flows (IFRS 1 para 40). In practice, this may require significant disclosure of adjustments to the financial statements for accounting policy differences.

If the entity mentioned above presents two years of comparative information, the reconciliations required by the standard would mean reconciling equity at 1 January 2007 (date of transition) and 31 December 2006 (end of last period presented under previous GAAP), and reconciling profit or loss for the year ended 31 December 2008 (the period last presented under previous GAAP). This leaves a gap in the reconciliations and our view is that in order to give full information to users of the financial statements such entities should give additional reconciliations of equity as at 31 December 2007 and of profit and loss for the year ended 31 December 2007.

Figure 4.4 represents an example of disclosures made by a company which prepared its 2009 annual report in accordance with IFRS for the first time.

Management's discussion and analysis (extract)

CHANGE IN ACCOUNTING POLICIES

Adoption of IFRS

Our 2009 annual financial statements represent our first annual financial statements prepared in accordance with IFRS. We adopted IFRS in accordance with IFRS 1, *First-time Adoption of International Financial Reporting Standards*. The first date at which we applied IFRS was January 1, 2008. In accordance with IFRS 1, we have:

- provided comparative financial information;
- applied the same accounting policies throughout all periods presented;
- retrospectively applied all effective IFRS standards as of December 31, 2009, as required; and
- applied certain optional exemptions and certain mandatory exceptions as applicable for first-time IFRS adopters.

We initially filed our first quarter 2009 report under Canadian GAAP. In July 2009, we filed amended first quarter 2009 financial statements to present our interim financial statements in accordance with International Accounting Standard 34, *Interim Financial Reporting* (IAS 34), with the accounting policies we expected to adopt in our December 31, 2009 financial statements. There was no material effect on our previously issued 2009 interim financial statements under IFRS from subsequently issued IFRS or IFRIC pronouncements, which have an effective date on or before December 31, 2009.

In 2008, the Canadian Accounting Standards Board confirmed that Canadian publicly accountable enterprises will be required to adopt IFRS by 2011 to replace Canadian GAAP. The Canadian securities regulatory authorities approved our application to early adopt IFRS in 2009.

For additional information on our IFRS adoption, please see note 34 to our 2009 annual financial statements.

Notes to Consolidated Financial Statements (extract)

NOTE 34: TRANSITION TO IFRS

These consolidated financial statements represent the first annual financial statements of the Company and its subsidiaries prepared in accordance with IFRS, as issued by the IASB. The Company adopted IFRS in accordance with IFRS 1, First-time Adoption of International Financial Reporting Standards. The first date at which IFRS was applied was January 1, 2008 ('Transition Date'). In accordance with IFRS, the Company has:

Figure 4.4 Transition to IFRS and changes in accounting policies

- provided comparative financial information;
- applied the same accounting policies throughout all periods presented;
- retrospectively applied all effective IFRS standards as of December 31, 2009, as required, and
- applied certain optional exemptions and certain mandatory exceptions as applicable for first time IFRS adopters.

The Company's consolidated financial statements were previously prepared in accordance with Canadian GAAP.

Initial elections upon adoption

Set forth below are the IFRS 1 applicable exemptions and exceptions applied in the conversion from Canadian GAAP to IFRS.

IFRS Exemption Options

1. **Business combinations** – IFRS 1 provides the option to apply IFRS 3, Business Combinations, retrospectively or prospectively from the Transition Date. The retrospective basis would require restatement of all business combinations that occurred prior to the Transition Date. The Company elected not to retrospectively apply IFRS 3 to business combinations that occurred prior to its Transition Date and such business combinations have not been restated. Any goodwill arising on such business combinations before the Transition Date has not been adjusted from the carrying value previously determined under Canadian GAAP as a result of applying these exemptions. Further, the Company did not early adopt IFRS 3 Revised and instead has adopted that standard upon its effective date which, for the Company, was January 1, 2010.
2. **Employee benefits** – IFRS 1 provides the option to retrospectively apply the corridor approach under IAS 19, Employee Benefits, for the recognition of actuarial gains and losses, or recognize all cumulative gains and losses deferred under Canadian GAAP in opening retained earnings at the Transition Date. The Company elected to recognize all cumulative actuarial gains and losses that existed at its Transition Date in opening retained earnings for all of its employee benefit plans.
3. **Currency translation differences** – Retrospective application of IFRS would require the Company to determine cumulative currency translation differences in accordance with IAS 21, The Effects of Changes in Foreign Exchange Rates, from the date a subsidiary or equity method investee was formed or acquired. IFRS 1 permits cumulative translation gains and losses to be reset to zero at transition date. The Company elected to reset all cumulative translation gains and losses to zero in opening retained earnings at its Transition Date.
4. **Share-based payments** – IFRS 2, Share-based Payments, encourages application of its provisions to equity instruments granted on or before November 7, 2002, but permits the application only to equity instruments granted after November 7, 2002 that had not vested by the Transition Date. The Company elected to avail itself of the exemption provided under IFRS 1 and applied IFRS 2 for all equity instruments granted after November 7, 2002 that had not vested by its Transition Date. Further, the Company applied IFRS 2 for all liabilities arising from share-based payment transactions that existed at its Transition Date. As a result of the transition method elected, the Company reversed the historical Canadian GAAP share-based compensation charges impacting shareholders' equity from retained earnings to capital.
5. **Borrowing costs** – IAS 23, Borrowing Costs, requires an entity to capitalize the borrowing costs related to all qualifying assets for which the commencement date for capitalization is on or after January 1, 2009. Early adoption is permitted. The Company elected not to early adopt this policy. Therefore, borrowing costs prior to January 1, 2009 are expensed.

IFRS Mandatory Exceptions

Set forth below are the applicable mandatory exceptions in IFRS 1 applied in the conversion from Canadian GAAP to IFRS.

1. **Hedge accounting** – Hedge accounting can only be applied prospectively from the Transition Date to transactions that satisfy the hedge accounting criteria in IAS 39, Financial Instruments: Recognition and Measurement, at that date. Hedging relationships cannot be designated retrospectively and the supporting documentation cannot be created retrospectively. As a result, only hedging relationships that satisfied the hedge accounting criteria as of its Transition Date are reflected as hedges in the Company's results under IFRS. All derivatives, whether or not they meet the IAS 39 criteria for hedge accounting, were fair valued and recorded in the statement of financial position.
2. **Estimates** – Hindsight is not used to create or revise estimates. The estimates previously made by the Company under Canadian GAAP were not revised for application of IFRS except where necessary to reflect any difference in accounting policies.

Figure 4.4 (*Cont'd*)

Summary

- IAS 8 – *Accounting Policies, Changes in Accounting Estimates and Errors* defines accounting policies as the specific principles, bases, conventions, rules and practices applied by an entity in preparing and presenting its financial statements.

- IFRS issued by the IASB do not generally permit any choice for accounting treatment but some of the IAS (issued earlier by the IASC) do offer a choice. Therefore an entity's accounting policies will usually be a mixture of policies required by standards and policies chosen by the entity.

- IAS 8 provides guidance on the selection of accounting policies. Accounting policies should be applied consistently and should be changed only if the change is required by an international standard or an interpretation, or if it results in reliable and more relevant information. A change in accounting policy should generally be accounted for retrospectively and disclosed in the notes to the financial statements. An exception to the requirement for retrospective application arises in the case of PPE and intangible assets where an entity changes from the cast model to the revaluation model.

- When an entity corrects a material prior period error it should disclose the nature of this error and the amount of the correction for each financial statement line item affected.

- IFRS 1 – *First-Time Adoption of International Financial Reporting Standards* sets out the procedure which should be followed when an entity adopts IFRS for the first time.

Research and references

The IASB documents relevant for this chapter are:

- IAS 8 – *Accounting Policies, Changes in Accounting Estimates and Errors*.
- IFRS 1 – *First-Time Adoption of International Financial Reporting Standards*.

The following are examples of books that take the issues of this chapter further:

- Alfredson, K., Leo, K., Picker, R., Loftus, J., Clark, K. and Wise, V. (2008) *Applying International Financial Reporting Standards*, 2nd edn. Wiley, Chapter 17.
- Epstein, B.J. and Jermakowicz, E.K. (2009) *IFRS 2009: Interpretation and Application of International Accounting and Financial Reporting Standards*. Wiley, Chapters 21 and 27.
- PricewaterhouseCoopers (2009) *IFRS Manual of Accounting – 2010. Global Guide to International Financial Reporting Standards*. CCH, Chapters 3 and 5.

Discussion questions and exercises

4.1 Accounting policies and accounting estimates

(a) Distinguish between accounting policies and accounting estimates.
(b) Explain how a change in an accounting policy should be accounted for.
(c) Explain how a change in an accounting estimate should be accounted for.

4.2 Changes in accounting policies

(a) In what circumstances may an entity change one of its accounting policies?
(b) Explain how an entity should select its accounting policy in relation to an item if there is no applicable international standard or interpretation.

4.3 Disclosures

List the disclosures which should be made when an accounting policy is changed.

4.4 Material prior period error

(a) Explain what is meant by a 'material prior period error' and explain how such an error should be corrected.
(b) List the disclosures which should be made when a material prior period error is corrected.

4.5 Change in accounting policy and related restatements

Harris plc began trading on 1 January 2006, preparing financial statements ended 31 December each year. During 2009, the company decided to change its accounting policy with regard to depreciation of property, plant and equipment. Depreciation charges calculated using the previous accounting policy and shown in the company's financial statements for the first three years of trading were as follows:

	€000
Year ended 31 December 2006	460
Year ended 31 December 2007	540
Year ended 31 December 2008	580

If the new accounting policy had been applied in the previous years, depreciation charges would have been:

	€000
Year ended 31 December 2006	780
Year ended 31 December 2007	620
Year ended 31 December 2008	460

The company's income statement for the year ended 31 December 2009 (before adjusting comparative figures to reflect the change in accounting policy) shows the following:

	2009 €000	2008 €000
Profit before depreciation	5,020	4,900
Depreciation of property, plant and equipment	(380)	(580)
Profit before taxation	4,640	4,320
Taxation	(1,392)	(1,296)
Profit after taxation	3,248	3,024

Retained earnings were reported as EUR 5,886,000 on 31 December 2007. No dividends have been paid in any year. It may be assumed that the company's tax expense is each year equal to 30 per cent of the profit before taxation.

(a) Restate the above income statement to reflect the change in accounting policy, in accordance with the requirements of IAS 8.
(b) Compute the company's retained earnings at 31 December 2009 and the restated retained earnings at 31 December 2007 and 2008.

4.6 Change in accounting policy and related restatements

Whilst preparing its financial statements for the year ended 30 June 2010, Ibex plc discovers that the sales figure for the year ended 30 June 2009 had been understated by EUR 200,000 as a result of a mathematical error. Trade receivables at 30 June 2009 had been understated by the same amount. This error is regarded as material.

The company's draft income statement for the year ended 30 June 2010, before correcting this error, is as follows:

	2010 €000	2009 €000
Sales	3,320	3,480
Cost of sales	(1,340)	(1,460)
Gross profit	1,980	2,020
Expenses	(1,180)	(1,120)
Profit before taxation	800	900
Taxation	(160)	(180)
Profit after taxation	640	720

Retained earnings at 30 June 2008 were EUR 1,720,000. No dividends were paid during the two years to 30 June 2010. It may be assumed that the company's tax expense each year is equal to 20 pre cent of the profit before taxation.

(a) Prepare an income statement for the year ended 30 June 2010, showing restated comparative figures for the year ended 30 June 2009.
(b) Compute the company's retained earnings at 30 June 2010 and the restated retained earnings at 30 June 2009.

Part Three Income statement and balance sheet items

5 Revenue (IAS 18) and construction contracts (IAS 11)

Contents

Objectives

When you have completed this chapter you should be able to:

- Explain what revenue is and how it relates to net income
- Distinguish between revenue and income
- Explain how to measure revenue
- Determine when revenue from sale of goods and from rendering of services is normally recognised
- Understand exceptions to these normal revenue-recognition principles
- Determine amounts to be disclosed in financial statements relating to construction contracts
- Explain how revenue can be misstated by creative accounting
- Explain the impact of the percentage of completion method on financial statements and ratio analysis.

5.1   Introduction

Because entities exist to earn revenue and make profit for their owners, revenue is typically the single largest item reported in an entity's financial statements. It is the top line in the income statement and is an important measure of the size and hence growth of an entity. Revenue is the key variable in a number of calculations and ratios that management and investors consider as key performance indicators (KPIs). Revenue directly impacts gross profit (or gross margin) and operating profit of an entity as well as the calculation of earnings per share (EPS) and a range of non-IFRS measures including EBITDA. As a result, it can be argued that the amount shown as revenue is the single most important item to the users of financial statements.

As you can see from Figure 5.1, revenue recognition is one of the biggest issues involved in restatements of financial statements for public companies registered with the SEC and listed on the New York Stock Exchange (NYSE), the National Association of Securities Dealers Automated Quotation (Nasdaq), or the American Stock Exchange (Amex).

5.2   Basic principles of IAS 18 – *Revenue* and IAS 11 – *Construction Contracts*

The objective of IAS 18 is to provide principles to be applied when accounting for revenue arising from transactions and events referred to below. The standard

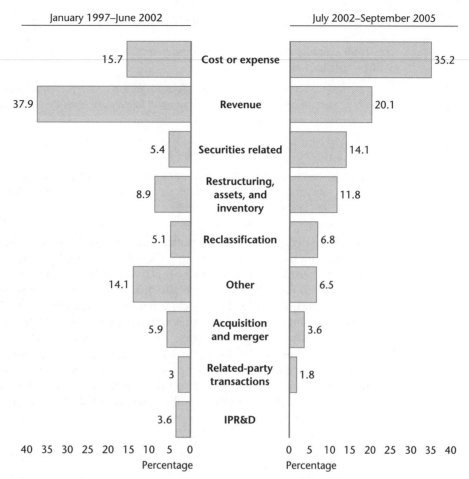

<u>January 1997–June 2002</u>   <u>July 2002–September 2005</u>

15.7 — Cost or expense — 35.2

37.9 — Revenue — 20.1

5.4 — Securities related — 14.1

8.9 — Restructuring, assets, and inventory — 11.8

5.1 — Reclassification — 6.8

14.1 — Other — 6.5

5.9 — Acquisition and merger — 3.6

3 — Related-party transactions — 1.8

3.6 — IPR&D

40 35 30 25 20 15 10 5 0   0 5 10 15 20 25 30 35 40
Percentage   Percentage

Figure 5.1 Restatement by reason: January 1997–June 2002 and
July 2002–September 2005
Source: US GAO (2006).

distinguishes 'revenue' from 'income' as explained in section 5.2.1. It sets out
detailed guidance for accounting for revenue from the following transactions and
events:

- sale of goods;
- rendering of services;
- use by others of assets belonging to the entity and giving rise to interest, royalties and dividends (this goes beyond the scope of this book and we will not deal
  with it);
- a number of specific transactions.

IAS 18 and IAS 11 give similar guidance on determining a transaction's stage of
completion. However, the guidance in IAS 18 relates to the rendering of services in
general, whereas IAS 11 specifically relates to the services provided under construction contracts (see section 5.4).

5.2.1 Definition of revenue and income

The IASB's *Framework for the Preparation and Presentation of Financial Statements* defines 'income' as:

> . . . *increases in economic benefits during the accounting period in the form of inflows or enhancements of assets or decreases of liabilities that result in increases in equity, other than those relating to contributions from equity participants.*

> *(Framework* para 7(a))

Revenue, a subset of income, is defined in IAS 18 as:

> . . . *the gross inflow of economic benefits during the period arising in the course of the ordinary activities of an entity when those inflows result in increases in equity, other than increases relating to contributions from equity participants.*

> (IAS 18 para 7)

From the above definitions, you will notice that 'revenue' includes economic benefits arising solely in the course of an entity's ordinary activities, whereas 'income' includes such benefits that arise from all activities whether ordinary or otherwise. The *Framework* in paras 74 and 75 explains that income encompasses both revenue and gains. Revenue is referred to by various names including sales, fees, interest, dividends, royalties and rent. Gains are other items that meet the definition of income but do not necessarily arise in the course of the entity's ordinary activities. Gains include those arising on the disposal of non-current assets, such as property, plant and equipment or long-term investments. They also include revaluation surpluses arising on revaluation of marketable securities or fixed assets (*Framework* para 76).

The distinction between revenue and income is not always clear as illustrated by the following example.

Example 5.1

'Revenue' vs 'income'

A car dealer, who sells both new and used cars, has demonstration cars available that can be used by potential customers for test drives. The cars are used for more than one year and then sold as used.

Does the sale represent the sale of a fixed asset, as the car was used by the dealer for the purpose of securing sales, or is the sale of the car the sale of an item of inventory resulting in the recording of revenue, as the dealer is in the business of selling new and used cars?

The car dealer is in the business of selling new and used cars. As selling used cars is part of his ordinary revenue generating activities, the sale of such used cars would represent revenue.

5.2.2 How to identify a transaction in order to recognise revenue

According to IAS 18 para 14, revenue from the ***sale of goods*** should be recognised when all the following conditions have been satisfied:

| Accounting Policies (extract) |
| Recognition of revenues |

Sales are recognised at the fair value of the consideration received or receivable, net of returns, trade discounts and volume rebates, when the significant risks and rewards of ownership of the goods are transferred to the buyer, and when it is probable that the economic benefits associated with the transaction will flow to the Group.

Royalty and commission income is recognised based on the contract terms on an accrual basis.

Figure 5.2 Recognition of sales revenue
Source: adidas Group Annual Report 2008.

(a) the entity has transferred to the buyer the significant risks and rewards of owner-ship of the goods (see Figure 5.2);

(b) the entity retains neither continuing managerial involvement to the degree usu-ally associated with ownership nor effective control over the goods sold;

(c) the amount of revenue can be measured reliably;

(d) it is probable that the economic benefits associated with the transaction will flow to the entity; and

(e) the costs incurred or to be incurred in respect of the transaction can be meas-ured reliably.

According to IAS 18 para 20, for a transaction involving the ***rendering of services***, when the outcome of the transaction can be estimated reliably, revenue should be recognised by reference to the stage of completion of the transaction at the end of the reporting period. The outcome of a transaction can be estimated reliably when all the following conditions are satisfied:

(a) the amount of revenue can be measured reliably;

(b) it is probable that the economic benefits associated with the transaction will flow to the entity;

(c) the stage of completion of the transaction at the end of the reporting period can be measured reliably;

(d) the costs incurred for the transaction and the costs to complete the transaction can be measured reliably.

The situations above (sale of goods and rendering of services) have the following conditions in common:

• reliable measurement of consideration;

• reliable measurement of costs;

• probability that the economic benefits from the transactions will flow to the entity.

These features are described below.

Reliable estimate of revenue

IAS 18 para 23 discusses the conditions necessary for a reliable estimate to be made of revenue in the context of rendering of services, but the three conditions below are equally valid for the sale of goods. In respect of the rendering of services, the entity should have agreed the following with the other party:

(a) each party's enforceable rights regarding the service to be provided and received by the parties;

(b) the consideration to be exchanged;

(c) the manner and terms of settlement.

It is also usually necessary for an entity to have an effective internal financial budgeting and reporting system. The entity reviews and, when necessary, revises the estimates of revenue as the service is performed. The need for such revisions does not necessarily indicate that the outcome of the transaction cannot be estimated reliably.

Reliable measurement of costs

In relation to the sale of goods produced by the entity, the costs incurred are generally manufacturing costs, which are calculated in accordance with IAS 2 – *Inventories*. Where goods are purchased for resale the costs generally comprise all costs of purchase. Measurement of each of these types of cost is usually relatively straightforward for an established business that is offering an existing product. It can be more difficult for a new business or an entity selling a new product. Costs such as those associated with setting up internal systems and processes and other start-up costs, should be segregated from the cost of the products to be manufactured. When a new business starts selling products or when an entity offers a new product, estimating the costs associated with returns or warranties can be difficult, because there is no experience upon which to estimate return rates and warranty costs.

Estimating the cost of providing services may be even less straightforward, especially where the contract for services spans several accounting periods and especially with reference to the future costs to be incurred. Given the difficulty inherent in such judgement, entities should consider the need to disclose the judgements made as a key source of *estimation uncertainty* in the financial statements in accordance with paragraph 125 of IAS 1 – *Presentation of Financial Statements*.

IAS 11 gives considerable guidance on the type of costs that should be included in a contract and on the type of costs that should be excluded. Identifying the costs to be included is the first stage in measuring the costs already incurred and to be incurred (this is discussed in section 5.4.4). Once the costs have been identified, measurement should be straightforward as it will generally be the price paid or the production costs. However, for a contract for services there will often be uncertainty about the extent of possible overruns. This is why IAS 11 and IAS 18 emphasise the need for a review of estimates as discussed in sections 5.4.4 and 5.4.6.

Probability that economic benefits will flow to the entity

One of the conditions for revenue recognition is that it is probable that the economic benefits associated with the transaction will flow to the entity. In some cases, this may not be probable until the consideration is received or until an uncertainty is removed. For example, it may be uncertain that a foreign governmental authority will grant permission to remit the sales consideration from that foreign country. When the permission is granted, the uncertainty is removed and revenue is recognised. However, when an uncertainty arises about the collectibility of an amount already included in revenue, the uncollectible amount is recognised as an expense, rather than as an adjustment of the amount of revenue originally recognised (IAS 18 para 18). In fact, any allowance recorded against any existing trade receivables is recorded as an expense (bad debt expense or bad debt provision).

5.2.3 Measurement of revenue

According to IAS 18 paras 9 and 10, revenue shall be measured at the fair value of the consideration received or receivable, taking into account the amount of any trade discounts and volume rebates allowed by the entity.

In most cases, the consideration is in the form of cash or cash equivalents and the amount of revenue is the amount of cash or cash equivalents received or receivable. However, when the inflow of cash or cash equivalents is deferred, the fair value of the consideration may be less than the nominal amount of cash received or receivable. For example, an entity may provide interest free credit to the buyer or accept a note receivable bearing a below-market interest rate from the buyer as consideration for the sale of goods. When the arrangement effectively constitutes a financing transaction, the fair value of the consideration is determined by discounting all future receipts using an imputed rate of interest.

The imputed rate of interest is the more clearly determinable of either:

(a) the prevailing rate for a similar instrument of an issuer with a similar credit rating; or

(b) a rate of interest that discounts the nominal amount of the instrument to the current cash sales price of the goods or services.

The difference between the fair value and the nominal amount of the consideration is recognised as interest revenue (IAS 18 para 11) (see Example 5.2).

Example 5.2

Fair value of revenue

On 1 January 2011, entity X sells entity Y goods for EUR 3,600, receivable on 1 January 2013.

Determine the fair value of revenue for entity X, assuming entity Y can borrow at 4.5 per cent a year.

Entity X should determine the fair value of revenue by calculating the present value of the cash flows receivable.

On 1 January 2011, revenue of EUR 3,297 is recorded, being EUR 3,600 discounted for 2 years. The discounted receivable should be updated at each balance sheet date to reflect the passage of time as shown in the table below. The resulting increase in the trade receivables represents interest income and should be recognised as such over the period from the date of sale to the expected date of receipt of cash.

Assuming that the year-end is 31 December, we would record the following:

	Opening balance (1 January)	Income statement for the accounting period		Closing balance (31 December)
	Trade receivables:	Interest income:	Revenue:	Trade receivables:
Year 2011	€3,297	€148	€3,297	€3,445
Year 2012	€3,445	€155	nil	€3,600

	Dr €	Cr €
1 January 2011		
Trade and other receivables	3,297	
Sales revenue		3,297
31 December 2011		
Trade and other receivables	148	
Interest income		148
31 December 2012		
Trade and other receivables	155	
Interest income		155
1 January 2013		
Cash and cash equivalents	3,600	
Trade and other receivables		3,600

5.3   Recognition of revenue from sale of goods

A contract for the sale of goods will normally give rise to revenue recognition when all the criteria set out in section 5.2.2 (IAS 18 para 14) have been satisfied, which is usually when delivery of the goods to the customer takes place. The application of the revenue recognition is illustrated in the following example.

Example 5.3

Application of revenue recognition criteria

Analyse the following transactions and explain when they give rise to revenue:

(a) In 2010, entity X purchases goods costing EUR 10,000 and sell (and deliver) them for EUR 16,000.

(b) In 2010, entity X purchases goods costing EUR 10,000. The goods will be sold (and delivered) in 2011 for EUR 16,000.

(c) In 2009, entity X purchased goods for EUR 10,000. Entity Y ordered the goods and paid EUR 4,000 in advance for the goods in 2010. The goods will be delivered and the balance of EUR 12,000 will be paid in 2011.

(a) There is a contract for sale in 2010 and the conditions for recognition of revenue are fulfilled in 2010 on delivery of goods. Therefore, EUR 16,000 is recognised as revenue. At the end of 2010, EUR 10,000 spent on purchasing the goods does not qualify as an asset as it does not give rights to future economic benefits (as those benefits have already been received in the form of the sales consideration). Therefore, EUR 10,000 is recorded in the income statement as cost of sales. In this way the matching concept is also applied.

	Dr €	Cr €
Inventory	10,000	
Cash and cash equivalents (or Trade payables)		10,000
Cash and cash equivalents (or Trade receivables)	16,000	
Sales revenue		16,000
Cost of sales	10,000	
Inventory		10,000

(b) At the end of 2010, there is no sale transaction, so no revenue is recognised. The cost of the goods (EUR 10,000) qualifies as an asset, because it provides a right or other access to future economic benefits controlled by the entity as a result of a past transaction. Therefore, EUR 10,000 is recorded as inventory in 2010.

In 2011, revenue of EUR 16,000 will be recognised. At the same time, the inventory will be derecognised, because there are no longer any future economic benefits to be derived from the asset and EUR 10,000 will be recognised as cost of sales.

	Dr €	Cr €
In 2010		
Inventory	10,000	
Cash and cash equivalents (or Trade payables)		10,000
In 2011		
Cash and cash equivalents (or Trade receivables)	16,000	
Sales revenue		16,000
Cost of sales	10,000	
Inventory		10,000

(c) At the end of 2009, there is no sale transaction, so no revenue is recognised. The cost of the goods (EUR 10,000) qualifies as an asset, because it provides a right or other access to future economic benefits controlled by the entity as a result of a past transaction. Therefore, EUR 10,000 is recorded as inventory.

In 2010, an order for the inventory is received. However, because the conditions for recognising revenue (we have assumed they are only met on delivery) have not been met by the end of 2010, no revenue is recognised. The customer has, however, paid EUR 4,000 in advance. This amount should be recorded as a liability (unearned revenue or deferred revenue) until such time as it is discharged by delivery of the goods. This applies whether or not the amount is refundable.

In 2011, delivery will be made and revenue of EUR 16,000 will be recognised (EUR 4,000 is released from liabilities and EUR 12,000 is expected to be received in 2011). The inventory of EUR 10,000 is derecognised because there are no longer any future benefits to be derived from it and EUR 10,000 is recognised as a cost of sales.

	Dr	Cr
	€	€
In 2009		
Inventory	10,000	
Cash and cash equivalents (or Trade payables)		10,000
In 2010		
Cash and cash equivalents	4,000	
Unearned revenue		4,000
In 2011		
Cash and cash equivalents	12,000	
Unearned revenue	4,000	
Sales revenue		16,000
Cost of sales	10,000	
Inventory		10,000

5.3.1 Transfer of significant risks and rewards of ownership

IAS 18 para 15 states that the assessment of when an entity has transferred the significant risks and rewards of ownership to the buyer requires an examination of the circumstances of the transaction. In most cases, the transfer of the risks and rewards of ownership coincides with the transfer of the legal title or the passing of possession to the buyer. This is the case for most retail sales.

IAS 18 notes that in some circumstances the transfer of risks and rewards of ownership occurs before or even after delivery. For example, in some jurisdictions the equitable interest in a property may pass to the buyer before legal title passes and, therefore, the risks and rewards also pass at that point.

Other examples of situations where the transfer of significant risks and rewards has not taken place include the following (IAS 18 para 15):

(a) When an entity retains an obligation for unsatisfactory performance not covered by normal warranty provisions. An example is where an entity supplies a new type of machine and guarantees that it will achieve a certain level of output or a refund will be given and it is uncertain whether the required level of output will be achieved.

(b) When the receipt of the revenue from a particular sale is contingent on the buyer deriving revenue from its sale of the goods. An example is a sale to a distributor where payment is due only if the distributor sells on the goods to a third party.

(c) When the goods are shipped subject to installation and the installation is a significant part of the contract which has not yet been completed by the entity. An example is the supply of a turnkey project where the seller is responsible for installing and making sure that the equipment is working to the customer's satisfaction.

(d) When the buyer has the right to rescind the purchase for a reason specified in the sales contract and the entity is uncertain about the probability of return (i.e. whether or not that right will be exercised and the goods returned). An example is goods supplied on a sale or return basis.

Another example of an entity retaining only an insignificant risk of ownership may be a retail sale when a refund is offered if the customer is not satisfied. Revenue in such cases is recognised at the time of sale provided the seller can reliably estimate future returns and recognises a liability for returns based on previous experience and other relevant factors (IAS 18 para 17).

5.3.2 Measurement of revenue from sale of goods: specific applications and examples

Table 5.1 below illustrates recognition criteria for sale of goods in a number of commercial situations.

Table 5.1 Sale of goods

Commercial situations	Revenue recognition criteria
'Bill and hold' sales, in which delivery is delayed at the buyer's request but the buyer takes title and accepts billing	Revenue should be recognised when the buyer takes title, provided: (a) it is probable that delivery will be made; (b) the item is on hand, identified and ready for delivery to the buyer at the time the sale is recognised; (c) the buyer specifically acknowledges the deferred delivery instructions; (d) the usual payment terms apply. Revenue should not be recognised when there is simply an intention to acquire or manufacture the goods in time for delivery.

Goods shipped subject to conditions	(a) *Installation and inspection* (See also Example 5.6).
	Revenue is normally recognised when the buyer accepts delivery, and installation and inspection are complete. However, revenue should be recognised immediately upon the buyer's acceptance of delivery when:
	
	    (i) the installation process is simple in nature, for example the installation of a factory tested television receiver which only requires unpacking and connection of power and antenna;
	    (ii) the inspection is performed only for the purpose of determining the contract prices, for example, shipments of iron ore, sugar or soya beans.
	
	(b) *When the buyer has negotiated a limited right of return.*
	If there is uncertainty about the possibility of return, revenue should be recognised when the shipment is formally accepted by the buyer or the goods have been delivered and the time period for rejection has elapsed.
	
	(c) *Consignment sales under which the recipient (buyer) undertakes to sell the goods on behalf of the shipper (seller).*
	Revenue should be recognised by the shipper when the goods are sold by the recipient to a third party.
	
	(d) *Cash on delivery sales.*
	Revenue should be recognised when delivery is made and cash is received by the seller or his agent.

Table 5.1 (*Cont'd*)

Commercial situations	Revenue recognition criteria
Lay away sales under which the goods are delivered only when the buyer makes the final payment in a series of instalments	Revenue from such sales should be recognised when the goods are delivered.
Sales with payment (or partial payment) to be received in advance of delivery for goods not presently held in inventory, for example, the goods are still to be manufactured or will be delivered directly to the customer by a third party	Revenue should be recognised when the goods are delivered to the buyer.
Sale and repurchase agreements under which the seller concurrently agrees to repurchase the same goods at a later date	The terms of the agreement need to be analysed to ascertain whether, in substance, the seller has transferred the risks and rewards of ownership to the buyer and hence revenue should be recognised. When the seller has retained the risks and rewards of ownership, even though legal title has been transferred, the transaction is a financing arrangement and does not give rise to revenue.
Sales to intermediate parties, such as distributors, dealers or others for resale	Revenue from such sales should be generally recognised when the risks and rewards of ownership have passed. However, when the buyer is acting, in substance, as an agent, the sale should be treated as a consignment sale.
Subscriptions to publications and similar items	When the items involved are of similar value in each time period, revenue should be recognised on a straight line basis over the period in which the items are despatched.
Instalment sales, under which the consideration is receivable in instalments	Revenue attributable to the sales price, exclusive of interest, should be recognised at the date of sale. The sale price is the present value of the consideration, determined by discounting the instalments receivable at the imputed rate of interest. The interest element should be recognised as revenue as it is earned, on a time proportion basis that takes into account the imputed rate of interest.
Real estate sales	Revenue should be normally recognised when legal title passes to the buyer.

5.4 Recognition of revenue from rendering of services and from construction contracts

5.4.1 Definitions relating to construction contracts

Before analysing the issues relating to revenue recognition for rendering of services and construction contracts, we should discuss certain definitions regarding construction contracts. These are contracts specifically negotiated for the construction of an asset or a combination of assets that are closely interrelated or interdependent in terms of their design, technology and function or their ultimate purpose or use

(IAS 11 para 3). They are formulated in a number of ways, which can be classified in the following two groups:

- Fixed price contracts are construction contracts in which the contractor agrees to a fixed contract price, or a fixed rate per unit of output, which in some cases is subject to cost escalation clauses.
- Cost plus contracts are construction contracts in which the contractor is reimbursed for allowable or otherwise defined costs, plus a percentage of these costs or a fixed fee.

A construction contract may be negotiated for the construction of a single asset such as a bridge, building, dam, pipeline, road, ship or tunnel. A construction contract may also deal with the construction of a number of assets which are closely interrelated or interdependent in terms of their design, technology and function or their ultimate purpose or use; examples of such contracts include those for the construction of refineries and other complex pieces of plant or equipment (IAS 11 para 4).

Combining and segmenting construction contracts

When a contract covers a number of assets, the construction of each asset shall be treated as a separate construction contract when (IAS 11 para 8):

(a) separate proposals have been submitted for each asset;
(b) each asset has been subject to separate negotiation and the contractor and customer have been able to accept or reject that part of the contract relating to each asset;
(c) the costs and revenues of each asset can be identified.

Example 5.4

Segmenting construction contracts

Entity A is negotiating with the local government to build a new bridge after demolishing the existing bridge near the city centre. At the initial meeting, it was indicated that the government would not be willing to pay for both components of the contract more than EUR 3m. The government representatives insisted that separate proposals should be submitted and negotiated; the contractor should maintain separate records for each component of the contract and upon request furnish details of the contract costs incurred by component. After submission of the separate proposals, it was agreed that the contract price of EUR 3m would be split in the ratio of 70 per cent for the construction of the new bridge and 30 per cent for demolishing the existing bridge.

Two questions arise whether the contract for the construction of the new bridge and the contract for demolishing the existing bridge should be treated as separate contracts or as a single contract.

In accordance with IAS 11, the two contracts should be *segmented* and treated as *separate contracts* because:

(a) separate proposals were submitted for the two contracts;
(b) the two contracts were negotiated separately;
(c) costs and revenue of each asset can be identified separately.

A group of contracts, whether with a single customer or with several customers, should be treated as a single construction contract when (IAS 11 para 9):

(a) the group of contracts is negotiated as a single package;

(b) the contracts are so closely interrelated that they are, in effect, part of a single project with an overall profit margin;

(c) the contracts are performed concurrently or in a continuous sequence.

Example 5.5

Combining construction contracts

New Essence plc is well known for its expertise in setting up underground waste removal systems. These systems remove waste twice a day, keeping the environment clean, supporting higher rates of recycling and reducing CO_2 emissions from refuse lorries by an estimated 90 per cent. Impressed by its track record, the local council authorities invited New Essence plc to submit a tender for a three-year contract to build a new waste removal system for the council civic offices and another tender for maintenance of the system for 10 years after completion of the construction.

Evaluate whether these two contracts should be segmented or combined into one contract for the purpose of IAS 11.

The two contracts should be *combined* and treated as a *single contract* because:

(a) the two contracts are very closely related to each other and, in fact, are part of a single contract with an overall profit margin;

(b) the contracts have been negotiated as a single package;

(c) the contracts are performed in a continuous sequence.

5.4.2 How to determine a stage of completion

The 'percentage of completion' method is used to recognise revenue for a transaction involving the rendering of services in accordance with IAS 18. The requirements of IAS 11 are generally applicable to recognise revenue and the associated expenses for transactions involving the rendering of services (IAS 18 para 21).

IAS 11 recognises the percentage of completion method as the only valid method of accounting for construction contracts. Under an earlier version of IAS 11, both the percentage of completion method and the completed contract method were recognised as being the acceptable alternative methods of accounting for long-term construction activities.

In accordance with IAS 18 and IAS 11, various methods may be used to determine the stage of completion. The key to the determination of which method to use is that revenue should relate only to work that has been performed and should not include any element relating to work that has yet to be carried out.

Depending on the nature of the transaction, the methods may include (IAS 18 para 24 and IAS 11 para 30):

(a) surveys of work performed method;

(b) services/works performed to date as a percentage of total services/work to be performed (also called units-of-work-performed method);

(c) the proportion that costs incurred to date bear to the estimated total contract costs (also referred to as the cost-to-cost method). Only costs that reflect services/ work performed to date are included in costs incurred to date. Only costs that reflect services/work performed and/or to be performed are included in the estimated total costs of the transaction.

Each of these methods of measuring progress on a contract can be identified as being either an input or an output measure. The *input measures* attempt to identify progress in a contract in terms of the efforts devoted to it. The cost-to-cost method is an example of an input measure. Under the cost-to-cost method, the percentage of completion would be estimated by comparing total costs incurred to date to total costs expected for the entire job. *Output measures* are made in terms of results by attempting to identify progress towards completion by physical measures. The units-of-work-performed method is an example of an output measure. Under this method, an estimate of completion is made in terms of achievements to date. Output measures are usually not considered to be as reliable as input measures.

Progress payments and advances received from customers often do not reflect the services/work performed.

When performance of a single contract takes place over time, then revenue should be recognised as performance takes place. For example, under a maintenance contract for six months, revenue should be recognised over the six months, as the service is provided over that period. It is not appropriate to record all the revenue upfront and provide for the costs expected to be incurred in providing the services, because to do this would be to recognise revenue before the seller had performed any part of the contract.

The application of the percentage of completion method where the provision of services straddles a year-end is considered in the following examples.

Example 5.6

Application of percentage of completion method

An entity has entered into fixed rate contracts with local authorities to inspect and report on local property values. Analyse the two following situations:

1 Valuation reports were completed and sent out before the year-end, but due to administrative problems, invoicing was delayed until after the year-end.

2 Valuation reports were not completed until after the year-end, although other work (i.e. site visits) had been completed.

1 Since the work has been completed, as evidenced by the submission of the valuation reports and since the contracts are at a fixed rate, the entity has completed its contractual performance and should recognise the revenue and profit on the work performed before the year-end.

2 Revenue should be recognised at the year-end according to the percentage of completion method. If writing of the reports does not constitute a *significant act* under the contract, then an appropriate percentage of the total contract price, should be taken to revenue, provided the outcome can be assessed with reasonable certainty.

Determining the stage of completion may, in some situations, be a matter of whether a contract may be broken down into separate components. For example, in the shipping industry, ships may be engaged in journeys to more than one port, which are not completed at the year-end. In these circumstances, revenue is often recognised by reference to the last leg of the journey completed before the year-end, as long as it is probable that benefits will flow to the entity. This is on the basis that the contract is capable of being broken into separable components.

When the stage of completion is determined by reference to the contract costs incurred to date, only those contract costs that reflect work performed are included in costs incurred to date. Examples of contract costs which are excluded are set out below. The examples relate to physical construction contracts, but the principle is the same for service contracts.

(a) contract costs that relate to future activity on the contract, such as costs of materials that have been delivered to a contract site or set aside for use in a contract but not yet installed, used or applied during contract performance, unless the materials have been made specially for the contract;

(b) payments made to subcontractors in advance of work performed under the subcontract (IAS 11 para 31).

For practical purposes, when services are performed by an indeterminate number of acts over a specified period of time, revenue is recognised on a straight-line basis over the specified period unless there is evidence that some other method better represents the stage of completion. When a specific act is much more significant than any other acts, the recognition of revenue is postponed until the significant act is executed (IAS 18 para 25).

When the outcome of the transaction involving the rendering of services cannot be estimated reliably, revenue should be recognised only to the extent of the expenses recognised that are recoverable (IAS 18 para 26). IAS 11 para 32 contains a similar requirement in respect of construction contracts: When the outcome of a construction contract cannot be estimated reliably:

(a) revenue should be recognised only to the extent of contract costs incurred that it is probable will be recoverable; and

(b) contract costs should be recognised as an expense in the period in which they are incurred.

IAS 18 para 27 explains that, in the early stages of a transaction, it is often the case that the outcome of the transaction cannot be estimated reliably. Nevertheless, it may be probable that the entity will recover the transaction costs incurred. Therefore, revenue should be recognised only to the extent of costs incurred that are expected to be recoverable. As the outcome of the transaction cannot be estimated reliably, no profit should be recognised.

Where the outcome of a transaction cannot be reliably estimated and costs already incurred are not expected to be recoverable, IAS 18 para 28 states that revenue should not be recognised and such costs should be expensed immediately. Similarly, IAS 11 para 34 states that contract costs that are not probable of being recovered should be recognised as an expense immediately. Examples of circumstances in which the recoverability of contract costs incurred may not be probable and in which contract costs may need to be recognised as an expense immediately include contracts:

(a) that are not fully enforceable, i.e. their validity is seriously in question;

(b) the completion of which is subject to the outcome of pending litigation or legislation;

(c) relating to properties that are likely to be condemned or expropriated;

(d) where the customer is unable to meet its obligations; or

(e) where the contractor is unable to complete the contract or otherwise meet its obligations under the contract.

5.4.3 Measurement of revenue from rendering of services: specific applications and examples

Table 5.2 below illustrates recognition criteria for rendering of services in a number of commercial situations.

Table 5.2 Rendering of services

Commercial situations	Revenue recognition criteria
Installation fees	Installation fees are recognised as revenue by reference to the stage of completion of the installation, unless they are incidental to the sale of a product in which case they should be recognised when the goods are sold.
Servicing fees included in the price of the product	When the selling price of a product includes an identifiable amount for subsequent servicing (for example, after sales support and product enhancement on the sale of software), that amount should be deferred and recognised as revenue over the period during which the service is performed.
Advertising commissions	Media commissions should be recognised when the related advertisement or commercial appears before the public.
Insurance agency commissions	Insurance agency commissions received or receivable which do not require the agent to render further service should be recognised as revenue by the agent on the effective commencement or renewal dates of the related policies. However, when it is probable that the agent will be required to render further services during the life of the policy, the commission, or part thereof, should be deferred and recognised as revenue over the period during which the policy is in force.
Admission fees	Revenue from artistic performances, banquets and other special events should be recognised when the event takes place.
Tuition fees	Revenue should be recognised over the period of instruction.
Initiation, entrance and membership fees	Revenue recognition depends on the nature of the services provided. If the fee permits only membership, and all other services or products are paid for separately, or if there is a separate annual subscription, the fee should be recognised as revenue. If the fee entitles the member to services or publications to be provided during the membership period, or to purchase goods or services at prices lower than those charged to non members, it should be recognised on a basis that reflects the timing, nature and value of the benefits provided.

Table 5.2 (*Cont'd*)

Commercial situations	Revenue recognition criteria
Franchise fees	Franchise fees may cover the supply of initial and subsequent services, equipment and other tangible assets, and know-how. Accordingly, franchise fees should be recognised as revenue on a basis that reflects the purpose for which the fees were charged. The following methods of franchise fee recognition are appropriate:
	(a) Supplies of equipment and other tangible assets – the amount, based on the fair value of the assets sold, should be recognised as revenue when the items are delivered or title passes.
	(b) Supplies of initial and subsequent services – fees for the provision of continuing services, whether part of the initial fee or a separate fee should be recognised as revenue as the services are rendered. When the separate fee does not cover the cost of continuing services together with a reasonable profit, part of the initial fee, sufficient to cover the costs of continuing services and to provide a reasonable profit on those services, should be deferred and recognised as revenue as the services are rendered.
	The franchise agreement may provide for the franchisor to supply equipment, inventories, or other tangible assets, at a price lower than that charged to others or a price that does not provide a reasonable profit on those sales. In these circumstances, part of the initial fee, sufficient to cover estimated costs in excess of that price and to provide a reasonable profit on those sales, should be deferred and recognised over the period the goods are likely to be sold to the franchisee. The balance of an initial fee should be recognised as revenue when performance of all the initial services and other obligations required of the franchisor (such as assistance with site selection, staff training, financing and advertising) has been substantially accomplished.
	The initial services and other obligations under an area franchise agreement may depend on the number of individual outlets established in the area. In this case, the fees attributable to the initial services should be recognised as revenue in proportion to the number of outlets for which the initial services have been substantially completed.
	If the initial fee is collectable over an extended period and there is a significant uncertainty that it will be collected in full, the fee should be recognised as cash instalments are received.
	(c) Continuing franchise fees – fees charged for the use of continuing rights granted by the agreement, or for other services provided during the period of the agreement, should be recognised as revenue as the services are provided or the rights used.
	(d) Agency transactions – transactions may take place between the franchisor and the franchisee which, in substance, involve the franchisor acting as agent for the franchisee. For example, the franchisor may order supplies and arrange for their delivery to the franchisee at no profit. Such transactions do not give rise to revenue.
Fees from the development of customised software	Fees from the development of customised software should be recognised as revenue by reference to the stage of completion of the development, including completion of services provided for post delivery service support.

5.4.4 Definition and determination of revenue, costs and profit for construction contracts

Contract revenue

According to IAS 11 para 11, contract revenue should comprise:

(a) the initial amount of revenue agreed in the contract; and

(b) variations in contract work, claims and incentive payments:

  (i) to the extent that it is probable that they will result in revenue; and
  (ii) they are capable of being reliably measured.

Contract revenue should be measured at the fair value of the consideration received or receivable. The measurement of contract revenue is affected by a variety of uncertainties that depend on the outcome of future events. The estimates often need to be revised as events occur and uncertainties are resolved. Therefore, the amount of contract revenue may increase or decrease from one period to the next.

For example:

(a) a contractor and a customer may agree variations or claims that increase or decrease contract revenue in a period subsequent to that in which the contract was initially agreed;

(b) the amount of revenue agreed in a fixed price contract may increase as a result of cost escalation clauses;

(c) the amount of contract revenue may decrease as a result of penalties arising from delays caused by the contractor in the completion of the contract; or

(d) when a fixed price contract involves a fixed price per unit of output, contract revenue increases as the number of units is increased (IAS 11 para 12).

As stated above, contract revenue should be measured at the fair value of the consideration received or receivable. This means that where payment is received in arrears to such an extent that the fair value of the consideration is less than the nominal amount of cash received or receivable, it would be necessary to discount the revenue (and the related receivable) to fair value as shown in the following example.

Example 5.7

Fair value of revenue from construction contracts

Entity A entered into a contract with entity B to construct a mobile telecom network. The total revenue for the contract is estimated at EUR 200,000. Entity A will take three years (2007–9) to construct the network.

The contract states that although progress billings will be made at the end of each year, entity B will only settle the invoices when the contract is 100 per cent completed.

Progress billings are invoiced at the end of each year to reflect the revenue that entity A should recognise on the contract for the year in accordance with the stage of completion method. The stage of completion is determined by the proportion that the costs incurred to date bear to the estimated total costs of the transaction. Progress billings invoiced by entity A were as follows:

(c) depreciation of plant and equipment used on the contract;

(d) costs of moving plant, equipment and materials to and from the contract site;

(e) costs of hiring plant and equipment;

(f) costs of design and technical assistance that is directly related to the contract;

(g) the estimated costs of rectification and guarantee work, including expected warranty costs; and

(h) claims from third parties.

These costs may be reduced by any incidental income that is not included in contract revenue, for example income from the sale of surplus materials and the disposal of plant and equipment at the end of the contract.

Costs that may be attributable to contract activity in general and can be allocated to specific contracts include:

(a) insurance;

(b) costs of design and technical assistance that are not directly related to a specific contract; and

(c) construction overheads.

Such costs should be allocated using methods that are systematic and rational and should be applied consistently to all costs having similar characteristics. The allocation should be based on the normal level of construction activity. Construction overheads include costs such as the preparation and processing of construction personnel payroll. Costs that may be attributable to contract activity in general and can be allocated to specific contracts also include borrowing costs.

Costs that are specifically chargeable to the customer under the terms of the contract may include some general administration costs and development costs for which reimbursement is specified in the terms of the contract.

IAS 11 para 20, lists the costs that cannot be attributed to contract activity and therefore should be excluded from the costs of a construction contract. These are:

(a) general administration costs for which reimbursement is not specified in the contract;

(b) selling costs;

(c) research and development costs for which reimbursement is not specified in the contract;

(d) depreciation of idle plant and equipment that is not used on a particular contract.

Under the percentage of completion method, contract revenue should be recognised as revenue in the income statement in the accounting periods in which the work is performed. Contract costs should usually be recognised as an expense in the income statement in the accounting periods in which the work to which they relate is performed. However, any expected excess of total contract costs over total contract revenue for the contract should be recognised as an expense immediately (IAS 11 para 26).

5.4.5 Presentation and disclosures for construction contracts

An entity should disclose:

(a) the amount of contract revenue recognised as revenue in the period;

(b) the methods used to determine the contract revenue recognised in the period; and

(c) the methods used to determine the stage of completion of contracts in progress (IAS 11 para 39).

An entity should disclose each of the following for contracts in progress at the end of the reporting period (IAS 11 para 40):

(a) the aggregate amount of costs incurred and recognised profits (less recognised losses) to date;

(b) the amount of advances received;

(c) the amount of retentions.

Retentions are amounts of progress billings that are not paid until the satisfaction of conditions specified in the contract for the payment of such amounts or until defects have been rectified. Progress billings are amounts billed for work performed on a contract whether or not they have been paid by the customer. Advances are amounts received by the contractor before the related work is performed (IAS 11 para 41).

An entity should present the gross amount due from/to customers for contract work as an asset/liability (IAS 11 para 42).

The gross amount due *from* customers for contract work is equal to:

> Costs incurred
> + recognised profits
> − the sum of recognised losses and progress billings

Accounting Principles, Basis for Preparation, and Estimates (extract)
Construction contracts

Revenues related to construction contracts are recognized using the percentage of completion method, based primarily on contract costs incurred to date, compared to estimated overall contract costs.

If the final outcome of a contract cannot be estimated reliably, contract revenue is recognized only to the extent costs incurred are expected to be recovered. Any projected losses on future work done under existing contracts are expensed and classified as accrued costs/provisions in the balance sheet under current provisions.

Losses on contracts are recognized in full when identified. Recognized contract profit includes profit derived from change orders and disputed amounts when, in management's assessment, realization is probable and reasonable estimates can be made. Project costs include costs directly related to the specific contract and indirect costs attributable to the contract.

Project revenue is classified as operating revenue in the profit and loss account. Work in progress is classified as projects under construction in the balance sheet. Advances from customers are deducted from the value of work in progress for the specific contract or, to the extent advances exceed this value, recorded as customer advances. Customer advances that exceed said contract offsets are classified as trade and other payables.

Figure 5.3 Accounting policy for construction contracts
Source: Aker ASA Annual Report 2008.

for all contracts in progress for which costs incurred plus recognised profits less recognised losses exceeds progress billings.

The gross amount due *to* customers for contract work is equal to:

> Costs incurred
> + recognised profits
> − the sum of recognised losses and progress billings

for all contracts in progress for which progress billings exceed costs incurred plus recognised profits less recognised losses.

Example 5.8

Construction contracts: calculation of gross amount due from customers

Assume that under the percentage of completion method revenue recognised is EUR 10,000, attributable costs recognised are EUR 6,000 and amounts billed in respect of work completed at the balance sheet date are EUR 7,000. In that case, the gross amount due from customers is EUR 3,000 (costs of EUR 6,000 + attributable profit of EUR 4,000 − amount billed of EUR 7,000). This is illustrated below:

	€
Costs incurred to date	6,000
Add: recognised profit	4,000
Deduct: recognised loss	–
Deduct: progress billings	(7,000)
Gross amount due from customers	**3,000**

If of the EUR 7,000 progress billings EUR 5,000 has been paid by the customer at the balance sheet date, the balance sheet would then include 'gross amount due from customers' of EUR 3,000 (as shown above) and 'trade receivables' of EUR 2,000 (= EUR 7,000 − EUR 5,000). There is no specific requirement in the standard to disclose separately EUR 2,000 included in trade receivables.

Assume now that there were two separate contracts, which had costs to date of EUR 6,000 and EUR 4,000 respectively and revenue had been recognised for EUR 10,000 and EUR 4,000 and expected losses of EUR 2,000 had been recognised for the second contract; progress billings were EUR 7,000 and EUR 1,000 respectively. The gross amount due from customer would be EUR 4,000 as demonstrated in Table 5.4 below.

Table 5.4 Gross amount due from customer

	Contract 1 €	Contract 2 €	Total €
Costs incurred to date	6,000	4,000	10,000
Add: recognised profits	4,000	–	4,000
Deduct: recognised losses	–	(2,000)	(2,000)
Deduct: progress billings	(7,000)	(1,000)	(8,000)
Gross amount due from customer	**3,000**	**1,000**	**4,000**

5.4.6 Construction contracts: practical applications

Revision of estimates

The figures to be included in the income statement will be both the appropriate amount of revenue and the associated costs of achieving that revenue, to the extent that these exceed amounts recognised in previous years. The estimated outcome of a contract that extends over several accounting periods will nearly always vary in the light of changes in circumstances and, for this reason, the result of the year will not necessarily represent the profit on the contract that is appropriate to the amount of work carried out in the period. It may also reflect the effect of changes in circumstances during the year that affect the total profit estimated to accrue on completion. This is illustrated in Example 5.9.

Example 5.9

Construction contracts: revision of estimates

A construction contractor has a fixed price contract for EUR 23,000. The initial estimate of costs is EUR 15,000 and the contract is expected to take four years (2006–9). In 2007 the contractor's estimate of total costs increases by EUR 1,000 to EUR 16,000. Of the EUR 1,000 increase, EUR 600 is to be incurred in 2008 and EUR 400 in 2009.

The contractor determines the stage of completion of the contract by comparing the costs of work performed to date with the estimated total costs, as shown in Table 5.5 (below).

Table 5.5 Stage of completion of the contract

	2006 €	2007 €	2008 €	2009 €
Revenue agreed in contract	23,000	23,000	23,000	23,000
Contract costs incurred to date	6,000	9,000	13,350	16,000
Contract costs to complete	9,000	7,000	2,650	–
Total estimated costs	15,000	16,000	16,000	16,000
Estimated profit	8,000	7,000	7,000	7,000
Stage of completion	40% (6,000 ÷ 15,000)	56.3% (9,000 ÷ 16,000)	83.4% (13,350 ÷ 16,000)	100%

The amount of revenue, costs and profit recognised in the income statement in 2006 through 2009 is shown in Table 5.6.

The profit margin in 2007 (20 per cent) is lower than in the subsequent years (30 per cent) because it takes account of the fact that in the light of the revised

Table 5.6 Revenue, costs and profit recognised for the construction contract

	To date €	Prior years €	Current year €	Margin
2006				
Revenue = €23,000 × 40% =	9,200		9,200	
Deduct: Costs = €15,000 × 40% =	6,000		6,000	
				3,200 ÷ 9,200
Profit	3,200		3,200	= 35%
2007				
Revenue = €23,000 × 56.3% =	12,950	9,200	3,750	
Deduct: Costs = €16,000 × 56.3% =	9,000	6,000	3,000	
				750 ÷ 3,750
Profit	3,950	3,200	750	= 20%
2008				
Revenue = €23,000 × 83.4% =	19,182	12,950	6,232	
Deduct: Costs = €16,000 × 83.4% =	13,350	9,000	4,350	
				1,882 ÷ 6,232
Profit	5,832	3,950	1,882	= 30%
2009				
Revenue	23,000	19,182	3,818	
Deduct: Costs	16,000	13,350	2,750	1,068 ÷ 3,818
Profit	7,000	5,832	1,068	= 30%

estimates, too much profit had been taken in 2006 when the total estimated cost was lower.

If the initial cost estimate was EUR 16,000, then the percentage of completion at the end of 2006 would have been 37.5 per cent (= EUR 6,000 ÷ EUR 16,000). This means that revenue of EUR 8,626 (= EUR 23,000 × 37.5%) would have been attributed to the costs incurred to date of EUR 6,000 giving a profit of EUR 2,626 compared with the reported profit of EUR 3,200. The revenue recognised in 2007 is that attributed to the total costs incurred to date, calculated on the basis of the revised estimate, less the revenue of EUR 9,200 reported in 2006. Therefore, the results for 2007 reflect the adjustment necessary in respect of 2006.

Inefficiencies

Contract costs are usually recognised as an expense in the period in which the work to which they relate is performed. Only if the costs relate to future activity should they be carried forward as work in progress. Equally, if costs incurred to date are used to determine the percentage of completion, then revenue attributed to work carried out should not be increased to offset additional costs incurred where these represent inefficiencies. This is illustrated in Example 5.10.

Example 5.10

Construction contracts: inefficiencies

A construction contractor has a fixed price contract for EUR 23,000. The initial estimate of costs is EUR 15,000 and the contract is expected to take four years (2006–9). In 2007 the contractor's estimate of total costs increases by EUR 1,000 to EUR 16,000 as a result of inefficiencies in 2007.

The contractor determines the stage of completion of the contract by comparing the costs of work performed to date with the estimated total costs, as shown in Table 5.7.

Table 5.7 Stage of completion of the contract – first method

	2006	2007	2008	2009
Revenue agreed in contract	23,000	23,000	23,000	23,000
Contract costs incurred to date	6,000	10,000	13,750	16,000
Contract costs to complete	9,000	6,000	2,250	–
Total estimated costs	15,000	16,000	16,000	16,000
Estimated profit	8,000	7,000	7,000	7,000
Stage of completion	40%	62.5%	85.94%	100%
	(6,000 ÷ 15,000)	(10,000 ÷ 16,000)	(13,750 ÷ 16,000)	

The amount of revenue, costs and profit recognised in the income statement in 2006 through 2009 under this method would be as shown in Table 5.8.

Table 5.8 Revenue, costs and profit recognised for the construction contract – first method

	To date	Prior years	Current year	Margin
2006				
Revenue = €23,000 × 40% =	9,200		9,200	
Deduct: Costs = €15,000 × 40% =	6,000		6,000	
Profit	3,200		3,200	3,200 ÷ 9,200 = 35%
2007				
Revenue = €23,000 × 62.5% =	14,375	9,200	5,175	
Deduct: Costs = €16,000 × 62.5% =	10,000	6,000	4,000	
Profit	4,375	3,200	1,175	1,175 ÷ 5,175 = 23%
2008				
Revenue = €23,000 × 85.94% =	19,766	14,375	5,391	
Deduct: Costs = €16,000 × 85.94% =	13,750	10,000	3,750	
Profit	6,016	4,375	1,641	1,641 ÷ 5,391 = 30%
2009				
Revenue	23,000	19,766	3,234	
Deduct: Costs	16,000	13,750	2,250	
Profit	7,000	6,016	984	984 ÷ 3,234 = 30%

As already pointed out in section 5.1, revenue recognition represented one of the biggest issues in restatements of financial statements of listed companies in the USA. Only after 2002 cost- or expense-related issues surpassed revenue recognition issues as the most frequently identified cause of restatements. However, revenue recognition remained the second most frequently identified reason for restatements from July 2002 through September 2005, accounting for 20 per cent of all the restatements (as shown in Figure 5.1). Revenue recognition is a major source of creative accounting in most countries.

Revenue misstatement usually takes one of two forms – recording revenues early or overstating them.

Premature recognition is a problem in both the manufacturing and the service sectors. In the case of goods, it usually arises because entities bring forward the delivery date artificially or recognise revenue before delivery. A US maker of household appliances provides an example of this. It achieved notoriety in the 1990s for its policy of 'bill and hold'. Under this policy, a retailer agreed to buy the appliances subject to later delivery and payment. The company recognised revenue on the contract date and stored the goods in a warehouse until the retailer called for them. This accounting policy came to light in 1998 and the company was forced to restate its 1996 and 1997 results (it later filed for bankruptcy protection in 2001).

In the case of services, long-term contracts are often the reason for early recognition of revenue. The supplier books revenue in full when a service contract is signed or the customer makes non-refundable payments, even though it has continuing obligations under the contract. Instances of premature revenue recognition have increased in recent years because of the growth of outsourcing. Companies now contract out many activities previously performed in-house and these contracts often extend over several accounting periods.

Revenue misstatement can also be traced to aggressive measurement practices. The dotcom bubble of 1999–2000 produced some interesting examples. Priceline, an internet company that offered discounted airline tickets and hotel rooms, reported as revenues the gross amount of the booking (e.g. the price of the hotel room or airline ticket) even though most of the cash went to the hotel or airline. By contrast, travel agencies report as revenue only their commission on the booking. Priceline claimed that, unlike a travel agent, it assumed the risks of owing the ticket/hotel booking, even if for a short period, and its commission was not fixed (the SEC accepted this argument). Promotional discounts offer another means of revenue inflation. For example, an online flower service offers all customers an electronic coupon that cuts twenty per cent off EUR 25 posted price of a floral bouquet. What is the revenue from a sale, EUR 25 (and marketing expenses of EUR 5) or EUR 20? Note that, in both examples, operating profit/loss is not affected.

Why do companies misstate revenue? 'Channel stuffing' (i.e. pushing goods onto distributors) and 'bill and hold' practices can often be traced to sales-based compensation schemes. Divisional managers are awarded bonuses based on meeting sales targets. Top management stretch the targets to outperform. Top managers themselves have an economic interest in inflating sales. Higher revenues usually result in higher profit and their remuneration is linked either directly (via profit-related bonuses) or indirectly (e.g. value of share options) to the amount and rate of increase in their company's profits. For start-up companies that make losses and have negative cash flows, the link between revenues and management wealth is more direct. These companies cannot be valued on the basis of current earnings or cash flows. A practice common in the dotcom bubble years was to use a price/revenue multiple to value them. To the extent that top management believe their firms should be valued in this way, they have an incentive to boost reported revenues, even if there is no impact on the bottom line.

Summary

- Revenue is a subset of income and is defined as the gross inflow of economic benefits arising in the course of the ordinary activities of an entity when those inflows result in increases in equity, other than increases relating to contributions from equity participants.

- Revenue should be recorded based on the substance, not the form, of a transaction.

- Revenue from the sale of goods should be recognised when: (a) an entity has transferred to the buyer the significant risks and rewards of ownership of the goods; (b) the entity retains neither continuing managerial involvement to the degree usually associated with ownership nor effective control over the goods sold; (c) the amount of revenue can be measured reliably; (d) it is probable that the economic benefits associated with the transaction will flow to the entity; and (e) the costs incurred or to be incurred in respect of the transaction can be measured reliably.

- Construction contracts are contracts specifically negotiated for the construction of an asset or a combination of assets that are closely interrelated or interdependent in terms of their design, technology and function or their ultimate purpose or use. They can be fixed price contracts or cost plus contracts.

- When a contract covers a number of assets, the construction of each asset should be treated as a separate construction contract when separate proposals have been submitted for each asset and each asset has been subject to separate negotiation. On the other hand, a group of contracts, whether with a single customer or with several customers, shall be treated as a single construction contract when the group of contracts is negotiated as a single package, the contracts are closely interrelated and the contracts are performed concurrently or in a continuous sequence.

- The 'percentage of completion' method is used to recognise revenue for construction contracts and for transactions involving the rendering of services. Depending on the nature of the transaction, the methods may include: (a) surveys of work performed method; (b) services/works performed to date as a percentage of total services/work to be performed (also called units-of-work-performed method); (c) the proportion that costs incurred to date bear to the estimated total contract costs (also referred to as the cost-to-cost method).

- Revenue recognition can be a major source of creative accounting. Misstatement of revenue usually takes one of two forms: recording revenues early or overstating them.

Research and references

The IASB documents relevant for this chapter are:

- *Framework for the Preparation and Presentation of Financial Statements.*
- IAS 18 – *Revenue.*
- IAS 11 – *Construction Contracts.*

The following are examples of books, research and discussion papers that take the issues of this chapter further:

- Alexander, D., Britton, A. and Jorissen, A. (2007) *International Financial Reporting and Analysis*, 3rd edn. Thomson, Chapters 16 and 18.
- Elliott, B. and Elliott, J. (2009) *Financial Accounting and Reporting*, 13th edn. Financial Times-Prentice Hall, Chapter 19.
- Epstein, B.J. and Jermakowicz, E.K. (2009) *IFRS 2009: Interpretation and Application of International Accounting and Financial Reporting Standards.* Wiley, Chapter 7.
- PricewaterhouseCoopers (2009) *IFRS Manual of Accounting – 2010. Global Guide to International Financial Reporting Standards.* CCH, Chapter 9.
- Stolowy, H. and Lebas, M.J. (2006) *Corporate Financial Reporting. A Global Perspective*, 2nd edn. Thomson, September, Chapter 6.
- Sutton, T. (2004) *Corporate Financial Accounting and Reporting*, 2nd edn. Financial Times-Prentice Hall, Chapter 10.
- US GAO (2006) *Financial Restatements. Update of Public Company Trends, Market Impacts, and Regulatory Enforcement Activities*, July (pdf file available from http://www.gao.gov/new.items/d06678.pdf).

Discussion questions and exercises

5.1   Basic principles of revenue recognition

(a) What is the difference between revenue and income?

(b) Which criteria does IAS 18 require for recognising revenue from the sale of goods?

(c) What is the basic principle for measuring revenue under IAS 18?

(d) To induce a buyer to make a major purchase, the seller allows the buyer to defer payment for one year, with no interest. IAS 18 requires the seller to 'impute' interest in recognising revenue. What does it mean?

(e) For what type of revenue does IAS 18 require the percentage of completion method?

5.2   Definition of key terms relating to construction contracts

(a) What is a construction contract?

(b) How and why should construction contracts be combined or segmented?

(c) How is the stage of completion determined?

(d) What is the effect of variations and claims on revenue recognition for construction contracts?

(e) How is the gross amount due to/from customers determined in relation to construction contracts?

5.3 Revenue from bill and hold sales

Entity E entered into a contract in 2009 to supply video game consoles to customer G. The contract is for 50,000 game consoles at EUR 100 each. The contract contains specific instructions from customer G with regard to the timing and location of the delivery. Entity E should deliver the consoles to customer G in 2010 at a date to be specified by the customer. Usual payment terms apply. Entity E's year-end is 31 December.

At 31 December 2009, entity E has inventory of 60,000 game consoles, including the 50,000 relating to the contract with customer G. However, entity E cannot use the 50,000 game consoles to satisfy other sales orders and at 31 December 2009 the title to the 50,000 consoles has passed to customer G. Delivery is expected to take place in 2010.

When should entity E recognise revenue?

5.4 Goods shipped subject to conditions

A clothing retailer sells T-shirts at a price of EUR 10 each. The T-shirts cost the retailer EUR 5 each. Customers have the right to return T-shirts within four weeks of purchase, provided that the T-shirts are unworn and undamaged. Based on the historical evidence, the retailer expects that 10 per cent of the T-shirts will be returned, of which half will be subsequently resold by the retailer.

When and what revenue should be recognised?

5.5 Continuing managerial involvement

Entity J sells a racehorse to entity K. As part of the arrangement entity J continues to house and train the horse, determine which races the horse will enter and set stud fees for the horse.

Should entity J recognise revenue on the sale of the horse to entity K?

5.6 Application of revenue recognition to an agency arrangement

Entity X distributes entity Y's products under a distribution agreement. The terms and conditions of the contract are such that entity X:

- Obtains title to the goods and sells them to third-party retailers.
- Stores, repackages, transport and invoices the goods sold to third-party retailers.
- Earns a fixed margin on the products sold to the retailers, but has no flexibility in establishing the sales price.
- Has the right to return the goods to entity Y without penalty.
- Is responsible for the goods while the goods are stored in entity X's warehouse, but entity Y bears the risk of obsolete goods.

Entity Y retains product liability. Entity Y is, therefore, responsible for manufacturing defects. Also, the credit risk rests with entity Y.

(a) Should entity Y recognise revenue on the transfer of the goods to entity X?
(b) What revenue should entity X recognise?

5.7 Combining and segmenting construction contracts

A contractor is negotiating two contracts with a single customer. The customer should either accept both contracts or reject both. The first contract will be for the design of a chemical plant and the second for the plant's construction. The planned profit margin on the design contract is 20 per cent and the planned profit margin on constructing the plant is 10 per cent.

How should the contracts be accounted for?

5.8 Revenue and costs attributable to the stage of completion

Company X is executing a gigantic project of constructing the tallest building in the country. The project is expected to take three years to complete. The company has signed a fixed price contract of EUR 36m for the construction of this prestigious tower. The details of the costs incurred to date in the first year are listed below:

Site labour costs	€ 3,000,000
Cost of construction material	€ 9,000,000
Depreciation of special plant and equipment used in contracting to build the tallest building	€ 1,500,000
Marketing and selling costs to get the tallest building in the country the right exposure	€ 3,000,000
Total	€16,500,000

Additional contract costs estimated to complete amount to EUR 16,500,000.

Calculate the percentage of completion and the amounts of revenue, costs and profit to be recognised under IAS 11.

5.9 Expected losses on a construction contract

Entity A is constructing a building for its customer. The construction is in the second year of a three year project.

Management had originally assessed the contract to be profitable and recognised a profit in year 1 of EUR 40,000 based on the percentage of the contract that had been completed at that time. Management now believe the contract will incur a loss of EUR 60,000.

Management have proposed that the loss of EUR 60,000 on the contract is recognised in year 2, but have questioned how the profit of EUR 40,000 recognised in year 1 should be treated.

What would you suggest?

5.10 Disclosures for construction contracts

In 2006 entity X was invited to tender for the construction of a residential block and connected shopping arcade with common plaza and garden and play areas. Tenders were required to detail the costs of each element separately, but it was clear that only one contractor would win the entire contract due to the interrelated aspect of the development.

During 2006, entity X management travelled to Canada to visit three possible designers in order to obtain their preliminary design proposals, of which only one would be selected. The cost of the visit was EUR 40,000. Later in 2006, having selected one designer, entity X management returned to Canada to clarify design details and request construction of a scale model in order to make a presentation of the tender to the ultimate customer. The cost of the second trip was EUR 30,000.

During 2007, but before the 2006 annual report was issued, entity X was notified that it had been awarded the contract. However, the contract was not signed until after the 2006 annual report was issued.

The contract was for a total of EUR 32m, comprising EUR 18m for the residential block, EUR 10m for the shopping arcade and EUR 4m for the common plaza, garden and play area. A mobilization advance of EUR 2m was paid at the outset, EUR 2m was payable at the end of 2007, EUR 10m at the end of 2008 and EUR 16m was payable at the end of 2009, at which point the development would be complete and EUR 2m was to be held back as a retention for one year (IAS 11 para 41 defines retentions as *amounts of progress billings that are not paid until the satisfaction of conditions specified in the contract for the payment of such amounts or until defects have been rectified*).

Entity X initially estimated that the total costs of the project would be EUR 24m, of which EUR 14m would be for the residential block, EUR 8m for the shopping arcade and EUR 2m for the plaza, garden and play area. Included in this cost is EUR 2m of plant acquired specifically for the project that could not be used subsequently. The estimated residual value of this plant at the end of the contract was EUR 200,000. Also included in the overall cost was 30 months of depreciation on general plant and equipment already owned by entity X at EUR 100,000 per month. The on-site accounts staff cost included in the estimate was EUR 10,000 per month. Their role was to maintain and record time cards of workers and receive and issue materials.

Costs incurred at each year-end were:

	2007 €000	2008 €000	2009 €000	Total €000
Residential block	2,000	6,000	6,000	14,000
Shopping arcade	1,000	3,600	3,400	8,000
Plaza, gardens and play area	–	400	1,600	2,000
Total	3,000	10,000	11,000	24,000

The costs at the end of 2007 include EUR 500,000 of materials delivered to the site for use in 2008.

In 2008, EUR 400,000 was paid to sub-contractors in advance for the work to be performed in 2009 on the plaza, gardens and play area.

During 2008 due to a fire at the neighbouring plot, the police cordoned off the whole area for a month while investigations were conducted. During this time all plant and equipment remained idle on site. However, work continued at entity X's workshop and yard.

During 2008, the customer requested a variation in the contract for EUR 2m; the cost of the variation was estimated at EUR 1.5m. However, the variation was not approved by the customer until after entity X's 2008 annual report was authorised for issue. Entity X incurred the extra costs for the variation in 2008.

Prepare entity X's income statement and the amounts that should be presented in the balance sheet for 2006 through 2009.

6 Inventories (IAS 2)

Contents

Although temporary changes in the load of activity can be ignored, persistent variation from the range of normal activity should lead to revision of the previous normal level of activity.

Where there is abnormally high production, the allocation of overheads is decreased so that inventory is not measured above cost (IAS 2 para 12). To include a 'normal' level of overhead in such a case would overstate inventory. For example, say, normal production is 20 and normal overhead (fixed) is EUR 20 so that 1 is allocated to each unit. If there are three items in inventory, then EUR 3 of overhead is carried forward. If, however, 30 are actually produced, then only EUR 0.667 (= EUR 20 ÷ 30 units) should be allocated to each item, so if there are three items in inventory at end of the year, EUR 2 of overhead is carried forward. Allocating EUR 1 to each inventory item, where 30 are produced would be recording above cost. Classifying overheads for the purpose of the allocation takes the function of the overhead as its distinguishing characteristic (for example, whether it is a function of production, marketing, selling or administration), rather than whether the overhead varies with time or with volume. The costs of general management, as distinct from functional management, are not directly related to the current production and are, therefore, excluded from costs of conversion.

A company should not include in the cost of inventory external distribution costs such as those relating to the transfer of goods from a sales depot to an external customer. It may, however, include a proportion of the costs that a company incurs in distributing goods from its factory to its sales depot, as these are costs incurred in bringing the inventory to its present location. Furthermore, distribution costs should be taken into account when assessing the net realisable value (see section 6.2.3).

IAS 2 allows borrowing costs to be included in the cost of inventory. However, this is limited to those circumstances where the allowed alternative treatment for borrowing costs, set out in IAS 23 – *Borrowing Costs*, applies (IAS 2 para 17). Under the allowed alternative treatment in IAS 23 borrowing costs should be expensed as incurred except to the extent that those borrowing costs directly attributable to the acquisition, construction or production of a *qualifying asset* are capitalised as part of that asset's cost. A qualifying asset is one which takes a substantial period of time to get ready for its intended use or sale. Inventory items would rarely meet this criterion.

A production process may result in more than one product being produced simultaneously. This is the case, for example, when joint products are produced or when there is a main product and a by-product. When the costs of conversion of each product are not separately identifiable, they are allocated between the products on a rational and consistent basis. The allocation may be based, for example, on the relative sales value of each product either at the stage in the production process when the products become separately identifiable, or at the completion of production. Most by-products, by their nature, are immaterial. When this is the case, they are often measured at net realisable value and this value is deducted from the cost of the main product. As a result, the carrying amount of the main product will not be materially different from its cost (IAS 2 para 14) (see Figure 6.3 for an example of an accounting policy for by-products).

Other costs

Other costs are included in the cost of inventories only to the extent that they are incurred in bringing the inventories to their present location and condition. For

> ### Inventories
>
> Inventories are valued at the lower of cost (which includes the applicable proportion of production overheads) and net realisable value.
>
> Platinum Group Metals (PGMs) inventory is valued by allocating costs, based on the joint cost of production, apportioned according to the relative sales value of each of the three main metals produced.
>
> By-product metals are valued at the incremental cost of production from the point of split-off from the PGM processing stream.
>
> In the process of initially developing the ore reserve it is common that metal is produced, although not at normal operating levels. Development is split into different phases according to the mining method used with differing levels of production expected in each phase. The Group recognises the metal produced in each development phase in inventory with an appropriate proportion of cost as operating costs. This allocation is calculated by reference to the produced volumes in relation to the total volumes expected from the development.

Figure 6.3 Example of an accounting policy for by-products
Source: Lonmin Plc Annual Report 2008.

example, it may be appropriate to include non-production overheads or the costs of designing products for specific customers in the cost of inventories (IAS 2 para 15).

Examples of costs excluded from the cost of inventories and recognised as expenses in the period in which they are incurred are (IAS 2 para 16):

- abnormal amounts of wasted materials, labour or other production costs;
- storage costs, unless those costs are necessary in the production process before a further production stage;
- administrative overheads that do not contribute to bringing inventories to their present location and condition;
- selling costs.

Figure 6.4 highlights examples of the types of costs that can be included in the cost of inventories.

Examples 6.2 and 6.3 illustrate the type of costs that may or may not be included in inventories.

Example 6.2

Storage costs

The production of whisky involves the distilling of aged whisky in a cask prior to bottling. Should storage cost be included in the cost of inventory?

Capitalisation of storage costs is allowed only if the storage is necessary in the production process prior to a further production stage (see IAS 2 para 16). Therefore, in this situation, the storage cost the entity incurs during the distilling process should be capitalised, as ageing is integral to making the finished product saleable.

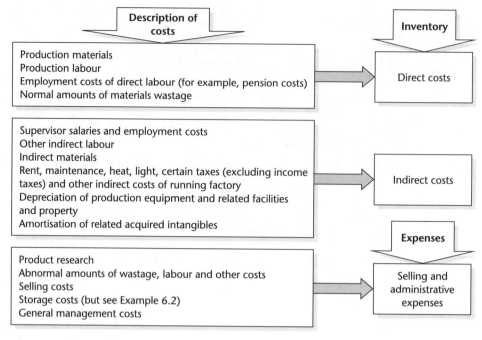

Figure 6.4 Cost of inventories

Example 6.3

Editing and translation costs

A publisher produces travel guides. Part of the costs of producing the guides includes the costs of editing, translating and collecting the data for the travel guides.

Should the editing and translation costs be included in the cost of inventory held by a publisher?

The costs incurred in editing, translating and collecting data should be included in the cost of inventories, as they are direct costs related to producing the travel guides for sale. The cost of inventories comprises all costs of purchase, costs of conversion and other costs incurred to bring the inventories to their present location and condition (IAS 2 para 10).

An entity may purchase inventories on deferred settlement terms. When the arrangement effectively contains a financing element, that element, for example, the difference between the purchase price for normal credit terms and the amount paid, is recognised as interest expense over the period of the financing (IAS 2 para 18).

Cost of inventories of a service provider

To the extent that service providers have inventories, they should measure them at their production costs. Normally, these costs consist primarily of labour and other

> Notes on consolidated financial statements (extract)
> Inventories
>
> Raw materials and consumables are measured at cost assigned by using the first-in, first-out method.
>
> Work in progress and finished goods are stated at cost assigned by using the first-in, first-out method. Cost comprises direct production costs such as raw materials, consumables, energy and labour, and production overheads such as employee costs, depreciation, maintenance etc. The production overheads are measured based on a standard cost method which is reviewed regularly in order to ensure relevant measures of utilisation, production lead time etc.
>
> If the expected sales price less completion costs and costs to execute sales (net realisable value) is lower than the carrying amount, a write-down is recognised for the amount by which the carrying amount exceeds its net realisable value.

Figure 6.5 Example of the use of standard costs
Source: Novo Nordisk Annual Report 2008.

costs of personnel directly engaged in providing the service, including supervisory personnel, and attributable overheads. Labour and other costs relating to sales and general administrative personnel are not included but are recognised as expenses in the period in which they are incurred (IAS 2 para 19).

Techniques for the measurement of cost

Techniques for the measurement of the cost of inventories, such as the standard cost method or the retail method, may be used for convenience if the results approximate cost. Standard costs take into account normal levels of materials and supplies, labour, efficiency and capacity utilisation. They should be regularly reviewed and, if necessary, revised in the light of current conditions (IAS 2 para 21) (see Figure 6.4).

The retail method is often used in the retail industry for measuring inventories of large numbers of rapidly changing items with similar margins for which it is impracticable to use other costing methods. The cost of inventory is determined by reducing the sales value of the inventory by an appropriate percentage gross margin. The percentage used should take into consideration inventory that has been marked down to below its original selling price. An average percentage for each retail department is often used (IAS 2 para 22).

6.2.2 Cost formulas

The cost of inventories of items that are not ordinarily interchangeable and goods or services produced and segregated for specific projects should be assigned by using specific identification of their individual costs (IAS 2 para 23).

Specific identification of cost means that specific costs are attributed to identified items of inventory. This is appropriate for items that are segregated for a specific project, regardless of whether they have been bought or produced. However, specific identification of costs is inappropriate when there are large numbers of items of inventory that are ordinarily interchangeable. In such circumstances, the method of selecting those items that remain in inventories could be used to obtain predetermined effects on the income statement (IAS 2 para 24).

The cost of inventories, other than those not ordinarily interchangeable, should be assigned by using the first-in, first-out (FIFO) or weighted average cost (AVCO) formula. An entity should use the same cost formula for all inventories having similar nature and use in the entity. For inventories with a different nature or use, different cost formulas may be justified (IAS 2 para 25).

For example, inventories used in one operating segment may have a use to the entity different from the same type of inventories used in another operating segment. However, a difference in geographical location of inventories (or the respective tax rules), by itself, is not sufficient to justify the use of different cost formulas (IAS 2 para 26).

The FIFO formula assumes that the items of inventory that were purchased or produced first are sold first, and consequently the items remaining in inventory at the end of the period are those most recently purchased or produced. Under the AVCO formula, the cost of each item is determined from the weighted average of the cost of similar items at the beginning of a period and the cost of similar items purchased or produced during the period. The average may be calculated on a periodic basis, or as each additional shipment is received, depending upon the circumstances of the entity (IAS 2 para 27).

Example 6.4 illustrates these cost formulas.

Example 6.4

Application of cost formulas

Positano Parts uses the perpetual inventory method and its reporting date is 31 December. Table 6.1 reports information extracted from its records about one of Positano Parts' products.

Table 6.1 Inventory movements of Positano Parts

2010		No. of units	Unit cost €	Total cost €	Total revenue €
01/01	Beginning balance	800	14.00	11,200	
06/01	Purchased	300	14.10	4,230	
05/02	Sold @ €24.00 per unit	1,000			24,000
19/03	Purchased	1,100	14.70	16,170	
24/03	Purchase returns	80	14.70	1,176	
10/04	Sold @ €24.20 per unit	700			16,940
22/06	Purchased	8,400	15.00	126,000	
31/07	Sold @ €26.50 per unit	1,800			47,700
04/08	Sales returns @ €26.50 per unit	20			(530)
04/09	Sold @ €27.00 per unit	3,500			94,500
06/10	Purchased	500	16.00	8,000	
27/11	Sold @ €30.00 per unit	3,100			93,000

We will illustrate:

1 The calculation of the cost of inventory on hand at 31 December 2010 and the cost of sales for the year ended 31 December 2010, using:
   (a) the FIFO cost formula (see Table 6.2 below);
   (b) the (moving) AVCO formula (we round the average unit cost to the nearest cent, and round the total cost amounts to the nearest euro) (see Table 6.3 on page 184).

2 The trading section of the income statement for the year ended 31 December 2010, using:
   (a) the FIFO cost formula (see Table 6.4 on page 184);
   (b) the (moving) AVCO formula (see Table 6.4).

Because the purchase price has been rising throughout the year, using the FIFO formula produces a lower cost of sales (higher gross profit) and a higher inventory balance than the (moving) AVCO formula. However, the difference is not significant.

Table 6.2 Cost of sales determined using the FIFO cost formula

Date	Details	Purchases			Cost of sales			Balance*		
		No. units	Unit cost €	Total cost €	No. units	Unit cost €	Total cost €	No. units	Unit cost €	Total cost €
01/01	Inventory balance							800	14.00	11,200
06/01	Purchases	300	14.10	4,230				800	14.00	11,200
								300	14.10	4,230
05/02	Sales				800	14.00	11,200			
					200	14.10	2,820	100	14.10	1,410
19/03	Purchases	1,100	14.70	16,170				100	14.10	1,410
								1,100	14.70	16,170
24/03	Purchase returns	(80)	14.70	(1,176)				100	14.10	1,410
								1,020	14.70	14,994
10/04	Sales				100	14.10	1,410			
					600	14.70	8,820	420	14.70	6,174
22/06	Purchases	8,400	15.00	126,000				420	14.70	6,174
								8,400	14.70	126,000
31/07	Sales				420	14.70	6,174			
					1,380	15.00	20,700	7,020	15.00	105,300
04/08	Sale returns**				(20)	15.00	(300)	7,040	15.00	105,600
04/09	Sales				3,500	15.00	52,500	3,540	15.00	53,100
06/10	Purchases	500	16.00	8,000				3,540	15.00	53,100
								500	16.00	8,000
27/11	Sales				3,100	15.00	46,500	440	15.00	6,600
								500	16.00	8,000
				153,224			149,824			

Notes:
* As it is assumed the earliest purchases are sold first, a separate balance of each purchase at a different price should be maintained.
** The principle of 'last out-first in' is applied to sales returns.

Inventories

Inventories and work in progress are valued at the lower of acquisition cost, at normal capacity utilization, and net realizable value. Net realizable value is defined as the estimated selling price in the ordinary course of business less the estimated costs of completion and the estimated costs necessary to make the sale at market value. The cost of inventories is assigned by using the weighted average cost formula. The cost of inventories are recognized as expense and included in cost of goods sold. Provisions for obsolescence are included in the value for inventory.

Note 14 Inventories

	Group December 31		Parent Company December 31	
	2008	2007	2008	2007
Raw materials	3,029	3,131	114	124
Products in progress	127	172	4	3
Finished products	9,440	9,048	119	234
Advances to suppliers	84	47	–	–
Total	12,680	12,398	237	361

Figure 6.7 Example of disclosures on inventory

Source: Electrolux Annual Report 2008.

- an increase in the estimated costs of completion or the estimated costs of making the sale (e.g. air-conditioning plants).

Inventories are usually written down to the NRV item by item. In some circumstances, however, it may be appropriate to group similar or related items. This may be the case for items of inventory relating to the same product line that have similar purposes or end uses, are produced and marketed in the same geographical area, and cannot be practicably evaluated separately from other items in that product line (IAS 2 para 29).

Example 6.5

Lower of cost and NRV test

On 31 March 2010 Ballata had items in its inventory as shown in Table 6.5.

Table 6.5 Ballata inventories as at 31 March 2010

Type of product	No. of products on hand	Cost/unit €	Selling price/unit €	Estimated cost of realisation/unit €
'Ping' irons No. 3	120	49	72	35
doz golf balls	475	18	21	2
High velocity shotguns	17	420	680	68
9 mm Uzi	18	370	740	37
Terminator 2 videos	10	79	270	13
Return to the Blue Lagoon	100	8	7	1

To determine the lower of cost and NRV to be shown in Ballata's financial statements as at 31 March 2010, we need to compare these two values item by item as shown in Table 6.6.

Table 6.6 Ballata inventories at the lower of cost and NRV as at 31 March 2010

Type of product	No. of products on hand	Cost/unit €	Selling price/unit €	Estimated cost of realisation/unit €	NRV/unit €	Total NRV €	Total cost €	Lower of cost and NRV €
'Ping' irons No. 3	120	49	72	35	37	4,440	5,880	4,440
doz golf balls	475	18	21	2	19	9,025	8,550	8,550
High velocity shotguns	17	420	680	68	612	10,404	7,140	7,140
9 mm Uzi	18	370	740	37	703	12,654	6,660	6,660
Terminator 2 videos	10	79	270	13	257	2,570	790	790
Return to the Blue Lagoon	100	8	7	1	6	600	800	600
						39,693	29,820	28,180

Therefore, the value of inventory as at 31 March 2010 is EUR 28,180.

Estimates of NRV should be based on the most reliable information available at the time the estimates are made (i.e. balance sheet date), of the amount the inventories are expected to realise. Thus, estimates should be made of:

- expected selling price
- estimated cost of completion, if any
- estimated selling costs.

These estimates should take into consideration fluctuations of price or costs directly relating to events occurring after the end of the period to the extent that such events confirm conditions existing at the end of the period.

The calculation of NRV should also take account of the intended use of the inventory. For example, the NRV of inventories held to satisfy a particular sales or service contract should be based on the contract price. Contracts for future sales or for future purchases of raw materials may give rise to provisions where such contracts are onerous. An example of the former is where a future sales contract is set at a price that is below the entity's cost of production of the relevant goods. An example of the latter is where an entity has a purchase commitment for goods or raw materials that is at a price above the price at which the entity can sell on the goods or manufacture the finished product from the raw materials. Onerous contracts are accounted for under IAS 37 – *Provisions, Contingent Liabilities and Contingent Assets* (IAS 2 para 31).

Materials and other supplies held for use in the production of inventories should not be written-down below cost if the finished products in which they will be incorporated are expected to be sold at or above cost. However, when a decline in the price of materials indicates that the cost of the finished products exceeds NRV, the materials should be written down to NRV. In such circumstances, the replacement cost of the materials may be the best available measure of their NRV (IAS 2 para 32).

Example 6.6

Net realisable value (NRV)

Entity B manufactures telecommunication equipment in three stages. There is a market for the semi-finished product for each stage, but the entity only sells the completed product. The following are details of the cost structure of the tele-communication equipment as at 31 December 2010 (financial year-end):

	Cost/unit	Selling price/unit
	€	€
Stage 1	300	240
Stage 2 – conversion costs	80	180
	380	420
Stage 3 – conversion costs	120	140
	500	560

Assuming that the selling costs are immaterial, what is the NRV of the semi-finished product at stage 1 as at 31 December 2010?

Although the selling price per unit at stage 1 is EUR 240, the calculation of the NRV of work in progress should consider the expected selling price of the finished products in which it will be incorporated (IAS 2 para 32). The profit margin on the estimated cost of completion should, therefore, be considered when calculating the NRV of work in progress if the entity has the ability to dispose of the finished product at a price that exceeds the production cost.

Therefore, the NRV of the semi-finished product at stage 1 is:

	€
Selling price of completed product	560
Deduct stage 3 conversion costs	(120)
Deduct stage 2 conversion costs	(80)
NRV at stage 1	360

A new assessment should be made of NRV at each subsequent period end. When the circumstances that previously caused inventories to be written down below cost no longer exist or when there is clear evidence of an increase in NRV because of changed economic circumstances, the amount of the write-down should be reversed (i.e. the reversal is limited to the amount of the original write-down) so that the new carrying amount represents the lower of the cost and the revised NRV. This occurs, for example, when an item of inventory that is carried at NRV, because its selling price had declined, is still on hand in a subsequent period and its selling price has increased (IAS 2 para 33).

6.2.4 Derecognition

When inventories are sold, the carrying amount of those inventories should be recognised as an expense in the period in which the related revenue is recognised. The amount of any write-down of inventories to NRV and all losses of inventories should be recognised as an expense in the period the write-down or loss occurs. The amount of any reversal of any write-down of inventories, arising from an increase in NRV, should be recognised as a reduction of the cost of sales for the corresponding amount in the period in which the reversal occurs (IAS 2 para 34).

Some inventories may be allocated to other asset accounts, for example, inventory used as a component of self-constructed property, plant or equipment. Inventories allocated to a fixed asset in this way should be depreciated and recognised as an expense during the useful life of that asset (IAS 2 para 35).

6.3 Financial analysis and interpretation

Inventories are items held for sale or used to manufacture products that will be sold. A retail entity would list only one category of inventory on the balance sheet: merchandise inventories purchased for resale to the public. A manufacturing entity, in contrast, would carry three main categories of inventories: raw materials and consumable supplies, work in progress (WIP) and finished goods. Exceptions would be service-oriented companies that carry little inventory as seen in section 6.1. Table 6.7 illustrates the proportion of inventories at the manufacturing, wholesale and retail levels. For these industries – drugs, household furniture and sporting goods – the percentage of inventories to total assets ranges from 20.4 to 39.6 per cent for manufacturing companies, to 34.6 to 57.8 per cent for retail firms.

Table 6.7 Inventories as a percentage of total assets

Industries	%
Manufacturing	
Pharmaceutical preparations	20.4
Household furniture	33.3
Sporting and athletic goods	39.6
Wholesale	
Drugs	30.4
Furniture	30.1
Sporting and recreational goods	44.8
Retail	
Pharmacies and drug stores	34.6
Furniture stores	48.9
Sporting goods stores	57.8

Source: Data from The Risk Management Association, Annual Statement Studies, Philadelphia, PA, 2007. © '2008' by RMA-The Risk Management Association. All Rights Reserved. No part of this table may be reproduced or utilized in any form or by any means without permission in writing. Refer to www.rmahq.org for further information.

Given the relative magnitude of inventory, the accounting method chosen to value inventory and the associated measurement of cost of sales have a considerable impact on an entity's financial position and operating results. Understanding the fundamentals of inventory accounting and the effect that different methods have on an entity's financial statements is essential to the user of financial statement information.

The method chosen by an entity to account for inventory determines the value of inventory in the balance sheet and the amount of expense recognised for cost of sales in the income statement with significant implications for tax payments. Section 6.2.2 illustrates that inventory valuation is based on the *assumption* regarding the flow of goods and has nothing to do with the *actual* order in which products are sold (or entered into the production process). The cost flow assumption (FIFO, LIFO or AVCO) is made in order to match the cost of products sold during an accounting period to the revenue generated from the sales and to assign a value to the inventory remaining unsold at the end of the accounting period. IAS 2 does not allow the use of LIFO, because it does not faithfully represent inventory flows. The IASB noted that the use of LIFO is often tax driven and concluded that tax considerations do not provide a conceptual basis for selecting an accounting treatment; and that it is therefore not acceptable to allow such an accounting treatment purely because of tax considerations.

Although LIFO is not allowed by IAS 2, we will use it in the examples set out below to illustrate the impact of these three methods on the financial statements.

6.3.1 Gross profit resulting from different valuation methods

In the following example we illustrate how gross profit changes depending on the method used for inventory accounting.

Example 6.7

Inventory cost formulas and gross profit

An entity that supplies coal to factories has the transactions shown in Table 6.8 during the first week of March 2010.

Table 6.8 Transactions involving inventories in the first week of March 2010

		Tonnes	Cost/selling price per tonne €
1 March	Beginning inventory	3,000	10
2 March	Purchases	4,000	11
3 March	Purchases	7,000	12
		14,000	
6 March	Sales	(9,000)	15
	Ending inventory	5,000	

The gross profit and gross profit margin for the first week of March under FIFO, LIFO and AVCO are shown in Table 6.9 below.

Table 6.9 Gross profit and gross profit margin under different cost formulas

	FIFO		LIFO		AVCO	
	€	%	€	%	€	%
Sales	135,000	100	135,000	100	135,000	100
Cost of sales	98,000	73	106,000	79	101,570	75
Gross profit	37,000	27	29,000	21	33,430	25
Ending inventory	60,000		52,000		56,430	

FIFO will give the highest gross profit during a period of rising prices, because sales are matched with the earlier (and cheaper) purchases. LIFO will give the lowest gross profit because sales are matched against the more recent (and dearer) purchases. The AVCO formula will normally give a figure that is closer to the FIFO cost formula.

The ending inventory figure in the balance sheet will be the highest under FIFO, because the cost of goods unsold and in stock will be based on the more recent (and dearer) purchases.

LIFO will give the lowest ending inventory figure as the goods unsold and in stock at the end of an accounting period will be based on the earlier (and cheaper) purchases.

Once again, the AVCO formula will normally give a figure that is closer to FIFO than to LIFO.

Nothing in our choice of cost formulas affects trade payables. We record purchases at cost and account for the related liability in the same way under all three cost formulas. All that changes is how we allocate those costs between inventory and cost of sales.

During a period of rising prices, FIFO yields higher inventory and higher gross profit than does LIFO. This result is consistent with the accounting equation that requires that:

Assets = Liabilities + Owners' equity.

If inventory is higher under FIFO (higher assets), either liabilities or owners' equity would be higher, as the equation should balance. Higher gross profit under FIFO implies higher net profit and, therefore, higher owner's equity.

6.3.2 Effects of inventory misstatements on financial analysis

Inventory errors can arise as a result of a number of factors. For example, incorrect physical counts might have been taken because goods that were in receiving or shipping areas instead of in the warehouse were erroneously omitted. A clerk might type a 5 on the key board instead of a 6.

other costs of personnel directly engaged in providing the service, including supervisory personnel, and attributable overheads.

- When inventories are sold, the carrying amount of those inventories should be recognised as an expense in the period in which the related revenue is recognised. The amount of any write-down of inventories to NRV and all losses of inventories should be recognised as an expense in the period the write-down or loss occurs. Some inventories may be allocated to other asset accounts, for example, inventory used as a component of self-constructed property, plant or equipment. In this case, they should be depreciated and recognised as an expense over the useful life of that asset.

- Given the relative magnitude of inventory, the accounting method chosen to value inventory and the associated measurement of cost of sales have a considerable impact on an entity's operating results and financial position. Understanding the fundamentals of inventory accounting and the effect that different methods have on an entity's financial statements is essential to the user of financial information.

- Inventory errors can arise as a result of a number of factors. For example, incorrect physical counts might arise because goods that are in receiving or shipping areas instead of in the warehouse are erroneously omitted. An inventory error usually affects two reporting periods. Amounts will be either overstated or understated in the period in which the error occurs, and the effect will then be counterbalanced by identical offsetting amounts in the following period.

- LIFO reserve is the difference between inventories valued at LIFO and what they would be under FIFO.

Research and references

The IASB document relevant for this chapter is IAS 2 – *Inventories*.

The following are examples of books that take the issues of this chapter further:

- Alexander, D., Britton, A. and Jorissen, A. (2007) *International Financial Reporting and Analysis*, 3rd edn. Thomson, Chapter 16.
- Alfredson, K., Leo, K., Picker, R., Loftus, J., Clark, K. and Wise, V. (2009) *Applying International Financial Reporting Standard*, 2nd edn. Wiley, Chapter 8.
- Elliott, B. and Elliott, J. (2009) *Financial Accounting and Reporting*, 13th edn. Financial Times-Prentice Hall, Chapter 18.
- Epstein, B.J. and Jermakowicz, E.K. (2009) *IFRS 2009: Interpretation and Application of International Accounting and Financial Reporting Standards*. Wiley, Chapter 6.
- Fraser, L.M. and Ormiston, A. (2010) *Understanding Financial Statements*, 9th edn. Prentice-Hall, Chapter 2.
- Kothari, J. and Barone, E. (2006) *Financial Accounting. An International Approach*. Financial Times-Prentice Hall, Chapter 6.
- PricewaterhouseCoopers (2009) *IFRS Manual of Accounting – 2010. Global Guide to International Financial Reporting Standards*. CCH, Chapter 20.
- Stolowy, H. and Lebas, M.J. (2006) *Corporate Financial Reporting. A Global Perspective*, 2nd edn. Thomson, September, Chapters 5 and 9.
- Sutton, T. (2004) *Corporate Financial Accounting and Reporting*, 2nd edn. Financial Times-Prentice Hall, Chapter 9.

Discussion questions and exercises

6.1 Definitions

(a) Define 'cost' in relation to inventory.
(b) What is meant by NRV?
(c) Explain the rule of lower of cost and NRV for inventory.

6.2 Cost formulas

(a) In what circumstances should assumptions be made in order to assign a cost to inventory items when they are sold?
(b) What is the difference between FIFO, LIFO and AVCO cost formulas?
(c) Compare and contrast the impact on the reported profit and asset value for an accounting period of the three cost formulas.

6.3 Cost of inventory

Entity A purchases motorcycles from Italy, Germany and Japan. It sells to domestic and foreign customers. Entity A incurred the following expenses during 2010:

(a) cost of purchases (based on vendors' invoices);
(b) trade discounts on purchases;
(c) import duties;
(d) freight insurance on purchases;
(e) other handling costs relating to imports;
(f) salaries of accounting department;
(g) brokerage commission payable to indenting agents for arranging imports;
(h) sales commission payable to sales agents;
(i) after-sales warranty costs.

Entity A seeks your advice on which costs are permitted under IAS 2 to be included in the cost of inventory.

6.4 FIFO cost formula

Entity B is a newly established international trading company. It commenced its operations in 2008. Entity B imports goods from China and sells in the local market. It uses the FIFO method to value its inventory. Listed below are purchases and sales made by the entity during 2009:

Purchases
January 2009	10,000 units @ €50 each
March 2009	15,000 units @ €60 each
September 2009	20,000 units @ €70 each

Sales
May 2009	15,000 units
November 2009	20,000 units

Based on the FIFO cost assumption, compute the value of inventory at 31 May 2009, 30 September 2009 and 31 December 2009.

6.5   AVCO formula

Entity C, a newly incorporated company, uses the latest version of a software package (EXODUS) to cost and value its inventory. The software uses the AVCO formula to value inventory. The following are the purchases and sales made by entity C during 2009 (being a newly set up company, entity C has no beginning inventory):

Purchases

15 January	100 units @ €500 per unit
10 March	150 units @ €600 per unit
25 September	400 units @ €700 per unit
	650 units

Sales

15 March	150 units
15 December	170 units
	320 units

Entity C has approached you to help value its inventory and the cost per unit of the inventory at 31 March 2009, 30 September 2009, and 31 December 2009, using the AVCO formula.

6.6   Application of cost formulas

The following information has been extracted from the records of entity D about one of its products. Entity D's reporting date is 30 September 2010.

		No. units	Unit cost €	Total cost €
2009				
01/10	Beginning balance	1,600	28.00	44,800
06/10	Purchased	600	28.20	16,920
05/11	Sold @ €48.00 per unit	2,000		
19/12	Purchased	2,200	29.40	64,680
24/12	Purchases returns	160	29.40	4,704
2010				
10/01	Sold @ €48.40 per unit	1,400		
22/03	Purchased	16,800	30.00	504,000
30/04	Sold @ €53.00 per unit	3,600		
04/05	Sales returns @ €53.00 per unit	40		
04/06	Sold @ €54.00 per unit	7,000		
06/08	Purchased	1,000	32.00	32,000
27/09	Sold @ €60.00 per unit	6,200		

Determine the cost of inventory on hand at 30 September 2010 and the cost of sales for the year ended 30 September 2010, using:

(a) the FIFO cost formula;

(b) the (moving) AVCO formula (round the average unit costs to the nearest cent, and round the total cost amounts to the nearest euro).

6.7 Application of cost formulas

Assume that entity E's beginning inventory on 1 March 2010 is nil. All inventory is finished goods and is of the same type. Details of the inventory received and sent out by entity E are shown below:

	Quantity (unit)	Cost per unit €
Batch 1 received on 1 March 2010	2	6.00
Batch 2 received on 15 March 2010	4	9.00

Assuming that on 25 March 2010 the entity sold 5 units, determine the value of its ending inventory on 31 March 2010 using:

(a) FIFO cost formula;
(b) AVCO formula.

6.8 Lower of cost and NRV

The following information relates to the inventory on hand at 30 June 2010 held by entity F.

Item no.	Quantity	Cost per unit €	Cost to replace €	Estimated selling price €	Cost of completion and disposal €
A1458	600	4.60	4.82	7.50	0.98
A1965	815	6.80	6.52	7.00	1.10
B6730	749	14.68	14.70	20.00	1.90
D0943	98	2.46	2.28	2.00	0.24
G8123	156	7.12	7.12	11.40	1.34
W2167	1492	12.24	12.30	15.32	0.72

Calculate the value of inventory on hand at 30 June 2010 in accordance with IAS 2.

6.9 Lower of cost and NRV

Entity G is a retailer of Italian furniture and has five major product lines: sofas, dining tables, beds, closets, and lounge chairs. As at 30 June 2010, quantity on hand, cost per unit, and NRV per unit of the product lines are as follows:

Product line	Quantity on hand	Cost per unit (€)	NRV per unit (€)
Sofas	100	2,000	2,040
Dining tables	200	1,000	900
Beds	300	3,000	3,200
Closets	400	1,500	1,540
Lounge chairs	500	500	400

Compute the value of inventory of entity G as at 30 June 2010, under IAS 2 using the 'lower of cost and NRV' rule.

6.10 Inventory misstatements

The financial statements of entity H for 2009 and 2010 had the following errors:

	2009	2010
Ending inventory	€8,000 overstated	€16,000 understated
Rent expense	€4,800 understated	€2,600 overstated

By what amount will the 2009 and 2010 profit before taxes be overstated or understated if these errors are not corrected?

7

Property, plant and equipment (IAS 16) and investment property (IAS 40)

Contents

Objectives

When you have completed this chapter you should be able to:

- Define the term 'property, plant and equipment' (PPE) in accordance with IAS 16
- State the criteria which should be satisfied for an item of PPE to be recognised as an asset
- Determine the cost of an item of PPE
- Distinguish between the cost model and the revaluation model for the measurement of PPE after initial recognition
- Compute depreciation for PPE using various depreciation methods
- Explain the requirements of IAS 23 relating to borrowing costs incurred for the acquisition, construction or production of a qualifying asset
- Define the term 'investment property' and explain the requirements of IAS 40 relating to investment properties.

7.1   Introduction

The objective of IAS 16 is to set out the accounting treatment for *Property, Plant and Equipment* (PPE) so that users can obtain information on an entity's investment in PPE and the changes in that investment. The principal issues it considers are the timing of recognition of the assets (recognition), the determination of their carrying amounts (measurement), depreciation and impairment (IAS 16 para 1).

Property, plant and equipment are tangible assets that:

(a) are held by an entity for use in the production or supply of goods or services, for rental to others, or for administrative purposes; and

(b) are expected to be used for more than one period (IAS 16 para 6).

IAS 40 – *Investment Property* deals with property (land or a building – or part of a building – or both) held to earn rentals or for capital appreciation or both, rather than for:

(a) use in the production or supply of goods or services or for administrative purposes; or

(b) sale in the ordinary course of business (IAS 40 para 5).

7.2   Initial recognition of property, plant and equipment and
elements of cost

An item of PPE, such as machinery, motor vehicles, furniture and fixtures, office equipment, ships, aircraft, etc. should initially be measured at its cost.

The cost of an item of PPE includes:

- the purchase price, including all non-refundable duties and taxes. Any trade discount and rebates are deducted in arriving at the purchase price;
- costs directly attributable to bringing the asset to working condition for its intended use. Directly attributable costs include:
  - ❐ site preparation; initial delivery and handling costs; installation and assembly costs;
  - ❐ professional fees such as for architects and engineers;
  - ❐ an initial estimate of the cost of dismantling and removing the item and site restoration costs, where an entity has an obligation to return the site to its original condition, for example the decommissioning of a nuclear power plant;
  - ❐ borrowing costs that are directly attributable to the acquisition, construction or production of an asset, in accordance with IAS 23 – *Borrowing Costs*.

Another type of cost sometimes put forward as a candidate for capitalisation, is the cost of training operatives for new machinery or computer equipment. IAS 16 para 19(c) does not permit capitalisation of such costs as they are operating costs rather than directly attributable to the item of PPE. This is because operatives may leave at short notice, their training costs would not meet the definition of an asset

---

Property, plant and equipment are measured at cost, including directly attributable borrowing costs, less accumulated depreciation and any impairment losses. Software used in the production process is considered to be an integral part of the related hardware and is capitalized as plant and machinery. Property and plant under construction is valued at the expense already incurred, including interest during the installation period. To the extent a legal or constructive obligation to a third party exists, the acquisition cost includes estimated costs of dismantling and removing the asset and restoring the site. The cost of replacing a part of an item of property, plant and equipment is recognized in the carrying value of the item if it is probable that the future economic benefits embodied within the item will flow to TeliaSonera and the cost of the item can be measured reliably. All other replacement costs are expensed as incurred. A change in estimated expenditures for dismantling, removal and restoration is added to and/or deducted from the carrying value of the related asset. To the extent that the change would result in a negative carrying value, this effect is recognized as income. The change in depreciation charge is recognized prospectively.

Capitalized interest is calculated, based on the Group's estimated average cost of borrowing. However, actual borrowing costs are capitalized if individually identifiable, such as interest paid on construction loans for buildings.

Government grants, initially measured at fair value, reduce the carrying value of related assets and are recognized as income over the assets' useful life by way of a reduced depreciation charge.

Figure 7.1 Capitalisation of costs

Source: TeliaSonera Annual Report 2008.

and, therefore, should not be capitalised, since the access to future economic benefits is not controlled by an entity.

The carrying amount of PPE may be reduced by the amount of government grants (IAS 16 para 28). Government grants are dealt with in IAS 20 – *Accounting for Government Grants and Disclosure of Government Assistance*. They are not dealt with in this book.

Figure 7.1 gives an example of disclosures in relation to the costs of PPE.

Example 7.1

Cost of PPE

On 1 January 2010, Zetajane Ltd acquired production equipment for EUR 250,000. The following further costs were incurred:

Delivery	€18,000
Installation	€24,000
Training costs	€2,500
General administration costs	€3,000

The installation and setting-up period took three months, and a further amount of EUR 21,000 was spent on costs directly related to bringing the asset to its working condition. The equipment was ready for use on 1 April 2010.

Monthly managerial reports indicated that for the first five months, the production quantities from this equipment resulted in an initial operating loss of EUR 15,000 because of small quantities produced. The months thereafter showed much more positive results.

The equipment has an estimated useful life of 14 years and a residual value of EUR 18,000. Estimated dismantling costs amount to EUR 12,500.

Determine the cost of the asset to be capitalised.

Historical cost of equipment

	€
Invoice price	250,000
Delivery	18,000
Installation	24,000
Other costs directly related to bringing the asset to its working condition	21,000
Initial estimate of dismantling costs	12,500
Cost of the equipment	325,500

Start-up costs and similar pre-production costs do not form part of the cost of an asset. Initial operating losses incurred prior to an asset achieving its planned performance are recognised as an expense. The same would apply to operating losses that occur because a revenue earning activity has been suspended during the construction of an item of PPE. Such losses should also be expensed. An example might be where a hotel is being refurbished and is, therefore, closed for a period. Any loss incurred in that period (rents, wages, etc.) would be expensed as incurred as it would not form part of the cost of improvements.

Example 7.2

Operating costs incurred in the start-up period

On 1 April 2010, an amusement park has a 'soft' opening to the public, to trial run its attractions. Tickets are sold at a 50 per cent discount during this period and the operating capacity is 80 per cent. The official opening day of the amusement park is 1 July 2010.

The management claims that the soft opening is a trial run necessary for the amusement park to be in the condition capable of operating in the intended manner. Accordingly, the net operating costs incurred should be capitalised.

The net operating costs should not be capitalised, but should be expensed in the income statement. Running at 80 per cent operating capacity is sufficient evidence that the amusement park is capable of operating in the manner intended by management.

7.2.1 Self-constructed assets

The cost of a self-constructed asset is determined using the same principles as for an acquired asset. If an entity makes similar assets for sale in the normal course of business, the cost of the asset is usually the same as the cost of constructing an asset for sale as determined in accordance with IAS 2 – *Inventories*. Therefore, any internal profit is eliminated in arriving at such costs (IAS 16 para 22).

As explained in Chapter 6, IAS 16 prohibits capitalisation of general and administrative overheads and start-up costs. One exception to this rule, however, might be self-constructed assets that are of a kind that an entity produces for sale, the cost of which is, therefore, determined in accordance with IAS 2. In fact, according to IAS 2 paras 10 and 12, the cost of inventories includes cost of conversion. Costs of conversion include a systematic allocation of fixed and variable production overheads. Fixed production overheads are indirect costs of production and include depreciation and maintenance of factory buildings and equipment and the cost of factory management and administration. In this specific and special case, therefore, a proportion of overheads relating to factory (but not office) management and administration should be included as cost.

Similarly, the cost of abnormal amounts of wasted material, labour, or other resources incurred in self-constructing an asset should not be included in the cost of the asset (IAS 16 para 22). Other specific types of abnormal costs that should also be excluded are costs related to design errors, industrial disputes, idle capacity and production delays.

Sometimes operations are performed in connection with the construction or development of an item of PPE but are not necessary to bring the item to the location and condition necessary for it to be capable of operating in the manner intended by management. These incidental operations may occur before or during the construction or development activities. For example, income may be earned through using a building site as a car park until construction starts. Because incidental

Property, plant and equipment is carried at the cost of acquisition or construction depreciated over its estimated useful life. A write-down (impairment loss) is recognized in addition if an asset's value falls below the depreciated cost of acquisition or construction.

The cost of acquisition comprises the acquisition price plus ancillary and subsequent acquisition costs, less any reduction received on the acquisition price. The cost of self-constructed property, plant and equipment comprises the direct cost of materials, direct manufacturing expenses and appropriate allocations of material and manufacturing overheads. Where an obligation exists to dismantle or remove an asset or restore a site to its former condition at the end of its useful life, the present value of the related future payments is capitalized along with the cost of acquisition or construction upon completion and a corresponding liability is recognized.

Figure 7.2 Accounting policy for self-constructed items of PPE
Source: Bayer Annual Report 2008.

operations are not necessary to bring an item to the location and condition necessary for it to be capable of operating in the manner intended by management, the income and related expenses of incidental operations should be recognised in the income statement (IAS 16 para 21).

Figure 7.2 gives an example of accounting policy for self-constructed assets.

7.2.2 Capitalisation of borrowing costs (IAS 23)

Views differ on whether finance costs should be included in the production cost of an asset or whether they should be expensed as incurred. Some regard such costs as forming part of the cost of the particular asset with which they can be either directly or indirectly identified. Others regard them as essentially period costs that should be charged to income regardless of how the borrowing is applied.

The previous version of IAS 23 permitted either treatment and included further requirements where a policy of capitalisation of finance costs was adopted.

In March 2007 the IASB issued a revised version of IAS 23, which removed the choice available and accordingly borrowing costs attributable to certain assets should be capitalised as part of the cost of the asset. This revised standard is applicable to periods beginning on or after 1 January 2009; earlier application is permitted.

Borrowing costs are interest and other costs that an entity incurs in connection with the borrowing of funds (IAS 23 (revised) para 5).

Examples of borrowing costs include (IAS 23 (revised) para 6):

(a) interest on bank overdrafts and short-term and long-term borrowings;

(b) amortisation of discounts or premiums relating to borrowings;

(c) amortisation of ancillary costs incurred in connection with the arrangement of borrowings;

(d) finance charges in respect of finance leases recognised in accordance with IAS 17 – *Leases*; and

(e) exchange differences arising from foreign currency borrowings to the extent that they are regarded as an adjustment to interest costs.

An entity should adopt a policy of capitalising borrowing costs on qualifying assets. A qualifying asset is an asset that necessarily takes a substantial period of time to get ready for its intended use or sale (IAS 23 (revised) para 5). Under the revised standard, capitalisation of borrowing costs for qualifying assets is mandatory.

Borrowing costs eligible for capitalisation

Only directly attributable borrowing costs should be capitalised. The borrowing costs that are directly attributable to the acquisition, construction or production of a qualifying asset are those borrowing costs that would have been avoided (for example, by avoiding additional borrowings or by using the funds paid out for the asset to repay existing borrowings) if the expenditure on the qualifying asset had not been made (IAS 23 (revised) paras 8 and 10).

It may be difficult to identify a direct relationship between particular borrowings and a qualifying asset and to determine the borrowings that could otherwise have been avoided. Such a difficulty occurs, for example, when the financing activity of an entity is coordinated centrally. Difficulties also arise when a group uses a range of debt instruments to borrow funds at varying rates of interest, and lends those funds on various bases to other entities in the group. As a result, the determination of the amount of borrowing costs that are directly attributable to the acquisition of a qualifying asset is difficult and the exercise of judgement is required (IAS 23 (revised) para 11).

To the extent that an entity borrows funds specifically for the purpose of obtaining a qualifying asset, the entity should determine the amount of borrowing costs to be capitalised as the actual borrowing costs incurred on that borrowing (IAS 23 (revised) para 12).

To the extent that an entity borrows funds generally and uses them for the purpose of obtaining a qualifying asset, the entity should determine the amount of borrowing costs to be capitalised by applying a capitalisation rate to the expenditures for that asset. The capitalisation rate should be the weighted average of the borrowing costs applicable to the borrowings of the entity that are outstanding during the period, other than borrowings made specifically for the purpose of obtaining a qualifying asset (IAS 23 (revised) para 14). The determination of the weighted average capitalisation rate is explained in the following example.

Example 7.3

Borrowing costs: weighted average capitalisation rate

An entity is constructing a new warehouse commencing on 1 September, which continues without interruption until after the year-end on 31 December. Directly attributable expenditure on this asset is EUR 200,000 in September and EUR 500,000 in each of the months of October to December. Therefore, the weighted average carrying amount of the asset during the period is:

$$(€200,000 + €700,000 + €1,200,000 + €1,700,000) \div 4 = €950,000$$

The entity has not taken out any specific borrowing to finance the construction of the asset, but has incurred finance costs on its general borrowings during the construction period. During the year the entity had 10 per cent debentures in issue with a face value of EUR 4m and an overdraft of EUR 1m which increased to EUR 1.5m in December on which interest was paid at 15 per cent until 1 October, when the rate was increased to 16 per cent.

The capitalisation rate of the general borrowings of the entity during the period of construction is calculated in Table 7.1.

Table 7.1 Capitalisation rate of general borrowings

	€
Finance cost on €4m 10% debentures during September–December	133,333
Interest at 15% on overdraft of €1m in September	12,500
Interest at 16% on overdraft of €1m in October and November	26,667
Interest at 16% on overdraft of €1.5m in December	20,000
Total finance costs in September–December	192,500

Weighted average borrowings during the period	=	$\dfrac{(€4m \times 4) + (€1m \times 3) + (€1.5m \times 1)}{4 \text{ months}}$
	=	€5,125,000
Capitalisation rate	=	Total finance costs in the period ÷ weighted average borrowings during period
	=	€192,500 ÷ €5,125,000
	=	3.756%

The capitalisation rate, therefore, reflects the weighted average cost of borrowings for the four-month period that the asset was under construction. On an annualised basis 3.756 per cent gives a capitalisation rate of 11.268 per cent per annum, which is what would be expected on the borrowings profile.

Therefore, the total amount of borrowing costs to be capitalised is calculated as follows:

Weighted average carrying amount of asset × capitalisation rate
= €950,000 × 11.268% × 4 ÷ 12
= €35,682

Borrowing costs

Borrowing costs directly attributable to the acquisition, construction or production of qualifying assets are added to the cost of the assets until such time the assets are substantially ready for their intended use. Where funds are borrowed specifically for the purpose of obtaining a qualifying asset, any investment income earned on temporary surplus funds is deducted from borrowing costs eligible for capitalisation.

All other borrowing costs are recognised as an expense when incurred.

Figure 7.3 Accounting policy for borrowing costs
Source: The Emirates Group, Annual Report 2008–9.

7.3   Subsequent costs

Once an item of PPE is recognised and capitalised in the books, an entity may incur further costs on that asset at a later date. Routine repairs and maintenance costs should normally be expensed in the income statement as costs are incurred (IAS 16 para 12). However, in instances where subsequent expenditure extends the useful life of an item of PPE, or increases its capacity, or achieves a substantial improvement in the quality of output, the additional expenditure should be recognised as part of the cost of the asset.

Significant components

An asset may consist of several different and significant physical components. Under IAS 16, if an item of PPE comprises two or more significant components, with substantially different useful lives, then each component should be treated separately for depreciation purposes (that is, as if each component was a separate asset in its own right) and depreciated over its individual useful life (IAS 16 para 43). It follows that when a component is replaced or restored, the old component should be written off, to avoid double counting and the new component capitalised, if its cost is recoverable.

Although the standard requires significant components to be treated as separate assets for depreciation purposes, the rules on the treatment of subsequent costs of replacing significant components do not actually require that the component that is replaced should have been separately identified on acquisition and separately depreciated since then. Normally this will have been done, but there may be instances where it has not. Instead the rules regarding subsequent costs of replacing components apply generally to parts that are replaced (both parts that have been separately identified for depreciation purposes and other material parts or components) and recognition of such costs as an asset depends on whether the costs meet the standard's asset recognition criteria.

The standard requires that the cost of a replacement component is recognised as an asset if it meets the recognition criteria (i.e. it is probable that future economic benefits associated with the item will flow to the entity and the cost of the item can be measured reliably). If such a cost meets those criteria and is capitalised, the carrying amount of the part or parts that are replaced is derecognised (e.g. the accumulated cost and depreciation of the replaced parts are eliminated). This applies whether or not the replaced part or component had been separately depreciated. If the cost and deprecation of the replaced part or component cannot be identified it is acceptable to use the cost of the replacement as a proxy for the cost of the replaced part when it was acquired or constructed (IAS 16 paras 13 and 70).

Examples of parts that may require replacement are the lining of a blast furnace that may require replacement after a specified number of hours of use, or aircraft interiors such as seats and galleys that may require replacement several times during the airframe's life. Other examples of parts that may require replacement less frequently are the interior walls of a building or a non-recurring replacement (IAS 16 para 13). A non-recurring replacement might be, for example, the replacement of a ventilation system with a new system that meets current health and safety requirements.

7.4 Measurement subsequent to initial recognition: cost model and depreciation

Subsequent to initial recognition as an asset, the carrying amount (or net book value, NBV) of an item of PPE is represented by its cost less any accumulated depreciation and any impairment losses (IAS 16 para 30). We deal with impairment losses in Chapter 10. In this section we illustrate how to determine depreciation.

To calculate depreciation of an asset, four factors need to be considered:

- cost;
- useful life;
- residual value;
- depreciation method.

7.4.1 Cost

As we have seen in section 7.2, this includes all directly attributable costs of bringing the asset to working condition for its intended use.

7.4.2 Useful life

This is either:

(a) the period of time over which an asset is expected to be used by an entity; or

(b) the number of production or similar units expected to be obtained from the asset by an entity.

When we talk about the useful life of an asset, we should take into account both its physical and economic lives:

- the *physical life of an asset* will be exhausted through wear and tear and/or the passage of time, although it is possible for the physical life to be extended considerably through careful maintenance, improvements and so on;
- the *economic life of an asset* is determined by the effects of technological progress and changes in demand. After a while, in fact, the asset may be unable to compete with newer assets or may no longer be relevant to the needs of the entity.

7.4.3 Residual value

Also known as disposal value, terminal value, scrap value or salvage, this is the net amount which an entity expects to obtain for an asset at the end of its useful life after deducting the expected costs of disposal.

To calculate the total amount to be depreciated with regard to an asset, the residual value should be deducted from the cost of the asset. The likely amount to be received on disposal is often difficult to predict. So in practice, residual value which is hardly significant is ignored by entities.

Depreciable amount = cost − estimated residual value

7.4.4 Depreciation methods

A variety of depreciation methods can be used to allocate the depreciable amount of an asset on a systematic basis over its useful life. These methods include:

- straight-line method;
- diminishing-balance method; and
- sum-of-the-units method.

Straight-line depreciation results in a constant charge over the useful life of the asset.

Diminishing-balance method results in a decreasing charge over the useful life of an asset. If the expected productivity or revenue-earning power of the asset is relatively greater during the earlier years of its life or where maintenance charges tend to increase during later years, this method may provide the most satisfactory allocation of cost.

Sum-of-the-units method results in a charge based on the expected use or output of the asset.

The method used for an asset should be selected based on the expected pattern of economic benefits and should be consistently applied from period to period unless there is a change in the expected pattern of economic benefits from the asset.

Sometimes an entity selects the method used by other companies in its industry to enhance comparability. Sometimes one method provides better matching of expense and revenue. Sometimes the method is chosen to present the life-cycle cost of an asset. Moreover, entities do not necessarily use the same depreciation methods for all types of depreciable assets.

Example 7.4

Calculation of depreciation

We are given the following information:

Cost of a machine acquired on 1 January 2006	€80,000
Estimated residual value at the end of its useful life	€2,048
Estimated useful life	4 years

Units expected to be produced during 2006	2,260
Units expected to be produced during 2007	2,430
Units expected to be produced during 2008	2,550
Units expected to be produced during 2009	2,504
Total units produced over 4 years	9,744

Now we will determine the depreciation charge for each year using:

(a) the straight-line method;

(b) the diminishing-balance method using a depreciation rate of 60 per cent;

(c) the sum-of-the-units method.

As we have seen earlier, these methods approach differently annual depreciation charges, but the total depreciation over the useful life of the asset is the same under each method. Table 7.2 summarises the data we will use for the asset purchased and placed in service on 1 January 2006.

Table 7.2 Data for recording depreciation for an asset

Data item	Amount
Cost of the machine	€80,000
Deduct: Estimated residual value	€2,048
Depreciable amount	€77,952
Estimated useful life:	
Years	4 years
Units	9,744

(a) Straight-line method

Annual depreciation charge = (cost – estimated residual value) ÷ useful life
= (€80,000 – €2,048) ÷ 4 years = €19,488

Since the asset was placed in service on the first day of the year, the entry to record each year's depreciation is as follows:

Dr Depreciation expense   €19,488
    Cr Accumulated depreciation   €19,488

A straight-line depreciation schedule for this asset is shown in Table 7.3.

Table 7.3 Straight-line depreciation

Date	Asset cost €	Depreciation rate	Depreciable amount €	Depreciation expense €	Accumulated depreciation €	Carrying amount (or NBV) €
01/01/2006	80,000				0	80,000
31/12/2006		0.25 ×	77,952 =	19,488	19,488	60,512
31/12/2007		0.25 ×	77,952 =	19,488	38,976	41,024
31/12/2008		0.25 ×	77,952 =	19,488	58,464	21,536
31/12/2009		0.25 ×	77,952 =	19,488	77,952	2,048 ← Residual value

The final column shows the asset's net book value, which is cost less accumulated depreciation. As the asset is used, the accumulated depreciation increases and the net book value decreases. At the end of 2009, the asset is fully depreciated and the asset's final net book value is its residual value of EUR 2,048.

(b) Diminishing-balance method

Cost of the machine	€80,000
Estimated residual value	€2,048
Fixed percentage to be applied	60%

The calculation will be as follows:

	€
Cost of machine	80,000
2006 depreciation charge (60% of cost)	(48,000)
Carrying amount (or NBV)	32,000
2007 depreciation charge (60% of carrying amount)	(19,200)
Carrying amount	12,800
2008 depreciation charge (60% of carrying amount)	(7,680)
Carrying amount	5,120
2009 depreciation charge (60% of carrying amount)	(3,072)
Residual amount	**2,048**

The fixed percentage to be applied has been derived using the following formula:

$$P = (1 - \sqrt[n]{R \div C}) \times 100\%$$

where: P = percentage rate for depreciation
 n = number of years of useful life of the asset
 R = residual value of the asset
 C = cost, or fair value, of the asset

The percentage rate for depreciation is applied to the cost of the machine and not to the depreciable amount. A diminishing-balance depreciation schedule for this asset is shown in Table 7.4.

Table 7.4 Diminishing-balance depreciation

Date	Asset cost €	Depreciation for the year			Accumulated depreciation €	Carrying amount (or NBV) €
		Depreciation rate	Depreciable amount €	Depreciation expense €		
01/01/2006	80,000				0	80,000
31/12/2006		0.6 ×	80,000 =	48,000	48,000	32,000
31/12/2007		0.6 ×	32,000 =	19,200	67,200	12,800
31/12/2008		0.6 ×	12,800 =	7,680	74,880	5,120
31/12/2009		0.6 ×	5,120 =	3,072	77,952	2,048 ← Residual value

(c) Sum-of-the-units method

Under the sum-of-the-units depreciation method, a fixed amount of depreciation is allocated to each unit of output. A unit of output can be miles, units, hours or output, depending on which unit type best defines the asset's use.

Depreciation charge per unit of output = (Cost – estimated residual value) ÷ number of units produced = €77,952 ÷ 9,744 units = €8 per unit produced

Sum-of-the-units depreciation for this machine is illustrated in Table 7.5.

Table 7.5 Sum-of-the-units depreciation

Date	Asset cost €	Depreciation per unit €	Number of units €	Depreciation expense €	Accumulated depreciation €	Carrying amount (or NBV) €
		Depreciation for the year				
01/01/2006	80,000				0	80,000
31/12/2006		8 ×	2,260 =	18,080	18,080	61,920
31/12/2007		8 ×	2,430 =	19,440	37,520	42,480
31/12/2008		8 ×	2,550 =	20,400	57,920	22,080
31/12/2009		8 ×	2,504 =	20,032	77,952	2,048 ← Residual value

Comparison of depreciation methods
Table 7.6 and Figure 7.4 show annual depreciation for the three methods.

Table 7.6 Comparison of depreciation methods

Year	(a) Straight-line €	(b) Diminishing-balance €	(c) Sum-of-the-units €
	Amount of depreciation per year		
2006	19,488	48,000	18,080
2007	19,488	19,200	19,440
2008	19,488	7,680	20,400
2009	19,488	3,072	20,032
Total accumulated depreciation	77,952	77,952	77,952

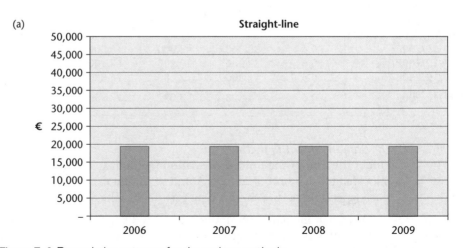

(a)

Straight-line

50,000
45,000
40,000
35,000
30,000
€ 25,000
20,000
15,000
10,000
5,000
—

2006   2007   2008   2009

Figure 7.4 Depreciation patterns for the various methods

(b)

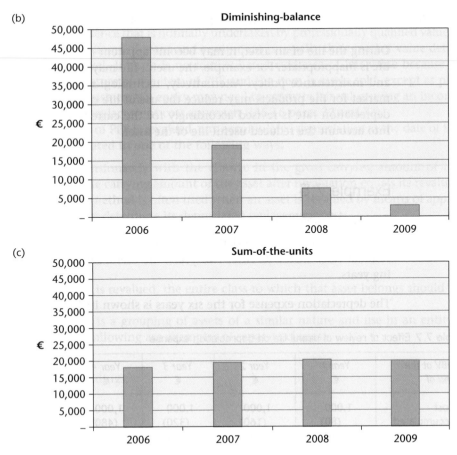

(c)

Figure 7.4 (*Cont'd*)

Figure 7.5 shows the depreciation charges for the four years under the three methods in one graph.

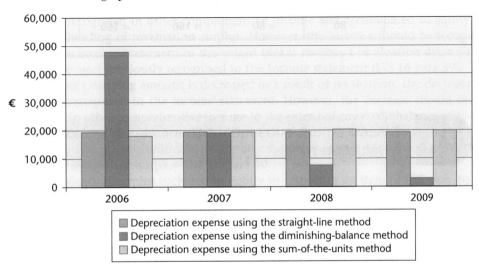

Figure 7.5 Annual depreciation by method

surplus to retained earnings are not made through the income statement (IAS 16 para 41).

Example 7.6

Revaluation increments and depreciable assets

On 30 June 2010, an item of plant has a carrying amount of EUR 84,000, being the original cost of EUR 140,000 less accumulated depreciation of EUR 56,000. The fair value of the asset is EUR 100,000. The tax rate is 30 per cent. The entries are shown in Figure 7.6 below.

The revaluation may be effected in two steps			
Step 1: Revalue the asset, disregarding the tax effect, and eliminate the accumulated depreciation.			
		€	€
Accumulated depreciation	Dr	56,000	
Plant	Cr		40,000
Asset revaluation surplus (Revaluation of asset)	Cr		16,000
Step 2: Adjust for the tax effect of the revaluation.			
Asset revaluation surplus	Dr	4,800	
Deferred tax liability	Cr		4,800
(Recognition of deferred tax liability as a direct adjustment against the asset revaluation surplus: 30% × EUR 16,000)			
The two entries could be *combined* as follows:			
Accumulated depreciation	Dr	56,000	
Plant	Cr		40,000
Deferred tax liability	Cr		4,800
Asset revaluation surplus (Revaluation of asset net of tax effect)	Cr		11,200

Figure 7.6 Journal entries for asset revaluation

Example 7.7

Transferring revaluation surplus to retained earnings

Assume an item of plant was acquired for EUR 200,000. The asset was immediately revalued to EUR 240,000. The asset has an expected useful life of 10 years, and the tax rate is 30 per cent.

The revaluation entry is:

Dr Plant	€40,000	
Cr Deferred tax liability		€12,000
Cr Asset revaluation surplus		€28,000
(Revaluation of plant)		

At the end of the first year, depreciation expense of EUR 24,000 would be recorded. As the asset is being used up at 10 per cent per annum, the entity may transfer 10 per cent of the asset revaluation surplus to retained earnings:

Dr Asset revaluation surplus	€2,800	
Cr Retained earnings		€2,800
(Transfer from asset revaluation surplus to retained earnings)		

7.6   Investment property (IAS 40)

As mentioned earlier (see section 7.1), an investment property is property (land or a building – or part of a building – or both) held (by the owner or by the lessee under a finance lease) to earn rentals or realise capital gains or both (IAS 40 para 5).

The following are examples of an investment property:

(a) Land held for long-term capital appreciation rather than for short-term sale in the ordinary course of business.

(b) Land held for currently undetermined future use. (If an entity has not determined that it will use the land as owner-occupied property or for short-term sale in the ordinary course of business, the land is regarded as held for capital appreciation.)

(c) A building owned by the entity (or held by the entity under a finance lease) and leased out under one or more operating leases.

(d) A building that is vacant but is held to be leased out under one or more operating leases (IAS 40 para 8).

An investment property generates cash flows largely independent of other assets held by an entity. This distinguishes an investment property from owner-occupied property, which is held by the owner for use in the production or supply of goods or services, for administrative purposes or for sale in the ordinary course of business. The definition of an investment property includes a building that is currently vacant but is held with a view to it being let out and an existing investment property that is being redeveloped with a view to its continued use as an investment property (IAS 40 para 5).

IAS 40 makes it clear that where a property is being constructed for future use as an investment property it does not meet the investment property definition until the construction or development is complete. During construction the property should be accounted for in accordance with IAS 16.

The chosen accounting policy should generally be consistently applied to the entity's all investment properties (i.e. it is not permitted to measure one property at cost and another at fair value). There is an assumption that an entity will be able to determine an investment property's fair value reliably. However, in exceptional cases this may not be possible, so the individual property should be measured at cost even where the entity has an accounting policy of measuring investment properties at fair value. Where an entity has this mixed accounting for investment properties, it should disclose why this is the case and if possible provide a range of estimates for fair value (IAS 40 paras 53 and 78).

Where an investment property is measured at fair value, the entity should continue to apply this accounting policy to it (IAS 40 para 55).

Where the fair value model is adopted following the initial recognition of investment properties, the properties should be valued at fair value at each balance sheet date.

A gain or loss arising from a change in the fair value of investment property should be recognised in the income statement for the period in which it arises (IAS 40 para 35).

The fair value of an investment property is the price at which the property could be exchanged between knowledgeable and willing parties in an arm's length transaction (IAS 40 para 5).

The fair value of an investment property should reflect market conditions at the balance sheet date. The best evidence of fair value is given by current prices in an active market for similar properties in the same location and condition. It is important to appreciate that the fair value is time specific (since market conditions change), so the valuation should take place at each balance sheet date.

The fair value of an investment property should reflect market conditions at the end of the reporting period (IAS 40 para 38). Figure 7.9 on page 224 shows an example of disclosure of fair value of an investment property carried at cost.

Example 7.9

Accounting for investment property

Sunny Village SpA is a manufacturer of toys. The following information relates to the property owned by the company:

Table 7.8 Property held by Sunny Village SpA

	€000
Land in Varese	1,600
Buildings thereon (acquired 30 June 2009)	4,200
Improvements to the building to extend rented floor capacity	800
Repairs and maintenance to investment property for the year	100
Rentals received for the year	320

The property is used as the administrative head office of the company (approximately 6 per cent of the floor space). The property can only be sold as a complete unit. The remainder of the building is leased out under operating leases. The company provides lessees with security services.

The company values investment properties using the fair value model. On 31 December 2009, the balance sheet date, Carlo Proper (an independent valuer) valued the property at EUR 7.2m.

To account for the property in the financial statements of Sunny Village SpA as at 31 December 2009, the property should first be classified as either investment property or owner-occupied property. It is classified as an investment property and is accounted for on the fair value model. The motivation is that the portion occupied by the company for administrative purposes is deemed to be insignificant (6 per cent) and portions of the property cannot be sold separately. In addition, the majority of the floor space of the property is used to generate rental income and the security services rendered to the lessees is insignificant.

The accounting treatment and disclosure of the property in the financial statements of Sunny Village SpA are shown in Figure 7.8 below.

Balance sheet as at 31 December 2009 (extract)		
	Note	€000
Assets		
Non-current assets		
Property, plant and equipment		xxx
Investment property	(4)	7,200

Notes to the financial statements (extract)
Accounting policies
The investment property is held to earn rentals and is stated at fair value, determined at each balance sheet date by an independent valuer based on market evidence of the most recent prices achieved in arms length transactions of similar properties in the same area.

(4) Investment property	
	€000
Opening balance	–
Additions	5,800
Improvements to building	800
Gain representing fair value adjustments	600
Closing balance at fair value	7,200

Calculation

Carrying amount of investment property	
	€000
Land	1,600
Building	4,200
Improvements to building	800
	6,600
Fair value	7,200
Gain shown in the income statement	600

Figure 7.8 Disclosures relating to the investment property made by Sunny Village SpA

> Investment properties are stated at amortized cost. Transaction costs are included on initial measurement. The fair values of investment properties are disclosed in the Notes. These are assessed using internationally accepted valuation methods, such as taking comparable properties as a guide to current market prices or by applying the discounted cash flow method. Like property, plant and equipment, investment properties are depreciated using the straight-line method.
>
> The fair values of investment properties are measured using internationally accepted valuation procedures, such as taking comparable properties as a guide to current market prices or the discounted cash flow method, and came to EUR 63,281,000 (2007: EUR 60,354,000) as of December 31, 2008. EUR 30,655,000 (2007: EUR 27,492,000) of this total is accounted for by fair value adjustments following independent external appraisals.

Figure 7.9 Disclosure of fair value of investment property carried at cost
Source: HOCHTIEF Aktiengesellschaft Annual Report 2008.

7.6.3 Transfers following a change in usage

A change in the use of a property may lead to it being derecognised as an investment property. The following Table 7.9 sets out where there might be evidence that a change in use has occurred and how the property should be treated following the change in use (IAS 40 para 57).

7.6.4 Disposal of investment properties

An investment property should be eliminated from the balance sheet when it is disposed of, either through sale or by entering into a finance lease. An investment property which is permanently withdrawn from use and will not generate any future economic benefits, even on its ultimate disposal, should be eliminated from the balance sheet (IAS 40 para 66).

When an investment property is disposed of or permanently withdrawn from use and no future benefit will accrue to the entity, a gain or loss should be calculated and recognised directly in the income statement in the period in which the disposal or retirement takes place. The gain or loss should normally be determined as the difference between the net disposal proceeds and the carrying amount of the asset (IAS 40 para 69).

Example 7.10

Disposal of an investment property

An entity purchased an investment property on 1 January 2006, for a cost of EUR 800,000. The property has a useful life of 50 years, with no residual value and at 31 December 2008 had a fair value of EUR 1,120,000. On 1 April 2009 the property was sold for net proceeds of EUR 1,080,000.

The amount that should be recognised in the income statement for the year ended 31 December 2009 regarding the disposal of the property is shown below:

	Cost model	Fair value model
	€	€
(a) Carrying amount €800,000 – (€800,000 ÷ 50 years × 3) =	752,000	
(b) Fair value		1,120,000
Net proceeds	1,080,000	1,080,000
Profit (loss) on disposal	328,000	(40,000)

Table 7.9 Accounting treatment for change in use of investment property

Evidence of change in use	Accounting treatment
Occupation of the property by the entity itself.	The property is now owner-occupied and should therefore be recognized as property in use by the entity in accordance with IAS 16.
	Where the investment property was measured at fair value, its fair value at the date of change in use should be treated as the deemed cost for future accounting (IAS 40 para 60).
Development of the property commences with the intention that it will then be sold by the entity.	The property is being held for sale in the normal course of business and should therefore be reclassified as inventory and accounted for in accordance with IAS 2 – Inventories.
	Where the investment property was measured at fair value, its fair value at the date of change in use should be treated as the deemed cost (IAS 40 para 60).
Development of the property commences with the intention that it will continue to be let after completion of the development works.	The property should continue to be held as an investment property under IAS 40.
A building that was occupied by the entity is vacated so that it can be let to third parties.	The property is no longer owner-occupied and therefore should be transferred to investment property and accounted for in accordance with IAS 40.
	Where an investment property is measured at fair value, the property should be revalued at the date of change in use and any difference should be recognized as a revaluation under IAS 16 (IAS 40 para 61).
A property that was originally held as inventory has now been let to a third party.	The property is no longer held for resale and is instead held to generate future rental income and therefore should be transferred to investment properties in accordance with IAS 40.
	Where an investment property is measured at fair value the property should be revalued at the date of change in use and any difference should be recognized in the income statement (IAS 40 para 65).
An entity has constructed a property that it now intends to let out to a number of third parties.	Whilst the property is being constructed it should be accounted for in accordance with IAS 16. However, on completion it should be transferred to investment property.
	Where an investment property is measured at fair value the property should be revalued at the date of change in use and any difference should be recognised in the income statement (IAS 40 para 65).

| 7.7 | Financial analysis and interpretation |

Management should make a number of choices when deciding about recognition and depreciation of assets. They should decide on, *inter alia*:

- the capitalisation policy;
- methods of depreciation;
- useful lives;
- residual values.

These choices are determined by the application of the principles set out in IAS 16. These choices affect the asset values reported in the balance sheet and depreciation charges in the income statement. They also affect several key financial ratios and the classification of cash flows in the statement of cash flows. An analyst should monitor the effects of these choices. Table 7.10 summarises the effects of capitalisation policy (i.e. capitalising versus expensing costs) on the financial statements and related key ratios.

Table 7.10 Effects of capitalising vs expensing costs

Item	Expensing	Capitalising
Equity	Lower because of a lower net profit	Higher because of a higher net profit
Net profit	Lower because of higher expenses	Higher because of lower expenses
Pretax cash generated from operating activities	Lower because of higher expenses	Higher because of lower expenses
Cash generated from investing activities	None because no effect on non-current assets	Lower because a non-current asset is acquired (invested in) for cash
Pretax total cash flow	None because depreciation is not a cash expense	None because deprecation is not a cash expense
Profit margin	Lower because of a lower net profit	Higher because of a higher net profit
Asset turnover	Higher because of lower total assets	Lower because of higher total assets
Current ratio	No effect on a pretax basis	No effect on a pretax basis
Debt-to-equity	Higher because of a lower equity	Lower because of a higher equity
Return on assets	Lower because earnings are lower percentage wise than reduced assets	Higher because earnings are higher percentage wise than increased assets
Return on equity	Lower because earnings are lower percentage wise than reduced equity	Higher because earnings are higher percentage wise than equity

The easiest way to understand the impact of using straight-line versus diminishing balance depreciation method is as follows: a diminishing balance depreciation method will increase the depreciation expense in the early years of an asset's useful life relative to what it would be if the straight-line method was used. This lowers reported income and also causes the book value of the PPE reported in the balance sheet to decline more quickly relative to what would be reported under the straight-line method. As a result, the shareholders' equity will be lower in the early years of an asset's life if diminishing-balance depreciation is used compared with what it would be if the straight-line method is used. Furthermore, the percentage impact falls more heavily on the smaller income value than on the larger asset and shareholders' equity values. Many of the key financial ratios that are based on income, asset values, or equity values will be affected by the choice of a depreciation method.

No matter which depreciation method is chosen, the total accumulated depreciation will be the same over the entire useful life of an asset. Thus, the effects shown in Table 7.11 for the earlier years of an asset's life reverse over time. However, these reversals apply to the depreciation effects associated with an individual asset. If

Table 7.11 Impact of changes in depreciation methods on financial statements and ratios (change made in the first years of the asset's useful life)

Item	Change from straight-line to diminishing-balance depreciation method	Change from diminishing-balance to straight-line depreciation method	Increase (Decrease) in asset's useful life	Increase (decrease) in residual value
Net profit	Lower because of higher depreciation charge	Higher because of lower depreciation charge	Higher (lower) because of lower (higher) depreciation charge	Higher (lower) because of lower (higher) depreciation charge
Equity	Lower because of higher asset write-down (i.e. lower carrying amount of assets)	Higher because of lower asset write-down	Higher (lower) because of lower (higher) asset write-down	Higher (lower) because of lower (higher) asset write-down
Cash flow Profit margin	No effect Lower because of lower earnings	No effect Higher because of higher earnings	No effect Higher (lower) because of higher (lower) earnings	No effect Higher (lower) because of higher (lower) earnings
Current ratio	None	None	None	None
Asset turnover	Higher because of lower assets	Lower because of higher assets	Lower (higher) because of higher (lower) assets	Lower (higher) because of higher (lower) assets
Debt-to-equity ratio	Higher because of lower equity	Lower because of higher equity	Lower (higher) because of higher (lower) equity	Lower (higher) because of higher (lower) equity
Return on assets	Lower because of a larger percentage decline in profit versus asset decline	Higher because of a larger percentage increase in profit versus asset increase	Higher (lower) because of a bigger (smaller) percentage increase in earnings versus asset increase	Higher (lower) because of a bigger (smaller) percentage increase in earnings versus asset increase
Return on equity	Lower because of a larger percentage decrease in profit versus equity decrease	Higher because of a larger percentage increase in profit versus equity increase	Higher (lower) because of a bigger (smaller) percentage increase in profit versus equity increase	Higher (lower) because of a bigger (smaller) percentage increase in profit versus equity increase

an entity's asset base is growing, the depreciation applicable to the most-recently acquired assets tends to dominate the overall depreciation expense of the entity. The effects described in Table 7.11 will normally apply over time because the reversal process is overshadowed by the depreciation charges of newer assets. Only if an entity is in decline and its capital expenditures are low will the reversal effects be noticeable in the aggregate.

As mentioned before, the choice of the useful life of an asset affects financial statement values and key financial ratios. All other factors being equal, shorter the useful life of an asset, higher will be its depreciation over its depreciable life. This will increase the depreciation expense, lower reported income, reduce asset values, and reduce the shareholders' equity relative to what they would be if a longer useful life was chosen.

Reported cash flow, however, will not be affected, because depreciation is not a cash expense. Key financial ratios that have income, asset values, and shareholders' equity as numerator or denominator will, however, be affected. A shorter useful life tends to lower profit margins and return on equity, while at the same time raising asset turnover and debt-to-equity ratios.

Choosing a high residual value has the opposite effect of choosing a short useful life. All other factors being equal, a high salvage (residual) value will lower the depreciation expense, increase reported income, and increase the book values of assets and shareholders' equity relative to what they would be if a lower salvage value had been chosen. Cash flow, however, is unaffected because depreciation is a noncash expense. As a result of a high salvage value, an entity's profit margin and return on equity increase, whereas its asset turnover and debt-to-equity ratios decrease.

When depreciation is based on the historical cost of the assets, it presents a problem during periods of inflation. When the prices of capital goods increase over time, the depreciation accumulated over the life of such assets will fall short of the amount needed to replace them when they wear out.

To understand this concept, consider an equipment that costs EUR 20,000, has a five-year useful life, and has no salvage value. If the straight-line depreciation is used, this asset will be depreciated at a rate of EUR 4,000 per year for its five-year life. Over the life of the equipment, this depreciation will accumulate to EUR 20,000. If there had been no inflation in the intervening period, the original equipment could then be replaced with a new EUR 20,000 piece of equipment. Historical-cost depreciation makes sense in a zero or low inflation environment, because the amount of depreciation expensed matches the cost to replace the asset.

However, suppose the inflation rate over the equipment's depreciable life had been 10 per cent per year, instead of zero. Then, when it comes time to replace the asset, everything else being equal, its replacement will cost EUR 32,210 (EUR $20,000 \times 1.10^5$). The accumulated depreciation of EUR 20,000 is EUR 12,210 less than what is required to physically restore the entity to its original operating capacity. In other words, the entity will not have enough retained earnings to replace the equipment at the end of five years.

This analysis illustrates that, during periods of high inflation, depreciating physical assets on the basis of historical cost, in accordance with the financial capital maintenance theory of income, tends to understate the true depreciation expense. As such, it overstates the true earnings of an entity from the point of view of the physical capital maintenance (replacement cost) theory of income.

Table 7.11 provides an overview of the impact of changes in depreciation methods, useful lives and residual or salvage values on financial statements and ratios. Comparisons of a company's financial performance with industry competitors would be similar to the effects of changes in Table 7.11's variables if competitors use different depreciation methods, higher (lower) depreciable asset lives, and relatively higher (lower) residual values.

Example 7.11

Net profit and depreciation methods

Use the data of the Example 7.7. Assuming that profit before depreciation for each of the four years in which the machine was held is respectively EUR 40,000, EUR 36,000, EUR 44,000 and EUR 48,000, we will calculate the net profit for the entity for each year under each depreciation method.

As we can see from Table 7.12, over the four years the total net profit is the same (i.e. EUR 90,048) regardless of the depreciation method used. What changes is the allocation of the cost of the asset and thus the depreciation charge and the profit.

Table 7.12 Net profit (loss) and depreciation methods

Year	Profit before depreciation €	Straight-line depreciation expense €	Net profit €	Diminishing-balance depreciation expense €	Net profit (loss) €	Sum-of-the-units depreciation expense €	Net profit €
2006	40,000	19,488	20,512	48,000	(8,000)	18,080	21,920
2007	36,000	19,488	16,512	19,200	16,800	19,440	16,560
2008	44,000	19,488	24,512	7,680	36,320	20,400	23,600
2009	48,000	19,488	28,512	3,072	44,928	20,032	27,968
Total	168,000	77,952	90,048	77,952	90,048	77,952	90,048

Under the straight-line depreciation method the depreciation expenses are equally allocated over the four years. While under the diminishing-balance depreciation method, the depreciation expense being higher in the first year, the net profit increases over the years from a loss of EUR 8,000 in 2006 to a net profit of EUR 44,928 in 2009.

The sum-of-the-units depreciation method leads to similar results as the straight-line method (see Figure 7.10).

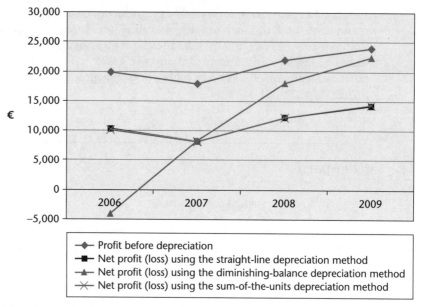

Figure 7.10 Net profit (loss) and depreciation methods

Summary

- Property, plant and equipment (PPE) are tangible assets that are held by an entity for use in the production or supply of goods or services, for rental to others, or for administrative purposes; and are expected to be used for more than one period.

- An item of PPE should initially be measured at its cost. This includes: the purchase price (less any trade discount and rebates) and costs directly attributable to bringing the asset to working condition for its intended use, such as site preparation; initial delivery and handling costs; installation and assembly costs; professional fees such as for architects and engineers; and the initial estimate of the cost of dismantling and removing the item and site restoration costs, where the entity has an obligation to return the site to its original condition, for example the decommissioning of a nuclear power plant.

- Routine repairs and maintenance costs should be expensed in the income statement as costs are incurred. However, where subsequent expenditure extends the useful life of an item of PPE, or increases its capacity, or achieves a substantial improvement in the quality of output, such additional expenditure should be recognised as part of the cost of the asset.

- Subsequent to initial recognition as an asset, the carrying amount of an item of PPE is represented by its cost less accumulated depreciation and any impairment losses. To calculate depreciation, four factors need to be considered: (i) cost of the asset; (ii) useful life of the asset; (iii) residual value; (iv) depreciation method.

- After recognition as an asset, an item of PPE whose fair value can be measured reliably should be carried at a revalued amount, being its fair value at the date of the revaluation less any subsequent accumulated depreciation and impairment losses. Revaluations should be made with sufficient regularity to ensure that the carrying amount does not differ materially from that which would be determined using fair value at the end of the reporting period.

- An investment property is a property (land or a building – or part of a building – or both) held to earn rentals or for capital appreciation or both, rather than for use in the production or supply of goods or services or for administrative purposes; or sale in the ordinary course of business. An investment property generates cash flows largely independent of other assets held by an entity.

- An investment property should be recognised as an asset when the normal conditions for asset recognition are satisfied. It should be measured initially at its cost, which is its purchase price and transaction costs such as professional fees for legal services, property transfer taxes and so on. Start-up costs, operating losses incurred before the investment property achieves the planned level of occupancy, abnormal amounts of wasted material, labour or other resources incurred in constructing or developing the property are excluded from the cost of an investment property.

- Following the initial measurement at cost, an investment property is either held at cost less accumulated depreciation (the cost model) or measured at fair value (the fair value model).

- Management should make a number of choices when deciding about recognition and depreciation of assets. They should decide on, *inter alia*, the capitalisation policy, methods of depreciation that will be used, the useful lives of the assets, and residual values of the assets. These choices affect the asset values reported in the balance sheet and depreciation charges in the income statement. They also affect several key financial ratios and the classification of cash flows in the statement of cash flows.

Research and references

The IASB documents relevant for this chapter are:

- IAS 8 – *Accounting Policies, Changes in Accounting Estimates and Errors.*
- IAS 16 – *Property, Plant and Equipment.*
- IAS 20 – *Accounting for Government and Disclosure of Government Assistance.*
- IAS 23 – *Borrowing Costs.*
- IAS 40 – *Investment Property.*

The following are examples of books that take the issues of this chapter further:

- Alexander, D., Britton, A. and Jorissen, A. (2007) *International Financial Reporting and Analysis*, 3rd edn. Thomson, Chapter 12.
- Elliott, B. and Elliott, J. (2009) *Financial Accounting and Reporting*, 13th edn. Financial Times-Prentice Hall, Chapter 15.

- the straight-line method;
- the diminishing balance method (at a rate of 30 per cent).

How should the entity choose between these methods?

7.7 Depreciation methods

On 1 January 2010, an entity, which prepares financial statements to 31 December each year, buys a machine at a cost of EUR 92,600. The machine's useful life is estimated at four years with a residual value of EUR 12,000. The machine is expected to achieve 50,000 units of production over its useful life, as follows:

Year to 31 December 2010	10,000 units
Year to 31 December 2011	20,000 units
Year to 31 December 2012	15,000 units
Year to 31 December 2013	5,000 units

Calculate depreciation charges for each of these four years using:

(a) the straight-line method;
(b) the diminishing-balance method (at a rate of 40 per cent);
(c) the units-of-production method.

7.8 Capitalisation of borrowing costs

(a) Define the term 'borrowing costs' and explain the accounting treatment of such costs in accordance with IAS 23.
(b) During the year ended 31 December 2009, an entity started work on the construction of a manufacturing plant and incurred expenditure as follows:

	€000
1 April 2009	3,000
1 August 2009	4,800
1 December 2009	3,600

All of these payments were made out of general borrowings. Construction work was still underway at 31 December 2009. The entity had the following general borrowings outstanding throughout the year 2009.

	Amount of loan	Interest for the year
	€000	€000
Loan A	20,000	2,300
Loan B	16,000	1,440
Loan C	10,000	860

Calculate the amount of borrowing costs that may be capitalised for the construction of the manufacturing plant during the year.

7.9 Investment property

(a) Define the term 'investment property' and explain the two models permitted by IAS 40 for the measurement of investment property after its initial recognition.

(b) How do these two models differ from the two models permitted by IAS 16 in relation to the measurement of PPE?

7.10 Carrying amount of a complex asset

Golden leisure is a private limited liability entity that operates a single cruise ship. The chip was acquired on 1 October 2000. Details of the cost of the ship's components and their estimated useful lives are:

Component	Original cost	Depreciation basis
	€m	
Ship's fabric (hull, decks etc)	600	25 years straight-line
Cabins and entertainment area fittings	300	12 years straight-line
Propulsion system	200	Useful life of 40,000 hours

At 30 September 2008 no further capital expenditure had been incurred on the ship.

In the year ended 30 September 2008 the ship experienced a high level of engine trouble which had cost the entity considerable lost revenue and payroll costs. At 30 September 2008 the propulsion system was expected to work for 30,000 hours. Due to the unreliability of the engines, a decision was taken in early October 2008 to replace the whole propulsion system at a cost of EUR 280m. The expected life of the new propulsion system was 50,000 hours and in the year ended 30 September 2009 the ship had used its engines for 5,000 hours.

At the same time as the propulsion replacement, the entity took the opportunity to do a limited upgrade to the cabin and entertainment facilities at a cost of EUR 120m and repaint the ship's fabric at a cost of EUR 40m. After the upgrade of the cabin and entertainment area fittings, it was estimated that their remaining life was five years (from the date of upgrade). For the purpose of calculating depreciation, all the work on the ship can be assumed to have been completed on 1 October 2008. All residual values can be taken as nil.

Calculate the carrying amount of Golden Leisure's cruise ship at 30 September 2009 and its related expenditure in the income statement for the year ended 30 September 2009. Your answer should explain the treatment of each item.

8 Leases (IAS 17)

Contents

Objectives

When you have completed this chapter you should be able to:

- Distinguish between a finance and an operating lease
- Account for finance leases from the perspective of a lessee
- Allocate finance charges over the term of a finance lease
- Account for finance leases from the perspective of a lessor
- Account for operating leases from the perspective of both lessors and lessees
- Recognise and account for sale and leaseback transaction.
- Discuss possible future changes to lease accounting.

8.1   Introduction

Leasing has long been a popular financing option for the acquisition of business property. During the past few decades, however, the business of leasing has experienced a staggering growth. The tremendous popularity of leasing is quite understandable, as it offers great flexibility, often coupled with a range of economic advantages over ownership.

The accounting treatment of lease transactions involves a number of complexities, which derive partly from the range of alternative structures that are available to the parties (lessor and lessee). The accounting treatment should be based on the premise that, when a lease transfers substantially all risks and rewards incidental to ownership to the lessee, that lease is in *substance* equivalent to the acquisition of an asset on credit by the lessee, and to a sale and financing by the lessor as shown in the following example.

Example 8.1

Substance over form applied to lease arrangements

Let us consider two entities, ABC and XYZ. The former borrowed EUR 20m and bought PPE with this money. XYZ borrowed no money, but leased PPE that would have cost EUR 20m to buy. If XYZ accounts for the transaction on the basis of the legal form of the arrangement, its profitability and financial condition would look unfairly better than ABC's. That is, XYZ will seem to have a better profit in relation to asset used (because assets seem smaller) and show smaller liabilities (see the first two balance sheets below). Key ratios significantly affected by this accounting treatment are return on total assets and gearing.

	ABC's balance sheet
Non-current assets + €20m	Loans + €20m

	XYZ's balance sheet (*form*)

	XYZ's balance sheet (*substance*)
Non-current assets + €20m	Lease liabilities + €20m

Therefore, when a finance lease agreement exists, a lessee should recognise the finance lease as an asset and a liability in its balance sheet at an amount equal to the fair value of the leased property or, if lower, the present value of the minimum lease payments, each determined at the inception of the lease as we will see later.

As shown briefly in the example above, the mandatory recognition of the asset/liability relating to the lease is justified by two arguments:

- Although the legal form of a lease agreement is such that the lessee may acquire no legal title to the leased asset, in the case of finance leases the substance and financial reality are such that the lessee acquires economic benefits of the use of the leased asset for the major part of its economic life in return for entering into an obligation to pay for that right an amount approximating, at the inception of the lease, the fair value of the asset and the related finance charge (IAS 17 para 21).

- If such lease transactions are not reflected in the lessee's statement of financial position, the economic resources and the level of obligations of an entity are understated, thereby distorting financial ratios (IAS 17 para 22).

These justifications represent the concept of *substance over form*:

> *To be useful in financial reporting, information should be a faithful representation of the economic phenomenon that it purports to represent. Faithful representation is attained when the depiction of an economic phenomenon is complete, neutral, and free from material error. Financial information that faithfully represents an economic phenomenon depicts the economic substance of the underlying transaction, event, or circumstance, which is not always the same as its legal form.*
>
> (*Framework* ED QC7)

This rationale views a lease transaction as a quasi-purchase of an asset, in the sense that the transaction is recorded as the acquisition of an asset even though no transfer of legal title takes place.

According to the *World Leasing Yearbook 2009*, in 2007 the annual volume of leases amounted to US$760 bn. However, the assets and liabilities arising from many of those contracts cannot be found in entities' balance sheets. This is because the current version of IAS 17 – *Leases* splits leases into two categories: finance leases and operating leases. If a lease is classified as a finance lease, assets and liabilities are recognised in the balance sheet. For an operating lease the lessee simply recognises lease payments as an expense over the lease term.

This current approach in IFRS is based on the assumption that a finance lease, unlike operating lease, is similar to the purchase of an underlying asset that is financed by a loan and should therefore be recognised in the balance sheet. This split into finance and operating leases has given rise to a number of problems:

- *Users (such as investors and analysts) complain that financial statements do not depict clearly the effects of operating leases.* Many users think that operating leases also give rise to assets and liabilities. Therefore they think lessees should recognise operating leases in their financial statements. As a result, they routinely adjust the recognised amounts in an attempt to understand the effect of those assets and liabilities on the balance sheet.

- *Similar transactions can be accounted for very differently.* The split between finance leases and operating leases means that economically similar transactions can be accounted for very differently. This reduces both the transparency of accounts and comparability for investors.

- *IAS 17 provides opportunities to structure transactions so as to achieve a particular lease classification.* If a lease is classified as an operating lease the lessee obtains a source of off balance sheet financing that can be difficult for investors to understand.

In March 2009 the IASB issued a discussion paper (DP) on lease accounting jointly with the FASB. The aim of the DP is to develop a model for recognising and measuring assets and liabilities under lease contracts in the same way independently of the lease classification (finance or operating). The two Boards justified this proposal on the grounds that recording all leases on the balance sheet would significantly increase the transparency and the comparability of lease accounting. If this principle is adopted in a new standard on lease accounting, it would result in the lessee recognising both:

- an asset for its right to use the leased item (the right-of-use asset); and

- a lease liability for its obligation to pay rentals (the present value of the lease payments will be obtained by discounting the lease payments using the lessee's incremental rate for leased borrowing instead of the interest rate implicit in the lease).

This proposal has been widely resisted.

8.2 Classification of leases

A lease is an agreement whereby the lessor conveys to the lessee the right to use an asset for an agreed period of time in return for a payment or a series of payments (IAS 17 para 4).

Thus, under a lease agreement the lessee acquires, not the asset itself, but the *right* to use the asset for a set time. Leased assets range from physical assets such as land, plant and vehicles, to intangible assets such as patents, copyright and mineral rights.

Lease agreements may also result in the eventual transfer of ownership from a lessor to a lessee. For example, under a hire purchase agreement, the lessee uses the asset while paying for its acquisition through installments. The agreed period of time may vary from a short period, such as the daily hire of a motor vehicle, to a longer period, such as the rental of office space by a company. The key feature of a lease is the existence of an asset owned by one party (the lessor) but used, for some or all of its economic life, by another party (the lessee).

Accounting for leases is complicated by the fact that there are two parties involved: the lessor and the lessee.

IAS 17 para 8 requires both lessees and lessors to classify each lease arrangement as either an *operating lease* or a *finance lease* at the inception of the lease, which is 'the earlier of the date of the lease agreement and the date of commitment by the parties to the principal provisions of the lease' (IAS 17 para 4). This classification process is vitally important because the accounting treatment and disclosures prescribed by the standard for each type of lease differ significantly.

The key criterion of a finance lease is the transfer of substantially all of the risks and rewards without the transfer of ownership of the asset.

Title may or may not eventually be transferred (IAS 17 para 4). An operating lease is simply defined as a lease other than a finance lease.

The *risks* of ownership include: possibilities of losses from idle capacity or technological obsolescence and of variations in return because of changing economic conditions.

Rewards are represented by the expectation of profitable operations over the asset's economic life and of gain from appreciation in value or realisation of a residual value (IAS 17 para 7).

To assist with the classification in the financial statements, IAS 17 paras 10 and 11 provide the following series of situations that individually or in combination would normally lead to a lease transaction being classified as a finance lease:

- The lease transfers ownership of the asset by the end of the lease term.

- The lessee has the option to purchase the asset at a price that is expected to be sufficiently lower than the fair value at the date the option becomes exercisable.

- The lease term is for the major part of the economic life of the asset even if title is not transferred.

- At the inception of the lease, the present value (PV) of the minimum lease payments (MLP) amounts to at least substantially all of the fair value of the leased asset.

- The leased assets are of such a specialised nature that only the lessee can use them without major modification.

- If the lessee can cancel the lease, the lessor's losses associated with the cancellation are borne by the lessee.

- Gains or losses from the fluctuation in the fair value of the residual accrue to the lessee (for example, in the form of a rent rebate equal to most of the sales proceeds at the end of the lease).

- The lessee has the ability to continue the lease for a secondary period at a rental that is substantially less than the market rent.

Note that these pointers are guidelines in assessing whether substantially all the risks and rewards are transferred. Each pointer relates to some measure of risk or rewards. For the purpose of analysis the guidelines have been restated as five main questions, as represented in Figure 8.1, to aid in classifying lease arrangements as either operating leases or finance leases.

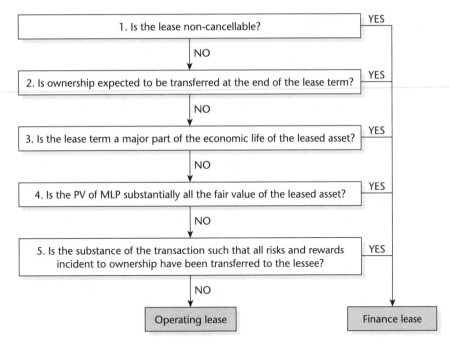

Figure 8.1 Guidelines for classifying a lease

8.3   Accounting for finance leases by lessees[1]

Once an arrangement has been classified as a finance lease, the asset and liability arising from it should be determined and recognised in the accounts.

In accounting for a finance lease it is necessary to record the lease in the balance sheet as both an asset and a liability (the obligation to pay future rentals). The amount at which the asset and liability are initially recorded should be the fair value of the leased property, or – if lower – the present value of the minimum lease payments discounted at the interest rate implicit in the lease.[2] Rentals paid under a finance lease should be apportioned between a finance charge (in the income statement) and a reduction in the outstanding liability (in the balance sheet). The finance charge should be allocated to time periods to give a constant periodic rate of interest on the remaining balance of liability. This is best achieved by use of the 'actuarial method' as illustrated in Example 8.2, which is identical to the 'effective interest' or 'amortised cost' method used for ordinary long-term fixed interest borrowings such as debentures.

Depreciation should also be charged on the leased asset under a finance lease. If it is not reasonably certain that the lessee will obtain ownership of the leased asset by the end of the lease term, the asset should be depreciated over the shorter of the lease term and its useful economic life; if it is likely that the lessee will obtain ownership it should be depreciated over its useful life. Depreciation should be charged to income in the usual way.

In the balance sheet, the outstanding liability under finance leases should be apportioned between current liabilities and non-current liabilities (see Example 8.2).

8.3.1 Initial recognition

When a lease is classified as a finance lease, IAS 17 para 20 requires a lessee to recognise, at the commencement of the lease term, an asset and a liability, each determined at the inception of the lease, equal to the fair value of the leased property or, if lower, the present value of the minimum lease payments (PV of MLP). The journal entry is:

Dr Leased asset	PV of MLP	
Cr Lease liability		PV of MLP

If not already determined as part of the classification process, the value of the asset or liability should be calculated at the inception of the lease by reference to the terms of the lease agreement. If the lessee incurs initial direct cost (IDC) associated with the negotiation and securing of the lease arrangements then, according to IAS 17 para 24, such costs should be added to the amount recognised as an asset. The journal entry is:

Dr Leased asset	PV of MLP + IDC	
Cr Lease liability		PV of MLP
Cr Cash		IDC

8.3.2 Subsequent measurement

After initial recognition, IAS 17 prescribes different accounting treatments for the leased asset and the lease liability.

Leased asset

IAS 17 para 27 states that:

The depreciation policy for depreciable leased assets should be consistent with that for depreciable assets that are owned, and the depreciation recognised should be calculated in accordance with IAS 16 – Property, Plant and Equipment and IAS 38 – Intangible Assets.

Depreciable assets are those whose future benefits are expected to expire over time or by use. The asset is depreciated over its useful life in a pattern reflecting the consumption or loss of the rewards embodied in the asset. The length of a leased asset's useful life depends on whether or not ownership of the asset will transfer at the end of the lease term. If the asset is to be returned to the lessor, then its useful life is the lease term. If it is reasonably certain that the ownership will be transferred to the lessee, then the useful life is the asset's economic life. Additionally, to determine whether a leased asset has become impaired, the lessee should apply IAS 36 – *Impairment of Assets* (see Chapter 10).

Lease liability

Because lease payments are made over the lease term, IAS 17 para 25 requires the payments to be divided into the following components:

- reduction in the lease liability;
- interest expense incurred;
- reimbursement of lessor costs;
- payment of contingent rent.

The latter two are easily determined by reference to the lease agreement, but the first two need to be calculated. The lease liability recognised at the commencement of the lease term represents the present value of future lease payments relating to the use of the asset. This present value is determined by applying the interest rate implicit in the lease as explained in Example 8.2. Thus, the interest expense can be obtained by applying the same rate to the outstanding lease liability at the beginning of the payment period. A payments schedule can be used to determine the interest expense and the reduction in the liability over the lease period.

IAS 17 para 25 requires that contingent rent should be recognised as an expense of the year in which it is incurred. The accounting standard is silent about the component of lease payments that represents a reimbursement of costs incurred by the lessor. However, as the cost of such items is effectively borne by the lessee, the payment should be recognised as an expense.

Example 8.2

Accounting for finance leases by lessees

An asset which could be purchased for EUR 23,450 is leased by Lessee Co for five years (its useful economic life, at the end of which it will have no residual value). Lessee Co is responsible for all maintenance and insurance costs. The lease provides for six half-yearly payments of EUR 4,500 in advance, the first payment being made on 1 January 2009. Show the amounts that will appear in respect of this leased asset in the profit and loss account of Lessee Co for the year ended 31 December 2009 and in its balance sheet at that date[3].

Since the lease covers the whole of the economic life of the asset, and Lessee Co is required to maintain and insure it, it may be deemed to transfer substantially all of the risks and rewards of ownership.

To allocate the finance charge using the actuarial method it is necessary to find the rate of interest which when applied to the outstanding liability during the period will result in a finance charge that represents a constant rate of interest on the outstanding liability over the whole term of the liability. This may be done as follows:

(i) Find the value of the annuity factor for five periods that sets the minimum lease payments equal to the amount of the opening obligation, that is:

$$€23{,}450 = €4{,}500 + €4{,}500a_{\overline{5}|r\%}$$

Note the annuity factor here is calculated for only five periods since the first payment under the lease is made in advance, i.e. on the first day of each six-month period.[4]

$$€23{,}450 - €4{,}500 = €4{,}500a_{\overline{5}|r\%} \rightarrow \frac{€18{,}950}{€4{,}500} = a_{\overline{5}|r\%} \rightarrow a_{\overline{5}|r\%} = 4.21\%$$

Table 8.1 Analysis of rental payments

Period starting	Obligation at start of period €	Rental payment €	Obligation during period €	Finance charge for the period €	Obligation at end of period €
1 Jan 2009	23,450	4,500	18,950	1,137	20,087
1 July 2009	20,087	4,500	15,587	935	16,522
1 Jan 2010	16,522	4,500	12,022	721	12,743
1 July 2010	12,743	4,500	8,243	495	8,738
1 Jan 2011	8,738	4,500	4,238	254	4,492
1 July 2011	4,492	4,500	–	–	–

(Rounding difference of €8)

Reading from the 'five periods' column of annuity tables (see Appendix to Chapter 2) it can be seen that this annuity factor relates to an interest rate of 6 per cent per half-year period (a little over 12 per cent p.a. [12.36 per cent]).

Because of the assumptions made here (that there is no guaranteed or unguaranteed residual value and no initial direct costs) the interest rate determined above is also equal to the interest rate implicit in the lease.

(ii) The analysis of rental payments under the lease may be made as shown in Table 8.1.

The amount shown as finance charge is calculated at 6 per cent per half-year period on the amount of the obligation outstanding during each period. Since in this example lease payments are made in advance, the obligation during each period is less than the amount outstanding at the start of each period.

In the income statement for the year ended 31 December 2009 a finance charge of EUR 2,072 will be shown. This is made up of the amounts of EUR 1,137 and EUR 935 covering the periods 1 January to 30 June 2009 and 1 July to 31 December 2009. In the balance sheet at 31 December 2009 obligations under the finance lease amounting to EUR 16,522 will be shown. This will be split between current liabilities and non-current liabilities.

There are different ways in which entities may make the split between current and non-current liabilities. The proper way to calculate the current liability is to discount the payments to be made in the next 12 months using the rate of interest used to allocate the finance charge. In this case, since the first of those payments is made on 1 January 2010, that payment will not be discounted; the payment due on 1 July 2010 will be discounted for one period at 6 per cent giving a value of EUR 4,245 and a total current liability of EUR 8,745. The balance of EUR 7,777 (= EUR 16,522 – EUR 8,745) will be a non-current liability, representing the present value now (i.e. at 31 December 2009) of the final two payments of EUR 4,500 each to be made in 2011.

The asset will be included amongst non-current assets at an amount equal to the initial obligation under the finance lease (EUR 23,450) and will be depreciated over its useful economic life which coincides here with the lease term. It should be depreciated on a basis consistent with that used for assets which are owned. Assuming the use of the straight-line basis, depreciation of EUR 7,817 (rounded) per annum will be charged to the income statement and the net book value of the asset in the balance sheet at 31 December 2009 will be EUR 15,633.

Where property, plant and equipment have been financed by lease agreements under which substantially all of the risks and rewards incidental to ownership are transferred to Emirates, they are classified as finance leases. Finance leases are capitalised at the commencement of the lease at the lower of the present value of the minimum lease payments or the fair value of the leased asset. The corresponding lease obligations are included under liabilities. Lease payments are treated as consisting of capital and interest elements. The interest element is charged to the consolidated income statement over the lease term so as to produce a constant periodic rate of interest on the remaining balance of the liability. Property, plant and equipment acquired under finance leases are depreciated in accordance with Emirates' policies.

10. Property, plant and equipment (continued)

The net book amount of property, plant and equipment includes AED 10,469.4 million (2008: AED 6,385.4 million) in respect of aircraft and AED 369.3 million (2008: AED 431.7 million) in respect of aircraft engines held under finance leases.

23. Lease liabilities

Finance leases

	2009 AED'000	2008 AED'000
Gross lease liabilities:		
Within one year	1,503,058	1,253,094
Between 2 and 5 years	3,972,214	3,121,403
After 5 years	6,746,519	3,697,934
	12,221,791	**8,072,431**
Future interest	(2,893,297)	(1,898,464)
Term deposits	–	(116,354)
Present value of finance lease liabilities	**9,328,494**	**6,057,613**
The present value of finance lease liabilities is repayable as follows:		
Within one year (Note 20)	**1,248,306**	**1,022,979**
Between 2 and 5 years	2,609,859	2,093,306
After 5 years	5,470,329	2,941,328
Total over one year (Note 20)	**8,080,188**	**5,034,634**
The present value of finance lease liabilities are denominated in the following currencies:		
US Dollars	9,174,131	5,879,139
Others	154,363	178,474

The lease liabilities are secured on the related aircraft and aircraft engines. In the event of these finance leases being terminated prior to their expiry, penalties are payable. Had these leases been cancelled at 31 March 2009, the penalties would have been AED 77.9 million (2008: AED 171.7 million).

Figure 8.2 Lessee finance lease disclosures

Source: The Emirates Group Annual Report 2008–9.

8.4   Accounting for finance leases by lessors

When a lease is classified as a finance lease, the lessor should 'derecognise' the leased asset and record a lease receivable.

8.4.1 Initial recognition

IAS 17 para 36 requires the lessor to recognise assets held under a finance lease in its balance sheet and present them as a receivable at an amount equal to the net investment in the lease. The net investment in the lease is defined as the gross investment in the lease discounted at the interest rate implicit in the lease.

The gross investment is equal to:

(a) the minimum lease payments receivable by the lessor under a finance lease; and

(b) any unguaranteed residual value accruing to the lessor (IAS 17 para 4).

and will normally be equal to the fair value of the asset at the inception of the lease. Initial direct costs, except those incurred by manufacturer or dealer lessors should be included in the initial measurement of the finance lease receivable and should reduce the amount of interest revenue recognised over the lease term. The definition of interest rate implicit in the lease automatically includes initial direct costs in the finance lease receivable, so there is no need to add them separately (IAS 17 para 38). Lessees are required to recognise assets and liabilities associated with finance leases at the commencement of the lease term but no date for recognition is specified for lessors; however, it would be the same date.

8.4.2 Subsequent measurement

As the lease payments are received from the lessee over the lease term, the receipts need to be analysed into the following components:

- reduction in the lease receivable;
- interest revenue earned;
- reimbursement of costs paid on behalf of the lessee;
- receipt of contingent fee.

The latter two are easily determined by reference to the lease agreement, but the first two need to be calculated in a similar fashion to that used by the lessee. The lease receivable recognised at the commencement of the lease term represents the present value of future lease payments relating to the use of the asset. This present value is determined by applying the interest rate implicit in the lease. Thus, the interest revenue can be obtained by applying the same rate to the outstanding lease receivable at the beginning of the payment period. A receipts schedule can be used to determine the interest revenue and the reduction in the receivable over the lease period.

The method for allocating gross earnings to accounting periods is referred to as the 'actuarial method'. This method allocates rentals between finance income and repayment of capital in each accounting period in such a way that finance income will emerge at a constant rate of return on the lessor's net investment in the lease.[5]

Accounting for executory costs and contingent rentals

IAS 17 is silent on the treatment of contingent rent and reimbursements of costs incurred on behalf of the lessee. However, as receipts meet the definition of income in the *Framework*, contingent rents should be recognised as revenue in the period they are earned, and reimbursements should be offset against the related expenses incurred.

Example 8.3

Accounting for finance leases by lessor

You are given the following information:

Lease term	7 years from 31 March 2004
Rental payments	€3,574 payable annually in advance
Asset cost	€20,000
Expected residual value	nil
Lessor's year-end date	30 September

Determine the finance income for each accounting period.

The first step is to calculate the interest rate implicit in the lease.

$$(€20,000 - €3,574) = €3,574 \ a_{\bar{\delta}|r\%}$$

$$a_{\bar{\delta}|r\%} = 4.5959709$$

Using the table in Appendix to Chapter 2 and linear interpolation,[6] we determine an annual interest rate of 8.1928 per cent as shown in Table 8.2. This equates a half-yearly interest rate of 4.0158 per cent:

$$(1.081928)^{1/2} - 1 = 1.040158 - 1 = 4.0158\%$$

Table 8.2 Implicit interest rate

	Cash flow €	Interest @ 8.1928% €	Balance €
31 March 2004	20,000	–	20,000
31 March 2004	(3,574)	–	16,426
31 March 2005	(3,574)	1,346	14,198
31 March 2006	(3,574)	1,163	11,787
31 March 2007	(3,574)	966	9,179
31 March 2008	(3,574)	752	6,357
31 March 2009	(3,574)	521	3,303
31 March 2010	(3,574)	271	–
	(5,018)	5,018	

Once the interest rate implicit in the lease is known, finance income can be allocated to the appropriate accounting periods as shown in Table 8.3.

Table 8.3 Analysis of rental payments

Date	Net investment at start of period	Interest income @ 4.0158%	Rental	Net investment at end of period	Annual finance income
30 September 2004	16,426	660	–	17,086	660
31 March 2005	17,086	686	3,574	14,198	–
30 September 2005	14,198	570	–	14,768	1,256
31 March 2006	14,768	593	3,574	11,787	–
30 September 2006	11,787	473	–	12,260	1,066
31 March 2007	12,260	492	3,574	9,179	–
30 September 2007	9,179	369	–	9,547	861
31 March 2008	9,547	383	3,574	6,357	–
30 September 2008	6,357	255	–	6,612	639
31 March 2009	6,612	266	3,574	3,303	–
30 September 2009	3,303	133	–	3,436	398
31 March 2010	3,436	138	3,574	0	–
30 September 2010	–	–	–	–	138
					5,018

8.5   Accounting for operating leases

Operating leases are straightforward and present no major accounting problems. Since the lessee has not taken on the risks and rewards of ownership, the leased item is not shown as an asset in the lessee's balance sheet. The lease payments are simply recognised as an expense, generally on a straight-line basis over the lease term.

The lessor has retained the risks and rewards of ownership, so the leased item is shown as an asset in the lessor's balance sheet and is depreciated in accordance with IASs 16 and 38. The lease payments are recognised as income. Any direct costs incurred by the lessor for arranging an operating lease should be added to the carrying amount of the asset concerned and then written off over the lease term as shown below:

	€
Asset	XXX
Deduct Accumulated depreciation	XXX
	XXX
Add Initial direct costs	XXX
	XXX

Example 8.4

Accounting for operating leases

On 1 July 2009, Medicine Hat Ltd leased a bobcat from Yellowknife Finance Ltd. The bobcat cost Yellowknife Finance Ltd EUR 71,932 on that same day. The finance lease agreement, which cost Yellowknife Finance Ltd EUR 762 to have it drawn up, contained the following clauses:

17 OTHER RECEIVABLES AND OTHER ASSETS

MILLION EURO	2008	2007
Receivables under finance leases	178	208
Claims for tax refunds	61	60
Receivables against AgfaPhoto Group companies (note 15)	32	24
Accrued interest on loans receivable	1	1
Other	57	70
TOTAL	329	363

Lease agreements in which the other party, as lessee, is to be regarded as the economic owner of the leased assets give rise to accounts receivable in the amount of the discounted future lease payments. These receivables amounted to 190 million Euro as of December 31, 2008 (2007: 219 million Euro) and will bear interest income until their maturity dates of 22 million Euro (2007: 26 million Euro). As of December 31, 2008, the write-downs on the receivables under finance leases amounted to 12 million Euro (2007: 11 million Euro).

The receivables under finance leases are as follows:

	2008			2007		
MILLION EURO	Total future payments	Unearned interest income	Present value	Total future payments	Unearned interest income	Present value
Not later than one year	84	10	74	95	13	82
Between one and five years	127	12	115	149	13	136
Later than five years	1	–	1	1	–	1
TOTAL	212	22	190	245	26	219

The Group leases out its commercial equipment under finance leases mainly via Agfa Finance (i.e. Agfa Finance NV and its subsidiaries) and via Agfa Corporation (USA).

At the inception of the lease, the present value of the minimum lease payments generally amounts to at least 90% of the fair value of leased assets.

The major part of the leases concluded with Agfa Finance typically run for a non-cancellable period of four years. The contracts generally include an option to purchase the leased equipment after that period at a price that generally lies between 2% and 5% of the gross investment at the inception of the lease. Sometimes, the fair value of the leased asset is paid back by means of a purchase obligation for consumables at a value higher than its market value, in such a way that this mark-up is sufficient to cover the amount initially invested by the lessor. In these types of contracts the mark-up and/or the lease term can be subject to change.

Agfa Finance offers its products via its subsidiaries in the USA, Canada, Australia, France, Italy and Poland and its branches in Europe (Spain, Switzerland, Benelux, Germany, UK and the Nordic countries) and Japan. As of December 31, 2008, the present value of the total future lease payments for Agfa Finance amounted to 168 million Euro (2007: 187 million Euro).

Agfa Corporation has a lease portfolio with an average remaining term of 20 months. The options at the end of these contracts are to purchase, to renew or to return the leased equipment at a value which is expected to be the fair value at the date the option becomes exercisable. As of December 31, 2008, the present value of the total future lease payments amounted to 22 million Euro (2007: 32 million Euro).

Figure 8.3 Lessor finance lease disclosures
Source: Agfa-Gevaert NV Annual Report 2008.

Lease term	3 years
The lease is cancellable	
Annual rental payment, in arrears (commencing 1 July 2009)	€7,800
Residual value at the end of the lease term	€49,000
Residual guaranteed by Medicine Hat Ltd	€0
Interest rate implicit in lease	6%

The estimated economic life of the bobcat is 10 years.

How should Medicine Hat Ltd account for this lease agreement?

IAS 17 requires that the lease should be classified as either a finance or an operating lease based on the extent to which the risks and rewards associated with the vehicle have been effectively transferred between Medicine Hat Ltd and Yellowknife Finance Ltd.

In order to classify this lease agreement as operating or finance we can use the guidelines set out in Figure 8.1.

- *Is the lease non-cancellable?*

The lease agreement is cancellable; either party can walk away from the arrangement without penalty.

- *Is ownership expected to be transferred at the end of the lease term?*

Medicine Hat Ltd expects to return the bobcat to Yellowknife Finance Ltd.

- *Is the lease term a major part of the economic life of the leased asset?*

The lease term is three years, which is only 30 per cent of the bobcat's economic life of 10 years. Therefore, the lease arrangement is not for the major part of the asset's life.

- *Is the present value of the minimum lease payments substantially all of the fair value of the leased asset?*

The minimum lease payments consist of three payments, in arrears, of EUR 7,800. There are no contingent rentals, executory costs or a guaranteed residual value.

Present value of minimum lease payments:

$$\text{PV of MLP} = \text{EUR } 7{,}800 \times a_{\overline{3}|6\%} = \text{EUR } 7{,}800 \times 2.6730 = \text{EUR } 20{,}850$$

This represents less than one third of the fair value of the asset (EUR 20,850 ÷ EUR 71,932 = 29%).

- *Is the substance of the transaction such that substantially all of the risks and rewards incident to the ownership have been transferred to the lessee?*

The shortness of the lease term compared to the asset's economic life indicates that it is in substance an operating lease.

Classification of the lease

On the basis of the evidence available, there has not been an effective transfer of substantially all of the risks and rewards associated with the bobcat to the lessee. Hence, the lease should be classified and accounted for as an operating lease.

Journal entries

The following journal entries should be passed in the books of both the lessor and the lessee for the year ended 30 June 2010:

Medicine Hat Ltd – lessee General journal			
30 June 2010			
Lease expense	Dr	7,800	
Cash	Cr		7,800
(Payment of the first year's rental)			

Yellowknife Finance Ltd – lessor General journal			
1 July 2009			
PPE	Dr	71,932	
Cash	Cr		71,932
(Purchase of bobcat)			
Deferred initial direct costs – PPE (prepayment)	Dr	762	
Cash	Cr		762
(Initial direct costs incurred for lease)			
30 June 2010			
Cash	Dr	7,800	
Lease income	Cr		7,800
(Receipt of first year's rental)			
Lease expense	Dr	254	
Deferred initial direct costs – PPE	Cr		254
(Recognition of initial direct cost: €762 ÷ 3 years)			
Depreciation expense	Dr	7,193	
Accumulated depreciation	Cr		7,193
(Depreciation charge for the year: €71,932 ÷ 10 years)			

Figure 8.4 Journal entries of the lessee and the lessor

Leases, where a significant portion of risks and rewards of ownership are retained by the lessor, are classified as operating leases. Lease rental charges, including advance rentals in respect of operating leases, are charged to the consolidated income statement on a straight-line basis over the period of the lease.

6. Operating costs (continued)

(b) Aircraft operating lease charges include AED 3,273.4 million (2008: AED 2,908.8 million) in respect of ninety four aircraft (2008: eighty five) and AED 523.2 million (2008: AED 670.0 million) in respect of wet leases of freighter aircraft.

(c) Corporate overheads includes non-aircraft operating lease charges amounting to AED 308.0 million (2008: AED 176.3 million), net foreign exchange loss of AED 708.4 million (2008: Nil) and AED 143.5 million (2008: Nil) loss on realisation of available-for-sale financial assets.

Figure 8.5 Lessee operating lease disclosures
Source: The Emirates Group Annual Report 2008–9.

Step 3 – record the rental payments

Entity A General journal		
Years 1–20	€	€
Dr Deferred gain on sale	30,000	
Cr Gain on disposal of non-current asset		30,000
(To release the deferred income over the lease term: €600,000 ÷ 20 years)		
Dr Depreciation expense	100,000	
Cr PPE		100,000
(To recognise depreciation on the leased asset: €2m ÷ 20 years)		
Dr Interest expense	X	
Dr Lease obligations	(176,436 – X)	
Cr Cash		176,436
(To record the rental payment due on the leased asset)		

Figure 8.8 Journal entries over the lease term

8.7 Financial analysis and interpretation

The effects of accounting for a lease in the financial statements of a lessee as an operating lease versus a finance lease can be summarised as follows:

- Lease payments under an operating lease are accounted for as a rental expense in the income statement.

- The balance sheet is only impacted indirectly for the rental expense which flows through to retained earnings via net profit.

- The rental expense is reported as an operating cash outflow (as a part of the entity's net profit) in the statement of cash flows.

- The total reported expense over the lease term would normally be the same for a finance lease as the total reported expense over the lease term would be under the operating lease. However, costs are higher in the early years under the finance lease.

- Under the finance lease both the asset and the net amount of debt are recorded in the balance sheet, whereas no such asset or debt is reported under the operating lease.

- Under finance lease accounting, the total lease payment is divided into an interest component and principal; a depreciation charge also arises when the asset represented by the principal (capital portion) is depreciated in accordance with IAS 16. Under the operating lease the payment is simply a rental expense.

- Under the operating lease, lease payments are reported as operating cash outflows (interest may be classified as a financing cash outflow), whereas under the finance lease, the cash outflow is normally allocated between operating and financing.

- The interest portion of the finance lease payment is normally reported as an operating cash outflow, whereas the repayment of the lease obligation portion is treated as a financing cash outflow. However, the net effect on total cash is the same under both methods.

- That portion of the lease obligation that is paid within one year or one operating cycle, whichever is longer, is classified as a current liability. The remainder is classified as a long-term liability.

Why do entities lease assets and under what conditions will they favour operating or finance leases? Several possible answers can be given to this question, but it should be considered within the context of a specific situation:

- Operating leases are advantageous when management compensation depends on return on assets or invested capital.

- An operating lease is advantageous when an entity wants to keep debt off of its balance sheet. This can help it if it has indenture covenants requiring low debt-to-equity ratio or high interest coverage ratio.

- Finance leases are favoured if an entity wants to show a higher cash flow from operations.

Table 8.4 summarises the effects of operating and finance leases on the financial statements of a lessee and its key financial ratios.

Summary

- A lease is an agreement whereby the lessor conveys to the lessee the right to use an asset for an agreed period of time in return for a payment or a series of payments.

- Lease arrangements can be either an *operating lease* or a *finance lease*. This distinction at the time of inception is important because the accounting treatment and disclosures prescribed for each type of lease differ significantly.

- There are situations that individually or in combination would normally lead to a lease transaction being treated as a finance lease: (a) ownership of the asset is transferred at the end of the lease term; (b) the lessee has the option to purchase the asset at the end of the lease term; (c) the lease term is for the major part of the economic life of the asset even if the title is not transferred; (d) at the inception of the lease, the present value of the minimum lease payments amounts to at least substantially all of the fair value of the leased asset; (e) the leased asset is of such a specialised nature that only the lessee can use it without a major modification.

- In accounting for a finance lease, the lessee should record the lease in the balance sheet as both an asset and a liability (the obligation to pay future rentals). The

Table 8.4 Effect of operating and finance leases on lessee financial statements and key financial ratios

Item or ratio	Operating lease	Finance lease
Balance sheet	No effect because no assets or liabilities are created.	A leased asset (for example, PPE) and a lease obligation are created when a lease is recorded.
Income statement	The lease payment is recorded as an expense. These payments are usually constant over the life of the lease.	Both interest expense and depreciation charge are incurred. In the early years of the lease, they combine to produce a higher expense than would be reported under an operating lease. However, over the life of the lease, the interest expense declines, causing the total expense to decline. This produces a positive trend in earnings. In the later years, earnings are higher under a finance lease than under an operating lease.
Statement of cash flows	The cash paid on the lease is recorded as an operating cash outflow.	The cash outflow from the lease payments is allocated partly to an operating or financing cash outflow (interest expense) and partly to a financing cash outflow (repayment of the lease obligation principal). Depreciation of the lease asset is not a cash expense, and therefore, it is not a cash flow item.
Profit margin	Higher in the early years because the rental expense is normally less than the total expense reported under a finance lease. However, in later years, it will be lower than under a finance lease.	Lower in the early years because the total reported expense under a finance lease is normally higher than the operating lease payment. However, the profit margin will trend upward over time, so in the later years it will be higher than the one for an operating lease.
Asset turnover	Higher because there are no leased assets recorded.	Lower because of the leased asset that is recorded. The ratio rises over time as the asset is depreciated.
Current ratio	Higher because no short-term debt is added to the balance sheet.	Lower because the current portion of the lease obligation created under a finance lease is a current liability. The current ratio deteriorates over time as the current portion of the lease obligation increases.
Debt-to-equity ratio	Lower because an operating lease creates no debt.	Higher because under a finance lease a lease obligation (liability) is created. However, the debt-to-equity ratio decreases over time as the lease obligation decreases.
Return on assets	Higher in the early years because profits are higher and assets are lower.	Lower in the early years because earnings are lower and assets are higher. However, the return on asset ratio improves over time because the earnings trend is positive and the assets decline as they are depreciated.
Return on equity	Higher in the early years because earnings are higher.	Lower in the early years because earnings are lower.
Interest coverage	Higher because no interest expense is incurred.	Lower because interest expense is created under a finance lease. However, the interest coverage ratio improves over time because the interest expense declines over time.

amount at which the asset and liability are initially recorded should be the fair value of the leased property, or, if lower, the present value of the minimum lease payments discounted at the interest rate implicit in the lease. Rentals paid under a finance lease should be apportioned between a finance charge (in the income statement) and a reduction in the outstanding liability (in the balance sheet). The finance charge should be allocated to time periods to give a constant periodic rate of interest on the remaining balance of liability. This is best achieved by using the 'actuarial method'. Depreciation should also be charged on the leased asset under a finance lease.

- When a lease is treated as a finance lease, the lessor should 'derecognise' the leased asset and record a lease receivable. The lease receivable recognised at the commencement of the lease term represents the present value of future lease payments relating to the use of the asset. This present value is determined by applying the interest rate implicit in the lease. Thus, the interest revenue can be obtained by applying the same rate to the outstanding lease receivable at the beginning of the payment period.

- If a lease arrangement is treated as operating, (a) the leased item is not shown as an asset in the lessee's balance sheet. The lease payments are simply recognised as an expense, generally on a straight-line basis over the lease term; (b) the leased item is shown as an asset in the lessor's balance sheet and is depreciated. The lease payments are recognised as income.

- A *sale and leaseback* is a lease transaction which involves the sale of an asset that is then leased back from the purchaser for all or part of its remaining economic life. Hence, the original owner becomes the lessee but the asset itself does not move. In substance, the lessee gives up legal ownership but still retains control over some or all of the asset's future economic benefits via the lease agreement.

- Operating leases are advantageous when management compensation depends on return on assets or invested capital, and when an entity wants to keep debt off from its balance sheet. This can help it if it has indenture covenants requiring low debt-to-equity ratios or high interest coverage ratios.

- The IASB and FASB are reviewing lease accounting with a view to develop a model for recognising and measuring assets and liabilities under operating and finance leases in the same way.

Research and references

The IASB documents relevant for this chapter are:

- IAS 17 – *Leases*.
- IAS 16 – *Property, Plant and Equipment*.
- Discussion Paper (DP): *Leases* March 2009.
- SIC 15 – *Operating Lease Incentives*.
- SIC 27 – *Evaluating the Substance of Transactions Involving the Legal form of a Lease*.
- IFRIC 4 – *Determining Whether an Arrangement Contains a Lease*.

The following are examples of books and papers that take the issues of this chapter further:

- Alexander, D., Britton, A. and Jorissen, A. (2007) *International Financial Reporting and Analysis*, 3rd edn. Thomson, Chapter 15.
- Alfredson, K., Leo, K., Picker, R., Loftus, J., Clark, K. and Wise, V. (2009) *Applying International Financial Reporting Standards*, 2nd edn. Wiley, Chapter 13.
- Australian Accounting Standards Board, Canadian Accounting Standards Board, International Accounting Standards Committee, New Zealand Financial Reporting Standards Board, UK ASB and US FASB (2000) 'Leases: Implementation of a New Approach', Position Paper, February.
- Elliott, B. and Elliott, J. (2009) *Financial Accounting and Reporting*, 13th edn. Financial Times-Prentice Hall, Chapter 16.
- Epstein, B.J. and Jermakowicz, E.K. (2009) *IFRS 2009: Interpretation and Application of International Accounting and Financial Reporting Standards*. Wiley, Chapter 14.
- PricewaterhouseCoopers (2009) *IFRS Manual of Accounting – 2010. Global Guide to International Financial Reporting Standards*. CCH, Chapter 19.

Discussion questions and exercises

8.1 Classification of leases

IAS 17 distinguishes between finance leases and operating leases and prescribes the accounting treatment for each type of lease.

(a) Define terms 'finance lease' and 'operating lease'.

(b) List the main situations in which a lease would normally be classified as a finance lease.

(c) Jon and Shabila Ltd is the lessee of the following leases:

    (i) Item A is leased at a cost EUR 10,000 per annum with a minimum lease term of five years. The item has a useful life of five years and would cost EUR 36,000 if bought for cash.

    (ii) Item B is leased at a cost of EUR 1,000 per month. The leased item has a useful life of 10 years and would cost EUR 80,000 to buy outright. The lease may be terminated at any time.

Determine whether each of these leases is an operating lease or a financial lease.

8.2 Operating and finance leases

(a) Leases are classified on the basis of 'substance over form'. What does this criterion mean and how does it relate to finance leases?

(b) What are 'minimum lease payments'?

(c) What is meant by 'the interest rate implicit in a lease'?

(d) Where a lessor incurs initial direct costs in establishing a lease agreement, how should such costs be accounted for by the lessor?

(e) How should operating leases be accounted for by lessors, in accordance with IAS 17?

8.3 Classification of leases

For the following arrangements, explain whether they are operating or finance lease transactions:

(a) Entity A leases an asset to entity B, and obtains a loan from a financial institution using the lease rentals and asset as collateral. Entity A sells the asset subject to the lease and the loan to a trustee, and leases the same asset back.

(b) Entity A enters into an agreement to buy petroleum products from entity B. The products are produced in a refinery built and operated by entity B on a site owned by entity A. While entity B could provide the products from other refineries that it owns, it is not practical to do so. Entity B retains the right to sell products produced by the refinery to other customers, but there is only a remote possibility that it will do so. The arrangement requires entity A to make both fixed, unavoidable payments, and variable payments based on input costs at a target level of efficiency to entity B.

(c) Entity A leases an asset to entity B for its entire economic life, and leases the same asset back under the same terms and conditions as the original lease. The two entities have a legally enforceable right to set off the amount owing to one another, and an intention to settle these amounts on a net basis.

(d) Entity A enters into a non-cancellable four year lease with entity B for an asset with an expected economic life of ten years. Entity A has an option to renew the lease for a further four years at the end of the lease term. At the conclusion of the lease arrangement, the asset will revert back to entity B. In a separate agreement, entity B is granted a put option to sell the asset to entity A should its market value at the end of the lease be less than the residual value.

8.4 Operating lease

On 1 January 2010, Qalam Ltd leases a machine to Shabs plc. The lease is for a term of three years and lease payments of EUR 2,000 per month are required. The machine has a useful life of eight years and would cost EUR 100,000 if bought for cash.

(a) Explain why the lease is an operating lease.

(b) Explain how the machine and the lease payments should be dealt with in the financial statements of Qalam Ltd, assuming that the company prepares its financial statements to 30 June each year.

8.5 Finance leases

On 1 July 2008, Huge & Co Ltd entered into a finance lease to acquire a machine. The cash price of the machine would have been EUR 264,000. The lease agreement specified that the company would make four lease payments, each of EUR 90,606, on 30 June 2009, 2010, 2011 and 2012. The interest rate implicit in the lease was 14 per cent per annum. Huge & Co Ltd prepares its financial statements on 30 June each year.

Determine the finance charge which should be shown in the company's income statement for each of the years to 30 June 2009, 2010, 2011 and 2012. Also show how the liability to the lessor should be presented in the balance sheet of Huge & Co Ltd as at 30 June 2009.

8.6   Finance lease

You are given the following information:

Cost of leased asset	€200,000
Lease term	5 years
Rental paid every six months in advance	€24,000
Expected residual on disposal at the end of the lease term	€20,000
Lessee's interest in residual proceeds	97%
Economic life	8 years
Inception and commencement date	1 January 2008
Lessee's financial year-end	31 December

Determine:

(a) the interest rate implicit in the lease;

(b) the finance charge to be allocated in each accounting period using the actuarial method;

(c) the effect on the lessee's balance sheet and income statement of this lease transaction.

8.7   Accounting for a finance lease by lessees

Sabrina Ltd prepares financial statements at 31 December each year. On 1 January 2009, the company acquired an asset by means of a finance lease. Details of the lease agreement are as follows:

Cash price of leased asset	€55,000
Lease term	5 years
Payments due annually in advance	€13,190
Useful life of asset	7 years
Residual value	€6,000
Rate of interest implicit in lease	10% per annum

Sabrina Ltd will obtain legal ownership of the asset at the end of the lease term. The company calculates depreciation on a straight-line basis.

(a) Determine the finance and depreciation charges which should be shown in the company's income statements for each of the years to 31 December 2009, 2010, 2011, 2012 and 2013.

(b) Calculate the liability to the lessor at the end of each of these years and show how this liability should be split between current liabilities and non-current liabilities.

8.8   Accounting for a finance lease by lessees

On 1 July 2009, Moose Jaw Ltd leased a plastic moulding machine from Winnipeg Ltd. The machine cost Winnipeg Ltd EUR 260,000 to manufacture and had a fair value of EUR 308,218 on 1 July 2009. The lease agreement contained the following clauses:

Lease term	4 years
Annual rental payment, in advance on 1 July each year	€83,000
Residual value at end of the lease term	€30,000
Residual guaranteed by lessee	Nil
Interest rate implicit in lease	8%
The lease is cancellable only with the agreement of the lessor	

The expected useful life of the machine is six years. Moose Jaw Ltd intends to return the machine to the lessor at the end of the lease term. Included in the annual rental payment is an amount of EUR 3,000 to cover the costs of maintenance and insurance paid for by the lessor.

(a) Classify the lease for both lessee and lessor based on the guidance provided in IAS 17 (refer to Figure 8.1).
(b) Prepare:

    (i) the lease schedules for the lessee (show all workings);
    (ii) the journal entries in the books of the lessee for the year ended 30 June 2010.

8.9   Accounting for a finance lease by lessee and lessor

On 1 July 2009, Haines Ltd leased a processing plant to Kitmat Ltd. The plant was purchased by Haines Ltd on 1 July 2009 at fair value of EUR 934,224. The lease agreement contained the clauses shown below:

Lease term	3 years
Economic life of plant	5 years
Annual rental payment, in arrears (commencing 30/06/2010)	€300,000
Residual value at end of the lease term	€180,000
Residual guaranteed by lessee	120,000
Interest rate implicit in lease	7%
The lease is cancellable only with the agreement of the lessor	

Kitmat Ltd intends to return the processing plant to the lessor at the end of the lease term. The lease has been classified as a finance lease by both the lessee and the lessor.

Prepare:

(a) the lease payment schedule for the lessee (show all workings);
(b) the journal entries in the books of the lessee for the year ending 30 June 2011;

(c) the lease receipt schedule for the lessor (show all workings);

(d) the journal entries in the books of the lessor for the year ending 30 June 2011.

8.10 Accounting for finance lease by lessee and lessor

On 1 July 2007, Vancouver Ltd leased a photocopier from Kamloops Ltd, a company that manufactures, retails and leases copiers. The photocopier had cost Kamloops Ltd EUR 60,000 to make but had a fair value on 1 July 2007 of EUR 70,160. The lease agreement contained the following provisions:

Lease term	3 years
Annual rental payment, payable in advance on 1 July each year	€29,000
Economic life of the copier	4 years
Estimated residual value at end of the lease term when the copier is returned to Kamloops Ltd	€6,000
Residual guaranteed by Vancouver Ltd	€3,000
Interest rate implicit in the lease	10%
The lease is cancellable, provided another lease is immediately entered into	

The annual payment included an amount of EUR 5,000 per annum to reimburse Kamloops Ltd for the cost of paper and toner supplied to Vancouver Ltd. Kamloops Ltd's solicitor prepared the lease agreement for a fee of EUR 2,730.

At the end of the lease term on 30 June 2010, Vancouver Ltd returned the copier to Kamloops Ltd, who sold the copier for EUR 6,000.

(a) Classify the lease for both the lessor and the lessee. Explain your answer.

(b) Prepare the following:

(i) For the lessee: the lease payment schedule and the journal entries for the year ended 30 June 2010.

(ii) For the lessor: the lease receipts schedule and the journal entries for the year ended 30 June 2008.

Notes

1 In accounting for leases by lessees the following definitions in summarised form should be borne in mind (see IAS 17 for precise definitions):

- *Lease term.* The period for which the lessee has contracted to lease the asset together with any further term for which it has the option to continue the lease and it is reasonably certain at the inception of the lease that the lessee will exercise such option.
- *Minimum lease payments.* The minimum payments over the lease term that the lessee is required to make together with any residual amounts guaranteed by the lessee (or a party related to the lessee) to the lessor.
- *Interest rate implicit in the lease.* This is the discount rate which at the inception of the lease makes the present value of the minimum lease payments and unguaranteed residual value equal to the fair value of the leased asset plus any initial direct costs of the lessor.

2 If this interest rate cannot be determined, the lessee's incremental borrowing rate should be used, e.g. the rate of interest payable on a similar lease.

3 For the sake of simplicity, we have assumed that there will be no guaranteed or unguaranteed residual values and no initial direct costs of the lessor, hence, the interest rate implicit in the lease is calculated simply by reference to the minimum payments over the lease term. It follows from this that the present value of the minimum lease payments discounted at the interest rate implicit in the lease is also equal to the fair value.

4 The effective loan is for EUR 18,950 as Lessee Co paid EUR 4,500 of the initial cost of the asset on 1 Jannary 2009.

5 A lessor's net investment in a lease is its gross investment in the lease discounted at the interest rate implicit in the lease.

6 4.4859%   9%

4.5959709%   r%

4.6229%   8%

$$(4.6229\% - 4.4859\%) : (8\% - 9\%) = (4.5959709\% - 4.4859\%) : (r - 9\%)$$
$$\rightarrow 0.137\% : (-1\%) = 0.1100709\% : (r - 9\%)$$
$$\rightarrow (r - 9\%) = [(-1\%) \times 0.1100709\%] \div 0.137\%$$
$$\rightarrow r = -0.8034372\% + 9\% = 8.1965628\% \text{ rounded to } 8.1928\%$$

9 Intangible assets (IAS 38)

Contents

Objectives

When you have completed this chapter you should be able to:

- Explain why accounting for intangibles has become important today
- Describe the key characteristics of an intangible asset
- Explain the criteria relating to the initial recognition and measurement of intangible assets
- Account for internally generated assets, particularly research and development
- Discuss potential inconsistencies between the recognition criteria for internally generated and acquired intangibles
- Explain how to account for intangibles subsequent to initial recognition
- Explain how to account for retirement and disposal of intangible assets.

9.1   Introduction

When a traditional commodity manufacturer wants to signal its long-term strength, it needs to demonstrate that it generates an adequate return on its investment in fixed assets and that it is a low cost manufacturer. When a technology entity wants to signal its future prospects, however, it faces a challenge of communicating the strength and value of its intellectual capital. In contrast to physical assets, intellectual capital derives much of its value from the fact that it can be deployed simultaneously in multiple tasks and that it can have increasing returns to scale, as knowledge is cumulative.

Even though intangibles have very different attributes compared to traditional fixed assets, they could still be valued if there were an organised exchange where they could be traded. This is not typically the case. Even if a pricing mechanism existed, the issue of intellectual property rights would remain. Except in the case where intellectual property is protected by a watertight patent, the ownership of such assets is often in question, making them inherently more risky than fixed assets.

The complexity of today's world and the increasing importance of intangibles to business entities, make the accounting treatment for them problematic.

Entities frequently expend resources or incur liabilities on the acquisition, development, maintenance or enhancement of intangible resources such as scientific or technical knowledge, design and implementation of new processes or systems, licences, intellectual property, market knowledge and trademarks (including brand names and publishing titles). Common examples of items encompassed by these broad headings are computer software, patents, copyrights, motion picture films, customer lists, mortgage servicing rights, fishing licences, import quotas, franchises, customer or supplier relationships, customer loyalty, market share and marketing rights (IAS 38 – *Intangible Assets* para 9). This is by no means an exhaustive list. IFRS 3 – *Business combinations* contains a further list of types of intangible assets that can be acquired in a business combination.

The criteria that should be satisfied before an item qualifies as an intangible asset under IAS 38 are discussed in section 9.2. However, some items may not be recognised as assets under IAS 38, even if they meet the criteria. These mainly include certain internally generated intangible assets.

In this chapter we will consider the accounting requirements affecting two different categories of intangible assets:

- Separately acquired intangible assets;
- Internally generated intangible assets.[1]

For these two categories of intangible assets, we deal with the following issues:

- key characteristics of intangible assets;
- recognition criteria;
- initial measurement of intangible assets and subsequent expenditure;
- measurement after recognition;
- derecognition of intangible assets;
- financial analysis and interpretation.

The advent of the internet has created new ways of communicating information that was unknown in the past, so we also deal with website development costs as they have many characteristics of intangible assets (see section 9.6).

9.2   Key characteristics of intangible assets

IAS 38 defines an intangible asset as *an identifiable non-monetary asset without physical substance*.

The key characteristics of intangible assets may be summarised as follows:

- They are resources controlled by an entity from which the entity expects to derive future economic benefits.
- They lack physical substance.
- They are identifiable.

9.2.1 Control and future economic benefits

The first of the key characteristics noted above indicates that there is an asset, which is *a resource controlled by an entity as a result of past events and from which future economic benefits are expected to flow to the entity (Framework* para 49(a)). This definition contains two elements: control and expectation of future economic benefits. If the control test is not passed, no asset can be recognised.

An entity controls an asset if the entity has the power to obtain future economic benefits flowing from the underlying resource and to restrict access to others of those benefits. The capacity of an entity to control the future economic benefits from an intangible asset would normally stem from legal rights that are enforceable in a court of law. In the absence of legal rights, it is more difficult to demonstrate control. However, legal enforceability of a right is not a necessary condition for control because an entity may be able to control the future economic benefits in some other ways (IAS 38 para 13).

Market and technical knowledge may give rise to future economic benefits. An entity controls those benefits if, for example, that technical knowledge is protected by legal rights such as copyrights, a restraint of trade agreement or by a legal duty on the part of employees to maintain confidentiality (IAS 38 para 14).

An entity is usually not considered to exercise sufficient control over its workforce for the workforce to be recognised as an intangible asset (IAS 38 para 15).

Another potential intangible asset where the issue of control is difficult is that of customer relationships. Entities may have expended much effort on building customer relationships and loyalty. However, without legal rights to protect or other ways to control the relationship or loyalty of customers, the entity usually has insufficient control over the expected benefits for those relationships to meet the definition of an asset. In the absence of legal rights to protect customer relationships, it is only where there are exchange transactions for the same or similar non-contractual customer relationships (other than as part of a business combination) that there is sufficient evidence that the entity is nonetheless able to control the expected future economic benefits flowing from the customer relationships. Any such exchange transactions would also provide evidence that the relationships were separable and the relationships would, therefore, qualify for recognition as an intangible asset if separately acquired or acquired as part of a business combination (IAS 39 para 16). The incidence of exchange transactions for non-contractual customer relationships is rare in practice.

The future economic benefits flowing from an intangible asset may include revenue from the sale of products or services, cost savings, or other benefits resulting from the use of the asset by the entity. For example, the use of intellectual property in a production process may reduce future production costs rather than increase future revenues (IAS 38 para 17).

9.2.2 Lack of physical substance

It may be difficult to categorise an asset as tangible or intangible.

Some intangible assets may be contained in or on a physical substance such as a compact disc (in the case of computer software), legal documentation (in the case of a licence or patent) or film. In determining whether an asset that incorporates both intangible and tangible elements should be accounted for as a tangible asset (IAS 16 – *Property, Plant and Equipment*) or as an intangible asset (IAS 38), an entity should assess which element is more significant. For example, computer software for a computer-controlled machine tool that cannot operate without that specific software is an integral part of the related hardware and it is treated as property, plant and equipment. The same applies to the operating system of a computer. When the software is not an integral part of the related hardware, computer software is treated as an intangible asset (IAS 38 para 4).

There may be also situations where, although the tangible and intangible elements cannot operate independently of each other, their respective costs are significant. In such cases it may be appropriate to account for each element separately. For example, a database may be stored on expensive computer hardware and the costs of the hardware may be separately identifiable from those of the database. Each element may have a different useful life, for example the hardware may become obsolete and the database may be transferred to another computer system. In such a situation it would be appropriate to account for separately the two components of the computer database, classifying the hardware as tangible and the database itself as intangible, because they are both significant components.

9.2.3 Identifiability

The last characteristic of an intangible asset is that it should be identifiable. An asset is identifiable if it either:

(a) is separable, i.e. is capable of being separated or divided from the entity and sold, transferred, licensed, rented or exchanged, either individually or together with a related contract, identifiable asset or liability, regardless of whether the entity intends to do so; or

(b) arises from contractual or other legal rights, regardless of whether those rights are transferable or separable from the entity or from other rights and obligations (IAS 38 para 12).

For physical assets identifiability is straightforward, because they can be seen. For intangible assets identifiability is more difficult and requires clear and practical principles. Intangible assets that can be separately identified should be recognised separately from goodwill in a business combination.

An intangible asset can be distinguished from goodwill if it is separable, i.e. capable of being separated or divided from the entity and sold, transferred, licensed, rented or exchanged. Therefore, in the context of intangible assets, separability signifies identifiability, and intangible assets with that characteristic that are acquired in a business combination should be recognised as assets separately from goodwill.

However, separability is not the only indication of identifiability. In contrast to goodwill, the values of many intangible assets arise from rights conveyed legally by contract or statute. In the case of acquired goodwill, its value arises from the collection of assembled assets that make up an acquired entity or the value created by assembling a collection of assets through a business combination, such as the synergies that are expected to result from combining entities or businesses. Although many intangible assets are both separable and arise from contractual legal rights, some contractual legal rights establish property interests that are not readily separable from the entity as a whole. For example, under the laws of some jurisdictions certain licences granted to an entity are not transferable except by sale of the entity as a whole. The fact that an intangible asset arises from contractual or other legal rights is a characteristic that distinguishes it from goodwill. Therefore, intangible assets with that characteristic that are acquired in a business combination should be recognised as assets separately from goodwill (IAS 38 paras BC9 and BC10).

9.3   Recognition criteria

Recognition of an item as an intangible asset requires an entity to demonstrate that the item meets the definition of an intangible asset, if it is probable that future economic benefits will flow to the entity and the cost of the asset can be reliably measured (IAS 38 para 21).

This requirement applies to costs incurred initially to acquire or internally generate an intangible asset and those incurred subsequently to add to, replace part of, or service it. If the recognition criteria cannot be demonstrated the costs should be expensed as incurred.

The nature of intangible assets is such that, in many cases, there are no additions to such an asset or replacements of part of it. Accordingly, most subsequent expenditures are likely to maintain the expected future economic benefits embodied in an existing intangible asset rather than meet the definition of an intangible asset and the criteria for recognition as an asset. Moreover, it is often difficult to attribute subsequent expenditure directly to a particular intangible asset rather than to the business as a whole. Therefore, most subsequent expenditure – expenditure incurred after the initial recognition of an acquired intangible asset or after completion of an internally generated intangible asset – will not qualify as an asset and should be expensed as incurred. In particular, IAS 38 para 20 requires that subsequent expenditure on brands, mastheads, publishing titles, customer lists and items similar in substance (whether externally acquired or internally generated) is expensed as incurred. This is because such expenditure cannot be distinguished from expenditure to develop the business as a whole.

An entity should assess the probability of expected future economic benefits using reasonable and supportable assumptions that represent management's best estimate of the set of economic conditions that will exist over the useful life of the asset (IAS 38 para 22).

An entity should use judgement to assess the degree of certainty attached to the flow of future economic benefits that are attributable to the use of the asset on the basis of the evidence available at the time of initial recognition, giving greater weight to external evidence (IAS 38 para 23).

9.3.1   Recognition of intangible assets acquired separately

Normally, the price an entity pays to acquire separately an intangible asset will reflect expectations about the probability that the expected future economic benefits embodied in the asset will flow to the entity. In other words, the entity expects there to be an inflow of economic benefits, even if there is uncertainty about the timing or the amount of the inflow. Therefore, the probability recognition criterion is considered to be satisfied for separately acquired intangible assets (IAS 38 para 25).

9.3.2   Recognition of internally generated intangible assets

Intangible assets that are developed or generated internally must satisfy both criteria for recognition (see IAS 38 para 21). There will always be difficulties in identifying internally generated intangible assets and in distinguishing the expected future economic benefits that might be attributable to the internally generated intangible assets from those expected from the business as a whole. There is no exchange transaction that establishes a cost or fair value for internally generated intangible assets that is separate from the costs or fair values attributable to the business as a whole. Generally, the difficulties associated with identifying internally generated intangible assets and with satisfying the recognition and measurement criteria mean that such assets either are indistinguishable from the rest of the business or cannot be reliably measured. Therefore, IAS 38 sets out specific procedures that should be followed to determine whether certain internally generated intangible assets can be recognised. It also prohibits recognising specific types of intangible assets for which the standard concludes that the recognition criteria can never be satisfied.

It is sometimes difficult to assess whether an internally generated intangible asset qualifies for recognition because of problems in:

(a) identifying whether and when there is an identifiable asset that will generate expected future economic benefits; and

(b) determining the cost of the asset reliably. In some cases, the cost of generating an intangible asset internally cannot be distinguished from the cost of maintaining or enhancing the entity's internally generated goodwill or of running day-to-day operations (IAS 38 para 51).

Example 9.1

Recognition of an internally generated intangible asset

Entity A is a major supplier to airlines and has two lines of business: sweet and salty snacks. The sweet snack unit comprises six brands, and the salty snack unit has four brands.

Entity A is continually seeking to innovate and attract new customers. It incurs expenditure related to research and development of new products, such as design of variations to current products and designs of new products. Research and development expenditure of EUR 2m for the sweet snack unit, and EUR 3.5m for the salty snack unit was incurred during 2010. The expenditure cannot be allocated separately to any specific product, but can be associated with a line of business.

Should research and development costs be capitalised? Explain why.

The research and development costs should not be capitalised as an internally generated intangible asset. An intangible asset should be identifiable and attributable to a specific product or project in order to meet the recognition criteria for an intangible asset. Therefore, entity A should be able to identify the future economic benefits that will flow from each separate intangible asset that it recognises. It is not possible to meet the recognition criteria for an intangible asset if management is unable to identify the individual product or project.

Research and development

To assess whether an internally generated intangible asset meets the criteria for recognition, an entity should classify the generation of the asset into:

(a) a research phase; and

(b) a development phase (IAS 38 para 52).

If an entity cannot distinguish the research phase from the development phase of an internal project to create an intangible asset, the entity should treat the expenditure on that project as if it were incurred in the research phase only (IAS 38 para 53).

IAS 38 defines 'research' as *original and planned investigation undertaken with the prospect of gaining new scientific or technical knowledge and understanding* and 'development' as *the application of research findings or other knowledge to a plan or design for the production of new or substantially improved materials, devices, products, processes, systems or services before the start of commercial production or use.*

The terms 'research phase' and 'development phase' have a broader meaning and are applied to a single project to distinguish the period of time and the quantum of the total project cost that is attributable to each type of activity.

Examples of research activities are:

(a) activities aimed at obtaining new knowledge;

(b) the search for, evaluation and final selection of, applications of research findings or other knowledge;

(c) the search for alternatives for materials, devices, products, processes, systems or services; and

(d) the formulation, design, evaluation and final selection of possible alternatives for new or improved materials, devices, products, processes, systems or services (IAS 38 para 56).

Examples of development activities are:

(a) the design, construction and testing of pre-production or pre-use prototypes and models;

(b) the design of tools, jigs, moulds and dies involving new technology;

(c) the design, construction and operation of a pilot plant that is not of a scale economically feasible for commercial production; and

(d) the design, construction and testing of a chosen alternative for new or improved materials, devices, products, processes, systems or services (IAS 38 para 59).

An entity may incur expenditure in developing new products for sale, such as a new model of motor car. It may also develop systems for its own use to enable it to keep up with changes in technology, such as design and construction of its own website, or to enable it to remain competitive such as more efficient distribution, warehouse and electronic point of sale systems.

No intangible asset arising from research (or from the research phase of an internal project) should be recognised. Expenditure on research (or on the research phase of an internal project) should be recognised as an expense as incurred (IAS 38 para 54).

In the research phase of an internal project, an entity cannot demonstrate that an intangible asset exists that will generate probable future economic benefits. Therefore, this expenditure should be recognised as an expense as incurred (IAS 38 para 55).

Although research expenditure is not recognised as an asset, an entity may sometimes purchase patents and other rights over processes that are used in a research and development project. These rights would qualify for recognition as separately acquired intangible assets, even though they are used in the research activity. This is because, as explained above, the 'future economic benefits' criterion is assumed to be automatically satisfied in the separate acquisition of an intangible asset. Although using the patent in the research project may not give rise to future economic benefits, the fact that it has been bought for value means that it is probable that it could also be sold again for value.

Although IAS 38 defines research as related to scientific or technical knowledge, the same accounting treatment of expensing the costs as incurred would apply to other forms of enquiry commonly termed 'research', for example, market research or customer research. In the development phase of an internal project, an entity can, in some instances, identify an intangible asset and demonstrate that the asset will generate probable future economic benefits. This is because the development phase of a project follows the research phase (IAS 38 para 58) and therefore will be further advanced. Thus, IAS 38 para 57 sets out the criteria to assist in determining the point at which an entity moves from the research phase (when costs are expensed) to the development phase (when subsequent costs are recognised as an asset). If the criteria are met there is no choice between recognising expenditure as an asset or expensing it. An intangible asset should be recognised. In order to recognise an intangible asset an entity should be able to demonstrate all of the following criteria:

(a) technical feasibility of completing the intangible asset so that it will be available for use or sale;

(b) its intention to complete the intangible asset and use or sell it;

(c) its ability to use or sell the intangible asset;

(d) how future economic benefits will probably be generated. Among other things, the entity should demonstrate the existence of a market for the output of the intangible asset or the intangible asset itself or, if it is to be used internally, the usefulness of the intangible asset;

(e) availability of adequate technical, financial and other resources to complete the development and to use or sell the intangible asset;

(f) its ability to measure reliably the expenditure attributable to the intangible asset during its development.

In order to determine at what stage a project meets the criteria above, the entity will need to consider the product life cycle and then apply the criteria at each stage of that cycle, as illustrated in Example 9.2.

Example 9.2

Recognition of research and development

Entity B is developing a new technology to be used in a manufacturing plant. The process can be split into 14 stages as illustrated in the figure below.

1. Identify a need for/benefit of new technology

2. Commission a project to investigate the new technology

3. Investigate other technologies available in the market

4. Investigate competitors' use of other technologies

5. Commission the design of alternative types of new technology and get input for feasibility of other technologies from the manufacturing floor

6. Prepare a short list of alternatives from stage 5 and prepare costing

7. Prepare a budget for the new technology and agree to the shortlist and the replacement of technology

8. Send the shortlist to line managers for input and list three based on feedback

9. Present the final three to the board for final selection

10. Finalise a development plan for the final selection

11. Develop new technology

12. Test new technology

13. Train staff on new technology

14. Roll out new technology to the production

Figure 9.1 R&D process

At what stage should the entity start to capitalise the costs of the project?

To determine at what stage it should start to capitalise the costs of the project, the entity should apply the criteria illustrated above (IAS 38 para 57; see page 272) to each of the stages and determine at which stage the criteria have been met in full. From that point on the entity should capitalise costs (see also section 9.4 below for a description of costs that should be capitalised).

In the example above this can be done as follows:

Stage 5. Criteria (a) and (c) have been met because the feasibility of completing the intangible asset for use and the entity's ability to use it have been confirmed.

Stage 7. Criteria (a), (c), (d) and (e) have been met at the end of this stage as a budget has been produced, it has been agreed to proceed with replacing the technology and adequate resources exist to complete development.

Stage 10. All the criteria have been met at this stage as, in addition to the above, the board has approved the project (evidence of the entity's intention to complete the asset – criterion (b)) and the development plan, based on the budgets, evidences the entity's ability to measure the expenditure reliably (criterion (f)).

This example is a simple illustration of how the process should work. In practice, the product life cycle may well be more complex and it may be difficult for the entity to assess which of the recognition criteria have been met at each stage.

Non-recognition of certain internally generated intangible assets

Internally generated brands, mastheads, publishing titles, customer lists and items similar in substance should not be recognised as intangible assets (IAS 38 para 63).

Expenditure on internally generated brands, mastheads, publishing titles, customer lists and items similar in substance cannot be distinguished from the cost of developing the business as a whole. Therefore, such items should not be recognised as intangible assets (IAS 38 para 64).

Expenditure that cannot be recognised as an intangible asset should be expensed (IAS 38 para 70) when it is incurred, unless it forms part of the cost of an intangible asset that meets the criteria for recognition as an intangible asset (whether internally generated or acquired).

Other types of cost not recognised as an asset

IAS 38 gives examples of the types of cost that, being indistinguishable from the costs of developing the business as a whole, should be expensed as incurred. These include:

- Research expenditure (except where it forms part of the cost of a business combination).
- Start-up costs, unless such costs (for example, costs of commissioning) are included in the cost of a tangible fixed asset in accordance with IAS 16. Costs that should be expensed as incurred include preliminary expenses of establishing a legal entity, expenditure on opening a new facility or business (pre-opening costs) or expenditure on starting up a new operation or launching a new product or process.
- Training costs.
- Advertising and promotion costs.
- Relocation expenses.
- Re-organisation costs.

2.1.3.5 RESEARCH AND DEVELOPMENT EXPENSES

Since 2003, with the application of IAS 38 'Intangible Assets', EADS has assessed whether product-related development costs qualify for capitalisation as internally generated intangible assets. Criteria for capitalisation are strictly applied. All research and development costs not meeting the IAS 38 criteria are expensed as incurred in the consolidated income statement.

In 2006, €411 million of product-related development costs were capitalised in accordance with IAS 38 (including €335 million relating to the Airbus A380 programme). €93 million were capitalised in 2007 (with no further capitalisation relating to the Airbus A380 programme following its entry into the production phase at the end of 2006), and €87 million were capitalised in 2008.

Capitalised development costs are generally amortised over the estimated number of units produced. If the number of units produced cannot be estimated reliably, capitalised development costs are amortised over the estimated useful life of the internally generated intangible asset. Amortisation of capitalised development costs is recognised within 'Cost of sales'. Amortisation of capitalised development costs amounted to €46 million in 2007 and €56 million in 2008, most of which related to the MRTT and the Airbus A380 programme. Amortisation in respect of the Airbus A380 programme began in 2007 following its entry into the production phase at the end of 2006.

Internally generated intangible assets are reviewed for impairment annually when the asset is not yet in use and subsequently whenever events or changes in circumstances indicate that the carrying amount may not be recoverable.

Figure 9.2 Example of disclosures relating to research and development and to amortisation methods

Source: EADS Management's discussion and analysis of financial condition and results of operations in Annual Report, 2008.

Internally generated goodwill

In some cases, expenditure is incurred to generate future economic benefits, but it does not result in the creation of an intangible asset that meets the recognition criteria illustrated on page 269. Such expenditure is often described as contributing to internally generated goodwill. Internally generated goodwill is not recognised as an asset because it is not an identifiable resource (i.e. it is not separable nor does it arise from contractual or other legal rights) controlled by the entity that can be measured reliably at cost (IAS 38 paras 48 and 49).

9.4   Initial measurement of intangible assets

An intangible asset should be measured initially at cost (IAS 38 para 24).

IAS 38 defines *cost* as the amount of cash or cash equivalents paid or the fair value of other consideration given to acquire an asset at the time of its acquisition or construction.

9.4.1 Initial measurement of intangible assets acquired separately

The cost of a separately acquired intangible asset can usually be measured reliably. This is particularly so when the purchase consideration is in the form of cash or other monetary assets (IAS 38 para 26).

The cost of a separately acquired intangible asset comprises:

(a) its purchase price, including import duties and non-refundable purchase taxes, after deducting trade discounts and rebates; and

(b) any directly attributable cost of preparing the asset for its intended use, including employee benefits, professional fees and costs of testing the proper functioning of the asset. However, costs of introducing a new product or service including advertising and promotion costs, costs of conducting a business in a new location including staff training costs and administrative or other general overhead costs are not part of the cost of an intangible asset (IAS 38 paras 27 to 29).

It is worth mentioning that entities often spend huge sums of money on advertising campaigns to launch new products. Some multinational entities even hire famous performing artists or film stars to act as brand ambassadors of their new products. Because the amounts spent on these advertising campaigns are so huge, these entities believe that the benefits from such a promotion would last longer than a year and thus they would prefer to defer the costs of introducing new products over a period of two or three years. However, deferring of such costs is categorically disallowed.

Example 9.3

Entity X acquires copyrights to the original recording of a famous singer. The agreement with the singer allows the entity to record and rerecord the singer for a period of five years. During the initial six-month period of the agreement, the singer is very ill and consequently cannot record. The studio time that was booked by the entity had to be paid for the period the singer could not sing. The costs incurred by the entity were:

(a) Legal costs of acquiring the copyrights	€15m
(b) Operational costs (studio time lost, etc.) during the start-up period	€ 1m
(c) Advertising campaign to launch the artist	€ 1m

Which of the above is a cost that can be capitalised as an intangible asset?

(a) The legal costs of acquiring the copyright can be capitalised.

(b) Operational costs during the start-up period should be expensed and not capitalised.

(c) The cost of the advertising campaign to launch the artist should be expensed and not capitalised.

9.4.2 Initial measurement of internally generated intangible assets

The cost of an internally generated intangible asset comprises all directly attributable costs necessary to create, produce, and prepare the asset to be capable of operating in the manner intended by management. Examples of directly attributable costs are:

(a) costs of materials and services used or consumed in generating the intangible asset;

(b) costs of employee benefits incurred from the generation of the intangible asset;

(c) fees to register a legal right; and

(d) amortisation of patents and licences that are used to generate the intangible asset.

IAS 23 – *Borrowing Costs* specifies criteria for the recognition of interest as an element of the cost of an internally generated intangible asset (IAS 38 para 66).

The following are not components of the cost of an internally generated intangible asset:

(a) selling, administrative and other general overhead expenditure unless this expenditure can be directly attributed to preparing the asset for use;

(b) identified inefficiencies and initial operating losses incurred before the asset achieves planned performance; and

(c) expenditure for training of staff to operate the asset (IAS 38 para 67).

Recognition of an expense

Expenditure for an intangible item should be recognised as an expense as incurred (IAS 38 para 68). Examples of such expenditures include:

(a) expenditure for research;

(b) expenditure for start-up activities (i.e. start-up costs), unless this expenditure is included in the cost of an item of property, plant and equipment in accordance with IAS 16. Start-up costs may consist of establishment costs such as legal and secretarial costs incurred in establishing a legal entity, expenditure to open a new facility or business (i.e. pre-opening costs) or expenditures for starting new operations or launching new products or processes (i.e. pre-operating costs);

(c) expenditure for training activities;

(d) expenditure for advertising and promotional activities;

(e) expenditure for relocating or reorganising part or all of an entity (IAS 38 para 69).

Example 9.4

Expensing vs capitalising expenditure relating to intangible assets

In 2009, entity X incurred EUR 200,000 of research expenditure on a project to develop a new product. It expensed these costs in accordance with IAS 38.

In 2010, entity Y purchased the research project, including certain patents that were registered by entity X, for EUR 300,000 and recognised the cost as an intangible asset in accordance with the standard.

In the same year, entity Y incurred EUR 400,000 of expenditure on completing the research phase and decided to develop the product commercially.

In 2011, entity Y incurred further costs of EUR 450,000 to bring the product to a stage where the conditions in the standard for recognising development costs as an internally generated intangible asset were met. Further costs of EUR 2m were incurred to bring the product into a condition where it is ready for use in the manner that management intended.

In 2012, initial marketing costs and losses of EUR 500,000 were incurred before the product reached widespread distribution.

The table below shows the accounting treatment of the expenditure incurred by entity Y in connection with this project.

Table 9.1 Expenditure relating to an intangible asset to be capitalised or expensed

Year	Expenditure	Accounting treatment
2009	No expenditure incurred by entity Y	N/A
2010	Cost of the acquired research project of €300,000	Capitalised (IAS 38 paras 24 and 25) (*)
2010	Subsequent research costs of €400,000	Expensed as incurred (IAS 38 paras 42 and 54)
2011	Subsequent development costs of €450,000	Expensed as incurred as they do not meet the conditions for recognition (IAS 38 paras 42 and 57)
2011	Further development costs of €2m	These costs should be recognised (there is no option to expense these costs), because they meet the conditions for recognition as an intangible asset (IAS 38 paras 42(b) and 57). The previously written off development costs should not be reinstated (IAS 38 para 71).
2012	Marketing costs and initial losses of €500,000	Expensed as incurred (IAS 38 paras 67 and 69)

(*) In 2010, entity X has an income of €300,000 and no related expense.

The carrying amount of the intangible asset when production and sale of the product commenced is, therefore, €2.3m. Had the asset been internally generated by entity Y the carrying amount would have been only €2m, because there would have been no cost for the acquisition of the research project, so only the development costs which met IAS 38's recognition criteria would be capitalised.

9.5   Measurement after initial recognition

An entity should choose either the cost model or the revaluation model as its accounting policy. If an intangible asset is accounted for using the revaluation model, all other assets in its class should also be accounted for using the same model, unless there is no active market for those assets. If an intangible asset in a class of revalued intangible assets cannot be revalued because there is no active market for this asset, the asset should be carried at its cost less any accumulated amortisation and impairment losses (IAS 38 paras 72 and 81).

The cost model requires that, after initial recognition, intangible assets should be carried at cost less accumulated amortisation and impairment losses (IAS 38 para 74). The revaluation model requires that, after initial recognition, an intangible asset should be carried at a revalued amount, being its fair value at the date of the revaluation less any subsequent accumulated amortisation and any subsequent accumulated impairment losses. For the purpose of revaluations, the fair value should be determined by reference to an active market. Revaluations should be made with such regularity that at the end of the reporting period the carrying amount of the asset does not differ materially from its fair value (IAS 38 para 75).

9.5.1 Application of revaluation model

The revaluation model does not allow revaluation of intangible assets that have not previously been recognised as assets (IAS 38 para 76). For example, over the years an entity might have accumulated for nominal consideration a number of licences of a kind that are traded on an active market. The entity did not recognise an intangible asset as the licences were individually immaterial when acquired. Market prices for such licences have recently risen significantly and the value of the licences held by the entity has substantially increased. The entity, is however, prohibited by IAS 38 from applying the revaluation model to the licences, because they were not previously recognised as an asset.

The revaluation model does not allow:

(a) revaluation of intangible assets that were not previously recognised as assets; or

(b) initial recognition of intangible assets at amounts other than cost (IAS 38 para 76).

There is an important exception to the guidance above, although in practice it is rarely expected to occur. The exception relates to an asset where only part of it has been recognised because the asset did not meet the recognition criteria until part of the way through the process of developing or acquiring it. This might occur, for example, where a development project only meets the recognition criteria at a late stage in its development, when most costs have been expensed. The standard does not permit such costs to be reinstated under the cost or revaluation models. However, if only a part of the cost of an intangible asset is recognised as an asset because the asset did not meet the criteria for recognition until part of the way through the process, the revaluation model may be applied to the whole of that asset. This means that an element of the revalued amount relates to the costs that were written off (IAS 38 para 77).

If an intangible asset in a class of revalued intangible assets cannot be revalued because there is no active market for this asset, the asset should be carried at its cost less any accumulated amortisation and impairment losses. If the fair value of a revalued intangible asset can no longer be determined by reference to an active market, the carrying amount of the asset should be its revalued amount at the date of the last revaluation by reference to the active market less any subsequent accumulated amortisation and any subsequent accumulated impairment losses. The fact that an active market no longer exists for a revalued intangible asset may indicate that the asset may be impaired and that it needs to be tested for impairment in accordance with IAS 36. If the fair value of the asset can be determined by reference to an active market at a subsequent measurement date, the revaluation model should be applied from that date (IAS 38 paras 81 to 84).

The revaluation model is rarely used in practice. In fact an active market, as defined above, exists for only a few types of intangible assets and the revaluation model can only be used where such a market exists. The standard notes that in some jurisdictions an active market may exist for freely transferable taxi licences, fishing licences or production quotas. An example of the last of these might be emission rights, for which an active market is likely once the scheme is fully operational.

Frequency of revaluations

The frequency of revaluations depends on the volatility of the fair values of the intangible assets being revalued. If the fair value of a revalued asset differs materially from its carrying amount, a further revaluation is necessary. Some intangible assets may experience significant and volatile movements in fair value, thus necessitating annual revaluations. Such frequent revaluations are unnecessary for intangible assets with only insignificant movements in fair values (IAS 38 para 79).

Basis of valuation

The only valuation basis permitted by IAS 38 is fair value determined by reference to an 'active market'. An asset's fair value is the amount for which that asset could be exchanged between knowledgeable, willing parties in an arm's length transaction. The definition of active market is a market in which all of the following conditions exist:

- Items traded in the market are homogeneous (similar in kind or nature).
- Willing buyers and sellers are always available.
- Prices are publicly quoted (IAS 38 para 8).

An active market cannot exist for brands, newspaper mastheads, music and film publishing rights, patents or trademarks, because each such asset is unique. Also, although intangible assets are bought and sold, contracts are negotiated between individual buyers and sellers, and transactions are relatively infrequent. For these reasons, the price paid for one asset may not provide sufficient evidence of the fair value of another. Moreover, prices are often not available to the public (IAS 38 para 78). An example might be the purchase and sale of a cigarette brand name. Because there is no active market for such assets and because the brand is unique, i.e. not like any other cigarette brand, the price paid is not a reliable measure of the fair value of other cigarette brands. That applies regardless of whether the other brands are owned by one of the entities involved in the transaction or by some other entity.

Treatment of accumulated amortisation when intangible assets are revalued

If an intangible asset is revalued, any accumulated amortisation at the date of the revaluation is either:

(a) restated proportionately with the change in the gross carrying amount of the asset so that the carrying amount of the asset after revaluation equals its revalued amount; or

(b) eliminated against the gross carrying amount of the asset and the net amount restated to the revalued amount of the asset (IAS 38 para 80).

Revaluation gains and losses

If the carrying amount of an intangible asset increases as a result of a revaluation, the increase should be recognised in the statement of comprehensive income and at the same time in equity under the heading of revaluation surplus. However, the increase should be recognised in the income statement to the extent that it reverses a revaluation decrease of the same asset previously recognised in the income statement (IAS 38 para 85).

If the carrying amount of an intangible asset decreases as a result of a revaluation, the decrease should be recognised in the income statement. However, the decrease should be recognised as other comprehensive income to the extent of any credit balance in the revaluation surplus in respect of that asset. The decrease recognised as other comprehensive income reduces the amount accumulated in equity under the heading of revaluation surplus (IAS 38 para 86).

The accumulated revaluation surplus included in equity may be transferred directly to retained earnings when the surplus is realised. The whole surplus may be realised on the retirement or disposal of the asset (IAS 38 para 87).

9.5.2 Amortisation and impairment

Amortisation is a systematic allocation of the depreciable amount of an intangible asset over its useful life. Depreciable amount is the cost of an asset, or other amount substituted for cost, less its residual value (IAS 38 para 8).

The depreciable amount of an intangible asset with a finite useful life should be allocated on a systematic basis over its useful life. Amortisation should begin when the asset is available for use, i.e. when it is in the location and condition necessary for it to be capable of operating in the manner intended by management. Amortisation should cease at the earlier of the date that the asset is classified as held for sale (or included in a disposal group that is classified as held for sale) in accordance with IFRS 5 and the date that the asset is derecognised. The amortisation method used should reflect the pattern in which the asset's future economic benefits are expected to be consumed by the entity. If that pattern cannot be determined reliably, the straight-line method should be used. The amortisation charge for each period should be recognised in the income statement or included in the carrying amount of another asset (IAS 38 para 97).

An intangible asset with an indefinite useful life should not be amortised (IAS 38 para 107).

Example 9.5

Revaluation model for intangible assets

Active Asset SpA owns a freely transferable taxi operator's licence, which it acquired on 1 January 2008 for EUR 20,000. The useful life of the licence is five years. The entity uses the straight-line method to amortise its intangible assets.

Such licences are frequently traded either between existing operators or with aspiring operators. At the balance sheet date, on 31 December 2009, due to a government-permitted increase in fixed taxi fares, the traded value of such licence was EUR 24,000. The accumulated amortisation on 31 December 2009 amounted to EUR 8,000.

What journal entries are required at 31 December 2009, to reflect the increase in the carrying value (cost or revalued amount less accumulated amortisation) on the revaluation of the operating licence based on the traded value of similar licence?

What would be the resultant carrying value of the intangible asset after the revaluation?

The entries to be recorded in the general journal are as follows:

Dr Intangible asset-accumulated amortisation	€8,000	
Cr intangible asset – cost		€8,000
(Being elimination of accumulated amortisation against the cost of the asset)		

Dr Intangible asset-cost	€12,000	
Cr Revaluation reserve		€12,000
(Being increase in net book value for revalued amount)		

The revised carrying value of the asset is:

$$€20,000 - €8,000 + €12,000 = €24,000$$

Useful life – finite and indefinite

An entity should assess whether the useful life of an intangible asset is finite or indefinite and, if finite, the length of or the number of production or similar units constituting that useful life. An intangible asset should be regarded by the entity as having an indefinite useful life when, based on an analysis of all the relevant factors, there is no foreseeable limit to the period over which the asset is expected to generate net cash inflows for the entity (IAS 38 para 88).

The accounting for an intangible asset is based on its useful life. An intangible asset with a finite useful life is amortised, and an intangible asset with an indefinite useful life is not (IAS 38 para 89).

Factors considered in determining the useful life of an intangible asset include:

(a) the expected usage of the asset by the entity and whether the asset could be managed efficiently by another team;

(b) typical product life cycles for the asset and public information on estimates of useful lives of similar assets that are used in a similar way;

(c) technical, technological, commercial or other types of obsolescence;

(d) the stability of the industry in which the asset is used and changes in the market demand for the products or services resulting from the asset;

(e) expected actions by competitors or potential competitors;

(f) the level of maintenance expenditure required to obtain the expected future economic benefits from the asset and the entity's ability and intention to reach such a level;

(g) the period of control over the asset and legal or similar limits on the use of the asset, such as the expiry dates of related leases; and

(h) whether the useful life of the asset is dependent on the useful life of other assets of the entity (IAS 38 para 90).

The term 'indefinite' does not mean 'infinite'. The useful life of an intangible asset reflects only that level of future maintenance expenditure required to maintain the asset at its standard of performance assessed at the time of estimating the asset's useful life, and the entity's ability and intention to reach such a level. A conclusion that the useful life of an intangible asset is indefinite should not depend on planned future expenditure in excess of that required to maintain the asset at that standard of performance (IAS 38 para 91).

Given the history of rapid changes in technology, computer software and other intangible assets are susceptible to technological obsolescence. Therefore, it is likely that their useful life is short (IAS 38 para 92).

The useful life of an intangible asset may be very long or even indefinite. Uncertainty justifies estimating the useful life of an intangible asset on a prudent basis, but it does not justify choosing a life that is unrealistically short (IAS 38 para 93).

The useful life of an intangible asset that arises from contractual or other legal rights should not exceed the period of the contractual or other legal rights, but may be shorter depending on the period over which the entity expects to use the asset. If the contractual or other legal rights are conveyed for a limited term that can be renewed, the useful life of the intangible asset should include the renewal period(s) only if there is evidence to support renewal by the entity without significant cost (IAS 38 para 94).

There may be both economic and legal factors influencing the useful life of an intangible asset. Economic factors determine the period over which future economic benefits will be received by the entity. Legal factors may restrict the period over which the entity controls access to these benefits. The useful life is the shorter of the periods determined by these factors (IAS 38 para 95).

Existence of the following factors, among others, indicates that an entity would be able to renew the contractual or other legal rights without significant cost:

(a) there is evidence, possibly based on experience, that the contractual or other legal rights will be renewed. If renewal is contingent upon the consent of a third party, this includes evidence that the third party will give its consent;

(b) there is evidence that any conditions necessary to obtain renewal will be satisfied; and

(c) the cost to the entity of renewal is not significant when compared with the future economic benefits expected to flow to the entity from renewal.

If the cost of renewal is significant when compared with the future economic benefits expected to flow to the entity from renewal, the 'renewal' cost represents, in substance, the cost to acquire a new intangible asset at the renewal date (IAS 38 para 96).

Residual value

The residual value of an intangible asset with a finite useful life should be assumed to be zero unless:

> **Notes to the consolidated financial statements (extract)**
>
> Intangible assets having an indefinite useful life are not amortised but tested for impairment at the end of each financial year as well as whenever there is an indication that the carrying amount exceeds the recoverable amount of the respective asset (see below 'Impairment of non-financial assets'). For such intangible assets the assessment for the indefinite useful life is reviewed annually on whether it remains supportable. A change from indefinite to finite life assessment is accounted for as change in estimate.

Figure 9.3 Intangible assets having an indefinite useful life

Source: EADS Annual Report 2008.

(a) there is a commitment by a third party to purchase the asset at the end of its useful life; or

(b) there is an active market for the asset and:

    (i) the residual value can be determined by reference to that market; and

    (ii) it is probable that such a market will exist at the end of the asset's useful life (IAS 38 para 100).

The depreciable amount of an asset with a finite useful life is determined after deducting its residual value. A residual value other than zero implies that an entity expects to dispose of the intangible asset before the end of its economic life (IAS 38 para 101).

The residual value of an intangible asset is the estimated amount that an entity would currently obtain from the disposal of the asset, after deducting the estimated costs of disposal, if the asset were already of the age and in the condition expected at the end of its useful life (IAS 38 para 8).

An estimate of an asset's residual value is based on the amount recoverable from disposal using prices prevailing at the date of the estimate for the sale of a similar asset that has reached the end of its useful life and has operated under conditions similar to those in which the asset will be used. The residual value is reviewed at least at each financial year-end. A change in the asset's residual value is accounted for as a change in an accounting estimate in accordance with IAS 8 – *Accounting Policies, Changes in Accounting Estimates and Errors* (IAS 38 para 102).

The residual value of an intangible asset may increase to an amount equal to or greater than the asset's carrying amount. If it does, the asset's amortisation charge is zero unless and until its residual value subsequently decreases to an amount below the asset's carrying amount (IAS 38 para 103).

Amortisation methods

The amortisable amount of an intangible asset with a finite useful life should be allocated on a systematic basis over its useful life. Amortisation should begin when the asset is available for use, i.e. when it is in the location and condition necessary for it to be capable of operating in the manner intended by management. Amortisation should cease at the earlier of the date that the asset is classified as held for sale (or included in a disposal group that is classified as held for sale) in accordance with IFRS 5 and the date that the asset is derecognised. The amortisation method used should reflect the pattern in which the asset's future economic benefits are expected to be consumed by the entity. If that pattern cannot be determined reliably, the straight-line method should be used. The amortisation charge for each period should be recognised in the income statement (IAS 38 para 97).

Intangible assets other than goodwill

Intangible assets, except for goodwill, are recorded at cost less accumulated amortization and any impairment losses. All intangible assets other than goodwill are assigned a finite life. Cost for acquired assets represents the purchase price including transaction costs. Cost for internally generated assets, such as software, represents direct internal and external design, development, and testing costs incurred to make the asset ready for use in the manner intended by management.

Intangible assets are amortized on a straight-line basis over the following estimated useful lives, starting from the date the asset is ready for use:

Premiums for long-term leases	*Shorter of lease term and useful life of leased assets*
Product rights and related supply agreements	5 to 20 years
Trademarks and patents	10 to 20 years
Software	3 to 5 years
Customer relationships	10 to 15 years
In process Research and Development	10 to 11 years
Others	3 to 15 years

Useful lives of product rights are determined based on the period over which the assets are expected to generate economic benefits for Syngenta ('economic life').

Patents and trademarks are amortized on a straight-line basis over their estimated economic or legal life, whichever is shorter. Useful lives assigned to acquired product rights are based on the maturity of the product and the estimated economic benefit that such product rights can provide.

Business combinations give Syngenta access to the distribution channels and customer relationships of the acquired business. These relationships normally continue to generate economic benefit to Syngenta following the acquisition. The useful lives of customer relationships are determined from management estimates of customer attrition rates.

Under IFRS 3, 'In-Process Research & Development (IPR&D)', is valued as part of the process of allocating the purchase price in a business combination. IPR&D is recorded separately from goodwill. It is assessed for impairment annually until it has been successfully developed and is available for use. It is then amortized over its useful life. IPR&D on business combinations agreed before March 31, 2004, to which IFRS 3 has not been applied, is included in goodwill for IFRS purposes.

Assets attributable to long-term supply agreements are amortized as part of cost of goods sold over the period of the supply agreement.

Purchased software licenses are amortized on a straight-line basis over the remaining license term. Internally developed software is amortized from the date the related system goes live, over the period until it is expected to be replaced or significant costs are expected to be incurred to upgrade it.

Useful lives of intangible assets are reviewed annually.

A one year reduction in the useful lives of all intangible assets other than software would increase amortization expense by US$14 million.

Figure 9.4 Disclosures of amortisation methods

Source: Syngenta Financial Report 2008.

A variety of amortisation methods can be used to allocate the amortisable amount of an asset on a systematic basis over its useful life. These methods include the straight-line method, the diminishing balance method and the unit of production method. The method used is selected on the basis of the expected pattern of consumption of the expected future economic benefits embodied in the asset and is applied consistently from period to period, unless there is a change in the expected pattern of consumption of those future economic benefits (IAS 38 para 98). The amortisation method should be reviewed at least at each financial year-end. If there has been a change in the expected pattern of consumption of future economic benefits from an intangible asset, the amortisation method should be changed to reflect the changed pattern. In practice it is unlikely that the pattern of consumption of an intangible asset would vary significantly over its useful life so changes in method should be rare.

9.6   Website development costs

An issue that caused considerable debate in the past was whether costs of developing a website may be capitalised or not. SIC 32 – *Intangible Assets, Website Costs* provides guidance on this topic and is summarised below.

An entity may incur internal expenditure on the development and operation of its own website for internal or external access. A website designed for external access may be used for various purposes such as to promote and advertise an entity's own products and services, provide electronic services, and sell products and services. A website designed for internal access may be used to store company policies and customer details, and search relevant information (SIC 32 para 1).

The stages of a website's development can be described as follows (SIC 32 para 2):

(a) *Planning* includes undertaking feasibility studies, defining objectives and specifications, evaluating alternatives and selecting preferences.

(b) *Application and infrastructure development* includes obtaining a domain name, purchasing and developing hardware and operating software, installing developed applications and stress testing.

(c) *Graphical design development* includes designing the appearance of web pages.

(d) *Content development* includes creating, purchasing, preparing and uploading information, either textual or graphical in nature, on the website before the completion of the website's development. This information may either be stored in separate databases that are integrated into (or accessed from) the website or coded directly into the web pages.

Once development of a website has been completed, the operating stage begins. During this stage, an entity maintains and enhances the applications, infrastructure, graphical design and content of the website (SIC 32 para 3).

When accounting for internal expenditure on the development and operation of an entity's own website for internal or external access, the issues are:

(a) whether the website is an internally generated intangible asset that is subject to the requirements of IAS 38; and

(b) the appropriate accounting treatment for such expenditure (SIC 32 para 4).

An internally developed website should be recognised as an intangible asset only if an entity can demonstrate that its website will generate probable future economic benefits, when, for example, the website is capable of generating revenues, including direct revenues from orders received on the website (SIC 32 para 8).

Any internal expenditure on the development and operation of an entity's own website should be accounted for in accordance with IAS 38. The nature of each activity for which expenditure is incurred (e.g. training employees and maintaining the website) and the website's stage of development or post-development should be evaluated to determine the appropriate accounting treatment. For example:

(a) The planning stage is similar in nature to the research phase. Expenditure incurred in this stage should be recognised as an expense as incurred.

(b) The application and infrastructure development stage, the graphical design stage and the content development stage, to the extent that content is developed for purposes other than to advertise and promote an entity's own products and services, are similar in nature to the development phase. Therefore, expenditure incurred in these stages should be included in the cost of a website recognised as an intangible asset. For example, expenditure on purchasing or creating content (other than content that advertises and promotes an entity's own products and services) specifically for a website, or expenditure to enable use of the content (e.g. a fee for acquiring a licence to reproduce) on the website, should be included in the cost of development when this condition is met. However, expenditure on an intangible item that was initially recognised as an expense in previous financial statements should not be recognised as part of the cost of an intangible asset at a later date (e.g. if the costs of a copyright have been fully amortised, and the content is subsequently provided on a website).

(c) Expenditure incurred in the content development stage, to the extent that content is developed to advertise and promote an entity's own products and services (e.g. digital photographs of products), should be recognised as an expense as incurred. For example, when accounting for expenditure on professional services for taking digital photographs of an entity's own products and for enhancing their display, expenditure should be recognised as an expense as the professional services are received during the process, not when the digital photographs are displayed on the website.

(d) The operating stage begins once development of a website is complete. Expenditure incurred in this stage should be recognised as an expense as incurred (SIC 32 para 9).

The best estimate of a website's useful life should be short (SIC 32 para 10).

9.7   Derecognition

An intangible asset should be derecognised:

(a) on disposal; or

(b) when no future economic benefits are expected from its use or disposal (IAS 38 para 112).

The gain or loss arising from the derecognition of an intangible asset should be determined as the difference between the net disposal proceeds, if any, and the carrying amount of the asset. It should be recognised in the income statement in the period in which derecognition occurs (IAS 38 para 113).

The consideration receivable on disposal of an intangible asset is recognised at its fair value. If payment for the intangible asset is deferred, the consideration received is recognised initially at the cash price equivalent. The difference between the nominal amount of the consideration and the cash price equivalent is recognised as interest revenue in accordance with IAS 18 reflecting the effective yield on the receivable (IAS 38 para 116).

It is important to differentiate between derecognition and impairment of an internally generated intangible asset. Where no future economic benefits are expected from the continuing use or disposal of the intangible asset, the intangible asset should be derecognised. A reduction in future economic benefits expected from the continuing use or (future) disposal of the intangible asset would result in the asset's impairment.

Example 9.6

Derecognition vs impairment

An entity is developing two products (A and B) to go on a new aircraft. Both products have previously met the recognition criteria for capitalisation as an internally generated intangible asset. Two issues arise during the course of the product's development.

The anticipated cost of production of product A has increased due to weight problems with the prototypes. The entity has submitted a claim for a price increase for product A, but no response has been received as yet. The entity's current forecasts show that the forecast margin on product A has substantially reduced.

The entity was required by its customer to sub-contract to a third party for product B. Now, the customer has insisted that development of this element is taken in house and has agreed to compensate the entity for the costs incurred to date. Product B is customer specific and cannot be used elsewhere.

Each product should be considered separately. There is an impairment trigger in respect of product A, which requires an impairment test under IAS 36. Product A is still expected to have some use and generate some margin so the product is not derecognised. Any impairment charged in the current year may be reversed in the future if an increase in sales price is agreed in the following year.

The development costs in relation to product B should be derecognised, as the development has no future benefit to the entity following the customer's decision.

Figure 9.5 on pages 289–90 gives an example of disclosures relating to intangible assets.

9.8   Financial analysis and interpretation[2]

We introduced this chapter by pointing out that the different attributes of intangibles compared to fixed assets make it difficult to communicate the strength and value of an entity's intellectual capital (I.C.).

Research and development

All research expenditure is expensed as incurred. Development expenditure is expensed as incurred unless it meets the criteria for recognition as an intangible asset (see policy on Other intangible assets).

Other intangible assets

Other intangible assets are carried at cost less accumulated amortisation and accumulated impairment losses. The cost of intangible assets acquired in a business combination is the fair value at acquisition date. The cost of separately acquired intangible assets, including computer software, comprises the purchase price and any directly attributable costs of preparing the asset for use. Amortisation begins when an asset is available for use and is calculated on a straight-line basis to allocate the cost less residual value of assets over their estimated useful lives using the following annual rates:

Development costs	10 to 25%
Computer software costs	10 to 25%
Patents, trademarks and licenses	Shorter of period of the agreement or 15 years

Useful lives are examined on an annual basis and adjustments where applicable are made on a prospective basis. No intangible assets other than goodwill are considered to have indefinite useful lives.

Expenditure incurred on development projects is capitalised as an intangible asset if it meets the recognition criteria set out in IAS 38, Intangible Assets. These require it to be probable that the expenditure will generate future economic benefits and can be measured reliably. To meet these criteria, it is necessary to be able to demonstrate, among other things, the technical feasibility of completing the intangible asset so that it will be available for use or sale.

Costs incurred in the preliminary stage of a development project are considered to be research costs, and are recognised in the income statement as incurred. These costs are incurred to determine the product concepts and alternatives, evaluate the alternatives and related risks, assess the technical feasibility of concepts, make the final selection from the possible alternatives and prepare the high level design and project planning. The costs incurred in the following development stage for substantially new or improved products are assessed against the IAS 38 criteria and considered for recognition as an asset when they meet those criteria. These costs are generally incurred in developing the detailed product design, software configuration and software interfaces; the coding of software, building of prototypes and integration of the software with hardware; and testing and releasing the product to manufacture and pilot production.

Development expenditure directed towards incremental improvements in existing products does not qualify for recognition as an intangible asset.

In general the costs of developing software products that are sold in packaged form and not integrated and sold with hardware are not recognised as intangible assets. The uncertainties associated with the functionality of these products mean that technical feasibility is achieved only immediately prior to or after field trial tests at customer sites. As a result minimal or no costs are considered to meet the IAS 38 criteria for recognition.

Development costs

Development costs are capitalised in accordance with the Group's accounting policy for other intangible assets. Determining the amounts to be capitalised requires management to make assumptions and estimates regarding the expected future cash generation of the assets and the expected period of benefits. At 31 March 2008, the carrying amount of capitalised development costs was £81 million (2007: £76 million).

Figure 9.5 Example of disclosures relating to intangible assets
Source: Invensys Annual Report 2008.

NOTES TO THE FINANCIAL STATEMENTS (CONTINUED)

14 Intangible assets – other

	Note	Development costs £m	Computer software costs £m	Patents, trademarks and licences £m	Total £m
Cost					
At 1 April 2006		99	33	4	136
Additions		16	10	–	26
Disposals		–	(1)	(3)	(4)
Exchange adjustments		(3)	(4)	–	(7)
At 31 March 2007		112	38	1	151
Additions		14	7	–	21
Additions – acquired through business combinations	32	3	–	–	3
Disposals		(2)	–	–	(2)
Disposal of subsidiaries[1]		–	(15)	(1)	(16)
Exchange adjustments		4	–	–	4
At 31 March 2008		131	30	–	161
Accumulated amortisation					
At 1 April 2006		25	27	3	55
Charge for the year		12	2	–	14
Disposals		–	(1)	(3)	(4)
Exchange adjustments		(1)	(3)	–	(4)
At 31 March 2007		36	25	–	61
Charge for the year		15	4	–	19
Impairment losses for the year[2]		1	–	–	1
Disposals		(2)	–	–	(2)
Disposal of subsidiaries[1]		–	(11)	–	(11)
Exchange adjustments		–	1	–	1
At 31 March 2008		50	19	–	69
Net book value					
At 31 March 2007		76	13	1	90
At 31 March 2008		81	11	–	92

[1] Included in disposal of subsidiaries are assets with a net book value of £4 million classfied as held for sale in the half-yearly financial statements.

[2] Impairment losses of £1 million (2007: £nil) relate to the write-down of specific development assets in the Ral Group. The technology represented by these assets is no longer expected to be used as intended following the PPP settlement and its recoverable amount has been reassessed accordingly.

Figure 9.5 (*Cont'd*)

Figure 9.6 illustrates the importance of this issue. It highlights the mismatch between assets that are readily measurable and those that underpin competitive advantage.

Because of the strict rules of IAS 38 on the recognition of internally generated intangibles, the IASB has focused on evaluating tangible assets. The sources of competitive advantage in today's economy, however, lie firmly to the right in the

| Tangible assets where ownership is clear and enforceable | Rights that can be bought, sold, stocked and readily traded in disembodied form and (generally) protected | Non-price factors of competitive advantage | Potentially unique competition factors that are within the firm's capability to bring about |

'Hard' Commodities (disembodied) ←——————————————————————→ 'Soft' – difficult to isolate and value (embodied)

TANGIBLE ASSETS	INTANGIBLE GOODS	INTANGIBLE COMPETENCES	LATENT CAPABILITIES
PHYSICAL ASSETS	MATERIAL SUPPLY CONTRACTS	COMPETENCY MAP	CAPABILITIES
PPE		Distinctive competences	Leadership
Inventory	Licences, quotas & franchises	Core competences	Workforce calibre
Other	REGISTRABLE IPR (intellectual property rights)	Routine competences	Organizational (including networks)
FINANCIAL ASSETS			
Cash & cash equivalents	Copyright or patent protected originals – film, music, artistic, scientific, etc. including market software		Market/reputational
Securities			Innovation/R&D in-process
Investments			Corporate renewal
	Trademarks		
	Designs		
	OTHER IPR		
	Brands, know-how & trade secrets		

Figure 9.6 Resources of 21st century entities

Source: PRISM Report 2003, Report series 2, October 2003.
www.euintangibles.net/research_results/finalreport.pdf. © PRISM, 2003.

diagram. The very nature of these assets indicates that their value is highly unlikely to be communicated through the current financial reporting framework. Therefore, we need alternative methods for communicating the performance of companies across the full spectrum of assets that underpin value and growth today, with a view to drawing some strong conclusions about the structure and content of the information required to piece together a complete picture of a company's performance – to measure both the hard goods to the left in the diagram and to evaluate the sources of competitive advantage to the right.

Skandia, a Swedish company has developed an I.C. model which has been very popular in the last decade, in Sweden as well as globally. In 1998 Skandia issued its Intellectual Capital Prototype Report, entitled 'Human Capital in Transformation'. In this report Skandia described I.C. as an entity's intangible resources, which can be assessed as the difference between its market value and its book value. Skandia divided the market value of an entity into financial capital and I.C. The latter was further broken into customer capital, organisational capital and human capital (see www.skandia.com).

Summary

- An intangible asset is an identifiable, non-monetary asset without physical substance. An identifiable asset is one which arises from legal rights or which is capable of being separated from the entity and sold, transferred, licensed, rented or exchanged.

- The cost of separately acquired intangible asset includes its purchase price and any directly attributable costs of preparing the asset for use. General administrative or other overheads are excluded.

- All research expenditure should be written off as an expense as incurred. Development expenditure incurred in relation to an internally generated intangible asset should be recognised as an asset if certain conditions are satisfied.

- Entities may choose between the cost model and the revaluation model for measuring intangible assets after initial recognition. If the revaluation model is used, it should be applied to entire classes of intangible assets. Regular revaluations should be made. Revaluation gains are recognised as other comprehensive income and revaluation losses are recognised as an expense in the income statement.

- Intangible assets with finite useful lives should be systematically amortised over those lives. Intangible assets with indefinite useful lives should not be amortised but should be subject to impairment reviews.

- Intangible assets should be derecognised on disposal or if they are expected to yield no more economic benefits.

Research and references

The IASB documents relevant for this chapter are:

- *Framework for the Preparation and Presentation of Financial Statements*.
- IAS 38 – *Intangible Assets*.
- SIC 32 – *Intangible Assets, Website Costs*.
- IAS 36 – *Impairment of Assets*.
- IFRS 3 – *Business Combinations*.

The following are examples of books and reports that take the issues of this chapter further:

- Alexander, D., Britton, A. and Jorissen, A. (2007) *International Financial Reporting and Analysis*, 3rd edn. Thomson, Chapter 13.
- Alfredson, K., Leo, K., Picker, R., Loftus, J., Clark, K. and Wise, V. (2009) *Applying International Financial Reporting Standards*, 2nd edn. Wiley, Chapter 10.
- Edvinsson, L. (1997) 'Developing Intellectual Capital at Skandia', *Long Range Planning* 30(3) pp. 366–373.
- Elliott, B. and Elliott, J. (2009) *Financial Accounting and Reporting*, 13th edn. Financial Times-Prentice Hall, Chapter 17.
- Epstein, B.J. and Jermakowicz, E.K. (2009) *IFRS 2009: Interpretation and Application of International Accounting and Financial Reporting Standards*. Wiley, Chapter 9.
- PricewaterhouseCoopers (2009) *IFRS Manual of Accounting – 2010. Global Guide to International Financial Reporting Standards*. CCH, Chapter 15.
- PricewaterhouseCoopers (2004) *Trends in Corporate Reporting 2004 – Towards Value Reporting*.

- Skandia (1998) *Human Capital in Transformation*, Skandia Insurance Company, Sveavägen (pdf file available from: http://www.skandia.com).
- Stolowy, H. and Lebas, M.J. (2006) *Corporate Financial Reporting. A Global perspective*, 2nd edn. Thomson, Chapter 8.
- Sutton, T. (2004) *Corporate Financial Accounting and Reporting*, 2nd edn. Financial Times-Prentice Hall, Chapter 8.

Discussion questions and exercises

9.1 Accounting for intangible assets

(a) Explain the term 'identifiable', and list assets that would be excluded from intangible assets as a result of this criterion included in the definition of an intangible asset.

(b) What is an 'active' market?

(c) Discuss the use of the revaluation model in accounting for intangible assets.

(d) What measurement issues arise in accounting for intangible assets?

9.2 Research and development

Expenditure on research costs should be recognized as an expense when it is incurred [. . .] An intangible asset arising from development should be recognized if, and only if, an entity can demonstrate all of the following [. . .]

(IAS 38 – *Intangible Assets*)

(a) Explain why expenditure on research is treated differently from expenditure on development.

(b) State the criteria to be demonstrated for expenditure on development to be recognised as an intangible asset.

(c) An entity has incurred the following costs prior to commercial production of a new pollution filter for use on commercial vehicles:

	€
Marketing awareness campaign	50,000
Patent royalty payable to inventor of filter	12,000
Salaries of staff testing filter prototypes	38,500

Which costs should be included in the internally generated intangible asset?

(d) Describe how and when development expenditure should be amortised.

9.3 Amortisation of intangibles

Entity X holds a trade mark that is well known within consumer circles and has enabled entity X to be a market leader in this area. The trade mark has been held by the entity for nine years. The legal life of the trade mark is five years, but is renewable by the entity at little cost to it.

Discuss how entity X should determine the useful life of the trade mark, noting in particular what form of evidence it should collect to justify its selection of useful life.

9.4 Recognition and amortisation of intangibles

An entity that sells DVDs by sending emails to prospective customers has acquired a customer list from another entity that also markets its products in a similar fashion. The entity estimates that it will generate sales from the list for a minimum of two years, and a maximum of three years. The entity intends to add names to the list from answers to a questionnaire attached to each of the emails. This should extend the useful life of the list for another year.

Discuss how the entity should account for the cost of the customer list. If the cost is capitalised, discuss the determination of the useful life over which the asset will be amortised.

9.5 Internally generated intangible assets

Extreme SpA is a newly established entity. It was set up by an entrepreneur who is generally interested in the business of providing engineering and operational support services to aircraft manufacturers. Extreme SpA, through the contacts of its owner, received a confirmed order from a well-known aircraft manufacturer to develop new designs for ducting the air conditioning of their aircraft. For this project, Extreme SpA needed funds aggregating to EUR 2 million. It was able to convince two international venture capitalists of the validity of the project and obtained funding of EUR 2m from them.

The expenditures Extreme SpA incurred in carrying out its research and development project follow, in chronological order:

- 15 January 2009: paid EUR 350,000 for the salaries of the technicians (engineers and consultants).
- 31 March 2009: incurred EUR 500,000 for the cost of developing the duct and producing the test model.
- 15 June 2009: paid an additional EUR 600,000 for revising the ducting process to ensure that the product could be introduced in the market.
- 15 August 2009: developed, at a cost of EUR 160,000, the first model (prototype) and tested it with the air conditioners to ensure its compatibility.
- 30 October 2009: a focus group of other engineering providers was invited to a conference for the introduction of this new product. Cost of the conference aggregated to EUR 100,000.
- 15 December 2009: the development phase was completed and cash flow budget was prepared. Net profit for 2009 was estimated at EUR 1,800,000.

What is the proper accounting treatment for the various costs incurred in 2009?

9.6 Recognition of intangible assets

Costs incurred by an established entity include:

(a) pre-opening costs of a business facility;
(b) recipes, secret formulas, models and designs, prototype;
(c) training, customer loyalty, and market share;
(d) an in-house-generated accounting software;
(e) the design of a pilot plan;
(f) licensing, royalty, and stand-still agreements;
(g) operating and broadcast rights;

(h) goodwill purchased in a business combination;
(i) a company-developed patented drug approved for medical use;
(j) a licence to manufacture a steroid by means of a government grant;
(k) cost of courses taken by management in quality engineering management;
(l) a television advertisement that will stimulate the sales in the technology industry.

Which of the above-mentioned costs are eligible for capitalisation according to IAS 38, and which of them should be expensed as they are incurred?

9.7 Recognition of intangibles under different hypotheses

Soweto Ltd is unsure of how to obtain computer software. Four possibilities are:

(1) Purchase computer software externally, including packages for payroll and general ledger.
(2) Contract independent programmers to develop specific software for the company's own use.
(3) Buy computer software to incorporate into a product that the company will develop.
(4) Employ its own programmers to write software that the company will use.

Discuss whether the accounting will differ depending on which method is chosen.

9.8 Research and development

Autocar SpA, a motor vehicle manufacturer, has a research division that worked on the following projects during 2009:

Project 1 – the design of a steering mechanism that does not operate like a conventional steering wheel, but reacts to the impulses from a driver's fingers.
Project 2 – the design of a welding apparatus that is controlled electronically rather than mechanically.

The following is a summary of the expenses of the above research department:

Amounts in thousands of euro	General	Project 1	Project 2
Material and services	128	935	620
Labour			
• Direct labour	–	620	320
• Department head salary	400	–	–
• Administrative personnel	725	–	–
Overhead			
• Direct	–	340	410
• Indirect	270	110	60

The departmental head spent 15 per cent of his time on Project 1 and 10 per cent of his time on Project 2.

Determine the costs to be capitalised.

9.9 Amortisation of intangibles

An entity has acquired local broadcast rights to the 2010 World Cup. Management expect World Cup related advertising revenue to commence from 1 March 2010. Management propose that amortisation of these rights should begin at the start of the tournament in June 2010.

Do you consider management proposal appropriate? Explain why.

9.10 Customer relationships

Entity A, acquired entity B, which operated a TV channel. Entity B negotiates the sale of air time directly with advertisers who are mostly big companies. Advertisement contracts are negotiated annually and the management consider it likely that the relationships will continue indefinitely.

Entity A's management have concluded that the criteria have been met in order to recognise such customer relationships as intangible assets separately from goodwill and propose to treat the relationships as having an indefinite useful life.

Do you consider the management proposal appropriate? Explain why.

9.11 Accounting for intangible assets

Pretoria Ltd is a highly successful engineering company that manufactures filters for air-conditioning systems. Due to its dissatisfaction with the quality of the filters currently available, on 1 January 2010 it commenced a project to design a more efficient filter. The following notes record the events relating to that project.

2010

January	Spent €290,000 on the salaries of company engineers and consultants who conducted basic tests on available filters with varying modifications.
February	Spent €330,000 on developing a new filter system, including the production of a basic model. It became obvious that the model in its current form was not successful because the material in the filter was not as effective as required.
March	Acquired the fibres division of Durban Ltd for €660,000. The fair values of the tangible assets of this division were:

> Property, plant and equipment   €360,000
> Inventories   €120,000

This business was acquired because one of the products it produced was a fibrous compound, sold under the brand name Springbok, that Pretoria Ltd considered would be excellent for including in the filtration process.

By buying the fibres division, Pretoria Ltd acquired the patent for this fibrous compound. Pretoria Ltd valued the patent at €100,000 and the brand name at €80,000, using a number of valuation techniques. The patent had a further ten-year life but was renewable on application. Further costs of €108,000 were incurred on the new filter system during March.

2010	
April	Spent a further €270,000 on revising the filtration process to incorporate the fibrous compound. By the end of April, Pretoria Ltd was convinced that it now had a viable product because preliminary tests showed that the filtration process was significantly better than any other available on the market.
May	Developed a prototype of the filtration component and proceeded to test it within a variety of models of air-conditioners. The company preferred to sell the filtration process to current manufacturers of air-conditioners if the process worked with currently available models. If this proved not possible, the company would then consider developing its own brand of air-conditioners using the new filtration system. By the end of May, the filtration system had proved successful on all but one of the currently available commercial models. Costs incurred were €130,000.
June	Various air-conditioner manufacturers were invited to demonstrations of the filtration system. Costs incurred were €50,000, including €24,000 for food and beverages for the prospective clients. The feedback from a number of the companies was that they were prepared to enter into negotiations for acquiring the filters from Pretoria Ltd. The company now believed it had a successful model and commenced planning the production of the filters. Ongoing costs of €90,000 to refine the filtration system, particularly in the light of comments by the manufacturers, were incurred in the latter part of June.

Explain the accounting for the various expenses incurred by Pretoria Ltd.

Note

1 IAS 38 also deals with (1) intangible assets acquired as part of a business combination; (2) intangible assets acquired through a government grant and (3) internally generated goodwill. We deal with intangible assets and goodwill acquired as part of a business combination in Part Six.

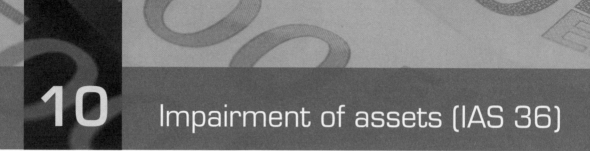

10 Impairment of assets (IAS 36)

Contents

When you have completed this chapter you should be able to:

- Explain what impairment means
- List the indicators that make an impairment test necessary
- Define the term 'cash-generating unit' and explain how a cash-generating unit is identified
- Undertake an impairment test for both an individual asset and for a cash-generating unit
- Calculate value in use
- Measure and recognise an impairment loss
- Account for reversal of impairment losses.

10.1   Introduction

Depreciation and amortisation are aimed at allocating the cost of a non-current asset (tangible or intangible) against revenue over the asset's useful life. However, events such as rapid economic obsolescence or physical damage of an asset may make this systematic allocation inadequate. In these cases, the carrying value of the asset may overstate the asset's worth to the entity.

Once impairment has been identified (see section 10.2.1), we should measure its size. In order to do so, the entity should compare the asset's carrying value with its *recoverable amount* (see section 10.2.2) as shown in the Figure 10.1.

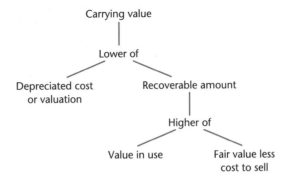

Figure 10.1 Carrying value of tangible and intangible (non-current) assets

If depreciated cost is higher than recoverable amount, an impairment loss should be recognised as an expense in the income statement immediately. After the recognition of an impairment loss, the depreciation (amortisation) charge for the asset should be adjusted in future periods to allocate the asset's revised carrying amount, less its residual value (if any), on a systematic basis over its remaining useful life.

An asset's *carrying value* is generally its depreciated cost (i.e. historical cost less accumulated depreciation).

An asset's *recoverable amount* is the higher of:

- *fair value less costs to sell* (the amount obtainable from the sale of an asset or cash-generating unit in an arm's length transaction between knowledgeable, willing parties, less the costs of disposal); and

- *value in use* (the present value of estimated future cash inflows and outflows to be derived from the continuing use of an asset and from its disposal at the end of its useful life). The determination of the value in use involves estimation of the appropriate discount rate to be applied to these future cash flows. Moreover, it may be impossible to make reasonable estimates for individual assets, so impairment tests should be carried out on groups of assets, called 'cash-generating units' (CGU) for which independent cash flows can be measured.

If the recoverable amount of an asset is less than its carrying amount, then the carrying amount of the asset should be reduced to its recoverable amount. That reduction is an *impairment loss*. An impairment cannot be avoided by arguing that the diminution in value is temporary and not permanent.

10.2   Key stages in the impairment process

Figure 10.2 shows the stages to be followed to account for an impairment loss.

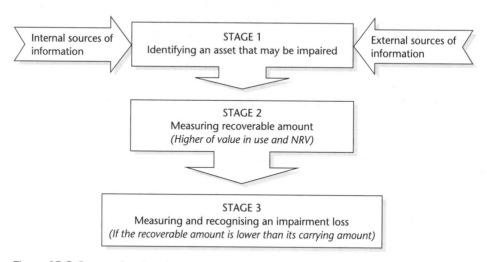

Figure 10.2 Stages of an impairment test

10.2.1 Stage 1: identifying an asset that may be impaired

IAS 36 – *Impairment of Assets* lists several sources of information (both external and internal to the entity) which should be considered when assessing whether there is any indication that an asset may be impaired (IAS 36 para 12).

External sources of information

(a) An asset's market value has declined significantly more than would be expected as a result of the passage of time or normal use.

(b) Significant changes with an adverse effect on the entity have taken place or will take place in the near future, in the technological, market, economic or legal environment in which the entity operates or in the market to which an asset is dedicated.

(c) Market interest rates or other market rates of return on investments have increased during the period, and those increases are likely to affect the discount rate used in calculating an asset's value in use and decrease the asset's recoverable amount materially.

(d) The carrying amount of the net assets of the entity exceeds its market capitalisation.

Internal sources of information

(a) There is evidence of obsolescence or physical damage to an asset.

(b) Significant and adverse changes have taken place or are expected to take place in the near future, to the extent to which, or manner in which, an asset is used or is expected to be used. These changes include:

- the asset becoming idle;
- plans to discontinue or restructure the operation to which an asset belongs;
- plans to dispose of an asset before the previously expected date; and reassessing the useful life of an asset as finite rather than indefinite.

(c) There is evidence that the economic performance of an asset is, or will be, worse than expected.

If any of these indications are present, the asset concerned should be tested for impairment by comparing its recoverable amount with its carrying amount.

Evidence from internal reporting that indicates that an asset may be impaired includes the existence of:

(a) cash flows for acquiring the asset, or subsequent cash needs for operating or maintaining it, that are significantly higher than those originally budgeted;

(b) actual net cash flows or an operating profit or loss flowing from the asset that are significantly worse than those budgeted;

(c) a significant decline in the budgeted net cash flows or operating profit, or a significant increase in budgeted loss, flowing from the asset; or

(d) operating losses or net cash outflows for the asset, when current period amounts are aggregated with budgeted amounts for the future (IAS 36 para 14).

The above list is not exhaustive. Other indicators may be apparent that are relevant to a business' particular circumstances (IAS 36 para 13). For example, changes in tax regulations, the impact of publicity over brand names, the change in the proposed use of an asset, an impairment recognised by an associate or the entrance of a new competitor to the market may require the recoverable amount of an entity's assets to be investigated.

Increases in market rates of interest are identified as an indicator for entities to consider. However, IAS 36 emphasises that increases in short-term interest rates would not necessarily trigger an impairment review. Changes in interest rates need to be considered in the context of the level of headroom indicated by previous impairment tests. A marginal increase in interest rates is unlikely to lead to an impairment charge where there was significant headroom in the last test.

Indicators that develop over time

Sometimes indicators assume more significance over time, perhaps as general market conditions worsen or an entity's performance gradually deteriorates. Entities should be alert to such trends and to their potential to becoming indicators of impairment.

Situations exist where impairments are the result of changes in economic conditions or other factors that develop over time. For example, industry trends that indicate a potential decrease in demand for an entity's product do not always develop to the point where an impairment indicator might be identified within one reporting cycle. A situation might exist where the trend in sales reflects a 5 per cent annual decrease for a few years, or where the market share of the entity's principal products has declined steadily. Any plans for reversing negative trends should be critically evaluated.

10.2.2 Stage 2: measuring recoverable amount

We have already defined *recoverable amount* as the higher of an asset's or cash-generating unit's fair value less costs to sell and its value in use (IAS 36 para 6). IAS 36 sets out the requirements for measuring the recoverable amount. These requirements use the term 'an asset' but they apply equally to an individual asset or a cash-generating unit.

It is not always necessary to determine both an asset's fair value less costs to sell and its value in use. If either of these amounts exceeds the asset's carrying amount, the asset is not impaired and it is not necessary to estimate the other amount (IAS 36 para 19).

It may be possible to determine fair value less costs to sell, even if an asset is not traded in an active market. However, sometimes it will not be possible to determine fair value less costs to sell because there is no basis for making a reliable estimate of the amount obtainable from the sale of the asset in an arm's length transaction between knowledgeable and willing parties. In this case, the entity may use the asset's value in use as its recoverable amount (IAS 36 para 20).

If there is no reason to believe that an asset's value in use materially exceeds its fair value less costs to sell, the asset's fair value less costs to sell may be used as its recoverable amount. This will often be the case for an asset that is held for disposal. This is because the value in use of an asset held for disposal will consist mainly of the net disposal proceeds, as the future cash flows from continuing use of the asset until its disposal are likely to be negligible (IAS 36 para 21).

Recoverable amount is determined for an individual asset or for a cash-generating unit (CGU) to which the asset belongs (IAS 36 para 22). Impairment losses for CGU are illustrated in section 10.4.

Example 10.1

Recoverable amount

An entity has seven assets (labelled A to G) for which there are indications of possible impairment. The carrying amount, fair value less costs to sell and value in use for each asset are shown in Table 10.1 below.

Table 10.1 Data available

	Carrying amount	Fair value less costs to sell	Value in use
	€	€	€
Asset A	20,000	24,000	36,000
Asset B	22,000	18,000	26,000
Asset C	14,000	23,000	n/d
Asset D	17,000	13,000	14,000
Asset E	25,500	n/d	37,600
Asset F	20,000	28,000	24,000
Asset G	42,000	30,000	20,000

Note: n/d = not determined.

Determine the amount of any impairment loss arising for each asset.

Table 10.2 Determination of impairment losses

	Carrying amount €	Recoverable amount €	Impairment loss €
Asset A	20,000	36,000	0
Asset B	22,000	26,000	0
Asset C	14,000	23,000 (at least)	0
Asset D	17,000	14,000	3,000
Asset E	25,500	37,600 (at least)	0
Asset F	20,000	28,000	0
Asset G	42,000	30,000	12,000

Notes:
(i)   In each case, the recoverable amount is the higher of fair value less costs to sell and value in use. For assets C and E, one of these figures has not been determined, so the recoverable amount cannot be calculated. However, the recoverable amount is higher than the carrying amount, so there is no impairment loss. However, assets D and G are impaired.
(ii) For most of the assets, the carrying amount is less than the recoverable amount, so there is no impairment loss. However, assets D and G are impaired.
(iii) Although value in use has not been determined for asset C and fair value less costs to sell has not been determined for asset E, it is still clear that these assets are not impaired. Therefore, it is not necessary to expend further effort to determine the missing figures.

Fair value less costs to sell

The best evidence of an asset's fair value is the price at which similar assets are currently changing hand in legally binding sales agreements. If an asset is of a type that is treated in an active market, the current market price provides evidence of fair value. In the absence of binding sales agreements or an active market, the asset's fair value will have to be estimated, based upon the best information available.

Costs of disposal are deducted when calculating fair value less costs to sell. These costs include items such as legal costs, stamp duty and costs that would be incurred to bring the asset into a condition suitable for sale.

Value in use

As stated above, an asset's value in use is calculated by discounting the future cash flows which the asset is expected to generate. These future cash flows should include:

(a) projections of future cash inflows from the use of the asset;

(b) projections of future cash outflows that will be necessarily incurred so as to generate cash inflows from the use of the asset (e.g. servicing and maintenance costs);

(c) net cash flows (if any) to be received or paid on disposal of the asset at the end of its useful life.

Future cash flows should be estimated for the asset in its current condition and should not take into account any cash flows that are expected to arise from improving or enhancing the asset's performance. Estimates of future cash flows should not include:

(a) cash outflows that relate to obligations that have already been recognized as liabilities (e.g. the payment of existing trade payables);

(b) cash inflows or outflows from financing activities (e.g. interest payable);

(c) tax receipts or payments.

It is clear that the calculation of value in use will involve making estimates of future cash flows. IAS 36 states that these estimates should be based on reasonable and supportable assumptions and that greater weight should be given to external evidence than to internal evidence. IAS 36 also states that cash flow projections should be based on management's most recent financial budgets or forecast. Short-term budgets may be extrapolated into the future using a steady or declining growth rate (unless an increasing rate is justified).

The discount rate used in calculating an asset's value in use should be a current pretax interest rate which reflects the time value of money.

Example 10.2

Value in use

Entity C estimates that an asset is expected to generate the following cash flows over its useful life of four years:

	Inflows €000	Outflows €000
Year 1	150	12
Year 2	200	14
Year 3	180	14
Year 4	120	12

All cash flows will occur at the end of the year concerned. At the end of the four-year period, the asset is expected to be sold for EUR 100,000. Assuming a discount rate of 12 per cent and working to the nearest €000, calculate the asset's value in use.

Table 10.3 Determination of value in use

	Inflows €000	Outflows €000	Net cash flow €000	Discount factor	Present value €000
Year 1	150	12	138	0.893	124
Year 2	200	14	186	0.797	148
Year 3	180	14	166	0.712	118
Year 4	120	12	208	0.636	132
Value in use					522

Notes:
(i)   The cash inflow for year 4 includes €100,000 disposal proceeds for the asset.
(ii) The discount factor for the first year is $1 \div 1.12 = 0.893$. The discount factor for the second year is $1 \div (1.12)^2$ and so forth.
(iii) The asset's value in use is €522,000.

Figure 10.3 below shows how Vodafone illustrated indicators that have triggered impairment losses being recognised in its annual report for the year ended 31 March 2010 and the key assumptions used in determining the value in use.

10.2.3 Stage 3: measuring and recognising an impairment loss

If the recoverable amount of an asset is less than its carrying amount, IAS 36 requires that the asset's carrying amount should be reduced to its recoverable amount. This reduction is an impairment loss. In general, an impairment loss should be recognised as an expense in the income statement. However, if the asset is carried at revalued amount, the impairment loss should be accounted for in the same way as a revaluation loss. This means that:

(a) The impairment loss is debited to the revaluation reserve and it is shown in the other comprehensive income section of the statement of comprehensive income.

(b) Any excess is then recognised as an expense in the income statement.

After an impairment loss has been recognised, subsequent depreciation or amortisation charges should allocate the asset's revised carrying amount (less residual value) over the reminder of its useful life.

Impairment reviews

IFRS requires management to undertake an annual test for impairment of indefinite lived assets and, for finite lived assets, to test for impairment if events or changes in circumstances indicate that the carrying amount of an asset may not be recoverable.

Impairment testing is an area involving management judgement, requiring assessment as to whether the carrying value of assets can be supported by the net present value of future cash flows derived from such assets using cash flow projections which have been discounted at an appropriate rate. In calculating the net present value of the future cash flows, certain assumptions are required to be made in respect of highly uncertain matters including management's expectations of:

- growth in EBITDA, calculated as adjusted operating profit before depreciation and amortisation;
- timing and quantum of future capital expenditure;
- long term growth rates; and
- the selection of discount rates to reflect the risks involved.

The Group prepares and approves formal five year management plans for its operations, which are used in the value in use calculations. In certain developing markets the fifth year of the management plan is not indicative of the long-term future performance as operations may not have reached maturity. For these operations, the Group extends the plan data for an additional five year period.

For businesses where the five year management plans are used for the Group's value in use calculations, a long-term growth rate into perpetuity has been determined as the lower of:

- the nominal GDP rates for the country of operation; and
- the long-term compound annual growth rate in EBITDA in years six to ten estimated by management.

For businesses where the plan data is extended for an additional five years for the Group's value in use calculations, a long-term growth rate into perpetuity has been determined as the lower of:

- the nominal GDP rates for the country of operation; and
- the compound annual growth rate in EBITDA in years nine to ten of the management plan.

Changing the assumptions selected by management, in particular the discount rate and growth rate assumptions used in the cash flow projections, could significantly affect the Group's impairment evaluation and hence results.

The Group's review includes the key assumptions related to sensitivity in the cash flow projections. Further details are provided in note 10 to the consolidated financial statements.

(from the Critical Accounting Estimates section)

10. Impairment

Impairment losses, net
The net impairment losses recognised in the consolidated income statement, as a separate line item within operating profit, in respect of goodwill and licences and spectrum fees are as follows:

Cash generating unit	Reportable segment	2010 £m	2009 £m	2008 £m
India	India	2,300	–	–
Spain	Spain	–	3,400	–
Turkey	Other Africa and Central Europe	(200)	2,250	–
Ghana	Other Africa and Central Europe	–	250	–
		2,100	5,900	–

Year ended 31 March 2010
The net impairment losses were based on value in use calculations. The pre-tax adjusted discount rate used in the most recent value in use in the year ended 31 March 2010 calculation are as follows:

	Pre-tax adjusted discount rate
India	13.8%
Turkey	17.6%

Figure 10.3 Impairment losses

Source: Vodafone Annual Report 2010.

India

During the year ended 31 March 2010 the goodwill in relation to the Group's operations in india was impaired by £2,300 million primarily due to intense price competition following the entry of a number of new operators into the market. The pre-tax risk adjusted discount rate used in the previous value in use calculation at 31 March 2009 was 12.3%.

Turkey

During the year ended 31 March 2010 impairment losses of £200 million, previously recognised in respect of intangible assets in relation to the Group's operations in Turkey, were reversed. The reversal was in relation to licences and spectrum and was as a result of favourable changes in the discount rate. The cash flow projections within the business plans used for impairment testing were substantially unchanged from those used at 31 March 2009. The pre-tax risk adjusted discount rate used in the previous value in use calculation at 31 March 2009 was 19.5%.

Year ended 31 March 2009

The impairment losses were based on value in use calculations. The pre-tax adjusted discount rate used in the most recent value in use in the year ended 31 March 2009 calculation are as follows:

	Pre-tax adjusted discount rate
Spain	10.3%
Turkey[1]	19.5%
Ghana	26.9%

Note:
(1) The pre-tax adjusted discount rate used in the value in use calculation at 30 September 2008 was 18.6%.

Spain

During the year ended 31 March 2009 the goodwill in relation to the Group's operations in Spain was impaired by £3,400 million following a fall in long-term cash flow forecasts resulting from the economic downturn. The pre-tax risk adjusted discount rate used in the previous value in use calculation at 31 January 2008 was 10.6%.

Turkey

During the year ended 31 March 2009 the goodwill and other intangible assets in relation to the Group's operations in Turkey was impaired by £2,250 million. At 30 September 2008 the goodwill was impaired by £1,700 million following adverse movements in the discount rate and adverse performance against previous plans. During the second half of the 2009 financial year, impairment losses of £300 million in relation to goodwill and £250 million in relation to licences and spectrum resulted from adverse changes in both the discount rate and a fall in the long-term GDP growth rate. The cash flow projections within the business plans used for impairment testing were substantially unchanged from those used at 30 September 2008. The pre-tax risk adjusted discount rate used in the previous value in use calculation at 31 January 2008 was 16.2%.

Ghana

During the year ended 31 March 2009 the goodwill in relation to the Group's operations in Ghana was impaired by £250 million following an increase in the discount rate. The cash flow projections within the business plan used for impairment testing was substantially unchanged from the acquisition business case in 2008.

Goodwill

The carrying value of goodwill at 31 March was as follows:

	2010 £m	2009 £m
Germany	12,301	12,786
Italy	14,786	15,361
Spain	10,167	10,561
	37,254	38,708
Other	14,584	15,250
	51,838	53,958

Figure 10.3 (*Cont'd*)

Example 10.3, based on one of the illustrative examples in the standard, considers vertical integration.

Example 10.3

Vertically integrated CGU

The reporting entity has two plants. Plant H produces raw material that is sold to plant I of the same entity. The raw material is sold by plant H to plant I at a price that transfers all the margins to plant H. 60 per cent of plant H's production is sold to plant I and 40 per cent is sold to external customers outside the reporting entity. 80 per cent of plant I's production is sold to external customers of the reporting entity.

We show how to determine the CGUs for plant H and plant I when:

- Plant H could sell its production in an active market instead of to plant I.
- There is no active market for the production of plant H.

In the first situation there is an active market for plant H's production so it is likely that plant H is a separate CGU. Plant I would also be a separate CGU, because it sells 80 per cent of its output externally and so generates cash flows that are largely independent of the cash flows from the other assets of the reporting entity. In the financial forecasts and budgets used for determining value in use for both plant H and plant I the internal transfer prices for production sold by plant H to plant I should be adjusted to arm's length prices.

In the second situation there is no active market for the output of plant H, and the cash inflows of plant H depend on the demand for the product sold by plant I. Plant H does not generate cash flows that are largely independent of the cash flows of assets operated by plant I. Also, the two plants are managed together, as the use of internal transfer prices demonstrates. Therefore, the two plants should be treated as one CGU.

Allocation of impairment loss

Any impairment loss calculated for a CGU should be allocated to reduce the carrying amount of the asset in the following order:

1 The carrying amount of goodwill should be first reduced, then the carrying amount of other assets of the unit should be reduced on a pro rata basis determined by the relative carrying value of each asset.

2 Any reductions in the carrying amount of the individual assets should be treated as impairment losses. The carrying amount of any individual asset should not be reduced below the highest of its fair value less cost to sell, its value in use, and zero.

If this rule is applied, the impairment loss not allocated to the individual asset will be allocated on a pro rata basis to the other assets of the group.

Example 10.4

Allocation of impairment loss of a CGU

A CGU has these net assets:

	€m
Goodwill	20
Property	40
Plant and equipment	60
Total	120

The recoverable amount has been determined at EUR 90m.

We show how to allocate the impairment loss to the net assets of the entity.

The impairment loss is EUR 30m (EUR 120m – EUR 90m). Of this loss, EUR 20m is used to eliminate the goodwill. The remaining EUR 10m is split between the other two assets in the ratio 40:60. Property is reduced by EUR 4m and plant and equipment by EUR 6m.

	Goodwill €m	Property €m	Plant €m	Total €m
Carrying value	20	40	60	120
Impairment loss	(20)	(4)	(6)	30
Carrying value after impairment	0	36	54	90

10.4   Reversing an impairment loss

A reversal of an impairment loss reflects an increase in the estimated service potential of an asset, either from use or from sale, since the date when an entity last recognised an impairment loss for that asset. An entity should identify the change in estimate that causes the increase in estimated service potential. Examples of changes in estimates include:

(a) a change in the basis for recoverable amount (i.e. whether recoverable amount is based on fair value less costs to sell or value in use);

(b) if the recoverable amount was based on value in use, a change in the amount or timing of estimated future cash flows or in the discount rate; or

(c) if the recoverable amount was based on fair value less costs to sell, a change in estimate of the components of fair value less costs to sell (IAS 36 para 115).

An asset's value in use may become greater than the asset's carrying amount simply because the present value of future cash inflows increases as they become closer due to the passage of time. However, the service potential of the asset has not increased.

Therefore, an impairment loss should not be reversed just because of the passage of time (sometimes called the 'unwinding' of the discount), even if the recoverable amount of the asset becomes higher than its carrying amount (IAS 36 para 116).

10.4.1 Reversing an impairment loss for an individual asset

The increased carrying amount of an asset other than goodwill attributable to a reversal of an impairment loss should not exceed the carrying amount that would have been determined (net of amortisation or depreciation) had no impairment loss been recognised for the asset in prior years (IAS 36 para 117).

Any increase in the carrying amount of an asset other than goodwill above the carrying amount that would have been determined (net of amortisation or depreciation) had no impairment loss been recognised for the asset in prior years is a revaluation. In accounting for such a revaluation, an entity should apply the IFRS applicable to the asset (IAS 36 para 118).

A reversal of an impairment loss for an asset other than goodwill should be recognised immediately in the income statement, unless the asset is carried at revalued amount. Any reversal of an impairment loss of a revalued asset should be treated as a revaluation increase (IAS 36 para 119).

A reversal of an impairment loss on a revalued asset is recognised in other comprehensive income and increases the revaluation surplus for that asset. However, to the extent that an impairment loss on the same revalued asset was previously recognised in the income statement, a reversal of that impairment loss is also recognised in the income statement (IAS 36 para 120).

After a reversal of an impairment loss is recognised, the depreciation (amortisation) charge for the asset should be adjusted in future periods to allocate the asset's revised carrying amount, less its residual value (if any), on a systematic basis over its remaining useful life (IAS 36 para 121).

10.4.2 Reversing an impairment loss for a cash-generating unit

A reversal of an impairment loss for a CGU should be allocated to the assets of the unit, except for goodwill, proportionally to the carrying amounts of those assets. Such increases in carrying amounts should be treated as reversals of impairment losses for individual assets and recognised in accordance with paragraph 119 (IAS 36 para 122).

In allocating a reversal of an impairment loss for a CGU, the carrying amount of an asset should not be increased above the lower of:

(a) its recoverable amount (if determinable); and

(b) the carrying amount that would have been determined (net of amortisation or depreciation) had no impairment loss been recognised for the asset in prior periods.

The amount of the reversal of the impairment loss that would otherwise have been allocated to the asset should be allocated pro rata to the other assets of the unit, except for goodwill (IAS 36 para 123).

Example 10.5

Reversal of an impairment loss

The calculation refers to an impairment loss suffered by subsidiary F as at 31 December 2008:

	Goodwill	Net assets	Total
	€m	€m	€m
Carrying value as at 31 December 2008	300	900	1200
Impairment	(300)	(200)	(500)
	–	700	700

There has been a favourable change in the estimates of the recoverable amount of entity F's net assets since the impairment loss was recognised. The recoverable amount is now EUR 800m as at 31 December 2009. The net assets' carrying value would have been EUR 720m as at 31 December 2009. Assets are depreciated at 20 per cent reducing balance.

Show the accounting treatment for the reversal of the impairment loss as at 31 December 2009.

The reversal of the impairment loss on goodwill should not be accounted for under IAS 36. The carrying amount of F can be increased up to the lower of the recoverable amount (EUR 800m) and the carrying value (EUR 720m) of the net asset. The carrying amount of F's net assets as at 31 December 2009 are shown below:

	Goodwill	Net assets	Total
	€m	€m	€m
Carrying value as at 31 December 2008 (after impairment loss)	Nil	700	700
Reversal of impairment loss	Nil	20	20
	Nil	720	720

Figure 10.4 on page 316 is an example of disclosures of accounting policy for impairment of goodwill and other long-lived assets.

10.5   Financial analysis and interpretation

An impaired asset is an asset that is going to be retained by the entity and whose book value is not expected to be recovered from future operations. Lack of recoverability is indicated by such factors as:

- a significant decrease in market value, physical change, or use of the asset;
- adverse changes in the legal or business climate;
- significant cost overruns; and
- Current, historical, and probable future operating or cash flow losses from the asset.

Goodwill

We do not amortize goodwill but test it for impairment at least annually and when events occur or changes in circumstances indicate that the recoverable amount of a cash-generating unit is less than its carrying value. In respect to at-equity investments, the carrying amount of goodwill is included in the carrying amount of the investment.

For the purpose of impairment testing, goodwill is allocated to our reportable segments Product, Consulting and Training which represent the lowest level of cash-generating units within the Group at which the goodwill is monitored for internal management purposes.

The carrying amount of goodwill by reportable segment at December 31, 2008, and 2007, is as follows:

Goodwill by Segments

€ millions	12/31/2008	Thereof Additions in 2008	12/31/2007	Thereof Additions in 2007
Segment				
Product	4,136	3,126	977	427
Consulting	692	280	409	76
Training	147	105	40	14
Total	4,975	3,511	1,426	517

Current-year additions to goodwill include adjustment to goodwill acquired in prior years in the amount of € – 35 million primarily for changes of tax positions.

For more information about our segments, see Note 28.

The impairment test for all three cash-generating units is based on the value in use determined by discounting the future cash flow expected to be generated from the continuing use of the unit. We project cash flows based on actual operating results and our 2-year business plan (2007: 3-year business plan). Cash flows for periods beyond this business plan were extrapolated. Our estimated cash flow projections are discounted to present value by means of a pre-tax discount rate between 10.78% and 10.86% (2007: 12.12% and 13.05%). The discount rate is based on a weighted averaged cost of capital approach (WACC).

Even when we applied a growth rate of only 0% for extrapolating cash flow projections beyond the years covered by our business plan (2007: value in use based on growth rates between 1.7% and 4.0%) for calculating the value-in-use for all cash-generating units the calculated amounts exceeded the carrying amounts. As a result more realistic values in use based on growth rates expected for post business plan periods were not needed.

Impairment of Long-Lived Assets

We review long-lived assets, such as property, plant, equipment, and acquired intangible assets for impairment whenever events or changes in circumstances indicate that the carrying amount of an asset or group of assets may not be recoverable. We assess recoverability of assets to be held and used by comparing their carrying amount to the recoverable amount, which is the higher of value in use and fair value less costs to sell. If an asset or group of assets is considered to be impaired, the impairment to be recognized is measured as the amount by which the carrying amount of the asset or group of assets exceeds its recoverable amount.

Figure 10.4 Disclosures of accounting policy for impairment of goodwill and long-lived assets
Source: SAP Annual Report 2008.

Management make the decisions about whether or not an asset's value is impaired by reference to internal and external sources of information, and use cash flow projections based on reasonable and supportable assumptions and their own most recent budgets and forecast.

According to IFRS, the need for a write-down, the size of the write-down, and the timing of the write-down should be determined by objective and supportable evidence rather than at management's discretion. Impairment losses therefore cannot easily be used to smooth or manipulate earnings in some other way. The discount rate used to determine the present value of future cash flow of the asset in its recoverability test should be determined objectively based on market conditions.

From an external analyst's perspective, it is difficult to forecast impairment losses. However, the impairment losses themselves and the related disclosures provide the analyst with useful information about management's projections of future cash flows.

When impairment losses are recognised the financial statements are affected in several ways:

- The carrying amount of an asset is reduced by the impairment loss. This reduces the carrying amount of the entity's total assets.
- Deferred tax liability is reduced and deferred tax income is recognised if the entity cannot take a tax reduction for the impairment loss until that asset is sold or fully used.
- Retained earnings and, hence, shareholder's equity, are reduced by the difference between the impairment loss and any associated reduction in the deferred tax liability.
- Profit before tax is reduced by the amount of the impairment loss.
- Profit is reduced by the difference between the impairment loss and any associated reduction in deferred tax expense.

In addition, an impairment loss affects the following financial ratios:

- Asset turnover ratios increase because of the lower asset base.
- The debt-to-equity ratios rise because of the lower equity base.
- Profit margins suffer a one-time reduction because of the recognition of an impairment loss.
- The book value (shareholders' equity) of the entity is reduced because of the reduction in equity.
- Future depreciation charges are reduced because the carrying amount of the asset is reduced.
- Lower future depreciation charges tend to cause the future profitability of the firm to increase (because losses are recognised in the current year).
- Higher future profitability and lower asset values tend to increase future returns on assets.
- Higher future profitability and lower equity values tend to increase future returns on equity.

Impairment losses do not directly affect cash flows because the cash outflows for the asset have already occurred and tax deductions, and hence tax payments, might not

10.3   Impairment indicator: change of asset's use

Entity C uses asset D to manufacture product X. There has been a significant reduction in demand for product X as a result of a change in consumer taste. Management have not assessed asset D for impairment because it can, subject to minimal reconfiguration, be used in the manufacture of its new product Y.

Should entity C review asset D for impairment?

10.4   Impairment indicator: introduction of a superior competitor product

Entity G produces mousetraps and has for some time been the market leader. Its chief competitor, Entity H has recently developed a new product that is widely acknowledged as being superior to entity G's mousetrap.

Entity G's management have not performed an impairment review on its plant on the grounds that the annual production and sales are ahead of budget.

Should entity G review its PPE for impairment?

10.5   Cash-generating units and impairment test

Entity E owns a large number of dairy farms in Italy. It has a number of factories that are used to produce milk products that are then sent to other factories to be converted into milk-based products such as yoghurt and custard. In applying IAS 36, the accountant of entity E is concerned about correctly identifying the cash-generating units (CGUs) for the entity, and has sought your advice on such questions as to whether the milk production section is a separate CGU even though the entity does not sell milk directly to other parties, or whether it should be included in the milk-based products CGU.

(a) Define CGU;
(b) Explain why impairment testing requires the use of CGU instead of a single asset;
(c) Explain the factors that should be considered in determining the CGUs for entity E.

10.6   Value in use – estimation of future cash flows

An entity is reviewing its business segments for impairment. The carrying value of its net assets is EUR 20m. Management have produced two computations for the value-in use of the business segment. The first value (EUR 18m) excludes the benefits to be derived from a future reorganisation, but the second value (EUR 22m) includes the benefits to be derived from the proposed future reorganisation. There is not an active market for the sale of the business segment.

Explain whether the business segment is impaired.

10.7   Value in use less than fair value less costs to sell

Entity F is involved in the generation and distribution of electricity. Management are reviewing all of its assets for impairment as a result of a fall in the market price of electricity. One of entity F's power stations, which is two years old, has a carrying value of EUR 5m and a value in use of EUR 4.4m taking into account the revised electricity price. The market for these assets is an active one, as investors are keen to enter the market to pursue the opportunities arising from market deregulation. A similar asset was recently sold to a US-based power utility for EUR 5.2m. The estimated incremental costs that would be directly attributable to the disposal are EUR 100,000. Management have no intention of selling the power station and are proposing to recognise an impairment charge based on its value in use.

Is this correct? Why?

10.8 Recoverable amount

The following information relates to individual equipment items of entity H at a balance sheet date:

	Carrying amount €	Fair value less costs to sell €	Value in use €
Item 1	119,000	121,000	114,000
Item 2 (note 1)	237,000	207,000	205,000
Item 3 (note 1)	115,000	117,000	123,000
Item 4	83,000	75,000	79,000
Item 5 (note 2)	31,000	26,000	–

Notes:

1 Items 2 and 3 are carried at revalued amounts, and the cumulative revaluation surpluses included in equity for the items are EUR 12,000 and EUR 6,000 respectively. Both items are manufacturing equipment.

2 Item 5 is a bus used for transporting employees in the mornings and evenings. It is not possible to determine the value in use of the bus separately because the bus does not generate cash inflows from continuing use that are independent of the cash flows from other assets.

Illustrate the major issues relating to the possible impairment of the five items.

10.9 CGU

A manufacturing entity owns several vehicles. The vehicles are several years old and could only be sold for scrap value. They do not generate cash independently from the entity.

How should the recoverable value of the vehicles be determined?

10.10 CGU

A railway entity has a contract with the government that requires service on each of 10 different routes. The trains operating on each route and the income from each route can be identified easily. Two of the routes make substantially more profit than the others. The entity also operates a taxi service, a bus company, and a travel agency.

What is the lowest level of CGUs that can be used by the entity?

10.11 Allocation of an impairment loss

A cash-generating unit has the following net assets:

	€m
Goodwill	10
Property	20
Plant and Equipment	30
	60

The recoverable amount has been determined at EUR 45m.

Allocate the impairment loss to the net assets of the entity.

10.12 Allocation of reversal of impairment losses for a CGU

Management of entity I are thinking of allocating the reversal of an impairment loss of a CGU. The original impairment was EUR 990 based on an original carrying amount of the CGU of EUR 2,790 less recoverable amount of EUR 1,800. Of the impairment loss EUR 600 was allocated to the write off of goodwill. Now the recoverable amount of the CGU is estimated at EUR 2,000. The carrying amount of the net assets of the CGU is EUR 1,600. There is thus a reversal of the impairment loss of EUR 400. Details of the original impairment allocation and the present carrying amounts, and the amounts that the assets would have been carried at had the original impairment not occurred are as follows:

Assets	Original carrying amount €	Impairment €	Original carrying amount after impairment €	Present carrying amount (after depreciation)* €	Carrying amount without impairment (after depreciation)* €
Goodwill	590	(590)	Nil	Nil	590
Property A	1,010	(10)	1,000	960	960
Machine A	180	(20)	160	120	140
Machine B	250	(92)	98	130	200
Machine C	260	(96)	164	130	220
Intangible A	500	(182)	318	260	460
Total	2,790	(990)	1,800	1,600	2,580

* The figures in the last two columns are not precise and assume in some cases changes in depreciation rates/useful lives following recognition of the original impairment.

Illustrate the revised estimates of recoverable amount and allocation of the reversal of the impairment loss.

11

Provisions, contingencies and events after the reporting period (IAS 37 and IAS 10)

Contents

Example 11.2

Provision versus contingent liability

In May 2008, ABC plc (which prepares financial statements to 30 June) guaranteed a EUR 200,000 bank loan provided to DEF Ltd. DEF Ltd was in a strong financial position at 30 June 2008, but this had worsened by 30 June 2009 and it seemed likely on that date that ABC plc would be required to honour its guarantee.

Explain how this guarantee should be treated in the financial statements of ABC plc at 30 June 2008 and 2009.

At 30 June 2008, there was a present obligation arising from a past event. However, an outflow of economic benefits did not seem probable, so no provision should be made. The guarantee falls within the definition of a contingent liability and should be disclosed in the notes to the financial statements, unless the possibility of an outflow of benefits was judged to be remote.

At 30 June 2009, there is still a present obligation arising from a past event, but now it seems probable that there will be an outflow of economic benefits. As long as a reliable estimate of the obligation can be made (which will almost certainly be the case) a provision should be made in relation to this obligation.

---

2. Summary of Significant Accounting Policies (extract)

2.24. Nuclear Provisions
The Group has recognized provisions for its obligations to decommission its nuclear power plants at the end of their operating lives, to store the related spent nuclear fuel and other radioactive waste initially on an interim basis and provision for its obligation to provide financing for subsequent permanent storage of spent fuel and irradiated parts of reactors (see Note 17).

The provisions recognized represent the best estimate of the expenditures required to settle the present obligation at the current balance sheet data. Such cost estimates, expressed at current price levels at the date of the estimate, are discounted using a long-term real rate of interest of 2.5% per annum to take into account the timing of payments. The initial discounted cost amounts are capitalized as part of property, plant and equipment and are depreciated over the lives of the nuclear plants. Each year, the provisions are increased to reflect the accretion of discount and to accrue an estimate for the effects of inflation, with the charges being recognized as a component of interest expense. At December 31, 2008 and 2007 the estimate for the effect of inflation is 2.5% and 2.0%, respectively.

The decommissioning process is expected to continue for approximately a fifty-year period for Temelin plant and sixty-year period for Dukovany plant subsequent to the final operation of the plants. It is currently anticipated that the permanent storage facility will become available in 2065 and the process of final disposal of the spent nuclear fuel will then continue until approximately 2075 when the process should be finished. While the Group has made its best estimate in establishing its nuclear provisions, because of potential changes in technology as well as safety and environmental requirements, plus the actual time scale to complete decommissioning and fuel storage activities, the ultimate provision requirements could vary significantly from the Group's current estimates.

Changes in a decommissioning liability that result from a change in the current best estimate of cash flows required to settle the obligation or a change in the discount rate are added to (or deducted from) the amount recognized as the related asset. However, to the extent that such a treatment would result in a negative asset, the effect of the change is recognized in the income for the current period.

Figure 11.2 Decommissioning provision disclosure under IAS 37
Source: CEZ Group Annual Report 2008.

2.25. Provisions for Decommissioning and Reclamation of Mines and Mining Damages

The Group has recognized provision for obligations to decommission and reclaim mines at the end of their operating lives (see Note 18). The provisions recognized represent the best estimate of the expenditures required to settle the present obligation at the current balance sheet date. Such cost estimates, expressed at current price levels, are discounted using a long-term real rate of interest of 2.5% per annum to take into account the timing of payments. The initial discounted cost amounts are capitalized as part of property, plant and equipment and are depreciated over the lives of the mines. Each year, the provisions are increased to reflect the accretion of discount and to accrue an estimate for the effects of inflation, with the charges being recognized as a component of interest expense. At December 31, 2008 and 2007 the estimate for the effect of inflation is 2.5% and 2.0%, respectively.

Changes in a decommissioning liability that result from a change in the current best estimate of cash flows required to settle the obligation or a change in the discount rate are added to (or deducted from) the amount recognized as the related asset. However, to the extent that such a treatment would result in a negative asset, the effect of the change is recognized in the income for the current period.

2.7. Property, Plant and Equipment

Property, plant and equipment are recorded at cost, net of accumulated depreciation and valuation allowances. Cost of plant in service includes materials, labor, payroll-related costs and the cost of debt financing used during construction. The cost also includes the estimated cost of dismantling and removing the asset and restoring the site, to the extent that is recognized as a provision under IAS 37, Provisions, Contingent Liabilities and Contingent Assets. Government grants received for construction of certain items of property, plant and equipment decrease the acquisition cost of the respective items.

Internally developed property, plant and equipment are recorded at their accumulated cost. The costs of completed technical improvements are capitalized. Upon sale, retirement or replacement of part of an item of property, plant and equipment the cost and related accumulated depreciation of the disposed item or its replaced part are derecognized from balance sheet. Any resulting gains or losses are included in profit or loss.

At each reporting date, the Company assesses whether there is any indication that an asset may be impaired. Where an indicator of impairment exists, the Company reviews the recoverable amounts of its property, plant and equipment to determine whether such amounts continue to exceed the assets' carrying values. Identified impairment of property, plant and equipment is recognized directly in profit or loss in the line item of Other operating expenses.

At each reporting date an assessment is made as to whether there is any indication that previously recognized impairment losses may no longer exist or may have decreased. If such indication exists, the Company makes an estimate of recoverable amount. A previously recognized impairment loss is reversed only if there has been a change in the estimates used to determine the asset's recoverable amount since the last impairment loss was recognized. If that is the case the carrying amount of the asset is increased to its recoverable amount. That increased amount cannot exceed the carrying amount that would have been determined, net of depreciation, had no impairment loss been recognized for the asset in prior years. Such reversal is recognized in profit or loss in the line item of Other operating expenses.

4. Property, Plant and Equipment (extract)

At December 31, 2008 and 2007, machinery and equipment included the capitalized costs of nuclear provisions as follows (in CZK millions):

	2008	2007
Cost	17,828	21,967
Accumulated depreciation	(5,319)	(4,802)
Net book value	12,509	17,165

16. Accumulated Provision for Nuclear Decommissioning and Fuel Storage

The Company operates two nuclear power plants. Nuclear power plant Dukovany consists of four 440 MW units which were put into service from 1985 to 1987. The second unclear power plant, Temelin, has two 1,000 MW units, which started commercial operation in 2002 and 2003. Czech parliament has enacted a Nuclear Act ('Act'), which defines certain obligations for the decontamination and dismantling ('decommissioning') of nuclear facilities and the disposal of radioactive waste and spent fuel ('disposal'). The Act requires that all nuclear parts of plant

Figure 11.2 *(Cont'd)*

and equipment be decommissioned following the end of the plant's operating life, currently 2027 for Dukovany and approximately 2042 for Temelin. An updated 2008 Dukovany and a 2004 Temelin decommissioning cost study estimate that nuclear decommissioning will cost CZK 17.3 billion and CZK 13.7 billion, respectively. The Company makes contributions to a restricted bank account in the amount of the nuclear provisions recorded under the Act. These restricted funds can be invested in government bonds and term deposits in accordance with the legislation and are shown in the balance sheet under other non-current financial assets (see Note 5).

The Ministry of Industry and Trade established the Radioactive Waste Repository Authority ('RAWRA') as the central organizer and operator of facilities for the final disposal of radioactive waste and spent fuel. The RAWRA centrally organizes, supervises and is responsible for all disposal facilities and for disposal of radioactive waste and spent fuel therein. The activities of the RAWRA are financed through a 'nuclear account' funded by the originators of radioactive waste (such as the Company). Contribution to the nuclear account was stated by a government resolution at 50 CZK per MWh produced at nuclear power plants. In 2008 and 2007, respectively, the payments to the nuclear account amounted to CZK 1,328 million and CZK 1,307 million, respectively. The originator of radioactive waste directly covers all costs associated with interim storage of radioactive waste and spent fuel. Actual costs incurred are charged against the accumulated provision for interim storage of spent nuclear fuel.

The Company has established provisions as described in Note 2.21, to recognize its estimated liabilities for decommissioning and spent fuel storage.

The following is a summary of the provisions for the years ended December 31, 2008 and 2007 (in CZK millions).

| | | Accumulated provisions | | |
| | Nuclear Decommissioning | Spent fuel storage | | Total |
		Interim	Long-term	
Balance at December 31, 2006	9,982	4,896	21,625	36,503
Movements during 2007				
Discount accretion	249	122	541	912
Effect of inflation	199	98	433	730
Provision charged to income statement	–	393	–	393
Effect of change in estimate charged to income statement	–	439	–	439
Effect of change in estimate added to (deducted from) fixed assets	(4)	32	1,467	1,495
Current cash expenditures	–	(168)	(1,307)	(1,475)
Balance at December 31, 2007	10,426	5,812	22,759	38,997
Movements during 2008				
Discount accretion	261	146	569	976
Effect of inflation	208	116	455	779
Provision charged to income statement	–	346	–	346
Effect of change in estimate charged to income statement	–	203	–	203
Effect of change in estimate added to (deducted from) fixed assets	(2,866)	23	(1,273)	(4,116)
Current cash expenditures	–	(435)	(1,328)	(1,763)
Balance at December 31, 2008	8,029	6,211	21,182	35,422

The current cash expenditures for the long-term storage of spent nuclear fuel represent payments to the state controlled nuclear account and the expenditures for interim storage represent mainly the purchase of interim fuel storage containers.

In 2007 the Company recorded the change in estimate for long-term fuel storage due to the modification of the expected output of the nuclear power plants.

In 2008 the Company recorded the change in estimate for nuclear decommissioning due to the update of the expert decommissioning study for nuclear power plant in Dukovany and the change in estimate in provision for long-term spent fuel storage due to the change in discount rate.

The actual decommissioning and spent fuel storage costs could vary substantially from the above estimates because of new regulatory requirements, changes in technology, increased costs of labor, materials, and equipment and/or the actual time required to complete all decommissioning, disposal and storage activities.

Figure 11.2 (Cont'd)

11.2   Measurement of a provision

As mentioned earlier, the amount of a provision should be the best estimate of the expenditure required to settle the obligation concerned. This is of course a matter of judgement and may require advice from independent experts. Note that:

(a) if the effect of the time value of money is material, the amount of the provision should be calculated as the present value of the expenditure required to settle the obligation;

(b) future events that may affect the amount required to settle an obligation should be taken into account when measuring a provision, so long as there is sufficient objective evidence that such events will occur. For instance, the estimated costs of cleaning up environmental damage might be reduced by anticipated changes in technology.

If a single obligation is being measured and there are several possible outcomes, each with a different cost, the best estimate of the required expenditure will usually be the cost of the most likely outcome. However, if most of the other possible outcomes would involve a higher cost, the best estimate of the expenditure will be a higher amount. Similarly, if most of the other possible outcomes would involve a lower cost, the best estimate of the expenditure will be a lower amount.

In cases where a provision relates to a large population of items, the amount of the provision should be estimated by calculating the 'expected value' of the obligation at the balance sheet date. This statistical method of estimation involves weighting all possible outcomes by their associated probabilities and is illustrated in the example below.

Example 11.3

Measurement of a provision

An entity sells goods with a six-month warranty. If minor defects were detected in all of the goods covered by warranties at the balance sheet date, the entity would incur costs of EUR 1m. If major defects were detected in all of the goods covered by warranties at the balance sheet date, the company would incur costs of EUR 4m. Experience shows that 75 per cent of goods sold have no defects, 20 per cent have minor defects and 5 per cent have major defects.

What is the expected value of the cost of repairs under warranties?

The expected value of the costs of repairs is:

$$(75\% \times € \text{ nil}) + (20\% \times €1m) + (5\% \times €4m) = €400,000$$

Changes in provisions and use of provisions

IAS 37 requires that a provision should be reviewed at each balance sheet date and adjusted to reflect the current best estimate of the required expenditure. If it is no longer probable that an outflow of economic benefits will be required to settle an obligation, the related provision should be reversed.

IAS 37 also requires that a provision should be used only for the purpose for which it was originally established.

11.3   Application of the recognition and measurement rules

Having established the recognition and measurement rules described above, IAS 37 then explains how these general rules should be applied in three specific cases. The three cases identified are future operating losses, onerous contracts and restructuring costs. A brief summary of the requirements of IAS 37 in respect of each of these is given below:

(a) *Future operating losses*. Future operating losses are not present obligations so they do not satisfy the recognition criteria for a provision. Therefore, provisions should not be recognised for future operating losses.

(b) *Onerous contracts*. An onerous contract is a contract 'in which the unavoidable costs of meeting the obligations under the contract exceed the economic benefits expected to be received under it'. If an entity has a contract that is onerous, the present obligation under that contract should be measured and recognised as a provision.

(c) *Restructuring costs*. A provision for restructuring costs (e.g. the costs of a major reorganisation) should be recognised only if the general recognition criteria set out in IAS 37 are satisfied. In particular:

(i)   A constructive obligation to restructure arises only when the entity has a detailed formal plan for the restructuring and has raised a valid expectation in those affected that it will carry out the restructuring, either by beginning to implement the plan or by announcing its main features.

(ii) If the restructuring involves the sale of an operation, no obligation for that sale arises until there is a binding sale agreement.

(iii) A provision for restructuring costs should include only direct costs arising from the restructuring.

The last of these rules means that staff retraining and relocation costs, marketing costs and the cost of investment in new systems should not be included in the amount of a provision for restructuring costs as these costs are associated with the ongoing activities of the entity.

Example 11.4

Recognition and measurement of a provision

The following information relates to an entity which prepares financial statements to 31 December each year:

(a) On 1 January 2009, the entity acquired new plant costing EUR 20 million. This plant will require a complete overhaul after five years of use, at an estimated cost of EUR 2 million. Accordingly, the entity wishes to make a provision of EUR 400,000 for plant overhaul costs in its financial statements for the year ended 31 December 2009 and then to increase this provision by EUR 400,000 in each of the next four years. This will have the effect of spreading the overhaul costs evenly over the years 2009 to 2013.

(b) On 31 December 2009, the entity moved from leased premises into new freehold premises. The lease on the old premises will continue for three more years at an annual cost of EUR 200,000. The lease cannot be cancelled and the premises cannot be sublet or used for any other purpose. The entity wishes to make a provision of EUR 600,000 in its financial statements for the year ended 31 December 2009.

(c) In November 2009, the entity decided to sell off one of its operations. No buyer had been found at 31 December 2009, but the sale is expected to result in a loss of EUR 1 million when it occurs. The entity wishes to provide for this loss in the financial statements for the year ended 31 December 2009.

Should any of these provisions be made in accordance with IAS 37?

(a) At 31 December 2009, there is no obligation to undertake the overhaul that is due in five years time. The plant could in fact be sold before the overhaul is required. Therefore, no provision should be made for the overhaul costs. IAS 16 – *Property, Plant and Equipment* prescribes the accounting treatment for this type of expenditure.

(b) In general, IAS 37 does not apply to leases. But this is an example of an onerous contract and IAS 37 does apply to such contracts. The obligation of EUR 600,000 is unavoidable and should be provided for.

(c) IAS 37 states that there is no present obligation in relation to the sale of an operation until a binding sale agreement exists. There is no such agreement at 31 December 2009 so there is no present obligation on that date. A provision should not be made.

11.4 Events after the reporing period (IAS 10)

IAS 10 defines events after the balance sheet date as 'those events, favourable and unfavourable, that occur between the balance sheet date and the date when the financial statements are authorised for issue'. Such events are classified into two types. These are:

(a) *Adjusting events*. Adjusting events are defined as 'those that provide evidence of conditions that existed at the balance sheet date'. An example of an adjusting event is the sale of inventories which were held at the balance sheet date. This event may provide useful evidence of their net realisable value on that date.

EUR 500,000. At 31 March 2010, the decision had not been announced and had not yet been acted upon.

(c) For the past few years, the company has been conducting two operations which cause environmental damage. One of these operations is in a country which by law requires companies to rectify any environmental damage which they cause. The other is in a country which has no such legislation. The costs of rectifying the damage caused to date by these two operations are estimated at EUR 10m and EUR 20m respectively.

(d) At 31 March 2010, the company owns a fleet of motor lorries, all of which require an annual service. This servicing work is expected to be performed during the year to 31 March 2011, at an estimated cost of EUR 100,000.

11.2 Measurement of provisions

(a) Explain how the amount of a provision should be measured.

(b) A company needs to make a provision for the cost of repairing a faulty product supplied to a customer some weeks previously. The company estimates that there is a 60 per cent chance that this repair will cost EUR 200,000. However, there is a 30 per cent chance that the cost will be EUR 300,000 and a 10 per cent chance that the cost will be EUR 400,000. How should the amount of the provision be measured?

11.3 Recognition of a provision

At its balance sheet date, an entity has each of the following:

(a) a present obligation which will probably require an outflow of resources;

(b) a present obligation which will probably not require an outflow of resources;

(c) a possible obligation arising from a disputed past event; the entity denies that this event occurred and a legal case is currently proceeding; it seems likely that the entity will win the case and that an outflow of resources will not be required;

(d) a possible obligation arising from another disputed past event; the entity again denies that this event occurred and again a legal case is currently proceeding; it seems likely that the entity will lose this case and that an outflow of resources will be required.

State, for each of these obligations, whether the entity should recognise a provision, disclose a contingent liability or do nothing. Assume that all of the obligations arise from past events and that reliable estimates can be made of the amounts concerned.

11.4 Recognition of a provision

Kenton Ltd prepares financial statements to 30 April each year. At 30 April 2010, the company is being sued by a customer who claims to have been harmed by one of the company's products. The case will come before the courts in late 2010.

Explain how this matter should be dealt with in the financial statements for the year ended 30 April 2010 if:

(a) the company's lawyers advise that the company will probably be found liable;

(b) the company's lawyers advise that the company will probably not be found liable.

11.5 Provisions

The annual accounting date of Lawson plc is 31 May. The following matter needs to be dealt with before the financial statements for the year ended 31 May 2010 can be finalised. The company operates an open-cast mine and is legally obliged to restore the environment when mine workings are complete. This is expected to occur in the year 2021. The estimated cost of rectifying the environmental damage so far is EUR 6m. The estimated total cost of rectifying the damage caused until mine workings are complete is EUR 50m.

Explain how this matter should be dealt with in the financial statements for the year ended 31 May 2010.

11.6 Events after the reporting period

An entity prepares financial statements to 31 December each year. The following events occurred after 31 December 2009 but before the financial statements for the year ended 31 December 2009 were authorised for issue:

(a) Inventory held at 31 December 2009 was sold to a customer.
(b) The entity made a major investment in plant and equipment.
(c) The entity made a take-over bid for another entity.
(d) A customer who owed an amount of money to the entity on 31 December 2009 was declared bankrupt.
(e) The entity announced a major restructuring plan.
(f) It was discovered that cash shown as an asset in the balance sheet at 31 December 2009 had been stolen on 28 December 2009.
(g) It was discovered that an item of equipment shown as an asset in the balance sheet at 31 December 2009 had been stolen on 12 January 2010.
(h) In February 2010 the government announced a change in tax rates that will have a significant effect on the entity's tax liability at 31 December 2009.

Classify each of these events as either an adjusting event or a non-adjusting event and explain how each event should be dealt with in the entity's financial statements for the year ended 31 December 2009. Assume that all the above events are material.

11.7 IAS 10 and IAS 37 requirements

Triangle, a public listed company, is in the process of finalising its draft financial statements for the year ended 31 March 2010. The following matters have been brought to your attention:

(i) On 1 April 2009 the company brought into use a new processing plant that had cost EUR 30m to construct and had an estimated life of ten years.

The plant uses hazardous chemicals which are put in containers and shipped abroad for safe disposal after processing. The chemicals have contaminated the plant itself which occurred as soon as the plant was used. It is a legal requirement that the plant is decontaminated at the end of its life. The estimated present value of this decontamination, using a discount rate of 8 per cent per annum, is EUR 10m. EUR 3m (EUR 30m/ 10 years) for plant depreciation and a provision of EUR 1m (EUR 10m/ 10 years) towards the cost of the decontamination have been accounted for in the draft financial statements as at 31 March 2010.

(ii) On 15 May 2010 the company's auditors discovered a fraud in the material requisitions department. A senior member of staff who took up employment with Triangle in August 2009 had been authorising payments for goods that had never been received. The payments were made to a fictitious company that cannot be traced. The member of staff was immediately dismissed. Calculations show that the total amount of the fraud to the date of its discovery was EUR 480,000 of which EUR 420,000 related to the year ended 31 March 2010. (Assume the fraud is material.)

(iii) The company has contacted its insurers in respect of the above fraud. Triangle is insured for theft, but the insurance company maintains that this is a commercial fraud and is not covered by the theft clause in the insurance policy. Triangle has not yet had an opinion from its lawyers.

Explain how the items in (i) and (ii) above should be treated in Triangle's financial statements for the year ended 31 March 2010 in accordance with IFRS. Your answer should quantify the amounts where possible.

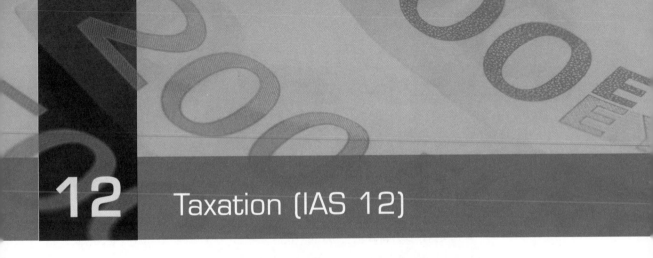

12 Taxation (IAS 12)

Contents

Objectives

When you have completed this chapter you should be able to:

- Understand differences between accounting and tax treatment for a range of transactions
- Calculate and account for current tax expense
- Explain the concept of deferred taxation
- Calculate and account for movements in deferred taxation accounts
- Account for changes in tax rates.

12.1   Introduction

Accounting profit is defined in IAS 12 – *Income Taxes* as *'profit or loss for a period before deducting tax expense'* (IAS 12 para 5), profit or loss being the excess (or deficiency) of revenues over expenses for that period. Such revenues and expenses would be determined and recognised in accordance with IAS/IFRS and the IASB *Framework*. Taxable profit is defined as *'the profit for a period, determined in accordance with the rules established by the taxation authorities, upon which income taxes are payable'* (IAS 12 para 5). Taxable profit is the excess of taxable income over taxable deductions allowable against that income. Thus, accounting profit and taxable profit – because they are determined by different principles and rules – are unlikely to be the same figure in any one period. Tax expense cannot be determined by simply multiplying the accounting profit by the applicable tax rate. Instead, accounting for income taxes involves identifying and accounting for the differences between accounting profit and taxable profit. These differences arise for a number of transactions and may be either permanent or temporary (see section 12.3 below).

12.2   Accounting for current taxes

IAS 12 does not cover current tax to the same degree of detail that it deals with deferred tax. However, a number of issues arise in respect of current tax, such as recognition and measurement of current tax liabilities and current tax assets in the balance sheet, uncertain tax positions, presentation and disclosure of current tax.

12.2.1 Recognition of current tax liabilities and current tax assets

IAS 12 defines current tax as *'the amount of income taxes payable (recoverable) in respect of the taxable profit (tax loss[1]) for a period'*. The term 'income taxes' refers to any tax payable on an entity's profits, regardless of the name given to that tax in the country concerned. The main requirements of IAS 12 with regard to current tax may be summarised as follows:

(a) The amount of current tax for an accounting period should generally be recognised as an expense (or as an income in the case of tax recoverable) and shown in the income statement. However, any current tax that arises on a transaction or event which is recognised directly in equity should also be recognised in equity. Items are 'recognised directly in equity' if they are excluded from the income statement but are shown instead in other comprehensive income. Examples include:

  • revaluation gains (see Chapter 7);
  • retrospective adjustments arising from a change in accounting policy or the correction of a prior period error (see Chapter 4).

  Any amount of tax which is due or recoverable relating to such items should not be shown in the income statement but should be shown in other comprehensive income (see Chapter 3).

  Note that there will usually be a single figure for income taxes in the income statement, made up of both current tax and (if any) deferred tax. An analysis of this single figure should be provided in the notes to the financial statements.

(b) The amount of any current tax that remains unpaid at the balance sheet date should be recognised as a liability. If the amount already paid exceeds the amount due, the excess should be recognised as an asset.

  Current tax assets and liabilities should be offset in the balance sheet only if there is a legally enforceable right to set off the amounts concerned and the entity intends to do so. This would not apply if, for example, the entity owed tax in one country and a refund of a tax was receivable in another country.

(c) Current tax should be measured using tax rates and tax laws *'that have been enacted or substiatially enacted by the balance sheet date'*. Tax rates and laws which have been announced but not enacted by the balance sheet date can be treated as 'substiantially enacted' if their enactment (which may occur several months after the announcement) is regarded as more or less a formality.

  Tax rates and laws which are announced after the balance sheet date are dealt with as non-adjusting events in accordance with international standard IAS 10 – *Events after the balance sheet date*.

(d) Any adjustments necessary to reflect underestimates or overestimates of current tax in previous periods should be included in the tax expense for the current period.

Example 12.1

Current taxes

The following information relates to entity A which prepares accounts to 30 June each year and is now completing its financial statements for the year ended 30 June 2010:

(a) The entity estimates that current tax for the year ended 30 June 2010 is EUR 750,000. This figure takes into account the new tax rates which were announced in March 2010 and which are confidently expected to be enacted in August 2010. If the new tax rates were disregarded, the amount due would be EUR 810,000.

(b) Payments on account totalling EUR 390,000 were made during the year ended 30 June 2010 relating to the current tax for the year.

(c) The current tax for the year ended 30 June 2009 was overestimated by EUR 30,000.

We illustrate below how to determine the amount of the current tax expense which should be shown in the income statement for the year ended 30 June 2010 and the amount of the current tax liability which should be shown in the balance sheet at the same date.

The new tax rates can be regarded as substiantially enacted so the current tax for the year is EUR 750,000. However, the income statement should show a current tax expense of EUR 720,000, so as to adjust for the previous year's overestimate of EUR 30,000.

Payments on account of EUR 390,000 reduce the current tax liability in the balance sheet to EUR 360,000 (EUR 750,000 – EUR 390,000).

12.2.2 Uncertain tax position

There may be situations when an entity's tax position is uncertain; for example, the tax treatment of an item of expense has been challenged by the tax authorities. Uncertainties relating to income taxes are not addressed specifically in IAS 12. IAS 37 – *Provisions, Contingent Liabilities and Contingent Assets*, excludes income taxes from its scope so no guidance is provided to measure uncertain tax positions. The general measurement principles, therefore, should be applied: 'Current tax liabilities (assets) for the current and prior periods should be measured at the amount expected to be paid to (recovered from) the taxation authorities using the tax rates (and tax laws) that have been enacted or substantially enacted at the balance sheet date' (IAS 12 para 46). An entity may choose to consider uncertain tax positions at the level of the individual uncertainty or a group of related uncertainties. Alternatively, it may choose to consider tax uncertainties at the level of its total tax liability to each tax authority.

In Example 12.2 below we have assumed that the entity has elected to consider tax uncertainties at the level of each uncertainty and that it is probable (more likely that not) that the tax will be payable.

Example 12.2

Uncertain tax positions

(a) Entity B included deductions in a tax return that may be challenged by the tax authorities resulting in an uncertain tax position. Entity B and its tax consultants estimate the probability of the potential outcomes for additional tax payable as shown in Table 12.1 below.

Table 12.1 Probability of potential outcomes for additional tax payable (case a)

Potential tax payable €	Individual probability %	Cumulative probability %	Probability-weighted calculation €
1,600	15	15	240
1,200	30	45	360
800	20	65	160
400	20	85	80
0	15	100	–
			840

- Most likely outcome: EUR 1,200 (probability of 30 per cent).
- Probability weighted outcome: EUR 840.

(b) Entity B takes a deduction in its tax return that may be subject to challenge by the tax authorities. It is estimated that there is a 40 per cent probability that an additional tax of EUR 240 will be payable and a 60 per cent probability that an additional tax of EUR 160 will be payable.

- Most likely outcome: EUR 160.
- Probability weighted outcome: EUR 192 (EUR 240 × 40% + EUR 160 × 60%).

(c) A deduction of EUR 600 may be subject to challenge. Table 12.2 shows how entity B and its tax consultants estimate the probability of the potential outcomes for the additional tax payable.

Table 12.2 Probability of potential outcomes for additional tax payable (case c)

Potential tax payable €	Individual probability %	Cumulative probability %	Probability-weighted calculation €
200	45	45	90
160	10	55	16
100	25	80	25
0	20	100	0
			131

- Probability weighted outcome: EUR 131.
- It would not be logical to use EUR 200 as the most likely outcome in this case, as it is more likely than not that some of the deductions will be accepted by the tax authorities. Whilst there is a 45 per cent chance that the full amount of EUR 200 will be payable, there is a 55 per cent chance of reduced tax being payable on the basis of the information given above. In this scenario, measurement using the probability weighted average method would be appropriate.

12.3 Accounting for deferred taxes

12.3.1 Temporary and permanent differences between taxable profit and accounting profit

When determining taxable profit, an entity may be allowed or required by the tax code to use accounting rules that are different from those that comply with IFRS. The resulting differences might increase or decrease profit. For example, an entity may be allowed to apply diminishing-balance depreciation to compute taxable profit and thereby defer its current tax liability, while at the same time it is required to use the straight-line depreciation method for determining the accounting profit in accordance with IFRS.

There are two main reasons why accounting profit and taxable profit can be different:

- *Permanent differences* are those differences between accounting profit and taxable profit that arise when income is not taxed or expenses are not tax deductible. For example, tax-free interest income is not included in taxable profit, even though it is part of the accounting profit.

- *Temporary differences* are those differences between accounting profit and taxable profit for an accounting period that arise whenever the measurement of assets and liabilities for income tax purposes differ from the measurement of assets and liabilities in accordance with IFRS. For example, if an entity uses the straight-line depreciation method for accounting purposes and diminishing-balance depreciation for income tax purposes, the book carrying amount of the assets will differ from the tax carrying amount of those assets. For income tax purposes, tax depreciation will be greater than IFRS depreciation in the early years and lower than IFRS depreciation in the later years of the asset's useful life.

Permanent differences affect the current accounting period's effective income tax rate (the ratio of the reported income tax expense to pretax profit), but do not have any impact on future income taxes. Temporary differences, on the other hand, affect the current year's income taxes and the income taxes that will be paid in future years because they represent a deferral of taxable profit from the current to subsequent accounting periods (or bringing forward of taxable profit from the future periods to the current accounting period).

Example 12.3

Temporary and permanent differences between accounting profit and taxable profit

In the year just ended, Engine Works generated earnings from operations before depreciation and income taxes of EUR 6,000. In addition, it earned EUR 100 of tax-free municipal bond interest income. It has only two assets subject to depreciation: one machine that was purchased at the beginning of last year for EUR 5,000, and another one that was purchased at the beginning of this year for EUR 10,000. Both machines are being depreciated over 10 years. Engine Works uses diminishing-balance depreciation method to compute depreciation for income tax purposes (worth EUR 3,000 this year) and the straight-line method to calculate depreciation for financial reporting purposes. The tax rate is 35 per cent.

Based on the information provided, Engine Works's income tax return and income statement for the **current** year would be as shown in Table 12.3.

Table 12.3 Taxable profit and accounting profit

Income tax return	€	Income statement	€
Income from operations before depreciation and income taxes	6,000	Income from operations before depreciation and income taxes	6,000
Tax-free interest income*		Tax-free interest income	100
Depreciation	(3,000)	Depreciation**	(1,500)
Taxable profit	3,000	Pretax profit	4,600
Income taxes payable to tax authorities (35% of 3,000)	1,050	Income tax expense	1,575***
		• Current	1,050
		• Deferred	525
			1,575***

* Tax-free interest income is excluded from taxable profit.
** (€5,000 ÷ 10 years) + (€10,000 ÷ 10 years) = €1,500.
*** €4,600 − €100 = €4,500 × 35% = €1,575

Based on the income tax return, the income tax that is payable to the tax authorities is EUR 1,050 whereas the income tax expense based on the accounting pretax profit is EUR 1,575. How is it determined?

As you can see from Table 12.3, there is a difference between pretax accounting profit and taxable profit of EUR 1,600. This difference consists of:

- EUR 100 of tax-free interest income that will never be taxed, but is part of pretax accounting profit. This is a *permanent difference* because this income is permanently excluded from taxation; the amount of tax that should be paid now or in the future is nil for both income tax and financial accounting purposes.
- EUR 1,500. The difference between the diminishing-balance depreciation (EUR 3,000) and the straight-line depreciation (EUR 1,500) is a *temporary difference* because the taxes that are 'saved' in the current year are deferred until the temporary differences start reversing. Over the life of the equipment the total depreciation expense will be the same for income tax and accounting purposes. The amount of EUR 1,500 represents the difference between the amounts of depreciation for the two machines based on the two depreciation methods. The income statement has a lower depreciation charge than the tax return and consequently a higher pretax profit. This difference will reverse over time when the straight-line depreciation will be higher than the reducing-balance depreciation.

If income tax expense is charged to the income statement without regard to the entity's actual tax obligation and the cash is reduced based on the payment of that actual obligation, then the dual aspect principle of accounting would be violated as shown in the journal entry below. Engine Works reports EUR 4,600 accounting profit (before tax) and income tax expense of EUR 1,050 (i.e. 35 per cent of its taxable profit) in its income statement, but only EUR 3,000 taxable profit to the tax authorities.

Assuming that all taxes need to be paid by the end of the period, the journal entry for these transactions would be as follows:

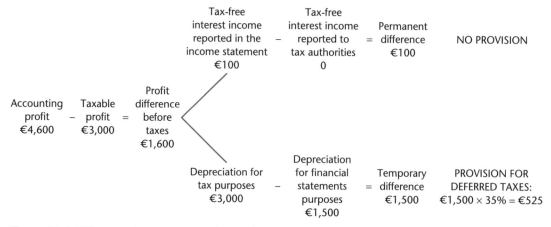

Figure 12.1 Differences between accounting profit and taxable profit and deferred taxes

Dr Tax expense	€1,575
Cr Cash	€1,050

However, as this entry does not balance, we may ask whether the difference of EUR 525 (= EUR 1,575 – EUR 1,050) represents a further reduction in assets, or an increase in a liability account or a component of profit.

The answer is that EUR 525 represents an increase in the liability (Deferred tax liability). In the balance sheet it is shown separately from Taxes Payable, which is the amount actually payable to the tax authorities in the current period.

Therefore the journal entry would be as follows:

Dr Current income tax expense	€1,050	
Dr Deferred income tax expense	€525	
Cr Cash		€1,050
Cr Deferred tax liability		€525

12.3.2 Deferred tax liabilities and deferred tax assets

Temporary differences give rise to deferred tax liabilities when they derive from a 'favourable' tax treatment (i.e. accelerated depreciation for tax purposes as opposed to economic depreciation for accounting purposes). A temporary difference will give rise to a deferred tax asset when an expense is recognised for book purposes in a period earlier than it is allowable or recognised for tax purposes.

In some circumstances the difference between accounting profit and taxable profit may result in a deferred tax asset. For example, IAS/IFRS require an entity to charge estimated future warranty costs as an expense of the period in which the warranted goods are sold, but tax rules generally do not permit deduction of such costs until they are actually incurred. This means that the entity which accrues warranty costs based on the best estimate of such costs will have a higher amount of accrued liability in its books or financial statements than in its tax return.

According to IAS 12, the carrying amount of a deferred tax asset should be reviewed at each balance sheet date. The carrying value of a deferred tax asset should be reduced to its net realisable value to the extent that it is no longer probable that sufficient taxable profit will be available to utilise the asset. Therefore, an asset should only be recognised when an entity expects to receive a benefit from its existence. The existence of a deferred tax liability (in the same jurisdiction) is strong evidence that the asset will be recoverable.

Example 12.4

Deferred tax assets

Consider the following situations:

	Situation 1	Situation 2
	€	€
Deferred tax liability	10,000	5,000
Deferred tax asset	(8,000)	(8,000)
Net position	2,000	(3,000)

- In situation 1 the existence of the liability ensures the recoverability of the asset and the asset should be provided.
- In situation 2 the company would provide for EUR 5,000 of the asset but would need to consider carefully the recoverability of the balance of EUR 3,000.

The measurement of deferred taxes should take place in two steps:

1 The first step consists of calculating the difference between the tax basis[2] and the book value of an individual taxable item in the balance sheet;

2 The second step consists of calculating the deferred income tax expense. This figure also represents the change in the 'Deferred tax liability' account for the period.

We illustrate this procedure in the next example. We show temporary differences created by the use of different depreciation methods for accounting and tax purposes, which is one of the most common sources of temporary differences in practice.

Example 12.5

Deferred tax measurement

On 1 January 2006, Huskes Ltd purchased for EUR 1.2m a single depreciable asset. For tax purposes it is depreciated over three years while for financial reporting purposes it is depreciated over five years using the straight-line method with residual value of nil. There are no other differences between accounting and tax rules for this entity. Assume that its profit before depreciation and taxes is EUR 1m each year and that the applicable tax rate is 40 per cent.

Table 12.4 shows the calculation of income taxes to be paid to the tax authorities in each of the five years to 31 December 2010.

Table 12.4 Income taxes payable

Year	Income before depreciation and taxes €000	Depreciation charge €000	Taxable income €000	Taxes due (at 40% rate) €000
2006	1,000	400	600	240
2007	1,000	400	600	240
2008	1,000	400	600	240
2009	1,000	–	1,000	400
2010	1,000	–	1,000	400
	5,000	**1,200**	**3,800**	**1,520**

Table 12.5 shows depreciation of the asset for tax purposes and its tax basis – balance of the asset account for tax purposes at the end of each year.

Table 12.5 Tax basis of the asset

Year	Original cost €000	Annual tax depreciation €000	Cumulative tax depreciation €000	Tax basis €000
2006	1,200	400	400	800
2007	1,200	400	800	400
2008	1,200	400	1,200	-0-
2009	1,200	-0-	1,200	-0-
2010	1,200	-0-	1,200	-0-

Table 12.6 presents depreciation for accounting purposes and the net book value of the asset at the end of each year.

Table 12.6 Depreciation for accounting purposes

Year	Original accounting cost €000	Accumulated depreciation €000	Net book value €000	Tax basis €000
2006	1,200	240	960	800
2007	1,200	480	720	400
2008	1,200	720	480	-0-
2009	1,200	960	240	-0-
2010	1,200	1,200	-0-	-0-

Table 12.7 shows the calculation of Huske Ltd's deferred income tax liability (first step described above) and deferred income tax expense (second step).

Table 12.7 Determination of deferred taxes

Year	Net book value €000	Tax basis €000	Net book value less tax basis €000	Deferred income tax liability (40%) €000	Deferred income tax expense €000
2006	960	800	160	64	64
2007	720	400	320	128	64
2008	480	-0-	480	192	64
2009	240	-0-	240	96	(96)
2010	-0-	-0-	-0-	-0-	(96)

Figure 12.2 shows the journal entries for each of the five years.

	Dr	Cr
2006		
Dr PPE	€1,200	
Cr Cash		€1,200
(Purchase of the asset)		
Dr Depreciation expense	€240	
Cr PPE		€240
(Depreciation expense)		
Dr Deferred taxes	€64	
Dr Current taxes	€240	
Cr Cash		€240
Cr Deferred tax liability		€64
(Determination of current and deferred taxes)		
2007		
Dr Depreciation expense	€240	
Cr PPE		€240
(Depreciation expense)		
Dr Deferred taxes	€64	
Dr Current taxes	€240	
Cr Cash		€240
Cr Deferred tax liability		€64
(Determination of current and deferred taxes)		
2008		
Same entries as Year 2		
2009		
Dr Depreciation expense	€240	
Cr PPE		€240
(Depreciation expense)		
Dr Deferred tax liability	€96	
Dr Current taxes	€400	
Cr Cash		€400
Cr Deferred taxes		€96
(Determination of current and deferred taxes)		
2010		
Same entries as 2009		

Figure 12.2 Journal entries (amounts in thousands of euro)

At the end of the life of the asset, the balance of the 'Deferred tax liability' account is nil.

12.3.3 Tax rate changes

Up to now we have assumed that the tax rate would remain constant indefinitely. What happens if income tax rates change? According to IAS 12, the balance in a deferred income tax account should be adjusted for a change in the tax rate. This adjustment affects accounting profit in the year in which the tax rate change is enacted; the adjustment is a component of income tax expense as shown in Example 12.6.

Example 12.6

Tax rate changes

On 31 December 2010, the balances of deferred tax accounts for Sabrina srl were as follows:

Deferred tax asset	€44,400
Deferred tax liability	€109,200

In June 2011, the tax authorities reduced the tax rate from 40 per cent to 30 per cent, effective from 1 January 2011.

As the deferred tax balances are now overstated, they should be adjusted as follows:

	Deferred tax asset	Deferred tax liability
Opening balance	€44,400	€109,200
Adjustment for change in tax rate: (40–30) ÷ 40	(€11,100)	(€27,300)
Restated balance	€33,300	€81,900

The adjusting journal entry is:

Dr Deferred tax liability	€27,300	
Cr Deferred tax asset		€11,100
Cr Income tax expense		€16,200

(Recognition of the impact of a change in tax rate on deferred tax amounts)

12.4 Financial analysis and interpretation

The first step in understanding how income taxes are accounted for in the financial statements according to the IFRS is to realise that the taxable profit and accounting profit have very different meanings. Taxable profit is computed using procedures that comply with the tax rules and is the basis upon which income taxes are paid. Accounting profit is computed using accounting policies that comply with IFRS.

Accounting policies (extract)

18. Deferred taxation assets and liabilities

Deferred taxation is recognised using the balance sheet liability method for all temporary differences, unless specifically exempt, at the tax rates that have been enacted or substantially enacted at the balance sheet date.

A deferred taxation asset represents the amount of income taxes recoverable in future periods in respect of deductible temporary differences, the carry forward of unused tax losses and the carry forward of unused tax credits (including unused credits for Secondary Taxation on Companies). Deferred taxation assets are only recognised to the extent that it is probable that taxable profits will be available against which deductible temporary differences can be utilised.

A deferred taxation liability represents the amount of income taxes payable in future periods in respect of taxable temporary differences. Deferred taxation liabilities are recognised for taxable temporary differences, unless specifically exempt.

Deferred taxation assets and liabilities are not recognised if the temporary difference arises from goodwill or from the initial recognition (other than in a business combination) of other assets and liabilities in a transaction that affects neither taxable income nor accounting profit.

Deferred taxation arising on investments in subsidiaries, associates and joint ventures is recognised except where the group is able to control the reversal of the temporary difference and it is probable that the temporary difference will not reverse in the foreseeable future.

Deferred taxation assets and liabilities are offset when there is a legally enforceable right to offset current taxation assets against current taxation liabilities and it is the intention to settle these on a net basis.

33. Taxation

The charge for current taxation is based on the results for the year as adjusted for income that is exempt and expenses that are not deductible using tax rates that are applicable to the taxable income.

Deferred taxation is recognised in profit or loss except when it relates to items credited or charged directly to equity, in which case it is also recognised in equity.

Secondary Taxation on Companies (STC) is recognised as part of the current taxation charge when the related dividend is declared. Deferred taxation is recognised if dividends received in the current year can be offset against future dividend payments to the extent of the reduction of future STC.

Figure 12.3 Tax and deferred tax accounting policies

Source: Barloworld Limited Annual Report 30 September 2008.

In determining taxable profit, an entity should comply with the tax rules which would be different to those that comply with IFRS. The resulting differences would either increase or decrease profits. For example, an entity may be allowed to use diminishing-balance depreciation to compute its taxable profit and thereby reduce and defer its tax liability, while at the same time it probably would use straight-line depreciation in determining its accounting profit under IFRS.

The second step is to understand the difference between current taxes, deferred tax assets and liabilities, and income tax expense. Current taxes represent the income tax owed to the tax authorities in accordance with the tax rules. Deferred taxes represent tax consequences of the recovery of assets and settlement of liabilities. Income tax expense is the expense reported in the income statement and includes

13

Employee benefits (IAS 19)

Contents

Objectives

When you have completed this chapter you should be able to:

- Describe the main categories of employee benefits
- Explain and apply the required accounting treatment for short-term employee benefits
- Explain the term 'post-employment benefit plan' and distinguish between defined contribution plans and defined benefit plans
- Explain and apply the required accounting treatment for defined contribution plans and defined benefit plans
- Outline the requirements of IAS 19 relating to other long-term benefits and termination benefits.

13.1   Introduction

IAS 19 – *Employee Benefits* identifies four categories of employee benefits:

(a) short-term employee benefits, such as wages, salaries and social security contributions, paid annual leave and paid sick leave, profit-sharing and bonuses (if payable within 12 months of the end of the period) and non-monetary benefits (such as medical care, housing, cars and free or subsidised goods or services) for current employees;

(b) post-employment benefits such as pensions, other retirement benefits, post-employment life insurance and post-employment medical care;

(c) other long-term employee benefits, including long-service leave or sabbatical leave, jubilee or other long-service benefits, long-term disability benefits and, if they are payable 12 months or more after the end of the period, profit-sharing, bonuses and deferred compensation; and

(d) termination benefits (IAS 19 para 4).

13.2   Short-term employee benefits

Short-term employee benefits are employee benefits (other than termination benefits) which should be expensed when incurred and the related liability falls due wholly within 12 months after the end of the period in which the employees render the related service (IAS 19 para 7).

The definition of short-term employee benefits covers items such as:

(a) wages, salaries and social security contributions;

(b) short-term compensated absences (such as paid annual leave and paid sick leave);

(c) profit-sharing and bonuses payable within twelve months after the end of the period in which the employees render the related service; and

(d) non-monetary benefits (such as medical care, housing, cars and free or sub-sidised goods or services) for current employees (IAS 19 para 8).

Accounting for short-term employee benefits does not generally present great difficulties (see IAS 19 para 9). In fact, if an employee has rendered services to an employer during an accounting period, the employer's financial statements for that period should recognise:

• an expense equal to the amount of the short-term employee benefits payable in exchange for those services, and

• a liability (accrued expense) after deducting any amount already paid.

An exception to the requirement to recognise an expense arises if another standard requires or permits the cost of the benefits to be recognised as an asset (see, for example, IAS 2 – *Inventories* and IAS 16 – *Property, Plant and Equipment*).

Note that short-term employee benefits are measured on an undiscounted basis, since the required payments are made either during the relevant accounting period or within 12 months of its end, so that the effect of discounting would be minimal.

13.2.1 Short-term compensated absences

IAS 19 para 11 uses the expression 'short-term compensated absences' to refer to paid employee absences (e.g. paid holidays and paid sick leave) which occur during the period in which the related employee services are performed or which are expected to occur within 12 months of the end of that period. Entitlement to compensated absences falls into two categories: *accumulating* and *non-accumulating*.

(a) *Accumulating compensated absences* are those that are carried forward and can be used in future periods if the current period's entitlement is not used in full. Accumulating compensated absences may be either vesting (in other words, employees are entitled to a cash payment for unused entitlement on leaving the entity) or non-vesting (when employees are not entitled to a cash payment for unused entitlement on leaving). An obligation arises as employees render services that increase their entitlement to future compensated absences. The obligation exists, and is recognised, even if the compensated absences are non-vesting, although the possibility that employees may leave before they use an accumulated non-vesting entitlement affects the measurement of that obligation (IAS 19 para 13).

(b) *Non-accumulating compensated absences* should not be carried forward: they lapse if the current period's entitlement is not used in full and do not entitle employees to a cash payment for unused entitlement on leaving the entity. This is commonly the case for sick pay (to the extent that unused past entitlement does not increase future entitlement), maternity or paternity leave and compensated absences for jury service or military service. An entity should not recognise any liability or expense until the time of the absence, because employee service does not increase the amount of the benefit (IAS 19 para 16).

Example 13.1

Accumulating compensated absences

An entity has 2,000 employees, each of whom is entitled to 10 days of paid sick leave in each calendar year. Unused sick leave at the end of each year may be carried forward for up to one further calendar year. Sick leave is taken first out of the current year's ten-day entitlement and then out of any unused entitlement brought forward.

At 31 December 2009, the average unused entitlement is six days per employee. Based on past experience, the entity expects that 85 per cent of employees will take no more than 10 days of sick leave in the forthcoming year but the remaining 15 per cent of employees will each take an average of 13 days.

Assuming an average cost to the entity of EUR 180 per day of paid sick leave, determine the liability which should appear on the entity's balance sheet as at 31 December 2009 in relation to paid sick leave.

1,700 employees are not expected to make use of their unused entitlement and therefore the amount expected to be accrued and paid for these employees is nil. The remaining 300 employees are each expected to use three days of their unused entitlement. Thus, the liability which should appear on the entity's balance sheet as at 31 December 2009 is EUR 162,000 (= 300 employees $\times$ 3 days $\times$ EUR 180).

13.2.2 Profit-sharing and bonus plans

IAS 19 para 17 states that an entity should recognise the expected cost of profit-sharing and bonus payments as short-term employee benefits when, and only when:

(a) the entity has a present legal or constructive obligation to make such payments as a result of past events; and

(b) a reliable estimate of the obligation can be made.

A *present obligation* exists when the employer has no realistic alternative but to make the payments concerned. This may be a legal obligation or it may be that the employer has a practice of making profit-sharing or bonus payments and this practice gives rise to a 'constructive' obligation. For example, an entity may have no legal obligation to pay a bonus. Nevertheless, in some cases, an entity has a practice of paying bonuses. In such cases, the entity has a constructive obligation to pay the bonuses. The measurement of a constructive obligation reflects the possibility that some employees may leave without receiving a bonus (IAS 19 para 19).

An obligation under profit-sharing and bonus plans arises as a result of employee service and not from a transaction with the entity's owners. Therefore, an entity should recognise the cost of profit-sharing and bonus plans not as a distribution of profit but as an expense (IAS 19 para 21).

If profit-sharing and bonus payments are not due wholly within twelve months after the end of the period in which the employees render the related service, those payments are other long-term employee benefits (IAS 19 para 22).

13.3   Post-employment benefits

Post-employment benefits consist mainly of retirement benefits, such as pensions. In some cases, the post-employment benefits scheme is administered directly by the employer. In other cases, a separate entity (a pension fund) is set up to receive contributions and pay employee benefits.

IAS 19 paras 24 to 28 distinguish between two types of pension scheme or 'plan':

- defined contribution plans; and
- defined benefit plans.

13.3.1 Defined contribution plans

Under defined contribution plans an employer pays fixed contributions into a pension fund each year and is not obliged to make any further contributions, even if the pension fund's assets are insufficient to pay the expected level of employee benefits. The risk that benefits will be less than expected falls upon the employees, not the employer.

Accounting for such a plan is generally straightforward and the required accounting treatment is similar to that required for short-term benefits. In general, if an employee has rendered services to an employer during an accounting period, the employer's financial statements for that period should recognise:

- an expense equal to the amount of the contributions payable by the employer into the defined contribution plan in exchange for those services; and
- a liability (accrued expense) equal to any part of this expense that has not been paid by the end of the period.

If the contributions already paid exceed the amount due to date, the excess should be recognised as an asset (prepaid expense) to the extent that this prepayment will lead to either a reduction in future payments or a cash refund.

13.3.2 Defined benefit plans

Defined benefit plans are post-employment benefit plans where the employer is obliged (either legally or constructively) to provide an agreed level of post-employment benefits. The employer's contributions are not limited to any fixed amount and these contributions may need to be increased if the pension fund has insufficient assets to pay the agreed level of benefits. The risk of having to make further contributions is borne by the employer, not the employee.

Accounting for defined benefit plans is highly complex and involves several steps which are illustrated below. The complexity arises because the expense recognised in each accounting period should be the cost to the employer of the retirement benefits that will eventually be paid to employees as a result of the services that they have received during that period. The problem is that these benefits may be payable in many years' time and their cost will depend upon a number of factors which are difficult to determine in advance, such as employee mortality rates and future returns on investments. The employer is exposed to both the 'actuarial risk' that employees will live longer than expected (which increases the cost of providing benefits) and the 'investment risk' that assets invested in the plan will be insufficient to pay the required benefits.

In these circumstances, the calculation of the expense which should be recognised for a defined benefit plan is not straightforward. Furthermore, the liability (or asset) should be calculated and shown in the employer's balance sheet relating to the plan. A simplified summary of the main features of the calculations is given below (IAS 19 para 50):

(a) At the end of each accounting period, reliable estimates should be made to determine the amount of the benefits that employees have earned in return for their services in prior periods ('the defined benefit obligation') and in the current period (the 'current service cost').

These estimates involve the making of assumptions with regard to such matters as employee mortality, employee turnover and future salary increase. Employers are encouraged (but not required) by IAS 19 to engage a qualified actuary to make the necessary estimates.

(b) These estimates are discounted so as to determine the present value of the defined benefit obligation and the present value of the current service cost.

(c) The 'interest cost' for the period is calculated. This is equal to the increase during the current accounting period of the present value of the defined benefit obligation calculated at the end of the previous period. This increase arises because the accumulated benefits which the employees had earned at the end of the previous period are now one period closer to being paid.

(d) 'Actuarial gains and losses' with regard to the defined obligation may now be calculated. These comprise:

(i) adjustments arising from differences between actuarial assumptions which were made at the end of the previous periods and actual events which occurred during the current period;

(ii) the effect of changes in actuarial assumptions between the start and end of the current period.

The overall actuarial gain or loss with regard to the defined benefit obligation for an accounting period is calculated by summarising the changes in that obligation during the period and inserting a balancing figure, as illustrated below:

2. SIGNIFICANT ACCOUNTING POLICIES (extract)

Leave benefits

Annual leave entitlement is provided for over the period that the leave accrues and is subject to a cap of 22 days.

Deferred bonus incentives

Employees of the wholly owned subsidiaries of Vodacom, including executive directors, are eligible for compensation benefits in the form of a Deferred Bonus Incentive Scheme. The benefit is recorded at the present value of the expected future cash outflows.

Short-term employee benefits

The cost of all short-term employee benefits is recognised during the year the employees render services, unless the Group uses the services of employees in the construction of an asset and the benefits received meet the recognition criteria of an asset, at which stage it is included as part of the related property, plant and equipment or intangible asset item.

	2007 Rm	2008 Rm	2009 Rm
29. PROVISIONS	1,443	1,675	1,875
Employee related	3,005	3,186	3,169
Annual leave	413	438	428
Balance at beginning of year	356	413	438
Transferred to disposal groups	–	–	(67)
Charged to employee expenses	66	44	72
Leave paid	(9)	(19)	(15)
Post-retirement medical aid (refer to note 30)	1,139	1,356	1,745
Balance at beginning of year	2,607	1,139	1,356
Interest cost	286	322	428
Current service cost	83	84	95
Expected return on plan asset	(188)	(257)	(223)
Actuarial loss	149	129	157
Termination settlement	–	–	(5)
Plan asset – initial recognition	(1,720)	–	–
Contributions paid	(78)	(61)	(63)
Telephone rebates (refer to note 30)	282	287	325
Balance at beginning of year	198	282	287
Interest cost	19	22	39
Current service cost	4	3	6
Past service cost	76	2	2
Actuarial loss	5	–	14
Benefits paid	(20)	(22)	(23)
Bonus	1,090	992	671
Balance at beginning of year	1,071	1,090	992
Transferred to disposal groups	–	–	(397)
Charged to employee expenses	965	797	577
Payment	(946)	(895)	(501)

Annual leave

In terms of Telkom's policy, employees are entitled to accumulate vested leave benefits not taken within a leave cycle, to a cap of 22 days which must be taken within an 18 month leave cycle. The leave cycle is reviewed annually and is in accordance with legislation.

Bonus

The Telkom bonus scheme consists of performance bonuses which are dependent on achievement of certain financial and non-financial targets. The bonus is to all qualifying employees payable bi-annually after Telkom's results have been made public.

Deferred bonus incentives

Employees of the wholly owned subsidiaries of Vodacom, including executive directors, are eligible for compensation benefits in the form of a Deferred Bonus Incentive Scheme. The benefit is recorded at the present value of the expected future cash outflows.

Figure 13.2 Example of disclosure of annual leave and bonus policies

Source: Telkom SA Limited Annual Report to 31 March 2009.

13.5   Termination benefits

Termination benefits are employee benefits payable as a result of either:

(a) an employer's decision to terminate an employee's employment before the normal retirement date; or

(b) an employee's decision to accept voluntary redundancy in exchange for those benefits (IAS 19 para 7).

In broad terms, termination benefits are amounts payable when an employee ceases to work for an employer. In this context they are similar to post-employment benefits, such as pensions. However, whereas post-employment benefits are earned throughout an employee's working life, termination benefits arise as a result of an event, such as a factory closure. The event that gives rise to an obligation is the termination, rather than employee service. Termination benefits are not earned in a literal sense, although their magnitude may be set by reference to an employee's period of service.

Typically termination benefits comprise lump sum payments, although they could take other forms such as retention of an entity car. Termination benefits also include:

- pension enhancements;
- 'gardening leave', that is, a salary until the end of a specified notice period during which the employee renders no further service that provides economic benefit to the reporting entity (IAS 19 para 135).

Example 13.3

Gardening leave

An entity is in the process of finalising the negotiation of the termination of one of its senior salesmen's contracts. The terms of the contract are that he will receive 12 months' notice. To avoid him working for any of their competitors (which is a significant risk to the entity) the intention is that he will go on 'gardening leave' for 12 months on full pay, paid monthly over the next year. He will not be replaced. The likelihood is that the agreement will be reached before the year-end.

IAS 19 para 133 requires that a provision should be made for termination benefits where an entity is demonstrably committed to either:

(a) terminate the employment of an employee or a group of employees before the normal retirement date; or

(b) provide termination benefits as a result of an offer made to encourage voluntary redundancy.

Thus, if agreement is reached by the year-end, the entity should make a provision.

13.6   Financial analysis and interpretation

The complexity of the accounting standards applicable to pensions and other retirement benefits results in a wide range of differences among the entities offering such plans. As a result of this complexity and the fundamental differences in the two types of plans described below, analysts have a difficult time discerning the underlying economic substance of an entity's reported pension and other retirement benefits.

*   *Defined contribution plans*, in which the employer agrees to contribute a specific amount to a pension plan each year. The employee's retirement income is largely determined by the performance of the portfolio into which the contributions are made.

*   *Defined benefit plans* require the employer to pay specified pension benefits to retired employees. The investment risk is borne by the employer.

For *defined contribution plans*, the employer's annual pension expense is the amount that the entity plan would contribute to the plan each year according to the contribution formula. Pension expense and cash outflow are the same, and there are no assets or liabilities recorded by the employer. A defined contribution pension plan only obliges the employer to make annual contributions to the pension plan based on a prescribed formula. Once the annual contributions have been made, the entity has no further obligation.

For *defined benefit plans*, the annual pension expense and employer's liability are determined by calculating the present value of future benefits to be paid to retirees. Forecasting future benefits involves actuarial studies and assumptions about future events, including life expectancies of plan participants, labour turnover rates, future wage levels, discount rates, rates of return on plan assets, etc. Benefits promised to participants are defined by a specific formula that reflects these estimated future events. The estimated benefits are allocated to the years of service worked by employees to develop the annual pension expense. Companies with defined benefit pension plans accrue obligations to pay benefits, according to the benefit formula, as the employee performs work. However, these obligations are not discharged until after the employee retires.

Because pension *benefit formulas* relate to the future benefits for the aggregate work performed by employees for the entity until their retirement, there are several alternative ways of determining the size of future obligations, and their current values. These are:

*   *Actuarial estimates and defined benefit formulas.* Entities use actuaries to perform complex calculations in order to estimate the size of future obligations and their present value. Included in the computations are projections of employee salary growth, mortality, employee turnover, and retirement dates. These estimates are combined with the plan's benefit formula to generate a forecast of benefits to be paid in the future. This future benefit stream is discounted to present value, which is the pension obligation.

*   *Measures of the defined benefit pension obligation* are:
    *   Accumulated Benefit Obligation (ABO) – the present value of pension benefits earned based on current salaries.

❏ Projected Benefit Obligation (PBO) – the present value of pension benefits earned, including projected salary increases.

❏ Vested Benefit Obligation (VBO) – the portion of the benefit obligation that does not depend on future employee service. Alternatively, it is the vested portion of the ABO.

Financial impact of assumptions. For pay-related plans PBO will be higher than ABO due to the inclusion of future salary increases. PBO and ABO will be the same for non-pay-related plans because salary increases have no effect on calculations. However, for non-pay-related plans, if there is enough evidence that the past increases in benefits will be extended into the future, PBO will be higher than ABO after adjusting computations. For all defined benefit plans, calculations of PBO, ABO, and VBO should include automatic increases in benefits such as cost-of-living adjustments.

Accounting standards assume that pensions are forms of deferred compensation for work currently performed and, as such, pension expenses are recognised on an accrual basis as earned by employees.

There are many *actuarial assumptions* that affect pension obligations. These are:

- the discount rate assumption;
- the wage growth rate assumption;
- the expected return on plan assets assumption;
- the age distribution of the workforce;
- the average service life of employees.

In *analysing actuarial assumptions*, analysts need to determine whether the current assumptions are appropriate, particularly compared to the entity's competitors. In addition, if the assumptions have been changed, analysts need to determine the effect on the financial statements of a change in the following parameters:

- *Discount rate assumption.* If the discount rate is increased, pension obligations will decrease, producing an actuarial gain for the year. If the discount rate is decreased, however, pension obligations will increase, resulting in an actuarial loss for the year.

- *Wage growth rate assumption.* The wage growth rate assumption directly affects pension obligations and the service cost component of the reported pension expense. Therefore, a higher (lower) wage growth rate assumption will result in a higher (lower) pension obligation and a higher (lower) service component of its reported pension expense.

- *Expected rate of return on fund assets.* Because all funds should earn the same risk-adjusted return in the long run. If the market is efficient, deviations in this assumption from the norm that is unrelated to changes in a pension portfolio's asset mix might suggest that the pension expense is overstated or understated. In general, if the expected return on plan assets is too high the pension expense would be understated, boosting reported earnings; if the expected return on plan assets is too low the pension expense is overstated, reducing reported earnings. Again, manipulating the expected return on plan assets will distort reported earnings and may be used to smooth earnings per share.

Table 13.1 Summary of assumptions and their impact

	Higher (Lower) discount rate	*Higher (Lower) compensation rate*	*Higher (Lower) expected rate of return on plan assets*
PBO	Lower (Higher)	Higher (Lower)	No impact
ABO	Lower (Higher)	No impact	No impact
VBO	Lower (Higher)	No impact	No impact
Pension expense	Lower (Higher)	Higher (Lower)	Lower (Higher)
Earnings	Higher (Lower)	Lower (Higher)	Higher (Lower)

Summary

- *Short-term employee benefits* are employee benefits (other than termination benefits) which should be expensed as incurred and the related liability should be payable within 12 months after the end of the period in which the employees render the related service.

- An employer's balance sheet should show a liability for the expected amount payable relating to the unused entitlement to accumulating short-term compensated absences.

- Post-employment benefits consist largely of pensions. A pension scheme or plan may be a defined contribution plan or a defined benefit plan.

- A defined contribution plan is one where the employer's contributions are fixed. The employer's financial statements should show an expense equal to the agreed amount of contributions for the period.

- A defined benefit plan is one where the employer is obliged to provide an agreed level of post-employment benefits. In order to account for defined benefit plans, it is necessary to make actuarial estimates of the accumulated post-employment benefits which employees have earned to date and the extra amount of such benefits that employees have earned during the current accounting period.

- Actuarial gains and losses may arise with regard to the defined benefit obligation or with regard to plan assets. These gains and losses may be caused by changes in actuarial assumptions or by the fact that returns on plan assets have been higher or lower than expected.

- The defined benefit expense for an accounting period is basically equal to the present value of the extra benefits that employees have earned during that period. But this figure will need to be adjusted or reflect actuarial gains or losses, the return on plan assets and a number of other factors.

- The defined benefit liability at the end of an accounting period is equal to the present value of the defined benefit obligation at the balance sheet date less the fair value of the plan assets on that date.

- Actuarial gains and losses within the '10 per cent corridor' may be carried forward rather than being reflected in the income statement.

- Termination benefits (such as redundancy pay) should be recognised as an expense when the employer is demonstrably committed to terminate the employment of an employee and provide termination benefits.

Research and references

The IASB documents relevant for this chapter is IAS 19 – *Employee Benefits*.

The following are examples of books, research and discussion papers that take the issues of this chapter further:

- Alexander, D., Britton, A. and Jorissen, A. (2007) *International Financial Reporting and Analysis*, 3rd edn. Thomson, Chapter 21.
- Elliott, B. and Elliott, J. (2009) *Financial Accounting and Reporting*, 13th edn. Financial Times-Prentice Hall, Chapter 13.
- Epstein, B.J. and Jermakowicz, E.K. (2009) *IFRS 2009: Interpretation and Application of International Accounting and Financial Reporting Standards*. Wiley, Chapter 16.
- PricewaterhouseCoopers (2009) *IFRS Manual of Accounting – 2010. Global Guide to International Financial Reporting Standards*. CCH, Chapters 11 and 12.
- Stolowy, H. and Lebas, M.J. (2006) *Corporate Financial Reporting. A Global Perspective*, 2nd edn. Thomson, September, Chapter 12.
- Sutton, T. (2004) *Corporate Financial Accounting and Reporting*, 2nd edn. Financial Times-Prentice Hall, Chapter 16.

Discussion questions and exercises

13.1 Categories of employment benefits

List the four categories of employee benefits which are identified by IAS 19 and give examples of each category.

13.2 Short-term employee benefits

An entity has 10,000 employees. Each employee is entitled to 20 days of paid holiday per calendar year. Up to five days of this entitlement may be carried forward and taken in the following year but cannot be carried forward any further. Employees are not paid for any holidays which they fail to take.

As at 31 December 2009, 9,130 employees had used in full their holiday entitlement for 2009. The remaining employees are carrying forward an average of three days per employee. Based on past experience, it is expected that these employees will each use an average of two of these three days before the end of 2010.

Each day of paid holiday costs the entity on average EUR 300.

Calculate the liability which should be stated in the entity's balance sheet as at 31 December 2009 with regard to paid holiday entitlement.

13.3 Post-employment benefits

(a) Distinguish between defined contribution pension plans and defined benefit pension plans.

(b) An entity's agreed contributions to a defined contribution plan for 2009 are EUR 700,000. Of this sum, the entity had paid EUR 640,000 by the end of the year. It is becoming clear that the pension fund assets will be insufficient to finance the expected level of employee benefits and that the entity would have to increase its annual contributions by 50 per cent if employee expectations are to be met.

Calculate the expense which should be charged to the entity's income statement for the year ended 31 December 2009 relating to this plan. Also calculate the amount of the liability which should be reflected in the entity's balance sheet.

(c) Explain why accounting for a defined benefit plan is much more difficult than accounting for a defined contribution plan.

13.4 Defined benefit pension plans

(a) With regard to defined benefit pension plans, explain each of the following terms:

(i)   defined benefit obligation;
(ii) current service cost;
(iii) interest cost;
(iv) actuarial gains and losses.

(b) List the main components of the defined benefit expense which should be shown in an employer's income statement. Also list the main components of the defined benefit liability which should be recorded in the employer's balance sheet.

13.5 Defined benefit obligation and plan assets

Northern plc prepares its financial statements to 31 December each year and has operated a defined benefit pension scheme for many years. At 31 December 2008, the present value of the defined benefit obligation was calculated at EUR 45m and the fair value of plan assets was EUR 43.8m. The following information relates to the year ended 31 December 2009:

(a) Expected return on plan assets was EUR 4.6m but actual returns was EUR 5.4m.

(b) Northern plc made contributions of EUR 7.6m into the plan. Employees contributed a further EUR 3m.

(c) The plan paid out benefits to past employees amounting to EUR 3.8m.

(d) The present value of the current service cost for the year (before deducting employee contributions) was EUR 7.4m.

(e) At 31 December 2009, the present value of the defined benefit obligation was calculated at EUR 54.8 million and the fair value of plan assets was EUR 16.4 million.

A discount rate of 8 per cent should be used in calculating the interest cost for the year.

Calculate the defined benefit expense which should be recorded in the entity's income statement for the year ended 31 December 2009 and the defined benefit liability or asset which should be recorded in the balance sheet at that date. Also reconcile the expense for the year to the employer contributions made during the year.

13.6 Accounting treatments of actuarial gains and losses

Outline the accounting treatments that are permitted by IAS 19 for actuarial gains and losses in connection with defined benefit pension plans.

Part Four Accounting for financial instruments

14 Financial instruments: classification

Contents

Objectives

When you have completed this chapter you should be able to:

- Define the term 'financial instrument'
- Define the terms 'financial asset', 'financial liability' and 'equity instrument'
- Identify the four categories of financial assets
- Classify financial instruments as either liabilities or equity
- Determine the liability and equity components of a compound financial instrument.

14.1 Introduction

Financial markets have experienced and continue to experience significant developments since the 1980s. As foreign exchange rates, interest rates and commodity prices became increasingly volatile, a need arose to manage the commercial risks arising from the instability of these markets. Primary financial instruments, such as bonds and shares, that comprised much of the traditional financing and risk management activities, gave way to derivative products, such as futures, options, forward contracts and swaps, for managing risks. Entities were able to change significantly their financial risk profile, virtually instantaneously, by entering into interest rate or foreign exchange swaps, or by acquiring options or forward contracts to hedge or take positions on future price movements. With the globalisation of financial markets, growth in international commerce, advancement in financial risk management and information technology, the development and use of cost effective innovative derivative products and complex financial instruments for managing risk and improving return on assets became commonplace.

However, it became apparent that this growth in the use of financial instruments had outstripped the development of guidance for their accounting. Traditional realisation and cost-based measurement concepts were no longer adequate to portray effectively their impact and risks, as some derivatives (for example, forward contracts and swaps) with no initial cost were simply not recognised in the financial statements until settlement. Deficiencies in current accounting practices, inconsistent treatment of economically similar transactions and the lack of visibility in the financial statements caused difficulty for both preparers and users of financial statements. This caused an atmosphere of uncertainty, which many people believed might discourage the legitimate use of derivative instruments. Concern about inadequate accounting for derivatives was also heightened by the public awareness surrounding large derivative-instrument losses at several companies. As a result, a pervasive need to develop a single, comprehensive standard for accounting and disclosure of financial instruments and hedging activities became a necessity.

The three international standards dealing with financial instruments which have been developed over the last decade are:

- IAS 32 – *Financial Instruments: Presentation;*
- IAS 39 – *Financial Instruments: Recognition and Measurement;*
- IFRS 7 – *Financial Instruments: Disclosures.*

As mentioned earlier, the EU Regulation required listed groups to prepare their consolidated financial statements using IFRS for periods commencing on or after 1 January 2005. For this to happen, IFRS had to be brought into EU law through a complex endorsement mechanism. Although most of the IASB standards were endorsed, IAS 39 was not endorsed in full. Some aspects of IAS 39, namely the option to fair value all liabilities and certain aspects of hedge accounting that troubled banks and regulators, did not find favour with the EU and were removed. This 'carve out' version was endorsed by the EU in November 2004. The 'carve out' relating to the fair value option was removed as a result of a subsequent amendment to IAS 39 and endorsement by the EU in November 2005.

IAS 39 has been in place for over 10 years and during this time it has been amended several times. As a result of the recent global financial crisis, the IASB and FASB have been working closely with the aim of ensuring a globally consistent and appropriate response. In July 2009 the IASB issued the ED *Financial Instruments: Classification and Measurement* as phase 1 of its project to replace IAS 39.

This area of accounting is renowned for its complexity and difficulty. In fact, the three standards listed above occupy nearly 450 pages of fine print. Accordingly, a detailed coverage of financial instruments is well beyond the scope of this book; so the aim of this chapter is to provide a basic introduction to the topic, where in Chapter 15 we illustrate how to recognise and measure financial assets and financial liabilities.

14.2   Definitions relating to financial instruments

Financial instruments embrace a broad range of assets and liabilities. They include:

- *Primary financial instruments*:
  - ❑ financial assets such as cash, receivables and equity securities of another entity;
  - ❑ financial liabilities such as debt.
- *Derivative financial instruments* such as financial options, forwards, swaps and futures.

IAS 32 para 11 provides four key definitions which apply throughout the standards dealing with financial instruments:

A financial instrument is any contract that gives rise to a financial asset of one entity and a financial liability or equity instrument of another entity.

A financial asset is any asset that is:

(a) cash;

(b) an equity instrument of another entity;

(c) a contractual right:

(i) to receive cash or another financial asset from another entity; or

(ii) to exchange financial assets or financial liabilities with another entity under conditions that are potentially favourable to the entity; or

(d) a contract that will or may be settled in the entity's own equity instruments and is:

(i) a non-derivative for which the entity is or may be obliged to receive a variable number of the entity's own equity instruments; or

(ii) a derivative that will or may be settled other than by the exchange of a fixed amount of cash or another financial asset for a fixed number of the entity's own equity instruments. For this purpose the entity's own equity instruments do not include instruments that are themselves contracts for the future receipt or delivery of the entity's own equity instruments.

A financial liability is any liability that is:

(a) a contractual obligation:

(i) to deliver cash or another financial asset to another entity; or

(ii) to exchange financial assets or financial liabilities with another entity under conditions that are potentially unfavourable to the entity; or

(b) a contract that will or may be settled in the entity's own equity instruments and is:

(i) a non-derivative for which the entity is or may be obliged to deliver a variable number of the entity's own equity instruments; or

(ii) a derivative that will or may be settled other than by the exchange of a fixed amount of cash or another financial asset for a fixed number of the entity's own equity instruments. For this purpose the entity's own equity instruments do not include instruments that are themselves contracts for the future receipt or delivery of the entity's own equity instruments.

An equity instrument is any contract that evidences a residual interest in the assets of an entity after deducting all of its liabilities.

The term *entity* includes individuals, partnerships, incorporated bodies, trusts and government agencies (IAS 32 para 14). Examples of equity instruments include non-puttable ordinary shares, some types of preference shares and share warrants or written call options that allow the holder to subscribe for or purchase a fixed number of non-puttable ordinary shares in the issuing entity in exchange for a fixed amount of cash or another financial asset.

Example 14.1

Primary financial instruments

Explain why each of the transactions listed below gives rise to a financial instrument as defined by IAS 32:

(a) an entity issues loan stock;

(b) an entity sells goods to a customer on credit;

(c) an entity buys goods from a supplier on credit;

(d) an entity deposits money into its bank account;

(e) an entity overdraws its bank account;

(f) an entity issues ordinary shares;

(g) an entity invests in newly-issued ordinary shares of another entity.

(a) The issue of loan stock creates a contractual obligation on the part of the entity to repay the loan at some time in the future. The contract between the entity and the lenders is a financial instrument because:

   • the lenders now have the right to be repaid (a financial asset);
   • the entity is now under an obligation to repay the loan (a financial liability).

(b) A sale on credit creates a contractual obligation on the part of the customer to pay for the goods. The contract with the customer is a financial instrument because:

   • the entity now has a trade receivable (a financial asset);
   • the customer now has a trade payable (a financial liability).

(c) A purchase on credit creates a contractual obligation on the part of the entity to pay for the goods. The contract with the supplier is a financial instrument because:

   • the supplier now has a trade receivable (a financial asset);
   • the entity now has a trade payable (a financial liability).

(d) In effect, a bank deposit is a loan to the bank and the bank is contractually obliged to repay this money. The contract with the bank is a financial instrument because:

   • the entity now has the right to withdraw its cash (a financial asset);
   • the bank is now under an obligation to repay the cash (a financial liability).

(e) A bank overdraft is a form of bank loan and the entity is contractually obliged to repay this loan. The contract with the bank is a financial instrument because:

   • the bank now has the right to be repaid (a financial asset);
   • the entity is now under an obligation to repay the overdraft (a financial liability).

(f) Ordinary shares are an equity instrument, as defined by IAS 32. The issue of ordinary shares creates a contract between the entity and its shareholders. This contract is a financial instrument because:

   • the shareholders now own the shares (a financial asset);
   • the entity now has extra share capital (an equity instrument).

(g) This purchase of ordinary shares creates a contract between the investing entity and the issuing entity. This contract is a financial instrument because:

   • the investing entity now owns the shares (a financial asset);
   • the issuing entity now has extra share capital (an equity instrument).

Classification of financial instruments

IAS 39 requires all financial assets and financial liabilities to be classified into specific categories. The need to classify financial instruments into specific categories arises from the mixed measurement model in IAS 39, under which some financial instruments are carried at amortised cost whilst others are carried at fair value. Consequently, a particular financial instrument's classification that is carried out at initial recognition drives the subsequent accounting treatment. IAS 39 prescribes four categories for financial assets and two categories for financial liabilities.

The four clearly defined categories of financial assets, as follows:

- financial assets at fair value through income statement[1], measured at fair value;
- held-to-maturity investments, measured at amortised cost;
- loans and receivables, measured at amortised cost;
- available-for-sale financial assets, measured at fair value.

The two categories of financial liabilities are as follows:

- financial liabilities at fair value through income statement;
- other financial liabilities, measured at amortised cost.

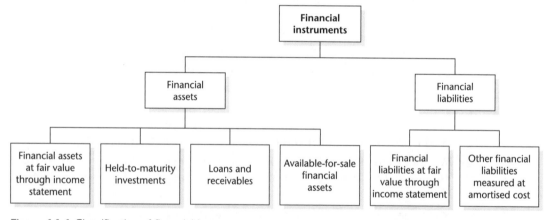

Figure 14.1 Classification of financial instruments

As stated above, the classification is important as it dictates how the financial assets and liabilities are subsequently measured in the financial statements.

14.3.1 Financial assets at fair value through income statement

A *financial asset at fair value through income statement* is a financial asset that meets either of the following conditions.

(a) It is classified as held for trading.

(b) Upon initial recognition it is designated by the entity at fair value through the income statement (IAS 39 para 9).

A financial asset is classified as *held for trading* if it is:

(i)   acquired or incurred principally for the purpose of selling or repurchasing it in the near term;

(ii) part of a portfolio of identified financial instruments that are managed together and for which there is evidence of a recent actual pattern of short-term profit-taking; or

(iii) a derivative (except for a derivative that is a financial guarantee contract or a designated and effective hedging instrument) (IAS 39 para 9).

Financial assets held for trading include:

- debt and equity securities that are actively traded by the entity;
- loans and receivables acquired by the entity with the intention of making a short-term profit from price or dealer's margin;
- securities held under repurchase agreements.

Derivatives are always categorised as held for trading, unless they are accounted for as effective hedging instruments.

According to IAS 39 para 9, an entity may designate a *financial asset at fair value through income statement* on initial recognition only in the following three circumstances:

1 The designation eliminates or significantly reduces a measurement or recognition inconsistently (sometimes referred to as an 'accounting mismatch') that would otherwise arise.

2 A group of financial assets, financial liabilities or both is managed and its performance is evaluated on a fair value basis, in accordance with a documented risk management or investment strategy.

3 The item proposed to be designated at fair value through income statement is a hybrid contract that contains one or more embedded derivatives unless:

 ❐ the embedded derivative(s) does(do) not significantly modify the cash flows that otherwise would be required by the contract; or

 ❐ it is clear with little or no analysis when a similar hybrid (combined) instrument is first considered that separation of the embedded derivative(s) is (are) prohibited, such as a prepayment option embedded in a loan that permits the holder to prepay the loan for approximately its amortised cost (IAS 39 para 11A).

14.3.2 Held-to-maturity investments

Held-to-maturity investments are non-derivative financial assets with fixed or determinable payments and fixed maturity that an entity has the positive intention and ability to hold to maturity other than:

(a) those that the entity upon initial recognition designates as at fair value through income statement;

(b) those that the entity designates as available for sale; and

(c) those that meet the definition of loans and receivables (IAS 39 para 9).

Intent to hold to maturity

An entity does not have a positive intention to hold to maturity an investment in a financial asset with a fixed maturity if:

(a) The entity intends to hold the financial asset for an undefined period. In other words, as the entity has not actually defined a period, the positive intent to hold-to-maturity does not exist.

(b) The entity stands ready to sell the financial asset (other than if a situation arises that is non-recurring and could not have been reasonably anticipated by the entity) in response to changes in market interest rates or risks, liquidity needs, changes in the availability of and the yield on alternative investments, changes in financing sources and terms or changes in foreign currency risk. All these situations are indicative that the entity intends to profit from changes in the asset's fair value and has no intention of holding the financial asset to maturity.

(c) The issuer has a right to settle the financial asset at an amount significantly below its amortised cost. Where this is the case and the issuer is expected to exercise that right, the entity cannot demonstrate a positive intent to hold the financial asset to maturity (IAS 39 para AG 16).

Ability to hold to maturity

It is not sufficient for the entity to demonstrate a positive intent to hold a financial asset to maturity; the entity must also demonstrate its ability to hold such an asset to maturity. An entity cannot demonstrate that ability if:

(a) It does not have the financial resources available to continue to finance the investment until maturity; or

(b) It is subject to an existing legal or other constraint that could frustrate its intention to hold the financial asset to maturity. (However, an issuer's call option does not necessarily frustrate an entity's intention to hold a financial asset to maturity) (IAS 39 para AG 23).

For example, it is unlikely that an open ended fund would be able to classify any financial asset as held-to maturity. Management might intend to hold the investments to maturity, but calls for redemption of shares or units could constrain the fund's ability to hold its investments to maturity.

The tainting rules

An entity should assess its intention and ability to hold its held-to-maturity investments to maturity not only when those financial assets are initially recognised, but also at each subsequent balance sheet date (IAS 39 para AG 25). Because an entity is expected not to change its *intent* about held-to-maturity security, the requirement to reassess the appropriateness of a security's classification would necessarily focus on the entity's *ability* to hold a security to maturity. As facts and circumstances may change, the entity may lose its ability to hold a debt security to maturity and thus would be forced to reclassify its held-to-maturity investments to available-for-sale.

Because management should assert that the criteria for a held-to-maturity investment has been met for each investment, the sale, reclassification or exercise of a put option of certain held-to-maturity securities will call into question ('taint') management's intent to hold all securities in the held-to-maturity category. As a result, when an entity during the current financial year has sold or reclassified more than an insignificant amount of held-to-maturity investments before maturity (more than insignificant in relation to the total amount of held-to-maturity investments), it is prohibited from classifying any financial asset as held-to-maturity for a period of two years after the occurrence of this event. Furthermore, all the entity's held-to-maturity investments, not just investments of a similar type, should be classified into the available-for-sale category and measured at fair value. In a sense a penalty is imposed for a change in management intention. When the prohibition ends (at the end of the second financial year following the tainting), the portfolio becomes 'cleansed' and the entity is once more able to assert that it has the intent and ability to hold debt securities to maturity (IAS 39 paras 9 and 54).

The tainting rules do not apply if only an insignificant amount of held-to-maturity investments is sold or reclassified. The standard does not define what an insignificant amount means, except that it should be measured by reference to the total amount of held-to-maturity investments. Therefore, judgement is needed to assess what is insignificant in each particular situation.

Example 14.2

Application of the tainting rules

An entity's held-to-maturity portfolio consists of a mixture of sterling corporate bonds, treasury bonds and Eurodollar bonds. The entity prepares its financial statements to 31 December 2007. During September 2007, the entity sold a certain Eurodollar bond to realise a large gain.

The fact that the entity sold one Eurodollar investment (not considered insignificant in relation to the total held-to-maturity portfolio) does not mean that only the Eurodollar sub-category has been tainted. The tainting rule is very clear. If an entity has sold or reclassified more than an insignificant amount of held-to-maturity investments, the entire portfolio and all remaining investments should be reclassified to the available-for-sale category (IAS 39 para IG B20). It follows that sub-classification of securities for the purpose of limiting the impact of sales or transfers of held-to-maturity securities is not an acceptable practice.

The reclassification is recorded in the reporting period in which the sales occurred (that is, the year ended 31 December 2007). Furthermore, as explained above, the entity is prohibited from reclassifying any investments in the held-to-maturity category for two full financial years after 31 December 2007 (i.e. 2008 and 2009). This means that any fixed interest securities acquired during 2008 and 2009, which could qualify for held-to-maturity classification, should not be classified as such in those years. The earliest date that the entity is able to classify investments as held-to-maturity is 1 January 2010 as shown in Figure 14.2 below.

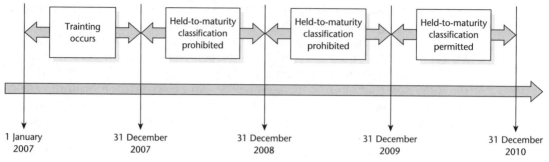

Figure 14.2 Application of the tainting rules

On 1 January 2010 when the portfolio becomes cleansed, and once again it becomes appropriate to carry securities at held-to-maturity, the fair value of the affected securities on 1 January 2010 becomes the new amortised cost. Furthermore, as tainting occured in the year ended 31 December 2007, the held-to-maturity classification for the comparative period to 31 December 2006 is not affected.

A decision tree for classifying financial assets as held-to-maturity is shown in Figure 14.3.

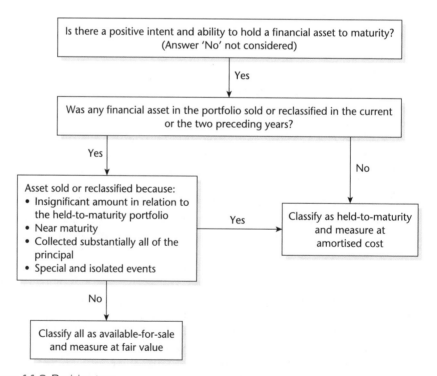

Figure 14.3 Decision tree

14.3.3 Loans and receivables

Loans and receivables are non-derivative financial assets with fixed or determinable payments that are not quoted in an active market other than:

(a) those that an entity intends to sell immediately or in the near term, which should be classified as held for trading, and those that the entity upon initial recognition designates as at fair value through income statement;

(b) those that an entity upon initial recognition designates as available for sale; or

(c) those for which a holder may not recover substantially all of its initial investment, other than because of credit deterioration, which should be classified as available for sale (IAS 39 para 9).

Loans and receivables typically arise when an entity provides money, goods or services directly to a debtor with no intention of trading the receivable. Examples include trade receivables, bank deposits and loan assets originated by the entity either directly or by way of syndication/participation arrangements. It also includes loans that are *purchased* in a secondary market that is not active and the loans are not quoted. Investments in debt securities that are quoted in a non-active market can also be classified as loans and receivables.

Example 14.3

Bank deposits in other banks

Banks make term deposits with a central bank or other banks. Sometimes, the proof of deposit is negotiable, sometimes not. Even if negotiable, the depositor bank may or may not intend to sell it. Such a deposit meets the definition of loans and receivables, whether or not the proof of deposit is negotiable, unless the depositor bank intends to sell the instrument immediately or in the near term, in which case the deposit should be classified as a financial asset held-for-trading (IAS 39 para IG B23).

14.3.4 Available-for-sale financial assets

Available-for-sale financial assets are those non-derivative financial assets that are designated as available for sale or are not classified as:

(a) loans and receivables;

(b) held-to-maturity investments; or

(c) financial assets at fair value through income statement (IAS 39 para 9).

Discussion questions and exercises

14.1 Definitions relating to financial instruments

(a) Define the terms 'financial instrument', 'financial asset', 'financial liability' and 'equity instrument'.

(b) Which of the following is a 'financial instrument' as defined by IAS 32? Give reasons for your answer.

(i) Cash

(ii) Investment in a debt instrument

(iii) Investment in a subsidiary

(iv) Provision for restoration of a mine site

(v) Buildings owned by a reporting entity

(vi) Leases

(vii) Trade receivables

(viii) An investment in an associate

(ix) A non-controlling interest in a partnership

(x) Provision for employee benefits.

14.2 Financial liabilities and equity instruments

Explain how IAS 32 distinguishes between financial liabilities and equity instruments.

14.3 Compound financial instruments

(a) Explain what is meant by a 'compound' financial instrument.

(b) Illustrate the accounting treatment of such an instrument.

14.4 Classification of financial instruments

IAS 39 classifies financial assets into four categories. Identify and explain each of these categories. Also explain the way in which each category of financial asset should be measured subsequent to initial recognition.

14.5 The tainting rule

Explain what the tainting rule is.

14.6 Separation of a convertible bond

On 1 January 2010, an entity issued EUR 400,000 of 7 per cent bond at par. Interest on this loan stock is payable on 31 December each year. The stock is due for redemption at par on 31 December 2013 but may be converted into ordinary shares on that date instead. Assuming that the market rate of interest to be used in discounted cash flow calculations is 9 per cent p.a., calculate the liability component and the equity component of this bond.

14.7 Mandatorily convertible bonds

An entity issues 300,000 convertible bonds at the start of year 2010. The bonds have a three-year term, and are issued at par with a face value of EUR 100 per bond, resulting in total proceeds of EUR 30m, which is also the fair value of the bonds. Interest is payable annually in arrears at a nominal annual interest rate of 6 per cent. Each EUR 100 nominal bond is mandatorily convertible at the end of 2012 into 25 ordinary shares. The entity incurs an issue cost of 1 per cent on the nominal value of the bond amounting to EUR 300,000.

Assuming that when the bonds are issued, the prevailing market interest rate for similar debt without conversion options is 9 per cent, determine the liability component and the equity component of this bond.

Notes

1 Although IAS/IFRS use the term *'financial assets/financial liabilities at fair value through profit or loss'*, we use *'through income statement'* throughout this chapter to be consistent with the terminology we have adopted.
2 The effective interest rate can be calculated on an Excel sheet.

15

Financial instruments: recognition, derecognition, measurement and disclosures

Contents

Objectives

When you have completed this chapter you should be able to:

- Explain the circumstances in which a financial asset or liability should be recognised

- Understand and apply the two approaches to derecognition of financial assets: 'risks and rewards' approach and 'control' approach

- Understand and apply the derecognition rules for financial liabilities

- Calculate the amounts at which financial assets and financial liabilities should be measured on initial recognition and subsequently

- List the main disclosure requirements relating to financial instruments.

15.1   Introduction

In Chapter 14 we dealt with what qualifies as financial assets and financial liabilities and how such assets and liabilities should be classfied. The next step is to determine when and how financial assets and financial liabilities should be recognised, measured and disclosed in an entity's financial statements.

The rights or obligations that comprise financial assets or financial liabilities are derived from the contractual provisions that underlie them. As a result, an entity should only recognise a financial asset or a financial liability at the time it becomes a party to a contract (IAS 39 para 14). That is the point at which it has the contractual rights or contractual obligations. As the above discussion suggests, recognition issues for financial assets and financial liabilities tend to be straightforward and are dealt with in section 15.2.

Once an entity recognises a financial asset or a financial liability, it is necessary to measure those contractual rights and obligations on initial recognition. Under IAS 39, all financial instruments should be measured initially by reference to their fair value, which is normally the transaction price, that is, the fair value of the consideration given or received. However, this will not always be the case, as we will see in section 15.5.1.

Subsequent to initial recognition, IAS 39's measurement approach is best described as a 'mixed attribute' model with certain assets and liabilities measured at cost and others at fair value. The model depends upon an instrument's classification into one of the four categories of financial assets or one of the two categories of financial liabilities discussed in sections 14.3 and 14.4. For example, depending on the nature of the instrument and management's intentions, a fixed interest security intended to be held-to-maturity would be measured at amortised cost and not at fair value. Notwithstanding this, the standard gives an entity the option to classify financial instruments that meet certain special criteria at fair value with all gains and losses taken to the income statement. The possibility for entities to use the fair value option simplifies the application of IAS 39 by mitigating certain anomalies that result from the use of the mixed measurement model.

15.2   Recognition of financial assets and liabilities

According to IAS 39 para 14, an entity is required to recognise a financial asset or liability in its balance sheet when, and only when, it becomes a party to the instrument's contractual provisions.

Examples of situations where an entity becomes a party to the contractual provisions of a financial instrument are many and varied. We consider below regular way transactions.

15.2.1 Regular way transactions

A regular way purchase or sale is a purchase or sale of a financial asset under a contract whose terms require delivery of the asset within the time frame established generally by regulation or convention in the marketplace concerned (IAS 39 para 9). Marketplace is not limited to a formal stock exchange or organised over-the-counter market. Rather, it means the environment in which the financial asset is customarily exchanged. An acceptable time frame in such a marketplace would be the period reasonably and customarily required for the parties to complete the transaction, prepare, and execute closing documents (IAS 39 para IG B28).

In many regulated financial markets, a settlement mechanism will exist under which transactions in financial instruments (particularly quoted equities and bonds) entered into at a particular date are settled a few days after this transaction date. The date on which the transaction is entered into is called the 'trade date'. It is the trade in which the entity commits to purchase or sell an asset. The date on which the transaction is settled by delivery of the underlying asset is called the 'settlement date'. For example, the standard settlement periods on the London Stock Exchange for equity market securities and wholesale gilts are the trade date plus three business days (T + 3) and the trade date plus one business day (T + 1) respectively. A contract with an individual or through a broker to buy or sell a financial asset that is normally traded on a regulated financial market, but with a settlement period that differs from that established by regulation in that financial marketplace, does not qualify as a regular way transaction (IAS 39 paras IG B29 and B30).

15.2.2 Trade date versus settlement date accounting

IAS 39 provides that a regular way purchase or sale of financial assets should be recognised and derecognised, as applicable, using either trade date accounting or settlement date accounting. Either method is acceptable, but it is an accounting policy choice that should be disclosed and applied consistently for all purchases and sales that belong to the same category of financial assets as set out in section 14.3. For this purpose assets that are held for trading form a separate category from assets designated at fair value through the income statement (IAS 39 para AG 53).

Where an entity adopts *trade date accounting* (the date on which an entity commits itself to purchase or sell an asset), the accounting treatment is as follows:

- In respect of a purchase of a financial asset, the asset received and the liability to pay for it are recognised on the trade date. After initial recognition, the financial asset is subsequently measured either at amortised cost or at fair value depending on its initial classification as explained in section 14.3.

- In respect of a sale of a financial asset, the asset is derecognised and the receivable from the buyer for the payment together with any gain or loss on disposal are recognised on the trade date.

IAS 39 notes that, generally, interest does not start to accrue on the asset and corresponding liability until the settlement date when the title passes (IAS 39 para AG 55).

Where an entity adopts *settlement date accounting* (the date on which an asset is delivered to the buying entity or by the selling entity), the accounting treatment is as prescribed by IAS 39 para AG 56:

- In respect of a purchase of a financial asset, the asset is recognised on the day it is received by the entity. Any change in the asset's fair value during the period between the trade date and the settlement date is accounted for in the same way as the acquired asset. In other words:
  - ❐ for assets carried at cost or amortised cost, the change in value is not recognised;
  - ❐ for assets classified as financial assets at fair value through income statement, the change in value is recognised in the income statement;[1] and
  - ❐ for available-for-sale assets, the change in value is recognised in other comprehensive income (OCI).

- In respect of a sale of a financial asset, the asset is derecognised and the receivable from the buyer for the payment together with any gain or loss on disposal are recognised on the day that it is delivered by the entity. Any change in the fair value of the asset between trade date and settlement date is not recognised, as there is an agreed upon sale price at the trade date, making subsequent changes in fair value irrelevant from the seller's perspective. In other words, the seller's right to changes in the fair value ceases on the trade date.

The following examples illustrate the application of trade date and settlement date accounting to the various categories of financial assets identified by IAS 39. These examples are taken from IAS 39's implementation guidance (IAS 39 paras IG D2.1 and D2.2).

Example 15.1

Regular way purchase of a financial asset

On 29 December 2009, an entity committed to purchase a financial asset for EUR 2,000, which is its fair value on commitment (trade) date. Transaction costs are immaterial. On 31 December 2009 (financial year-end) and on 4 January 2010 (settlement date) the fair value of the asset was EUR 2,004 and EUR 2,006, respectively.

The amounts to be recorded for the asset will depend on how it is classified and whether trade date or settlement date accounting is used, as shown in Figure 15.1, below (any interest that might have accrued on the asset is disregarded).

(a) Trade date accounting

Date	Held-to-maturity investments – carried at amortised cost €	Available-for-sale assets – remeasured to fair value with changes in OCI €	Assets at fair value through income statement – remeasured to fair value with changes in the income statement €
29 December 2009 Dr Financial asset Cr Liability for payment To record asset and liability for payment	2,000 (2,000)	2,000 (2,000)	2,000 (2,000)
31 December 2009 Dr Financial asset Cr Equity Cr Income statement To recognise change in fair value	– – –	4 (4) –	4 – (4)
4 January 2010 Dr Financial asset Cr Equity Cr Income statement To recognise change in fair value	– – –	2 (2) –	2 – (2)
4 January 2010 Dr Liability for payment Cr Cash To record settlement of liability	2,000 (2,000)	2,000 (2,000)	2,000 (2,000)
Asset's carrying value at 4 January 2010	2,000	2,006	2,006

Figure 15.1 Trade date accounting vs settlement date accounting for a regular way purchase of a financial asset: journal entries

(b) Settlement date accounting

Date	Held-to-maturity investments – carried at amortised cost €	Available-for-sale assets – remeasured to fair value with changes in OCI €	Assets at fair value through income statement – remeasured to fair value with changes in the income statement €
29 December 2009 *No entries are recorded at the commitment date*			
31 December 2009 Dr Financial asset Cr Equity Cr Income statement To recognise change in fair value	– – –	4 (4) –	4 – (4)
4 January 2010 Dr Financial asset Cr Equity Cr Income statement To recognise change in fair value	– – –	2 (2) –	2 – (2)
4 January 2010 Dr Financial asset Cr Cash To record the asset's purchase at the contracted cash amount plus changes in fair value since trade date.	2,000 –	2,000 (2,000)	2,000 (2,000)
Asset's carrying value at 4 January 2010	2,000	2,006	2,006

Figure 15.1 *(Cont'd)*

Example 15.2

Regular way sale of a financial asset

On 29 December 2009 (trade date) an entity entered into a contract to sell a financial asset at its current fair value of EUR 2,020. The asset was acquired one year earlier for EUR 2,000 and its amortised cost was EUR 2,000. On 31 December 2009 (financial year-end), the fair value of the asset was EUR 2,024. On 4 January 2010 (settlement date), the fair value was EUR 2,026.

The amounts to be recorded will depend on how the asset is classified and whether trade date or settlement date accounting is used as shown in Figure 15.2, below (any interest that might have accrued on the asset is disregarded).

A regular way sale is accounted for as a sale on the trade date if trade date accounting is used and on the settlement date if settlement date accounting is used.

(a) Trade date accounting

Date	Held-to-maturity investments – carried at amortised cost €	Available-for-sale assets – remeasured to fair value with changes in OCI €	Assets at fair value through income statement – remeasured to fair value with changes in the income statement €
Carrying value prior to 29 December 2009	2,000	2,020	2,020
29 December 2009 Dr Receivable Cr Asset Dr Equity Cr Income statement	2,020 (2,000) (20)	2,020 (2,020) 20 (20)	2,020 (2,020) – –
To record the disposal of the asset and the 'recycling' of cumulative gain from equity to the income statement on disposal of the available-for-sale asset on the trade date.			
31 December 2009			
A change in the fair value of a financial asset that is sold on a regular way basis is not recorded in the financial statements between the trade date and the settlement date because the seller's right to changes in the fair value ceases on the trade date.			
4 January 2010 Dr Cash Cr Receivable	2,020 (2,020)	2,020 (2,020)	2,020 (2,020)
To record settlement of sales contract			

(b) Settlement date accounting

Date	Held-to-maturity investments – carried at amortised cost €	Available-for-sale assets – remeasured to fair value with changes in OCI €	Assets at fair value through income statement – remeasured to fair value with changes in the income statement €
Carrying value prior to 29 December 2009	2,000	2,020	2,020
31 December 2009			
A change in the fair value of a financial asset that is sold on a regular way basis is not recorded in the financial statements between trade date and settlement date, even if the entity applies settlement date accounting, because the seller's right to changes in the fair value ceases on the trade date.			
4 January 2010 Dr Cash Cr Asset Dr Equity Cr Income statement	2,020 (2,000) (20)	2,020 (2,020) 20 (20)	2,020 (2,020) – –
To record the disposal of the asset and the recycling of cumulative gain on the available for-sale asset recognised in equity to the income statement on the settlement date.			

Figure 15.2 Trade date accounting vs settlement date accounting for a regular way sale of a financial asset: journal entries

It is fairly common for entities to raise finance by selling financial assets, such as portfolios of trade receivables, loans, etc. No special problem arises where a transferor sells financial assets for cash or other assets, with no continuing involvement with the asset sold or with the transferee. The accounting for such transactions as sales and the corresponding derecognition of the asset is well established.

At the other extreme is a transfer of a financial asset where the buyer has an unconditional right and obligation to return the asset at the original price, usually with interest as in a repurchase transaction. Again, the accounting in this situation is fairly straightforward. The transaction is treated as a financing, with both the asset and the liability in the balance sheet, because the risk and rewards of ownership of the asset have not been transferred.

Problems begin to surface, however, when transfers are undertaken between the above two extremes in circumstances where the seller retains certain interests in the assets transferred. Examples include transfers that are subject to recourse and agreements to acquire the transferred asset or make additional payments that reflect the performance of the transferred asset.

IAS 39 specifies one set of requirements that apply to the derecognition of all financial assets, from the simple maturity of an instrument to the more complex securitisation transactions. Most of them are such complex transactions that go beyond the scope of this book and therefore they are not illustrated.

There are two separate approaches to derecognition under IFRS:

- the 'risks and rewards' approach (see situations 1 and 2 described below); and

- the 'control' approach (see situation 3, below).

The control approach is only used where the risks and rewards approach does not provide a clear answer. Hence, the risks and rewards approach should be evaluated first. When focusing on the risks and rewards, IAS 39 distinguishes among three types of transfers as explained above and which are illustrated below.

15.3.1 'Risks and rewards' approach: situation 1

An entity may *retain* substantially all risks and rewards of ownership of the transferred financial asset. In this situation, IAS 39 requires the entity to continue to recognise the financial asset in its entirety. No gain or loss is recognised as a result of the transfer. This situation is sometimes referred to as a failed sale. Examples of such transactions include:

- a sale of a financial asset where the asset will be returned to the transferor for a fixed price at a future date (e.g. a sale and repurchase transaction or repo)

- a sale of a group of short-term trade receivables where the transferor issues a guarantee to compensate the buyer for any credit losses incurred in the group and there are no other substantive risks transferred;

- a sale of a financial asset where the transferor retains a call option to repurchase the transferred asset, at the transferor's option, where the option is deep-in-the-money (i.e. it is highly probable that the option will be exercised);
- a sale of a financial asset where the transferor issues (writes) a put option that obligates it to repurchase the transferred asset, at the transferee's option, where the option is deep-in-the-money;
- a sale of a financial asset where the transferor enters into a total return swap with the transferee that returns all increases in fair value of the transferred asset to the transferor and provides the transferee with compensation for all decreases in fair value.

Example 15.3

Transfer of a financial asset while retaining substantially all risks and rewards of ownership

An entity sells an asset for a fixed price but simultaneously enters into a forward contract to repurchase the transferred financial asset in one year at the same price plus interest. In this case, even though the entity has transferred the financial asset, there has been no significant change in the entity's exposure to risks and rewards of the asset. Due to the agreement to repurchase the asset for a fixed price on a future date, irrespective of what the market price of the asset may be on that date, the entity continues to be exposed to any increases or decreases in the value of the asset in the period between the sale and the repurchase. In substance, therefore, a repurchase transaction is similar to a borrowing of an amount equal to the fixed price plus interest with the transferred asset serving as collateral to the transferee.

For example, if an entity sells a financial asset for EUR 28,600 in cash and at the same time enters into an agreement with the buyer to repurchase the asset in three months for EUR 29,000, the sale would not qualify for derecognition. The asset would continue to be recognised, and the seller would instead recognise a borrowing from the buyer, as follows:

Dr Cash	€28,600	
Cr Borrowing		€28,600

In the period between the sale and repurchase of the financial asset, the entity would accrue interest expense on the borrowing for the difference between the sale price (EUR 28,600) and repurchase price (EUR 29,000):

Dr Interest expense	€400	
Cr Borrowing		€400

On the date of repurchase, the entity would record the repurchase as follows:

Dr Borrowing	€29,000	
Cr Cash		€29,000

15.3.2 'Risks and rewards' approach: situation 2

An entity may *transfer* substantially all risks and rewards of ownership of the transferred asset. In such a situation, the entity should derecognise the financial asset in its entirety. On derecognition, if there is a difference between the consideration received and the carrying amount of the financial asset, the entity should recognise a gain or loss on the sale in the income statement. For a derecognised financial asset classified as available for sale, the gain or loss is adjusted for any unrealised holding gains or losses that previously have been included in OCI for that financial asset. Examples of transactions where an entity has transferred substantially all risks and rewards of ownership include:

- a sale of a financial asset where the seller (transferor) does not retain any rights or obligations (e.g. an option or guarantee) associated with the sold asset;
- a sale of a financial asset where the transferor retains the right to repurchase the financial asset, but the repurchase price is set as the current fair value of the asset on the repurchase date;
- a sale of a financial asset where the transferor retains a call option to repurchase the transferred asset, at the transferor's option, but that option is deep-out-of-the-money (i.e. it is not probable that the option will be exercised);
- a sale of a financial asset where the transferor writes a put option that obliges it to repurchase the transferred asset, at the transferee's option, but that option is deep-out-of-the-money.

Example 15.4

Transfer of a financial asset with all risks and rewards of ownership

If the carrying amount of a financial asset is EUR 29,000 and the entity sells it for cash at EUR 30,000 in a transfer that qualifies for derecognition, an entity should make these entries:

Dr Cash	€30,000	
Cr Financial asset		€29,000
Cr Gain on sale		€1,000

If the asset sold was an available-for-sale financial asset, the entries would be different. Changes in fair value of available-for-sale financial assets are not recognised in the income statement, but as a separate component of equity until realised. If changes in fair value of EUR 3,000 had previously been recognised in OCI, the entity would make these entries on derecognition, assuming the carrying amount was EUR 29,000 and the sale price EUR 30,000:

Dr Cash	€30,000	
Dr Available-for-sale gains recognised in OCI	€3,000	
Cr Financial asset		€29,000
Cr Gain on sale		€4,000

15.3.3 'Control' approach: situation 3

An entity may neither retain nor transfer substantially all risks and rewards of ownership of the transferred asset (i.e. cases that fall between situations 1 and 2, above). In this case derecognition depends on whether the entity has retained *control* of the transferred financial asset. An entity has lost control if the other party (the transferee) has the practical ability to sell the asset in its entirety to a third party without attaching any restriction to the transfer.

- If the transferor has *lost control* of the transferred asset, the financial asset is derecognised in its entirety. If there is a difference between the asset's carrying amount (adjusted for any deferred unrealised holding gains and losses in OCI) and the consideration received a gain or loss is recognised in the same way as described under situation 2.

- If the transferor has *retained control* over the transferred asset, the entity continues to recognise the asset to the extent of its continuing involvement. The continuing involvement is determined based on the extent to which the entity continues to be exposed to changes in amounts and timing of the net cash flows of the transferred asset (i.e. based on its nominal or maximum exposure to changes in net cash flows of the transferred asset).

An example of a transaction where an entity neither retains nor transfers substantially all risks and rewards of ownership is a sale of a group of receivables where the transferor issues a guarantee to compensate the buyer for any credit losses incurred in the group up to a maximum amount that is less than the expected credit losses in the group.

Example 15.5

Retention of control of the transferred financial asset

If an entity sells for EUR 195,000 a loan portfolio that has a carrying amount of EUR 200,000 and provides the buyer with a guarantee to compensate the buyer for any impairment losses up to EUR 5,000 when expected losses based on historical experience is EUR 11,000, the entity may determine that it has neither retained nor transferred substantially all risks and rewards of ownership. Therefore, it should evaluate whether it has retained control of the transferred asset. If the entity has retained control, the seller would continue to recognise EUR 5,000 as an asset and a corresponding liability to reflect its continuing involvement in the asset (i.e. the maximum amount it may pay under the guarantee) and derecognise the remainder of the carrying amount of the loan portfolio of EUR 195,000.

Table 15.1 summarises the accounting treatment for the three types of transfers just described.

Table 15.1 Accounting treatment of transfers of financial assets

Situations		Accounting treatment
(1) The transferor has retained substantially all risks and rewards		Continued recognition of the transferred asset. Any consideration received is recognised as a borrowing.
(2) The transferor has transferred substantially all risks and rewards		Derecognition. The transferor recognises any resulting gain or loss.
(3) The transferor has neither retained nor transferred substantially all risks and rewards.	The transferor has retained control.	Continued recognition of the transferred asset to the extent of the transferor's continuing involvement in the asset. The transferor recognises a gain or loss for any part that qualifies for derecognition.
	The transferor has lost control.	Derecognition. The transferor recognises any resulting gain or loss.

15.4 Derecognition of financial liabilities

Derecognition rules for financial liabilities are somewhat different from those relating to financial assets. Whereas derecognition rules for financial assets tend to focus on risks and rewards and may not lead to derecognition even though legal transfer has occurred, derecognition rules for financial liabilities focus solely on the legal release of the contractual obligations. The rules in IAS 39 deal with extinguishment of financial liabilities, their modification by lenders and the recognition and measurement of any gains and losses that arise from extinguishment and modification. These issues are considered in detail below.

15.4.1 Extinguishment of a financial liability

A financial liability (trading or other) is removed from the balance sheet when it is extinguished, i.e. when the obligation is discharged, cancelled or expired (IAS 39 para 39). This condition is met when the debtor either:

(a) discharges the liability (or part of it) by paying the creditor, normally with cash, other financial assets, goods or services; or

(b) is legally released from the primary responsibility for the liability (or part of it) either by process of law or by the creditor. (If the debtor has given a guarantee this condition may still be met) (IAS 39 para AG 57).

The condition for extinguishment is also met if an entity repurchases a bond that it has previously issued, even if the entity is a market maker or intends to resell it in the near term (IAS 39 para AG 58). This is consistent with the treatment of treasury

an extinguishment, the carrying amount of the liability should be adjusted for any costs or fees incurred and amortised over the remaining term of the modified liability (IAS 39 para AG 62).

Example 15.8

Renegotiation of debt

An entity borrowed EUR 2m from a bank on 1 January 2000 at a fixed rate of 9 per cent per annum for 10 years. The entity incurred issue costs of EUR 200,000. Interest on the loan is payable yearly in arrears. As a result of deteriorating financial condition during 2005, the entity approached its bank for a modification of the loan terms. The following terms were agreed with effect from 1 January 2006 (all interest paid to date):

• the interest rate is reduced to 7.5 per cent payable yearly in arrears;

• the original amount payable on maturity is reduced to EUR 1.9m;

• the maturity of the loan is extended by two years to 31 December 2011;

• renegotiation fees of EUR 60,000 are payable on 1 January 2006.

The loan would be recorded initially at 1 January 2000 at net proceeds of EUR 1.8m and would be amortised using the effective interest rate method. The effective interest rate is 10.6749 per cent as shown in the Table 15.2, below.

Table 15.2 Annual interest charges and the carrying value of the loan using the effective interest rate method

	Interest @ 10.6749% €	Payments €	Carrying value €
1 January 2000			1,800,000
31 December 2000	192,148	180,000	1,812,148
31 December 2001	193,445	180,000	1,825,593
31 December 2002	194,880	180,000	1,840,474
31 December 2003	196,469	180,000	1,856,943
31 December 2004	198,227	180,000	1,875,170
31 December 2005	200,172	180,000	**1,895,342**
31 December 2006	202,326	180,000	1,917,668
31 December 2007	204,709	180,000	1,942,377
31 December 2008	207,347	180,000	1,969,724
31 December 2009	210,266	2,180,000	–
			(–10 rounding difference)

On 1 January 2006, the remaining cash flows on the old debt comprise four annual interest payments of EUR 180,000 each and the EUR 2m of principal payable at redemption. The present value of these remaining cash flows on that date amounts to EUR 1,895,342 as shown in the Table 15.2, above. The present value of the cash flows under the revised terms discounted at the original effective interest rate of 10.6749 per cent is shown in Table 15.3, below.

Table 15.3 Present value of cash flows under the revised terms

		Cash flows €	Present value €
1 January 2006	Fees	60,000	60,000
31 December 2006	Revised interest	150,000	135,532
31 December 2007	Revised interest	150,000	122,460
31 December 2008	Revised interest	150,000	110,648
31 December 2009	Revised interest	150,000	99,976
31 December 2010	Revised interest	150,000	90,333
31 December 2011	Revised interest + principal	2,050,000	1,115,473
			1,734,421

The present value of EUR 1,734,421 represents 91.5 per cent of the present value of previous cash flows (EUR 1,734,421 ÷ EUR 1,895,342). As the difference in present values of EUR 160,921 (EUR 1,895,342 – EUR 1,734,421) is less than 10 per cent of the present value of the previous cash flows, the modification is not accounted for as extinguishment.

The question arises as to how to account for the present value difference of EUR 160,921 arising from the renegotiation:

- one approach would be to recognise the difference immediately in the income statement by adjusting the previous carrying value of the liability from EUR 1,895,342 to EUR 1,734,421;
- another approach would be to recognise the difference over the remaining life of the instrument by adjusting the effective interest rate so that the previous carrying value of EUR 1,895,342 accretes to the redemption amount of EUR 1.9m by 31 December 2011.

The effective interest rate that amortises the previous carrying value, as adjusted for fees incurred of EUR 60,000, is 8.6453 per cent as shown in the Table 15.4, below.

Table 15.4 Interest charges and the previous carrying value adjusted for the amount of fees incurred

	Interest @ 8.6453% €	Payments €	Carrying value €
			1,895,342
Fees paid			(60,000)
1 January 2006			1,835,342
31 December 2006	158,672	150,000	1,844,014
31 December 2007	159,421	150,000	1,853,435
31 December 2008	160,235	150,000	1,863,670
31 December 2009	161,120	150,000	1,874,789
31 December 2010	162,081	150,000	1,886,871
31 December 2011	163,126	2,050,000	(−4 rounding difference)
	964,654	2,800,000	

15.5   Measurement of financial assets and liabilities

An entity recognises a financial asset or a financial liability when it first becomes a party to the contractual rights and obligations in the contract. It is, therefore, necessary to measure those contractual rights and obligations on initial recognition. Under IAS 39, all financial instruments are measured initially by reference to their fair value, which is normally the transaction price, that is, the fair value of the consideration given or received. However, this will not always be the case.

Subsequent to initial recognition, IAS 39's measurement approach is best described as a 'mixed attribute' model with certain assets and liabilities measured at cost and others at fair value. The model depends upon an instrument's classification into one of the four categories of financial assets or one of the two categories of financial liabilities discussed in section 14.3.5. For example, depending on the nature of the instrument and management's intentions, a fixed interest security intended to be held-to-maturity would be measured at amortised cost and not at fair value. Notwithstanding this, as explained in section 14.3.5, the standard gives entities an option to classify financial instruments that meet certain special criteria at fair value with all gains and losses taken to the income statement. The possibility for entities to use the fair value option simplifies the application of IAS 39 by mitigating certain anomalies that result from the use of the mixed measurement model.

This section deals with IAS 39's basic measurement requirements and addresses the concepts of fair value and amortised cost, including the use of the effective interest method and the standard's impairment model.

15.5.1 Initial measurement

Initial fair value

When a financial asset or financial liability is recognised initially, IAS 39 para 43 requires the entity to measure it at its 'fair value' including, in certain situations, transaction costs. The standard defines fair value as the amount for which an asset could be exchanged, or a liability settled, between knowledgeable willing parties in an arm's length transaction (IAS 39 para 9). The concept of fair value and requirements for determining the fair value of financial instruments are discussed later in this chapter.

Given that fair value is the price that arm's length market participants would pay or receive in a routine transaction under the market conditions at the date at which the asset or liability is to be measured for accounting purposes (the measurement date), it follows that a financial instrument's initial fair value will normally be the transaction price, that is, the fair value of the consideration given or received (IAS 39 para AG 64).

Example 15.9

Interest free loan to an employee

Entity A grants an interest free loan of EUR 10,000 to Mr X, one of its employees, for a period of three years. The market rate of interest to this individual for a three year loan with payment of interest at maturity is 5 per cent.

The consideration given to Mr X consists of two assets:

- The fair value of the loan:

$$\frac{€10,000}{(1.05)^3} = €8,638$$

- The difference of EUR 1,362 is accounted for as employee compensation in accordance with IAS 19 – *Employee Benefits*.

Transaction costs

Transaction costs are incremental costs that are directly attributable to the acquisition or issue or disposal of a financial asset or financial liability. An incremental cost is one that would not have been incurred if the entity had not acquired, issued or disposed of the financial instrument (IAS 39 para 9).

Transaction costs include fees and commissions paid to agents (including employees acting as selling agents), advisers, brokers and dealers, levies by regulatory agencies and securities exchanges, and transfer taxes and duties. Transaction costs do not include debt premiums or discounts, financing costs or internal administrative or holding costs (IAS 39 para AG 13).

According to IAS 39 para IG E1.1, the above fees together with the related direct origination costs are accounted for in a financial instrument's initial measurement as follows:

- When a financial asset or financial liability is recognised initially and not designated at fair value through the income statement, transaction costs (net of fees received) that are directly attributable to the acquisition or issue are included in the initial fair value. For financial assets, such costs are added to the amount originally recognised. For financial liabilities, such costs are deducted from the amount originally recognised. This applies to financial instruments carried at amortised cost and available-for-sale financial assets (IAS 39 para 43).

- For financial instruments that are measured at fair value through the income statement, transaction costs (net of any fees received) are not added to the initial fair value, but are immediately recognised in the income statement on initial recognition.

- Transaction costs expected to be incurred on a financial instrument's transfer or disposal are not included in the financial instrument's measurement.

Settlement date accounting for regular way transactions

When an entity uses settlement date accounting for an asset that is subsequently measured at cost or amortised cost, the asset is recognised initially at settlement date, but measured at the fair value on trade date (IAS 39 para 44). This is an exception to the general rule referred to at the beginning of this section (see page 418) that a financial asset should be recognised at its fair value on initial recognition. The accounting for regular way trades is considered in section 15.2.

15.5.2 Subsequent measurement of financial assets

As set out in Chapter 14, financial assets are classified in one of four categories. Following their initial recognition, the classification determines how the financial asset is subsequently measured, including any recognition of profit or loss. Table 15.9 on page 427 summarises the requirements that are considered in the remainder of this section.

Financial assets at fair value through the income statement

After initial recognition, financial assets falling within this category (including assets held for trading and derivative assets not designated as effective hedging instruments and assets designated on initial recognition at fair value through the income statement) are measured at fair value, without the deduction of transaction costs that the entity may incur on sale or other disposal (IAS 39 para 46). Such transaction costs are future costs that relate to the sale or the disposal and are not relevant for determining fair value. Therefore, they should properly be included in the period in which the sale or the disposal takes place.

The standard's requirements for determining the fair value of instruments that are measured on this basis are considered in section 15.6. Investments in equity instruments that do not have a quoted market price in an active market and whose fair value cannot be reliably measured and derivatives that are linked to and must be settled by delivery of such unquoted equity instruments, should be measured at cost (IAS 39 para 46(c)).

All gains and losses arising from changes in fair value of financial assets falling within this category are recognised, not surprisingly, in the income statement (IAS 39 para 55(a)). This means that assets falling within this category are not subject to review for impairment as losses due to fall in value (including impairment) would automatically be reflected in the income statement.

Loans and receivables

Loans and receivables, as defined in Chapter 14, are measured at *amortised cost* using the effective interest method (IAS 39 para 46(a)). They are measured on this basis whether they are intended to be held-to-maturity or not (IAS 39 para AG 68).

The *effective interest method* is a method of calculating the amortised cost of a financial asset or a financial liability and of allocating the interest income or interest expense over the relevant period. The effective interest rate is the rate that exactly discounts estimated future cash payments or receipts through the expected life of the financial instrument. When calculating the effective interest rate, an entity should estimate cash flows considering all contractual terms of the financial instrument but should not consider future credit losses. The calculation includes all fees paid or received between parties to the contract that are an integral part of the effective interest rate, transaction costs, and all other premiums or discounts (IAS 39 para 9).

The amortised cost method of accounting is illustrated in Example 15.10, below.

Example 15.10

Amortised cost method

On 1 January 2008, a company buys EUR 200,000 of 6 per cent loan stock for EUR 187,860. Interest will be received on 31 December each year and the stock will be redeemed at par on 31 December 2012. The company intends to hold the stock until maturity and calculates the effective interest rate to be 7.5 per cent per annum. Financial statements are prepared at 31 December each year.

(a) State the amount at which this loan stock should be measured on 1 January 2008.

(b) Calculate the amount at which the loan stock should be measured on 31 December 2008, 2009, 2010, 2011 and 2012.

(c) Show that the effective rate of 7.5 per cent 'exactly discounts estimated future cash receipts to the initial carrying amount of the asset' as required by IAS 39.

(a) The loan stock is measured initially at EUR 187,860.

(b) The amortised cost of the loan stock at the end of each year is calculated as shown in Table 15.5.

Table 15.5 Calculation of the amortised cost of the loan stock

Year	Balance b/f €	Interest @ 7.5% €	Amount received €	Amortised cost €
2008	187,860	14,090	(12,000)	189,950
2009	189,950	14,246	(12,000)	192,196
2010	192,196	14,414	(12,000)	194,610
2011	194,610	14,596	(12,000)	197,206
2012	197,206	14,794	(212,000)	0
		72,140		

Notes:

(i)   The interest earned each year is 7.5 per cent on the balance brought forward. This is credited to the company's income statement. Interest at 7.5 per cent for 2012 in fact would be EUR 14,790, but this has been adjusted to EUR 14,794 to ensure that the balance remaining at the end of the year is EUR nil. It would appear that the effective rate of interest is actually very slightly more than 7.5 per cent.

(ii) The effective interest rate (7.5 per cent) is higher than the rate (6 per cent) at which annual interest payments are calculated because the company will receive a premium of EUR 12,140 (EUR 200,000 – EUR 187,860) when the loan stock is redeemed. The effective interest method spreads this premium fairly over the life of the loan stock.

(iii) The total credit to the income statement is EUR 72,140. This is equal to annual interest of EUR 12,000 for five years plus the premium of EUR 12,140.

(c) If the amounts receivable during the life of the loan stock are discounted at an annual rate of 7.5 per cent, the present value of each amount is as shown in Table 15.6.

Table 15.6 Present value of the cash flows receivable during the life of the loan stock

	Workings (amount receivable ÷ discount factor)	Present value €
Receivable 31 December 2008	€12,000 ÷ 1.075	11,162
Receivable 31 December 2009	€12,000 ÷ $(1.075)^2$	10,384
Receivable 31 December 2010	€12,000 ÷ $(1.075)^3$	9,660
Receivable 31 December 2011	€12,000 ÷ $(1.075)^4$	8,986
Receivable 31 December 2012	€212,000 ÷ $(1.075)^5$	147,670
Total present value		187,862

Apart from a small rounding difference, an effective rate of 7.5 per cent does indeed discount estimated future cash receipts to the initial carrying amount of EUR 187,860.

Held-to-maturity investments

Held-to-maturity investments are also measured at amortised cost using the effective interest method. Gains and losses are accounted for in the same way as loans and receivables.

Available-for-sale assets

Available-for-sale financial assets should be measured at fair value. As with assets designated at fair value through the income statement, transaction costs that will be incurred on the sale or disposal of such assets should not be deducted. However, there is an exemption from measurement at fair value of an available-for-sale asset if its fair value cannot be measured reliably. This exemption only applies to unquoted equity instruments and derivative contracts based on those instruments. These instruments should be measured at cost (IAS 39 para 46(c)).

As explained above (see page 419), transaction costs that are directly attributable to the acquisition or issue of an available-for-sale financial asset are added to the initial fair value. For available-for-sale financial assets, transaction costs are recognised in OCI as part of a change in fair value at the subsequent measurement. If an available-for-sale financial asset has fixed or determinable payments and does not have an indefinite life, the transaction costs are amortised through the income statement using the effective interest method (see section 15.5.3, below). If an available-for-sale financial asset does not have fixed or determinable payments and has an indefinite life, the transaction costs are recognised in the income statement when the asset is derecognised or becomes impaired (IAS 39 para AG 67).

All gains and losses arising from changes in fair value of available-for-sale financial assets are recognised directly in OCI, except as follows:

- Interest calculated using the effective interest method is recognised in the income statement. Dividends on available-for-sale equity instruments are recognised in the income statement when the entity's right to receive payment is established (IAS 18 para 30(c));
- Foreign exchange gains and losses on monetary financial assets are recognised in the income statement;
- Impairment losses are recognised in the income statement (see also section 15.7.2). Reversals of impairment of a debt instrument are also recognised in the income statement, but reversals of impairment on equity instruments are not (see also section 15.7.3) (IAS 39 para 55(b)).

When an available-for-sale financial asset is derecognised as a result of a sale or is impaired, the cumulative gain or loss previously recognised in OCI is recycled and recognised in the income statement (IAS 39 paras 55(b) and 67). For example, assume that an entity acquires an equity security for EUR 1,000 that has a fair value at the end of the year of EUR 1,200. A gain of EUR 200 is recognised in OCI. In the following year, the entity sells the security for EUR 1,100. In the year of sale a profit of EUR 100, being the difference between proceeds of EUR 1,100 and original cost of EUR 1,000 is recognised. This represents the difference between the proceeds of EUR 1,100 and the previous carrying value of EUR 1,200 (EUR 100 loss) and the recycling to the income statement of EUR 200 gain previously recognised in OCI.

In the above example, a single security is used to illustrate the accounting for recycling. In practice, the entity may have acquired the same security in tranches at different dates and at different prices over a period of time. IAS 39 does not specify whether such fungible assets (or indeed any other fungible financial assets) should be considered individually or in aggregate, and, if in aggregate, which measurement basis (AVCO, FIFO, etc.) is appropriate for calculating the gain or loss on a partial disposal. This is in contrast to IAS 2 – *Inventories*, which specifies the use of AVCO or FIFO in most circumstances. In practice, entities may opt, as an accounting policy choice, for any one of the methods. The method used should be applied consistently and disclosed in the accounting policy.

The subsequent measurement of available-for-sale financial assets with fixed and determinable payments is complicated by the fact that fair value changes are recognised in OCI, but interest income is recognised in each period in the income statement using the effective interest method. In order to ensure that the change in fair value is correctly calculated at the measurement date, it would be necessary to compare the instrument's clean price (the fair value of the instrument less accrued interest) with its amortised cost, excluding accrued interest, at that date. Therefore, although the instrument is measured at fair value, the amortised cost should still be calculated using the effective interest method in order to determine interest income.

of EUR 3 per share. At 31 December 2009, the quoted ex-dividend price of the shares amounts to EUR 42 per share. The entity receives payment of the dividend on 6 January 2010.

At 31 December 2009, the entity will recognise the dividend income in the income statement and the change in the fair value of the shares in OCI as noted below:

	Dr	Cr
	€	€
Dividend receivable	3,000	
Income statement – dividend income – 1,000 @ €3		3,000
Available-for-sale financial asset	2,000	
Other comprehensive income – 1,000 @ (€42 – €40)		2,000

The shares' quoted price prior to the dividend adjustment would have been EUR 45 giving a total fair value change of EUR 5,000. However, as part of this change (EUR 3,000) is realised as a result of the dividend income recognised in the income statement; there is an equal and offsetting change in OCI.

15.5.3 Subsequent measurement of financial liabilities

After initial recognition, an entity should measure financial liabilities (other than those falling in the category of financial liabilities at fair value through the income statement) at amortised cost using the effective interest method as illustrated in Example 15.13.

Example 15.13

Effective interest rate method of amortisation

On 1 July 2008, a company issues EUR 2m of 8 per cent loan stock. The stock is issued at a 10 per cent discount (so only EUR 1,800,000 is received from the lenders) and issue costs of EUR 78,600 are incurred. Interest is payable in arrears on 30 June each year and the loan stock is redeemable at par on 30 June 2011. The effective interest rate is calculated to be 14 per cent per annum. The company prepares financial statements to 30 June each year.

(a) State the amount at which this loan stock should be measured on 1 July 2008.

(b) Calculate the amount at which the loan stock should be measured on 30 June 2009, 2010 and 2011.

(a) The loan stock should be measured initially at EUR 1,721,400 (EUR 1,800,000 – EUR 78,600). This is the amount of the consideration received when the stock was issued, less directly attributable transaction costs.

(b) The loan stock should be measured at amortised cost using the effective interest method. Amortised cost at the end of each year is calculated in Table 15.8.

Table 15.8 Measurement of the loan stock using the effective interest method

Year to 30 June	Balance b/f €	Interest @ 14% €	Amount paid €	Amortised cost €
2009	1,721,400	240,996	(160,000)	1,802,396
2010	1,802,396	252,336	(160,000)	1,894,732
2011	1,894,732	265,268	(2,160,000)	0
		758,600		

Notes:

(i) The interest each year is 14 per cent of the balance brought forward. This is charged to the company's income statement. Interest at 14 per cent for 2011 is actually EUR 265,263 but this has been adjusted to EUR 265,268 to ensure that the balance remaining at the end of 2011 is EUR nil. The effective rate of interest is in fact very slightly more than 14 per cent.

(ii) The effective interest rate (14 per cent) is higher than the rate (8 per cent) at which annual interest payments are calculated because the loan was issued at a discount and the company has had to pay transaction costs. The effective interest method spreads these two items fairly over the life of the loan stock.

(iii) The total charge to the income statement is EUR 758,600. This is equal to annual interest of EUR 160,000 for three years plus the discount of EUR 200,000 and issue costs of EUR 78,600: €480,000 + €200,000 + €78,600.

Table 15.9 Subsequent measurement of financial assets and financial liabilities

Classification	Initial measurement	Subsequent measurement	Changes in carrying amount	Impairment
Financial asset or financial liability at fair value through income statement	Fair value	Fair value	Income statement	Not applicable as any impairment will be taken to the income statement as part of the change in fair value
Loans and receivables	Fair value plus transaction costs	Amortised cost	Income statement	Yes
Held-to-maturity investments	Fair value plus transaction costs	Amortised cost	Income statement	Yes
Available-for-sale financial assets	Fair value plus transaction costs (1)	Fair value (2)	OCI (3)	Yes
Other financial liabilities	Fair value plus transaction costs	Amortised cost	Income statement	Not applicable

Notes:
(1) Cost for equity instruments that do not have any quoted market price in an active market and whose fair value cannot be reliably measured and derivative assets that are linked to and should be settled by delivery of such unquoted equity instruments.
(2) Cost when fair value is not reliably measurable.
(3) Income statement for those financial assets without an active market.

loan more cheaply and so carry two identical securities in the same not-for-sale account at vastly different prices.

Financial assets, even complex pools of assets, trade continuously in markets. Markets function best when companies disclose valid information about the values of their assets and future cash flows. If companies choose not to disclose their best estimates of the fair values of their assets, market participants will make their own judgments about future cash flows and subtract a risk premium for non-disclosure. Good accounting should reduce such dead-weight losses.

This already happens in another financial sector. Mutual funds in the US now use models, rather than the last traded price, to provide estimates of the fair values of their assets that trade in overseas markets. The models forecast the prices at which these overseas assets would have traded at the close of the US market, based on the closing prices of similar assets in the US market. In this way, the funds ensure that their shareholders do not trade at biased net asset values calculated from stale prices. Banks can similarly use models to update the prices that would be paid for various assets. Trading desks in financial institutions have models that allow them to predict prices to within 5 per cent of what would be offered for even their complex asset pools.

Obtaining fair-value estimates for complex pools of asset-backed securities, of course, is not trivial. But these days it is possible for a bank's analysts to use recent market transaction prices as reference points and then adjust for the unique characteristics of the assets they actually hold, such as the specific local housing prices underlying their mortgage assets.

For fair-value estimates made by internal bank analysts to be credible, they need to be independently validated by external auditors. Many certified auditors, however, have little training or experience in the models used to calculate fair-value estimates. In this case, auditing firms can use outside experts, much as they do today with actuaries and lawyers who provide an independent attestation to other complex estimates disclosed in a company's financial statements. The higher cost of using independent experts is part of the price of originating and investing in complex, infrequently traded financial instruments.

Legislators and regulators fear that marking banks' assets down to fair-value estimates will trigger automatic actions as capital ratios deteriorate. But using accounting rules to mislead regulators with inaccurate information is a poor policy. If capital calculations are based on inaccurate values of assets, the ratios are already lower than they appear. Banks should provide regulators with the best information about their assets and liabilities and, separately, allow them the flexibility and discretion to adjust capital adequacy ratios based on the economic situation. Regulators can lower capital ratios during downturns and raise them during good economic times.

No system of disclosing the fair value of complex securities is perfect. Models can be misused or misinterpreted. But reasonable and auditable methods exist today to incorporate the information in the most recent market prices. Investors, creditors, boards and regulators need not base decisions on biased values of a company's financial assets and liabilities.

Robert Kaplan, Robert Merton and Scott Richard, 'Disclose the fair value of complex securities', *Financial Times*, 17 August 2009.

15.7 Impairment of financial assets

A financial asset measured at amortised cost is impaired when its carrying value exceeds the present value of the future cash flows discounted at the financial asset's original effective interest rate. A financial asset that is carried at fair value through the income statement does not give rise to any impairment issues as diminution in value due to impairment would already be reflected in the fair value and, hence, in the income statement. It follows that impairment issues are only relevant to financial assets that are carried at amortised cost and available-for-sale financial assets whose fair value changes are recognised in equity.

IAS 39 deals with impairment of financial assets through a two-step process:

1 First, an entity should carry out an impairment review of its financial assets at each balance sheet date. The aim of this review is to determine whether there is objective evidence that impairment exists for a financial asset (IAS 39 para 58). This is considered below.

2 Secondly, if there is objective evidence of impairment, the entity should measure and record the impairment loss in the reporting period (IAS 39 para 58). The measurement of impairment losses differs between financial assets carried at amortised cost, financial assets carried at cost and available-for-sale financial assets (see section 15.7.2, below). There is also a difference on whether impairment losses can be reversed depending on whether the available-for-sale instrument is debt or equity (see section 15.7.3, below).

15.7.1 Objective evidence of impairment

IAS 39 para 59 provides examples of factors that may, either individually or taken together, provide sufficient objective evidence that an impairment loss has been incurred in a financial asset or group of financial assets. They include observable data that comes to the attention of the holder of the asset about the following loss events:

(a) significant financial difficulty of the issuer;

(b) a breach of contract, such as a default or delinquency in interest or principal payments;

(c) the lender, for economic or legal reasons relating to the borrower's financial difficulty, granting to the borrower a concession that the lender would not otherwise consider;

(d) it becomes probable that the borrower will enter bankruptcy or other financial reorganisation;

(e) the disappearance of an active market for that financial asset because of financial difficulties[2];

(f) observable data indicating that there is a measurable decrease in the estimated future cash flows from a group of financial assets since the initial recognition of those assets, although the decrease cannot yet be identified with the individual financial assets in the group, including:

(i) adverse changes in the payment status of borrowers in the group (i.e., an increased number of delayed payments or an increased number of credit card borrowers who have reached their credit limit and are paying the minimum monthly amount); or

(ii) national or local economic conditions that correlate with defaults on the assets in the group (i.e., an increase in the unemployment rate in the geographical area of the borrowers, a decrease in property prices for mortgages in the relevant area, a decrease in oil prices for loan assets to oil producers, or adverse changes in industry conditions that affect the borrowers in the group).

Evidence of impairment for equity instruments

IAS 39 includes additional guidance about impairment indicators that are specific to investments in equity instruments. They apply in addition to the impairment indicators described above, which focus on the assessment of impairment in debt instruments.

In addition to the types of events listed above, objective evidence of impairment for an investment in an equity instrument includes information about significant changes with an adverse effect that have taken place in the technological, market, economic or legal environment in which the issuer operates, and indicates that the cost of the investment in the equity instrument may not be recovered. A significant or prolonged decline in the fair value of an investment in an equity instrument below its cost is also objective evidence of impairment (IAS 39 para 61).

15.7.2 Measurement of impairment losses

As mentioned earlier, the measurement of impairment losses differs depending on the classification of financial assets.

Measurement of impairment losses for financial assets carried at amortised cost

Financial assets carried at amortised cost are classified as either loans and receivables or held-to-maturity. If there is objective evidence that an impairment loss on such an asset has been incurred, the amount of the loss should be measured as the difference between the asset's carrying amount and the present value of estimated future cash flows. The expected cash flows should exclude future credit losses that have not been incurred and should be discounted at the financial asset's original effective interest rate (that is, the effective interest rate computed at initial recognition) (IAS 39 para 63).

The standard allows the carrying amount of the asset to be reduced either directly by writing it down or through the use of an allowance account such as a loan loss provision or provision for bad and doubtful debts. However, the amount of the loss should be recognised in the income statement (IAS 39 para 63).

The asset's carrying amount in the entity's balance sheet is stated net of any related allowance (IAS 39 para AG 84).

In some circumstances, it may not be practicable to make a reasonably reliable direct estimate of the present value of future cash flows expected from an impaired financial asset measured at amortised cost. As a practical expedient, the carrying amount of the impaired asset may be determined in these circumstances on the basis of an instrument's fair value using an observable market price (IAS 39 para AG 84).

A loan's observable market price is the loan's quoted price that can be obtained from reliable market sources. For example, loans with an active secondary market could be measured based on the observable market price. Similarly, an entity that has a viable plan to dispose of loans in a bulk sale could measure impairment by comparison to the net proceeds received on similar loan sales. However, it is likely that the use of the observable market price will be infrequent, because either there may not be a market for the loans or the market may be illiquid.

The expected future cash flows that are included in the calculation are the contractual cash of the instrument itself, reduced or delayed based on the current expectations of the amount and timing of these cash flows as a result of losses incurred at the balance sheet date. In circumstances where the amount outstanding is expected to be collected in full, but the collection period is delayed, an impairment loss should still be recognised, unless the creditor receives full compensation (for instance, in the form of penalty interest) for the period of the delinquency, as illustrated in Example 15.14.

Example 15.14

Impairment arising from changes in the amount and timing of cash flows

Because of Customer B's financial difficulties, Entity A is concerned that Customer B will not be able to make all principal and interest payments due on a loan in a timely manner. It negotiates a restructuring of the loan. Entity A expects that Customer B will be able to meet its obligations under the restructured terms in any of the following cases.

- Customer B will pay the full principal amount of the original loan five years after the original due date, but none of the interest due under the original terms.
- Customer B will pay the full principal amount of the original loan on the original due date, but none of the interest due under the original terms.
- Customer B will pay the full principal amount of the original loan on the original due date with interest only at a lower interest rate than the interest rate inherent in the original loan.
- Customer B will pay the full principal amount of the original loan five years after the original due date and all interest accrued during the original loan term, but no interest for the extended term.
- Customer B will pay the full principal amount of the original loan five years after the original due date and all interest, including interest for both the original term of the loan and the extended term (IAS 39 para IG E4.3).

Given that customer B is in financial difficulties, an impairment loss has been incurred, as there is objective evidence of impairment. The amount of the impairment loss for a loan measured at amortised cost is the difference between the loan's carrying amount and the present value of future principal and interest payments discounted at the loan's original effective interest rate.

In the first four scenarios above, the present value of the future principal and interest payments discounted at the loan's original effective interest rate will be lower than the loan's carrying amount. Therefore, an impairment loss should be recognised in those cases.

In the final scenario, even though the timing of payments has changed, the lender will receive interest on interest, and the present value of the future principal and interest payments discounted at the loan's original effective interest rate will equal the carrying amount of the loan. Therefore, there is no impairment loss. However, this is unlikely given customer B's financial difficulties.

Where an impaired financial asset is secured by collateral, the calculation of the present value of the estimated future cash flows of the collateralised financial asset should reflect the cash flows that may result from foreclosure less costs for obtaining and selling the collateral, whether or not foreclosure is probable (IAS 39 para AG 84). As the measurement of the impaired financial asset reflects the collateral asset's fair value, the collateral is not recognised as an asset separately from the impaired financial asset, unless it meets the recognition criteria for an asset in another standard (IAS 39 IG para E4.8).

Measurement of impairment losses for financial assets carried at cost

An unquoted equity instrument that is not carried at fair value because its fair value cannot be reliably measured, or on a derivative asset that is linked to and must be settled by delivery of such an unquoted equity instrument, are measured at cost. For such instruments, if there is objective evidence that an impairment loss has been incurred, the amount of the impairment loss should be measured as the difference between the carrying amount of the financial asset and the present value of estimated future cash flows discounted at the current market rate of return for a similar financial asset. Such impairment losses are not permitted to be reversed (IAS 39 para 66).

Measurement of impairment losses for available-for-sale financial assets

When a decline in the fair value of an available-for-sale financial asset has been recognised directly in OCI and there is objective evidence that the asset is impaired, the cumulative loss that had been recognised directly in OCI should be reclassified from OCI and recognised in the income statement even though the financial asset has not been derecognised (IAS 39 para 67).

The amount of cumulative loss that is recycled to the income statement is the difference between the acquisition cost (net of any principal repayment and amortisation) and current fair value, less any impairment loss on that financial asset previously recognised in the income statement (IAS 39 para 68).

Any portion of the cumulative net loss that is attributable to foreign currency changes on that asset that had been recognised in equity is also recognised in the income statement. Any subsequent losses, including any portion attributable to foreign currency changes, are also recognised in the income statement until the asset is derecognised (IAS 39 para IG E4.9).

15.7.3 Reversal of impairment losses

It is possible that after an impairment loss has been recognised for an available-for-sale financial asset circumstances change in a subsequent period such that the fair value of the available-for-sale financial instrument increases. In those circumstances, the treatment required by the standard for reversals of impairment losses on available-for-sale debt instruments is different from those on available-for-sale equity instruments as described below:

- If, in a subsequent period, the fair value of a debt instrument classified as available-for-sale increases and the increase can be objectively related to an event occurring after the impairment loss was recognised in the income statement, the impairment loss should be reversed, with the amount of the reversal recognised in the income statement (IAS 39 para 70).

- Impairment losses recognised in the income statement for an investment in an equity instrument classified as available-for-sale should not be reversed through the income statement (IAS 39 para 69). This means that subsequent increases in fair value including those that have the effect of reversing earlier impairment losses should be recognised in equity. This is a significant change from the previous version of the standard.

Example 15.15

Impairment of an available-for-sale financial asset

On 1 July 2010, entity A invested in a financial instrument. At this date the cost and fair value of the instrument was EUR 1m. The instrument is classified as available-for-sale and therefore is measured at fair value, and changes in fair value are recorded in OCI.

Changes in the fair value of this instrument are set out below:

Year	Fair value changes	Nature of change
2011	€100,000	No objective evidence of impairment
2012	€200,000	Objective evidence of impairment
2013	€150,000	Objective evidence of reversal of impairment

We will illustrate the accounting treatment of the above changes in the fair value, assuming that the financial instrument is:

(a) a debt instrument

(b) an equity instrument.

We ignore interest income.

Summary

- An entity is required to recognise a financial asset or liability on its balance sheet when it becomes a party to the instrument's contractual provisions. Examples of such situations are represented by regular way transactions: a regular way purchase or sale is a purchase or sale of a financial asset under a contract whose terms require delivery of the asset within the time frame established generally by regulation or convention in the marketplace concerned.

- Under IAS 39, all financial instruments should be measured initially by reference to their fair value, which is normally the transaction price.

- Subsequent to initial recognition, IAS 39's measurement approach is best described as a 'mixed attribute' model with certain assets and liabilities measured at cost and others at fair value. The model depends upon an instrument's classification into one of the four categories of financial assets or one of the two categories of financial liabilities.

- The effective interest method is a method of calculating the amortised cost of a financial asset or a financial liability and of allocating the interest income or interest expense over the relevant period. The effective interest rate is the rate that discounts estimated future cash receipts or payments over the expected life of the financial instrument.

- After initial recognition, financial assets at fair value through the income statement should be measured at fair value. All gains and losses arising from changes in fair value of financial assets falling within this category should be recognised in the income statement.

- Loans and receivables and held-to-maturity investments should be measured at amortised cost using the effective interest method.

- Available-for-sale financial assets should be measured at fair value. There is an exemption from measurement at fair value of an available-for-sale asset if its fair value cannot be measured reliably. This exemption only applies to unquoted equity instruments and derivative contracts based on those instruments. These instruments should be measured at cost. All gains and losses arising from changes in fair value of available-for-sale financial assets should be recognised in OCI. When an available-for-sale financial asset is derecognised as a result of a sale or impairment, the cumulative gain or loss previously recognised in OCI should be recycled and recognised in the income statement.

- After initial recognition, an entity should measure financial liabilities (other than those falling in the category of financial liabilities at fair value through the income statement) at amortised cost using the effective interest method.

- A financial asset measured at amortised cost is impaired when its carrying value exceeds the present value of the future cash flows discounted at the financial asset's original effective interest rate. A financial asset that is carried at fair value through the income statement does not give rise to any impairment issues as diminution in value due to impairment would already be reflected in the fair value and, hence, in the income statement. It follows that impairment issues are only relevant to financial assets that are carried at amortised cost and available-for-sale financial assets whose fair value changes are recognised in OCI.

- An entity should disclose information that enables users of its financial statements to evaluate the nature and extent of risks arising from financial instruments to which the entity is exposed at the end of the reporting period statement. These risks typically include, but are not limited to, credit risk, liquidity risk and market risk.

Research and references

The IASB documents relevant for this chapter are:

- IAS 32 – *Financial Instruments: Presentation*.
- IAS 39 – *Financial Instruments: Recognition and Measurement*.
- IFRS 7 – *Financial Instruments: Disclosures*.

The following are examples of books, research and discussion papers that take the issues of this chapter further:

- Alexander, D., Britton, A. and Jorissen, A. (2007) *International Financial Reporting and Analysis,* 3rd edn. Thomson, Chapter 17.
- Barth, M.E. and Landsman, W.R. (1995) 'Fundamental issues related to using fair value accounting for financial reporting', *Accounting Horizons*, 9(4), December, pp. 97–107.
- Butler, C. (2009) *Accounting for Financial Instruments*. Wiley.
- Dealy, N. and Singleton-Green, B. (2007) 'What's fair?', *Accountancy*, June, p. 77.
- Deans, S. (2007) 'Discussion of "Is fair value accounting information relevant and reliable? Evidence from capital market research"', *Accounting and Business Research*, International Accounting Policy Forum special issue, pp. 31–2.
- Elliott, B. and Elliott, J. (2009) *Financial Accounting and Reporting,* 13th edn. Financial Times-Prentice Hall, Chapter 12.
- Epstein, B.J. and Jermakowicz, E.K. (2009) *IFRS 2009: Interpretation and Application of International Accounting and Financial Reporting Standards*. Wiley, Chapter 13.
- Hairs, C.J., Belsham, D.J., Bryson, N.M., George, C.M., Hare, D.J.P., Smith, D.A. and Thompson, S. (2002) 'Fair valuation of liabilities', *British Actuarial Journal*, 8(2), pp. 203–340.
- Hitz, J.M. (2007) 'The decision usefulness of fair value accounting. A theoretical perspective', *European Accounting Review*, 16(2), pp. 323–62.
- Horton, J. and Macve, R. (2000) '"Fair value" for financial instruments: how erasing theory is leading to unworkable global accounting standards for performance reporting', *Australian Accounting Review*, July, pp. 26–39 (available at http://www2.lse.ac.uk/accounting/pdf/HortonandMacverevisedFairValueForFinancialInstruments.pdf)
- Horton, J. and Macve, R. (2007) *An Experiment in 'Fair Value' Accounting?* ICAEW, October.
- International Accounting Standards Board (2008) *Reducing Complexity in Reporting Financial Instruments* (Discussion Paper). London: IASC Foundation.
- Landsman, W.R., Peasnell, K.V. and Shakespeare, C. (2008) 'Are asset securitizations sales or loans?', *The Accounting Review*, 83(5), September, pp. 1251–72.
- Laux, C. and Leuz, C. (2009) 'The crisis of fair-value accounting: making sense of the recent debate', *Accounting, Organizations and Society*, 34(6–7), October, pp. 826–34.

- Penman, S.H. (2007) 'Financial reporting quality: is fair value a plus or a minus?', *Accounting and Business Research*, Special Issue: International Accounting Policy Forum, pp. 33–44.
- PricewaterhouseCoopers (2009) *IFRS Manual of Accounting – 2010. Global Guide to International Financial Reporting Standards*. CCH, Chapter 6.
- Rayman, R.A. (2007) 'Fair value accounting and the present value fallacy: the need for an alternative conceptual framework', *British Accounting Review*, 39(3), September, pp. 211–25.
- Ryan, S.G. (2008) 'Accounting in and for the subprime crisis', *The Accounting Review*, 83(6), December, pp. 1605–38.
- Securities and Exchange Commission (2008) *Final Report of the Advisory Committee on Improvements to Financial Reporting to the United States Securities and Exchange Commission*. Washington, DC: SEC.
- Securities and Exchange Commission (2008) *Report and Recommendations Pursuant to Section 133 of the Emergency Economic Stabilization Act of: Study on Mark-to-Market Accounting*. Washington, DC: SEC.
- Sutton, T. (2004) *Corporate Financial Accounting and Reporting*, 2nd edn. Financial Times-Prentice Hall, Chapter 13.
- Turner, A. (2009) *The Turner Review: A Regulatory Response to the Global Banking Crisis*. London: Financial Services Authority.
- Walton, P. (ed.) (2007) *The Routledge Companion to Fair Value in Financial Reporting*. London: Routledge.

Discussion questions and exercises

15.1 Recognition and derecognition of financial assets and financial liabilities

(a) When should a financial asset or liability be recognised?

(b) What are the approaches to derecognition of financial assets under IFRS?

(c) What are the provisions of IAS 39 relating to derecognition of financial liabilities?

15.2 Impairment of financial assets

(a) To which financial assets does impairment refer to? When are such financial assets impaired?

(b) List examples of evidence of an impairment loss.

(c) If there is objective evidence that an impairment loss has been incurred, how should it be measured?

15.3 Financial instrument risk disclosures

(a) Explain the terms 'credit risk', 'liquidity risk' and 'market risk' used in IFRS 7.

(b) List the main disclosures required by IFRS 7 in relation to each of these three types of risk.

15.4 Derecognition of a financial asset in its entirety

Entity A holds a small number of shares in entity B. The shares are classified as available-for-sale. On 31 March 2010, the shares' fair value is EUR 2,400 and the cumulative gain recognised in OCI is EUR 400. On the same day, entity B is acquired by entity C, a large listed company. As a result, entity A receives shares in entity C at a fair value of EUR 2,600.

What should entity A do in connection with the transactions described above?

15.5   Sale and repurchase transactions

An entity purchases EUR 20m, 10 per cent five-year government bonds on 1 January 2009 with semi-annual interest payable on 30 June and 31 December for EUR 21.6m that results in a premium of EUR 1.6m. The entity classifies the bonds as held-to-maturity investments at amortised cost. The amortisation of the bonds to maturity using the effective interest method is shown below:

	Cash received	Interest income @ 4.0130325%	Carrying amount
1 January 2009			21,600,000
1 July 2009	1,000,000	866,815	21,466,815
1 January 2010	1,000,000	861,470	21,328,285
1 July 2010	1,000,000	855,911	21,184,196
1 January 2011	1,000,000	850,129	21,034,325
1 July 2011	1,000,000	844,114	20,878,439
1 January 2012	1,000,000	837,859	20,716,298
1 July 2012	1,000,000	831,352	20,547,650
1 January 2013	1,000,000	824,584	20,372,233
1 July 2013	1,000,000	817,544	20,189,778
31 December 2013	1,000,000	810,222	20,000,000
	10,000,000	8,400,000	

On 1 July 2010, the entity sells the bonds at its fair value of EUR 21.2m to a third party with an agreement to repurchase the bonds on 1 July 2011 for EUR 21.3m.

(a) Does this sale qualify for derecognition? If so, how would you account for it?
(b) Suppose now that the repurchase contract is to be settled net in cash and that the fair value of the asset at the date of repurchase amounts to EUR 21.31m (i.e. the entity will pay an additional EUR 10,000 to the bank). How would your answer to question (a) change?

15.6   Derecognition of part of a liability

On 1 January 2006, an entity issued 1 million 8 per cent EUR 100 nominal ten-year term bonds with interest payable each 30 June and 31 December. The bonds, which are traded in the market, were issued at par. Issue costs of EUR 2m were incurred.

On 31 December 2009, the entity repurchased 600,000 bonds at the then market value of EUR 96 per EUR 100 nominal. The amortised cost of the bonds at 31 December 2009 amounted to EUR 98,655,495.

Determine the gain (loss) arising on repurchase.

15.7 Exchange and modification of debt instrument

An entity issued a five-year bond that is listed and traded on a stock exchange. In the following year, the entity proposes a modification of the bond's repayment terms, to extend the maturity. The proposed modification becomes effective if it achieves approval of more than 75 per cent of the bondholders, in accordance with the terms set out in the offering circular. Dissenting bondholders are entitled to have their bonds purchased by the entity (or any other party) at fair value, being the market price immediately prior to the proposed modification being put to the bondholders for consideration. The entity appoints an investment bank to stand ready to acquire any bonds from the dissenting bondholders and the bank will hold the bonds afterwards as principal. The proposed modification of the repayment terms was accepted by 80 per cent of the bondholders. The dissenting 20 per cent sold their bonds to an investment bank at fair value.

Would you consider this situation as an extinguishment or modification of a debt instrument?

15.8 Measurement of a loan stock using the effective interest method

On 1 January 2008, an entity bought EUR 200,000 of 6 per cent loan stock for EUR 187,860. Interest is receivable on 31 December each year and the stock will be redeemed at par on 31 December 2012. The company intends to hold the stock until maturity and calculates the effective interest rate to be 7.5 per cent per annum. Financial statements are prepared on 31 December each year.

(a) State the amount at which this loan stock should be measured on 1 January 2008.
(b) Calculate the amount at which the loan stock should be measured on 31 December 2008, 2009, 2010, 2011 and 2012.
(c) Show that the effective rate of 7.5 per cent 'exactly discounts estimated future cash receipts to the initial carrying amount of the asset' as required by IAS 39.

15.9 Measurement of a loan stock using the effective interest method

On 1 July 2008, a company issued EUR 2m of 8 per cent loan stock. The stock was issued at a 10 per cent discount (so only EUR 1,800,000 is received from the lenders) and issue costs of EUR 78,600 were incurred. Interest is payable in arrears on 30 June each year and the loan stock is redeemable at par on 30 June 2011. The effective interest rate is calculated to be 14 per cent per annum. The company prepares financial statements to 30 June each year.

(a) State the amount at which this loan stock should be measured on 1 July 2008.
(b) Calculate the amount at which the loan stock should be measured on 30 June 2009, 2010 and 2011.

15.10 Fixed interest loan asset repayable at maturity

On 1 January 2005 entity A originated a ten-year 7 per cent EUR 2m loan. The loan carried an annual interest rate of 7 per cent payable at the end of each year and is repayable at par at the end of 2014. Entity A charged a 1.25 per cent (EUR 25,000) non-refundable loan origination fee to the borrower and also incurred EUR 50,000 in direct loan origination costs.

The contract specifies that the borrower has an option to prepay the instrument and that no penalty will be charged for prepayment. At inception, the entity expects the borrower not to prepay.

The initial carrying amount of the loan asset is calculated as follows:

	€
Loan principal	2,000,000
Origination fees charged to borrower	(25,000)
Origination costs incurred by lender	50,000
Carrying amount of loan	2,025,000

(a) Should the prepayment option be separately accounted for?
(b) Determine the carrying amount of the loan at the end of each year until its maturity.

15.11 Fixed interest loan asset repayable in equal instalments

On 1 January 2005, entity A originated a ten-year 7 per cent EUR 2m loan. The loan is repaid in equal annual payments of EUR 284,756 through to maturity date at 31 December 2014. Entity A charged a 1.25 per cent (EUR 25,000) non-refundable loan origination fee to the borrower and also incurred EUR 50,000 in direct loan origination costs.

The contract specifies that the borrower has an option to prepay the instrument and that no penalty will be charged for prepayment. At inception, the entity expects the borrower not to prepay.

The initial carrying amount of the loan is calculated as follows:

	€
Loan principal	2,000,000
Origination fees charged to borrower	(25,000)
Origination costs incurred by lender	50,000
Carrying amount of loan	2,025,000

(a) Should the prepayment option be separately accounted for?
(b) Determine the carrying amount of the loan at the end of each year until its maturity.

Notes

1 Although IAS/IFRS use the term *'financial assets/financial liabilities at fair value through profit or loss'*, throughout this chapter we use *'through income statement'* to be consistent with the terminology we have adopted.
2 However, the disappearance of an active market because an entity's financial instruments are no longer publicly traded is not an evidence of impairment (IAS 39 para 60).

3 The question arises as to whether the further decrease of EUR 181,818 should be taken to the available-for-sale reserve in equity or recognised as a further impairment loss in the income statement for the year ending 31 December 2010. Both accounting treatments are acceptable. An entity should make an accounting policy choice as to which treatment it accepts and will apply it to all similar transactions. If material, the entity should disclose this policy in its financial statements.

4 IAS 1 (revised) sets out the requirements for the presentation of an asset or a liability as current or non-current in the balance sheet and specifically states that the presentation should be in such a format that provides useful information about the liquidity and solvency of an entity. In May 2007, the IFRIC was asked to provide guidance on whether derivatives that may be settled more than one year after the balance sheet date but are classified as held-for-trading in accordance with IAS 39, should be presented as current or non-current in the balance sheet. The IFRIC did not take this issue onto its agenda, but recommended the IASB to remove the implication in IAS 1 (revised) that such derivative should always be presented as current. The IASB subsequently provided clarity as part of the annual improvements to IFRS published in May 2008. IAS 1 (revised) clarified that some financial assets and liabilities classified as held for trading in accordance with IAS 39 are examples of current assets and liabilities respectively.

Part Five Reporting and disclosures

16 Statement of cash flows (IAS 7)

Contents

Objectives

When you have completed this chapter you should be able to:

- Explain the objectives of a statement of cash flows and why it is important
- Define 'cash and cash equivalents'
- Classify activities affecting cash as operating, investing, and financing
- Use indirect and direct methods to calculate cash flows from operating activities
- Determine cash flows from financing and investing activities
- Prepare a statement of cash flows in accordance with IAS 7

16.1   Introduction

Despite their indispensable usefulness, the income statement and balance sheet do not stress the importance of liquidity.

The accruals-based nature of the income statement tends to obscure the question of how and where the business is generating the cash it needs to continue its operations and thereby generate more cash.

People and organisations will not normally accept other than cash in settlement of their claims against an entity. If an entity wants to employ people, it must pay them in cash. If it wants to buy a new equipment, the seller of the asset will normally insist on being paid in cash, probably after a short period of credit. When entities fail, it is their inability to find the cash to pay claimants that really drives them under.

The above-mentioned factors lead to cash being the pre-eminent business asset and, therefore, the one that analysts and others watch most carefully in trying to assess the ability of entities to survive and/or to take advantage of commercial opportunities as they arise.

The old business adage says: *cash is king*. This reflects the fact that it is possible to make a profit and still run into cash flow problems. A successful entity is one which actively manages its cash flow.

16.2   Objectives of a statement of cash flows and its relationship with the income statement and balance sheet

Information about the cash flows of an entity is useful in providing users of financial statements with a basis to assess the entity's ability to generate cash (cash includes cash equivalents) and its need to utilise those cash flows. The economic decisions that are taken by users require an evaluation of an entity's ability to generate cash and the timing and certainty of its generation (IAS 7 Objective).

A statement of cash flows, when used in conjunction with the rest of the financial statements, provides information that enables users to determine the following:

- the ability of an entity to generate cash from its operations;
- the cash consequences of investing and financing decisions;
- the sustainability of an entity's cash-generating capability;
- how well an entity's operating cash flow correlates to net income;
- information about the liquidity and long-term solvency of an entity;
- the ability of an entity to finance its growth from internally generated funds.

A statement of cash flows reports an entity's cash receipts or cash inflows and cash payments or cash outflows during a given period. It shows the relationship of net profit to changes in cash balances. Cash balances can decline despite net profit and vice versa. It explains where the cash came from during a period and where it went.

A statement of cash flows confines itself to cash movements, while an income statement is concerned with movements in wealth.

Increases and decreases in wealth do not necessarily involve cash. For example, a business making a sale (generating revenue) increases its wealth, but if the sale is made on credit, no cash changes hands – not at the time of sale, at least. Here the increase in wealth is reflected in another asset: trade receivables.

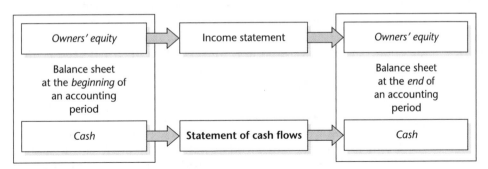

Figure 16.1 Relationship between the balance sheet, income statement and statement of cash flows

16.3   Cash and cash equivalents

Cash equivalents are held for the purpose of meeting short-term cash commitments rather than for investment or other purposes. For an investment to qualify as a cash equivalent it should be 'readily convertible' into cash and be subject to an insignificant risk of changes in value. Thus, an investment normally qualifies as a cash equivalent only when it has a short maturity of, say, three months or less from the date of acquisition. Equity investments are excluded from cash equivalents unless they are, in substance, cash equivalents (IAS 7 para 7).

Cash flows exclude movements between items that constitute cash or cash equivalents because these components are part of the cash management of an entity

> ### 36. Cash and cash equivalents
>
> Cash and cash equivalents comprise cash, checks and balances with banks and public-sector entities. In accordance with IAS 7 (Cash Flow Statements) this item also includes securities with original maturities of up to three months, reflecting their high liquidity. Cash and cash equivalents amounted to €2,094 million as of December 31, 2008 (2007: €2,581 million). Cash of €57 million (2007: €755 million) has been deposited in escrow accounts for payments relating to civil law settlements in antitrust proceedings.

Figure 16.2 Cash and cash equivalents
Source: Bayer Annual Report 2008.

rather than part of its operating, investing and financing activities. Cash management includes the investment of excess cash in cash equivalents (IAS 7 para 9).

16.3.1 Meaning of 'readily convertible'

The term 'readily convertible' implies that the investment can be convertible into cash without notice, meaning that it is not subject to any time restriction. Consequently, monies deposited in a bank account for an unspecified period of time, but which can only be withdrawn by giving notice, would not necessarily be treated as cash equivalents under the definition. Even so, such funds can usually be withdrawn by paying a penalty. However if the penalty incurred on withdrawal is not significant enough to cause any appreciable change in the capital amount withdrawn and the notice period for withdrawal by incurring a penalty payment is short, for example, seven days, the exclusion of such a deposit from cash equivalents may give an incongruous result, as it is nearer to cash than a deposit treated as a cash equivalent because it has a maturity of, say, two or three months. That is, without a doubt, not the intended effect of the definition and the phrase 'readily convertible' should generally be interpreted as 'convertible without an undue period of notice and without the incidence of a significant penalty on withdrawal'. This means that the facts of each circumstance should take into account the way in which such deposits are viewed and used. Cash deposits with, say, up to one month's notice that could be withdrawn without significant penalty would, therefore, fall within cash equivalents without violating the essence of the definition.

16.3.2 Maturity threshold

Companies normally use a range of instruments for cash management, investment and financing purposes. Such instruments may include bank borrowings, gilts, money market instruments, commercial paper, euronotes, etc. Although many of these instruments are readily convertible and can be held for the short-term, only those highly liquid instruments that are subject to insignificant risk of changes in value should be considered cash equivalents.

Clarification of this point is given in IAS 7, which states that an investment with a short maturity from the date of acquisition will generally qualify as a cash equivalent, provided it is used for cash management purposes. The standard specifies that a short maturity period would be a three-month period or less from the date of acquisition (IAS 7 para 7). Although any limit on maturity is somewhat subjective, it implies that investments that are so near cash will not have a significant risk that they will change in value in response to risks such as interest rate risks.

The three-month maturity period begins from the time the investment was acquired (IAS 7 para 7). Any investment, such as a gilt or a certificate of deposit, purchased with a maturity period of more than three months will not be a cash equivalent as the maturity of these instruments exposes them to fluctuations in capital value. Furthermore, they will not become a cash equivalent when their remaining maturity period, measured from a subsequent balance sheet date, becomes three months or less, as maturity period is measured from the date of acquisition.

Example 16.1

Cash equivalent and maturity threshold

On 1 July 2010, entity A purchased a government bond with a maturity date of 30 November 2010.

Entity A's financial year end is 30 September.

Should the bond be classified as cash equivalent in the balance sheet as at 30 September 2010?

The bond should not be classified as cash equivalent. At the date of acquisition, 1 July 2010, the maturity of the bond is five months. This does not comply with the short maturity of three months or less from the date of acquisition, suggested in IAS 7. The fact that the bond matures less than three months from the balance sheet date (30 September) will not result in its classification as a cash equivalent at that point. The maturity period is assessed from the *date of acquisition* not from the balance sheet date.

IAS 7 specifically excludes equity investments from cash equivalents, unless they are cash equivalents in substance. This is due to the high risk of changes in capital value, despite the fact that they can be readily marketable and convertible into cash. The example given in the standard where an investment in shares could be classified as a cash equivalent is where preference shares have been acquired within a short period of their maturity and with a specified redemption date (IAS 7 para 7).

Where the counterparty to any short-term investment demonstrates that it is experiencing financial problems, there may be doubt over its ability to fulfil the requirements of the agreement. In such circumstances the entity should not classify this investment as a cash equivalent as there is a risk that the investment will not be readily convertible or that the maturity date will not be met.

16.3.3 Treatment of borrowings

Bank borrowings are generally considered to be financing activities. However, in some countries, bank overdrafts which are repayable on demand form an integral part of an entity's cash management. In these circumstances, bank overdrafts are included as a component of cash and cash equivalents. A characteristic of such banking arrangements is that the bank balance often fluctuates from being positive to overdrawn (IAS 7 para 8).

Another instance where borrowings may be classified as cash equivalents is where an entity has an invoice discounting facility with a lending institution, which is not a registered bank, such as a debt factor. The cash extended to the entity by the debt factor may be repayable on demand. So, if this forms an integral part of the entity's cash management, it may be appropriate to show it within cash and cash equivalents. If the invoice discounting facility is so classified, this fact should be disclosed.

Examples of companies which include bank overdrafts in cash and cash equivalents are given in Figure 16.3, while an example of a company which excludes bank overdrafts from cash and cash equivalents is given in Figure 16.4.

(a)

Cash and cash equivalents reported in the cashflow statement include all liquid assets disclosed in the balance sheet; i.e., cash in hand, checks and bank balances.

Source: Puma Annual Report 2008.

(b)

Cash and Cash Equivalents

For the purposes of the Group Cash Flow Statement cash and cash equivalents at 31 December comprise cash at bank and in hand net of bank overdrafts.

	2008	2007	2006
	($ million)		
Cash and bank	145	170	346
Bank overdrafts	(23)	(61)	(55)
Cash and cash equivalents	122	109	291

Source: Smith & Nephew plc Annual Report 2008.

(c)

Cash and cash equivalents

Cash and cash equivalents includes cash in hand, call deposits and other short-term liquid investments with original maturities of three months or less.

Cash and short-term deposits at the balance sheet date are offset against bank loans and overdrafts where formal rights of set-off exist and there is an intention to settle on a net basis.

Source: Invensys Annual Report 2008.

Figure 16.3 Examples of bank overdrafts included in cash and cash equivalents

---

	Notes	2008 EURm	2007 EURm	2006 EURm
Financial year ended December 31				
Cash and cash equivalents comprise of:				
Bank and cash		1,706	2,125	1,479
Current available-for-sale investments, cash equivalents	15, 35	3,842	4,725	2,046
		5,548	6,850	3,525

Figure 16.4 Bank overdrafts excluded from cash and cash equivalents

Source: Nokia Annual Report 2008.

16.4   Activities affecting cash

The statement of cash flows should report cash flows during the period classified by operating, investing and financing activities. An entity should present its cash flows from operating, investing and financing activities in a manner which is most appropriate to its business. Classification by activity provides information that allows users to assess the impact of those activities on the financial position of the entity and the amount of its cash and cash equivalents. This information may also be used to evaluate the relationships among those activities. A single transaction may include cash flows that are classified differently. For example, when the cash repayment of a loan includes both interest and capital, the interest element is classified as an operating activity and the capital element is classified as a financing activity (IAS 7 paras 10 to 12).

16.4.1 Operating activities

The amount of cash flows arising from operating activities is a key indicator of the extent to which the operations of the entity have generated sufficient cash flows to repay loans, maintain the operating capability of the entity, pay dividends and make new investments without recourse to external sources of financing. Information about the specific components of historical operating cash flows is useful, in conjunction with other information, in forecasting future operating cash flows (IAS 7 para 13).

Cash flows from operating activities are primarily derived from the principal revenue-producing activities of the entity. Therefore, they generally result from the transactions and other events that enter into the determination of profit or loss. Examples of cash flows from operating activities are:

(a) cash receipts from the sale of goods and rendering of services;

(b) cash receipts from royalties, fees, commissions and other revenue;

(c) cash payments to suppliers for goods and services;

(d) cash payments to and on behalf of employees;

(e) cash receipts and cash payments of an insurance entity for premiums and claims, annuities and other policy benefits;

(f) cash payments or refunds of income taxes unless they can be specifically identified with financing and investing activities; and

(g) cash receipts and payments from contracts held for dealing or trading purposes (IAS 7 para 14).

Some transactions, such as the sale of an item of plant, may give rise to a gain or loss which is included in the determination of profit or loss. However, the cash flows relating to such transactions are cash flows from investing activities (IAS 7 para 14).

An entity may hold securities and loans for dealing or trading purposes, in which case they are similar to inventory acquired specifically for resale. Therefore, cash flows arising from the purchase and sale of dealing or trading securities are classified as operating activities. Similarly, cash advances and loans made by financial institutions are usually classified as operating activities since they relate to the main revenue-producing activity of that entity (IAS 7 para 15).

16.4.2 Investing and financing activities

Investing activities involve providing and collecting cash as a lender or as an owner of securities, and acquiring and disposing of plant, and equipment, and other long-lived assets.

The separate disclosure of cash flows arising from investing activities is important because such cash flows represent the extent to which expenditures have been made for resources intended to generate future income and cash flows.

Examples of cash flows arising from investing activities are:

- cash payments to acquire property, plant and equipment, intangibles and other long-term assets;

- cash receipts from sales of property, plant and equipment, intangibles and other long-term assets;

- cash payments to acquire equity or debt instruments of other entities and interests in joint ventures;

- cash receipts from sales of equity or debt instruments of other entities and interests in joint ventures;

- cash advances and loans made to third parties;

- cash receipts from repayment of advances and loans made to third parties;

- cash payments for futures contracts, forward contracts, option contracts and swap contracts except when the contracts are held for dealing or trading purposes, or the payments are classified as financing activities (IAS 7 para 16).

Financing activities involve obtaining resources as a borrower or issuer of securities and repaying creditors and owners.

The separate disclosure of cash flows arising from financing activities is important for predicting claims on future cash flows by providers of capital to the entity.

Examples of cash flows arising from financing activities are:

- cash proceeds from issuing shares or other equity instruments;

- cash payments to owners to acquire or redeem the entity's shares;

- cash proceeds from issuing debentures, loans, notes, bonds, mortgages and other short or long-term borrowings;

- cash repayments of amounts borrowed; and

- cash payments by a lessee for the reduction of the outstanding liability relating to a finance lease (IAS 7 para 17).

16.5   How to prepare a statement of cash flows

According to IAS 7, the statement of cash flows is a primary financial statement which, together with the income statement and balance sheet, should be prepared by all entities. As mentioned in section 16.4, an entity should classify changes in cash and cash equivalents into operating, investing, and financing activities.

There are two methods to determine *cash flows from operating activities*:

- The *direct method*, which computes cash flows from operating activities as collections less operating disbursements. This means that only the cash part of each item in the income statement is taken into account.

- The *indirect method*, which computes cash flows from operating activities by adjusting the net profit or loss on an accrual basis to reflect only cash receipts and outlays.

16.5.1   Cash flows from operating activities – direct method

The *direct method* reports the major classes of *gross* operating cash receipts (for example, cash collected from customers) and gross operating cash payments (for example, cash paid to suppliers and employees). These gross operating cash flows are aggregated to produce the net operating cash flow of the entity. This presentation is consistent with that of investing and financing activities. Table 16.1 is an extract, based on the example in Appendix A to IAS 7, from the statement of cash flows of an entity that presents its cash flows from operating activities using the direct method.

There are essentially two ways in which gross operating cash receipts and payments may be derived under the direct method. They may be captured directly from a separate cash-based accounting system that records amounts paid or received in any transaction. Alternatively, this may be determined indirectly by adjusting operating items from the income statement for non-cash items, changes in working capital and other items that relate to investing and financing cash flows (IAS 7 para 19). For example, cash collected from customers may be derived indirectly by adjusting sales for the changes in amounts receivable from customers during the

Table 16.1 Cash flows from operating activities – direct method

Cash flows from operating activities	
Cash receipts from customers	x
Cash paid to suppliers and employees	(x)
Cash generated from operations	x
Interest paid	(x)
Income taxes paid	(x)
Net cash from operating activities	x

period. Similarly, cash paid to suppliers for goods used in manufacture or resale may be determined indirectly by adjusting cost of sales for changes in inventory and amounts due to suppliers during the period.

The standard encourages, but does not require, reporting entities to use the direct method (IAS 7 para 19). This is because the direct method produces a statement of cash flows in its purest form with new information that is not otherwise available from the income statement and the balance sheet. However, in spite of its theoretical soundness, the direct method may involve implementation costs. Many companies may not collect information that will allow them to determine gross cash receipts and payments directly from the accounting system. Although the information under the direct method could be obtained under the alternative method discussed above by making appropriate adjustments, it is considered that the more detailed the categories of operating cash receipts and payments to be reported, the more complex will be the procedure for determining them. Therefore, this approach may require incremental work to be performed compared to that required for the indirect method, because it would involve the sub-categorisation of debtors and creditors. Few companies have the need to derive cash receipts and payments for operating cash flows in this way. For the reasons stated above, the direct method is not popular and, the indirect method, described below, is more commonly used.

16.5.2 Cash flows from operating activities – indirect method

Under the *indirect method*, the cash flows from operating activities are determined by adjusting the profit or loss to remove the effects of non-cash items (such as depreciation and provisions), changes in working capital (such as accruals and prepayments and changes in receivables and payables in the period) and items that relate to investing and financing activities (IAS 7 para 20). The main adjustments mentioned above are summarised by Melville (2009) as follows:

(i) Non-cash expenses which are debited to the income statement but have not involved an outflow of cash (e.g. depreciation) are added back.

(ii) Non-cash income which is credited to the income statement but has not involved an inflow of cash (e.g. a decrease in the allowance for doubtful trade receivables) is deducted.

(iii) Increases or decreases in the following items between the beginning and the end of the accounting period are adjusted for as indicated in Table 16.2, below.

Table 16.2 Cash flows from operating activities – indirect method: adjustments in working capital

	Increase	*Decrease*
Inventories	Deduct	Add
Trade receivables	Deduct	Add
Prepaid expenses	Deduct	Add
Trade payables	Add	Deduct
Accrued expenses	Add	Deduct

The effect of these adjustments is to change the basis of the income statement from the accrual basis required by IAS 1 – *Presentation of Financial Statements* to a cash basis. For instance, an increase in trade payables causes the purchases figure shown in the income statement to be higher than the amount actually paid to suppliers. Adding this increase back to the profit for the period shows what the profit would have been if purchases had been accounted for on a cash basis.

A simple way of remembering the correct adjustment for each of the increases and decreases listed above is to consider what would happen if the increase or decrease occurred and nothing else changed in the balance sheet other than cash. For instance, a decrease in trade receivables would generate extra cash as customers paid their debts. This would have a beneficial effect on cash and so a decrease in trade receivables should be added to profit when calculating the total amount of cash generated from operations.

(iv) Any items of income or expense which have been included in the calculation of profit or loss before tax but which represent cash flows from either investing or financing activities are deducted (income) or added back (expenses). Interest payable is also added back.

(v) Interest and tax paid should be presented on the face of the statement of cash flows (IAS 7 paras 32 and 35). This means that when we use the indirect method, we should show interest and taxes actually paid as with the direct method.

Table 16.3 is an extract, based on the example in Appendix A to IAS 7, from the statement of cash flows of an entity that presents its cash flows from operating activities using the indirect method.

Table 16.3 Cash flows from operating activities – indirect method

Cash flows from operating activities	
Profit before taxation	x
Adjustments for:	
Depreciation	x
Foreign exchange loss	x
Loss on disposal of PPE	x
Investment income	(x)
Interest expense	x
	x
Adjustments in working capital:	
Increase in trade and other receivables	(x)
Decrease in inventories	x
Decrease in trade payables	(x)
Cash generated from operations	x
Interest received	x
Interest paid	(x)
Income taxes paid	(x)
Net cash from operating activities	x

IAS 7 describes the indirect method as a method '. . . *whereby profit or loss is adjusted for the effects of transactions of a non-cash nature, any deferrals or accruals of past or future operating cash receipts or payments, and items of income or expense associated with investing or financing cash flows'* (IAS 7 para 18(b)). Profit or loss under international standards generally means profit after tax or net income. However, the example in the appendix to IAS 7 begins the reconciliation, not with profit for the period, but with profit before taxation. This ambiguity in the standard seems to give some flexibility in choosing a starting point for the reconciliation. Puma and Rolls Royce, for example, use profit before taxes as the starting point for the reconciliation, while Roche uses net profit. PwC (2009) considers that it is acceptable to use net profit, pretax profit or another operating result as a starting point for the reconciliation. Judgement should be exercised to ensure that the starting point is not misleading and that the outcome properly reflects the cash flows.

Section 16.6 sets out a comprehensive example of a statement of cash flows with explanatory notes. This example illustrates cash flows from operating activities under both direct and indirect methods and the starting point for reconciling profit to cash from operating activities is profit before tax.

16.5.3 Cash flows from investing and financing activities

Determining cash flows from investing and financing activities are identical under both direct and indirect methods of preparing the statement of cash flows.

Cash flows from investing activities primarily represent changes in long-term asset accounts and their effect on cash as explained above in section 16.4.2.

Example 16.2

Cash flows from operating activities vs investing activities

How should the cash flows in respect of the purchase of land and buildings be classified by a property developer that purchases land and buildings:

(a) to redevelop and sell them?

(b) for the purpose of earning rental income from the properties?

The property developer should classify the cash outflows in respect of the purchase of land and buildings as:

(a) operating cash flows. A developer's purchase of property is similar to inventory acquired by a manufacturer;

(b) investing cash flows. The purchase represents an investment on which a return (rental income) will be earned.

The cash payments disclosed for the acquisition of long-term assets will include any capitalised development costs and costs incurred for the construction of an asset by the entity for its own use.

The amount paid in respect of fixed assets during the year may not be the same as the amount of additions shown in the fixed asset note. The difference may be due to a number of reasons. For example, fixed assets may be purchased on credit, in which case the amounts for additions shown in the fixed asset note would need to be adjusted for the outstanding payable to arrive at the cash paid. Furthermore, the change in fixed asset creditors should be eliminated from the total change in creditors, to arrive at the movement in operating creditors, a figure needed for the reconciliation of profit to net cash flow where the indirect method is used to report cash flows from operating activities. In addition, where interest has been capitalised during the period and included within the fixed assets, the amount so capitalised would need to be deducted to arrive at the correct amount of cash paid for the acquisition or construction of a fixed asset. The amount of capitalised interest that has been paid during the period should be included in the total of interest paid during the period and separately disclosed. Another example is where fixed assets have been acquired in foreign currencies. In this situation, the functional currency equivalent of the foreign currency amount paid in cash that is reported in the cash flow statement is not necessarily the same as the functional currency equivalent of the cost recorded at the date of the transaction and included in the balance sheet, because of changes in exchange rates during the period of credit.

A further example is that of assets acquired under finance leases. Most companies do not show assets acquired under finance leases separately, but include them in the total additions figure in their fixed assets movements note. Since assets acquired under finance leases may not involve any cash outlay at the inception of the lease, it will be necessary to eliminate the whole amount in respect of leased assets that is included in the figure for fixed assets additions so that the actual cash outflow for fixed assets purchased can be reflected in the statement of cash flows. Any finance lease rental payments should be separated out into their separate components for capital and interest payments. The cash payment in relation to the capital element should be classified under financing activities (IAS 7 para 17(e)). The cash payment in relation to the interest element should be treated in the same manner as other interest payable.

Companies may invest to maintain the existing level of operations (for example, routine replacement of plant and machinery for normal wear and tear) or to expand the level of operations (such as, by investing in new products or services). In practice, there is no clear distinction between these two types of capital expenditures and the criteria used may also differ from company to company. However, some entities may find it useful to make such a distinction. IAS 7, therefore, encourages that the aggregate amount of cash flows that represent increases in operating capacity be disclosed separately from those cash flows that are required to maintain operating capacity (IAS 7 para 50(c)).

Cash flows from financing activities show the cash flows to/from providers of capital, which would include related long-term liabilities and shareholders' equity accounts as explained above in section 16.4.2.

Transaction costs arising on obtaining debt financing, such as fees paid to banks or lawyers on arrangement, are a form of finance cost and are accounted for using the effective interest method (see section 15.5.3). These costs would, therefore, be treated in the same way as any interest payable on debt finance and classified as financing activity cash flows. No guidance is given in IAS 7 in relation to whether cash flows for equity transactions should be shown gross or net of transaction costs. However, we consider that where transaction costs of an equity transaction are material, they should be disclosed separately from the proceeds of the equity

(a)
Consolidated Cash Flow Statement for the year ended 31 December (extract)

	2008 €m	2007 €m
Financing activities		
Finance revenue received	**2.0**	5.5
Finance costs paid	**(59.4)**	(67.8)
Finance cost element of finance lease payments	**(19.2)**	(17.5)
Net capital element of finance lease payments	**(53.5)**	(57.6)
Purchase of own shares	**–**	(2.7)
Cash flow on derivative financial instruments – debt	**0.2**	(35.3)
Proceeds from bank and other loans	**129.1**	141.6
Net cash used in financing activities	**(0.8)**	(33.8)

Source: Avis Europe Annual Report 2008.

(b)
Consolidated cash flow statement
For the year ended December 31, 2008 (extract)

	2008 £m	2007 £m
Cash flows from financing activities		
Borrowings due within one year – repayment of loans	**(1)**	(350)
Borrowings due after one year – repayment of loans	**(22)**	–
Capital element of finance lease payments	**(4)**	(5)
Net cash outflow from decrease in borrowings	**(27)**	(355)
Interest received	**52**	95
Interest paid	**(53)**	(93)
Interest element of finance lease payments	**(1)**	(3)
Decrease/(increase) in government securities and corporate bonds	**39**	(6)
Issue of ordinary shares	**17**	29
Purchase of ordinary shares	**(44)**	(77)
Other transactions in ordinary shares	**(4)**	34
Redemption of B Shares	**(200)**	(97)
Net cash outflow from financing activities	**(221)**	(473)

Source: Roll Royce Annual Report 2008.

Figure 16.5 Examples of finance lease payments classified as cash flows from financing activities

instrument under financing activity. This is in keeping with the principle that, in general, cash inflows and outflows should be reported gross. This is particularly relevant where transaction costs relate to the issue of compound instrument that contains both a liability and an equity element.

Interest and dividend cash flows – The cash flows arising from dividends and interest receipts and payments should be classified in the statement of cash flows under the activity appropriate to their nature. Classification should be on a consistent basis from period to period. Additionally, these items are required to be disclosed separately on the face of the statement of cash flows. For total interest paid, the standard requires disclosure on the face of the statement of cash flows, regardless of whether the interest has been expensed or capitalised (IAS 7 paras 31 and 32).

Example 16.3

Cash inflows from dividend income

How should cash flows in respect of dividend income be classified by a venture capital entity? Consider two different situations:

(a) The entity has an investment of 10 per cent in an entity in which it does not have significant influence. Dividend income of EUR 1m has been received in the year.

(b) The entity has invested some surplus cash in an entity, acquiring a 10 per cent interest, in the hope of achieving a better return than in a bank savings account. Dividend income of EUR 1m has been received in the year.

Management should classify the cash inflows as:

(a) An operating cash flow. A venture capital entity's primary objective is to invest in entities to achieve a return in the form of dividend income or capital growth.

(b) An investing cash flow. The purchase of shares is not the entity's primary business activity. The purchase has been made to achieve a return on surplus funds.

IAS 7 para 34 permits companies to classify dividends paid as a component of cash flows from operating activities, because this allows users to determine the ability of an entity to pay dividends out of operating cash flows. Nevertheless, it is likely that most entities would categorise interest paid in operating and dividends paid to parent and minority shareholders in financing on the grounds that, although both are payments to providers of capital, interest paid is contractual and has to be paid when due, whereas dividends are discretionary and payments may vary according to the amount legally available for distribution, the cash available and the dividend policy of the entity.

Figures 16.6 and 16.7 give two examples of different treatment of interest and dividends paid.

16.5.4 Classification of taxation cash flows

Cash flows relating to taxation on income should be separately disclosed under operating activities in the statement of cash flows, unless it can be specifically attributed to financing or investing activities (IAS 7 para 35). It may be inappropriate and rather misleading to allocate tax flows between the three economic activities. A payment of income or corporation tax usually involves only one cash flow that is arrived at by applying the rate of tax to the entity's total taxable profit (taxable income). The total taxable income is the result of aggregation of taxable income arising from all sources, including taxable gains arising on the disposal of assets. The taxation rules under which total taxable income is calculated often do not easily lend themselves to subdivision between operating, investing and

Consolidated cash flow statements, IFRS

Financial year ended December 31	2008 EURm	2007 EURm	2006 EURm
Cash flow from operating activities			
Profit attributable to equity holders of the parent	**3,988**	7,205	4,306
Adjustments, total	**3,469**	1,269	1,857
Change in net working capital	**−2,546**	605	−793
Cash generated from operations	**4,911**	9,079	5,370
Interest received	**416**	362	235
Interest paid	**−155**	−59	−18
Other financial income and expenses, net received	**−195**	−43	54
Income taxes paid, net received	**−1,780**	−1,457	−1,163
Net cash from operating activities	**3,197**	7,882	4,478

32. Notes to cash flow statement

EURm	2008	2007	2006
Adjustments for:			
Depreciation and amortization	**1,617**	1,206	712
(Profit)/loss on sale of property, plant and equipment and available-for-sale investments	**−11**	−1,864	−4
Income taxes	**1,081**	1,522	1,357
Share of results of associated companies	**−6**	−44	−28
Minority interest	**−99**	−459	60
Financial income and expenses	**2**	−239	−207
Impairment charges	**149**	63	51
Retirements	**186**	–	–
Share-based compensation	**74**	228	192
Restructuring charges	**448**	856	–
Customer financing impairment charges and reversals	**–**	–	−276
Finnish pension settlement	**152**	–	–
Other income and expenses	**−124**	–	–
Adjustments, total	**3,469**	1,269	1,857
Change in net working capital			
Increase in short-term receivables	**−534**	−2,146	−1,770
Decrease (+)/increase (−) in inventories	**321**	−245	84
Decrease (−)/increase (+) in interest-free short-term liabilities	**−2,333**	2,996	893
Change in net working capital	**−2,546**	605	−793

Figure 16.6 Example of interest classified as an operating cash flow

Source: Nokia Annual Report 2008.

Roche Group consolidated cash flow statement	in millions of CHF	

	Year ended 31 December	
Cash flow from financing activities	2008	2007
Proceeds from issue of long-term debt instruments	–	719
Repayment and redemption of long-term debt instruments	(2,188)	(1,908)
Increase (decrease) in other long-term debt	(234)	4
Increase (decrease) in short-term borrowings	(190)	(389)
Transactions in own equity instruments	(98)	1,085
Change in ownership interest in subsidiaries		
– Chuga	(934)	–
– Ventana	(1,285)	–
Interest and dividends paid	(4,267)	(3,324)
Exercises of equity-settled equity compensation plans	598	450
Genentech and Chugal share repurchases	(844)	(1,895)
Other financing cash flows	–	(12)
Total cash flows from financing activities	**(9,442)**	**(5,270)**

Notes

Cash flows from financing activities

Cash flows from financing activities are primarily the proceeds from the issue and repayment of the Group's equity and debt instruments. They also include interest payments and dividend payments on these instruments. Cash flows from short-term financing, including finance leases, are also included. These cash flows indicate the Group's transactions with the providers of its equity and debt financing. Cash flows from short-term borrowings are shown as a net movement, as these consist of a large number of transactions with short maturity.

Interest and dividends paid	in millions of CHF	
	2008	2007
Interest paid	(216)	(297)
Dividends paid	(4,051)	(3,027)
Total	**(4,267)**	**(3,324)**

Figure 16.7 Example of interest and dividends paid classified as financing cash flows
Source: Roche Annual Report 2008.

financing activities. Consequently, any allocation that attempts to segregate the taxation cash flows in this manner may result in the reporting of hypothetical figures in the statement of cash flows. For example, in many tax regimes the tax effects of investing activities (for example, tax deductions arising on the acquisition of plant and machinery) are set-off against profits arising from operating activities (trading profits). The reporting of a theoretical tax refund due to tax deductions on the acquisition of plant and equipment under investing activities will require grossing up the actual tax paid on operating activities. A similar situation arises where the tax effects of trading losses are set-off against taxable gains arising on the disposal of assets.

Clearly, this is not what happens in practice and to present it as such in the statement of cash flows would be misleading. Moreover, as taxation cash flows generally arise from activities in an earlier period, apportioning the taxation cash flows would not necessarily report the taxation cash flows along with the transactions that gave rise to them. Therefore, in general, an entity would report a single tax cash flow in the statement of cash flows under operating activities.

Where taxation cash flows are disclosed under different activities, the standard requires that the total amount of tax paid in relation to income is disclosed (IAS 7 para 36).

16.5.5 Reconciliation with balance sheet items

IAS 7 para 45 requires that the components making up the total opening and closing balance of cash and cash equivalents in the statement of cash flows should be disclosed and that these should be reconciled to the appropriate balance sheet items.

Moreover, where the reporting entity holds foreign currency cash and cash equivalent balances, then any exchange difference arising on their retranslation at the balance sheet date will have increased or decreased such cash and cash equivalent balances. As such exchange differences do not give rise to any cash flows, they will not be reported as part of the movement in cash and cash equivalents. Consequently, it is necessary to consider such exchange differences in any analysis where movements in cash and cash equivalents are related to opening and closing balances.

In fact, IAS 7 para 28 requires the effect of exchange rate changes on cash and cash equivalents held or due in a foreign currency (those arising from the retranslation of opening balances of cash and cash equivalents and those arising from translating the cash flows at rates other than the year-end rate) to be reported in the statement of cash flows to reconcile cash and cash equivalents at the beginning and the end of the period. The treatment of exchange differences in the context of the statement of cash flows is considered in the example below.

Example 16.4

Foreign currency and cash flows

A French company which accounts in euro was set up in January 2008 and raised EUR 400,000 by issuing shares. It purchased goods for resale from the USA in February 2008 for US$ 400,000, when the exchange rate was €1 = $1.5. The company settled the debt in October 2008 when the exchange rate was €1 = $1.6.

Assuming that there are no other transactions during the year, how would you disclose these transactions in the statement of cash flows?

The company should enter the purchase in its inventory records as:

$$\$400,000 \div 1.5 = €266,667$$

The amount paid in settlement was:

$$\$400,000 \div 1.6 = €250,000$$

The company would, therefore, record an exchange gain in its income statement for 2006 of:

$$€266,667 - €250,000 = €16,667$$

Assuming that there are no other transactions during the year and the inventory remained unsold at the balance sheet date at 31 December 2008, a simplified statement of cash flows is given below in Table 16.4.

Table 16.4 Simplified statement of cash flows

Statement of cash flows		
	€	€
Cash flows from operating activities		
Profit	16,667	
Adjustment for:		
Increase in inventories	(266,667)	
Net cash flows used in operating activities		(250,000)
Cash flows from financing activities		
Issue of shares	400,000	
Net cash flows from financing activities		400,000
Net increase in cash and cash equivalents*		150,000

* Represented by ending cash balance (= Proceeds from share issue €400,000 – payments for inventory €250,000).

It is obvious that the net cash flows used in operating activities comprise the payment of €250,000 for inventory. Because the outstanding payables for €266,667 was settled during the year for €250,000, the exchange gain of €16,667 is already reflected in the payment and, therefore, no adjustment for the exchange gain is necessary in reconciling the profit to the operating cash flow as illustrated above. Therefore, as a general rule, exchange differences on settled transactions relating to operations will not appear as a reconciling item in the reconciliation of profit to net cash flow from operating activities using the indirect method.

An example of disclosure in respect of cash and cash equivalents is shown in Figure 16.8, below.

Cash and cash equivalents

Cash and cash equivalents consist of cash in hand, cash at bank, short-term deposits with financial institutions with original maturity periods of three months or less and bank overdrafts.

Cash and cash equivalents included in the statement of cash flows comprise the following balance sheet amounts:

	2009	2008
	€	€
Cash at bank and in hand	X	X
Short-term bank deposits	X	X
Bank overdrafts	(X)	(X)
Cash and cash equivalents	X	X

Figure 16.8 Example of disclosure of cash and cash equivalents

16.6   Statement of cash flows: a comprehensive example

The income statement for the year ended 31 December 2008 and balance sheets as at 31 December 2007 and 2008 for Sunny Beach are shown in Tables 16.5 and 16.6, respectively.

Table 16.5 Sunny Beach income statement for the year ended 31 December 2008

	€	€
Revenue		
Sales revenue	1,600,000	
Interest	10,000	
Gain on sale of plant	8,000	
		1,618,000
Expenses		
Cost of sales	960,000	
Wages and salaries	240,000	
Depreciation – plant and equipment	50,000	
Interest	8,000	
Other expenses	152,000	
		1,410,000
Profit before tax		208,000
Income tax expense		60,000
Net profit for the year		148,000

Table 16.6 Sunny Beach comparative balance sheets as at 31 December 2007 and 2008

	31 December 2007 €	31 December 2008 €	Increase (decrease) €
Cash at bank	120,000	109,100	(10,900)
Trade receivables	140,000	158,000	18,000
Inventory	130,000	140,000	10,000
Prepayments	16,000	19,000	3,000
Interest receivable	300	200	(100)
A Plant	300,000	330,000	30,000
B Investments	24,000	28,000	4,000
B Intangibles	–	30,000	30,000
	730,300	814,300	
Trade payables	84,000	90,000	6,000
Wages and salaries payable	8,000	10,000	2,000
Accrued interest	–	400	400
Other expense payable	6,000	3,600	(2,400)
E Current tax payable	28,000	32,000	4,000
E Deferred tax	10,000	16,000	6,000
C Long-term borrowings	120,000	140,000	20,000
Share capital	400,000	400,000	–
D Retained earnings	74,300	122,300	48,000
	730,300	814,300	

Additional information extracted from the company's records is reported below:

A Plant that had a written-down value of EUR 20,000 was sold for EUR 28,000 cash. New equipment purchased for cash amounted to EUR 100,000.

B Investments (EUR 4,000) and intangibles (EUR 30,000) were acquired for cash.

C A borrowing of EUR 20,000 was obtained in cash during the year.

D Dividends paid in cash were EUR 100,000.

E Income tax expense for the year comprises:

Current income taxes	€54,000
Increase in deferred taxes	€6,000
	€60,000

Step 1 – Determine cash receipts from customers

The starting point for determining how much cash was received from customers is the sales revenue reported in the income statement. However, this figure reflects sales made by the entity during the period irrespective of whether the customers have paid for the sales. Credit sales are recorded by a debit to trade receivables and a credit to sales revenue. On the other hand, the cash received from customers includes sales made in the previous period that were not collected in cash until the current period, and excludes sales made in the current period that remain unpaid at the end of the period. Hence, the cash received from customers (assuming that no bad debts have been written off or settlement discounts given) equals:

Beginning trade receivables + Sales revenue – Ending trade receivables

Using the Sunny Beach information from Tables 16.5 and 16.6, the amount of cash receipts from customers is determined as follows:

Beginning trade receivables	€140,000
Add: Sales revenue	1,600,000
Cash collectable from customers	1,740,000
Deduct: Ending trade receivables	(158,000)
Cash receipts from customers	€1,582,000

If any debts had been written off during the period, cash collectable from customers would be further reduced by the amount of the write-offs in calculating the cash received from customers. A similar adjustment would be necessary if settlement discounts were given to customers for the payment of their accounts within prescribed credit terms. Such discounts reduce the cash received from customers, and necessitate the inclusion of a non-cash expense (discounts allowed) in the income statement.

The logic of this calculation is apparent from the following summarised trade receivables account in the general ledger for the year:

Trade receivables

	€		€
Opening balance	140,000	Bad debts expense	–
Sales	1,600,000	Discounts allowed	–
		Cash receipts	1,582,000
		Closing balance	158,000
	1,740,000		1,740,000

The above summarised general ledger account can be reconstructed from the balance sheet (the opening and closing balances) and income statement (bad debts expense, discount allowed and sales). The cash receipts amount is then determined by the difference in the trade receivables account.

The above approach may be simplified by working with the change in receivables over the period. Under this approach, the cash received from customers (assuming there are no bad debts written off or discounts allowed) equals:

Sales revenue – Increase in trade receivables

or

+ Decrease in trade receivables

Thus, the cash received from the Sunny Beach customers can alternatively be determined as:

€1,600,000 – €18,000 = €1,582,000

Step 2 – Determine interest received

A similar approach is used to determine interest received, because interest received equals:

Interest revenue – Increase in interest receivable

or

+ Decrease in interest receivable

Thus, Sunny Beach's interest received is:

€10,000 + €100 = €10,100

Step 3 – Determine cash paid to suppliers and employees

Payments to suppliers may comprise purchases of inventory and payments for services. However, not all inventory purchased during the year is reflected in the income statement as cost of sales, because cost of sales includes beginning inventory and excludes ending inventory. Purchases of inventory made during the period equals:

Cost of sales – Beginning inventory + Ending inventory

Alternatively, this could be expressed as:

Cost of sales + Increase in inventory

or

– Decrease in inventory

Using a similar approach to that outlined for cash receipts from customers, it is then necessary to adjust for trade payables at the beginning and end of the period to arrive at cash paid to suppliers for purchases of inventory. Thus, cash paid to suppliers of inventories is calculated as:

Beginning trade payables + Purchases of inventory – Ending trade payables

Alternatively, this could be expressed as:

Purchases of inventory   +   Decrease in trade payables

or

–   Increase in trade payables

Sunny Beach's comparative balance sheets report an increase in inventory of EUR 10,000 and in trade payables of EUR 6,000. Hence, cash paid to suppliers for purchases is calculated as follows:

Cost of sales	€960,000
Add: Increase in inventory	10,000
Purchases for the year	970,000
Deduct: Increase in trade payables	(6,000)
Payments to suppliers for purchases of inventory	€964,000

The logic of the previous calculations is apparent from the following summarised inventory and trade payables (for inventory) accounts in the general ledger for the year:

Inventory

	€		€
Opening balance	130,000	Cost of sales	960,000
Purchases	970,000	Closing balance	140,000
	1,100,000		1,100,000

Trade payables

	€		€
Cash payments	964,000	Opening balance	84,000
Closing balance	90,000	Purchases	970,000
	1,054,000		1,054,000

The above summarised general ledger accounts can be reconstructed from the information contained in the balance sheet (the opening and closing balances) and the income statement (cost of sales). The purchases amount is then determined by the difference in the inventory account and inserted in the trade payables account. The amount of cash payments is then determined by the difference in the trade payables account.

A similar approach is taken to determine the amount of payments made to suppliers for services and to employees. Adjustments must be made to the relevant expenses recognised in the income statement for changes in the beginning

Step 6 – Prepare the operating section of the statement of cash flows using the direct method

Table 16.7 Sunny Beach statement of cash flows (extract) – direct method

Cash flows from operating activities	
Cash receipts from customers	€1,582,000
Cash paid to suppliers and employees	(1,359,400)
Cash generated from operations	222,600
Interest received*	10,100
Interest paid**	(7,600)
Income tax paid	(50,000)
Net cash from operating activities	€175,100

* May be classified as investing.
** May be classified as financing.

Step 7 – Prepare the operating section of the statement of cash flows using the indirect method

Table 16.8 Sunny Beach statement of cash flows (extract) – indirect method

Cash flows from operating activities	
Profit before tax	€208,000
Adjustments for:	
Depreciation	50,000
Interest income	(10,000)
Gain on sale of plant	(8,000)
Interest expense	8,000
Increase in trade receivables	(18,000)
Increase in inventory	(10,000)
Increase in prepayments	(3,000)
Increase in trade payables	6,000
Decrease in other payables	(400)
Cash generated from operations	222,600
Interest received*	10,100
Interest paid**	(7,600)
Income taxes paid	(50,000)
Net cash from operating activities	€175,100

* May be classified as investing.
** May be classified as financing.

Step 8 – Determine cash flows from investing activities

Determining cash flows from investing activities requires identifying cash inflows and outflows relating to the acquisition and disposal of long-term assets and other investments not included in cash equivalents.

The comparative balance sheets of Sunny Beach show that plant has increased by EUR 30,000 (A), investments by EUR 4,000 (B) and intangibles by EUR 30,000 (B). To determine the cash flows relating to these increases, it is necessary to analyse the underlying transactions.

The net increase in plant reflects the recording of acquisitions, disposals and depreciation. Using the data provided, the analysis of the plant movement (which is net of accumulated depreciation) is as follows:

Beginning balance	€300,000
Acquisitions	100,000
Disposals	(20,000)
Depreciation for year	(50,000)
Ending balance	€330,000

The additional information states that the acquisitions were made for cash during the period, so no adjustment is necessary for the year-end payables. Assuming that there were no outstanding payables for plant purchases at the beginning of the year, the cash outflow for plant acquisitions for the year is EUR 100,000 (A). (If payables for plant purchases were outstanding at the beginning of the period, the amount would need to be included in plant purchases paid during the period.)

The proceeds on the sale of plant can be calculated as:

Net book value of plant disposed of   +   Gain on disposal
or
−   Loss on disposal of plant

For Sunny Beach, the calculation is as follows:

$$€20,000 + €8,000 = €28,000$$

However, the proceeds from the sale of plant equal the cash inflow for the year only if there are no receivables outstanding arising from the sale of plant at either the beginning or end of the year. If receivables exist, the cash inflow is determined using the approach previously outlined for sales revenue and interest receivable. For simplicity, it is assumed that Sunny Beach had no receivables outstanding, at the beginning or end of the year, arising from the sale of plant.

Issues similar to those outlined for the acquisition of plant arise in respect of investments and intangibles. The comparative balance sheets for Sunny Beach show that the movement in investment and intangibles equal the additional cash acquisitions made during the period. Note, however, that the movements in these items equal the cash outflows for the year only if it is assumed that there were no outstanding trade payables at the beginning of the year that were settled during the year. If payables exist, the cash outflow is determined using the approach that was previously outlined for cash paid to suppliers and employees.

Using the above information, Sunny Beach's statement of cash flows showing the cash flows from investing activities for the current year is presented in Table 16.9.

Table 16.9 Sunny Beach statement of cash flows (extract) – investing activities section

Cash flows from investing activities	
Purchases of intangibles	€(30,000)
Purchases of investments	(4,000)
Purchases of plant	(100,000)
Proceeds from sale of plant	28,000
Net cash used in investing activities	€(106,000)

Step 9 – Determine cash flows from financing activities

Determining cash flows from financing activities requires identifying cash flows that resulted in changes in the size and composition of equity capital and borrowings.

The additional information (C) confirms that the increase in borrowings of EUR 20,000 derived from the comparative balance sheets of Sunny Beach arose from an additional borrowing. It would normally be necessary to analyse the net movement in borrowings in order to identify whether the movement reflects repayments and additional borrowings, and whether any new borrowings arose from non-cash transactions.

Share capital is unchanged at EUR 400,000. The movement in retained earnings of EUR 48,000 reflects:

Net profit for the year	€148,000
Dividends (paid in cash) (D)	100,000
Net movement	€48,000

Table 16.10 Sunny Beach statement of cash flows (extract) – financing activities section

Cash flows from financing activities	
Proceeds from borrowings	€20,000
Dividends paid*	(100,000)
Net cash used in financing activities	€(80,000)

* Dividends paid may be classified as an operating cash flow.

Table 16.11 Sunny Beach statement of cash flows for the year ended 31 December 2008

	€	€
Cash flows from operating activities		
Cash receipts from customers	1,582,000	
Cash paid to suppliers and employees	(1,359,400)	
Cash generated from operations	222,600	
Interest received	10,100	
Interest paid	(7,600)	
Income tax paid	(50,000)	
Net cash from operating activities		175,100
Cash flows from investing activities		
Purchase of intangibles	(30,000)	
Purchase of investments	(4,000)	
Purchase of plant	(100,000)	
Proceeds from sale of plant	28,000	
Net cash used in investing activities		(106,000)
Cash flows from financing activities		
Proceeds from borrowings	20,000	
Dividends paid	(100,000)	
Net cash used in financing activities		(80,000)
Net decrease in cash and cash equivalents		(10,900)
Cash and cash equivalents at the beginning of the year		(120,000)
Cash and cash equivalents at the end of the year		109,000

Step 10 – Put all the pieces together

The complete statement of cash flows for Sunny Beach (using the direct method for reporting cash flows from operating activities) is shown in Table 16.11.

The balance of cash at year-end of EUR 109,000, shown in Table 16.11, agrees with the cash at bank balance shown in the balance sheet at 31 December 2008 in Table 16.6. There are no cash equivalents such as a short-term deposit or bank overdraft. Where there are cash equivalents, IAS 7 para 45 requires that the cash and cash equivalents be disclosed, with the amounts reconciled in the statement of cash flows and the equivalent items reported in the balance sheet.

Summary

- Information about the cash flows of an entity is useful in providing users of financial statements with a basis to assess the ability of the entity to generate cash and cash equivalents and the needs of the entity to use those cash flows.

- Cash and cash equivalents comprise investments readily convertible into cash and subject to an insignificant risk of changes in value. Bank overdrafts are often included as a negative component of cash and cash equivalents.

- A statement of cash flows focuses on the change, i.e. increase or decrease in cash and cash equivalents and the activities that cause that increase or decrease, i.e. operating, investing and financing activities.

- Cash flows from operating activities may be calculated using either the direct or indirect method. The former restates each income statement item to reflect the movement of cash. The latter starts with the operating profit and adjusts it for the effects of changes in inventories, receivables and payables and non-cash items such as depreciation, amortisation and long-term provisions.

- Cash flows from investing activities primarily represent changes in non-current assets and their effects on cash, such as the acquisition or disposal of PPE, equity and debt instruments of other entities, advances and loans made to, or repayments from, third parties.

- Cash flows from financing activities show the cash flows to/from providers of capital, such as receipts from an issue of share or other equity securities; payments made to redeem such securities; proceeds from the issue of debentures and repayments of such securities.

Research and references

The IASB document relevant to this chapter is IAS 7 – *Statement of Cash Flows*.

The following are examples of articles and books that take the issues of this chapter further:

- Alexander, D., Britton, A. and Jorissen, A. (2007) *International Financial Reporting and Analysis*, 3rd edn. Thomson, Chapter 23.
- Chartered Accountants of Canada (2008) *Improved Communication with Non-GAAP Financial Measures. General Principles and Guidance for Reporting EBITDA and Free Cash Flow.* February.
- Elliott, B. and Elliott, J. (2009) *Financial Accounting and Reporting*, 13th edn. Financial Times-Prentice Hall, Chapter 26.
- Epstein, B.J. and Jermakowicz, E.K. (2009) *IFRS 2009: Interpretation and Application of International Accounting and Financial Reporting Standards.* Wiley, Chapter 4.
- Melville, A. (2009) *International Financial Reporting*, 2nd edn. Financial Times Press.
- PricewaterhouseCoopers (2009) *IFRS Manual of Accounting – 2010. Global Guide to International Financial Reporting Standards.* CCH, Chapter 30.
- Reilley, P. (2008) 'Standard-Setters Need to Focus on Cash Flow', *Financial Times*, 14 May.
- Stolowy, H. and Lebas, M.J. (2006) *Corporate Financial Reporting. A Global Perspective*, 2nd edn. Thomson, September, Chapter 14.
- Sutton, T. (2004) *Corporate Financial Accounting and Reporting*, 2nd edn. Financial Times-Prentice Hall, Chapter 18.
- Van Greuning, H. (2005) *International Financial Reporting Standards. A Practical Guide*, revised edition. Washington, DC: World Bank, Chapter 4.
- Walsh, C. (2008) *Key Management Ratios, Master the Management Metrics that Drive and Control Your Business*, 3rd edn. Financial Times-Prentice Hall, Part Three.

Discussion questions and exercises

16.1 Statement of cash flows (IAS 7)

(a) What is the objective of a statement of cash flows?

(b) How might a statement of cash flows be used?

(c) What is the meaning of 'cash equivalent'?

(d) Explain the classification of cash flows required under IAS 7.

16.2 Cash flows from operating activities

(a) Explain the differences between the presentation of cash flows from operating activities under the direct method and their presentation under the indirect method.

(b) Do you consider one method to be more appropriate than the other? Why?

16.3 Profit (loss) and cash flows

(a) An entity may report a considerable net profit for a year and still report (net) negative cash flows from its operating activities. How can this happen?

(b) An entity may report a considerable net loss for a year and still report (net) positive cash flows from operating activities over the same period. How can this happen?

16.4 Movements in cash equivalents

Entity A, as part of its cash management activities, invested EUR 20 million in redeemable preference shares (within three months from the date of their redemption). To do so, entity A instructed its bank to use a maturing time deposit (a two-month fixed deposit) with the bank.

Explain how entity A would treat in its statement of cash flows the cash out-flows resulting from the investment of funds in redeemable preferred shares and the cash inflows resulting from the use of a maturing time deposit.

16.5 Cash flows from operating activities – direct method

Entity E prepares its statement of cash flows under the direct method and has provided this information:

Net credit sales	€10,000,000
Trade receivables, end of the year	3,000,000
Trade receivables, beginning of the year	5,000,000
Purchases (on account)	8,000,000
Trade payables, end of the year	3,800,000
Trade payables, beginning of the year	4,000,000
Operating expenses (including depreciation)	6,000,000
Accrued expenses, beginning of the year	1,000,000
Accrued expenses, end of the year	800,000
Depreciation of property, plant and equipment	1,200,000

For the purposes of the statement of cash flows under the direct method, you are required to compute the cash collections from customers, payments to suppliers, and cash paid for operating expenses.

16.6 Cash flows from operating activities – indirect method

Entity F has provided you with the following information to prepare the operating activities of the statement of cash flows under the indirect method:

Profit before taxes	€800,000
Depreciation of property, plant and equipment	400,000
Loss on sale of building	200,000
Interest expense	300,000
Interest payable, beginning of the year	200,000
Interest payable, end of the year	100,000
Income taxes paid	200,000
Trade receivables, beginning of the year	1,000,000
Trade receivables, end of the year	1,700,000
Inventory, beginning of the year	1,000,000
Inventory, end of the year	800,000
Trade payables, beginning of the year	400,000
Trade payables, end of the year	1,000,000

Prepare the operating activities section of the statement of cash flows using the indirect method.

16.7 Cash flows from investing activities

The accounting records of entity H at 31 December 2008 and 31 December 2009 showed the following information in relation to its non-current assets:

	31 December 2008	31 December 2009
	€	€
Land, at independent valuation	200,000	240,000
Plant, at cost	140,000	170,000
Accumulated depreciation	(40,000)	(56,000)
Available-for-sale listed investments,		
at fair value	60,000	80,000
Goodwill	50,000	40,000
Land revaluation reserve	40,000	68,000
Investments revaluation reserve	10,000	22,000
Impairment of goodwill	–	10,000

Additional information:

- There were no acquisitions or disposal of land.
- There were no disposals of plant or investments.
- The land revaluation reserve increment is net of deferred tax of EUR 12,000.
- The investments revaluation reserve increment for the year is net of deferred tax of EUR 4,000.

Determine the amount of net investing cash flows entity H would report in its statement of cash flows for the year ended 31 December 2009, and prepare the investing section of the statement of cash flows.

16.8 Cash flows from financing activities

The following information has been extracted from the accounting records of entity I:

	30 June 2008	30 June 2009
	€	€
Borrowings	200,000	400,000
Share capital	400,000	500,000
Property revaluation reserve	100,000	120,000
Retained earnings	150,000	190,000

Additional information:

- Borrowings of EUR 40,000 were repaid during the year ended 30 June 2009. New borrowings include EUR 160,000 vendor finance for the acquisition of a property.
- The increase in share capital includes EUR 60,000 arising from the company's dividend reinvestment scheme.
- The movement in retained earnings comprises profit for the year for EUR 180,000, net of dividends for EUR 140,000.
- There were no dividends payable reported in the balance sheet at either 30 June 2008 or 30 June 2009.

Determine the amount of financing cash flows entity I would report in its statement of cash flows for the year ended 30 June 2009, and prepare the financing section of the statement of cash flows.

16.9 Foreign currency transactions and cash flows

A UK company which accounts in sterling (£) was set up in January 2009 and raised £400,000 by issuing shares. It purchased goods for resale from Italy in February 2009 for EUR 400,000, when the exchange rate was £1 = EUR 1.5.

At the year-end, 31 December 2009, the trade payable was not settled. At the same date, the exchange rate was £1 = EUR 1.55.

Assuming that there are no other transactions during the year, how would you disclose these transactions in the statement of cash flows?

16.10 Foreign currency transactions and cash flows

The opening balance sheet at 1 January 2009 of an Italian company, which accounts in euro consists of cash of EUR 200,000 and share capital of EUR 200,000. The company takes out a long-term loan on 30 June 2009 of US$ 540,000 when the rate of exchange is EUR 1 = US$1.4. The proceeds are immediately converted to euro, that is, EUR 385,714. There are no other transactions during the year. The exchange rate at the balance sheet date, 31 December 2009, is EUR 1 = US$1.6.

Prepare the statement of cash flows for 2009.

16.11 Statement of cash flows – direct method

A summarised comparative balance sheet of entity N is presented below, together with the income statement for the year ended 30 September 2009:

	30 September 2008	30 September 2009
	€	€
Cash	60,000	126,000
Trade receivables	92,000	140,000
Inventory	60,000	64,000
Investments	70,000	80,000
Plant	250,000	300,000
Accumulated depreciation	(46,000)	(70,000)
Total assets	486,000	640,000
Trade payables	78,000	86,000
Accrued interest	6,000	10,000
Current tax payable	20,000	24,000
Borrowings	120,000	200,000
Share capital	200,000	200,000
Retained earnings	62,000	120,000
Total liabilities and equity	486,000	640,000

Income statement
for the year ended 30 September 2009

	€
Sales	€1,380,000
Cost of sales	966,000
Gross profit	414,000
Distribution costs	104,000
Administration costs	148,000
Interest	12,000
Profit before tax	150,000
Income tax expense	46,000
Net profit for the year	€104,000

Additional information:

- There were no disposals of investments or plant during the year.
- There are no deferred tax balances.
- A dividend of EUR 46,000 was paid during the year.

Using the direct method of presenting cash flows from operating activities, prepare a statement of cash flows in accordance with IAS 7 for the year ended 30 September 2009.

16.12 Statement of cash flows – indirect method

A summarised comparative balance sheet of entity O is presented below:

	31 December 2008 €	31 December 2009 €
Cash	192,000	98,000
Trade receivables	294,000	326,000
Prepayments	40,000	30,000
Inventory	120,000	208,000
Land	80,000	80,000
Plant	736,000	840,000
Accumulated depreciation	(90,000)	(140,000)
Deferred tax	40,000	48,000
Total assets	1,412,000	1,490,000
Trade payables	280,000	304,000
Accrued liabilities	72,000	84,000
Current tax payable	48,000	62,000
Dividends payable	112,000	100,000
Borrowings	146,000	150,000
Share capital	670,000	690,000
Retained earnings	84,000	100,000
Total liabilities and equity	1,412,000	1,490,000

Additional information:

- Plant additions amounted to EUR 144,000. Plant with a written-down value of EUR 30,000 (cost EUR 40,000, accumulated depreciation EUR 10,000) was sold for EUR 44,000. The proceeds were outstanding at 31 December 2009.
- Trade payables at 31 December 2008 include EUR 68,000 arising from the acquisition of plant.
- Accrued liabilities include accrued interest of EUR 6,000 at 31 December 2008 and EUR 8,000 at 31 December 2009.
- The share capital increase of EUR 20,000 arose from the reinvestment of dividends.
- The net profit for the year was EUR 184,000, after interest expense of EUR 12,000 and income tax expense of EUR 92,000.
- Dividends declared out of profits for the year were: interim dividend EUR 68,000, final dividend EUR 100,000.

Using the indirect method of presenting cash flows from operating activities, prepare a statement of cash flows in accordance with IAS 7 for the year ended 31 December 2009.

16.13 Statement of cash flows – direct and indirect methods

Financial information for Tremendous SpA for the year ended 31 December 2009 follows:

Tremendous SpA
Balance sheet as at 31 December 2009 and 2008

	2009 €	2008 €
Assets		
Cash and cash equivalents	9,000	3,000
Trade receivables	15,000	7,500
Inventory	6,000	4,500
Intangible asset, net	3,000	4,500
Due from associates	57,000	57,000
Property, plant and equipment, cost	36,000	67,500
Accumulated depreciation	(15,000)	(18,000)
Property, plant and equipment, net	21,000	49,500
Total assets	111,000	126,000
Liabilities		
Trade payables	€15,000	€37,500
Income taxes payable	6,000	3,000
Deferred taxes payable	9,000	6,000
Total liabilities	30,000	46,500
Shareholders' equity		
Share capital	19,500	19,500
Retained earnings	61,500	60,000
Total shareholders' equity	81,000	79,500
Total liabilities and shareholders' equity	111,000	126,000

Tremendous SpA
Income statement for the year ended 31 December 2009

	€
Sales	90,000
Cost of sales	(30,000)
Gross profit	60,000
Administrative and selling expenses	(6,000)
Interest expenses	(6,000)
Depreciation of property, plant and equipment	(6,000)
Amortisation of intangible assets	(1,500)
Investment income	9,000
Profit before tax	49,500
Income tax expense	(12,000)
Net profit for the year	37,500

Additional information:

This additional information is relevant to the preparation of statement of cash flows:

1 All sales made by Tremendous SpA are credit sales. All purchases are on account.

2 Interest expense for the year 2009 was EUR 6,000, which was fully paid during the year.

3 The company pays salaries and other employee dues before the end of each month. All administration and selling expenses incurred were paid before 31 December 2009.

4 Investment income comprised dividend income from investments in shares of blue chip companies. This was received before 31 December 2009.

5 Equipment with a net book value of EUR 22,500 and original cost of EUR 31,500 was sold for EUR 22,500.

6 The company declared and paid dividends of EUR 36,000 to its share-holders during 2009.

7 Income tax expense for the year 2009 was EUR 12,000, against which the company paid EUR 6,000 during 2009 as an estimate.

Prepare the statement of cash flows for Tremendous SpA, according to the requirements of IAS 7 under both the direct and indirect methods.

17

Other issues relating to reporting and disclosures

Contents

Operating segments that do not meet any of the quantitative thresholds may be considered reportable, and separately disclosed, if management believe that information about the segment would be useful to users of the financial statements (IFRS 8 para 13).

If the total external revenue reported by operating segments constitutes less than 75 per cent of the entity's revenue, additional operating segments should be identified as reportable segments (even if they do not meet the criteria set out above) until at least 75 per cent of the entity's revenue is included in reportable segments (IFRS 8 para 15).

If an operating segment is identified as a reportable segment in the current period in accordance with the quantitative thresholds, segment data for a prior period presented for comparative purposes should be restated to reflect the newly reportable segment as a separate segment, even if that segment did not satisfy the criteria for reportability in paragraph 13 in the prior period, unless the necessary information is not available and the cost to develop it would be excessive (IFRS 8 para 18).

The flow chart in Figure 17.1 illustrates how to apply the main provisions for identifying reportable segments as defined above.

17.1.3 Disclosure

An entity should disclose information to enable users of its financial statements to evaluate the nature and financial effects of the business activities in which it engages and the economic environments in which it operates (IFRS 8 para 20).

According to IFRS 8 paras 21–24, an entity should disclose the following:

(a) *General information:*

- factors used to identify the entity's reportable segments, including the basis of organisation (for example, whether management have chosen to organise the entity around differences in products and services, geographical areas, regulatory environments, or a combination of factors and whether operating segments have been aggregated); and
- types of products and services from which each reportable segment derives its revenues.

(b) *Information about reported segment profit or loss, segment assets, segment liabilities and the basis of measurement:*

- revenues from external customers;
- revenues from transactions with other operating segments of the same entity;
- interest revenue;
- interest expense;
- depreciation and amortisation;
- material items of income and expense disclosed in accordance with IAS 1 (revised);
- the entity's interest in the profit or loss of associates and joint ventures accounted for by the equity method;
- income tax expense or income; and
- material non-cash items other than depreciation and amortisation.

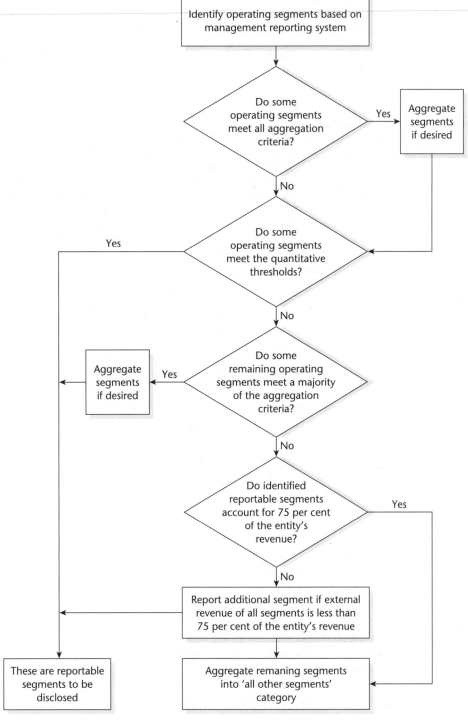

Figure 17.1 Diagram for identifying reportable segments
Source: IFRS 8 IG7.

(c) *Reconciliations* of the totals of segment revenues, reported segment profit or loss, segment assets, segment liabilities and other material segment items to corresponding entity amounts as described in section 17.1.3, below.

Figure 17.2 represents an example of the information relating to reportable segments.

- *Description of the types of products and services from which each reportable segment derives its revenues*

  Diversified Company has five reportable segments: car parts, motor vessels, software, electronics and finance. The car parts segment produces replacement parts for sale to car parts retailers. The motor vessels segment produces small motor vessels to serve the offshore oil industry and similar businesses. The software segment produces application software for sale to computer manufacturers and retailers. The electronics segment produces integrated circuits and related products for sale to computer manufacturers.

  The finance segment is responsible for portions of the company's financial operations including financing customer purchases of products from other segments and property lending operations.

- *Measurement of operating segment profit or loss, assets and liabilities*

  The accounting policies of the operating segments are the same as those described in the summary of significant accounting policies except that pension expense for each operating segment is recognised and measured on the basis of cash payments to the pension plan. Diversified Company evaluates performance on the basis of profit or loss from operations before tax expense excluding non-recurring gains and losses and foreign exchange gains and losses.

  Diversified Company accounts for intersegment sales and transfers as if the sales or transfers were to third parties, i.e. at current market prices.

- *Factors that management used to identify the entity's reportable segments*

  Diversified Company's reportable segments are strategic business units that offer different products and services. They are managed separately because each business requires different technology and marketing strategies. Most of the businesses were acquired as individual units, and the management at the time of the acquisition were retained.

Figure 17.2 Descriptive information about an entity's reportable segments

Figure 17.3 shows a suggested format for disclosing information about reportable segment profit or loss, assets and liabilities. The same type of information is required for each year for which a statement of comprehensive income is presented. Diversified Company does not allocate tax expense (tax income) or non-recurring gains and losses to reportable segments.

In addition, not all reportable segments have material non-cash items other than depreciation and amortisation in the income statement. The amounts in this example are assumed to be the amounts in reports used by the chief operating decision maker.

Information about geographical areas

If an entity's activities are not organised on the basis of differences in related products and services or if its reportable segments hold assets in different geographical areas and report revenues from customers in different geographical areas, that entity should report the following geographical information:

	Car parts €	Motor vessels €	Software €	Electronics €	Finance €	All other €	Totals €
Revenues from external customers	3,000	5,000	9,500	12,000	5,000	1,000(a)	35,500
Intersegment revenues	–	–	3,000	1,500	–	–	4,500
Interest revenue	450	800	1,000	1,500	–	–	3,750
Interest expense	350	600	700	1,100	–	–	2,750
Net interest revenue(b)	–	–	–	–	1,000	–	1,000
Depreciation and amortisation	200	100	50	1,500	1,100	–	2,950
Reportable segment profit	200	70	900	2,300	500	100	4,070
Other material non-cash items:							
Impairment of assets	–	200	–	–	–	–	200
Reportable segment assets	2,000	5,000	3,000	12,000	57,000	2,000	81,000
Expenditures for reportable segment							
non-current assets	300	700	500	800	600	–	2,900
Reportable segment liabilities	1,050	3,000	1,800	8,000	30,000	–	43,850

(a) Revenues from segments below the quantitative thresholds are attributable to four operating segments of Diversified Company. Those segments include a small property business, an electronics equipment rental business, a software consulting practice and a warehouse leasing operation. None of those segments has ever met any of the quantitative thresholds for determining reportable segments.

(b) The finance segment derives a majority of its revenue from interest. Management primarily rely on net interest revenue, not the gross revenue and expense amounts, in managing that segment. Therefore, as permitted by paragraph 23, only the net amount is disclosed.

Figure 17.3 Information about reportable segment profit or loss, assets and liabilities for Diversified Company

(a) revenues from external customers:

    (i)   attributed to the entity's country of domicile; and

    (ii) attributed to all foreign countries in total from which the entity derives revenues. If revenues from external customers attributed to an individual foreign country are material, those revenues should be disclosed separately. An entity should disclose the basis for attributing revenues from external customers to individual countries.

(b) PPE:

    (i)   located in the entity's country of domicile; and

    (ii) located in all foreign countries in total in which the entity holds assets. If assets in an individual foreign country are material, those assets should be disclosed separately.

Figure 17.4 illustrates the geographical information required above.

Geographical information	Revenues* €	Non-current assets €
United States	19,000	11,000
Canada	4,200	–
China	3,400	6,500
Japan	2,900	3,500
Other countries	6,000	3,000
Total	35,500	24,000

Figure 17.4 Geographical information

* Revenues of Diversified Company are attributed to countries on the basis of the customer's location.

17.1.4 Measurement

The amount of each segment item reported should be the measure reported to the chief operating decision maker for the purposes of making decisions about allocating resources to the segment and assessing its performance. Adjustments and eliminations made in preparing an entity's financial statements and allocations of revenues, expenses, and gains or losses should be included in determining reported segment profit or loss only if they are included in the measure of the segment's profit or loss that is used by the chief operating decision maker. Similarly, only those assets and liabilities that are included in the measures of the segment's assets and segment's liabilities that are used by the chief operating decision maker should be reported for that segment. If amounts are allocated to reported segment profit or loss, assets or liabilities, those amounts should be allocated on a reasonable basis (IFRS 8 para 25).

If the chief operating decision maker uses only one measure of an operating segment's profit or loss, the segment's assets or the segment's liabilities in assessing segment performance and deciding how to allocate resources, segment profit or loss, assets and liabilities should be reported at those measures. If the chief operating decision maker uses more than one measure of an operating segment's profit or loss, the segment's assets or the segment's liabilities, the reported measures should be those that management believe are determined in accordance with the measurement principles most consistent with those used in measuring the corresponding amounts in the entity's financial statements (IFRS 8 para 26).

Reconciliations

An entity should provide reconciliations of all of the following:

(a) the total of the reportable segments' revenues to the entity's revenue;

(b) the total of the reportable segments' measures of profit or loss to the entity's profit or loss before tax expense (tax income) and discontinued operations. However, if an entity allocates to reportable segments items such as tax expense (tax income), the entity should reconcile the total of the segments' measures of profit or loss to the entity's profit or loss after those items;

(c) the total of the reportable segments' assets to the entity's assets;

(d) the total of the reportable segments' liabilities to the entity's liabilities;

(e) the total of the reportable segments' amounts for every other material item of information disclosed to the corresponding amount for the entity.

All material reconciling items should be separately identified and described. For example, the amount of each material adjustment needed to reconcile reportable segment profit or loss to the entity's profit or loss arising from different accounting policies should be separately identified and described (IFRS 8 para 28).

Figure 17.5 illustrates reconciliations of reportable segment revenues, profit or loss, assets and liabilities to the entity's corresponding amounts for Diversified Company.

Revenues	€
Total revenues for reportable segments	39,000
Other revenues	1,000
Elimination of intersegment revenues	(4,500)
Diversified Company's revenues	35,500

Profit or loss	€
Total profit or loss for reportable segments	3,970
Other profit or loss	100
Elimination of intersegment profits	(500)
Unallocated amounts:	
Litigation settlement received	500
Other corporate expenses	(750)
Adjustment to pension expense in consolidation	(250)
Income before income tax expense	3,070

Assets	€
Total assets for reportable segments	79,000
Other assets	2,000
Elimination of receivable from corporate headquarters	(1,000)
Other unallocated amounts	1,500
Diversified Company's assets	81,500

Liabilities	€
Total liabilities for reportable segments	43,850
Unallocated defined benefit pension liabilities	25,000
Diversified Company's liabilities	68,850

Other material items	Reportable segment totals	Adjustments	Entity totals
	€	€	€
Interest revenue	3,750	75	3,825
Interest expense	2,750	(50)	2,700
Net interest revenue (finance segment only)	1,000	–	1,000
Expenditures for assets	2,900	1,000	3,900
Depreciation and amortisation	2,950	–	2,950
Impairment of assets	200	–	200

The reconciling item to adjust expenditures for assets is the amount incurred for the corporate headquarters building, which is not included in segment information. None of the other adjustments are material.

Figure 17.5 Reconciliation of reportable segment revenues, profit or loss, assets and liabilities for Diversified Company

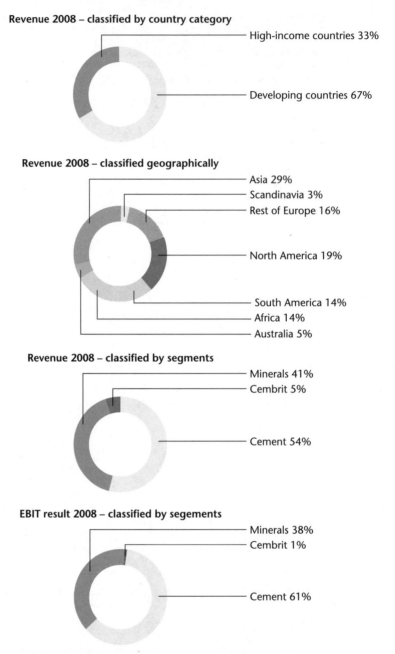

Figure 17.6 Revenue and EBIT classified geographically and by segment

Source: FLSmidth Annual Report 2008.

17.2   Earnings per share (IAS 33)

Earnings per share (EPS) is a ratio that is widely used by financial analysts, investors and others to gauge a company's profitability and to value its shares. Its purpose is to indicate how effective a company has been in using the resources provided by the ordinary equity holders. The allocation of earnings accruing to other providers of finance, such as preference shareholders is a prior charge and is often fixed. Therefore, the income remaining after making allocations to those parties is attributable to ordinary shareholders. This amount, when presented on the face of the profit and loss account on a cent per share basis, assists the ordinary shareholders to gauge the company's current net earnings and changes in its net earnings from period to period. It can, therefore, be relevant as a measure of company performance and in evaluating management's effectiveness. Another reason for the popularity of EPS is that it forms the basis for calculating the 'price-earnings ratio', which is a standard stock market indicator. Price-earnings ratios relating to both past and prospective profits are widely used by investors and analysts in valuing shares.

EPS is simply a ratio of the numerator – earnings measured in terms of profits available to ordinary shareholders – to the denominator – the number of ordinary shares. Therefore, it is very simple in concept, but it is the determination of the numerator and, in particular, the denominator that can make the calculation of this ratio rather complex in practice. Also if the ratio is to be meaningful it must be calculated on a similar basis for every entity so as to facilitate comparisons between different accounting periods for the same entity and between different entities in the same period.

17.2.1 How to determine basic EPS

Basic EPS should be calculated by dividing the profit or loss for the period attributable to the parent entity's ordinary equity holders by the weighted average number of ordinary shares outstanding during the period (IAS 33 para 10).

The term 'ordinary share' is defined as an equity instrument that is subordinate to all other classes of equity instrument. An equity instrument is any contract that evidences a residual interest in the assets of an entity after deducting all of its liabilities (IAS 33 para 5 and IAS 32 para 11). Ordinary shares participate in profit only after other types of shares such as preference shares have participated (IAS 33 para 6).

The computation of the EPS figure requires a calculation of the earnings as the numerator and the relevant number of ordinary shares as the denominator. If no adjustments are required to the numerator or the denominator, the profit or loss attributable to the ordinary equity holders and the relevant number of ordinary shares can be obtained directly from the financial statements and the figure computed. However, care is required to ensure that the number of shares is stated consistently to avoid distortions arising from changes in the capital structure that has changed the number of shares outstanding without a corresponding change in resources during the whole or part of a year. Such changes occur, for example, with bonus issues and share splits, new issues during the year, etc. In such cases (i.e., bonus issues, share splits, exercise of conversion rights, etc.) the number of shares used in the basic EPS calculation should be adjusted as illustrated in Examples 17.1 to 17.4.

Bonus issues

A bonus issue arises when an entity capitalises reserves to give existing shareholders more shares. In effect, a simple transfer is made from reserves to issued share capital. In real terms, neither the shareholder receives any immediate financial benefit nor does the entity suffer any immediate financial consequence. The process indicates that the reserves will remain invested in the assets of the company and therefore are no longer available for distribution. There are, however, more shares in circulation.

Example 17.1

Adjusting the number of shares used in the basic EPS calculation in a bonus issue

Assume that XYZ had a net profit for 2009 of EUR 1,250,000 and an issued share capital of EUR 1,500,000 comprising 1,000,000 ordinary shares of EUR 0.50 each and 1,000,000 10 per cent preference shares of EUR 1 each.

Now assume that XYZ increased its shares in 2009 by the issue of 1,000,000 new ordinary shares and achieved identical earnings in 2009 as in 2008.

- Determine the basic EPS for 2009 for XYZ.
- How would you restate the basic EPS of 2008 in order to achieve the comparison of performance between the two years?

The EPS reported in 2009 would be immediately halved from EUR 1.15 to EUR 0.575. Clearly, this does not provide a useful comparison of performance between 2009 and 2008. The solution is to restate the EPS for 2008 that appears in the 2009 financial statements, using the number of shares in issue at 31 December 2009:

Basic EPS for 2008 (restated) = €1,150,000 ÷ 2,000,000 shares = **€0.575**

Share splits

When the market value of a share becomes high some entities decide to increase the number of shares held by each shareholder by changing the nominal value of each share. The effect is to reduce the market price per share but each shareholder owns the same total value in shares. However, as a result of a share split, shares become more marketable. A share split would be treated in the same way as a bonus issue, as illustrated in Example 17.2.

Example 17.2

Adjusting the number of shares used in the basic EPS calculation in a share split

Refer to the data provided in Example 17.1. Assume that XYZ split the 1,000,000 shares of EUR 0.50 each into 2,000,000 shares of EUR 0.25 each. As 2009 basic EPS would be calculated using 2,000,000 shares, it would seem that the basic EPS had halved in 2009.

This is misleading and 2008 basic EPS is therefore restated using 2,000,000 shares. However, the total market capitalisation of XYZ would remain unchanged. For example if prior to the split, each share had a market value of EUR 4 and the company had a total market capitalisation of EUR 4,000,000, after the split each share would have a market price of EUR 2 and the company market capitalisation would remain unchanged at EUR 4,000,000.

New issue of shares

Issuing more shares to raise additional capital should generate additional earnings. In this situation we have a real change in the company's capital and there is no need to adjust any comparative figures. However, a problem arises in the year in which the issue takes place. Unless the issue occurs on the first day of the financial year, the new funds would be available to generate profits for only a part of the year. It would therefore be misleading to calculate the EPS figure by dividing the earnings generated during the year by the number of shares in issue at the end of the year. The method adopted to counter this is to use a time-weighted average for the number of shares, as illustrated in Example 17.3.

Example 17.3

Time-weighted number of shares for the basic EPS calculation

Assume that the following information is available for XYZ:

Number of shares (nominal value EUR 0.50 each) in issue at 1 January 2009:	1,000,000
Number of shares issued for cash at market price on 30 September 2009:	500,000

Determine the time-weighted number of shares for EPS calculation at 31 December 2009.

Number of shares in issue for nine months to date of issue: 1,000,000 × 9/12 months	750,000
Number of shares in issue for 3 months from date of issue: 1,500,000 × 3/12 months	375,000
Time-weighted shares to calculate basic EPS	*1,125,000*

Earnings per share (EPS) and diluted earnings per share (EPS diluted) are measured according to IAS 33.

Notes to the consolidated financial statements (extract)

Accounting policies (extract)

36. Earnings per share (EPS)

DKKm	2008	2007
Earnings		
FLSmidth & Co. shareholders' share of profit/loss for the year	1,515	1,294
FLSmidth & Co. Group earnings from discontinuing activities	59	1
Net effect after tax of purchase price allocations regarding GL&V Process	195	94
Number of shares, average		
Number of shares issued	53,200,000	53,200,000
Adjustment for own shares	(822,142)	(838,921)
Potential increase of shares in circulation, options in the money	166,152	278,504
	52,544,010	52,639,583
Earnings per share		
• Continuing and discontinuing activities per share, DKK	28.9	24.7
• Continuing and discontinuing activities, diluted, per share, DKK	28.8	24.6
• Continuing and discontinuing activities, diluted, before the effect of purchase price allocations regarding GL&V Process, per share, DKK	32.5	26.4
• Continuing activities per share, DKK	27.8	24.7
• Continuing activities, diluted, per share, DKK	27.7	24.6

> Non-diluted earnings per share in respect of discontinuing activities amount to DKK 1.1 (2007: DKK 0.0) and diluted earnings per share in respect of discontinuing activities amount to DKK 1.1 (2007: DKK 0.0). These earnings are calculated based on the Group's earnings from discontinuing activities which amount to DKK 59m (2007: DKK 1m).

Figure 17.7 (*Cont'd*)

17.3 Related party disclosures (IAS 24)

Related party transactions can take a variety of forms. Many of them include transactions in the normal course of business, for example, purchases or sales of goods at market values. However, others can include significant one-off transactions that may be at a fair value on an arm's length basis or which may be at book value or some other amount that differs from market prices. The stated objective of IAS 24 – *Related Party Disclosures*, is to ensure that an entity's financial statements contain the disclosures necessary to draw attention to the possibility that its financial position and profit or loss may have been affected by the existence of related parties and by transactions and outstanding balances with such parties (IAS 24 para 1).

The reasons for the disclosure of related party transactions by explaining the effect on a reporting entity of the existence of related party relationships may be summarised as follows (IAS 24 paras 5–8):

- Related party relationships are a normal feature of commerce and business. For example, entities frequently carry on parts of their activities through subsidiaries, joint ventures and associates. In these circumstances, the entity's ability to affect the financial and operating policies of the investee is through the presence of control, joint control or significant influence.

- A related party relationship could have an effect on the income statement and financial position of an entity. Related parties may enter into transactions that unrelated parties would not. For example, an entity that sells goods to its parent at cost might not sell on those terms to another customer. Also, transactions between related parties may not be made at the same amounts as between un-related parties.

- The net profit (loss) and financial position of an entity may be affected by a related party relationship even if related party transactions do not occur. For example, a subsidiary may terminate relations with a trading partner on acquisition by the parent of a fellow subsidiary engaged in the same activity as the former trading partner. Alternatively, one party may refrain from acting because of the significant influence of another – for example, a subsidiary may be instructed by its parent not to engage in research and development.

- For these reasons, knowledge of related party transactions, outstanding balances and relationships may affect assessments of an entity's operations by users of financial statements, including assessments of the risks and opportunities facing the entity.

These are relatively straightforward examples given in the standard. However, there are many more extreme examples where related party transactions (often concealed from shareholders) have significantly distorted results and financial position and led to the entity's collapse and subsequent investigation by regulatory bodies. Examples are:

- borrowing by the entity from the entity's pension funds;
- artificial sales and other transactions with 'special purpose entities' (SPEs) that are related to the entity;
- loans to key management personnel.

The purpose of IAS 24 is to ensure that entities have a duty to make disclosure of all related party transactions so that shareholders are aware that such transactions may have affected the financial performance and position.

17.3.1 Related parties

IAS 24 requires transactions between a reporting entity and its related parties to be disclosed in its financial statements. The *reporting entity* is the entity, where it is preparing its individual or separate financial statements. However, if the entity is a parent entity and is preparing consolidated financial statements, the reporting entity is the group headed by the parent entity. Under IAS 27 – *Consolidated and Separate Financial Statements*, a parent should prepare consolidated financial statements comprising itself and its subsidiaries. The criteria for establishing related party relationships between an entity and its related parties and the group and its related parties should, therefore, be applied at the individual entity level and, in the case of consolidated financial statements, at the group level.

Criteria for related party relationships

A related party can be either an individual or an entity. IAS 24 para 9 specifies that certain parties are related parties. The list that follows includes general criteria that encompass relationships involving control, joint control and significant influence and which require the identification of parties that fall within those criteria. It also includes specifically identified parties, which are classed as related without resort to the more general criteria. Specifically a party is related to an entity if:

(a) directly, or indirectly through one or more intermediaries, the party:
  (i) controls, is controlled by, or is under common control with, the entity (this includes parents, subsidiaries and fellow subsidiaries);
  (ii) has an interest in the entity that gives it significant influence over the entity; or
  (iii) has joint control over the entity;

(b) the party is an associate of the entity;

(c) the party is a joint venture in which the entity is a venturer;

(d) the party is a member of the key management personnel of the entity or its parent;

(e) the party is a close member of the family of any individual referred to in (a) or (d);

(f) the party is an entity that is controlled, jointly controlled or significantly influenced by, or for which significant voting power in such entity resides with, directly or indirectly, any individual referred to in (d) or (e); or

(g) the party is a post-employment benefit plan for the benefit of employees of either the reporting entity, or an entity related to the reporting entity.

Also included are entities in which such persons have directly, or indirectly, significant voting power.

In respect of the most specific list above there is likely to be little difficulty in identifying related parties. The more general criteria involve the application of the terms 'control', 'joint control' and 'significant influence'.

Control

Control is the power to govern the financial and operating policies of an entity so as to obtain benefits from its activities (IAS 24 para 9).

One of the main purposes of the related parties standard is to make users aware of the possibility that the financial performance and position may have been affected by the existence of related parties. Most related party transactions are carried out in the normal course of an entity's business, but entities do also sometimes act improperly or illegally through the medium of related parties and it is particularly in those circumstances that disclosure is important.

Of course, it would be naïve to think that an entity that indulged in improper or illegal activities would willingly disclose the fact. However, the existence of rules in the standard gives authority to both employees involved in preparing the financial statements, and to auditors, to resist any suppression of disclosure. In addition, regulators and other authorities are able to use the standard's provisions when investigating and punishing the illegality after it has been revealed.

The definition appears to have the effect that control exists, for the purpose of IAS 24, where, for example, another entity or an individual holds more than half an entity's voting rights, whether or not that voting power is actually used to direct the entity's policies. There must also be some potential benefit for the controlling party as a result of such direction. For instance, venture capitalists with over 50 per cent of the shares with voting rights in an entity will generally have 'control' of that entity. Another example where control would exist would be where an entity or an individual has less than 50 per cent of voting rights, but has the power to control the financial and operating policies of another entity by, for example, agreement with the other shareholders. Based on IAS 27 para 14, the existence and effect of potential voting rights that are currently exercisable or convertible, including potential voting rights held by another entity or individual, are considered when assessing whether an entity has the power to govern the financial and operating policies of another entity.

The definition of control encompasses control by individuals and, for example, partnerships, as well as parent entities. An example of control by a partnership would be where a limited partnership controls over 50 per cent of the voting rights in a reporting entity.

Where control exists, even though no transactions have taken place, IAS 24 requires disclosure of the parent entity and, if different, the ultimate controlling party.

Common control and joint control

Entities subject to common control by the same source are included in the definition of related party, because of the potential effect on transactions between them and on their financial position. The most usual example of common control is within a group where two fellow subsidiaries are both under the control of the parent. Common control also arises, for example, when two entities are subject to common control by an individual.

Joint control is the contractually agreed sharing of control over an economic activity (IAS 24 para 9). For the purpose of IAS 24, we can refer to IAS 31 paras 9 and 10:

- The existence of a contractual arrangement distinguishes interests that involve joint control by investments in associates in which the investor has significant influence. Activities that have no contractual arrangement to establish joint control are not joint ventures for the purposes of this Standard.

- The contractual arrangement may be evidenced in a number of ways, for example by a contract between the venturers or minutes of discussions between the venturers. In some cases, the arrangement is incorporated in the articles or other by-laws of the joint venture. Whatever its form, the contractual arrangement is usually in writing and deals with such matters as:

  (a) the activity, duration and reporting obligations of the joint venture;
  (b) the appointment of the board of directors or equivalent governing body of the joint venture and the voting rights of the venturers;
  (c) capital contributions by the venturers; and
  (d) the sharing by the venturers of the output, income, expenses or results of the joint venture.

This definition means that where the entity is a joint venture between two or more venturers that share joint control over the entity, each of the venturers is a related party of the entity. Where the entity is itself a venturer, a party that is a joint venture of the entity is also a specifically identified related party to the entity.

Significant influence

Significant influence is the power to participate in the financial and operating policy decisions of an entity, but it is not control over those policies. Significant influence may be gained by share ownership, statute or agreement (IAS 24, para 9).

This is similar to the definition in IAS 28 – *Investment in associates*. IAS 28 para 7 gives more detail than IAS 24 on how the term should be interpreted. The existence of significant influence by an investor is usually evidenced in one or more of the following ways:

(a) representation on the board of directors or equivalent governing body of the investee;

(b) participation in policy-making processes, including participation in decisions about dividends or other distributions;

(c) material transactions between the investor and the investee;

(d) interchange of managerial personnel; or

(e) provision of essential technical information.

The definition means that where the entity is an associate of another party, that other party is a related party of the entity. In other words, where the entity itself has a significant influence over another party, that other party is its associate and is, therefore, also a specifically identified related party of the entity.

Substance of the relationship

IAS 24 contains an important overriding principle: in considering each possible related party relationship, attention should be directed to the substance of the relationship and not merely the legal form (IAS 24 para 10). An example of how this principle might be applied to a situation involving common control is given below. In addition the following sections describe how the principle might be applied in some less straightforward situations.

Example 17.6

Parties related in substance

Consider the following related party relationship and indicate the disclosure that should be made by entity A and entity C.

- Entity A is in financial difficulties. It is owned by Mr Xerox who is its sole director.
- Entity A sells for EUR 500,000 PPE having a book value of EUR 1m to entity B, which is owned by Mr Zapatos who is also entity B's sole director, for EUR 500,000.

- Entity B then sells the same PPE for EUR 500,000 to entity C which is also owned by Mr Xerox, who is its sole director.

The relationships between Messrs Xerox and Zapatos and entities A, B and C is represented in the figure below.

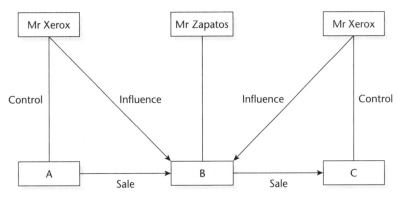

Figure 17.8 Representation of related party relationship

Entity A has sold a property to a third party (entity B), unconnected to its director, at an amount below its book value. It might be understandable that the sale is below book value as it might be a forced sale: in fact, entity A is in financial difficulties. However, entity B makes neither profit nor loss on the deal and appears to be an agent or intermediary for the transfer from entity A to entity C. Taking the transaction as a whole, the substance of this arrangement appears to be that a transaction has occurred between entity A and entity C. This has been facilitated via an intermediary: entity B. As entity A and entity C are subject to common control, they are related parties. In substance, a transaction has occurred between these two parties and this should be disclosed in accordance with IAS 24.[2] In the financial statements of both entity A and entity C details of the transaction should be disclosed alongside the fact that the transaction has been undertaken via an intermediary.[3]

Despite the absence of specific guidance in IAS 24, an entity preparing its financial statements should be guided by the substance of its relationships.

Significant influence and control by the same source

IAS 24 para 10 requires that in considering each possible related party relationship, attention should be directed to the substance of the relationship and not merely the legal form. This may be applied in two ways:

- First, it may be applied to a situation where, for example, a special purpose entity (SPE) is formed in which an entity would appear to have no ownership interest (using perhaps a trust arrangement to hold the investor's interest), but where the entity, in fact, exercises control. In such a situation, the substance is that the entity has control and, thus, the investee falls within the definition of a related party in the standard.

27. Related Parties (extract)

The Group purchases products, goods and services from related parties in the ordinary course of business.

At December 31, 2006 and 2005, the receivables from related parties and payables to related parties are as follows (in CZK millions):

	Receivables		Payables	
	2006	2005	2006	2005
Associates and other affiliates				
AFRAS Energo s.r.o.	1	–	6	3
AZ Elektrostav, a.s.	7	21	20	1
Coal Energy, a.s.	394	432	2	–
CEZ ENERGOSERVIS spol. s.r.o.	4	2	45	–
Elektrovod Holding, a.s.	–	1	–	25
ELTRAF, a.s.	4	2	11	1
Energetická montážní spolecnost Ceská Lípa, s.r.o.	60	7	31	1
Energetická montážní spolecnost Liberec, s.r.o.	20	2	13	–
Energetická montážní spolecnost Ústí nad Labem, s.r.o.	39	10	17	1
KNAUF POCERADY, spol. s.r.o.	8	8	–	–
KOTOUC ŠTRAMBERK, spol. s.r.o.l)	–	8	–	10
LOMY MORINA spol. s.r.o.	–	1	14	11
OSC, a.s.	–	–	9	22
Plzenská energetika a.s.2)	–	34	–	38
PRODECO, a.s.	13	1	36	13
SEG s.r.o.	3	6	60	12
SHD – KOMES a.s.	14	–	71	43
SIGMA – ENERGO s.r.o.	–	–	16	11
Others	30	24	54	37
Total associates and other affiliates	**597**	**559**	**405**	**229**
Companies under the control of Company's majority owner				
CEPS, a.s.	219	271	782	233
Ceská pošta s.p.	–	1	12	28
Ceské dráhy, a.s.	21	242	171	171
Ministry of Finance of the Czech Republic	2,854	5,671	–	–
Others	1	3	–	2
Total companies under the control of Company's majority owner	**3,095**	**6,188**	**965**	**434**
Total	**3,692**	**6,747**	**1,370**	**663**

Figure 17.10 (Cont'd)

Summary

- An operating segment is a component of an entity: (a) that engages in business activities from which it may earn revenues and incur expenses; (b) whose operating results are regularly reviewed by the entity's chief operating decision maker to make decisions about resources to be allocated to the segment and assess its performance, and (c) for which discrete financial information is available.

- An entity should report separately information about each operating segment that exceeds certain quantitative thresholds: (a) its reported revenue, including both sales to external customers and intersegment sales or transfers, is 10 per cent or more of the combined revenue, internal and external, of all operating segments; (b) the absolute amount of its reported profit or loss is 10 per cent or more of the greater, in absolute amount, of (i) the combined reported profit of all operating segments that did not report a loss and (ii) the combined reported loss of all operating segments that reported a loss; (c) its assets are 10 per cent or more of the combined assets of all operating segments.

- A popular means of measuring an entity's performance is earnings per share (EPS). This ratio is produced by dividing net profit for the year after deducting minority interests and any non-voting share dividend by the average number of equity shares in issue.

- When an entity has issued securities which carry the right to be converted into equity shares at some future date, it should disclose its diluted EPS, which is calculated assuming that this conversion has taken place, showing the position as if all the possible options are taken up and shares are issued. When an entity has potential ordinary shares it should add them to the basic weighted average number if they are dilutive. Where there are convertible bonds or convertible preference shares, an entity should adjust the net profit for: any dividends on dilutive potential ordinary shares that have been deducted in arriving at the net profit attributable to ordinary shareholders; interest recognised in the period for the dilutive potential ordinary shares; and any other changes in income or expense that would result from the conversion of the dilutive potential ordinary shares, e.g. the reduction of interest expense related to convertible bonds results in a higher net profit.

- Related party relationships are a normal feature of commerce and business. A related party relationship could have an effect on the income statement and financial position of an entity. Related parties may enter into transactions that unrelated parties would not. For example, an entity that sells goods to its parent at cost might not sell on those terms to another customer. Also, transactions between related parties may not be made at the same amounts as between unrelated parties. For these reasons, knowledge of related party transactions, outstanding balances and relationships may affect assessments of an entity's operations by users of financial statements, including assessments of the risks and opportunities facing the entity.

- A party is related to an entity if: the party controls, is controlled by, or is under common control with, the entity; the party is an associate of the entity; the party is a joint venture in which the entity is a venturer; the party is a member of the key management personnel of the entity or its parent; the party is a post-employment benefit plan for the benefit of employees of the entity, or of any entity that is a related party of the entity; etc.

- A related party transaction is a transfer of resources, services or obligations between related parties, regardless of whether a price is charged. IAS 24 lists examples of transactions that should be disclosed if they are with a related party.

17.7 EPS

The issued share capital of Edwards plc consists of 800,000 ordinary shares. There are no preference shares. Some years ago, the entity issued EUR 2m of 10 per cent convertible loan stock. The entity's net income for the year ended 31 March 2010 is EUR 1,280,000.

(a) Calculate basic EPS for the year ended 31 March 2010.
(b) Calculate diluted EPS for the year ended 31 March 2010, assuming that the entity pays tax at 30 per cent.
(c) Rework both of the above calculations, assuming now that the loan stock was not issued 'some years ago' but was in fact issued on 1 October 2009.

17.8 EPS

The net income attributable to the ordinary shareholders of Frobisher plc is as follows:

	€000
year ended 31 December 2008	3,600
year ended 31 December 2009	4,950

For many years, the entity's issued share capital consisted of 9 million ordinary shares. However, on 1 April 2009, the company made a 1 for 4 rights issue at EUR 1 per share. The market value of the entity's shares just before this rights issue was EUR 2 per share.

(a) Calculate EPS for the year ended 31 December 2009.
(b) Calculate restated EPS for the year ended 31 December 2008.

17.9 EPS

On 1 January 2008, an entity issued EUR 4m of 7 per cent convertible loan stock. The holders of this stock may choose to convert the stock to ordinary shares on 1 January 2012, 2013 or 2014. The number of ordinary shares into which the stock will be converted is as follows:

Date of conversion	Number of shares issued
1 January 2012	400 shares per EUR 2,000 of stock
1 January 2013	420 shares per EUR 2,000 of stock
1 January 2014	440 shares per EUR 2,000 of stock

The entity's net income for the year ended 30 September 2009 was EUR 4.4m. The comparative figure for the year ended 30 September 2008 was EUR 4.8m. The entity pays tax at 30 per cent.

On 1 October 2007, the entity's issued share capital consisted of 1.5 million 12 per cent preference shares of EUR 2 each and 5 million ordinary shares of EUR 0.40 each. On 1 April 2009 the entity issued a further 500,000 ordinary shares at market price.

The preference dividend was paid in full in both the year ended 30 September 2008 and the year ended 30 September 2009.

(a) Calculate basic EPS and diluted EPS for the year ended 30 September 2008.

(b) Calculate basic EPS and diluted EPS for the year ended 30 September 2009.

17.10 Related parties

The following information relates to Z plc:

(a) Alan owns 27 of the ordinary shares of Z plc. Elaine is his wife.
(b) Z plc owns 60 per cent of the ordinary shares of Y plc.
(c) Z plc owns 15 per cent of the ordinary shares of X plc.
(d) Barbara is a director of Z plc. She owns 75 per cent of the ordinary shares of W Ltd. David is her husband. He owns 10 per cent of the ordinary shares of V Ltd.
(e) Colin works for Z plc as a manager but he is not a director. Fiona is his daughter.
(f) Z plc has established a pension scheme for the benefit of its employees.

Identify those parties (if any) which are related to Z plc.

17.11 Related party transactions

Apex plc owns 55 per cent of the ordinary shares of Mitchell Ltd. Brown Ltd owns 30 per cent of the ordinary shares of Mitchell Ltd. During the accounting period under review, there are no transactions between Apex plc and Mitchell Ltd, but there are transactions between Brown Ltd and Mitchell Ltd and between Apex plc and Brown Ltd.

Explain the related party disclosures which will be required in the individual financial statements of each entity.

Notes

1 The term 'chief operating decision maker' identifies a function, not necessarily a manager with a specific title. That function is to allocate resources to and assess the performance of the operating segments of an entity. Often the chief operating decision maker of an entity is its chief executive officer or chief operating officer or a group of executive directors (IFRS 8 para 7).

2 It may also be necessary to consider whether Mr Zapatos and entity B are also related parties of both entity A and entity C. This is because entity B and Mr Zapatos are unlikely to have agreed to participate in the transaction, unless they were controlled or influenced by Mr Xerox. If this is the case, any transactions between entity A or entity C and Mr Zapatos or entity B should also be disclosed.

3 If it is determined that Mr Zapatos or entity B is a related party, disclosure should also be made of the fact that the intermediary company was a related party. This is because the standard requires disclosure of information *necessary for an understanding of the potential effect of the relationship on the financial statements*.

Part Six Group reporting

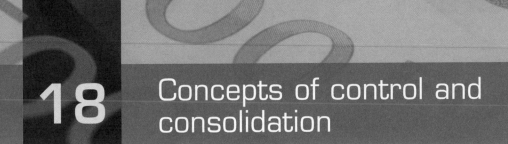

18 Concepts of control and consolidation

Contents

Objectives

When you have completed this chapter you should be able to:

- Describe the alternative concepts of consolidation
- Explain the nature and various forms of controlled entities
- Define the term 'control' for determining a parent–subsidiary relationship
- Describe the factors to consider in determining whether an entity has the power to govern the policies of another entity
- Discuss the importance of ownership in determining parent–subsidiary relationships
- Identify the entities that should prepare consolidated financial statements
- Explain the differences in report format between single entities and consolidated entities.

18.1   Introduction

To grow or expand entities can either form wholly owned domestic or foreign entities (organic growth) or invest in other entities by acquiring their equity. These investments are typically long-term investments; when they are large enough, they allow the investing entities varying degrees of control over the investee company.

A group exists when an entity (a parent or holding company) controls, either directly or indirectly, another entity (a subsidiary). Therefore a *group* comprises a parent and all its subsidiaries (IAS 27 para 4) (see Figure 18.1).

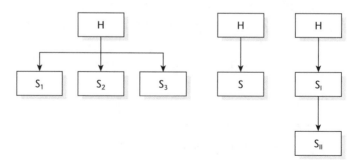

Figure 18.1 Different forms of groups

Note: H represents the parent or holding company; S_1, S_2, S_3, S and S_I represent directly controlled subsidiaries, while S_{II} represents a subsidiary controlled through another one.
Source: Kothari and Barone (2006).

The reasons for such complex structures are summarised below:

- The combination of two businesses may result in economies of scale and scope, that is to say the cost of producing the combined output will be less than the sum of the costs of producing outputs separately or, alternatively, the combined output will be greater for the same total cost. Such economies may be achieved not only in production but also in administration, research and development and financing.

- Combining with another business may be one way of eliminating or reducing competition. Although integration may occur for many reasons, one reason may be that it is possible to reduce competition both by vertical integration, that is by combining with an entity at an earlier or later stage of the production cycle, or by horizontal integration, that is by combining with a firm at the same stage in the production cycle;

- By combining with another entity which makes different products, an entity is often able to reduce risk. Thus one reason for a combination involving businesses in different industries may be a desire to generate an earnings stream which is less variable than the separate earnings streams of the two individual businesses.

- The various entities in the group need to be legally separate when they operate in several countries under several different laws.

- Sometimes there are tax advantages in being separate or there may be tax disadvantages in combining formerly separate entities.

- The legal structures may partially reflect a hierarchical organisational structure.

- The (financial and non-financial) performances may improve thanks to a better integration of different activities carried out by the various entities forming the group.

18.2 Form of consolidated financial statements

IAS 27 – *Consolidated and Separate Financial Statements* requires the financial statements of a group to be in the form of consolidated financial statements, unless the parent is exempt from preparing such financial statements. Consolidated financial statements are the financial statements of a group presented as those of a single economic entity. In preparing consolidated financial statements, an entity combines the financial statements of the parent and its subsidiaries line by line by adding together like items of assets, liabilities, equity, income and expenses [IAS 27 paras 4 and 22].

Paragraph 10 of IAS 1 (revised) – *Presentation of Financial Statements* requires that consolidated financial statements should include:

- a consolidated statement of financial position or balance sheet dealing with the parent and its subsidiaries;

- a consolidated statement of comprehensive income or income statement dealing with the profit or loss of the parent and its subsidiaries;

- a consolidated statement of changes in equity;

1 control of the financial and operating policies

2 benefits obtained from that control for a subsidiary relationship to exist.

Financial and operating policies

It will be necessary to analyse an entity's financial and operating policies in some detail to find out where control lies. There is little guidance in IAS 27 as to the specific policies an investor must control. The two key financial and operating policies of an entity that will often give the best indication of who has control are the 'distribution and reinvestment' policy and approval of the annual business plan. Other important financial and operating policies that should be considered include: the entity's strategic direction; ability to approve capital expenditure; and raising of finance.[1]

Benefits

The second part of the IAS 27 definition of control is concerned with a parent's ability to use that power to obtain benefits from the activities of its subsidiary. Apart from the obvious benefits related to an ownership interest (that is, dividends flows or an interest in the entity's residual net assets, there are other benefits that can accrue to the controlling entity, such as:

- benefits from structuring transactions with a subsidiary to obtain scarce raw materials on a priority basis, at strategic locations, or at reduced costs of delivery

- benefits from gaining access to the subsidiary's distribution network, patents, or production techniques

- benefits from combining certain functions of the parent and subsidiary to create economies of scale in, for example, costs of management, employee benefits or insurance

- benefits from denying or regulating access to a subsidiary's assets by its non-controlling investors, creditors, competitors and others.

The 'benefit test' is rarely failed in circumstances when the 'power to govern the financial and operating policies' test is passed.

18.4.3 Five situations of control

IAS 27 para 13 lists five situations where a parent has control over another entity – its subsidiary.

1 Control is presumed to exist when the parent owns, directly or indirectly through subsidiaries, more than half of the voting power of an entity unless, in exceptional circumstances, it can be clearly demonstrated that such ownership does not constitute control.

Control also exists when the parent owns half or less of the voting power of an entity when there is:

2 power over more than half of the voting rights by virtue of an agreement with other investors;

3 power to govern the financial and operating policies of the entity under a statute or an agreement;

4 power to appoint or remove the majority of the members of the board of directors or equivalent governing body and control of the entity is by that board or body; or

5 power to cast the majority of votes at meetings of the board of directors or equivalent governing body and control of the entity is by that board or body.

In practice, control often arises through a combination of factors noted above. Control often arises through a combination of factors described above. For example, an investor can control an entity by both majority ownership of the voting power (situation 1) and agreement of the board (situation 5). There may also be situations in practice where an investor controls an entity by both majority ownership of the voting power and agreement of the board.

1 Majority of voting rights

Under IAS 27's requirements, a parent or its subsidiaries have to have ownership of the voting power of an entity before the control provisions apply. For entities, ownership of voting power would normally be gained by having an ownership interest in the entity. However, it would be possible to gain ownership of voting power by other means.

An entity is a subsidiary when the parent owns, directly or indirectly through subsidiaries, more than half of the voting power of it (IAS 27 para 13). This is the control provision that is applied most frequently in practice to identify subsidiaries. While ownership (equity shares) and voting rights (that is, voting power) are usually held in equal proportions, there are situations where an entity may own a majority of the equity shares in another entity and yet not hold more than one half of its voting power. In such a situation, the entity will not be a subsidiary (unless it is a subsidiary by virtue of one of the other control provisions set out above).

'Voting power' can be taken to mean the ability to exercise the rights conferred on shareholders in respect of their shares to vote at the entity's general meetings on all, or substantially all, matters. This would apply also where an entity does not have share capital. If the entity does not have general meetings where matters are decided by exercising voting rights, 'voting power' can be taken to mean having the ability to exercise the right under the undertaking's constitution to direct its overall policy, or to alter the terms of its constitution.

Voting rights that relate to shares held as security would be treated as held by the entity providing the security where those rights (excluding any right to exercise them to preserve the value of the security, or to realise it) are only exercisable in accordance with that entity's instructions. This situation might arise for example, where entity A grants a loan to entity B, entity B gives entity A shares in entity C as security for the loan. However, entity A does not gain the voting rights on the shares in entity C, unless entity B defaults on the loan. Hence, entity B retains control of the voting rights in entity C (unless it defaults) even though they are held by entity A.

Control is presumed to exist when the parent owns, directly or indirectly through subsidiaries, more than half of the voting power of an entity unless, in exceptional circumstances, it can be clearly demonstrated that such ownership does not constitute control (IAS 27 para 13).

It is very unusual that an entity that holds more than one half of another entity's voting rights will be unable to exercise control. However, this might be the case where another party clearly does control the entity. These situations might include surrender of the right to control by contract (for example, in a joint venture), or legal restrictions on an acquirer's ability to exercise all of the voting rights acquired.

Virtually all entities are subject to some form of government regulation and the existence of regulation does not necessarily rebut the presumption that control exists. For example, an entity that owns more than half of the voting rights of a regulated utility will not be prevented from governing the utility's financial and operating policies because the regulator imposes price controls.

Only regulation that prevents the acquirer from governing an entity's financial and operating policies will rebut the presumption of control. For example, the law might require that the state appoints half of the board of directors of certain defence contractors and exercises a casting vote if the board is deadlocked. This regulation would prevent an entity that owned more than half the voting rights from governing the financial and operating policies.

An acquiree's charter might also restrict an acquirer's ability to exercise all of the voting rights acquired. It may restrict the right to appoint the board of directors to the holders of a certain class of voting shares or restrict the circumstances in which the acquirer can exercise its voting rights.

Example 18.2

Acquirer's voting rights restricted by acquiree's charter

Entity A entered into an agreement on 31 December 2009, to sell 80 per cent of a wholly-owned subsidiary B, to entity C. Entity A's representatives on the board of subsidiary B will immediately resign and will be replaced by the new majority owners.

Entity A has also provided subsidiary B with a short-term loan. Entity C has agreed to apply certain operating decisions defined by entity A, as stated in a memorandum of understanding, during the period when the loan is outstanding. Any operating decision proposed by entity C, which differs from the memorandum of understanding, is subject to entity A's veto, during that period.

Entity A retains control over subsidiary B and should consolidate it, despite the fact that entity C owns 80 per cent of subsidiary B.

Entity A has determined subsidiary B's operating decisions, stated in the memorandum of understanding as part of the purchase agreement. It is entitled to veto any different decision proposed by entity C, as long as the subordinated loan is outstanding.

An entity might appear to control over 50 per cent of another entity's voting rights by having a holding of more than 50 per cent of the share capital, but an agreement with the other shareholders might significantly restrict this control. It could, for example, require unanimous agreement between the shareholders before it could: pay a dividend; change direction of the entity's business; incur capital expenditure over a specified level; pay its directors and other employees; change other major operating and financial policies, etc. In this type of situation, the entity holding more than 50 per cent of the share capital would not control the other entity. However, it might still have joint control or significant influence (see Chapter 20 for additional discussion).

Control can be contrasted with joint control. Joint control is the contractually agreed sharing of control over an economic activity, and exists only when the strategic financial and operating decisions relating to the activity require the unanimous consent of the parties sharing control (the venturers) (IAS 31 para 3). Where joint control exists over an entity, it falls within the requirements of IAS 31 (see Chapter 20 for additional discussion).

2 Majority of voting rights by agreement with other shareholders

An entity will be a subsidiary where its parent can exercise power over more than half of the voting rights by virtue of an agreement with other investors (IAS 27 para 13(a)).

Example 18.3

Majority of voting rights by agreement with other shareholders

Entity A owns 45 per cent of the voting shares of entity B. Entity A also has an agreement with other shareholders that they will always vote a further 20 per cent holding in the same way as entity A.

The agreement between entity A and the other shareholders provides entity A with control over 65 per cent of the voting rights of entity B. This is because the other shareholders will vote in accordance with the instructions of entity A. Entity A, therefore, controls entity B and entity B is its subsidiary and should be consolidated in entity A's consolidated financial statements.

---

3 Power to govern under a statute or an agreement

An entity will be a subsidiary where the parent has the power to govern the financial and operating policies of the entity under a statute or an agreement (IAS 27 para 13(b)).

It is likely that a parent will have such a power to govern where it has a right to give directions with respect to the operating and financial policies of another entity, which that entity's directors are obliged to follow whether or not they are for the benefit of that entity.

Example 18.4

Power to govern under a statute or an agreement

Three entities A, B and C invest in entity D to manufacture footballs. Entity A has considerable experience in manufacturing footballs and has developed new technology to improve their production. Entity B and entity C are both banks that have previously financed entity A's operations.

Entity A will contribute technology and know-how to entity D, whilst entity B and entity C will contribute finance. The share ownership will be entity A: 40 per cent, entity B: 30 per cent and entity C: 30 per cent. Each entity will appoint directors in proportion to their ownership percentage. An agreement between the shareholders states that all directors will be non-executive except for the managing director and the finance director, both of whom will be appointed by entity A in recognition of its expertise in the area of football manufacture.

The shareholder agreement delegates to entity A's managing director and its finance director the power to set entity D's operating policies and operating budget. However, any requests for additional financing should be considered by the full board.

The delegation of powers over the entity's operating policies and operating budget to the directors appointed by entity A, provides entity A with effective control of entity D. Although there are some powers retained by the full board, including decisions over changes to financing and share structure, these are limited and provide rights that are more protective in nature.

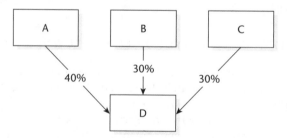

Figure 18.3 Structure of the group

The decisions concerning financial and operating policies represent a substantial part of the total range of decisions to be taken in respect of the operating entity. In particular, entity A has control over the distribution policy and can determine whether surplus funds are distributed or reinvested. Control over these financial and operating decisions, therefore, provides participative control over entity D.

4 and 5 Control of the board

According to IAS 27 para 13(c) and (d), there are two control situations relating to the board:

* power to appoint or remove the majority of the members of the board of directors or equivalent governing body and control of the entity is by that board or body;

- power to cast the majority of votes at meetings of the board of directors or equivalent governing body and control of the entity is by that board or body.

The first circumstance 'power to appoint or remove the majority of the members of the board of directors' makes no reference to their voting power. Usually directors have equal voting rights at board meetings, so that power to appoint or remove the majority of the board will mean control of the board and the entity. However, it is conceivable that sometimes some directors may have more votes than others at board meetings. If an entity controlled the appointment and removal of a majority of directors, but those directors did not have a majority of votes at board meetings, the entity might still appear to meet the definition under IFRS for it to have control. In this situation, it would be necessary to consider carefully whether in such highly unusual but possible circumstances this would prevent the first entity from having control even though it appeared to meet the definition. If, for example, another entity could appoint a minority of the directors, but those directors had a majority of votes at board meetings, that other entity might well have control. Where it appears that two unrelated entities could be identified as the parent only one can have control in practice.

The second circumstance, 'power to cast the majority of votes at meetings' can be taken to mean the power to cast the majority of the voting rights at board meetings on all, or substantially all, matters (without the need for any person's consent or agreement).

Where there are restrictions placed on the rights or the ability of the parent to exercise control, this would indicate that there is a loss of control and the entity is no longer a subsidiary (see section 18.6). Alternatively, in a situation where there is effectively deadlock in voting rights there might be joint control, in which case this might indicate the existence of a joint venture (see Chapter 20).

Example 18.5

Control via right to appoint majority of the board

Entity A owns 45 per cent of the shares in entity B but, based on the shareholders agreement, controls the composition of its board of directors by having the power to appoint or remove the majority of entity B's directors.

Amendments to entity B's articles of incorporation state that acquisitions and disposals of assets for amounts higher than 50 per cent of the fair value of entity B's total assets, and the decision to liquidate entity B, are reserved for shareholder vote.

The ability of entity A to control the composition of entity B's board, therefore, confers control of entity B to entity A. Although certain decisions are reserved for shareholder vote, where entity A has control of only 45 per cent of the votes, such decisions tend to be protective in nature. Provided the decisions reserved for shareholder vote do not interfere with the operations of entity B, entity A will be able to control entity B's operating and financial policies so as to obtain benefits from its activities. Hence, entity B would be regarded as entity A's subsidiary.

Example 18.6

Intervention by government (minority shareholder) in operation and financial policy decisions

A government does not have a controlling shareholding in a company, but has a golden share that enables it to replace the board of directors with its nominees should the government disagree with the operating and financial policy decisions taken by the other shareholder.

Whilst the golden share exists to enable the government to protect its national interest, the power that this share gives the government extends beyond this as there are no restrictions on the circumstances in which it can intervene. The share gives the government power to control the board, which means the operating and financial policies are controlled by the government so as to obtain benefits from its activities. Conversely, if there were restrictions on when the government could intervene, for example only in preventing the issuance of additional shares or the sale of a material ownership interest to foreign shareholders, then this would indicate that the government does not control the company.

Where an entity has the right to appoint a director with a casting vote in the event of a board deadlock and because of this that entity controls more than half of the voting power on the board, it will effectively control the board and can, therefore, control any board decision.

Example 18.7

Control via the power to direct the board's votes

Entity A owns 50 per cent of the voting shares of entity B. The board of directors consist of eight members. Entity A appoints four directors and two other investors appoint two directors each. One of the entity A's nominated directors always serves as a chairperson of entity B's board and has the casting vote at board meetings.

Entity A has the casting vote at board meetings in the event that the directors cannot reach a majority decision. This provides entity A with control of board decisions and, therefore, control of entity B. Hence entity B is a subsidiary of entity A and would be consolidated into entity A's consolidated financial statements.

In practice a further complication can arise. Many 50/50 joint ventures are set up in the form of companies with each party owing 50 per cent of the equity, holding 50 per cent of the voting rights in general meetings and having the right to appoint directors with 50 per cent of the votes on the board. In order to avoid total deadlock in the event of a disagreement a 'rotating' chairperson is appointed with a casting vote. The chairperson, who is chosen from the directors, is appointed in alternate years by each party to the joint venture. Therefore, in theory, by virtue of the casting vote, in years one, three and five the undertaking is a subsidiary of one of the parties while in years two, four and six it is a subsidiary of the other.

The two parties appear to control the venture in alternate years. Such problems can be resolved in practice by considering the substance of the arrangement. There may be other arrangements in place that give one of the parties control or both parties joint control. It is likely that the arrangement outlined above would be treated as a joint venture with shared control.

18.4.4 Indirect control

In determining whether a power should be attributed to a parent, similar rights held by a subsidiary should be treated as if they are held by the parent.

Example 18.8

Indirect control of a subsidiary

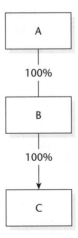

Figure 18.4 Structure of the group

Entity A's subsidiary B is an investor of entity C. In this circumstance, even where the parent is not a direct investor of entity C itself (for the purposes of determining whether entity C is a subsidiary of the parent), entity A, the parent, is treated as an investor of entity C.

In addition, where a group has intermediate parents their subsidiaries will also be regarded as subsidiaries of any parent undertakings further up the group structure. Consequently, subsidiaries of all parents within a group are subsidiaries of the ultimate parent. In other words 'control' means both direct and indirect control through entities that are themselves controlled by the parent.

18.4.5 *De facto* control

De facto control describes the situation where an entity owns less than 50 per cent of the voting shares in another entity, but is deemed to have control for reasons other than potential voting rights, contract or other statutory means.

18.5   Dissimilar activities and severe long-term restrictions

A subsidiary should not be excluded from consolidation because its business activities are dissimilar from those of the other entities within the group. Relevant information should be provided by consolidating such subsidiaries and disclosing additional information in the consolidated financial statements about the different business activities of subsidiaries (IAS 27 para 20).

A parent is not permitted to exclude from consolidation an entity it continues to control simply because that entity is operating under severe long-term restrictions that significantly impair its ability to transfer funds to the parent. Control must be lost for exclusion to occur (IAS 27 para IN 9). The existence of severe long-term restrictions over the transfers of funds, do not in themselves preclude control. In order for the entity not to be consolidated, control needs to be lost so that it is no longer a subsidiary.

In general, restrictions on control should be dealt with by disclosure. The over-riding principle is that a parent *should* consolidate an entity that it controls and *should not* consolidate an entity that it does not control.

18.6   Loss of control

A parent will lose control of an entity (its subsidiary) when it no longer has the power to control the financial and operating policies of that entity and, hence, cannot gain the benefits from its activities. Such a loss in control might arise even where there has not been a change in the ownership interest in the subsidiary. There are a number of situations where a parent's control over its subsidiary may be lost and hence it should no longer be treated as a subsidiary. These could include the following situations:

- A power of veto is granted to a third party.
- The parent enters into an agreement with a minority shareholder that gives both parties joint control.

- A subsidiary becomes subject to the control of a government.

- Insolvency or administration procedures are in progress.

A parent might lose control over a foreign subsidiary when it becomes subject to the control of a government of a particular country. A government that has merely imposed restrictions over the funds that can be repatriated out of the country to the parent does not have the appropriate level of control for the parent to avoid consolidation. But where another party has the power to impose its will on the entity by gaining control of voting power or the board, the mere existence of that power will indicate that the entity is not a subsidiary.

Where a subsidiary is subject to an insolvency procedure and control over the entity has passed to a designated official, the effect will be that the entity will no longer be a subsidiary. Whether formal insolvency procedures in a particular country represent such loss of control will depend on the nature of legislation in the jurisdiction in question.

The income and expenses of a subsidiary are included in the consolidated financial statements until the date on which the parent ceases to control the subsidiary (IAS 27 para 30). An investment in an entity should be accounted for in accordance with IAS 39 – *Financial Instruments: Recognition and Measurement* from the date that it ceases to be a subsidiary, provided that it does not become an associate as defined in IAS 28 or a jointly controlled entity as described in IAS 31 (IAS 27 para 31).

18.7   Concepts of group and consolidation

We have seen that for a variety of legal, tax and other reasons businesses generally choose to conduct their activities not through a single legal entity, but through several entities under the ultimate control of the group's parent. For this reason the financial statements of a parent by itself do not present a complete picture of its economic activities or financial position. Users of financial statements want information about the financial position, as well as results of operations and changes in the financial position, of the group as whole. Hence, there is a need for consolidated financial statements that present financial information about a group as a whole.

The accounting literature makes reference to different concepts or models on how a group is established and how the financial statements of the companies forming the group are consolidated. The most common consolidation models are:

- the economic entity model;

- the parent entity model; and

- the proprietary model.

All these models are explained below through an example. Current IFRS have elements of two models: the parent company model and the economic entity model.

Differences in consolidation arise under these models only if the parent does not own all the equity in a subsidiary; in other words if a non-controlling interest (NCI) exists. NCI is that portion of the profit or loss and net assets of a subsidiary

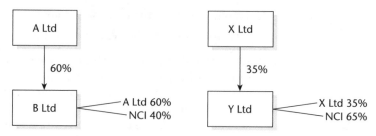

Figure 18.5 Non-controlling interest (NCI)

attributable to equity interests that are not owned by the parent directly or indirectly through subsidiaries (IAS 27 para 4).

In Figure 18.5, it can be seen that the parent A has a 60 per cent (ownership) interest in B and there is a NCI of 40 per cent. Similarly the parent X has a 35 per cent interest in Y while there is a NCI of 65 per cent. Even though it is termed a 'minority interest', the percentage interest could be greater than that of the parent because the criterion for consolidation is control and not ownership interest. The meaning and measurement of the NCI are discussed in more detail in Chapter 19.

The main areas affected in the preparation of consolidated financial statements by the choice of model of consolidation are:

- *The assets and liabilities of a subsidiary included in the consolidated financial statements.* This relates to whether all the net assets of a subsidiary are included in the consolidated group or just those attributable to the parent.
- *The classification (and the measurement) of the NCI as equity or liability.* The consolidated assets consist of the sum of the assets of the parent and those of the subsidiaries. The choice of model affects the amount shown as total consolidated liabilities and equity, since the choice of model affects the category into which the NCI is placed as well as the calculation of the amount of the NCI.
- *The adjustment for the effects of transactions within the group.* The consolidated financial statements show the performance and financial position of the group in its dealings with parties external to the group. Where, for example, profits are made by one part of the group, such as a subsidiary, in selling inventory to another part of the group, such as the parent, the effects of these transactions should be eliminated with adjustments being made to the profits recorded by the subsidiary. The choice of model affects whether all the profit on such transactions is adjusted for or whether only part of the profit is eliminated[3].

18.7.1 Economic entity model of consolidation

The economic entity model considers the group as a single entity. In this model the reporting entity comprises 100 per cent of the entire group of entities under the parent's control. This means that as well as recording 100 per cent of subsidiaries' net assets, it is necessary also to record 100 per cent of their goodwill.

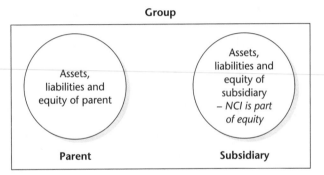

Figure 18.6 Group under the economic entity model
Source: Alfredson *et al.* (2009).

NCI is recognised under this model, but it is treated as part of shareholders' funds (i.e. contributor of capital to the group in the same capacity as the equity holders of the parent), thereby emphasising the control that the parent and its shareholders have over a subsidiary.

Diagrammatically, the group under the economic entity model is as shown in Figure 18.6.

The implications of adopting the economic entity model of consolidation for the preparation of the consolidated financial statements are as follows (Alfredson et al. 2009):

- Where there are transactions between members of the group, the effects of these transactions are adjusted in full, as required by IAS 27 para 20 (see Chapter 19 for a detailed discussion). This is consistent with the view that the consolidated financial statements should show the results of transactions between the group and parties external to the group. The adjustments are then unaffected by the extent of the parent's ownership interest in the subsidiary.

- As the NCI is classified as a contributor of equity to the group, it is disclosed in the equity section of the consolidated financial statements, as per IAS 1 (revised) para 54(q) and IAS 27 para 27.

- Because of the classification of the NCI as equity, its measurement is based on the share of consolidated equity and not on the share of the recorded equity of the subsidiary in which the NCI is held.

18.7.2 Parent entity model of consolidation

The parent company model considers the group from the parent's perspective. In this model, the reporting entity compromises 100 per cent of the entire group of entities under the parent's control as its base, even if the parent has less than 100 per cent of the shares in the subsidiary. However, the goodwill that arises on consolidation relates only to the parent's share of the subsidiary and not to the NCI's share of goodwill.

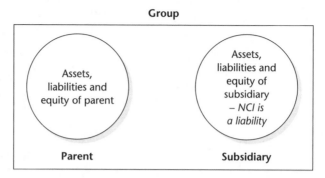

Figure 18.7 Group under the parent entity model
Source: Alfredson *et al.* (2009).

The parent company members' interest is limited to their shareholding in subsidiaries. NCI is not regarded as shareholders' funds and is shown separately either before or after shareholders' funds.

Diagrammatically, the group under the parent company model is as shown in Figure 18.7.

Under this model (Alfredson et al. 2009):

- Adjustments for transactions within the group involve both partial (i.e. to the extent of the parent's interest in the subsidiary) and total elimination procedures. Only the parent's share of the intragroup profit is eliminated where the subsidiary is the selling entity, but all the profit is eliminated where the parent is the seller. The rationale for this is based on the classification of the NCI as a liability, and the need to increase the share of the NCI when the subsidiary makes a profit on transactions with the parent. The justification is based on the need to report accurately the liability to the NCI.

- The NCI is reported in the liability section of the consolidated balance sheet.

- The NCI is calculated as its proportionate share of the recorded equity of the subsidiary, with no adjustments for transactions within the group.

The focus of the parent entity model is on the parent's equity holders as the prime user group. All controlled assets and liabilities are included in the consolidated financial statements, but the claim by the parent's equity holders is net of the liability claim of the NCI.

18.7.3 Proprietary model of consolidation

This model is sometimes referred to as proportional consolidation or pro-rata consolidation. Under the proprietary model (Alfredson et al. 2009):

- The group consists of the assets and liabilities of the parent and the parent's proportional share of the assets and liabilities of the subsidiary. Hence, the consolidated financial statements do not include all the net assets of a subsidiary, only the parent's share.

Group

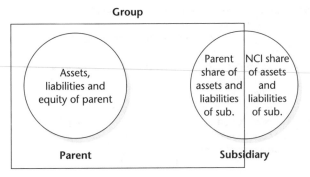

Figure 18.8 Group under the proprietary model
Source: Alfredson *et al.* (2009).

- As the NCI is outside the group, the NCI share of subsidiary equity is not disclosed, and neither is the NCI share of the net assets of the subsidiary.

Diagrammatically, the group under the proprietary model is as shown in Figure 18.8.

Under this model:

- Transactions between the parent and the subsidiary are adjusted proportionally (i.e. to the extent of the parent's ownership interest in the subsidiary).

- NCI is not disclosed.

18.7.4 Model used in IFRS

IFRS incorporates elements of both economic entity and parent entity models. The basis for recognising NCI is consistent with the parent entity model as the goodwill that arises on consolidation relates only to the parent's share of the subsidiary; the share of goodwill relating to the NCI is excluded (see section 19.3, Method 1). However, NCI is shown within equity in the balance sheet[4].

The income statement reflects the profit or loss for the financial year and the profit or loss is analysed between:

- profit or loss attributable to NCI; and
- profit or loss attributable to equity holders of the parent.

In other words, NCI is an allocation of the group profit and not a deduction in arriving at the profit or loss for the financial year.

Table 18.1 Concepts of group and differences in consolidation

Concepts of group	Accounting treatment in consolidated financial statements			
	Fair value of assets and liabilities of subsidiary	Goodwill	Classification of NCI	Adjustments for transactions within the group
Economic entity model (see section 18.7.1)	100% included in the consolidated financial statements	100% (both parent's and NCI's share of the goodwill)	Equity	Transactions adjusted in full (adjustment unaffected by parent's ownership interest in the subsidiary)
Parent entity model (see section 18.7.2)	100% included in the consolidated financial statements	Only the parent's share of goodwill (excluding NCI's share)	Liability	Transactions adjusted in full when the parent is the seller; or partially (i.e. to the extent of the parent's interest in the subsidiary) when the subsidiary is the selling entity
Proprietary model (see section 18.7.3)	Only parent's share included in the consolidated financial statements	Only the parent's share of goodwill	Not disclosed	Transactions adjusted partially (i.e. to the extent of the parent's interest in the subsidiary)
Model adopted by the IASB (see sections 18.7.4 and 19.3)	100% included in the consolidated financial statements	Only the parent's share of goodwill*	Consistent with the parent company model, but shown in equity*	Transactions adjusted in full as for the economic entity model

* Note that this accounting treatment relates to Method 1 as illustrated in section 19.3 Under Method 2, 100 per cent of goodwill is recognised and therefore also the NCI's share of the goodwill (see Chapter 19).

Example 18.9

Consolidation models

The balance sheet of Halbert SpA (H) as at 31 December 2009 is shown below:

	H €
Non-current assets	25,000
Net current assets	23,000
Net assets	**48,000**
Share capital	16,000
Retained earnings	27,000
Non-current liabilities	5,000
	48,000

On 1 January 2010, Halbert SpA (H) acquired 80 per cent of the 10,000 EUR 1 ordinary shares in Settimo SpA (S) for EUR 1.60 per share in cash and gained control. The fair value of the non-current assets of Settimo SpA at that date was EUR 12,400. The balance sheets of H and S on 1 January 2010 or at the acquisition date were as follows:

Table 18.2 H's and S's balance sheets as at 1 January 2010

	H €	S €
Non-current assets	25,000	12,000
Investment in S	12,800	–
Net current assets	10,200(*)	3,000
Net assets	**48,000**	**15,000**
Share capital	16,000	10,000
Retained earnings	27,000	5,000
Non-current liabilities	5,000	
Shareholders' equity and liabilities	**48,000**	**15,000**

(*) EUR 23,000 before the acquisition *less* EUR 12,800 for the consideration paid to acquire S.

1 *Economic entity model of consolidation*

Table 18.3 Consolidated balance sheet under the economic entity model

	H	S		Adjustments Dr	Cr		Consolidated balance sheet
	€	€		€	€		€
Non-current assets	25,000	12,000	(i) (ii)	320 80			37,400
Investment in S	12,800				12,800	(i)	–
Goodwill			(i) (ii)	480 120			600
Net current assets	10,200	3,000					13,200
Net assets	*48,000*	*15,000*					*51,200*
Equity							
Share capital	16,000	10,000	(i) (ii)	8,000 2,000			
Retained earnings	27,000	5,000	(i) (ii)	4,000 1,000			
NCI					3,200	(ii)	
Total equity							*46,200*
Non-current liabilities	5,000						5,000
Shareholders' equity and liabilities	*48,000*	*15,000*		*15,880*	*15,880*		*51,200*

Notes

- All assets and liabilities of S are included in the consolidated balance sheet.
- Non-current assets have been revalued to their fair value. Therefore, the total revaluation taken into account is EUR 400 (EUR 320 relating to the parent's share and EUR 80 relating to NCI).
- Goodwill is EUR 600 of which EUR 480 paid by H when acquiring 80 per cent of S. Though NCI has not paid anything for the remaining 20 per cent of goodwill, EUR 120 is nevertheless added.
- NCI is considered part of the group's equity.

2 Parent entity model of consolidation

Table 18.4 Consolidated balance sheet under the parent entity model

	H	S		Dr	Cr		Consolidated balance sheet
	€	€		€	€		€
Non-current assets	25,000	12,000	(i)	320			37,320
Investment in S	12,800				12,800	(i)	–
Goodwill			(i)	480			480
Net current assets	10,200	3,000					13,200
Total assets	*48,000*	*15,000*					*51,000*
Equity							
Share capital	16,000	10,000	(i)	8,000			16,000
			(ii)	2,000			
Retained earnings	27,000	5,000	(i)	4,000			27,000
			(ii)	1,000			
Total equity							*43,000*
Liabilities							
NCI					3,000	(ii)	3,000
Non-current liabilities	5,000						5,000
Total liabilities							*8,000*
Shareholders' equity and liabilities	*48,000*	*15,000*		*15,800*	*15,800*		*51,000*

Notes

- All assets and liabilities of S are included in the consolidated balance sheet.
- Non-current assets have been revalued by EUR 320 (i.e. the revaluation relating to the parent's share of 80 per cent).
- The goodwill recognised is EUR 480 actually paid by H.
- NCI is considered a liability.

3 *Proprietary model of consolidation*

Table 18.5 Consolidated balance sheet under the proprietary model

	H	S	80% of S's assets and liabilities		Adjustments Dr	Cr		Consolidated balance sheet
	€	€	€		€	€		€
Non-current assets	25,000	12,000	9,600	(i)	320			34,920
Investment in S	12,800					12,800	(i)	–
Goodwill				(i)	480			480
Net current assets	10,200	3,000	2,400					12,600
Total assets	*48,000*	*15,000*	12,000					*48,000*
Equity								
Share capital	16,000	10,000	8,000	(i)	8,000			16,000
Retained earnings	27,000	5,000	4,000	(i)	4,000			27,000
Non-current liabilities	5,000							5,000
Shareholders' equity and liabilities	*48,000*	*15,000*	12,000		*12,800*	*12,800*		*48,000*

Notes

- Only 80 per cent of S's assets and liabilities are included in the consolidated balance sheet.
- Non-current assets have been revalued by EUR 320 (i.e. the revaluation relating to the parent's share of 80 per cent).
- The goodwill recognised is H's share only (i.e. EUR 480).
- NCI is not taken into account.

4 *Consolidation under IFRS*

Table 18.6 Consolidated balance sheet in accordance with IFRS[5]

	H	S		Adjustments Dr	Cr		Consolidated balance sheet
	€	€		€	€		€
Non-current assets	25,000	12,000	(i) (ii)	320 80			37,400
Investment in S	12,800				12,800	(i)	–
Goodwill			(i)	480			480
Net current assets	10,200	3,000					13,200
Net assets	*48,000*	*15,000*					*51,080*
Equity							
Share capital	16,000	10,000	(i) (ii)	8,000 2,000			
Retained earnings	27,000	5,000	(i) (ii)	4,000 1,000			
NCI					3,080	(ii)	
Total equity							46,080
Non-current liabilities	5,000						5,000
Shareholders' equity and liabilities	*48,000*	*15,000*		*15,880*	*15,880*		*51,080*

Notes

- All assets and liabilities of S are included in the consolidated balance sheet at their fair values. Therefore, the NCI in S's is stated at its proportion of the net fair value of those assets. The total revaluation taken into account is EUR 400 (EUR 320 relating to the parent's share and EUR 80 relating to NCI). This is consistent with the economic entity model.

- The goodwill recognised is EUR 480 which was actually paid by H. This is consistent with the parent entity model.

- NCI is classified as equity.

Summary

- A group exists when an entity (a parent or holding company) controls, either directly or indirectly, another entity (a subsidiary).

- A subsidiary is an entity that is controlled by another entity (known as the parent). The definition of control is not based solely on legal ownership but refers to control of the financial and operating policies and benefits obtained from that control for a subsidiary relationship to exist.

- IAS 27 specifies five situations where a parent has control over another entity. Control is presumed to exist when the parent owns, directly or indirectly through subsidiaries, more than half of the voting power of an entity. Control also exists when the parent owns half or less of the voting power of an entity when there is: power over more than half of the voting rights by virtue of an agreement with other investors; power to govern the financial and operating policies of the entity under a statute or an agreement; power to appoint or remove the majority of the members of the board of directors or equivalent governing body and control of the entity is by that board or body; or power to cast the majority of votes at meetings of the board of directors or equivalent governing body and control of the entity is by that board or body.

- Consolidated financial statements are the financial statements of a group presented as those of a single economic entity. In preparing consolidated financial statements, an entity combines the financial statements of the parent and its subsidiaries line by line by adding together like items of assets, liabilities, income and expenses. Consolidated financial statements should include: a consolidated balance sheet, a consolidated income statement, a consolidated statement of changes in equity, a consolidated statement of cast flows and explanatory notes.

- A parent need not present consolidated financial statements if and only if: (a) the parent is itself a wholly-owned subsidiary, or is a partially-owned subsidiary of another entity and its other owners, including those not otherwise entitled to vote, have been informed about, and do not object to, the parent not presenting consolidated financial statements; (b) the parent's debt or equity instruments are not traded in a public market; (c) the parent did not file its financial statements with a securities commission or other regulatory organisation for the purpose of issuing any class of instruments in a public market; and (d) the ultimate or any intermediate parent of the ultimate parent produces consolidated financial statements available for public use that comply with IFRS.

- A subsidiary should not be excluded from consolidation because its business activities are dissimilar from those of the other entities within the group. Relevant information should be provided by consolidating such subsidiaries and disclosing additional information in the consolidated financial statements about the different business activities of subsidiaries.

- The most common consolidation concepts/models are: the economic entity model, the parent entity model and the proprietary model. Differences in consolidation arise under these models only if the parent does not own all the equity in a subsidiary (i.e. if a NCI exists). The main areas affected in the preparation of consolidated financial statements by the choice of model for consolidation are: the assets and liabilities of a subsidiary included in the consolidated financial statements; the classification (and the measurement) of the NCI as equity or liability; and the adjustments for the effects of transactions within the group.

- IFRS has elements of both economic entity and parent entity models. The basis for recognising NCI is consistent with the parent entity model as the goodwill that arises on consolidation relates only to the parent's share of the subsidiary; the share of goodwill relating to the minority shareholder(s) is excluded. However, NCI is shown within equity in the balance sheet. In the consolidated income statement the profit or loss is analysed between profit or loss attributable to NCI and profit or loss attributable to equity holders of the parent.

Research and references

The IASB documents relevant for this chapter are:

- IAS 1 (revised) – *Presentation of Financial Statements*.
- IAS 27 – *Consolidated and Separate Financial Statements*.
- IAS 31 – *Interests in Joint Ventures*.
- SIC 12 – *Consolidation. Special Purpose Entities*.

The following are examples of books, research and discussion papers that take the issues of this chapter further:

- Alexander, D., Britton, A. and Jorissen, A. (2007) *International Financial Reporting and Analysis*, 3rd edn. Thomson, Chapters 25 and 26.
- Alfredson, K., Picker, R., Loftus, J., Clark, K., Wise, V. and Dyki, M. (2009) *Applying International Financial Reporting Standards*, 2nd edn. Wiley, Chapter 21.
- Elliott, B. and Elliott, J. (2009) *Financial Accounting and Reporting*, 13th edn. Financial Times-Prentice Hall, Chapter 20.
- Epstein, B.J. and Jermakowicz, E.K. (2009) *IFRS 2009: Interpretation and Application of International Accounting and Financial Reporting Standards*. Wiley, Chapter 11.
- Kothari, J. and Barone, E. (2006) *Financial Accounting. An International Approach*. Financial Times-Prentice Hall, Chapter 11.
- Leo, K.J. (1987) *Consolidated Financial Statements. Discussion Paper No. 11*, Australian Accounting Research Foundation, Melbourne.
- Pacter, P. (1991) *Consolidated Policy and Procedures. Discussion Memorandum*, Financial Accounting Standards Board, Norwalk CT.
- PricewaterhouseCoopers (2009) *IFRS Manual of Accounting – 2010. Global Guide to International Financial Reporting Standards*. CCH, Chapter 24.

- Stolowy, H. and Lebas, M.J. (2006) *Corporate Financial Reporting. A Global Perspective*, 2nd edn. Thomson, September, Chapter 13.
- Sutton, T. (2004) *Corporate Financial Accounting and Reporting*, 2nd edn. Financial Times-Prentice Hall, Chapter 14.

Discussion questions and exercises

18.1 Groups and consolidated statements

(a) Define a group and the reasons why groups exist.

(b) Which entities should prepare consolidated financial statements?

(c) Which entities are exempted?

18.2 Subsidiaries

(a) Define a subsidiary.

(b) When should a subsidiary be excluded from consolidation?

18.3 Control

(a) What does 'control' mean?

(b) Describe the situations of control listed by IAS 27.

18.4 *De facto* control

(a) Define *de facto* control.

(b) Entity P has a 45 per cent interest in entity S. The remaining 55 per cent is owned by a single investor, who does not attend general meetings.

Does entity P have *de facto* control over entity S?

18.5 *De facto* control

A parent company, P, has a 51 per cent interest in subsidiary S, a listed company. The other shareholders are dispersed and tend not to attend meetings or appoint proxies to represent them.

Entity P has been consolidating the subsidiary S through its 51 per cent ownership interest. Subsidiary S is highly leveraged, begins to make losses and the parent P decides to sell a 6 per cent interest in entity S to an investment bank.

Entity P plans to continue to determine the operating and financial policies of entity S and protect its investment by managing entity S's operations. The 49 per cent interest will enable entity P to continue to control the appointment of entity S's board and its operations (as it will still hold a majority of the votes actually cast at entity S's general meetings). The market in entity S's shares is deep and liquid and it will not be difficult for entity P to reacquire a voting controlling interest in the future. There is no history of shareholder activism in entity S.

Does entity P have *de facto* control over entity S?

18.6 Concepts of groups and consolidation

(a) Illustrate the most common consolidation models.

(b) Which model has been adopted by the IASB?

18.7 Consolidation models

The balance sheet of entity H as at 31 December 2009 is shown below:

	€
Non-current assets	75,000
Net current assets	69,000
Net assets	*144,000*
Share capital	48,000
Retained earnings	81,000
Liabilities	15,000
Total equity and liabilities	*144,000*

On 1 January 2010, entity H acquired 80 per cent of the 30,000 EUR 1 ordinary shares in entity S for EUR 1.60 per share in cash and gained control. The fair value of the non-current assets of entity S at that date was EUR 37,200. The balance sheets of H and S on 1 January 2010, after the acquisition, were as follows:

	H	S
	€	€
Non-current assets	75,000	36,000
Investment in S	38,400	–
Net current assets	30,600	9,000
Net assets	*144,000*	*45,000*
Share capital	48,000	30,000
Retained earnings	81,000	15,000
Non-current liabilities	15,000	–
Total equity and liabilities	*144,000*	*45,000*

Prepare the consolidated balance sheet as at 1 January 2010 under the:

(a) economic entity model of consolidation;

(b) parent entity model of consolidation;

(c) proprietary model of consolidation.

Explain which model the IASB has adopted and prepare a consolidated balance sheet at the same date accordingly.

Notes

1 It is also useful to determine whether an investor's rights enable effective participation in the entity's financial and operating policies and whether this enables it to control that investee. Examples of participating rights include rights relating to:

- Selecting, terminating and setting the compensation of management responsible for implementing the investee's policies and procedures
- Establishing operating and capital decisions of the investee, including budgets in the ordinary course of business (for example, approval of the annual business plan)
- Decisions covering acquisitions and disposals of assets
- Decisions relating to financing requirements in the ordinary course of business
- Blocking customary or expected dividends.

2 In this example it is assumed that the ownership of shares equals voting power.

3 In this section, only a brief outline of the alternative models of consolidation is given. A more detailed analysis can be found in Leo (1987) and Pacter (1991).

4 NCI does not fit into the definition of a liability under the *Framework*. The group has no obligation to transfer resources to NCI. In the Basis for Conclusion on IAS 27, the IASB made the following comments in relation to the NCI:

BC30: The Board decided to require NCI to be presented in the consolidated balance sheet within equity, separately from the equity of the shareholders of the parent. The Board concluded that a NCI is not a liability of a group because it does not meet the definition of a liability in the *Framework*.

BC31: *Framework* para 49 (b) states that a liability is a present obligation of the entity arising from past events, the settlement of which is expected to result in an outflow from the entity of resources embodying economic benefits. *Framework* para 60 further indicates that an essential characteristic of a liability is that the entity has a present obligation and that an obligation is a duty or responsibility to act or perform in a particular way. The Board noted that the existence of a NCI in the net assets of a subsidiary does not give rise to a present obligation of the group, the settlement of which is expected to result in an outflow of economic benefits from the group.

BC32: Rather, the Board noted that a NCI represents the residual interest in the net assets of those subsidiaries held by some of the shareholders of the subsidiaries within the group, and therefore meet the *Framework's* definition of equity. *Framework* para 49 (c) states that equity is the residual interest in the assets of the entity after deducting all its liabilities.

5 Note that we have applied Method 1 as illustrated in Chapter 19.

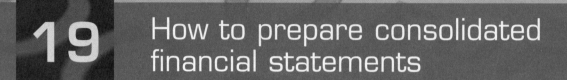

19 How to prepare consolidated financial statements

Contents

Objectives

When you have completed this chapter you should be able to:

- Define a business combination
- Prepare a consolidated balance sheet at the date of acquisition
- Calculate goodwill and explain its treatment in the consolidated financial statements
- Account for non-controlling interests under the two options available in IFRS 3
- Explain the need for fair value adjustments and prepare consolidated financial statements reflecting such adjustments
- Account for post-acquisition profits of a subsidiary
- Eliminate intragroup balances and deal with reconciling items
- Account for unrealised profits on intragroup transactions
- Prepare a consolidated income statement
- Prepare a consolidated statement of changes in equity.

19.1   Business combinations

In March 2004, the IASB issued IFRS 3 – *Business Combinations*. In January 2008, the IASB published a revised version of IFRS 3. IFRS 3 has introduced significant changes to accounting for business combinations by prohibiting merger accounting and ruling that all business combinations are acquisitions. It requires that an acquirer should be identified for every business combination. Other changes are set out below:

- Goodwill should not be amortised, but should be subject to an annual impairment test.
- Negative goodwill should be recognised immediately in the income statement.
- Contingent liabilities should be recognised at fair value.
- Detailed disclosures about business combinations are required to be made.

A business combination is a transaction or an event in which an *acquirer* obtains control of one or more *businesses*. A *business* is an integrated set of activities and assets that is capable of being conducted and managed for the purpose of providing a return in the form of dividends, lower costs or other economic benefits directly to investors or other owners, members or participants (IFRS 3 (revised) Appendix A).

Example 19.1

What constitutes a business?

Some examples of what constitutes a business under IFRS 3 definition are given below.

1 A banking group with its headquarters in Canada operates throughout the Caribbean with a branch of the Canadian company in each territory. The branches are not separate legal entities, but the Caribbean banking operation is managed as a separate profit centre within the Canadian entity. It has access to all of the inputs and processes necessary to provide services and generate revenues. The Caribbean banking operation is a business.

2 A multinational industrial chemicals group based in Finland operates a resins business throughout the world. The group structure is organised to be tax efficient and the resins business is made up of a group of companies in some countries, a separate subsidiary in some countries and a division of a larger company in some other countries. The resins business has its own management team and is managed as a separate profit centre. It has access to all of the inputs and processes necessary to manufacture resins and generate revenues. The resins business is a business.

3 A multinational consumer products group owns the rights and patents for a large number of brands. The brands are exploited in different ways by subsidiaries throughout the world. The group is managed by reference to geographically determined profit centres. The brands do not have all the inputs and processes needed to generate revenues. For example, an individual brand does not have access to manufacturing or distribution facilities. Hence, an individual brand or group of brands is not a business.

19.2 Acquisition method

IFRS 3 states that an entity should account for each business combination by applying the acquisition method (IFRS 3 (revised) para 4).

Application of the acquisition method requires:

(a) identifying the acquirer;

(b) determining the *acquisition date*;

(c) recognising and measuring the identifiable assets acquired, the liabilities assumed and any non-controlling interest (NCI) in the acquiree; and

(d) recognising and measuring goodwill or a gain from a bargain purchase (IFRS 3 (revised) para 5).

19.2.1   Identifying the acquirer

The acquisition method views a business combination from the acquirer's perspective. It assumes that one of the parties to the transaction can be identified as the acquirer. Consequently, IFRS 3 (revised) requires an acquirer to be identified for all business combinations (IFRS 3 (revised) para 6). The acquirer is the combining entity that obtains control of the acquiree (IFRS 3 Appendix A). Control is defined in IAS 27 (revised) as "the power to govern the financial and operating policies of an entity or business so as to obtain benefits from its activities" (see Chapter 18).

An example of a group that identified an acquirer under IFRS, where the acquirer was not identified under previous GAAP, is T&F Informa plc. The combination of Taylor & Francis Group plc and Informa Group plc in May 2004 was accounted for as a merger under previous GAAP. However, this combination took place after the group's date of transition to IFRS and, therefore, did not qualify for the business combinations exemption in IFRS 1. This means that the business combination should be restated to comply with IFRS 3. In a press release issued in June 2005, explaining how the group's previously reported financial performance and position are reported under IFRS, the group announced that the merger accounting had been reversed under IFRS and the combination had been accounted for as an acquisition, with Informa Group plc as the acquirer: 'The principal changes to T&F Informa plc's reported financial information under UK GAAP arising from the adoption of IFRS are as a result of the adoption of the acquisition accounting method, rather than merger accounting, for the combination of Taylor & Francis Group plc and Informa Group plc on 10 May 2004. Under IFRS 3, this results in the recognition of significant additional intangible assets, goodwill and deferred taxation as well as the exclusion of the results of Taylor & Francis Group plc for the pre-acquisition period from 1 January 2004 to 10 May 2004. Certain costs, treated as merger costs under UK GAAP, have been reclassified as costs of acquisition and added to goodwill in the balance sheet. Informa Group plc (subsequently renamed T&F Informa plc) is deemed to be the acquiring company; (. . .) The Group has elected not to apply IFRS 3 retrospectively to business combinations that took place before the date of transition, 1 January 2004. As a result, goodwill arising from past business combinations has not been amortised during 2004 except for an impairment provision of £15.00m. All other business combinations since 1 January 2004 have been accounted for under IFRS 3. The most notable impact of this has been the reversal of the Merger accounting rules applied to the combination of Taylor & Francis Group plc and Informa Group plc on 10 May 2004 which has now been accounted for under the Acquisition accounting method. (. . .)'

19.2.2   Determining the acquisition date

The acquirer should identify the acquisition date, which is the date on which it obtains control of the acquiree (IAS 3 (revised) para 8).

The date on which the acquirer obtains control of the acquiree is generally the date on which the acquirer legally transfers the consideration, acquires the assets and assumes the liabilities of the acquiree – the closing date. However, the acquirer might obtain control on a date that is either earlier or later than the closing date. For example, the acquisition date precedes the closing date if a written agreement provides that the acquirer obtains control of the acquiree on a date before the closing date. An acquirer should consider all pertinent facts and circumstances in identifying the acquisition date (IAS 3 (revised) para 9).

Example 19.2

Determining the date control passes – not date of agreement

Entity P acquires 100 per cent of entity S for cash. The sale agreement specifies that the acquisition date is 10 June. Directors are nominated by entity P and appointed in place of the existing directors on 1 July, the date when all of the conditions in the sale agreement are satisfied. The shares in entity S are transferred to entity P when the consideration is paid in cash on 20 July.

What is the date of acquisition?

Based on the facts given above, the date of acquisition is 1 July, the date from which entity P is able to govern entity S's financial and operating policies. This is the date on which entity P is able to appoint the directors.

The consideration in this case is an obligation to make payment at a later date. The consideration is exchanged on 1 July when control of entity S was transferred to entity P. The payment of cash on 20 July does not affect the acquisition's recognition.

The date established in the sale agreement is not binding for accounting purposes. The date when control passes to the acquirer will often differ from the date set in the agreement.

19.2.3 Recognising and measuring the assets acquired and the liabilities assumed

Recognition principle

As of the acquisition date, the acquirer should recognise, separately from goodwill, the identifiable assets acquired, the liabilities assumed and any non-controlling interest in the acquiree (IFRS 3 (revised) para 10).

Recognition conditions

To qualify for recognition as part of applying the acquisition method, the identifiable assets acquired and liabilities assumed should meet the definitions of assets and liabilities in the *Framework for the Preparation and Presentation of Financial Statements* at the acquisition date. For example, costs the acquirer expects but is not obliged to incur in the future to effect its plan to exit an activity of an acquiree or to terminate the employment of or relocate an acquiree's employees are not liabilities at the acquisition date. Therefore, the acquirer should not recognise those costs as part of applying the acquisition method (IFRS 3 (revised) para 11).

In addition, to qualify for recognition as part of applying the acquisition method, the identifiable assets acquired and liabilities assumed should be part of what the acquirer and the acquiree (or its former *owners*) exchanged in the business combination transaction rather than the result of separate transactions (IFRS 3 (revised) para 12).

The acquirer's application of the recognition principle and conditions may result in recognising some assets and liabilities that the acquiree had not previously recognised as assets and liabilities in its financial statements. For example, the acquirer recognises the acquired identifiable intangible assets, such as a brand name, a patent or a customer relationship, that the acquiree did not recognise as assets in its financial statements because it developed them internally and charged the related costs to expense (IFRS 3 (revised) para 13).

Measurement principle

The acquirer should measure the identifiable assets acquired and the liabilities assumed at their fair values at the acquisition date (IFRS 3 (revised) para 18).

19.2.4 Recognising and measuring goodwill

The acquirer should recognise goodwill as of the acquisition date measured as the excess of (a) over (b) below:

(a) the cost of acquisition;

(b) the net amounts of the identifiable assets acquired and the liabilities assumed measured at fair value at the acquisition date (IFRS 3 (revised) para 32).

(a) Cost of acquisition		
Expenses of acquisition	Purchase consideration	
Goodwill	(b) Fair value of assets, liabilities and contingent liabilities	
Goodwill	Revaluation to fair value	Book value of assets, liabilities and contingent liabilities

Figure 19.1 How to determine goodwill on acquisition

Bargain purchases

Occasionally, an acquirer will make a bargain purchase, which is a business combination in which the net fair value of the identifiable assets acquired and the liabilities assumed at the date of acquisition exceeds the consideration paid. In that case, the acquirer should recognise the resulting gain in its income statement on the acquisition date. A bargain purchase might happen, for example, in a business

---

Notes to the Consolidated Financial Statements (extract)

Consolidation Principles

The consolidated financial statements were prepared as of the December 31, 2008 reporting date of the annual financial statements of the Puma AG parent company on the basis of uniform accounting policies pursuant to IFRS.

The capital consolidation of subsidiaries acquired after January 1, 2005 is based on the acquisition method. The acquisition costs of the business combination also include the costs directly allocable to the purchase, as well as all debts arising within the scope of the acquisition transaction. Upon initial consolidation, assets, debts and contingent liabilities identified in the context of a business combination are stated at the fair value applicable at the acquisition date, independent of the scope of minority interests.

The surplus of the acquisition costs arising from the purchase that exceeds the Group's share in the net assets (stated at fair value) is reported as Goodwill. If acquisition costs are below the amount of the net assets stated at fair value, the difference is reported directly in the income statement.

Goodwill

Goodwill is derived from the difference between the purchase price and fair value of the acquired asset and liability items. The goodwill from acquisitions is largely attributable to the infrastructure acquired and the pertaining opportunity to make a positive contribution to corporate value. An impairment test per cash generating unit is to be performed at least once a year, and in the event of indications of impairment. The impairment test may lead to an impairment expense.

Figure 19.2 Acquisition method and calculation of goodwill
Source: Puma Annual Report 2008.

combination that is a forced sale in which the seller is acting under compulsion (IFRS 3 (revised) paras 34 and 35).

Example 19.3

Acquisition analysis

As noted above, the parent should record its investment in the subsidiary at the cost of the business combination, which is the fair value of the consideration paid. Where the cost of the business combination is greater than the acquirer's interest in the net fair value of the identifiable assets, liabilities and contingent liabilities of the acquiree, goodwill should be recognised in the consolidated balance sheet. Where the reverse occurs, the excess should be recognised as a gain in the consolidated income statement. An acquisition analysis should be conducted at acquisition date because it is necessary to recognise the identifiable assets and liabilities of the subsidiary and any goodwill. As already noted, this may give rise to the recognition of assets, liabilities and contingent liabilities that are not recognised in the records of the subsidiary. For example, the business combination may give rise to intangibles that could not be recognised in the subsidiary's records.

The first step in the consolidation process is to undertake the above acquisition analysis in order to obtain the information necessary for making both the business combination valuation and pre-acquisition adjustments for the consolidated balance sheet.

On 1 July 2009, Gemma Ltd acquired all the issued share capital of Floud Ltd, giving in exchange 100,000 shares in Gemma Ltd, these having a fair value of EUR 10 per share.[1] At the acquisition date, the balance sheets of Gemma Ltd and Floud Ltd, and the fair values of Floud Ltd's assets and liabilities, were as shown in Table 19.1.

Table 19.1 Information at acquisition date

	Gemma Ltd	Floud Ltd	
	Carrying amount €	Carrying amount €	Fair value €
ASSETS			
Land	240,000	300,000	340,000
Equipment	1,240,000	960,000	660,000
Accumulated depreciation	(760,000)	(340,000)	
Shares in Floud Ltd	1,000,000		
Inventory	184,000	150,000	160,000
Cash	30,000	10,000	10,000
Total assets	1,934,000	1,080,000	
LIABILITIES AND EQUITY			
Liabilities			
Provisions	60,000	120,000	120,000
Payables	54,000	68,000	68,000
Tax liabilities	20,000	12,000	12,000
Total liabilities	134,000	200,000	
Equity			
Share capital	1,100,000	600,000	
Retained earnings	700,000	280,000	
Total equity	1,800,000	880,000	
Total equity and liabilities	1,934,000	1,080,000	

At the acquisition date, Floud Ltd had an unrecorded patent with a fair value of EUR 40,000 and a contingent liability with a fair value of EUR 30,000. The tax rate is 30 per cent.

An analysis at the acquisition date then consists of comparing the fair value of the consideration paid and the net fair value of the identifiable assets, liabilities and contingent liabilities acquired. The net fair value of the subsidiary could be calculated by revaluing the assets and liabilities of the subsidiary from the carrying amounts to fair value, remembering that under IAS 12 – *Income Taxes* revaluation of assets requires a recognition of the tax effect of the revaluation because there is no difference between the carrying amount and the tax base caused by the revaluation. However, in calculating the net fair value acquired, the calculation should be done by adding the recorded equity of the subsidiary (which represents the recorded net assets of the subsidiary) and the differences between the carrying amounts of the assets and liabilities and their fair values, adjusted for tax. The book equity of the subsidiary in the figure above consists of:

€600,000 capital + €280,000 retained earnings

The equity relating to the differences in fair value and the carrying amounts for assets and liabilities recorded by Floud Ltd – as well as for assets, liabilities and contingent liabilities not recognised by the subsidiary but recognised as being acquired as part of the business combination – is sometimes referred to as the *business combination valuation reserve* (BCVR). This reserve is not an account recognised in the subsidiary's records, but it is recognised in the consolidation process as part of the business combination. For example, for land there is a EUR 40,000 difference between the fair value and the carrying amount. On revaluation of the land to fair value, a business combination valuation reserve of EUR 28,000 [being EUR 40,000 × (1 − 30%)] should be recorded.

The acquisition analysis, including the determination of the goodwill of the subsidiary, is as shown below.

Table 19.2 Acquisition analysis at 1 July 2009

(a) Cost of combination	= 100,000 × €10 = €1,000,000
(b) Net fair value of identifiable assets, liabilities and contingent liabilities of Floud Ltd	= €600,000 + €280,000 (recorded equity) + (€340,000 − €300,000) (1 − 30%) (BCVR − land) + (€660,000 − €630,000) (1 − 30%) (BCVR − equipment) + (€160,000 − €150,000) (1 − 30%) (BCVR − inventory) + €40,000 (1 − 30%) (BCVR − patent) − €30,000 (1 − 30%) (BCVR − contingent liability) = €950,000
(c) Goodwill = (a) − (b)	= €1,000,000 − €950,000 = €50,000

Goodwill

Goodwill is the excess of the purchase cost over the fair value of acquired identifiable assets and liabilities. Goodwill arising from the acquisition of a foreign entity and any fair value adjustments to the carrying amounts of assets and liabilities of that foreign entity, are treated as assets and liabilities of the reporting entity respectively, and are translated at exchange rates prevailing at the date of the initial consolidation. Goodwill is carried in the functional currency of the acquired foreign entity.

Acquired goodwill is valued at cost less accumulated impairment losses. Effective January 1, 2005, scheduled amortisation of goodwill ceased due to changes in IFRS. Goodwill is tested annually for impairment, and additionally when there are indications of potential impairment.

Goodwill has been allocated for impairment testing purposes to three cash-generating units. The Group's cash-generating units are identified according to major brand of operations in line with the internal management approach. The adidas Group has thus defined the three segments adidas, Reebok and TaylorMade-adidas Golf as the relevant cash-generating units.

Figure 19.3 Goodwill and impairment test
Source: adidas Group Annual Report 2008.

The carrying amounts of acquired goodwill are allocated to the cash-generating units as follows:

Allocation of goodwill				
€ in millions				
	adidas	Reebok	TaylorMade-adidas Golf	Total goodwill
January 1, 2008	748	406	282	1,436
Additions	18	–	–	18
Currency effects	24	19	2	45
December 31, 2008	790	425	284	1,499

In 2008, the adidas Group determined that no impairment of goodwill was necessary.

The recoverable amount of a cash-generating unit is determined on the basis of value in use. This calculation uses cash flow projections based on the financial planning covering a five-year period in total in the case of the cash-generating unit Reebok and a four-year period in total in the case of the cash-generating units adidas and TaylorMade-adidas Golf. Cash flows beyond this period are extrapolated using steady growth rates of 1.7% (2007: 2.0% to 2.5%). These growth rates do not exceed the long-term average growth rate of the business in which each cash-generating unit operates.

Discount rates are based on a weighted average cost of capital calculation considering a five-year average debt/equity structure and financing costs including the Group's major competitors of each cash-generating unit. The discount rates used are after-tax rates and reflect the specific equity and country risk of the relevant cash-generating unit.

11 Goodwill

Goodwill primarily relates to the Group's acquisitions of the Reebok and TaylorMade businesses as well as recent and previous acquisitions of subsidiaries in the United States, Australia/New Zealand, Netherlands/Belgium and Italy.

Goodwill		
€ in millions		
	Dec. 31, 2008	Dec. 31, 2007
Goodwill, gross	1,499	1,436
Less: impairment	–	–
Goodwill, net	1,499	1,436

The majority of goodwill which primarily relates to the acquisition of the Reebok business in 2006 is denominated in US dollars. A positive currency translation effect of €45 million and negative €80 million was recorded for the years ending December 31, 2008 and 2007, respectively.

From January 1, 2005, goodwill is tested annually for impairment. There was no impairment expense for the years ending December 31, 2008 and 2007. The Group determines whether goodwill impairment is necessary at least on an annual basis. This requires an estimation of the value in use of the cash-generating units to which the goodwill is allocated. Estimating the value in use requires the Group to make an estimate of the expected future cash flows from the cash-generating unit and also to choose a suitable discount rate in order to calculate the present value of those cash flows.

Future changes in expected cash flows and discount rates may lead to impairments of the accounted goodwill in the future.

Figure 19.3 (*Cont'd*)

19.3   Non-controlling interest (NCI)

A parent company does not need to purchase all the shares of another company to gain control. We have seen in Chapter 18 that holders of the 'minority' shares are collectively referred to as the non-controlling interest (NCI). They are part owners of the subsidiary. Therefore, the parent does not own all the net assets of the acquired company but controls them.

One of the purposes of preparing consolidated financial statements is to show the effectiveness of that control. Thus, all of the assets and liabilities of the subsidiary should be included in the consolidated balance sheet and the NCI should be shown as partly financing those net assets.

IFRS 3 allows for two different methods of measuring the NCI in the consolidated balance sheet:

- *Method 1* requires that the non-controlling interest be measured at the proportionate share of the net assets of the subsidiary at the date of acquisition plus the relevant share of changes in the post-acquisition net assets of the acquired subsidiary. The practical effect of this method is that at each reporting date the NCI is measured as the share of the net assets of the subsidiary.

- *Method 2* requires that the NCI be measured at fair value at the date of acquisition, plus the relevant share of changes in the post-acquisition net assets of the acquired subsidiary. The practical effect of this method is that at each reporting date the NCI is measured as the share of the net assets of the subsidiary, plus the goodwill that is apportioned to the non-controlling interest.

In the consolidated income statement, the total profit of the subsidiary should be included and the NCI in it should be separately identified. The income statement is dealt with in more detail in section 19.6. The effect on the consolidated balance sheet is illustrated in Example 19.4, below.

Example 19.4

Non-controlling interest

On 1 January 2010 entity P acquired 80 per cent of the 5,000 EUR 4 ordinary shares of entity S for EUR 6 per cent in cash and gained control. The fair value of the net assets of S at that date was the same as the book value.

We will first use method 1 to compute the NCI. The individual balance sheets immediately after the acquisition and the consolidated balance sheet at that date are given in Table 19.3 below.

Table 19.3 Consolidated balance sheet at the date of acquisition applying method 1 for NCI

	P	S	Consolidated balance sheet	Notes
	€	€	€	
ASSETS				
Non-current assets	40,000	22,000	62,000	3
Goodwill	–	–	1,600	1
Investment in S	24,000	–	–	
Net current assets	22,000	6,000	28,000	3
Net assets	86,000	28,000	91,600	
Equity				
Share capital	32,000	20,000	32,000	4
Retained earnings	54,000	8,000	54,000	4
	86,000	28,000	86,000	
NCI			5,600	2
Total equity	86,000	28,000	91,600	

Note 1 Goodwill

	€	€
The parent company investment in S		24,000
Deduct: The parent's share of the subsidiary's share capital		
(80% × €20,000)	16,000	
The parent's share of the retained earnings		
(80% × €8,000)	6,400	
(Equivalent to the share of net assets: 80% × €28,000)		(22,400)
The difference is goodwill		1,600

Note 2 Non-controlling interest (NCI)

		€
NCI in the share capital of S	(20% × €20,000)	4,000
NCI in the retained earnings of S	(20% × €8,000)	1,600
NCI (Equivalent to the share of net assets: 20% × €28,000)		5,600

In the consolidated balance sheet the NCI should be shown as a separate item in the equity of the group as follows:

	€
Share capital	32,000
Retained earnings	54,000
P's share of equity	86,000
NCI	5,600
Total equity	91,600

NCI is shown as part of the ownership of the group rather than as a liability.

Note 3 Consolidated assets and liabilities

	€
Non-current assets other than goodwill (€40,000 + €22,000)	62,000
Goodwill as calculated in Note 1	1,600
Net current assets	28,000
	91,600

Note 4 Consolidated share capital and reserves

		€
Share capital	*(parent company only)*	32,000
Retained earnings	*(parent company only)*	54,000
		86,000

Let us measure the NCI by using method 2. In order to use this method, we need to know the fair value of the NCI in the subsidiary at the date of acquisition. Let us assume in this case that this fair value is EUR 5,800. The use of method 2 affects two figures – goodwill and NCI. The impact is the goodwill that is attributed to the NCI and it is computed as follows:

	€
Fair value of NCI at the date of acquisition	5,800
20% of the net assets at the date of acquisition (20% x €28,000)	(5,600)
Attributable goodwill	**200**

The consolidated balance sheet would now be as shown in Table 19.4, below.

Table 19.4 Consolidated balance sheet at the date of acquisition applying method 2 for NCI

	€
ASSETS	
Non-current assets	62,000
Goodwill (€1,600 + €200)	1,800
Net current assets	28,000
Net assets	91,800
EQUITY	
Share capital	32,000
Retained earnings	54,000
	86,000
NCI (€5,600 + €200)	5,800
Total equity	91,800

Treatment of fair values of subsidiary's assets at acquisition date

So far we have assumed that the book values of the non-current assets of the subsidiary is equal to their fair values. In practice, book values rarely equals fair values and it is necessary to revalue the assets and liabilities of the subsidiary prior to consolidation as shown in Example 19.5 below. Note that, when consolidating, the parent company's assets and liabilities remain unchanged at book value – it is only the subsidiary's that are adjusted for the purpose of consolidated financial statements.

Example 19.5

Differences between a subsidiary's fair values and book values

Assume that the non-current asset of S in Example 19.4 on page 562 had a fair value of EUR 23,200. In that case, the non-current assets would be increased by EUR 1,200 and a pre-acquisition revaluation reserve created of EUR 1,200. We will assume that NCI is measured using method 1.

Table **19.5** Consolidated balance sheet at the date of acquisition including the pre-acquisition revaluation reserve

	P	S	Consolidated balance sheet	Notes
	€	€	€	
ASSETS				
Non-current assets	40,000	22,000	63,200	3
Goodwill	–	–	640	1
Investment in S	24,000	–	–	
Net current assets	22,000	6,000	28,000	
Net assets	86,000	28,000	91,840	
Equity				
Share capital	32,000	20,000	32,000	
Retained earnings	54,000	8,000	54,000	
	86,000	28,000	86,000	
NCI	–	–	5,840	2
Total equity	86,000	28,000	91,840	

Note 1 Goodwill

	€	€
The parent company investment in S		24,000
Deduct: The parent's share of the subsidiary's share capital		
(80% × €20,000)	16,000	
The parent's share of the retained earnings		
(80% × €8,000)	6,400	
The parent's share of the revaluation (80% × €1,200)	960	
(Equivalent to the share of net assets: 80% × €29,200)		(23,360)
The difference is goodwill		**640**

Note 2 NCI

		€
NCI in the share capital of S	(20% × €20,000)	4,000
NCI in the retained earnings of S	(20% × €8,000)	1,600
NCI in the revaluation of S's assets	(20% × €1,200)	240
NCI (Equivalent to the share of net assets: 20% × €29,200)		**5,600**

Note 3 Non-current assets (€40,000 + €22,000 + €1,200)   **€63,200**

It should be noted that the revaluation of the subsidiary's assets is only necessary for the consolidated financial statements. No entries should be made in the individual accounts of the subsidiary or its books of accounts. The preparation of consolidated statements is a separate exercise that in no way should affect the records of the individual companies.

19.5 How to prepare a consolidated balance sheet after the date of acquisition

19.5.1 Pre- and post-acquisition profits/losses

Any profits or losses of a subsidiary made before the date of acquisition are referred to as *pre-acquisition profits/losses* in the consolidated financial statements. These are represented by the net assets that exist in the subsidiary as at the date of acquisition and, as we have seen in section 19.2.4, the fair values of these net assets will be dealt with in the goodwill calculation.

Any profits of losses made after the date of acquisition are referred to as *post-acquisition profits*. As these profits will have arisen whilst the subsidiary was under the control of the parent company, they should be included in the consolidated income statement and should appear in the retained earnings figure in the balance sheet. Example 19.6 illustrates the approach to dealing with pre- and post-acquisition profits.

Example 19.6

Accounting treatment of pre- and post-acquisition profits

On 1 January 2009, Princess plc acquired 80 per cent of the 100,000 EUR 1 ordinary shares of Sultan plc for EUR 1.50 per share in cash and gained control. The retained earnings of Sultan plc were EUR 40,000. The fair value of NCI at the date of acquisition was EUR 29,500 (we will use method 2 to compute the non-controlling interest). The fair value of the non-current assets in Sultan plc was EUR 6,000 above the book value.

The balance sheets of Princess plc and Sultan plc as well as the consolidated balance sheet are shown in Table 19.6.

Table 19.6 Consolidated balance sheet as at 31 December 2009 applying method 2 to compute NCI

	Princess	Sultan	Consolidated balance sheet	Notes
	€	€	€	
ASSETS				
Non-current assets	260,000	120,000	386,000	3
Goodwill	–	–	3,500	1
Investment in Surprise	120,000	–	–	
Net current assets	130,000	40,000	170,000	3
Net assets	510,000	160,000	559,500	
EQUITY				
Share capital	160,000	100,000	160,000	4
Retained earnings	350,000	60,000	366,000	4
	510,000	160,000	526,000	
NCI			33,500	2
Total equity	510,000	160,000	559,500	

Note 1 Goodwill as at 1 January 2009

	€	€
The parent company investment in Sultan		120,000
Deduct:		
The parent's share of the subsidiary's share capital (80% × €100,000)	80,000	
The parent's share of the retained earnings as at 1 January 2009 (80% × €40,000)	32,000	
The parent's share of the revaluation (80% × €6,000)	4,800	
		(116,800)
Goodwill attributable to Princess's shareholders		3,200
Fair value of non-controlling interest at the date of acquisition		29,500
20% of net assets at the date of acquisition (€100,000 + €40,000 + €6,000)		(29,200)
		300
Total goodwill (€3,200 + €300)		*3,500*

Note that retained earnings of Sultan of €40,000 represent pre-acquisition profits; this figure is used to calculate the goodwill of NCI.

Note 2 NCI as at 31 December 2009

		€
NCI in the share capital of Sultan	(20% × €100,000)	20,000
NCI in the retained earnings of Sultan as at 31 December 2009	(20% × €60,000)	12,000
NCI in the revaluation of Sultan's assets	(20% × €6,000)	1,200
NCI in the net assets of Sultan as at 31 December 2009		33,200
NCI in goodwill		300
		33,500

The non-controlling shareholders are entitled to their percentage share of the closing net assets. The pre- and post-acquisition division is irrelevant to the minority – they are entitled to their percentage share of the total retained earnings at any date the consolidated balance sheet is prepared.

Note 3 Consolidated assets and liabilities

	Princess €		Sultan €	Group €
Non-current assets other than goodwill	260,000	+	(120,000 + revaluation 6,000)	386,000
Goodwill		see Note 1		3,500
Net current assets	130,000	+	40,000	170,000
Total				**559,500**

Note 4 Consolidated equity

		€	€
Share capital	*(parent company only)*		160,000
Retained earnings			
* *Parent company*		350,000	
* *Parent's share of the post-acquisition retained earnings of Sultan: 80% × (retained earnings as at 31 December 2009 – retained earnings as at 1 January 2009)*		16,000	
			366,000
			526,000

19.5.2 Intragroup balances

We have seen above that we set off the parent's investment in a subsidiary against the parent's share of the subsidiary's share capital and reserves (retained earnings +/– revaluation changes) as at the date of acquisition.

However, after the acquisition there are likely to be other balances in the balance sheet of both the parent and the subsidiary arising from intercompany (or intragroup) transactions. These will require adjustments in order that the consolidated statements do not double count assets and/or liabilities. These are normally referred to as consolidation adjustments and would be authorised as consolidation journal entries by a manager or officer responsible for consolidation. The following are examples of intragroup transactions which will be considered below:

- preferred shares held by a parent in its subsidiary;
- bonds held by a parent in its subsidiary;
- intercompany balances arising from intragroup sales or other transactions such as intercompany loans;
- intragroup dividends payable/receivable.

Figure 19.4 shows Puma's consolidation principles in relation to intragroup transactions.

Notes to the Consolidated Financial Statements (extract)

Consolidation principles

Intra-group receivables and liabilities have been offset against one another. Any differences arising from exchange rate fluctuations are included in consolidated earnings to the extent that they accrued during the reporting period. If the receivables and liabilities are long-term in nature, a currency difference is included in equity with neutral effect on profits.

Within the course of income consolidation, internal sales revenue and intra-group income are offset against the expenses attributable to them. Interim profits not yet realized within the Group as well as intra-Group investment income are eliminated with an effect on profits.

Figure 19.4 Intragroup balances
Source: Puma Annual Report 2008.

Preferred shares

A parent company, in addition to the ordinary shares by which it gained control, may have acquired preferred shares in the subsidiary. If so, any amount paid by the parent company will be included within the investment in subsidiary figure that appears in the parent company's balance sheet. Just as the ordinary shares represent part of the net assets acquired, so the parent's share of the preferred shares in the subsidiary's balance sheet will represent part of the net assets acquired and will be included in the calculation of goodwill.

Any preferred shares not held by the parent are part of the non-controlling interest – this applies even though the parent might itself hold less than 50 per cent of the preferred shares – it is not necessary for the parent to hold a majority of the preferred shares.

Where preferred shares are recognised as liabilities of the subsidiary under IAS 32 – *Financial Instruments: Presentation and Disclosure*, they are accounted for in the same way as bonds. On consolidation the preferred shares purchased by the parent and included in the cost of investment will be cancelled out against the liability of the subsidiary.

Bonds

As with the preferred shares, any bonds in the subsidiary's balance sheet that have been acquired by the parent will represent part of the net assets acquired and will be included in the calculation of goodwill. However, the amount of bonds not held by the parent will not be part of the non-controlling interest as they do not bestow any rights of ownership on shareholders. They are, effectively, a form of long-term loan, and will be shown as such in the consolidated balance sheet.

Intragroup balances arising from sales or other transactions

IAS 27 para 20 requires intragroup balances to be eliminated in full. If entries in the parent's records and the subsidiary's records are up to date, the same figure will appear as a balance in the current assets of one company and in the current liabilities of the other. For example, if the parent company has supplied goods invoiced at EUR 10,000 to its subsidiary, there will be a trade receivable for EUR 10,000 in the parent's balance sheet and a trade payable for EUR 10,000 in the subsidiary's balance sheet. These need to be offset, i.e. eliminated before preparing the consolidated financial statements.

In practice, temporary differences may arise for such items as inventory or cash in transit that are recorded in one company's books but of which the other company is not yet aware, e.g. goods or cash in transit. In such a case, the records will require reconciling and updating before proceeding. In a multinational company, this is usually a time-consuming exercise.

Intragroup dividends payable/receivable

If the subsidiary has declared a dividend before the end of the year, this will appear in its current liabilities and in the current assets of the parent company and should be offset before preparing the consolidated balance sheet. If the subsidiary is wholly owned by the parent the whole amount will be eliminated. If, however, there is a non-controlling interest in the subsidiary, the non-cancelled amount of the dividend payable in the subsidiary's balance sheet will be the amount payable to the minority and will be reported as part of the NCI in the consolidated balance sheet. Where a dividend has not been declared by the end of the year, there is no liability under IAS 10 – *Events after the Balance Sheet Date* and, thus, there should be no liability reported under IFRS.

Unrealised profit on intragroup sales

Where sales have been made between two companies within the group, there may be an element of profit that has not been realised by the group if the goods have not then been sold on to a third party before the end of the accounting period. Example 19.7, below, explains how to eliminate intragroup profit.

Example 19.7

Unrealised profit on intragroup sales

Assume that entity X buys EUR 10,000 worth of goods for resale and sells them to its subsidiary Y for EUR 15,000 making a profit of EUR 5,000. At the balance sheet date, if the subsidiary Y still has these goods in inventory, the group has not yet made any profit on these goods and the EUR 5,000 is therefore 'unrealised'. It should be removed from the balance sheet by:

- reducing the retained earnings of entity X by EUR 5,000;
- reducing the inventory of the subsidiary Y by EUR 5,000.

EUR 5,000 is called a provision for unrealised profit.

If these goods are eventually sold by the subsidiary Y to customers outside the group for EUR 22,000, the profit made by the group will be EUR 12,000 (i.e. the difference between the original cost of the goods to entity X, EUR 10,000, and the eventual sale price of EUR 22,000). It follows from this that it is only necessary to provide for an unrealised profit from intragroup sales to the extent that the goods are still in the inventories of the group at the balance sheet date.

Example 19.8

How to prepare a consolidated balance sheet after the date of acquisition

On 1 January 2010 Mother plc acquired 80 per cent of the ordinary shares of Son plc for EUR 42,200, 20 per cent of the preferred shares for EUR 4,000 and 10 per cent of the bonds for EUR 1,800, and gained control. The retained earnings as at 1 January 2010 were EUR 8,000. The fair value of the land in Son plc was EUR 2,000 above book value.

During the year, Mother plc sold some of its inventory to Son plc for EUR 6,000 which represented cost plus a mark-up of 25 per cent. Half of these goods are still in the inventory of Son plc at 31 December 2010.

The balance sheets of the two companies are shown in Table 19.7.

Prepare a consolidated balance sheet as at 31 December 2010. Note that depreciation is not charged on land. Use method 1 to compute NCI.

Note 1 Goodwill (note that this calculation will be the same as at the date of acquisition)

	€	€
The cost of Mother's investment for ordinary shares, preferred shares and bonds		48,000
Deduct:		
The parent's share of the subsidiary's share capital (80% × €22,000)	17,600	
The parent's share of the retained earnings as at 1 January 2010 (80% × €8,000)	6,400	
The parent's share of the land revaluation (80% × €2,000)	1,600	
The parent's share of preferred shares (20% × €16,000)	3,200	
The parent's share of bonds (10% × €14,000)	1,400	
		(30,200)
Goodwill attributable to Mother's shareholders		*17,800*

As method 1 is applied, this is also the goodwill that will be shown in the consolidated balance sheet.

Table 19.7 Balance sheets of Mother plc and Son plc as at 31 December 2010

	Mother €	Son €
ASSETS		
Non-current assets		
PPE	51,840	86,800
Investment in Son	48,000	–
Current assets		
Inventories	19,200	8,000
Son current account	16,000	–
Bond interest receivable	70	–
Other current assets	3,930	6,700
TOTAL ASSETS	139,040	101,500
EQUITY AND LIABILITIES		
Equity		
Share capital	48,000	22,000
Preferred shares	8,000	16,000
Retained earnings	60,000	17,000
	116,000	55,000
Non-current liabilities		
Bonds	10,000	14,000
Current liabilities		
Mother current account	–	16,000
Bond interest payable	–	700
Other current liabilities	13,040	15,800
TOTAL EQUITY AND LIABILITIES	139,040	101,500

Note 2 Intergroup adjustments

2a The current accounts of €16,000 between the two companies are eliminated (note that the accounts are equal which indicates that there are no items such as goods in transit or cash in transit which would have required a reconciliation).

2b The bond interest receivable by Mother plc is eliminated with €70 (= 10% × €700) of the bond interest payable by Son plc leaving €630 (= 90% × €700) payable to outsiders. This is not part of the non-controlling interest as bond holders have no ownership rights in the company.

2c Provision for unrealised profit on the inventory of Son plc:
- The mark-up on the intragroup sales was: €6,000 × 25 ÷ 125 = €1,200
- Half the goods are still in inventories at the balance sheet date so we should provide: ½ × €1,200 for the unrealised profit = **€600**

Table 19.8 Consolidated balance sheet as at 31 December 2010 applying method 1 to compute NCI

	Mother	Son	Consolidated balance sheet	Notes
	€	€	€	
ASSETS				
Non-current assets				
PPE	51,840	86,800	140,640	4
Goodwill	–	–	17,800	1
Investment in Son	48,000	–	–	1
Current assets				
Inventories	19,200	8,000	26,600	2c
				4
Son current account	16,000	–	–	2a
Bond interest receivable	70	–	–	2b
Other current assets	3,930	6,700	10,630	4
TOTAL ASSETS	139,040	101,500	195,670	
EQUITY AND LIABILITIES				
Equity				
Share capital	48,000	22,000	48,000	5
Preferred shares	8,000	16,000	8,000	5
Retained earnings	60,000	17,000	66,600	5
	116,000	55,000	122,600	
NCI			21,000	3
Total equity			143,600	
Non-current liabilities				
Bonds	10,000	14,000	22,600	6
Current liabilities				
Mother current account		16,000		2a
Bond interest payable		700	630	2b
Other current liabilities	13,040	15,800	28,840	4
TOTAL EQUITY AND LIABILITIES	139,040	101,500	195,670	

Note 3 NCI as at 31 December 2010

		€
NCI in the share capital of Son	(20% × €22,000)	4,400
NCI in the retained earnings of Son as at 31 December 2010	(20% × €17,000)	3,400
NCI in the land revaluation	(20% × €2,000)	400
NCI in the preferred shares of Son	(80% × €16,000)	12,800
NCI		*21,000*

Note 4 Consolidated assets and liabilities

	Mother	Son	Group
	€	€	€
PPE	51,840 +	(86,800 + revaluation 2,000)	= 140,640
Inventories	19,200 +	(8,000 – provision for unrealised profit 600)	= 26,600
Other current assets	3,930 +	6,700	= 10,630
Other current liabilities	13,040 +	15,800	= 28,840

Note 5 Consolidated equity

		€	€
Share capital	(parent company's only)		**48,000**
Preferred shares	(parent company's only)		**8,000**
Retained earnings:			
* parent company's		60,000	
deduct: provision for unrealised profit		(600)	
			59,400
* parent's share of the post-acquisition profit of Son: 80% × €17,000		13,600	
deduct: 80% of pre-acquisition profit: (80% × €8,000)		(6,400)	
			7,200
			66,600

Note 6 Bonds

	Mother	Son	Group
	€	€	€
Bonds	10,000 +	(14,000 – intragroup 1,400)	= **22,600**

19.5.3 Provision for unrealised profit affecting NCI

Where a subsidiary with a non-controlling interest sells goods to a parent company at a mark-up, the non-controlling interest should be charged with its share of any provision for unrealised profit. For example, if entity Mother plc in Example 19.8 above had sold goods to the subsidiary Son plc for EUR 6,000 including a mark-up of 25 per cent, the non-controlling interest would have been charged with 20 per cent of the provision for unrealised profit (= 20% × €600 = €120). The parent would have been charged with the remaining EUR 480.

19.5.4 Uniform accounting policies and reporting dates

Uniform accounting policies

Consolidated financial statements should be prepared using uniform accounting policies for like transactions and other events in similar circumstances (IAS 27 para 24). Hence, on consolidation adjustments should be made to the amounts that have been reported by subsidiaries in their individual financial statements, when their accounting policies differ from those of the group.

If a member of the group uses accounting policies other than those adopted in the consolidated financial statements for like transactions and events in similar circumstances, appropriate adjustments should be made to its financial statements in preparing the consolidated financial statements (IAS 27 para 25).

Where a new subsidiary is acquired by a group and the two have different accounting policies, the new subsidiary has sufficient reason to change its accounting policy and make a prior year adjustment in accordance with IAS 8 – *Accounting Policies, Changes in Accounting Estimates and Errors*. Alternatively, the new subsidiary may continue with its original accounting policy in its entity financial statements, in which case the group would need to make an adjustment on consolidation to reflect the subsidiary's results in accordance with the group's accounting policy.

Problems can arise for subsidiaries in certain jurisdictions to apply uniform accounting policies. It may not always be practicable for the parent to insist that the subsidiaries change their accounting policies to bring them into line with the group's accounting policies for reasons of company law or tax law. For this reason, today groups have reporting packages for consolidation purposes. In such reporting packages, a subsidiary's financial statements will be reported in accordance with the group's accounting policies. Reporting packages would also include all other information required for the group's annual report.

Subsidiary year-ends

The financial statements of the parent and its subsidiaries used in the preparation of the consolidated financial statements should be prepared as of the same reporting date (IAS 27 para 22). They should also cover the same financial period.

When the reporting dates of the parent and a subsidiary are different, the subsidiary should prepare, for consolidation purposes, additional financial statements (reporting package) as of the same date as the financial statements of the parent unless it is impracticable to do so (IAS 27 para 22). If it is not practicable to use additional financial statements, the subsidiary's financial statements should be used, provided that its year-end is not more than three months before or after the relevant year-end of the parent. One practical reason sometimes given for having different year-ends is to avoid delays in presenting the consolidated financial statements. In this situation, any changes that have taken place in the intervening period that materially affect the view given by the financial statements should be taken into account by adjusting the consolidated financial statements. The length of the reporting periods and any difference in the reporting dates should be the same from period to period (IAS 27 para 23).

Consolidation adjustments for non-coterminous year-ends might be required for dividends paid by the subsidiary to the parent and settlement of intragroup balances outstanding at the subsidiary's year-end, which would obviously have to be dealt with as part of the consolidation process. Other transactions might not be so obvious, such as a post balance sheet event in the subsidiary. For example, an adjustment should be made for a substantial loss on a contract undertaken by a subsidiary that has occurred in between the subsidiary's year-end and that of its parent. Another example is that of a subsidiary incorporated overseas and there has been a devaluation of the currency in which it trades between its year-end date and that of its parent.

Example 19.9 illustrates the options that are available when consolidating a subsidiary with a non-coterminous year-end.

Example 19.9

Subsidiary year-end

A parent company has a year-end of 30 June 2010. One of its subsidiaries has a year-end of 31 December 2009 and another has a year-end of 31 March 2010.

What figures should the parent include in its consolidated financial statements in respect of these subsidiaries?

The first subsidiary should prepare additional financial statements covering the year ended 30 June 2009 (that is, coinciding with that of its parent). It should not prepare additional financial statements to, for example, 31 May, despite this date being within three months of the parent's year-end. Under no circumstances (unless the subsidiary is immaterial) may the parent consolidate the subsidiary's actual financial statements, as the subsidiary's year-end is more than three months before that of the parent.

With respect to the second subsidiary, the parent should consolidate additional financial statements prepared by the subsidiary for the year ended 30 June 2010, but if this is not practicable the parent may consolidate the financial statements of the subsidiary for the year ended 31 March 2010 (as it ends no more than three months prior to the parent's year-end). If the financial statements for the year ended 31 March 2010 are used, consideration should be given to the requirement to adjust for material transactions between the subsidiary's year-end and that of the parent.

The following information should be given for each subsidiary that is included in the consolidated financial statements and whose financial information refers to a different date or different accounting period from that of the parent:

- its name;
- its reporting date;
- the reason for using a different reporting date or period (IAS 27 para 41(c)).

19.6   How to prepare a consolidated income statement

When preparing a consolidated income statement we should take into account all the adjustments necessary for the intragroup transactions and unrealised profit as explained in sections 19.5.2 and 19.5.3. Moreover, adjustment is required to attribute the profit for the year to the shareholders of the parent and to NCI. The disclosure relating to this attribution is shown in the income statement of Puma in Figure 19.5, below.

How to prepare a consolidated income statement is illustrated in Example 19.10.

	2008 € million	2007 € million
Sales	2,524.2	2,373.5
Cost of sales	1,217.6	1,131.8
Gross profit	**1,306.6**	**1,241.7**
Royalty and commisssion income	25.7	35.6
	1,332.4	1,277.2
Other operating income and expenses	1,007.0	905.2
EBIT	**325.4**	**372.0**
Financial result	1.1	10.5
EBT	**326.4**	**382.5**
Taxes on income	94.8	110.9
Net earnings before attribution	**231.6**	**271.6**
attributable to: Minorities	−1.1	2.6
Equity holders of the parent (net earnings)	**232.8**	**269.0**

Figure 19.5 Puma's consolidated income statement
Source: Puma Annual Report 2008.

Example 19.10

Consolidated income statement

Information at the date of acquisition

- On 1 January 2008 Ante plc acquired 75 per cent of the ordinary shares and 20 per cent of the preferred shares in Post plc.
- At that date the retained earnings of Post were EUR 60,000.
- Ante paid EUR 20,000 more than the fair value of the net assets acquired. Method 1 has been used to measure the non-controlling interest.

Information relating to 2008

- Ante sold Post goods at their cost (EUR 18,000) plus a mark-up of one third. These were the only intragroup sales.
- At the end of 2008, half of these goods were still in the inventory of Post.
- At the end of 2008 Ante realised that the acquisition of Post was a bad one and decided to write off 20 per cent of the goodwill as an impairment loss.
- Dividends paid in 2008 by Ante and Post were as follows:

	Ante €	Post €
On ordinary shares	80,000	10,000
On preferred shares	–	6,000

Table 19.9 shows the individual income statements of Ante and Post together with the consolidated income statement for the year ended 31 December 2009. Explanatory notes are set out below.

Table 19.9 Consolidated income statement for the year ended 31 December 2009

	Ante €	Post €	Consolidated income statement €	Notes
Sales	400,000	240,000	616,000	1-3
Cost of sales	120,000	120,000	219,000	1-2-3
Gross profit	280,000	120,000	397,000	
Operating expenses	118,164	80,000	198,164	4
Impairment of goodwill	–	–	4,000	5
Operating profit	161,836	40,000	194,836	
Dividends received (ordinary shares)	7,500			6
Dividends received (preferred shares)	1,200			6
Profit before tax	170,536	40,000	194,836	
Tax expense	28,008	12,000	40,008	7
Profit for the year	142,528	28,000	154,828	
Attributable to:				
Ordinary shareholders of Ante (balance)			144,528	8
Non-controlling shareholders in Post			10,300	8
			154,828	

Operating profit: EUR 194,836 (see notes 1 to 5)

Adjustments are required to establish the operating profit. This entails eliminating the effects of intragroup sales and inventory transferred within the group with a profit loading but not sold at the balance sheet date and charging goodwill impairment.

Note 1 Eliminate intragroup sales on consolidation

Cancel the intragroup sales of EUR 24,000 (EUR 18,000 + $^1/_3$) by:

(i) Reducing the sales of Ante from EUR 400,000 to EUR 376,000

(ii) Reducing the cost of sales of Post by the same amount from EUR 120,000 to EUR 96,000

Note 2 Eliminate unrealised profit on intragroup sales of goods still in closing inventory

(i) Ante has sold the goods to Post at a mark-up of EUR 6,000

(ii) Half of the goods remain in the inventory of Post at the end of 2009

(iii) From the group's point of view there is an unrealised profit of half of the mark-up, i.e. EUR 3,000. Therefore,
- Deduct: EUR 3,000 from the gross profit of Ante by adding this amount to the cost of sales.
- Add this amount to a provision for unrealised profit.
- Reduce the inventory in the consolidated balance sheet by the amount of the provision.

Note 3 Aggregate the adjusted sales and cost of sales figures for items in Notes 1 and 2

(i) Add the adjusted sales figures:

$$(€400,000 - \text{intragroup sales } €24,000) + €240,000 = €616,000$$

(ii) Add the adjusted cost of sales figures:

€120,000 + (€120,000 − €24,000) + provision for
unrealised profit €3,000   = €219,000

Note 4 Aggregate expenses

No adjustment is required to the parent or subsidiary total figures.

Note 5 Deduct impairment loss

Goodwill paid on acquisition was EUR 20,000 and it has been estimated that there has been a EUR 4,000 impairment loss.

Note 6 Accounting for intragroup dividends

Adjustments are required to establish the profit after tax earned by the group as a whole. This entails eliminating dividends and interest that have been paid to the parent by the subsidiary. If this were not done, there would be a double counting as these would appear in the operating profit of the subsidiary, which has been included in the consolidated operating profit, and again as dividends and interest received by the group.

(i)   Dividends on ordinary shares of EUR 7,500 received by Ante is 75 per cent of the EUR 10,000 dividend paid by Post.

(ii) Cancel the intragroup dividend of EUR 7,500 received by Ante from Post, leaving EUR 2,500 dividend paid by Post to the NCI.

(iii) The dividend on preferred shares of EUR 1,200 received by Ante is 20 per cent of EUR 6,000 paid by Post.

(iv) Cancel EUR 1,200 dividend on preferred shares received by Ante from Post.

(v)   The balance of EUR 4,800 was paid to the NCI.

Note 7 Aggregate the taxation figures

No adjustment is required to the parent or subsidiary total figures (we ignore tax effect on the unrealised profit).

Note 8 Allocation of net profit to parent's shareholders and non-controlling interest

Adjustment is required to establish how much of the profit after tax is attributable to the parent's shareholders. This entails allocating the NCI in the subsidiary as a percentage of the subsidiary's net profit figure, as adjusted for any dividends on preferred shares.

		€
Preferred shares – dividends on these shares:		
* Non-controlling shareholders hold 80% of preferred shares	(80% × €6,000)	= 4,800
Ordinary shares – net profit of the subsidiary *less* dividends on preferred shares:		
* Non-controlling shareholders hold 25% of ordinary shares	25% × (€28,000 − €6,000)	= 5,500
Total NCI in the net profit of the subsidiary		*10,300*

19.7   How to prepare a consolidated statement of changes in equity

We will prepare extracts of the consolidated statement of changes in equity for the Ante group using the same data as in Example 19.10.

Example 19.11

Consolidated statement of changes in equity (retained earning columns only)

In order to prepare the consolidated statement of changes in equity, we need the opening balances of retained earnings. These are as follows:

Ante: EUR 138,642
Post: EUR 108,000

The statement will be as shown in Table 19.10.

Table 19.10 Consolidated statement of changes in equity (retained earnings column)

	Ante group	Non-controlling interest	Total	Notes
Opening balance	174,672	27,000	201,672	1-2
Comprehensive income for the year	144,528	10,300	154,828	
Deduct: Dividends paid on:				
– ordinary shares	(80,000)	(2,500)	(82,500)	3
– preferred shares	–	(4,800)	(4,800)	
Closing balance	239,200	30,000	269,200	

Note 1 Opening balance for Ante group

		€
Opening balance of Ante's retained earnings		138,672
Group share of Post's retained earnings	75% × (€108,000 – €72,000)	36,000
Since acquisition		174,672

Note 2 Opening balance for NCI

$$€108,000 × 25\% = €27,000$$

Note 3 Dividends paid

In the Ante group column the dividends paid are those of the parent only. The parent's share of Post's dividends cancels out with the parent company's investment income. The non-controlling share is dealt with in the column 'Non-controlling interest'. The dividends paid to NCI are:

$$25\% × €10,000 + 80\% × €6,000 = €7,300$$

Changes in Equity in € million	Subscribed capital	Group reserves				Retained earnings	Treasury stock	Total equity before minorities	Minorities	Total
		Capital reserves	Profit reserves	Difference from currency conversion	Cashflow hedges					
Dec. 31, 2006	**44.1**	**170.7**	**291.8**	**-34.7**	**-4.5**	**799.3**	**-225.6**	**1,041.3**	**7.7**	**1,049.0**
Dividend payment						-39.9		-39.9	-1.2	-41.1
Unrecognized net actuarial gain/loss						-0.3		-0.3		-0.3
Currency changes				-38.3				-38.3	-1.2	-39.5
Release to the income statement					3.4			3.4		3.4
Market value for cashflow hedges					-25.0			-25.0		-25.0
Capital increase	0.2	12.8						12.9		12.9
Net Earnings						269.0		269.0	2.6	271.6
Reduction of subscribed capital due to cancellation of own shares according to § 237 Abs. 3 AktG	-3.3		-222.3			-41.6	225.6	-41.6		-41.6
Purchase of treasury stock							-34.7	-34.7		-34.7
Dec. 31, 2007	**41.0**	**183.5**	**69.5**	**-73.0**	**-26.1**	**986.7**	**-34.7**	**1,146.8**	**8.0**	**1,154.8**
Dividend payment						-42.5		-42.5		-42.5
Unrecognized net actuarial gain/loss						-1.3		-1.3		-1.3
Currency changes/others				-19.0				-19.0	-4.4	-23.4
Release to the income statement					26.1			26.1		26.1
Market value for cashflow hedges					11.1			11.1		11.1
Capital increase	0.0	0.9						0.9		0.9
Value of employees services		1.2						1.2		1.2
Net Earnings						232.8		232.8	-1.1	231.6
Purchase of treasury stock							-181.4	-181.4		-181.4
Dec. 31, 2008	**41.0**	**185.5**	**69.5**	**-92.0**	**11.1**	**1,175.6**	**-216.1**	**1,174.7**	**2.5**	**1,177.2**

Figure 19.6 Consolidated statement of changes in equity

Source: Puma Annual Report 2008.

Figure 19.6 shows the statement of changes in equity of Puma. Note the impact of dividend payment and allocation of net profit (or net earnings) on the retained earnings attributable to the parent's shareholders and to NCI (minorities).

19.8   Dividends or interest paid by a subsidiary out of pre-acquisition profits

In Example 19.11 above, we illustrated the accounting treatment where a dividend was paid by a subsidiary out of post-acquisition profit. This showed that, when dividends and interest are received by a parent company from its subsidiary, they will normally be credited as income in the income statement of the parent company.

However, this treatment will not be appropriate where the dividends or interest have been paid out of profits earned by the subsidiary before acquisition. The reason is that the dividends or interest are paid out of the net assets acquired at the date of acquisition and these were a part of the consideration paid for the investment. The dividends or interest received by the parent, therefore, do not represent income but a return of the purchase price, which should be reported as such in the parent's balance sheet. This is illustrated in Example 19.12 below.

Example 19.12

Dividends paid out of pre-acquisition profits

On 1 October 2009, Trevelyan plc acquired 75 per cent of the shares in Shabila plc for EUR 240,000 when the balance of the retained earnings of Shabila was EUR 120,000. There was no goodwill.

On 14 November 2009, Trevelyan received a dividend of EUR 9,000 from Shabila out of the profit of the year ended 30 September 2009.

There were no intragroup transactions, other than the dividend.

The EUR 9,000 dividend received from Shabila plc is not income and should not therefore appear in Trevelyan plc's income statement. The correct treatment is to deduct it from the investment in Shabila plc, which will then become €231,000 (= €240,000 – €9,000). The consolidation would then proceed as usual.

Summary

- Business combinations should be accounted for applying the acquisition method. This requires: (a) identifying the acquirer; (b) determining the acquisition date; (c) recognising and measuring the assets, liabilities and any NCI in the acquiree; and (d) recognising and measuring goodwill (or gain from a bargain purchase).

- The acquirer (i.e. parent company) should record its investment in the acquiree (i.e. subsidiary) at the cost of the business combination, which is the fair value of the consideration paid. Where the cost of the business combination is higher the acquirer's interest in the net fair value of the identifiable assets, liabilities and contingent liabilities of the acquiree, goodwill should be recognised in the consolidated balance sheet. Where the reverse occurs, the excess should be recognised as a gain in the consolidated income statement.

- When a subsidiary is not fully owned by the parent company, the parent should account for NCI in the consolidated financial statements. All the assets and liabilities of the subsidiary should be included in the consolidated balance sheet and the NCI should be shown as partly financing those net assets.

- Any profits or losses of a subsidiary made before the date of acquisition are referred to as pre-acquisition profits/losses in the consolidated financial statements. Any profit or losses made after the date of acquisition are referred to as post-acquisition profits/losses.

- Examples of intragroup transactions that require consolidation adjustments are: preferred shares and/or bonds held by a parent in its subsidiary; intercompany loans; intragroup dividends payable/receivables. Where sales have been made between two companies within the group, there may be an element of profit that has not been realised by the group if the goods have not been sold to a third party before the end of the accounting period. This profit should be eliminated when preparing consolidated financial statements.

- Uniform group accounting policies should be used to determine the amounts to be included in the consolidated financial statements for like transactions and other events in similar circumstances. Hence, on consolidation adjustments should be made to the amounts that have been reported by subsidiaries in their individual financial statements, when their accounting polices differ from those of the group.

- The financial statements of all subsidiaries to be used in preparing the consolidated financial statements should be prepared to the same financial year-end as those of the parent. They should also cover the same financial period. When the reporting date of a subsidiary differs from that of the parent, additional financial statements should be prepared to the same date as those of the parent. If it is not practicable to use additional financial statements, the subsidiary's financial statements should be used, providing that its year ended not more than three months before or after the relevant year-end of the parent.

19.7 Consolidated balance sheet after the acquisition date

On 31 March 2010, entity P acquired 75 per cent of the ordinary shares, 30 per cent of the preferred shares and 20 per cent of the bonds in entity S and gained control. The balance of retained earnings as at 31 March 2010 was EUR 160,000. The fair value of the land owned by entity S was EUR 30,000 above its book value. No adjustment had been made for this revaluation.

The balance sheets of entities P and S as at 30 June 2010 were as follows:

	P	S
	€	€
ASSETS		
Non-current assets		
PPP (including land)	823,000	1,085,500
Investment in S	460,000	–
	1,283,000	1,085,500
Current assets		
Inventory	232,000	100,000
S current account	200,000	–
Bond interest receivable	1,750	–
Other current assets	50,000	75,000
	483,750	175,000
Total assets	**1,766,750**	**1,260,500**
EQUITY AND LIABILITIES		
Equity		
Ordinary shares	600,000	276,000
Preferred shares	100,000	200,000
Retained earnings	750,000	212,000
	1,450,000	688,000
Non-current liabilities (bonds)	125,000	175,000
Current liabilities		
P current account	–	200,000
Bond interest payable	6,250	8,750
Other current liabilities	185,500	188,750
	191,750	397,500
Total equity and liabilities	**1,766,750**	**1,260,500**

Additional information:

(i) 20 per cent of the goodwill is to be written off as an impairment loss.
(ii) During the quarter to 30 June 2010, entity P sold some of its inventory to entity S for EUR 30,000 with a mark-up of 25 per cent. Half of those goods were still in the inventory of entity S at 30 June 2010.
(iii) Land is not depreciated.
(iv) There has been no movement in share capital since the acquisition.
(v) Method 1 is used to compute the non-controlling interest.

Prepare a consolidated balance sheet as at 30 June 2010.

19.8 Consolidated income statement

Entity P acquired 80 per cent of the ordinary shares and 10 per cent of the preferred shares in entity S on 30 June 2007 when entity S's retained earnings were EUR 90,000.

During the year ended 30 June 2010 entity P sold entity S goods for EUR 24,000 with a mark-up of 50 per cent. Half of these goods were still unsold at the end of the accounting year. There was goodwill impairment loss of EUR 6,000. Non-controlling interest is measured using method 1.

The income statements of the two entities for the year ended 30 June 2010 were as follows:

	P €	S €
Sales revenue	600,000	360,000
Cost of sales	(180,000)	(180,000)
Gross profit	420,000	180,000
Expenses	(177,246)	(120,000)
Dividends received (ordinary shares)	12,000	–
Dividends received (preferred shares)	900	–
Profit before taxes	255,654	60,000
Income taxes	(42,012)	(18,000)
Net profit for the year	*213,642*	*42,000*

Prepare a consolidated income statement for the year ended 30 June 2010.

19.9 Consolidated statements

The balance sheets of entities P and S as at 31 March 2010 are as follows:

	P €	S €
ASSETS		
Non-current assets		
PPE at cost	1,100,000	450,000
Accumulated depreciation	(440,000)	(135,000)
	660,000	315,000
Investment in S	375,000	–
	1,035,000	315,000
Current assets		
Inventory	450,000	135,000
Trade receivables	360,000	180,000
Current account – S	45,000	–
Cash and cash equivalents	72,000	36,000
	927,000	351,000
Total assets	*1,962,000*	*666,000*
EQUITY AND LIABILITIES		
Equity		
Share capital	392,000	180,000
Reserves	490,000	63,000
Retained earnings	450,000	270,000
	1,332,000	513,000
Current liabilities		
Trade payables	567,000	81,000
Taxes payable	63,000	27,000
Current account – P	–	45,000
	630,000	153,000
Total equity and liabilities	*1,962,000*	*666,000*

The income statements of entities P and S for the year ended 31 March 2010 are as follows:

	P	S
	€	€
Sales revenue	2,880,000	540,000
Cost of sales	(2,090,000)	(270,000)
Gross profit	790,000	270,000
Expenses	(247,000)	(180,000)
Dividends received	18,000	–
Profit before taxes	561,000	90,000
Income taxes	(63,000)	(27,000)
Profit for the year	**498,000**	**63,000**

Additional information:

(i)   Entity P acquired 80 per cent of the shares in entity S when S's retained earnings were EUR 160,000 and S's reserves were EUR 36,000.

(ii) Non-controlling interest is measured using method 1.

(iii) During the year ended 31 March 2010 entity P sold entity S goods for EUR 36,000 which represented cost plus a 50 per cent mark-up. Half of these goods were still in stock on 31 March 2010.

(iv) During the year ended 31 March 2010, entities P and S paid dividends of EUR 360,000 and EUR 22,500 respectively. On 1 April 2009, the opening balances of retained earnings for the two entities were EUR 312,000 and EUR 229,500 respectively.

Prepare:

(a) a consolidated income statement for the year ended 31 March 2010;

(b) a consolidated balance sheet as at 31 March 2010;

(c) a consolidated statement of changes in equity for the year ended 31 March 2010.

Note

1 Shares in another company can be purchased for cash or through an exchange of shares. In the former case, the cash will be reduced and exchanged for another asset, 'Investment in the subsidiary company'. If there is an exchange of shares there will be an increase in the share capital and, probably, the share premium of the acquiring company rather than a decrease in cash. There is no effect in either case on the accounts of the acquired company. The purchase price may contain a mixture of cash and shares and possibly other assets as well.

20 Investments in associates (IAS 28) and interests in joint ventures (IAS 31)

Objectives

When you have completed this chapter you should be able to:

- Define an associate
- Account for an associate in the consolidated financial statements using the equity method
- Account for transactions between a group and its associate
- Define a joint venture
- Describe the different forms of a joint venture
- Account for jointly controlled operations
- Account for jointly controlled assets
- Account for jointly controlled entities.

20.1 Investments in associates

20.1.1 Definition of an associate and significant influence

The definition of an *associate* in IAS 28 hinges on the investing company having significant influence.

The definitions given in IAS 28 para 2 are as follows:

An associate is an entity, including an unincorporated entity such as a partnership, over which the investor has significant influence and that is neither a subsidiary nor an interest in a joint venture.

Significant influence is the power to participate in the financial and operating policy decisions of the investee but is not control or joint control over those policies.

Control is the power to govern the financial and operating policies of an entity so as to obtain benefits from its activities.

Joint control is the contractually agreed sharing of control over an economic activity, and exists only when the strategic financial and operating decisions relating to the activity require the unanimous consent of the parties sharing control (the venturers).

The key to the definition of an associate is ***significant influence***, which is 'the power to participate in the financial and operating policy decisions of the investee but is not control or joint control over those policies' (IAS 28 para 2). Hence it is the power to participate and have influence, rather than the actual exercise of influence. For example, it would not be necessary for an investor to exercise its power if the investee always happened to do what the investor wanted by accident or by design, but the investor would have the power if needed. If an investor elected to be passive, significant influence would still exist as long as it had the power to participate in the financial and operating policy decisions when it so wished.

If an investor holds, directly or indirectly (e.g. through subsidiaries), 20 per cent or more of the voting power of the investee, it is presumed that the investor has significant influence, unless it can be clearly demonstrated that this is not the case. Conversely, if the investor holds, directly or indirectly (e.g. through subsidiaries), less than 20 per cent of the voting power of the investee, it is presumed that the investor does not have significant influence, unless such influence can be clearly demonstrated. A substantial or majority ownership by another investor does not necessarily preclude an investor from having significant influence (IAS 28 para 6).

The standard gives no further definition or guidance as to what it means by voting *power*. We consider voting power to mean the rights that shareholders have to vote at general meetings of the entity on all, or substantially all, matters. This does not include voting rights held in a fiduciary capacity or voting rights held as nominee that can only be exercised with the consent of another party.

Demonstrating existence of significant influence

IAS 28 para 7 gives examples of how an investor could demonstrate that it has significant influence.

- representation on the board of directors or equivalent governing body of the investee;

- participation in policy-making processes, including participation in decisions about dividends or other distributions;
- material transactions between the investor and the investee;
- interchange of managerial personnel; or
- provision of essential technical information.

Any one of the examples could evidence the existence of significant influence; it is not necessary for all of the examples to apply. In practice, the best evidence of an entity having significant influence is the fact that it is exercising such influence. However, it is having the power to be able to participate in the policy decisions that matters not the actual exercise of that power. An investor may be on the board of the investee, but elect to be passive by not actively participating at meetings or abstaining from voting (although in practice this might be difficult to demonstrate). It is the power that comes with this board representation that matters not the fact that the investor is participating or not participating in the policy-making process.

A practical problem may arise in judging the amount of influence the investor has over its investment where the investment has only just been made. In these circumstances, the actual relationship usually becomes clear fairly soon after an investment is acquired. However, as stated above, it is the power to exercise significant influence that matters and not the actual exercise of that influence and, therefore, factors such as the number of board members the investor may nominate and the proposed decision-taking process should be used to evaluate the relationship before its record is established. If the actual relationship were to develop differently from that assumed from the arrangements on making the investment, it may be necessary subsequently to change the way in which the investment is accounted if, in practice, the investor was not able to exercise significant influence.

Significant influence might be called into question if the investor has failed in an attempt to gain board representation or to obtain timely financial information from the investee or if the investee is actively opposing the investor's attempts to exercise influence over it. This is demonstrated by the following example.

Example 20.1

Demonstrating significant influence

Entity A owns 20 per cent of the voting rights in entity B and is entitled to appoint one director to the board, which consists of five members. The remaining 80 per cent of the voting rights are held by two entities, each of which is entitled to appoint two directors.

A quorum of four directors and a simple majority of those present is required to make decisions. The other shareholders frequently call board meetings at short notice and make decisions in the absence of entity A's representative. Entity A has requested financial information from entity B, but this information has not been provided. Entity A's representative has attended board meetings, but suggestions for items to be included on the agenda have been ignored and the other directors oppose any suggestions made by entity A.

Despite the fact that the investor owns 20 per cent of the voting rights and has representation on the board, the existence of other shareholders holding a significant proportion of the voting rights prevent the investor from exercising significant influence. Whilst it appears that entity A should have the power to participate in the financial and operating policy decisions, the other shareholders frustrate entity A's efforts and are preventing entity A from actually having any influence.

In this situation, entity B would not be an associate of entity A.

In Example 20.1, the other investors were able to achieve a majority vote by working together. This enabled them to actively oppose entity A's attempts to exercise influence and thereby removed its power. However, the standard says that a substantial or majority ownership by another investor does not necessarily preclude an investor from having significant influence (IAS 28 para 6).

An associate relationship can also arise where an entity has more than a 50 per cent interest in another entity, but does not control the operating and financial policies of the undertaking. Figure 20.1 provides an example of this.

> **3 Developments in the relations with partner of the group in its subsidiary Wahaha in China (extract)**
>
> **Accounting Treatment**
> As a result of the development of the events since June 30, 2007, the continued restricted access to the financial information and the lack of any concrete development in the second half of 2007, the Group considers that it is no longer able to exercise its control over the Subsidiaries. Nevertheless, the Group considers that it exercises a significant influence over the Subsidiaries, notably due to its holding in the capital and its presence at the board meetings, and has therefore accounted for the holdings in the Subsidiaries under the equity method as from July 1, 2007.

Figure 20.1 Associate relationship where investor has more than a 50 per cent interest but no control

Source: Groupe Danone Annual Report 2007.

On the contrary, an entity having less than a 20 per cent interest in an associate can still have significant influence through representation on key decision-making bodies. An example of such a situation is given in Figure 20.2.

20.1.2 The equity method

IAS 28 requires that an investment in an associate should normally be accounted for using the 'equity method'. The equity method is defined as '*a method of accounting whereby the investment is initially recognised at cost and adjusted thereafter for the post-acquisition change in the investor's share of the investee*'. The definition goes on to state that the income statement of the investor should include the investor's share of the investee's income or loss. In general, equity accounting should be used whether or not the investor also has subsidiaries and so presents consolidated financial statements.

> **Notes to the accounts (extract)**
> **19 Investments (extract)**
>
> The Group accounts for its investment in Iberia as an associate although the Group holds less than 20 per cent of the issued share capital as the Group has the ability to exercise significant influence over the investment due to the Group's voting power (both through its equity holding and its representation on key decision-making committees) and the nature of the commercial relationships with Iberia. On November 15, 2006 the Group acquired the minority interest held by American Airlines in BA & AA Holdings Ltd, the subsidiary that holds the interest in Iberia (see note 34).
>
> In February 2008, the Group purchased 28.7 million additional shares in Iberia at an average price of €2.34 per share (£54 million), taking its holding to 13.15 per cent (2007: 9.95 per cent). The acquisition of additional shares in Iberia resulted in goodwill of £9 million, which has been reflected in investment in associates.

Figure 20.2 Less than a 20 per cent interest but significant influence

Source: British Airways Plc Annual Report 2007–8.

Application of the equity method

Under the equity method of accounting, the investment made by the investing company is recorded initially at cost. This will include goodwill if the cost of the investment is greater than the investor's share of the fair value of the investee's identifiable net assets. However, any goodwill included in the cost of an investment accounted for by the equity method is not separately recognised (see Figure 20.2 above). Nor is it separately tested for impairment. But the amount paid for goodwill should be determined in case there is a negative goodwill. Negative goodwill should be recognised as income in the investor's income statement.

In subsequent years, the required accounting treatment is as follows:

(a) The investor's share of the investee's profit or loss for the year is recognised in the investor's income statement and is either added to or subtracted from the carrying amount of the investment in the investor's balance sheet.

(b) Any dividends received from the investee are subtracted from the carrying amount of the investment.

(c) The carrying amount of the investment is also adjusted for the investor's share of any changes in the investee's equity (such as revaluation surpluses) that have not passed through the investee's income statement. The investor's share of such items should be recognised in other comprehensive income.

It is important to grasp the difference between the equity method which is used in relation to associates and the acquisition method which is used in relation to subsidiaries. With the equity method, only *the investor's share* of the associate's income or loss is shown in the investor's income statement (or consolidated income statement) and this is shown as a single figure. With the acquisition method, *all* of the subsidiary's sales, cost of sales, expenses etc. are incorporated line by line into the consolidated income statement and then the profit attributable to the non-controlling interest (NCI) (if any) is subtracted.

Similarly, under the equity method, an investment in an associate is shown in the investor's balance sheet (or consolidated balance sheet) as a single non-current asset. With the acquisition method, all of the subsidiary's assets and liabilities are incorporated line by line into the consolidated balance sheet. Any NCI is then shown in equity.

Example 20.2

Equity method

Alpha plc is the parent of a group of companies. On 1 January 2009, Alpha plc acquired 25 per cent of the ordinary share capital of Beta Ltd at a cost of EUR 200,000. This was precisely equal to 25 per cent of the fair value of Beta Ltd's identifiable net assets on that date. During the year ended 31 December 2009, Beta Ltd made a profit after tax of EUR 84,000 and paid an ordinary dividend of EUR 54,000. Explain how these transactions should be reflected in the consolidated financial statements of Alpha plc for the year ended 31 December 2009.

In the consolidated income statement of Alpha plc, 'share of profit of associates' is shown as EUR 21,000 (25% × EUR 84,000). IAS 1 (revised) – *Presentation of Financial Statements* suggests that this amount should be shown just before the group's pretax profit.

The investment is recognised initially at cost. The group's share of the associate's profit is added and the dividend of EUR 13,500 (25% × 54,000) is deducted. So in the consolidated balance sheet, the figure for 'investments in associates' is EUR 207,500 (200,000 + 21,000 – 13,500). This is shown as a non-current asset.

Example 20.3

Equity method and consolidated financial statements

Gamma plc is the parent of several wholly-owned subsidiaries. On 1 July 2008, Gamma plc acquired 30 per cent of the ordinary shares of Delta Ltd at a cost of EUR 140,000. Delta Ltd had retained earnings of EUR 100,000 on that date and all of its assets and liabilities were carried at fair value. Delta Ltd has issued no shares since Gamma plc acquired its 30 per cent holding.

The draft consolidated financial statements of Gamma plc for the year ended 30 June 2009 (before applying the equity method) and the financial statements of Delta Ltd for that year are shown in Tables 20.1–20.6.

Prepare a consolidated income statement for the year ended 30 June 2009 and a consolidated balance sheet at that date. Also prepare an extract from the consolidated statement of changes in equity, showing the changes in the group's retained earnings.

Delta Ltd is an associate of Gamma plc. The cost of the investment was EUR 140,000 and the fair value of 30% of the net assets of Delta Ltd on 1 July 2008 was 30% × EUR 300,000 = EUR 90,000. Therefore, there is a goodwill of EUR 50,000. This is not shown separately, but it was necessary to do this calculation so as to be sure that there was no negative goodwill.

Table 20.1 Income statements for the year ended 30 June 2009

	Gamma plc and subsidiaries €000	Delta Ltd €000
Sales revenue	1,860	640
Cost of sales	(680)	(340)
Gross profit	1,180	300
Operating expenses	(430)	(210)
Operating profit	750	90
Dividend received from Delta Ltd	12	–
Profit before tax	762	90
Taxation	(150)	(30)
Net profit for the year	612	60

Table 20.2 Balance sheets as at 30 June 2009

	Gamma plc and subsidiaries €000	Delta Ltd €000
Assets		
Non-current assets		
Property, plant and equipment	1,020	310
Investment in Delta Ltd, at cost	140	
	1,160	
Current assets	450	80
Total assets	1,610	390
Equity		
Share capital	600	200
Retained earnings	780	120
	1,380	320
Liabilities		
Current liabilities	230	70
Total equity and liabilities	1,610	390

Table 20.3 Statements of changes in equity (retained earnings only) for the year ended 30 June 2009

	Gamma plc and subsidiaries €000	Delta Ltd €000
Balance at 30 June 2008	408	100
Profit for the year	612	60
	1,020	160
Dividends paid	(240)	(40)
Balance at 30 June 2009	780	120

The investment in associate at 30 June 2009 is EUR 140,000 + (30% × EUR 60,000) − EUR 12,000 = EUR 146,000. The dividend received of EUR 12,000 should be removed from the group income statement and replaced by the group's EUR 18,000 share of the associate's profit for the year. The group retained earnings increase by EUR 6,000 in consequence. The final consolidated financial statements are as shown in the following tables.

Table 20.4 Consolidated income statement for the year ended 30 June 2009

	€000
Sales revenue	1,860
Cost of sales	(680)
Gross profit	1,180
Operating expenses	(430)
Operating profit	750
Share of profit of associate	18
Profit before tax	768
Taxation	(150)
Net profit for the year	618

Table 20.5 Consolidated balance sheet as at 30 June 2009

	€000
Assets	
Non-current assets	
Property, plant and equipment	1,020
Investment in associate	146
	1,166
Current assets	450
Total assets	1,616
Equity	
Share capital	600
Retained earnings	786
	1,386
Liabilities	
Current liabilities	230
Total equity and liabilities	1,616

Table 20.6 Consolidated statement of changes in equity (retained earnings only) for the year ended 30 June 2009

	€000
Balance at 30 June 2008	408
Profit for the year	618
	1,026
Dividends paid	(240)
Balance at 30 June 2009	786

Upstream and downstream transactions

'Upstream' and 'downstream' transactions are transactions between an investor and an associate. An example of an upstream transaction is the sale of goods by the associate to the investor. An example of a downstream transaction is the sale of goods by the investor to the associate. IAS 28 requires that unrealised profits resulting from such transactions should be eliminated to the extent of the investor's interest in the associate. This differs from the IAS 27 requirement that unrealised profits on intragroup transactions should be fully eliminated, whether or not the subsidiary concerned is wholly-owned.

Accounting entries which eliminate the unrealised profits resulting from upstream and downstream transactions are as follows:

(a) **Upstream**. In the investor's income statement, the unrealised profit on the transaction is deducted from the investor's share of profit from associates. This automatically reduces the figure for the investment in associates shown in the investor's balance sheet.

(b) **Downstream**. The unrealised profit on the transaction is subtracted from the investor's gross profit (usually by increasing cost of sales) and is also deducted from the figure for the investment in associates shown in the investor's balance sheet.

Example 20.4

Upstream and downstream transactions

An investor company has a 25 per cent interest in an associate. During the year ended 31 December 2009, the investor bought goods from the associate on which the associate earned a profit of EUR 20,000. One-half of these goods remained unsold by the investor at the year-end.

(a) Calculate the unrealised profit on this transaction and explain how this is eliminated from the investor's financial statements.

(b) Explain how the required accounting treatment would differ if the goods had been sold by the investor to the associate rather than the other way around.

(a) The unrealised profit is EUR 2,500 (25% × 50% × EUR 20,000). In the investor's income statement, the share of profit from associate is reduced by EUR 2,500. In the investor's balance sheet, the investment in associate is reduced by EUR 2,500.

(b) In the investor's income statement, the cost of sales figure is increased by EUR 2,500. In the investor's balance sheet, the investment in associate is reduced by EUR 2,500.

Losses of an associate

As stated earlier in this chapter, the investor's share of an associate's loss is recognised in the investor's income statement and is deducted from the carrying amount of the investment in the investor's balance sheet. However, if the investor's share of an associate's loss is greater than the carrying amount of the investment, that amount is reduced to zero and the investor should normally recognise no further losses. But further losses should be recognised if the investor has incurred legal or constructive obligations on behalf of the associate. This situation might occur if the investor has guaranteed the associate's debts.

If the carrying amount of the investment is reduced to zero but the associate then eventually returns to profit, the investor should not resume recognition of its share of the associate's profits until after those profits have cancelled out all the losses which were not being recognised whilst the carrying amount of the investment was zero.

Impairment losses

Any goodwill which is included in the carrying amount of an investment in an associate is not separately recognised and is not separately tested for impairment. However, the entire carrying amount of the investment should be tested for impairment whenever there is an indication that impairment may have occurred. IAS 39 – *Financial Instruments: Recognition and Measurement* sets out a list of such indications. As usual, an impairment test involves comparing the carrying amount of the investment with the higher of its value in use and its fair value less costs to sell.

Reporting dates and accounting policies

IAS 28 specifies rules with regard to reporting dates and accounting policies that are similar to their IAS 27 counterparts. In summary:

(a) If the reporting date of an investor and an associate are different, the associate should prepare additional financial statements for the use of the investor, using the same reporting date as the investor. If this is impracticable, the financial statements of the associate should be adjusted to take account of any significant transactions or events between the associate's reporting date and the investor's reporting date. In any case, the difference between the reporting date of the associate and that of the investor should not exceed three months.

(b) The investor's financial statements should be prepared using uniform accounting policies. If an associate uses different accounting policies from those adopted by the investor, its financial statements should be adjusted to conform with the investor's accounting policies before the equity method is applied.

20.2   Interests in joint ventures

An entity may enter into a joint venture with another party for many reasons. The joint venture partners may have complementary skills, it may be necessary to share the risk of a project, the project may benefit from economies of scale if two or more venturers are involved or the size of the project may be beyond a single entity's capabilities. The purpose of joint ventures may be to share costs or there may be a profit motive. Joint ventures may appear in unincorporated or incorporated form. In its simplest form, a joint venture need not result in the creation of a separate entity at all. 'Strategic alliances' in which companies agree to work together to promote each other's products or services may also be considered joint ventures.

The following are examples of joint ventures:

- shared distribution network;
- consortia to jointly produce products (for example, aircraft and ships);
- property development;
- property management;
- property investment;
- pharmaceutical companies sharing research;
- shared use of an asset (such as an oil field or pipeline or football teams sharing a ground).

Under IAS 31, jointly controlled entities are accounted for using either proportionate consolidation or equity accounting. Currently, the IASB has a short-term project with the objective of removing the option for proportionate consolidation for jointly controlled entities. This would remove one of the main differences between IAS 31 and US GAAP.

20.2.1 Definition of a joint venture and joint control

IAS 31 para 3 defines a joint venture in the following terms:

> *A joint venture is a contractual arrangement whereby two or more parties undertake an economic activity that is subject to joint control.*

This definition is not restricted by legal structure but, as can be seen from the definition, there must be a contractual arrangement giving joint control. Joint control is defined in the standard as follows:

> *Joint control is the contractually agreed sharing of control over an economic activity, and exists only when the strategic financial and operating decisions relating to the activity require the unanimous consent of the parties sharing control (the venturers).*

This definition can be contrasted with 'control', which is defined in IAS 31 para 3 as:

> *. . . the power to govern the financial and operating policies of an economic activity so as to obtain benefits from it.*

IAS 31 uses the term *economic activity* rather than entity. This is because joint ventures take many different forms and structures, and the standard does not limit itself to only those joint arrangements housed in a legal entity.

In this definition of joint control the standard requires the strategic financial and operating decisions relating to the activity to be agreed upon unanimously by the venturers. The standard does not give examples of the type of strategic decisions that require unanimous consent, but the decisions would include matters such as:

- issuing shares;
- capital expenditure;
- significant asset disposals;
- approving a business plan;
- changing the strategic direction of the business such as changes in products, markets and activities;

- remuneration policy;
- major financing;
- distributions and investment;
- appointment, revocation of governing bodies' members.

A joint venture agreement must require unanimity for these important decisions of strategy, but not for lesser issues that arise in the day-to-day management of the business. It is impractical for the venturers to unanimously agree to every decision required in carrying out an economic activity. Consideration should be given to the nature of the decisions that are subject to unanimous consent. To qualify as strategic financial and operating decisions, rights should be over substantive operating and financial decisions in the ordinary course of business.

The key characteristic of a joint venture is an economic activity in which two or more parties exercise, by contract, joint control. This does not mean that every venturer must have an equal financial interest in the venture. Venturers may have different interests in the net assets and profit and loss of a venture, but still be equal in terms of exercising joint control.

An example of a disclosure concerning the determination of the existence of joint control is given in Figure 20.3.

---

2. Summary of consolidation and accounting policies (extract)

Joint ventures
Millicom determines the existence of joint control by reference to the joint venture agreements, articles of association, structures and voting protocols of the Boards of Directors of those ventures.

Figure 20.3 Determining the existence of joint control

Source: Millicom International Cellular SA Annual Report 2008.

20.2.2 Forms of joint venture

Joint ventures may take many different forms and structures. IAS 31 identifies three broad types of joint venture:

- jointly controlled operations;
- jointly controlled assets;
- jointly controlled entities.

Whatever their form, however, all joint ventures share the common characteristics that two or more venturers are bound by a contractual arrangement that establishes joint control (IAS 31 para 7).

Jointly controlled operations and assets

Jointly controlled operations or jointly controlled assets are somewhat similar in nature to jointly controlled entities in that two or more participants will form them and there will be an agreement covering the arrangement. But they differ in that these joint ventures do not involve the establishment of a corporation, partnership, entity, or a financial structure that is separate from the venturers themselves.

The standard notes that some joint ventures involve the use of the assets and other resources of the venturers themselves. This is a jointly controlled operation whereby:

> *Each venturer uses its own property, plant and equipment and carries its own inventories. It also incurs its own expenses and liabilities and raises its own finance, which represent its own obligations. The joint venture activities may be carried out by the venturer's employees alongside the venturer's similar activities. The joint venture agreement usually provides a means by which the revenue from the sale of the joint product and any expenses incurred in common are shared among the venturers.*

> (IAS 31 para 13)

Therefore, in a joint operation each venturer uses its own resources and carries out its own part of a joint operation separately from the activities of the other venturer(s). Each venturer owns and controls its own resources that it uses in the joint operation, and incurs its own expenses and raises its own financing. The contractual arrangement governing the operation would be expected to specify how the goods or service outputs of the joint operation, and any revenues from their sale, and any common expenses, are to be shared among the venturers.

Such an operation is one when two or more venturers combine their operations, resources and expertise in order to manufacture, market and distribute jointly a particular product. Different parts of the manufacturing process are carried out by each of the venturers (IAS 31 para 14). As an example, a number of venturers may carry out different parts of a manufacturing process, each using their own resources and expertise in order to manufacture, market and distribute a product jointly. An example is a consortium of aerospace companies jointly manufacturing an aircraft. They carry responsibility for different areas of expertise such as:

- manufacturing engines;
- manufacturing fuselage and wings;
- aerodynamics.

They share the revenues from the sale of aircraft and jointly incur expenses. The revenues and common costs are shared as contractually agreed among themselves. Venturers incur their own separate costs such as labour costs, manufacturing costs, supplies, inventory of unused parts and work in progress.

The standard notes that some joint ventures involve joint control, and often joint ownership, of one or more assets contributed to, or acquired for the purpose of, a joint venture and dedicated to the purposes of a joint venture. This is a jointly controlled asset whereby:

> *The assets are used to obtain benefits for the venturers. Each venturer may take a share of the output from the assets and each bears an agreed share of the expenses incurred.*

> (IAS 31 para 18)

This type of joint venture involves the joint ownership of a single asset that is not a separate entity (IAS 31 para 19).

Many activities in the oil, gas and mineral extraction industries involve jointly controlled assets (IAS 31 para 20). A common example is where two oil companies

- Any expenses that it has incurred in respect of its interest in the venture, for example those related to financing the venturer's interest in the assets and selling its share of the output (IAS 31 paras 21 and 22).

The share to be accounted for is determined by the contractual agreement between the venturers that governs the venture. The contractual agreement will typically specify the quantities and timing of the physical output. The venturer should apply its own accounting policies developed under IAS 18 – *Revenue*, in order to account for its share.

A venturer may appear to have an 'intragroup' balance with its jointly controlled operation or asset. In principle, a jointly controlled operation or asset is not a separate legal entity so there should be no assets or liabilities in the venturer's accounts in respect of any of its own 'intragroup' balances. In a simple scenario where each venturer has contributed equal amounts to the jointly controlled operation or asset then the venturer's share of the total balance in the joint controlled operation's or asset's books (if any) will equal the asset in the venturer's books and these balances will then cancel with the result that there is nothing to be shown in the venturer's financial statements. This is consistent with the principle that there should be no intragroup balance with the jointly controlled operation (or asset) as it is not a separate entity from the venturer.

Example 20.5

Transactions with jointly controlled operations

Two entities decide to undertake a joint road construction project. They agree to supply different assets and staff to the jointly controlled operation. One of the venturers has opened a separate bank account for the purposes of the joint operation. The venturers charge rental for their plant used in the project to the bank account and also have an agreed staff cost per hour, which is also charged to that account. No other costs are permitted to be charged to that account. The venturers fund the account and invoice the customer in their joint names. Any surplus is shared 50/50.

The joint operation transactions that need to be reflected in each venturer's accounts are not a straight share of the transactions that go through the joint operation's bank account. Each venturer accounts for the costs it has borne itself. Although the venturer is charging a rental to the joint operation for the use of its plant, the plant is already accounted for as a fixed asset in the venturer's balance sheet and its profit and loss account will already bear a normal depreciation charge for the asset's use. The rental charged to the joint operation needs to be eliminated. Similarly, the venturer is charging its actual staff costs in its income statement, so it will need to eliminate any charge made to the joint operation on a different basis. The joint operation will bill its customers for the work undertaken by the venture and it would be appropriate for the venturer to recognise its share (50 per cent in this case) in its revenue. Arrangements might also be in place between the venturers whereby any costs incurred in excess of a predetermined budget are in part passed on to the other venturer. Such arrangements would be set out in the joint venture agreement. Therefore, it might be necessary to book an additional charge or credit if the actual costs incurred by the venturer are different from the costs under the joint venture agreement. Consequently, the venturer may in part be funding the costs of its joint operation partner (or *vice versa*).

Example 20.6

Jointly controlled operation

Entity A and entity B have entered into a joint operation to produce products for sale. Entity A manufactures the product and provides the day-to-day management of the production. Entity A makes a 10 per cent margin on the products it sells to the joint operation. Entity B identified the opportunity and contributed EUR 80,000. Entity A contributed EUR 20,000. Profits are shared 50/50.

During the joint operation's first year, entity A incurred costs of EUR 140,000 in respect of work in progress, of which EUR 100,000 was charged to the joint operation at EUR 110,000. The joint operation made product sales to third parties of EUR 80,000 and the cost of those sales in the joint operation was EUR 60,000. There are no third party debtors or creditors at the year-end as all transactions have been settled.

Table 20.7 Entity A's adjusted balance sheet

	Entity A €000	JO €000	50% JO €000	Adjustments €000	Entity A adjusted €000
Balance sheet					
Contribution	20.0	–	–	(20.0)[c]	
Finished products and work in progress					
Costs	140.0	110.0	55.0	(55.0)[a]	140.0
Transfer to cost of sales	(100.0)	(60.0)	(30.0)	(50.0)[b]	(80.0)
	60.0	50.0	25	(25)	60.0
Cash/loan	(50.0)	70.0	35	–	(15.0)
	10.0	120.0	60.0	(25)	(45.0)
Liability to entity B	–	100.0	50.0	(20.0)[c]	30.0
Net profit	10.0	20.0	10.0	(5.0)	15.0
	10.0	120.0	60.0	(25.0)	45.0
Income statement					
Sales	110.0	80.0	40.0	(55.0)[a]	95
Cost of sales	(100.0)	(60.0)	(30.0)	50.0[b]	(80.0)
Net profit[d]	10.0	20.0	10.0	(5)	15

Notes

(a) Half of entity A's sales have in effect been made to entity B and these can continue to be recognised by entity A. But EUR 55,000 of entity A's sales need to be eliminated and replaced by its share of the sales made by the joint operation (that is, EUR 40,000).

(b) Similarly, half of the entity A's cost of sales relates to sale made in effect to entity B, the other half (that is, EUR 50,000) relate to the goods sold to the joint operation at a profit margin of 10 per cent and these need to be eliminated. The balance of inventory of EUR 60,000 is made up of entity A's finished products and work in progress of EUR 40,000 together with the share outstanding in the joint operation of EUR 25,000, less the profit element included in this inventory of EUR 5,000, which has been eliminated.

(c) There is a disparity in the amount of capital contributed by both of the parties to the joint operation. In effect this means that entity A has an obligation under the operation to fund part of the repayment of entity B's contribution out of its share of the resources of the joint operation. This obligation is likely to be settled eventually out of entity A's share of the cash resources of the joint operation.

(d) Taxation is ignored.

Jointly controlled entities

A venturer's interest in a jointly controlled entity should be recognised using proportionate consolidation or the equity method. The equity method is the same method as used when accounting for an investment in an associate (see section 20.1.2). Examples of the accounting policies of companies that use the equity method to account for jointly controlled entities are given in Figure 20.4 (a) and (b).

Proportionate consolidation is an accounting method whereby *'a venturer's share of each of the assets, liabilities, income and expenses of a jointly controlled entity is combined line by line with similar items in the venturer's financial statements or reported as separate line items in the venturer's financial statements'* (IAS 31 para 3). The consolidation procedure is similar to that which is used when preparing group accounts but differs in that only the venturer's share of the assets etc. of the jointly controlled entity are brought into account. This means that no minority interest is shown in either the income statement or the balance sheet.

In general, an interest in a jointly controlled entity should be accounted for by one of these two methods, regardless of whether or not the venturer also has subsidiaries and so presents consolidated financial statements. However, since the publication of IAS 31 there has been a change in perspective. The IASB has proposed in its Exposure Draft (ED) 9 – *Joint Arrangements* to remove the option of proportionate consolidation for jointly-controlled entities. The likely removal of this accounting option may encourage entities using IAS 31 for the first time to adopt the equity method for their jointly-controlled entities as this would remove the need to change from proportionate consolidation to equity accounting after the option is removed.

(a)

B. SUMMARY OF SIGNIFICANT ACCOUNTING POLICIES (extract)
B.I. Basis of consolidation

The consolidated financial statements include the accounts of sanofi-aventis and subsidiaries controlled by sanofi-aventis, using the full consolidation method. The existence of effectively exercisable or convertible potential voting rights is taken into account in determining whether control exists.

Joint ventures are accounted for by the equity method in accordance with the option in IAS 31 (Interests in Joint Ventures).

Source: Sanofi-Aventis S.A., Annual Report 2007.

(b)
Accounting policies (extract)
B. Basis of consolidation

The consolidated financial statements incorporate the financial statements of the Company and its subsidiaries, together with a share of the results, assets and liabilities of jointly controlled entities (joint ventures) and associates using the equity method of accounting, where the investment is carried at cost plus post-acquisition changes in the share of net assets of the joint venture, less any provision for impairment.

A subsidiary is defined as an entity controlled by the Company Control is achieved where the Company has the power to govern the financial and operating policies of an entity so as to obtain benefits from its activities. A joint venture is an entity established to engage in economic activity, which the Company jointly controls with its fellow venturers. An associate is an entity which is neither a subsidiary nor a joint venture, but over which the Company has significant influence. Losses in excess of the consolidated interest in joint ventures are not recognised, except where the Company or its subsidiaries have made a commitment to make good those losses.

Where necessary, adjustments are made to bring the accounting policies used under UK generally accepted accounting principles (UK GAAP), US generally accepted accounting principles (US GAAP) or other framework used in the individual financial statements of the Company, subsidiaries and joint ventures into line with those used by the Company in its consolidated financial statements under IFRS. Inter-company transactions are eliminated.

The results of subsidiaries and joint ventures acquired or disposed of during the year are included in the consolidated income statement from the effective date of acquisition or up to the effective date of disposal, as appropriate.

Acquisitions are accounted for using the purchase method, where the purchase price is allocated to assets and liabilities on a fair value basis and the remainder recognised as goodwill.

Source: National Grid Annual Report 2008.

Figure 20.4 Equity method for jointly controlled entities

Application of proportionate consolidation

Venturers that use proportionate consolidation to account for interests in jointly controlled entities may use either of two reporting formats. These are:

(a) **Line-by-line.** If this format is used, venturers combine their share of each of the assets, liabilities, income and expenses of the jointly controlled entity with similar items, line by line, in their own financial statements.

Transactions between a venturer and a jointly controlled entity

When a venturer sells assets to a jointly controlled entity, any unrealised profit on the sale should be recognised only to the extent that it is attributable to the interests of the other venturers. For instance, if the venturer has a 30 per cent interest in the jointly controlled entity, 30 per cent of the profit on a sale of assets to that entity should not be recognised until the assets are sold on to a third party. The remaining 70 per cent of the profit should be recognised immediately. But when a venturer sells assets to a jointly controlled entity at a loss, the full amount of that loss should be recognised immediately if the sale provides evidence of a reduction in the net realisable value of current assets or an impairment loss (IAS 31 para 48).

When a venturer buys assets from a jointly controlled entity, the venturer should not recognise its share of the entity's profit on the sale until the assets are sold on to a third party. But the venturer's share of any losses arising on such transactions should be recognised immediately if they provide evidence of a reduction in the net realisable value of current assets or an impairment loss (IAS 31 para 49).

An example of an accounting policy that describes the accounting treatment for trading transactions with jointly controlled entities is given in Figure 20.5.

---

2. Summary of consolidation and accounting policies (extract)

Joint ventures
The Group recognizes the portion of gains or losses on the sale of assets by the Group to the joint venture that is attributable to the other parties in the joint venture. The Group does not recognize its share of profits or losses that results from the purchase of assets by the Group from the joint venture until it resells the assets to an independent party. However, if a loss on the transaction provides evidence of a reduction in the net realizable value of current assets or an impairment loss, the loss is recognized immediately.

Figure 20.5 Trading transactions with jointly controlled entities
Source: Millicom International Cellular SA Annual Report 2008.

Summary

- An associate is an entity over which the investor has significant influence (i.e. the power to participate in the financial and operating policy decisions of the investee). This will usually be the case if the investor owns at least 20 per cent of the investee's voting power.

- An investment in an associate should be accounted for by the equity method. The investment is initially recognised at cost and is then adjusted for the post-acquisition change in the investor's share of the associate's net assets. The investor's income statement shows the investor's share of the associate's income or loss.

- Unrealised profits resulting from upstream and downstream transactions between an investor and an associate should be eliminated to the extent of the investor's interest in the associate.

- A joint venture is a contractual arrangement whereby two or more venturers share joint control over an economic activity. IAS 31 distinguishes between three categories of joint venture. These are jointly controlled operations, jointly controlled assets and jointly controlled entities.

- The accounting method for jointly controlled operations effectively treats the operations as if the venturer conducted them independently. Consequently, a venturer accounts for the assets it controls and the liabilities and expenses it incurs independently. The accounting entries are booked in the venturer's own financial statements and, therefore, they flow through into the consolidated financial statements should the venturer prepare them. No further adjustments or consolidation procedures are required. The venturer is also required to account for the share of the income it earns from the sale of the product by the jointly controlled operation; the share being determined in accordance with the contractual agreement. Therefore, each venturer accounts for its interest in the arrangement in its own financial statements.

- The accounting method for a jointly controlled asset apportions to each venturer the venture's share of revenues, expenses, assets and liabilities. The venturer recognises its share in its own financial statements and its accounting records. Consequently, as for jointly controlled operations, the accounting entries flow through into the consolidated financial statements, should the venturer prepare them, and no further adjustments or consolidation procedures are required.

- An interest in a jointly controlled entity may be accounted for by either the equity method or proportionate consolidation. The option of proportionate consolidation is expected to be removed fairly soon.

Research and references

The IASB documents relevant for this chapter are:

- IAS 1 (revised) – *Presentation of Financial Statements*.
- IAS 27 – *Consolidated and Separate Financial Statements*.
- IAS 28 – *Investments in Associates*.
- IAS 31 – *Interests in Joint Venturers*.
- *Improvements to IFRSs*, May 2008.
- Exposure Draft (ED) 9: *Joint Arrangements*.

The following are examples of books, research and discussion papers that take the issues of this chapter further:

- Alexander, D., Britton, A. and Jorissen, A. (2007) *International Financial Reporting and Analysis*, 3rd edn. Thomson, Chapters 25 and 26.
- Elliott, B. and Elliott, J. (2009) *Financial Accounting and Reporting*, 13th edn. Financial Times-Prentice Hall, Chapter 23.
- Epstein, B.J. and Jermakowicz, E.K. (2009) *IFRS 2009: Interpretation and Application of International Accounting and Financial Reporting Standards*. Wiley, Chapter 10.
- PricewaterhouseCoopers (2009) *IFRS Manual of Accounting – 2010. Global Guide to International Financial Reporting Standards*. CCH, Chapters 27 and 28.
- Sutton, T. (2004) *Corporate Financial Accounting and Reporting*, 2nd edn. Financial Times-Prentice Hall, Chapter 14.

directors to the board of B. A intends to hold the investment for a significant period of time. The entities prepare their financial statements to 31 December each year. The abbreviated balance sheet of B on 31 December 2009 follows:

Sundry net assets	€6m
Issued share capital	€1m
Share premium	€2m
Retained earnings	€3m

B had made no new issues of shares since the acquisition of the investment by A. The recoverable amount of net assets of B is deemed to be EUR 7m. The fair value of the net assets at the date of acquisition was EUR 5m.

What amount should be shown in A's consolidated balance sheets as at 31 December 2009 for the investment in B?

20.8 Accounting for an associate and a subsidiary

The balance sheets of Fiera Ltd, Cole Ltd and Jong Ltd as at 31 July 2009 are as follows:

	Fiera Ltd	Cole Ltd	Jong Ltd
Assets	€000	€000	€000
Non-current assets			
Property, plant and equipment	5,160	740	560
Investment in Cole Ltd	820		
Investment in Jong Ltd	180		
	6,160		
Current assets	2,300	440	340
Total assets	8,460	1,180	900
Equity			
Share capital	2,000	200	160
Retained Earnings	4,840	760	560
	6,840	960	720
Liabilities			
Current liabilities	1,620	220	180
Total equity and liabilities	8,460	1,180	900

Additional information:

(a) On 31 July 2006, Fiera Ltd paid EUR 820,000 to acquire 90 per cent of the share capital of Cole Ltd. The retained earnings of Cole Ltd on that date were EUR 440,000. The company's issued share capital has not changed since Fiera Ltd acquired its holding. On 31 July 2006, the fair value of the non-current assets of Cole Ltd was EUR 160,000 higher than their book value. This valuation has not been reflected in the books of Cole Ltd.

(b) On 31 July 2008, Fiera Ltd paid EUR 180,000 to acquire 25 per cent of the share capital of Jong Ltd. The retained earnings of Jong Ltd on that date were EUR 480,000 and all of its assets and liabilities were carried at fair value. The company's issued share capital has not changed since Fiera Ltd acquired its holding.

(c) There have been no impairment losses.

Prepare a consolidated balance sheet of Fiera Ltd as at 31 July 2009.

20.9 Accounting for an associate

In 2005, Torn Ltd paid EUR 280,000 to acquire 40 per cent of the share capital of Acre Ltd. At that time, the retained earnings of Acre Ltd were EUR 200,000 and all of its assets and liabilities were carried at fair value. Neither company has issued any shares since this acquisition occurred. The draft financial statements of the two companies for the year ended 30 September 2009 are as follows:

Income statements for the year ended 30 September 2009 (extract)

	Torn Ltd	Acre Ltd
	€000	€000
Operating profit	1,300	280
Dividend received from Acre Ltd	40	–
Profit before tax	1,340	280
Taxation	340	380
Net profit for the year	1,000	220

Balance sheets as at 30 September 2009

	Torn Ltd	Acre Ltd
	€000	€000
Assets		
Non-current assets		
Property, plant and equipment	3,200	800
Investment in Acre Ltd, at cost	280	
	3,480	
Current assets	1,560	580
	5,040	1,380
Equity		
Share capital	2,000	400
Retained earnings (1,980 + 100)	2,420	640
	4,420	1,040
Liabilities		
Current liabilities (940 + 1/3 of 360)	620	340
	5,040	1,380

Statement of changes in equity (retained earnings only) for the year ended 30 September 2009

	Torn Ltd	Acre Ltd
	€000	€000
Balance at 30 September 2008	1,420	520
Profit for the year	1,000	220
Dividends paid	–	(100)
Balance at 30 September 2009	2,420	640

During the year ended 30 September 2009, Torn Ltd bought goods from Acre Ltd for EUR 60,000 which cost Acre Ltd EUR 40,000. One-quarter of these goods were unsold by Torn Ltd at 30 September 2009.

Prepare the financial statements of Torn Ltd for the year ended 30 September 2009.

Glossary

This glossary primarily represents the terminology and language used by the International Accounting Standards Board. However, there are numerous cross-references to terminology commonly used in the United States and the United Kingdom.

Terms used in an entry that are defined elsewhere in the glossary are shown in small capitals.

A

AAA See AMERICAN ACCOUNTING ASSOCIATION.

ACCA See ASSOCIATION OF CHARTERED CERTIFIED ACCOUNTANTS.

Accelerated depreciation DEPRECIATION at a faster rate than an even allocation of cost over an asset's expected life. This is prevalent in many European countries, usually as tax concessions intended to encourage investment in certain class of fixed assets or regions.

Account See ACCOUNTS.

Accountability See STEWARDSHIP.

Accounting Process of identifying, measuring and communicating information to permit informed judgements and decisions by users of the information. It also relates to the preparation, presentation and interpretation of financial statements.

Accounting convention Another way of referring to the fundamental conceptual rules of accounting. See ACCOUNTING PRINCIPLES.

Accounting equation Mathematical representation of a transaction under the DOUBLE ENTRY system. The total of assets and expenses (all debits) equal the total of liabilities, capital and revenues (all credits).

Accounting period See FINANCIAL YEAR.

Accounting policies The specific principles, bases, conventions, rules and practices adopted by an entity in preparing and presenting its financial statements.

Accounting principles Fundamental rules or conventions as to how assets and liabilities should be measured or valued and accounting statements prepared.

Accounting Principles Board (APB)   APB was set up in 1959 in the USA and was replaced in 1973 by the FINANCIAL ACCOUNTING STANDARDS BOARD. It issued 31 opinions and four statements which mostly have not been replaced and therefore they are still an integral part of the GENERALLY ACCEPTED ACCOUNTING PRINCIPLES.

Accounting profit   The profit or loss for a period before deducting income tax expense.

Accounting records   See BOOKS.

Accounting standards   Technical accounting rules of valuation, measurement, recognition and disclosure. Each country today has its own denomination (i.e. UK FRS, US GAAP, IAS/IFRS, etc.).

Accounts   Records of the BOOKKEEPING entries dealing with a particular item. In the DOUBLE ENTRY system there is a DEBIT side (left) and a CREDIT side (right). Accounts also mean financial statements in the UK terminology.

Accounts payable   See TRADE AND OTHER PAYABLES.

Accounts receivable   See TRADE AND OTHER RECEIVABLES.

Accruals   See ACCRUED EXPENSES and ACCRUED REVENUES.

Accrual basis of accounting   The effects of transactions and events are recognised when they occur (and not as cash and cash equivalents are received or paid) and they are recorded in the accounting records and reported in the financial statements of the periods to which they relate. For example, accountancy fees or the cost of electricity consumed in an accounting period should be accounted for as a charge in the income statement and as liabilities in the balance sheet even though these costs have not been paid and invoices have not yet been received.

Accrued expenses   EXPENSES related to an accounting period and outstanding or unpaid at the end of it. Accrued expenses are paid or settled subsequent to the accounting period.

Accrued revenues   REVENUES related to an accounting period which will be cashed or settled subsequent to the accounting period.

Accumulated depreciation   Total amount by which the cost of FIXED ASSETS has been reduced to take account of the wear and tear and/or obsolescence at a given date (see DEPRECIATION).

Acid test   See QUICK RATIO.

Acquisition   Normal method of BUSINESS COMBINATION (see CONSOLIDATED FINANCIAL STATEMENTS).
   A business combination in which one of the entities, the acquirer, obtains control over the net assets and operations of another entity, the acquiree, in exchange for the transfer of assets, incurrence of liability or issue of equity.

AGM   See ANNUAL GENERAL MEETING.

AICPA   See AMERICAN INSTITUTE OF CERTIFIED PUBLIC ACCOUNTANTS.

Allowances   PROVISION in the US terminology. An allowance represents an amount charged against PROFIT or Income to recognise reductions in value of an asset (i.e. allowance for depreciation, allowance for doubtful debts, etc.).

American Accounting Association (AAA)   An organisation of accounting academics in the USA. It organises conferences annually and publishes The Accounting Review and Accounting Horizons.

American Institute of Certified Public Accountants (AICPA)   Founded in 1887, it is responsible for professional and ethical guidance for its members and the educational standards. It is also responsible for setting auditing standards which are known as Generally Accepted Auditing Standards.

Amortisation   The systematic allocation of the depreciable amount of an intangible asset (such as patents, licences, etc.) over its economic or contractual life.

Annual general meeting (AGM)   Annual meeting of the shareholders of a COMPANY which normally takes place after the end of the company's financial year to approve the annual financial statements and other matters, such as the appointment of directors and auditors.

Annual report   A document containing the financial statements, notes, the directors' report, the management discussion and analysis or operating and financial review, and the report by the auditors issued to shareholders and stakeholders after a COMPANY's year-end.

Articles of association   Regulations for the management of a COMPANY registered in the UK which sets out the rights and duties of the shareholders and directors, and the relationship between different types of shareholders. Together with the MEMORANDUM OF ASSOCIATION they form the COMPANY's constitution. Called BYLAWS in the USA or statutes in the mainland Europe.

Asset   A resource owned by an entity as a result of past events and from which future economic benefits are expected to flow to the entity. The NET ASSETS are determined by deducting the LIABILITIES from the total assets.

In a balance sheet the following categories of assets are distinguished: current assets – cash, bank deposits, inventories, trade receivables and trade investments; non-current (tangible) assets – land, buildings, plant and machinery, vehicles and furniture; non-current (intangible) assets – goodwill, patents, and so on. Financial assets can be either current or non-current assets.

Associated company   An entity in which an investor has significant influence and which is neither a subsidiary nor a joint venture of the investor. The significant influence is presumed when an investor holds 20 per cent or more of the voting power of the investee.

Association of Chartered Certified Accountants (ACCA)   The largest and fastest-growing international accountancy body in the world, with over 490,000 members and students in 170 countries. In 1904 eight people formed the London Association of Accountants. ACCA went through a number of mergers and amalgamations over the years. In 1984 it became the Chartered Association of Certified Accountants to reflect the fact that, a decade earlier, it had been granted a Royal Charter of Incorporation. In 1996 ACCA became the Association of Chartered Certified Accountants (ACCA). Its members, known as Chartered Certified Accountants, are employed in industry, financial services, the public sector, or in public practice.

Audit committee   A COMPANY committee, usually made of non-executive directors of the company, on all matters of internal control, accounting issues and disclosures in the financial statements. Such audit committee also is responsible for approving the auditors' fees.

Auditing   An examination conducted by auditors which involves checking the physical existence and valuation of ASSETS and examining the internal control's system to ensure the correct recording of transactions. The objective of an audit of financial statements is to enable the auditor to express an opinion whether the financial statements are prepared, in all material respects, in accordance with an applicable financial reporting framework and give a true and fair view of the entity.

Auditing practices board   The Consultative Committee of the Accountancy Bodies committee responsible for preparing AUDITING STANDARDS and guidelines in the UK.

Auditing standards   Regulations or standards to be observed by external auditors in preparing their work and issuing their AUDIT REPORT.

Audit report   The auditor's report contains a clear written expression of opinion on the financial statements. An unqualified opinion is expressed when the auditor concludes that the financial statements give a true and fair view or are presented fairly, in all material respects, in accordance with the applicable financial reporting framework.

Authorised share capital   The maximum amount of capital that a registered company is authorised to issue under its MEMORANDUM OF ASSOCIATION or bylaws or statutes.

AVCO   See AVERAGE COST.

Average cost (AVCO)   In the context of INVENTORY valuation, a method of determining the historical cost of an item of inventory. The cost is obtained by dividing all purchases for a period (i.e. month or year) by the total quantity bought in that period (weighted average cost). See FIFO and LIFO.

B

Bad debts   Amounts owed by customers which are or are expected to be uncollectible, probably because the customer has become insolvent. A bad debt is recorded as an EXPENSE against INCOME and the related amount in the Trade and other receivables is written down to nil.

Balance sheet   A statement of the ASSETS, LIABILITIES and CAPITAL of an ENTITY as at a given date, usually at the end of an accounting period, as distinct from income statement, which presents transactions for a period. The balance sheet is in two parts: assets on the left-hand side or at the top, and liabilities on the right-hand side or at the bottom. The assets of the company – receivables, property, cash – are equal to the claims or liabilities of the persons or organisations owing them: creditors, lenders and shareholders. This is the basis of double-entry bookkeeping.

According to the basic accounting equation, assets equal liabilities plus equity; therefore, assets minus liabilities equal equity.

Basic earnings per share   The amount of net profit for the period that is attributable to ordinary shareholders divided by the weighted average number of ordinary shares outstanding during the period.

Bear   Investor on the STOCK EXCHANGE who expects a fall in prices and so sells securities. A bear market is one in which investors are pessimistic as opposed to a Bull market in which investors expect share prices to rise.

Big Four   A title which describes the four remaining largest international accounting firms: Deloitte Touche Tohmatsu, Ernst & Young, KPMG and Pricewaterhouse-Coopers. Before the demise of Arthur Andersen, there were the 'Big Five' and at one time there were the 'Big Eight'.

Bill of exchange   Acknowledgement of a debt in the form of an order in writing addressed by one party to another requiring the latter to pay on demand or at a fixed time a specified amount. Can be transferred to others, i.e. they are negotiable. Bills of exchange are divided into the categories of bank bills, trade bills, fine trade bills and finance bills. Called notes in the USA.

Bonds   Represent long-term debentures issued under a contract by a COMPANY for a fixed term, normally a fixed INTEREST rate and a fixed redemption value.

Bonus shares   Shares issued for free to shareholders in proportion to their share-holding generally with the aim of lowering or diluting the share price. There is no transfer or movement of cash. An entity's retained earnings or reserves are 'converted' into share capital by an accounting entry.

Book value (gross)   Value of the ASSETS and LIABILITIES of a business as stated in its FINANCIAL STATEMENTS.

Book value (net)   Amount at which an Asset is stated in the Balance sheet depending on the system of accounting being used. It does not necessarily represent the amount for which the Asset can be sold.

The net book value of a long-lived asset is given by its historical cost less accumulated depreciation/amortisation and impairment loss.

Borrowing costs   Interest and other costs incurred by an entity in connection with the borrowing of funds.

Budget   A financial plan to guide a business to prepare, monitor and control its activities during the year.

Bull   Investor on a STOCK EXCHANGE who expects a rise in price and so buys securities with the aim to sell them again later at a profit. Also describes an optimistic state of the market as opposed to a BEAR market.

Business combination   The bringing together of separate entities into one economic entity as a result of one entity obtaining control over the net assets and operations of another entity. (see CONSOLIDATED FINANCIAL STATEMENTS).

Business reporting   Wide variety of information disclosed by economic entities about themselves in a number of different ways. An important feature of business reporting is that it is reporting by managers – that is, by those who run the business. In law, this will often mean the board of directors as a whole, which may well include non-executives. In practice, the preparation and disclosure of information are often delegated – by the board to executives, and by senior executives to more junior ones. Law and practice vary among jurisdictions, from one business to another, and from one type of reporting to another. Some of what managers disclose is accounting information and we refer to this as financial reporting.

Everything else they disclose we refer to as non-financial reporting. The boundary between financial reporting and non-financial reporting can be a grey area, as non-financial reporting often summarises or discusses information drawn from financial reporting. Some of these disclosures comply with rules or norms that govern what information should be disclosed and/or how it should be calculated. We refer to the key features of these rules or norms as reporting models.

Business segment   A distinguishable component of an entity that is engaged in providing an individual product or service or a group of related products or services and that is subject to risks and returns that are different from those of other business segments.

Bylaws   The rules concerning the operations of an entity in the USA. See MEMORANDUM OF ASSOCIATION.

C

Cadbury Committee   A UK government appointed committee, which in December 1992 put forward proposals for good corporate governance.

Called-up share capital   Amount of the capital due from the shareholders where the shares are being paid in instalments or in calls.

Capital employed   There is no universally agreed definition of the term. It is often referred to as the sum of owners' equity and non-current liabilities.

Capital gains tax   A tax levied on the gain realised on disposal of an asset.

Capital lease   US term for FINANCE LEASE.

Capital reserves   ACCOUNTS, such as the SHARE PREMIUM account, which can be distributed by a COMPANY only if certain conditions are met under the law. RESTRICTED SURPLUS in US terminology.

Capitalisation   What an entity is worth considering the total market value of all the SHARES (market capitalisation of an entity).
   Recognition of expenditure as an ASSET rather than an EXPENSE (capitalisation of development expenditure under IFRS).

Carrying value (or amount)   Amount at which an item is shown in a BALANCE SHEET. In the case of a long lived asset, it represents the amount at which the asset is recognised in the balance sheet after deducting accumulated depreciation (amortisation) and accumulated impairment losses thereon.

Cash   Cash on hand and demand deposits.

Cash equivalents   Short-term, highly liquid investments that are readily convertible to known amounts of cash and which are subject to an insignificant risk of changes in value.

Cash flow   Represents the flow of money entering (cash inflow) or leaving (cash outflow) the entity during a period of time.

Cash flow statement   See STATEMENT OF CASH FLOWS.

Chart of accounts   Detailed and standardised system of account codes adopted by an entity for its Assets, Liabilities, Capital, Revenues and Expenses.

Chartered Institute of Management Accountants (CIMA)   A UK professional body that offers a qualification in management accountancy, focusing on accounting for business. CIMA was founded in its current form in 1919 under the Title 'The Institute of Cost and Works Accountants' (ICWA). It specialised in the development of accounting technique for use in the internal control of manufacturing, service and public sector operations. It developed a position as the leading professional body in the areas of product costing, budgeting, management accounting, investment appraisal and business decision making. The Institute changed its name from ICWA to the Institute of Cost and Management Accountants (ICMA) in 1972 then to the Chartered Institute of Management Accountants (CIMA) in 1986 after the granting of a Royal Charter. Although based in the UK, it is active worldwide, with more than 172,000 members and students in 165 countries.

Class of assets   Grouping of assets of a similar nature and use in an entity's operations.

Closing rate method   In UK terminology, method of Currency translation under which the financial statements of foreign subsidiaries are translated into the parent company's currency at current exchange rates.

Commercial code   Code, a part of the legal system, containing specific accounting rules applicable to companies.

Common stock   US terminology for Ordinary shares, that represent equity capital of a company.

Companies' Acts   See Company law.

Company law   The law that deals with companies and their operations.

Conceptual framework for financial reporting   Establishes the concepts that underlie financial reporting. The framework is a coherent system of concepts that flow from an objective. The objective of financial reporting is the foundation of the framework. The other concepts provide guidance on identifying the boundaries of financial reporting; selecting the transactions, other events and circumstances to be represented; how they should be recognised and measured (or disclosed); and how they should be summarised and communicated in financial reports.

Conservatism   See Prudence.

Consistency   A concept whereby an entity should use each year identical rules for measurement, valuation and recognition in its Financial statements in order to allow for proper comparison of figures from year to year. The purpose of consistency is to ensure proper comparison of a year's profits and values with those of the previous years.

Consolidated financial statements   Presentation of the financial position and results of a Parent and its Subsidiaries (bringing together their balance sheets and income statements) as if they were a single entity. Generally, the Financial statements of all the enterprises in a Group are aggregated and consolidation adjustments are made to eliminate all intragroup transactions and their effects.

Contingent asset   A possible asset that arises from past events and whose existence will be confirmed only by the occurrence or non-occurrence of one or more uncertain future events not wholly within the control of the entity.

Contingent liability

(a) A possible obligation that arises from past events and whose existence will be confirmed only by the occurrence or non-occurrence of one or more uncertain future events not wholly within the control of the entity; or
(b) a present obligation that arises from past events but is not recognised because:
    (i) it is not probable that an outflow of resources embodying economic benefits will be required to settle the obligation; or
    (ii) the amount of the obligation cannot be measured with sufficient reliability.

Contract   An agreement between two or more parties that has clear economic consequences that the parties have little, if any, discretion to avoid, usually because the agreement is enforceable at law. Contracts may take a variety of forms and need not be in writing.

Control (of an asset)   The power to obtain the future economic benefits that flow from an asset.

Control (of an entity)   The power to govern the financial and operating policies of an entity so as to obtain benefits from its activities.

Corporate governance   How a company is managed, in terms of the institutional systems and protocols meant to ensure accountability and sound ethics. The concept encompasses a variety of issues, including disclosure of information to shareholders and board members, remuneration of senior executives, potential conflict of interest among managers and directors, supervisory structures etc.

Corporation tax   A tax levied on the taxable profits of companies.

Cost   The amount of cash or cash equivalent paid or the fair value of other consideration given to acquire an asset at the time of its acquisition or construction.

Cost method   A method of accounting for investments whereby the investment is recorded at cost. The income statement reflects income from the investment only to the extent that the investor receives distributions from accumulated net profits of the investee arising subsequent to the date of acquisition.

Cost of an acquisition   The amount of cash or cash equivalents paid or the fair value, at the date of exchange, of other purchase consideration given by the acquirer in exchange for control over the net assets of the other entity, plus any costs directly attributable to the acquisition.

Cost of capital   Cost of capital is a means by which an investor who provides capital can expect a return that is commensurate with the risk to which that capital is exposed. The term can also be used to describe the cost of raising money.

Cost of disposal   Incremental costs directly attributable to the disposal of an asset, excluding finance costs and income tax expense.

Cost of inventories   All costs of purchase, costs of conversion and other costs incurred in bringing the inventories to their present location and condition.

Creditors   See Trade and other payables.

Currency translation   See Foreign currency translation.

Current assets   Assets that are expected to turn into cash within one year. Such assets normally include Inventory, Trade and other receivables, and Cash.

Current cost accounting   Method of adjusting accounting to reflect the changing prices of the entity's Assets. It is often included under the generic heading Inflation accounting, although its normal form does not involve adjustments for inflation but for specific price changes relating to the entity's assets.

Current liabilities   Liabilities that will be paid within a year. Thus they will include Trade and other payables, certain Tax liabilities, and declared Dividends. Bank overdrafts are included on the grounds that they fluctuate in size and are technically repayable at short notice.

Current purchasing power accounting (CPP)   UK term for a method of adjusting Historical cost accounting financial statements to take into consideration inflation. The US equivalent is General price level adjusted or constant dollar.

Current ratio   Current assets divided by Current liabilities of an entity at a particular date.

D

Date of acquisition   The date on which control of the net assets and operations of an acquiree is effectively transferred to the acquirer.

Debentures   Loans, usually long-term and secured on company Assets.

Debt-equity ratio   See Gearing.

Debtors   Amount of money owed to the business by customers who have been invoiced for goods or services but who have not yet paid what they owe. Recorded as Current asset. See Trade and other receivables.

Deferred tax assets   The amounts of income taxes recoverable in future periods in respect of:

(a) deductible temporary differences;
(b) carryforward of unused tax losses; and
(c) carryforward of unused tax credits.

Deferred tax liabilities   The amounts of income taxes payable in future periods in respect of taxable temporary differences.

Depreciable amount   The cost of an asset, or other amount substituted for cost in the financial statements, less its residual value.

Depreciation   The systematic allocation of the Depreciable amount of an asset over its useful life. Annual depreciation can be determined using the straight-line method or the diminishing-balance method or the sum-of-the-units method.

Deprival value   The amount by which a business would be worse off if it were deprived of a particular asset. This is sometimes referred to as its 'value to the business' or 'value to the owner'.

Derivative   A financial instrument, such as financial options, futures and forwards, interest rate swaps and currency swaps, which creates rights and obligations that have the effect of transferring between the parties to the instrument one or more of the financial risks inherent in an underlying primary financial instrument. Derivative instruments do not result in a transfer of the underlying primary financial instruments on inception of the contract and such a transfer does not necessarily take place on maturity of the contract.

Development   The application of research findings or other knowledge to a plan or design for the production of new or substantially improved materials, devices, products, processes, systems or services prior to the commencement of commercial production or use.

Diluted earnings per share   The amount of net profit for the period that is attributable to ordinary shareholders divided by the weighted average number of ordinary shares outstanding during the period, both adjusted for the effects of all DILUTIVE POTENTIAL ORDINARY SHARES.

Dilutive potential ordinary shares   Potential ordinary shares whose conversion to ordinary shares would decrease net profit per share from continuing ordinary operations or increase loss per share from continuing ordinary operations.

Direct method of reporting cash flows from operating activities   A method which analyses major classes of gross cash receipts and gross cash payments.

Discontinued/discontinuing operation   A component of an entity:

(a) that the entity, pursuant to a single plan, is:
  (i) disposing of substantially in its entirety, such as by selling the component in a single transaction, by demerger or spin-off of ownership of the component to the entity's shareholders;
  (ii) disposing of piecemeal, such as by selling off the component's assets and settling its liabilities individually; or
  (iii) terminating through abandonment;
(b) that represents a separate major line of business or geographical area of operations; and
(c) that can be distinguished operationally and for financial reporting purposes.

Distributable profits and reserves   Usually covers the year's profit as well as any undistributed profit from previous years which is available for distribution to shareholders as DIVIDENDS.

Dividends   PROFIT after tax paid out to the shareholders (usually in the form of a half yearly or annual payment).

The company directors decide how much profit will be paid out as dividends, if any, and how much will be retained in the business to help finance future operations.

Dividend cover   Number of times the most recent annual dividend could have been paid out of the most recent PROFIT which indicates how secure future dividend payments are.

Dividend yield   Indication of the potential cash return on buying shares calculated by dividing the most recent total annual dividend per share by the market price.

(a) a statement of financial position (or balance sheet);

(b) a statement of comprehensive income (or income statement);

(c) a statement of changes in equity:

(d) statement of cash flows; and

(e) accounting policies and explanatory notes.

Financial year Period for which FINANCIAL STATEMENTS or ACCOUNTS are prepared in UK terminology. Also known in the USA as a FISCAL YEAR.

Financing activities Activities that result in changes in the size and composition of the equity capital and borrowings of the entity.

First-in, first-out (FIFO) The assumption that the items of inventory which were purchased first are sold first, and consequently the items remaining in inventory at the end of the period are those most recently purchased or produced.

Fiscal year US term for the period for which a company prepares FINANCIAL STATEMENTS. The date commonly selected is 31 December as it coincides with the year-end for tax purposes. See FINANCIAL YEAR.

Fixed assets Tangible assets intended for a continuous use in the entity, such as plant and machinery, buildings, furniture and fixture, subject to depreciation. Under US terminology, these are called PROPERTY, PLANT AND EQUIPMENT.

Fixed costs Fixed costs incorporate all business costs, which do not change, regardless of the volume of production or sale. Typically, fixed costs can be related to overheads, such as the rent of the premises, lease payments on equipment, or other predictable costs which remain static.

Foreign currency A currency other than the reporting currency of an entity.

Foreign currency transaction A transaction which is denominated in or requires settlement in a foreign currency.

Foreign currency translation (see currency translation) Accounting operation whereby the financial statements of a foreign SUBSIDIARY are 'translated' into the currency of the parent company (reporting currency) to facilitate the preparation of CONSOLIDATED FINANCIAL STATEMENTS.

Foreign entity A foreign operation, the activities of which are not an integral part of those of the reporting entity.

Foreign operation A subsidiary, associate, joint venture or branch of the reporting entity, the activities of which are based or conducted in a country other than the country of the reporting entity.

FRS See FINANCIAL REPORTING STANDARDS.

Fundamental errors Errors discovered in the current period that are of such significance that the financial statements of one or more prior periods can no longer be considered to have been reliable at the date of their issue.

Future economic benefit The potential to contribute, directly or indirectly, to the flow of cash and cash equivalents to the entity. The potential may be a productive one that is part of the operating activities of the entity. It may also take the form of convertibility into cash or cash equivalents or a capability to reduce cash outflows, such as when an alternative manufacturing process lowers the costs of production.

G

GAAP   See GENERALLY ACCEPTED ACCOUNTING PRINCIPLES.

Gearing   A measurement of the degree to which a business is funded by loans rather than SHAREHOLDERS' EQUITY. The US expression is LEVERAGE.

General price level adjusted accounting (GPLA)   A US term for a system of adjusting historical cost accounting by price indices to account for inflation. See GENERAL PURCHASING POWER APPROACH.

General purchasing power approach   The restatement of some or all of the items in the financial statements for changes in the general price level.

General-purpose financial statements   Financial statements intended to meet the needs of users who are not in a position to require an entity to prepare reports tailored to their particular information needs.

Generally accepted accounting principles (GAAP)   Mainly US technical term encompassing the ACCOUNTING STANDARDS of the FINANCIAL ACCOUNTING STANDARDS BOARD and rules of the predecessor bodies. The SEC requires companies registered with it to comply with GAAP when preparing their financial statements.

Generally accepted auditing standards   A US term for rules to be followed by auditors when carrying out an audit of financial statements.

Geographical segments   A distinguishable component of an entity that is engaged in providing products or services within a particular economic environment and that is subject to risks and returns that are different from those of components operating in other economic environments.

Going concern   An entity is normally viewed as a going concern, that is, as continuing in operation for the foreseeable future. It is assumed that the entity has neither the intention nor the necessity of liquidation or of curtailing materially the scale of its operations.

Golden share   The allocation of substantial voting rights to a particular shareholder so that possible takeover bids can be thwarted.

Goodwill   The amount paid for a business above the FAIR VALUE of its NET ASSETS upon ACQUISITION. This means that there is a premium in terms of its value compared with the business's existing and identifiable assets and liabilities. It can represent various things such as customer loyalty, knowledgeable and skilled management or its ability to earn more profit than similar newly formed businesses.

Government grants   Assistance by government in the form of transfer of resources to an entity in return for past or future compliance with certain conditions relating to the operating activities of the entity. They exclude those forms of government assistance which cannot reasonably have a value placed upon them and trans-actions with government which cannot be distinguished from the normal trading transactions of the entity.

GPLA See GENERAL PRICE LEVEL ADJUSTED ACCOUNTING.

Gross profit The difference between the value of sales and the related COST OF SALES.

Group A parent and all its subsidiaries.

Group accounts The financial statements of a group of companies, i.e. of a parent company and its subsidiaries. UK expression for CONSOLIDATED FINANCIAL STATEMENTS.

H

Hedging Designing one or more HEDGING INSTRUMENTS so that their change in fair value is an offset, in whole or in part to the change in fair value or cash flows of a hedged item.

Hedging instrument A designed derivative or (in limited circumstances) another financial asset or liability whose fair value or cash flows are expected to offset changes in the fair value or cash flows of a designed hedged item. A non-derivative financial asset or liability may be designated as a hedging instrument for hedge accounting purposes only if it hedges the risk of changes in foreign currency exchange rates.

Historical cost Assets are recorded at the amount of cash or cash equivalents paid or the fair value of the consideration given to acquire them at the time of their acquisition. Liabilities are recorded at the amount of proceeds received in exchange for the obligation, or in some circumstances (for example, income taxes), at the amounts of cash or cash equivalents expected to be paid to satisfy the liabilities in the normal course of business.

Historical cost accounting Conventional accounting system widely established throughout the world except in some countries where inflation is endemic and high. Even in the latter countries, the GENERAL PURCHASING POWER APPROACH is a set of simple adjustments carried out annually from historical cost records.

Holding company A company that owns or controls other companies, that does not itself actively trade but operates via its subsidiaries. CONSOLIDATED FINANCIAL STATEMENTS are required for the group. A holding company is also known as a PARENT Company.

Hyperinflation Loss of purchasing power of money at such a rate that comparison of amounts from transactions and other events that have occurred at different times, even within the same accounting period, is misleading.

I

IASB See INTERNATIONAL ACCOUNTING STANDARDS BOARD.

IASC See INTERNATIONAL ACCOUNTING STANDARDS COMMITTEE.

ICAEW See INSTITUTE OF CHARTERED ACCOUNTANTS IN ENGLAND & WALES (ICAEW).

ICMA See CHARTERED INSTITUTE OF MANAGEMENT ACCOUNTANTS (CIMA).

ICWA See CHARTERED INSTITUTE OF MANAGEMENT ACCOUNTANTS (CIMA).

Impairment   The loss of value of an ASSET below its book value (i.e. generally its depreciated cost). This is measured by comparing the book value with the RECOVER-ABLE AMOUNT.

Impairment loss   The amount by which the carrying amount of an asset exceeds its recoverable amount.

Income   Increases in economic benefits during the accounting period in the form of inflows or enhancements of assets or decreases in liabilities that result in increases in equity, other than those relating to contributions from equity participants.

Income statement   The statement of revenues and expenses of a particular period, leading to the determination of net income or net profit. The equivalent UK statement is the PROFIT AND LOSS ACCOUNT. See STATEMENT OF COMPREHENSIVE INCOME.

Indirect method of reporting cash flows from operating activities   Under this method, net profit or loss is adjusted for the effects of transactions of a non-cash nature, any deferrals or accruals of past or future operating cash receipts or payments, and items of income or expense associated with investing or financing cash flows.

Inflation accounting   Inflation accounting aims to provide financial comparisons over a period of time in which the value of money has changed, because of inflation.

Institute of Chartered Accountants in England & Wales (ICAEW)   The largest professional accountancy body in Europe with over 132,000 members. The Institute of Accountants in London was formed in 1870. In 1871, standards for membership were established with new members having to show knowledge and aptitude through successfully passing an oral examination. Initially the London Institute restricted its membership to that city, but as other institutes were established elsewhere (for example, in Manchester, Sheffield and Liverpool) it was decided to remove this restriction and as such in 1872 it simply became known as the Institute of Accountants to reflect its new national coverage. By 1878, these multitude of institutes were considering merging in a further bid to improve their status. This was finally achieved in 1880, when the ICAEW was incorporated by Royal Charter. The Institute received a Supplemental Charter in 1948.

Intangible assets   ASSETS, such as goodwill, patents, brand names, trademarks, copyrights and franchises, that are not physical or tangible.

Interest rate risk   A price risk – the risk that the value of a financial instrument will fluctuate due to changes in market interest rates.

Interim period   A financial reporting period shorter than a full financial year.

Interim financial report   A financial report containing either a complete set of financial statements or a set of condensed financial statements for an interim period.

International Accounting Standards Committee (IASC)   See International Accounting Standards Board.

International Organisation of Securities Commissions (IOSCO)   An international body of governmental regulators of stock exchanges.

Marking-to-market Accounting for investments or commodities by constantly updating their values to the current market value in the BALANCE SHEET and taking any resulting GAINS or LOSSES to INCOME immediately.

Matching of costs with revenues Expenses are recognised in the INCOME STATEMENT on the basis of a direct association between the costs incurred and the earning of specific items of income. This process involves the simultaneous or combined recognition of revenues and expenses that result directly and jointly from the same transactions or other events.

Materiality Information is material if its non-disclosure could influence the economic decisions of users taken on the basis of the financial statements.

Measurement The process of determining the monetary amounts at which the elements of the financial statements are to be recognised and carried in the balance sheet and income statement.

Monetary items (monetary assets; monetary financial assets and financial liabilities; monetary financial instruments) Money held and assets (financial assets) and liabilities (financial liabilities) to be received or paid in fixed or determinable amounts of money.

Money measurement convention Financial statements include only those items that can be measured in monetary terms with reasonable OBJECTIVITY. Thus the value (to the entity) of skilled management or of loyal staff or customers, is not normally shown in financial statements. This is because it is virtually impossible to measure reliably its worth in money terms. This convention is linked to the use of HISTORICAL COST ACCOUNTING, where ASSETS are measured at their purchase price or production cost.

N

NBV See NET BOOK VALUE.

Negative goodwill Any (remaining) excess, as at the date of the acquisition of an entity, of the acquirer's interest in the fair values of the identifiable assets and liabilities acquired over the cost of the acquisition.

Net assets The worth of an entity in accounting terms as measured or represented by its Balance Sheet. It is the total of all the recorded ASSETS less the LIABILITIES that are owed to outsiders. The net assets equal the SHAREHOLDERS' EQUITY.

Net book value (NBV) The net amount at which an asset is stated in the BALANCE SHEET of an entity.

Net current assets The net current assets or (accounting) working capital of an entity is the excess of the current assets (such as cash, inventories and accounts receivable) over the current liabilities (such as trade payables and overdrafts).

Net income See NET PROFIT OR LOSS.

Net investment in a foreign entity The reporting entity's share in the net assets of that entity.

Net present value (NPV) A current estimate of the present discounted value of the future net cash flows in the normal course of business.

Net profit (or loss)   The profit of an entity after operating expenses and all other charges including taxes, interest and depreciation have been deducted from total revenue. Also called net earnings or net income. If expenses and charges exceed revenue, the entity incurs a net loss.

Net realisable value (NRV)   Usually represents the net current selling price of the assets, net of the estimated costs of completion and selling costs.

Net selling price   The amount obtainable from the sale of an asset in an arm's length transaction between knowledgeable parties.

Net worth   See NET ASSETS.

Neutrality   Freedom from bias of the information contained in financial statements.

Nominal value   Most shares (and bonds) have a nominal or par value. When a company issues new shares the share capital is recorded at nominal value, any excess being recorded as SHARE PREMIUM.

Non-adjusting events after the balance sheet date   See EVENTS AFTER THE REPORTING DATE.

Non-controlling interest (NCI)   That part of the net results of operations and of net assets of a subsidiary attributable to interests which are not owned, directly or indirectly through subsidiaries, by the parent.

Non-profit   The description applied to an organisation whose main aims are not commercial; for example, a university or a charity. Depending on the legal structure of such bodies, they may not be subject to normal accounting rules.

NPV   See NET PRESENT VALUE.

NRV   See NET REALISABLE VALUE and LOWER OF COST AND NET REALISABLE VALUE.

O

Objectivity   An accounting measurement is said to be objective if it is reasonably independent of the judgement of management. There is a trade-off between objectivity and relevance. For example, today the price of a building acquired ten years ago is objective but may be irrelevant from the point of view of the current value of that building today or for a decision about what to do with it.

Obligation   A duty or responsibility to act or perform in a certain way. Obligations may be legally enforceable as a consequence of a binding contract or statutory requirement. Obligations also arise, however, from normal business practice, custom and a desire to maintain good business relations or act in an equitable manner.

Offsetting   See SET-OFF, LEGAL RIGHT OF.

Onerous contract   A contract in which the unavoidable costs of meeting the obligations under the contract exceed the economic benefits expected to be received under it.

Operating activities   The principal revenue-producing activities of an entity and other activities that are not investing or financing activities.

relating to a subsequent period (for example, rent or insurance premiums). The parallel accounting treatment for expenses paid in arrears gives rise to ACCRUED EXPENSES in the balance sheet.

Price/earnings ratio (P/E ratio)   This ratio compares the market price of an ORDINARY SHARE with the earnings per share of that company, based on the most recently available year's PROFIT after INTEREST, tax, MINORITY INTEREST and preference dividend.

Price risk   There are three types of price risk: currency risk, interest rate risk and market risk. The term 'price risk' embodies not only the potential for loss but also the potential for gain in terms of price.

Primary financial instruments   Financial assets such as cash, receivables and equity securities of another entity and financial liabilities such as debt.

Prior-year adjustment   This arises when an entity discovers an error of material size in its financial statements of previous years, or if there is a change in accounting policies.

Private company   A company which is not allowed to sell its shares or loan stock on an open market. See PRIVATE LIMITED COMPANY.

Private limited company   A company that is not allowed to create a market in its securities. It should be distinguished from a PUBLIC LIMITED COMPANY. In most countries where this distinction exists, private companies are much more numerous than public companies. Rules for disclosures, audit, profit distribution, etc. are normally less onerous for private companies.

Profit   The residual amount that remains after all expenses (including capital maintenance adjustments, where appropriate) have been deducted from income.

Profit and loss account   See INCOME STATEMENT.

Property, plant and equipment   Tangible assets that:

(a) are held by an entity for use in the production or supply of goods or services, for rental to others, or for administrative purposes; and
(b) are expected to be used during more than one period.

Proportional consolidation   See PROPORTIONATE CONSOLIDATION.

Proportionate consolidation   A method of accounting and reporting whereby a venturer's share of each of the assets, liabilities, income and expenses of a jointly controlled entity is combined on a line-by-line basis with similar items in the venturer's financial statements or reported as separate line items in the venturer's financial statements.

Provision   A liability which represents uncertain timing or amount. See ALLOWANCE.

Prudence   The inclusion of a degree of caution in the exercise of judgements needed in making the estimates required under conditions of uncertainty, such that assets or income are not overstated and liabilities or expenses are not understated.
   In the USA, CONSERVATISM is the word generally used for this concept.

Public company See PUBLIC LIMITED COMPANY.

Public limited company A company whose SECURITIES may legally be publicly traded. In the US it is a corporation that is registered with the SECURITIES AND EXCHANGE COMMISSION. Often, the expression PUBLIC COMPANY is used loosely to mean companies whose shares are traded on a stock exchange.

Purchase accounting A US term for the normal method of BUSINESS COMBINATION.

Q

Qualified audit report Report which states that the financial statements give a True and Fair View except for certain qualifying remarks. The qualifications may concern the under- or overstatement of profit (loss) and assets or liabilities, infringement of company law or accounting standards. See AUDIT REPORT.

Quarterly report Unaudited document, reporting the financial results for a quarter and noting any significant changes or events in the quarter. Quarterly reports contain financial statements, a discussion from the management, and a list of 'material events' that have affected the company's operations (such as a stock split or acquisition).

Quick ratio Measure of a company's liquidity. It compares CURRENT ASSETS (net of INVENTORY) to CURRENT LIABILITIES. An alternative measure comparing all Current Assets to all Current Liabilities is called the CURRENT RATIO.

Quoted company An alternative expression for a LISTED COMPANY.

R

R & D See RESEARCH AND DEVELOPMENT.

Rate of return Measure of the profitability of a business or an investment. It normally compares Profit of the business or on investment with the amount of CAPITAL invested in it.

Ratios A ratio expresses a relation between two items appearing in the financial statements. A ratio in isolation tells us little. To get an objective view of a situation we should use numerous ratios and apply appropriate benchmarks. These benchmarks can be derived from various sources, such as historical data, competitors' accounts and published data of all kinds. It is the trend over time rather than the absolute number that gives the most valuable information.

Realisable value The amount of CASH or CASH EQUIVALENTS that could currently be obtained by selling an asset in an orderly disposal.

Receivables An IFRS and US expression for amounts of money due to an entity. It is often known as Trade and other receivables or as ACCOUNTS RECEIVABLE. The UK term is DEBTORS.

Recognition The process of incorporating (recording) in the balance sheet or income statement an item that meets the definition of an element and satisfies the following criteria for recognition:

(a) it is probable that any future economic benefit associated with the item will flow to or from the entity; and

(b) the item has a cost or value that can be measured reliably.

Recoverable amount   The higher of an asset's net selling price and its value in use.

Related parties   Parties are considered to be related if one party has the ability to control the other party or exercise significant influence over the other party in making financial and operating decisions.

Related party transaction   A transfer of resources or obligations between related parties, regardless of whether a price is charged.

Relevance   Information has the quality of relevance when it influences the economic decisions of users by helping them evaluate past, present or future events or confirming, or correcting, their past evaluations.

Reliability   Information has the quality of reliability when it is free from material error and bias and can be depended upon by users to represent faithfully that which it either purports to represent or could reasonably be expected to represent.

Replacement cost accounting   A system of preparing financial statements in which all ASSETS (and expenses relating to them, such as DEPRECIATION) are valued at current REPLACEMENT COSTS (the amount a business would have to pay in order to replace an asset).

Replacement cost of an asset   Represents the current acquisition cost of a similar asset, new or used, or of an equivalent productive capacity or service potential.

Reportable segment   A business segment or a geographical segment for which segment information is required to be disclosed under IFRS or equivalent accounting standards.

Reporting currency   The currency used in presenting the financial statements.

Reporting entity   An entity for which there are users who rely on the financial statements as their major source of financial information about the entity.

Research   Original and planned investigation undertaken with the prospect of gaining new scientific or technical knowledge and understanding.

Research and development (R&D)   Examples of research activities are:

(a) activities aimed at obtaining new knowledge;

(b) search for, evaluation and final selection of, applications of research findings or other knowledge;

(c) search for alternatives for materials, devices, products, processes, systems or services; and

(d) formulation, design, evaluation and final selection of possible alternatives for new or improved materials, devices, products, processes, systems or services.

According to IFRS 38, expenditure on research should not be capitalised but recognised as an expense when it is incurred. No CAPITALISATION is permitted.

Example of development activities are:

(a) design, construction and testing of pre-production or pre-use prototypes and models;
(b) design of tools involving new technologies;
(c) design, construction and testing of a chosen alternative for new or improved materials, devices, products, processes, systems or services.

According to IFRS 38, expenditure relating to development activities can be capitalised as intangible assets under certain conditions.

Reserve   An amount voluntarily or compulsorily set aside out of profit. In the case of voluntarily allocation profits are retained in the entity for growth; whereas in the case of compulsory allocation profits are retained to protect generally the interests of the creditors.

Residual value   The net amount which an entity expects to obtain for an asset at the end of its useful life after deducting the expected costs of disposal.

Restricted surplus   US expression for amounts of retained earnings or profit that are unavailable for distribution to shareholders. See UNDISTRIBUTABLE RESERVES.

Retained earnings   US expression for RETAINED PROFIT. See RESERVE.

Retained profit   Amount of profit, earned in the current and prior years, that have not yet been paid out as Dividends, but retained in the entity. RETAINED EARNINGS is a typical US expression for such amounts.

Retirement benefit plans   Arrangements whereby an entity provides benefits for its employees on or after termination of service (either in the form of an annual income or as a lump sum) when such benefits, or the employer's contributions towards them, can be determined or estimated in advance of retirement from the provision of a document or from the entity's practices. See also POST-EMPLOYMENT BENEFIT PLANS.

Return on capital employed (ROCE)   EBIT divided by CAPITAL EMPLOYED.

Return on equity (ROE)   Net profit divided by EQUITY.

Revalued amount of an asset   The fair value of an asset at the date of a revaluation less any subsequent accumulated depreciation.

Revenue   The gross inflow of economic benefits during a period arising in the course of the ordinary activities of an entity when those inflows result in an increase in equity, other than increases relating to contributions from equity participants.

Revenue reserve   UK expression for RETAINED PROFIT.

Rights issue   The sale of additional SHARES by a company to its existing shareholders usually at a discount on market prices. The rights to buy the shares are given to the existing shareholders in proportion to their shareholdings. Rights issues should be distinguished from BONUS SHARES where no money is paid to the company, but where existing shareholders receive shares for 'free' in proportion to their shareholdings and the profits so 'distributed' are relabelled as share capital.

ROCE   See RETURN ON CAPITAL EMPLOYED.

ROE   See RETURN ON EQUITY.

S

Sale-and-leaseback transactions   The sale of an asset by a vendor and the leasing of the same asset back to the vendor. The rentals and the sale price are usually interdependent.

SEC   See SECURITIES AND EXCHANGE COMMISSION.

Securities and Exchange Commission (SEC)   The US government agency set up in 1934 after the Wall Street Crash of 1929. Its function is to control the issue and exchange of publicly traded shares, with the aim to protect US investors against malpractice in the securities market. Listed companies are required to register with the SEC, and then comply with a mass of detailed regulations about disclosure.

Security   An instrument representing ownership (SHARES), a debt agreement (BONDS), or the rights to ownership (DERIVATIVES).

Segmental reporting   The disclosure of SALES, PROFIT or ASSETS by line of business or by geographical area. See also GEOGRAPHICAL SEGMENT and REPORTABLE SEGMENT.

Set-off, legal right of   A debtor's legal right, by contract or otherwise, to settle or otherwise eliminate all or a portion of an amount due to a creditor by applying against that amount a receivable from the same creditor.

Shareholders' equity

1   The total of the shareholders' interest in a company. This will at a given date include the share capital, amounts contributed in excess of the PAR VALUE of shares (i.e. SHARE PREMIUM or PAID-IN SURPLUS), and retained earnings.
2   The difference between total assets and total liabilities.

Shareholders' funds   See SHAREHOLDERS' EQUITY.

Share premium   Amounts received by a company in excess of the NOMINAL VALUE of the shares from the shareholders on purchase of shares from the company.

SIC   See STANDING INTERPRETATIONS COMMITTEE.

Significant influence   The power to participate in the financial and operating policy decisions of an economic activity but not control or joint control over those policies. According to IFRSs this is presumed to exist when an investor has a 20 per cent or greater interest in the entity. See ASSOCIATED COMPANY.

Solvency   The availability of cash and cash equivalents on a continuous basis to meet financial commitments as they fall due.

SSAP   STATEMENTS OF STANDARD ACCOUNTING PRACTICE.

Standing Interpretations Committee (SIC)   Set up in 1997 by the INTERNATIONAL ACCOUNTING STANDARDS COMMITTEE (now the IASB) to publish interpretations of international accounting standards.

Statement of cash flows   A financial statement focusing on the cash flow of various activities of an entity such as operating, investing and financing activities for a period or year.

Statement of comprehensive income   An entity should present all items of income and expense recognised in a period:

(a) in a single statement of comprehensive income; or
(b) in two statements: a statement displaying components of profit or loss (separate INCOME STATEMENT) and a second statement beginning with profit or loss and displaying components of OTHER COMPREHENSIVE INCOME (statement of comprehensive income).

Statement of financial position   See BALANCE SHEET.

Statement of total recognised gains and losses   A financial statement required from the UK companies since 1993. It includes gains and losses that are not recorded in the PROFIT AND LOSS ACCOUNT, such as those on FOREIGN CURRENCY TRANSLATION and on the Revaluation of FIXED ASSETS. See COMPREHENSIVE INCOME.

Stewardship   One of the objectives of financial reporting. It refers to the accountability of management. Management are accountable to the entity's capital providers for the custody and safekeeping of the entity's economic resources and for their efficient and profitable use, including protecting them from unfavourable economic effects such as inflation and technological changes. Management are also responsible for ensuring compliance with laws, regulations and contractual provisions.

The stewardship objective is about providing information about the past (including, for example, the transactions entered into, the decisions taken and the policies adopted) at a level of detail and in a way that enables the entity's past performance to be assessed in its own right, rather than just as part of an assessment about likely future performance. And it is about providing information about how the entity has been positioned for the future.

Stock exchange   An organised market for the issue of new securities and the exchange of existing securities. Companies whose shares may be sold on such exchanges are called LISTED or QUOTED COMPANIES. In addition to accounting regulations, listed companies are required to comply with the listing requirements of their particular STOCK EXCHANGE.

Stockholders' equity   See SHAREHOLDERS' EQUITY.

Straight-line depreciation   A method of calculating the annual DEPRECIATION charge for a FIXED ASSET. Under this method, annual depreciation charge equals the cost of the asset less any estimated residual value divided by the number of years of useful life.

Subsidiary   An entity that is controlled by another entity (known as the PARENT). Control is presumed when an entity has a more than 50 per cent interest in another entity.

Substance over form   The principle that transactions and other events are accounted for and presented in accordance with their substance and economic reality and not merely their legal form.

Window dressing The manipulation of figures in financial statements in order to make them appear better than they otherwise would be. A company might wish to do this in order to influence the judgement of existing or potential shareholders or lenders, the government, or other readers of financial statements.

Working capital Represents either:

(a) the difference between CURRENT ASSETS and CURRENT LIABILITIES (accounting working capital) or
(b) Inventory plus TRADE RECEIVABLES less TRADE PAYABLES (trade or operating working capital).

Index